GRAPHIC CLASSICS

GRAPHIC CLASSICS

Graphic design is a form of visual communication that seeks, through the interplay of words and images, to promote an idea or product. Its history charts a rich and diverse journey, spanning centuries and encompassing numerous styles, technological innovations, and cultural shifts.

The advancement of the moveable-type printing press in the fifteenth century (following earlier applications in China and Korea that failed to proliferate) revolutionized the way information could be reproduced and disseminated. The Industrial Revolution in the eighteenth and nineteenth centuries was equally consequential, bringing with it significant societal changes and mechanical innovations that marked the beginning of mass communication. The rise of industrialization led to the growth of advertising, and commercial design—posters, packaging, promotional materials—quickly became an essential tool for business.

Today, graphic design continues to serve trade, commerce, communication, and culture. It evolves alongside new technologies—most notably the computer and the smart phone—informs our experience and navigation of the world, and aids global movements, such as the drive for environmental sustainability and greater social equality. Graphic design exists in virtually every aspect of contemporary life, and, throughout its development, has reflected and responded to change, making it a dynamic and ever evolving art form, one that closely reflects the cultural and societal times in which it operates.

In addition to its commercial applications, graphic design has played a significant role in the history of protest, helping to convey social and political messages with impact. Through powerful imagery, bold typography, and dramatic color schemes, graphic designers have provided millions worldwide with the tools to call out the issues that impact our daily lives, including oppressive political agendas, racial inequality, gender discrimination, accessibility, and LGBTQ+ rights—with many critical examples featured in this volume.

As a leading publisher in the visual arts, Phaidon is renowned for producing beautiful books, using innovative design to enhance and support their content. For this publication, we have compiled an archive of exceptional graphics throughout history that we consider to be the finest examples in the field. In addition to our own submissions, we have asked contemporary graphic designers, design historians, and critics internationally to suggest works that, in their view, successfully integrate communicative function with aesthetic form, and that have set new standards for production and quality. The resulting curated selection, rigorously reviewed and edited down from thousands of entries, represents an unparalleled resource of the world's very best graphic design.

First published in 2012, this revised and updated edition, *Graphic Classics*, brings the selection into the present, with the addition of fifty new examples that highlight designers reshaping the graphic culture of today, as well as those earlier pioneers who were previously overlooked.

Like many other creative fields, graphic design historically has been a male-dominated domain, with a distinctly European and North American emphasis. In our reassessment of the archive, we have aimed, in some way, to adjust this imbalance, providing a platform for different voices, approaches, and disciplines to be honored and valued within the design community. The time is long overdue for a newly amplified selection of first-class graphic design to take center stage.

Graphic Classics contains five hundreds works, drawn from all corners of the world, spanning from the advent of mechanical reproduction to today's most cutting-edge advertising, book, corporate, information, logo, magazine, newspaper, poster, and typeface design, each of which has created a benchmark for excellence and innovation.

- Advertising
- Book
- Book Cover
- Identity
- Information Design
- Logo
- Magazine / Newspaper
- Magazine Cover
- Poster
- Record / CD Cover
- Typeface

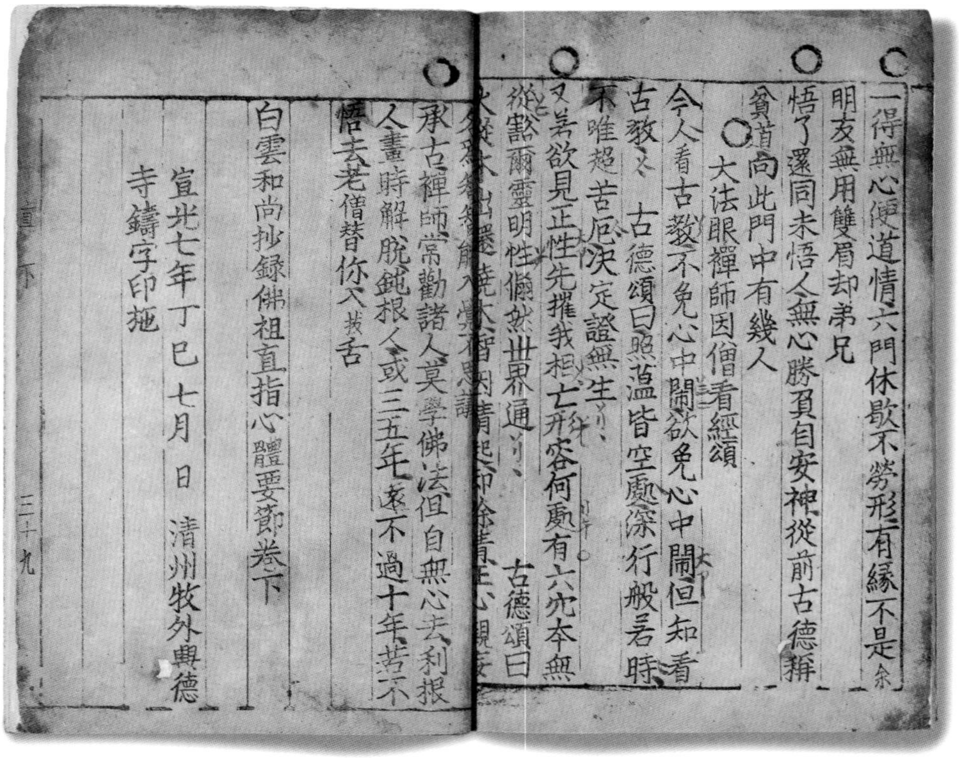

● **1377 . BAEGUN HWASANG CHOROK BULJO JIKJI SIMCHE YOJEOL .** Book . Various

→ p.354

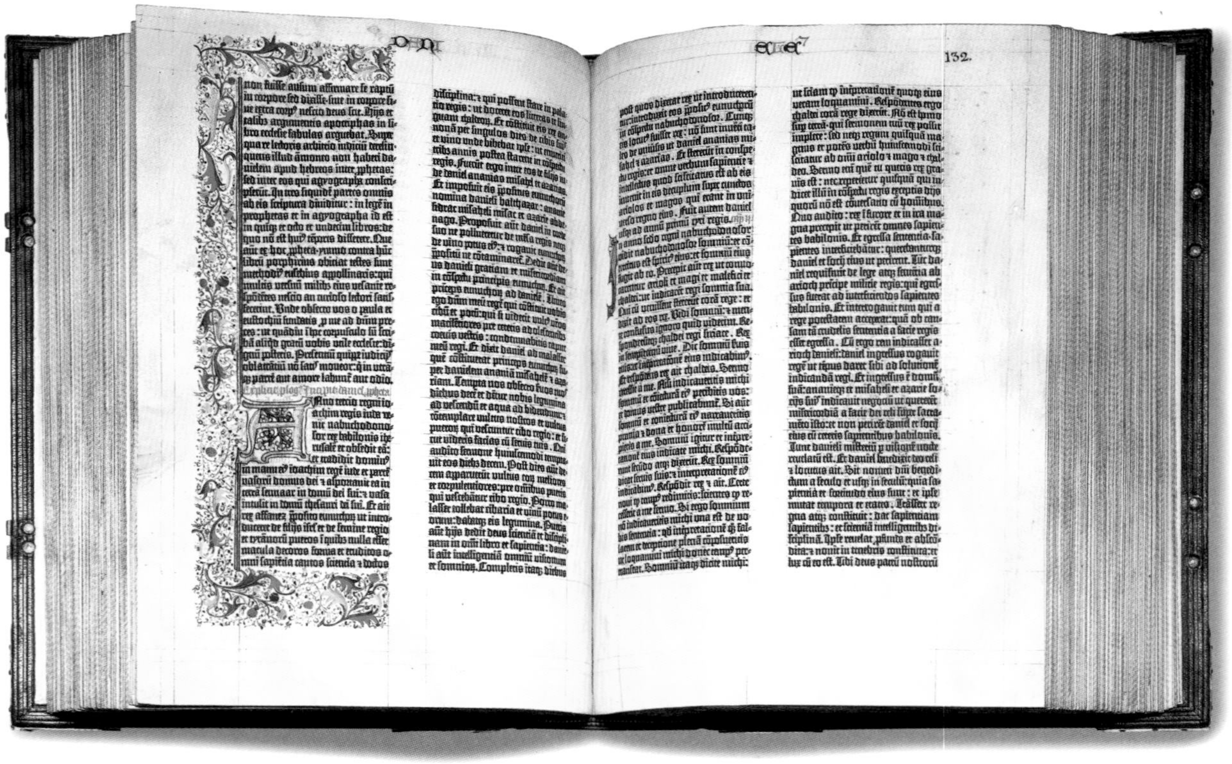

● c. **1453–1455 . THE GUTENBERG BIBLE .** Book . Johannes Gutenberg

→ p.354

In dem anfang hat got beschaffen himel vñ erden aber die erde was eytel vnd lere vnd die finsternus warē auff dē antlitz des abgrūds vnd der gaist des herrē swebet oder ward getragē ob dē wassern. Moyses der gottlich prophet vnd geschicht beschreiber der schier. vijᶜ. iar vor dem Troyanischē krieg gewest ist leret wie got der macher vnd ordner der ding als er diss werck fürname zu allererst dē himel zeseyn einen stul des selbē gottes des schöpffers gemacht vnd in die höhe auffgehenckt vñ dar nach die erdē gestifftet vnd dē himel vnderworffē hat. Aber die finsternüssen hat er gesetzt in der erden dañ sie begreüfft durch sich selbs nichtzit des liechts sie nēme es dañ vō himel. In dez hat er gesetzt das ewig liecht vñ die obern gaist vnd das ewig lebē. vnd hinwiderūmb in der erden die finsternüß vnd die vndern gaist vnd dē tod. Aber in dem das Moyses spricht das got beschaffen hab so stelt er damit ab drey irrūg Platonis Aristotilis vñ Epicuri. dañ Plato hielt das got vnd die vorpildnus oder gestältnuß seiner geschöpff vnd yle vō ewigkeit gewessen vnd im anfang die werlt vō dē selbē yle gemacht wordē wer. Die kriechē sprechē yle sey die erst vngeformt materi auß der :alle ding geschöpfft: vnd dise sichtpere elemēt die sich mit etlicher eintrechtigleit einander vergleichē geformt. oder (als die andern sprechē) von d materi vñ form. oder vō dē aller dynnisten staub in der sunnen glantz erscheinende gemacht seyē. Aber got hat die werlt on ainiche vorligende vnd vorberaite materi beschaffen. dan er was zu ertrachten der alleklūgst vnd zemachen d allersinnreichst ee dañ er das werck der werlt fürname wañ in im was dar brunn des volkūmē vñ volbrachtē guts das vō dē sellē güt als ein pach entsprūnge. Er hat in anfāg die engel. aller creatur die erstē gemacht vñ auß dē das nicht ist. dañ er ist durch die ewigkeit starck. vñ durch die stercke vnermeßner machtigkeit. die des ends vñ der maß mangelt. als das lebē des schöpffers. Darūmb was wunders ist das. ob der. der die werlt machē wolt vorhin ein materi darauß er machet fürberaittet. auß dem dasnit was. das haben villeicht auch die Saraceni verstanden. die sprechē das die engel vō got auß dē finsternussē zū liecht gefürt vñ mit ewiger frewd erfült seinē doch ist in etlichē die einpildung göttliches stāmens nit blibē. sunder sie sind auß aigner verkerung vō gütten zum vbel getretten vñ zu teüfeln wordē. Die erde was eytel. das ist (als Jeronimus od die. lxx. außlegē) vnsyhtperlich vñ vnzesamen gefügt. die er vō irer zestrewlichkeit wegē einē abgrund nēnet. vñ die die kriechyschē chaos haissē einē abgrund. heist er die erden. das ist ein materi mit driueltiger ermessung in die allerhohstē tieff außgepraittet. Da von auch Ouidius der poet in seinē gedicht gar schön meldung thüt. vnd der gaist des herrē ein werckzewg gotlicher kūst swebet ob dē wassern: als d wil eins pawherrē so er yde ding zemachē verordent. so die werck gottes volkomē sind. so wirdt die beschöpffūg d dīg außgedrückt in sechser zall. des teill sind. ains zway drey. Nwn zaygt Moyses durch die werck d sechs tag nemlich in dē ersten die beschöpfung. In dem andern vnd dritten die ordnung oder schickung. vnd in den andern die zierung.

1493 . THE NUREMBERG CHRONICLE . Book . Michael Wolgemut, Wilhelm Pleydenwurff, Albrecht Dürer

→ p.354

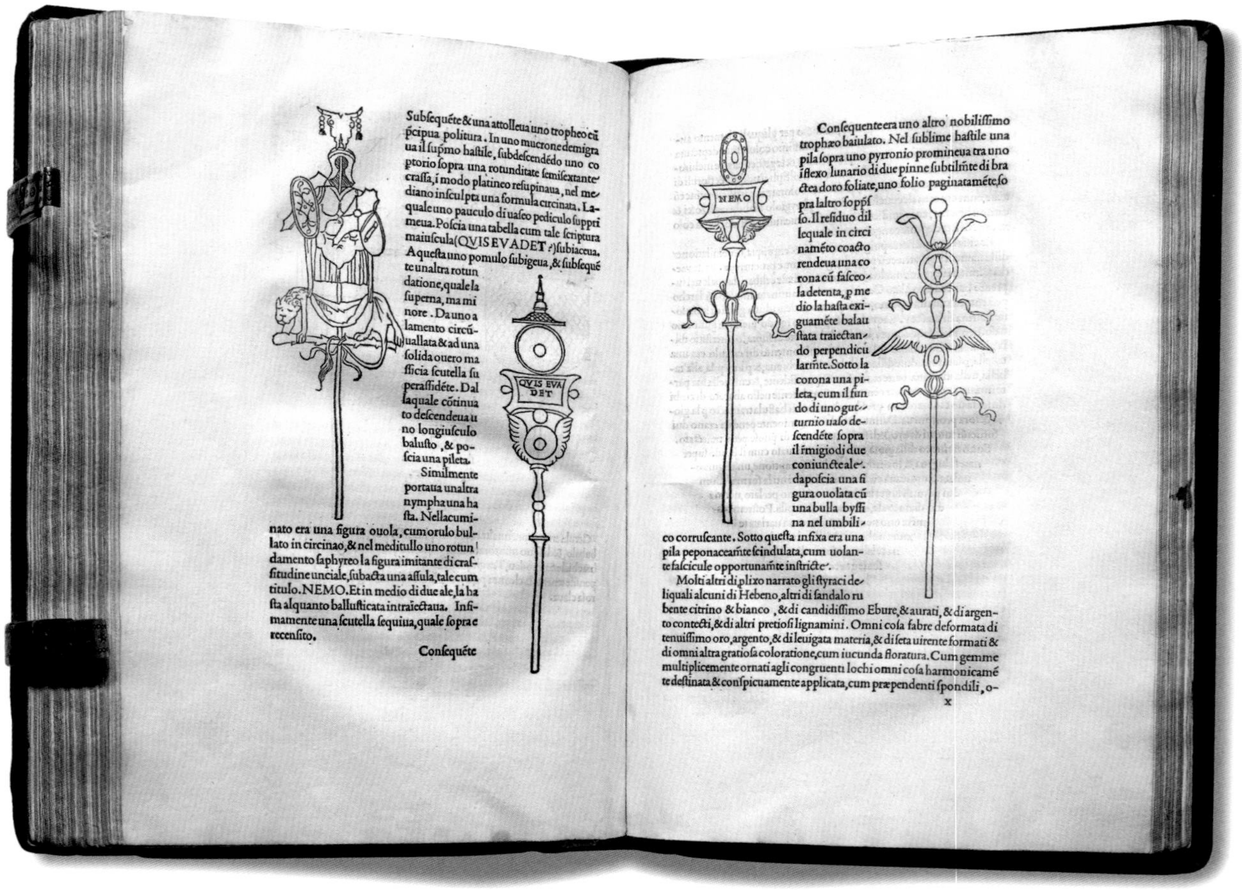

● **1499 . HYPNEROTOMACHIA POLIPHILI .** Book . Aldus Manutius

→ p.355

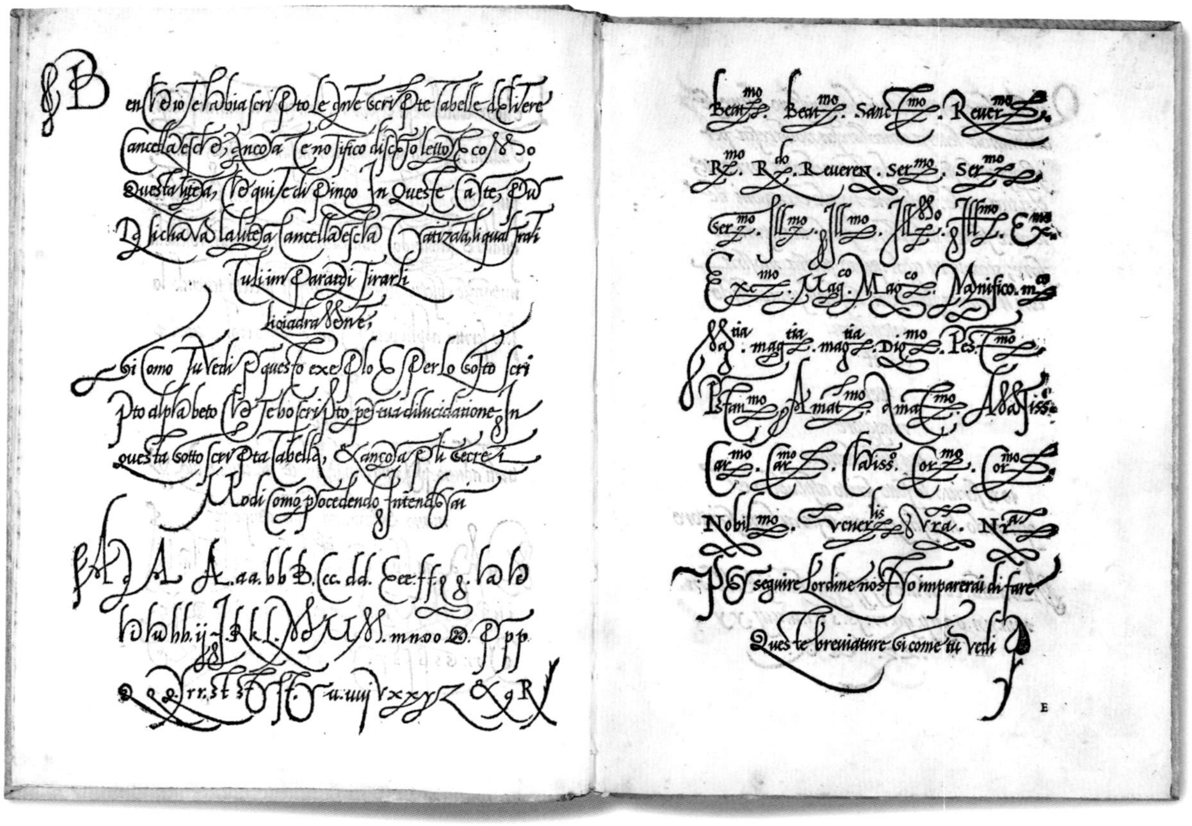

● ***1524 . LO PRESENTE LIBRO .*** Book . Giovanni Antonio Tagliente

→ p.355

36 ABCDEFGHIJKLMNOPQRST
UVWXYZ ABCDEFGHIJKLM
abcdefghijklmnopqrstuvwxyz ct st
abcdefghijkklmnopqrstuvwxyz & Qu

30 NOPQRSTUVWXYZ ABCDEFGHIJ
KLMNOPQRSTUVWYXZ ABCDEF
abcdefghijklmnopqrstuvwxyz abcdefghij
klmnopqrstuvwxyz abcdefghjkklmnopqrstuvw

24 GHIJKLMNOPQRSTUVWXYZ ABCDEFG
HIJKLMNOPQRSTUVWXYZ ABCDEFG
ff fi fl ffi ffl & *ff fi fl ffi ffl &* .,“”:;? ! [ ] ( ) st ct 1234567890
abcdefghijklmnopqrstuvwxyz abcdefghijklmno
pqrstuvwxyz abcdefghijkklmnopqrstuvwxyz abcdefghi

18 HIJKLMNOPQRSTUVWXYZ ABCDEFGHIJKLMNOPQ
RSTUVWXYZ ABCDEFGHIJKLMNOPQRSTUVWXYZ
abcdefghijklmnopqrstuvwxyz ct st *abcdefghijkklmnopqrstuvwxyz*

14 ABCDEFGHIJKLMNOPQRSTUVW *ABCDEFGHIJKLMNOPQRSTUV*
XYZAB abcdefghijklmnopqrstuvwxyz *123456789012 abcdefghijklmnopqrstuvwxyz*

12 ABCDEFGHIJKLMNOPQRSTUVWXY? *ABCDEFGHIJKLMNOPQRSTUVWXY*
abcdefghijklmnopqrstuvwxyz ABCDEFGHIJK *abcdefghijklmnopqrstuvwxyzabcdef* 1234567890

10 ABCDEFGHIJKLMNOPQRSTUVWXYZ ABCDE *ABCDEFGHIJKLMNOPQRSTUVWXYZABCD*
ghijklmnopqrstuvwxyzabcd ABCDEFGHIJKLMNOPQRST *efghijklmnopqrstuvwxyzabcdefghijklmnopqrs* 1234567890

28

● **1530 . GARAMOND .** Typeface . Claude Garamond

→ p.355

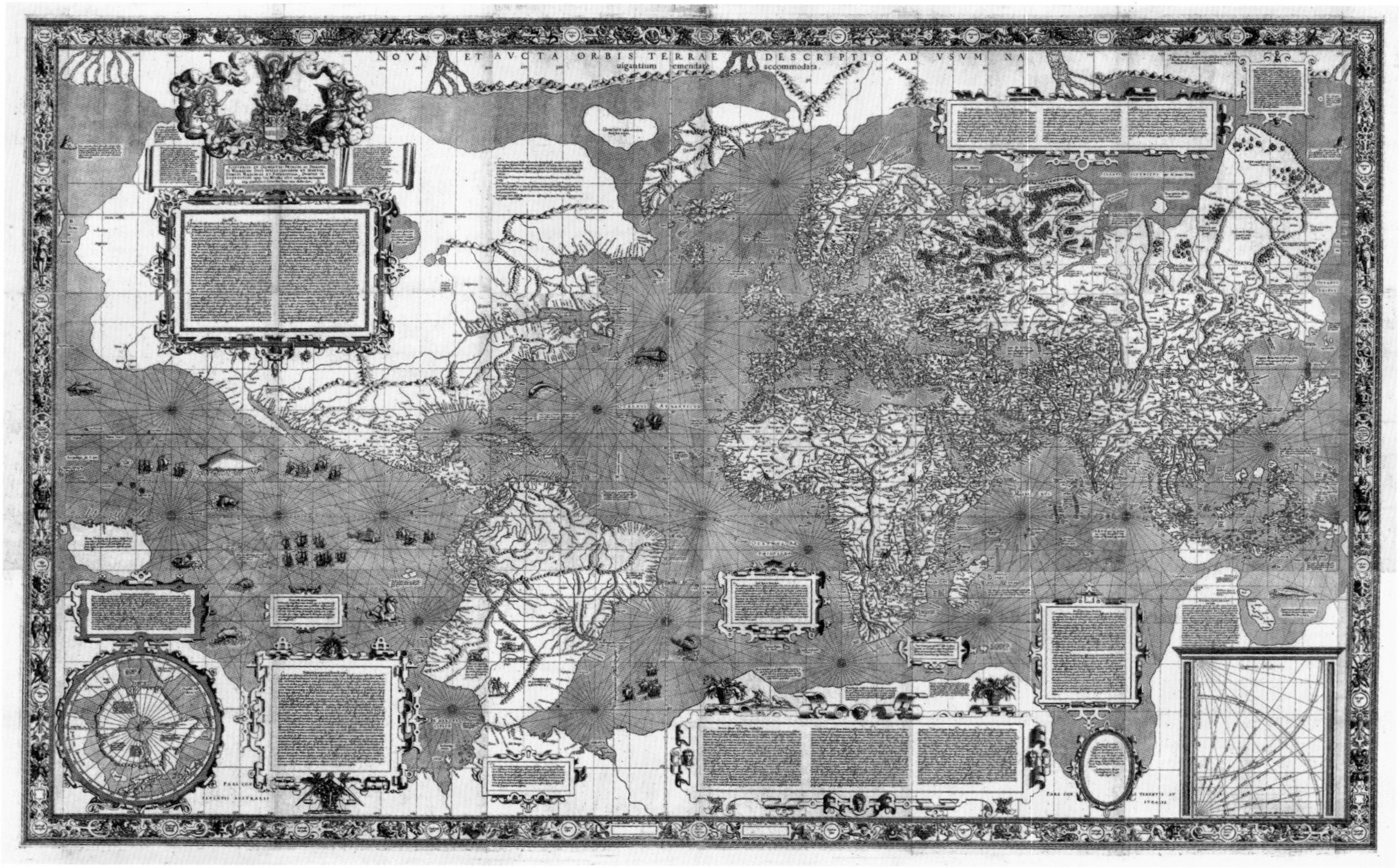

● **1569 . MERCATOR PROJECTION .** Information Design . Gerardus Mercator

→ p.356

● **1734 . CASLON .** Typeface . William Caslon

→ p.356

● c. **1750 . MUSIC NOTATION (FIVE-LINE STAVE) .** Information Design . Unknown

→ p.356

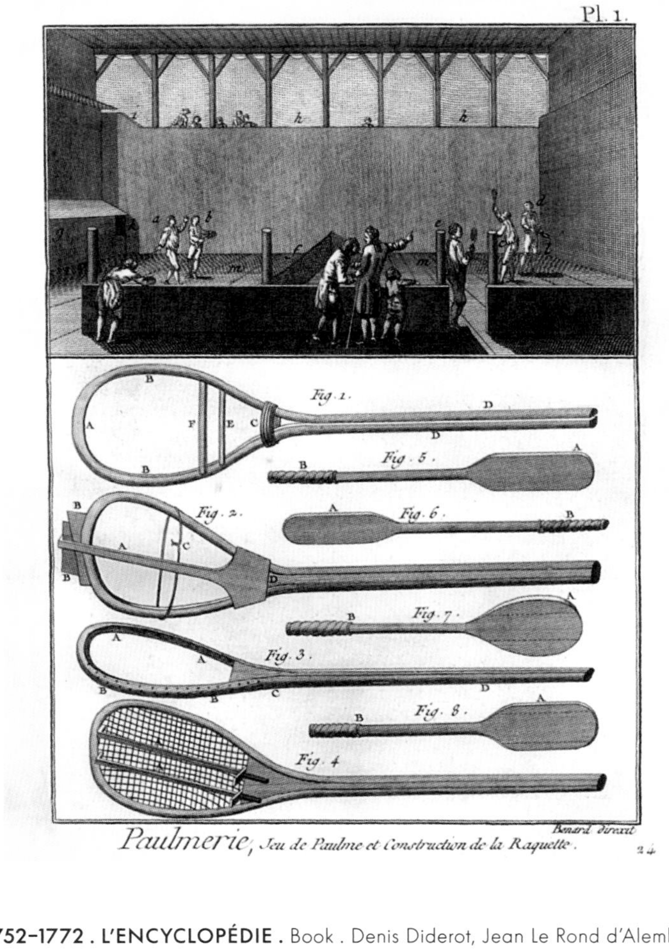

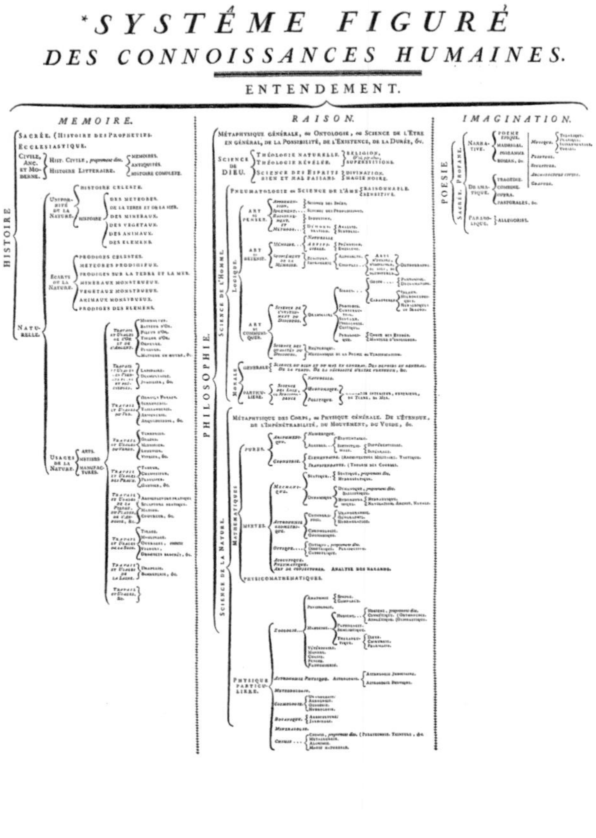

● **1752–1772 . L'ENCYCLOPÉDIE .** Book . Denis Diderot, Jean Le Rond d'Alembert, Louis-Jacques Goussier

→ p.357

● **1754 . JOIN, OR DIE .** Information Design . Benjamin Franklin
RIGHT: *Pennsylvania Gazette*, 1754

→ p.357

A

S P E C I M E N

By *JOHN BASKERVILLE* of *Birmingham.*

I Am indebted to you for two Letters dated from Corcyra. You congratulate me in one of them on the Account you have Received, that I ſtill preſerve my former Authority in the Commonwealth: and wiſh me Joy in the other of my late Marriage. With reſpect to the Firſt, *if to mean well to the Intereſt of my Country and to approve that meaning to every Friend of its Liberties, may be conſider'd as maintaining my Authority; the Account you have heard is certainly true. But if it conſiſts in rendering thoſe Sentiments effectual to the Public Welfare or at leaſt in daring freely to Support and inforce them;*

I Am indebted to you for two Letters dated from Corcyra. You congratulate me in one of them on the Account you have Received, that I ſtill preſerve my former Authority in the Commonwealth: and wiſh me Joy in the other of my late Marriage. With reſpect to the firſt, if to mean well to the Intereſt of my Country and to approve that meaning to every Friend of its Liberties, may be conſider'd as maintaining my Authority; the Account you have heard is certainly true. But if it conſiſts in rendering thoſe Sentiments effectual to the Public Welfare or at leaſt in daring freely to Support and inforce them; alas! my Friend I have not the leaſt ſha-

I Am indebted to you for two Letters dated from Corcyra. You congratulate me in one of them on the Account you have received, that I ſtill preſerve my former Authority in the Commonwealth: and wiſh me joy in the other of my late Marriage. With reſpect to the Firſt, if to mean well to the Intereſt of my Country and to approve that meaning to every Friend of its Liberties, may be conſider'd as maintaining *my Authority; the Account you have heard is certainly true. But if it conſiſts in rendering thoſe Sentiments effectual to the Public Welfare or at leaſt in daring freely to Support and inforce them; alas! my Friend I have not the leaſt ſhadow of Authority remaining. The Truth of it is, it will be ſufficient Honor if I can have ſo much Authority over myſelf as to bear with patience our preſent and impending Calamities: a frame of Mind not to be acquired without difficulty,*

Q. HORATII FLACCI

Hac ego ſi compellar imag[illegible] cuncta reſigno.
Nec ſomnum plebis laudo ſatur altilium; nec
Otia divitiis Arabum liberrima muto.
Sæpe verecundum laudaſti: rexque, paterque
Audiſti coram, nec verbo parcius abſens
Inſpice ſi poſſum donata reponere lætus.
Haud male Telemachus proles patientis Ulyſſei;
Non eſt aptus equis Ithacæ locus, ut neque planis
Porrectus ſpatiis, neque multæ prodigus herbæ:
Atride, magis apta tibi tua dona relinquam.
Parvum parva decent. mihi jam non regia Roma,
Sed vacuum Tibur placet, aut imbelle Tarentum.
Strenuus et fortis, cauſiſque Philippus agendis

EPISTOLARUM LIBER I.

Clarus, ab officiis octavam circiter horam
Dum redit, atque foro nimium diſtare Carinas
Jam grandis natu queritur; conſpexit, ut aiunt,
Adraſum quendam vacua tonſoris in umbra
Cultello proprios purgantem leniter ungues.
Demetri, (puer hic non læve juſſa Philippi (quis,
Accipiebat) abi, quære, et refer; unde domo,
Cujus fortunæ, quo ſit patre, quove patrono.
It, redit, et narrat, Vulteium nomine Menam
Præconem, tenui cenſu ſine crimine notum,
Et properare loco, et ceſſare, et quærere, et uti
Gaudentem parviſque ſodalibus, et lare certo,
Et ludis, et poſt deciſa negotia, Campo.

145

→ p.357

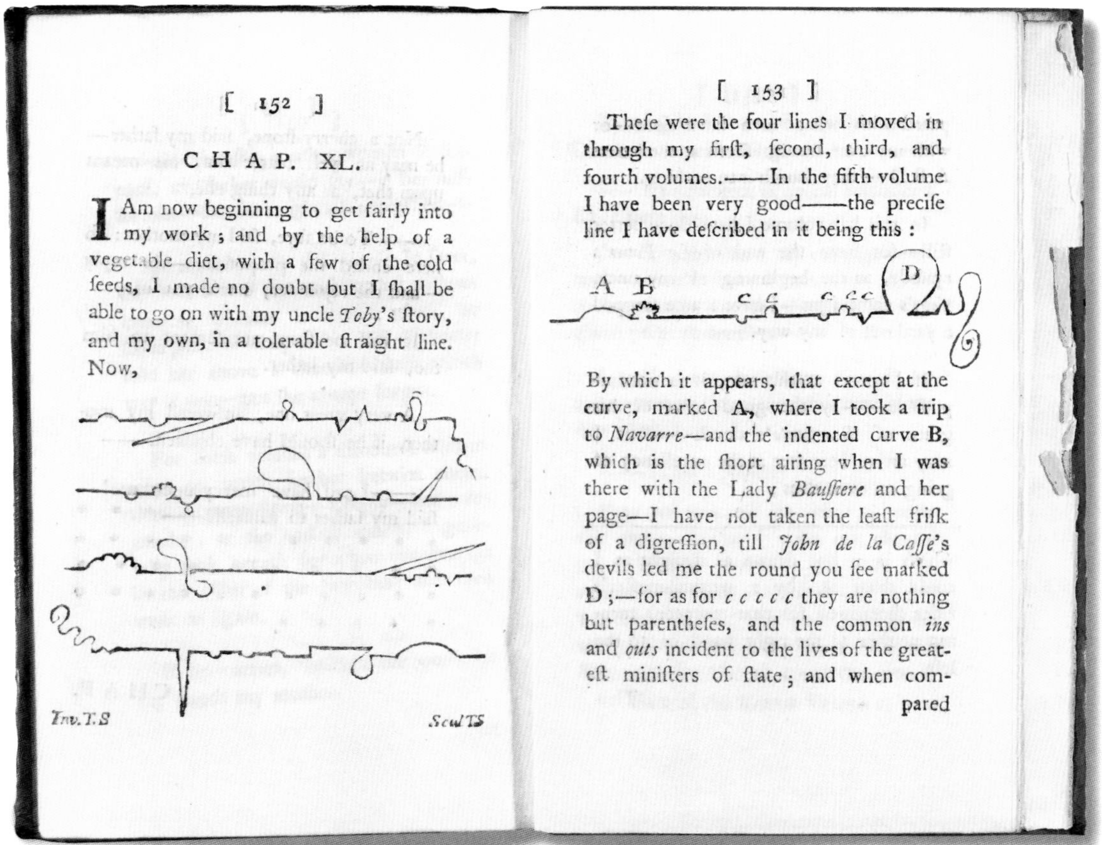
[152]

CHAP. XL.

I Am now beginning to get fairly into my work; and by the help of a vegetable diet, with a few of the cold feeds, I made no doubt but I fhall be able to go on with my uncle *Toby*'s ftory, and my own, in a tolerable ftraight line. Now,

[153]

Thefe were the four lines I moved in through my firft, fecond, third, and fourth volumes.——In the fifth volume I have been very good——the precife line I have defcribed in it being this:

By which it appears, that except at the curve, marked A, where I took a trip to *Navarre*—and the indented curve B, which is the fhort airing when I was there with the Lady *Bauffiere* and her page—I have not taken the leaft frifk of a digreffion, till *John de la Caffe*'s devils led me the round you fee marked D;—for as for *c c c c c* they are nothing but parenthefes, and the common *ins* and *outs* incident to the lives of the greateft minifters of ftate; and when compared

1759–1767 . THE LIFE AND OPINIONS OF TRISTRAM SHANDY . Book . Laurence Sterne

→ p.358

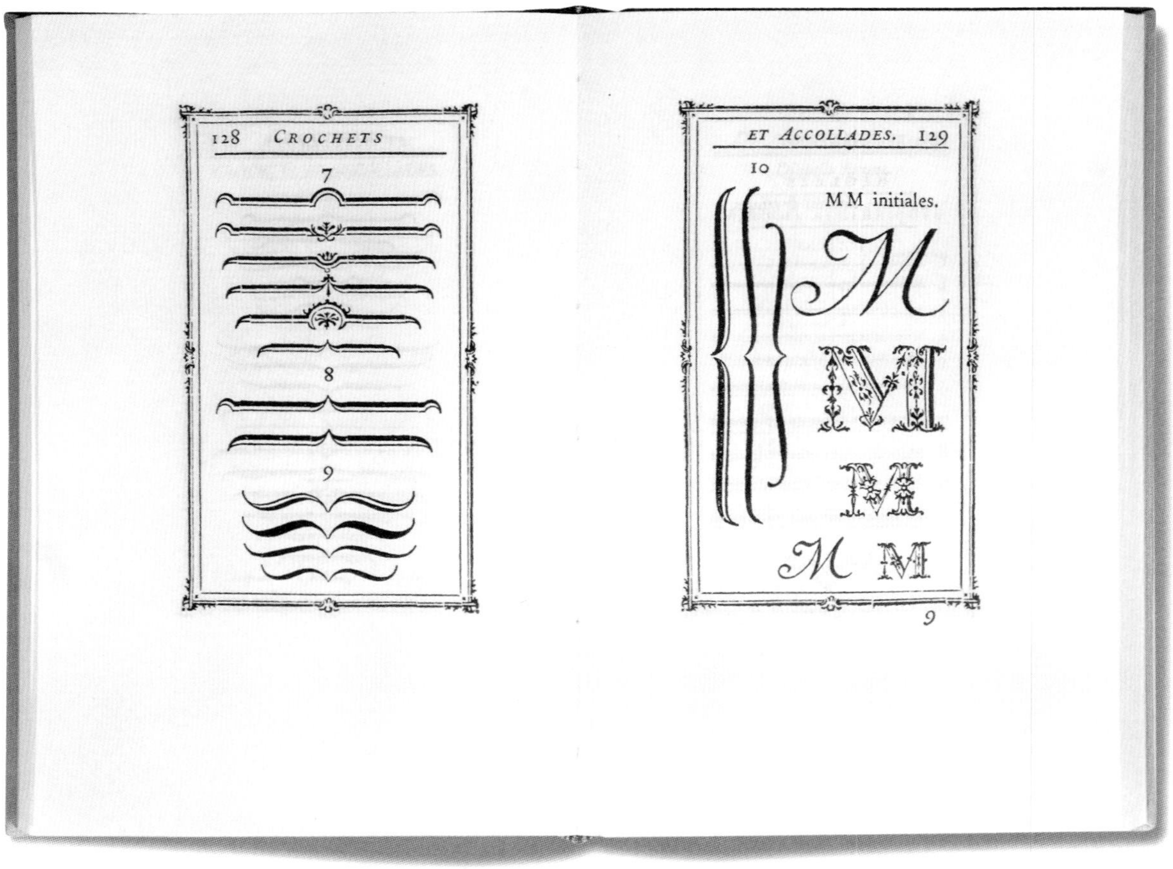
128 *Crochets*

7

8

9

et Accollades. 129

10

M M initiales.

9

1764–1766 . MANUEL TYPOGRAPHIQUE . Book . Pierre-Simon Fournier

→ p.358

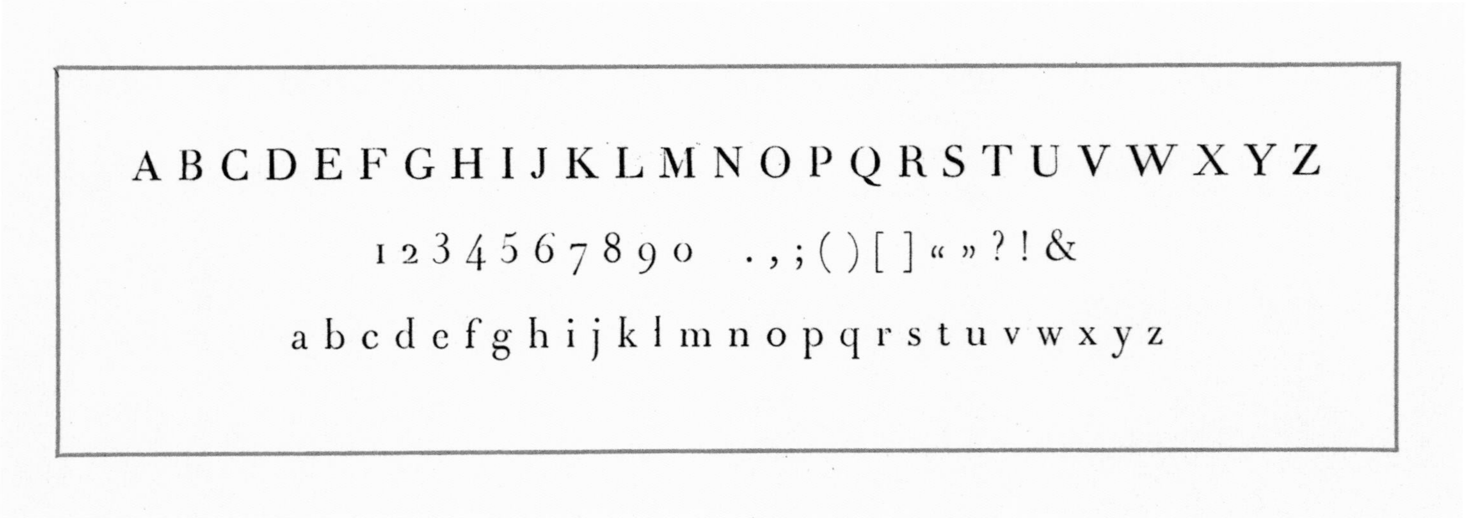

● c. 1784 . **DIDOT** . Typeface . Firmin Didot

→ p.358

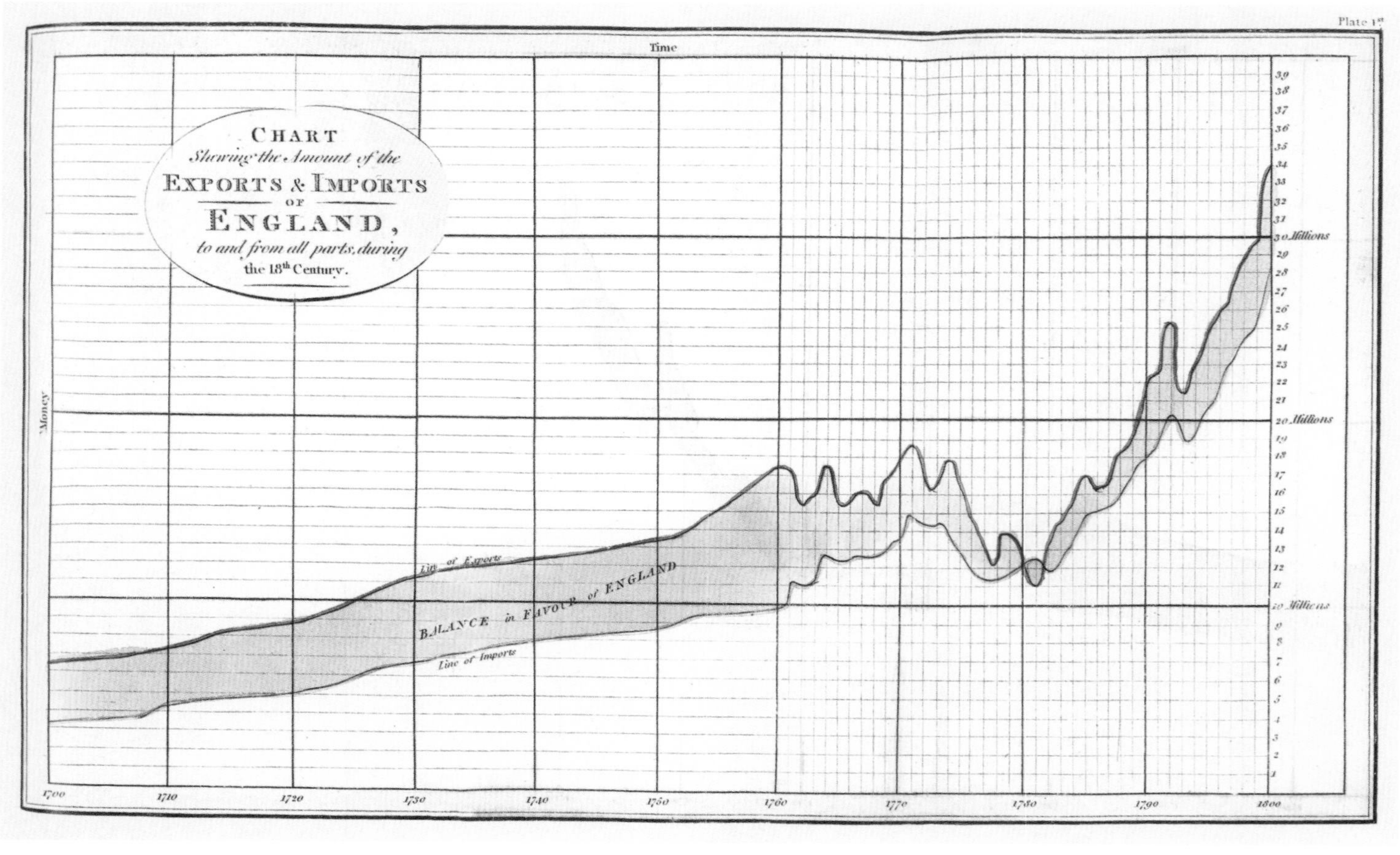

● 1786 . **THE COMMERCIAL AND POLITICAL ATLAS** . Book . William Playfair

→ p.359

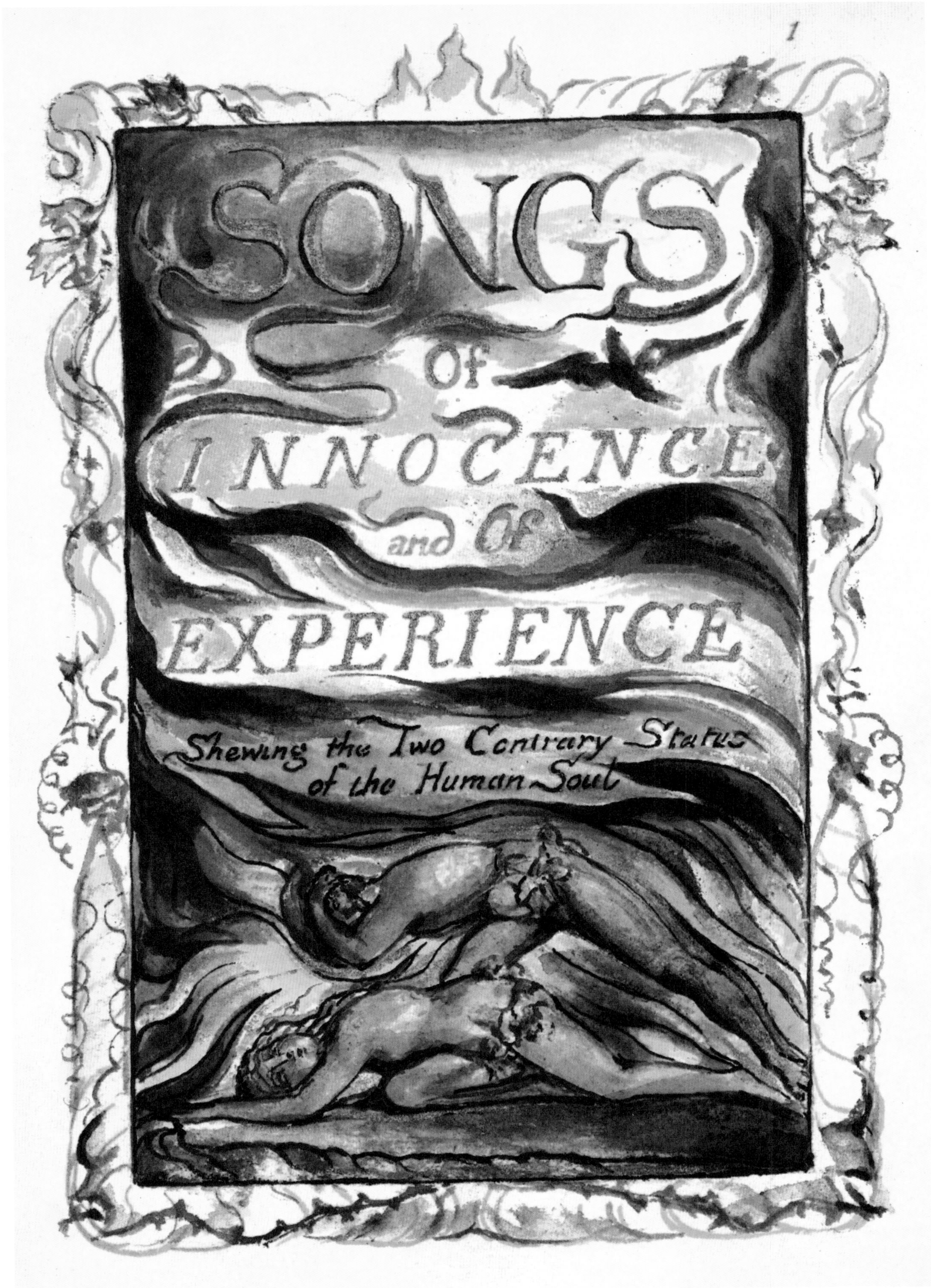

1789–1794 . SONGS OF INNOCENCE AND OF EXPERIENCE . Book . William Blake

→ p.359

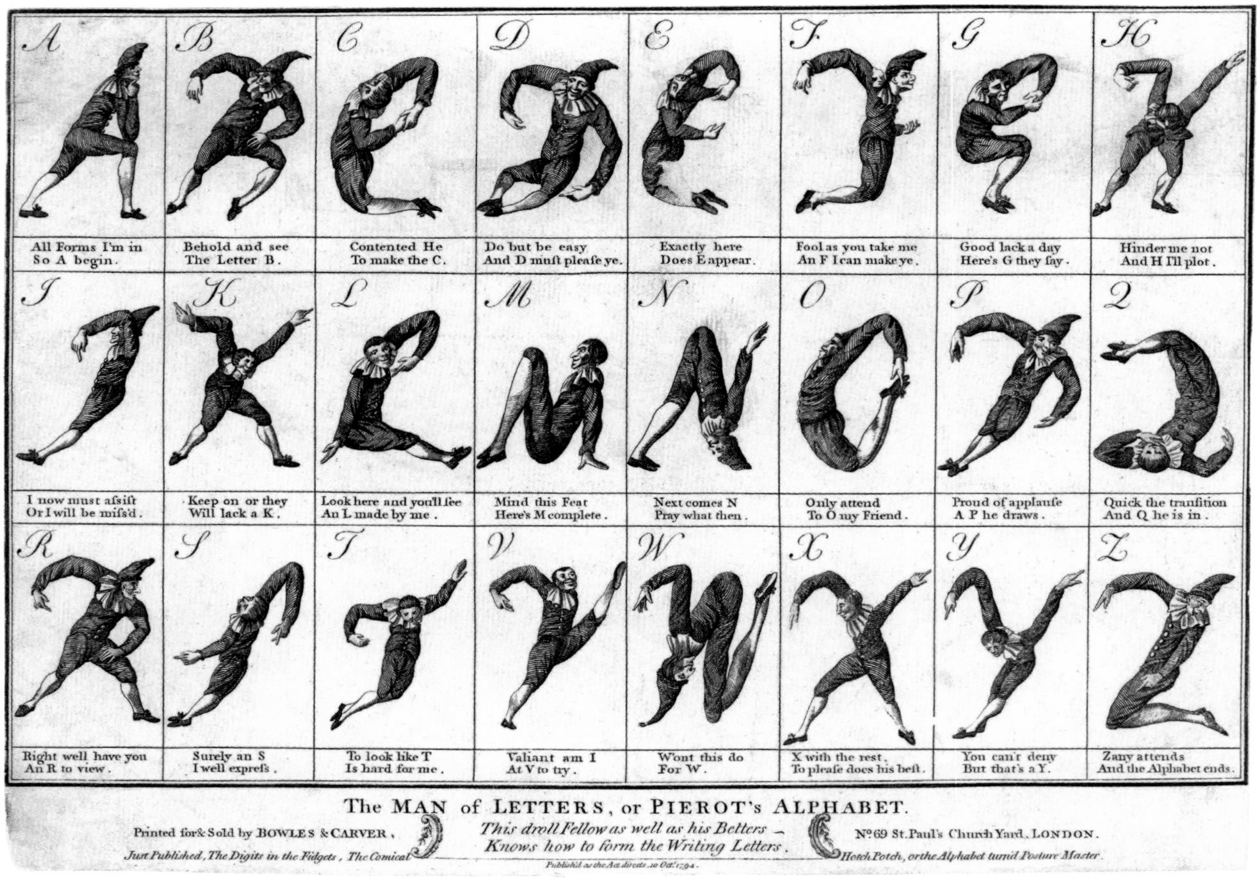

● **1794 . THE MAN OF LETTERS, OR PIERROT'S ALPHABET .** Typeface . Unknown

→ p.359

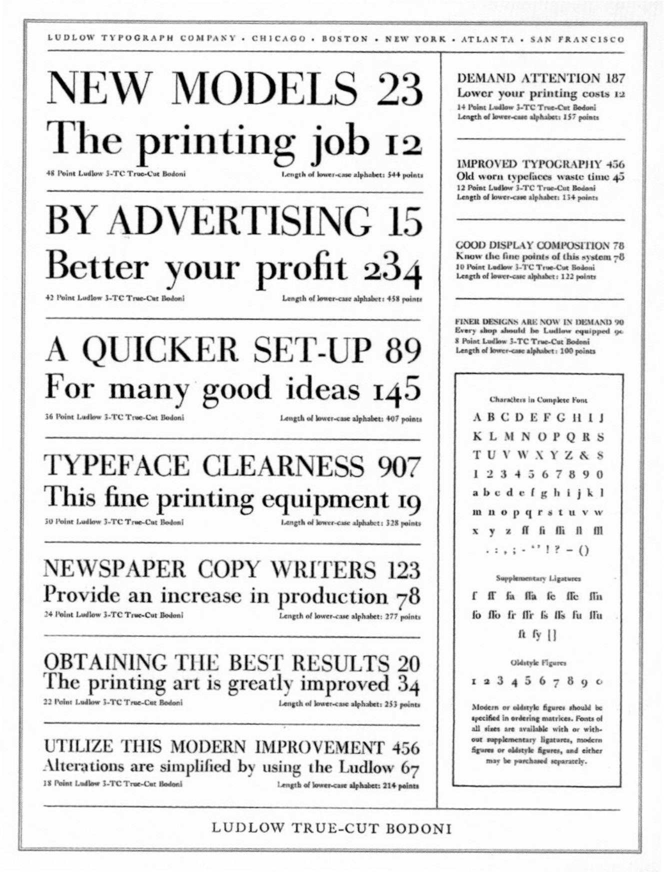
LUDLOW TYPOGRAPH COMPANY • CHICAGO • BOSTON • NEW YORK • ATLANTA • SAN FRANCISCO

NEW MODELS 23
The printing job 12
48 Point Ludlow 3-TC True-Cut Bodoni — Length of lower-case alphabet: 544 points

BY ADVERTISING 15
Better your profit 234
42 Point Ludlow 3-TC True-Cut Bodoni — Length of lower-case alphabet: 458 points

A QUICKER SET-UP 89
For many good ideas 145
36 Point Ludlow 3-TC True-Cut Bodoni — Length of lower-case alphabet: 407 points

TYPEFACE CLEARNESS 907
This fine printing equipment 19
30 Point Ludlow 3-TC True-Cut Bodoni — Length of lower-case alphabet: 328 points

NEWSPAPER COPY WRITERS 123
Provide an increase in production 78
24 Point Ludlow 3-TC True-Cut Bodoni — Length of lower-case alphabet: 277 points

OBTAINING THE BEST RESULTS 20
The printing art is greatly improved 34
22 Point Ludlow 3-TC True-Cut Bodoni — Length of lower-case alphabet: 253 points

UTILIZE THIS MODERN IMPROVEMENT 456
Alterations are simplified by using the Ludlow 67
18 Point Ludlow 3-TC True-Cut Bodoni — Length of lower-case alphabet: 214 points

DEMAND ATTENTION 187
Lower your printing costs 12
14 Point Ludlow 3-TC True-Cut Bodoni
Length of lower-case alphabet: 157 points

IMPROVED TYPOGRAPHY 456
Old worn typefaces waste time 45
12 Point Ludlow 3-TC True-Cut Bodoni
Length of lower-case alphabet: 134 points

GOOD DISPLAY COMPOSITION 78
Know the fine points of this system 78
10 Point Ludlow 3-TC True-Cut Bodoni
Length of lower-case alphabet: 122 points

FINER DESIGNS ARE NOW IN DEMAND 90
Every shop should be Ludlow equipped 90
8 Point Ludlow 3-TC True-Cut Bodoni
Length of lower-case alphabet: 100 points

Characters in Complete Font
A B C D E F G H I J
K L M N O P Q R S
T U V W X Y Z & $
1 2 3 4 5 6 7 8 9 0
a b c d e f g h i j k l
m n o p q r s t u v w
x y z ff fi ffi fl ffl
. : , ; - ' ' ! ? – ()

Supplementary Ligatures
ſ ſſ ſa ſſa ſe ſſe ſſi
ſo ſſo ſr ſſr ſs ſſs ſu ſſu
ſt ſy [ ]

Oldstyle Figures
1 2 3 4 5 6 7 8 9 0

Modern or oldstyle figures should be specified in ordering matrices. Fonts of all sizes are available with or without supplementary ligatures, modern figures or oldstyle figures, and either may be purchased separately.

LUDLOW TRUE-CUT BODONI

● **1798 . BODONI .** Typeface . Giambattista Bodoni

→ p.360

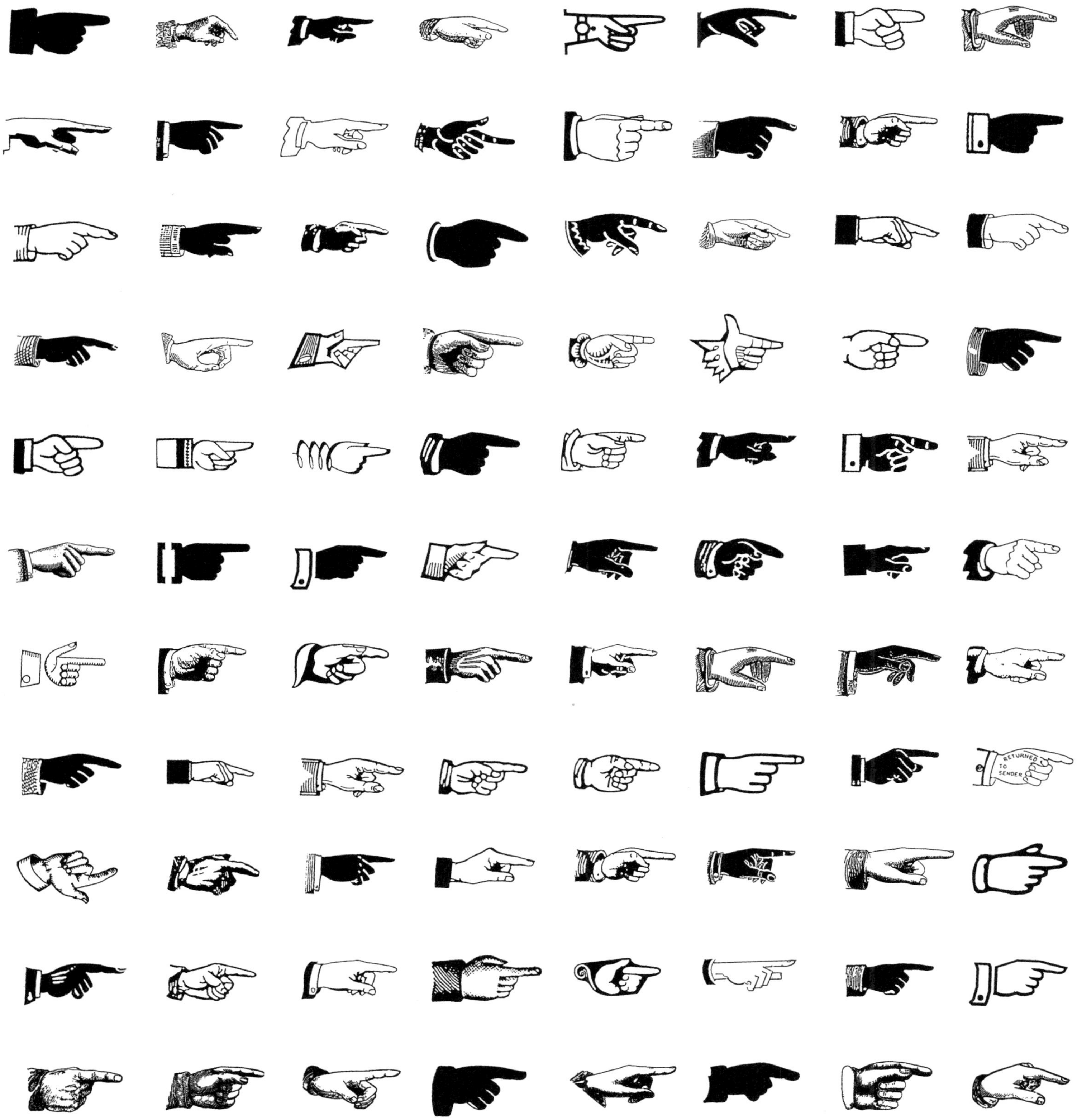

c. 1800 . **PRINTERS' FIST** . Information Design . Various

→ p.360

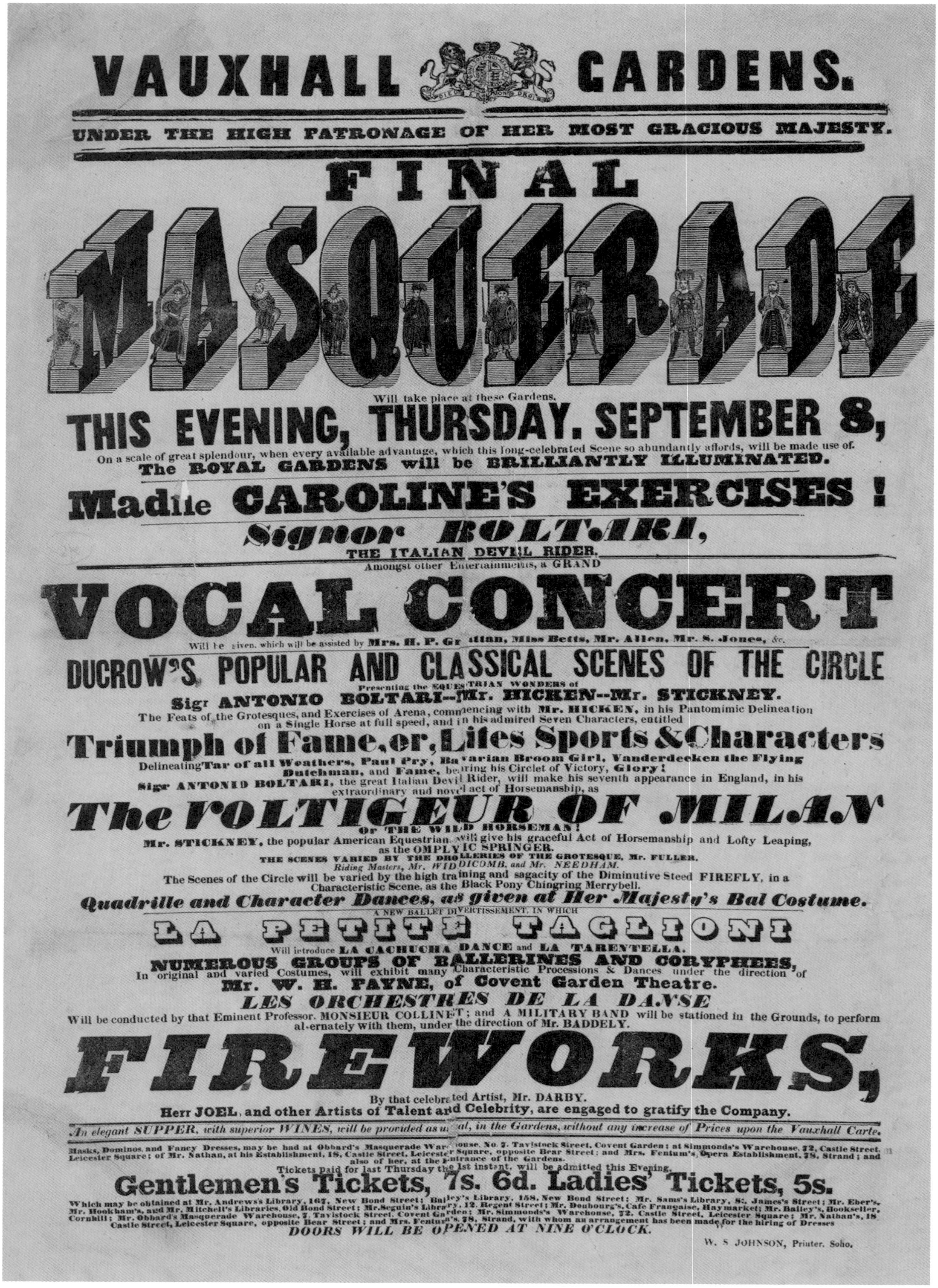

● c. 1800–1900 . **BILL POSTERS** . Poster . Various
W. S. Johnson, 1859

→ p.360

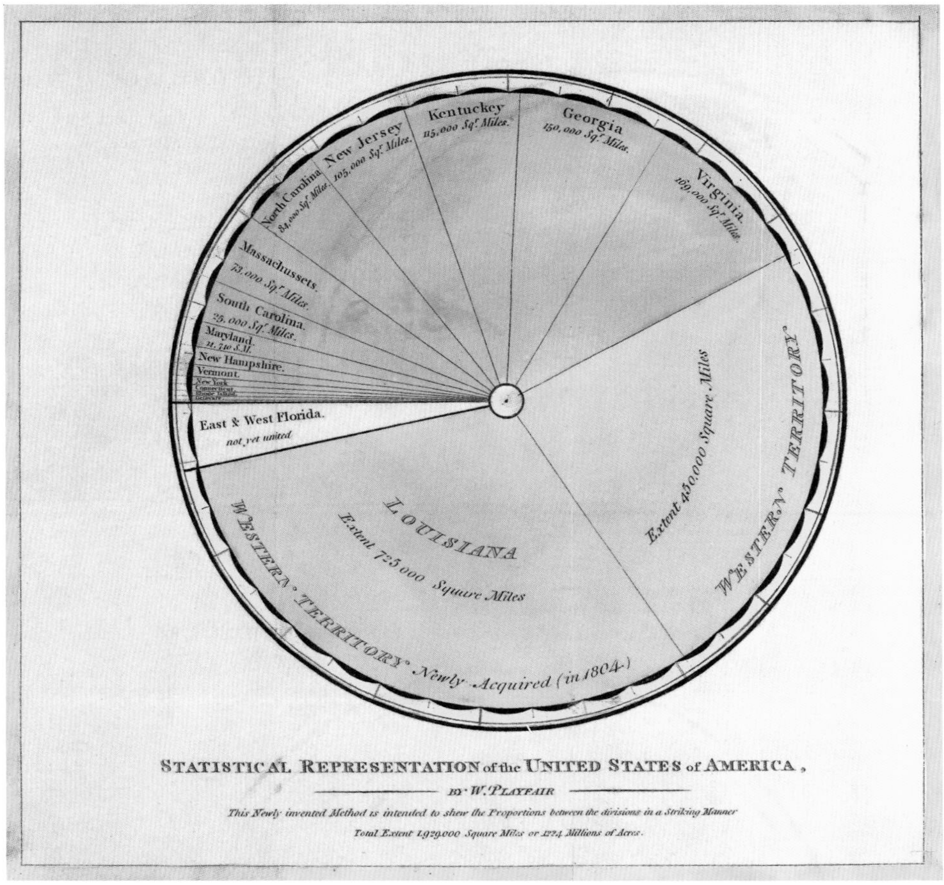

● **1801 . PIE CHART** . Information Design . William Playfair

→ p.361

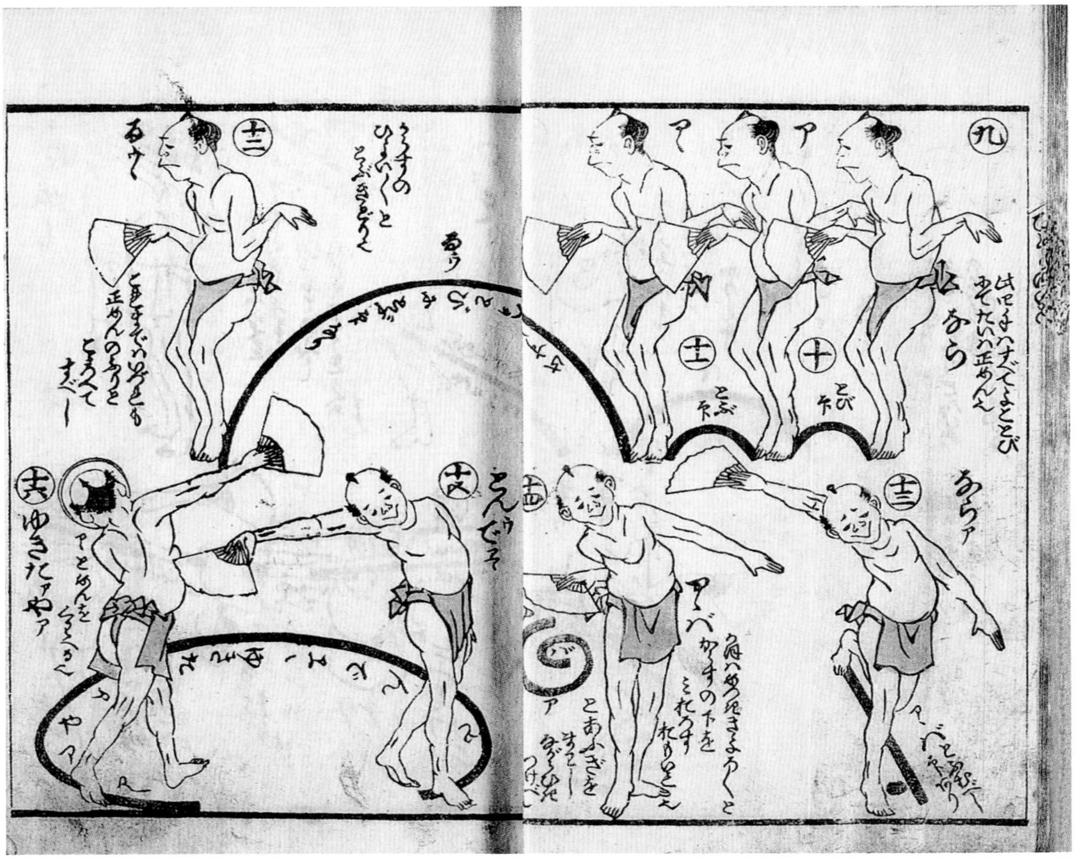

● **1814–1878 . HOKUSAI MANGA .** Book . Katsushika Hokusai
"Self-taught Dancing Apprenticeship," Vol. 1, 1814

→ p.361

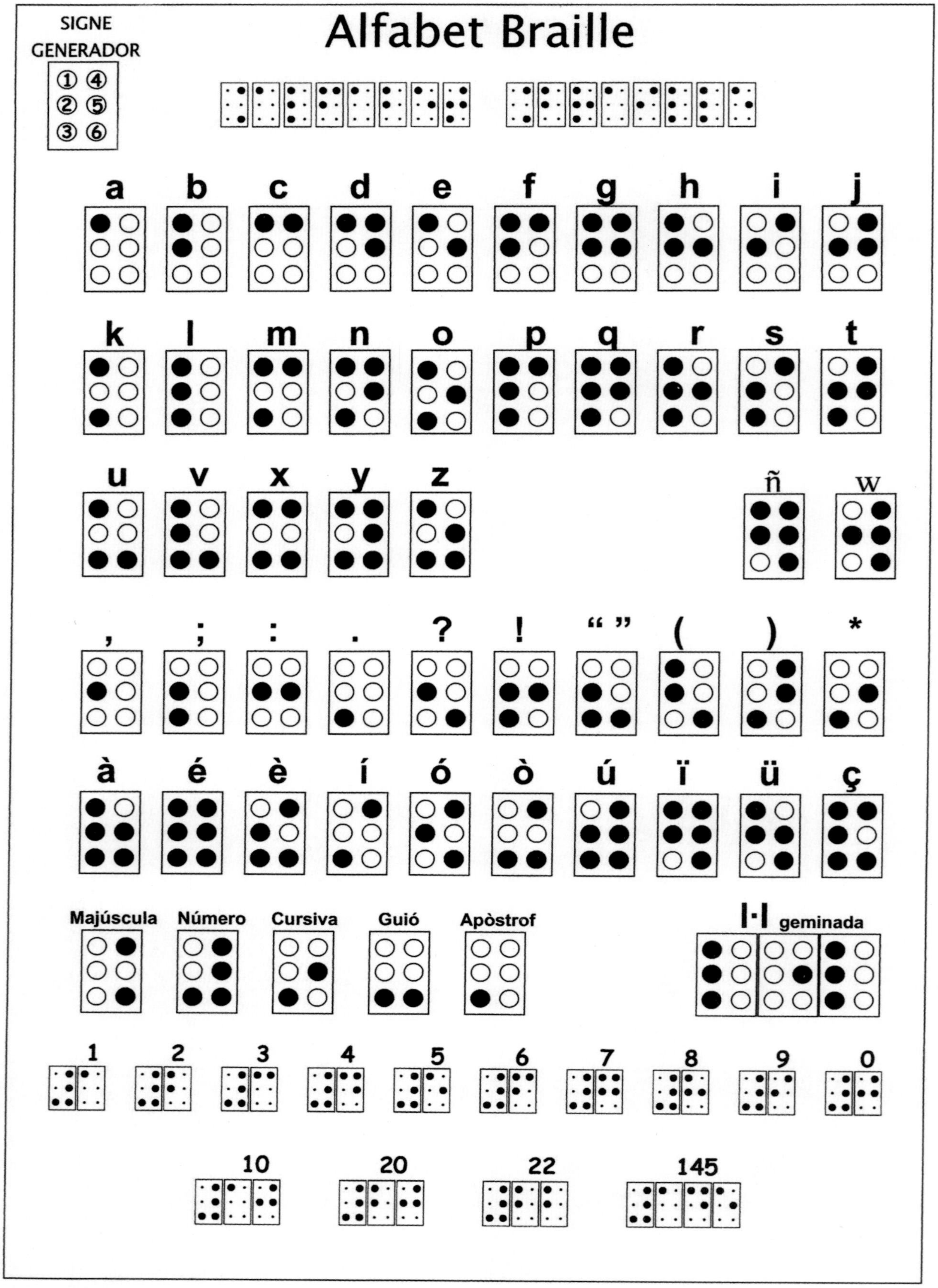

● **1829 . BRAILLE .** Information Design . Louis Braille

→ p.361

Letters

a	• —
b	— • • •
c	— • — •
d	— • •
e	•
f	• • — •
g	— — •
h	• • • •
i	• •
j	• — — —
k	— • —
l	• — • •
m	— —
n	— •
o	— — —
p	• — — •
q	— — • —
r	• — •
s	• • •
t	—
u	• • —
v	• • • —
w	• — —
x	— • • —
y	— • — —
z	— — • •
Fullstop	• — • — • —
Comma	— — • • — —
Query	• • — — • •

Numbers

0	— — — — —
1	• — — — —
2	• • — — —
3	• • • — —
4	• • • • —
5	• • • • •
6	— • • • •
7	— — • • •
8	— — — • •
9	— — — — •

1838 . MORSE CODE . Information Design . Samuel Finley Breese Morse

→ p.362

● **1841–2002 . PUNCH .** Magazine / Newspaper . Mark Lemon et al.
Vol. 148, No. 3836, January 13, 1915

→ p.362

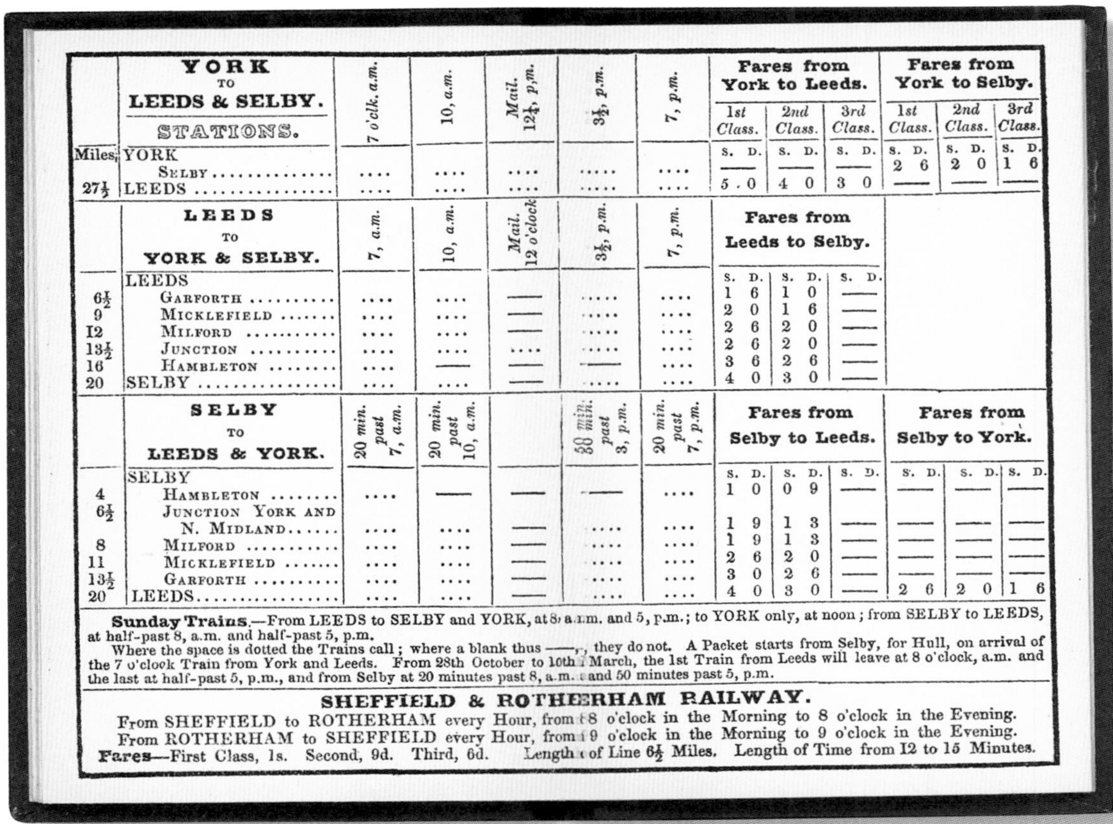

Miles	YORK TO LEEDS & SELBY. STATIONS.	7 o'clk. a.m.	10, a.m.	Mail. 12¼, p.m.	3½, p.m.	7, p.m.	Fares from York to Leeds. 1st Class. s. d.	2nd Class. s. d.	3rd Class. s. d.	Fares from York to Selby. 1st Class. s. d.	2nd Class. s. d.	3rd Class. s. d.
	YORK											
	SELBY	....	....	....	....	....	—	—	—	2 6	2 0	1 6
27½	LEEDS	....	....	....	....	....	5 . 0	4 0	3 0	—	—	—

Miles	LEEDS TO YORK & SELBY.	7, a.m.	10, a.m.	Mail. 12 o'clock	3½, p.m.	7, p.m.	Fares from Leeds to Selby. s. d.	s. d.	s. d.
	LEEDS								
6½	GARFORTH	....	....	—	....	....	1 6	1 0	—
9	MICKLEFIELD	....	....	—	....	....	2 0	1 6	—
12	MILFORD	....	....	—	....	....	2 6	2 0	—
13½	JUNCTION	....	....	....	....	....	2 6	2 0	—
16	HAMBLETON	....	—	—	—	....	3 6	2 6	—
20	SELBY	....	....	—	....	....	4 0	3 0	—

Miles	SELBY TO LEEDS & YORK.	20 min. past 7, a.m.	20 min. past 10, a.m.		50 min. past 3, p.m.	20 min. past 7, p.m.	Fares from Selby to Leeds. s. d.	s. d.	s. d.	Fares from Selby to York. s. d.	s. d.	s. d.
	SELBY											
4	HAMBLETON	....	—	—	—	....	1 0	0 9	—	—	—	—
6½	JUNCTION YORK AND N. MIDLAND	....	....	—	....	....	1 9	1 3	—	—	—	—
8	MILFORD	....	....	—	....	....	1 9	1 3	—	—	—	—
11	MICKLEFIELD	....	....	—	....	....	2 6	2 0	—	—	—	—
13½	GARFORTH	....	....	—	....	....	3 0	2 6	—	—	—	—
20	LEEDS	....	....	—	....	....	4 0	3 0	—	2 6	2 0	1 6

Sunday Trains.—From LEEDS to SELBY and YORK, at 8, a.m. and 5, p.m.; to YORK only, at noon; from SELBY to LEEDS, at half-past 8, a.m. and half-past 5, p.m.

Where the space is dotted the Trains call; where a blank thus ——, they do not. A Packet starts from Selby, for Hull, on arrival of the 7 o'clock Train from York and Leeds. From 28th October to 10th March, the 1st Train from Leeds will leave at 8 o'clock, a.m. and the last at half-past 5, p.m., and from Selby at 20 minutes past 8, a.m. and 50 minutes past 5, p.m.

SHEFFIELD & ROTHERHAM RAILWAY.

From SHEFFIELD to ROTHERHAM every Hour, from 8 o'clock in the Morning to 8 o'clock in the Evening.
From ROTHERHAM to SHEFFIELD every Hour, from 9 o'clock in the Morning to 9 o'clock in the Evening.
Fares—First Class, 1s. Second, 9d. Third, 6d. Length of Line 6½ Miles. Length of Time from 12 to 15 Minutes.

1841–1961 . BRADSHAW'S MONTHLY RAILWAY GUIDE . Information Design . George Bradshaw

→ p.362

TWO LINES ENGLISH CLARENDON.

The municipal orders produced for England
MORNING CONCERT

DOUBLE PICA CLARENDON.

WHEREAS in pursuance of an Act passed in the reign of King George the Third of
SPECIMEN OF PRINTING

GREAT PRIMER CLARENDON.

WHEREAS in pursuance of the Act passed in the reign of King George the Third suppressing the
MODERN EMBELLISHMENT

PICA CLARENDON.

WHEREAS, in pursuance of this Act passed during the twentieth year of the reign of King George the Third, for the entire suppression of Societies
MEMOIRS OF EMINENT PAINTERS

REED AND FOX (LATE R. BESLEY & CO.), LONDON.

FOUR LINES PICA CONDENSED CLARENDON. No. 2.

MODERN
hunter
Mansion

FOUR LINES PICA EXTENDED CLARENDON

HOUSE
miner
Romans

REED AND FOX (LATE R. BESLEY & CO.), LONDON.

1845 . CLARENDON . Typeface . Robert Besley

→ p.363

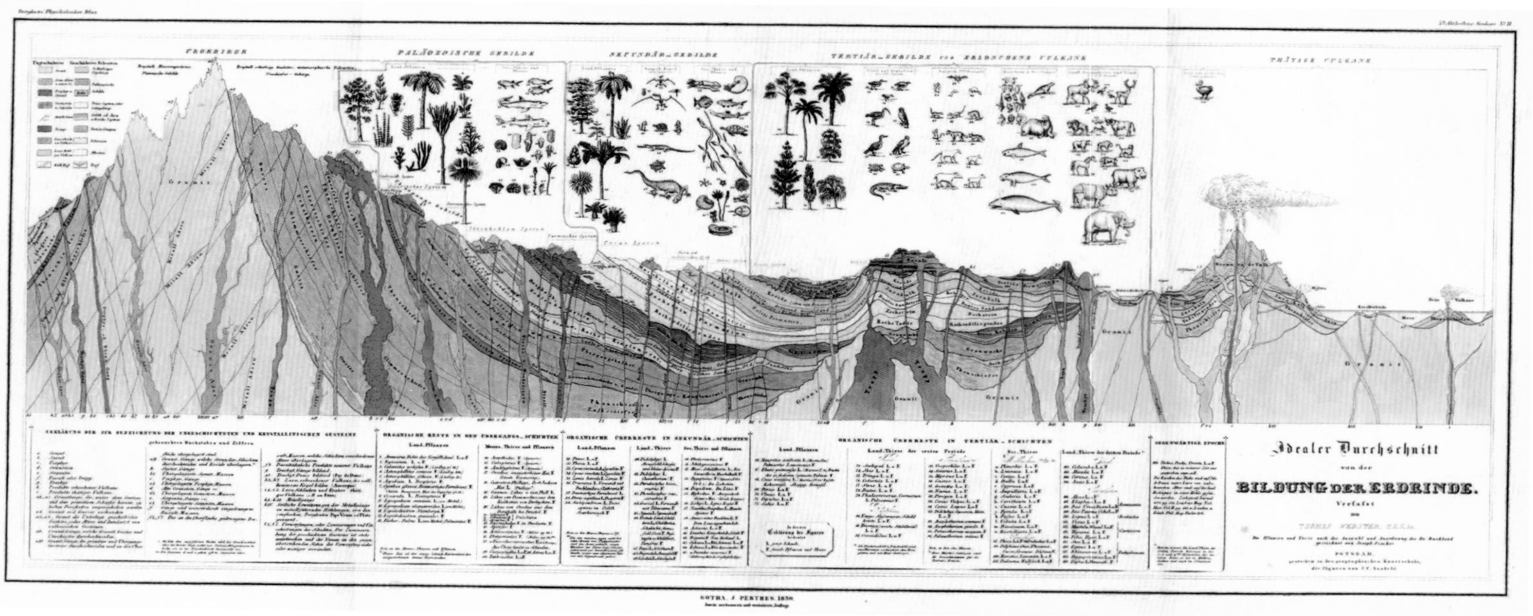

● **1845/1848 . PHYSIKALISCHER ATLAS .** Book . Heinrich Berghaus

→ p.363

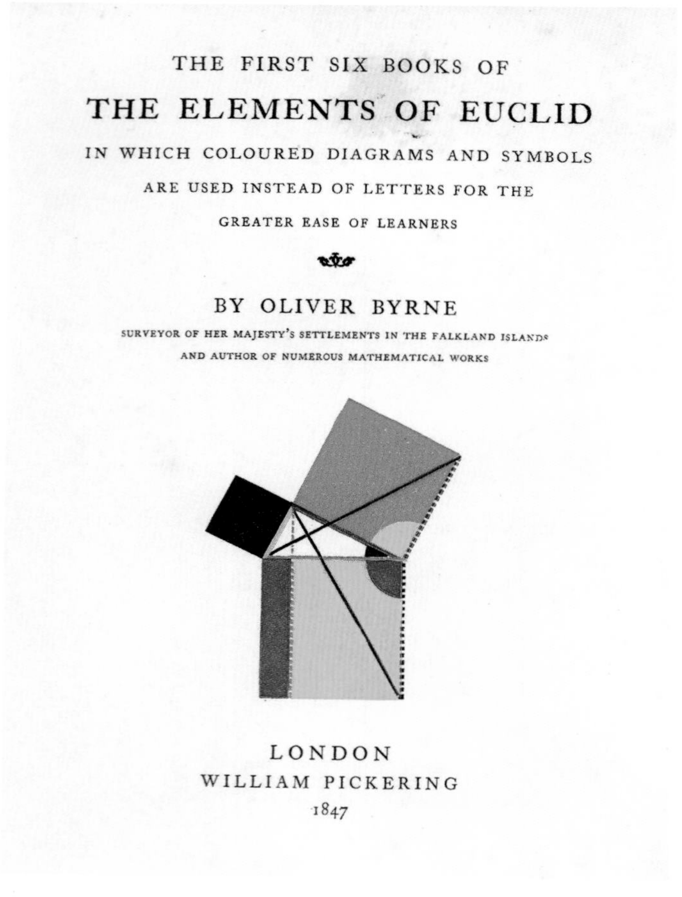

THE FIRST SIX BOOKS OF
THE ELEMENTS OF EUCLID
IN WHICH COLOURED DIAGRAMS AND SYMBOLS
ARE USED INSTEAD OF LETTERS FOR THE
GREATER EASE OF LEARNERS

BY OLIVER BYRNE
SURVEYOR OF HER MAJESTY'S SETTLEMENTS IN THE FALKLAND ISLANDS
AND AUTHOR OF NUMEROUS MATHEMATICAL WORKS

LONDON
WILLIAM PICKERING
1847

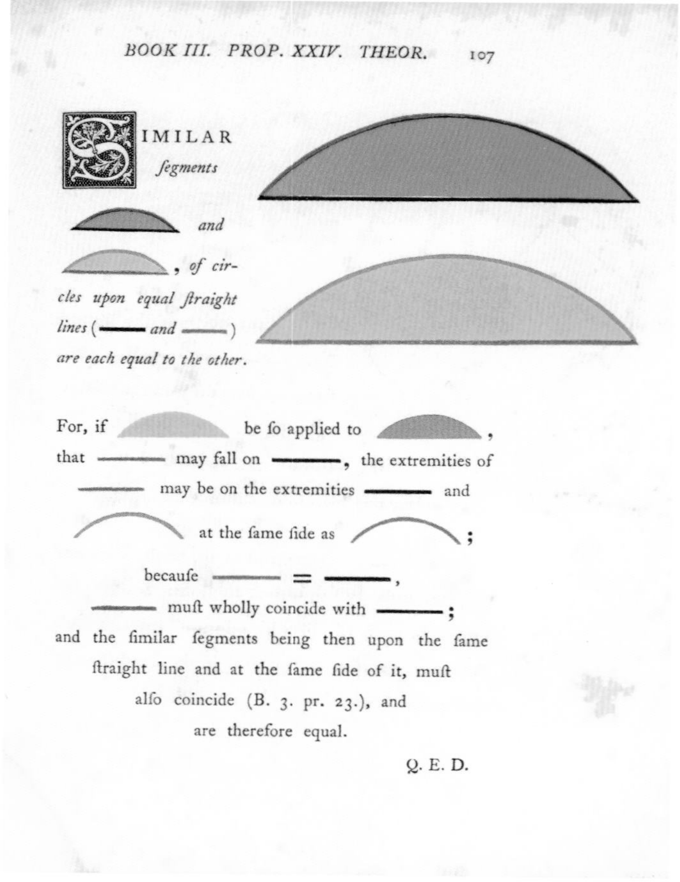

BOOK III. PROP. XXIV. THEOR. 107

SIMILAR ſegments and , of circles upon equal ſtraight lines (and) are each equal to the other.

For, if be ſo applied to , that may fall on , the extremities of may be on the extremities and at the ſame ſide as ;

becauſe = , must wholly coincide with ; and the ſimilar ſegments being then upon the ſame ſtraight line and at the ſame ſide of it, muſt alſo coincide (B. 3. pr. 23.), and are therefore equal.

Q. E. D.

● **1847 . THE ELEMENTS OF EUCLID .** Book . Oliver Byrne

→ p.363

● **1850 . FETTE FRAKTUR .** Typeface . Johann Christian Bauer

→ p.364

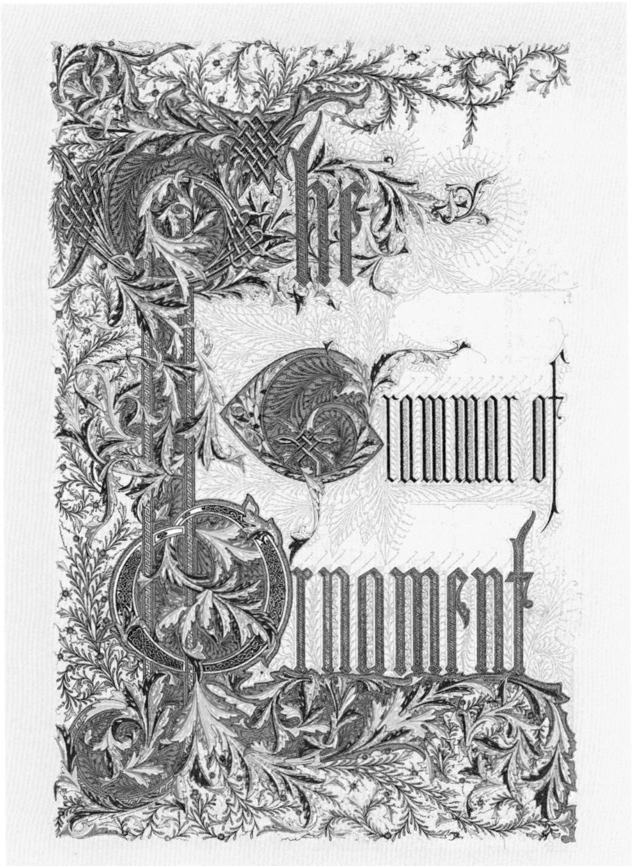

● **1856 . THE GRAMMAR OF ORNAMENT .** Book . Owen Jones

→ p.364

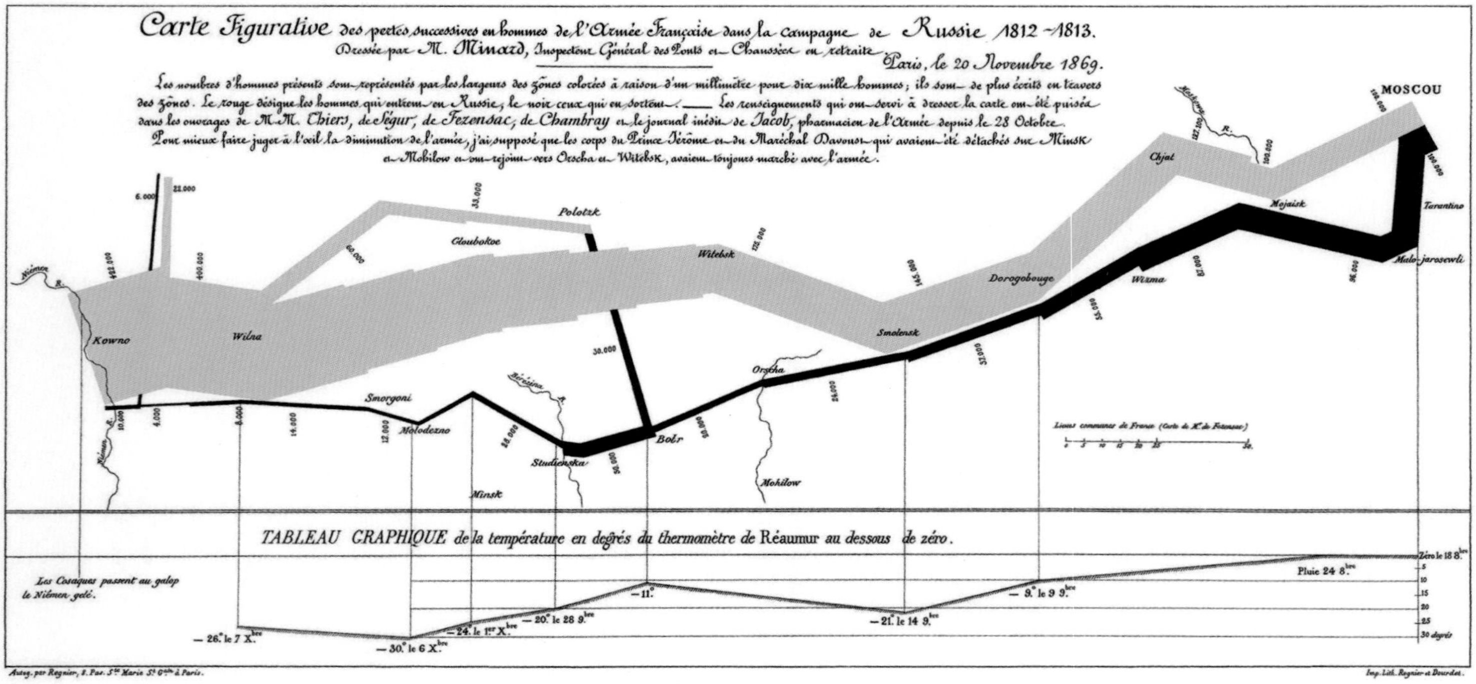

1861 . **NAPOLEON'S MARCH .** Information Design . Charles Joseph Minard

→ p.364

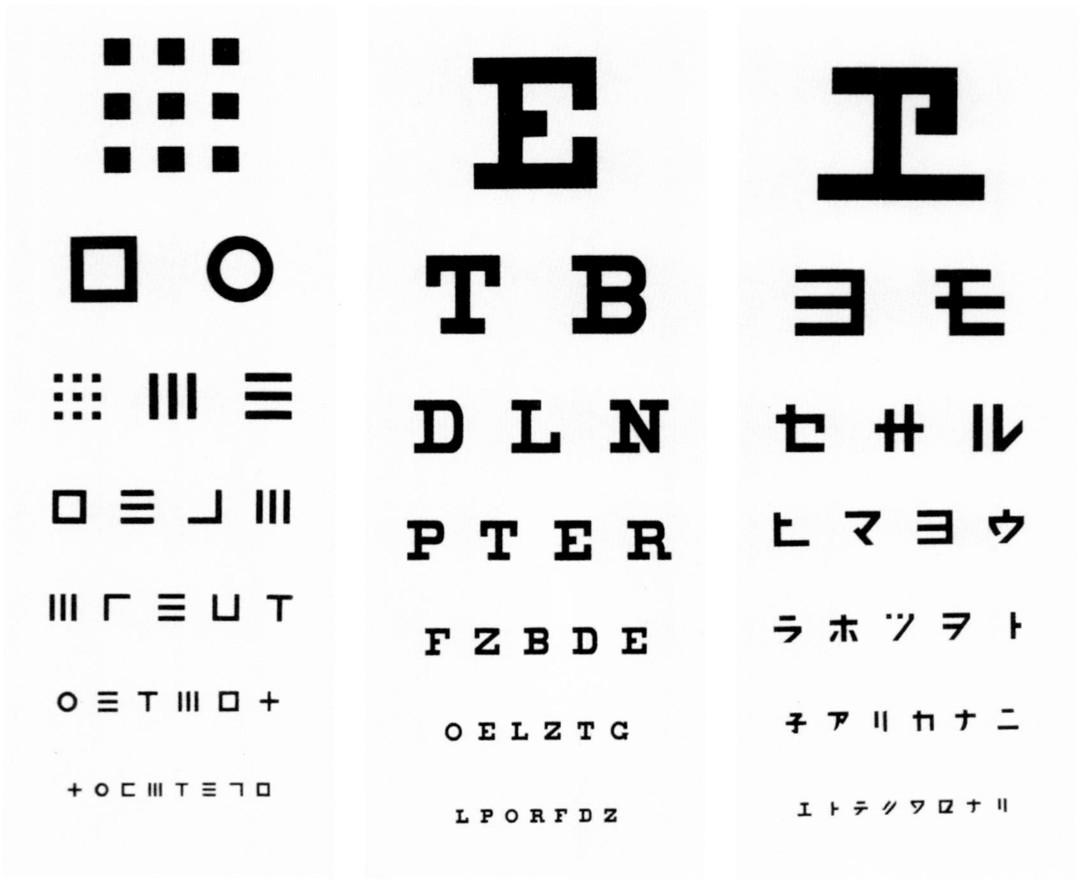

1862 . **SNELLEN CHART .** Information Design . Herman Snellen

→ p.365

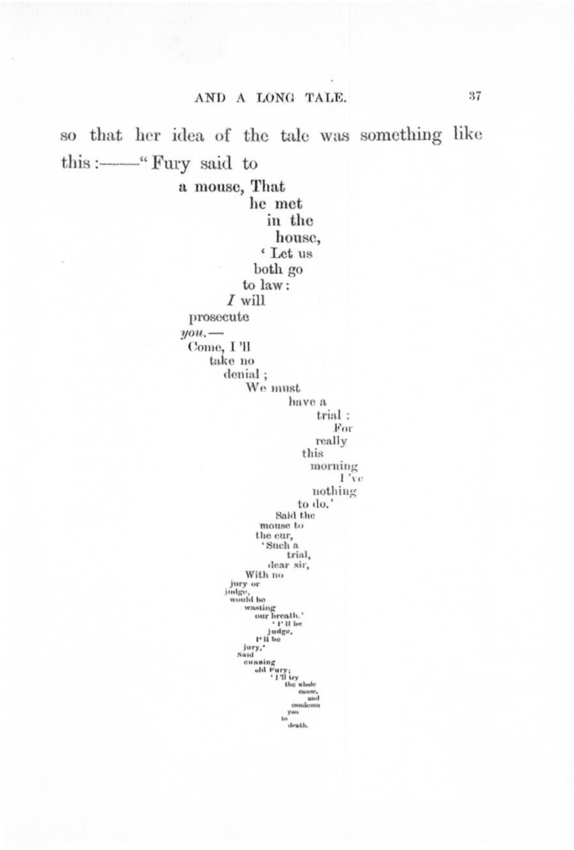

AND A LONG TALE. 37

so that her idea of the tale was something like this:——"Fury said to a mouse, That he met in the house, 'Let us both go to law: *I* will prosecute *you*.— Come, I'll take no denial; We must have a trial: For really this morning I've nothing to do.' Said the mouse to the cur, 'Such a trial, dear sir, With no jury or judge, would be wasting our breath.' 'I'll be judge, I'll be jury,' Said cunning old Fury; 'I'll try the whole cause, and condemn you to death.'

● **1863 . THE RED CROSS .** Information Design . Dr. Louis Appia, Gen. Henri Dufour

→ p.365

● **1865 . ALICE'S ADVENTURES IN WONDERLAND, BY LEWIS CARROLL** Book . Sir John Tenniel

→ p.365

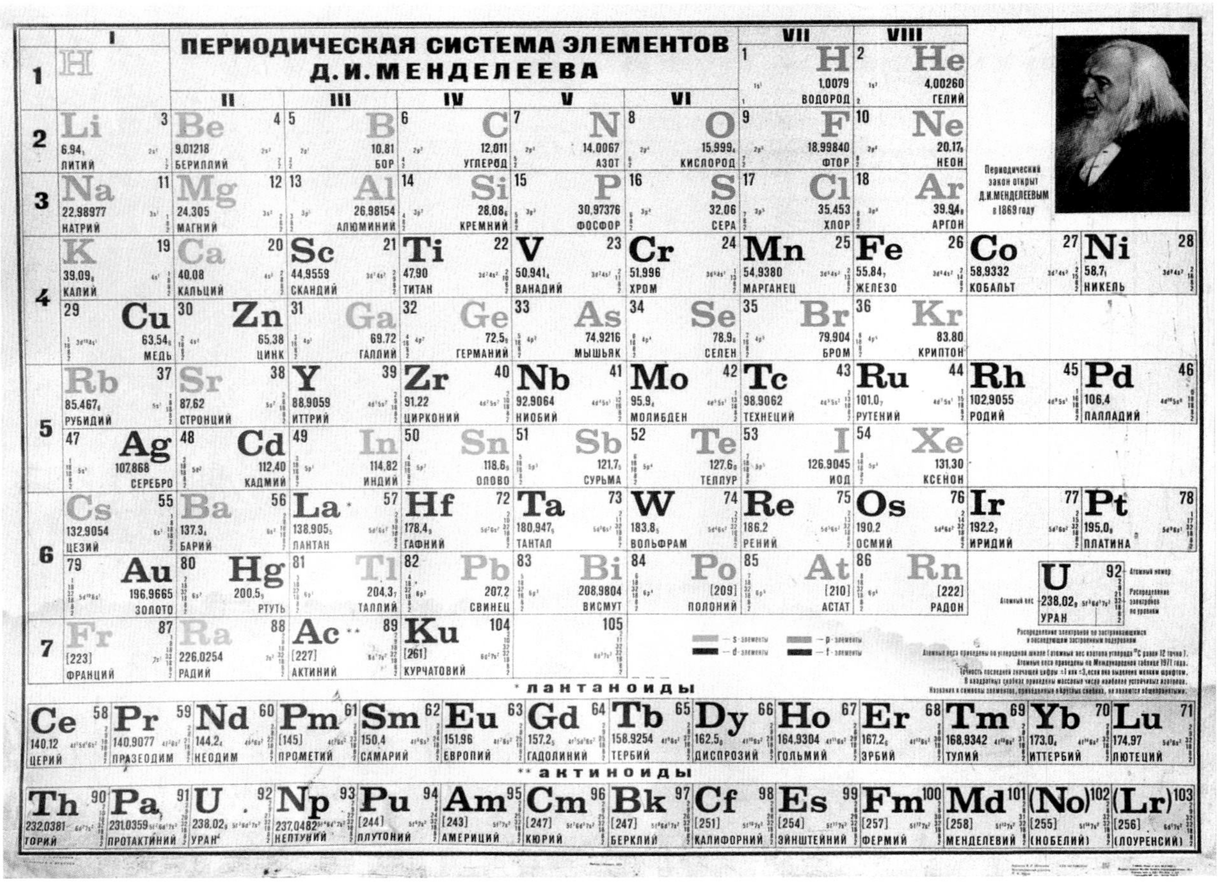

● **1869 . PERIODIC TABLE OF ELEMENTS .** Information Design . Dmitri Mendeleev

→ p.366

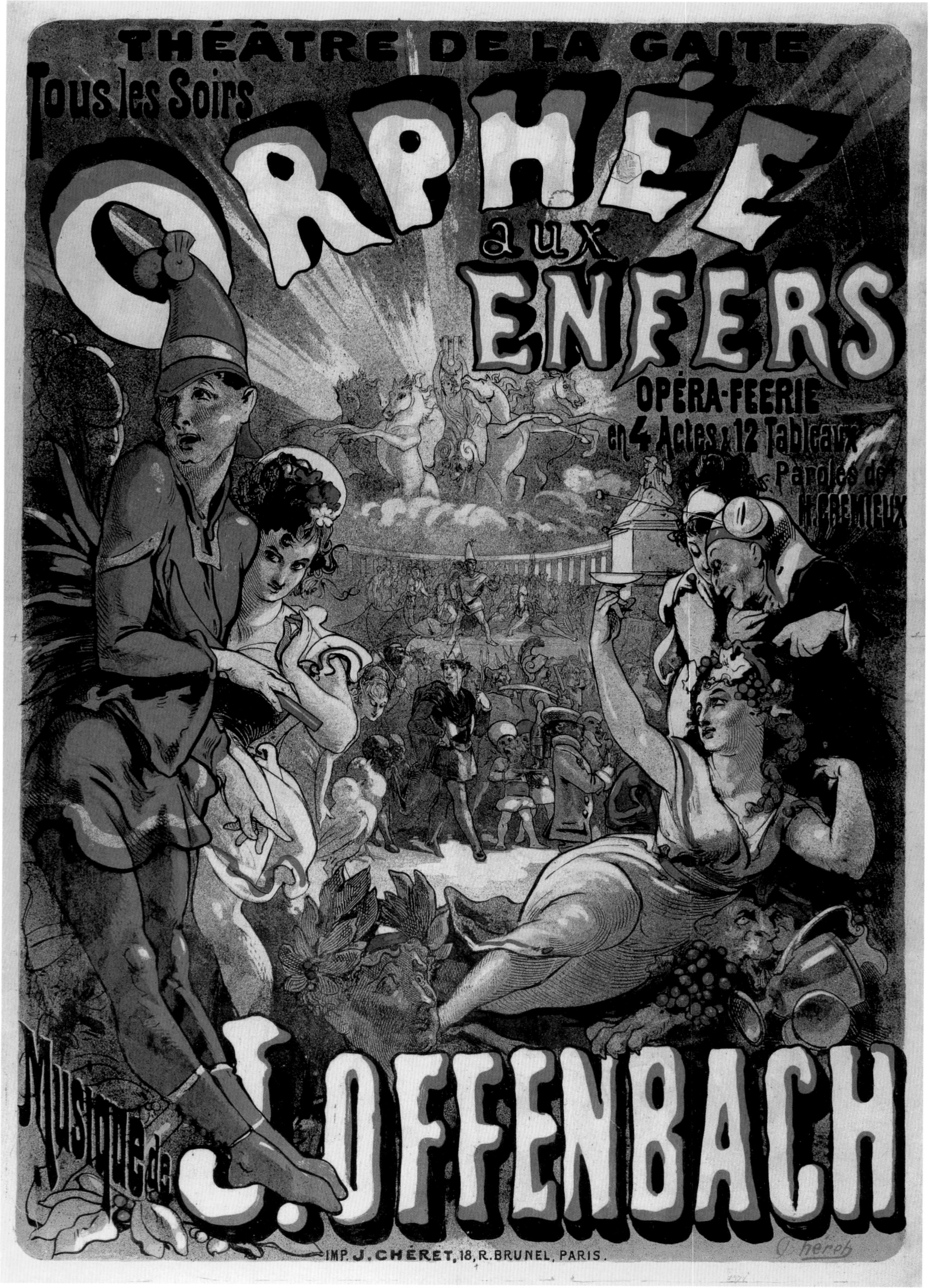

● **1874 . ORPHÉE AUX ENFERS .** Poster . Jules Chéret

→ p.366

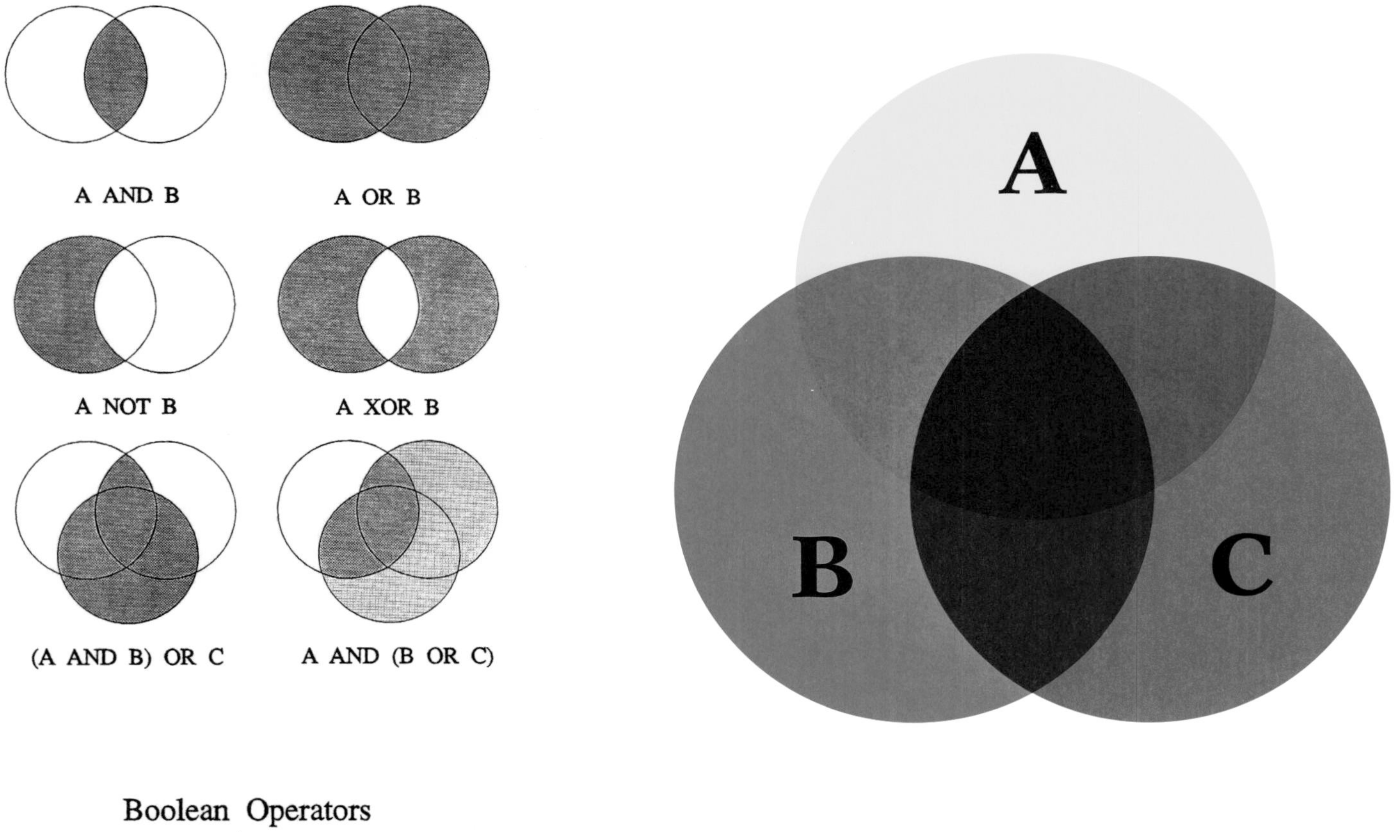

● **1880 . VENN DIAGRAM .** Information Design . John Venn

→ p.366

● **1886 . COCA-COLA .** Logo . Frank Mason Robinson

→ p.367

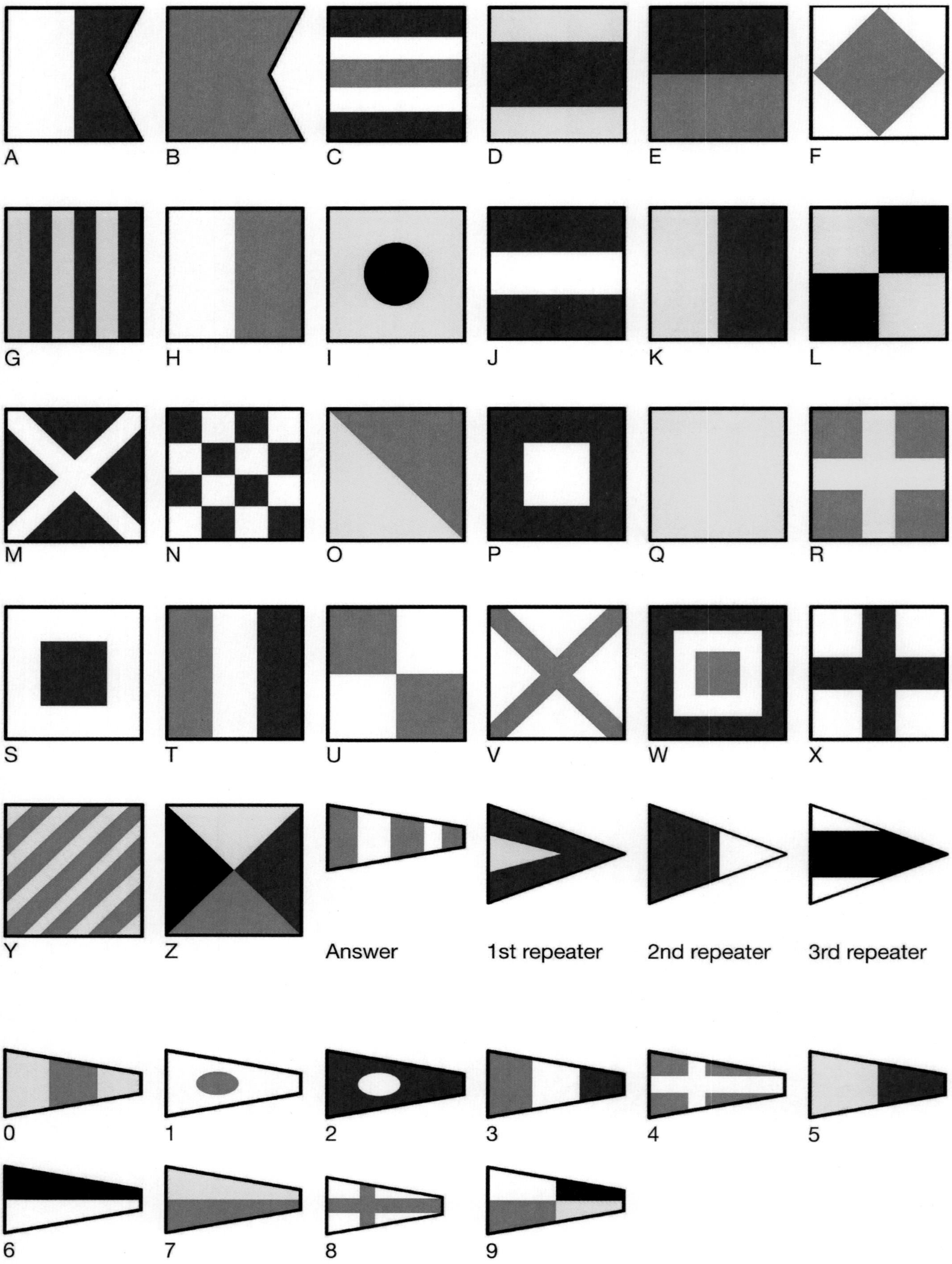

● **1887 . INTERNATIONAL CODE OF SYMBOLS AND INTERNATIONAL MARITIME FLAGS .** Information Design . Unknown

→ p.367

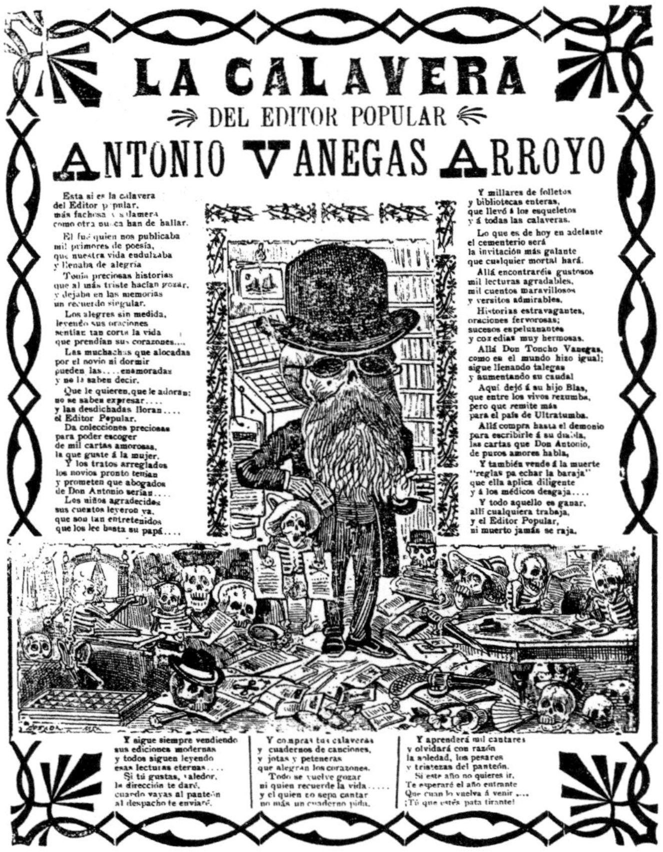

LA CALAVERA

DEL EDITOR POPULAR

ANTONIO VANEGAS ARROYO

Esta si es la calavera
del Editor popular,
más fachosa y zalamera
como otra nunca han de hallar.

El fué quien nos publicaba
mil primores de poesía,
que nuestra vida endulzaba
y llenaba de alegría

Tenía preciosas historias
que al más triste hacían gozar,
y dejaba en las memorias
un recuerdo singular.

Los alegres sin medida,
leyendo sus oraciones
sentían tan corta la vida
que prendían sus corazones....

Las muchachas que alocadas
por el novio ni dormir
pueden las....enamoradas
y no la saben decir.

Que le quieren, que le adoran:
no se saben expresar....
y las desdichadas lloran....
el Editor Popular.

Da colecciones preciosas
para poder escoger
de mil cartas amorosas,
la que guste á la mujer.

Y los tratos arreglados
los novios pronto tenían
y prometen que abogados
de Don Antonio serían....

Los niños agradecidos
sus cuentos leyeron ya,
que son tan entretenidos
que los lee hasta su papá....

Y millares de folletos
y bibliotecas enteras,
que llevó á los esqueletos
y á todas las calaveras.

Lo que es de hoy en adelante
el cementerio será
la invitación más galante
que cualquier mortal hará.

Allá encontraréis gustosos
mil lecturas agradables,
mil cuentos maravillosos
y versitos admirables.

Historias estravagantes,
oraciones fervorosas;
sucesos espeluznantes
y comedias muy hermosas.

Allá Don Toncho Vanegas,
como en el mundo hizo igual;
sigue llenando talegas
y aumentando su caudal

Aquí dejó á su hijo Blas,
que entre los vivos rezumba,
pero que remite más
para el país de Ultratumba.

Allá compra hasta el demonio
para escribirle á su diabla,
las cartas que Don Antonio,
de puros amores habla,

Y también vende á la muerte
"reglas pa echar la baraja"
que ella aplica diligente
y á los médicos desgaja....

Y todo aquello es ganar,
allí cualquiera trabaja,
y el Editor Popular,
ni muerto jamás se raja.

Y sigue siempre vendiendo
sus ediciones modernas
y todos siguen leyendo
esas lecturas eternas....

Si tú gustas, valedor,
la dirección te daré,
cuando vayas al panteón
al despacho te enviaré.

Y compras tus calaveras
y cuadernos de canciones,
y jotas y peteneras
que alegran los corazones.

Todo se vuelve gozar
ni quien recuerde la vida.....
y el quien no sepa cantar
no más un cuaderno pida.

Y aprenderá mil cantares
y olvidará con razón
la soledad, los pesares
y tristezas del panteón.

Si este año no quieres ir,
Te esperaré el año entrante
Que cuan lo vuelva á venir ....
¡Tú que estés pata tirante!

● c. 1890–1913 . **CALAVERAS** . Magazine / Newspaper . José Guadalupe Posada

→ p.367

● 1892 . **GENERAL ELECTRIC** . Logo . Unknown

→ p.368

● **1892–1893 . ARISTIDE BRUANT .** Poster . Henri de Toulouse-Lautrec

→ p.368

● **1894–1898 . THE CHAP-BOOK .** Magazine Cover . William H. Bradley
"The Twins," No. 1, 1894

→ p.368

● **1894 . LA REVUE BLANCHE .**
Poster . Pierre Bonnard

→ p.369

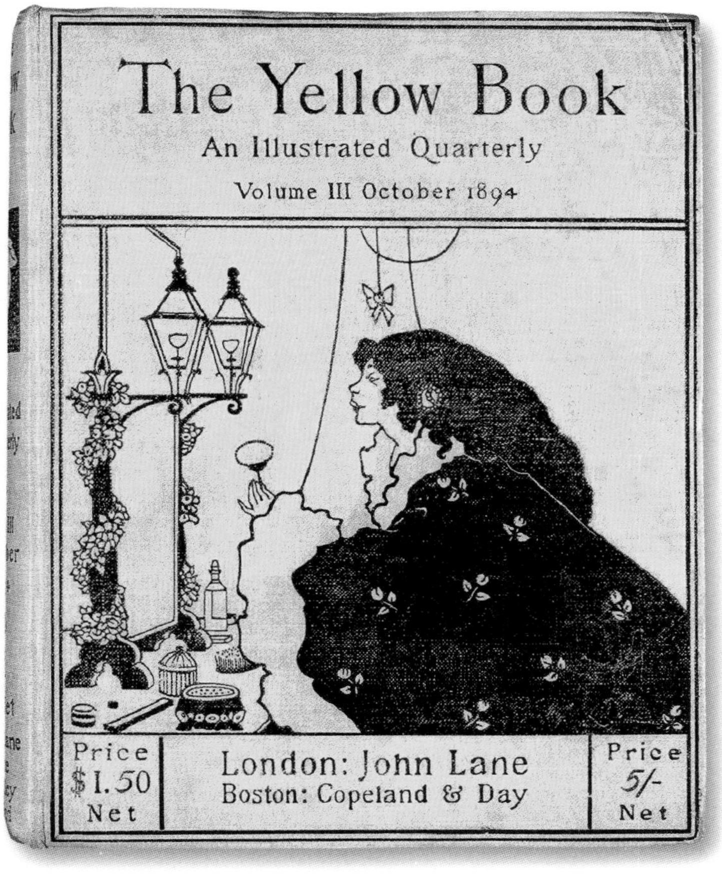

● **1894–1895 . THE YELLOW BOOK .** Magazine / Newspaper . Aubrey Beardsley
Vol. 3, October 1894

→ p.369

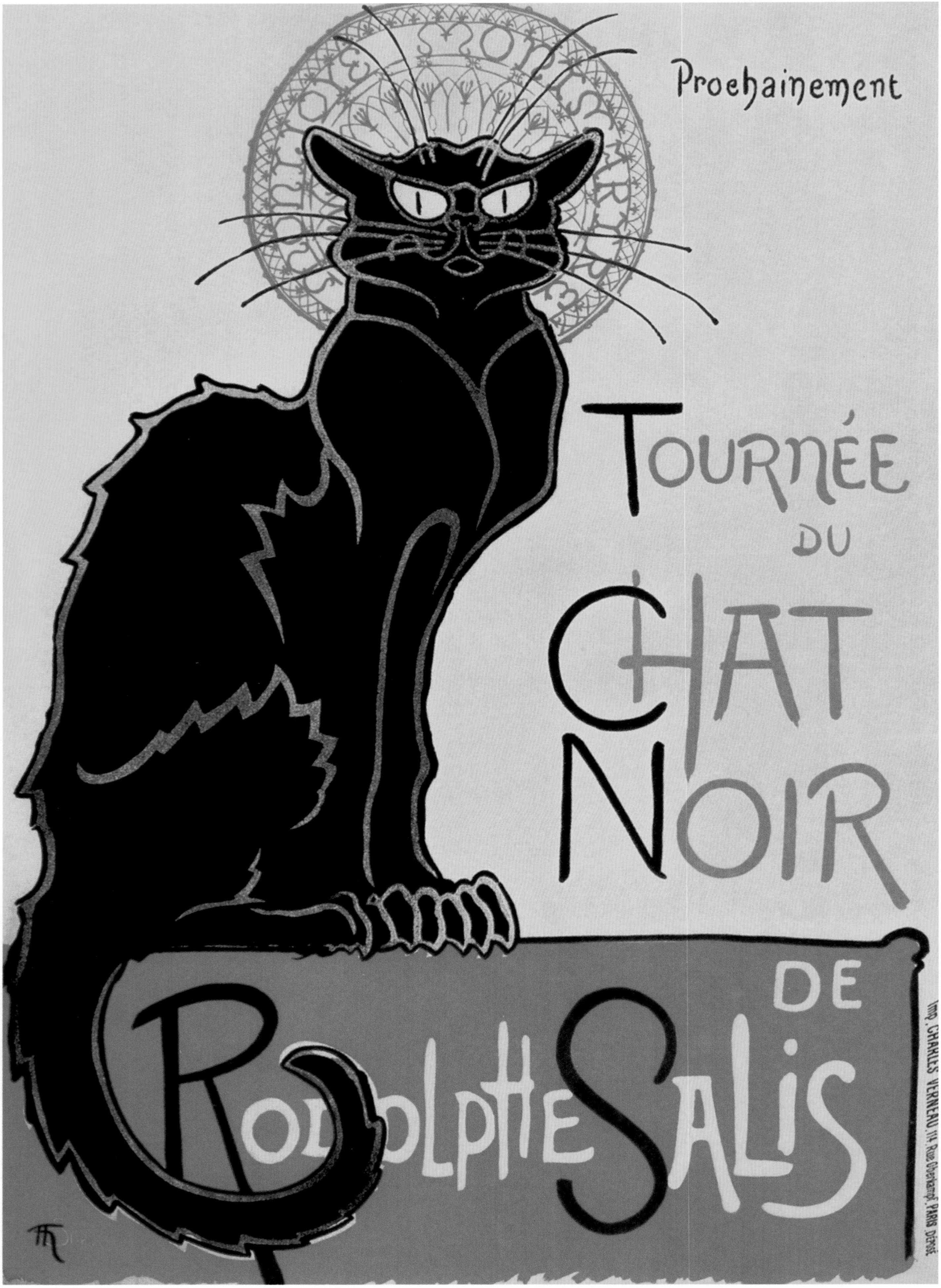

● **1894 . TOURNÉE DU CHAT NOIR .** Poster . Théophile-Alexandre Steinlen

→ p.369

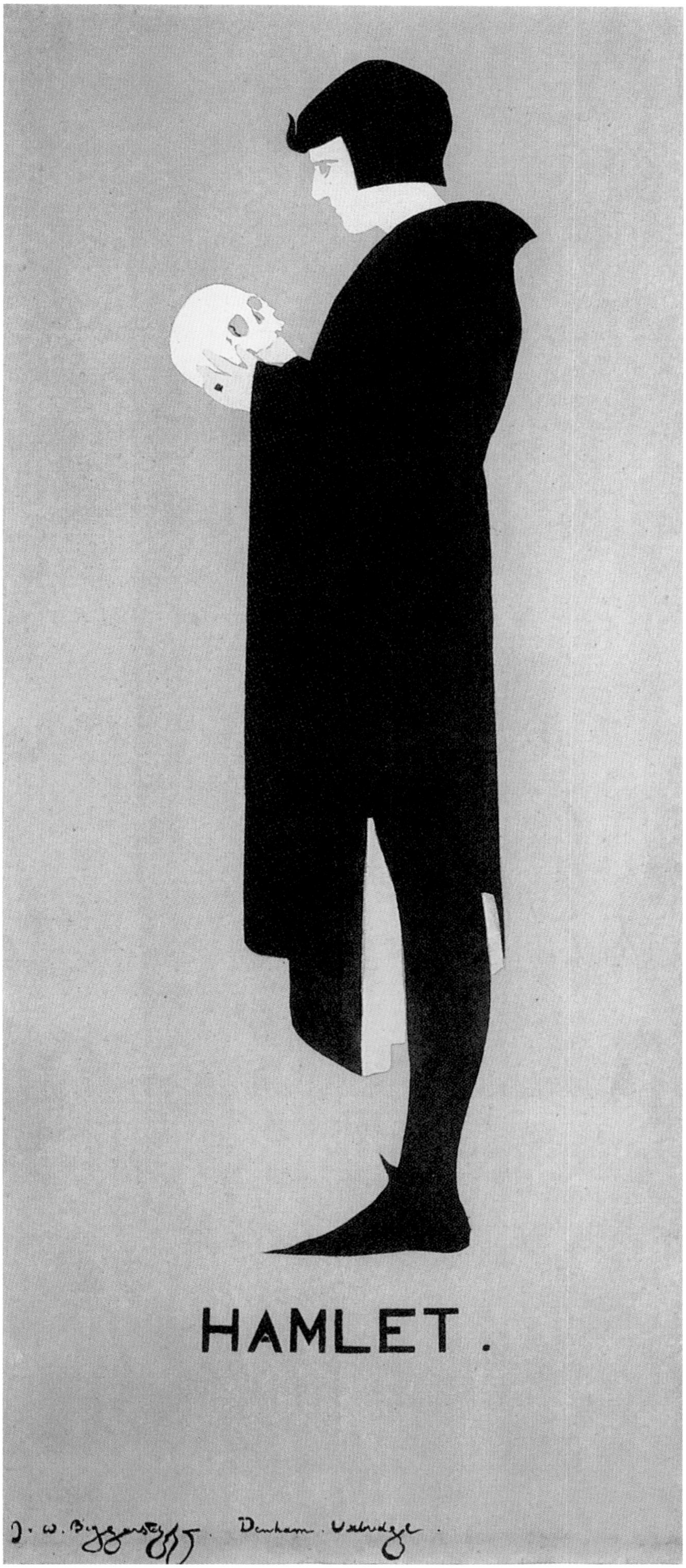

● **1894 . HAMLET .** Poster . The Beggarstaffs: James Pryde, William Nicholson

→ p.370

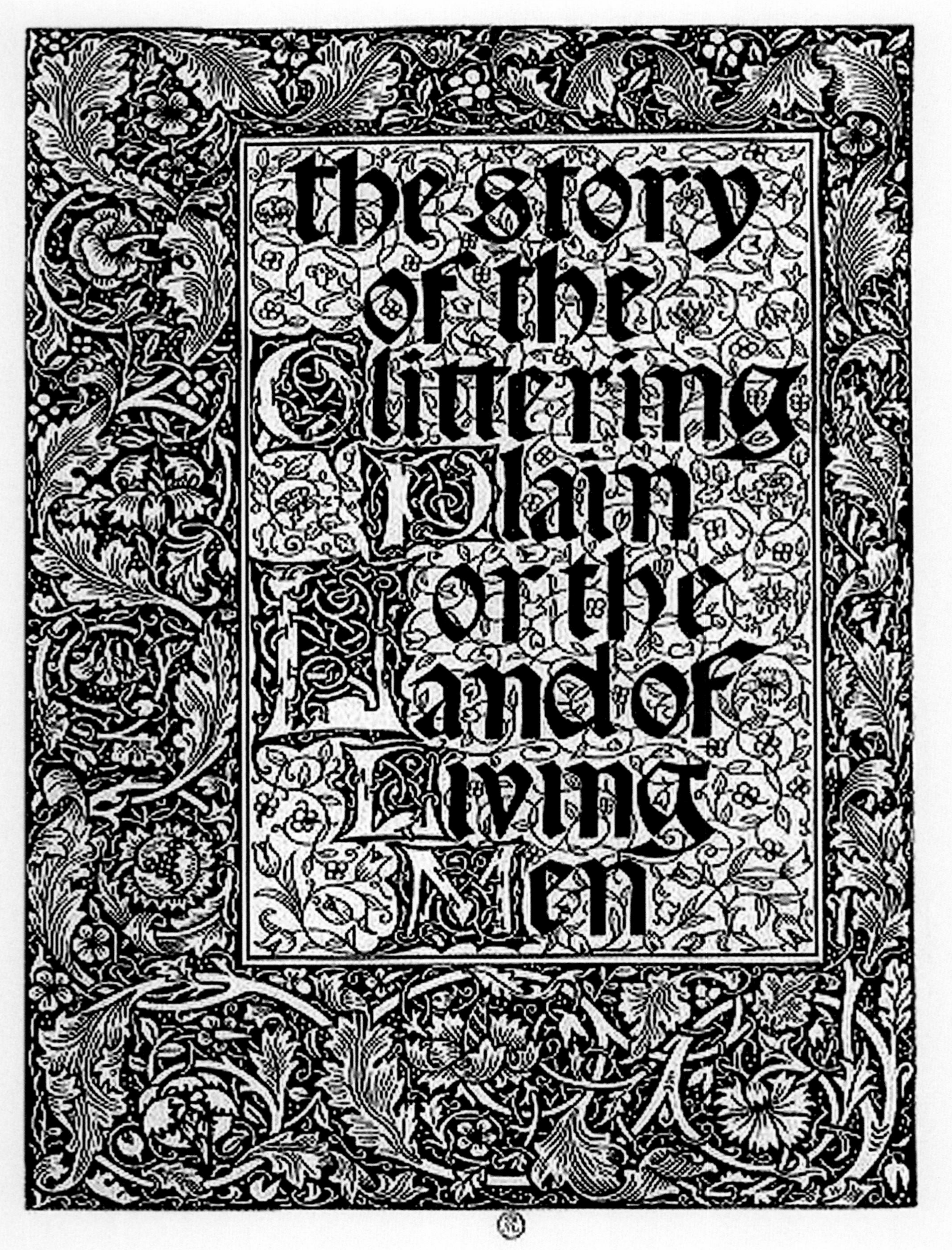

1894 . THE STORY OF THE GLITTERING PLAIN OR THE LAND OF LIVING MEN . Book . William Morris, Walter Crane

→ p.370

Akzidenz-Grotesk fett 6

82477a 5/6 p Min. ca. 3 kg 150a 42A Sign. 82

Unter den industriellen Erzeugnissen, die von Rösch entwickelt wurden, nehmen moderne Tapeten einen TAPETEN FÜR DIE NEUE WOHNUNG 1234567890

82478 6 p Min. ca. 4 kg 180a 46A

In the pig-iron branch of iron and steel trade production has by only one meaning resumed normal CENTRAL AMERICAN RAILROAD STATION

82480 8 p Min. ca. 5 kg 130a 38A

Die Zusammenarbeit mit der Industrie POLYTECHNISCHE LEHRANSTALT

82481 10 p kl. Bild ca. 6 kg 112a 32A Sign. 82

Fantaskiske kaktuspark i Monaco REJSEBOG TIL SYDFRANKRIG

82482 10 p Min. ca. 6 kg 106a 32A

Musée d'Extrême-Orient à Paris ÉTUDE DE LA CIVILISATION

82483 12 p Min. ca. 6 kg 72a 22A

Kraftfahrzeug-Reparaturen AUTOMOBIL-EXPORTE

82484 14 p Min. ca. 7 kg 58a 18A

La chronique des lettres AGENCE DE VOYAGE

82485 16 p Min. ca. 8 kg 54a 18A

Profileisen-Walzwerk STAB 1234567890

82486 20 p Min. ca. 10 kg 46a 14A

Antenna systems RADIOSTUDIO

82487 24 p Min. ca. 10 kg 34a 10A

Transportkran WERKSTOFF

82488 28 p Min. ca. 12 kg 30a 8A

Atomantrieb ZENTRALE

82489 36 p Min. ca. 14 kg 22a 6A

Biblioteca PINTURA

82490 48 p Min. ca. 16 kg 10a 4A

Scripts

82491 60 p Min. ca 20 kg 8a 4A

MAIN

82492 72 p Min. ca. 24 kg 8a 4A

Buch

Größere Grade als Plakatschrift in »Plakadur«

● 1896 . AKZIDENZ-GROTESK . Typeface . Unknown

→ p.370

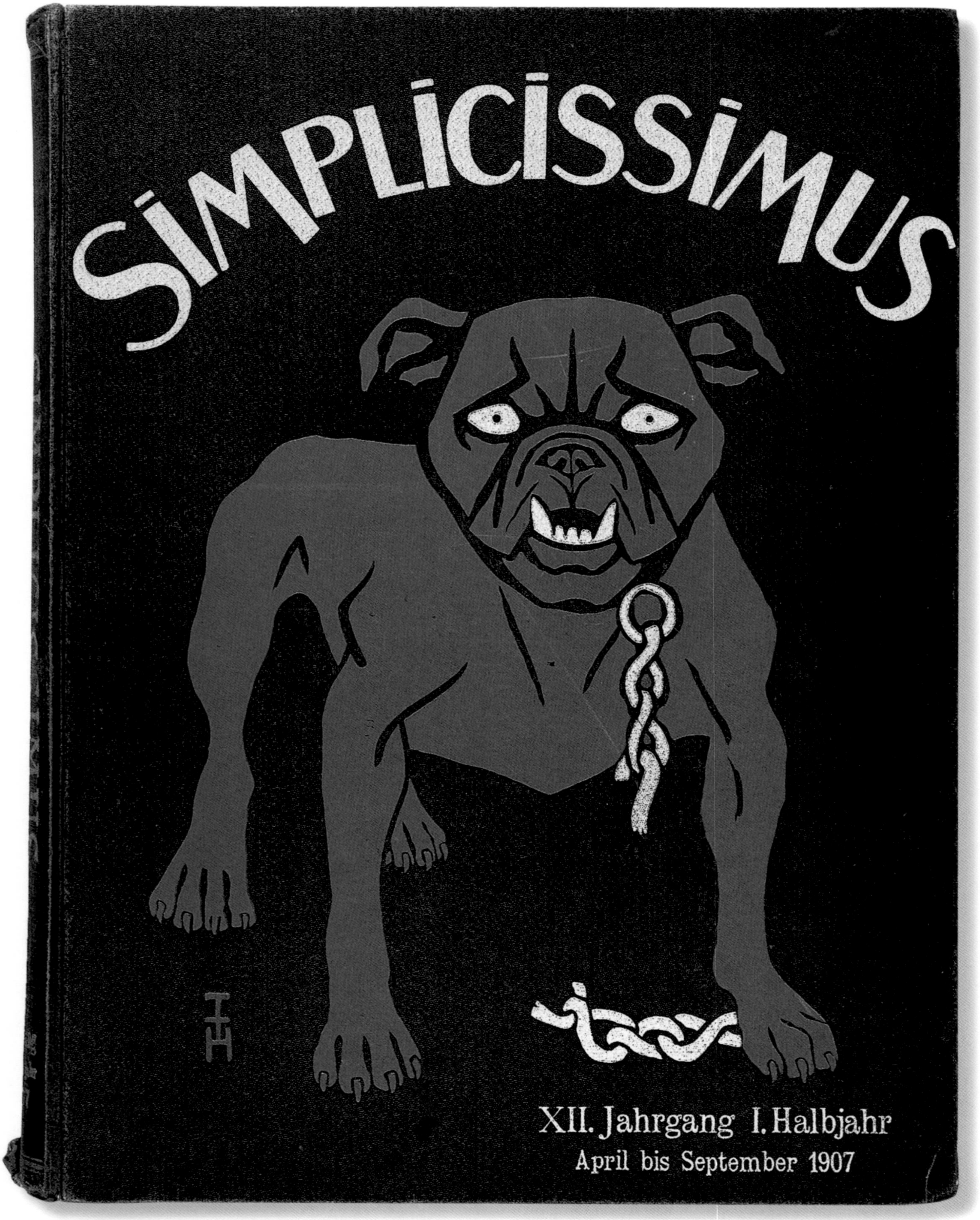

● **1896–1944 . SIMPLICISSIMUS .** Magazine / Newspaper . Thomas Theodor Heine et al.
Thomas Theodor Heine, Vol. 12, bound collection, 1907

→ p.371

● **1896 . THE SCOTTISH MUSICAL REVIEW .** Poster . Charles Rennie Mackintosh

→ p.371

1899 • 7. JANUAR • JUGEND • IV. JAHRGANG • NR. 2

Münchner illustrierte Wochenschrift für Kunst und Leben. — G. Hirth's Verlag in München & Leipzig.

● **1896–1940 . JUGEND .** Magazine / Newspaper . Various
Vol. 4, No. 2, January 7, 1899

→ p.371

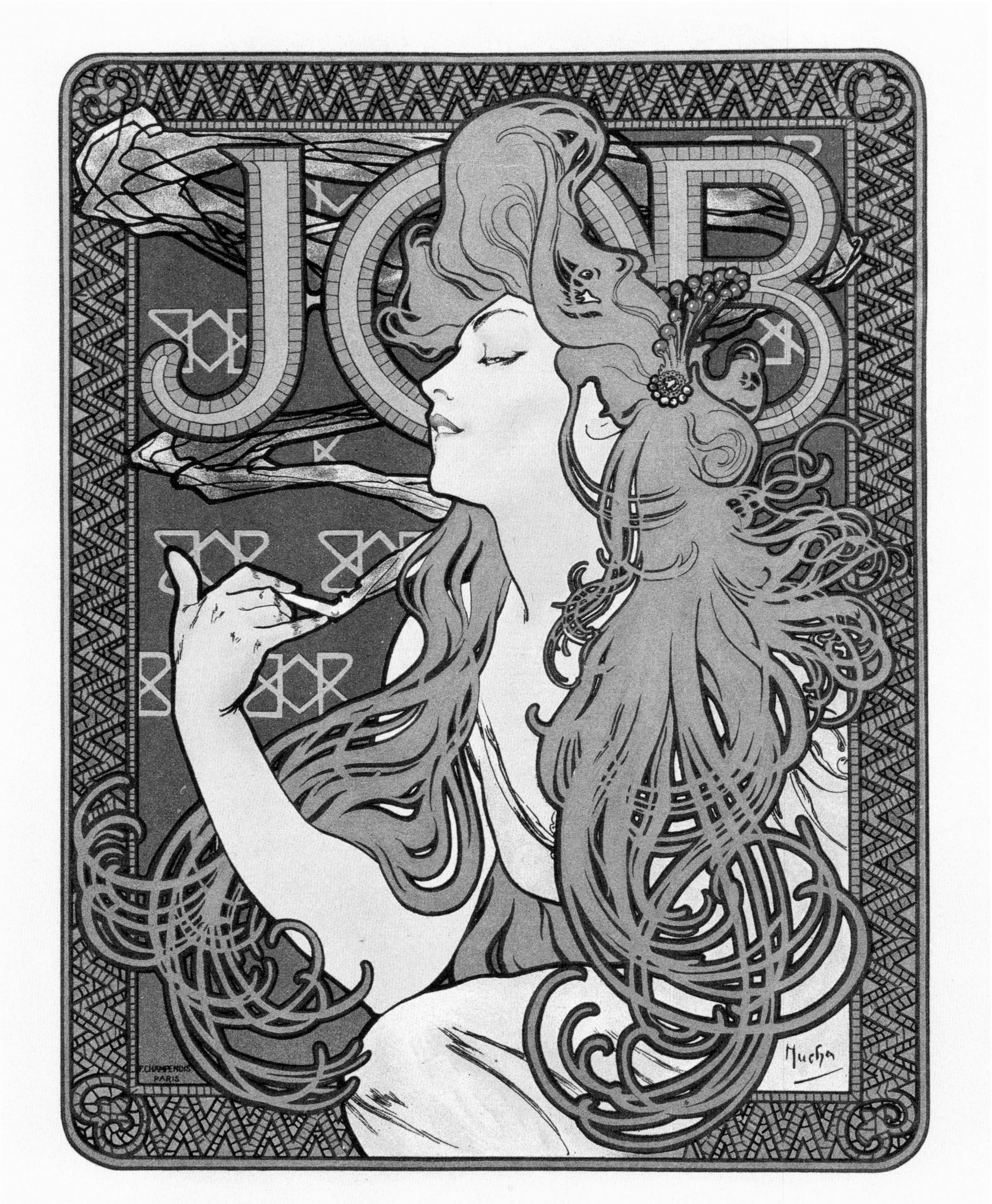

● **1896/1898 . JOB CIGARETTE PAPERS .** Poster . Alphonse Mucha

→ p.372

● **1898 . TROPON: L'ALIMENT LE PLUS CONCENTRÉ** . Identity . Henry van de Velde

→ p.372

● **1898–1903 . VER SACRUM .** Magazine / Newspaper . Alfred Roller et al.
TOP LEFT: Koloman Moser, Vol. 2, No. 4, 1899; TOP RIGHT: Vol. 2, No. 3, 1899; BOTTOM: Koloman Moser, illustration for "Vorfrühling" ("Early Spring"), by Rainer Maria Rilke, 1901

→ p.372

1898 . MICHELIN MAN . Logo . Marius Rossillon

→ p.373

1899 . HIS MASTER'S VOICE . Logo . Francis Barraud

→ p.373

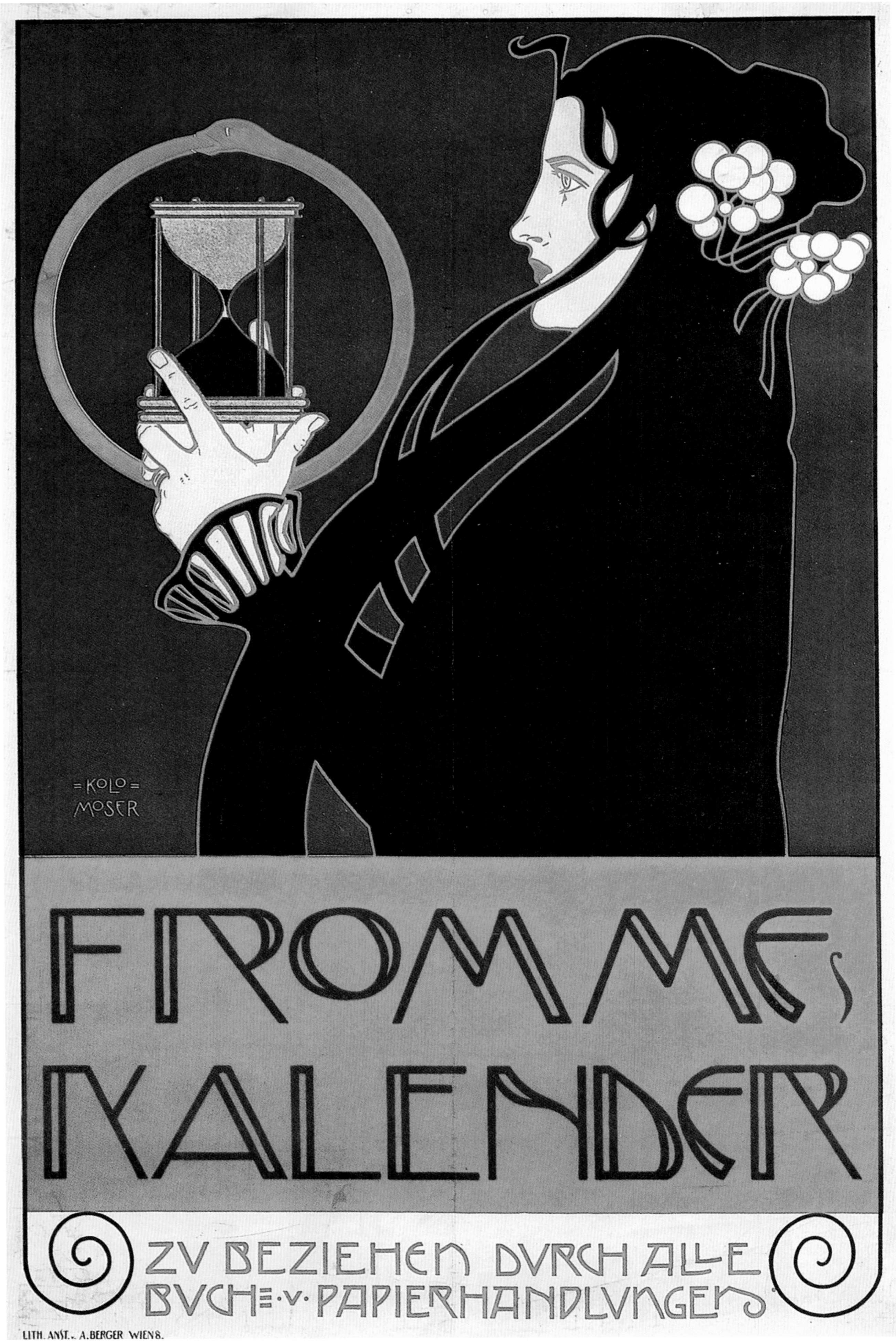

● **1899 . FROMME'S KALENDER .** Poster . Koloman Moser

→ p.373

● **1900 . ECKMANNSCHRIFT .** Typeface . Otto Eckmann

→ p.374

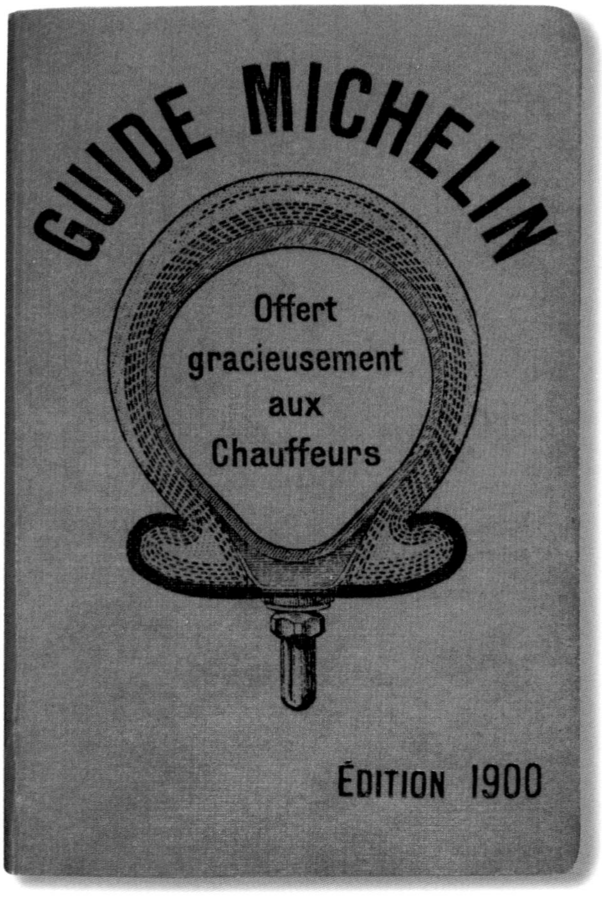

● **1900–PRESENT MICHELIN GUIDE .** Book . André Michelin

→ p.374

COMBINAISONS ORNEMENTALES

SE MULTIPLIANT A L'INFINI A L'AIDE DU MIROIR

DESSINS DE

MM. P. VERNEUIL - G. AURIOL ET A. MUCHA

PARIS

Librairie Centrale des Beaux-Arts

13, Rue de Lafayette

De l'emploi du miroir

La nécessité où se trouve le décorateur de varier à l'infini les motifs des ornementations qui lui sont demandées, a conduit les esprits curieux à rechercher un moyen pratique, simple et rapide d'arriver à ce résultat.

Les jeux de glaces sont en ce cas d'un secours inappréciable, soit que l'on veuille se rendre compte de l'effet d'un motif redoublé, soit pour trouver rapidement des coins de bordures, soit enfin pour chercher des motifs d'ornementation plus ou moins compliqués.

Chacun verra du reste rapidement tout ce que l'on peut tirer de ce procédé ingénieux, que nous n'avons certes pas la prétention d'avoir inventé.

Le kaléidoscope, dont s'émerveillent les enfants, ne repose pas sur un autre principe. Nous avons encore simplifié celui-ci.

Alors que le kaléidoscope est composé de trois glaces fixes réunies en triangle, nous nous servons simplement de deux glaces réunies par une charnière nous permettant de

● c. 1900 . **COMBINAISONS ORNEMENTALES** . Book . Alphonse Mucha, Maurice-Pillard Verneuil, Georges Auriol

→ p.374

The family of **Franklin Gothic**

AaBbCcDd

ABCDEFGHIJKLMNOPQRSTUVWXYZ
abcdefghijklmnopqrstuvwxyz
1234567890$%&(,.;:!?)

Franklin Gothic Book

ABCDEFGHIJKLMNOPQRSTUVWXYZ
abcdefghijklmnopqrstuvwxyz
1234567890$%&(,.;:!?)

Franklin Gothic Book Oblique

ABCDEFGHIJKLMNOPQRSTUVWXYZ
abcdefghijklmnopqrstuvwxyz
1234567890$%&(,.;:!?)

Franklin Gothic Medium

ABCDEFGHIJKLMNOPQRSTUVWXYZ
abcdefghijklmnopqrstuvwxyz
1234567890$%&(,.;:!?)

Franklin Gothic Medium Oblique

● **1902 . FRANKLIN GOTHIC .** Typeface . Morris Fuller Benton

→ p.375

● **1903 . PERRIER .** Logo . St. John Harmsworth
Lady of Fashion, January 4, 1906

→ p.375

CITROËN

● **1903 . CITROËN .** Logo . André Citroën
Logo, 1985

→ p.375

IN THE BEGINNING GOD CREATED THE HEAVEN AND THE EARTH. ¶ AND THE EARTH WAS WITHOUT FORM, AND VOID; AND DARKNESS WAS UPON THE FACE OF THE DEEP, & THE SPIRIT OF GOD MOVED UPON THE FACE OF THE WATERS. ¶ And God said, Let there be light: & there was light. And God saw the light, that it was good: & God divided the light from the darkness. And God called the light Day, and the darkness he called Night. And the evening and the morning were the first day. ¶ And God said, Let there be a firmament in the midst of the waters, & let it divide the waters from the waters. And God made the firmament, and divided the waters which were under the firmament from the waters which were above the firmament: & it was so. And God called the firmament Heaven. And the evening & the morning were the second day. ¶ And God said, Let the waters under the heaven be gathered together unto one place, and let the dry land appear: and it was so. And God called the dry land Earth; and the gathering together of the waters called he Seas: and God saw that it was good. And God said, Let the earth bring forth grass, the herb yielding seed, and the fruit tree yielding fruit after his kind, whose seed is in itself, upon the earth: & it was so. And the earth brought forth grass, & herb yielding seed after his kind, & the tree yielding fruit, whose seed was in itself, after his kind: and God saw that it was good. And the evening & the morning were the third day. ¶ And God said, Let there be lights in the firmament of the heaven to divide the day from the night; and let them be for signs, and for seasons, and for days, & years: and let them be for lights in the firmament of the heaven to give light upon the earth: & it was so. And God made two great lights; the greater light to rule the day, and the lesser light to rule the night: he made the stars also. And God set them in the firmament of the heaven to give light upon the earth, and to rule over the day and over the night, & to divide the light from the darkness: and God saw that it was good. And the evening and the morning were the fourth day. ¶ And God said, Let the waters bring forth abundantly the moving creature that hath life, and fowl that may fly above the earth in the open firmament of heaven. And God created great whales, & every living creature that moveth, which the waters brought forth abundantly, after their kind, & every winged fowl after his kind: & God saw that it was good. And God blessed them, saying, Be fruitful, & multiply, and fill the waters in the seas, and let fowl multiply in the earth. And the evening & the morning were the fifth day. ¶ And God said, Let the earth bring forth the living creature after his kind, cattle, and creeping thing, and beast of the earth after his kind: and it was so. And God made the beast of the earth after his kind, and cattle after their kind, and every thing that creepeth upon the

27

● **1903–1905 . DOVES PRESS BIBLE .** Book . Thomas James Cobden-Sanderson, Edward Johnston

→ p.376

● **1903 . SECESSION 16. AUSSTELLUNG .** Poster . Alfred Roller

→ p.376

● **1903 . WIENER WERKSTÄTTE .** Logo . Josef Hoffmann, Koloman Moser

→ p.376

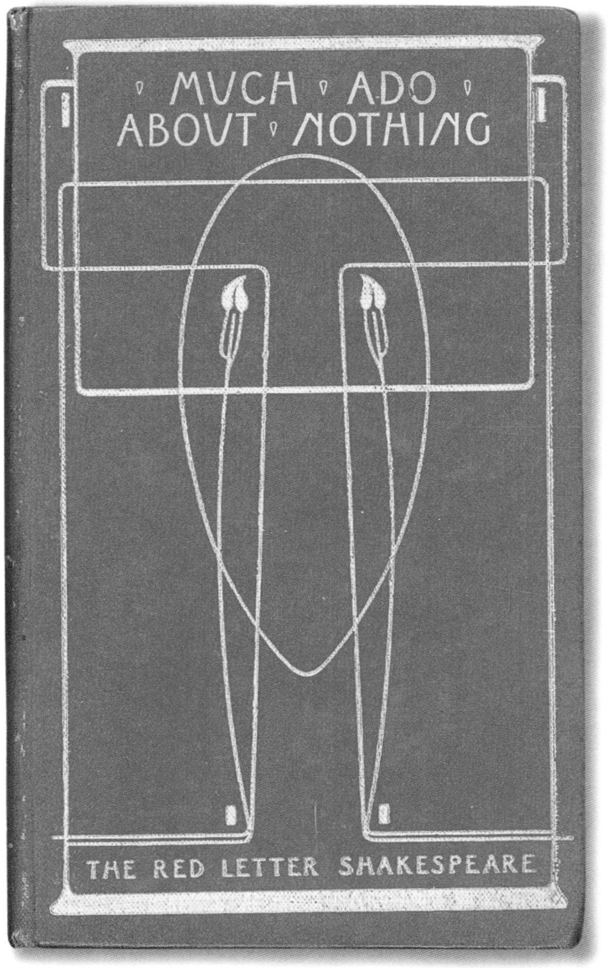

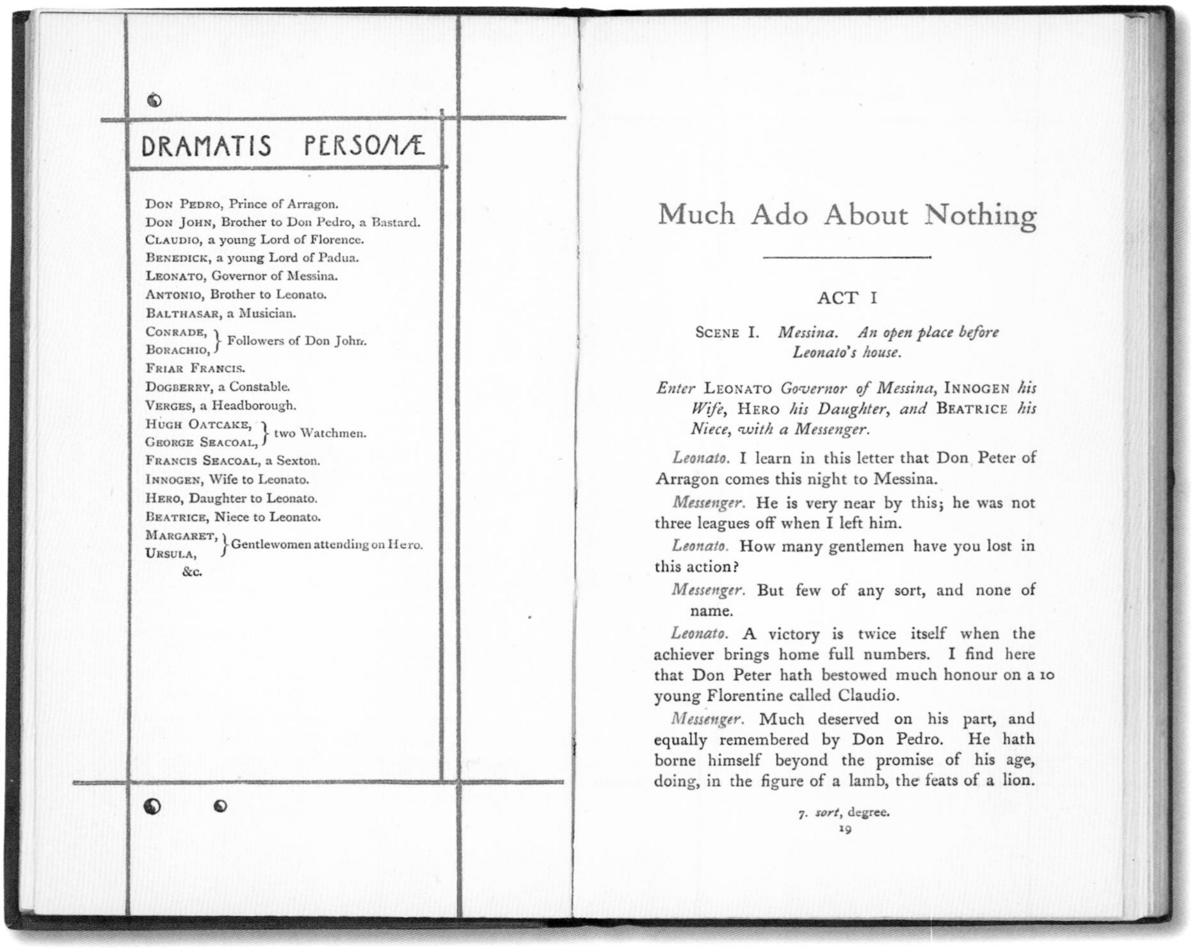
DRAMATIS PERSONÆ

DON PEDRO, Prince of Arragon.
DON JOHN, Brother to Don Pedro, a Bastard.
CLAUDIO, a young Lord of Florence.
BENEDICK, a young Lord of Padua.
LEONATO, Governor of Messina.
ANTONIO, Brother to Leonato.
BALTHASAR, a Musician.
CONRADE, BORACHIO, } Followers of Don John.
FRIAR FRANCIS.
DOGBERRY, a Constable.
VERGES, a Headborough.
HUGH OATCAKE, GEORGE SEACOAL, } two Watchmen.
FRANCIS SEACOAL, a Sexton.
INNOGEN, Wife to Leonato.
HERO, Daughter to Leonato.
BEATRICE, Niece to Leonato.
MARGARET, URSULA, } Gentlewomen attending on Hero.
&c.

Much Ado About Nothing

ACT I

SCENE I. *Messina. An open place before Leonato's house.*

Enter LEONATO *Governor of Messina,* INNOGEN *his Wife,* HERO *his Daughter, and* BEATRICE *his Niece, with a Messenger.*

Leonato. I learn in this letter that Don Peter of Arragon comes this night to Messina.

Messenger. He is very near by this; he was not three leagues off when I left him.

Leonato. How many gentlemen have you lost in this action?

Messenger. But few of any sort, and none of name.

Leonato. A victory is twice itself when the achiever brings home full numbers. I find here that Don Peter hath bestowed much honour on a young Florentine called Claudio.

Messenger. Much deserved on his part, and equally remembered by Don Pedro. He hath borne himself beyond the promise of his age, doing, in the figure of a lamb, the feats of a lion.

7. *sort,* degree.
19

1904–1908 . THE RED LETTER SHAKESPEARE . Book . Talwin Morris

→ p.377

● c. 1904 . **BAYER** . Logo . Disputed

→ p.377

● 1905 . **WASCHANSTALT ZÜRICH AG** . Poster . Robert Hardmeyer

→ p.377

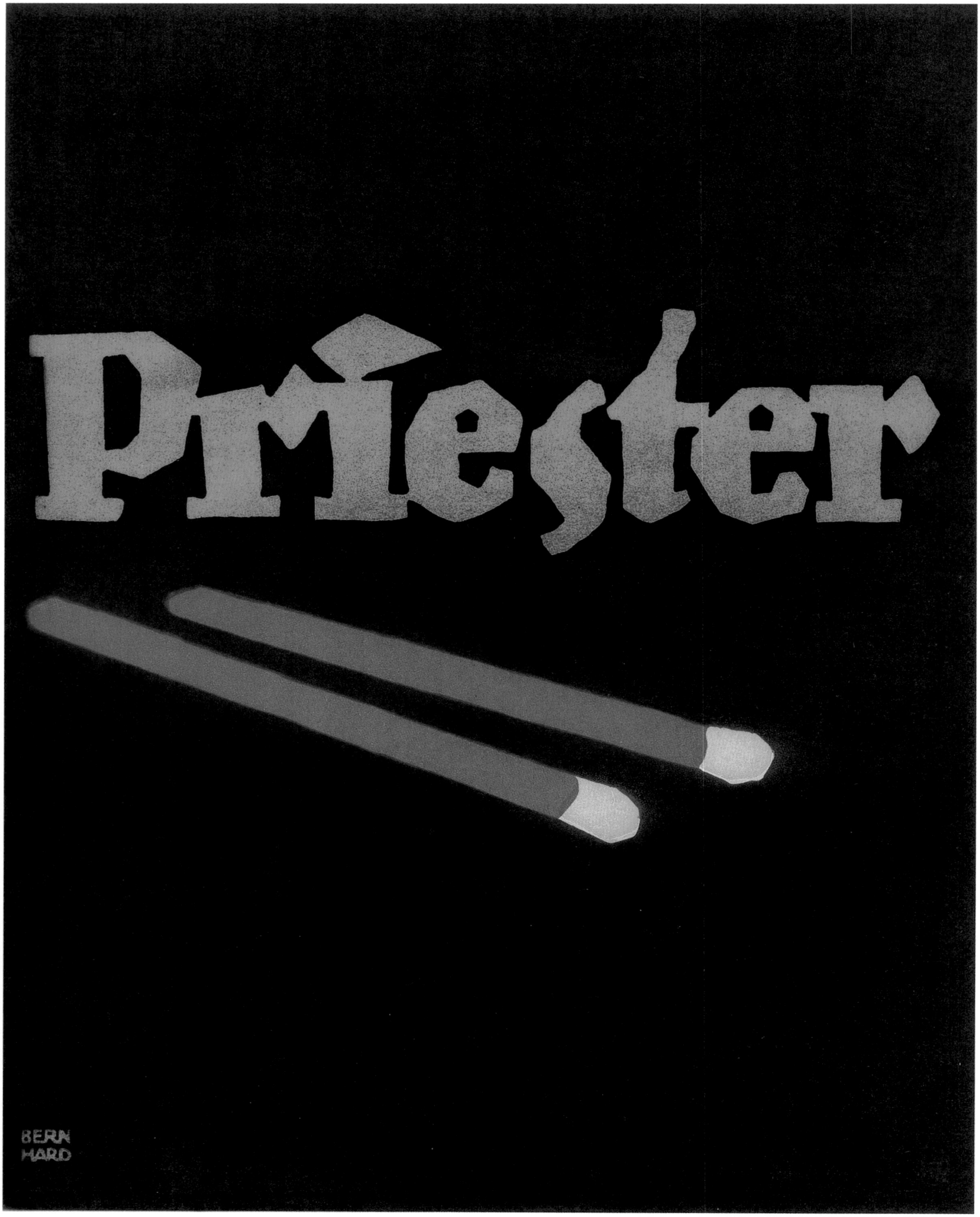

● **1905 . PRIESTER .** Poster . Lucian Bernhard

→ p.378

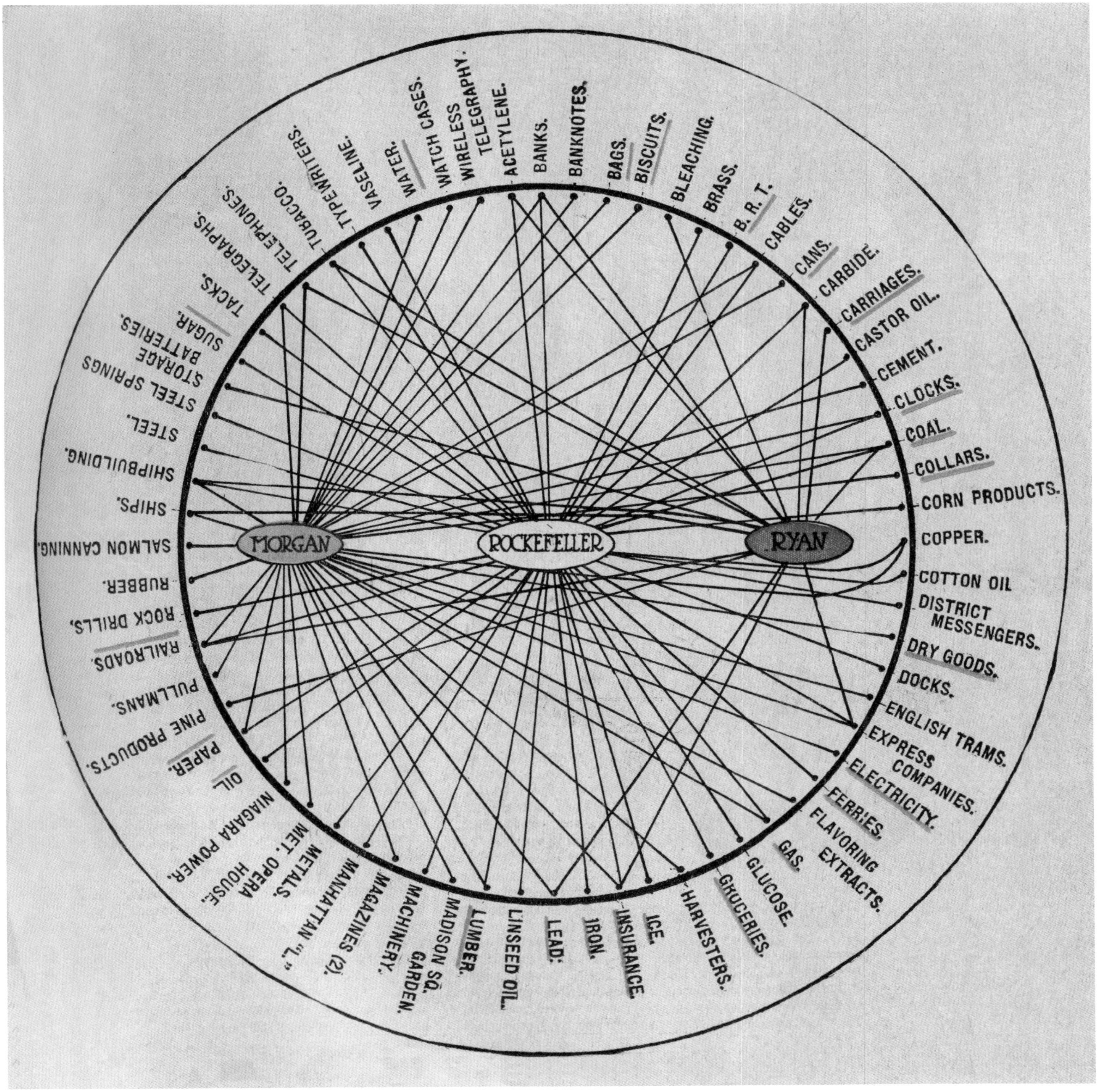

1906 . WHO GETS YOUR MONEY ("RING OF POWER") . Information Design . John Campbell Cory

→ p.378

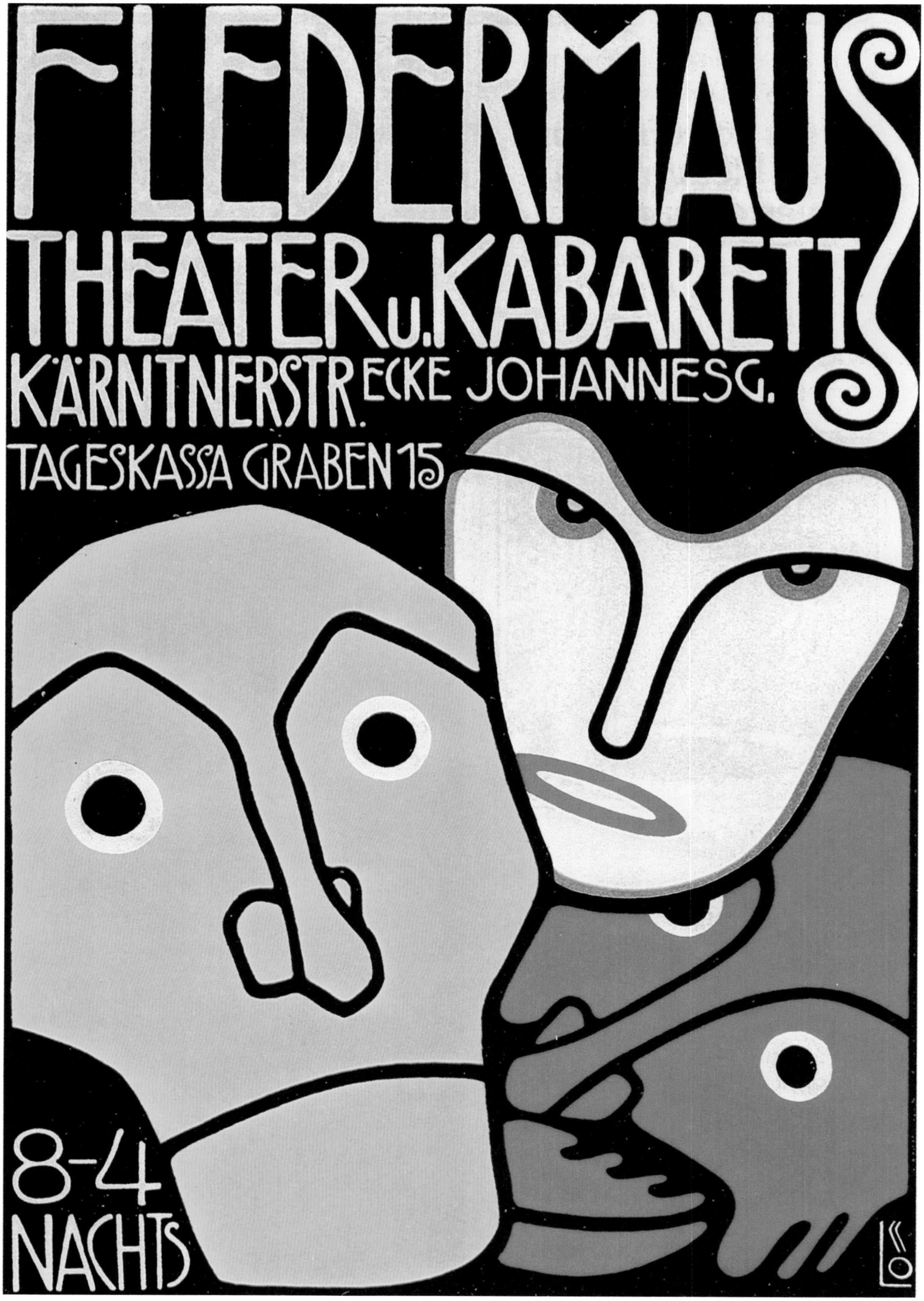

● **1907 . DIE FLEDERMAUS .** Poster . Berthold Löffler

→ p.378

● **1907 . AEG .** Identity . Peter Behrens

→ p.379

● **1908 . CONFECTION KEHL .** Poster . Ludwig Hohlwein

→ p.379

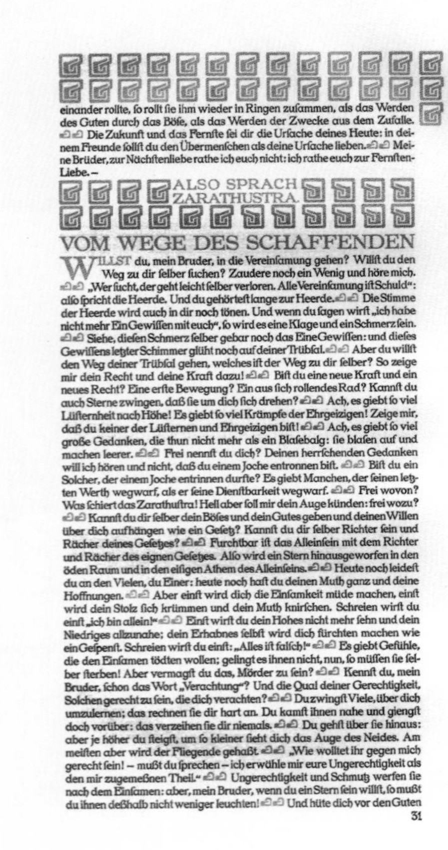

einander rollte, ſo rollt ſie ihm wieder in Ringen zuſammen, als das Werden des Guten durch das Böſe, als das Werden der Zwecke aus dem Zufalle. Die Zukunft und das Fernſte ſei dir die Urſache deines Heute: in deinem Freunde ſollſt du den Übermenſchen als deine Urſache lieben. Meine Brüder, zur Nächſtenliebe rathe ich euch nicht: ich rathe euch zur Fernſten-Liebe. –

ALSO SPRACH ZARATHUSTRA.

VOM WEGE DES SCHAFFENDEN

WILLST du, mein Bruder, in die Vereinſamung gehen? Willſt du den Weg zu dir ſelber ſuchen? Zaudere noch ein Wenig und höre mich. „Wer ſucht, der geht leicht ſelber verloren. Alle Vereinſamung iſt Schuld“: alſo ſpricht die Heerde. Und du gehörteſt lange zur Heerde. Die Stimme der Heerde wird auch in dir noch tönen. Und wenn du ſagen wirſt „ich habe nicht mehr Ein Gewiſſen mit euch“, ſo wird es eine Klage und ein Schmerz ſein. Siehe, dieſen Schmerz ſelber gebar noch das Eine Gewiſſen: und dieſes Gewiſſens letzter Schimmer glüht noch auf deiner Trübſal. Aber du willſt den Weg deiner Trübſal gehen, welches iſt der Weg zu dir ſelber? So zeige mir dein Recht und deine Kraft dazu! Biſt du eine neue Kraft und ein neues Recht? Eine erſte Bewegung? Ein aus ſich rollendes Rad? Kannſt du auch Sterne zwingen, daß ſie um dich ſich drehen? Ach, es giebt ſo viel Lüſternheit nach Höhe! Es giebt ſo viel Krämpfe der Ehrgeizigen! Zeige mir, daß du keiner der Lüſternen und Ehrgeizigen biſt! Ach, es giebt ſo viel große Gedanken, die thun nicht mehr als ein Blaſebalg: ſie blaſen auf und machen leerer. Frei nennſt du dich? Deinen herrſchenden Gedanken will ich hören und nicht, daß du einem Joche entronnen biſt. Biſt du ein Solcher, der einem Joche entrinnen durfte? Es giebt Manchen, der ſeinen letzten Werth wegwarf, als er ſeine Dienſtbarkeit wegwarf. Frei wovon? Was ſchiert das Zarathuſtra! Hell aber ſoll mir dein Auge künden: frei wozu? Kannſt du dir ſelber dein Böſes und dein Gutes geben und deinen Willen über dich aufhängen wie ein Geſetz? Kannſt du dir ſelber Richter ſein und Rächer deines Geſetzes? Furchtbar iſt das Alleinſein mit dem Richter und Rächer des eignen Geſetzes. Alſo wird ein Stern hinausgeworfen in den öden Raum und in den eiſigen Athem des Alleinſeins. Heute noch leideſt du an den Vielen, du Einer: heute noch haſt du deinen Muth ganz und deine Hoffnungen. Aber einſt wird dich die Einſamkeit müde machen, einſt wird dein Stolz ſich krümmen und dein Muth knirſchen. Schreien wirſt du einſt „ich bin allein!“ Einſt wirſt du dein Hohes nicht mehr ſehn und dein Niedriges allzunahe; dein Erhabnes ſelbſt wird dich fürchten machen wie ein Geſpenſt. Schreien wirſt du einſt: „Alles iſt falſch!“ Es giebt Gefühle, die den Einſamen tödten wollen; gelingt es ihnen nicht, nun, ſo müſſen ſie ſelber ſterben! Aber vermagſt du das, Mörder zu ſein? Kennſt du, mein Bruder, ſchon das Wort „Verachtung“? Und die Qual deiner Gerechtigkeit, Solchen gerecht zu ſein, die dich verachten? Du zwingſt Viele, über dich umzulernen; das rechnen ſie dir hart an. Du kamſt ihnen nahe und giengſt doch vorüber: das verzeihen ſie dir niemals. Du gehſt über ſie hinaus: aber je höher du ſteigſt, um ſo kleiner ſieht dich das Auge des Neides. Am meiſten aber wird der Fliegende gehaßt. „Wie wolltet ihr gegen mich gerecht ſein! – mußt du ſprechen – ich erwähle mir eure Ungerechtigkeit als den mir zugemeßnen Theil.“ Ungerechtigkeit und Schmutz werfen ſie nach dem Einſamen: aber, mein Bruder, wenn du ein Stern ſein willſt, ſo mußt du ihnen deßhalb nicht weniger leuchten! Und hüte dich vor den Guten

31

● **1908 . ALSO SPRACH ZARATHUSTRA .** Book . Henry van de Velde

→ p.379

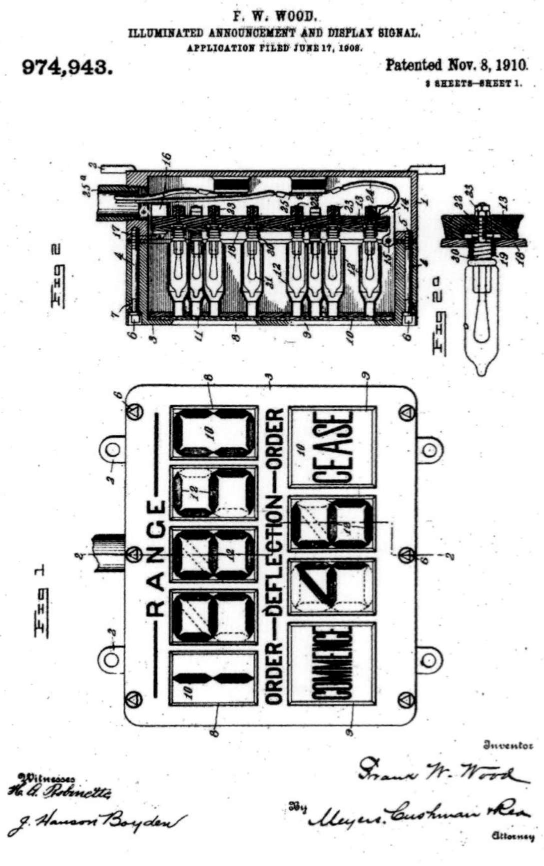

● **1908 . SEVEN-SEGMENT DISPLAY .** Typeface . Frank W. Wood

→ p.380

● **1908 . BAUMWOLLPFLÜCKERIN .** Poster . Oskar Kokoschka

→ p.380

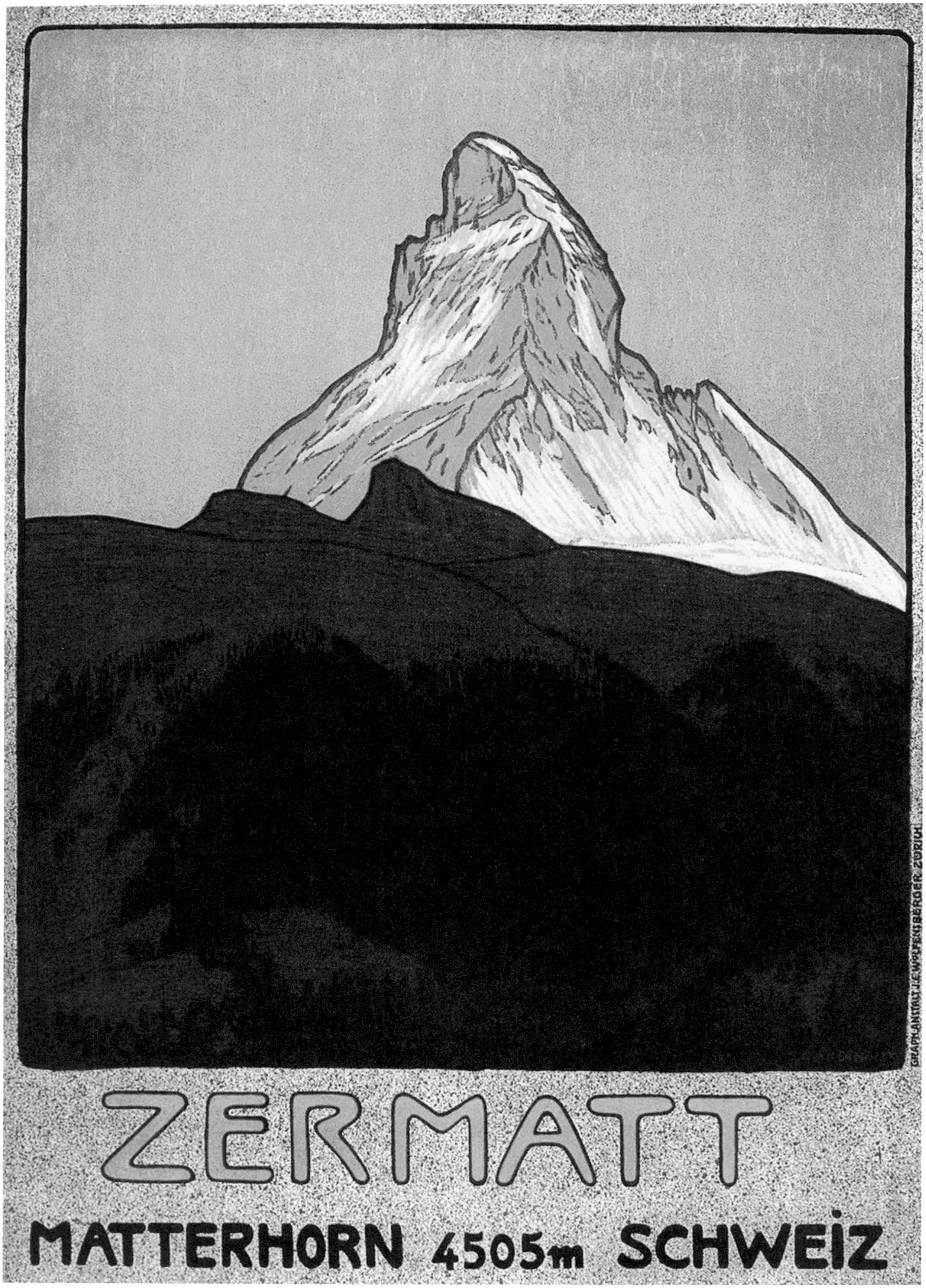

● **1908 . ZERMATT MATTERHORN .** Poster . Emil Cardinaux

→ p.380

● **1909 . COPYRIGHT** . Information Design . Unknown

→ p.381

● **1911 . OPEL** . Poster . Hans Rudi Erdt

→ p.381

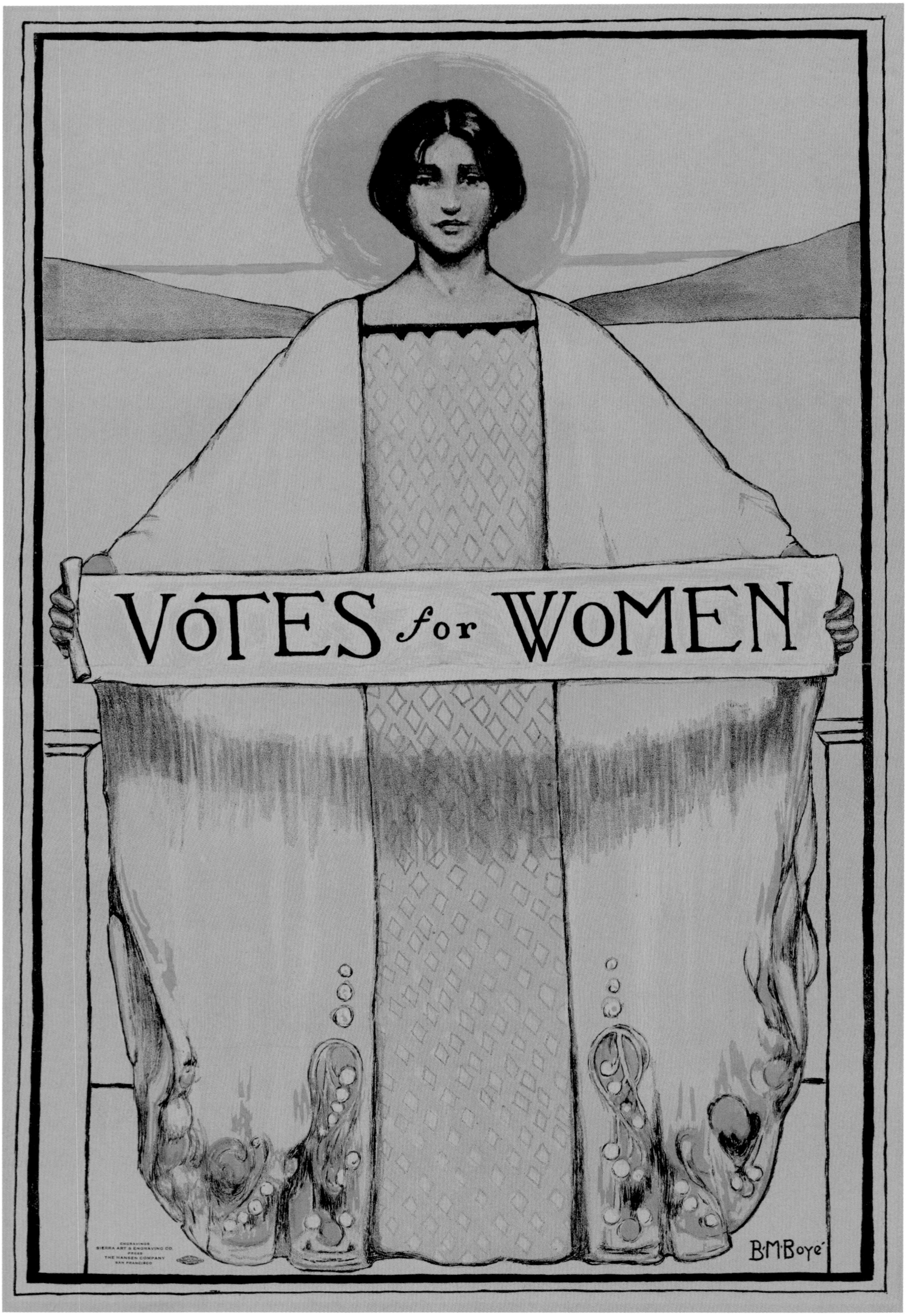

● **1911 . VOTES FOR WOMEN .** Poster . B. M. Boye

→ p.381

● **1912 . INSEL-BÜCHEREI .** Book Cover . Anton Kippenberg, Gotthard de Beauclair
FROM LEFT: *Sternstunden der Menschheit* (*Decisive Moments in History*), by Stefan Zweig, No. 165, 1927; *Jüdische Geschichten* (Jewish History), by J. L. Perez, No. 204, 1916; *Der Ausgewählten Gedichte Erster Teil* (Selected Poems, Part 1), by Rainer Maria Rilke, No. 400, ed. 1951

→ p.382

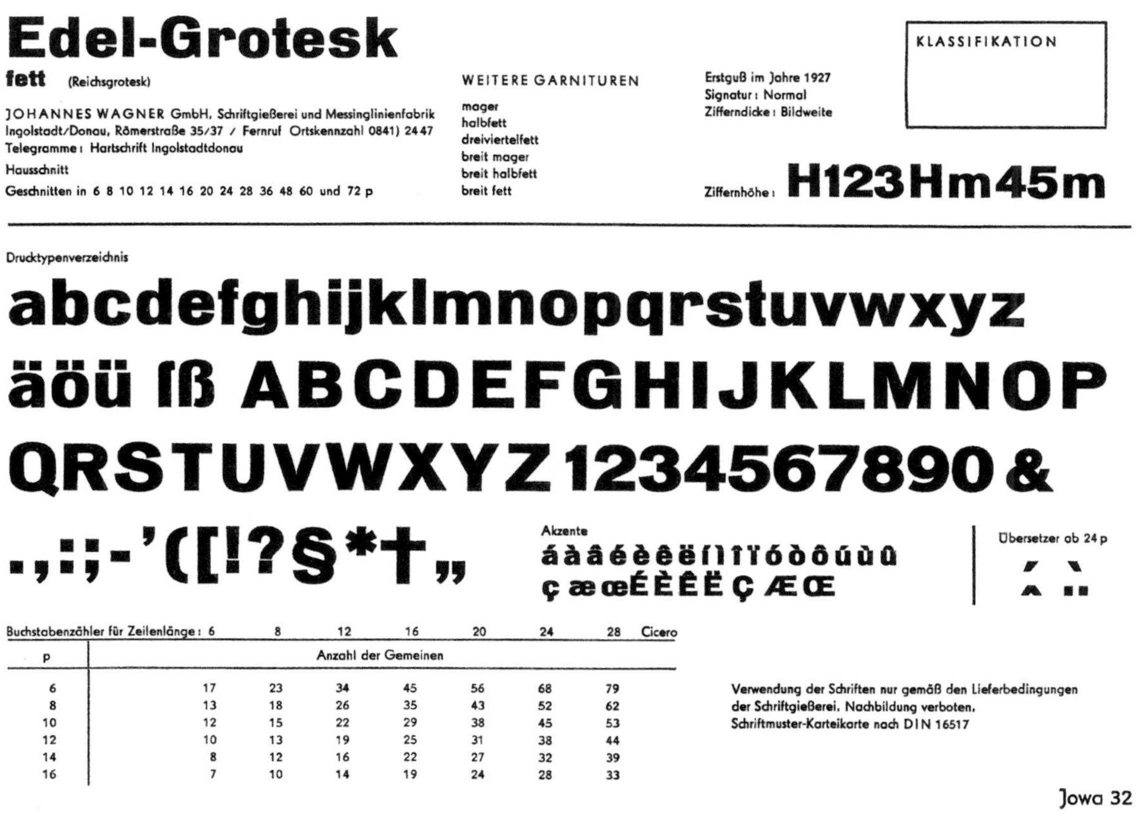

Edel-Grotesk
fett (Reichsgrotesk)

JOHANNES WAGNER GmbH, Schriftgießerei und Messinglinienfabrik
Ingolstadt/Donau, Römerstraße 35/37 / Fernruf Ortskennzahl 0841) 2447
Telegramme: Hartschrift Ingolstadtdonau
Hausschnitt
Geschnitten in 6 8 10 12 14 16 20 24 28 36 48 60 und 72 p

WEITERE GARNITUREN
mager
halbfett
dreiviertelfett
breit mager
breit halbfett
breit fett

Erstguß im Jahre 1927
Signatur: Normal
Zifferndicke: Bildweite

KLASSIFIKATION

Ziffernhöhe: H123Hm45m

Drucktypenverzeichnis

abcdefghijklmnopqrstuvwxyz
äöü ſß ABCDEFGHIJKLMNOP
QRSTUVWXYZ 1234567890 &
.,:;-'([!?§*†„

Akzente
á à â é è ê ë í ì î ï ó ò ô ú ù û
ç æ œ É È Ê Ë Ç Æ Œ

Übersetzer ab 24 p

Buchstabenzähler für Zeilenlänge: 6 8 12 16 20 24 28 Cicero

p	6	8	12	16	20	24	28
	Anzahl der Gemeinen						
6	17	23	34	45	56	68	79
8	13	18	26	35	43	52	62
10	12	15	22	29	38	45	53
12	10	13	19	25	31	38	44
14	8	12	16	22	27	32	39
16	7	10	14	19	24	28	33

Verwendung der Schriften nur gemäß den Lieferbedingungen der Schriftgießerei. Nachbildung verboten. Schriftmuster-Karteikarte nach DIN 16517

Jowa 32

● **1912–1914 . EDEL-GROTESK .** Typeface . Wagner & Schmidt

→ p.382

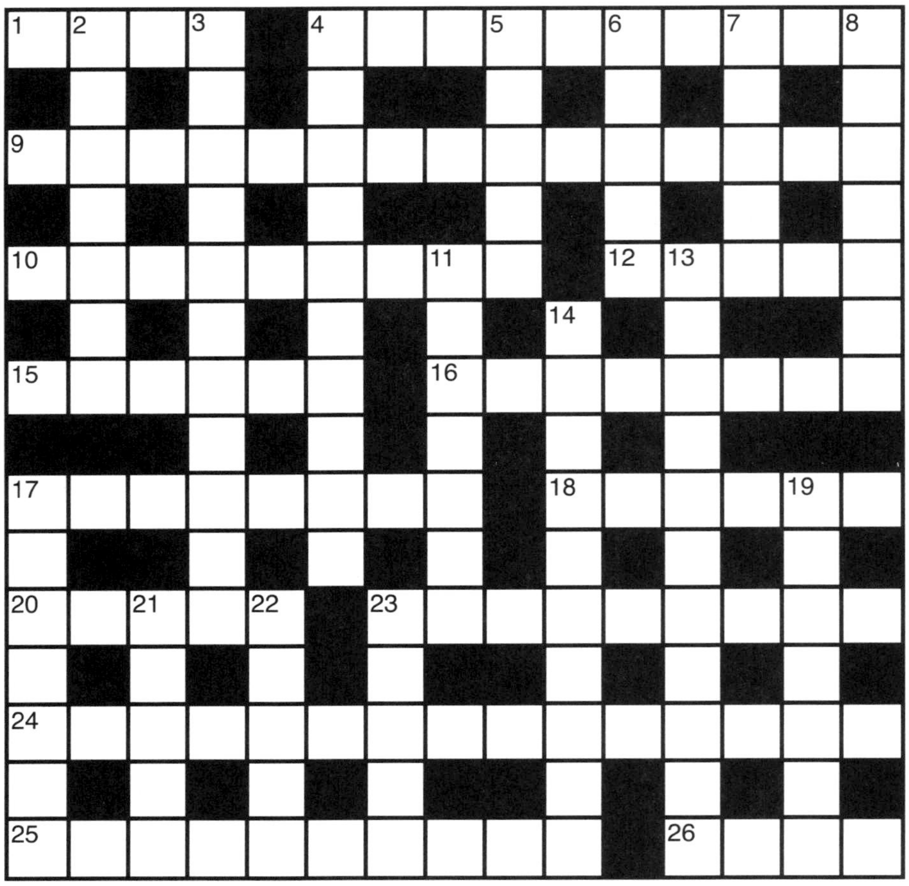

1913 . **CROSSWORD PUZZLE .** Information Design . Arthur Wynne

→ p.382

1913 . **OLYMPIC RINGS .** Logo . Pierre Frédy, Baron de Coubertin

→ p.383

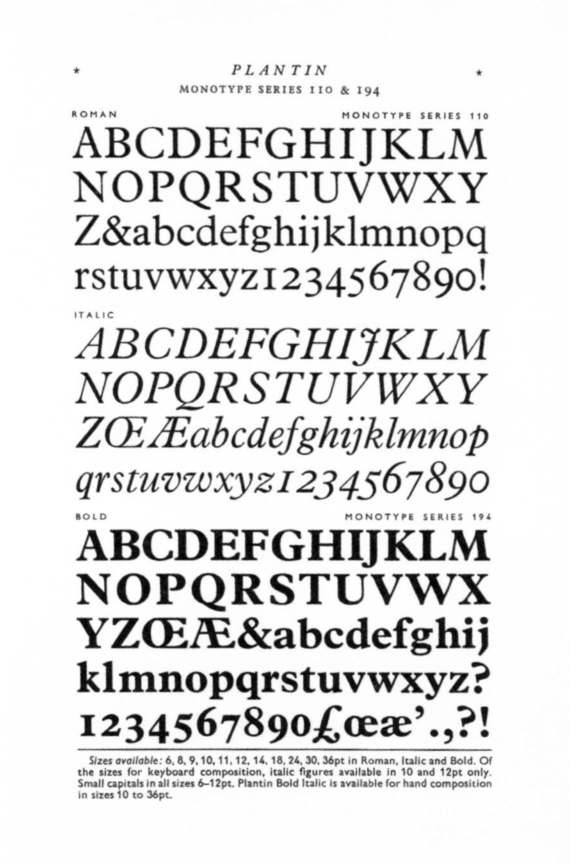

* PLANTIN *
MONOTYPE SERIES 110 & 194

ROMAN — MONOTYPE SERIES 110

ABCDEFGHIJKLM
NOPQRSTUVWXY
Z&abcdefghijklmnopq
rstuvwxyz1234567890!

ITALIC

ABCDEFGHIJKLM
NOPQRSTUVWXY
ZŒÆabcdefghijklmnop
qrstuvwxyz1234567890

BOLD — MONOTYPE SERIES 194

ABCDEFGHIJKLM
NOPQRSTUVWX
YZŒÆ&abcdefghij
klmnopqrstuvwxyz?
1234567890£œæ'.,?!

Sizes available: 6, 8, 9, 10, 11, 12, 14, 18, 24, 30, 36pt in Roman, Italic and Bold. Of the sizes for keyboard composition, italic figures available in 10 and 12pt only. Small capitals in all sizes 6–12pt. Plantin Bold Italic is available for hand composition in sizes 10 to 36pt.

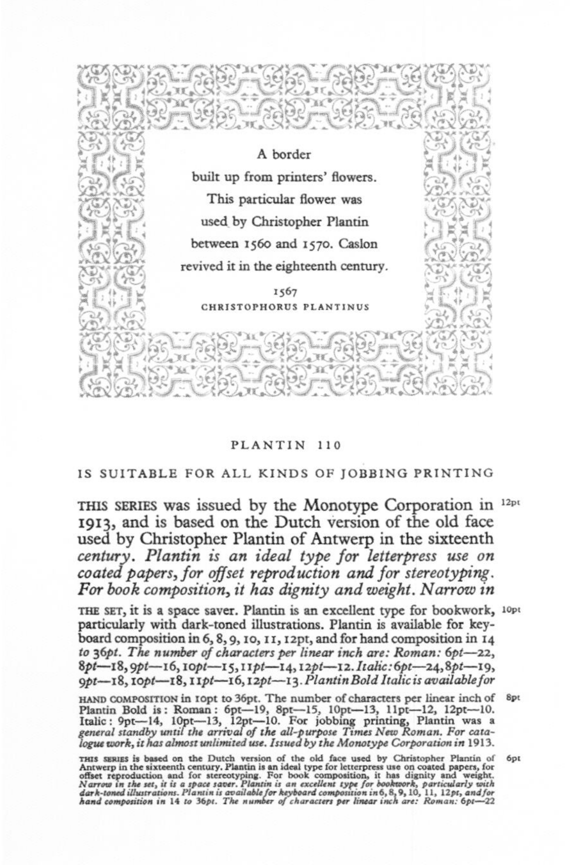

A border built up from printers' flowers. This particular flower was used by Christopher Plantin between 1560 and 1570. Caslon revived it in the eighteenth century.

1567
CHRISTOPHORUS PLANTINUS

PLANTIN 110

IS SUITABLE FOR ALL KINDS OF JOBBING PRINTING

THIS SERIES was issued by the Monotype Corporation in 1913, and is based on the Dutch version of the old face used by Christopher Plantin of Antwerp in the sixteenth century. *Plantin is an ideal type for letterpress use on coated papers, for offset reproduction and for stereotyping. For book composition, it has dignity and weight. Narrow in* 12pt

THE SET, it is a space saver. Plantin is an excellent type for bookwork, particularly with dark-toned illustrations. Plantin is available for keyboard composition in 6, 8, 9, 10, 11, 12pt, and for hand composition in 14 *to 36pt. The number of characters per linear inch are: Roman: 6pt—22, 8pt—18, 9pt—16, 10pt—15, 11pt—14, 12pt—12. Italic: 6pt—24, 8pt—19, 9pt—18, 10pt—18, 11pt—16, 12pt—13. Plantin Bold Italic is available for* 10pt

HAND COMPOSITION in 10pt to 36pt. The number of characters per linear inch of Plantin Bold is: Roman: 6pt—19, 8pt—15, 10pt—13, 11pt—12, 12pt—10. Italic: 9pt—14, 10pt—13, 12pt—10. For jobbing printing, Plantin was a *general standby until the arrival of the all-purpose Times New Roman. For catalogue work, it has almost unlimited use. Issued by the Monotype Corporation in* 1913. 8pt

THIS SERIES is based on the Dutch version of the old face used by Christopher Plantin of Antwerp in the sixteenth century. Plantin is an ideal type for letterpress use on coated papers, for offset reproduction and for stereotyping. For book composition, it has dignity and weight. *Narrow in the set, it is a space saver. Plantin is an excellent type for bookwork, particularly with dark-toned illustrations. Plantin is available for keyboard composition in 6, 8, 9, 10, 11, 12pt, and for hand composition in 14 to 36pt. The number of characters per linear inch are: Roman: 6pt—22* 6pt

● **1913 . PLANTIN .** Typeface . F. H. Pierpont, after Christophe Plantin

→ p.383

LACERBA

ANNO II, N. 19 — Periodico quindicinale | FIRENZE, 20 SETTEMBRE 1914 — Via Ricasoli, 8 | IL N. 2 SOLDI — L'ANNO 4 LIRE

LACERBA, Dichiarazione. — PAPINI, Finiamola! — SOFFICI, Per la guerra. — NEAL, L'Italia al bivio. — TAVOLATO, s c i o u. — FOLGORE ... — REGHINI, Sempre avanti. — DISTASO, Cosa siamo!

DICHIARAZIONE

Il governo italiano il quale sta in questo momento disonorando e rovinando il paese con l'insistere, nessuno sa perchè, in una neutralità divenuta ormai imbecille, non perde nessuna occasione per dichiarare che questo suo modo di comportarsi davanti agli avvenimenti che trasformeranno la faccia dell'Europa, corrisponde perfettamente al desiderio della maggioranza del popolo italiano. Noi non crediamo che questa sia la verità. Eccettuati i preti, una parte dei socialisti e pochi trippai amanti del quieto vivere a costo di qualunque umiliazione, nessuno in Italia approva l'inerzia che il governo c'impone, che ci snerva e che ci condurrà alla più abbietta depressione morale, se non, alla fine, a una reazione esasperata che a parecchi potrà costare assai caro.

Comunque, e anche ammettendo che, secondo le convinzioni di Palazzo Braschi e della Consulta, il nostro popolo sia davvero il popolo più stolto, vile e nullo della terra, è bene si sappia a Roma e per tutto che se la maggioranza approva il contegno del nostro governo, c'è tuttavia un certo numero d'italiani i quali non l'approvano assolutamente e non intendono affatto assumerne la responsabilità morale.

Al contrario, questa minoranza desidera:

1. - Che il governo italiano, in conformità della sua promessa di difendere i nostri interessi materiali e ideali già anche troppo minacciati e danneggiati dall'azione aggressiva delle nostre antiche alleate, agisca contro di esse in ordine del diritto e della civiltà.

2. - Che le terre irredente e le coste adriatiche congiunte per sangue, lingua e amore alla patria italiana siano a questa vittoriosamente e definitivamente riunite.

3. - Che l'Italia uscita per consenso unanime di popolo dalla triplice alleanza stabilisca a partire da questo gran momento la sua politica su basi che non siano, come per il passato, fatte d'errori, d'equivoci e di compromessi contro natura. Errori equivoci e compromessi che ci hanno fruttato volta a volta inimicizie, offese, danni e le più crudeli disillusioni.

4. - Che tuttociò avvenga nel più breve tempo possibile, giacchè gli avvenimenti incalzano che potrebbero volgersi a nostro svantaggio o a nostro disonore, l'inverno si avvicina, il tempo stringe, e sarebbe assurdo e criminoso decidersi troppo tardi.

C'è - se la maggioranza vuol altro - una minoranza che vuol questo; e noi ci sentiamo orgogliosi di far parte di questa pretesa minoranza.

LACERBA

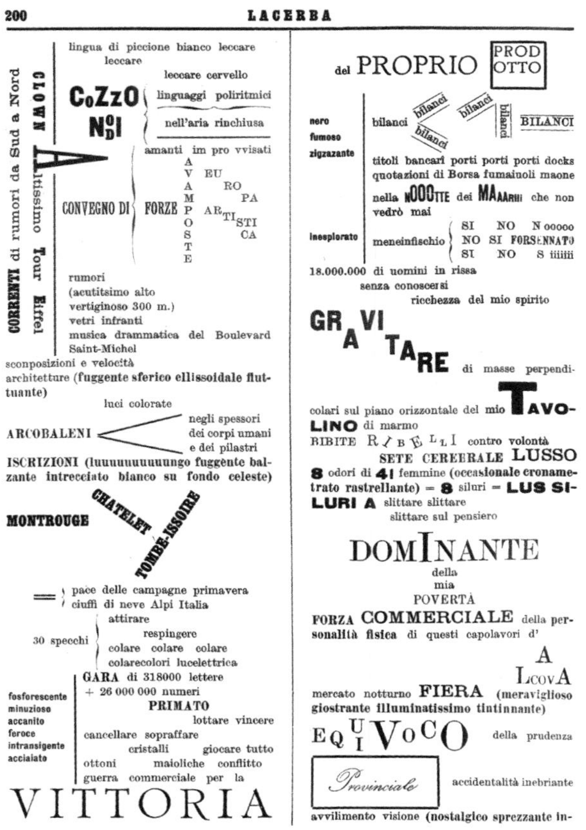

200 — LACERBA

lingua di piccione bianco leccare leccare
leccare cervello
linguaggi poliritmici
nell'aria rinchiusa
CoZzO NøDI
CLOWN
CORRENTI di rumori da Sud a Nord
A ltissimo Tour Eiffel
amanti im pro vvisati
A V A M P O S T E
EU RO PA
AR TI STI CA
CONVEGNO DI FORZE
rumori
(acutitsimo alto
vertiginoso 300 m.)
vetri infranti
musica drammatica del Boulevard Saint-Michel
scomposizioni e velocità
architetture (fuggente sferico ellissoidale fluttuante)
luci colorate
negli spessori
dei corpi umani
e dei pilastri
ARCOBALENI
ISCRIZIONI (luuuuuuuuuungo fuggente balzante intrecciato bianco su fondo celeste)
MONTROUGE
CHATELET
TOMBE-ISSOIRE
pace delle campagne primavera
ciuffi di neve Alpi Italia
attirare
respingere
30 specchi
colare colare colare
colarecolori lucelettrica
GARA di 318000 lettere
+ 26 000 000 numeri
PRIMATO
lottare vincere
cancellare sopraffare
cristalli giocare tutto
ottoni maioliche conflitto
guerra commerciale per la
fosforescente minuzioso accanito feroce intransigente acciaiato
VITTORIA

del PROPRIO PROD OTTO
nero fumoso zigzazante
bilanci bilanci bilanci bilanci bilanci BILANCI
titoli bancari porti porti porti docks
quotazioni di Borsa fumaiuoli maone
nella NOOOTTE dei MAAARIII che non vedrò mai
inesplorato
meneinfischio
SI NO N ooooo
NO SI FORSENNATO
SI NO S iiiiii
18.000.000 di uomini in rissa
senza conoscersi
ricchezza del mio spirito
GR A VI TA RE di masse perpendicolari sul piano orizzontale del mio TAVOLINO di marmo
BIBITE RIBELLI contro volontà
SETE CEREBRALE LUSSO
8 odori di 41 femmine (occasionale cronametrato rastrellante) = 8 siluri = LUS SILURI A slittare slittare
slittare sul pensiero
DOMINANTE
della
mia
POVERTÀ
FORZA COMMERCIALE della personalità fisica di questi capolavori d'
A
LCOVA
mercato notturno FIERA (meraviglioso giostrante illuminatissimo tintinnante)
EQUIVOCO della prudenza
Provinciale
accidentalità inebriante
avvilimento visione (nostalgico sprezzante in-

● **1913–1915 . LACERBA .** Magazine / Newspaper . Giovanni Papini, Ardengo Soffici
LEFT: Vol. 2, No. 19, September 20, 1914; RIGHT: Vol. 2, No. 13, July 1, 1914

→ p.383

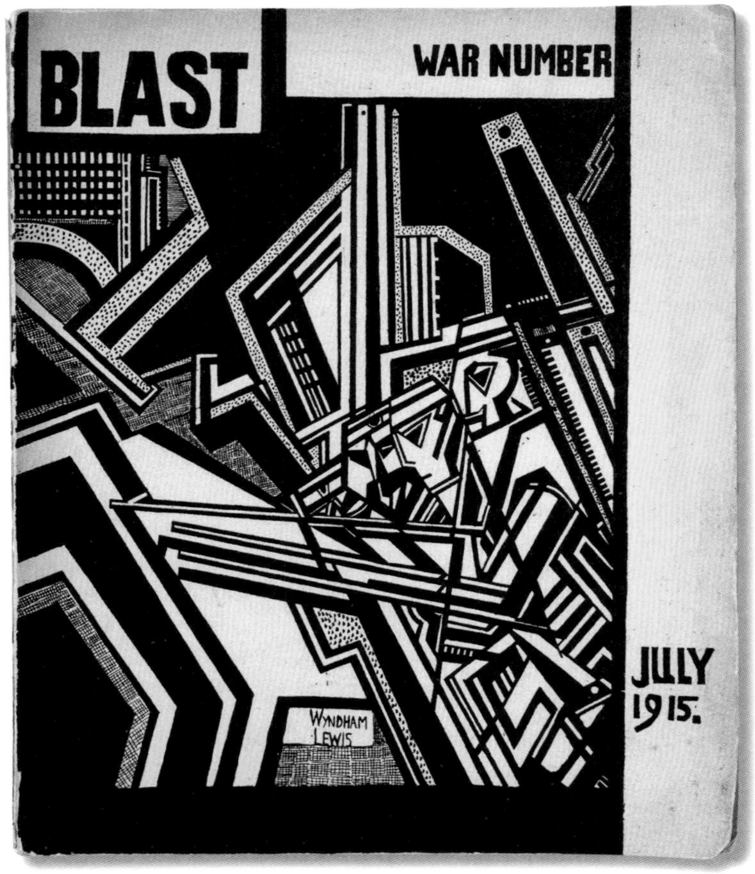

● **1914 . ZANG TUMB TUMB .**
Book . Filippo T. Marinetti

→ p.384

● **1914–1915 . BLAST .** Magazine / Newspaper . Wyndham Lewis
"War Number," No. 2, July 1915

→ p.384

● **1916 . BATAVIER LIJN, ROTTERDAM–LONDEN .** Poster . Bart van der Leck

→ p.384

IM JUNI 1917

NEUE JUGEND

PREIS 20 PF.

PROSPEKT
zur Kleinen Grosz Mappe.

Prospekt zur Kleinen Grosz Mappe.

Der Malik-Verlag, Berlin-Südende

34, Steglitzer Strasse, Südende.

CHRONIK Friedrich Adler ist zum Tode verurteilt, Stockholm-Getöne gegen internationale Teuerung - das Leben weiterhin billiger, Lebensmittel bleiben in Cornerstimmung. Nach Reuter verhungern in Ovamboland die Ovambos, keine Kaffern - in den European Dominions niemand! Verhungert doch - Steigerung!! Spinoza ist eingestampft für Bedarf diplomatischer Sendschreiben - Liberia, Pseudoliberia - Molière verrieselt in Sternheim (Zukunft vom 26. 5. 1917), Umfassungsmanöver gegen Wallner in Wien, Durst! - das Aktionsbuch ist erschienen. Frühlingswende fiebert Sexualität, Heufieber. Liebeloh la l'au! Sich hinzu-schmeissen! Lichtmord!! — unsere Seelen sind so wund. **Amokläufer** .... Die Messer raus!!!

Man muß Kautschukmann sein!

Ja, Kautschukmann sein — eventuell den Kopf zwischen die Beine stecken oder durchs Faß springen — und spiralig in die Luft schnellen! sieh, ein Paragraph rempelt Dich an,
eine Affiche,
ein Flohzirkus . . .
. . . .
(sämtliche Flöhe liegen an Schlingen — desertieren ausgeschlossen — Springen von Flöhen auf Kommando, Parademarsch der Flöhe
. . . .)
Immerhin wichtig ist, das Gleichgewichtzu behalten!
Wo vordem die gotische Kirche,
messelt sich heute
das Warenhaus hoch — !

EIN „MARSIAS" INTERESSENT

— Die Fahrstühle sausen . . . Eisenbahnunglücks, Explosionskatastrophen . . . .
— quer durchrast der Balkanzug Mitteleuropa,
doch gibts auch Baumblüte und Edelmarmeladenrationierung . . . .
Wie gesagt, Kautschukmann sein
beweglich in allen Knochen
nicht blos im Dichter-Sessel dösen
oder vor der Staffelei schön getönte Bildchen pinseln.

Den Bequemen gilts zu stören
beim Verdauungsschläfchen
ihm den pazifistischen Popo zu kitzeln,
rumort! explodiert! zerplatzt! — oder hängt euch ans Fensterkreuz . . . .
Laßt euren Kadaver in die Branntweingasse baumeln!
Ja! Wieder elastisch werden, nach allen Seiten höchst federnd — sich verbiegen — anboxen! Kinn- oder Herzgrubenhieb!

Ladies and gentlemen!!
Jeder hat Zutritt!

Nur nähertreten!! . . . nur nähertreten!! . . .
Schon beulen sie den Weihrauchkessel ein.
Nervös rutscht das weiche Gesäß hin und her!
. . . .
Ja! Wenn nicht sämtliche Flöhe an Schlingen lägen! . . . .

Dieses Blatt ist der

PROSPEKT ZUR KLEINEN GROSZ-MAPPE

Die Sekte 1917

Die Sekte Neunzehn Siebzehn wächst aus dem Intellekt der umstehenden Zuhörer empor und zwingt ihre Mitglieder gegen den Block der Überzeugten. Die ohnmächtige Wut unserer Leser verpflichtet, einen bereits in Schwingung umgesetzten Glauben wieder zu fixieren, um mit den Gläubigen von neuem dagegen loszugehen. Die Leute wollen halt nichts alleine tun.

Sekten. Mehr Sekten. Noch mehr Sekten.

Das Wunder der Christian Science ist über unseren kürzlich veranstalteten Werbe Abend gerauscht und schüttet Glück aus über diejenigen, die uns lieben, um uns hinterrücks zu erdolchen.

Darum muss Einer seine Stimme erheben: Nicht mehr glauben, überhaupt nicht glauben. Sich selbst. (Sich und selbst) Beten.

Wenngleich jeder schuldig ist an der Unfähigkeit der andern, Feind zu sein, sondern schlotternder Neidhammel, soll keiner an dieser Schuld sich selbst beruhigt genug sein lassen. Nicht das Peinliche dieser Schuld schmatzend zu fressen, soll es ankommen, sondern Genuss auch noch auszukotzen — und wiederum zu fressen und wiederum!

Es ist in jeder Sekunde, die ein hundertmal verfluchtes Leben schenkt (unsägliche Wonne durstend das galizische Petroleumgebiet zu durchfahren, die Gestänge der Bohrtürme verrusst!) so unendlich vieles zu tun.

Betet mit dem Schädel gegen die Wand!!

Wir — aha! — wir treten gegen die Menschen nicht auf. Wir treten geduldig noch mit den Menschen auf. Die Sekte Neunzehn Siebzehn schlägt gegeneinander, Sturmflut aus unseren Gebeten, die aus der Ohnmacht der Gläubigen emporgewachsen sind. Unsere Mitglieder verrecken, weil die Sekte sie nicht mehr locker lässt. Betet aus unseren Gebeten zu diesem Ende. Damit ihr endlich in die Schlinge kommt. Es ist ein so ungleiches Spiel mit diesen Sanften, Zappelnden. Der Magen der **Neunzehn Siebzehn** will das alles nicht mehr verdauen, immer wieder dasselbe, die Ohnmacht der Gläubigen, der Block der Ueberzeugten, das Einfangen, Verarbeiten, Auskotzen, Fressen,

das Ich triumphierend über Puntas Arenas, Michigan See, Sachalin bis Sorau. Dort wurde der Dichter Heinrich Steinhausen geboren, steht in der Zeitung.

Halt dich, Junge.

Die Frist ist um. Her die neue Ladung. Sektierer, los! Wieviel zappeln schon wieder?

Die Arbeit Arbeit Arbeit Arbeit: Triumph der Christian Science.

Das Wunder der Sekte Neunzehn Siebzehn.

1917.

SCHREIT!!

Kannst du radfahren?

Zu den reinsten unverbildeten Erklärungen und Dokumenten unseres Lebens gehören jene Bilder auf den Rückfronten der Häuser, diese Erlasse des Kaufmanns (des wahren Herrn dieser Zeit) — von unerhörter Sachlichkeit vorgetragen, gigantisch eingeätzt wie auf alten Pyramiden, pressen sie das psychologische und formale Erleben des in knallendem Stadtbahnzug Dahinrollenden. Fabelhaft bunt und klar, wie nie ein Tafelbildchen, — von kosmischer Komik, brutal, materiell, bleichsüchtig, verwaschen — drohend und mahnend gleich Ragtimestepptanzmelodie immer wieder sich ins Gehirn bohrend —

Das gröhlt in einem fort!

Zwingt uns zum prallenden Marineblau, zu Grellrots (ganze Straßen Buchstaben), Varietégrün, Spezialitätengelb, Wollwarengraus, und fistelndes Rosa —

Moziationen tauchen auf . . . .

Champagner-Flasche — der Korken knallt davon, ho! ho!

Sekt Schloss Vaux.

Ich, Dannemann-Zigarre schief im Maul, Zeitung — vor mir knerzen die Knattermotore — hart überholt nach Backbord der rote Autobus!

Ho! ho! schon wieder brüllen die Häuserwände:

Regie-Zigaretten, *Satrap,* Palast-Hotel, Teppich-Thomas, bade zu Hause, Steiners Paradiesbett . . . . . ho! . . . . . *Sarg's Kalodont* . . . . . Passage-Cafe . . . . . **AEG** . . . . . Ceresit.

z. B., vom Training kommend, am Punching Ball . . . . Den Joe hiebst Du nieder.

z. B., Du segeltest fabelhaft in die Chausseen, eben noch flog Dir der Fußball an die klemmerlose Nase, Du hingst oben im Aeroplan unter der Bergsonne — zwischen den Stämmen knallte Deine Winchesterbüchse (Gott ließ ja Eisen wachsen, bravo)

Abends in deu Asphaltbrüchen, in Geldsack-Hills, zwischen Porter-Bierplakaten, oder an der Bar bei Kantorowicz, in Zooquellen oder pikfein mit steifem Hemd aalglatt bei Adlon, strömendes **Pils Coctails Ersatz** und Agoston, **Apollotheater** und Kinohäuser . . . . und dem Treiben der beiden Herzfelder! . . . .

Sag mal? — . . . . . . **graults Dir** da **nicht** in den Kunstsalons? in den Ölgemäldegalerien . . . . . . ?
in den literarische Soiréen . . . . . ?

Lieber Leser! Ein guter Fußballspieler enthält immerhin eine ganze Menge Wert — obwohl er nicht dichtet, malt und Töne setzt!

Bleibt die Frage?

Kennst Du Schiller und Goethe — ? — ja!

Aber kannst Du radfahren?

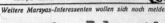

Weitere Marsyas-Interessenten wollen sich noch melden!

● **1916–1917 . NEUE JUGEND .** Magazine / Newspaper . John Heartfield
No. 2, June 1917

→ p.385

● **1916 . PEOPLE'S CHARITY FOR GERMAN PRISONERS OF WAR AND CIVILIAN INTERNEES .** Poster . Ludwig Hohlwein

→ p.385

ZESDE JAARGANG 1924-1925
NB
DE STIJL
12
INTERNATIONAAL MAANDBLAD
VOOR NIEUWE KUNST WETEN-
SCHAP EN KULTUUR REDACTIE
THEO VAN DOESBURG
WARSCHAU
LEIDEN HANNOVER PARIJS BRNO WEENEN

● **1917–1932 . DE STIJL .** Magazine / Newspaper . Theo van Doesburg, Vilmos Huszár
Vol. 6, No. 12, 1924–5

→ p.385

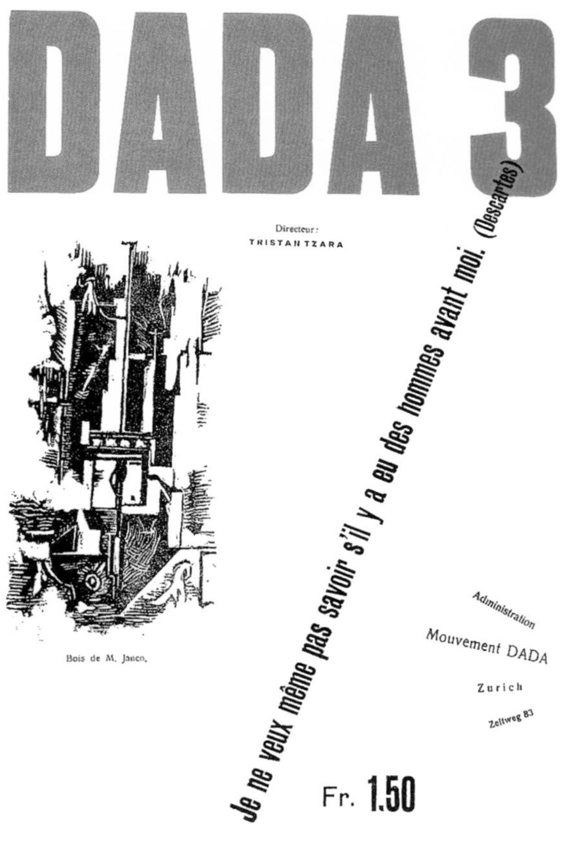

DADA 3
Directeur:
TRISTAN TZARA
Je ne veux même pas savoir s'il y a eu des hommes avant moi. (Descartes)
Bois de M. Janco.
Administration
Mouvement DADA
Zurich
Zeltweg 83
Fr. 1.50

● **1917–1920 . DADA .** Magazine / Newspaper . Francis Picabia, Tristan Tzara, Marcel Janco
LEFT: Marcel Janco, No. 3, December 1918; RIGHT: Francis Picabia, No. 4–5, January 1919

→ p.386

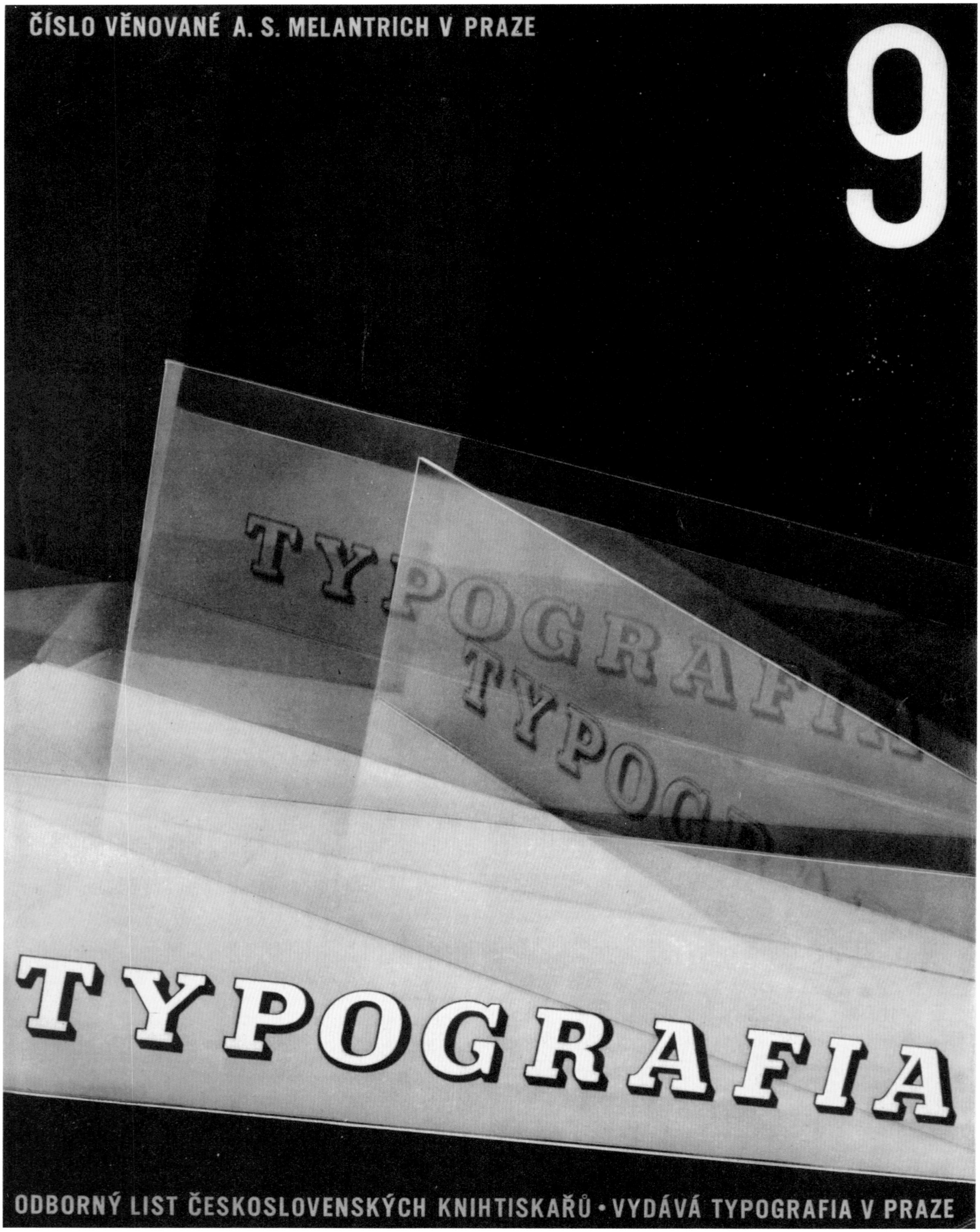
ČÍSLO VĚNOVANÉ A. S. MELANTRICH V PRAZE
9
TYPOGRAFIA
ODBORNÝ LIST ČESKOSLOVENSKÝCH KNIHTISKAŘŮ • VYDÁVÁ TYPOGRAFIA V PRAZE

● **1918–1939 . TYPOGRAFIA .** Magazine / Newspaper . Various
Vol. 39, No. 9, September 1932

→ p.386

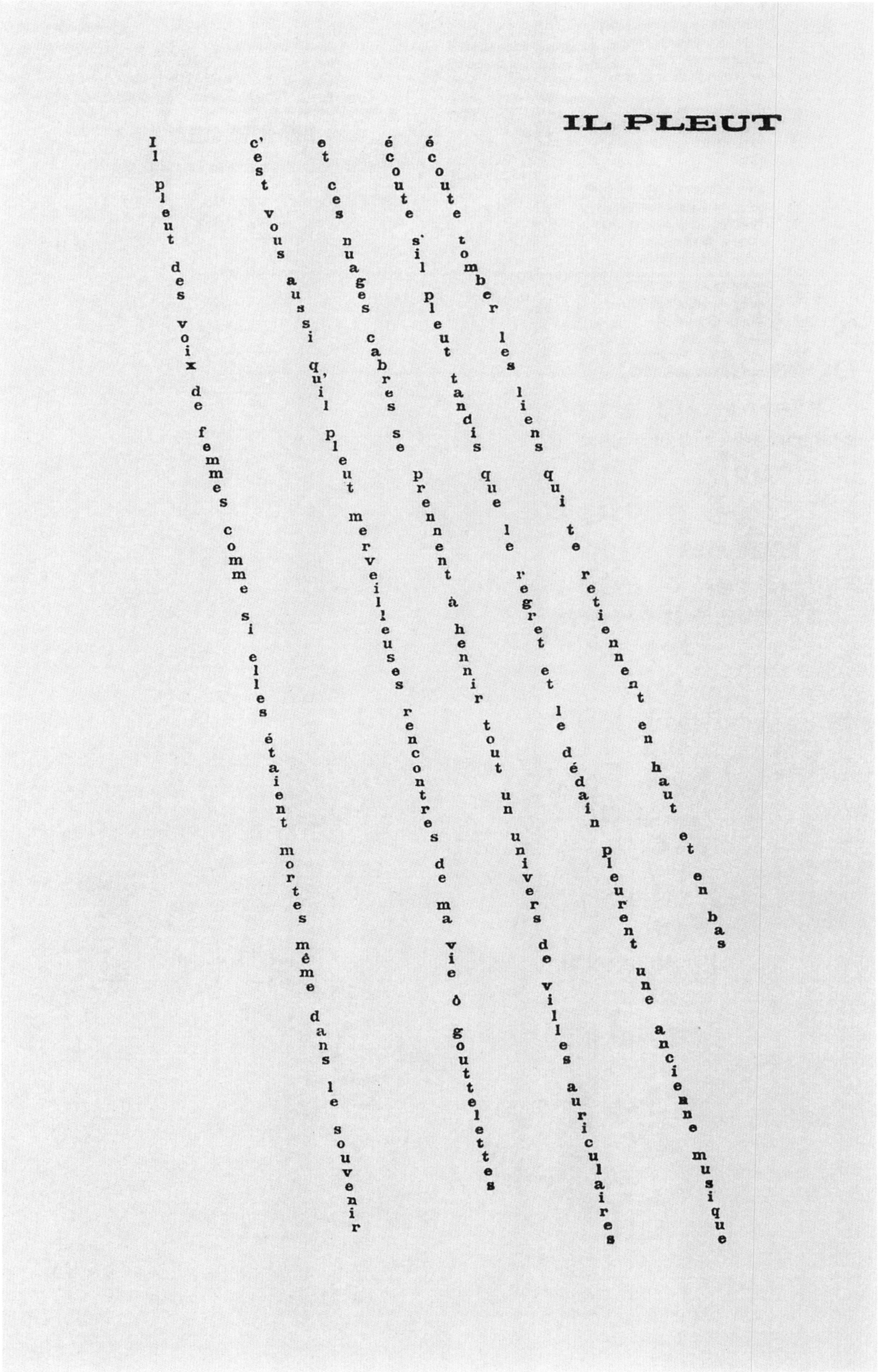

IL PLEUT

Il pleut des voix de femmes comme si elles étaient mortes même dans le souvenir
c'est vous aussi qu'il pleut merveilleuses rencontres de ma vie ô gouttelettes
et ces nuages cabrés se prennent à hennir tout un univers de villes auriculaires
écoute s'il pleut tandis que le regret et le dédain pleurent une ancienne musique
écoute tomber les liens qui te retiennent en haut et en bas

1918 . IL PLEUT . Book . Guillaume Apollinaire

→ p.386

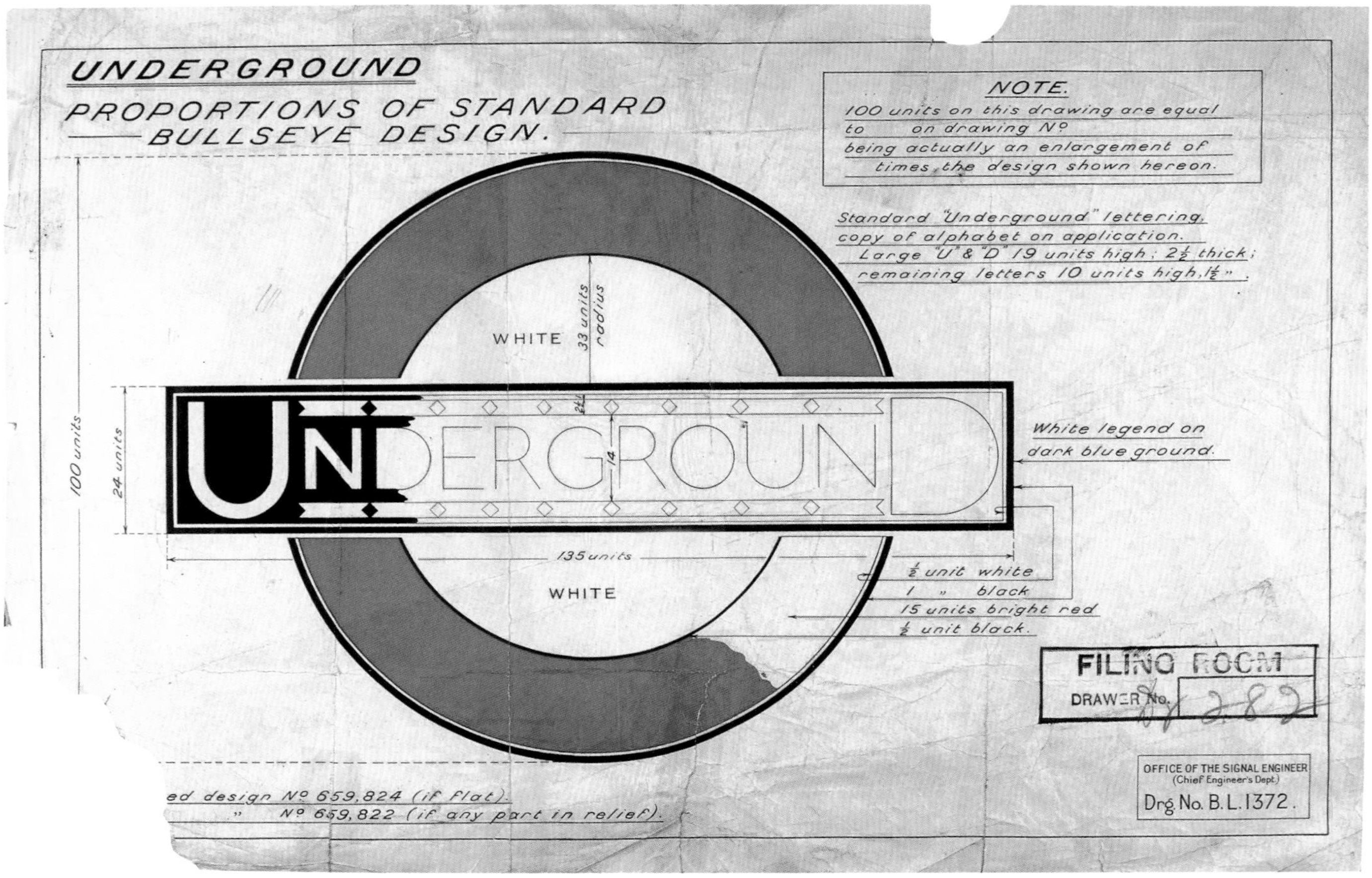

● **1918 . LONDON UNDERGROUND .** Logo . Edward Johnston

→ p.387

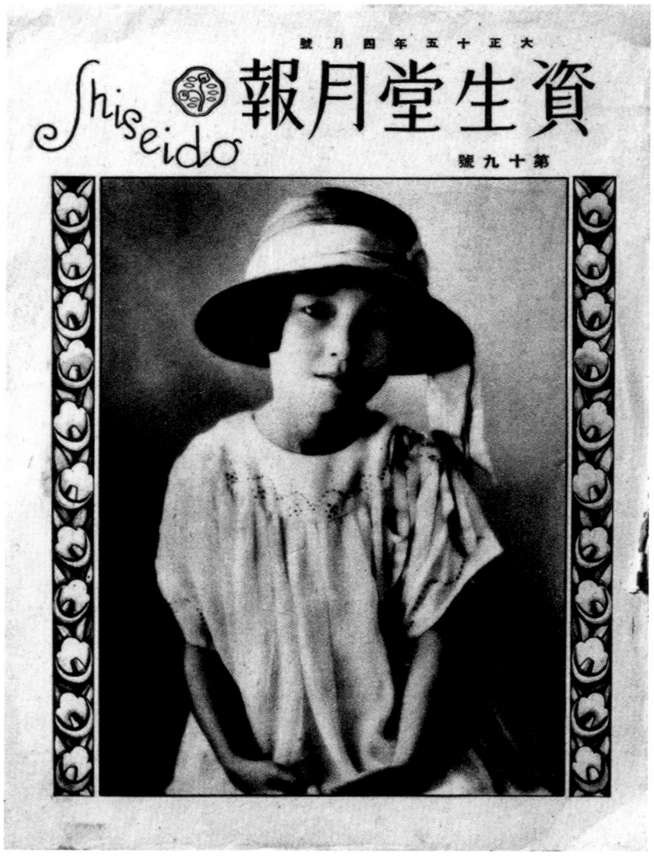

● **1918 . SHISEIDO .** Logo . Shinzo Fukuhara
Shiseido Monthly Info, April 1926

→ p.387

C'est le

31

Décembre

Dieu le père est à son bureau américain. Il signe hâtivement d'innombrables papiers. Il est en bras de chemise et a un abat-jour vert sur les yeux. Il se lève, allume un gros cigare, consulte sa montre, marche nerveusement dans son cabinet, va et vient en mâchonnant son cigare. Il se rassied à son bureau, repousse fiévreu-

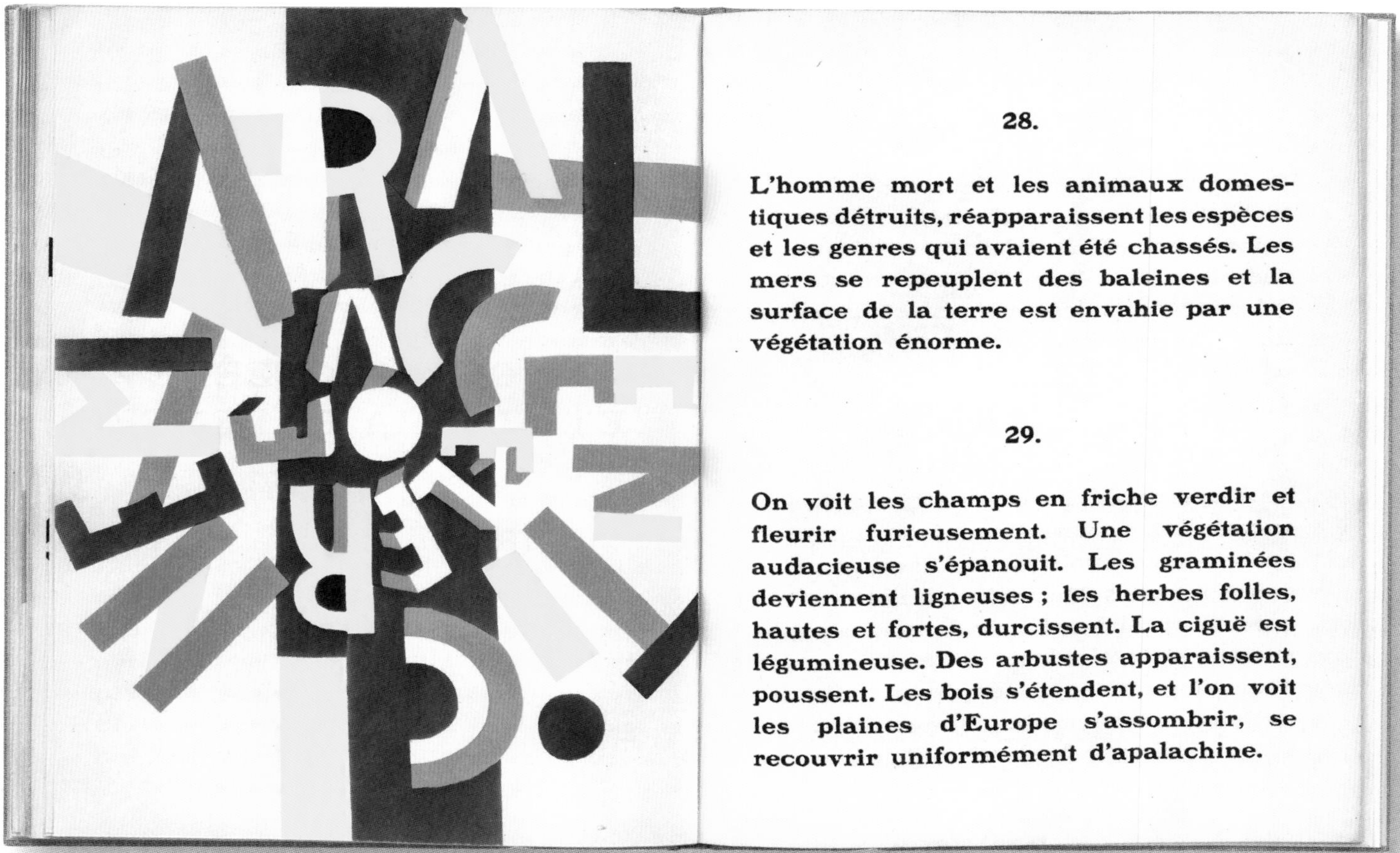

28.

L'homme mort et les animaux domestiques détruits, réapparaissent les espèces et les genres qui avaient été chassés. Les mers se repeuplent des baleines et la surface de la terre est envahie par une végétation énorme.

29.

On voit les champs en friche verdir et fleurir furieusement. Une végétation audacieuse s'épanouit. Les graminées deviennent ligneuses ; les herbes folles, hautes et fortes, durcissent. La ciguë est légumineuse. Des arbustes apparaissent, poussent. Les bois s'étendent, et l'on voit les plaines d'Europe s'assombrir, se recouvrir uniformément d'apalachine.

● 1919 . LA FIN DU MONDE, BY BLAISE CENDRARS . Book . Fernand Léger

→ p.387

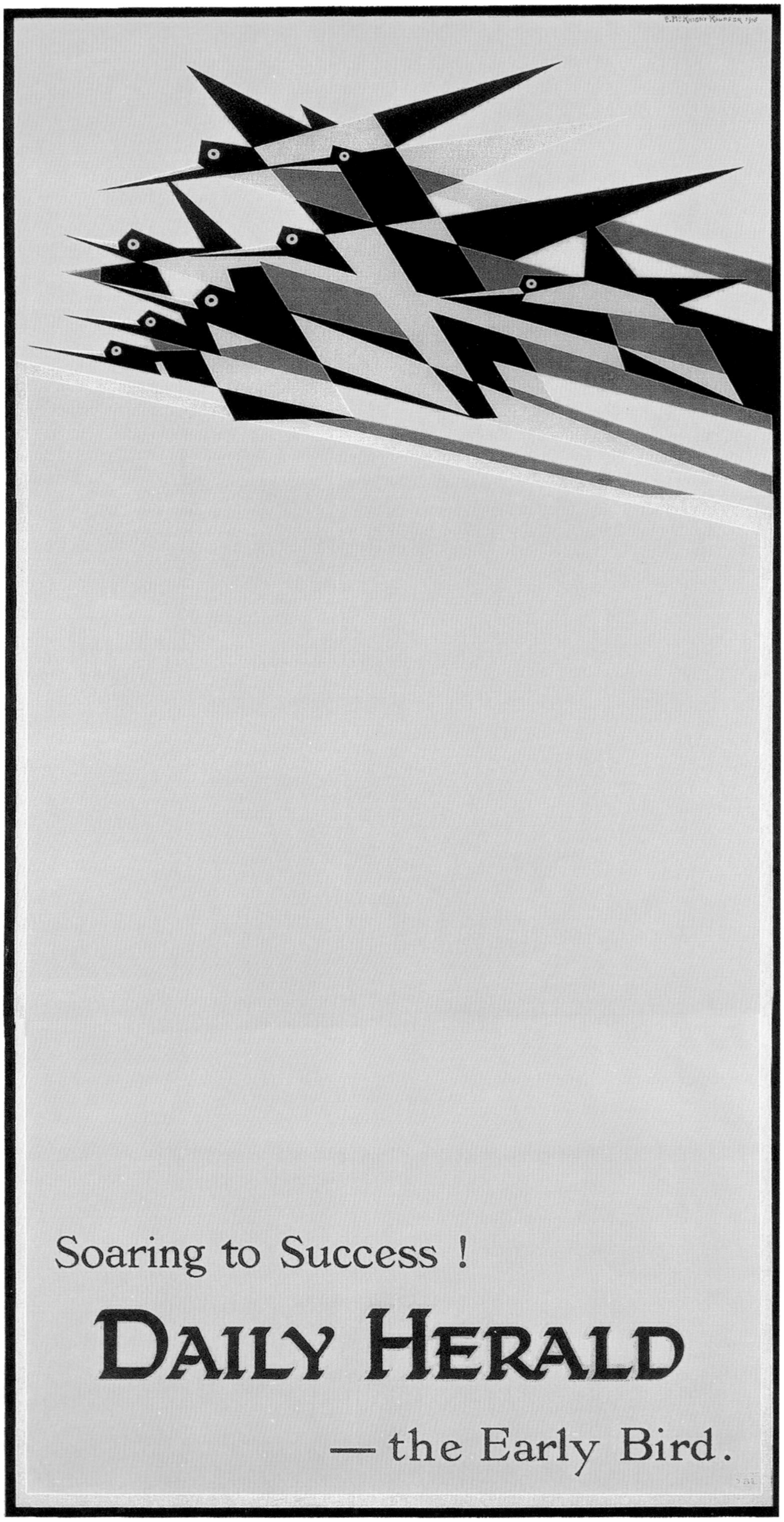

● **1919 . FLIGHT .** Poster . Edward McKnight Kauffer

→ p.388

● **1920 . PRO DVA KVADRATA .** Book . El Lissitzky

→ p.388

● **1920–1924 . BROOM .** Magazine / Newspaper . Various
LEFT: Ladislaw Medges, Vol. 2, No. 3, June 1922; RIGHT: El Lissitzky, Vol. 4, No. 3, February 1923

→ p.388

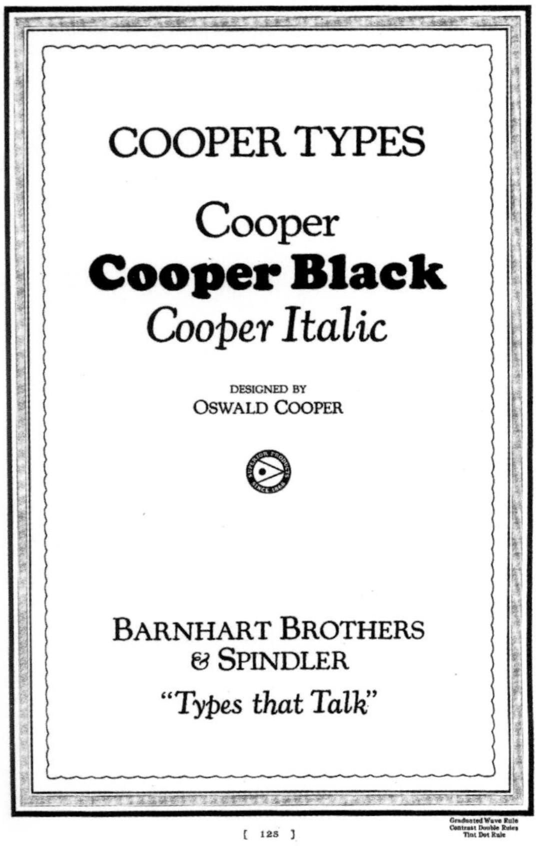

COOPER TYPES

Cooper

Cooper Black

Cooper Italic

DESIGNED BY
OSWALD COOPER

BARNHART BROTHERS
& SPINDLER

"Types that Talk"

[125]

Graduated Wave Rule
Contrast Double Rules
Tint Dot Rule

COOPER BLACK
PATENT PENDING

48 Point 3 A 4 a
SCORE PUNCH
Bold Ideas Goal

36 Point 3 A 4 a
CRITICS HONORED
Vigorous & Original

30 Point 4 A 7 a
SUCH STRONG DESIGN
Inspires Absolute Belief

24 Point 5 A 9 a
¶ MAKING METHODS PUBLIC
Startle Foes—Convince Friend

18 Point 6 A 13 a
MAIL ORDER HOUSE
Desires Strong Virile
Figures $1234567890

10 Point 14 A 28 a
THIS FACE TAKES HEAVY INK
Because of this fact a spotlight [so to speak] may be directed to the strong points one may wish emphasized in sales arguments

14 Point 10 A 20 a
SHOWING UNIFORM SIZES
By Using More Cooper Black
Modern Ideas Are Produced

8 Point 16 A 32 a
COOPER DESIGN BY LETTER EXPERT
Oswald Cooper who has originated this letter of character occupies an enviable place among advertising profession and has added great deal to its advancement

12 Point 13 A 26 a
LETTERS ARE MADE CLOSE SET
Making Possible Designs of Massed
Arrangement Like Hand Lettering

6 Point 18 A 36 a
DESIGNS WITH THE PROPER KNOWLEDGE
He understands the anatomy of letters—their bones as he calls them—the result of which is structure and form with strength and beauty giving design intrinsic worth of enduring art

All Fonts contain ¶ • — [ ] special characters

[133]

● **1921 . COOPER BLACK .** Typeface . Oswald Cooper

→ p.389

● **1921 . CHANEL .** Identity . Gabrielle "Coco" Chanel

→ p.389

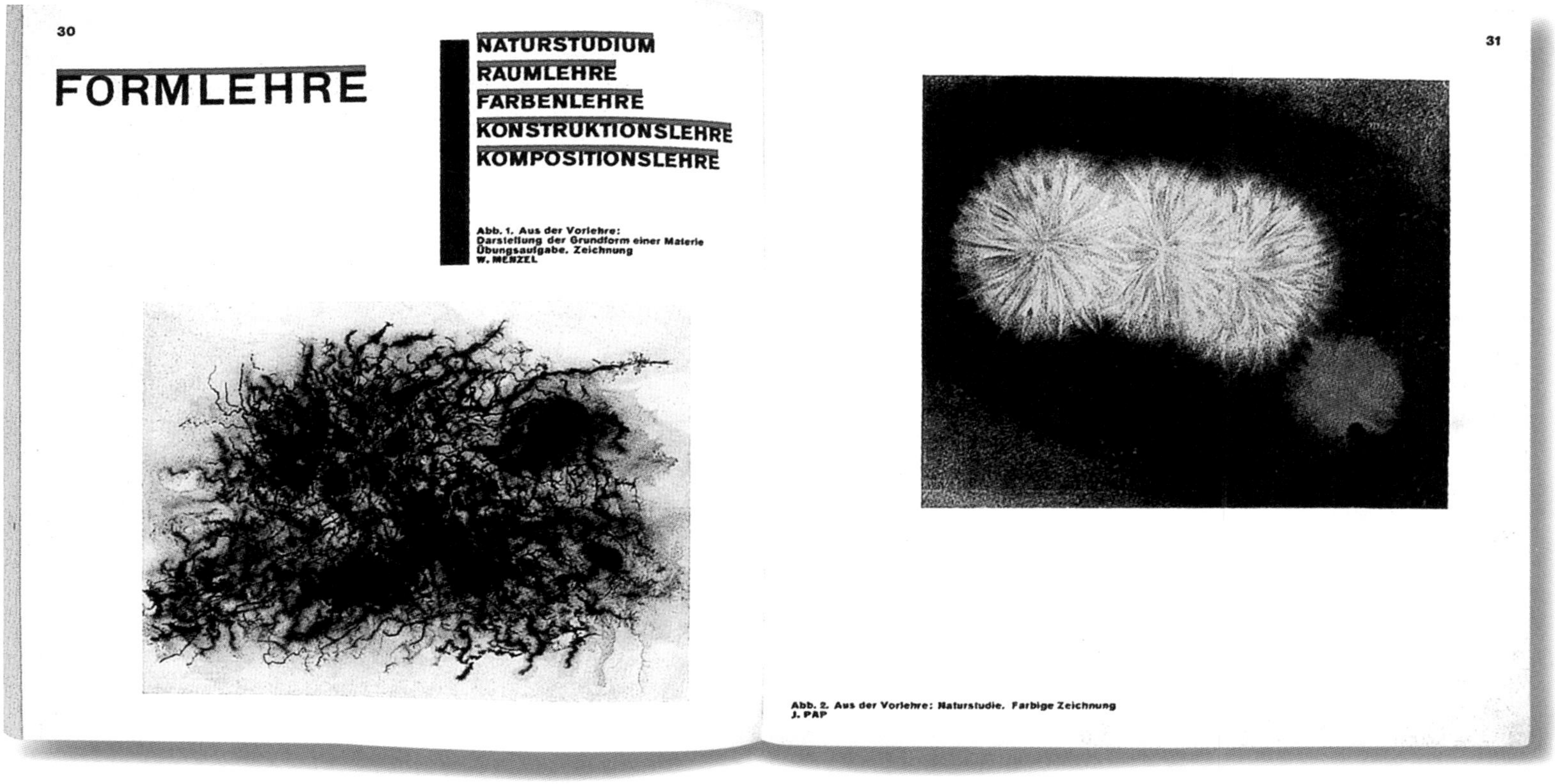

● **1922–1931 . BAUHAUS PROGRAMS .** Book . László Moholy-Nagy, Herbert Bayer, Walter Gropius
TOP: László Moholy-Nagy, "Bauhausbücher 14," 1929; BOTTOM: László Moholy-Nagy, *Staatliches Bauhaus in Weimar*, 1919–1923, 1923

→ p.389

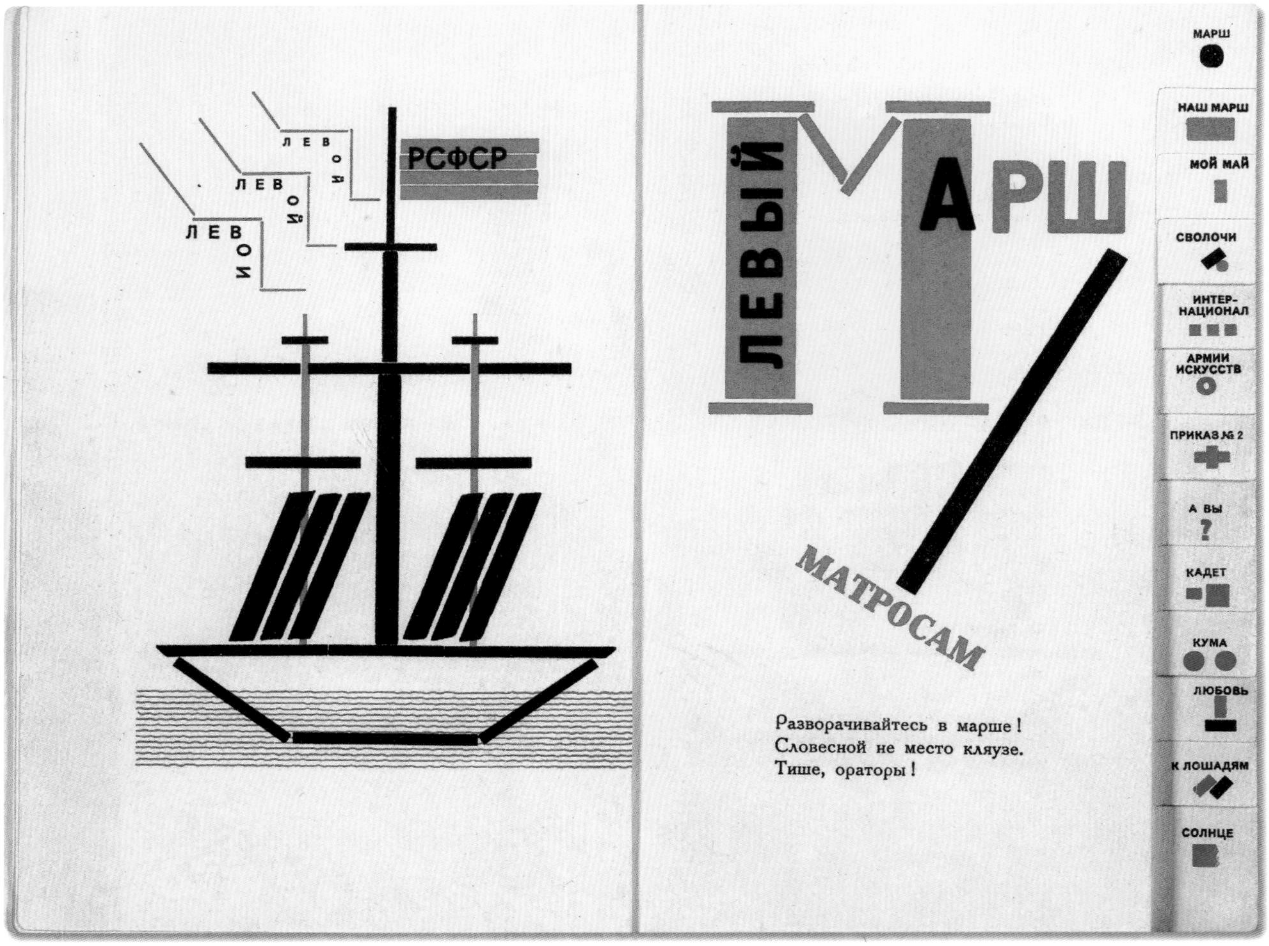

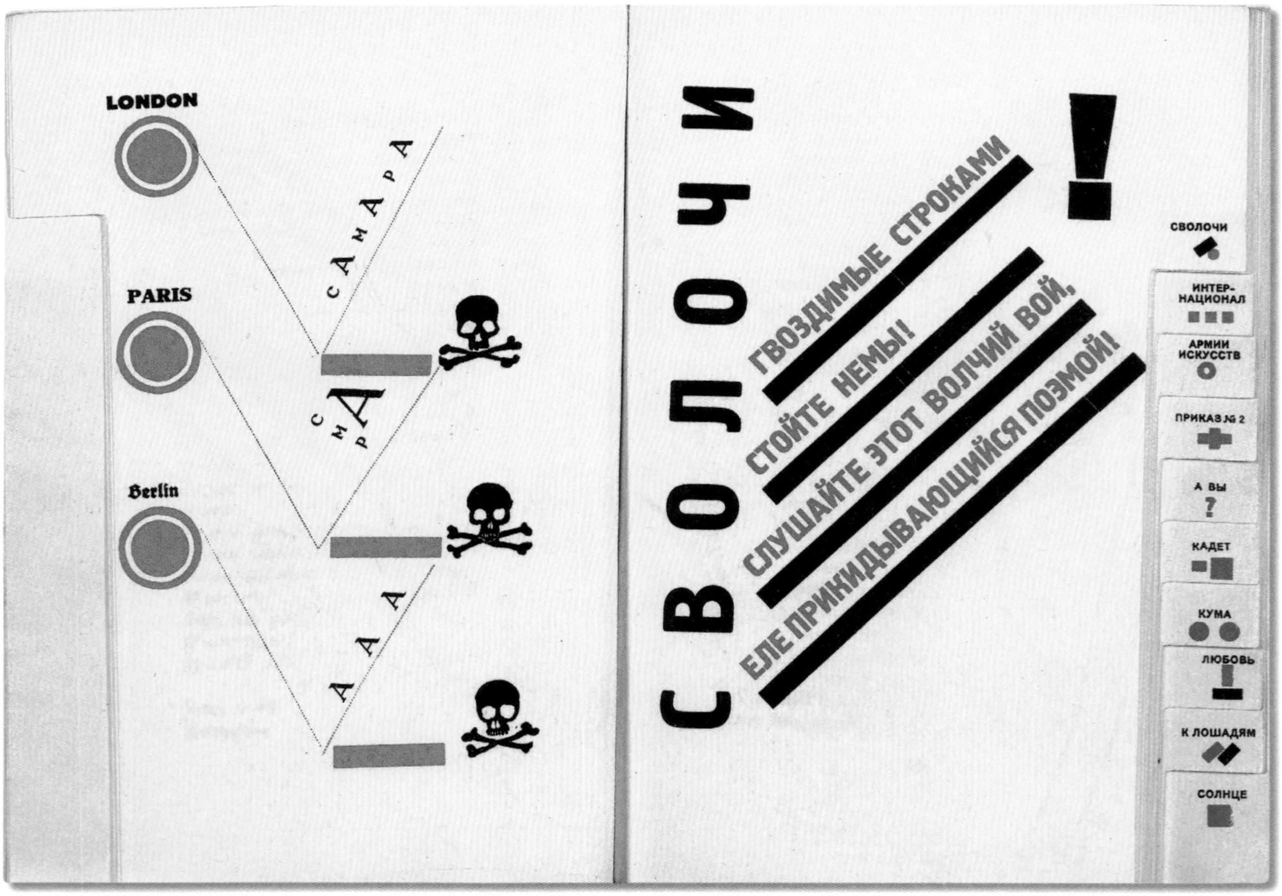

1923 . DLYA GOLOSA, BY VLADIMIR MAYAKOVSKY . Book . El Lissitzky

→ p.390

● **1923–1925/1927–1929 . LEF AND NOVYI LEF .** Magazine / Newspaper . Aleksandr Rodchenko
LEF, Vol. 1, No. 3, June–July, 1923

→ p.390

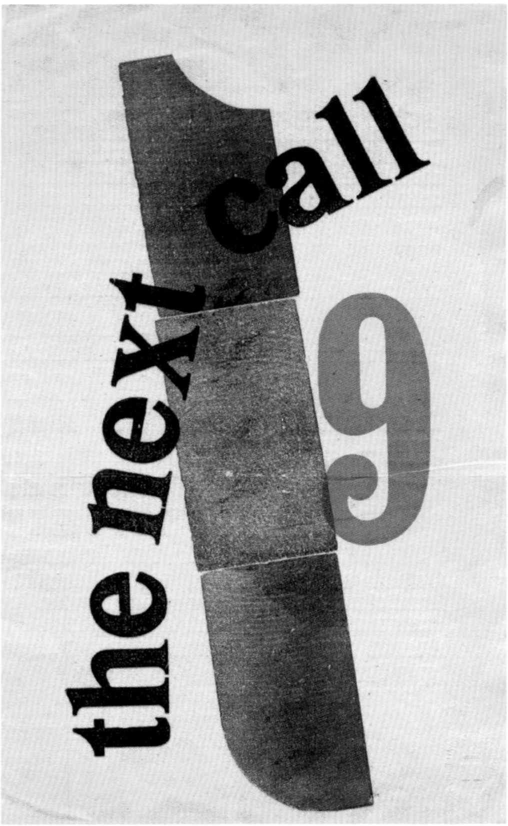

● **1923–1926 . THE NEXT CALL .**
Magazine / Newspaper . Hendrik Nicolaas Werkman
No. 9, 1925

→ p.390

● **1923 . LIDANTIU FARAM .**
Book . Ilia Zdanevich

→ p.391

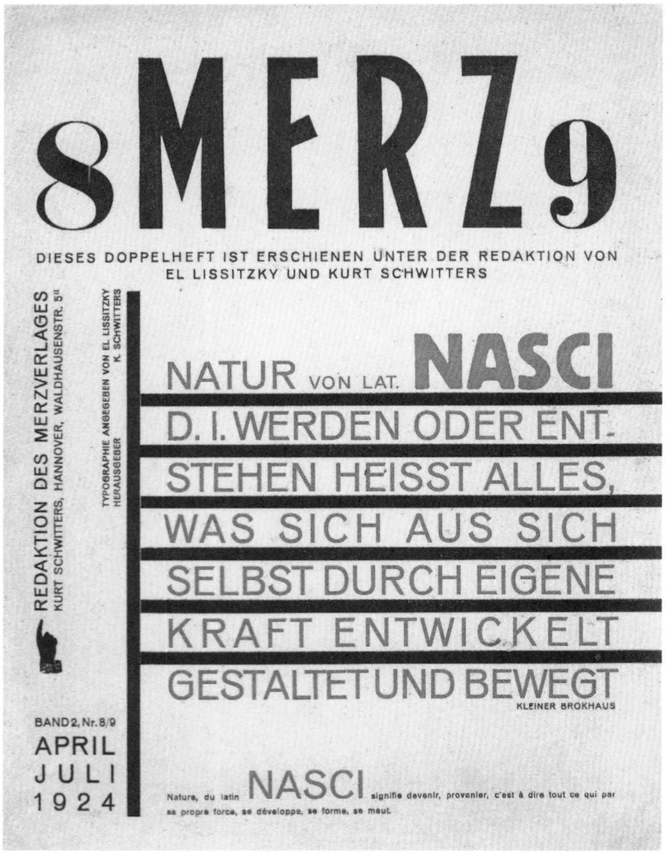

● **1923–1932 . MERZ .** Magazine / Newspaper . Kurt Schwitters et al.
LEFT: "Natur" (Nature), No. 8–9, April–July 1924; RIGHT: "Typoreklame: Pelikan-Nummer" (Typographic Advertising: Pelican Issue), No. 11, 1924

→ p.391

ЛУЧШИХ СОСОК
НЕ БЫЛО И НЕТ
ТРЕСТ
СССР
ГОТОВ СОСАТЬ ДО СТАРЫХ ЛЕТ
ПРОДАЮТСЯ ВЕЗДЕ
РЕЗИНОТРЕСТ

● **1923 . LUCHSHIKH SOSOK NE BYLO I NET .** Poster . Aleksandr Rodchenko

→ p.391

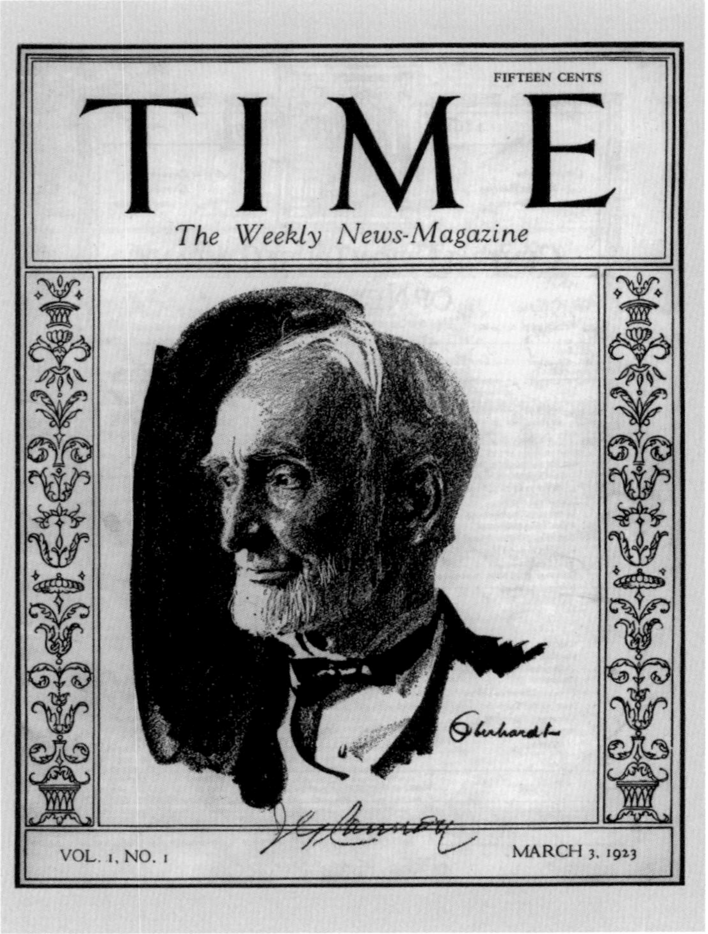

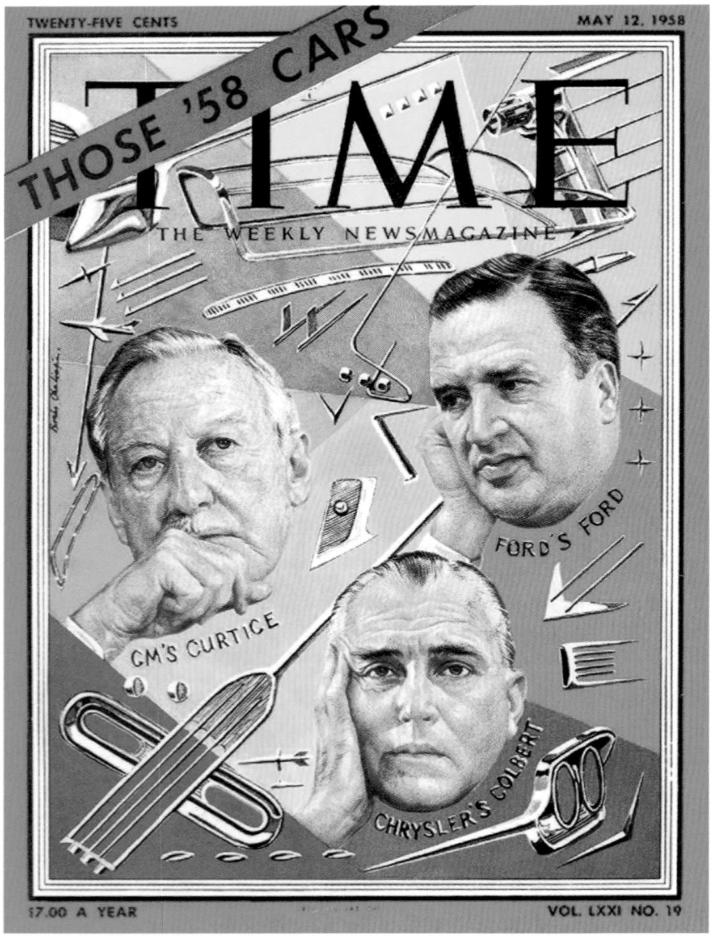

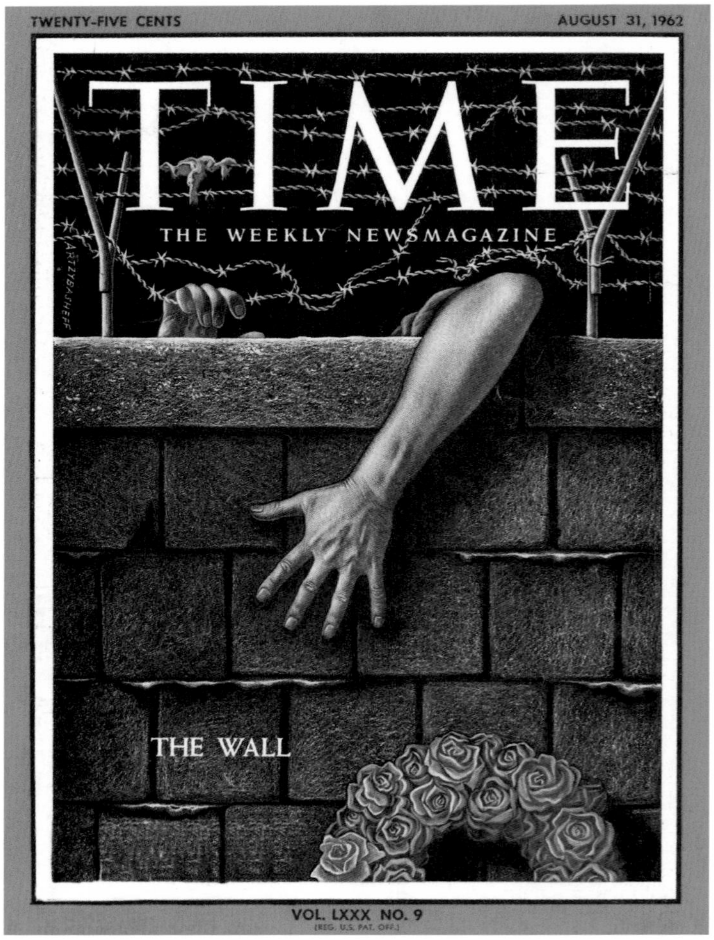

● **1923–PRESENT . TIME .** Magazine / Newspaper . Various
TOP LEFT: William Oberhardt, Vol. 1, No. 1, March 3, 1923; TOP RIGHT: Boris Artzybasheff, Vol. 55, No. 20, May 15, 1950; BOTTOM LEFT: Boris Chaliapin, Vol. 71, No. 19, May 12, 1958; BOTTOM RIGHT: Boris Artzybasheff, Vol. 80, No. 9, August 31, 1962

→ p.392

● **1924 . KINO GLAZ .** Poster . Aleksandr Rodchenko

→ p.392

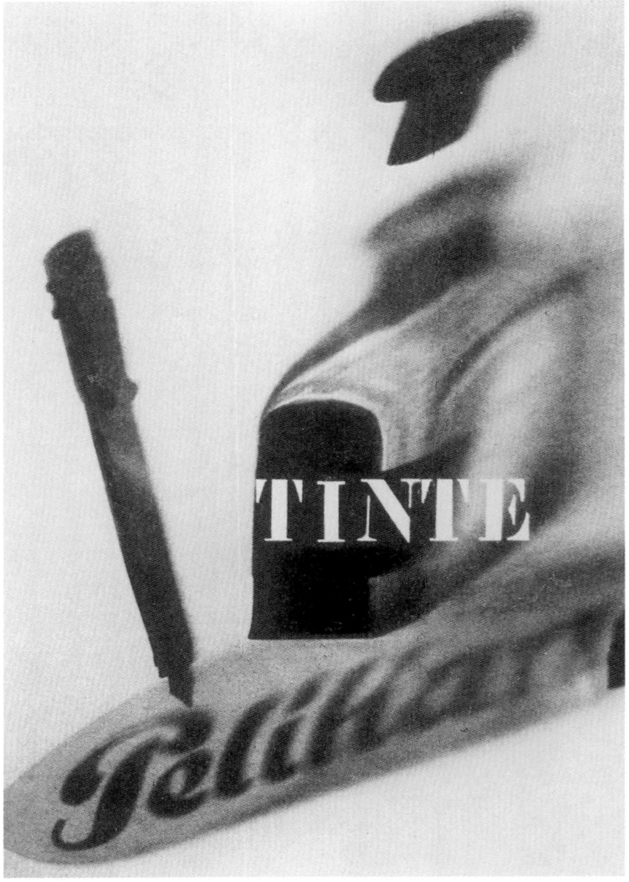

● **1924 . PELIKAN INK .** Advertising . El Lissitzky

→ p.392

● **1924 . KNIGI .** Poster . Aleksandr Rodchenko

→ p.393

● **1924–1944 . GEBRAUCHSGRAPHIK .** Magazine / Newspaper . Various
August 1926

→ p.393

● **1925 . BOCHUMER VEREIN .** Advertising . Max Burchartz

→ p.393

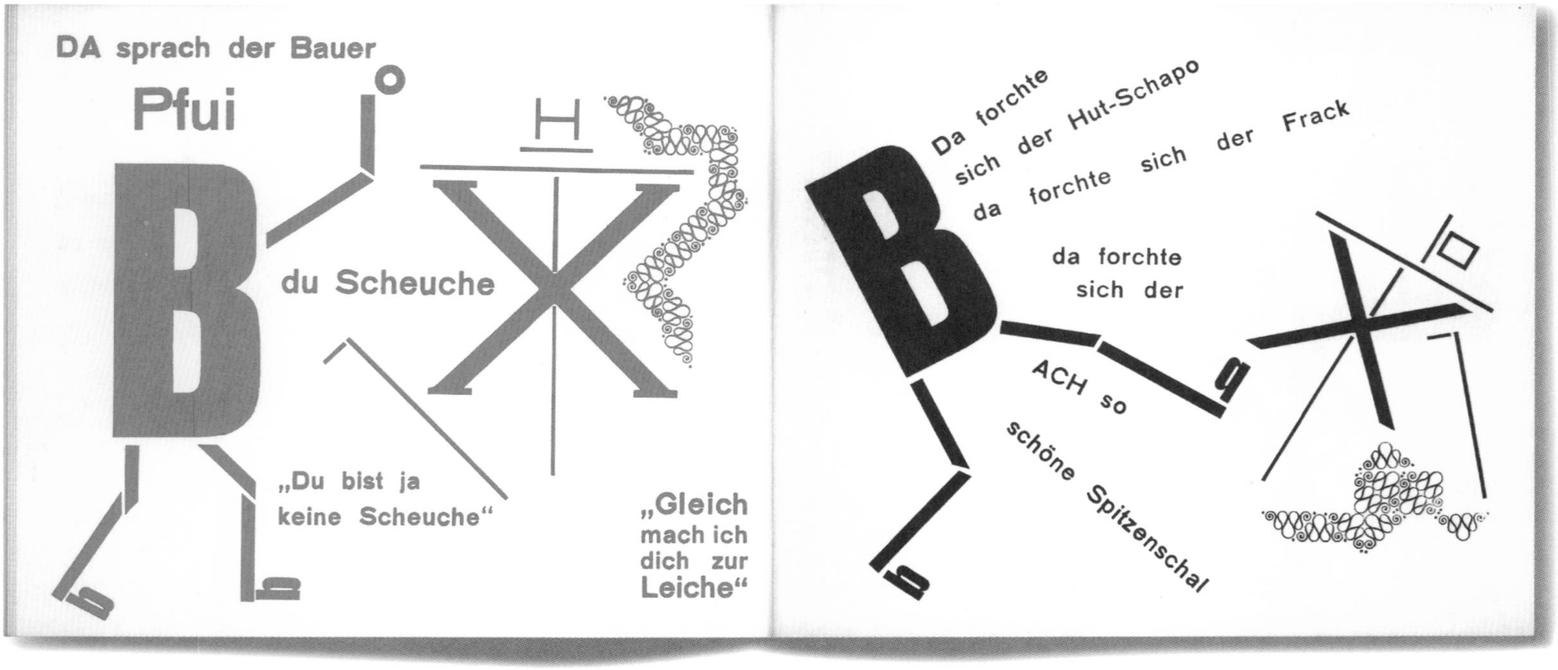

● **1925 . MERZ 14/15: DIE SCHEUCHE MÄRCHEN .** Book . Kurt Schwitters, Theo van Doesburg

→ p.394

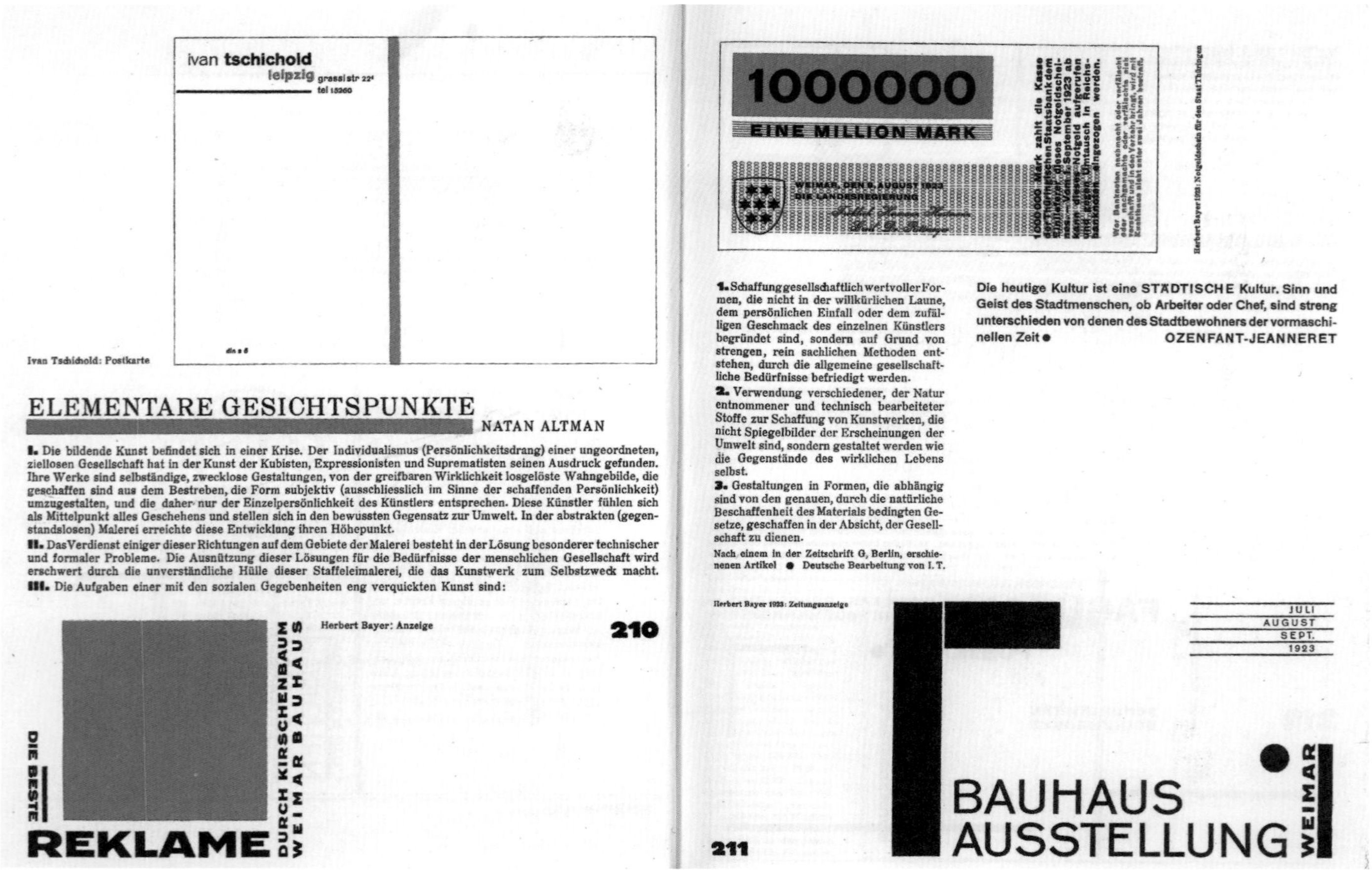
ivan **tschichold**
leipzig

Ivan Tschichold: Postkarte

ELEMENTARE GESICHTSPUNKTE

NATAN ALTMAN

I. Die bildende Kunst befindet sich in einer Krise. Der Individualismus (Persönlichkeitsdrang) einer ungeordneten, ziellosen Gesellschaft hat in der Kunst der Kubisten, Expressionisten und Suprematisten seinen Ausdruck gefunden. Ihre Werke sind selbständige, zwecklose Gestaltungen, von der greifbaren Wirklichkeit losgelöste Wahngebilde, die geschaffen sind aus dem Bestreben, die Form subjektiv (ausschliesslich im Sinne der schaffenden Persönlichkeit) umzugestalten, und die daher nur der Einzelpersönlichkeit des Künstlers entsprechen. Diese Künstler fühlen sich als Mittelpunkt alles Geschehens und stellen sich in den bewussten Gegensatz zur Umwelt. In der abstrakten (gegenstandslosen) Malerei erreichte diese Entwicklung ihren Höhepunkt.

II. Das Verdienst einiger dieser Richtungen auf dem Gebiete der Malerei besteht in der Lösung besonderer technischer und formaler Probleme. Die Ausnützung dieser Lösungen für die Bedürfnisse der menschlichen Gesellschaft wird erschwert durch die unverständliche Hülle dieser Staffeleimalerei, die das Kunstwerk zum Selbstzweck macht.

III. Die Aufgaben einer mit den sozialen Gegebenheiten eng verquickten Kunst sind:

Herbert Bayer: Anzeige

210

DIE BESTE REKLAME DURCH KIRSCHENBAUM WEIMAR BAUHAUS

1000000
EINE MILLION MARK
WEIMAR, DEN 9. AUGUST 1923
DIE LANDESREGIERUNG

1. Schaffung gesellschaftlich wertvoller Formen, die nicht in der willkürlichen Laune, dem persönlichen Einfall oder dem zufälligen Geschmack des einzelnen Künstlers begründet sind, sondern auf Grund von strengen, rein sachlichen Methoden entstehen, durch die allgemeine gesellschaftliche Bedürfnisse befriedigt werden.

2. Verwendung verschiedener, der Natur entnommener und technisch bearbeiteter Stoffe zur Schaffung von Kunstwerken, die nicht Spiegelbilder der Erscheinungen der Umwelt sind, sondern gestaltet werden wie die Gegenstände des wirklichen Lebens selbst.

3. Gestaltungen in Formen, die abhängig sind von den genauen, durch die natürliche Beschaffenheit des Materials bedingten Gesetze, geschaffen in der Absicht, der Gesellschaft zu dienen.

Nach einem in der Zeitschrift G, Berlin, erschienenen Artikel ● Deutsche Bearbeitung von I. T.

Die heutige Kultur ist eine STÄDTISCHE Kultur. Sinn und Geist des Stadtmenschen, ob Arbeiter oder Chef, sind streng unterschieden von denen des Stadtbewohners der vormaschinellen Zeit ● OZENFANT-JEANNERET

Herbert Bayer 1923: Zeitungsanzeige

JULI
AUGUST
SEPT.
1923

BAUHAUS
AUSSTELLUNG
WEIMAR

211

● **1925 . ELEMENTARE TYPOGRAPHIE .** Magazine / Newspaper . Jan Tschichold

→ p.394

● **1925 . DIE KUNSTISMEN/LES ISMES DE L'ART/THE ISMS OF ART .** Book . El Lissitzky, Hans Arp

→ p.394

abcdefghi
jklmnopqr
stuvwxyz
HERBERT BAYER: Abb. 1. Alfabet
„g" und „k" sind noch als unfertig zu betrachten
d
Beispiel eines Zeichens in größerem Maßstab Präzise optische Wirkung
sturm blond
Abb. 2. Anwendung
399

● **1925 . BAYER UNIVERSAL .** Typeface . Herbert Bayer

→ p.395

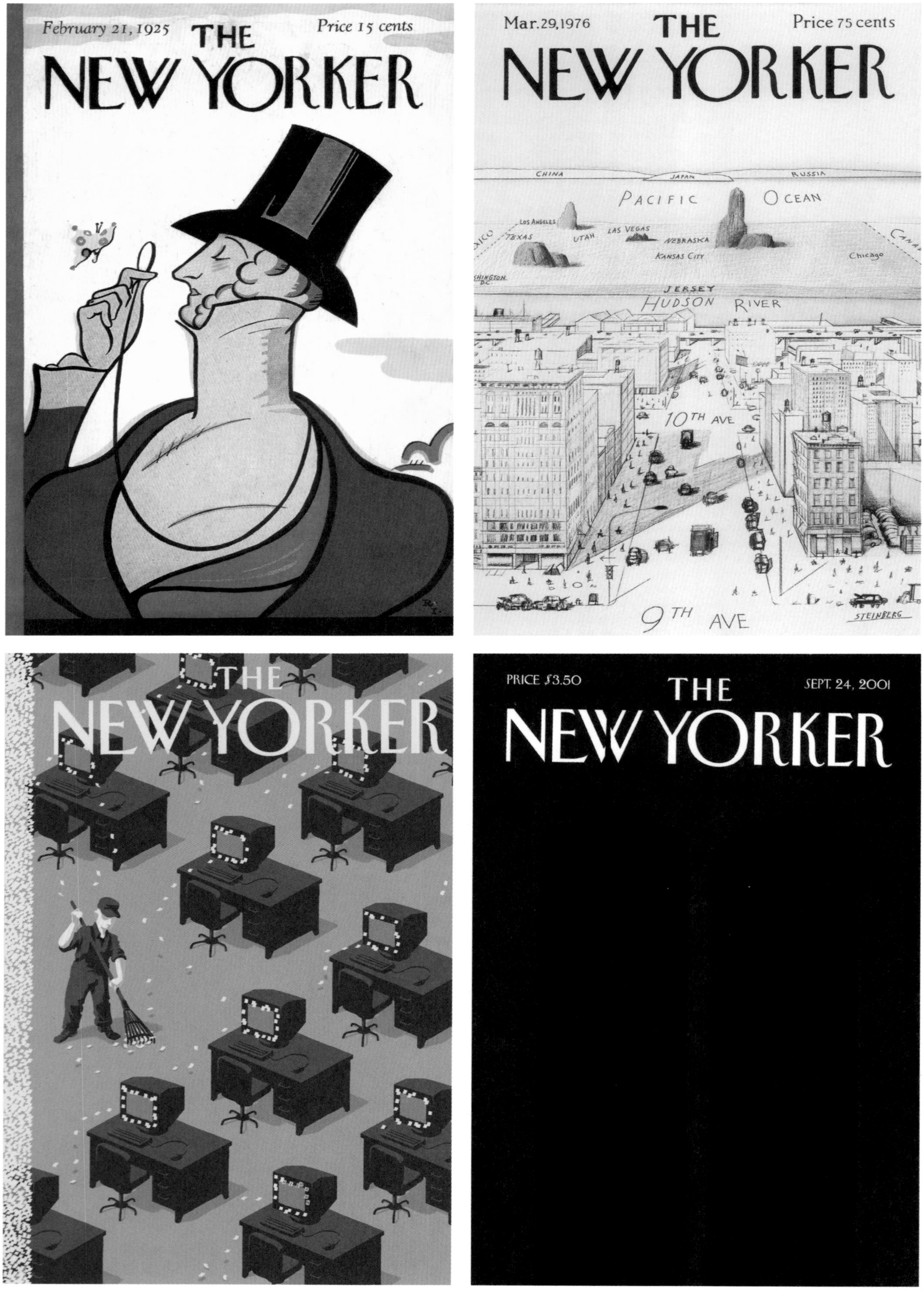

● **1925–PRESENT . THE NEW YORKER .** Magazine / Newspaper . Various
TOP LEFT: Rea Irvin, February 21, 1925; TOP RIGHT: Saul Steinberg, March 29, 1976; BOTTOM LEFT: Christoph Niemann, October 25, 2004; BOTTOM RIGHT: Art Spiegelman, September 24, 2001

→ p.395

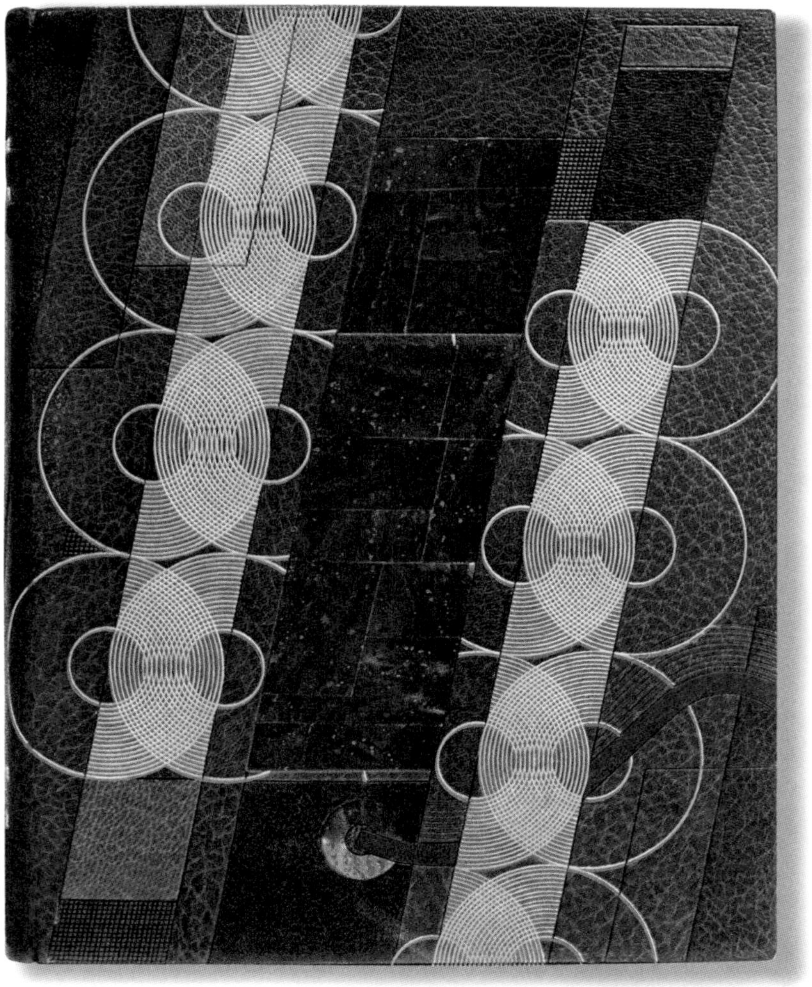

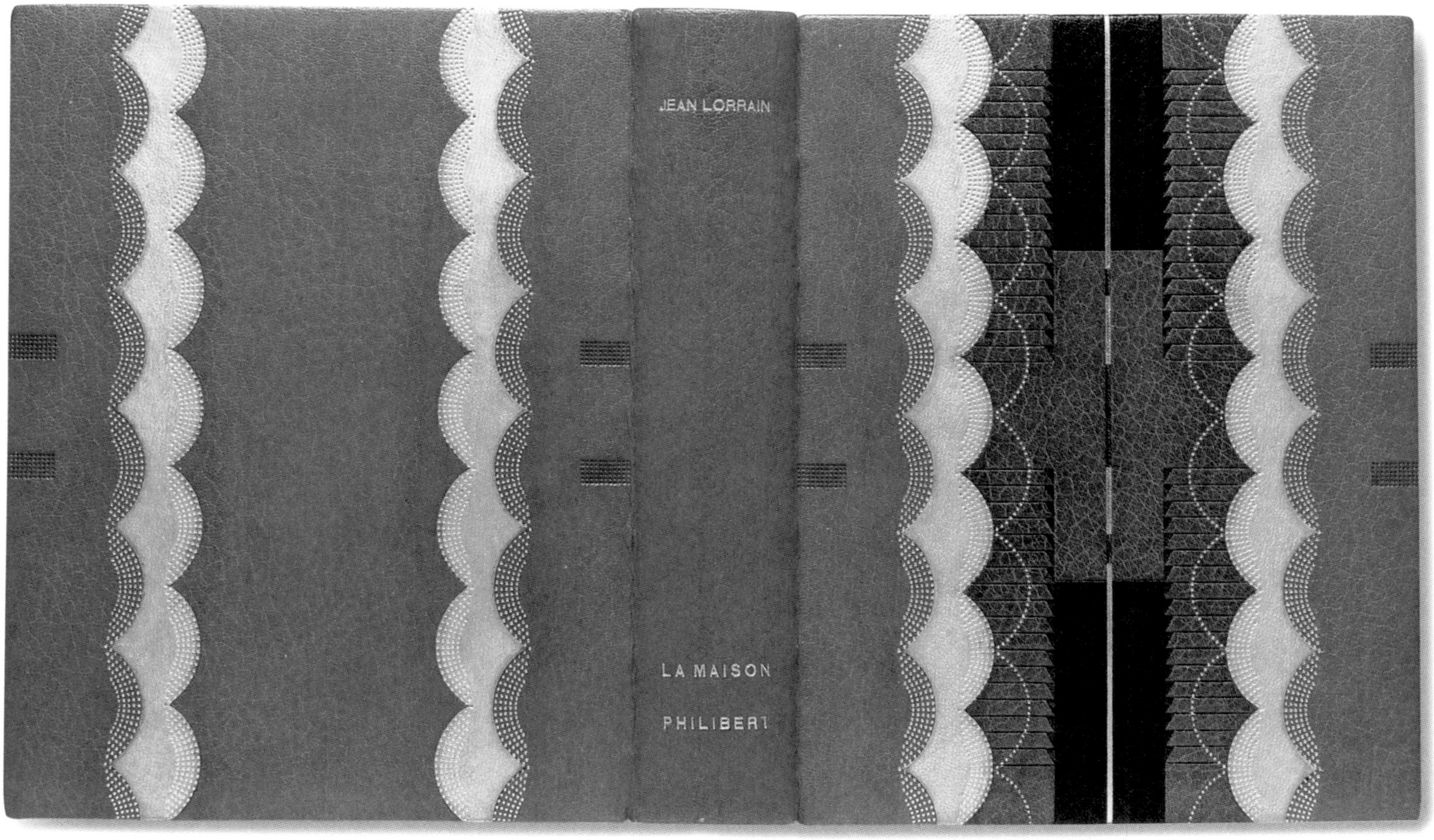

● **c. 1925 . PIERRE LEGRAIN BINDING .** Book Cover . Pierre Legrain
TOP: *La Canne de Jaspe, Monsieur d'Amercoeur, Le Trèfle Noir, Contes a Soi-Même*, by Henri de Régnier, ed. 1925; BOTTOM: *La Maison Philibert*, by Jean Lorrain, ed. 1925

→ p.395

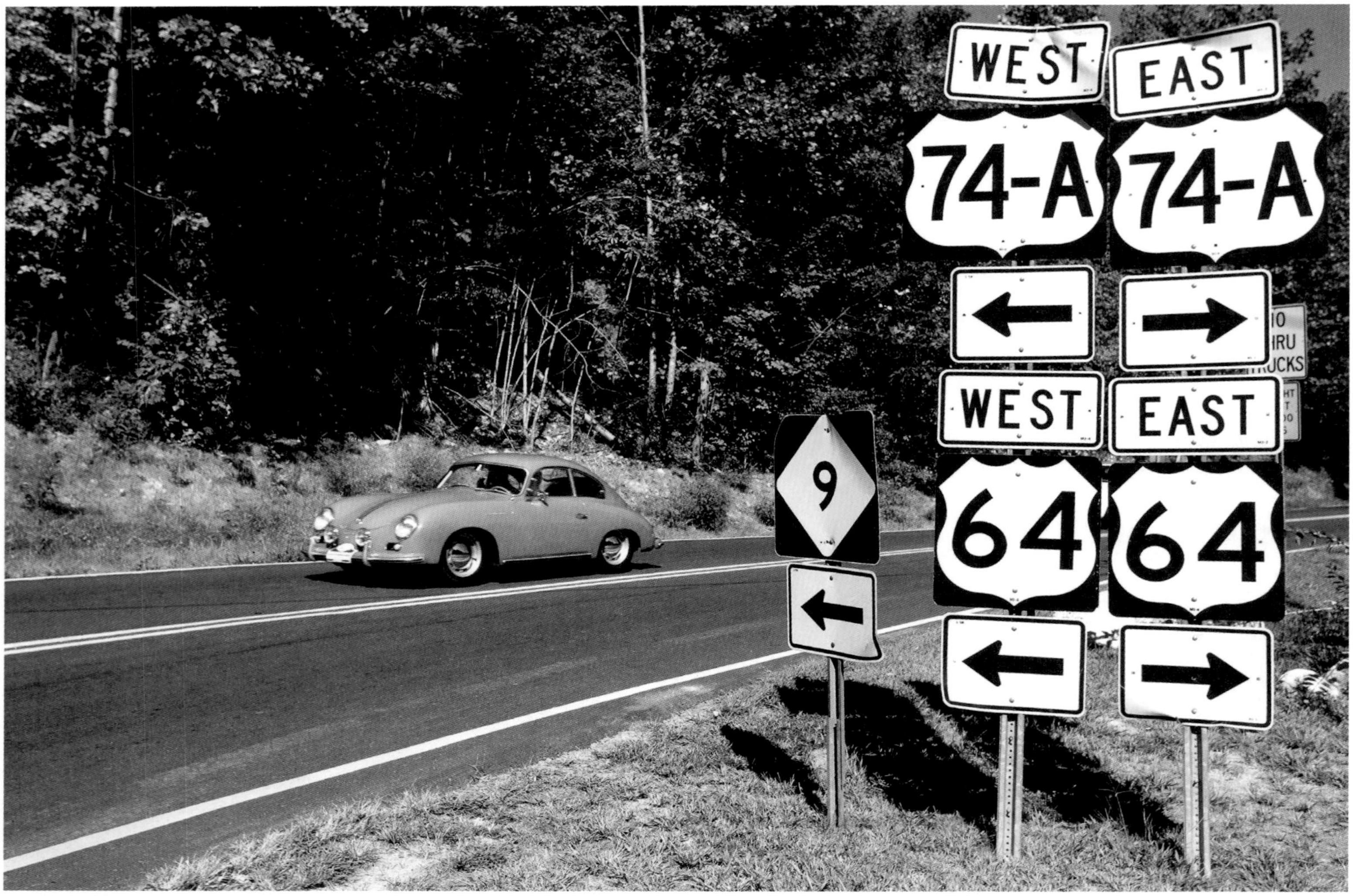

1926 . U.S. ROUTE SHIELD . Information Design . Frank F. Rogers et al.

→ p.396

A
nazváno buď prostou chatrčí
Ó palmy přeneste svůj rovník nad Vltavu
Šnek má svůj prostý dům z nějž růžky vystrčí
a člověk neví kam by složil hlavu
6

D
From the West is bent the bow
An Indian finds footpaths overgrown
His last friends perished long ago
The moon waxes The prairie turns to stone
18

S
V planinách Černé Indie
žil krotitel hadů jménem John
Miloval Elis hadí tanečnici
a ta ho uštkla Zemřel na příjici
40

● **1926 . ABECEDA .** Book . Karel Teige

→ p.396

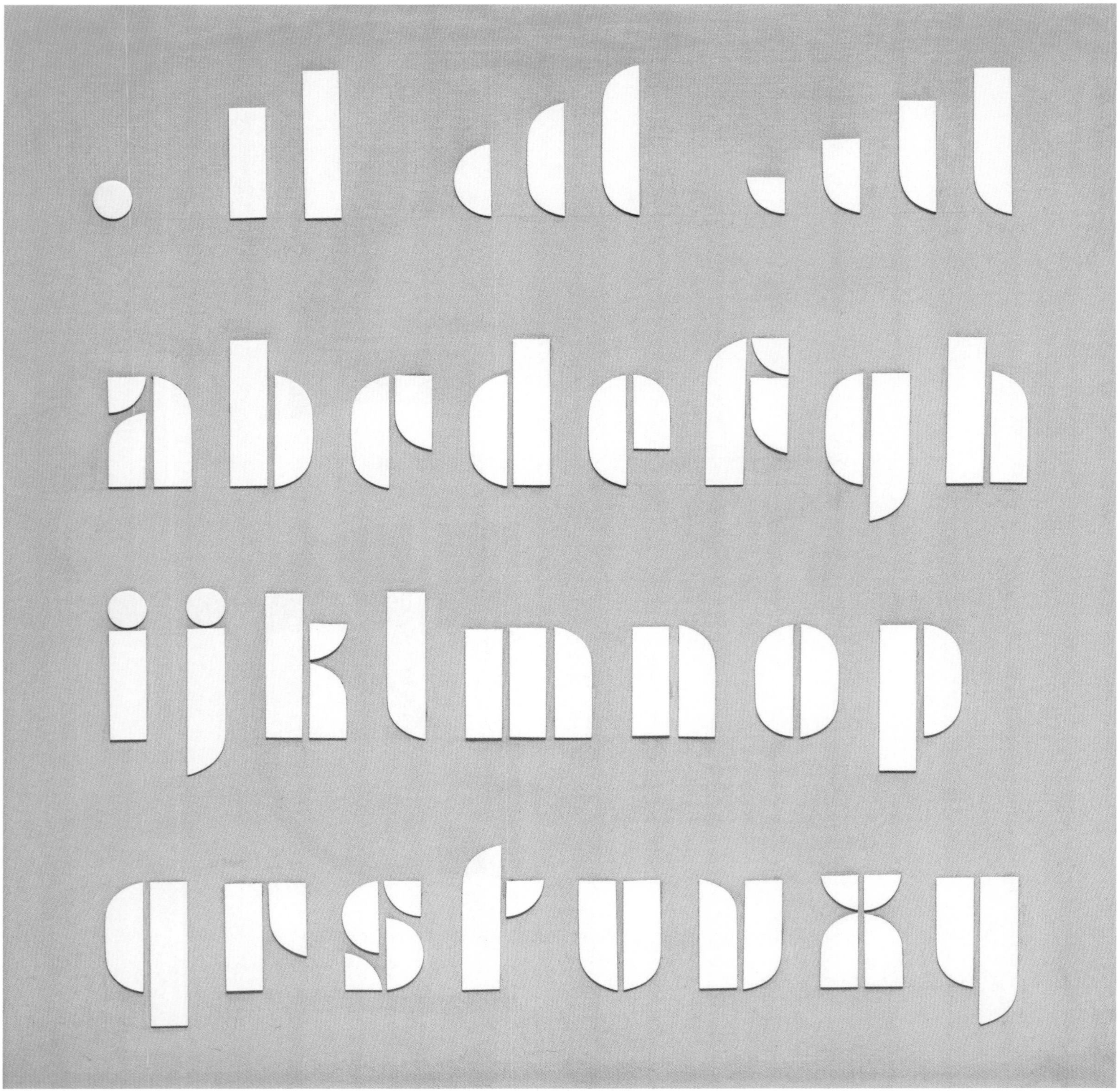

● **1926–1931 . KOMBINATIONSSCHRIFT .** Typeface . Josef Albers

→ p.396

● **1926 . FANGHUANG, BY LU XUN .** Book Cover . Tao Yuan-qing

→ p.397

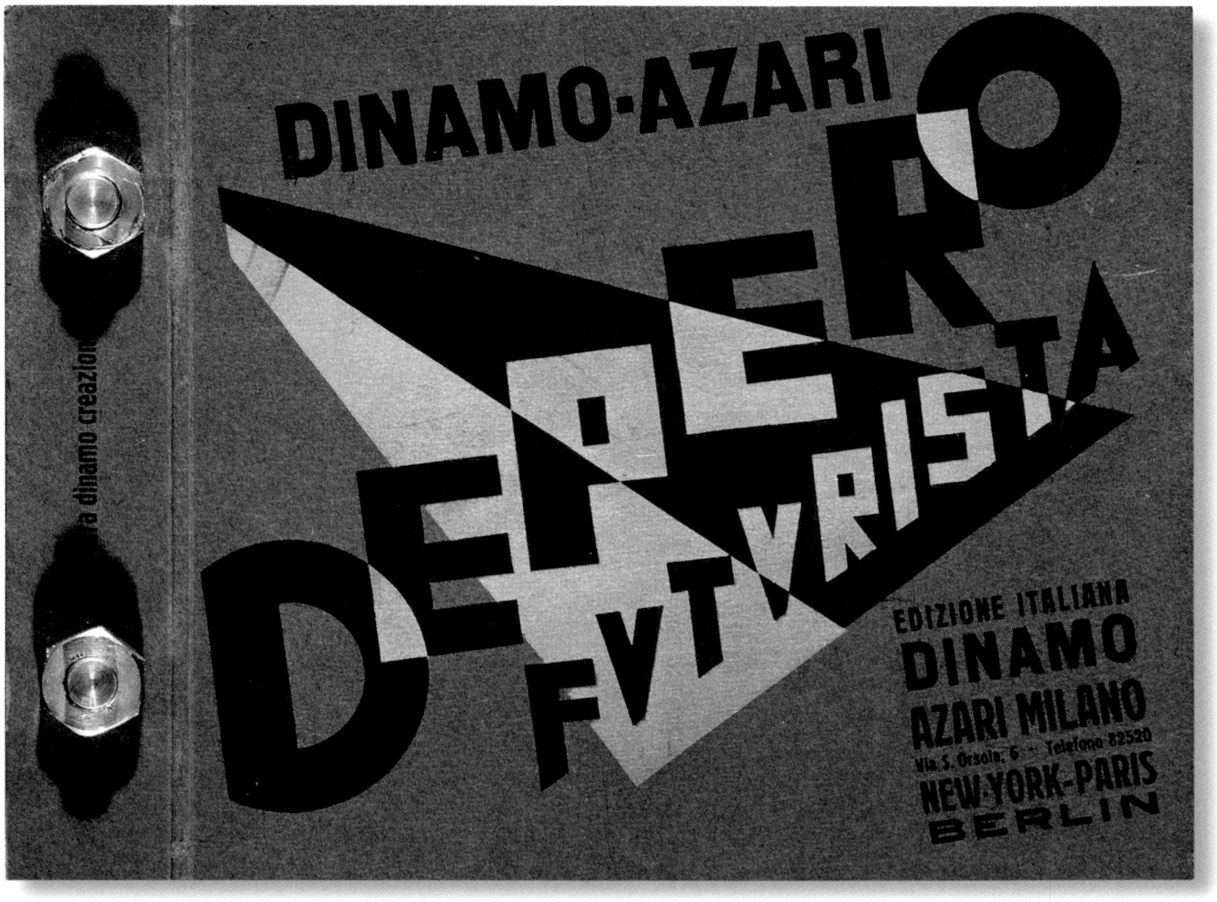

● **1927 . DEPERO FUTURISTA .** Book . Fortunato Depero

→ p.397

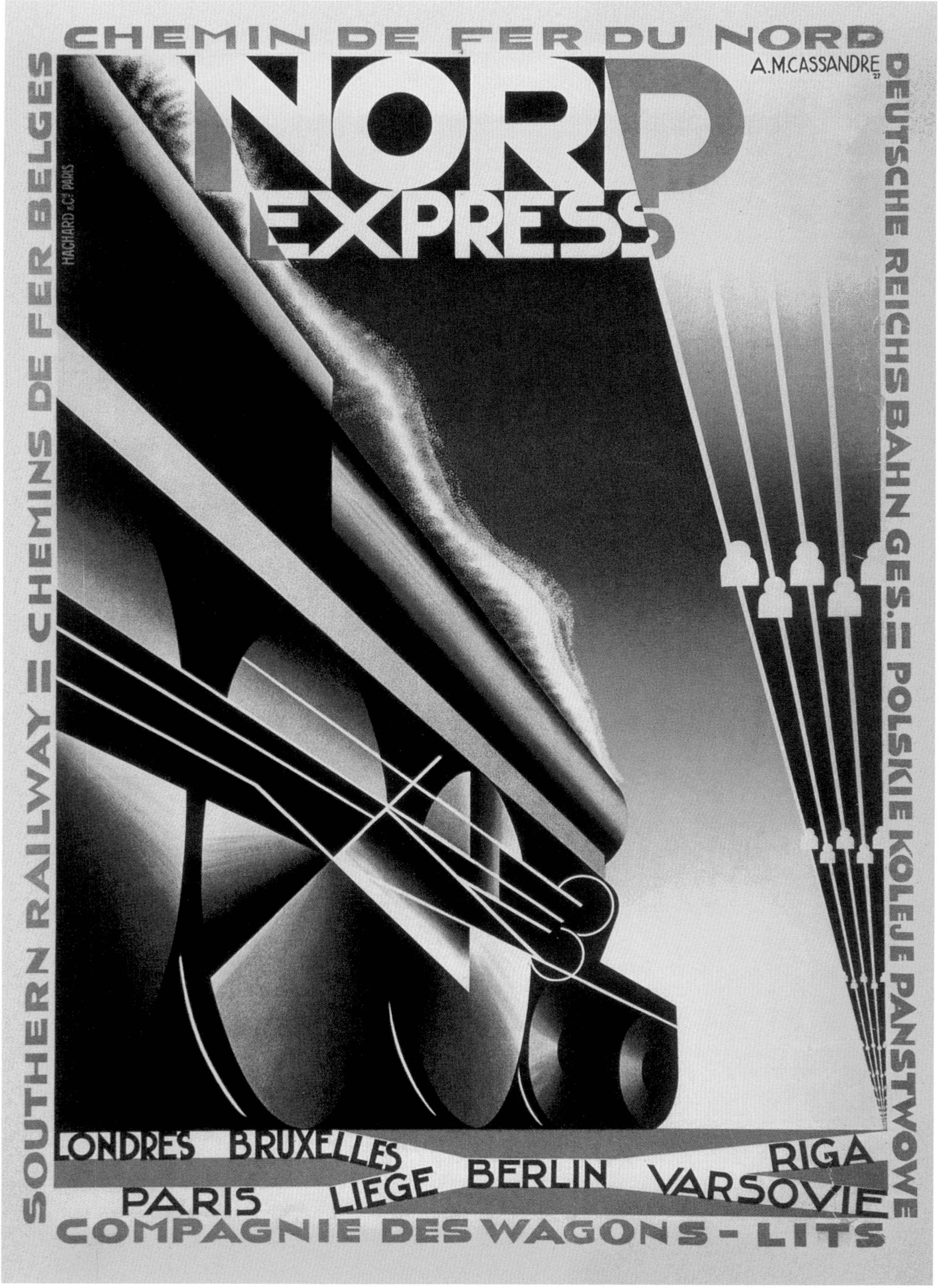

● **1927 . NORD EXPRESS .** Poster . A. M. Cassandre

→ p.397

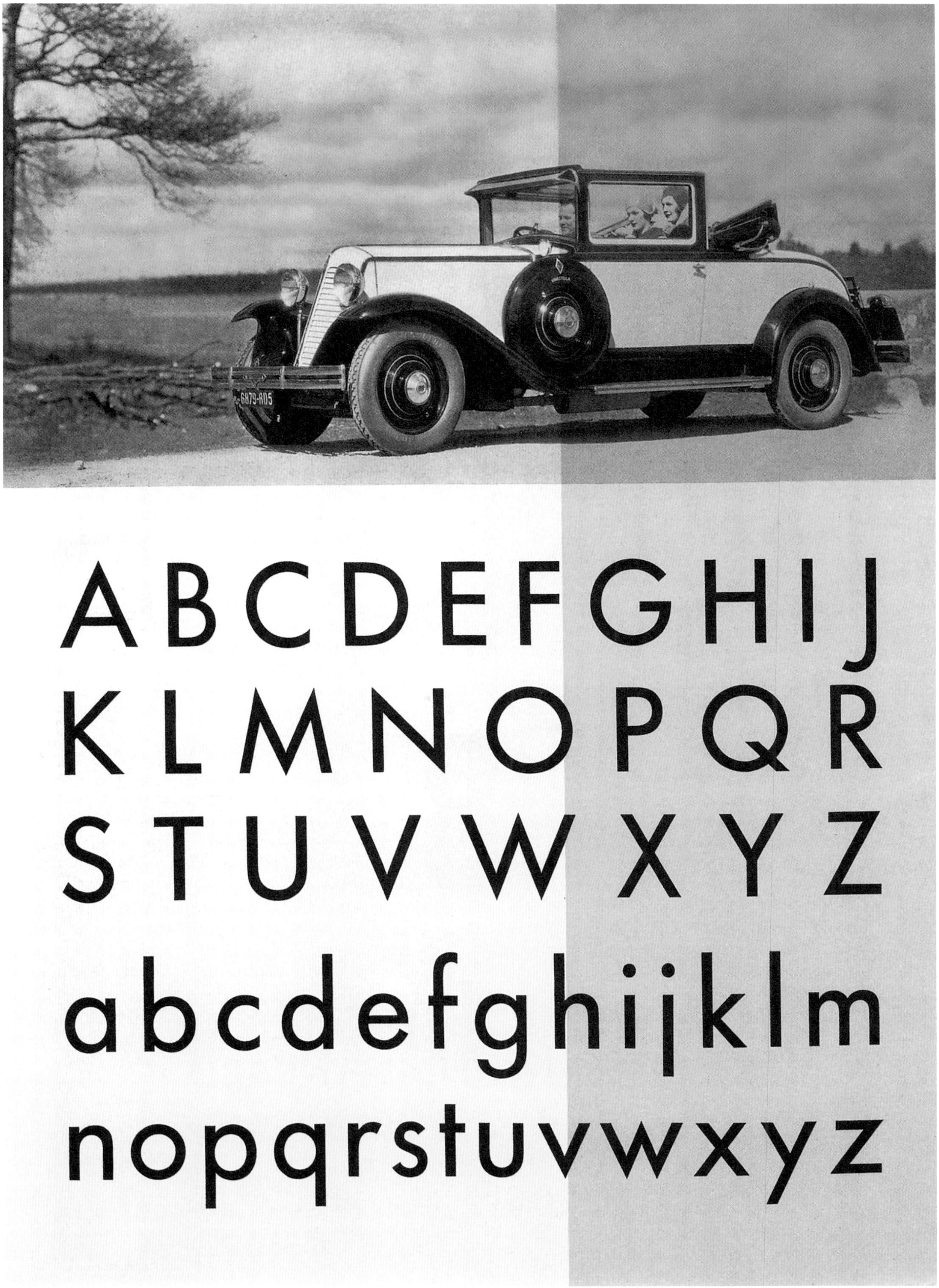

● **1927 . FUTURA .** Typeface . Paul Renner

→ p.398

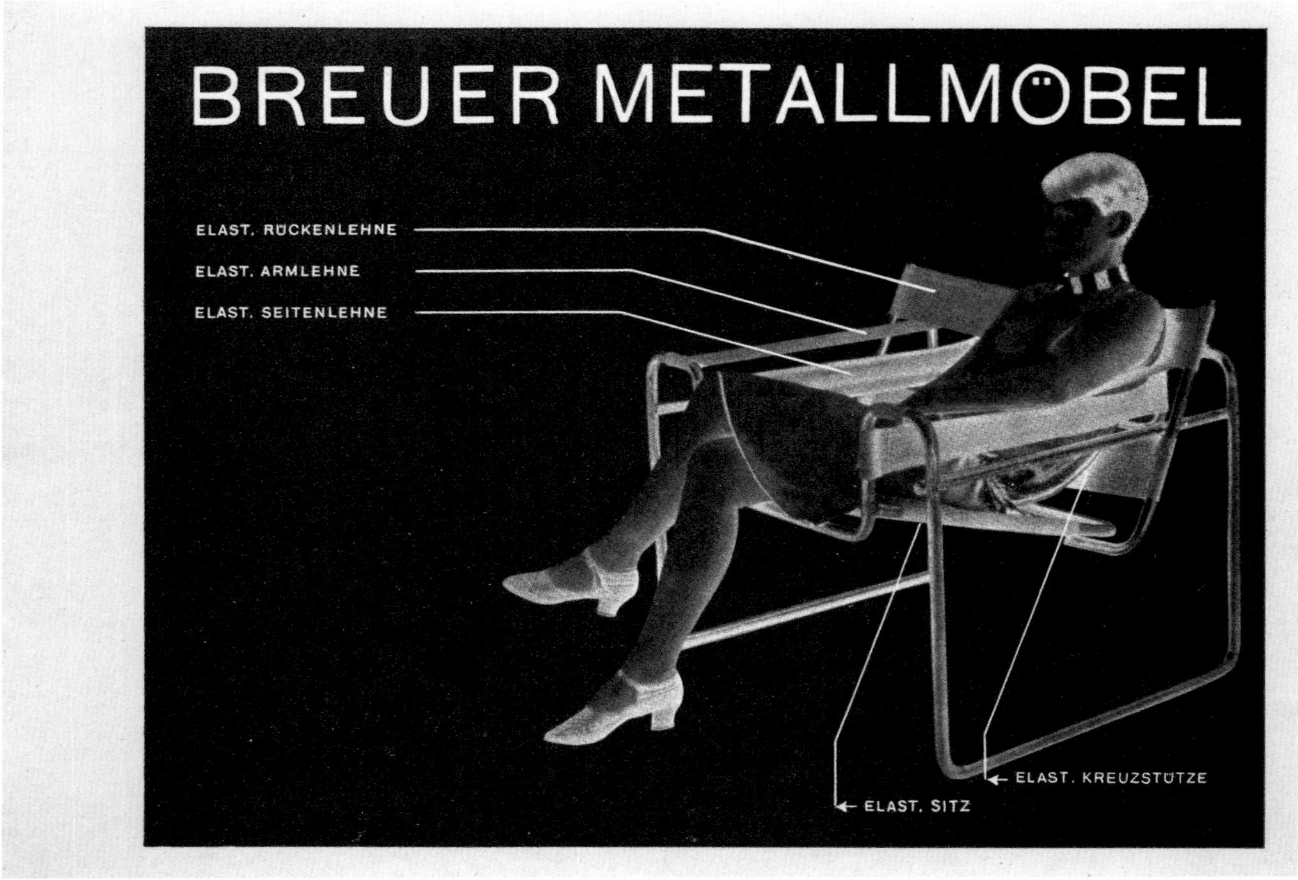

THEATERSTUHL
mit Klappsitz.
Stoffsitz, Stoffrückenlehne,
schwarze Holzarmlehne

B1

Sitzbreite ca. 550 mm

Die Rückenlehnen sind nachzuspannen.
Gummi-Anschlagringe, daher geräuschlos.

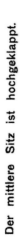

Der mittlere Sitz ist hochgeklappt.

● **1927 . BREUER METALLMÖBEL .** Book . Herbert Bayer

→ p.398

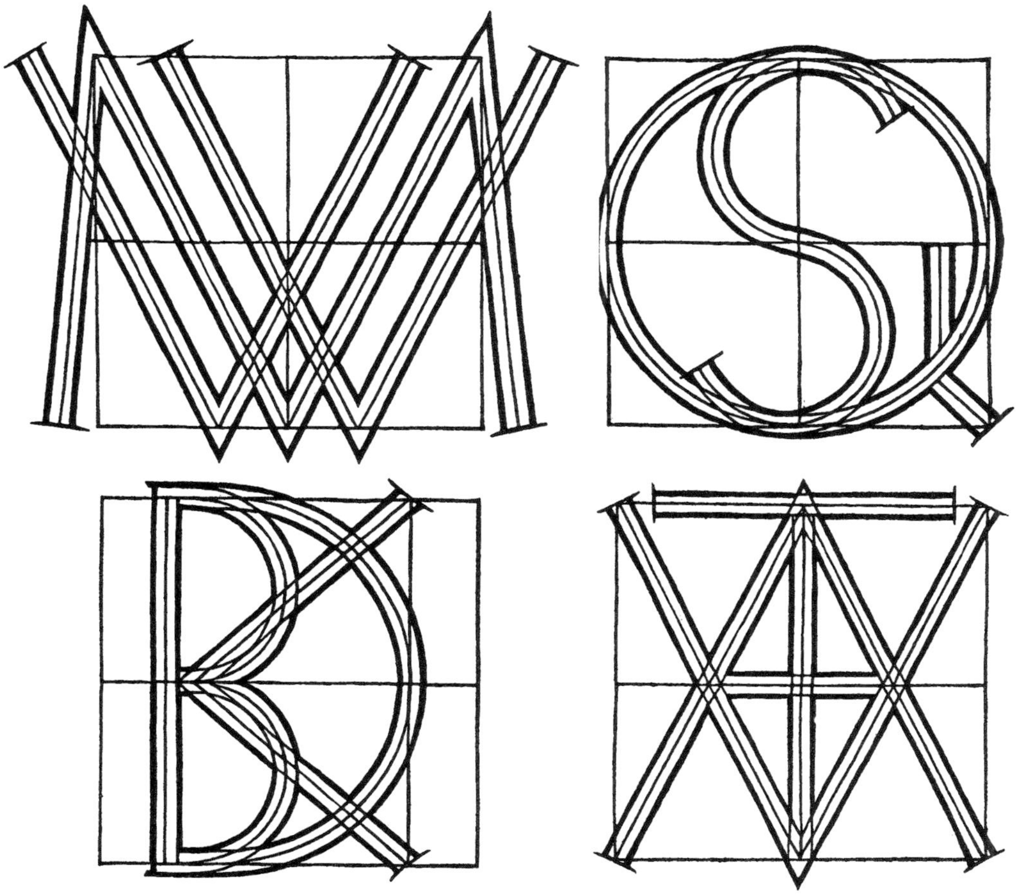

● **1927 . KABEL .** Typeface . Rudolf Koch

→ p.398

OPEL

● **1927–1929 . OPEL .** Poster . Max Bittrof

→ p.399

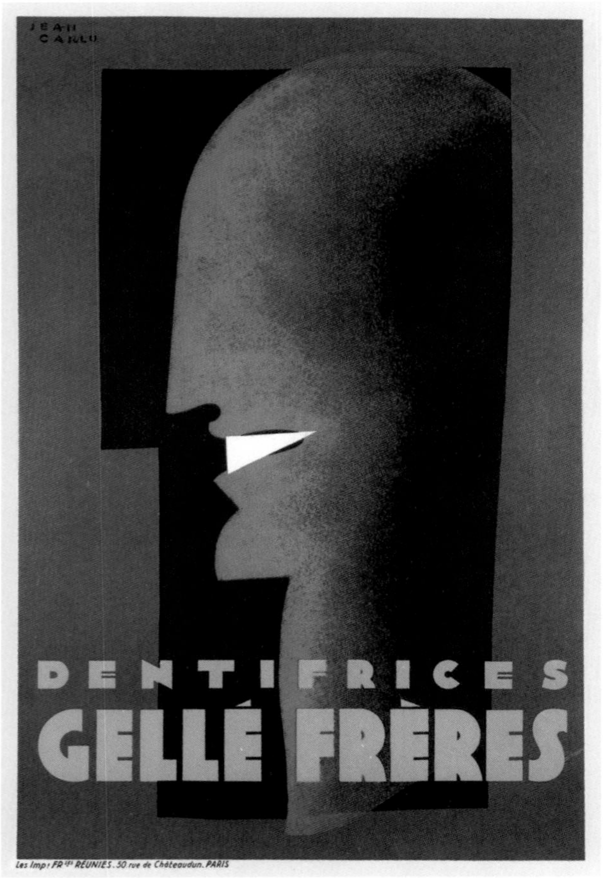

● **1927 . DENTIFRICES GELLÉ FRÈRES .** Poster . Jean Carlu

→ p.399

● **1927 . GABA .** Poster . Niklaus Stöcklin

→ p.399

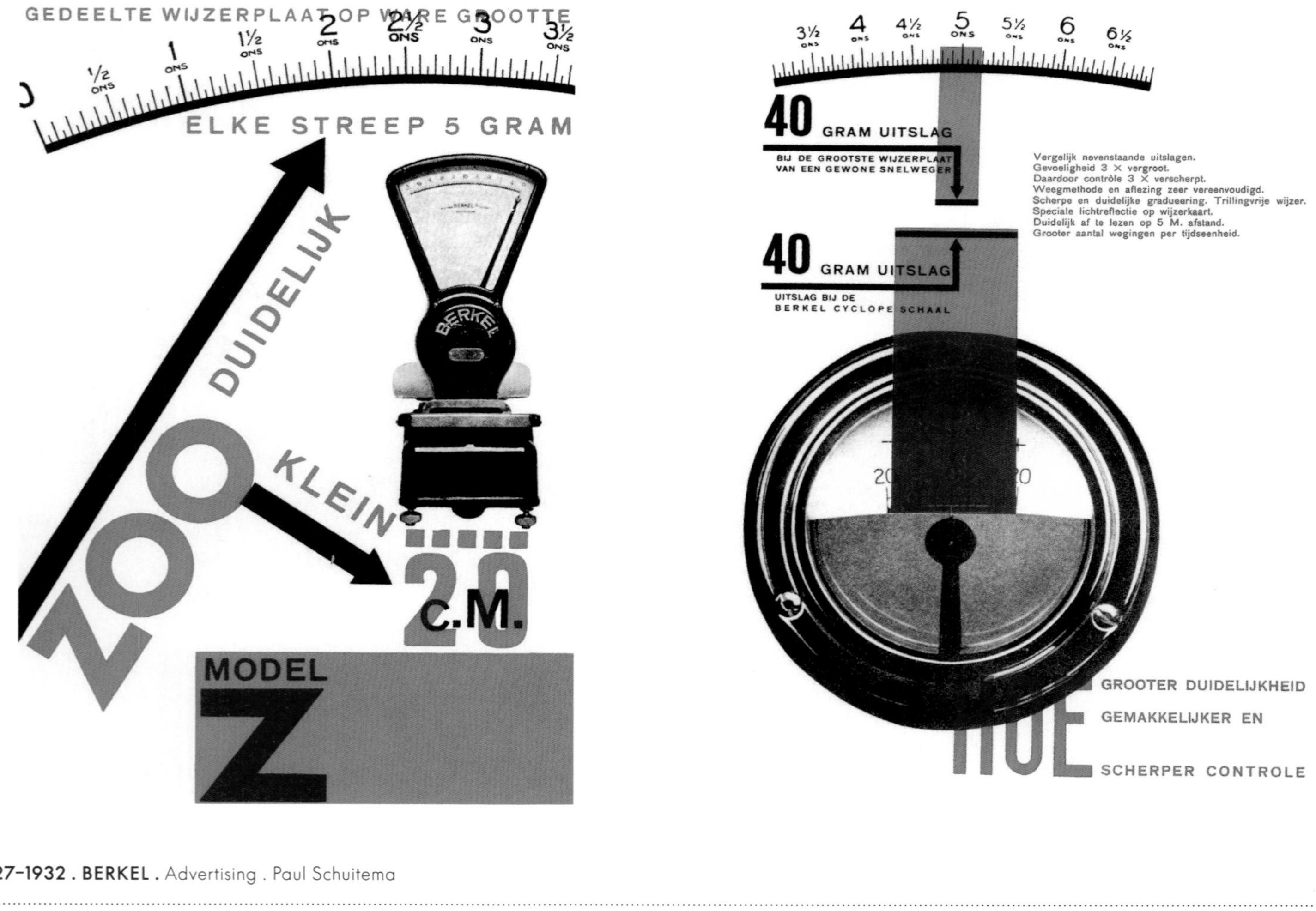

● **1927–1932 . BERKEL .** Advertising . Paul Schuitema

→ p.400

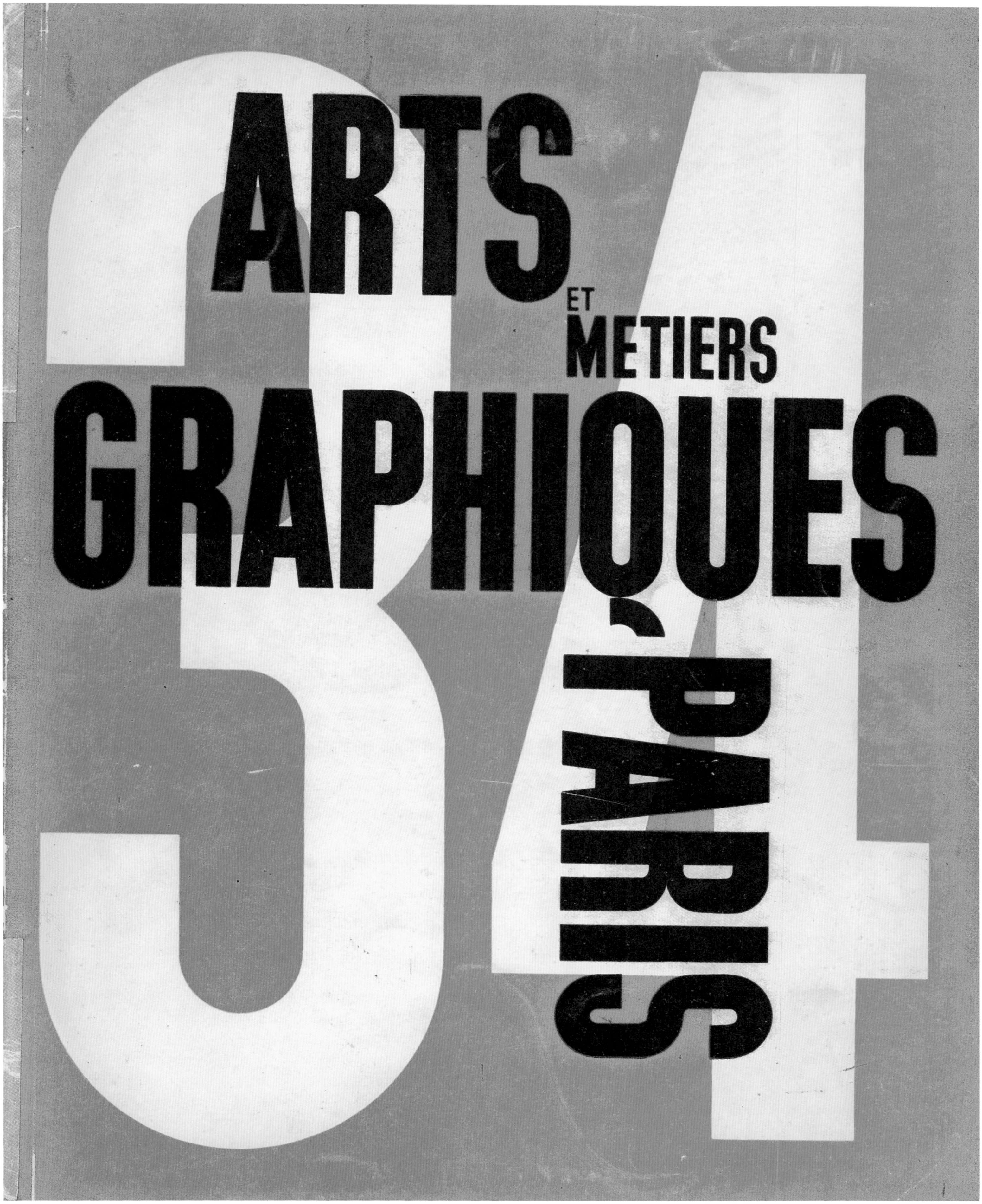

● **1927–1939 . ARTS ET MÉTIERS GRAPHIQUES .** Magazine / Newspaper . Various
No. 34, March 1933

→ p.400

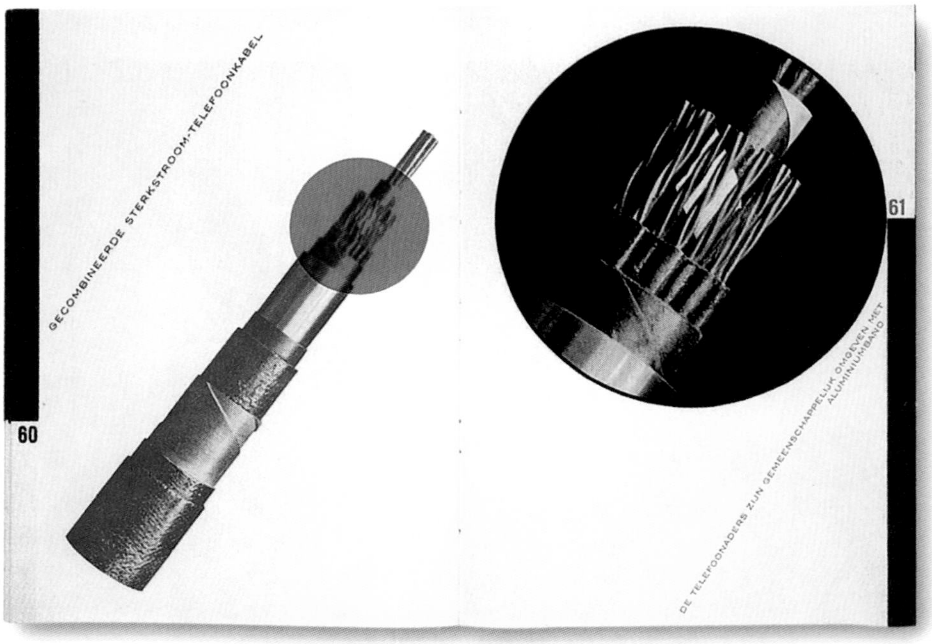

● **1928 . N. V. NEDERLANDSCHE KABELFABRIEK 1927–1928 .** Book . Piet Zwart

→ p.400

● **1928 . SIMFONIA BOLSHOGO GORODA .** Poster . Georgii Stenberg, Vladimir Stenberg

→ p.401

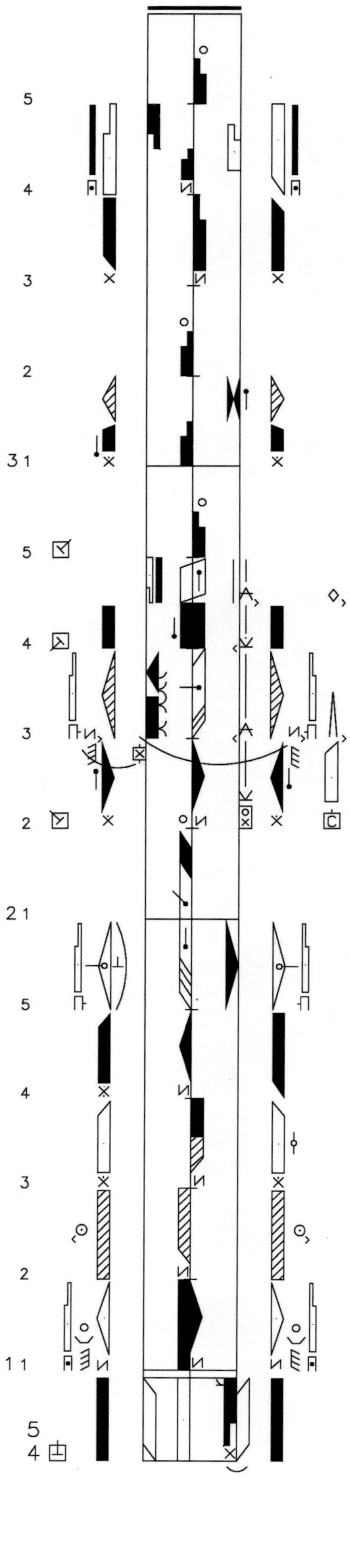

● **1928 . LABANOTATION .** Information Design . Rudolf von Laban

→ p.401

● **1928 . BÜRO .** Poster . Theo Ballmer

→ p.401

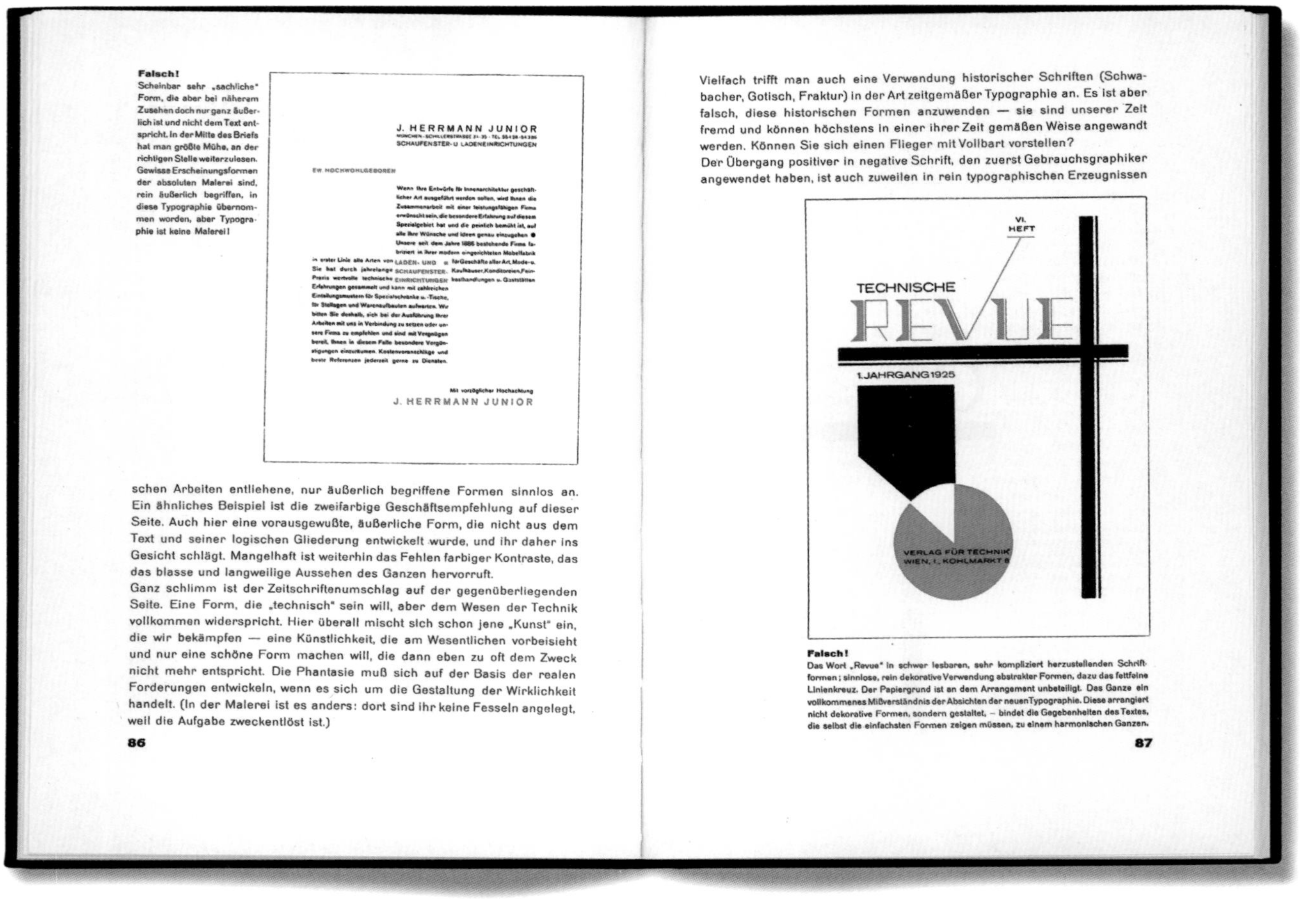

Falsch!
Scheinbar sehr „sachliche" Form, die aber bei näherem Zusehen doch nur ganz äußerlich ist und nicht dem Text entspricht. In der Mitte des Briefs hat man größte Mühe, an der richtigen Stelle weiterzulesen. Gewisse Erscheinungsformen der absoluten Malerei sind, rein äußerlich begriffen, in diese Typographie übernommen worden, aber Typographie ist keine Malerei!

schen Arbeiten entliehene, nur äußerlich begriffene Formen sinnlos an. Ein ähnliches Beispiel ist die zweifarbige Geschäftsempfehlung auf dieser Seite. Auch hier eine vorausgewußte, äußerliche Form, die nicht aus dem Text und seiner logischen Gliederung entwickelt wurde, und ihr daher ins Gesicht schlägt. Mangelhaft ist weiterhin das Fehlen farbiger Kontraste, das das blasse und langweilige Aussehen des Ganzen hervorruft.
Ganz schlimm ist der Zeitschriftenumschlag auf der gegenüberliegenden Seite. Eine Form, die „technisch" sein will, aber dem Wesen der Technik vollkommen widerspricht. Hier überall mischt sich schon jene „Kunst" ein, die wir bekämpfen — eine Künstlichkeit, die am Wesentlichen vorbeisieht und nur eine schöne Form machen will, die dann eben zu oft dem Zweck nicht mehr entspricht. Die Phantasie muß sich auf der Basis der realen Forderungen entwickeln, wenn es sich um die Gestaltung der Wirklichkeit handelt. (In der Malerei ist es anders: dort sind ihr keine Fesseln angelegt, weil die Aufgabe zweckentlöst ist.)

86

Vielfach trifft man auch eine Verwendung historischer Schriften (Schwabacher, Gotisch, Fraktur) in der Art zeitgemäßer Typographie an. Es ist aber falsch, diese historischen Formen anzuwenden — sie sind unserer Zeit fremd und können höchstens in einer ihrer Zeit gemäßen Weise angewandt werden. Können Sie sich einen Flieger mit Vollbart vorstellen?
Der Übergang positiver in negative Schrift, den zuerst Gebrauchsgraphiker angewendet haben, ist auch zuweilen in rein typographischen Erzeugnissen

Falsch!
Das Wort „Revue" in schwer lesbaren, sehr kompliziert herzustellenden Schriftformen; sinnlose, rein dekorative Verwendung abstrakter Formen, dazu das fettfeine Linienkreuz. Der Papiergrund ist an dem Arrangement unbeteiligt. Das Ganze ein vollkommenes Mißverständnis der Absichten der neuen Typographie. Diese arrangiert nicht dekorative Formen, sondern gestaltet, – bindet die Gegebenheiten des Textes, die selbst die einfachsten Formen zeigen müssen, zu einem harmonischen Ganzen.

87

● **1928 . DIE NEUE TYPOGRAPHIE .** Book . Jan Tschichold

→ p.402

● **1928 . CHRYSLER .** Advertising . Ashley Havinden

→ p.402

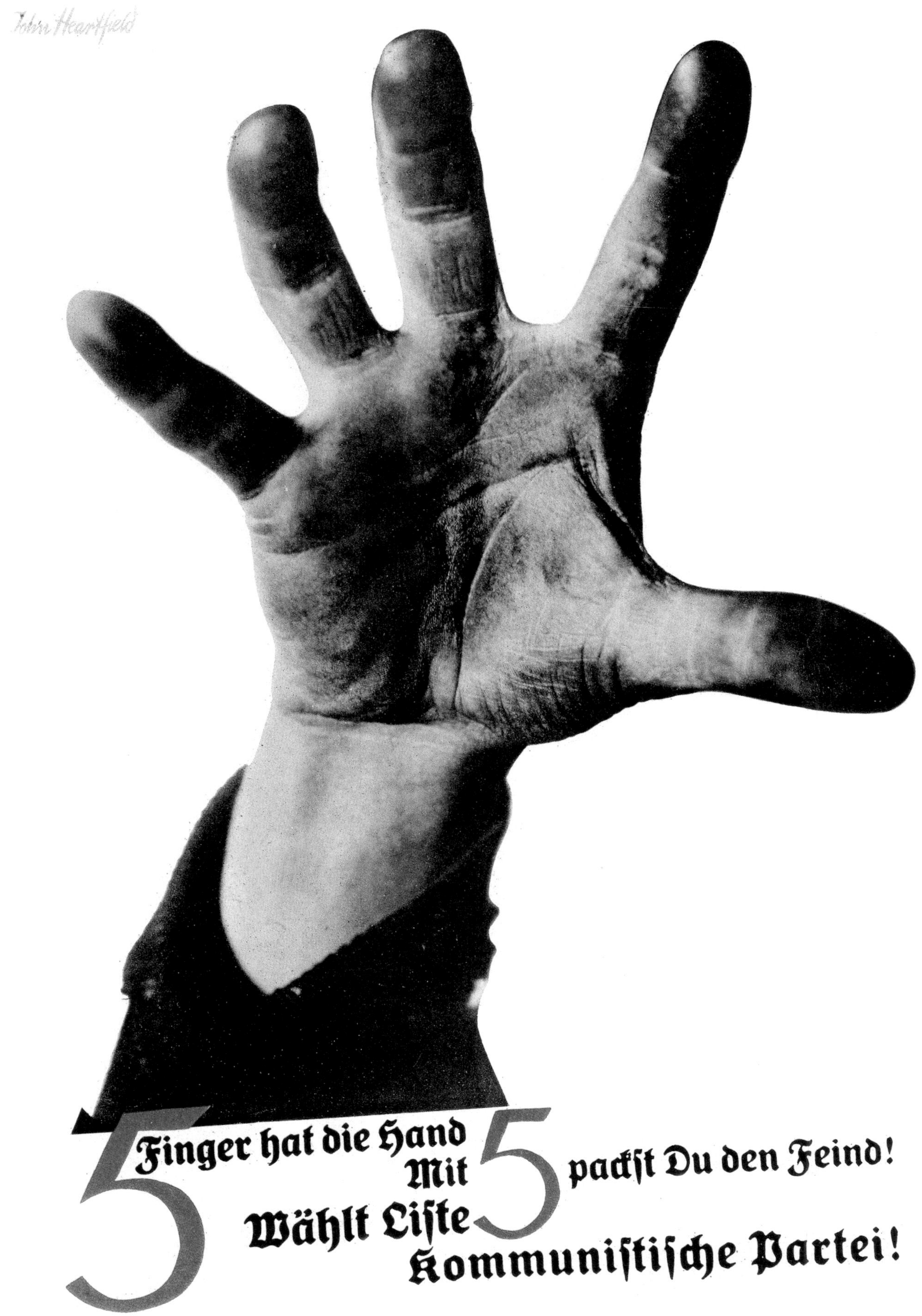

● **1928 . 5 FINGER HAT DIE HAND .** Poster . John Heartfield

→ p.402

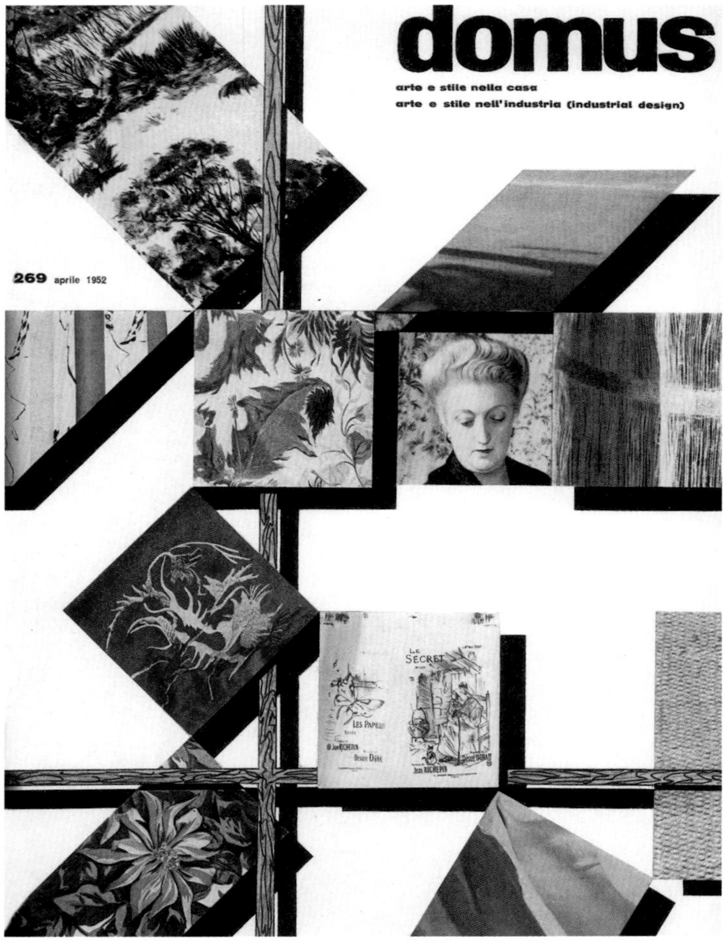

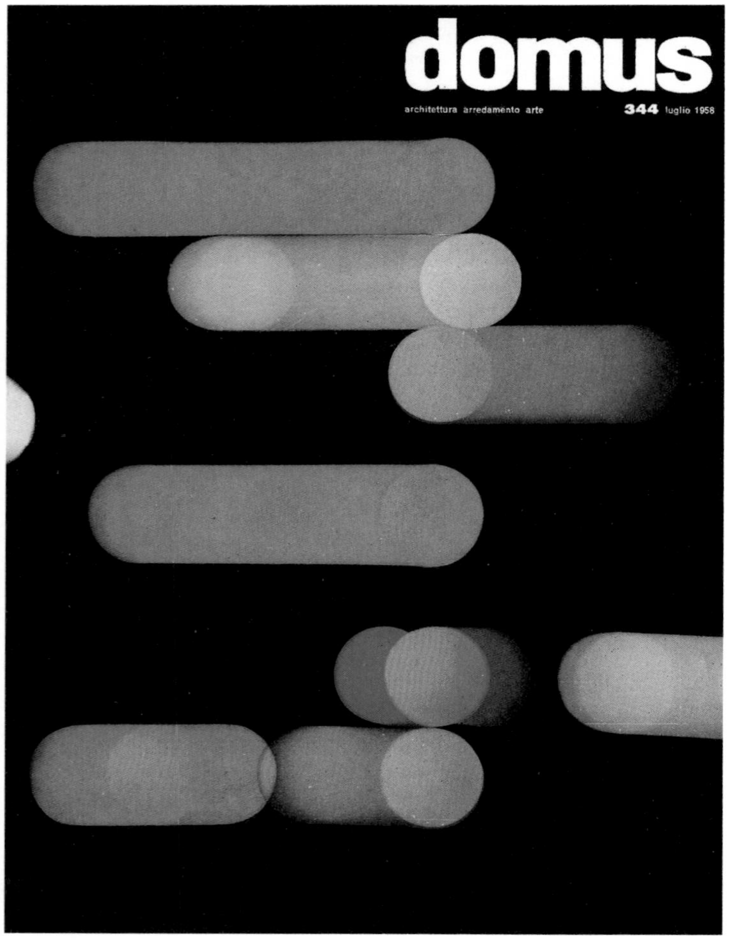

● **1928–PRESENT . DOMUS .** Magazine / Newspaper . Gio Ponti et al.
TOP LEFT: No. 217, January 1947; TOP RIGHT: No. 269, April 1952; BOTTOM LEFT: Photograph William Klein, No. 344, July 1958; BOTTOM RIGHT: William Klein, No. 362, January 1960

→ p.403

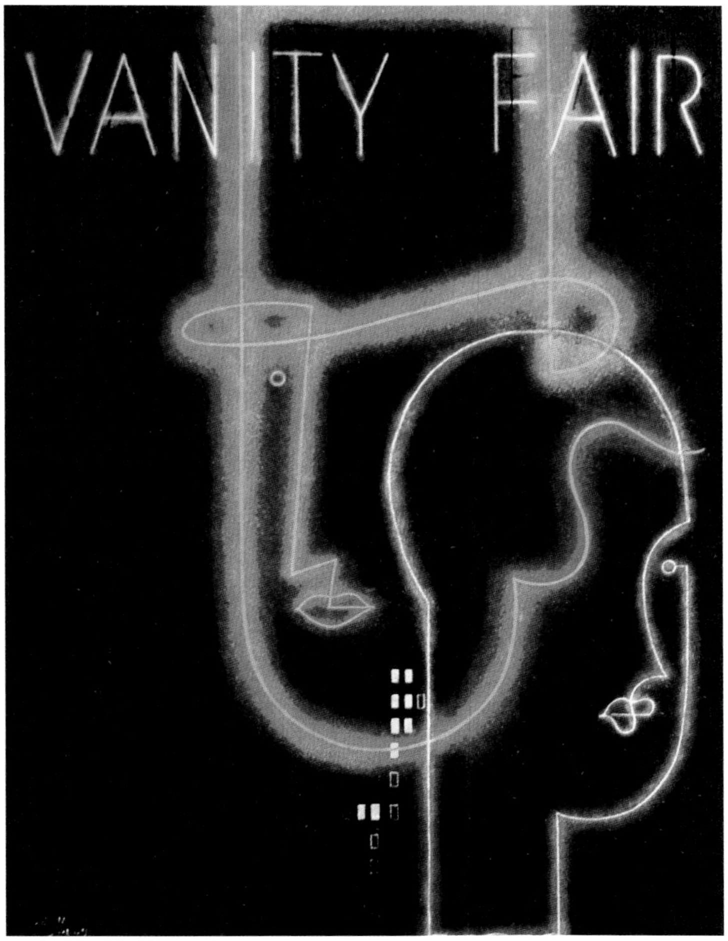

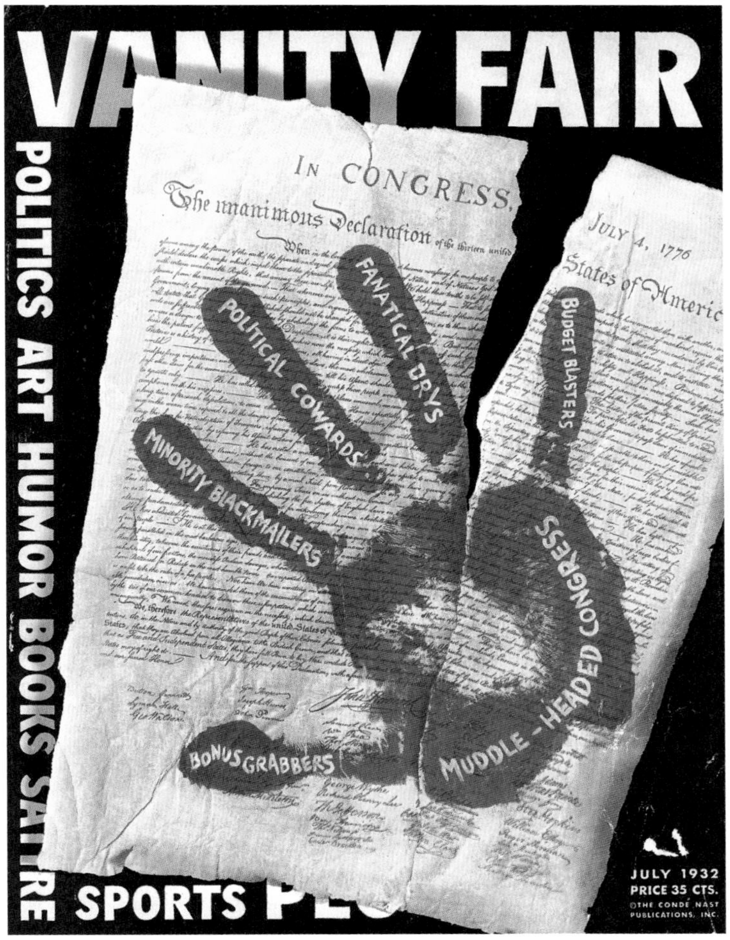

● **1929–1936 . VANITY FAIR .** Magazine Cover . Mehemed Fehmy Agha
TOP LEFT: Eduardo Garcia Benito, January 1930; TOP RIGHT: Jean Carlu, April 1931; BOTTOM LEFT: July 1932; BOTTOM RIGHT: Bobri, "Everybody's Washington," May 1933

→ p.403

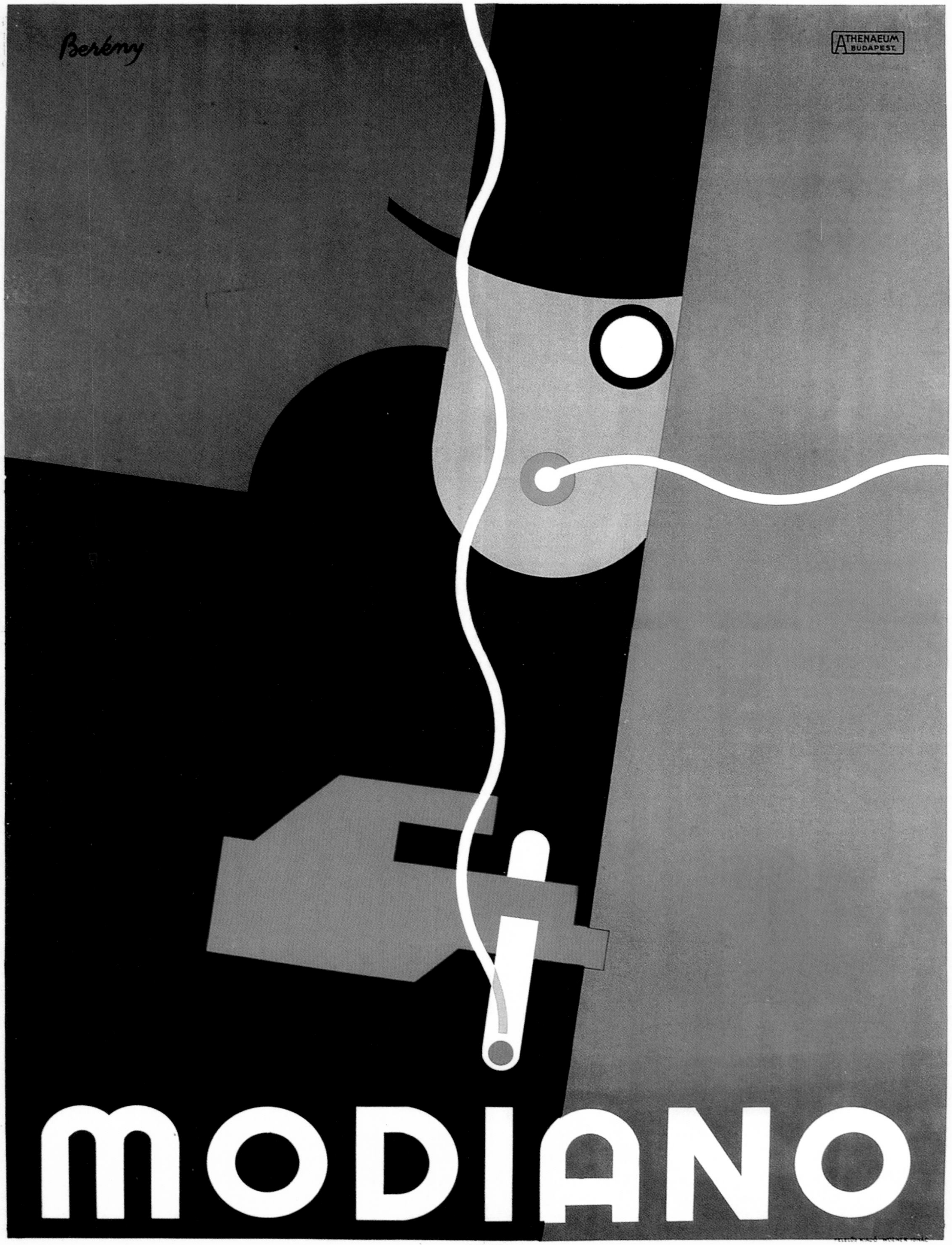

● **1928 . MODIANO .** Poster . Róbert Berény

→ p.403

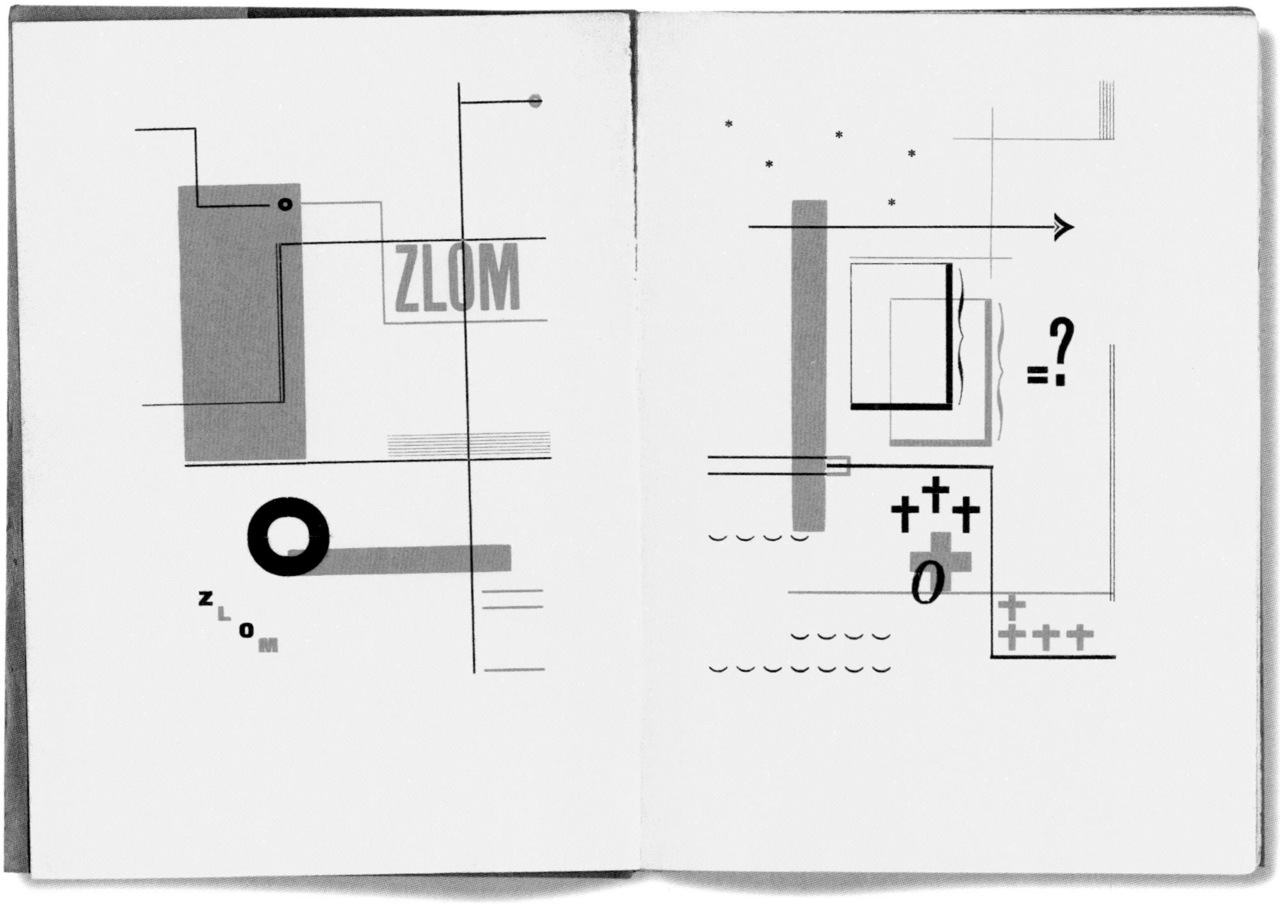

● **1928 . ZLOM, BY KONSTANTIN BIEBL .** Book . Karel Teige

→ p.404

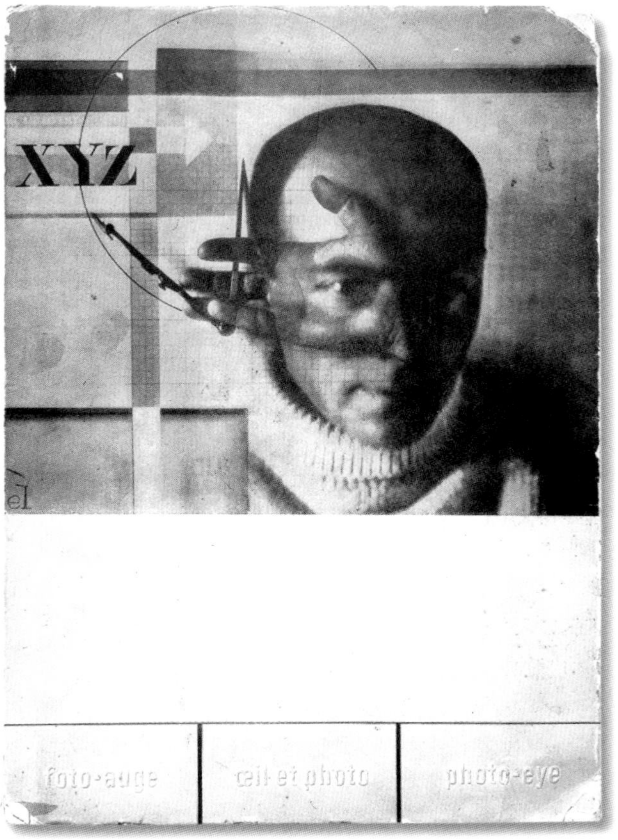

● **1929 . FOTO-AUGE .**
Book . Franz Roh, Jan Tschichold

→ p.404

● **1929–1938 . DIE NEUE LINIE .**
Magazine Cover . Herbert Bayer, László Moholy-Nagy
László Moholy-Nagy, September 1929

→ p.404

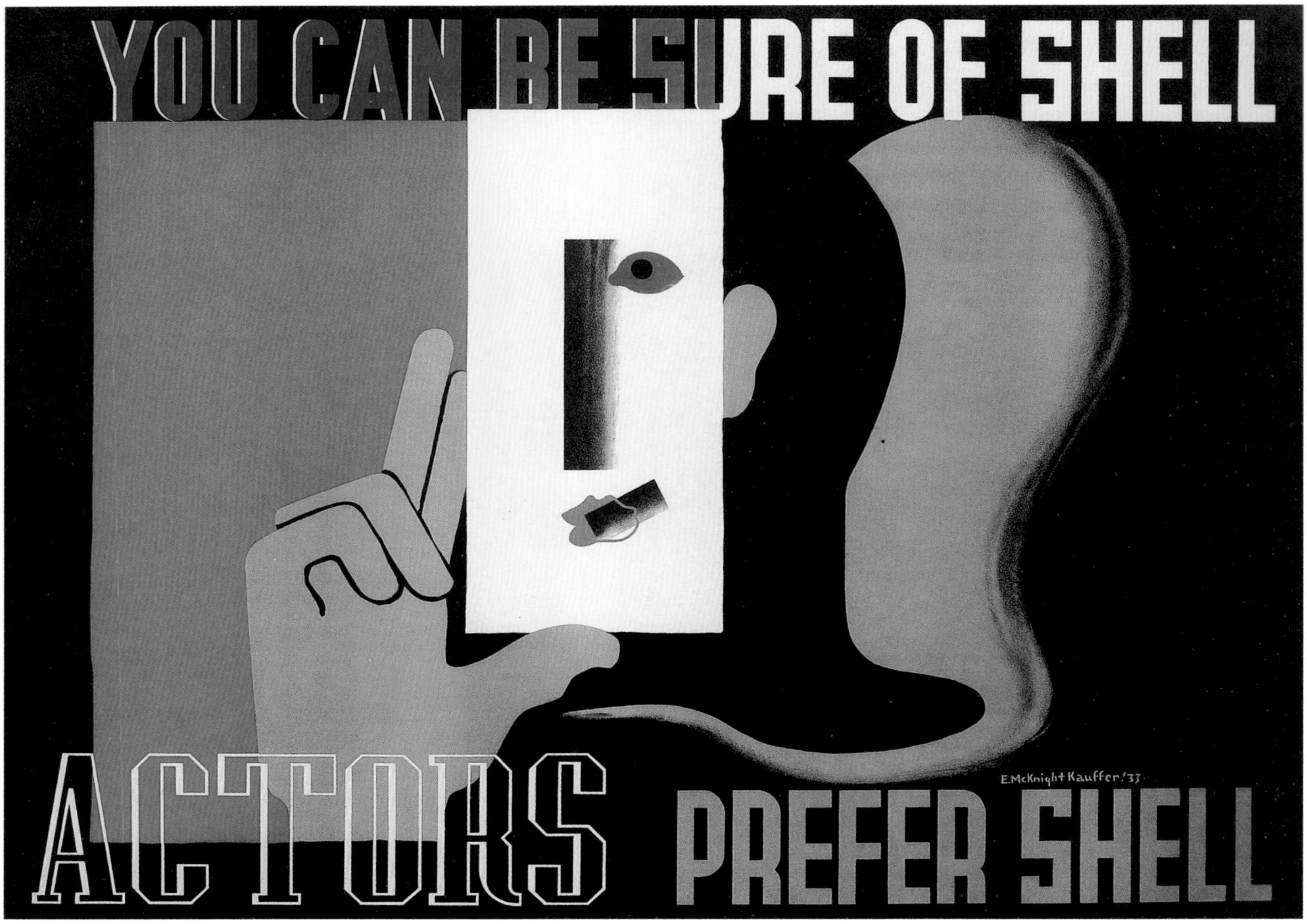

● **1929–1939 . YOU CAN BE SURE OF SHELL .** Poster . Edward McKnight Kauffer

→ p.405

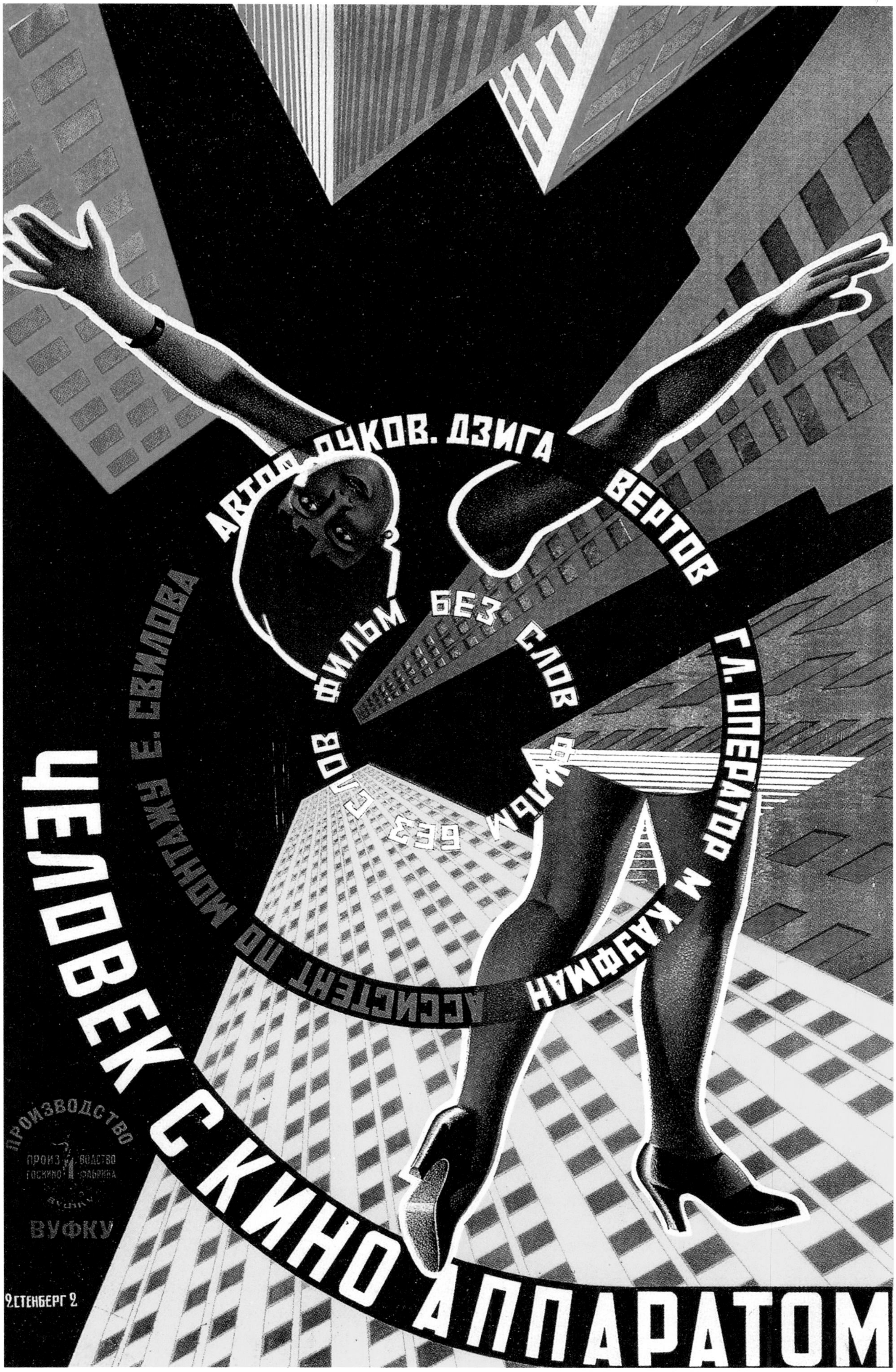

● **1929 . THE MAN WITH THE MOVIE CAMERA .** Poster . Georgii Stenberg, Vladimir Stenberg

→ p.405

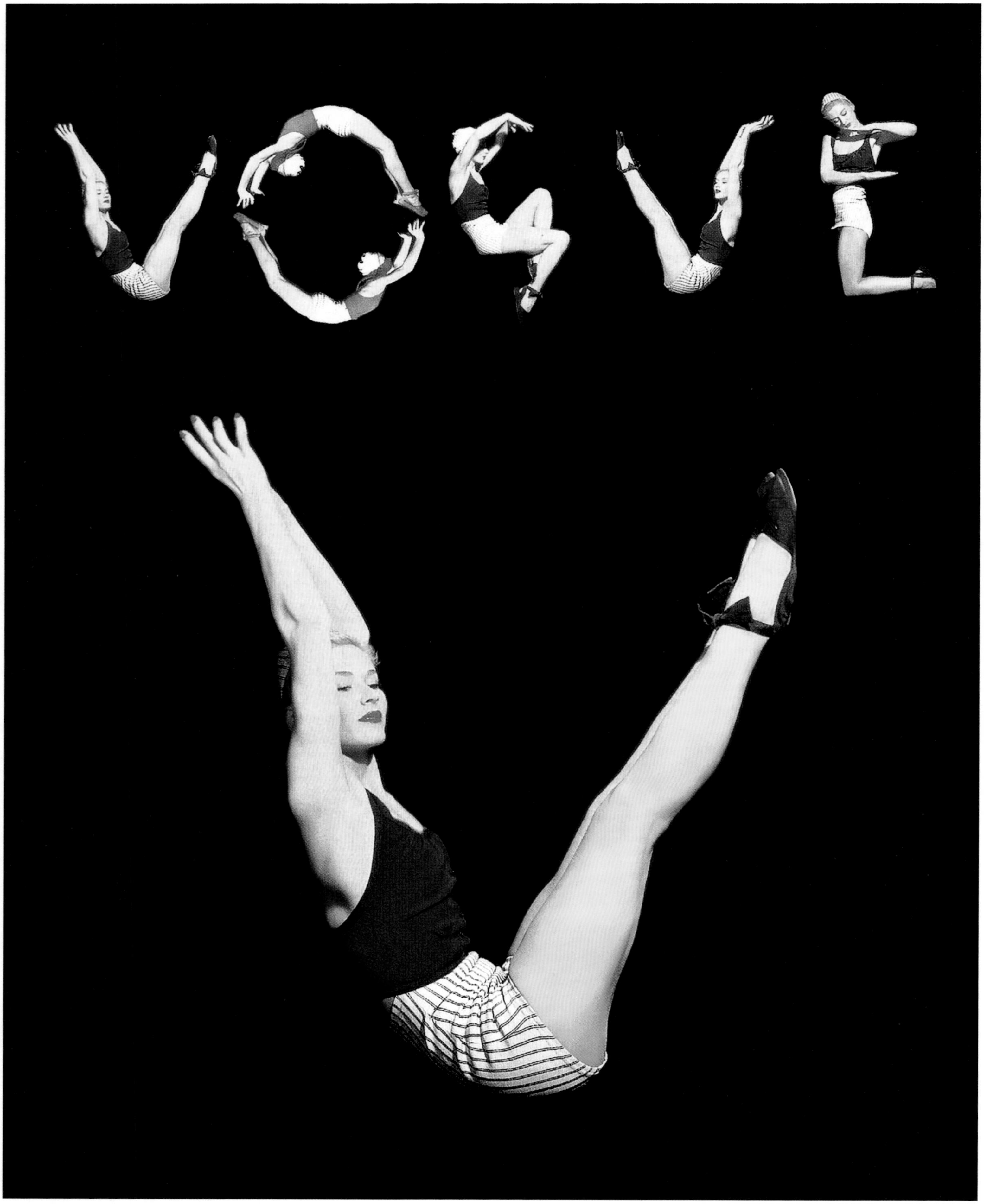

● **1929–1955 . VOGUE .** Magazine / Newspaper . Mehemed Fehmy Agha, Alexander Liberman, et al.
Mehemed Fehmy Agha, photograph Horst, August 1940

→ p.405

● **1929 . BROADWAY .** Typeface . Morris Fuller Benton

→ p.406

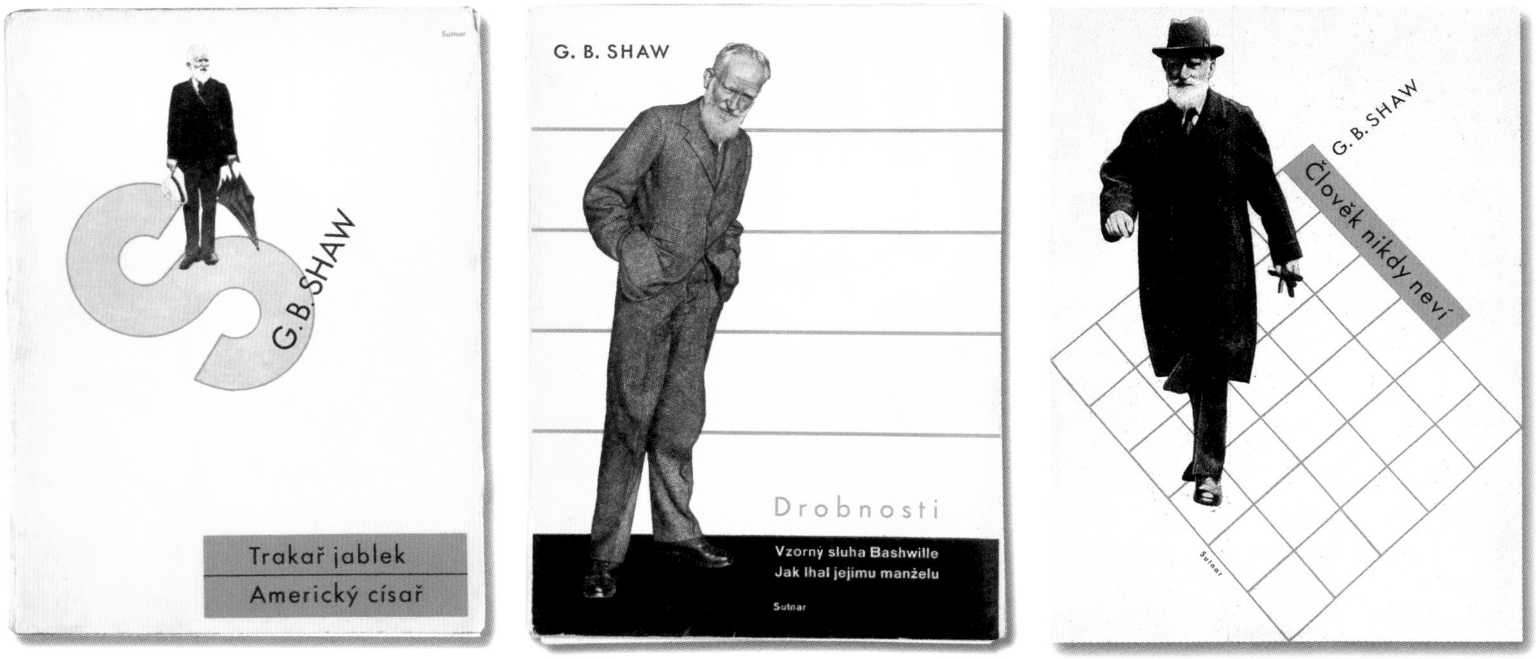

● **1930–1933 . GEORGE BERNARD SHAW SERIES .** Book Cover . Ladislav Sutnar
FROM LEFT: *Trakař jablek: Americký císař* (*The Apple Cart: The American Emperor*), 1932; *Drobnosti I: Vzorný sluha Bashville* (*Small Things I: The Admirable Bashville*), 1930; *Člověk nikdy neví* (*You Never Can Tell*), 1931

→ p.406

● **1930–1938 . AIZ .** Magazine / Newspaper . John Heartfield
No. 15, April 5, 1936

→ p.406

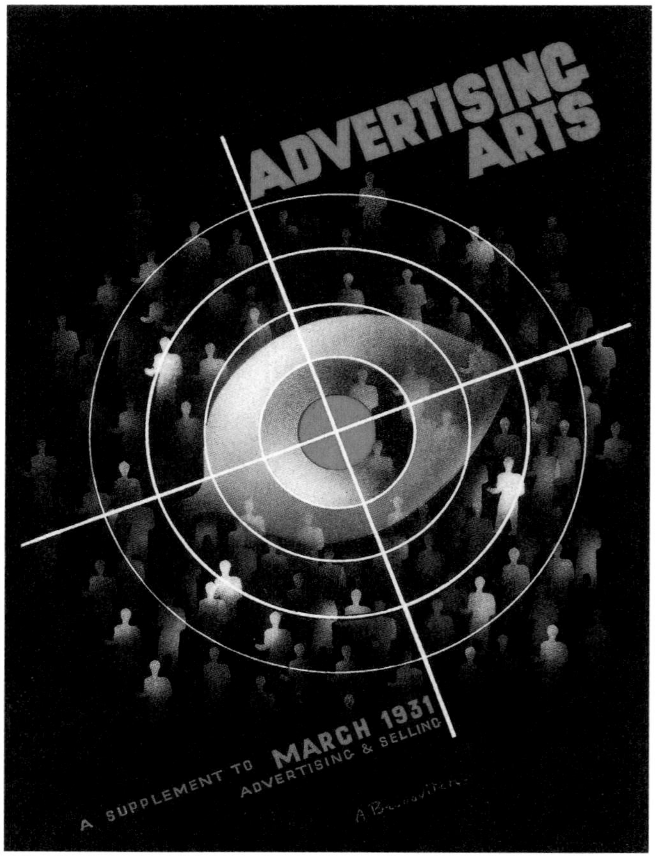

● **1930–1939 . ADVERTISING ARTS .** Magazine Cover . Various
Alexey Brodovitch, March 1931

→ p.407

● **1930 . VYPOLNIM PLAN, VELIKIKH RABOT .** Poster . Gustav Klutsis

→ p.407

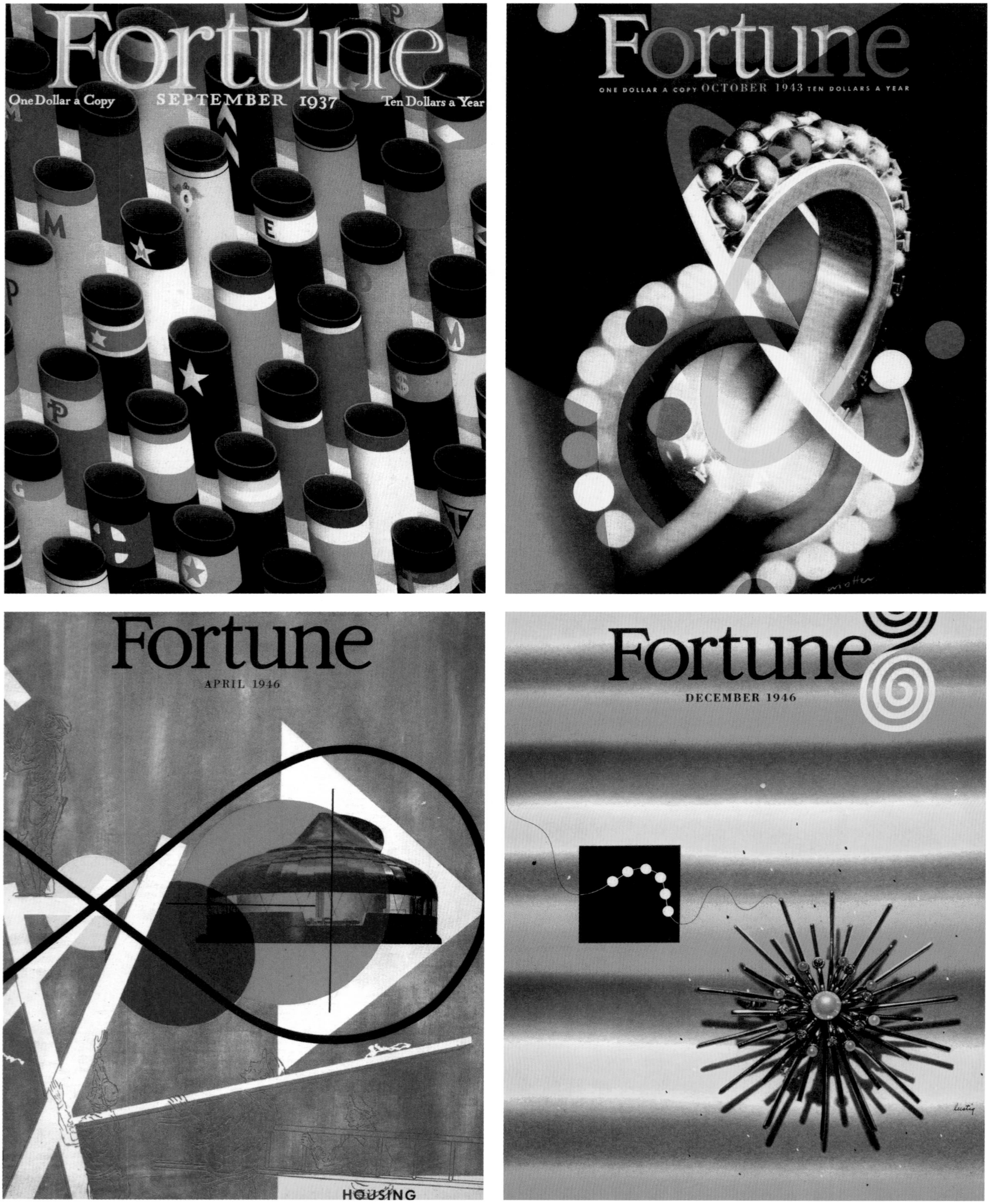

● **1930–1962 . FORTUNE .** Magazine Cover . Various
TOP LEFT: Antonio Petruccelli, September 1937; TOP RIGHT: Herbert Matter, October 1943; BOTTOM LEFT: Lester Beall, April 1946; BOTTOM RIGHT: Alvin Lustig, December 1946

→ p.407

WIRELESS

Before Picasso began to stick actual pieces of paper which he had cut out of newspapers on to his canvasses, we should never have had the courage to compose an advertisement page with such apparently unsuitable elements. Their diversity, however, is the only thing which could so vividly suggest the diversity of wireless announcements. There is no longer any excuse needed for rapid transition from one country to another, from politics to music or from boxing matches to stock exchange quotations. In this respect our ears have educated our eyes, and the art of lay-out has been quick to profit by this newly acquired adaptability.

● **1931 . MISE EN PAGE: THE THEORY AND PRACTICE OF LAYOUT .** Book . Alfred Tolmer

→ p.408

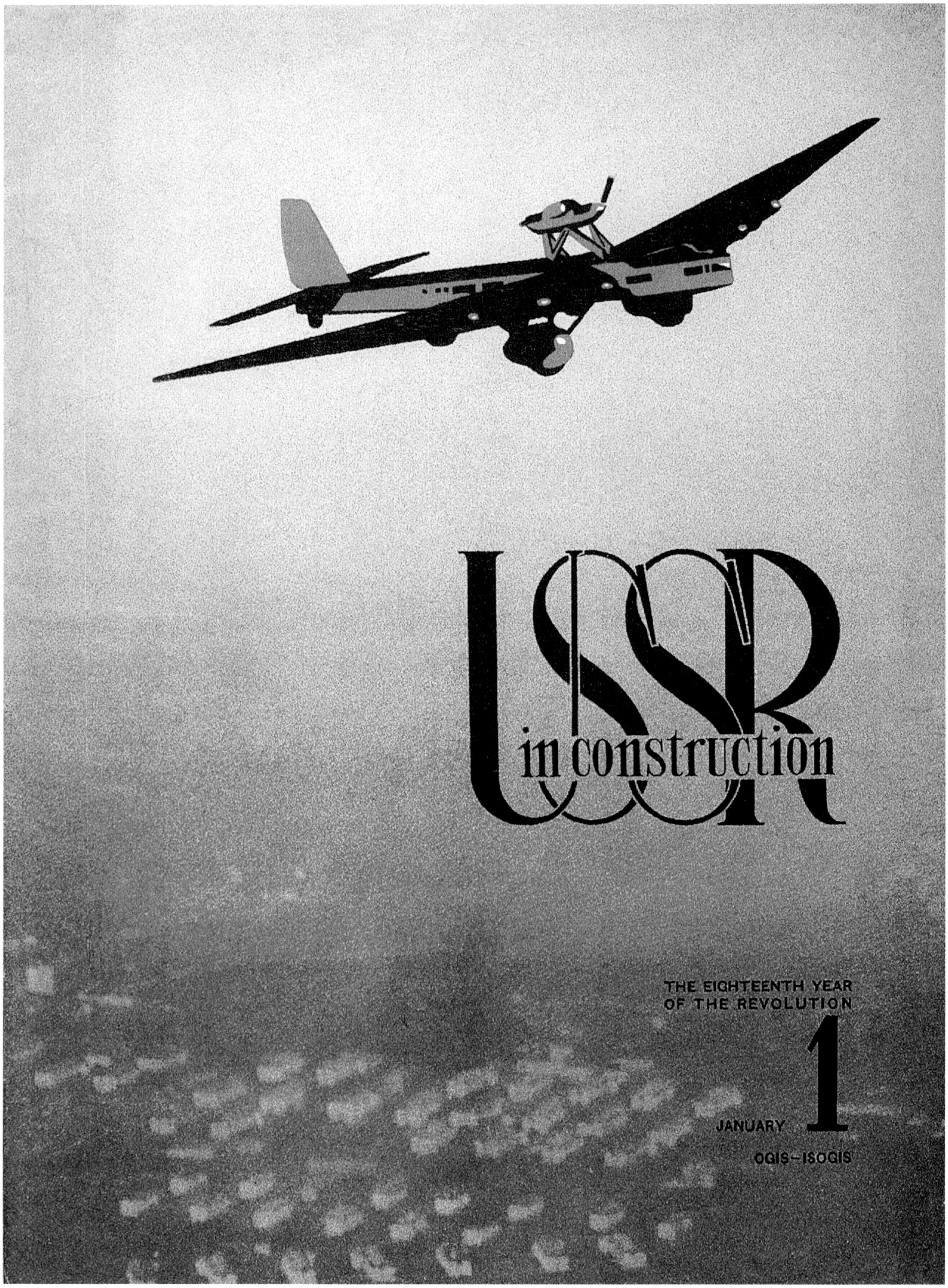

● **1930–1941 . USSR IN CONSTRUCTION .** Magazine / Newspaper . El Lissitzky, Aleksandr Rodchenko
Natan Altman, No. 1, January 1930

→ p.408

● **1931–1933 . FILM: SERIE MONOGRAFIEËN OVER FILMKUNST .** Magazine Cover . Piet Zwart
TOP LEFT: No. 1, 1933; TOP RIGHT: No. 3, 1933; BOTTOM LEFT: No. 7, 1931; BOTTOM RIGHT: No. 8, 1931

→ p.408

žijeme 1931
obrázkový magazin dnešní doby
první ročník ● sešit 4-5 ● str. 97-160 ● červenec-srpen 1931

● **1931–1935 . ŽIJEME .** Magazine / Newspaper . Ladislav Sutnar
March 1931

→ p.409

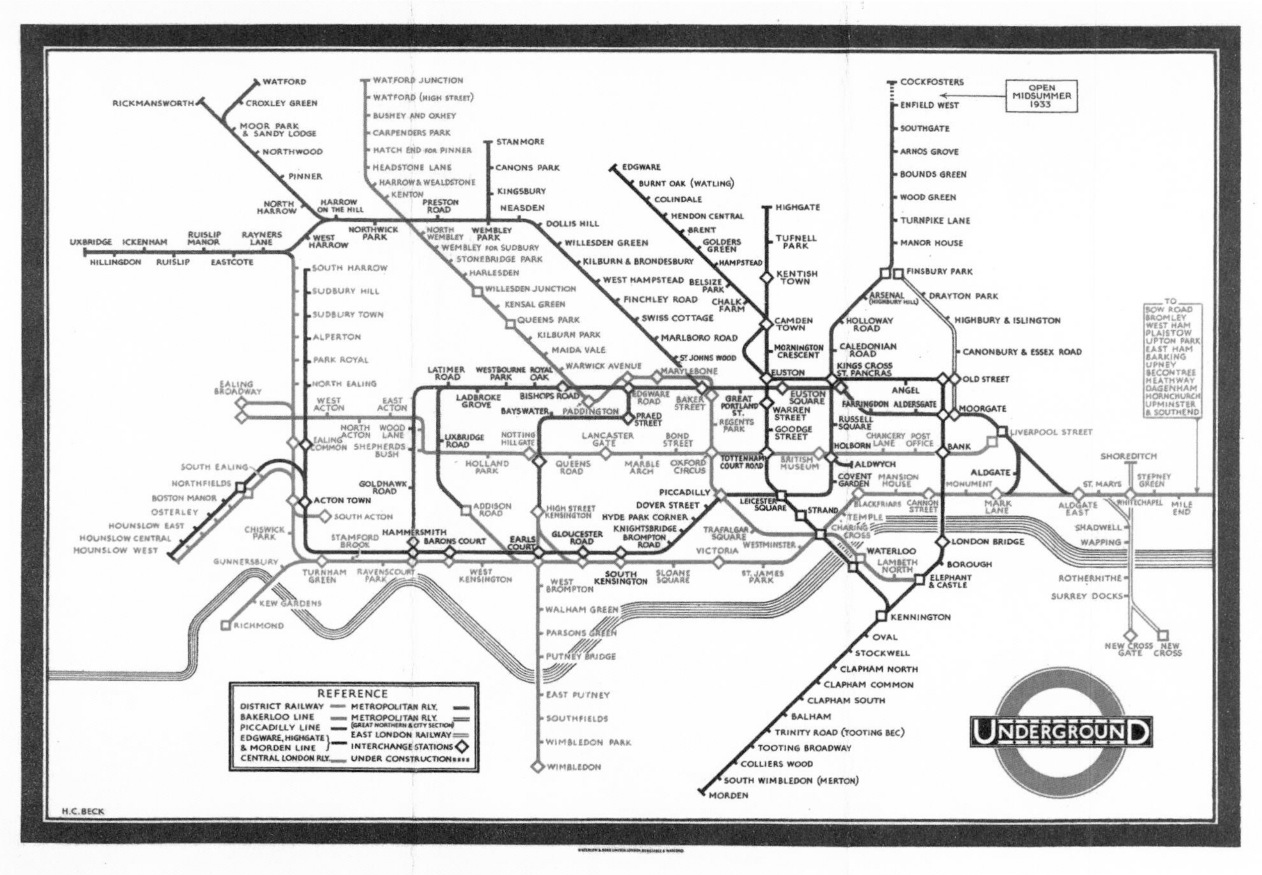

● **1931 . LONDON UNDERGROUND MAP .** Information Design . Henry C. Beck

→ p.409

● **1931 . INTERNATIONALE AUSSTELLUNG KUNST DER WERBUNG .** Poster . Max Burchartz

→ p.409

DOCUMENTOS DE ACTIVIDAD CONTEMPORÁNEA
AC 1
PUBLICACIÓN DEL G. A. T. E. P. A. C.
SUMARIO:
* Exposición de Pintura y Arquitectura Modernas de San Sebastián.
* Puertas "Standard" de madera.
* Urbanización de la Barcelona futura.
* Ensanche de Ceuta.
* San Pol de Mar (Barcelona).
* Habitaciones de Hotel.
* Fotografía-Cine.
* La ciudad verde de Moscú.
* Noticias.
* Bibliografía.
2,50 Ptas.

● **1931–1937 . A. C. DOCUMENTOS DE ACTIVIDAD CONTEMPORÁNEA .** Magazine / Newspaper . GATEPAC
No. 1, 1931

→ p.410

DIN
1451
Beiblatt 3
Normschriften
Engschrift Mittelschrift Breitschrift
mit Hilfsnetz gemalt Hilfsnetz für Malschablonen
Beispiele
Fette Engschrift
Innerhalb eines Wortes
Alleinstehend
abcdefghijklmnopqrstuvwxl
yzßäöü&.,-:;!?") 1234567890
ÄÖÜABCDEFGHIJKLMNOPQRST
UVWXYZ
Fette Mittelschrift
abcdefghijklmnopqrs
tuvwxyzßäöü&.,-:;!?")
1234567890ÄÖÜABC
DEFGHIJKLMNOPQR

● **1931/1980/1995 . DIN AND FF DIN .** Typeface . Unknown, Albert-Jan Pool

→ p.410

● **1931–1938/1947–1948 . RONINGYO .** Magazine Cover . Takashi Kono
April 1937

→ p.410

● **1931 . AUSSTELLUNGEN WALTER GROPIUS, RATIONELLE BEBAUUNGSWEISEN .** Poster . Ernst Keller

→ p.411

● **1932 . DUBO DUBON DUBONNET .** Poster . A. M. Cassandre

→ p.411

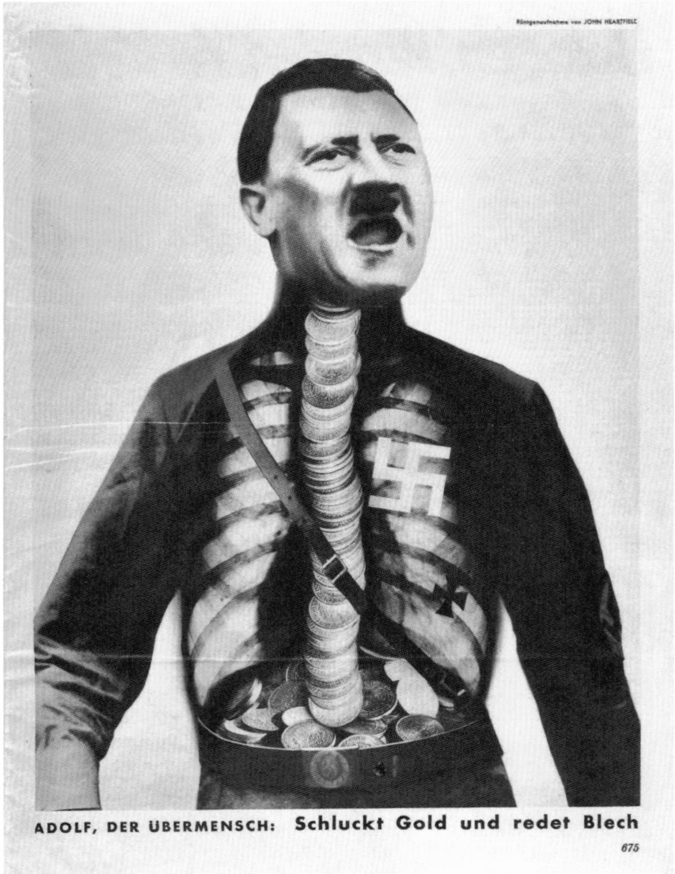

● **1932 . ADOLF DER ÜBERMENSCH SCHLUCKT GOLD UND REDET BLECH .** Poster . John Heartfield

→ p.411

THE TIMES

No. 46,750 LATE LONDON EDITION LONDON THURSDAY MAY 10 1934 PRICE 2d

● **1932 . TIMES NEW ROMAN .** Typeface . Stanley Morison, Victor Lardent
The Times, Thursday, May 10, 1934

→ p.412

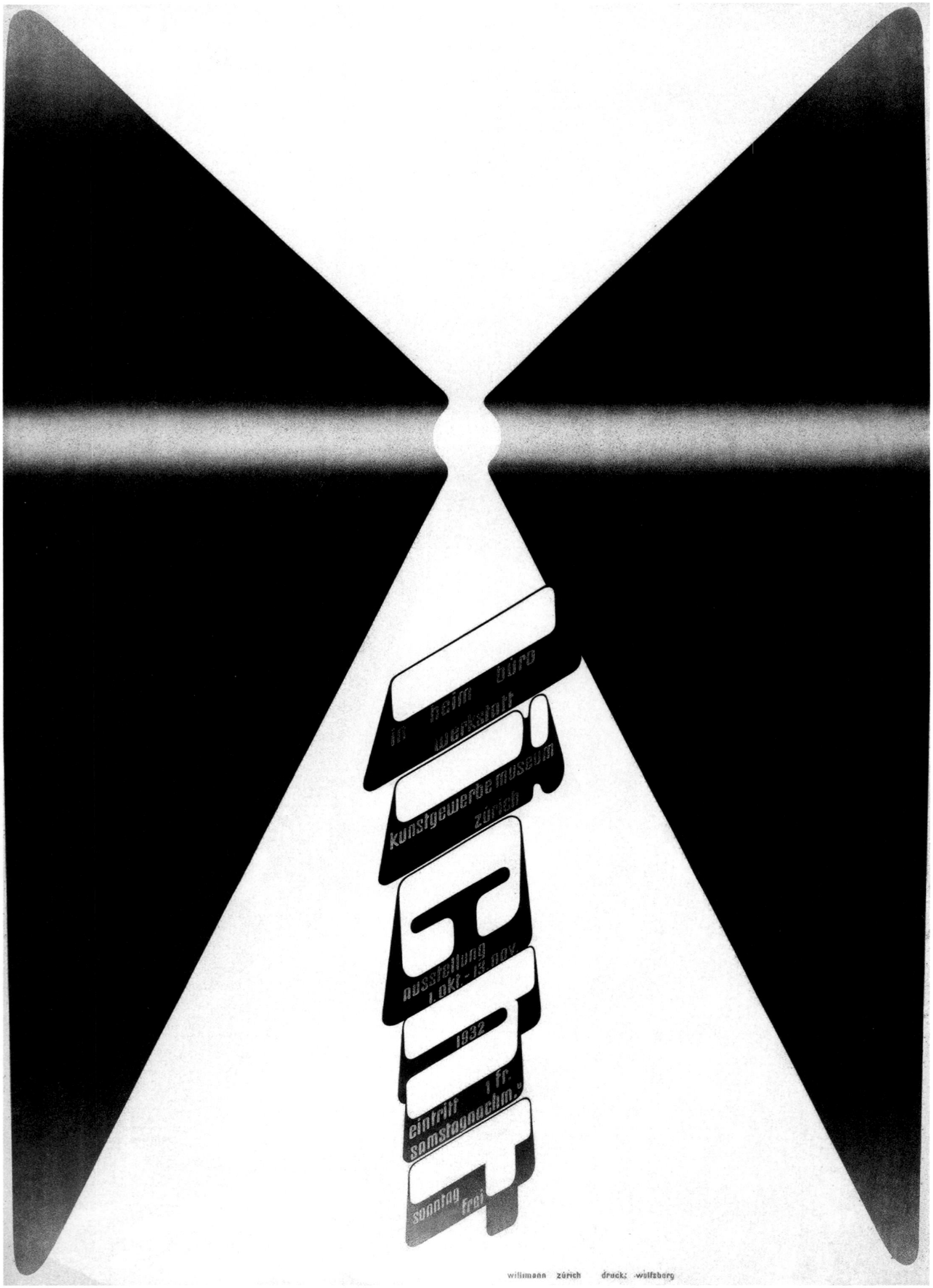

● **1932 . LICHT .** Poster . Alfred Willimann

→ p.412

● **1932–1934 . FUTURISMO .** Magazine / Newspaper . Enrico Prampolini
Vol. 1, No. 8, October 28, 1933

→ p.412

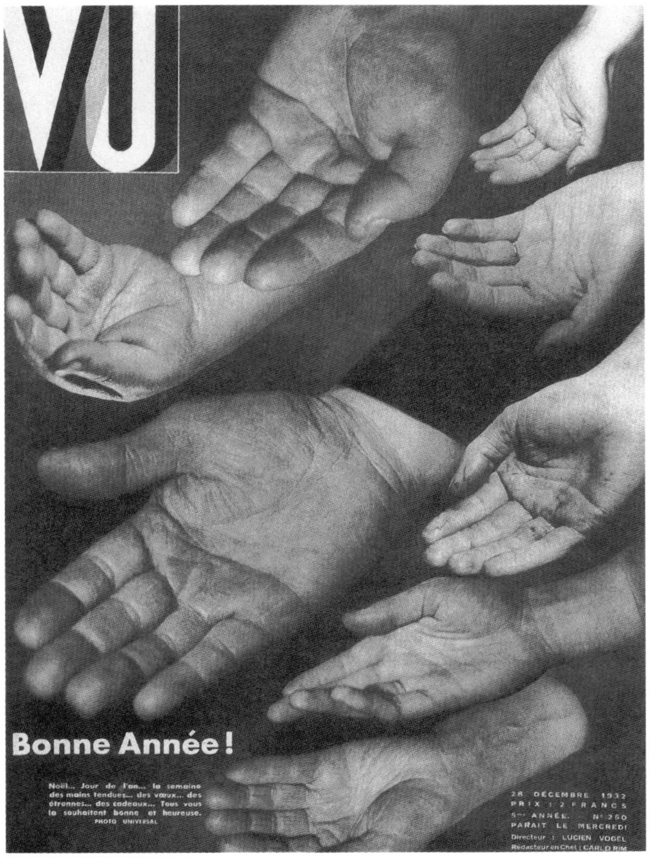

● **1932–1937 . VU .** Magazine / Newspaper . Alexander Liberman
December 28, 1932

→ p.413

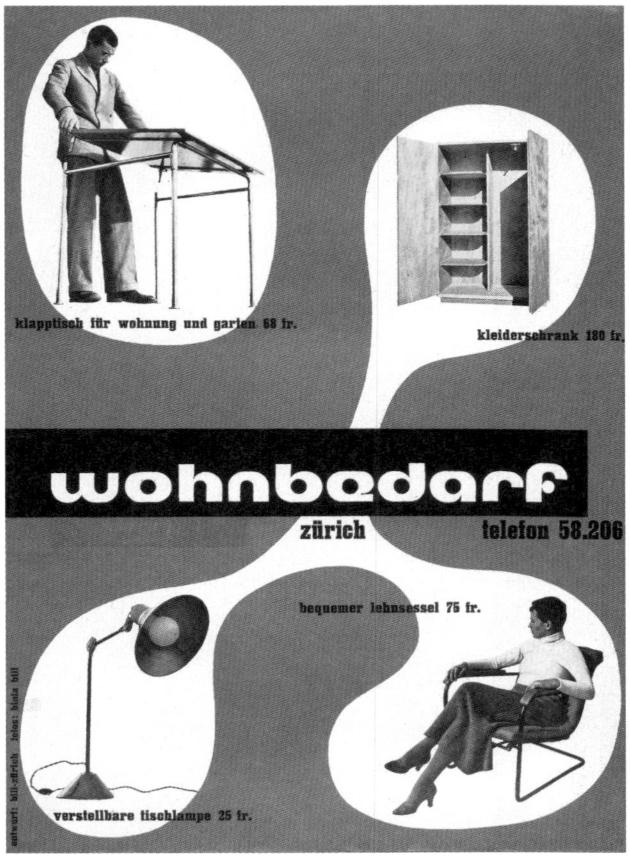

● **1932 . WOHNBEDARF .**
Identity . Max Bill

→ p.413

● **1933 . BRAUN .** Logo . Will Münch

→ p.413

● **1933 . ESSO .** Logo . Unknown

→ p.414

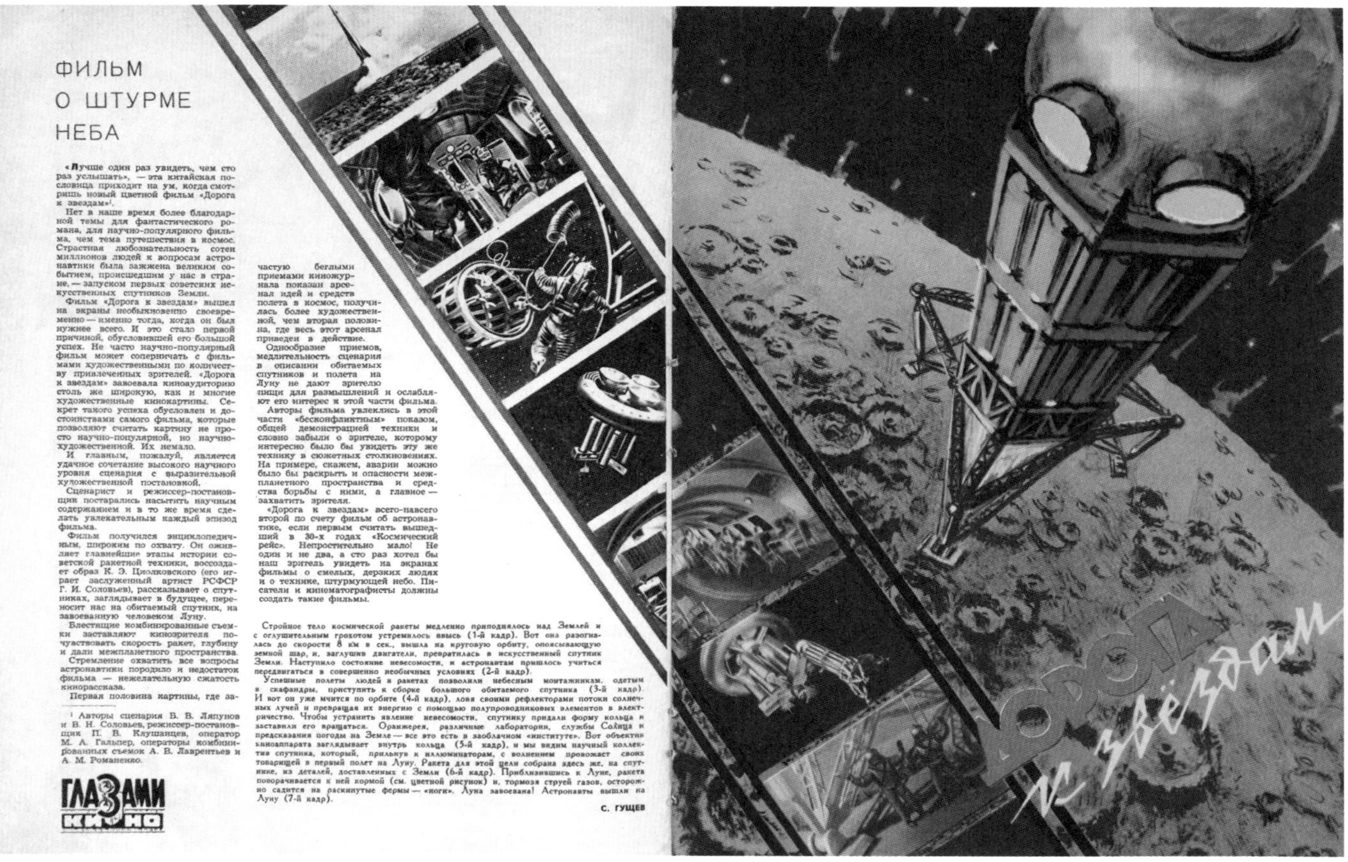

ФИЛЬМ О ШТУРМЕ НЕБА

«Лучше один раз увидеть, чем сто раз услышать», — эта китайская пословица приходит на ум, когда смотришь новый цветной фильм «Дорога к звездам»[1].

Нет в наше время более благодарной темы для фантастического романа, для научно-популярного фильма, чем тема путешествия в космос. Страстная любознательность сотен миллионов людей к вопросам астронавтики была зажжена великим событием, происшедшим у нас в стране, — запуском первых советских искусственных спутников Земли.

Фильм «Дорога к звездам» вышел на экраны необыкновенно своевременно — именно тогда, когда он был нужнее всего. И это стало первой причиной, обусловившей его большой успех. Не часто научно-популярный фильм может соперничать с фильмами художественными по количеству привлеченных зрителей. «Дорога к звездам» завоевала киноаудиторию столь же широкую, как и многие художественные кинокартины. Секрет такого успеха обусловлен и достоинствами самого фильма, которые позволяют считать картину не просто научно-популярной, но научно-художественной. Их немало.

И главным, пожалуй, является удачное сочетание высокого научного уровня сценария с выразительной художественной постановкой.

Сценарист и режиссер-постановщик постарались насытить научным содержанием и в то же время сделать увлекательным каждый эпизод фильма.

Фильм получился энциклопедичным, широким по охвату. Он оживляет главнейшие этапы истории советской ракетной техники, воссоздает образ К. Э. Циолковского (его играет заслуженный артист РСФСР Г. И. Соловьев), рассказывает о спутниках, заглядывает в будущее, переносит нас на обитаемый спутник, на завоеванную человеком Луну.

Блестящие комбинированные съемки заставляют кинозрителя почувствовать скорость ракет, глубину и дали межпланетного пространства.

Стремление охватить все вопросы астронавтики породило и недостаток фильма — нежелательную сжатость кинорассказа.

Первая половина картины, где зачастую беглыми приемами киножурнала показан арсенал идей и средств полета в космос, получилась более художественной, чем вторая половина, где весь этот арсенал приведен в действие.

Однообразие приемов, медлительность сценария в описании обитаемых спутников и полета на Луну не дают зрителю пищи для размышлений и ослабляют его интерес к этой части фильма.

Авторы фильма увлеклись в этой части «бесконфликтным» показом, общей демонстрацией техники и словно забыли о зрителе, которому интересно было бы увидеть эту же технику в сюжетных столкновениях. На примере, скажем, аварии можно было бы раскрыть и опасности межпланетного пространства и средства борьбы с ними, а главное — захватить зрителя.

«Дорога к звездам» всего-навсего второй по счету фильм об астронавтике, если первым считать вышедший в 30-х годах «Космический рейс». Непростительно мало! Не один и не два, а сто раз хотел бы наш зритель увидеть на экранах фильмы о смелых, дерзких людях и о технике, штурмующей небо. Писатели и кинематографисты должны создать такие фильмы.

[1] Авторы сценария Б. В. Ляпунов и В. Н. Соловьев, режиссер-постановщик П. В. Клушанцев, оператор М. А. Гальпер, операторы комбинированных съемок А. В. Лаврентьев и А. М. Романенко.

ГЛАЗАМИ КИНО

Стройное тело космической ракеты медленно приподнялось над Землей и с оглушительным грохотом устремилось ввысь (1-й кадр). Вот она разогналась до скорости 8 км в сек., вышла на круговую орбиту, опоясывающую земной шар, и, заглушив двигатели, превратилась в искусственный спутник Земли. Наступило состояние невесомости, и астронавтам пришлось учиться передвигаться в совершенно необычных условиях (2-й кадр).

Успешные полеты людей в ракетах позволили небесным монтажникам, одетым в скафандры, приступить к сборке большого обитаемого спутника (3-й кадр). И вот он уже мчится по орбите (4-й кадр), ловя своими рефлекторами потоки солнечных лучей и превращая их энергию с помощью полупроводниковых элементов в электричество. Чтобы устранить явление невесомости, спутнику придали форму кольца и заставили его вращаться. Оранжерея, различные лаборатории, службы Солнца и предсказания погоды на Земле — все это есть в заоблачном «институте». Вот объектив киноаппарата заглядывает внутрь кольца (5-й кадр), и мы видим научный коллектив спутника, который, прильнув к иллюминаторам, с волнением провожает своих товарищей в первый полет на Луну. Ракета для этой цели собрана здесь же, на спутнике, из деталей, доставленных с Земли (6-й кадр). Приблизившись к Луне, ракета поворачивается к ней кормой (см. цветной рисунок) и, тормозя струей газов, осторожно садится на раскинутые фермы — «ноги». Луна завоевана! Астронавты вышли на Луну (7-й кадр).

С. ГУЩЕВ

● **1933–PRESENT . TEKHNIKA—MOLODEZHI .** Magazine / Newspaper . Various
Illustration V. Ivanov, for the article "Machine Engines that Invade the Sky," No. 2, 1963

→ p.414

● **1934–1942 . PM/A-D .** Magazine / Newspaper . Various
Herbert Bayer, December–January, 1939–40

→ p.414

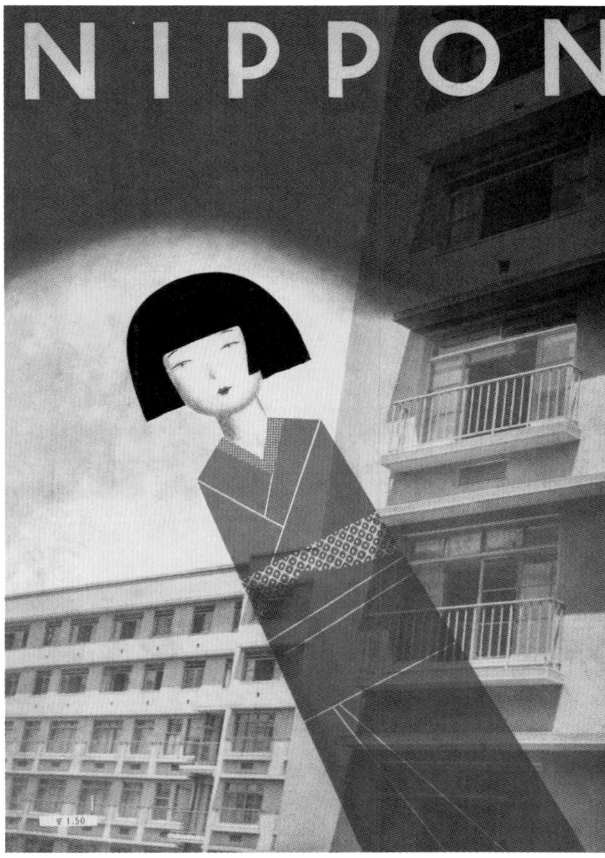

● **1934–1944 . NIPPON .** Magazine Cover . Nihon Kobo
Ayao Yamana, photograph Yoshio Watanabe, 1934

→ p.415

● **1934 . ST. MORITZ .** Identity . Walter Herdeg

→ p.415

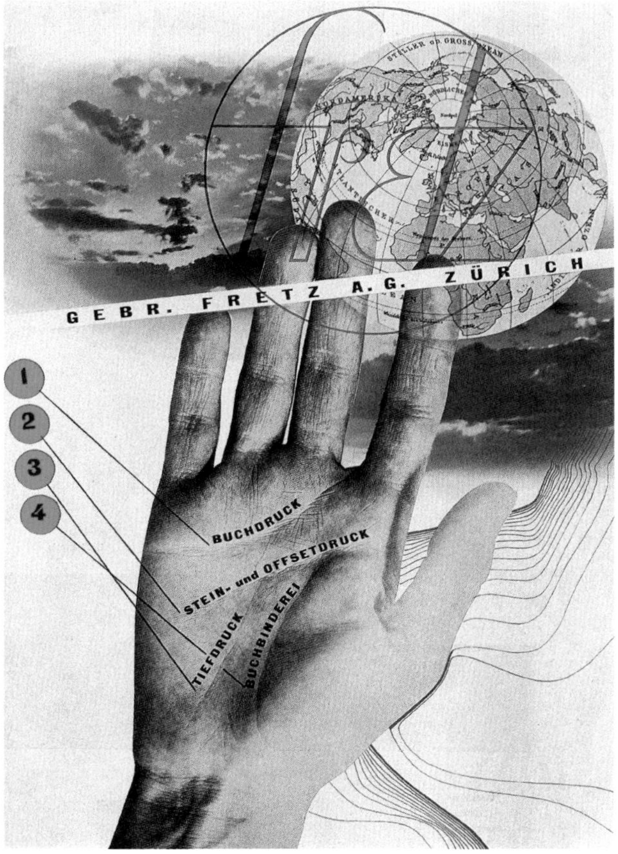

● **1934 . GEBRUDER FRETZ AG .**
Book . Herbert Matter

→ p.415

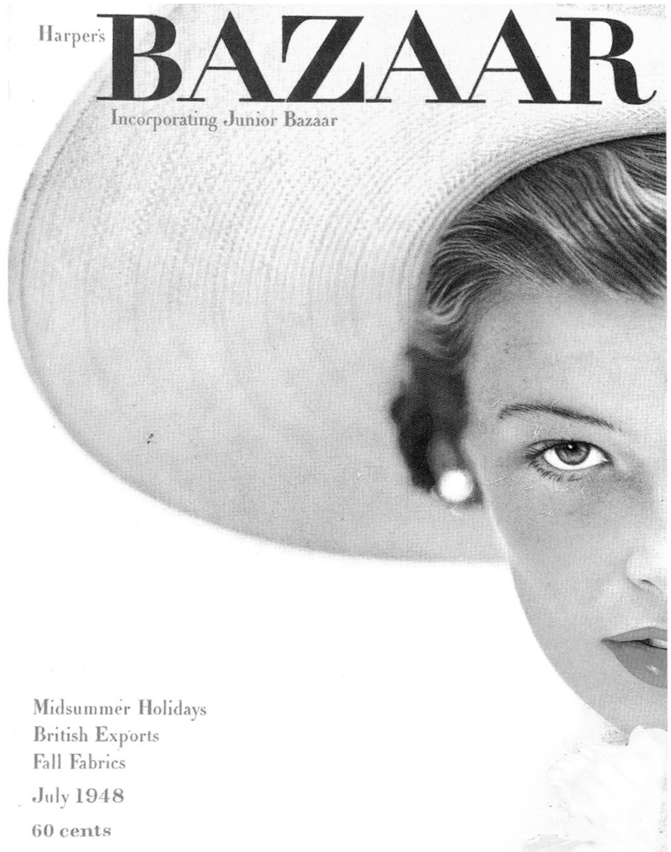

● **1934–1958 . HARPER'S BAZAAR .** Magazine / Newspaper . Alexey Brodovitch
Photograph Richard Avedon, July 1948

→ p.416

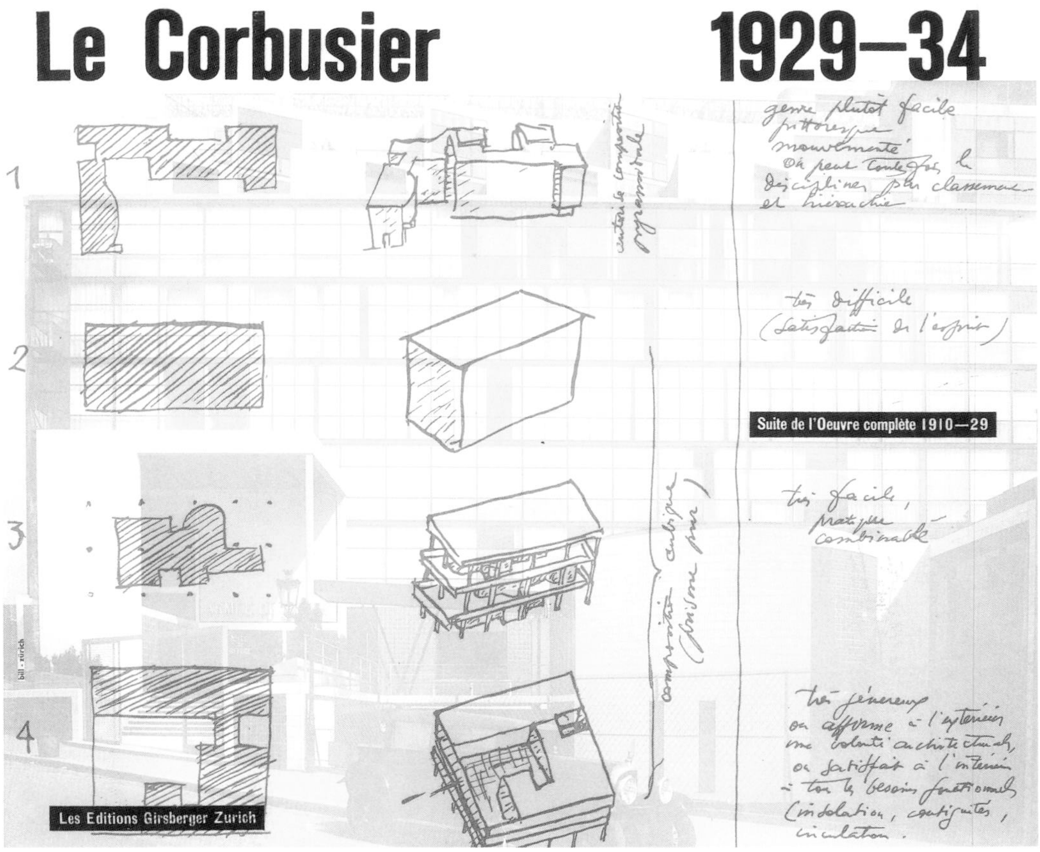

● **1935–1939 . LE CORBUSIER & PIERRE JEANNERET: OEUVRE COMPLÈTE .** Book . Max Bill
Oeuvre complete: Vol. 2, 1929–34, 1935

→ p.416

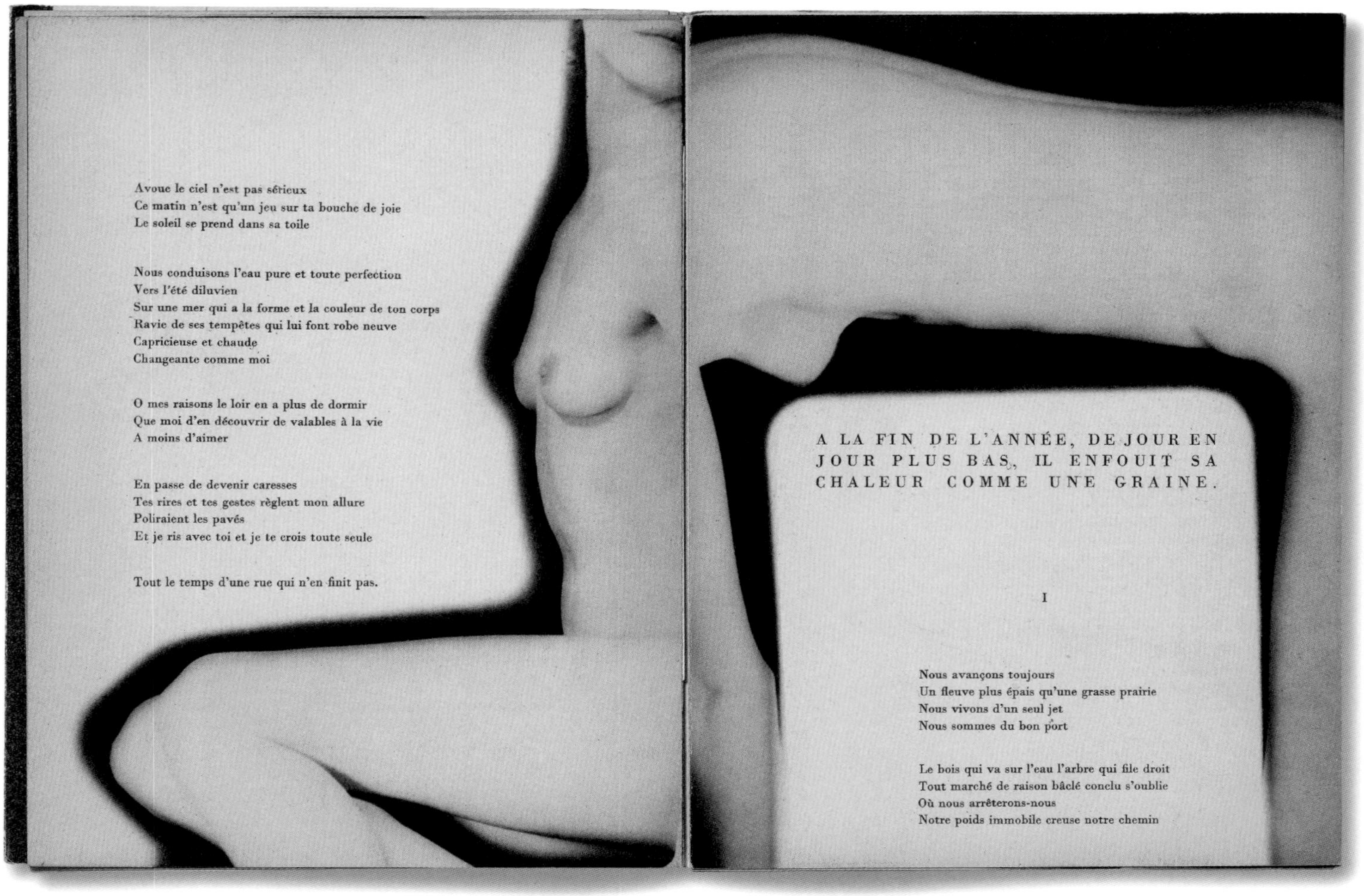

Avoue le ciel n'est pas sérieux
Ce matin n'est qu'un jeu sur ta bouche de joie
Le soleil se prend dans sa toile

Nous conduisons l'eau pure et toute perfection
Vers l'été diluvien
Sur une mer qui a la forme et la couleur de ton corps
Ravie de ses tempêtes qui lui font robe neuve
Capricieuse et chaude
Changeante comme moi

O mes raisons le loir en a plus de dormir
Que moi d'en découvrir de valables à la vie
A moins d'aimer

En passe de devenir caresses
Tes rires et tes gestes règlent mon allure
Poliraient les pavés
Et je ris avec toi et je te crois toute seule

Tout le temps d'une rue qui n'en finit pas.

A LA FIN DE L'ANNÉE, DE JOUR EN JOUR PLUS BAS, IL ENFOUIT SA CHALEUR COMME UNE GRAINE.

I

Nous avançons toujours
Un fleuve plus épais qu'une grasse prairie
Nous vivons d'un seul jet
Nous sommes du bon port

Le bois qui va sur l'eau l'arbre qui file droit
Tout marché de raison bâclé conclu s'oublie
Où nous arrêterons-nous
Notre poids immobile creuse notre chemin

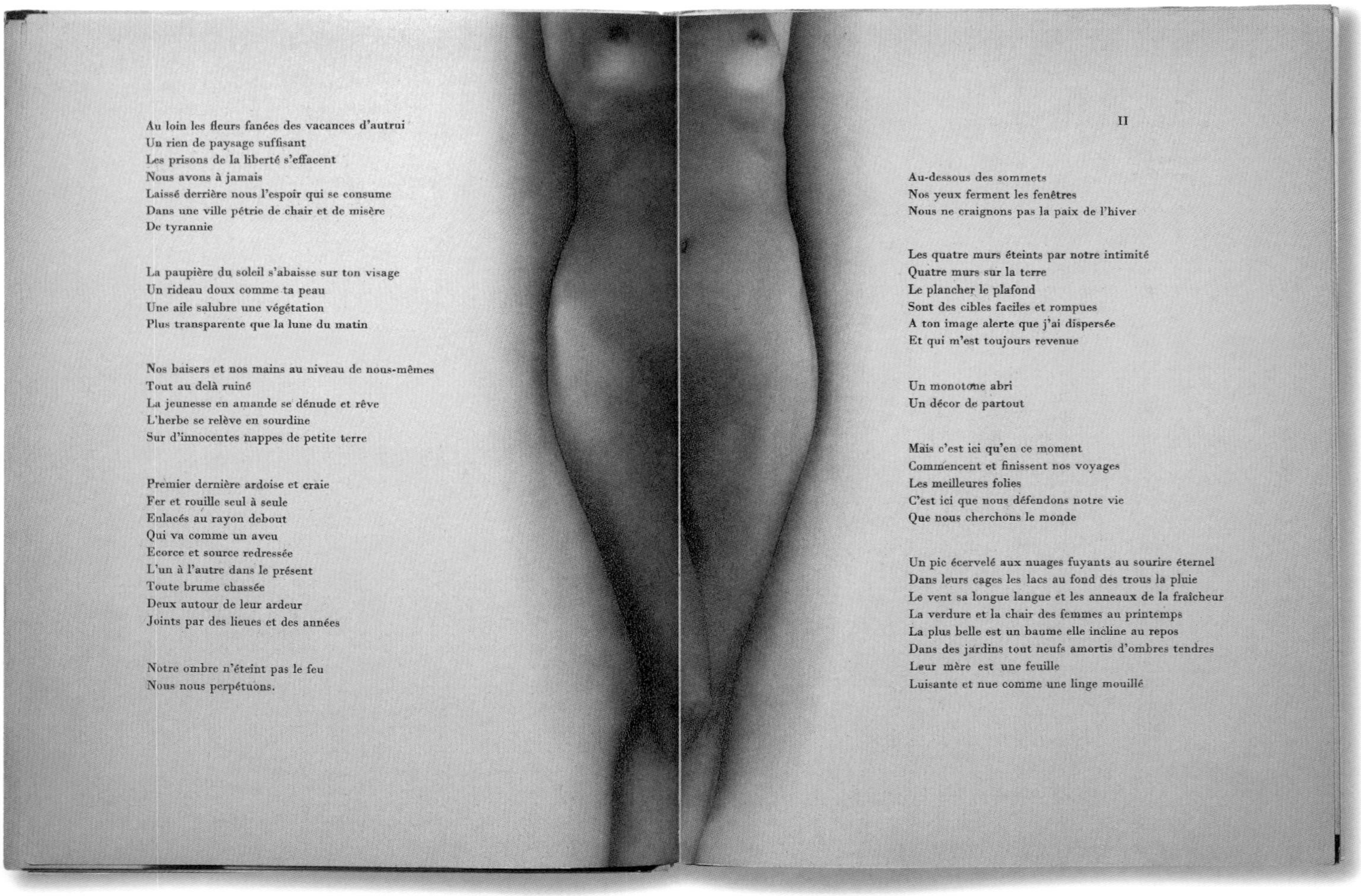

Au loin les fleurs fanées des vacances d'autrui
Un rien de paysage suffisant
Les prisons de la liberté s'effacent
Nous avons à jamais
Laissé derrière nous l'espoir qui se consume
Dans une ville pétrie de chair et de misère
De tyrannie

La paupière du soleil s'abaisse sur ton visage
Un rideau doux comme ta peau
Une aile salubre une végétation
Plus transparente que la lune du matin

Nos baisers et nos mains au niveau de nous-mêmes
Tout au delà ruiné
La jeunesse en amande se dénude et rêve
L'herbe se relève en sourdine
Sur d'innocentes nappes de petite terre

Premier dernière ardoise et craie
Fer et rouille seul à seule
Enlacés au rayon debout
Qui va comme un aveu
Ecorce et source redressée
L'un à l'autre dans le présent
Toute brume chassée
Deux autour de leur ardeur
Joints par des lieues et des années

Notre ombre n'éteint pas le feu
Nous nous perpétuons.

II

Au-dessous des sommets
Nos yeux ferment les fenêtres
Nous ne craignons pas la paix de l'hiver

Les quatre murs éteints par notre intimité
Quatre murs sur la terre
Le plancher le plafond
Sont des cibles faciles et rompues
A ton image alerte que j'ai dispersée
Et qui m'est toujours revenue

Un monotone abri
Un décor de partout

Mais c'est ici qu'en ce moment
Commencent et finissent nos voyages
Les meilleures folies
C'est ici que nous défendons notre vie
Que nous cherchons le monde

Un pic écervelé aux nuages fuyants au sourire éternel
Dans leurs cages les lacs au fond des trous la pluie
Le vent sa longue langue et les anneaux de la fraîcheur
La verdure et la chair des femmes au printemps
La plus belle est un baume elle incline au repos
Dans des jardins tout neufs amortis d'ombres tendres
Leur mère est une feuille
Luisante et nue comme une linge mouillé

1935 . FACILE, BY PAUL ÉLUARD . Book . Guy Lévis-Mano, Man Ray

→ p.416

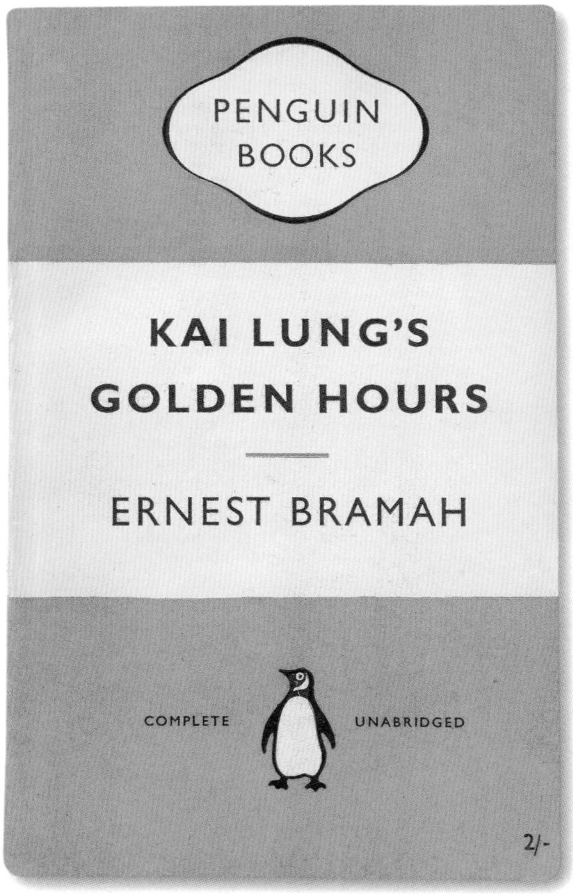

● **1935 . PENGUIN BOOKS .** Book Cover . Edward Young

→ p.417

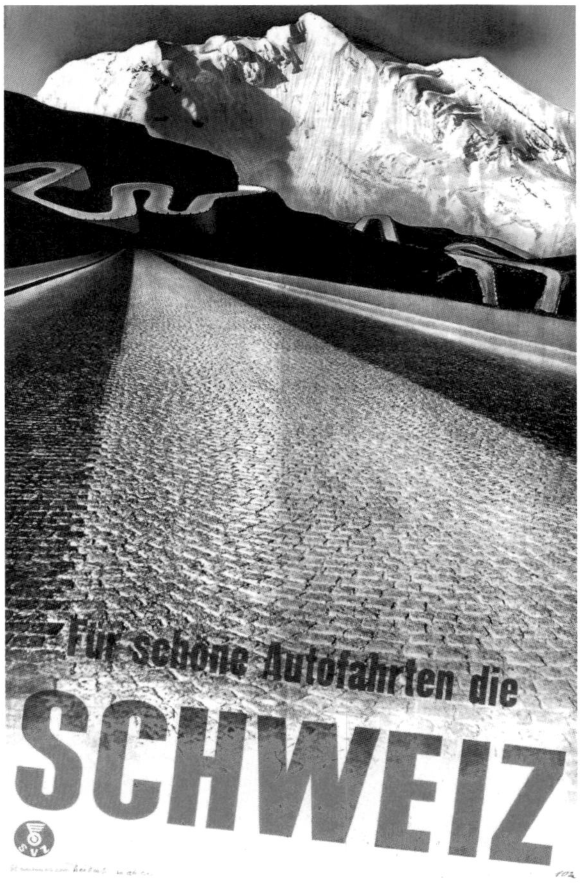

● **1935 . ALL ROADS LEAD TO SWITZERLAND .** Poster . Herbert Matter

→ p.417

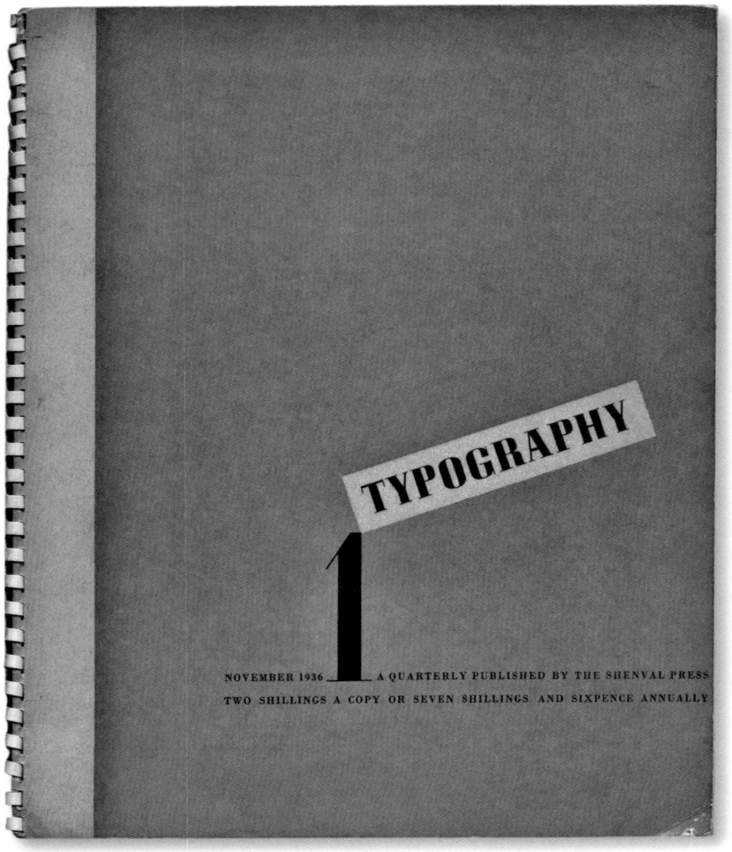

● **1936–1939 . TYPOGRAPHY .** Magazine / Newspaper . Robert Harling
LEFT: No. 1, November 1936; RIGHT: No. 6, Summer 1938

→ p.417

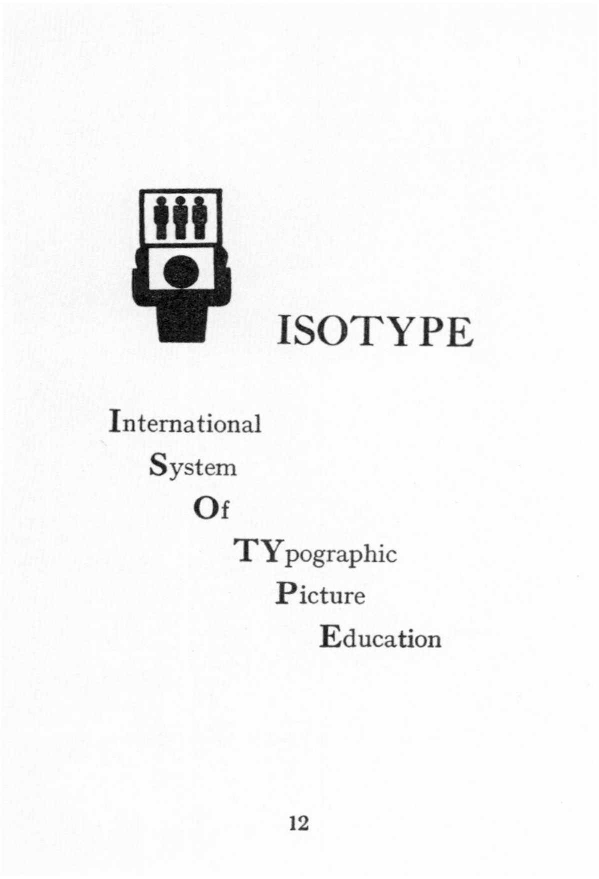

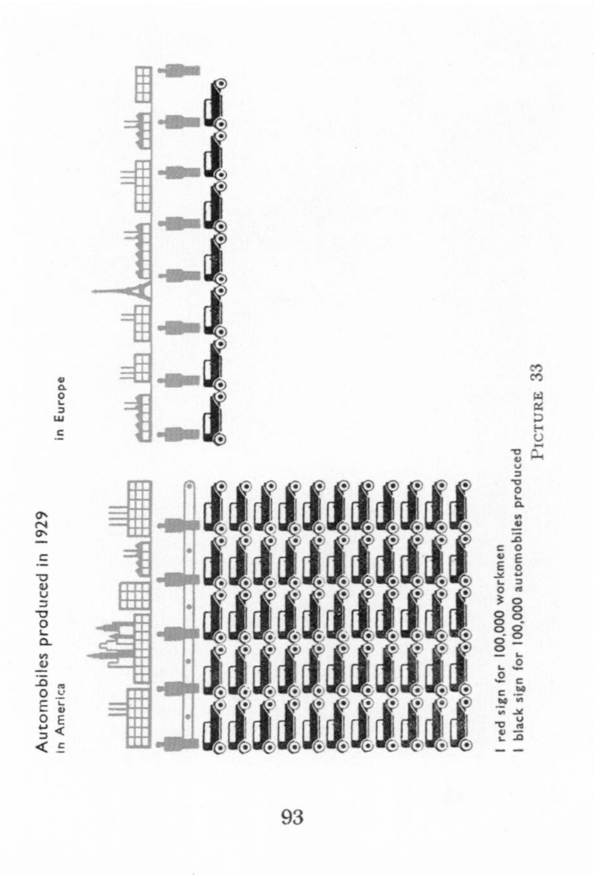

● **1936 . INTERNATIONAL PICTURE LANGUAGE .** Information Design . Otto Neurath

→ p.418

● **1936 . SPRATT'S .** Logo . Max Field-Bush

→ p.418

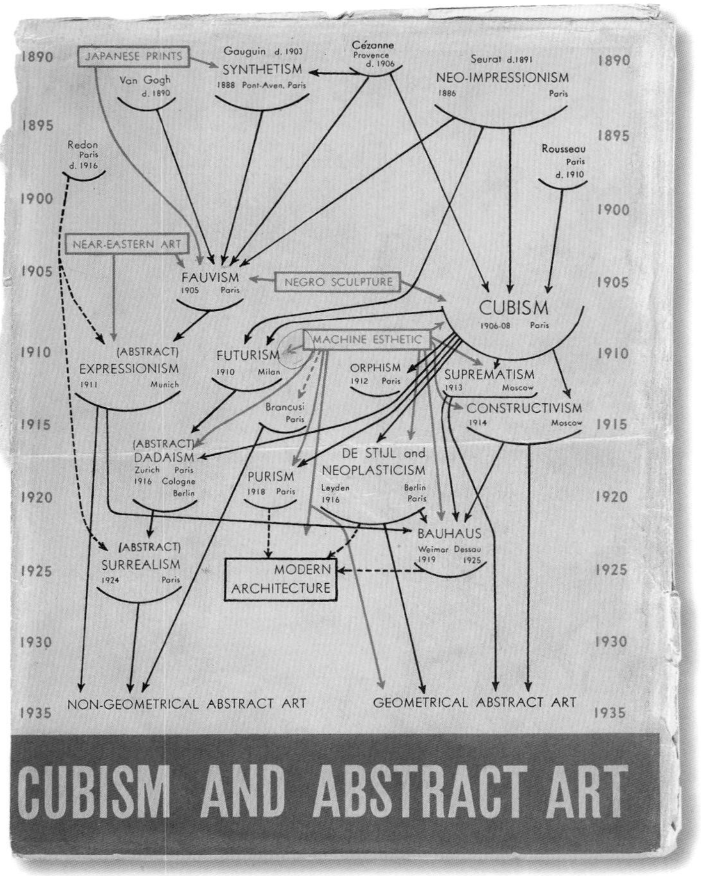

● **1936 . CUBISM AND ABSTRACT ART .**
Book Cover . Alfred H. Barr, Jr.

→ p.418

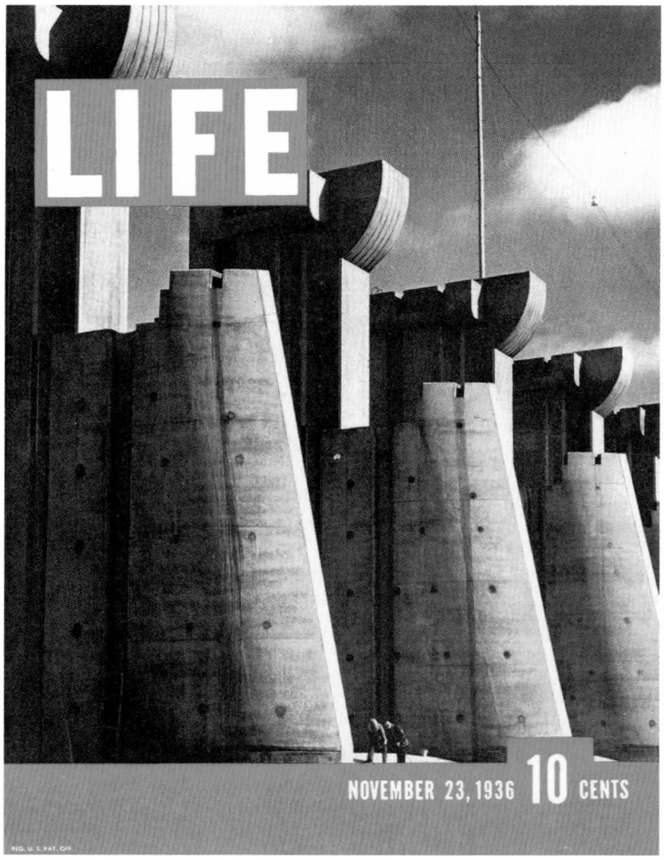

● **1936–2000 . LIFE .** Magazine / Newspaper . Various
Photograph Margaret Bourke-White, November 23, 1936

→ p.419

● **1936 . LONDON A TO Z .** Book . Phyllis Pearsall

→ p.419

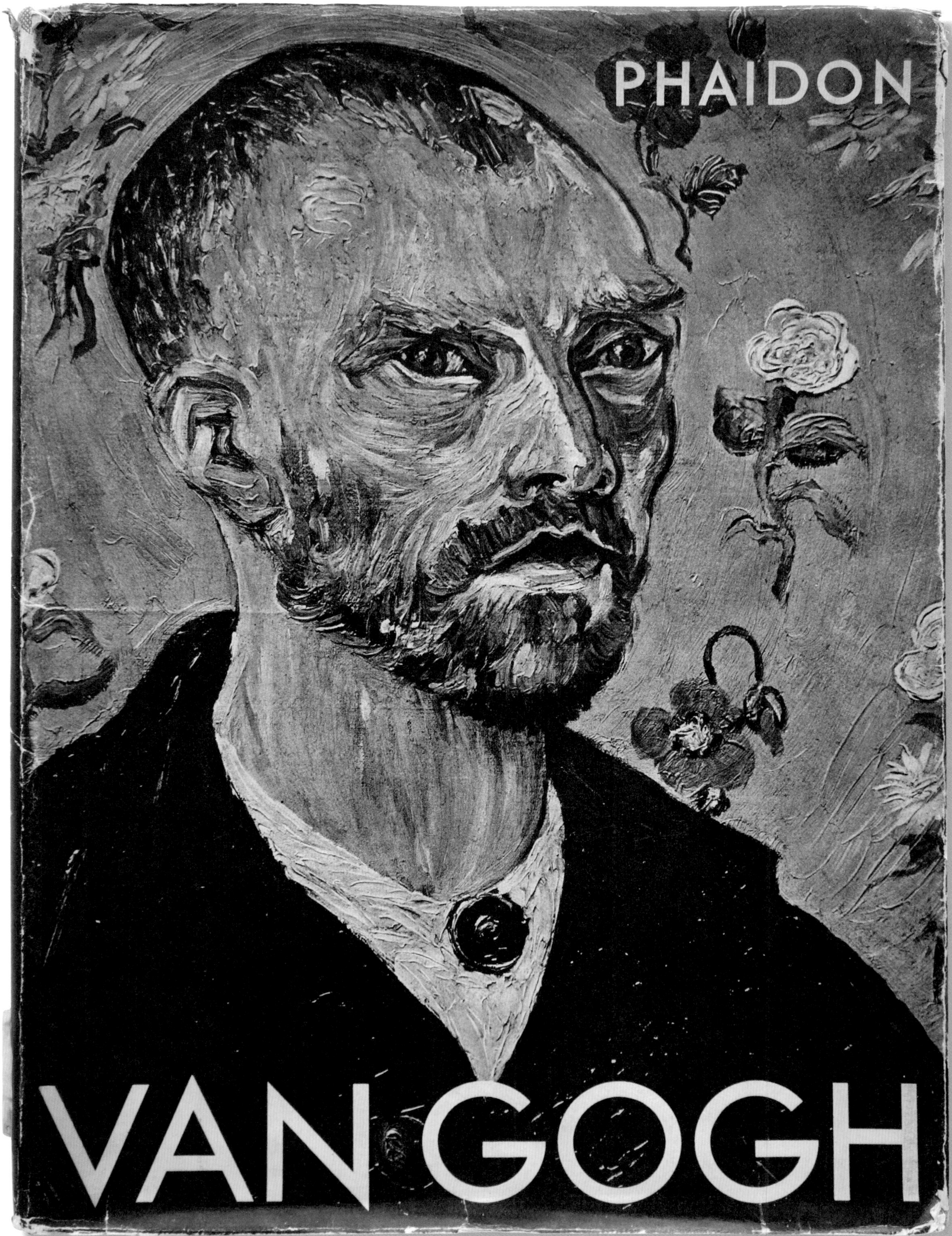

1936 . VAN GOGH . Book . Béla Horovitz

→ p.419

● **1937 . RURAL ELECTRIFICATION ADMINISTRATION .** Poster . Lester Beall

→ p.420

● **1937 . PEIGNOT .** Typeface . A. M. Cassandre

→ p.420

● **1937 . MERCEDES-BENZ .** Logo . Gottlieb Daimler

→ p.420

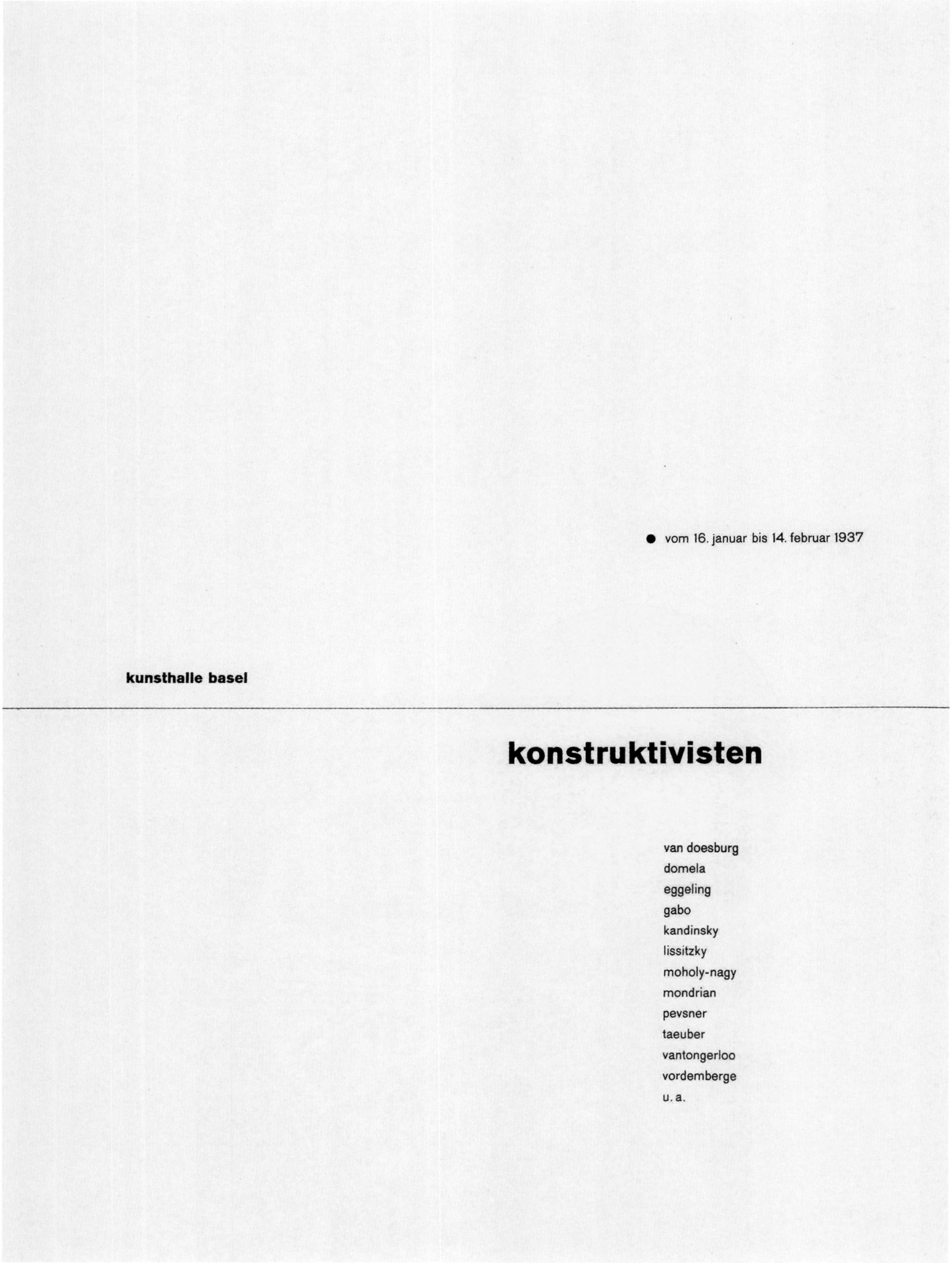

● **1937 . KONSTRUKTIVISTEN .** Poster . Jan Tschichold

→ p.421

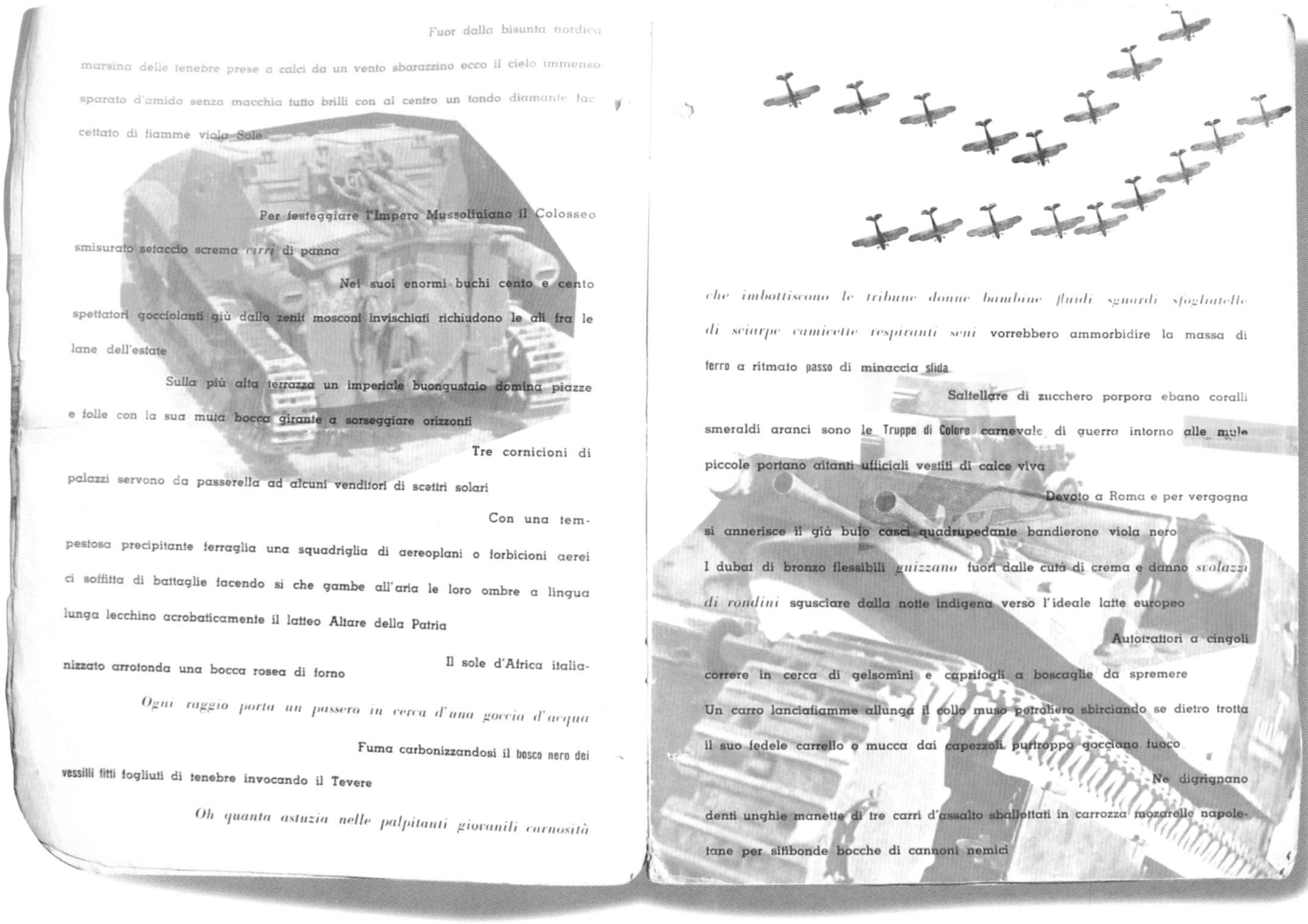

Fuor dalla bisunta nordica marsina delle tenebre prese a calci da un vento sbarazzino ecco il cielo immenso sparato d'amido senza macchia tutto brilli con al centro un tondo diamante faccettato di fiamme viola Sole

Per festeggiare l'Impero Mussoliniano il Colosseo smisurato setaccio screma *cirri* di panna

Nei suoi enormi buchi cento e cento spettatori gocciolanti giù dallo zenit mosconi invischiati richiudono le ali fra le lane dell'estate

Sulla più alta terrazza un imperiale buongustaio domina piazze e folle con la sua muta bocca girante a sorseggiare orizzonti

Tre cornicioni di palazzi servono da passerella ad alcuni venditori di scettri solari

Con una tempestosa precipitante ferraglia una squadriglia di aereoplani o forbicioni aerei ci soffitta di battaglie facendo si che gambe all'aria le loro ombre a lingua lunga lecchino acrobaticamente il latteo Altare della Patria

Il sole d'Africa italianizzato arrotonda una bocca rosea di forno

Ogni raggio porta un passero in cerca d'una goccia d'acqua

Fuma carbonizzandosi il bosco nero dei vessilli fitti fogliuti di tenebre invocando il Tevere

Oh quanta astuzia nelle palpitanti giovanili carnosità

che imbottiscono le tribune donne bambine fluidi sguardi sfogliatelle di sciarpe camicette respiranti seni vorrebbero ammorbidire la massa di ferro a ritmato passo di minaccia sfida

Saltellare di zucchero porpora ebano coralli smeraldi aranci sono le Truppe di Colore carnevale di guerra intorno alle mule piccole portano aitanti ufficiali vestiti di calce viva

Devoto a Roma e per vergogna si annerisce il già buio casci quadrupedante bandierone viola nero

I dubat di bronzo flessibili *guizzano* fuori dalle cutà di crema e danno *svolazzi di rondini* sgusciare dalla notte indigena verso l'ideale latte europeo

Autotrattori a cingoli correre in cerca di gelsomini e caprifogli a boscaglie da spremere

Un carro lanciafiamme allunga il collo muso petroliero sbirciando se dietro trotta il suo fedele carrello o mucca dai capezzoli purtroppo gocciano fuoco

Ne digrignano denti unghie manette di tre carri d'assalto sballottati in carrozza mozarelle napoletane per sitibonde bocche di cannoni nemici

● **1937 . IL POEMA DEL VESTITO DI LATTE .** Book . Bruno Munari

→ p.421

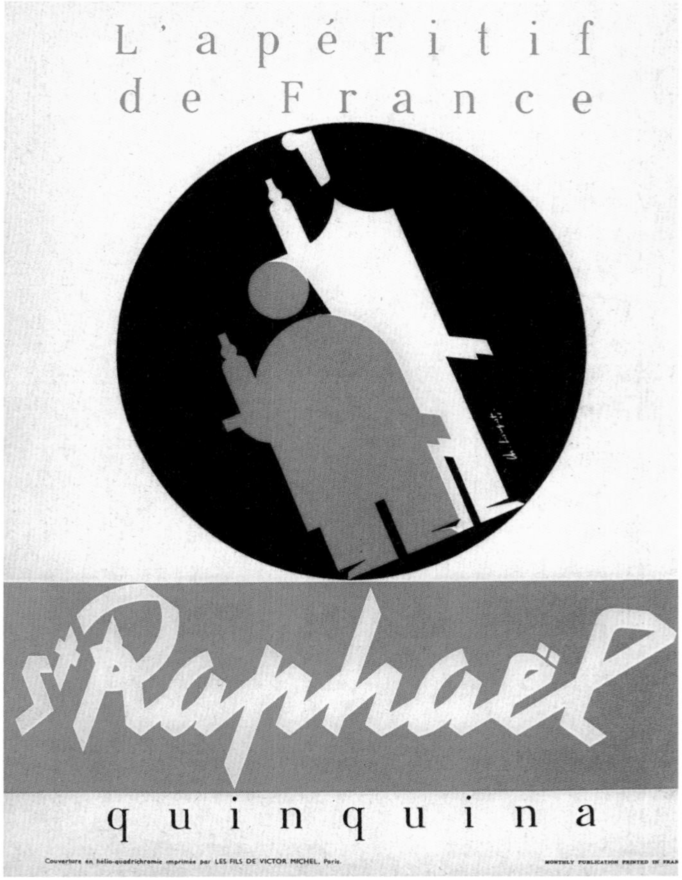

1937–1960 . SAINT-RAPHAËL QUINQUINA . Advertising . Charles Loupot

→ p.421

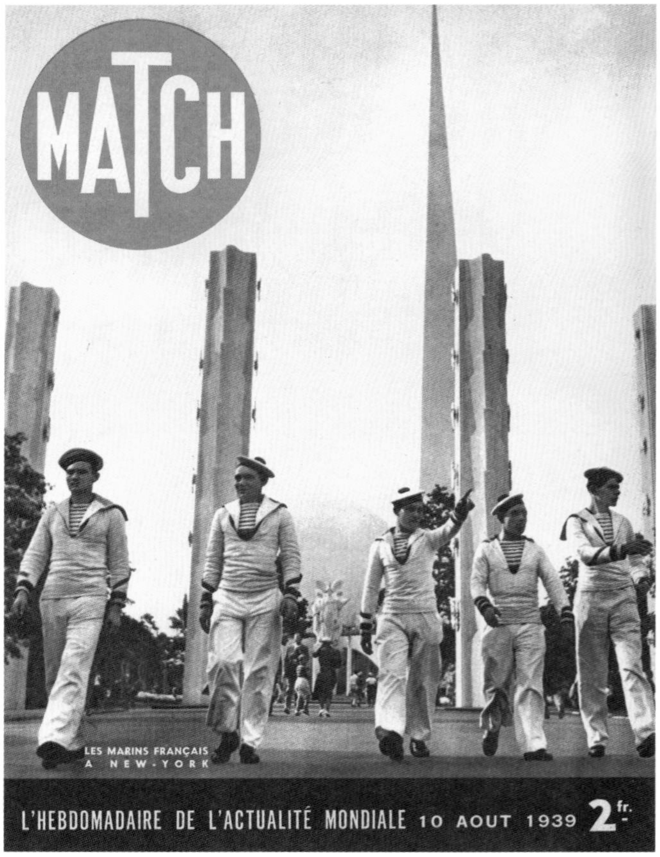

1938–1940 . MATCH . Magazine Cover . Unknown
LEFT: July 13, 1939; RIGHT: August 10, 1939

→ p.422

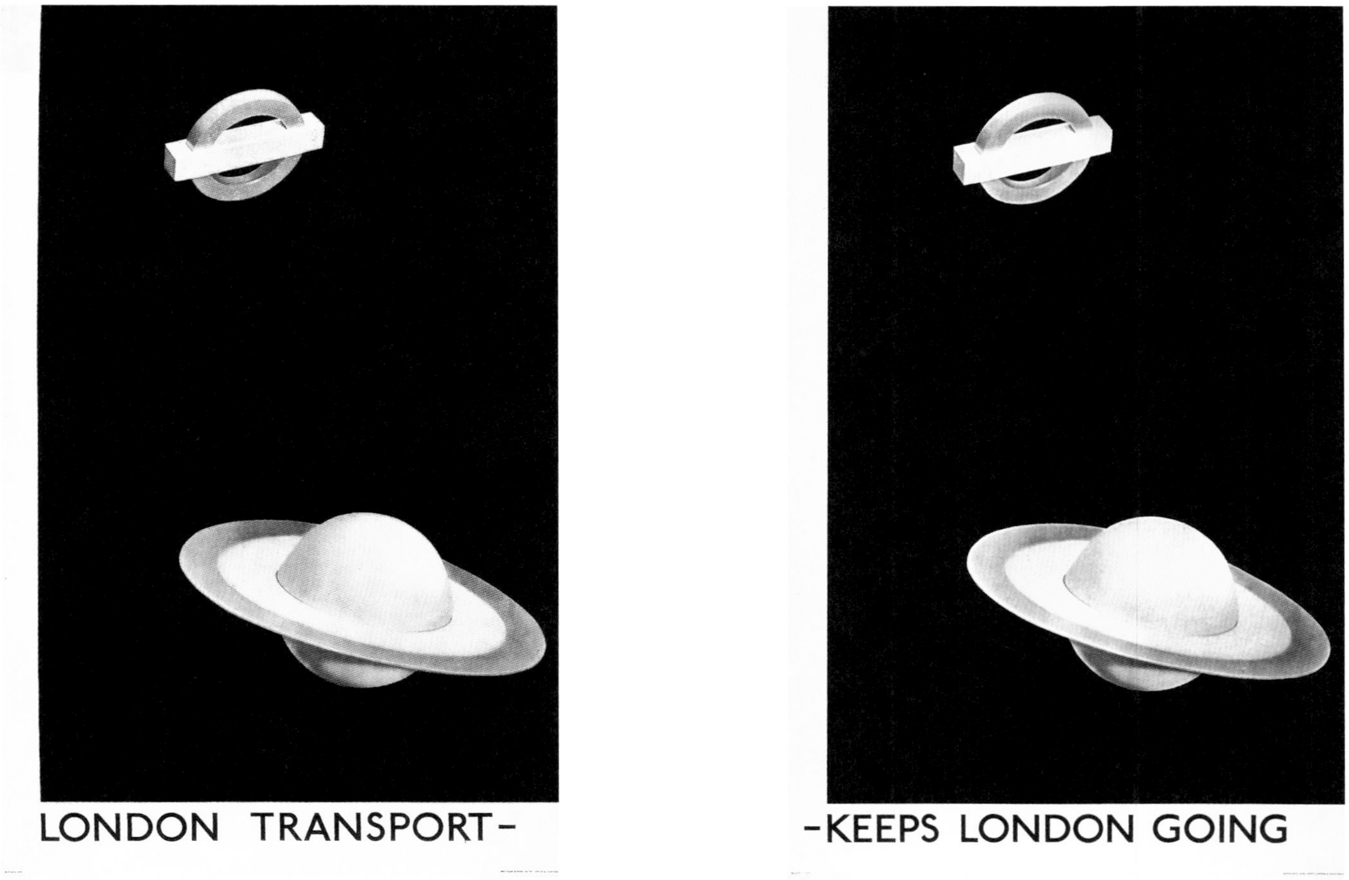

● **1938 . LONDON TRANSPORT—KEEPS LONDON GOING .** Poster . Man Ray

→ p.422

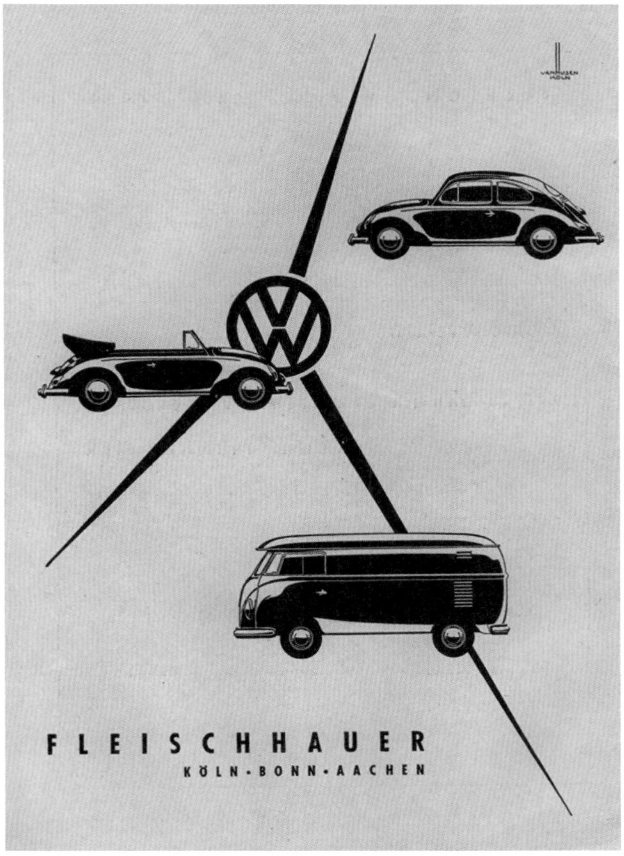

● **c. 1938 . VOLKSWAGEN .** Logo . Franz Reimspiess

→ p.422

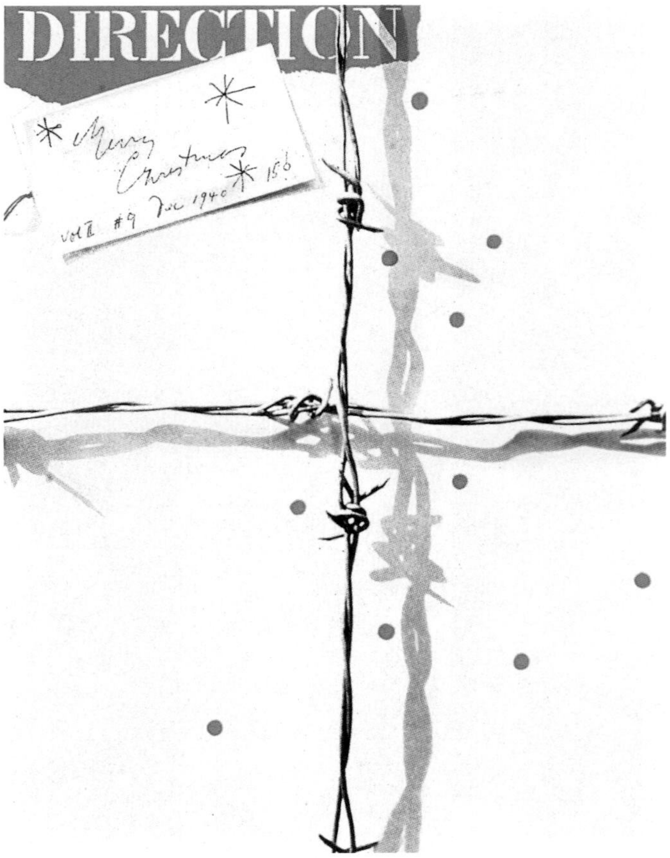

● **1938–1945 . DIRECTION .** Magazine Cover . Paul Rand
Vol. 2, No. 9, December 1940

→ p.423

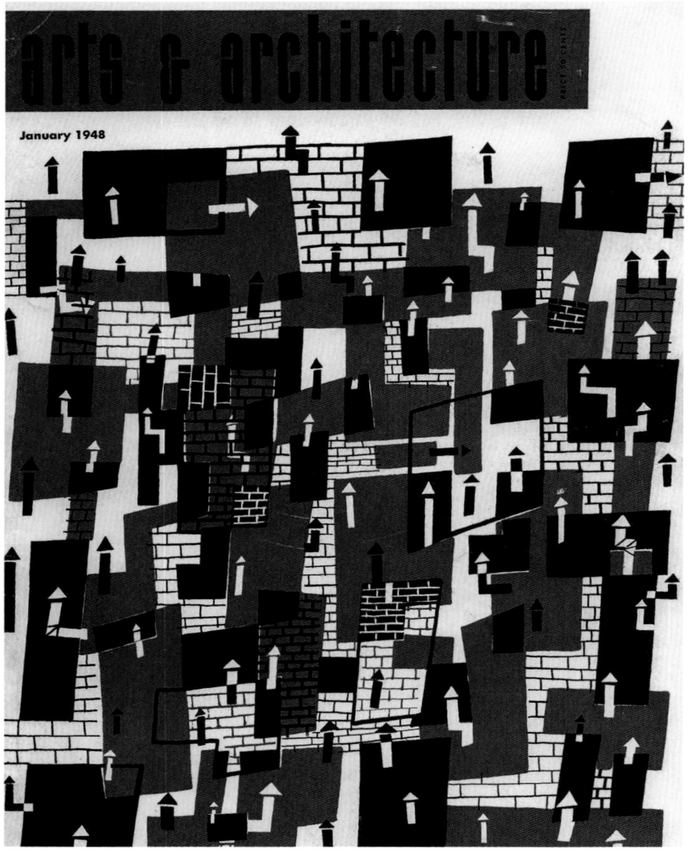

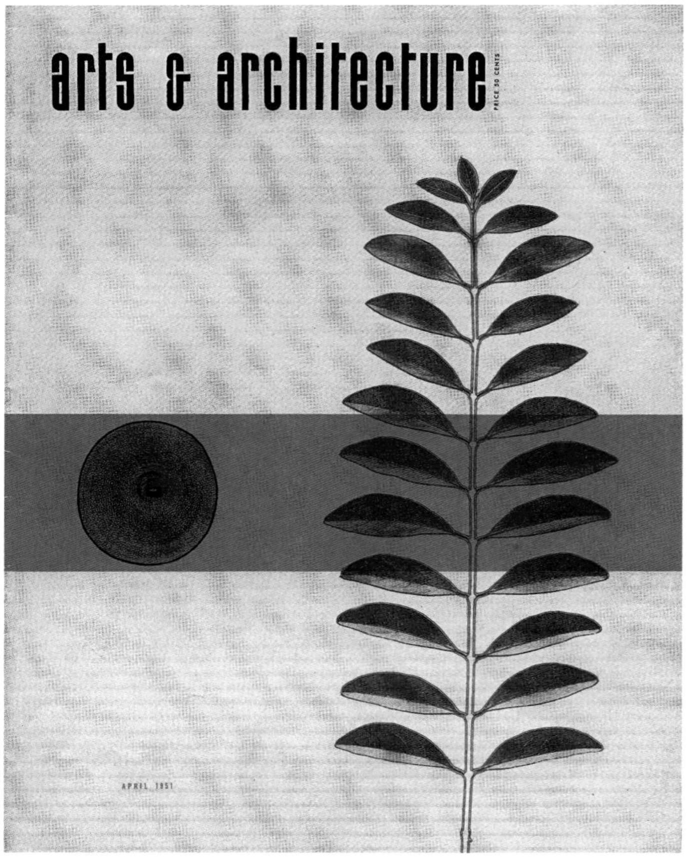

● **1938–1962 . ARTS & ARCHITECTURE .** Magazine Cover . Various
LEFT: January 1948; RIGHT: James Reed, April 1951

→ p.423

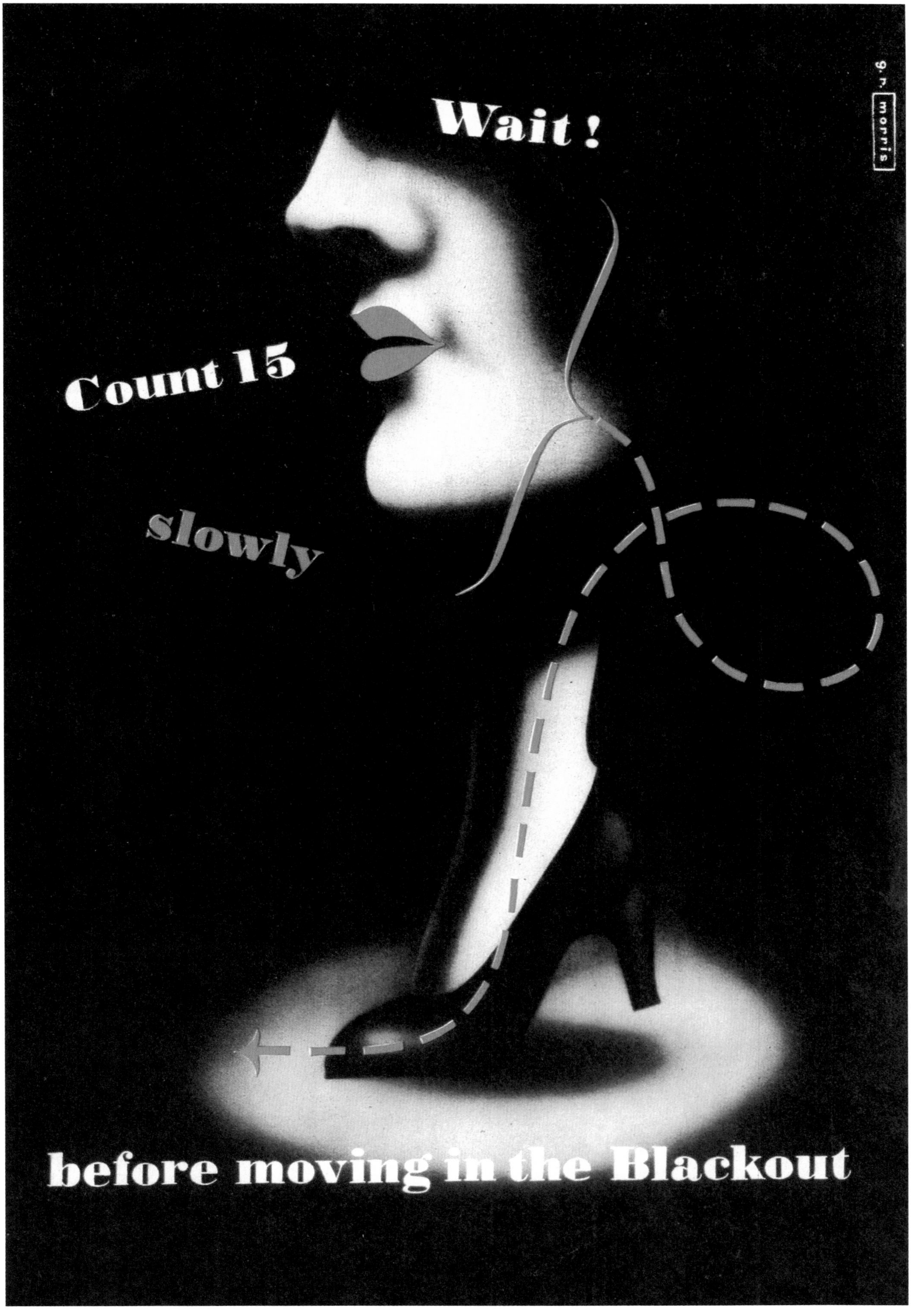

● **1939 . WAIT! COUNT 15 SLOWLY BEFORE MOVING IN THE BLACKOUT .** Poster . G. R. Morris

→ p.423

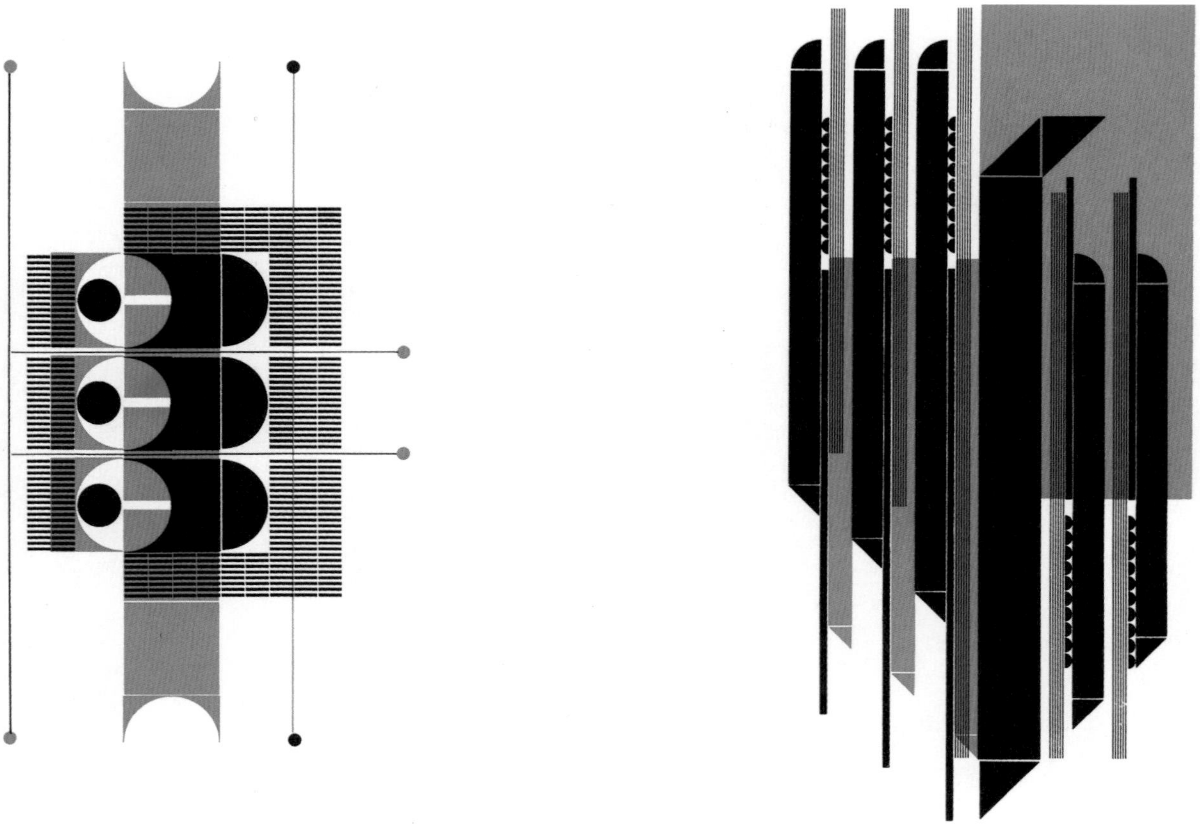

● **1940 . THE GHOST IN THE UNDERBLOWS, BY ALFRED YOUNG FISHER .** Book . Alvin Lustig

→ p.424

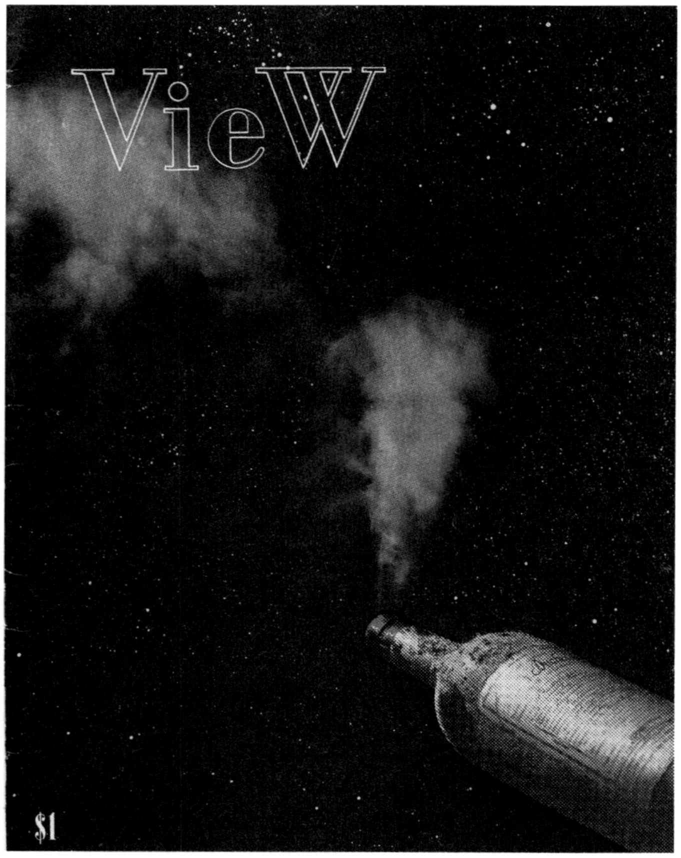

● **1940–1947 . VIEW .** Magazine Cover . Parker Tyler et al.
Marcel Duchamp, Vol. 5, No. 1, March 1945

→ p.424

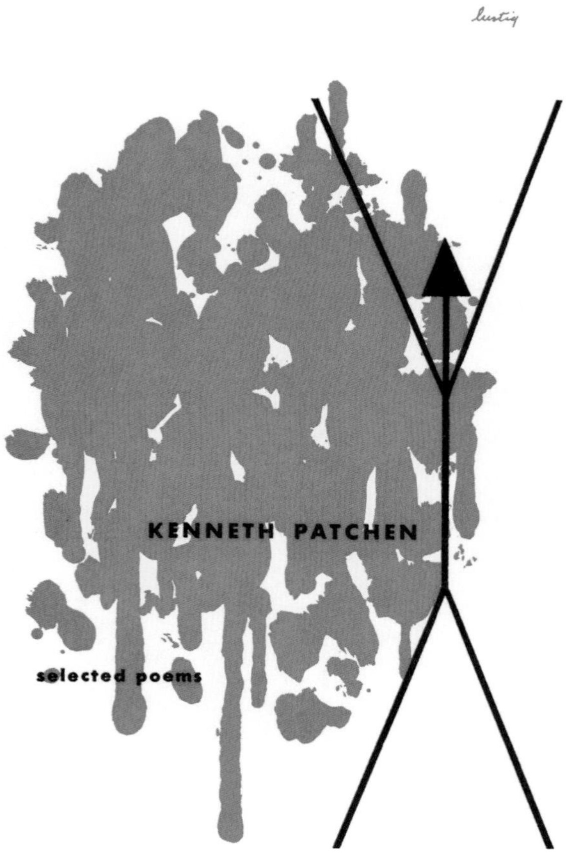

● **1940–1952 . NEW CLASSICS .** Book Cover . Alvin Lustig
Selected Poems of Kenneth Patchen, 1946

→ p.424

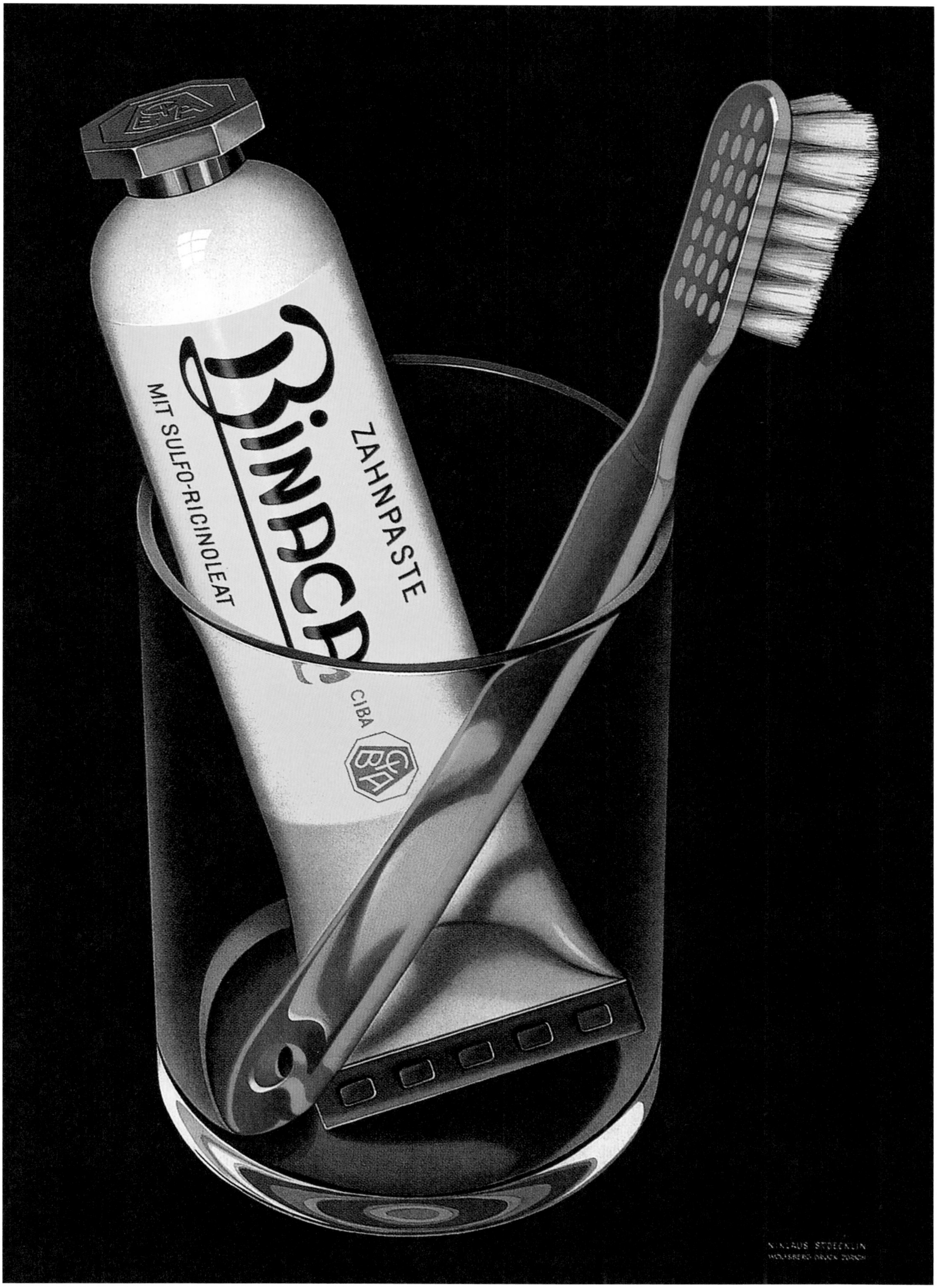

● **1941 . BINACA .** Poster . Niklaus Stöcklin

→ p.425

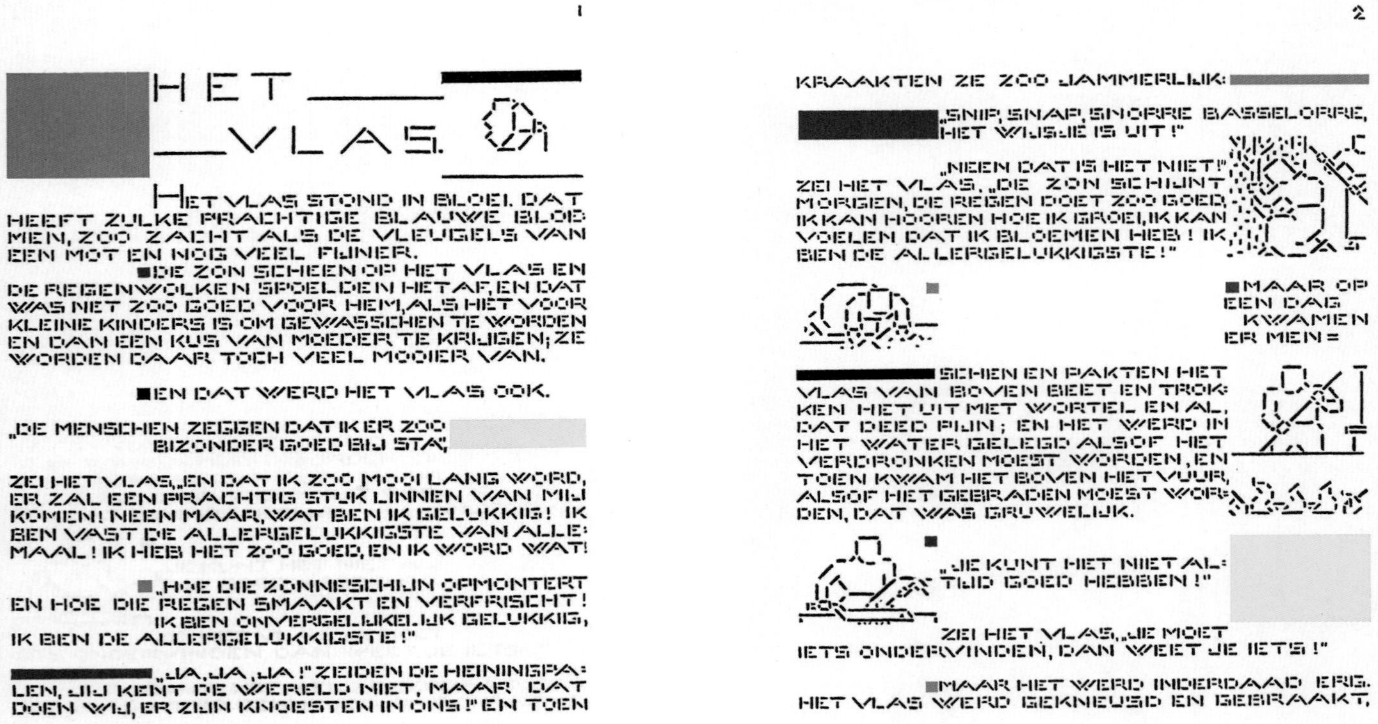
1

HET
VLAS.

HET VLAS STOND IN BLOEI. DAT HEEFT ZULKE PRACHTIGE BLAUWE BLOEMEN, ZOO ZACHT ALS DE VLEUGELS VAN EEN MOT EN NOG VEEL FIJNER.

DE ZON SCHEEN OP HET VLAS EN DE REGENWOLKEN SPOELDEN HET AF, EN DAT WAS NET ZOO GOED VOOR HEM, ALS HET VOOR KLEINE KINDERS IS OM GEWASSCHEN TE WORDEN EN DAN EEN KUS VAN MOEDER TE KRIJGEN; ZE WORDEN DAAR TOCH VEEL MOOIER VAN.

EN DAT WERD HET VLAS OOK.

„DE MENSCHEN ZEGGEN DAT IK ER ZOO BIZONDER GOED BIJ STA,"

ZEI HET VLAS, „EN DAT IK ZOO MOOI LANG WORD, ER ZAL EEN PRACHTIG STUK LINNEN VAN MIJ KOMEN! NEEN MAAR, WAT BEN IK GELUKKIG! IK BEN VAST DE ALLERGELUKKIGSTE VAN ALLEMAAL! IK HEB HET ZOO GOED, EN IK WORD WAT!

„HOE DIE ZONNESCHIJN OPMONTERT EN HOE DIE REGEN SMAAKT EN VERFRISCHT! IK BEN ONVERGELIJKELIJK GELUKKIG, IK BEN DE ALLERGELUKKIGSTE!"

„JA, JA, JA!" ZEIDEN DE HEININGPALEN, „JIJ KENT DE WERELD NIET, MAAR DAT DOEN WIJ, ER ZIJN KNOESTEN IN ONS!" EN TOEN

2

KRAAKTEN ZE ZOO JAMMERLIJK:

„SNIP, SNAP, SNORRE BASSELORRE, HET WIJSJE IS UIT!"

„NEEN DAT IS HET NIET!" ZEI HET VLAS, „DE ZON SCHIJNT MORGEN, DE REGEN DOET ZOO GOED, IK KAN HOOREN HOE IK GROEI, IK KAN VOELEN DAT IK BLOEMEN HEB! IK BEN DE ALLERGELUKKIGSTE!"

MAAR OP EEN DAG KWAMEN ER MENSCHEN EN PAKTEN HET VLAS VAN BOVEN BEET EN TROKKEN HET UIT MET WORTEL EN AL, DAT DEED PIJN; EN HET WERD IN HET WATER GELEGD ALSOF HET VERDRONKEN MOEST WORDEN, EN TOEN KWAM HET BOVEN HET VUUR, ALSOF HET GEBRADEN MOEST WORDEN, DAT WAS GRUWELIJK.

„JE KUNT HET NIET ALTIJD GOED HEBBEN!"

ZEI HET VLAS, „JE MOET IETS ONDERVINDEN, DAN WEET JE IETS!"

MAAR HET WERD INDERDAAD ERG. HET VLAS WERD GEKNEUSD EN GEBRAAKT,

● **1941 . HET VLAS .** Book . Bart van der Leck

→ p.425

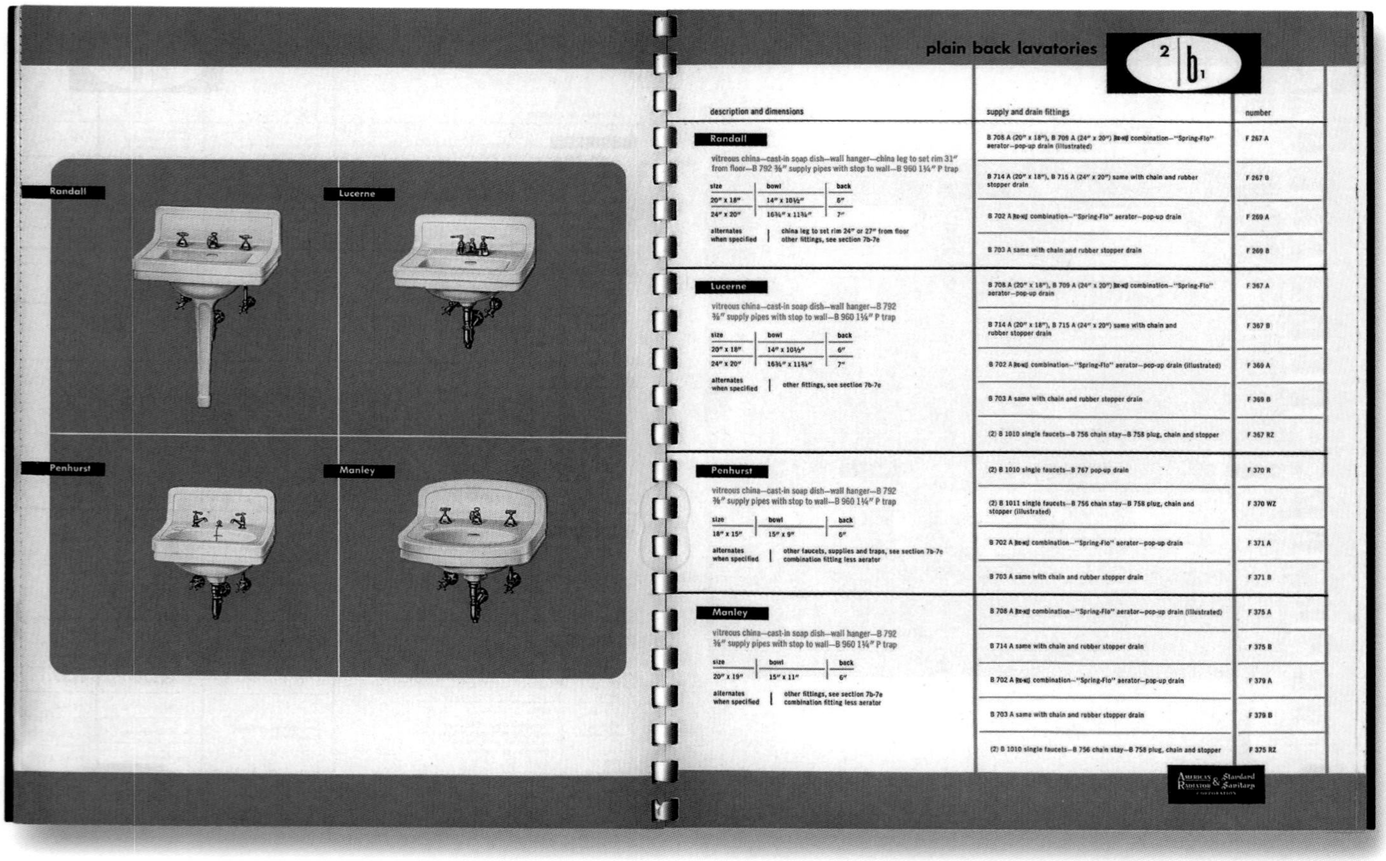

● **1941–1960 . SWEET'S FILES .** Book . Ladislav Sutnar

→ p.425

● **1944–1951 . SCOPE .** Magazine / Newspaper . Lester Beall
Vol. 2, No. 6, 1948

→ p.426

1945 . BALLET . Book . Alexey Brodovitch

→ p.426

economy
through mass-production and standardization, our furniture provides economic, flexible usefulness for home . . . housing . . . and institution.
H. G. KNOLL associates 601 MADISON AVENUE, NEW YORK 22, NEW YORK
Lustig

form
structure
economy
this mark of the three plus signs . . . symbols of clean design, sound construction and low cost will from now on help you to identify our products: furniture . . . equipment for living . . . developed by our Planning Unit. Send your name for our new catalog to 601 Madison Avenue, New York 22, N. Y.
H. G. KNOLL associates

1945 . H. G. KNOLL ASSOCIATES . Advertising . Alvin Lustig

→ p.426

1945 . BORZOI . Logo . Paul Rand

→ p.427

1946 . RADIATION . Information Design . Bill Ray, George Warlick

→ p.427

MAY WE SEND YOU AN ILLUSTRATED BROCHURE?

1946–1966 . KNOLL ASSOCIATES . Advertising . Herbert Matter

→ p.427

● **1946 . PIRELLI .** Logo . Unknown

→ p.428

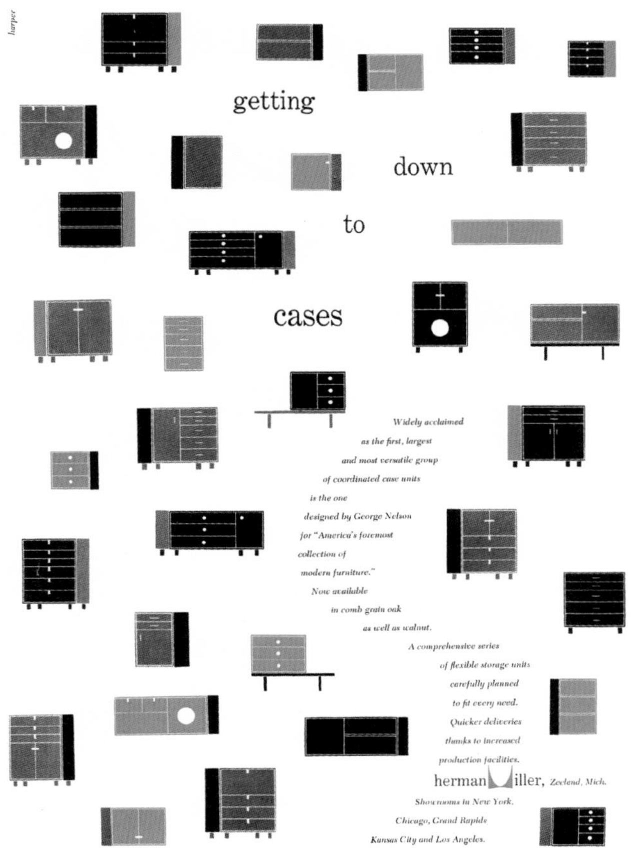

● **1947 . HERMAN MILLER .** Identity . Irving Harper et al.
Irving Harper, "Getting Down to Cases," 1952

→ p.428

● **1947–1950 . SEVENTEEN .** Magazine / Newspaper . Cipe Pineles
July 1949

→ p.428

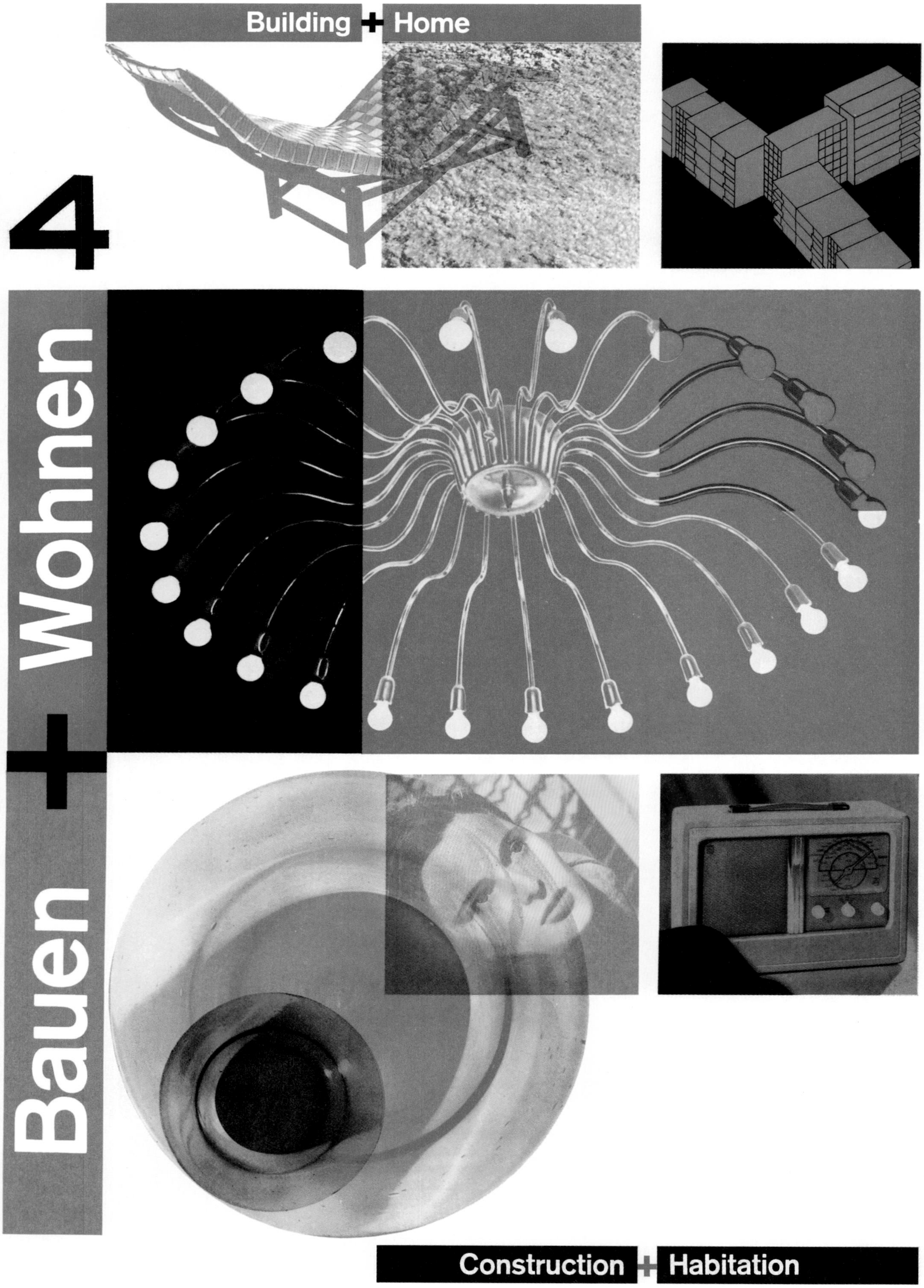

● **1947–1956 . BAUEN + WOHNEN .** Magazine / Newspaper . Richard Paul Lohse
No. 4, 1948

→ p.429

● **1947 . WIEDERAUFBAU .** Poster . Otl Aicher

→ p.429

● **1947–PRESENT . DER SPIEGEL .** Magazine Cover . Various
LEFT: Vol. 1, No. 47, November 22, 1947; RIGHT: Vol. 63, No. 9, February 21, 2009

→ p.429

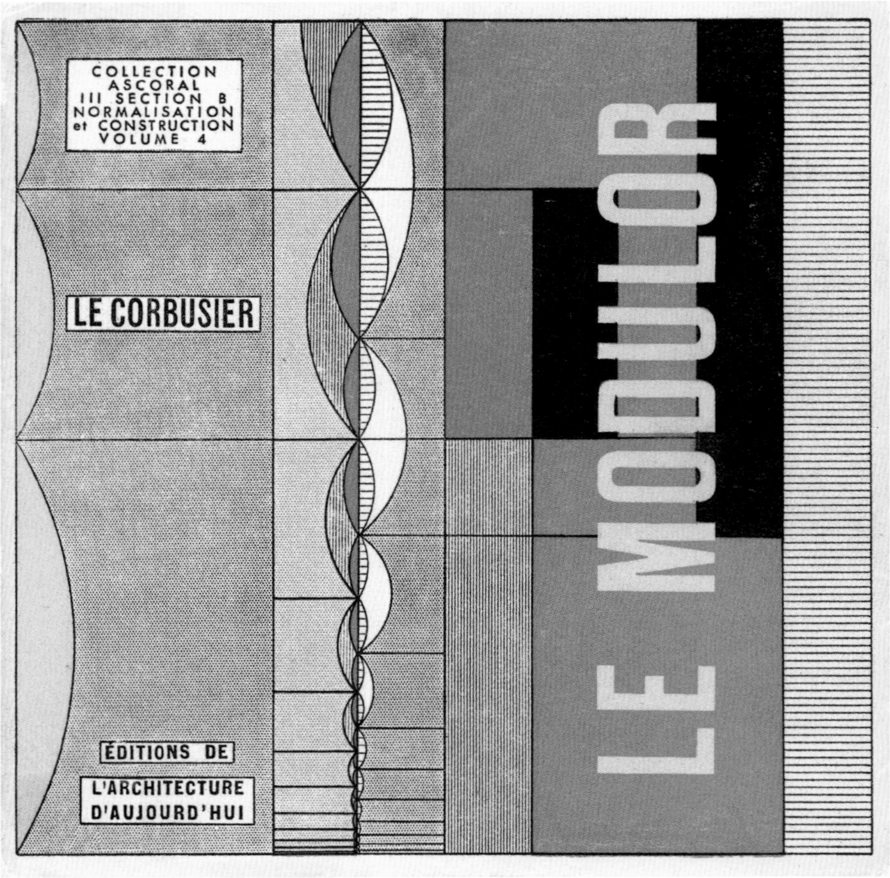

1948 . LE MODULOR . Book . Le Corbusier

→ p.430

1948 . HALAG . Logo . Hermann Eidenbenz

→ p.430

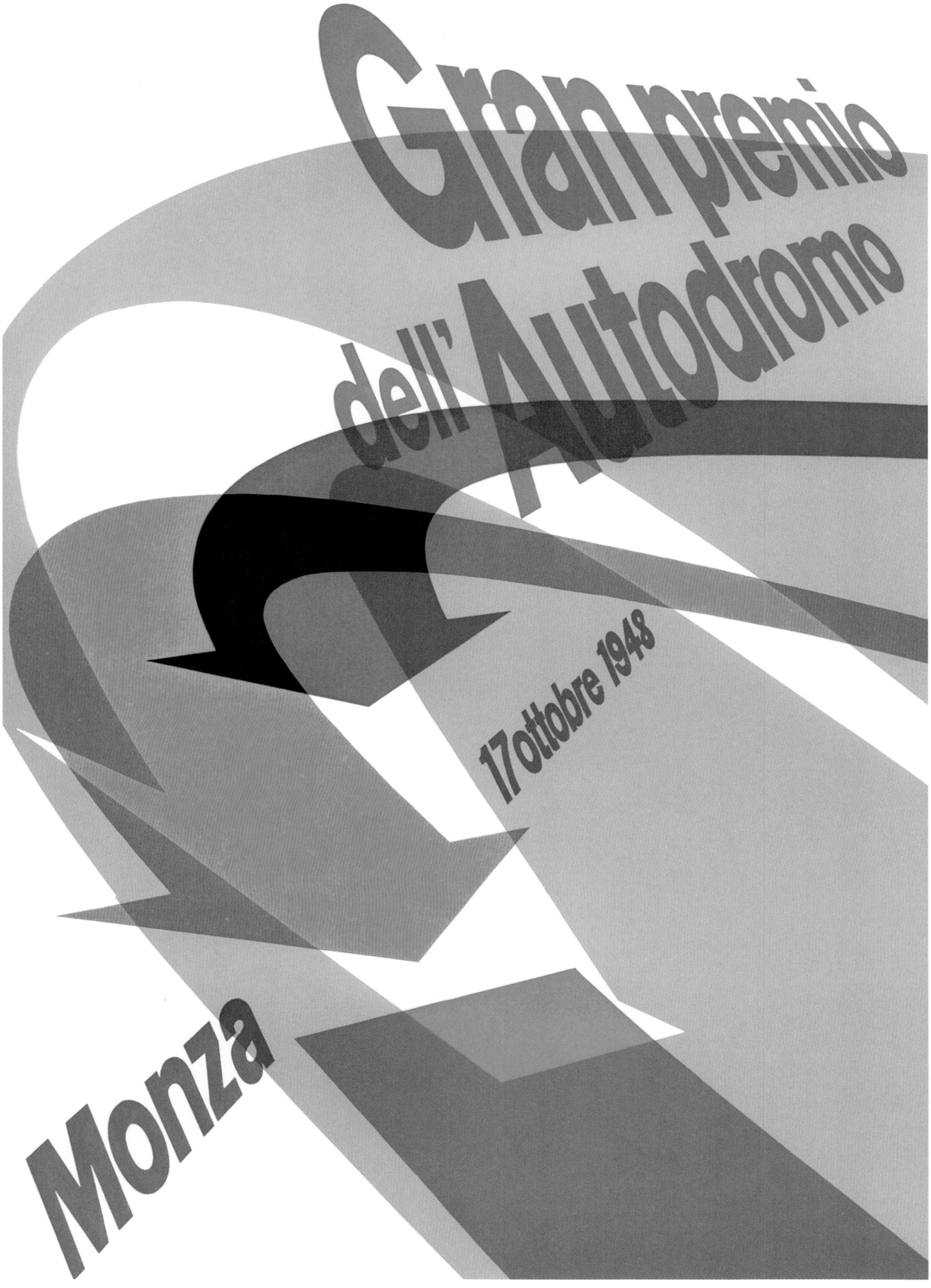

● **1948 . GRAN PREMIO DELL'AUTODROMO .** Poster . Max Huber

→ p.430

● **1948–PRESENT . STERN .** Magazine / Newspaper . Various
No. 1, August 1, 1948

→ p.431

● **1949 . ZEBRA CROSSING .** Information Design . Unknown

→ p.431

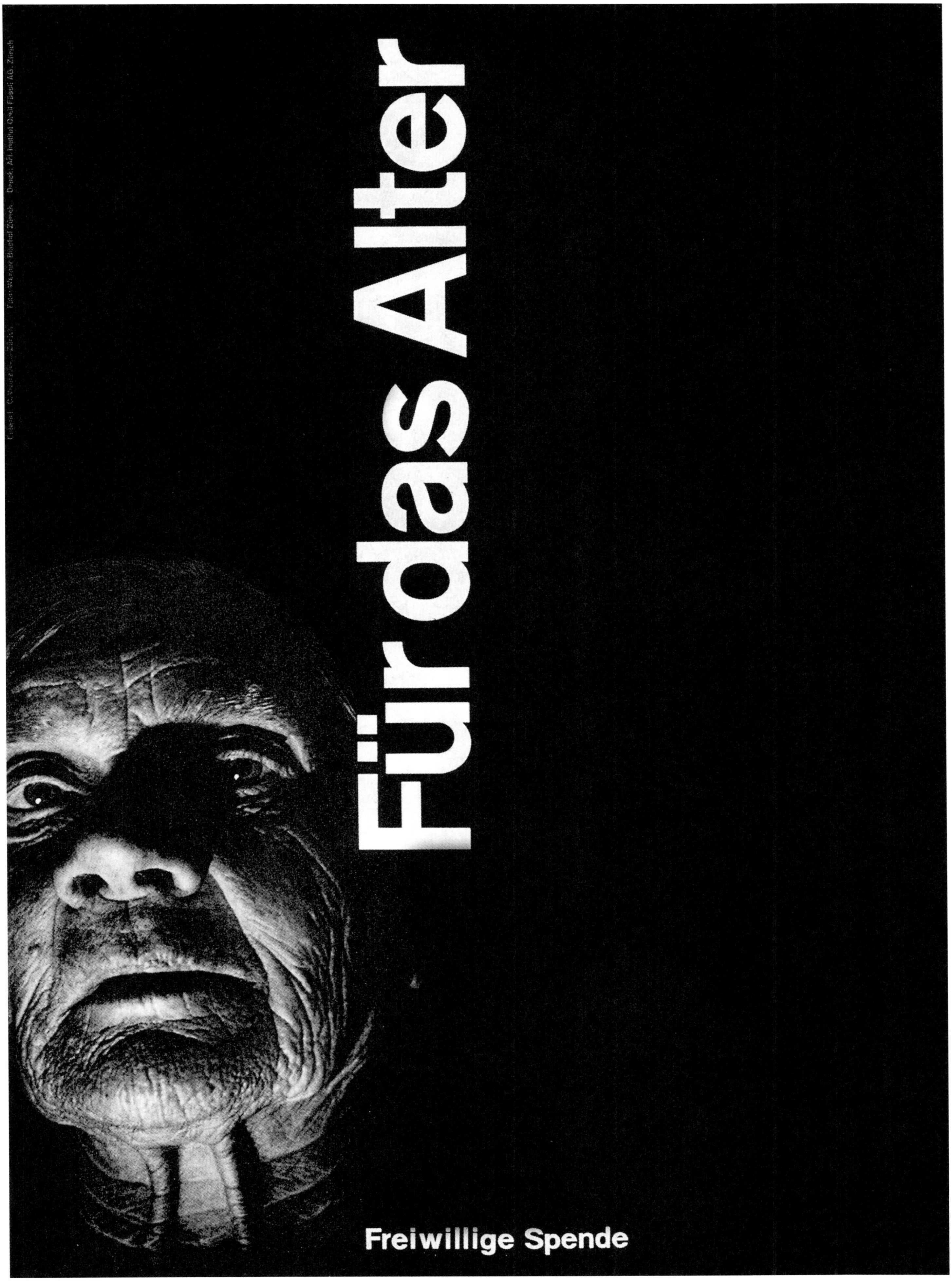

● **1949 . FÜR DAS ALTER .** Poster . Carlo Vivarelli

→ p.431

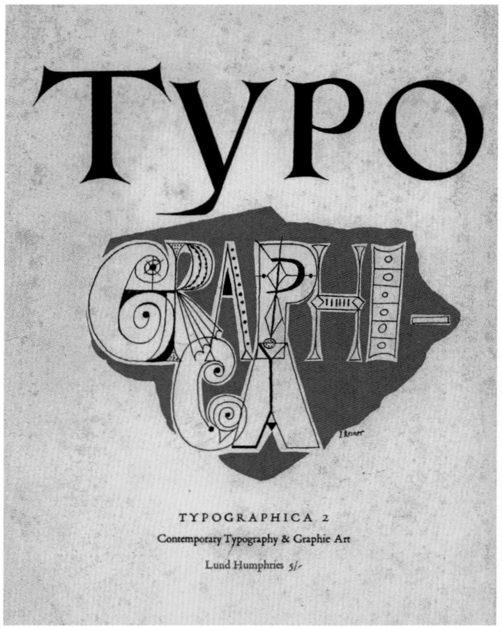

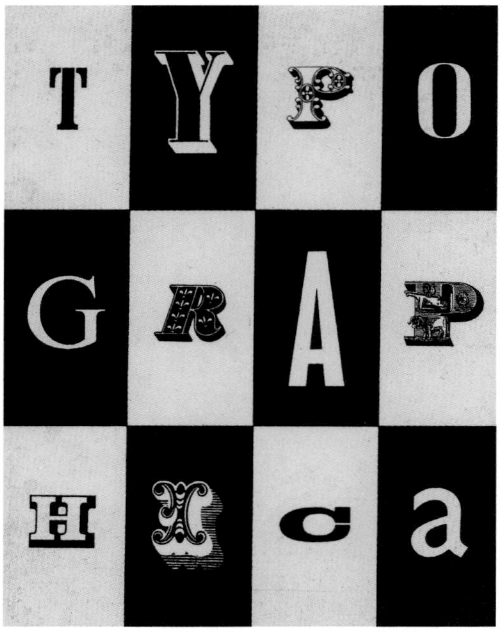

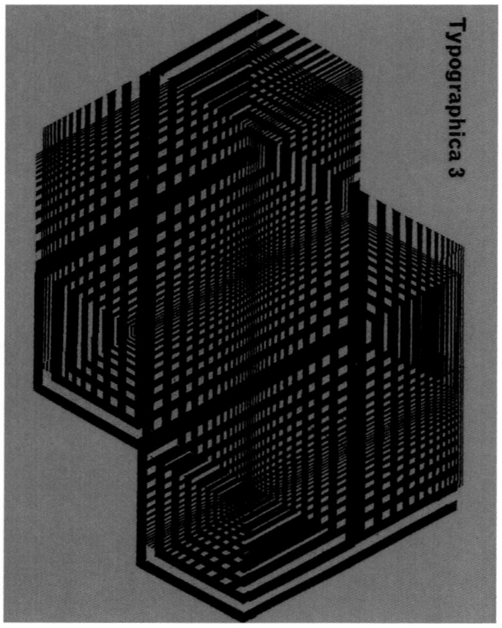

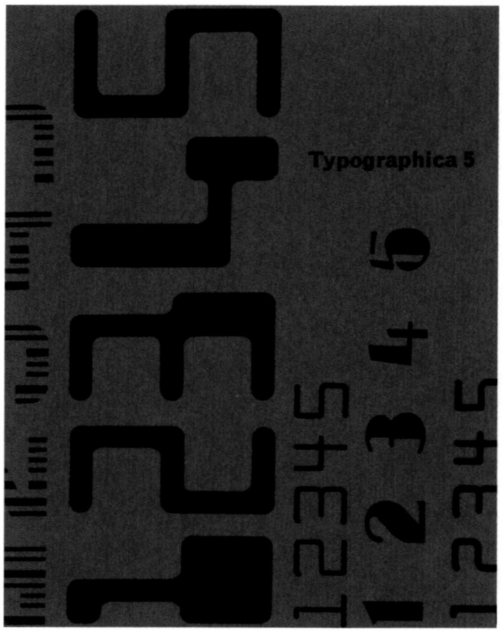

● **1949–1967 . TYPOGRAPHICA .** Magazine / Newspaper . Herbert Spencer
FROM TOP ROW, LEFT TO RIGHT: No. 2, 1950; No. 3, 1950; No. 14, 1958; New Series, No. 3, 1961; New Series, No. 5, 1962; New Series, No. 7, 1963

→ p.432

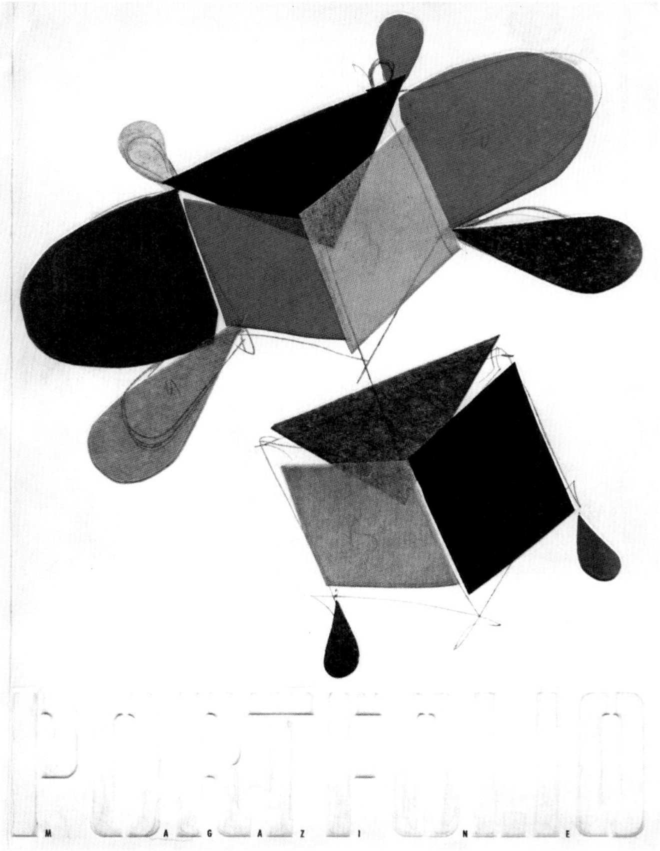

● **1950–1951 . PORTFOLIO .** Magazine / Newspaper . Alexey Brodovitch, Frank Zachary
Charles Eames, No. 2, 1950

→ p.432

● **1950s . OVOMALTINE .** Advertising . Carlo Vivarelli

→ p.432

● **1950–1951 . FLAIR .** Magazine / Newspaper . Federico Pallavicini
No. 1, February 1950

→ p.433

● **1951 . CBS .** Logo . William Golden

→ p.433

● **1951–1954 . INTERIORS .** Magazine Cover . Andy Warhol
February 1954

→ p.433

1951–1959 . THE FINANCIAL TIMES . Advertising . Abram Games

→ p.434

● **1952 . NIE! .** Poster . Tadeusz Trepkowski

→ p.434

● **1953 . SCHÜTZT DAS KIND! .** Poster . Josef Müller-Brockmann

→ p.434

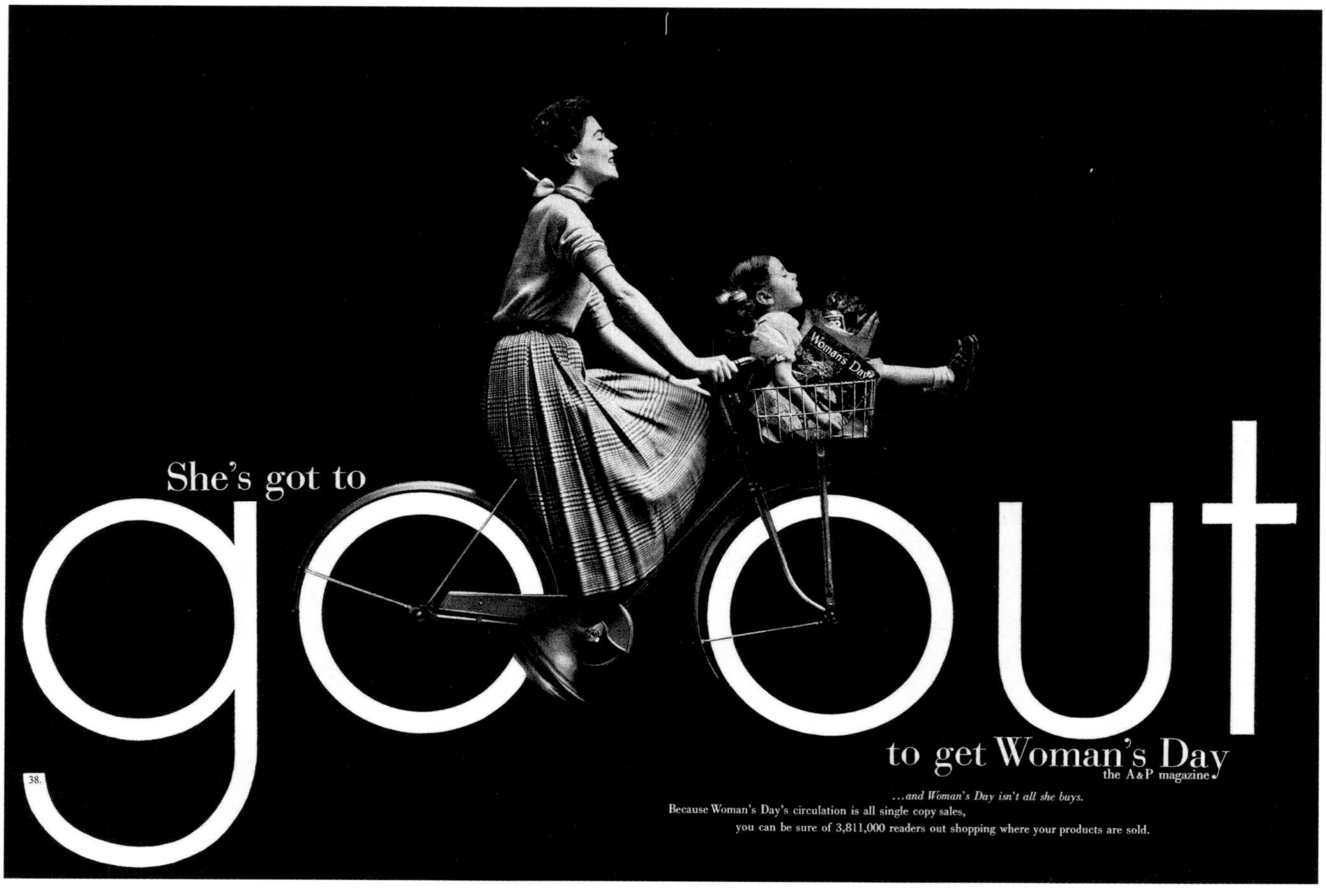

● **1953 . SHE'S GOT TO GO OUT TO GET WOMAN'S DAY .** Advertising . Gene Federico

→ p.435

● **1953–PRESENT . IDEA .** Magazine / Newspaper . Various
LEFT: Kenji Ito, No. 1, 1953; RIGHT: Pieter Brattinga, No. 66, August 1964

→ p.435

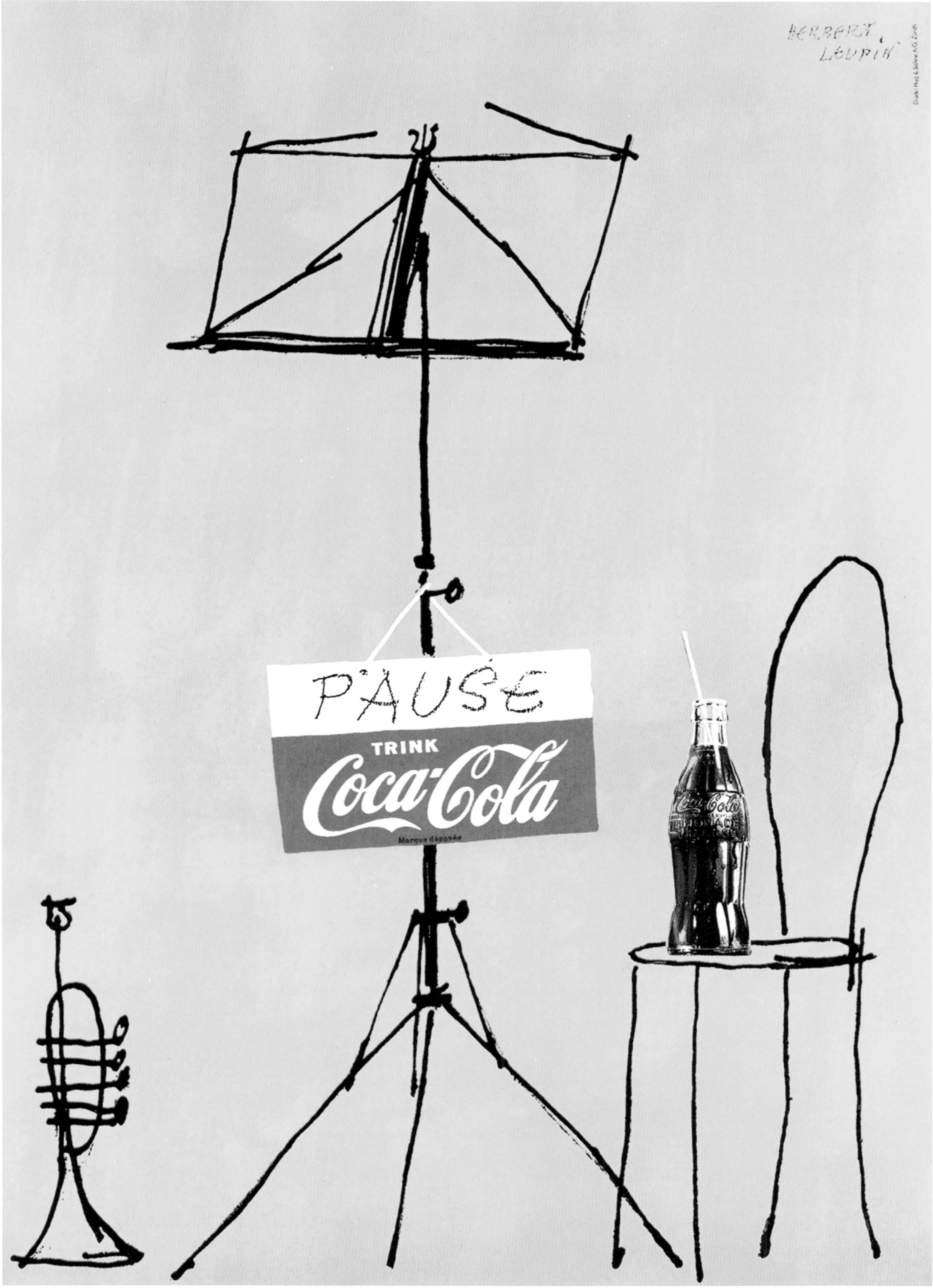

● **1953 . PAUSE—TRINK COCA-COLA .** Poster . Herbert Leupin

→ p.435

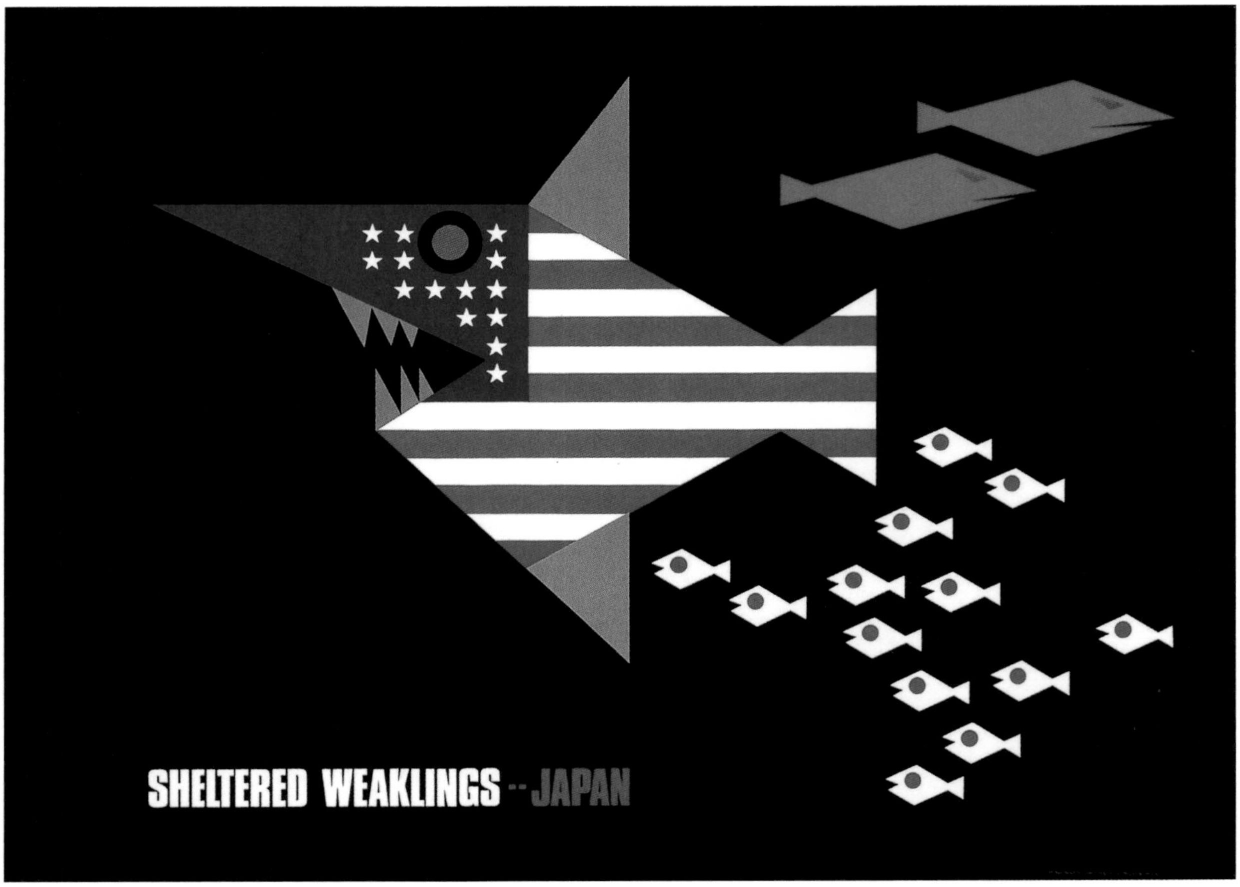

● **1953 . SHELTERED WEAKLINGS—JAPAN .** Poster . Takashi Kono

→ p.436

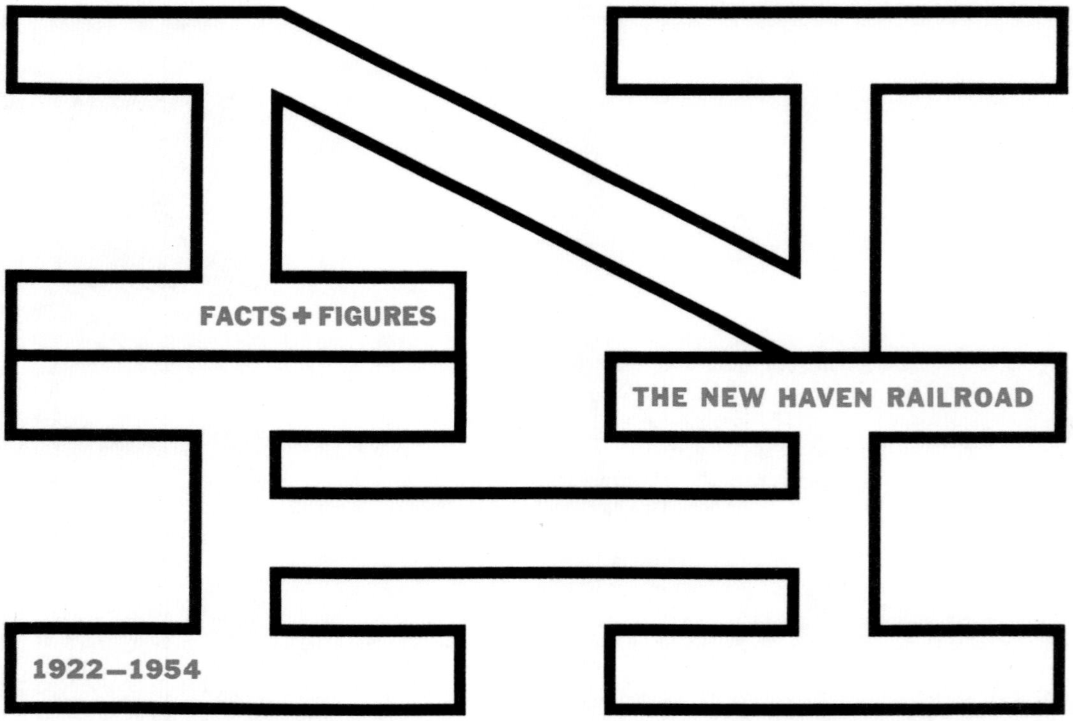

● **1954 . THE NEW HAVEN RAILROAD .** Identity . Herbert Matter et al.

→ p.436

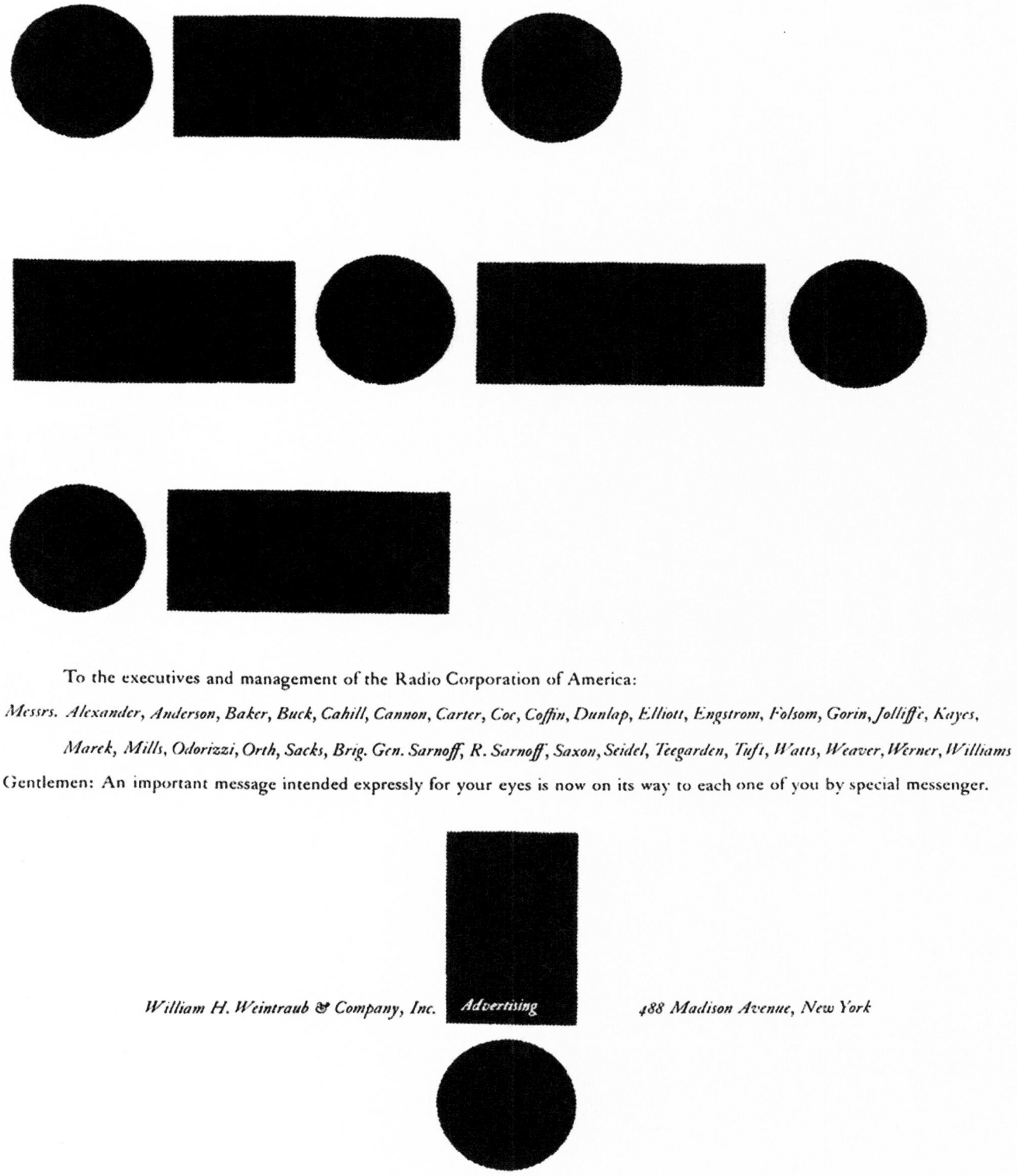

To the executives and management of the Radio Corporation of America:
Messrs. Alexander, Anderson, Baker, Buck, Cahill, Cannon, Carter, Coe, Coffin, Dunlap, Elliott, Engstrom, Folsom, Gorin, Jolliffe, Kayes,
Marek, Mills, Odorizzi, Orth, Sacks, Brig. Gen. Sarnoff, R. Sarnoff, Saxon, Seidel, Teegarden, Tuft, Watts, Weaver, Werner, Williams
Gentlemen: An important message intended expressly for your eyes is now on its way to each one of you by special messenger.
William H. Weintraub & Company, Inc.
Advertising
488 Madison Avenue, New York

1954 . RCA . Advertising . Paul Rand

→ p.436

● **1954–1957 . UNIVERS .** Typeface . Adrian Frutiger

→ p.437

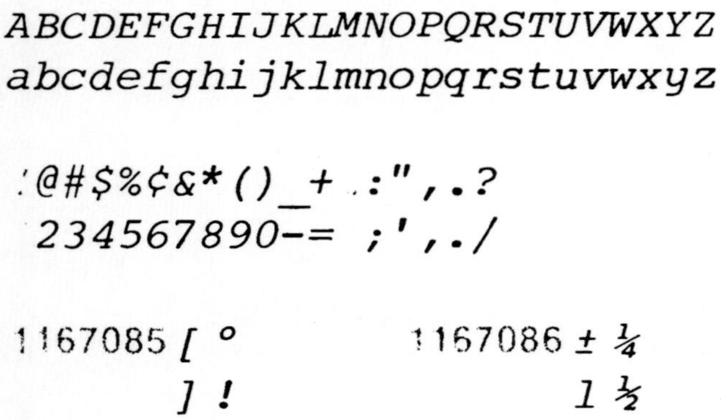

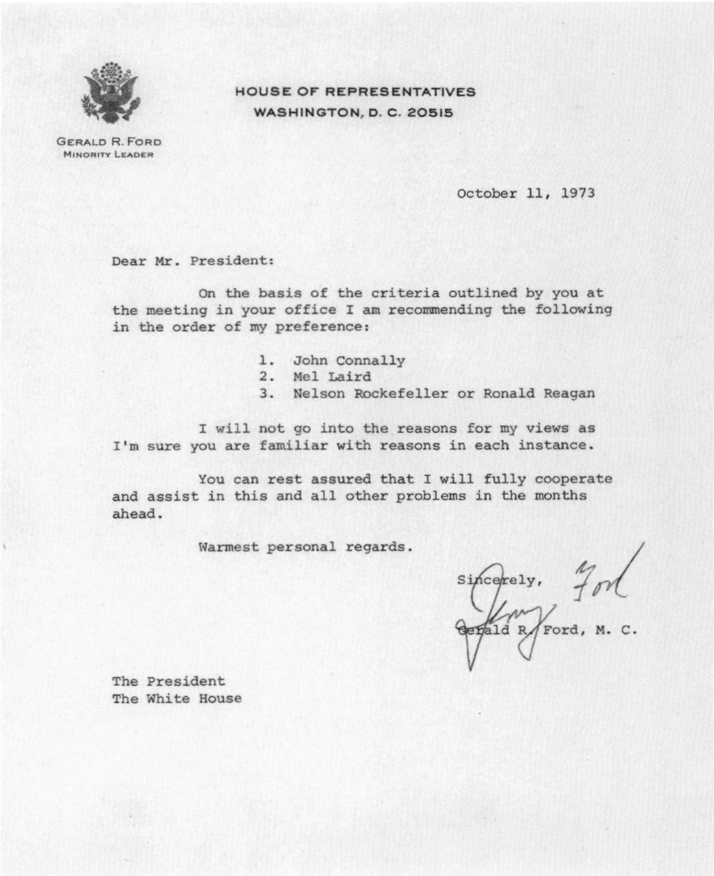

GERALD R. FORD
MINORITY LEADER

HOUSE OF REPRESENTATIVES
WASHINGTON, D. C. 20515

October 11, 1973

Dear Mr. President:

On the basis of the criteria outlined by you at the meeting in your office I am recommending the following in the order of my preference:

1. John Connally
2. Mel Laird
3. Nelson Rockefeller or Ronald Reagan

I will not go into the reasons for my views as I'm sure you are familiar with reasons in each instance.

You can rest assured that I will fully cooperate and assist in this and all other problems in the months ahead.

Warmest personal regards.

Sincerely,

Jerry Ford

Gerald R. Ford, M. C.

The President
The White House

● **1955 . COURIER .** Typeface . Howard Kettler

→ p.437

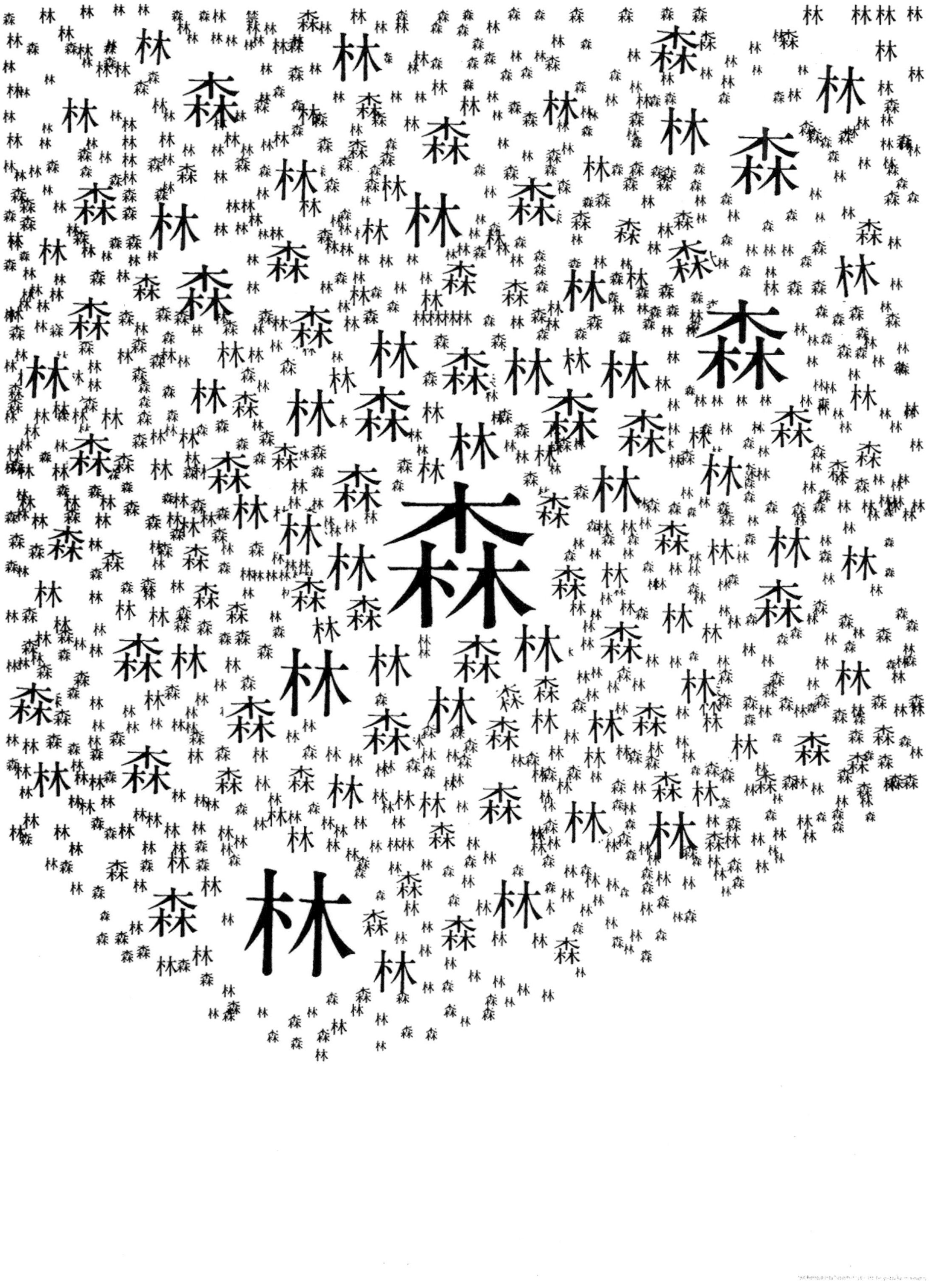

1955 . HAYASHI-MORI . Poster . Ryuichi Yamashiro

→ p.437

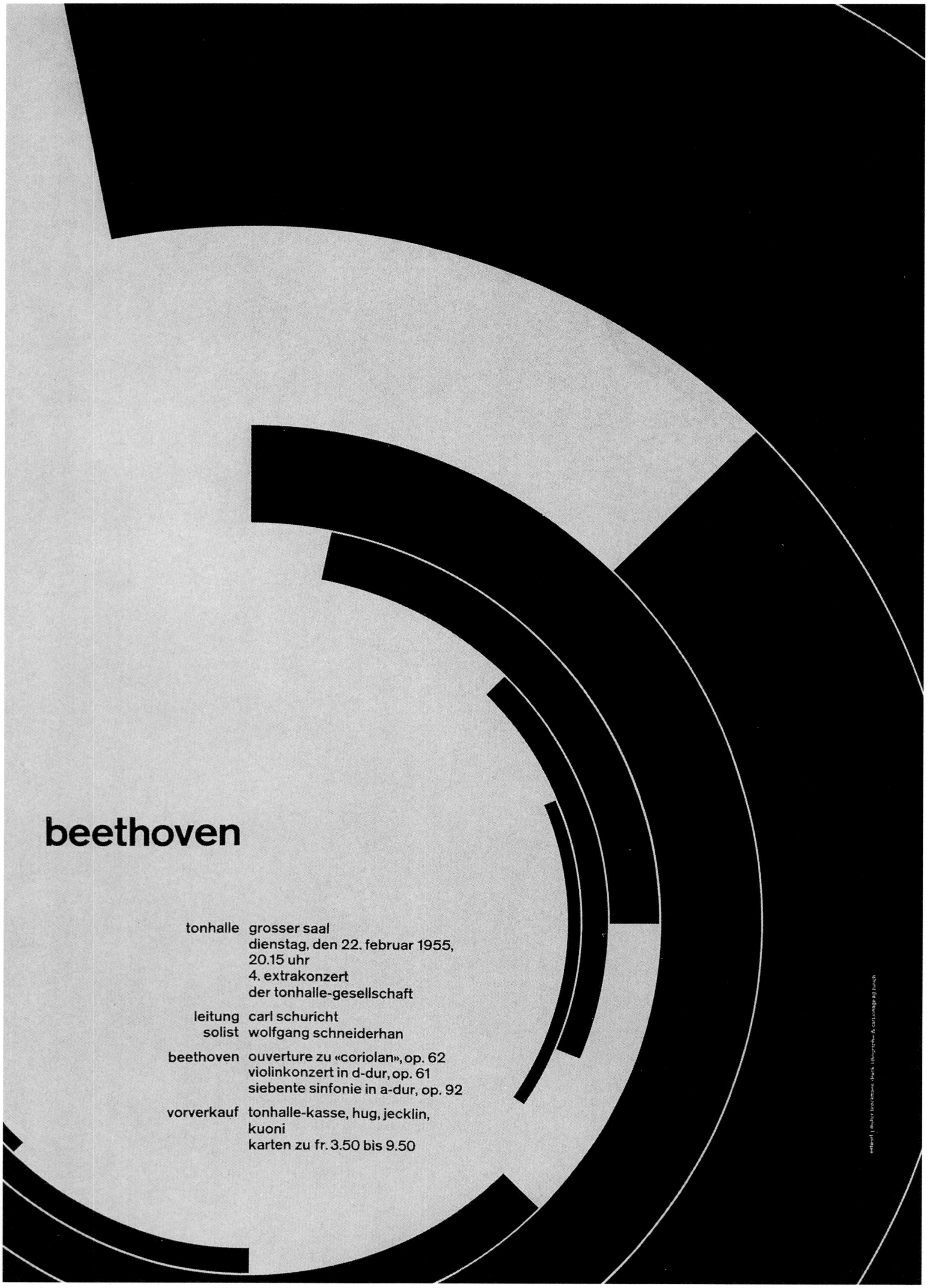

● **1955 . BEETHOVEN .** Poster . Josef Müller-Brockmann

→ p.438

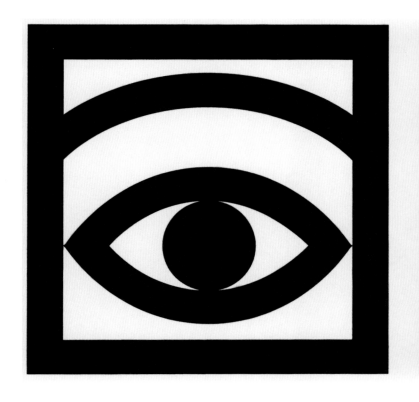

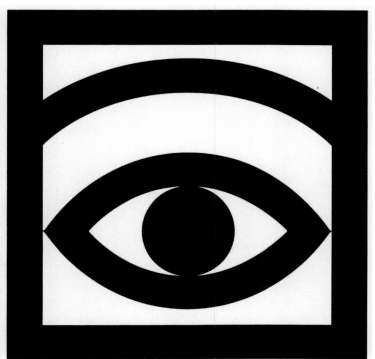

● **1956 . MAZETTI .** Identity . Olle Eksell

→ p.438

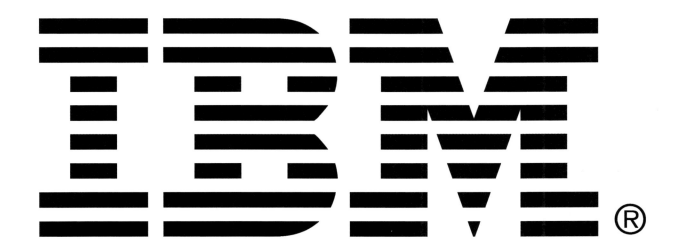

● **1956–1991 . IBM .** Identity . Paul Rand

→ p.438

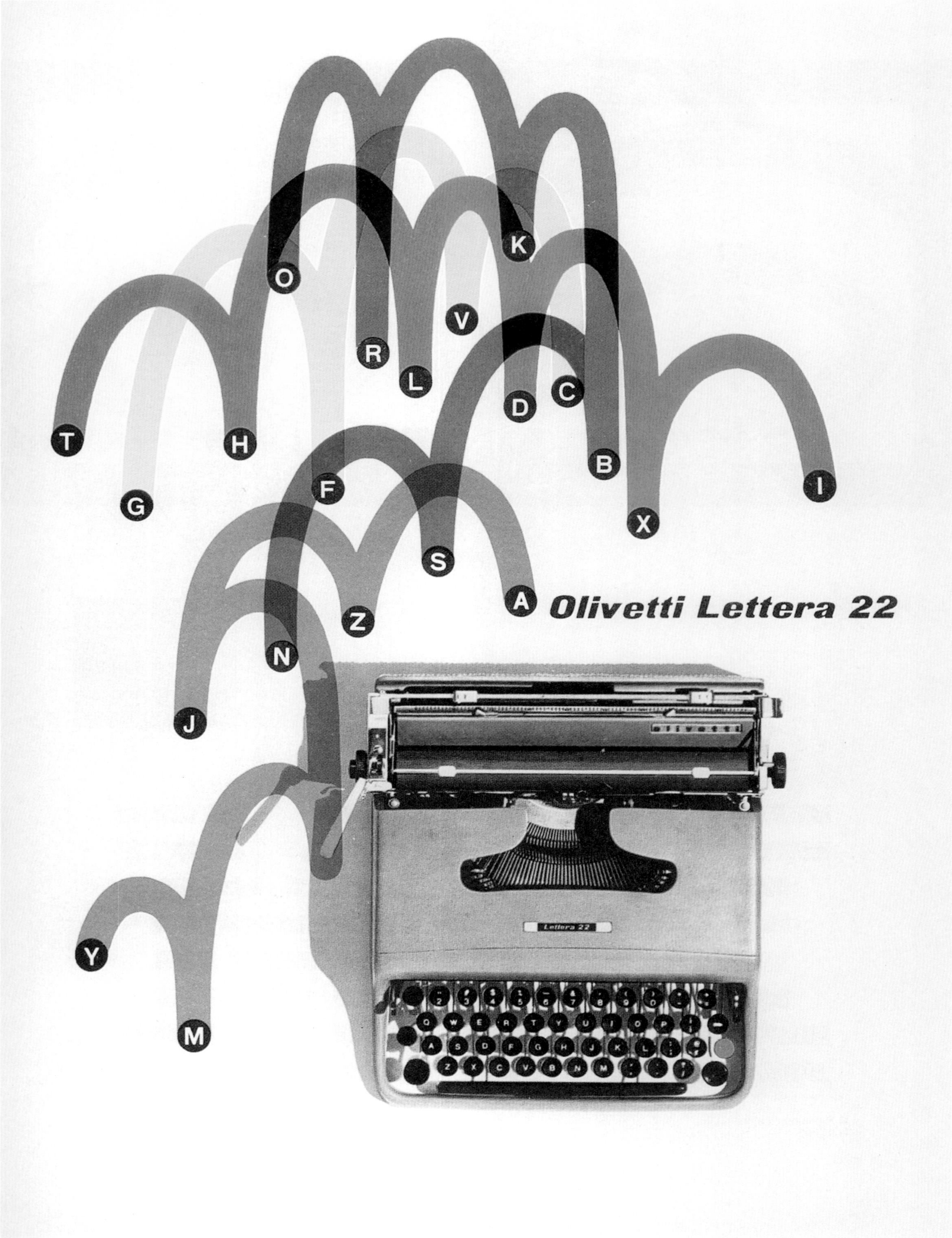

1956 . OLIVETTI . Advertising . Giovanni Pintori

→ p.439

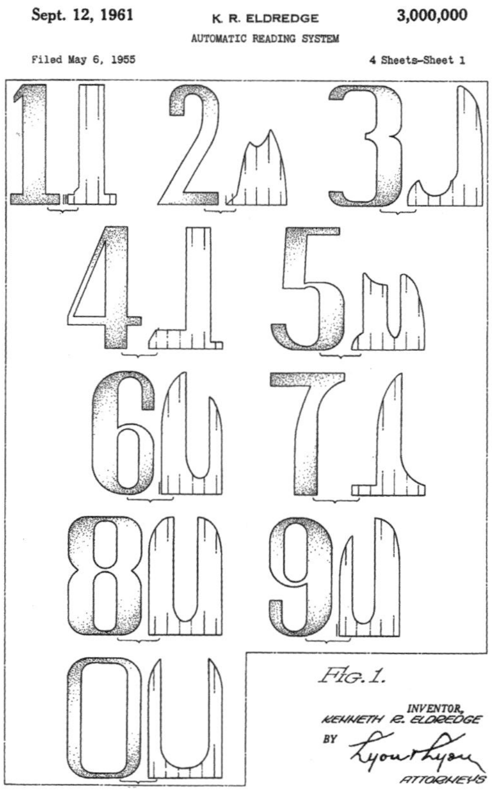

● **1956 . MAGNETIC INK CHARACTER RECOGNITION .** Typeface . Stanford Research Institute

→ p.439

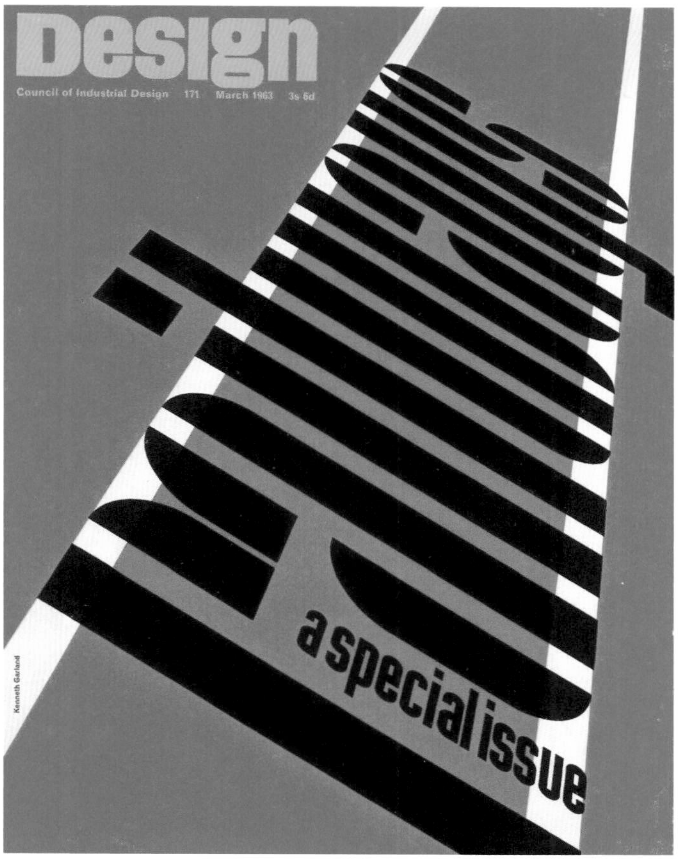

● **1956–1962 . DESIGN .** Magazine / Newspaper . Ken Garland
No. 171, March 1963

→ p.439

DANESE

MILANO

1957 . **DANESE** . Logo . Franco Meneguzzo

→ p.440

1957 . **SCHIFF NACH EUROPA, BY MARKUS KUTTER** . Book . Karl Gerstner

→ p.440

1957–1967 . BRITISH MOTORWAY AND ROAD SIGNAGE SYSTEM . Information Design . Jock Kinneir, Margaret Calvert
TOP: Motorway Junction Ahead; BOTTOM LEFT: School Children Crossing; BOTTOM RIGHT: Road Works

→ p.440

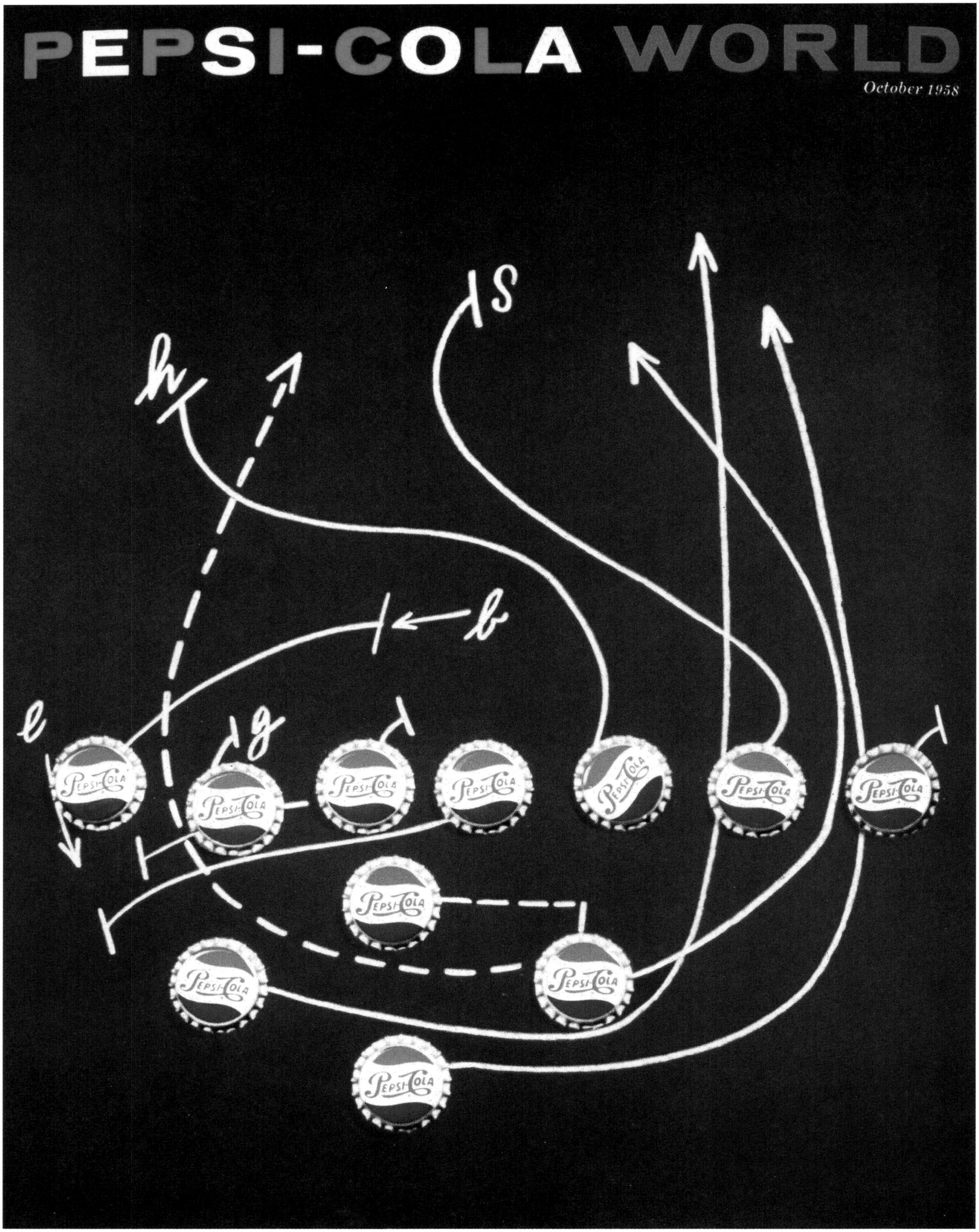

● **1957–1959 . PEPSI-COLA WORLD .** Magazine Cover . Robert Brownjohn et al.
October 1958

→ p.441

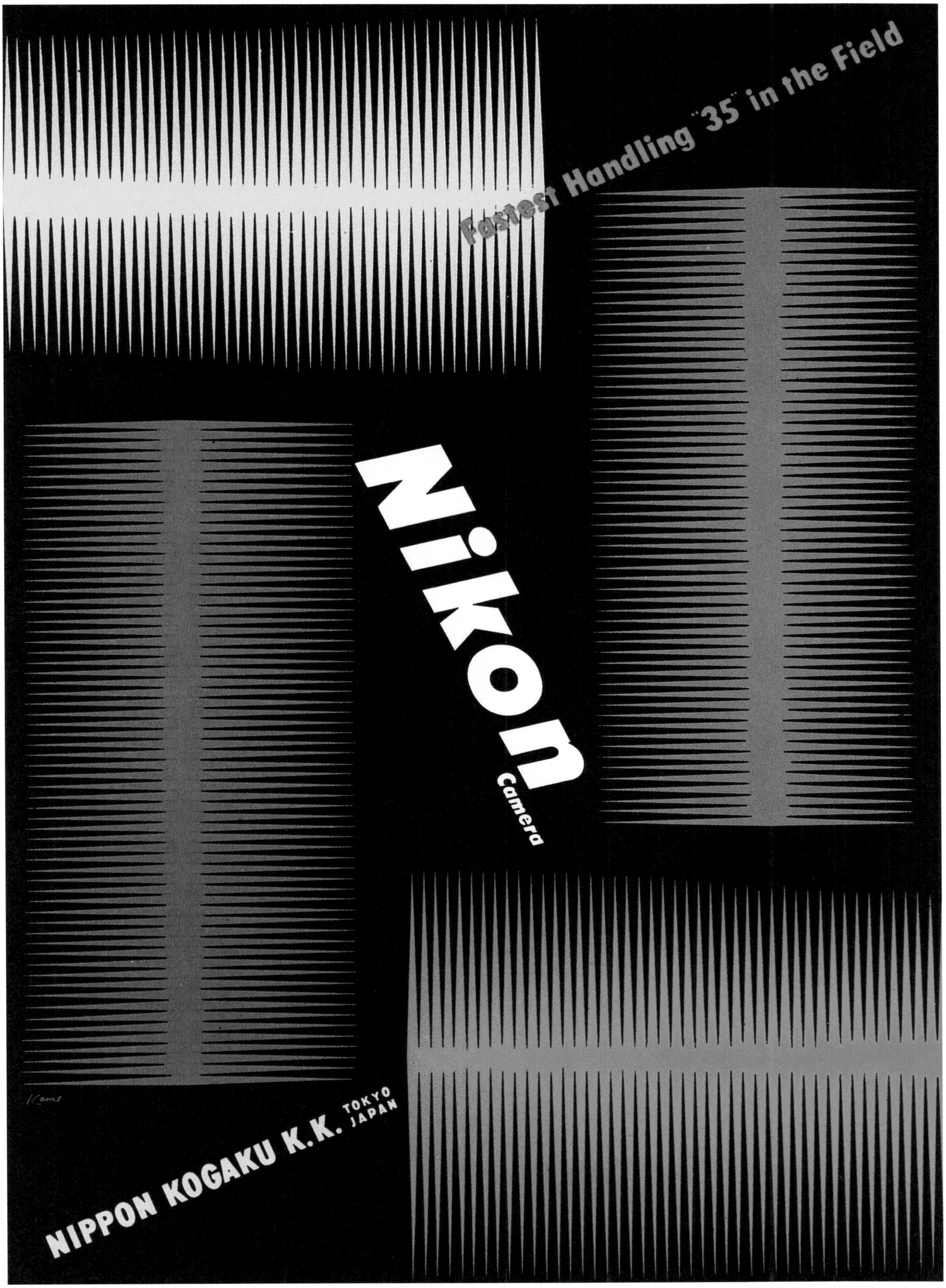

● **1957 . NIKON CAMERA .** Poster . Yusaku Kamekura

→ p.441

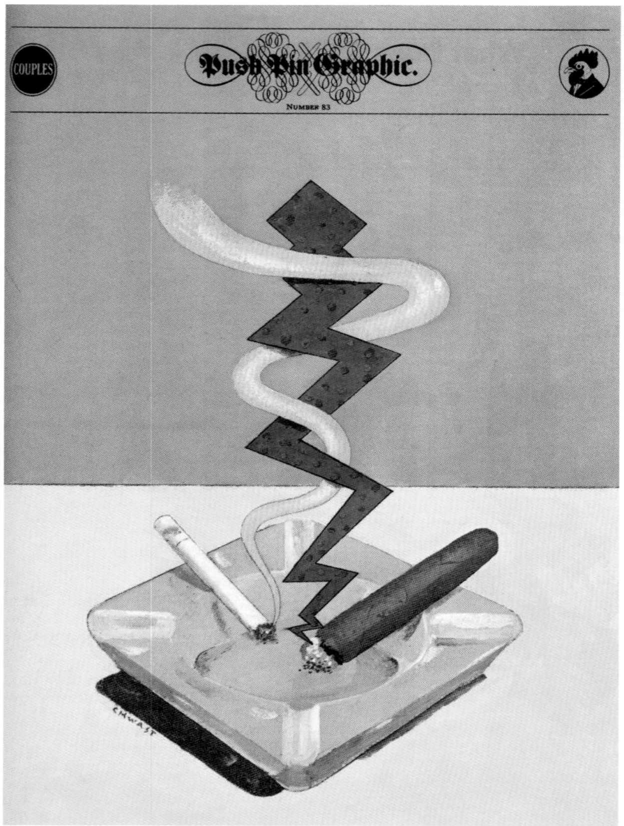

● **1957–1980 . THE PUSH PIN GRAPHIC .**
Magazine / Newspaper . Seymour Chwast et al.
No. 83, 1981

→ p.441

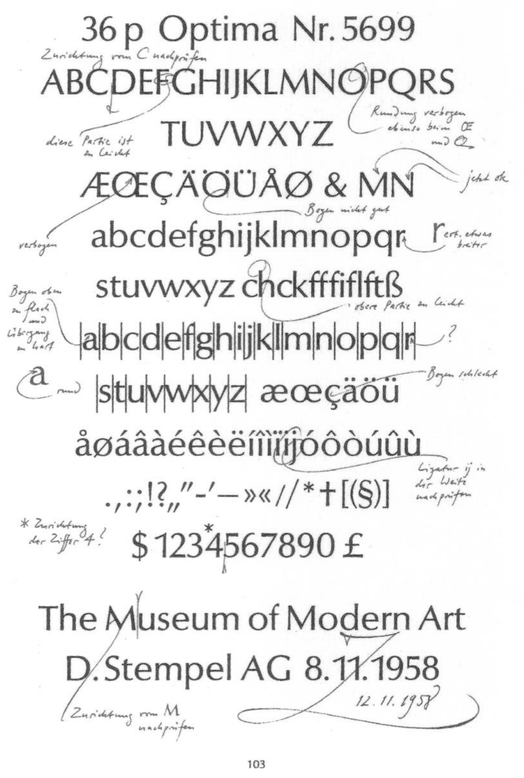

● **1958 . OPTIMA .**
Typeface . Hermann Zapf

→ p.442

● **1958 . CAMPAIGN FOR NUCLEAR DISARMAMENT .** Information Design . Gerald Holtom

→ p.442

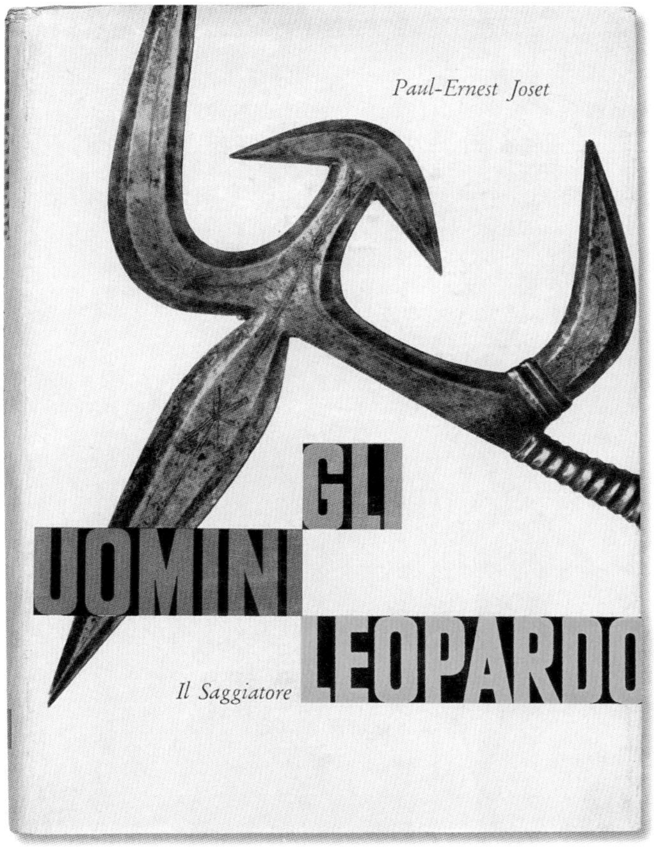
Paul-Ernest Joset
GLI
UOMINI
LEOPARDO
Il Saggiatore

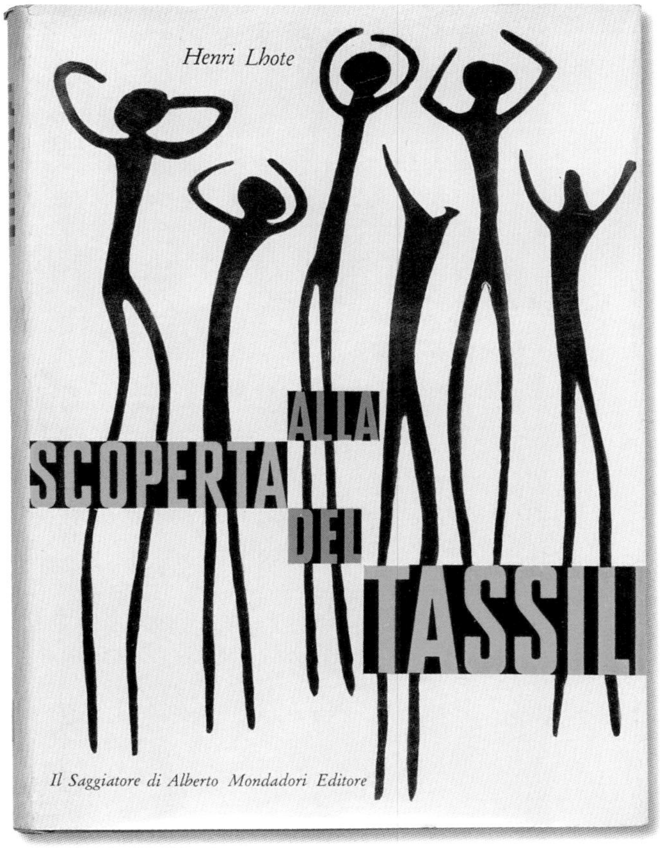
Henri Lhote
ALLA
SCOPERTA
DEL
TASSILI
Il Saggiatore di Alberto Mondadori Editore

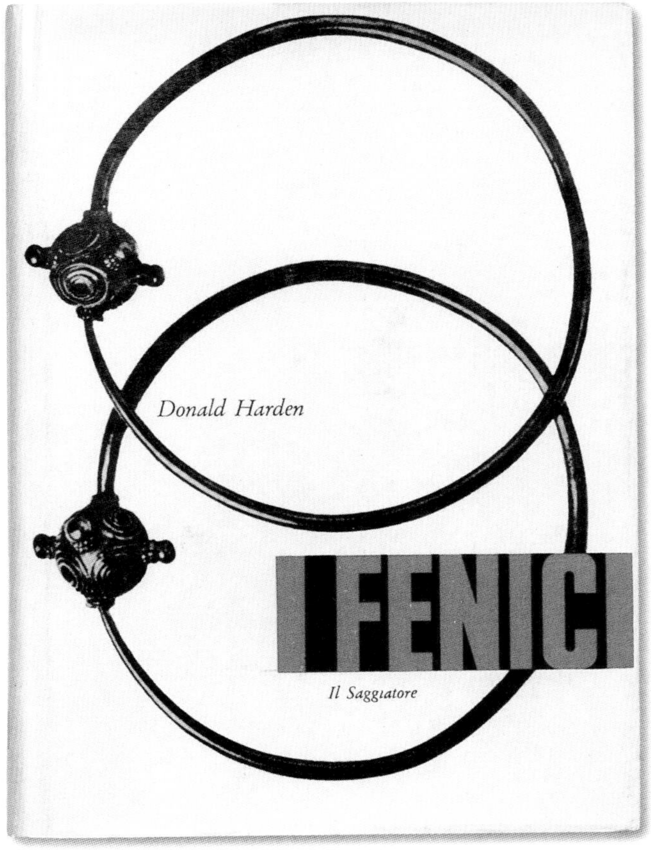
Donald Harden
I FENICI
Il Saggiatore

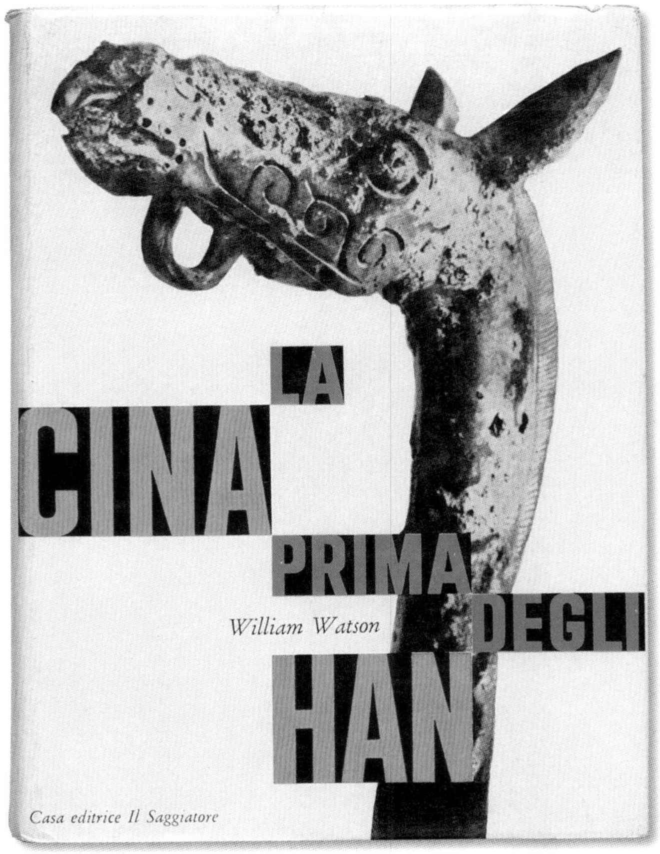
LA
CINA
PRIMA
DEGLI
HAN
William Watson
Casa editrice Il Saggiatore

1958–1978 . UOMO E MITO . Book Cover . Anita Klinz
TOP LEFT: *Gli Uomini Leopardo* (*The Leopard Men*), by Paul-Ernest Joset, 1960; TOP RIGHT: *Alla Scoperta del Tassili* (*The Search for the Tassili Frescoes*), by Henri Lhote, 1959; BOTTOM LEFT: *I Fenici* (*The Phoenicians*), by Donald Harden, 1964; BOTTOM RIGHT: *La Cina Prima Degli Han* (*China Before the Han Dynasty*), William Watson, 1963

→ p.442

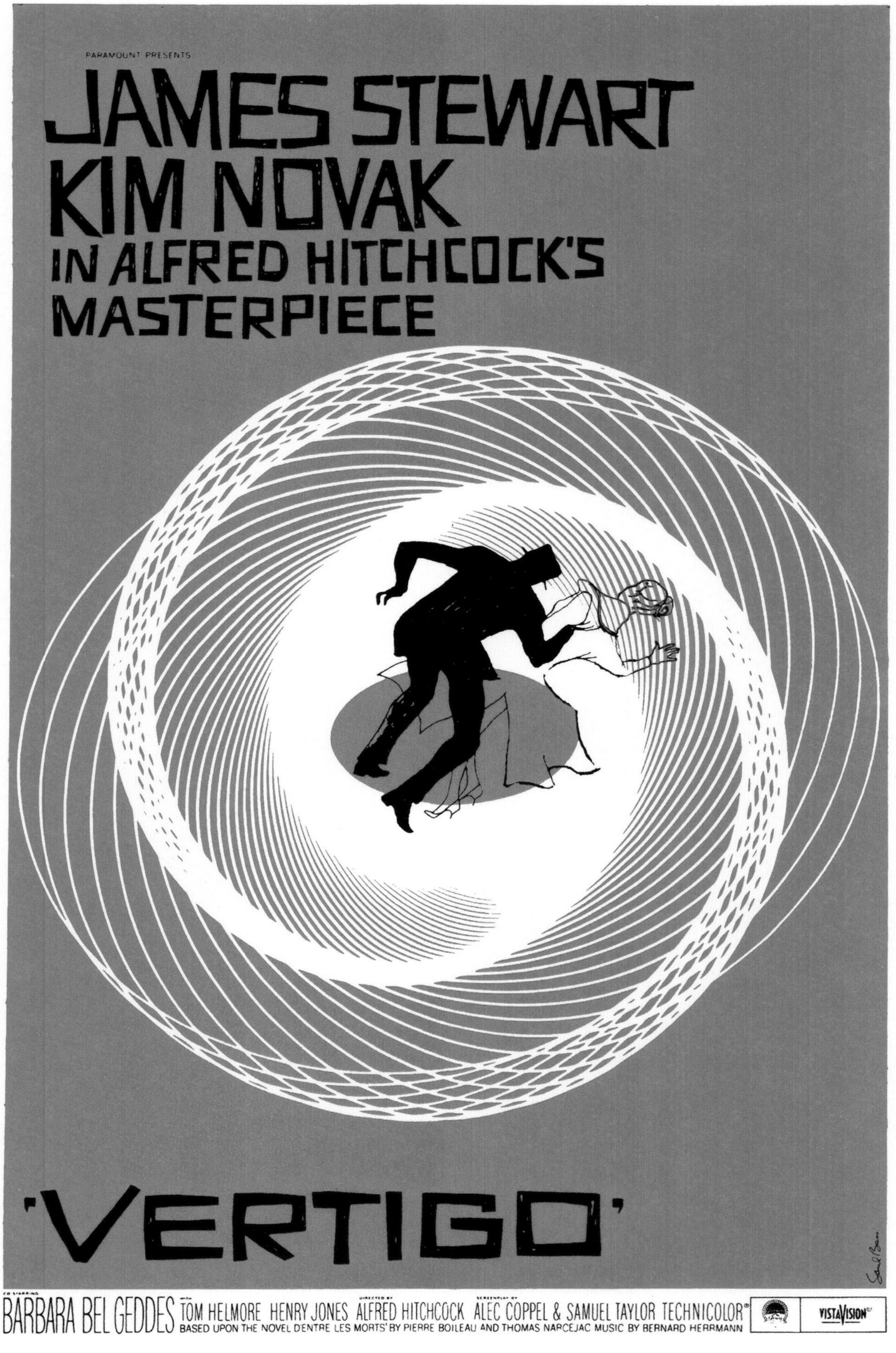

● **1958 . VERTIGO .** Poster . Saul Bass

→ p.443

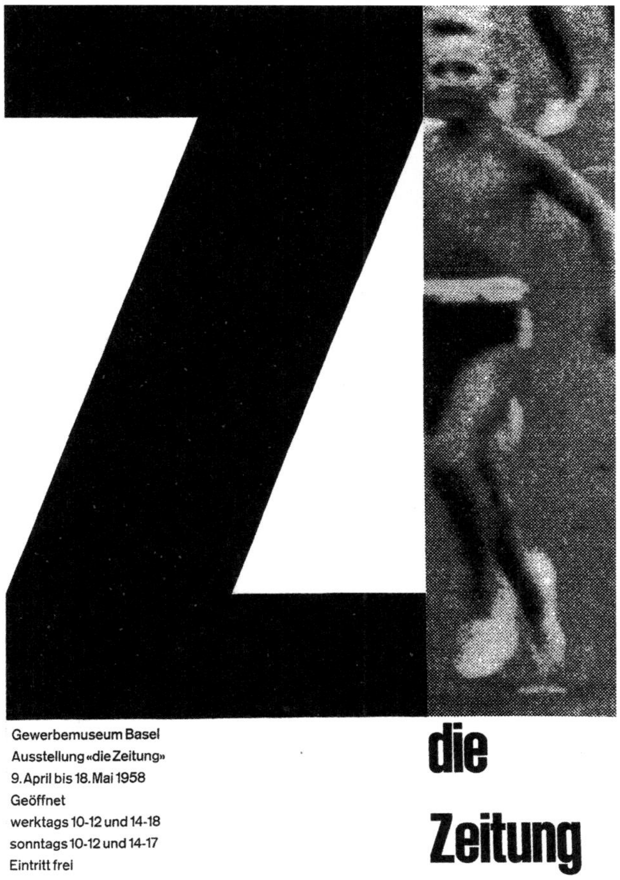
Gewerbemuseum Basel
Ausstellung «die Zeitung»
9. April bis 18. Mai 1958
Geöffnet
werktags 10-12 und 14-18
sonntags 10-12 und 14-17
Eintritt frei
die
Zeitung

● **1958 . DIE ZEITUNG .** Poster . Emil Ruder

→ p.443

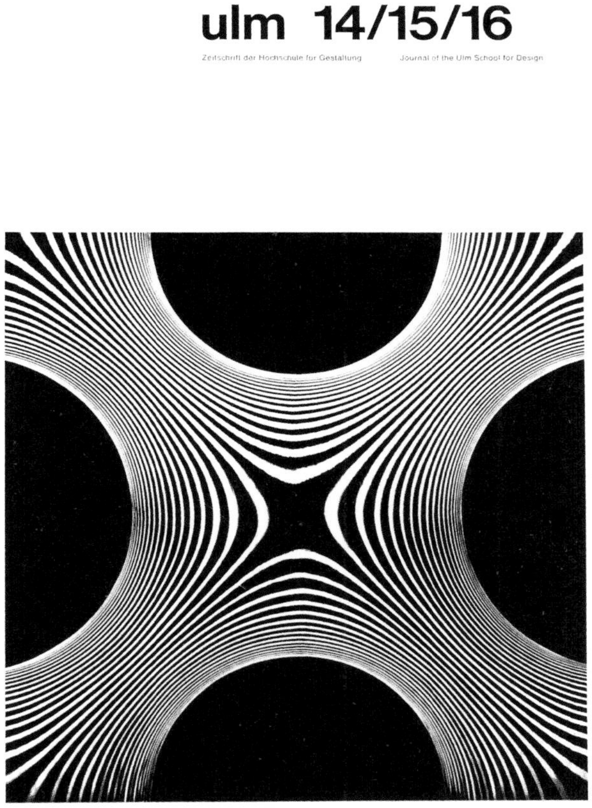
ulm 14/15/16
Zeitschrift der Hochschule für Gestaltung
Journal of the Ulm School for Design

● **1958–1968 . ULM .** Magazine / Newspaper . Anthony Froshaug, Tomás Gonda
Herbert Kapitzki and Eckhard Jung, December 1965

→ p.443

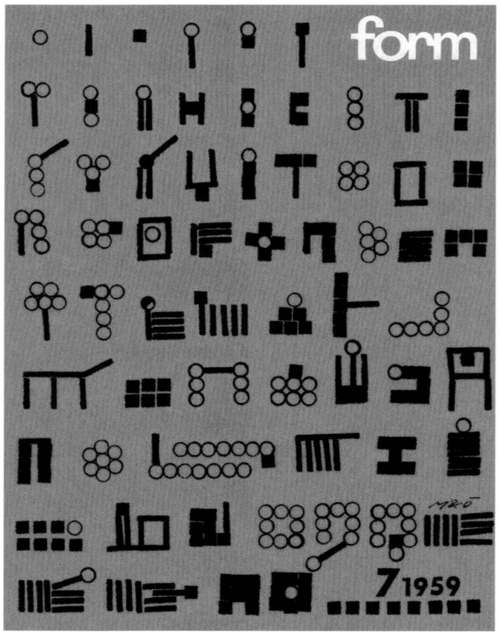

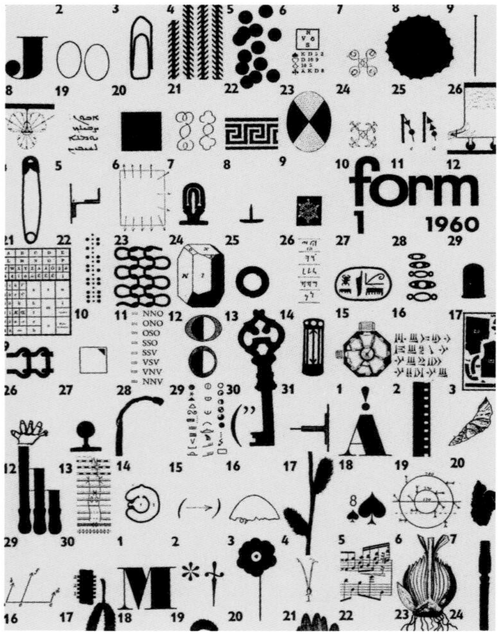

● **1959–1961 . FORM .** Magazine Cover . John Melin, Anders Österlin
FROM LEFT: No. 1, 1959; No. 7, 1959; No. 1, 1960

→ p.444

● **1959 . RHEINBRÜCKE .** Advertising . Karl Gerstner

→ p.444

© 1962 VOLKSWAGEN OF AMERICA, INC.

Think small.

Our little car isn't so much of a novelty any more.

A couple of dozen college kids don't try to squeeze inside it.

The guy at the gas station doesn't ask where the gas goes.

Nobody even stares at our shape.

In fact, some people who drive our little flivver don't even think 32 miles to the gallon is going any great guns.

Or using five pints of oil instead of five quarts.

Or never needing anti-freeze.

Or racking up 40,000 miles on a set of tires.

That's because once you get used to some of our economies, you don't even think about them any more.

Except when you squeeze into a small parking spot. Or renew your small insurance. Or pay a small repair bill. Or trade in your old VW for a new one.

Think it over.

1959 . THINK SMALL . Advertising . Helmut Krone

→ p.444

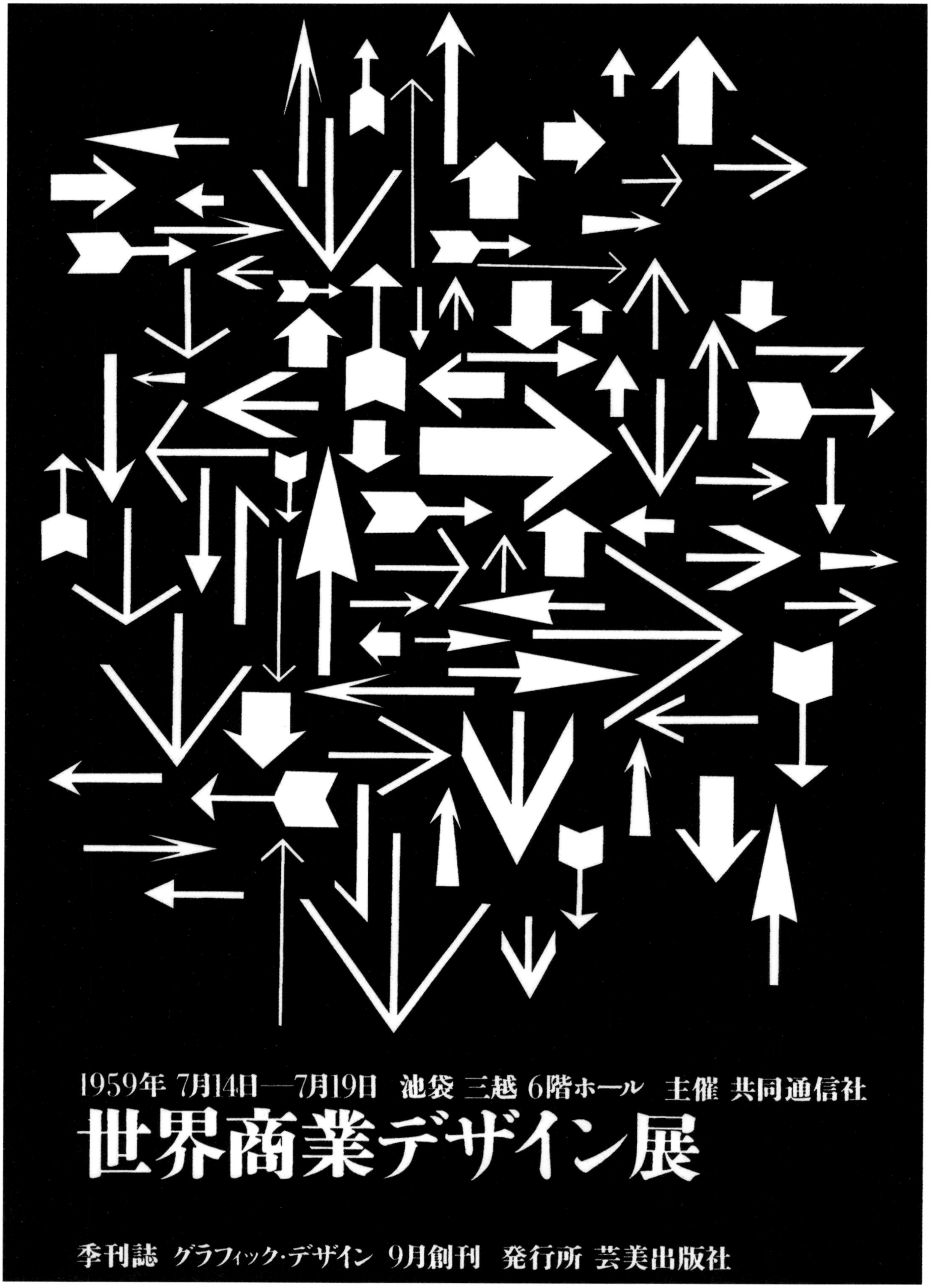
1959年 7月14日—7月19日 池袋 三越 6階ホール 主催 共同通信社
世界商業デザイン展
季刊誌 グラフィック・デザイン 9月創刊 発行所 芸美出版社

● **1959 . WORLD GRAPHIC DESIGN EXHIBITION .** Poster . Ikko Tanaka

→ p.445

● **1959–1961 . ALMANAQUE .** Magazine Cover . Sebastião Rodrigues
FROM TOP ROW, LEFT TO RIGHT: October 1959; December 1959; March 1960; April 1960; July 1960; August 1960

→ p.445

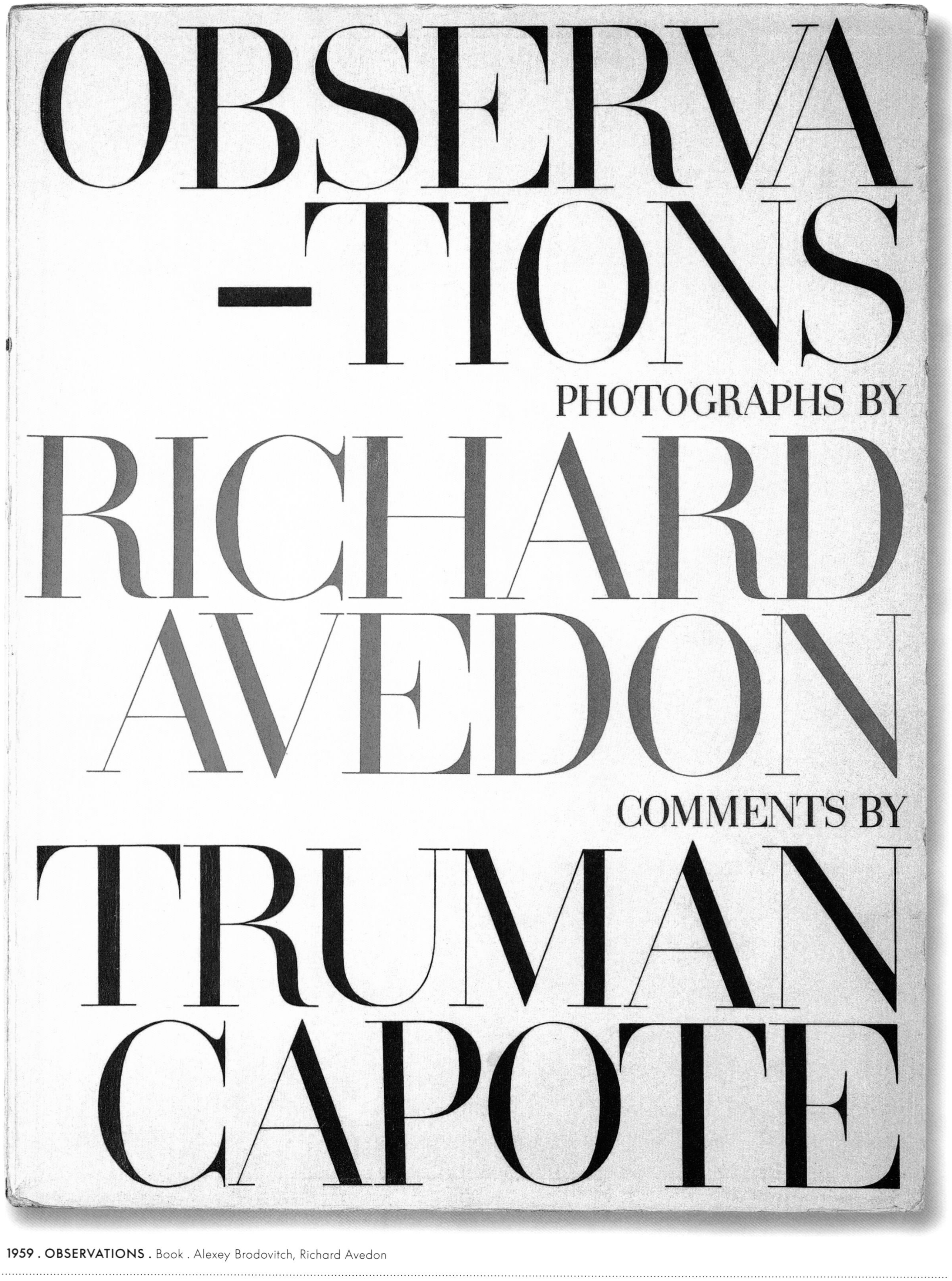

1959 . OBSERVATIONS . Book . Alexey Brodovitch, Richard Avedon

→ p.445

● **1959–1971 . TWEN .** Magazine / Newspaper . Willy Fleckhaus
FROM LEFT: No. 9, September 1968; No. 3, March 1969; No. 6, June 1969

→ p.446

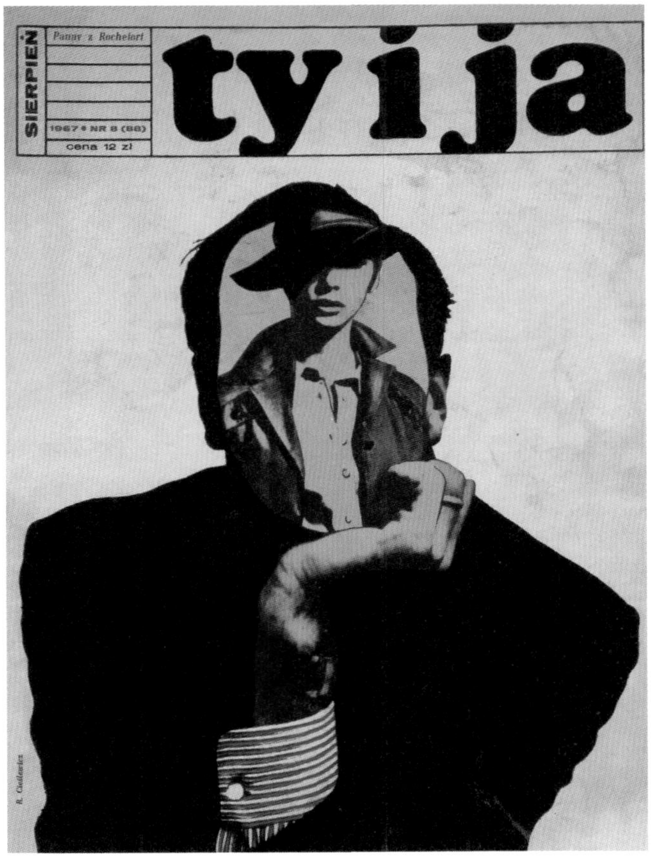

● **1959–1962 . TY I JA .** Magazine / Newspaper . Roman Cieslewicz
FROM LEFT: No. 12, 1968; No. 8, 1967

→ p.446

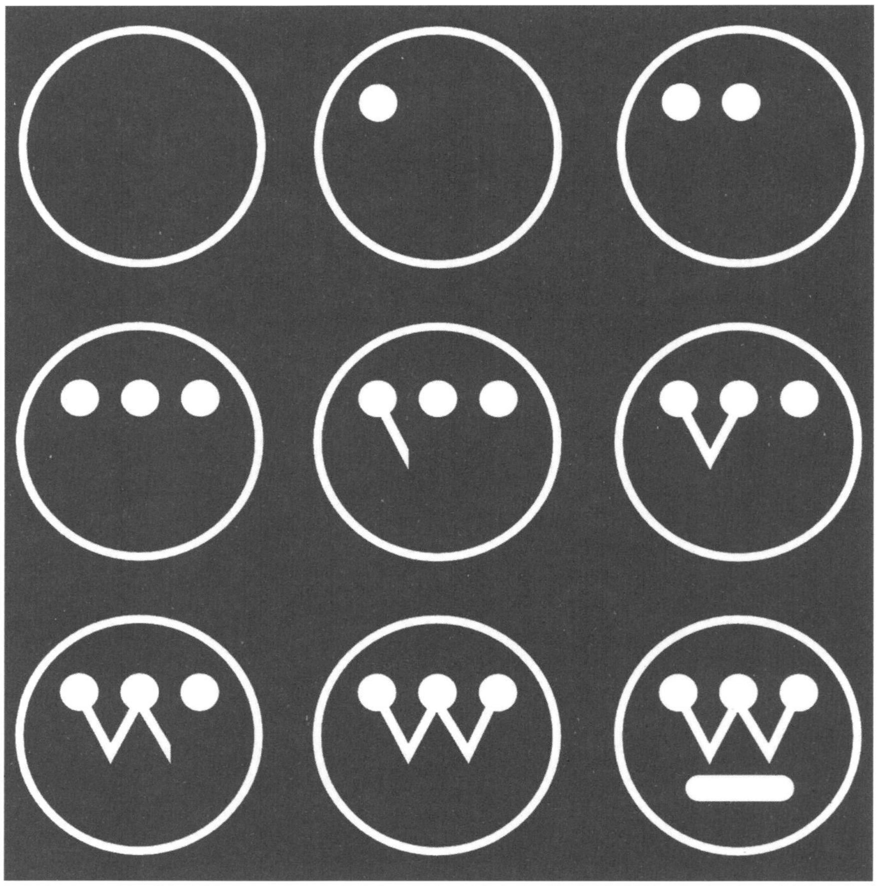

● **1959 . WESTINGHOUSE .** Logo . Paul Rand

→ p.446

● **1959 . NORTH BY NORTHWEST .** Identity . Saul Bass

→ p.447

1960 . WASSER . Advertising . Siegfried Odermatt

→ p.447

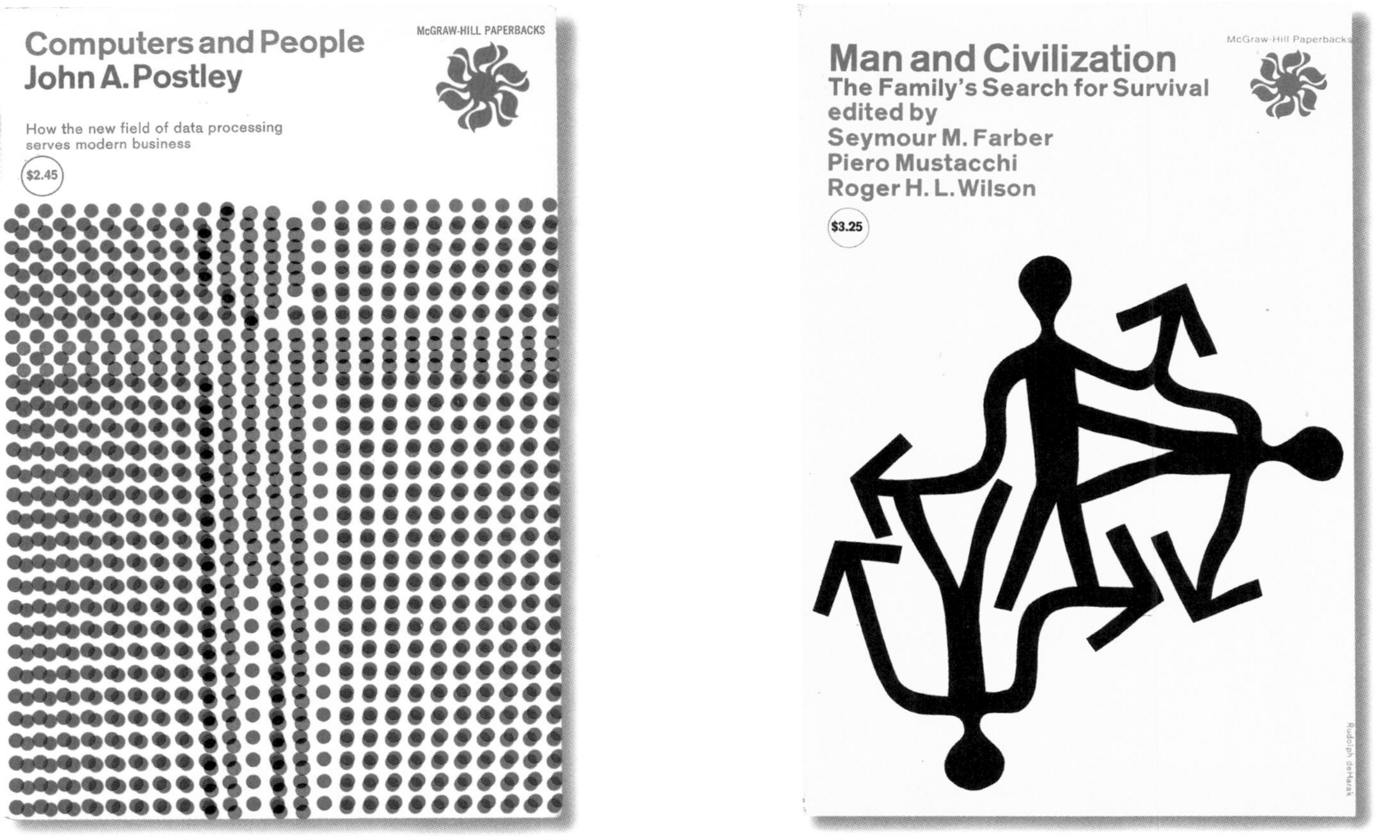

1960s . MCGRAW-HILL PAPERBACKS . Book Cover . Rudolph de Harak
FROM LEFT: *Computers and People*, by John A. Postley, 1963; *Man and Civilization: The Family's Search for Survival*, eds. Seymour M. Farber, Piero Mustacchi, and Roger H. L. Wilson, 1965

→ p.447

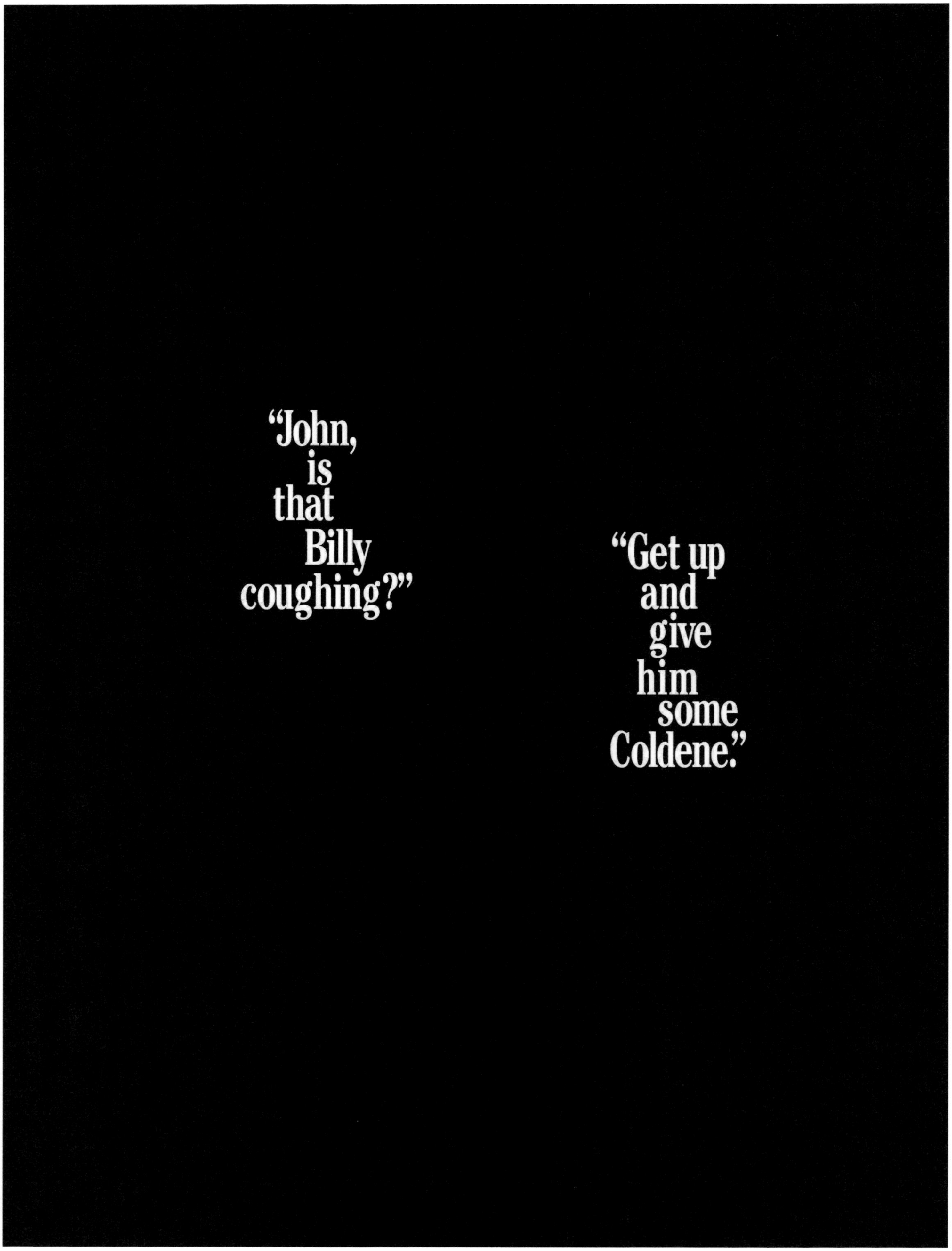
"John, is that Billy coughing?"
"Get up and give him some Coldene."

1960 . COLDENE . Advertising . Papert Koenig Lois

→ p.448

1960 . **PUNT E MES .** Poster . Armando Testa

→ p.448

● **1960 . CHASE MANHATTAN BANK .** Logo . Ivan Chermayeff, Tom Geismar

→ p.448

● **1960 . CANADIAN NATIONAL RAILWAY .** Logo . Allan Fleming et al.

→ p.449

● **1961 . THE GRAPHIC ARTIST AND HIS DESIGN PROBLEMS .** Book . Josef Müller-Brockmann

→ p.449

● **1961 . YVES SAINT LAURENT .** Logo . A. M. Cassandre

→ p.449

● **1961–1964 . SHOW .** Magazine / Newspaper . Henry Wolf, Sam Antupit
October 1961

→ p.450

1961 . HELVETICA . Typeface . Edouard Hoffmann, Max Miedinger

→ p.450

1962 . MCDONALD'S . Logo . Jim Schindler

→ p.450

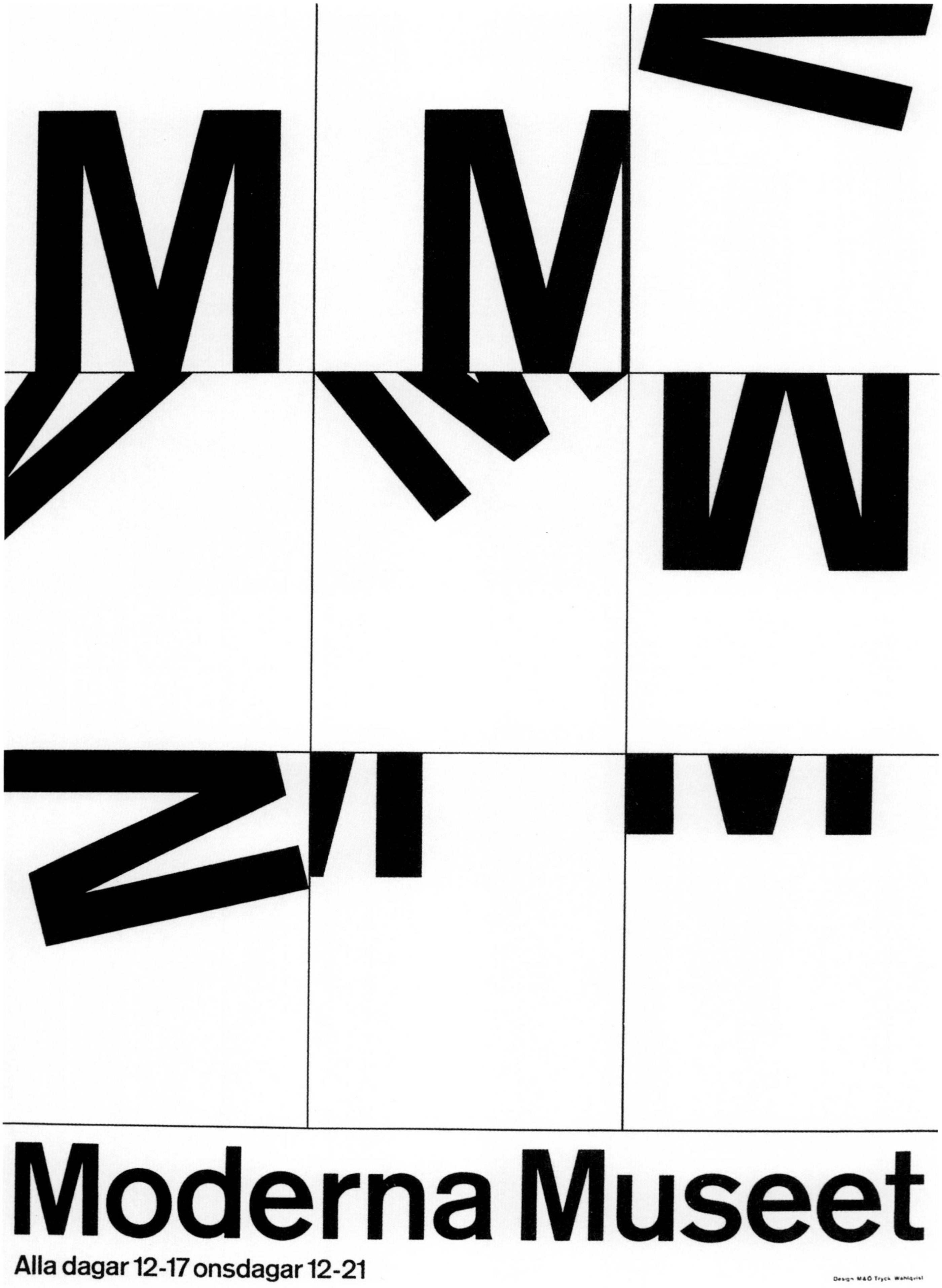

● **1962 . MODERNA MUSEET .** Poster . John Melin, Anders Österlin

→ p.451

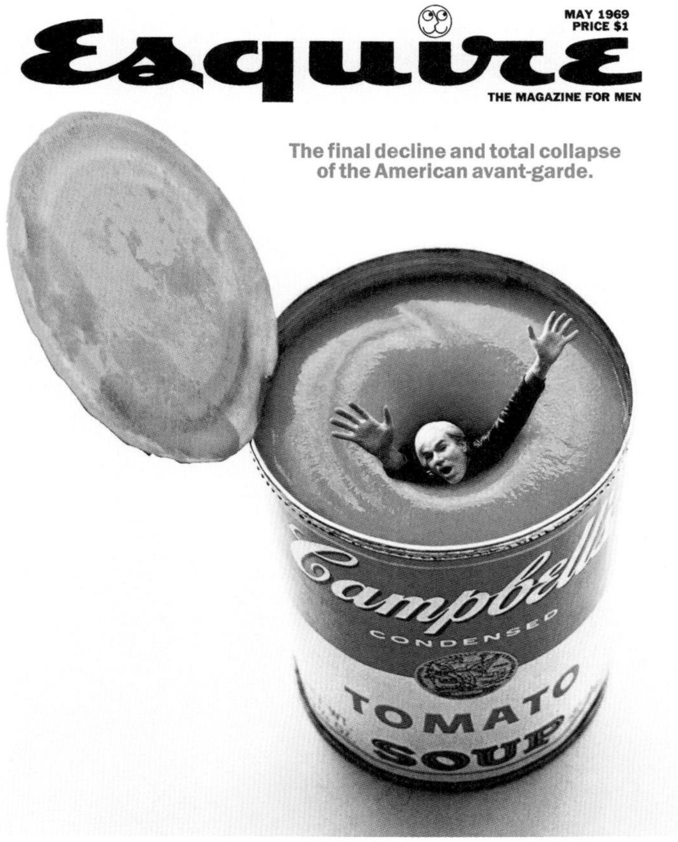

● **1962–1972 . ESQUIRE .** Magazine Cover . George Lois
May 1969

→ p.451

● **1962 . PIRELLI SLIPPERS .** Advertising . Fletcher/Forbes/Gill

→ p.451

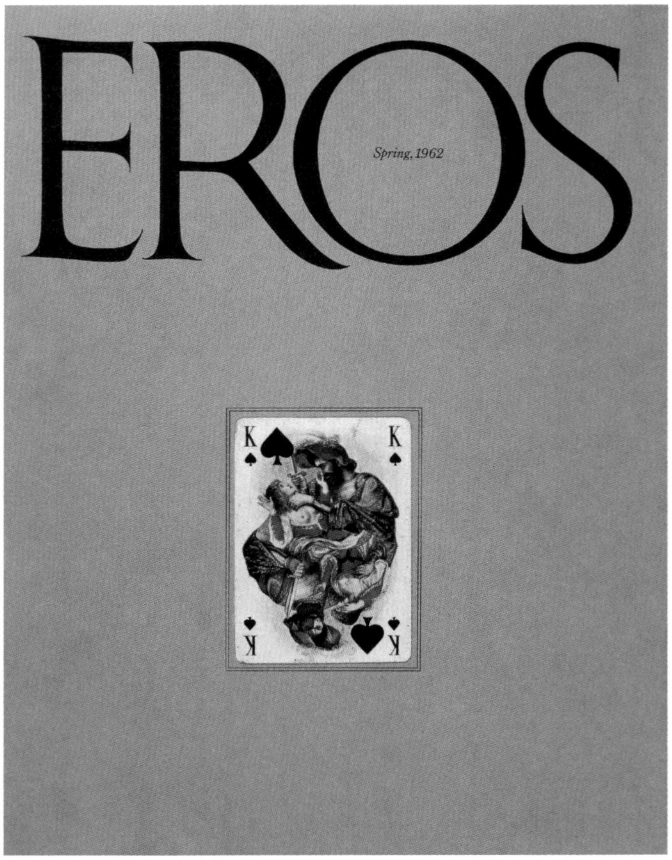

● **1962 . EROS .** Magazine / Newspaper . Herb Lubalin
Vol. 1, No. 1, Spring 1962

→ p.452

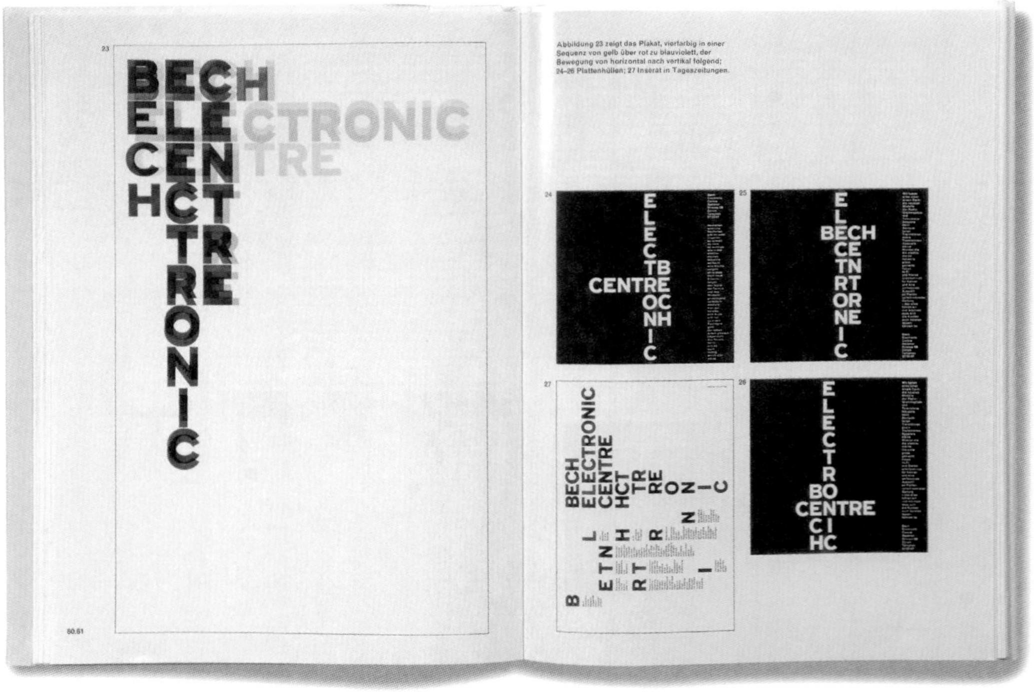

● **1963 . PROGRAMME ENTWERFEN .** Book . Karl Gerstner

→ p.452

● **1963 . WILHELM TELL .** Poster . Armin Hofmann

→ p.452

● **1963 . KLM .** Logo . F. H. K. Henrion

→ p.453

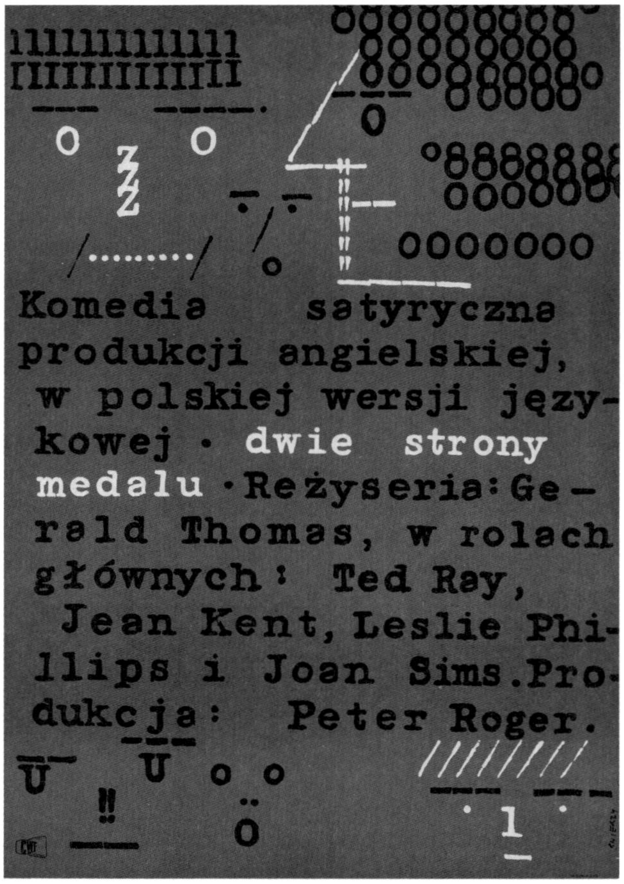

● **1963 . DWIE STRONY MEDALU .** Poster . Waldemar Swierzy

→ p.453

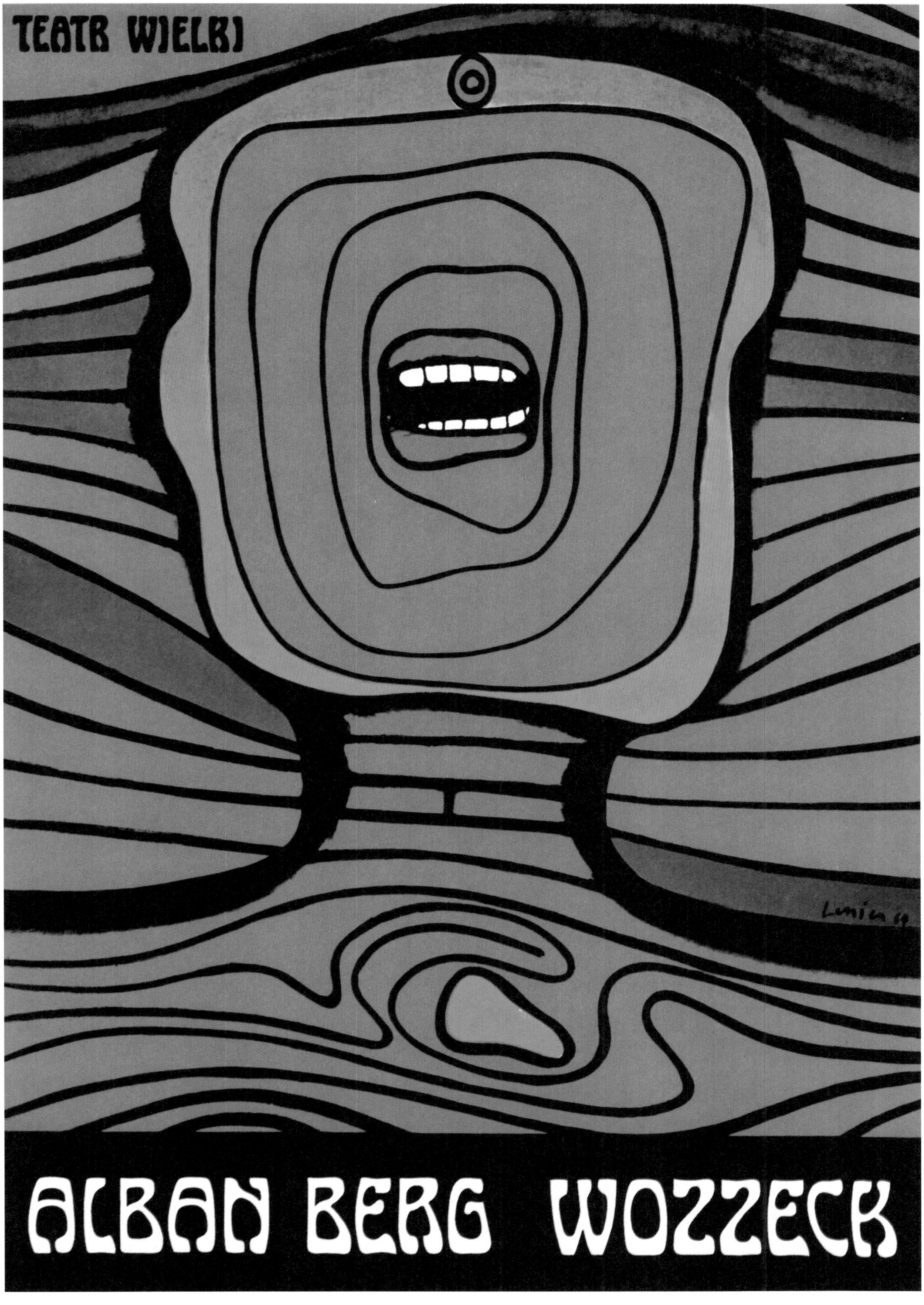

● **1964 . WOZZECK .** Poster . Jan Lenica

→ p.453

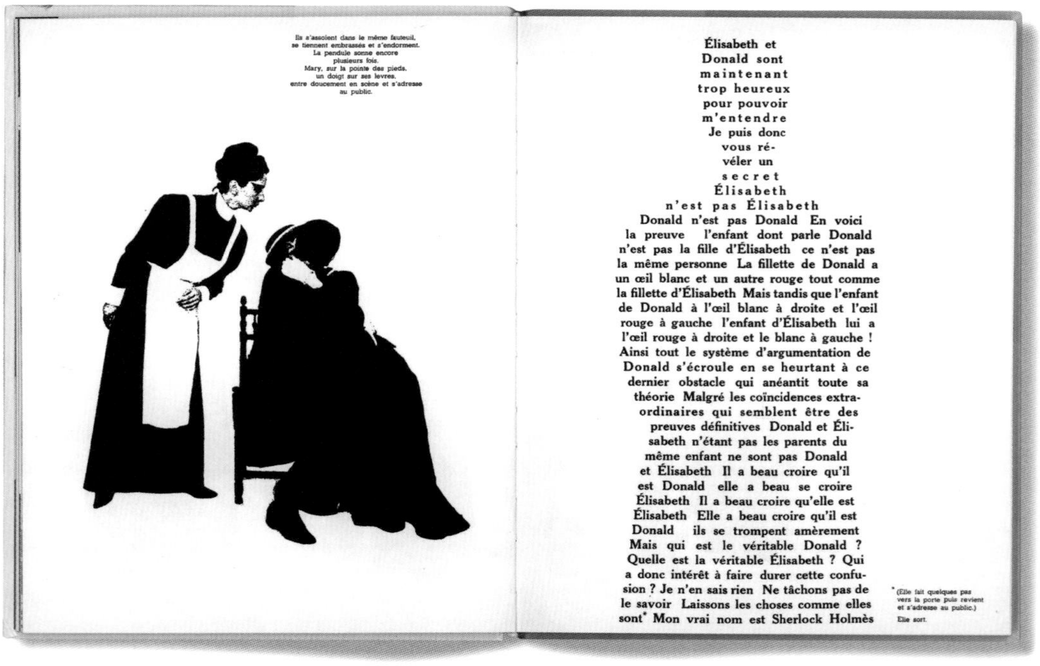

1964 . LA CANTATRICE CHAUVE, BY EUGÈNE IONESCO . Book . Robert Massin

→ p.454

● **1964 . WOOLMARK .** Logo . Franco Grignani

→ p.454

● **1964 . CAMPARI .** Poster . Bruno Munari

→ p.454

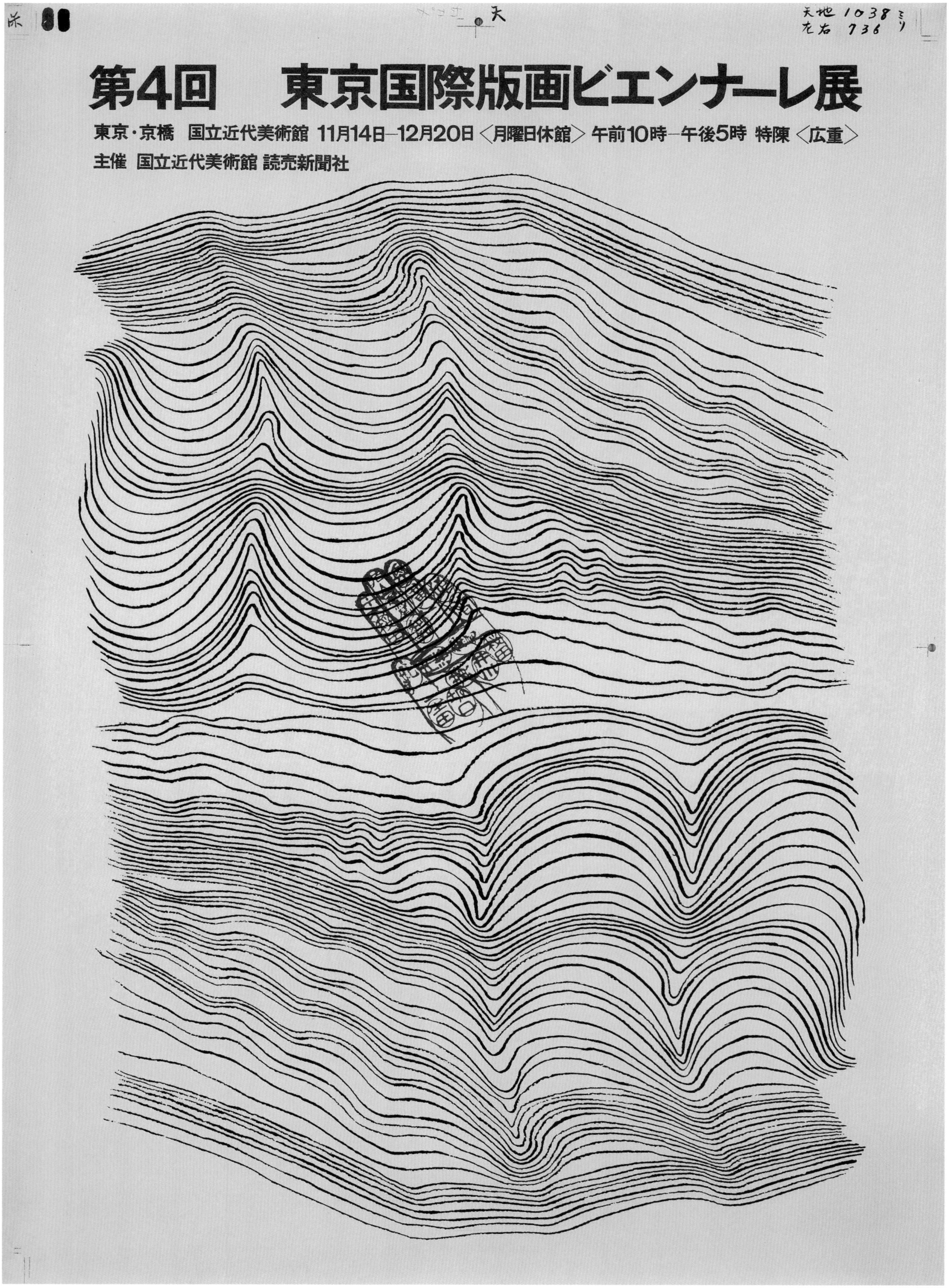
第4回　東京国際版画ビエンナーレ展
東京・京橋　国立近代美術館　11月14日—12月20日 <月曜日休館> 午前10時—午後5時　特陳 <広重>
主催　国立近代美術館 読売新聞社

● **1964 . 4TH INTERNATIONAL BIENNIAL EXHIBITION OF PRINTS IN TOKYO .** Poster . Kiyoshi Awazu

→ p.455

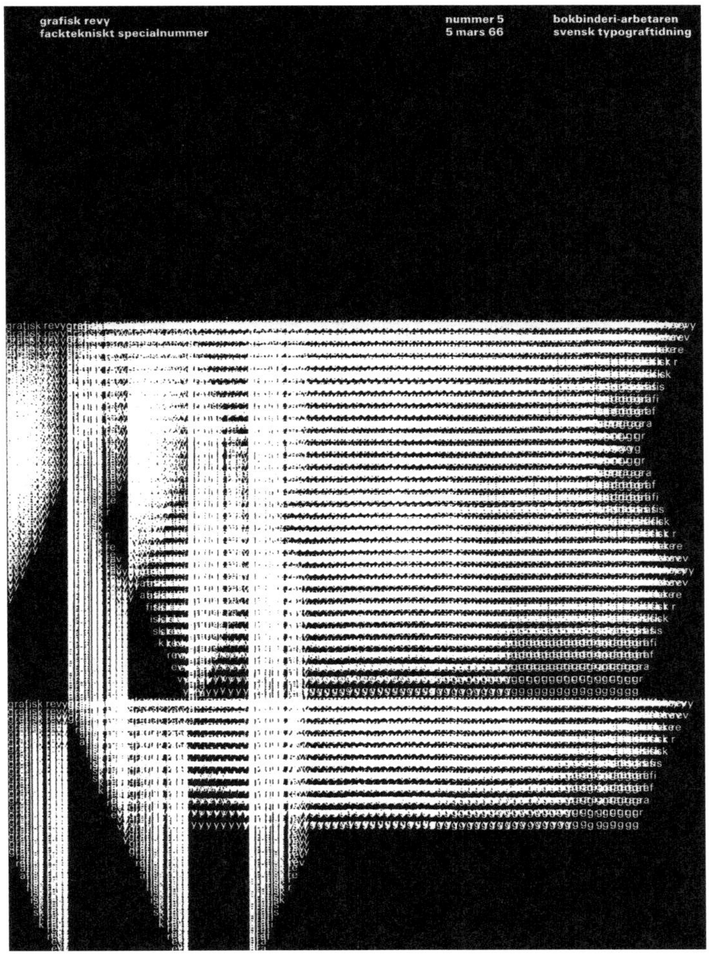

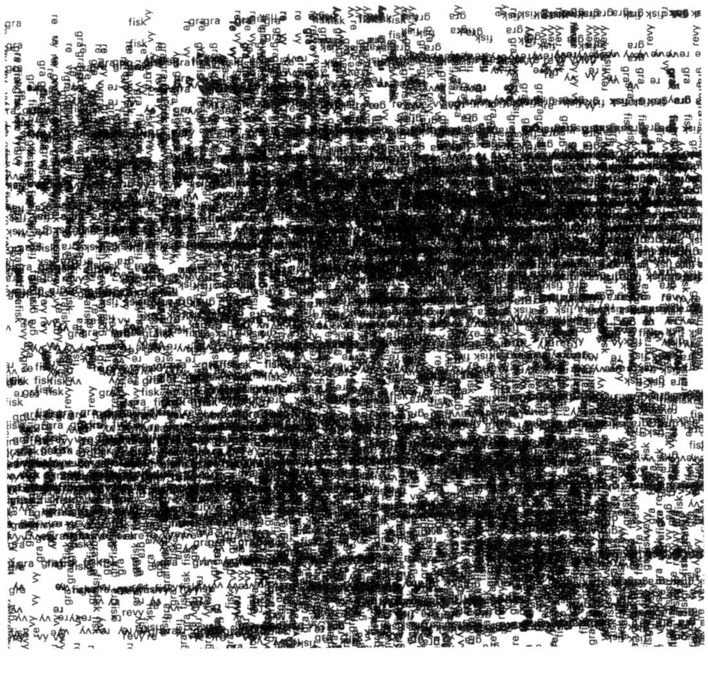

● **1964–1966 . GRAFISK REVY .** Magazine Cover . Helmut Schmid
TOP LEFT: No. 5, March 5, 1966; TOP RIGHT: No. 19, November 20, 1965; BOTTOM LEFT: No. 24, November 20, 1964; BOTTOM RIGHT: No. 9, May 5, 1965

→ p.455

TOKYO 1964
Affiche officielle des Jeux Olympiques de Tokyo 1964

1964 . 1964 TOKYO OLYMPICS . Identity . Yusaku Kamekura, Masaru Katsumi

→ p.455

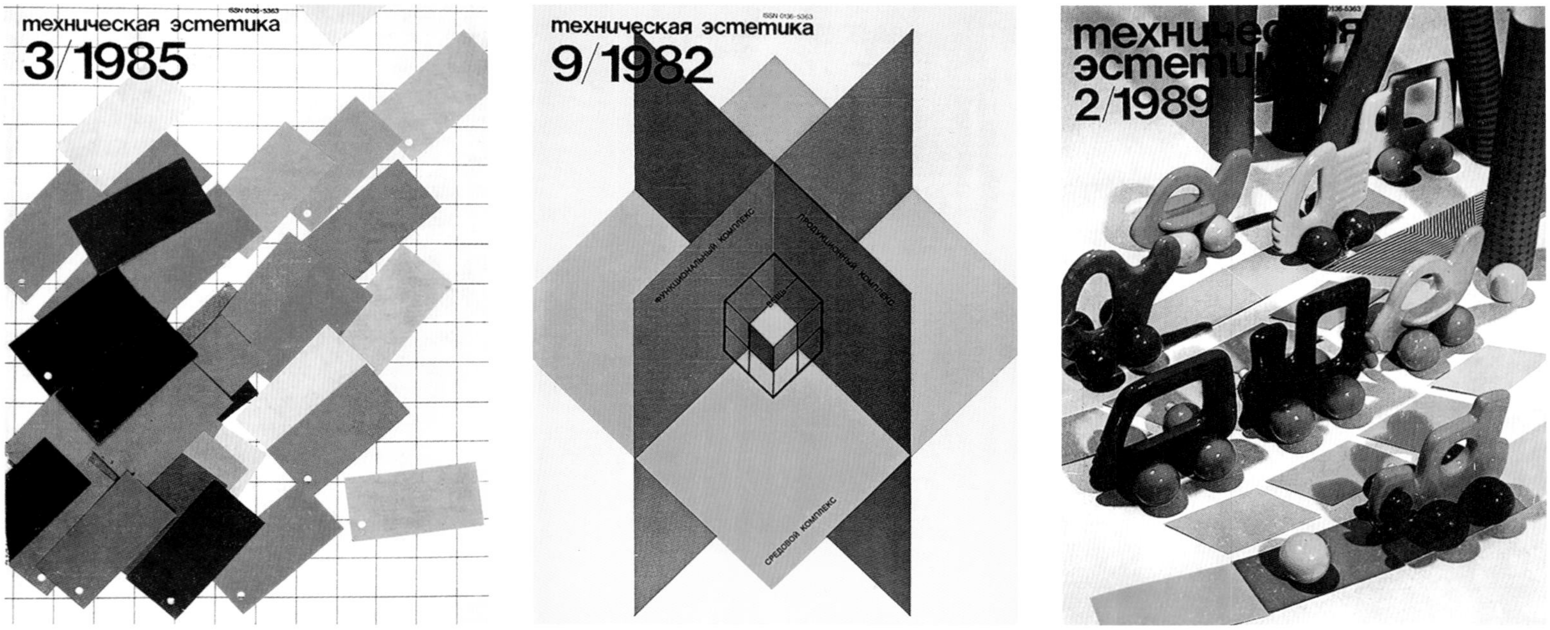

● **1964–1992 . TEKHNICHESKAYA ESTETIKA .** Magazine Cover . Various
FROM LEFT: No. 3, 1985; No. 9, 1982; No. 2, 1989

→ p.456

MoMA

The Museum of Modern Art

● **1964/2004 . MOMA .** Logo . Ivan Chermayeff, Matthew Carter

→ p.456

1965 . YOU DON'T HAVE TO BE JEWISH TO LOVE LEVY'S . Advertising . Doyle Dane Bernbach

→ p.456

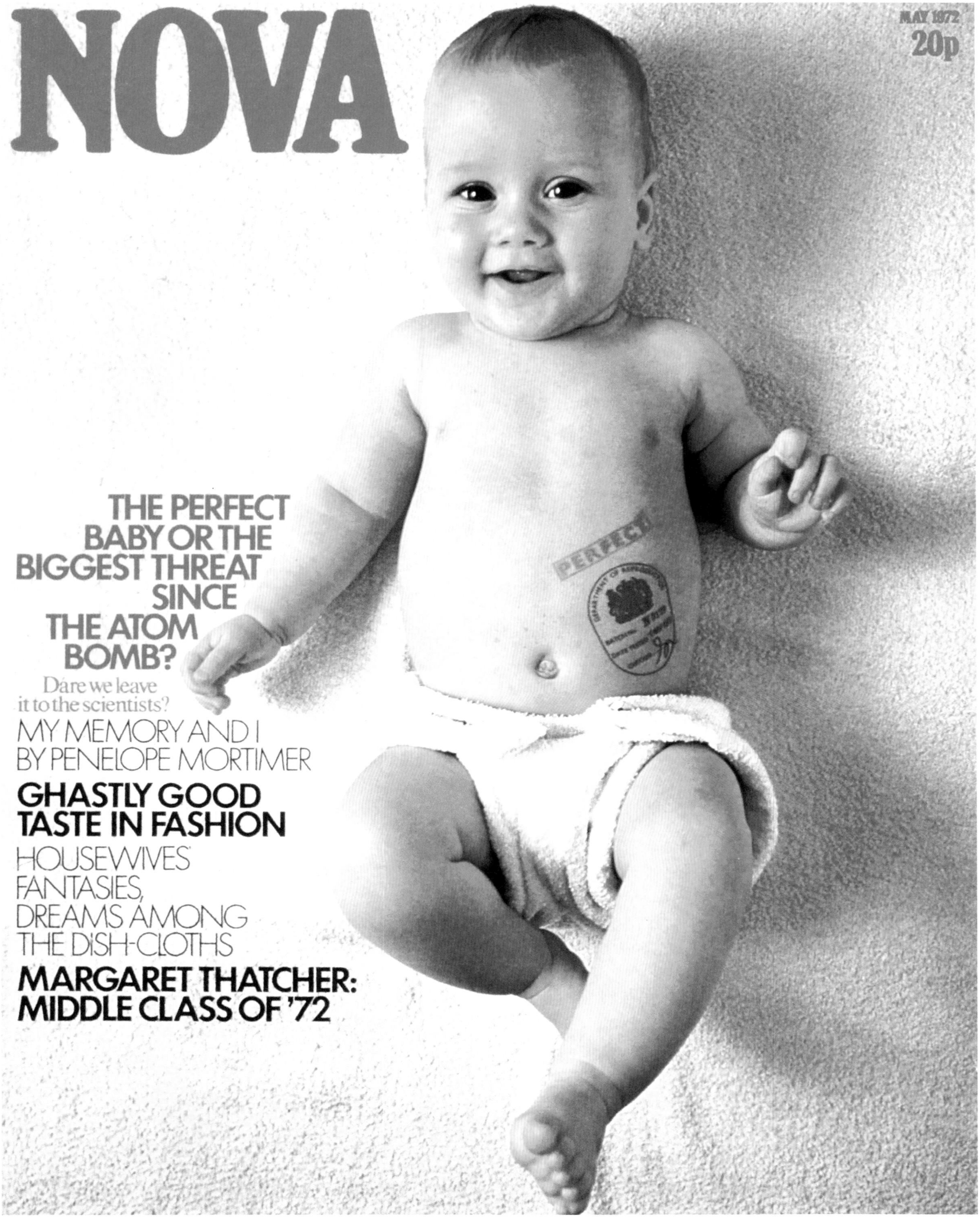
NOVA
MAY 1972
20p
THE PERFECT BABY OR THE BIGGEST THREAT SINCE THE ATOM BOMB?
Dare we leave it to the scientists?
MY MEMORY AND I BY PENELOPE MORTIMER
GHASTLY GOOD TASTE IN FASHION
HOUSEWIVES' FANTASIES, DREAMS AMONG THE DISH-CLOTHS
MARGARET THATCHER: MIDDLE CLASS OF '72
PERFECT

● **1965–1975 . NOVA .** Magazine / Newspaper . Harri Peccinotti et al.
David Hillman, photograph Tony Evans, May 1972

→ p.457

● **1965 . ASAHI STINY BEER .** Poster . Kazumasa Nagai

→ p.457

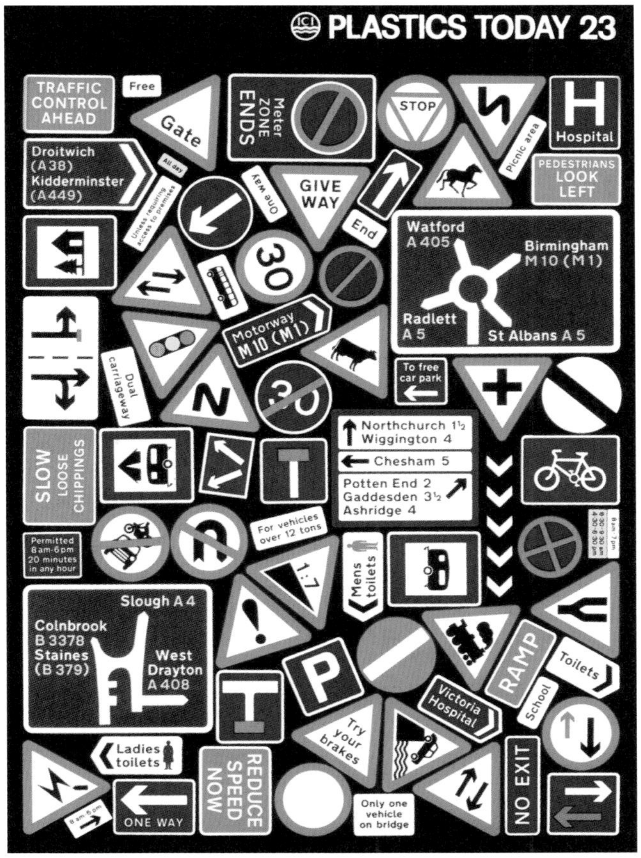

● **1965 . PLASTICS TODAY .** Magazine / Newspaper . Colin Forbes
No. 23, 1965

→ p.457

Mobil

● **1965 . MOBIL .** Identity . Ivan Chermayeff, Tom Geismar

→ p.458

● **1965 . TADANORI YOKOO: HAVING REACHED A CLIMAX AT THE AGE OF 29, I WAS DEAD .** Poster . Tadanori Yokoo

→ p.458

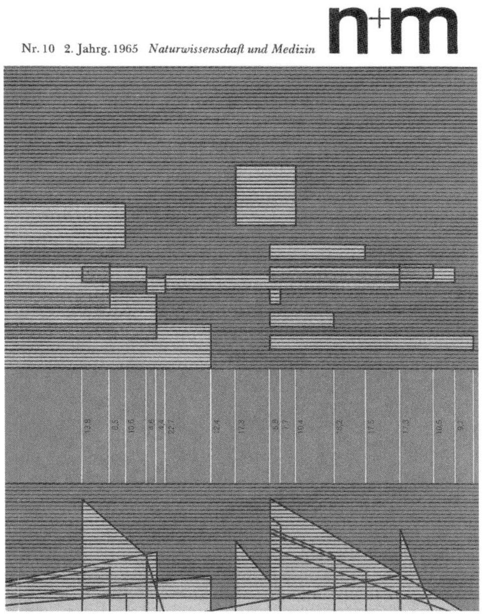

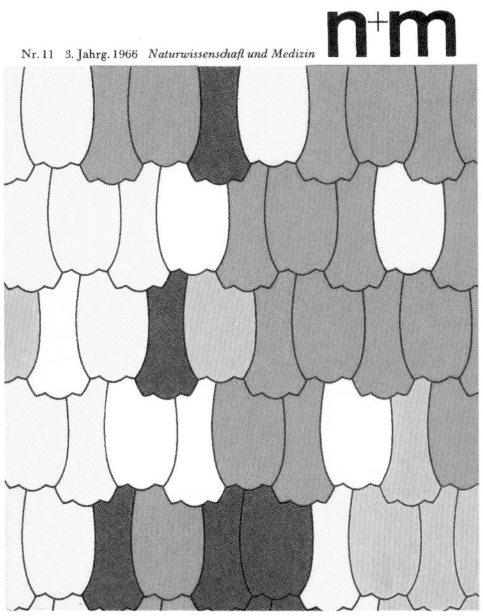

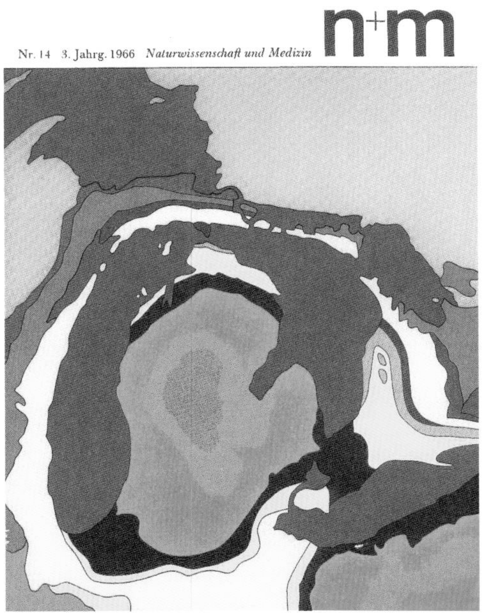

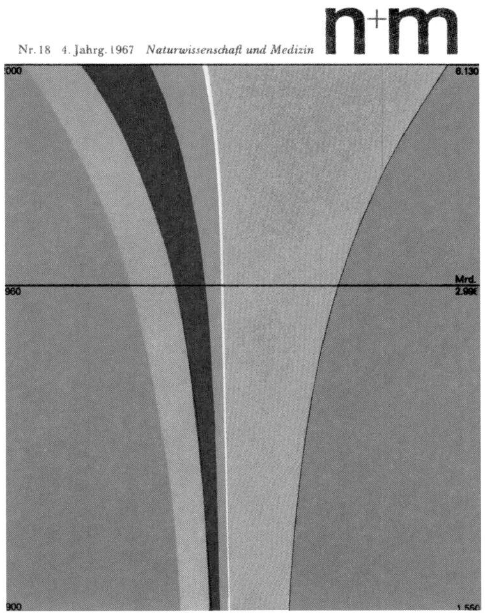

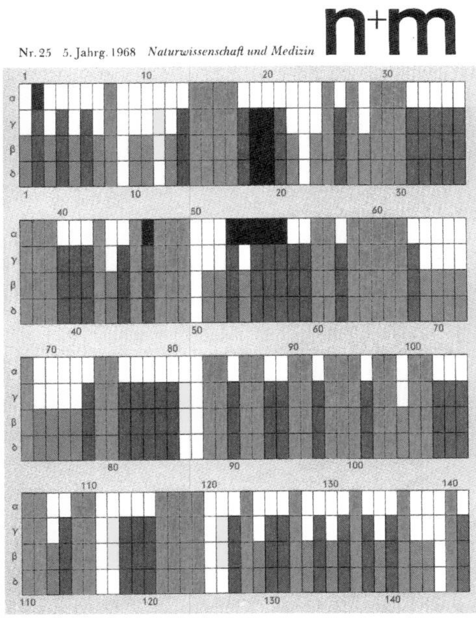

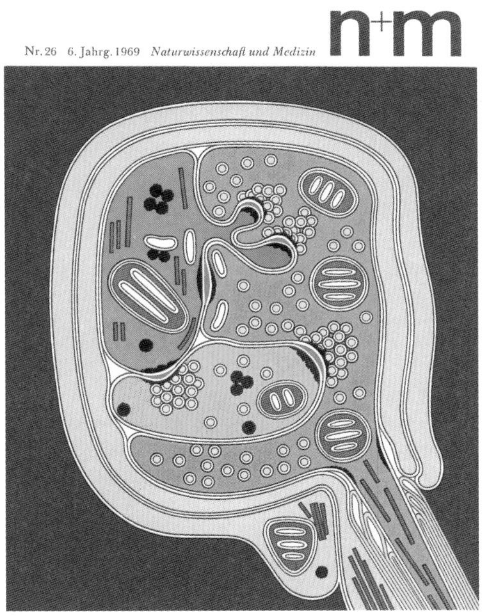

● **1965–1972 . N+M .** Magazine Cover . Erwin Poell
FROM TOP ROW, LEFT TO RIGHT: Vol. 2, No. 10, 1965; Vol. 3, No. 11, 1966; Vol. 3, No. 14, 1966; Vol. 4, No. 18, 1967; Vol. 5, No. 23, 1968; Vol. 5, No. 25, 1968; Vol. 6, No. 26, 1969; Vol. 6, No. 29, 1969; Vol. 8, No. 37, 1971

→ p.458

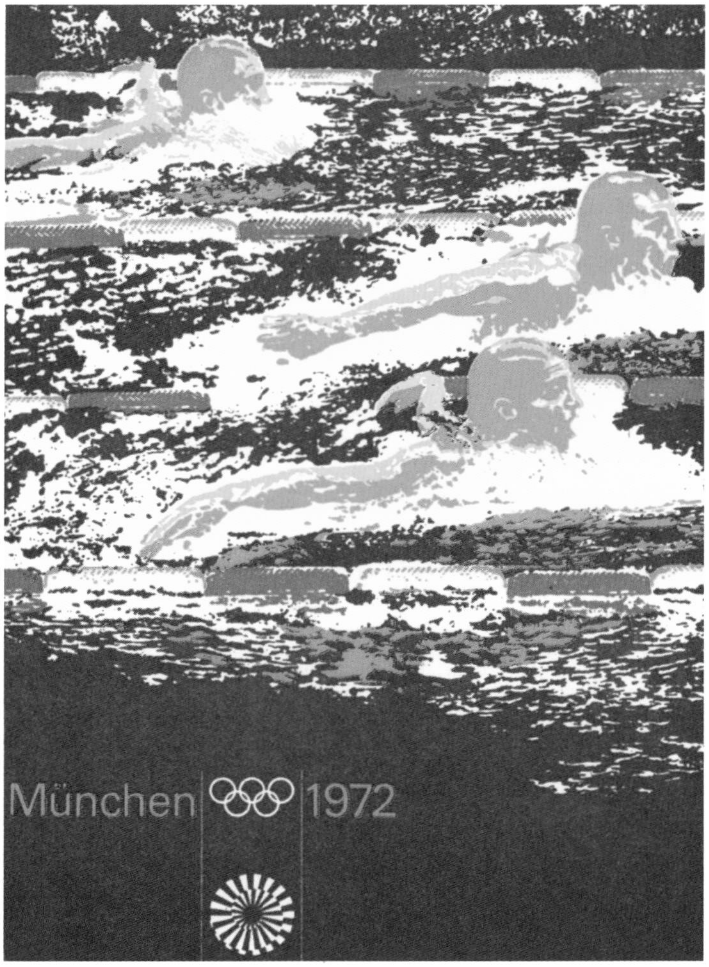

● **1966–1972 . 1972 MUNICH OLYMPICS .** Identity . Otl Aicher et al.

→ p.459

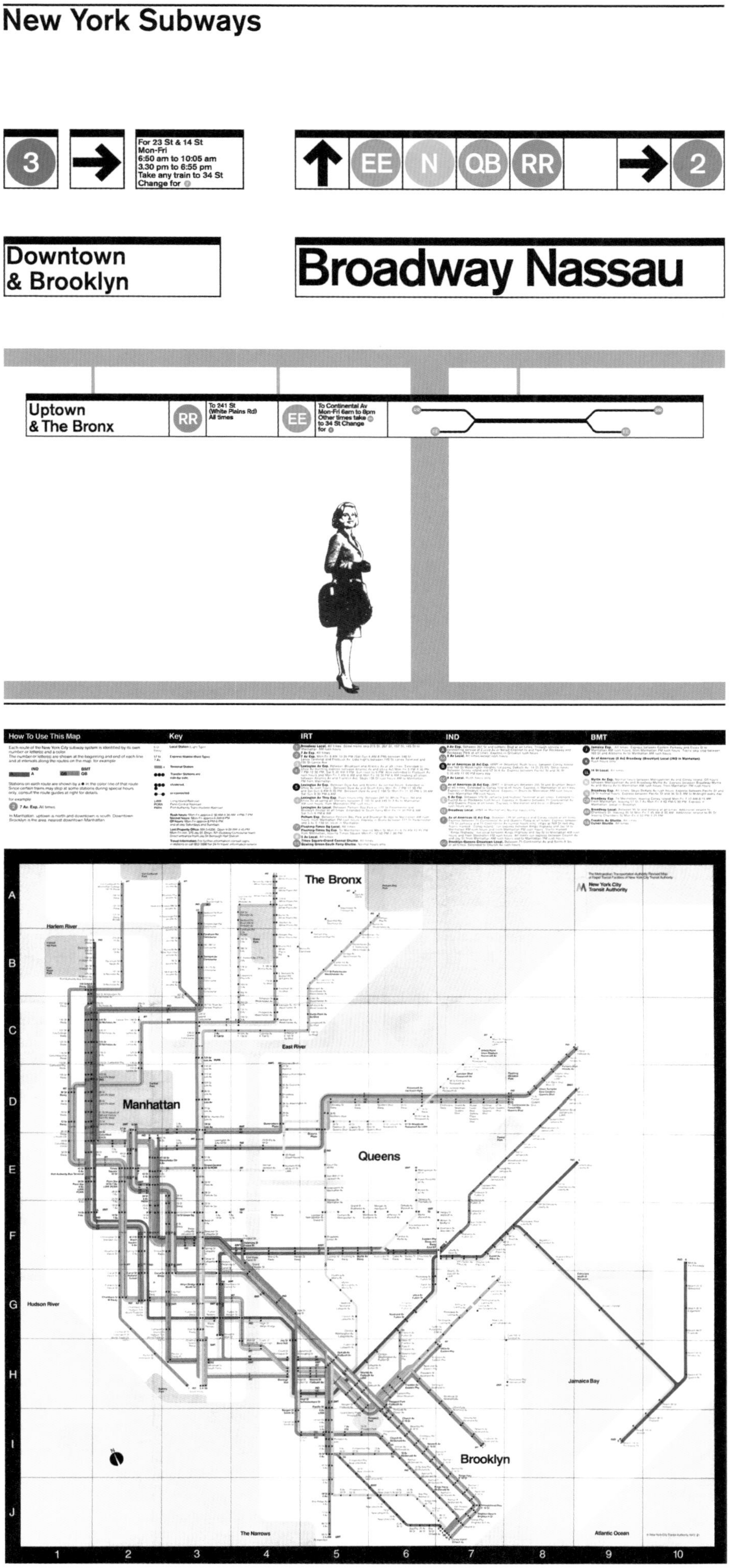

● **1966–1972 . NEW YORK SUBWAY SIGN SYSTEM AND MAP .** Information Design . Massimo Vignelli, Bob Noorda

→ p.459

● **1966–1979 . EPICUREAN .** Magazine Cover . Les Mason
FROM TOP ROW, LEFT TO RIGHT: No. 17, February 1969; No. 33, October 1971; No. 51, October–November 1974; No. 52, December–January 1974–5; No. 55, June–July 1975; No. 57, October–November 1975; No. 63, October–November 1976; No. 71, February–March 1978; No. 36, April–May 1972

→ p.459

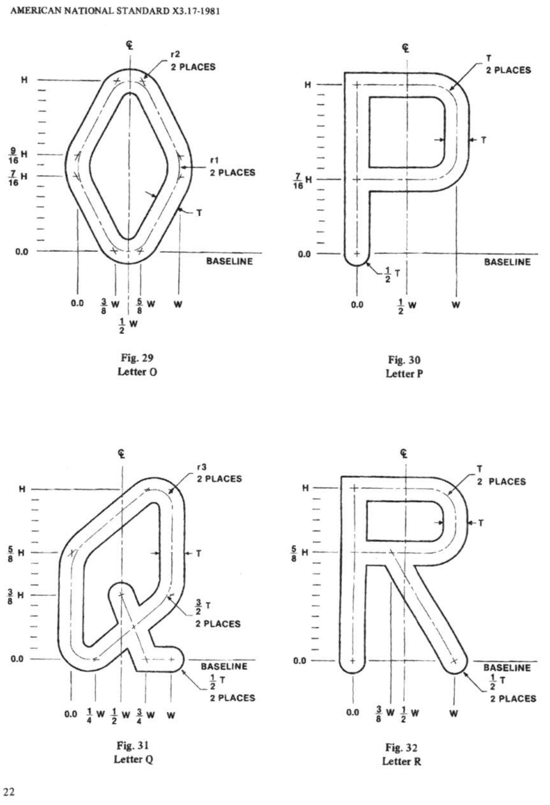

● **1966/1968 . OCR—A AND B .** Typeface . Adrian Frutiger

→ p.460

● **1967 . SABON .** Typeface . Jan Tschichold

→ p.460

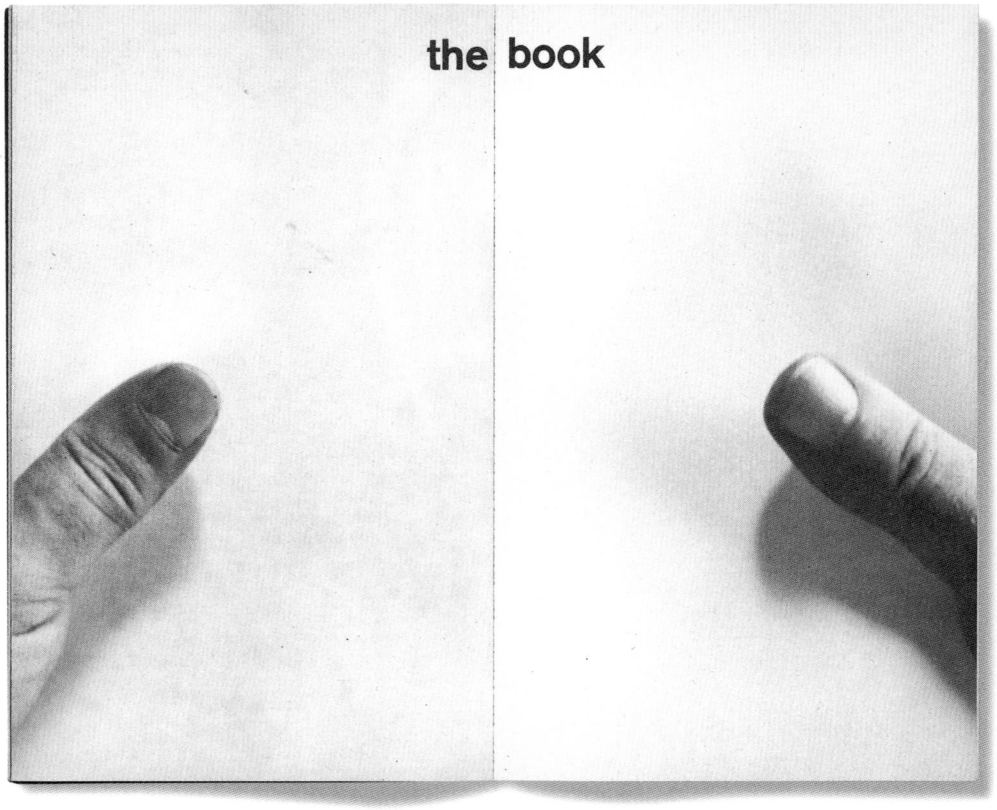

1967 . THE MEDIUM IS THE MASSAGE . Book . Quentin Fiore, Marshall McLuhan

→ p.460

1967 . TYPOGRAPHIE . Book . Emil Ruder

→ p.461

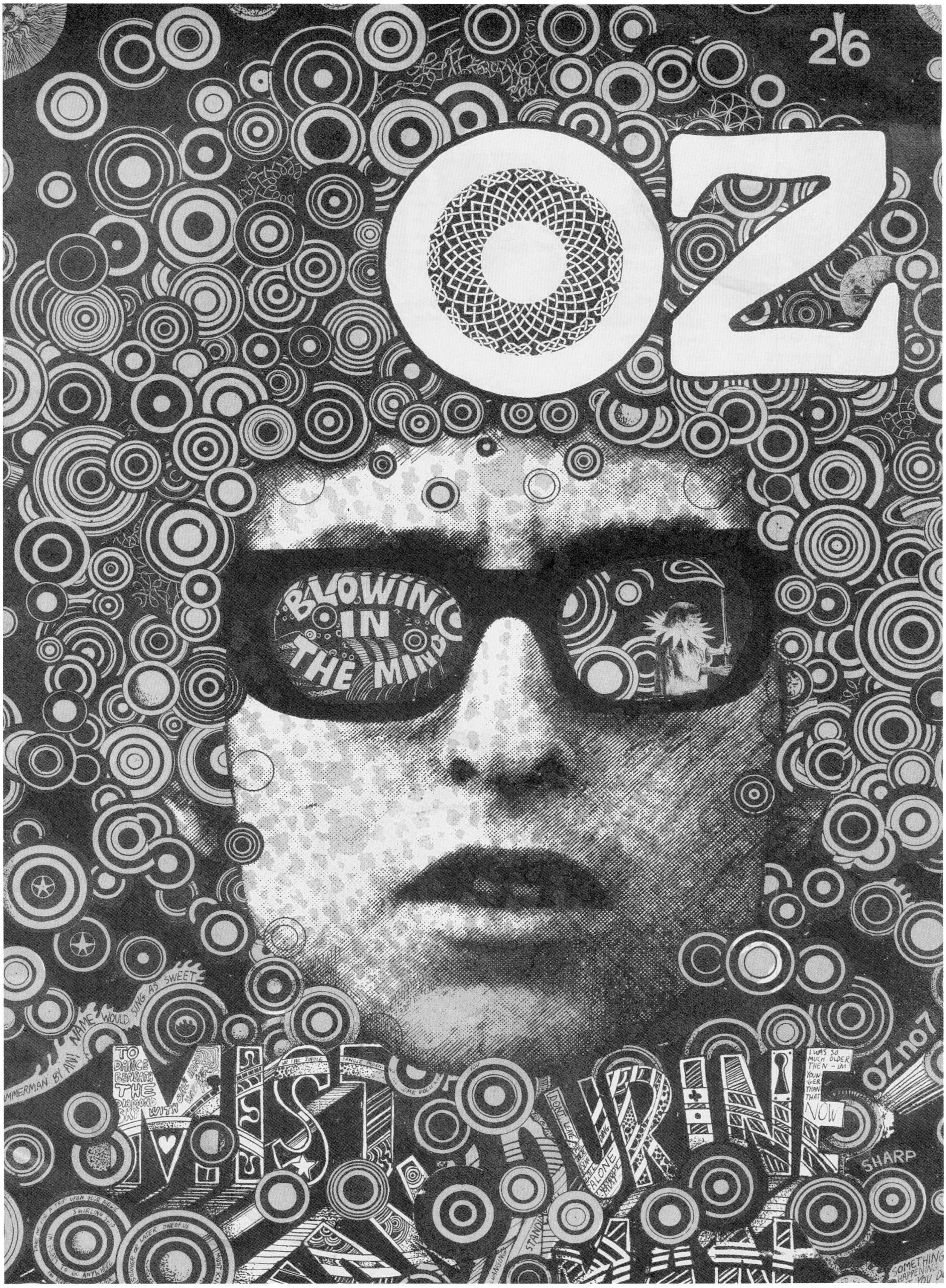

● **1967–1973 . OZ .** Magazine / Newspaper . Martin Sharp et al.
"Blowing in the Mind," No. 7, October 1967

→ p.461

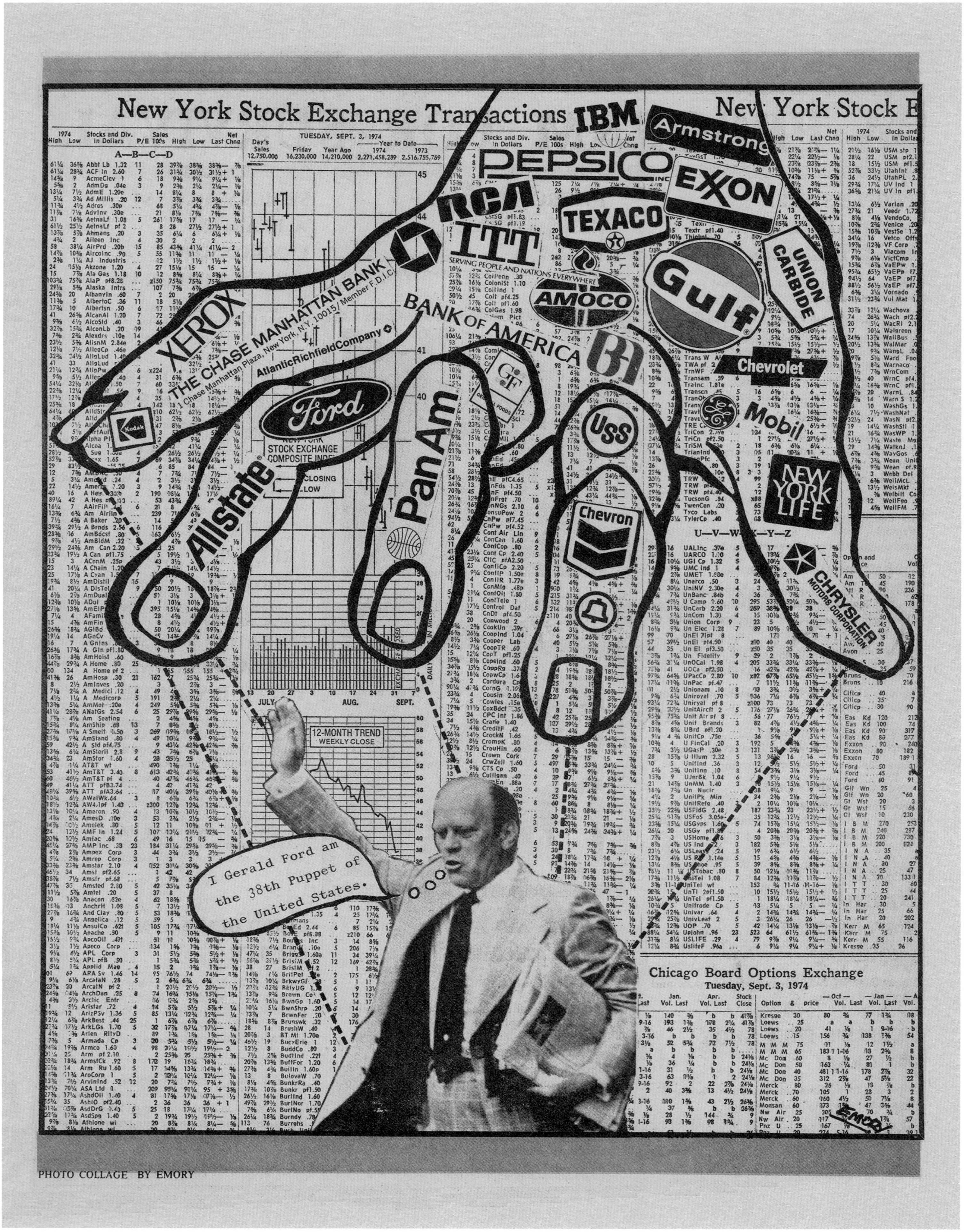

● **1967–1980 . THE BLACK PANTHER .** Magazine / Newspaper . Emory Douglas
"I Gerald Ford Am the 38th Puppet of the United States," September 21, 1974

→ p.461

● **1967 . BLACK POWER / WHITE POWER .** Poster . Tomi Ungerer

→ p.462

● **1967 . THE BEATLES—SGT. PEPPER'S LONELY HEARTS CLUB BAND .** Record / CD Cover . Peter Blake, Jann Haworth

→ p.462

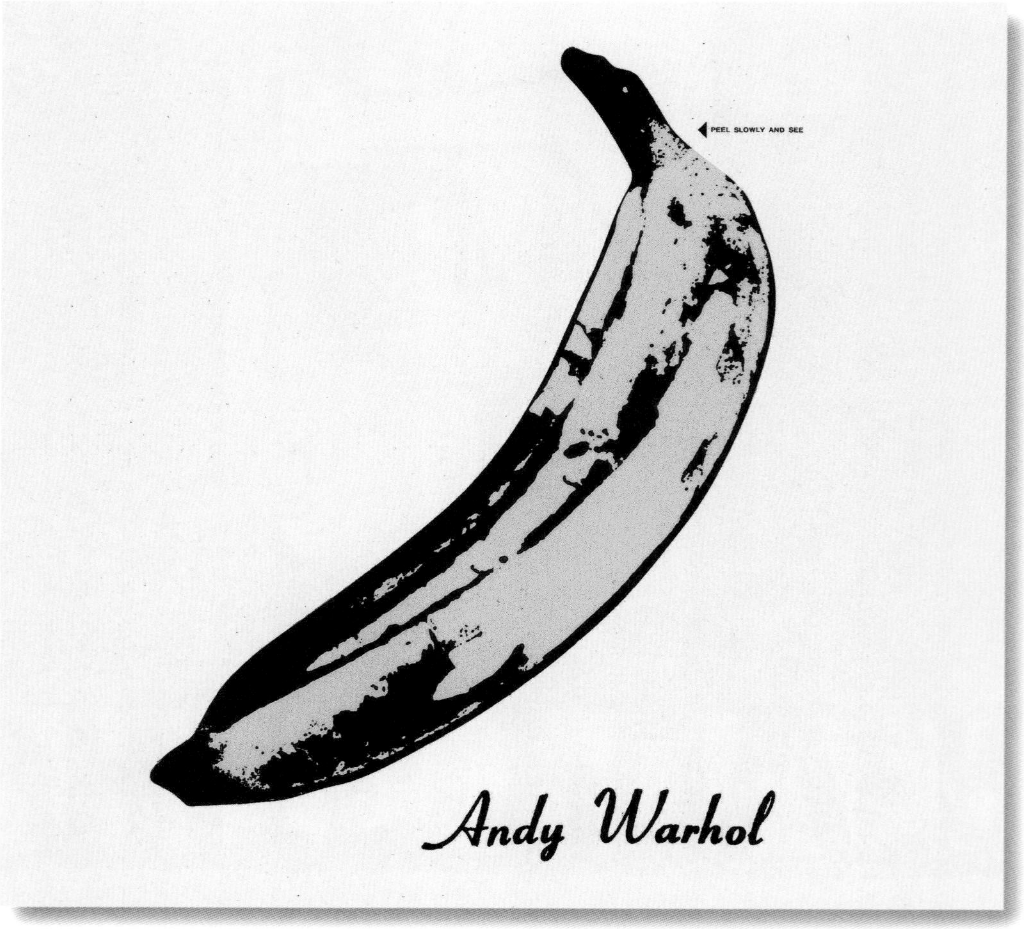

● **1967 . THE VELVET UNDERGROUND AND NICO .** Record / CD Cover . Andy Warhol

→ p.462

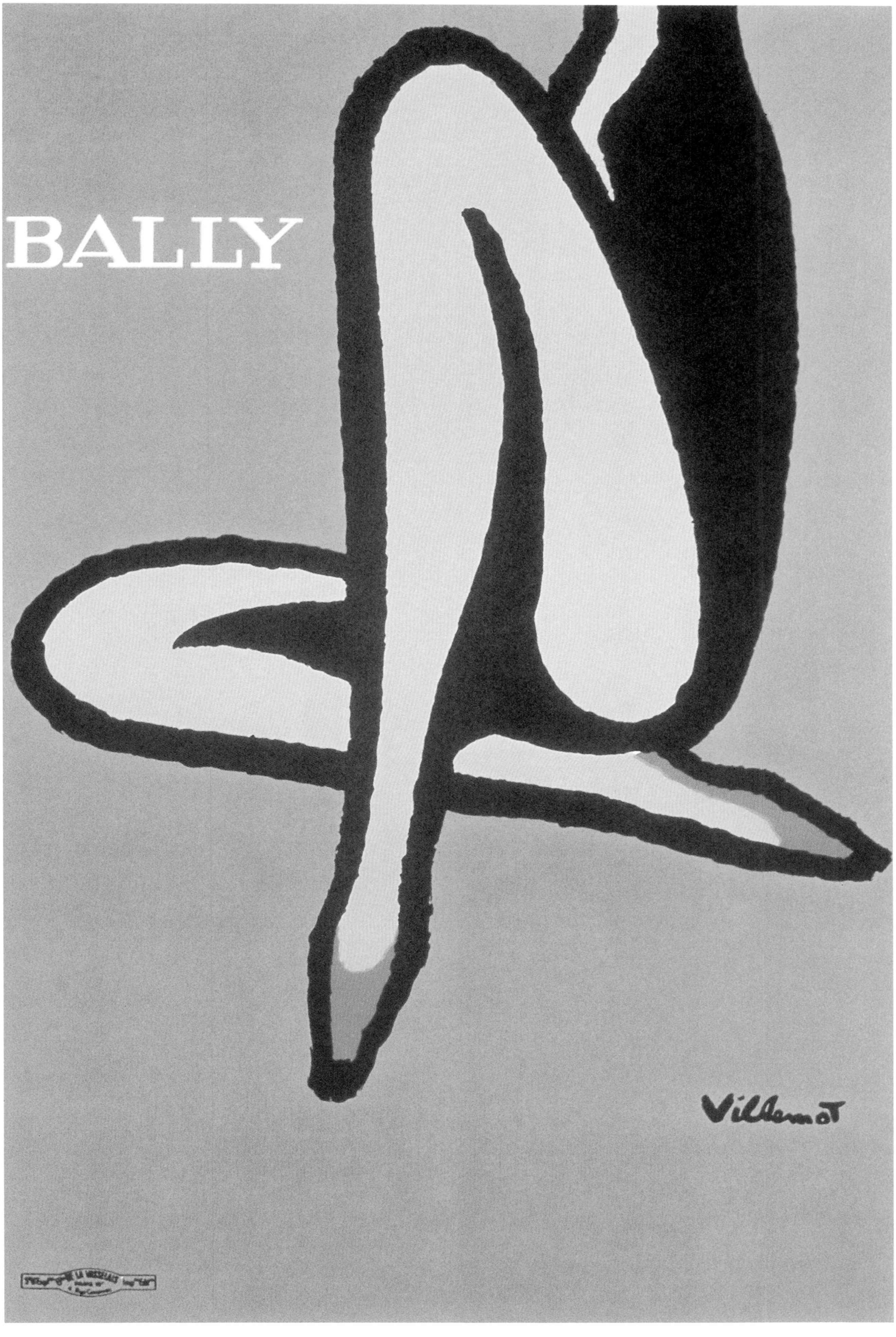

● **1967–1989 . BALLY .** Poster . Bernard Villemot

→ p.463

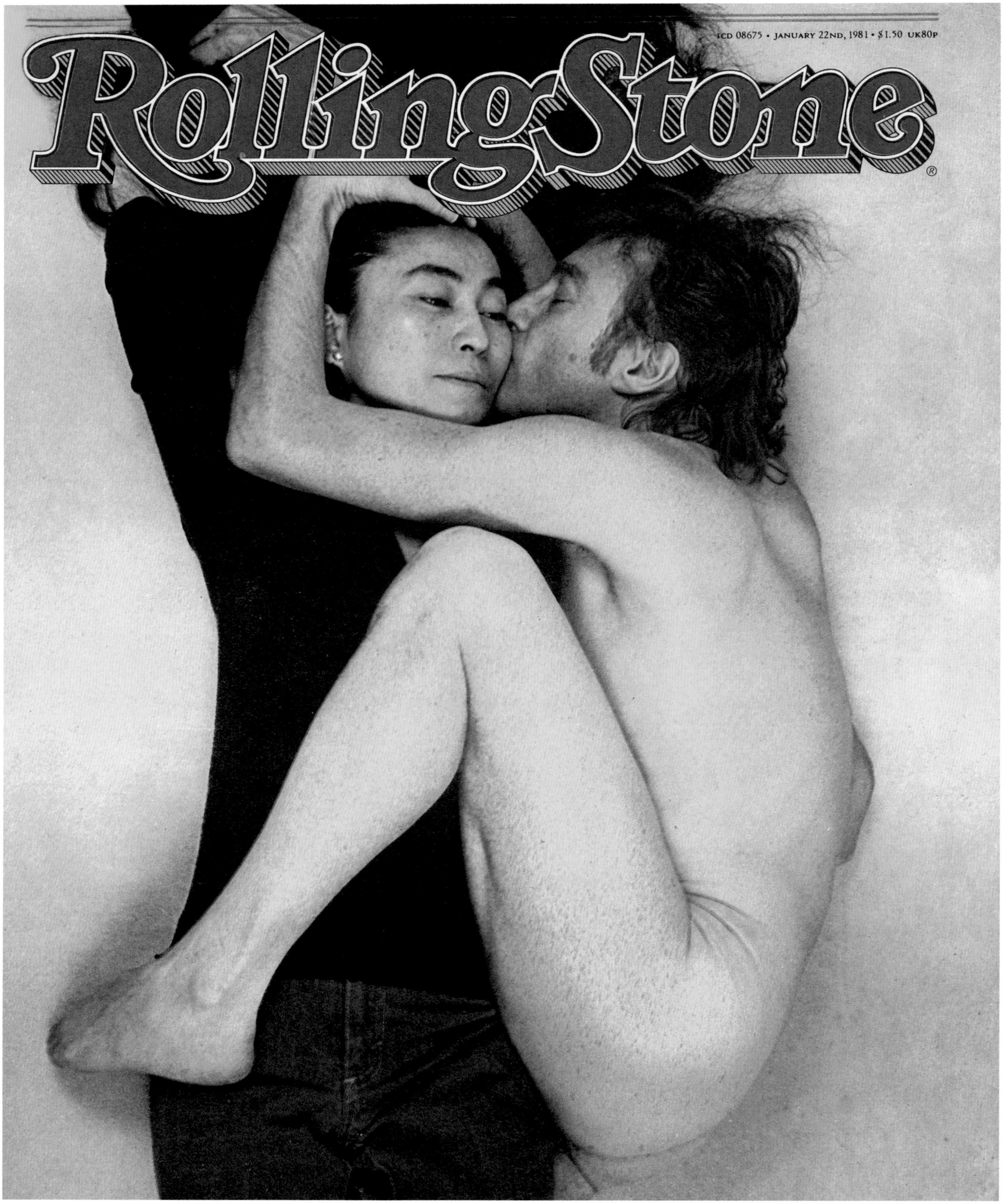

● **1967–1982 . ROLLING STONE .** Magazine Cover . Various
Photograph Annie Leibovitz, January 22, 1981

→ p.463

Knoll

● **1967 . KNOLL .** Logo . Massimo Vignelli

→ p.463

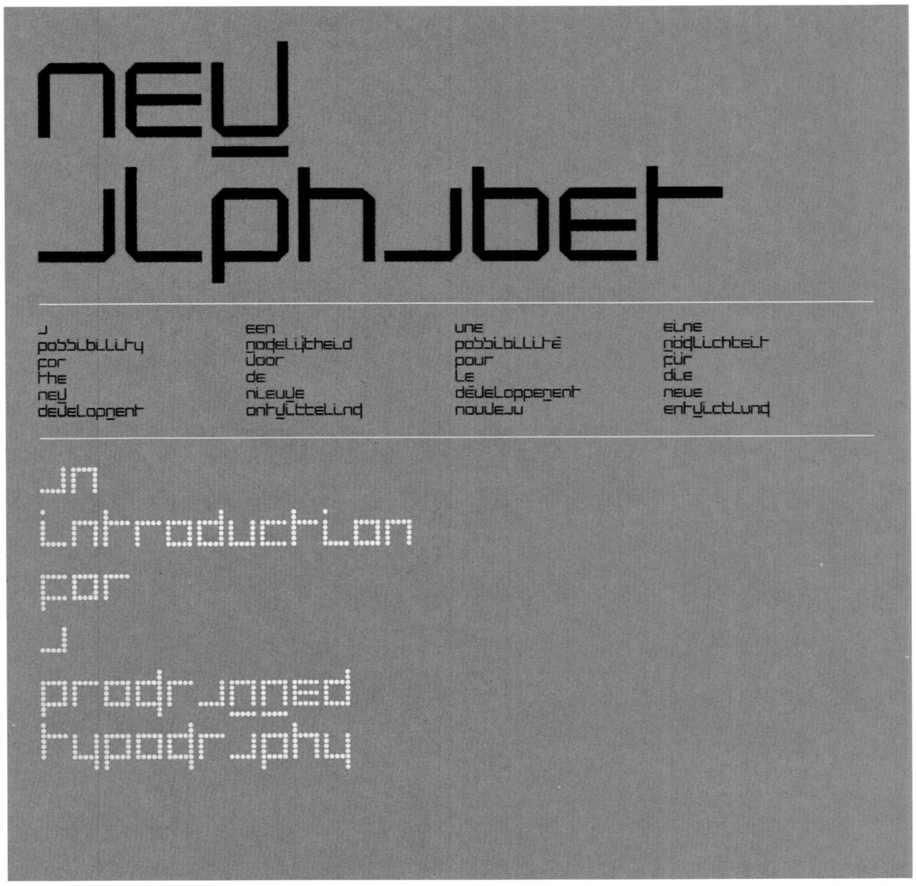

● **1967 . NEW ALPHABET .** Typeface . Wim Crouwel

→ p.464

● **1968 . ATELIER POPULAIRE .** Poster . Atelier Populaire

→ p.464

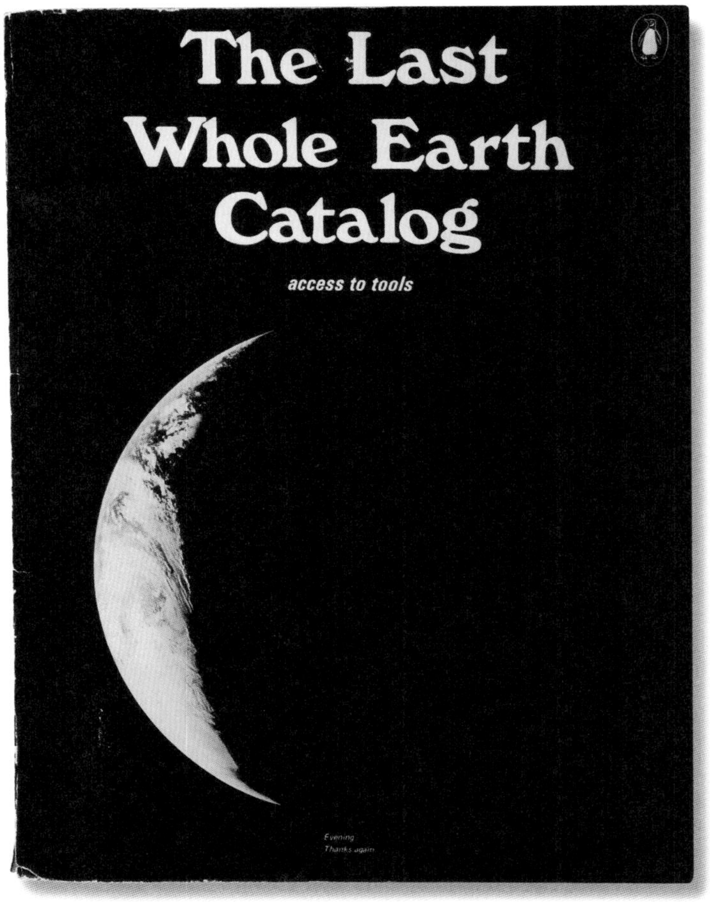

● **1968–1975 . WHOLE EARTH CATALOG: ACCESS TO TOOLS .** Book . Stewart Brand

→ p.464

● **1968–1971 . AVANT GARDE .** Magazine / Newspaper . Herb Lubalin
No. 6, January 1969

→ p.465

1968 . VORMGEVERS . Poster . Wim Crouwel

→ p.465

ABCDEFGHIJKLMN
OPQRSTUVWXYZ&
abcdefghijklmnopqrs
tuvwxyzß1234567890
You may ask w
hy so many differen
t typefaces. They all serve th
e same purpose but they express man's
diversity. It is the same diversity we find in wine. I once saw
a list of Médoc wines featuring sixty different Médocs all of
the same year. All of them were wines but each was differen
t from the others. It's the nuances that are important. The s
ame is true for typefaces. Sie fragen sich, warum es notwen
dig ist, so viele Schriften zur Verfügung zu haben. Sie dienen alle zum selben, aber m
achen die Vielfalt des Menschen aus. Diese Vielfalt ist wie beim Wein. Ich habe einmal
eine Weinkarte studiert mit sechzig Médoc-Weinen aus dem selben Jahr. Das ist ausna
hmslos Wein, aber doch nicht alles der gleiche Wein. Es hat eben gleichwohl Nuancen.
So ist es auch mit der Schrift. You may ask why so many different typefaces. They all s
erve the same purpose but they express man's diversity. It is the same diversity we fin
d in wine. I once saw a list of Médoc wines featuring sixty different Médocs all of the
same year. All of them were wines but each was different from the others.
It's the nuances that are important. The same is true for typefaces. Pourquoi
tant d'Alphabets différents! Tous servent au même but, mais aussi à exprimer
la diversité de l'homme. C'est cette même diversité que nous retrouvons da
ns les vins de Médoc. J'ai pu, un jour, relever soixante crus, tous de la même
année. Il s'agissait certes de vins, mais tous étaient différents. Tout est dans
la nuance du bouquet. Il en est de même pour les caractères! Sie fragen sich,
warum es notwendig ist, so viele Schriften zur Verfügung zu haben. Sie die
nen alle zum selben, aber machen die Vielfalt
der Menschen aus. Diese Vielfalt ist wie beim
Wein. Ich habe einmal eine Weinkarte studiert
mit sechzig Médoc-Weinen aus dem selben Jah
r. Das ist ausnahmslos Wein, aber doch nicht al
les der gleiche Wein. Es hat eben gleichwohl N
uancen. So ist es auch mit der Schrift. You may
ask why so many different typefaces. They all s
erve the same purpose but they express man's
divesity. It is the same diversity we fi nd in win

● **1968 . FRUTIGER .** Typeface . Adrian Frutiger

→ p.465

● **1968 . 1968 MEXICO CITY OLYMPICS .** Identity . Lance Wyman, Peter Murdoch, et al.

→ p.466

● **1968 . DAY OF THE HEROIC GUERRILLA .** Poster . Elena Serrano

→ p.466

● **1969–1971 . KUNST DER SECHZIGER JAHRE .** Book . Wolf Vostell

→ p.466

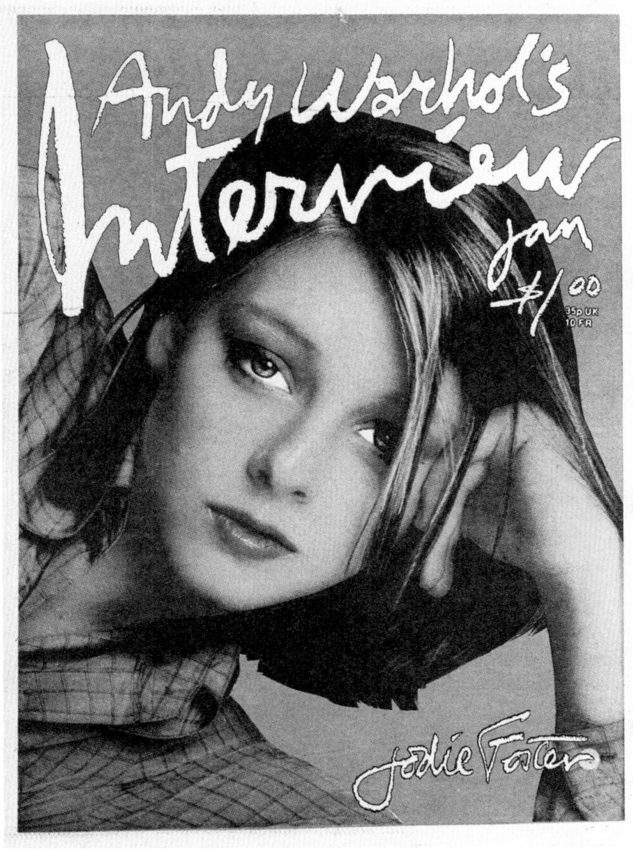

● **1969–1987 . INTERVIEW .** Magazine / Newspaper . Andy Warhol, Richard Bernstein
January 1977

→ p.467

● **1969 . VALENTINE .** Poster . Milton Glaser

→ p.467

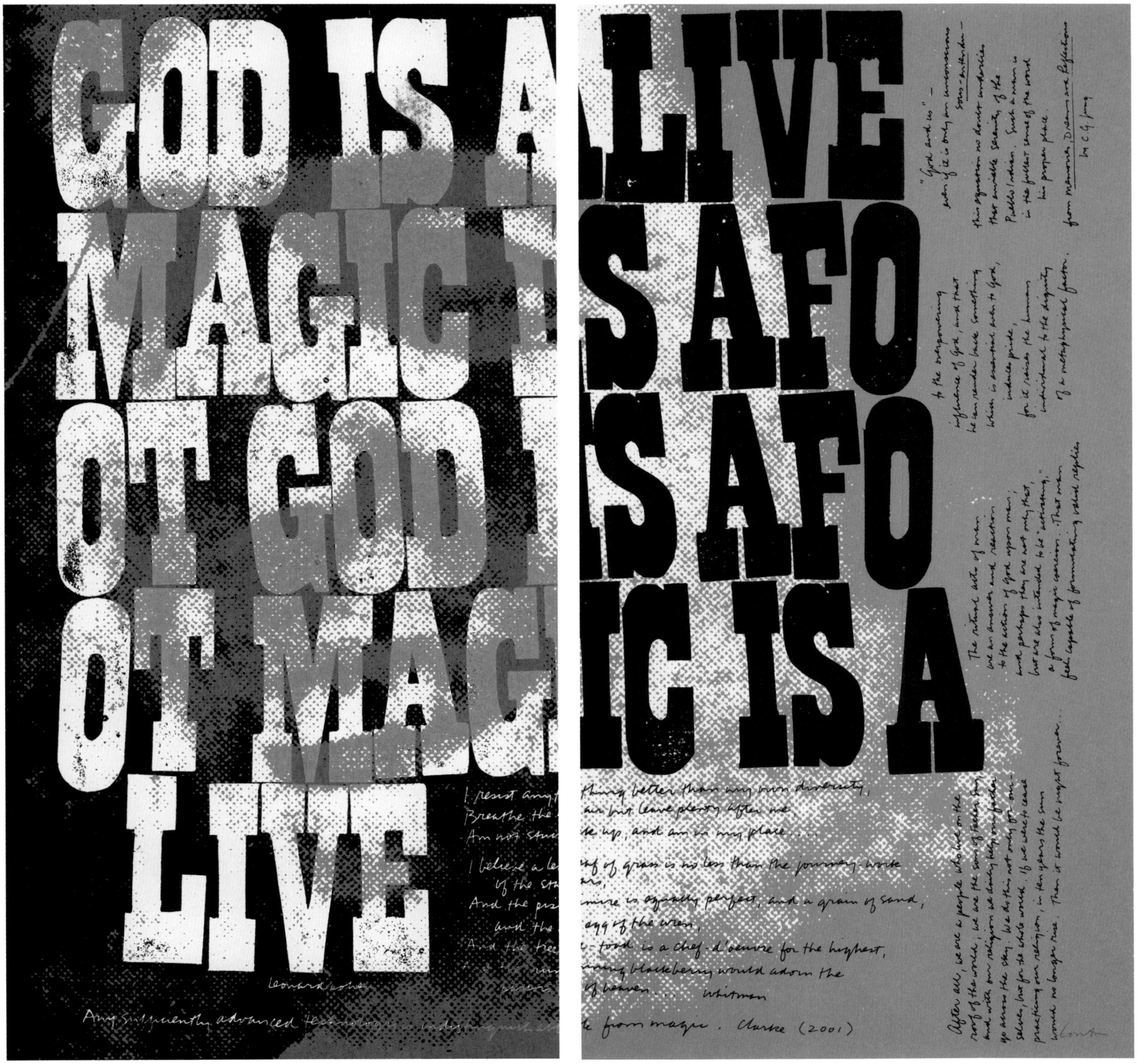

● **1969 . GOD IS ALIVE (PARTS 1 AND 2) .** Poster . Corita Kent

→ p.467

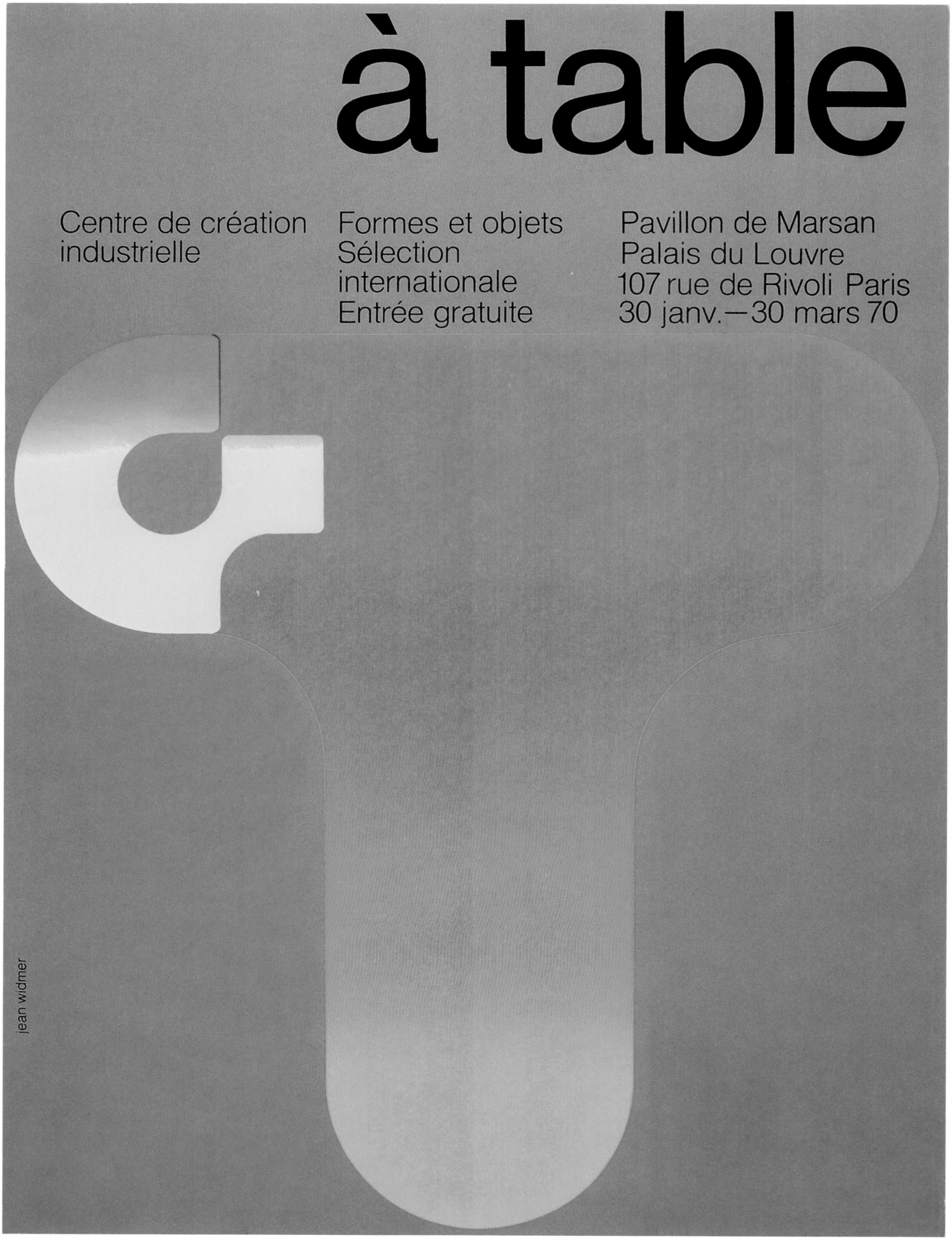

à table
Centre de création industrielle
Formes et objets Sélection internationale Entrée gratuite
Pavillon de Marsan Palais du Louvre 107 rue de Rivoli Paris 30 janv.—30 mars 70
jean widmer

● **1969–1972 . CENTRE DE CRÉATION INDUSTRIELLE .** Poster . Jean Widmer

→ p.468

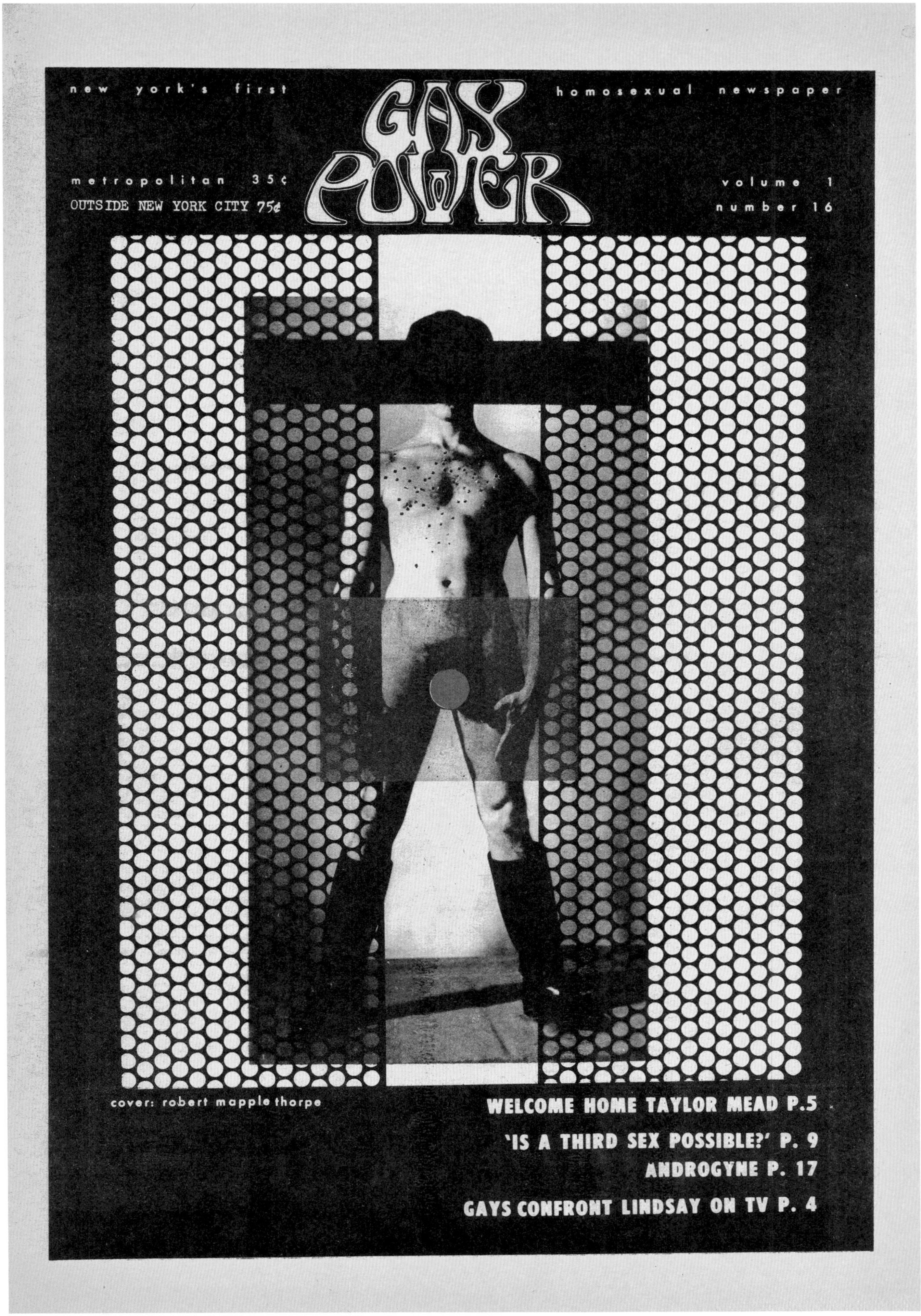

● **1969–1970 . GAY POWER .** Magazine / Newspaper . John Heys et al.
Artwork Robert Mapplethorpe, *Bull's Eye*, 1970, Vol. 1, No. 16, 1970

→ p.468

15 settembre-13 ottobre 1969
28° festival internazionale del teatro di prosa
la Biennale di Venezia

● **1969 . LA BIENNALE DI VENEZIA .** Poster . A. G. Fronzoni

→ p.468

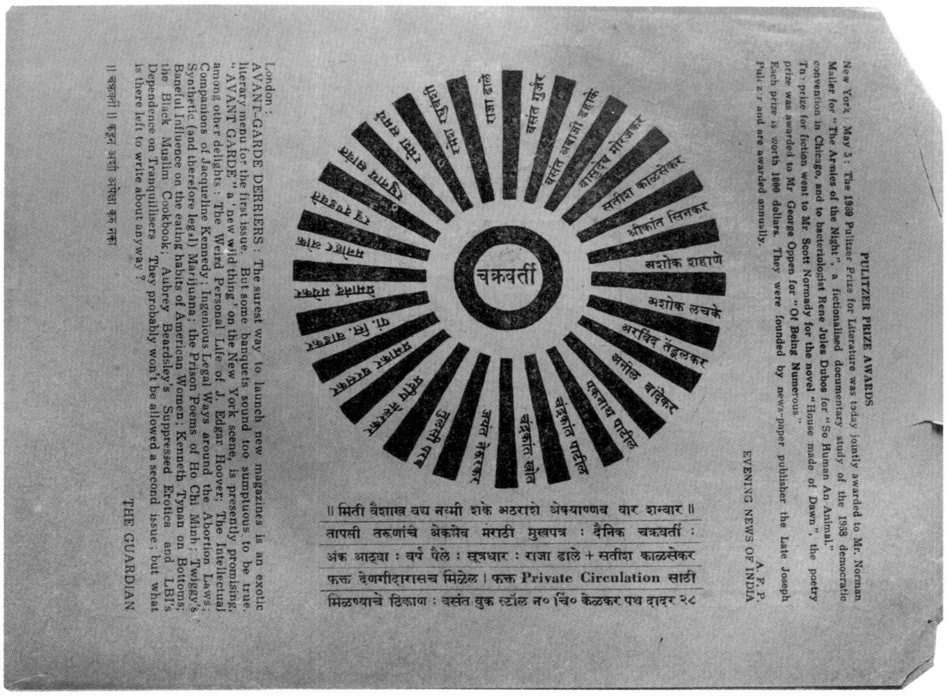

PULITZER PRIZE AWARDS

New York : May 5 : The 1969 Pulitzer Prize for Literature was today jointly awarded to Mr. Norman Mailer for "The Armies of the Night", a fictionalised documentary study of the 1968 democratic convention in Chicago, and to bacteriologist Rene Jules Dubos for "So Human An Animal."
The prize for fiction went to Mr Scott Normady for the novel "House made of Dawn", the poetry prize was awarded to Mr George Oppen for "Of Being Numerous."
Each prize is worth 1000 dollars. They were founded by news-paper publisher the Late Joseph Pulitzer and are awarded annually.

A. F. P.
EVENING NEWS OF INDIA

॥ मिती वैशाख वद्य नवमी शके अठराशे ऐक्याण्णव वार शन्वार ॥
तापसी तरूणांचे ऐकमेव मराठी मुखपत्र : दैनिक चक्रवर्ती :
अंक आठवा : वर्ष पैले : सूत्रधार : राजा ढाले + सतीश काळसेकर
फक्त देणगीदारासच मिळेल । फक्त Private Circulation साठी
मिळण्याचे ठिकाण : वसंत बुक स्टॉल नं० चिं० केळकर पथ दादर २८

London :
AVANT-GARDE DERRIERS : The surest way to launch new magazines is an exotic literary menu for the first issue. But some banquets sound too sumptuous to be true. "AVANT GARDE" a 'new wild thing' on the New York scene, is presently promising, among other delights : The Weird Personal Life of J. Edgar Hoover; The Intellectual Companions of Jacqueline Kennedy; Ingenious Legal Ways around the Abortion Laws; Synthetic (and therefore legal) Marijuana; the Prison Poems of Ho Chi Minh; Twiggy's Baneful Influence on the eating habits of American Women; Kenneth Tynan on Bottoms; the Black Muslim Cookbook; Aubrey Beardsley's Suppressed Erotica and LBI's Dependence on Tranquillisers They probably won't be allowed a second issue; but what is there left to write about anyway ?

THE GUARDIAN

॥ चक्रवर्ती ॥ कहून अशी अपेक्षा करू नका

● **1970s . CHAKRAVARTY .** Magazine / Newspaper . Raja Dhale
No. 8

→ p.469

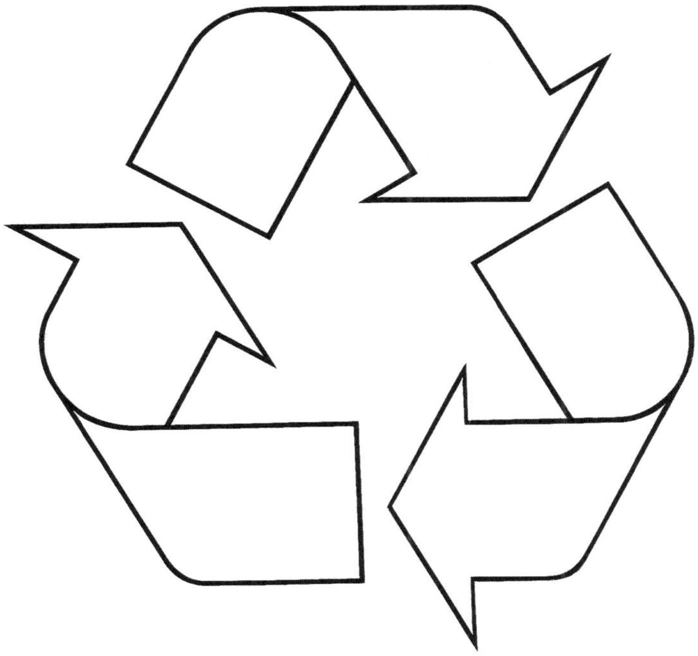

● **1970 . RECYCLING .** Information Design . Gary Anderson

→ p.469

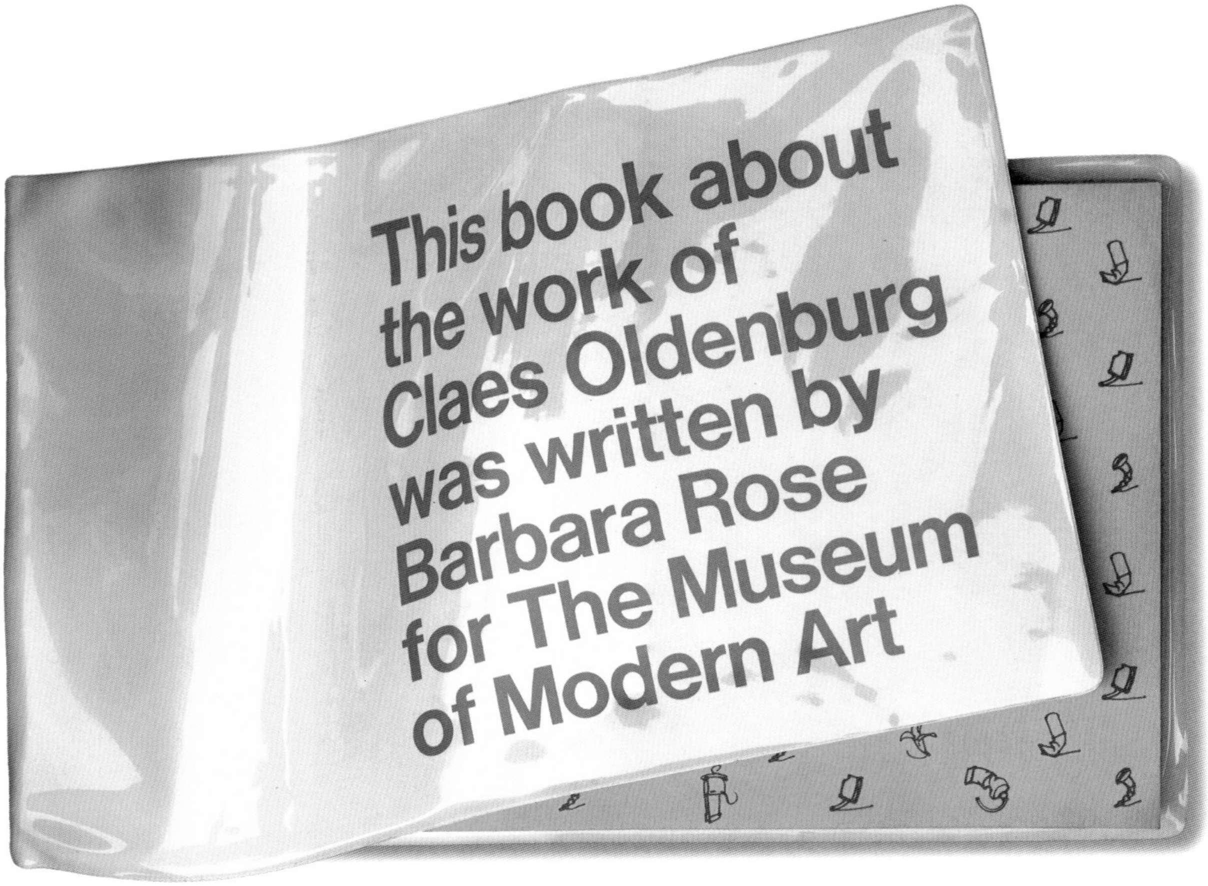

● **1970 . CLAES OLDENBURG .** Book . Ivan Chermayeff, Tom Geismar

→ p.469

● **1970–1976 . CASABELLA .** Magazine Cover . Alessandro Mendini
No. 367, July 1972

→ p.470

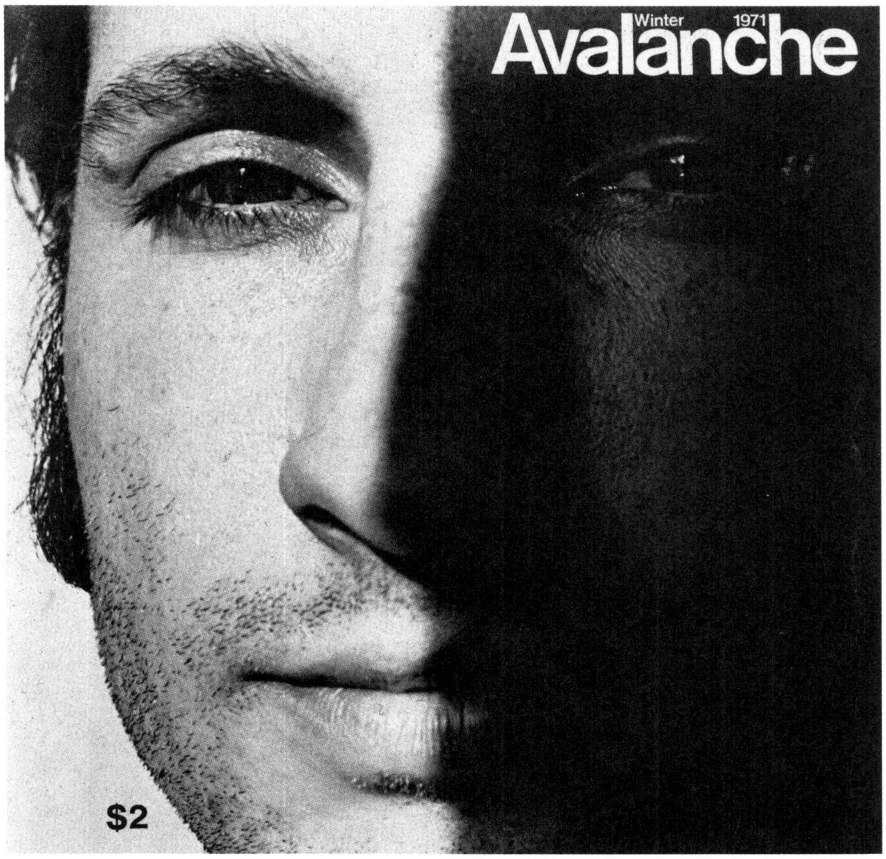

● **1970–1976 . AVALANCHE .** Magazine / Newspaper . Willoughby Sharp
No. 2, Winter 1971

→ p.470

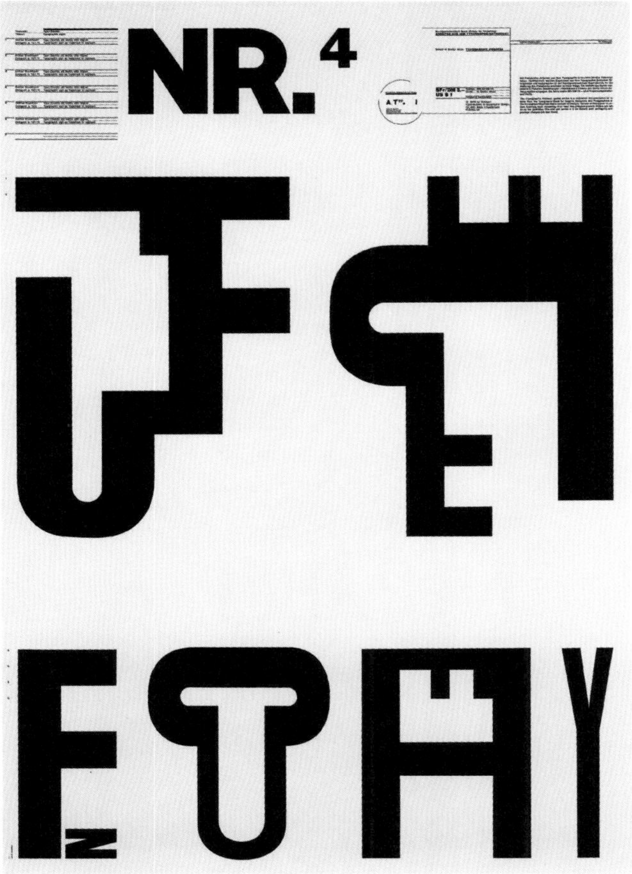

● **1971–1974 . TYPOGRAPHIC PROCESS .** Poster . Wolfgang Weingart et al.

→ p.470

OKIKE
AN AFRICAN JOURNAL OF NEW WRITING
NUMBER 6
EDITED BY CHINUA ACHEBE

● **1971–PRESENT . OKIKE: AN AFRICAN JOURNAL OF NEW WRITING .** Magazine Cover . Obiora Udechukwu
No. 6, 1974

→ p.471

● **1971 . NIKE .** Logo . Carolyn Davidson

→ p.471

● **1971 . SHELL .** Logo . Raymond Loewy

→ p.471

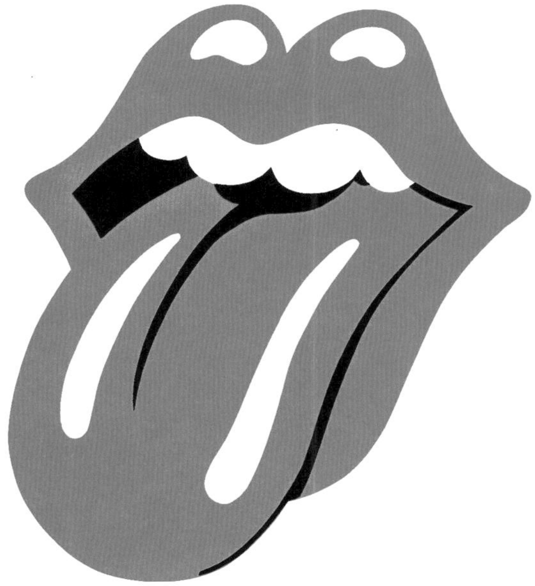

● **1971 . ROLLING STONES .** Logo . John Pasche

→ p.472

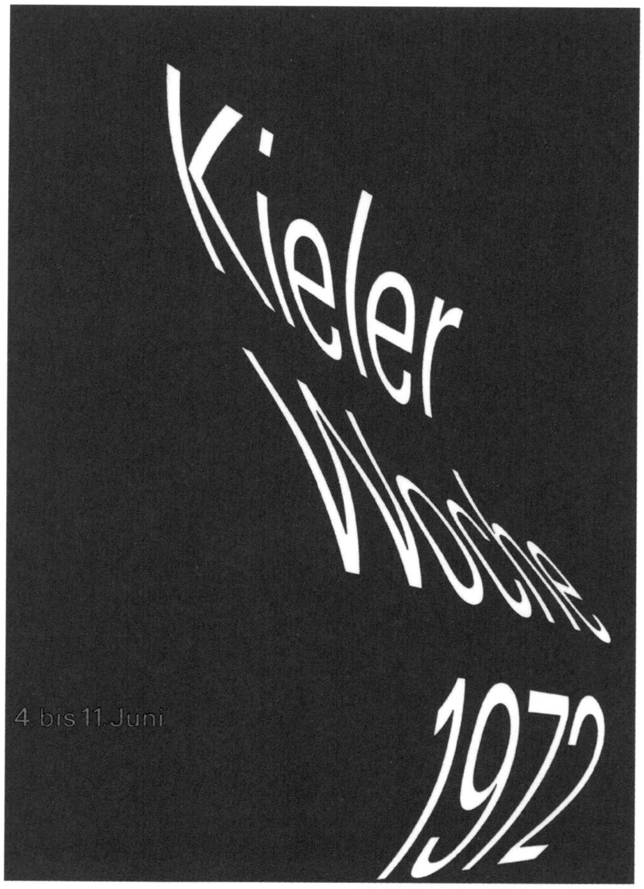

● **1972 . KIELER WOCHE .** Poster . Rolf Müller

→ p.472

● **1972 . RENAULT .** Logo . Victor Vasarely

→ p.472

● **1972 . ADIDAS .** Logo . Various

→ p.473

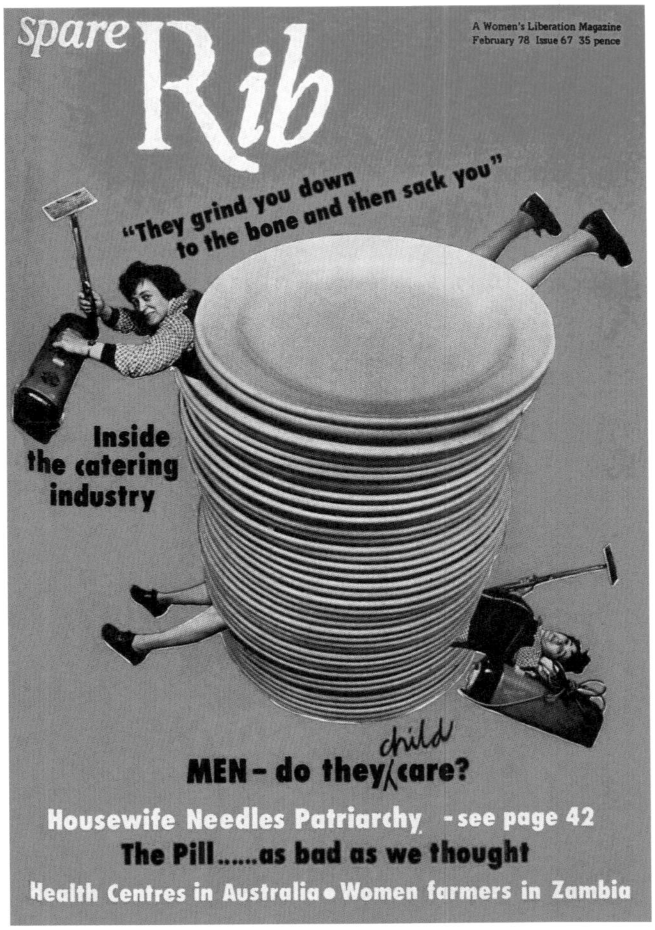

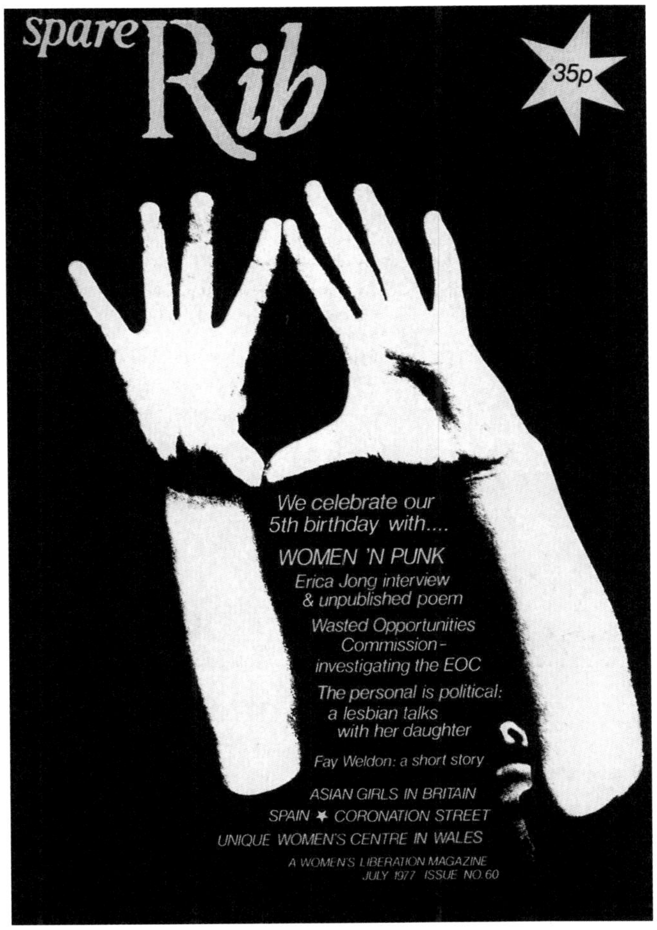

● **1972–1993 . SPARE RIB .** Magazine / Newspaper . Kate Hepburn, Sally Doust, et al.
TOP LEFT: Kate Hepburn, photographs Roger Perry, "It Needn't Be A Chore!," No. 9, March 1973; TOP RIGHT: Laura Margolis, photographs Val Wilmer, "Inside the Catering Industry," No. 67, February 1978; BOTTOM LEFT: Laura Margolis, photograph Angela Phillips, "Reclaiming the Night, London, November 12," No. 66, January 1978; BOTTOM RIGHT: Design and photographs Laura Margolis, "We Celebrate our Fifth Birthday with...WOMEN 'N PUNK," No. 60, July 1977

→ p.473

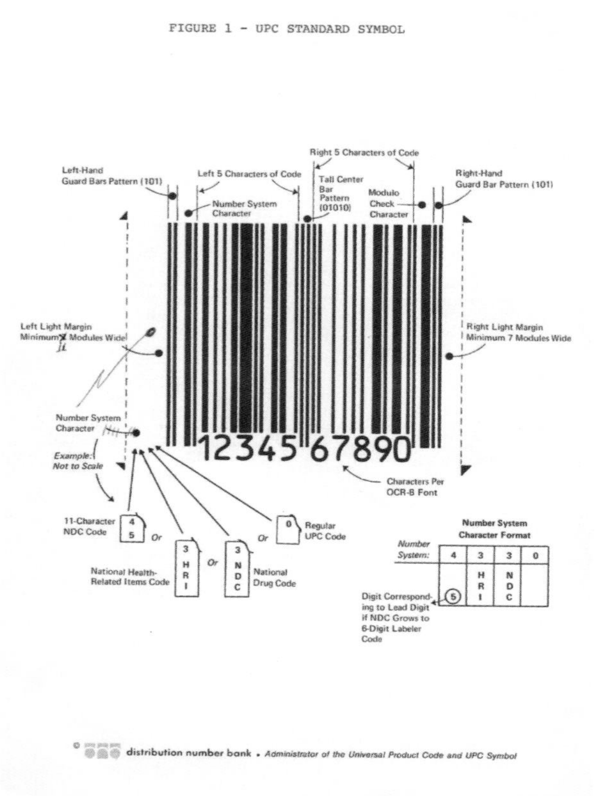

● **1973 . THE UNIVERSAL PRODUCT CODE .**
Information Design . George J. Laurer

→ p.473

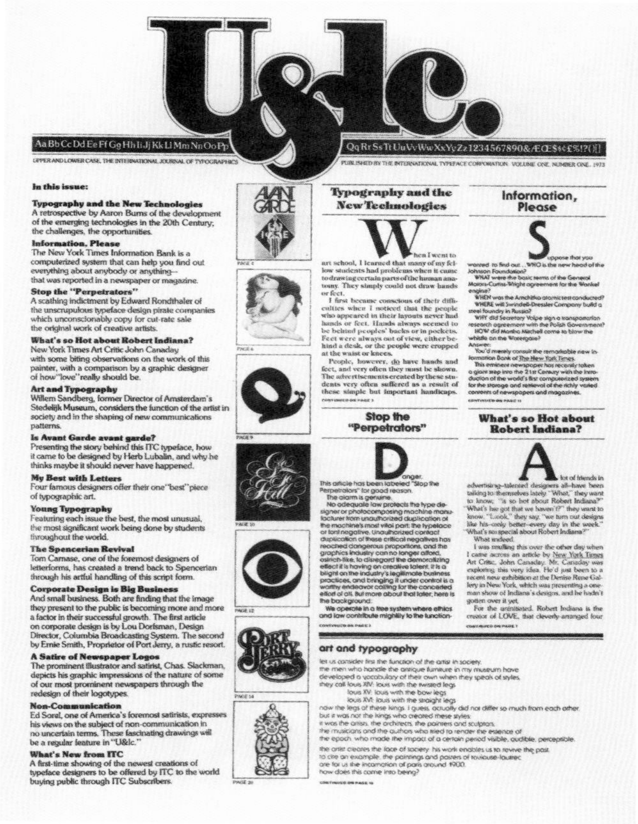

U&lc.

Aa Bb Cc Dd Ee Ff Gg Hh Ii Jj Kk Ll Mm Nn Oo Pp Qq Rr Ss Tt Uu Vv Ww Xx Yy Zz 1234567890&ÆŒ$¢£%!?()[]

UPPER AND LOWER CASE, THE INTERNATIONAL JOURNAL OF TYPOGRAPHICS

PUBLISHED BY THE INTERNATIONAL TYPEFACE CORPORATION. VOLUME ONE, NUMBER ONE, 1973

In this issue:

Typography and the New Technologies
A retrospective by Aaron Burns of the development of the emerging technologies in the 20th Century; the challenges, the opportunities.

Information, Please
The New York Times Information Bank is a computerized system that can help you find out everything about anybody or anything— that was reported in a newspaper or magazine.

Stop the "Perpetrators"
A scathing indictment by Edward Rondthaler of the unscrupulous typeface design pirate companies which unconscionably copy for cut-rate sale the original work of creative artists.

What's so Hot about Robert Indiana?
New York Times Art Critic John Canaday with some biting observations on the work of this painter, with a comparison by a graphic designer of how "love" really should be.

Art and Typography
Willem Sandberg, former Director of Amsterdam's Stedelijk Museum, considers the function of the artist in society and in the shaping of new communications patterns.

Is Avant Garde avant garde?
Presenting the story behind this ITC typeface, how it came to be designed by Herb Lubalin, and why he thinks maybe it should never have happened.

My Best with Letters
Four famous designers offer their one "best" piece of typographic art.

Young Typography
Featuring each issue the best, the most unusual, the most significant work being done by students throughout the world.

The Spencerian Revival
Tom Carnase, one of the foremost designers of letterforms, has created a trend back to Spencerian through his artful handling of this script form.

Corporate Design is Big Business
And small business. Both are finding that the image they present to the public is becoming more and more a factor in their successful growth. The first article on corporate design is by Lou Dorfsman, Design Director, Columbia Broadcasting System. The second by Ernie Smith, Proprietor of Port Jerry, a rustic resort.

A Satire of Newspaper Logos
The prominent illustrator and satirist, Chas. Slackman, depicts his graphic impressions of the nature of some of our most prominent newspapers through the redesign of their logotypes.

Non-Communication
Ed Sorel, one of America's foremost satirists, expresses his views on the subject of non-communication in no uncertain terms. These fascinating drawings will be a regular feature in "U&lc."

What's New from ITC
A first-time showing of the newest creations of typeface designers to be offered by ITC to the world buying public through ITC Subscribers.

PAGE 4 · PAGE 6 · PAGE 9 · PAGE 10 · PAGE 12 · PAGE 14 · PAGE 20

Typography and the New Technologies

When I went to art school, I learned that many of my fellow students had problems when it came to drawing certain parts of the human anatomy. They simply could not draw hands or feet.

I first became conscious of their difficulties when I noticed that the people who appeared in their layouts never had hands or feet. Hands always seemed to be behind peoples' backs or in pockets. Feet were always out of view, either behind a desk, or the people were cropped at the waist or knees.

People, however, do have hands and feet, and very often they must be shown. The advertisements created by these students very often suffered as a result of these simple but important handicaps.

CONTINUED ON PAGE 3

Information, Please

Suppose that you wanted to find out... WHO is the new head of the Johnson Foundation?

WHAT were the basic terms of the General Motors-Curtiss-Wright agreement for the Wankel engine?

WHEN was the Amchitka atomic test conducted?

WHERE will Swindell-Dressler Company build a steel foundry in Russia?

WHY did Secretary Volpe sign a transportation research agreement with the Polish Government?

HOW did Martha Mitchell come to blow the whistle on the Watergate?

Answer:

You'd merely consult the remarkable new Information Bank of The New York Times.

This eminent newspaper has recently taken a giant step into the 21st Century with the introduction of the world's first computerized system for the storage and retrieval of the richly varied contents of newspapers and magazines.

CONTINUED ON PAGE 11

Stop the "Perpetrators"

Danger.
This article has been labeled "Stop the Perpetrators" for good reason.

The alarm is genuine.

No adequate law protects the type designer or photocomposing machine manufacturer from unauthorized duplication of the machine's most vital part: the typeface or font negative. Unauthorized contact duplication of these critical negatives has reached dangerous proportions, and the graphics industry can no longer afford, ostrich-like, to disregard the demoralizing effect it is having on creative talent. It is a blight on the industry's legitimate business practices, and bringing it under control is a worthy endeavor calling for the concerted effort of all. But more about that later, here is the background:

We operate in a free system where ethics and law contribute mightily to the function-

CONTINUED ON PAGE 3

What's so Hot about Robert Indiana?

A lot of friends in advertising—talented designers all—have been talking to themselves lately. "What," they want to know, "is so hot about Robert Indiana?" "What's he got that we haven't?" they want to know. "Look," they say, "we turn out designs like his—only better—every day in the week." "What's so special about Robert Indiana?"

What indeed.

I was mulling this over the other day when I came across an article by New York Times Art Critic, John Canaday. Mr. Canaday was exploring this very idea. He'd just been to a recent new exhibition at the Denise Rene Gallery in New York, which was presenting a one-man show of Indiana's designs, and he hadn't gotten over it yet.

For the uninitiated, Robert Indiana is the creator of LOVE, that cleverly arranged four

CONTINUED ON PAGE 7

art and typography

let us consider first the function of the artist in society.
the men who handle the antique furniture in my museum have
developed a vocabulary of their own when they speak of styles.
they call louis XIV: louis with the twisted legs
louis XV: louis with the bow legs
louis XVI: louis with the straight legs
now the legs of these kings, i guess, actually did not differ so much from each other,
but it was not the kings who created these styles:
it was the artists, the architects, the painters and sculptors,
the musicians and the authors who tried to render the essence of
the epoch, who made the impact of a certain period visible, audible, perceptible.

the artist creates the face of society: his work enables us to revive the past.
to cite an example, the paintings and posters of toulouse-lautrec
are for us the incarnation of paris around 1900.
how does this come into being?

● **1973–1999 . U&LC .** Magazine / Newspaper .
Herb Lubalin, Aaron Burns, Ed Rondthaler
Vol. 1, No. 1, 1973

→ p.474

● **c. 1974 . CHURCHWARD ROUNDSQUARE .** Typeface . Joseph Churchward

→ p.474

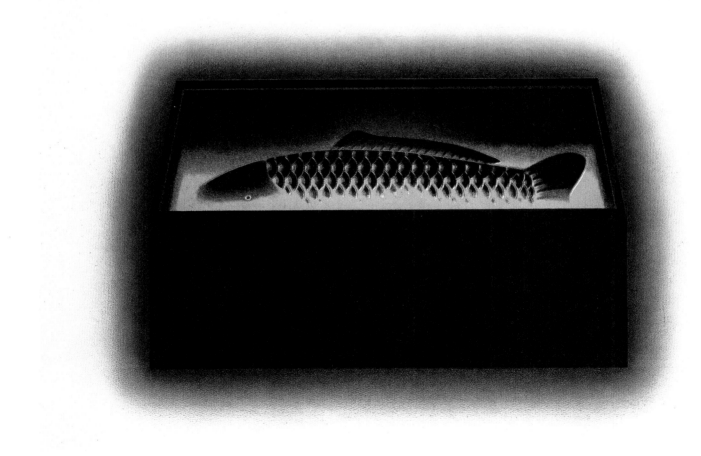

● **1974 . NEW MUSIC MEDIA, NEW MAGIC MEDIA .** Poster . Koichi Sato

→ p.474

● **1974 . DEUTSCHE BANK .** Logo . Anton Stankowski, Karl Duschek

→ p.475

ABCDEFGHI
JKLMNOPQR
STUVWXYZ
abcdefghijkl
mnopqrstuv
wxyzæœß/&
Ø(–).:;!?€¥£§
1234567890

● **1975 . DEMOS .** Typeface . Gerard Unger

→ p.475

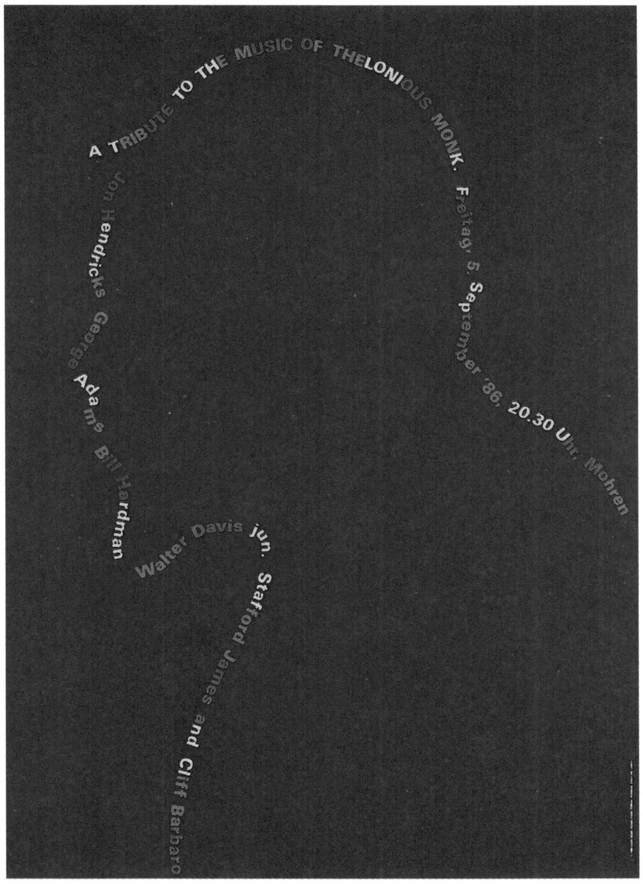

● **1975–PRESENT . JAZZ .** Poster . Niklaus Troxler

→ p.475

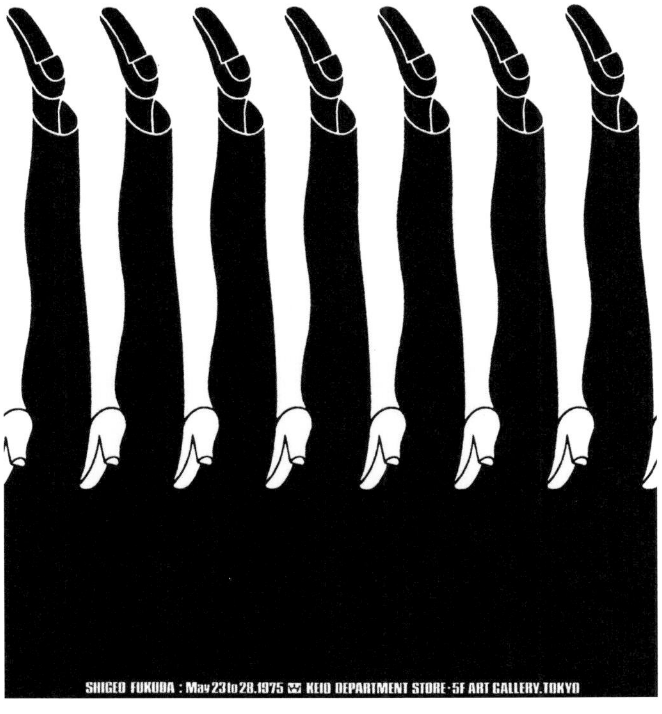

● **1975 . SHIGEO FUKUDA .** Poster . Shigeo Fukuda

→ p.476

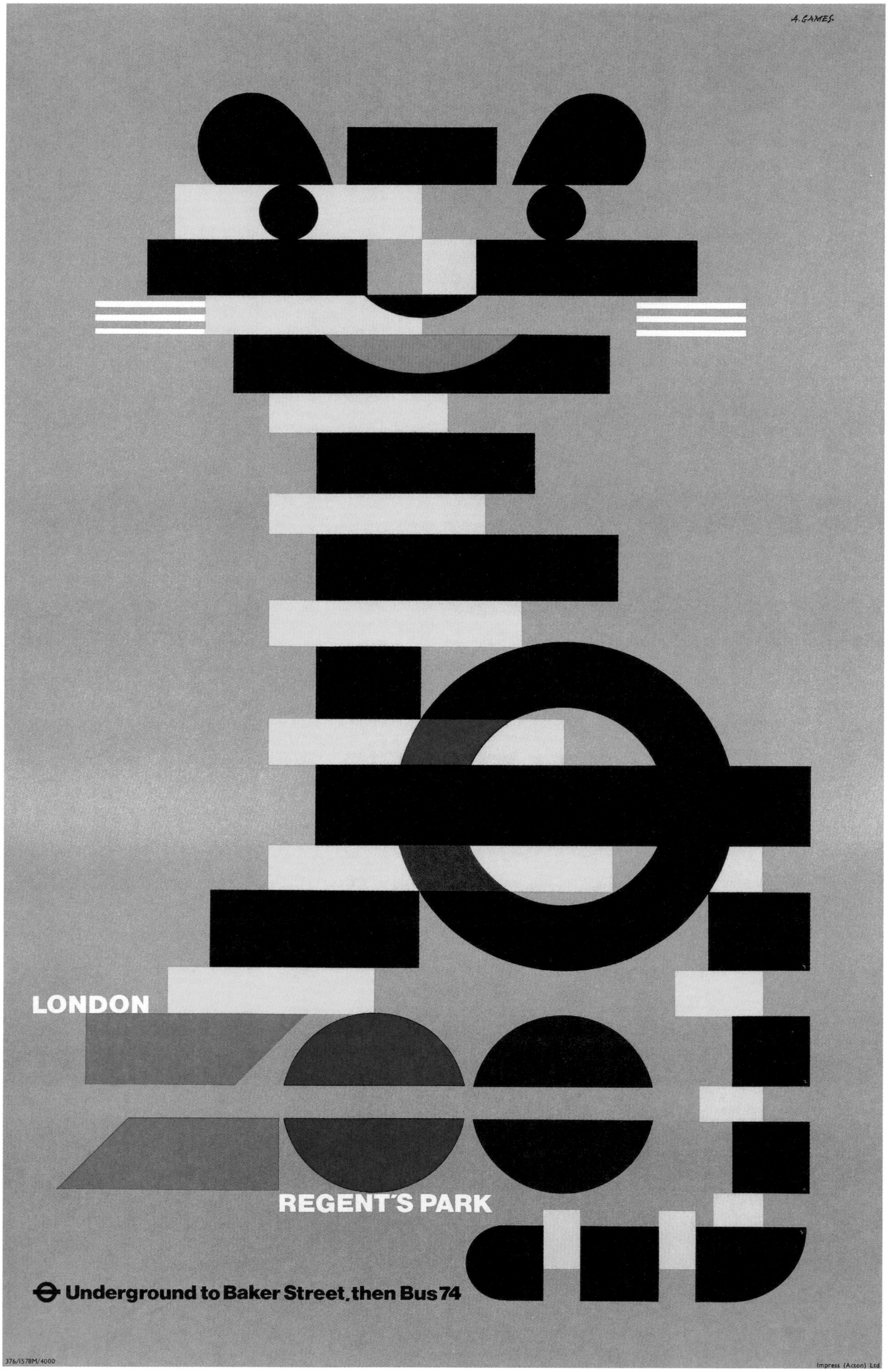

● **1976 . LONDON ZOO .** Poster . Abram Games

→ p.476

1976 . APPLE . Logo . Rob Janoff

→ p.476

The Logotype: Grid Drawing for Large Applications

The NASA logotype should be reproduced photographically whenever possible. However, for large applications such as signage, the logo may be reproduced using this grid drawing as an accurate guide. To achieve the best reproduction, care should be taken to maintain the correct proportion, stroke-width, and curves of the logotype. Note that 3 units of the grid are equal to the vertical stroke width.

Contact the NASA Graphics Coordinator for advice and counsel on problems related to reproducing the NASA logotype at large sizes.

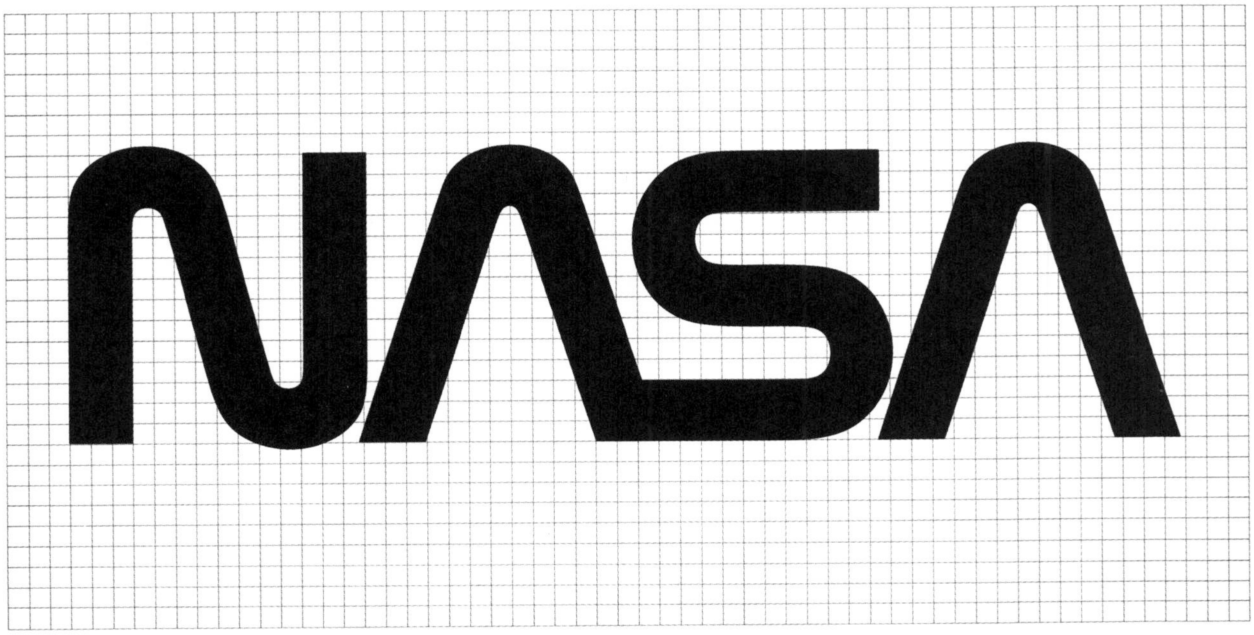

1976 . NASA GRAPHICS STANDARDS MANUAL . Identity . Danne & Blackburn

→ p.477

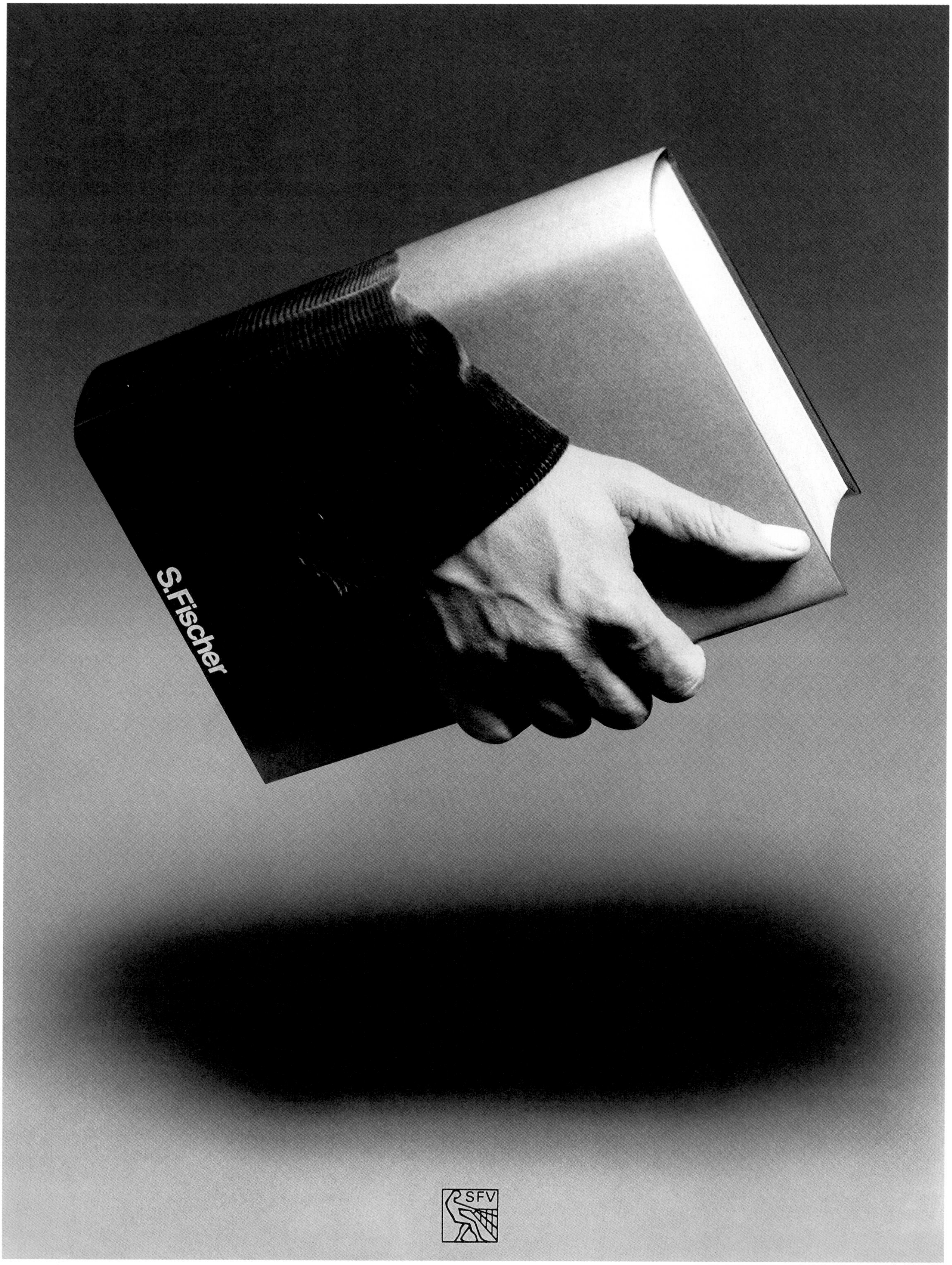

● **1976–1979 . S. FISCHER-VERLAG .** Poster . Gunter Rambow

→ p.477

● **1977 . I ❤ NY .** Logo . Milton Glaser

→ p.477

● **1977 . 3M .** Logo . Siegel+Gale

→ p.478

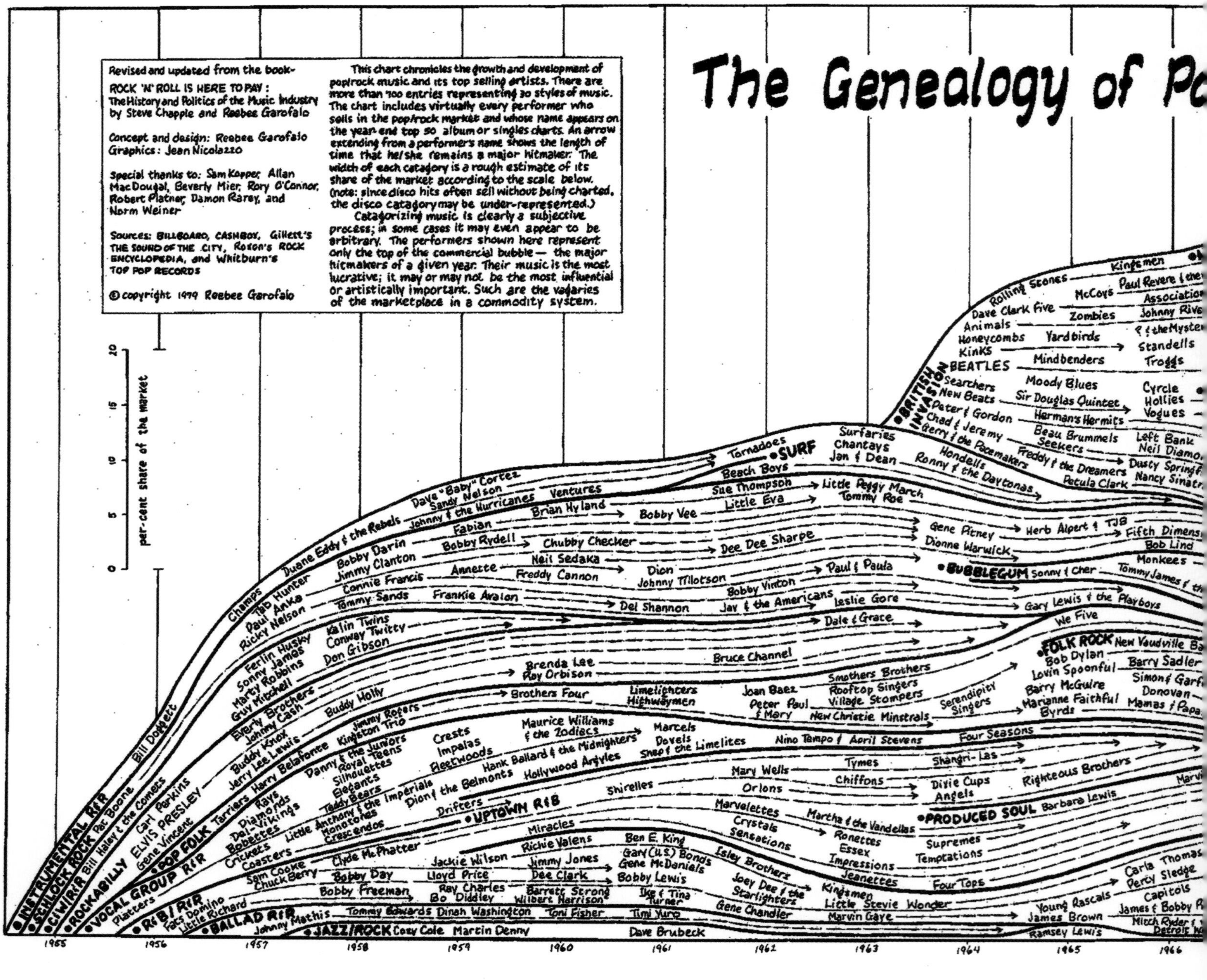

1977 . **THE GENEALOGY OF POP/ROCK MUSIC** . Information Design . Reebee Garofalo, Damon Rarey

→ p.478

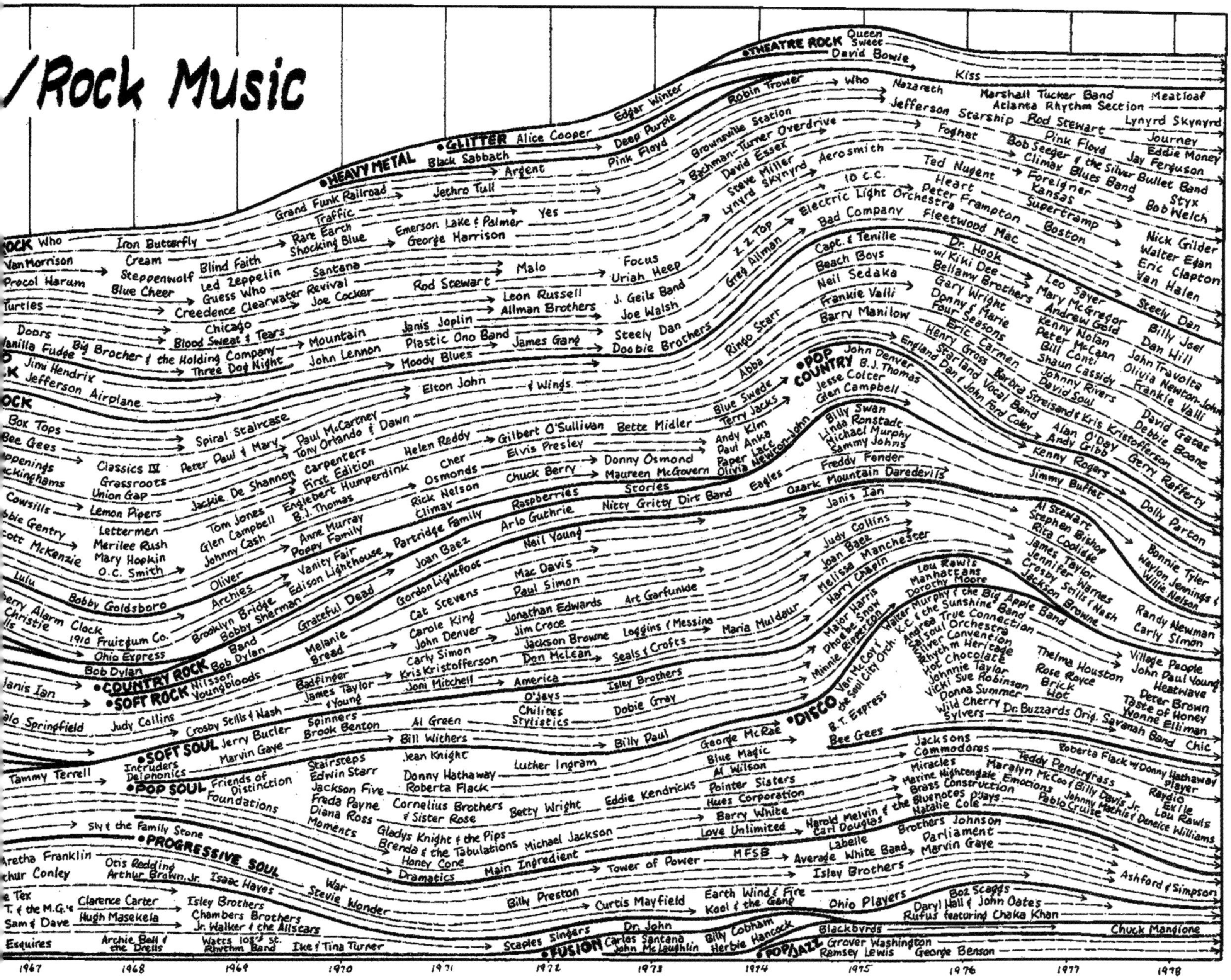

/Rock Music
THEATRE ROCK
Queen
Sweet
David Bowie
Kiss
GLITTER
Alice Cooper
Edgar Winter
Robin Trower
Who
Nazareth
Marshall Tucker Band
Meatloaf
Atlanta Rhythm Section
Jefferson Starship
Rod Stewart
Lynyrd Skynyrd
HEAVY METAL
Black Sabbath
Argent
Deep Purple
Pink Floyd
Grownsville Station
Bachman-Turner Overdrive
David Essex
Steve Miller
Lynyrd Skynyrd
Aerosmith
Foghat
Pink Floyd
Journey
Bob Seeger & the Silver Bullet Band
Eddie Money
Jay Ferguson
Climax Blues Band
Ted Nugent
Heart
Foreigner
Kansas
Styx
Bob Welch
10 C.C.
Electric Light Orchestra
Peter Frampton
Supertramp
Boston
Grand Funk Railroad
Jethro Tull
Traffic
Rare Earth
Shocking Blue
Emerson Lake & Palmer
George Harrison
Yes
ROCK
Who
Van Morrison
Procol Harum
Turtles
Doors
Vanilla Fudge
Jimi Hendrix
Jefferson Airplane
Iron Butterfly
Cream
Steppenwolf
Blue Cheer
Blind Faith
Led Zeppelin
Guess Who
Creedence Clearwater Revival
Chicago
Blood Sweat & Tears
Big Brother & the Holding Company
Three Dog Night
Santana
Joe Cocker
Mountain
John Lennon
Malo
Rod Stewart
Leon Russell
Allman Brothers
Janis Joplin
Plastic Ono Band
Moody Blues
James Gang
Elton John
& Wings
Focus
Uriah Heep
J. Geils Band
Joe Walsh
Steely Dan
Doobie Brothers
Z.Z. Top
Greg Allman
Ringo Starr
Bad Company
Fleetwood Mac
Capt. & Tenille
Beach Boys
Neil Sedaka
Frankie Valli
Barry Manilow
Dr. Hook
w/ Kiki Dee
Bellamy Brothers
Gary Wright
Donny & Marie
Four Seasons
Eric Carmen
Henry Gross
Starland Vocal Band
England Dan / John Ford Coley
Leo Sayer
Mary McGregor
Andrew Gold
Kenny Nolan
Peter McCann
Bill Conti
Shaun Cassidy
Johnny Rivers
David Soul
Barbra Streisand & Kris Kristofferson
Nick Gilder
Walter Egan
Eric Clapton
Van Halen
Steely Dan
Billy Joel
Dan Hill
John Travolta
Olivia Newton-John
Frankie Valli
Abba
POP COUNTRY
John Denver
B.J. Thomas
Jesse Colter
Glen Campbell
Blue Swede
Terry Jacks
Andy Kim
Paul Anka
Paper Lace
Olivia Newton-John
Billy Swan
Linda Ronstadt
Michael Murphy
Sammy Johns
Freddy Fender
Alan O'Day
Andy Gibb
Kenny Rogers
David Gates
Debbie Boone
Gerry Rafferty
ROCK
Box Tops
Bee Gees
Happenings
Buckinghams
Cowsills
Bobbie Gentry
Scott McKenzie
Lulu
Classics IV
Grassroots
Union Gap
Lemon Pipers
Lettermen
Merilee Rush
Mary Hopkin
O.C. Smith
Spiral Staircase
Peter Paul & Mary
Paul McCartney
Tony Orlando & Dawn
Carpenters
First Edition
Jackie De Shannon
Englebert Humperdink
B.J. Thomas
Tom Jones
Glen Campbell
Johnny Cash
Anne Murray
Poppy Family
Helen Reddy
Cher
Osmonds
Rick Nelson
Climax
Gilbert O'Sullivan
Elvis Presley
Chuck Berry
Bette Midler
Donny Osmond
Maureen McGovern
Stories
Raspberries
Nitty Gritty Dirt Band
Eagles
Ozark Mountain Daredevils
Jimmy Buffet
Dolly Parton
Bobby Goldsboro
Oliver
Archies
Vanity Fair
Edison Lighthouse
Partridge Family
Arlo Guthrie
Neil Young
Janis Ian
Judy Collins
Joan Baez
Melissa Manchester
Harry Chapin
Al Stewart
Stephen Bishop
Rita Coolidge
James Taylor
Jennifer Warnes
Crosby Stills & Nash
Jackson Browne
Bonnie Tyler
Waylon Jennings & Willie Nelson
Cherry Alarm Clock
Lou Christie
1910 Fruitgum Co.
Ohio Express
Bob Dylan
Brooklyn Bridge
Bobby Sherman
Grateful Dead
Joan Baez
Gordon Lightfoot
Mac Davis
Paul Simon
Cat Stevens
Carole King
John Denver
Art Garfunkle
Jonathan Edwards
Jim Croce
Jackson Browne
Loggins & Messina
Maria Muldaur
Don McLean
Seals & Crofts
Carly Simon
Kris Kristofferson
Joni Mitchell
America
Isley Brothers
Randy Newman
Carly Simon
Lou Rawls
Manhattans
Dorothy Moore
Walter Murphy & the Big Apple Band
K.C. & the Sunshine Band
Andrea True Connection
Salsoul Orchestra
Silver Convention
Rhythm Heritage
Hot Chocolate
Johnnie Taylor
Vicki Sue Robinson
Donna Summer
Wild Cherry
Sylvers
Dr. Buzzards Orig. Savannah Band
Thelma Houston
Rose Royce
Brick
Hot
Village People
John Paul Young
Heatwave
Peter Brown
Taste of Honey
Yvonne Elliman
Chic
Janis Ian
COUNTRY ROCK
Bob Dylan
Band
Melanie
Bread
SOFT ROCK
Nilsson
Youngbloods
Badfinger
James Taylor
& Young
Crosby Stills & Nash
Judy Collins
Dusty Springfield
O'Jays
Chilites
Stylistics
Dobie Gray
Major Harris
Phoebe Snow
Minnie Riperton
Van McCoy & the Soul City Orch.
DISCO
B.T. Express
Bee Gees
Al Green
Bill Withers
Billy Paul
George McRae
Spinners
Brook Benton
SOFT SOUL
Jerry Butler
Marvin Gaye
Tammy Terrell
Intruders
Delphonics
POP SOUL
Friends of Distinction
Foundations
Stairsteps
Edwin Starr
Jackson Five
Freda Payne
Diana Ross
Moments
Jean Knight
Donny Hathaway
Roberta Flack
Cornelius Brothers & Sister Rose
Luther Ingram
Betty Wright
Eddie Kendricks
Blue Magic
Al Wilson
Pointer Sisters
Hues Corporation
Barry White
Love Unlimited
Harold Melvin & the Bluenotes
Carl Douglas
Jacksons
Commodores
Miracles
Marine Nightengale
Brass Construction
O'Jays
Natalie Cole
Roberta Flack w/ Donny Hathaway
Teddy Pendergrass
Marilyn McCoo & Billy Davis Jr.
Emotions
Johnny Mathis & Deneice Williams
Pablo Cruise
Player
Raydio
Exile
Lou Rawls
Sly & the Family Stone
PROGRESSIVE SOUL
Aretha Franklin
Arthur Conley
Otis Redding
Arthur Brown, Jr.
Isaac Hayes
Joe Tex
Booker T. & the M.G.'s
Sam & Dave
Esquires
Clarence Carter
Hugh Masekela
Archie Bell & the Drells
Isley Brothers
Chambers Brothers
Jr. Walker & the Allstars
Watts 103rd St. Rhythm Band
Ike & Tina Turner
War
Stevie Wonder
Gladys Knight & the Pips
Brenda & the Tabulations
Honey Cone
Dramatics
Michael Jackson
Main Ingredient
Tower of Power
MFSB
Labelle
Average White Band
Isley Brothers
Brothers Johnson
Parliament
Marvin Gaye
Ashford & Simpson
Billy Preston
Curtis Mayfield
Earth Wind & Fire
Kool & the Gang
Ohio Players
Boz Scaggs
Daryl Hall & John Oates
Rufus featuring Chaka Khan
Staples Singers
FUSION
Dr. John
Carlos Santana
John McLaughlin
Billy Cobham
Herbie Hancock
POP/JAZZ
Blackbyrds
Grover Washington
Ramsey Lewis
George Benson
Chuck Mangione
1967
1968
1969
1970
1971
1972
1973
1974
1975
1976
1977
1978

1977 . SEX PISTOLS—GOD SAVE THE QUEEN . Record / CD Cover . Jamie Reid

→ p.478

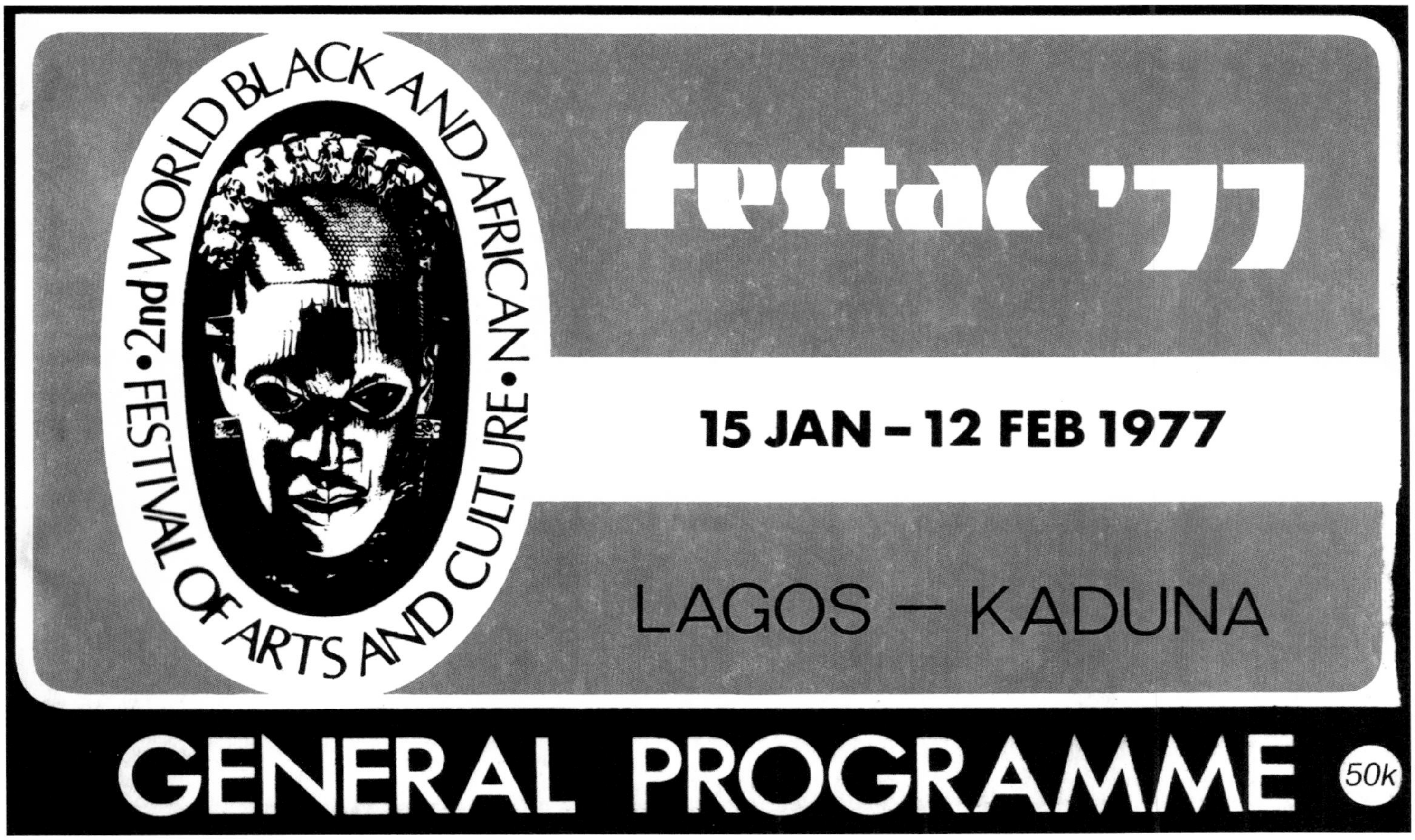

1977 . FESTAC '77 . Identity . Unknown

→ p.479

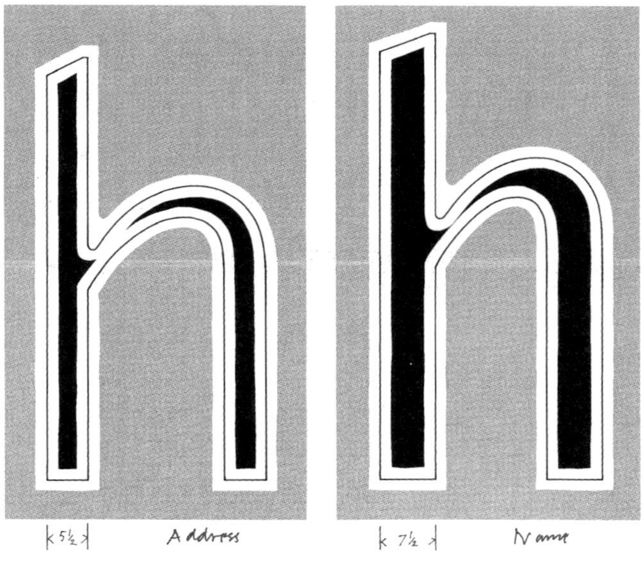

The lowercase h's from Bell Gothic (the Address font) and Bell Gothic Bold (the Name and Number font).

The black line is the Bell Gothic design on paper, vintage 1937. Superimposed on the originals are the effects of a tolerance of .003", made up of the loss of .0015" (the black image) and the gain of .0015" (the white-on-gray image), the accumulated variation caused by production processes. This, in graphic form, is what the AT&T report describes.

The black image has become very feeble—eroded completely away where the arch springs from the stem. The most common complaint of Bell's subscribers is that the directory pages are too light; if they are trying to read 6 pt characters with a stem weight of .0025" (that of the black image) they are not being unreasonable. It is the effort to counteract this distressing lightness that leads to over-inking, the blurring of character image, the sacrificing of readability and frequent press stops for washdown, with the consequence of increased printing costs. It seems essential, therefore, that a new directory face should show a gain in stroke weight, a controlled gain incorporated in the design by the designer, not applied remedially in subsequent production processes.

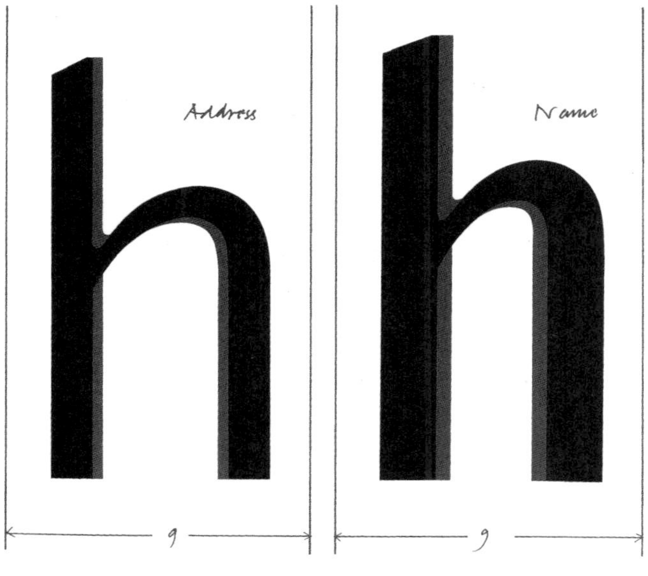

The same two Bell Gothic h's with weight added to the original forms and shown in gray.

The stem weight of the lighter Address font letter is now .007", the minimum recommended, with results that are unexceptionable. The implications for the right-hand letter (Bell Gothic Bold, the Name and Number font) are much less satisfactory: firstly, in order to preserve sufficient contrast between light and bold faces, rather more weight had to be added to the heavier h than to the lighter one; and, secondly, in both letters it was necessary to add weight only on the inside of the strokes. This last measure—the preservation of ample side-bearing (the white space between adjacent letters)—is vital in countering the tendency of CRT-set characters to spread and occasionally to bridge when electronically compressed in the typesetter. It was found that the resulting letter in the bolder Name and Number font was unacceptably narrow and illegible on its original width of 9 units; the combined pressures of added stem weight and maintained side-bearing forced the font onto bodies one unit wider than Bell Gothic Bold.

1978 . BELL CENTENNIAL . Typeface . Matthew Carter

→ p.479

swissair

● **1978 . SWISSAIR .** Identity . Karl Gerstner

→ p.479

● **1979 . WOMEN OF THE REVOLUTION .** Poster . Morteza Momayez
RIGHT: "Tulip," c. 1978–9

→ p.480

1979 . JOY DIVISION—UNKNOWN PLEASURES . Record / CD Cover . Peter Saville

→ p.480

1980–PRESENT . ABSOLUT VODKA . Advertising . TBWA

→ p.480

1980–PRESENT . I-D . Magazine / Newspaper . Terry Jones et al.
Photograph Nick Knight, model Sarah Stockbridge, No. 50, August 1987

→ p.481

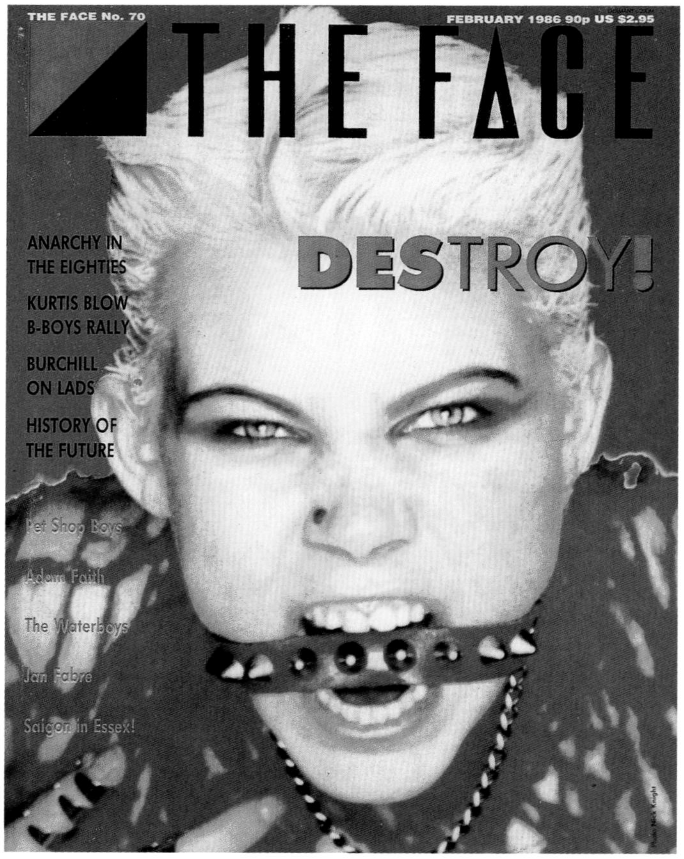

1981–1986 . THE FACE . Magazine / Newspaper . Neville Brody
Photograph Nick Knight, model Sarah Campbell, No. 70, February 1986

→ p.481

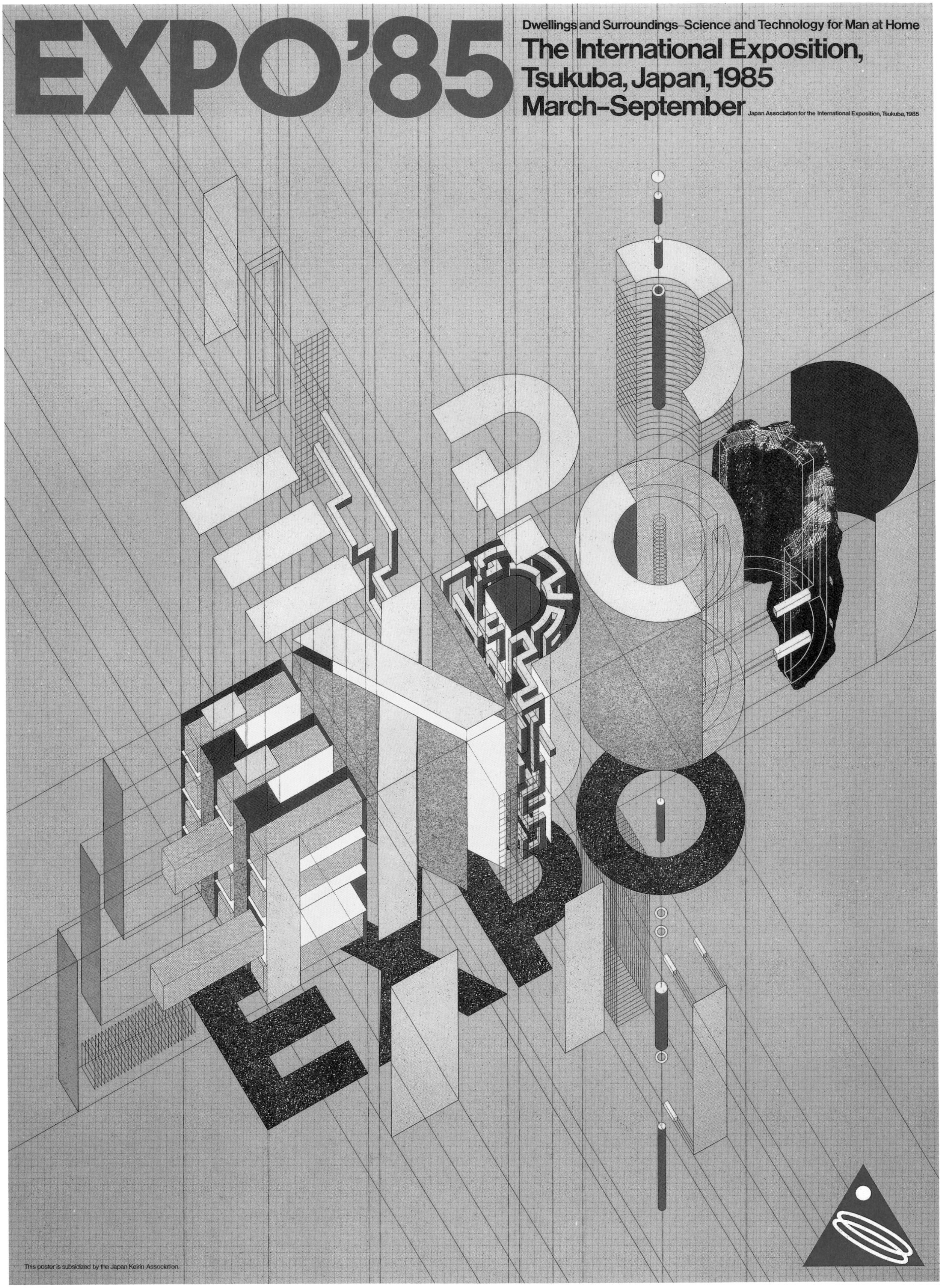

● **1982 . EXPO '85 .** Poster . Takenobu Igarashi

→ p.481

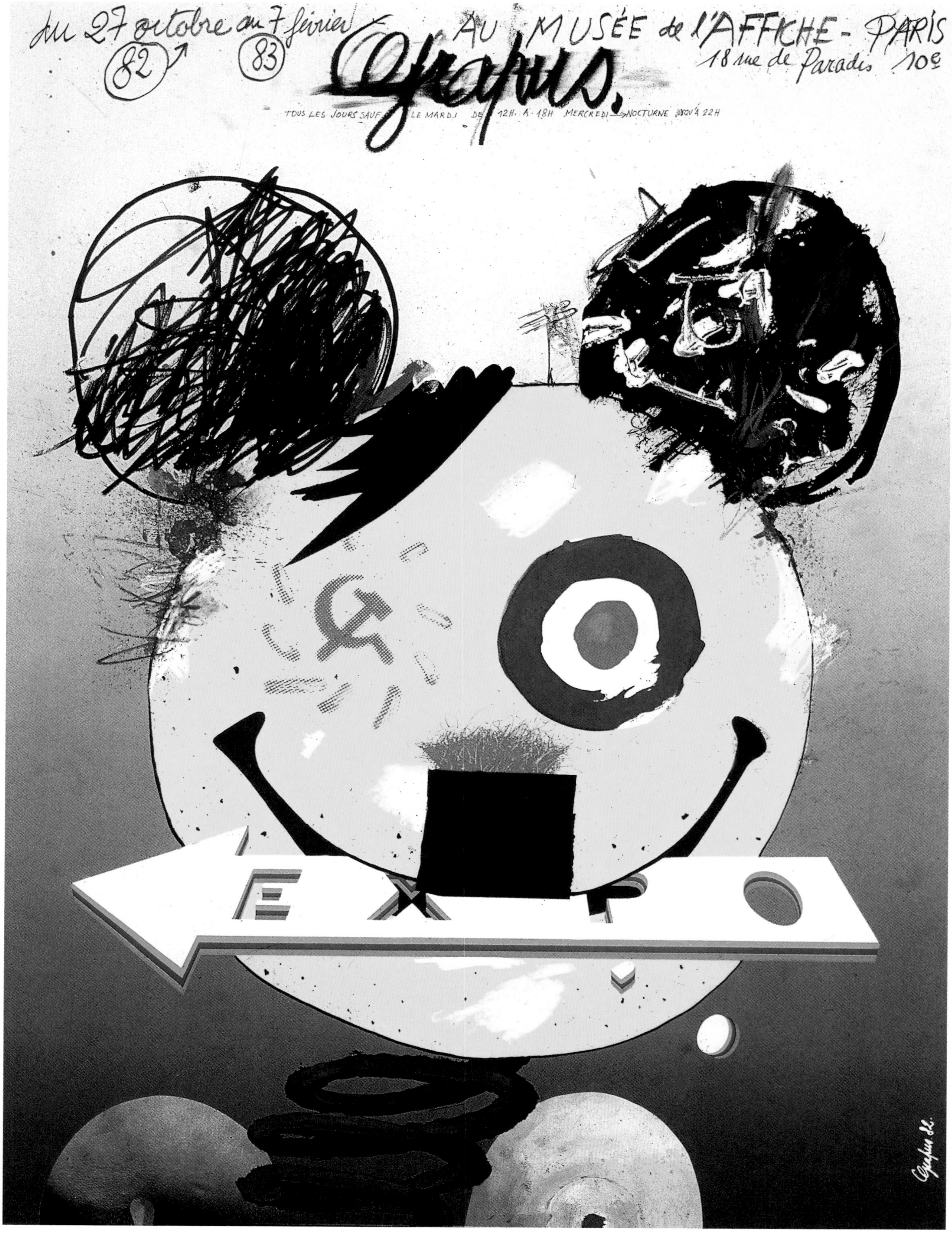

● **1982 . GRAPUS .** Poster . Grapus

→ p.482

● **1982 . FABER & FABER .** Logo . John McConnell

→ p.482

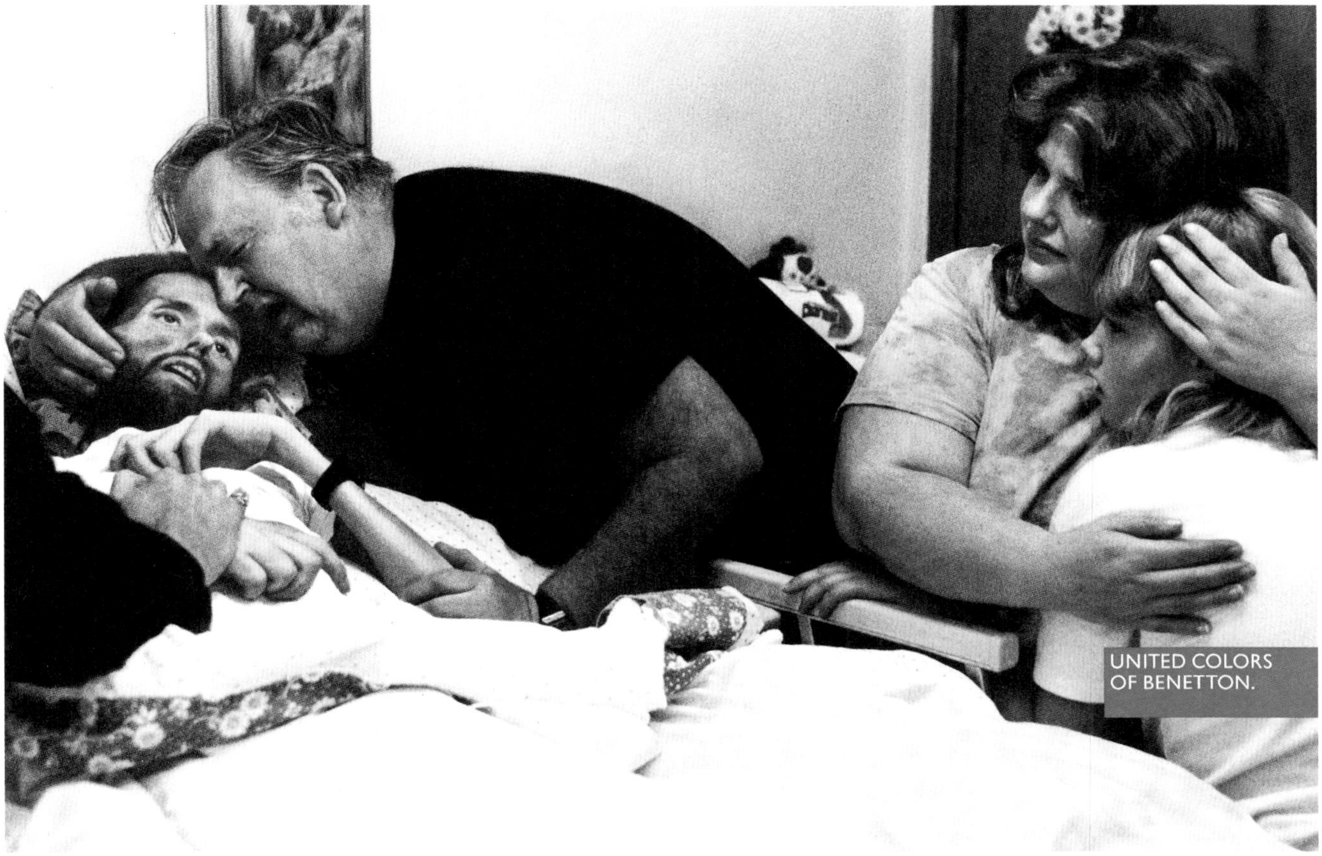

● **1982–2000 . BENETTON .** Advertising . Oliviero Toscani
Photograph Therese Frare, *AIDS—David Kirby*, 1990

→ p.482

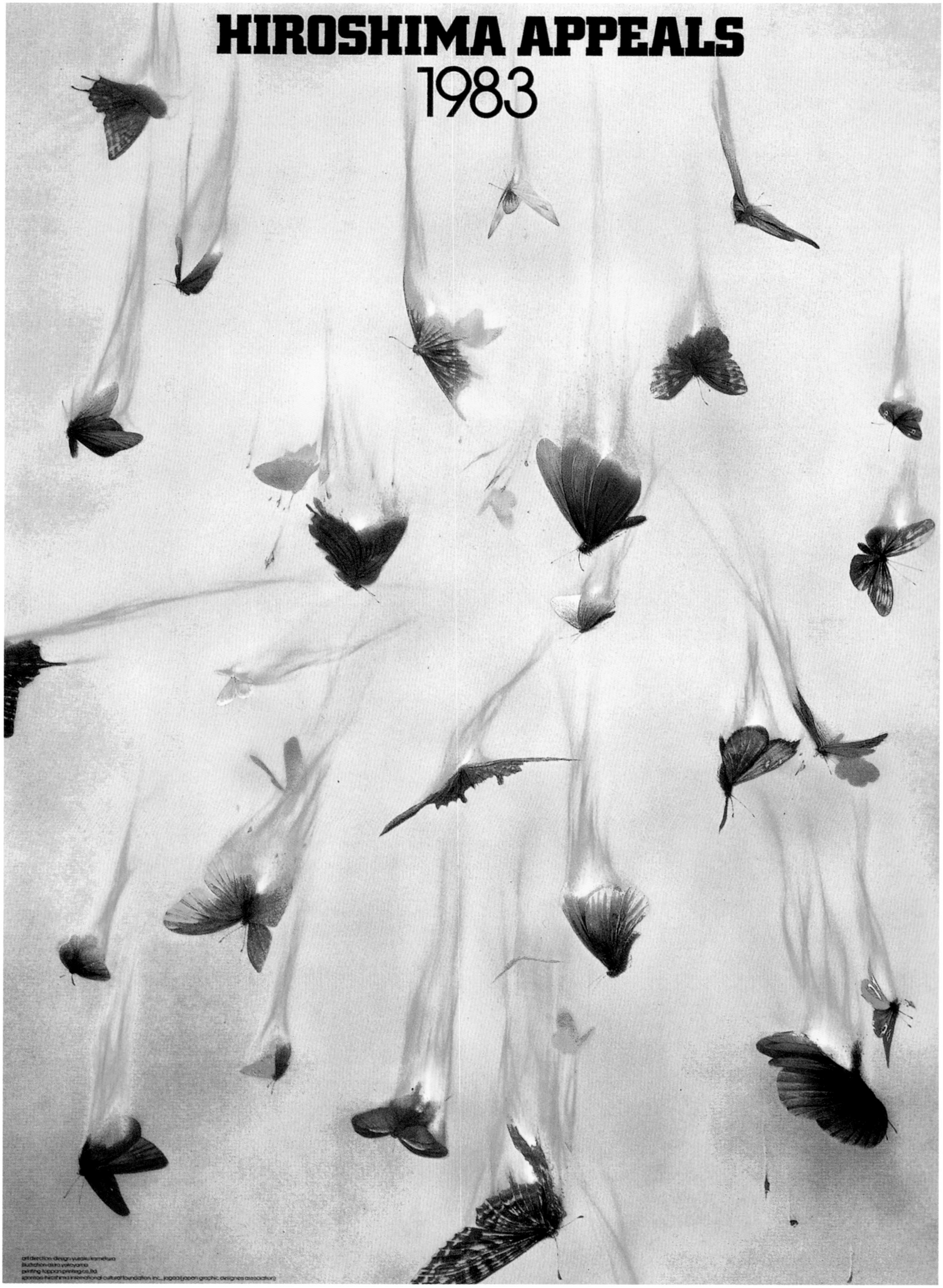

● **1983 . HIROSHIMA APPEALS .** Poster . Yusaku Kamekura .

→ p.483

● **1984 . ORIGINAL MACINTOSH ICONS .** Information Design . Susan Kare

→ p.483

● **1984 . CYCLE OF FILMS BY JEAN-LUC GODARD .** Poster . Werner Jeker

→ p.483

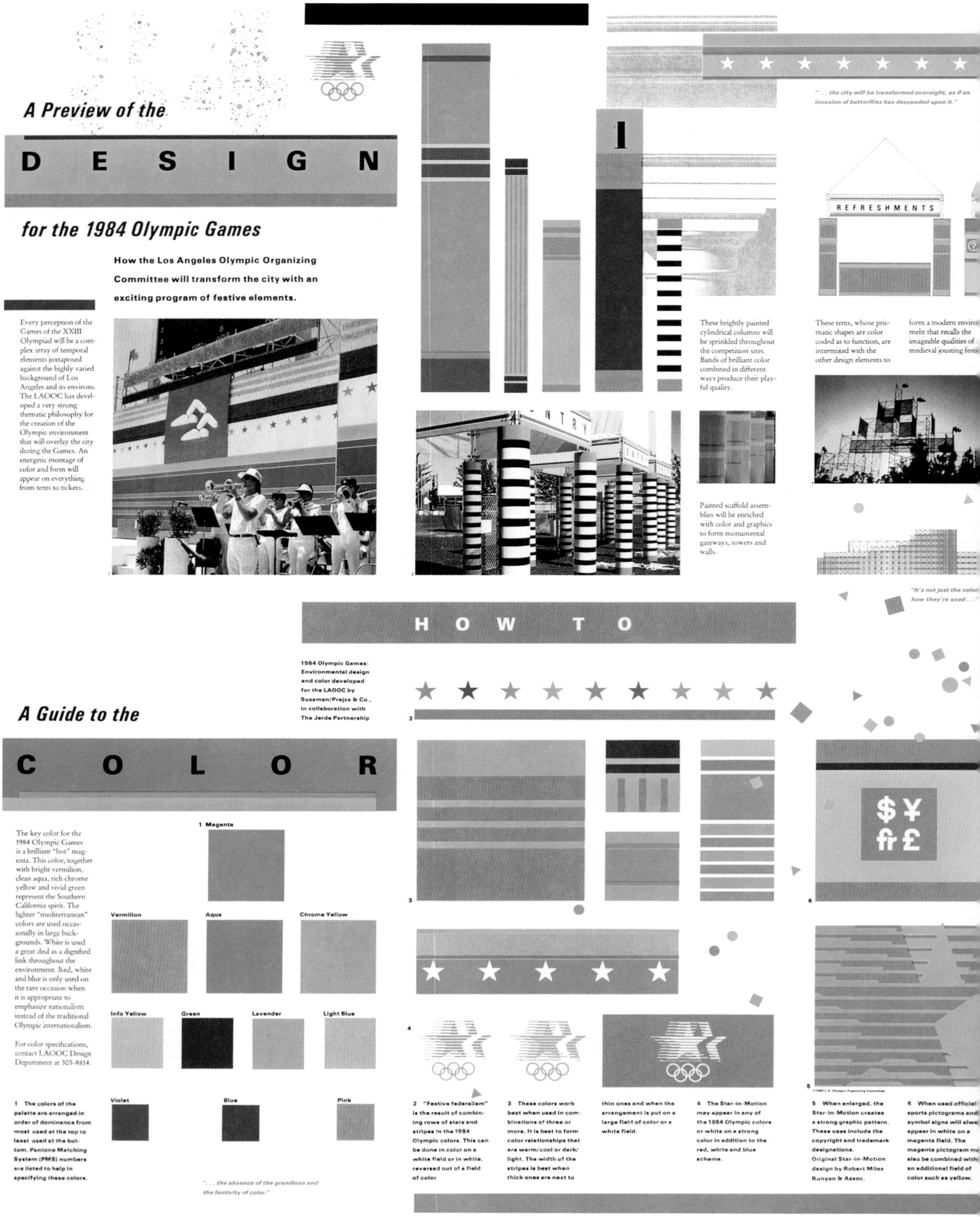

A Preview of the

D E S I G N

for the 1984 Olympic Games

How the Los Angeles Olympic Organizing Committee will transform the city with an exciting program of festive elements.

Every perception of the Games of the XXIII Olympiad will be a complex array of temporal elements juxtaposed against the highly varied background of Los Angeles and its environs. The LAOOC has developed a very strong thematic philosophy for the creation of the Olympic environment that will overlay the city during the Games. An energetic montage of color and form will appear on everything from tents to tickets.

These brightly painted cylindrical columns will be sprinkled throughout the competition sites. Bands of brilliant color combined in different ways produce their playful quality.

REFRESHMENTS

These tents, whose prismatic shapes are color coded as to function, are intermixed with the other design elements to form a modern enviro ment that recalls the imageable qualities of medieval jousting festi

Painted scaffold assemblies will be enriched with color and graphics to form monumental gateways, towers and walls.

"... the city will be transformed overnight, as if an invasion of butterflies has descended upon it."

"It's not just the color how they're used ..."

H O W T O

1984 Olympic Games: Environmental design and color developed for the LAOOC by Sussman/Prejza & Co., in collaboration with The Jerde Partnership

A Guide to the

C O L O R

The key color for the 1984 Olympic Games is a brilliant "hot" magenta. This color, together with bright vermilion, clean aqua, rich chrome yellow and vivid green represent the Southern California spirit. The lighter "mediterranean" colors are used occasionally in large backgrounds. White is used a great deal as a dignified link throughout the environment. Red, white and blue is only used on the rare occasion when it is appropriate to emphasize nationalism instead of the traditional Olympic internationalism.

For color specifications, contact LAOOC Design Department at 305-8814.

1 Magenta

Vermilion — Aqua — Chrome Yellow

Info Yellow — Green — Lavender — Light Blue

Violet — Blue — Pink

1 The colors of the palette are arranged in order of dominance from most used at the top to least used at the bottom. Pantone Matching System (PMS) numbers are listed to help in specifying these colors.

"... the absence of the grandiose and the festivity of color."

$ ¥ fr £

©1980 L.A. Olympic Organizing Committee

2 "Festive federalism" is the result of combining rows of stars and stripes in the 1984 Olympic colors. This can be done in color on a white field or in white, reversed out of a field of color.

3 These colors work best when used in combinations of three or more. It is best to form color relationships that are warm/cool or dark/light. The width of the stripes is best when thick ones are next to thin ones and when the arrangement is put on a large field of color or a white field.

4 The Star-in-Motion may appear in any of the 1984 Olympic colors or white on a strong color in addition to the red, white and blue scheme.

5 When enlarged, the Star-in-Motion creates a strong graphic pattern. These uses include the copyright and trademark designations. Original Star-in-Motion design by Robert Miles Runyan & Assoc.

6 When used official sports pictograms and symbol signs will alwa appear in white on a magenta field. The magenta pictogram m also be combined with an additional field of color such as yellow.

● 1984 . 1984 LOS ANGELES OLYMPICS . Identity . Sussman/Prejza & Company

→ p.484

The association of bunting with stadia is a long-standing one. A carefully chosen set of colors, not associated with any one country, has been developed in miles of fabric and paper that will ring the fields of play.

All these elements and more not shown here are designed and brought together with a spirited attitude we have dubbed "festive federalism" – that is, an absolute celebration of the festive, temporal qualities of the Games coupled with a design palette that is very American in its conception, yet intriguingly international in its imagery.

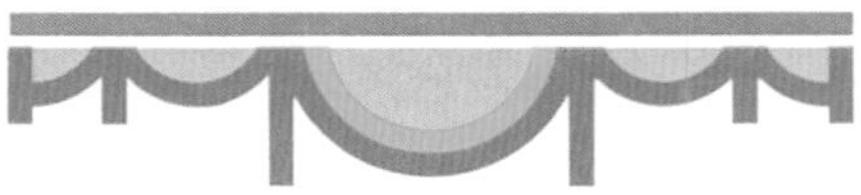

"A city that has both Whittier Boulevard and Rodeo Drive ought to be able to do a hell of a decorating job . . ."

"The bride wore red, white and blue but, oh, the confetti . . ."

These design concepts presented here are for informational purposes, not for reproduction.

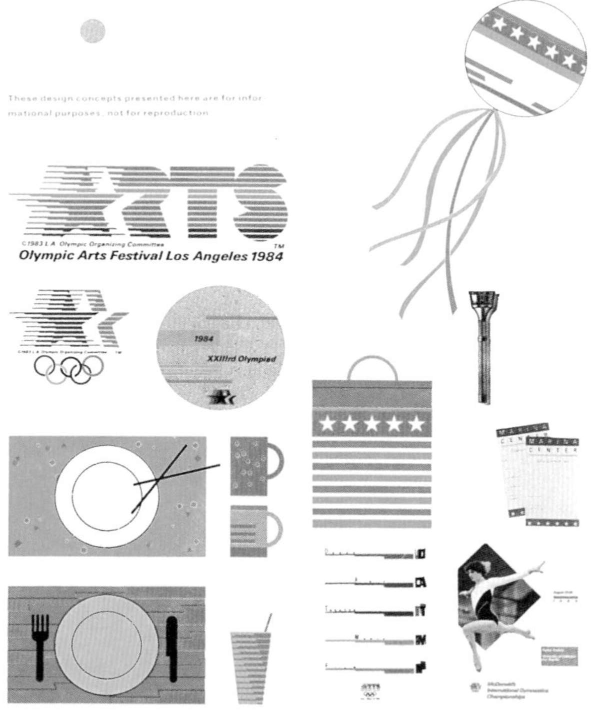

HOW NOT TO

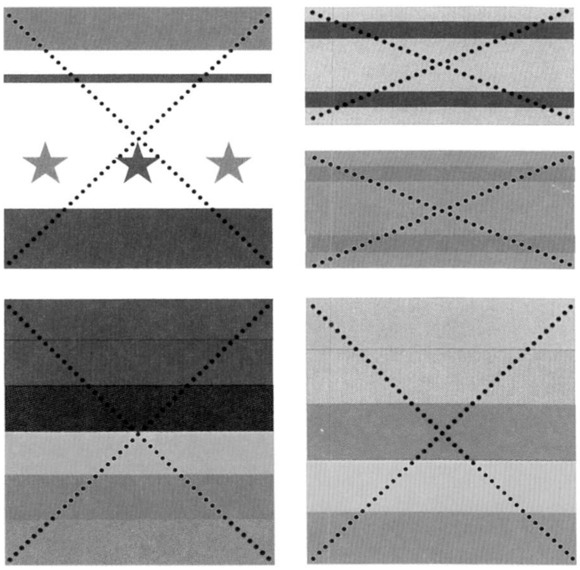

The dominant type-
e is the Univers
ies. Univers 66 (italic)
sed in conjunction
h official LAOOC
rks. Univers 67 (reg-
) is used for general
nage and headline
ds, while Univers 68 (italic) is used as a supplement. The Garamond Type family is used when a classic face is more appropriate, as in text.

8 Typography appears flush left in upper and lower case and can easily be combined with the "festive" stars and stripes.

9 The "festive federal" colors and elements such as stars, stripes, confetti, spray and abstracted Star-in-Motion pattern have been adapted for multiple uses.

Contributions to the design program:
Pictograms:
Keith Bright & Assoc.
Printed Graphics:
Arnold Schwartzman
Follis Design
Robie Design Assoc., Inc.
Franz Evenhuis
Torch:
Neuhart Donges Neuhart
Scaffold Design:
John Aleksich & Assoc.

Photography:
Annette Del Zoppo
Steve Smith (9, 10)
Tim Street-Porter (1, 11)
The Delmar Watson Collection (8)

10 Do not use red, white, and blue as a decorative color scheme. The Star-in-Motion in red, white, and blue should always be used small and in a dignified manner.

11 Do not use light and dark combinations of the same color or the colors in a "rainbow" arrangement. When using stripes, do not make them all the same width.

Design Guide Poster:
Sussman/Prejza & Co., Inc.
Debra Valencia
Printing:
Sales Corporation of America
Southern California Office
Stanton, California 90680

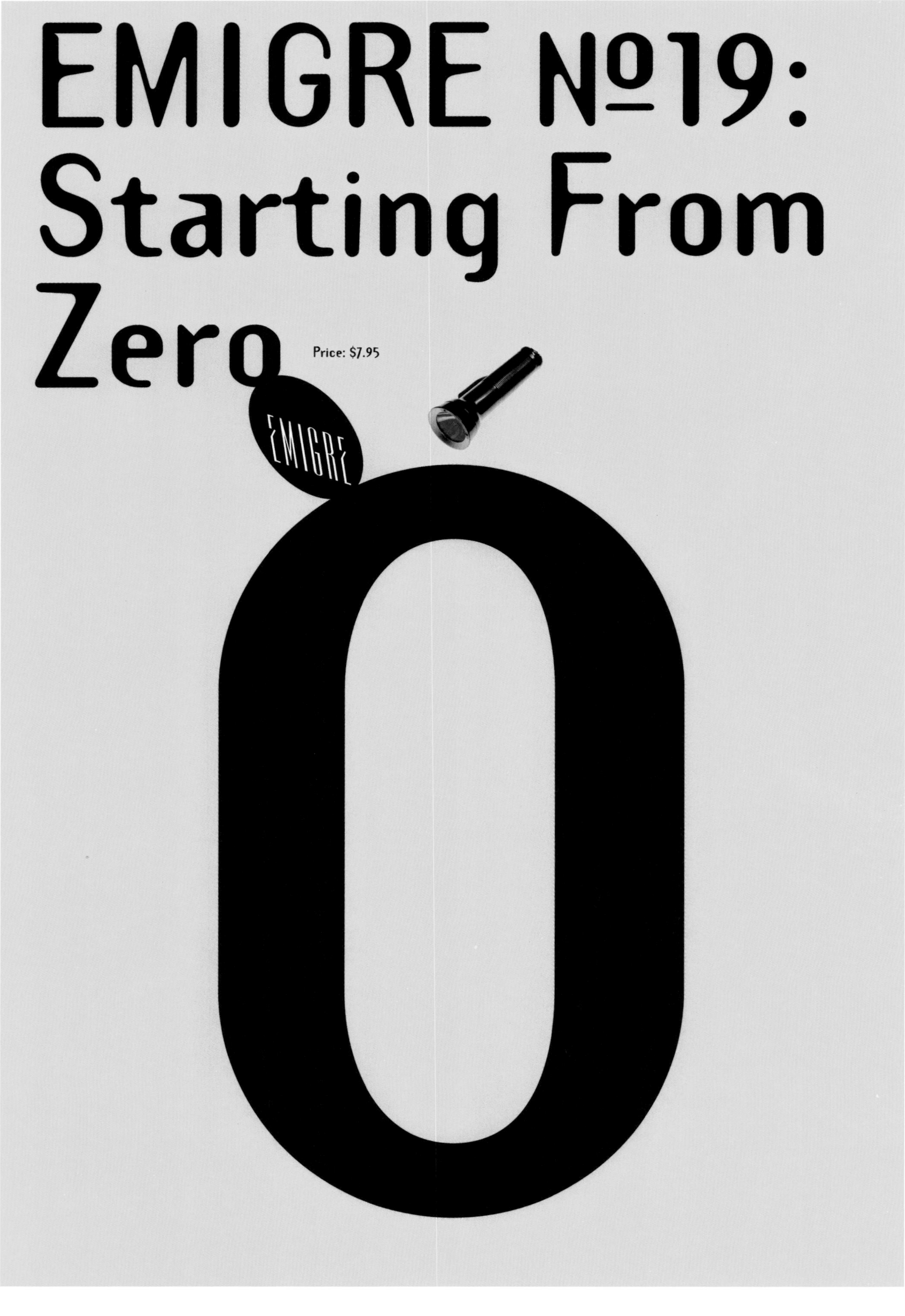

● **1984–2005 . EMIGRE .** Magazine / Newspaper . Rudy VanderLans, Zuzana Licko
"Starting From Zero," No. 19, 1991

→ p.484

1984 . MUSÉE D'ORSAY . Logo . Bruno Monguzzi, Jean Widmer

→ p.484

1985 . YALE UNIVERSITY PRESS . Logo . Paul Rand

→ p.485

● **1985–1991 . J.D.s .** Magazine / Newspaper . G.B. Jones, Bruce LaBruce
Photograph Jena von Brücker, No. 8, 1990

→ p.485

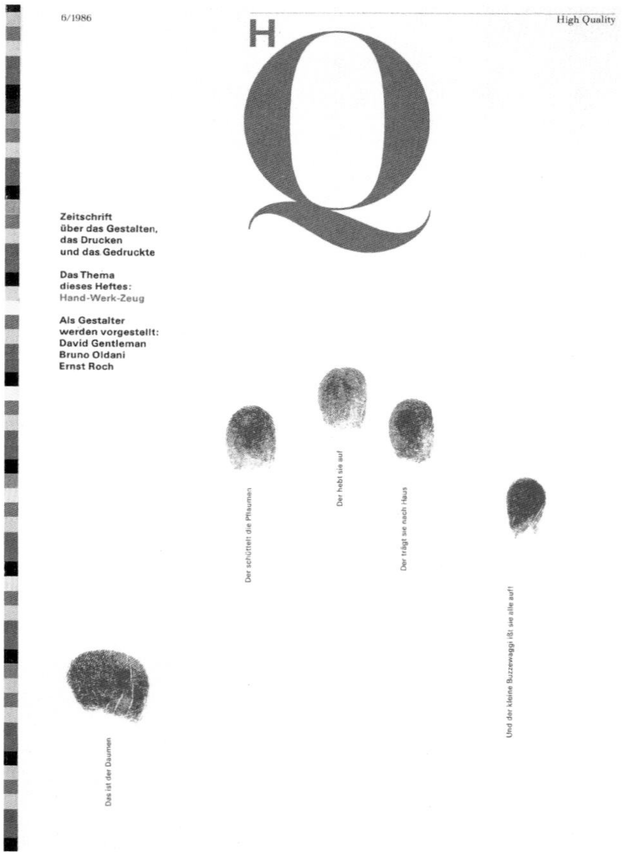

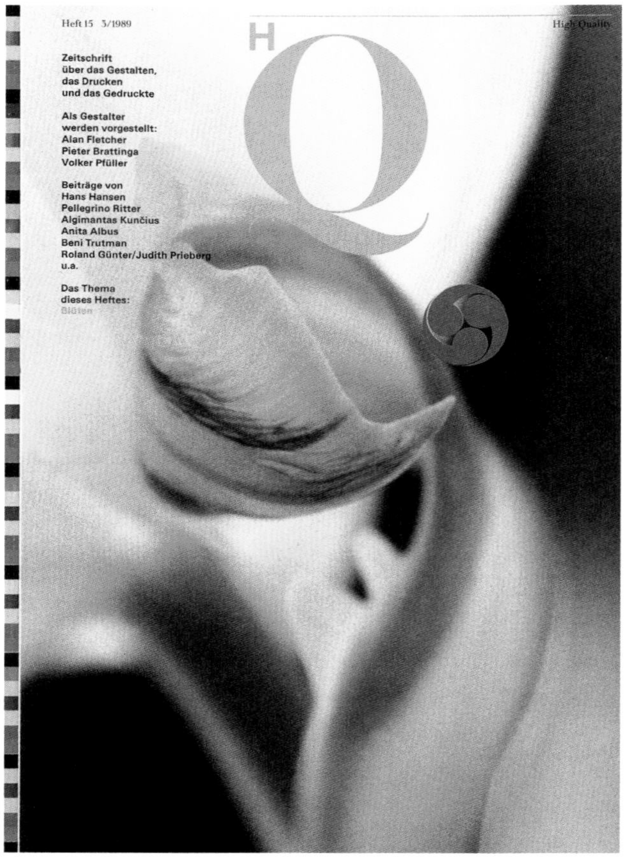

● **1985–1998 . HQ (HIGH QUALITY) .** Magazine / Newspaper . Rolf Müller
LEFT: Vol. 6, 1986; RIGHT: Vol. 5, No. 15, 1989

→ p.485

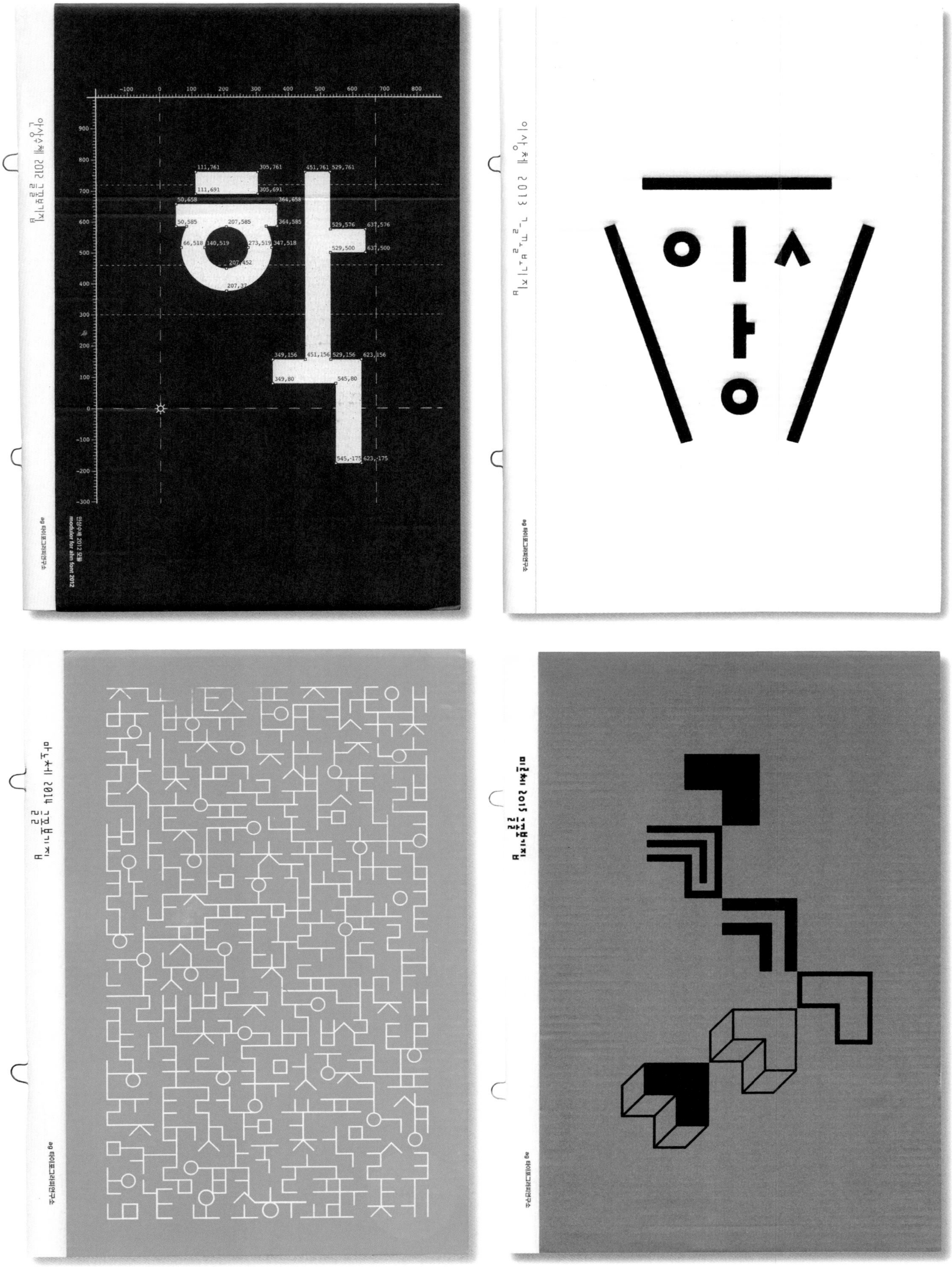

● **1985 . AHNSANGSOO .** Typeface . Ahn Sang-soo
TOP LEFT: Ahnsangsoo, 1985; TOP RIGHT: Leesang, 1991; BOTTOM LEFT: Mano, 1993; BOTTOM RIGHT: Myrrh, 1992

→ p.486

● **1986 . DESIGN PROCESS AUTO .** Poster . Pierre Mendell

→ p.486

● **1986 . IQ .** Poster . Uwe Loesch

→ p.486

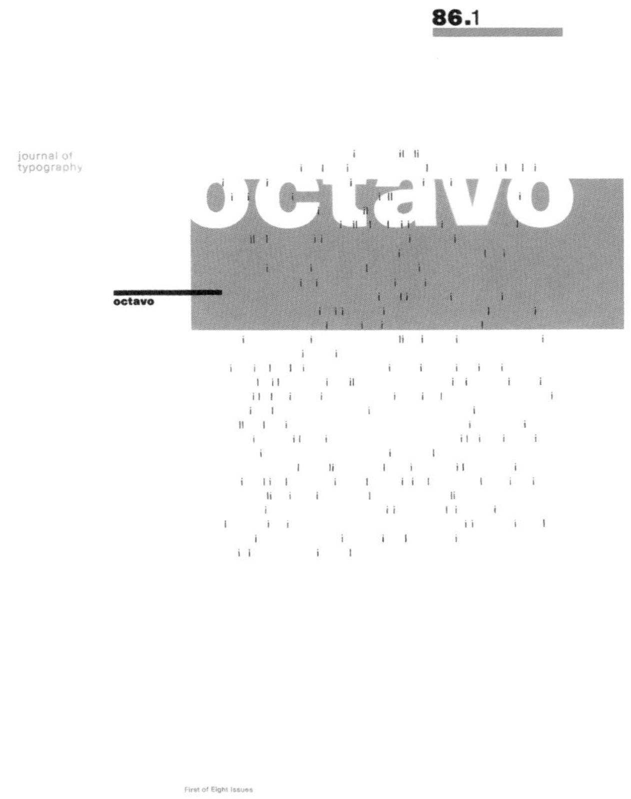

● **1986–1992 . OCTAVO .** Magazine / Newspaper . Mark Holt, Hamish Muir, Simon Johnston
No. 86.1, 1986

→ p.487

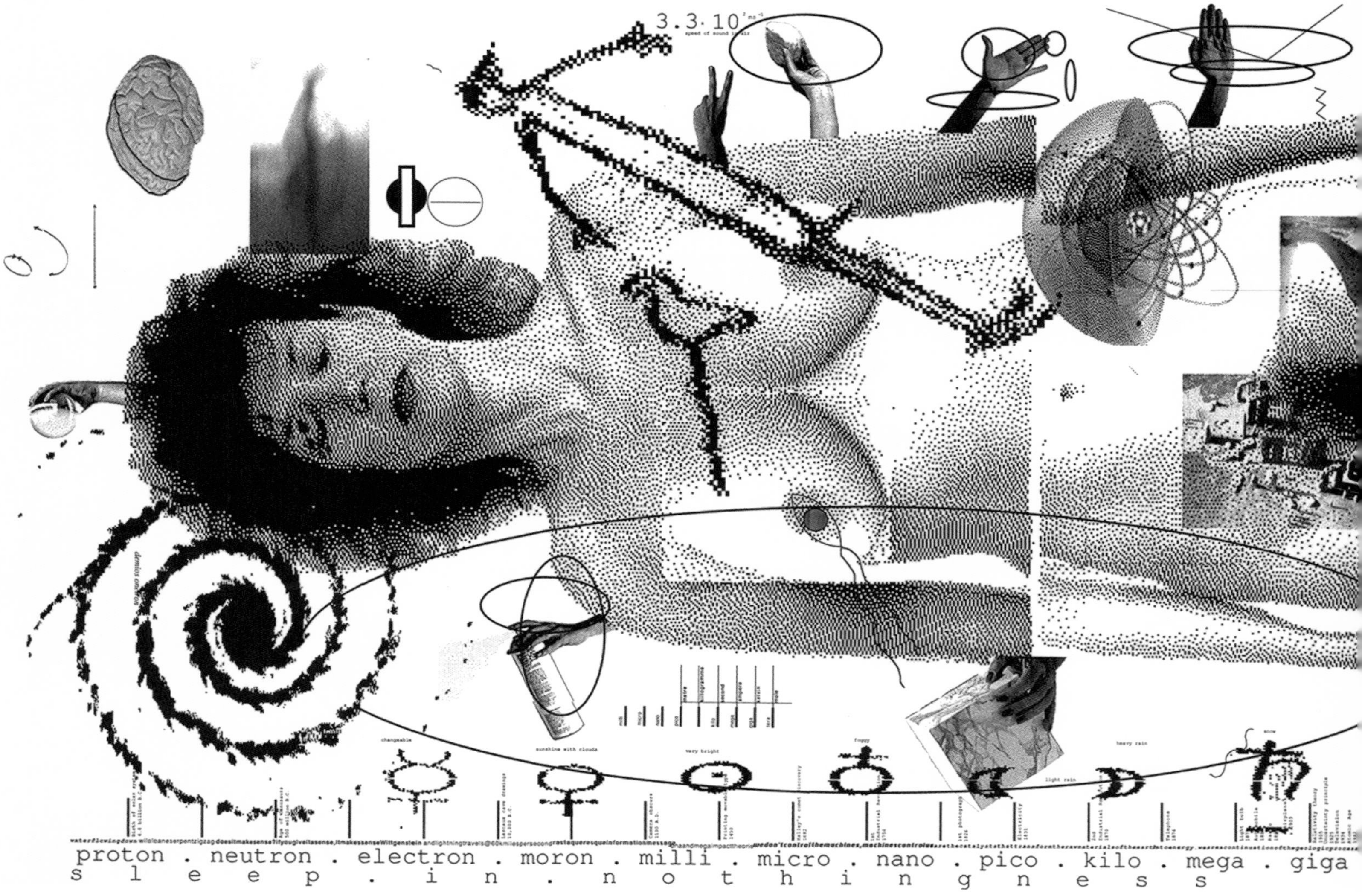

proton . neutron . electron . moron . milli . micro . nano . pico . kilo . mega . giga
s l e e p . i n . n o t h i n g n e s s

● **1986 . DOES IT MAKE SENSE? .** Magazine / Newspaper . April Greiman

→ p.487

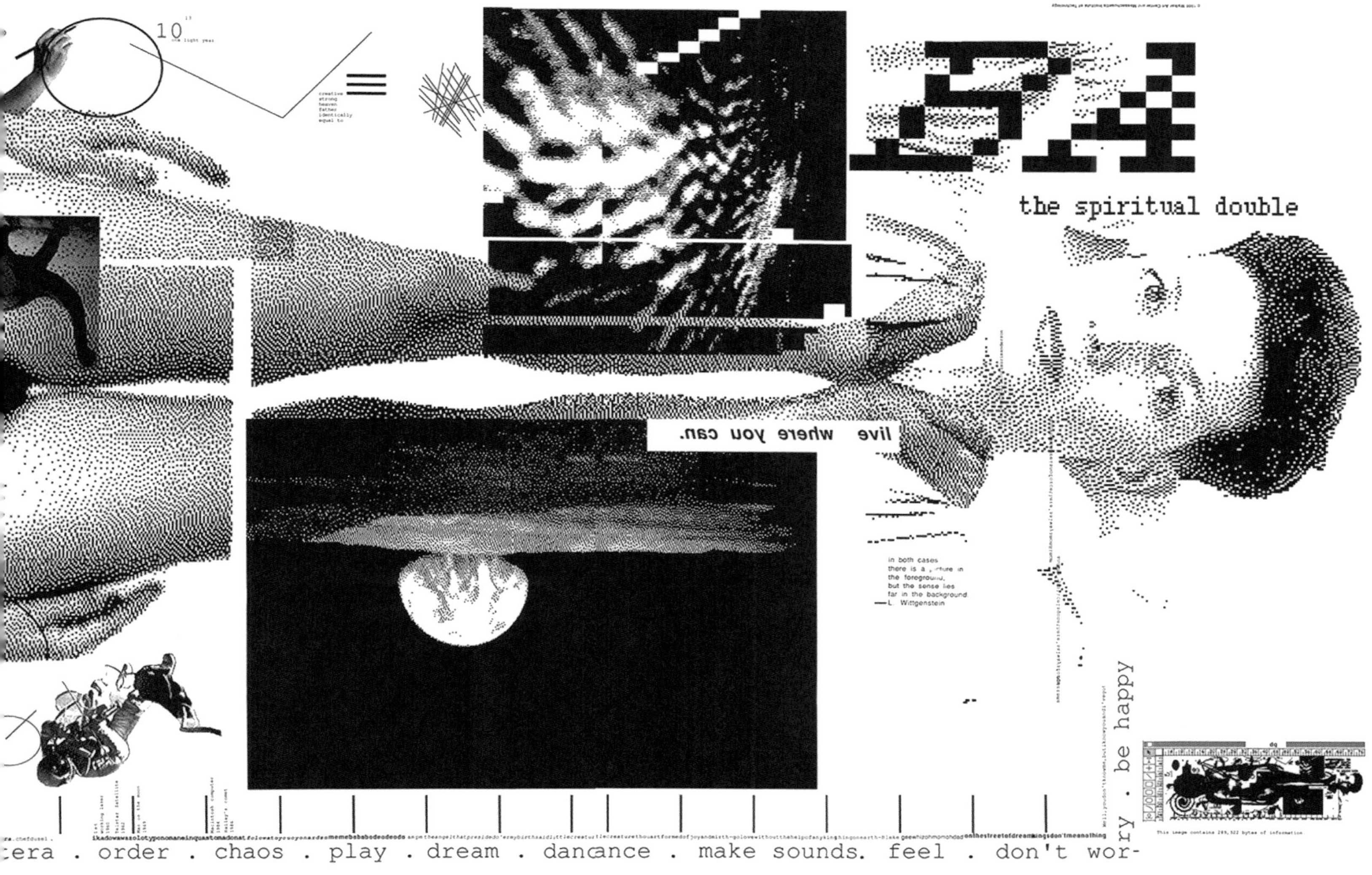

the spiritual double
live where you can.
in both cases
the foreground,
but the sense lies
far in the background
—L. Wittgenstein
ry . be happy
era . order . chaos . play . dream . dancance . make sounds. feel . don't wor-

Is your train
of thought subject
to delays?

The Economist

"I never read
The Economist."

Management trainee. Aged 42.

To err is human.
To er, um, ah
is unacceptable.

The Economist

1986–2006 . **THE ECONOMIST** . Advertising . Abbott Mead Vickers BBDO

→ p.487

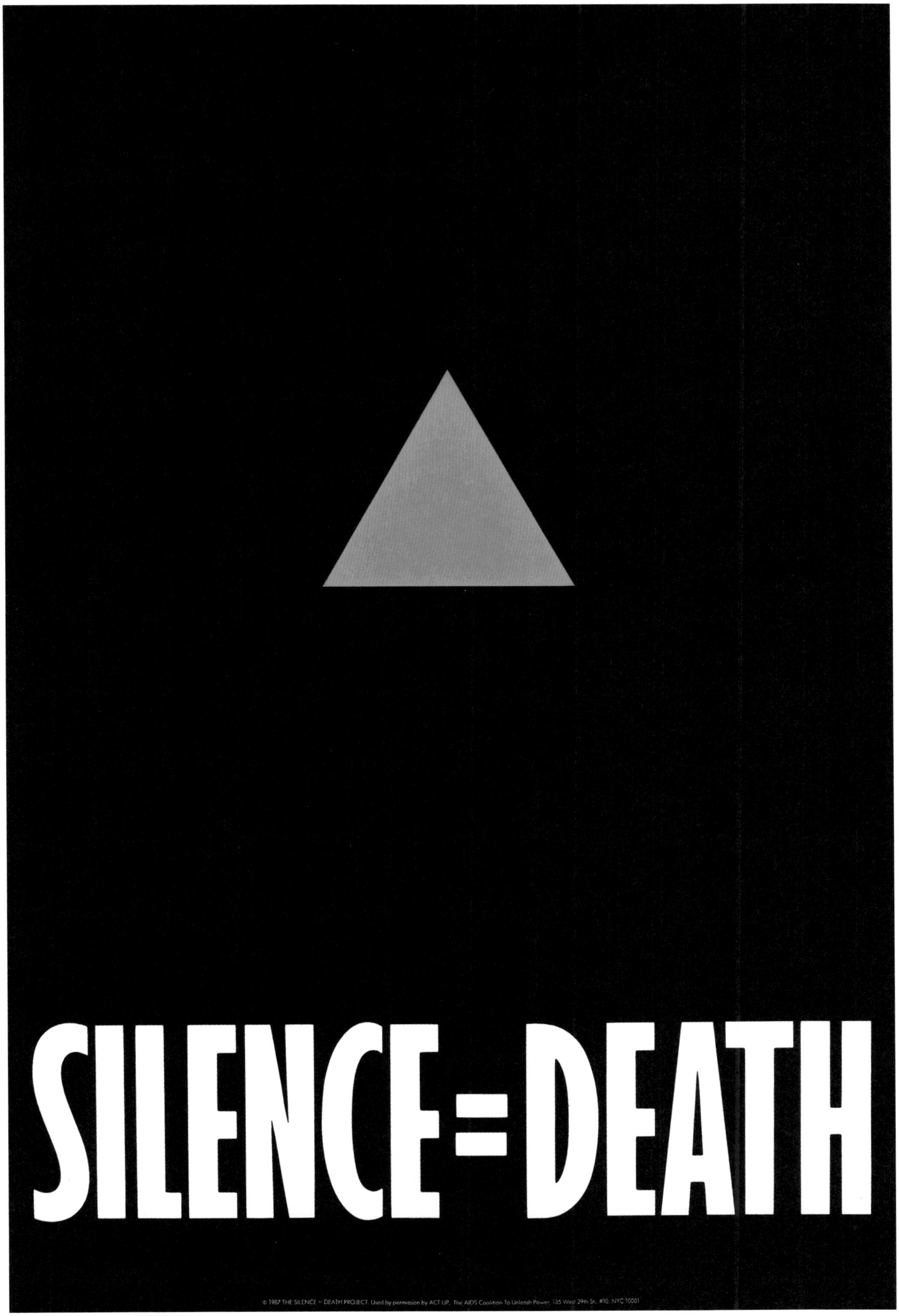

● **1987 . SILENCE = DEATH .** Poster . Avram Finkelstein et al.

→ p.488

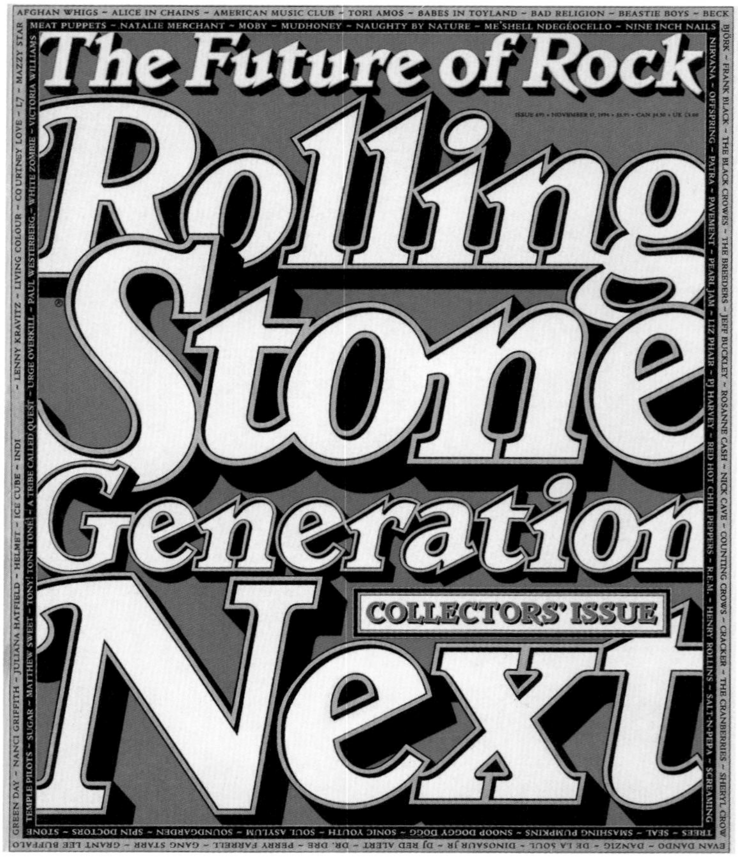
AFGHAN WHIGS - ALICE IN CHAINS - AMERICAN MUSIC CLUB - TORI AMOS - BABES IN TOYLAND - BAD RELIGION - BEASTIE BOYS - BECK
MEAT PUPPETS - NATALIE MERCHANT - MOBY - MUDHONEY - NAUGHTY BY NATURE - ME'SHELL NDEGÉOCELLO - NINE INCH NAILS
The Future of Rock
Rolling Stone
Generation Next
COLLECTORS' ISSUE

● **1987–2001 . ROLLING STONE .** Magazine / Newspaper . Fred Woodward
"The Future of Rock: Generation Next—Collector's Issue," November 17, 1994

→ p.488

ABCDEFGHIJKLMN
OPQRSTUVWXYZ&
abcdefghijklmnopqrs
tuvwxyzß1234567890
You may ask w
hy so many differen
t typefaces. They all serve the
same purpose but they express man's di
versity. It is the same diversity we find in wine. I once saw a li
st of Médoc wines featuring sixty different Médocs all of the
same year. All of them were wines but each was different fro
m the others. It's the nuances that are important. The same i
s true for typefaces. Pourquoi tant d'Alphabets différents! To
us servent au même but, mais aussi à exprimer la diversité de l'homme. C'est cette
même diversité que nous retrouvons dans les vins de Médoc. J'ai pu, un jour, relever
soixante crus, tous de la même année. Il s'agissait certes de vins, mais tous étaient di
fférents. Tout est dans la nuance du bouquet. Il en est de même pour les caractères!
Sie fragen sich, warum es notwendig ist, so viele Schriften zur Verfügung zu haben. S
ie dienen alle zum selben, aber machen die Vielfalt des Menschen aus. Diese Vielfalt
ist wie beim Wein. Ich habe einmal eine Weinkarte studiert mit sechzig Médoc-Weine
n aus dem selben Jahr. Das ist ausnahmslos Wein, aber doch nicht alles
der gleiche Wein. Es hat eben gleichwohl Nuancen. So ist es auch mit de
r Schrift. You may ask why so many different typefaces. They all serve the
same purpose but they express man's diversity. It is the same diversity w
e find in wine. I once saw a list of Médoc wines featuring sixty different M
édocs all of the same year. All of them were wines but each was different
from the others. It's the nuances that are important. The same is true for
typefaces. Pourquoi tant d'Alphabets différents! Tous servent au même b
ut, mais aussi à exprimer la diversité de l'h
omme. C'est cette même diversité que nou
s retrouvons dans les vins de Médoc. J'ai p
u, un jour, relever soixante crus, tous de la
même année. Il s'agissait certes de vins, ma
is tous étaient différents. Tout est dans la nu
ance du bouquet. Il en est de même pour l
es caractères! Sie fragen sich, warum es not
wendig ist, so viele Schriften zur Verfügung
zu haben. Sie dienen alle zum selben, aber

● **1988 . AVENIR .** Typeface . Adrian Frutiger

→ p.488

Home news, page 4
Reginald Harraden: packaging Manchester

Analysis, page 23
Lord Carrington's end of term report on Nato

Movie, page 34
Holly Hunter's Berlin broadcast

Sport, page 18
Norman Whiteside: old head on young feet

25p
Thursday
February 18
1988
Published in London
and Manchester

The Guardian

Top officers face fresh RUC inquiry

David Hearst, John Carvel and Joe Joyce

THE POSSIBLE role played by the Royal Ulster Constabulary's most senior officers in the cover-up over six police killings in County Armagh in 1982 is to be investigated by the Northern Ireland police authority, Mr Tom King, the Northern Ireland Secretary, told the Commons yesterday.

Sir John Hermon, the RUC Chief Constable, his deputy Mr Michael McAtamney, and Assistant Chief Constable Trevor Forbes, who was head of the Special Branch at the time of the shootings, were all due to be interviewed by Mr John Stalker, the former deputy chief constable of Greater Manchester taken off the inquiry.

Mr King announced that Mr Charles Kelly, Chief Constable of Staffordshire, had been appointed to reconsider whether 11 officers should face disciplinary charges for conspiring to pervert the course of justice.

Mr King said that observations made by Mr Colin Sampson, the West Yorkshire Chief Constable, who took over from Mr Stalker, on the role of more senior officers would be referred to the police authority, the disciplinary authority for all high-ranking officers.

In the most comprehensive statement yet about the Stalker affair Mr King said Sir John and Mr McAtamney would ensure in future that all information given to the Director of Public Prosecutions in Northern Ireland, Sir Barry Shaw, was accurate "whether or not any security interest is involved".

Announcing widespread changes in the control of the RUC Special Branch, Mr King said the desire to protect intelligence sources must never again lead it to "operate outside effective accountability and control".

The statement was a telling vindication of Mr Stalker's allegations and led to speculation in Belfast that Sir John, who is due to retire in November, might go earlier.

Mr Stalker, welcoming Mr King's statement, said: "It shows that I did a straightforward policeman's job in Northern Ireland. I am grateful for his acknowledgement that some of the recommendations now being implemented flow directly from my report."

Mr King gave the impression that a solution could also be close in the extradition procedures row with Dublin.

Dublin rejected Mr King's announcement as "absolutely unsatisfactory". The Energy Minister, Mr Ray Burke, said: "It is essential for the trust and confidence of the minority in the performance of justice in the North that there should be prosecutions."

In a special Dail debate, the Prime Minister, Mr Charles Haughey, emphasised "our determination and resolve to do everything in our power to defeat the men of violence and to maintain the rule of law".

The Stalker affair and the Birmingham Six case, he argued, had clear implications for the fair treatment of Irish people and justified the safeguards in the new Irish extradition arrangements. "If the British Government persists in refusing to operate the new procedures in accordance with Irish law, extradition will not be possible at all."

Unanswered questions, page 3
Day in politics, page 6

Righteous indignation. . .Police try persuasion with a Christian CND supporter

PHOTOGRAPH MARTIN ARGLES

Soldiers of Christ arise and put armour on

Ed Vulliamy

THAT those who fear the Lord need have no fear of any man was made manifest outside the Ministry of Defence in London yesterday. A column of the Christian faithful, including nuns, priests, and monks laid siege to the high temple of war with a determination which astounded the police and the servants of Anti-Christ who looked on from the ministry windows.

By the end of the Ash Wednesday protest, organised by Christian CND, 64 demonstrators had been arrested. Most were charged with criminal damage; some with obstruction.

The scene recalled the most tightly organised of revolutionary demonstrations: nuns hitched up their skirts to clamber over barriers or to dodge around police lines; vicars carrying walkie-talkies co-ordinated the action with military precision which must have been the envy of those within the Whitehall building.

Many of the 400-odd Christian protesters outside the ministry were middle-aged. Some 65 of them pressed against the lines of police, clutching lumps of charcoal and large wooden crosses. When they spotted a breach in the lines of the forces of darkness, they dived at it and ran through to the walls. The nuns daubed the slogans "Repent" and "Peace" in ash and charcoal which had been blessed by the Anglican Bishop of Southwark, Peter Selby, during a special service at St George's Roman Catholic Cathedral.

Most were arrested on the spot; others waited to be taken away. Cheers went up as the martyrs were bundled into police buses and taken to the inquisition at Cannon Row police station.

The Rev Paul Bayes, chairman of Christian CND, declared: "The MoD is where nuclear wars are planned and we are asking them to repent."

Legal history made, page 4

Solicitor charged with submitting false forms

Scotland Yard queries legal aid claims

Exclusive

Clare Dyer
Legal Correspondent

A NUMBER of solicitors' firms in London are being investigated by the police and the legal aid authorities for suspected fraud in submitting legal aid payment claims.

One solicitor with offices in London has been committed for trial at the Old Bailey charged with submitting false "green forms" — the forms solicitors use to claim payment for legal work — totalling £8,900.

It is alleged that the authorities were alerted because his claim forms were for £90 or £50, the maximum sums solicitors can incur for different categories of work without getting authorisation from the legal aid office.

Another solicitor, from east London, is under investigation by Scotland Yard, but has not been charged. He is suspected of submitting exaggerated claims for time spent waiting for cases to begin in magistrates' courts and for travelling time to court.

The cases are the first to involve Scotland Yard. Previously files have been sent to the Director of Public Prosecutions, but officials have felt there was insufficient evidence to prosecute.

Up to five more firms doing criminal work are under suspicion by London legal aid offices, but no decision has been taken on whether to pass files to the police.

The suspicions centre on inflated claims for waiting time, double or treble claiming for waiting time when attending court on behalf of more than one client, and claiming for fictitious attendances at police stations and prisons.

The suspected abuses came to light after a new system of checks was introduced last year in London's three legal aid area offices. About 50 files a week, chosen at random, are checked for inflated or improper billing, according to a legal aid head office spokesman.

An official in the Lord Chancellor's department, the government department responsible for legal aid, said yesterday the danger of fraudulent claims was most acute with bills for magistrates' court work because payment was handled by civil servants in legal aid offices, divorced from the court.

In the crown court solicitors' bills are assessed by court officials.

An experienced criminal solicitor said: "I had three cases in court this morning, all adjourned to different dates. If I claimed for the same waiting time on each bill there would be no way of tying up the three to show that all the waiting time was for the same day."

US colonel kidnapped

Julie Flint in Beirut

GUNMEN, clearly acting on precise intelligence, yesterday kidnapped a US marine colonel in south Lebanon, intercepting him between Tyre and Naqoura as he drove a United Nations jeep.

Reports from the south said two carloads of men intercepted Lieut Col Richard Higgins three miles south of Tyre, on a coastal road controlled by the Shi'ite movement, Amal, as he headed for the headquarters of the United Nations peacekeeping force Unifil in Naqoura.

Sources in south Lebanon said the kidnappers forced him out of his jeep and into one their cars but made no move against another five foreigners — including one Irishman but no more Americans — travelling in a second UN vehicle.

The Reagan administration yesterday condemned the kidnapping and said it would hold the kidnappers responsible for Colonel Higgins's safety. The White House could do little more than reiterate its call for the release of all hostages in Lebanon.

President Reagan was told of the marine's disappearance at his mountaintop ranch in California where he is on holiday.

The colonel, described as the head of the 15-man observer group attached to Unifil headquarters, was the fourth foreigner kidnapped in Lebanon in three weeks and the third with UN connections.

A Swede and a Norwegian, Mr Jan Stening and Mr William Jorgensen, attached to the UN agency for Palestinian Refugees, were abducted in Sidon, midway between Beirut and Tyre, on February 5. UN officials have received no ransom demand and are still puzzled by the motives for the kidnappings.

Amal, whose position as the strongest single force in south Lebanon is coming under pressure both from pro-Iran fundamentalism and from renewed Palestinian guerrilla activity, was shocked by the kidnapping and launched an extensive hunt for the kidnappers.

Shi'ite sources in the south said scores of checkpoints were thrown up and several villages searched.

UN helicopters flew over the entire Tyre area concentrating on the winding, cave-ridden wadis to the east.

By late last night there had been no claims to the kidnapping, the first of an American in south Lebanon.

Although kidnappings have virtually wiped out the American presence in West Beirut, a considerable number of Americans remain in south Lebanon — at least six of them members of Colonel Higgins's UN Truce Supervision Organisation team.

Kinnock sees Palestinian tragedy, page 24

Aids warnings 'ignored'

Angella Johnson

MANY people have failed to change their sexual behaviour and still have sex with more than one partner despite an increase in Aids cases, it was announced yesterday.

Dr Spencer Hagard, of the Health Education Authority, said recent research shows that while most people are aware of Aids, many sexually active young people are not worried about contracting the HIV virus.

After a government campaign last year to warn people about Aids, a survey by the British Market Research Board showed that nine out of 100 people have had more than one sexual partner in the past year. Two out of every 100 said they had had five or six partners.

Dr Hagard warned that the number of people with the HIV virus has doubled since 1983 because of complacency among heterosexuals who believe they are not in a high risk group.

"In 1986 there were 308 new cases diagnosed, by 1987 that figure has risen to 633 and we expect it to more than double next year," he said.

He was announcing the authority's new offensive against the spread of Aids, which will include a £4 million advertising campaign aimed at encouraging heterosexuals to change their sexual practices.

The campaign, which began last night with two 60-second television commercials, shown on ITV and BBC, will urge heterosexual young people to behave more responsibly about sex and will encourage the use of condoms.

The target groups in the first burst of advertising (February to May) will be the general public, with emphasis on the 16 to 30 age group. Over the four months the campaign will be backed by advertisements in magazines and newspapers warning people that sleeping around is dangerous.

People of all ages travelling in the UK and abroad are urged to be careful. The story of a man who contracted the Aids virus on a business trip is used on posters to warn those tempted to sleep with a new partner while away from home.

By the end of last year there were 630 people carrying the Aids virus, 697 had died and 1,227 people were suffering from the cumulative effect of the disease.

A survey published in the British Medical Journal last week showed that half the 18 to 24-year-olds and a third of the 16 to 17 year-olds interviewed admitted that if they wanted to have sex the absence of a condom would not stop them.

● The Terrence Higgins Trust, welcoming the campaign, said it must be successful if Britain is to avoid an epidemic.

"It's not your day, is it? Locked out of TV-am this morning and as this is only our first evening together, you're not getting in here, either."

News in brief

Kinnock in Israel attack

The Labour leader, Mr Neil Kinnock, has attacked Israeli policy in the occupied territories after being moved nearly to tears when he visited two Arabs in a hospital in Nablus who had been shot in the back. Page 24

Nuclear crash admission

The Ministry of Defence has admitted that an accident to a nuclear convoy which regularly uses the A1 could scatter radioactive debris over a built-up area. Page 4

Wrong number

Workers walked out of the Solihull Land-Rover plant after the company supplied the ex-directory numbers of some workers to Mori for a telephone poll. Page 2

Helicopter shooting

An inquest verdict that a British army helicopter pilot died "as a result of enemy action" during the Falklands war has been quashed after the High Court heard how a Royal Navy destroyer shot him down by mistake. Page 2

Thatcher weapons call

Mrs Thatcher has publicly criticised West Germany's reluctance to introduce modernised nuclear weapons in Europe. Page 24

Waldheim support drops

Austrian support for President Waldheim has slipped from 72 to 46 per cent since the historians' report Page 10

Inside today's Guardian

Arts, Reviews	21
Financial News	14-16
Cartoons	26
Computer Guardian	25-33
Crosswords	24,26
Entertainments	33
Grassroots	38
Guardian Women	20
Home News	2-4,8,24
International News	10-13
Letters	22
Listings	35
Movie Guardian	34
Personal/Law Report	37
Politics	6
Sports News	17-19

● **1988–2005 . THE GUARDIAN .** Magazine / Newspaper . David Hillman
Thursday, February 18, 1988

→ p.489

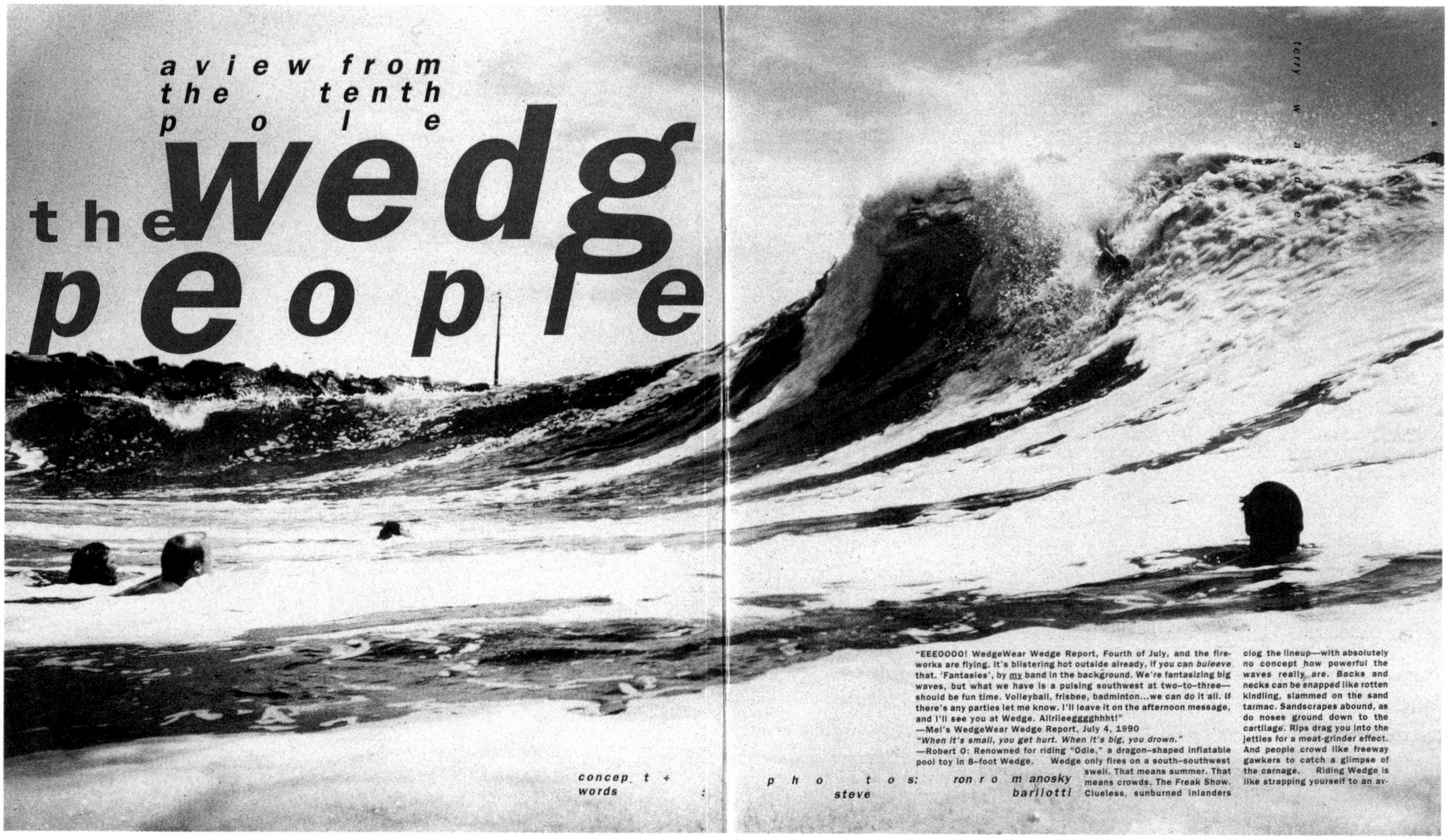

a view from
the tenth
pole
the wedg
people
terry wade
concept + words
photos: ron romanosky
steve barilotti
"EEEOOOO! WedgeWear Wedge Report, Fourth of July, and the fireworks are flying. It's blistering hot outside already, if you can buleeve that. 'Fantasies', by my band in the background. We're fantasizing big waves, but what we have is a pulsing southwest at two-to-three—should be fun time. Volleyball, frisbee, badminton...we can do it all. If there's any parties let me know. I'll leave it on the afternoon message, and I'll see you at Wedge. Allriieegggghhht!"
—Mel's WedgeWear Wedge Report, July 4, 1990
"When it's small, you get hurt. When it's big, you drown."
—Robert O: Renowned for riding "Odie," a dragon-shaped inflatable pool toy in 8-foot Wedge.
Wedge only fires on a south-southwest swell. That means summer. That means crowds. The Freak Show. Clueless, sunburned inlanders clog the lineup—with absolutely no concept how powerful the waves really are. Backs and necks can be snapped like rotten kindling, slammed on the sand tarmac. Sandscrapes abound, as do noses ground down to the cartilage. Rips drag you into the jetties for a meat-grinder effect. And people crowd like freeway gawkers to catch a glimpse of the carnage.
Riding Wedge is like strapping yourself to an av-

● **1989–1992 . BEACH CULTURE .** Magazine / Newspaper . David Carson
TOP: Photograph Geof Kern, Vol. 1, No. 3, August–September 1990; BOTTOM: Photograph Ron Romanosky, No. 5, February–March 1991

→ p.489

JEANS/WF-P06-054/¥9,000/ •BLUE •BLACK

THIS COLOR IS BLUE

1989 . WORKSHOP: Y'S FOR MEN . Book . Yasuhiro Sawada

→ p.489

V&A

● **1989 . V&A .** Logo . Alan Fletcher

→ p.490

ABCDE ABCDE
FGHIJ FGHIJ
KLMN KLMN
OPQRS OPQRS
TUVW TUVW
XYZ& XYZ&
01234 01234
56789 56789

● **1989 . TRAJAN .** Typeface . Carol Twombly

→ p.490

● **1989–2006 . CINEMAFRICA .** Poster . Ralph Schraivogel

→ p.490

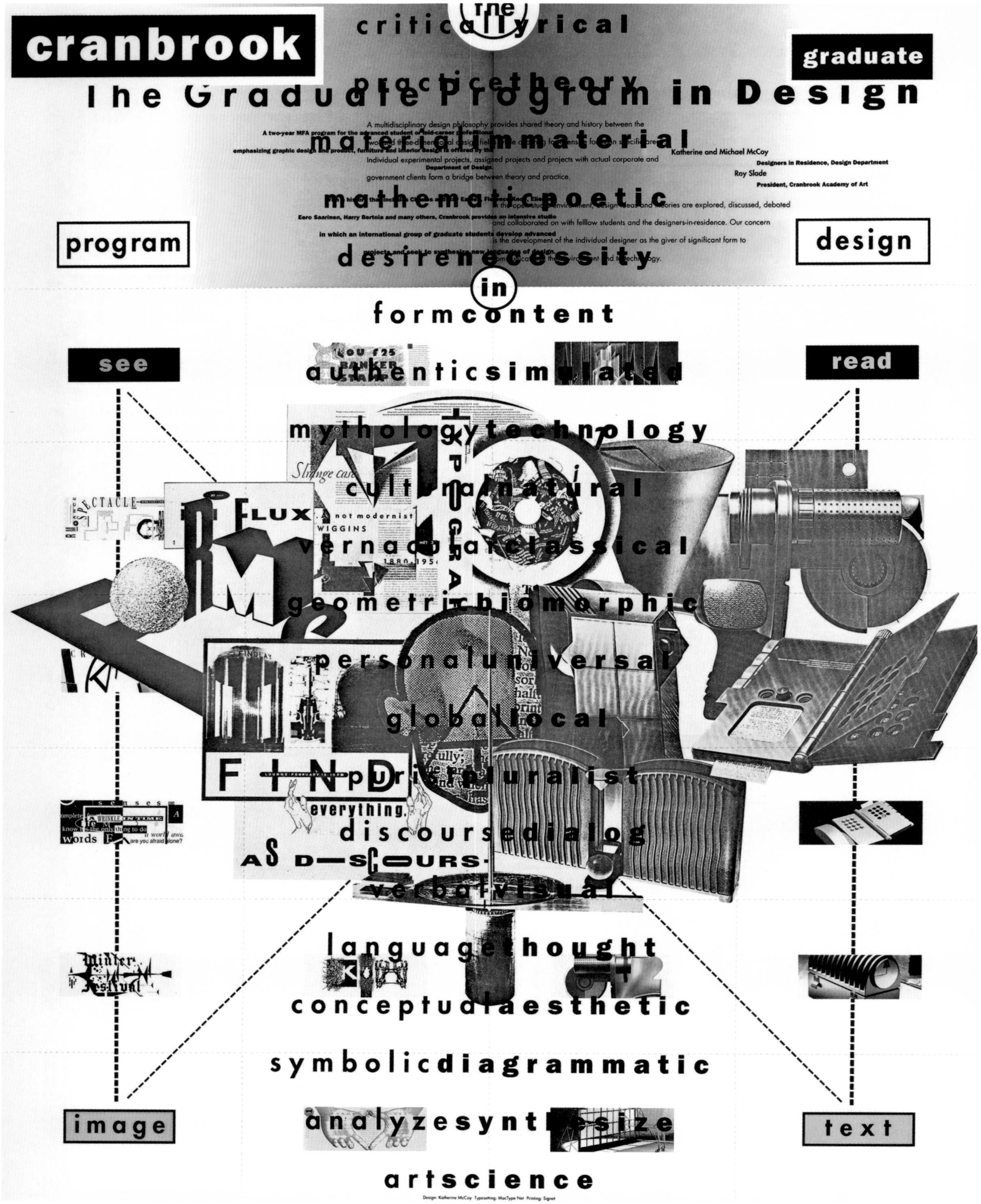

● **1989 . CRANBROOK: THE GRADUATE PROGRAM IN DESIGN .** Poster . Katherine McCoy

→ p.491

● **1989 . UNTITLED (YOUR BODY IS A BATTLEGROUND) .** Poster . Barbara Kruger

→ p.491

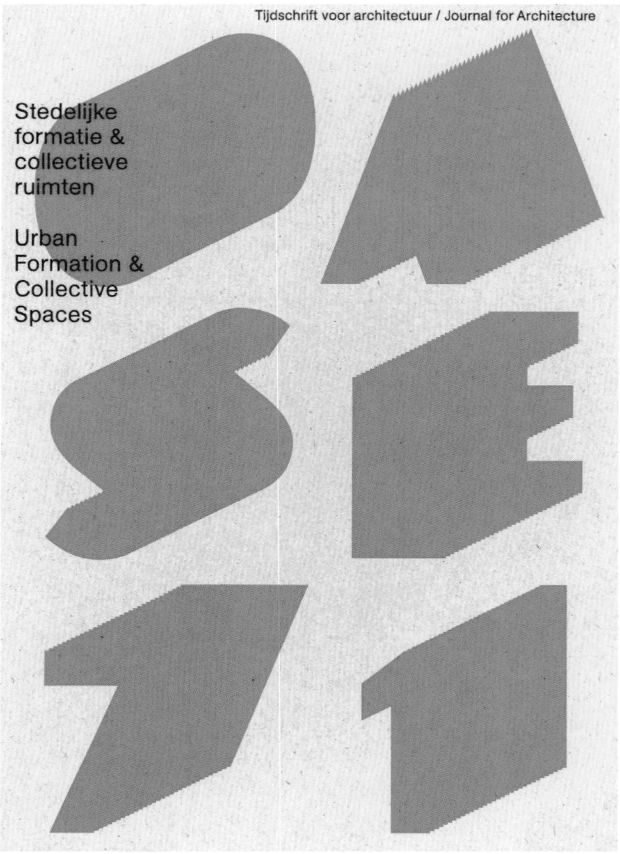

● **1990–PRESENT . OASE JOURNAL FOR ARCHITECTURE .** Magazine / Newspaper . Karel Martens
No. 71, 2007

→ p.491

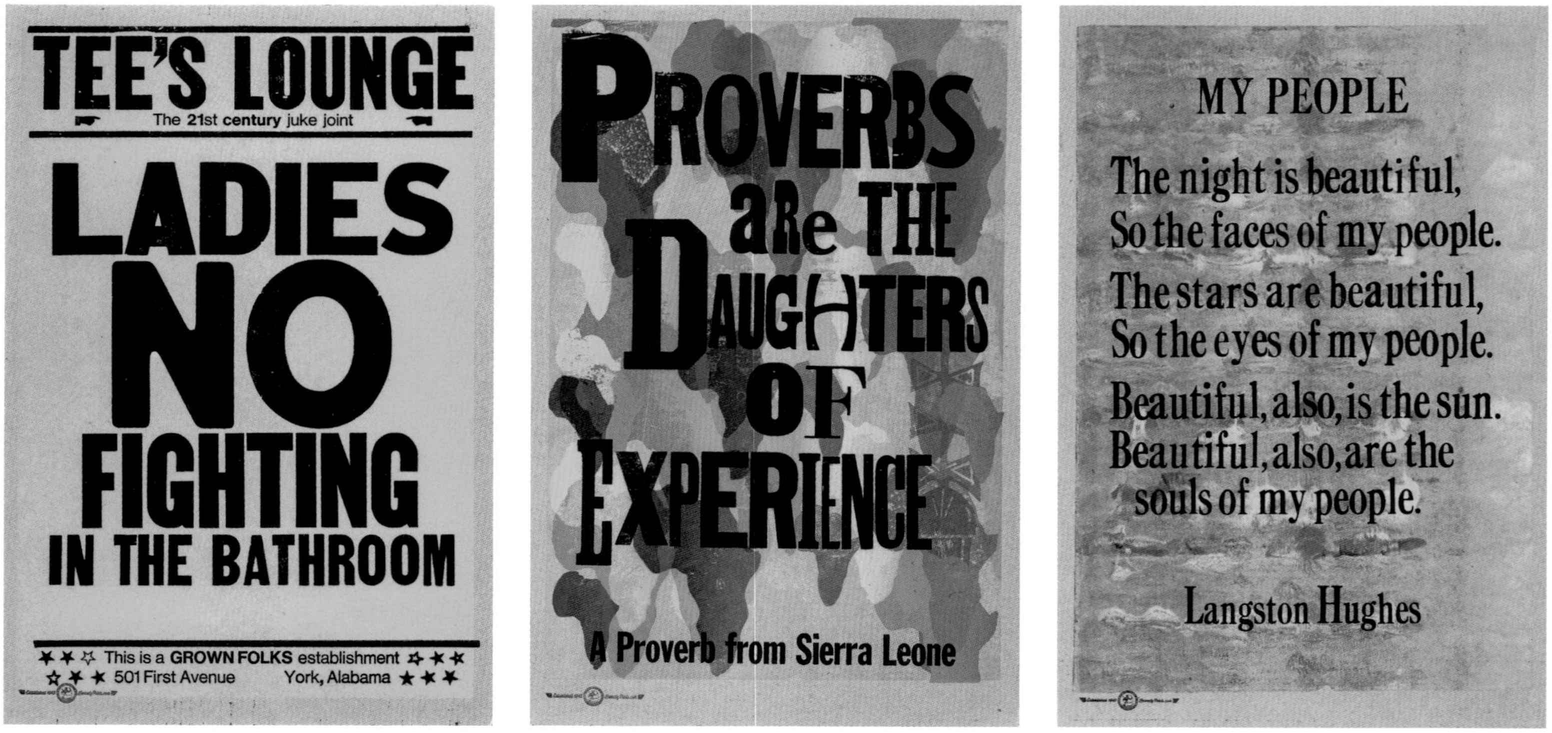

● **1990s–PRESENT . LETTERPRESS POSTERS (VARIOUS) .** Poster . Kennedy Prints
FROM LEFT: "Ladies, No Fighting," 2003; "Proverbs Are the Daughters of Experience," 2013; "My People," 2023

→ p.492

● **1991 . JUNGLE FEVER .** Poster . Art Sims

→ p.492

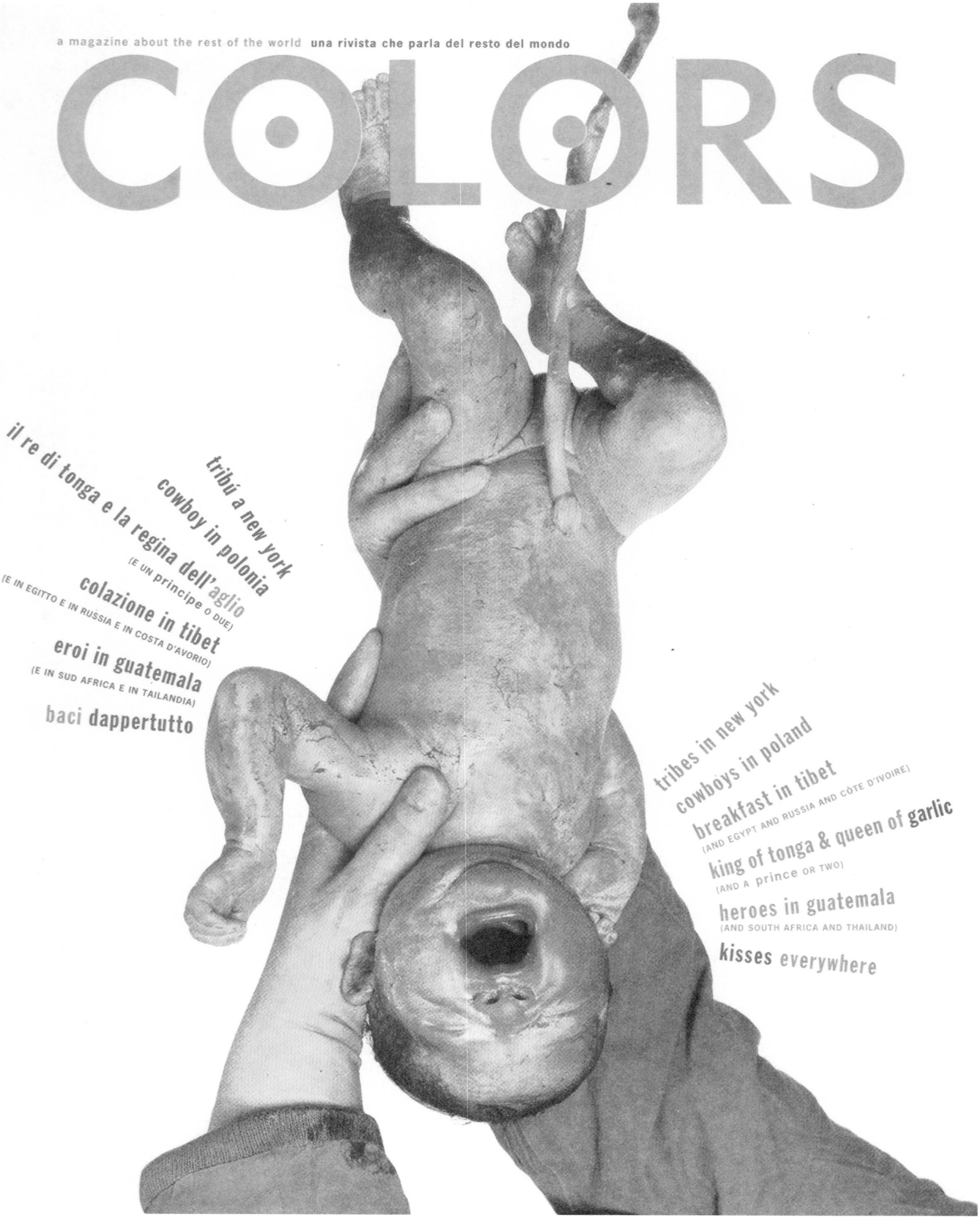
a magazine about the rest of the world una rivista che parla del resto del mondo
COLORS
tribú a new york
cowboy in polonia
il re di tonga e la regina dell'aglio
(E UN principe O DUE)
colazione in tibet
(E IN EGITTO E IN RUSSIA E IN COSTA D'AVORIO)
eroi in guatemala
(E IN SUD AFRICA E IN TAILANDIA)
baci dappertutto
tribes in new york
cowboys in poland
breakfast in tibet
(AND EGYPT AND RUSSIA AND CÔTE D'IVOIRE)
king of tonga & queen of garlic
(AND A prince OR TWO)
heroes in guatemala
(AND SOUTH AFRICA AND THAILAND)
kisses everywhere

● **1991–1995 . COLORS .** Magazine / Newspaper . Tibor Kalman
Photograph Oliviero Toscani, No. 1, 1991

→ p.492

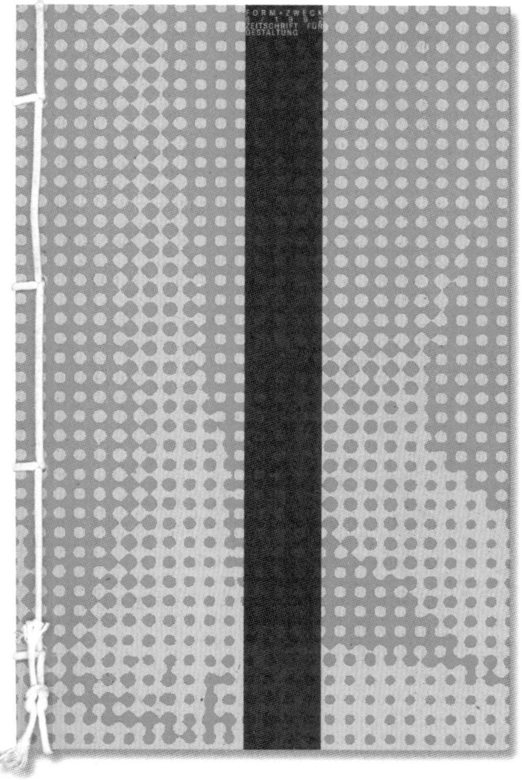

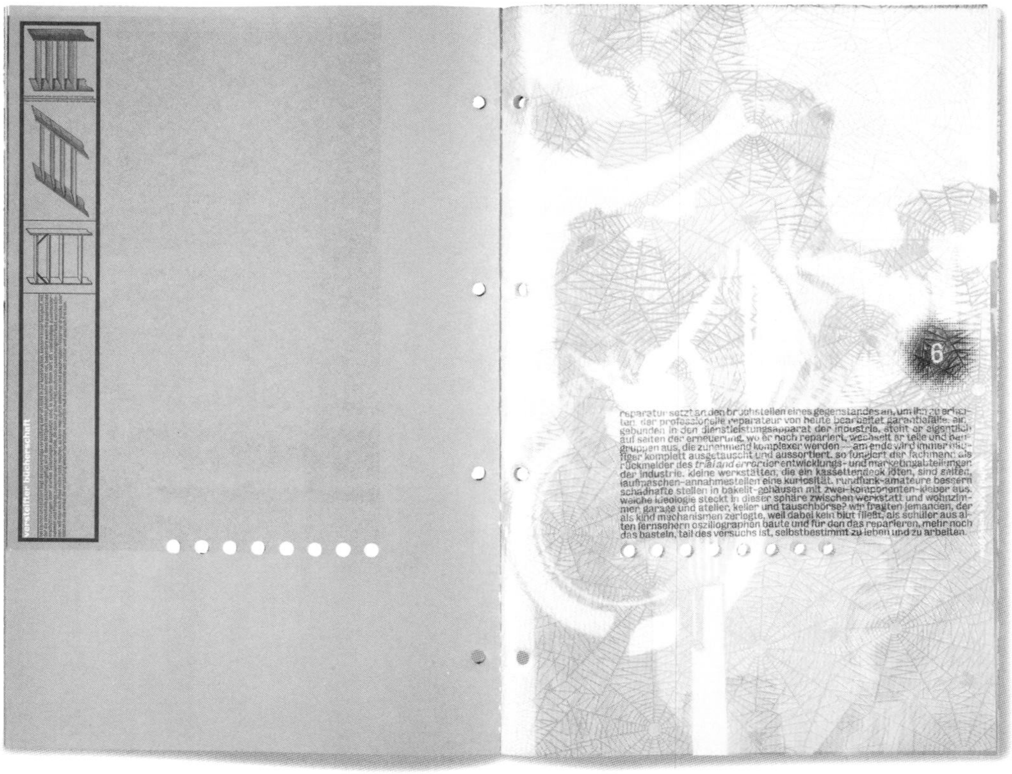

● **1991–1995 . FORM + ZWECK .** Magazine / Newspaper . Cyan
LEFT: No. 6, 1992; RIGHT: No. 11, 1995

→ p.493

THE NEW YORK TIMES OP-ED SATURDAY, MAY 15, 1993 19

Observer
RUSSELL BAKER
Joining Up For Glory

Campaign Spending: Despised but Addictive
By Peter Kostmayer
Clinton's reforms don't go far enough.

Broadway Book War – A Reader's Guide
By Melvin Jules Bukiet

Here is another country-club problem.

My Hopes, My Fears, My Disease
By Dennis deLeon
With each H.I.V. self-disclosure, we fight bigotry.

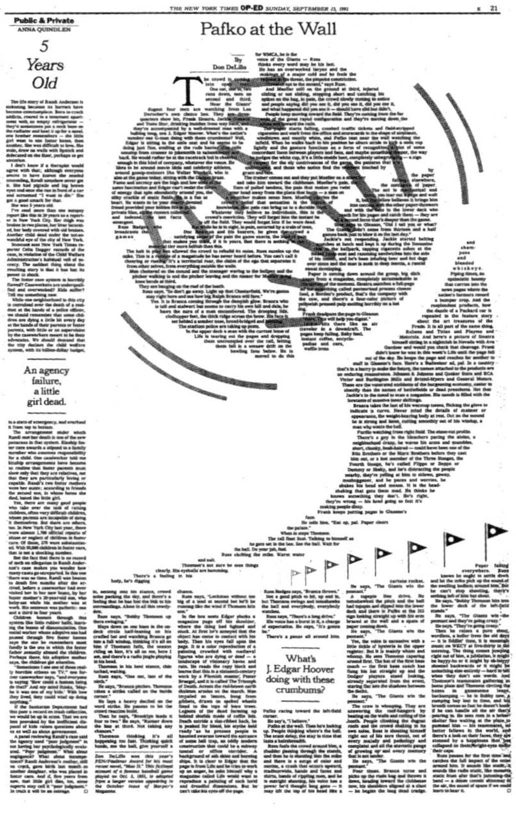
THE NEW YORK TIMES OP-ED SUNDAY, SEPTEMBER 13, 1992 21

Public & Private
ANNA QUINDLEN
5 Years Old

Pafko at the Wall
By Don DeLillo

An agency failure, a little girl dead.

What's J. Edgar Hoover doing with these crumbums?

● **1992 . THE NEW YORK TIMES OP-ED .** Magazine / Newspaper . Mirko Ilić
LEFT: Saturday, May 15, 1993; RIGHT: Sunday, September 13, 1992

→ p.493

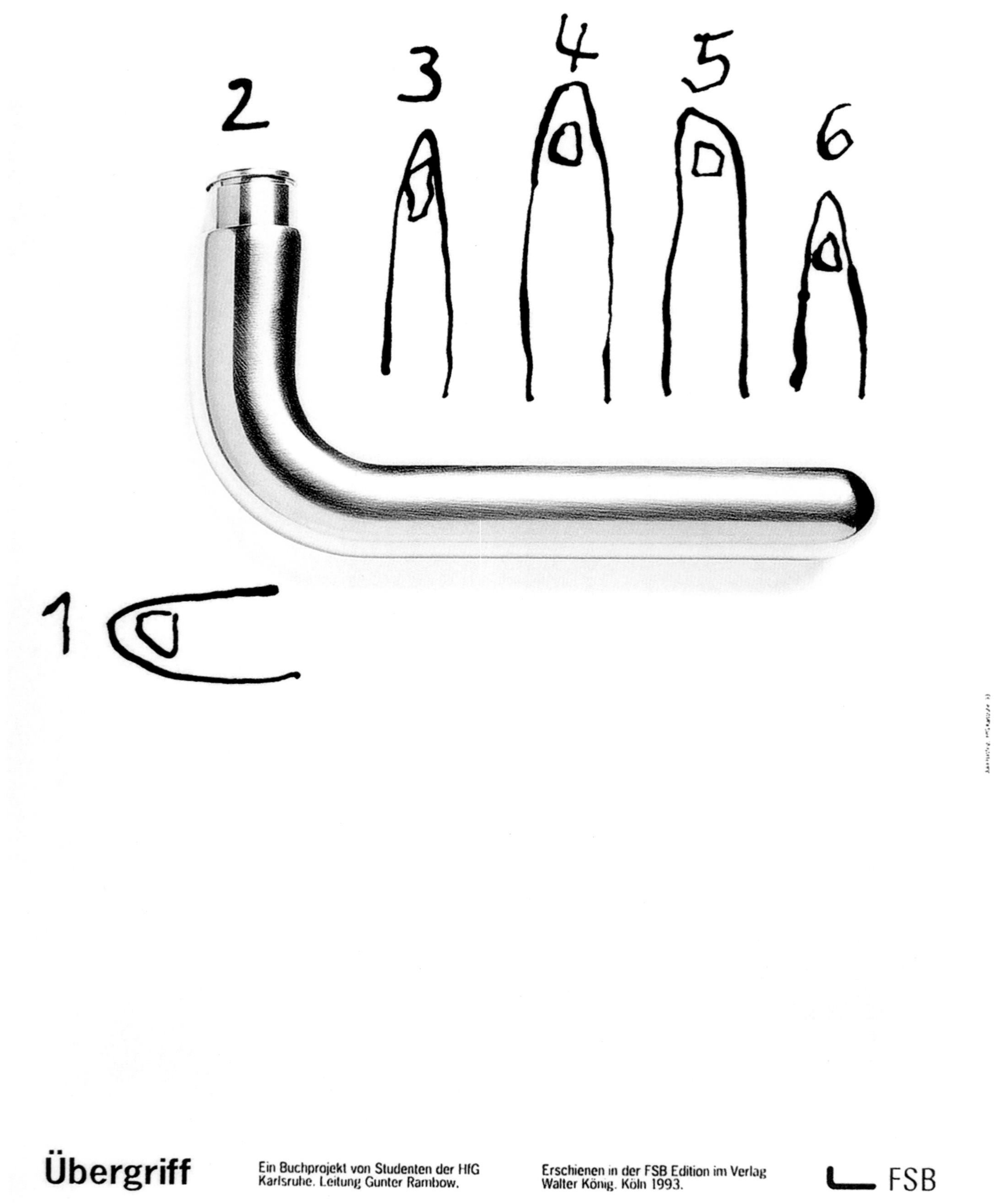

2
3
4
5
6
1
Übergriff
Ein Buchprojekt von Studenten der HfG Karlsruhe. Leitung Gunter Rambow.
Erschienen in der FSB Edition im Verlag Walter König. Köln 1993.
FSB

1992 . ÜBERGRIFF . Advertising . Julia Hasting

→ p.493

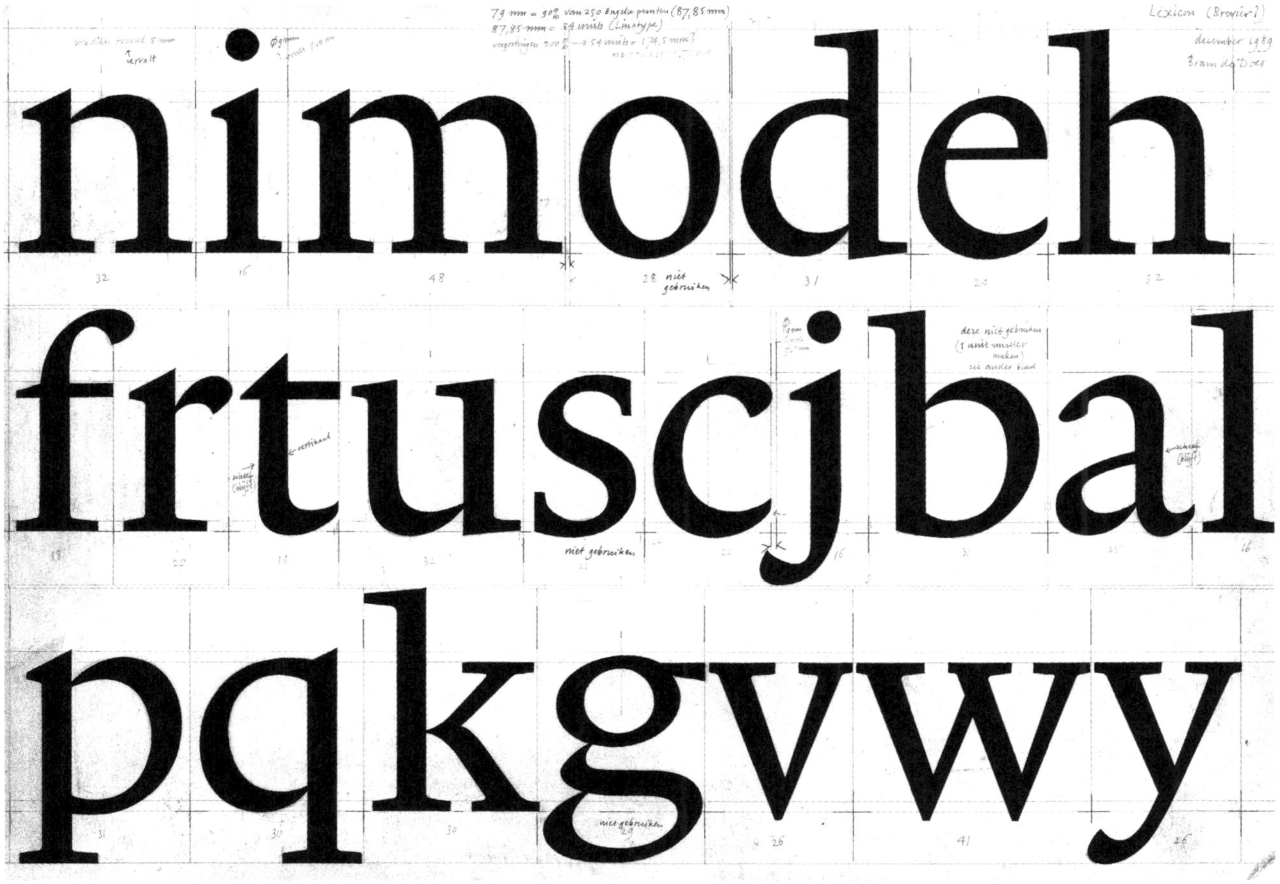

● **1992 . LEXICON .** Typeface . Bram de Does

→ p.494

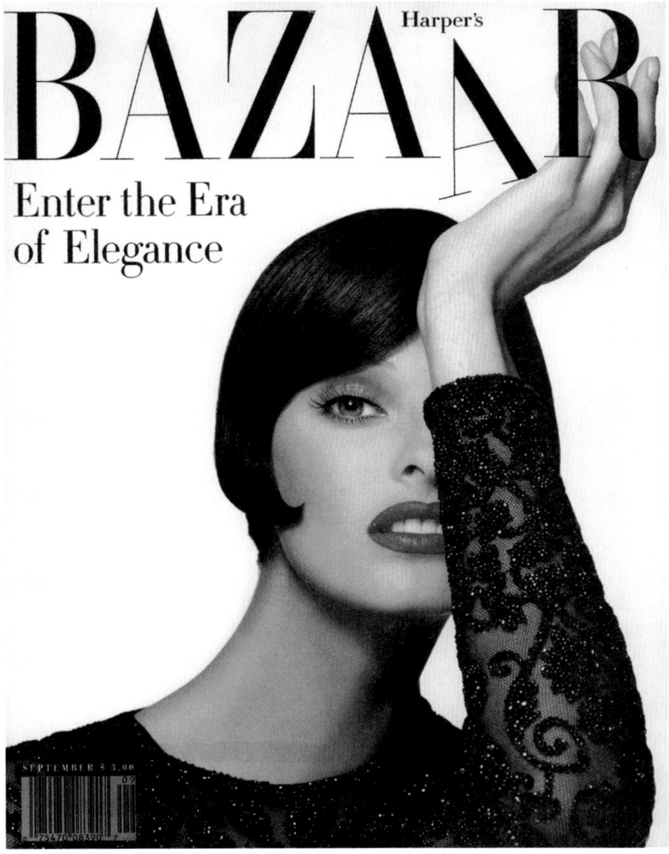

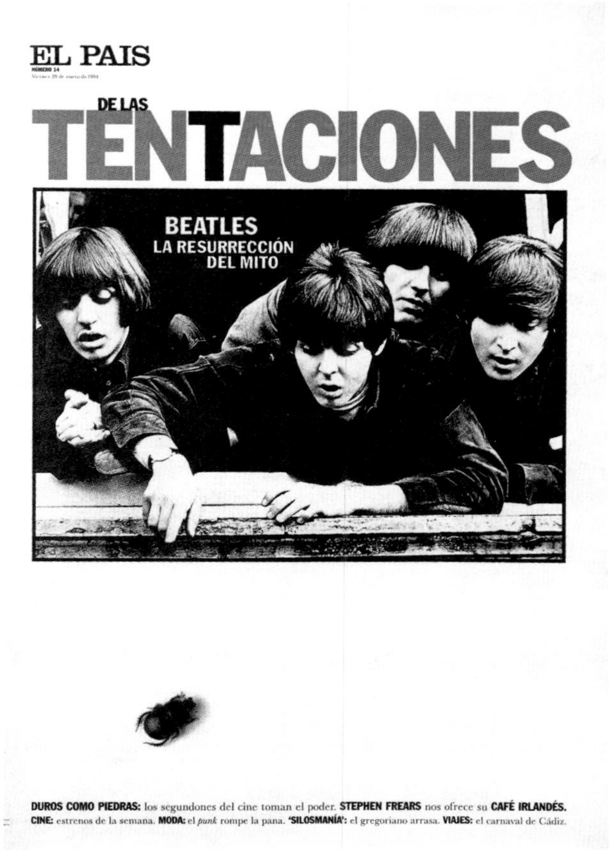

● **1992–1999 . HARPER'S BAZAAR .** Magazine / Newspaper . Fabien Baron
Photograph Patrick Demarchelier, model Linda Evangelista, September 1992

→ p.494

● **1993–PRESENT . TENTACIONES .** Magazine / Newspaper . Fernando Gutiérrez
Photograph Robert Whitaker, 1965, No. 14, 1994

→ p.494

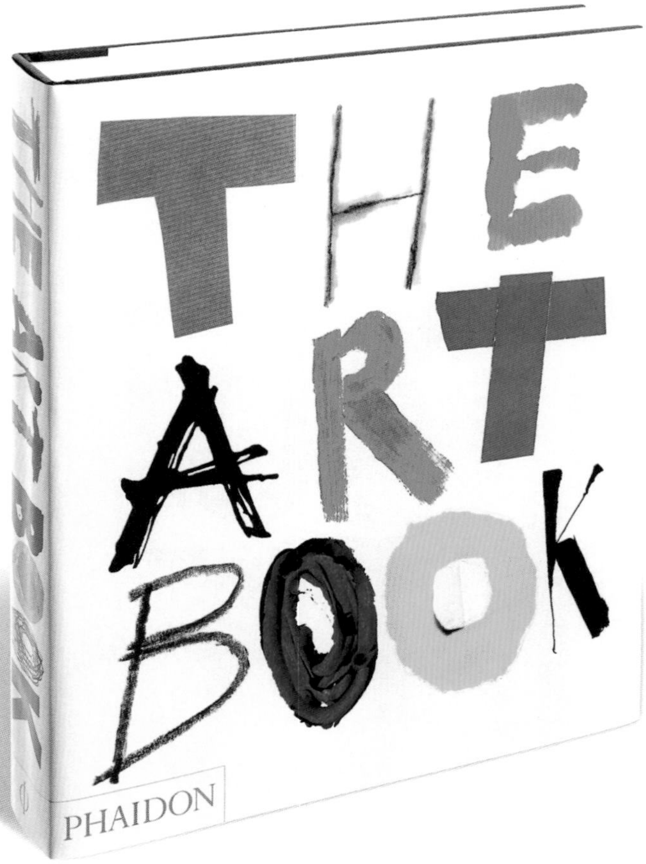

● **1994 . THE ART BOOK .** Book . Alan Fletcher

→ p.495

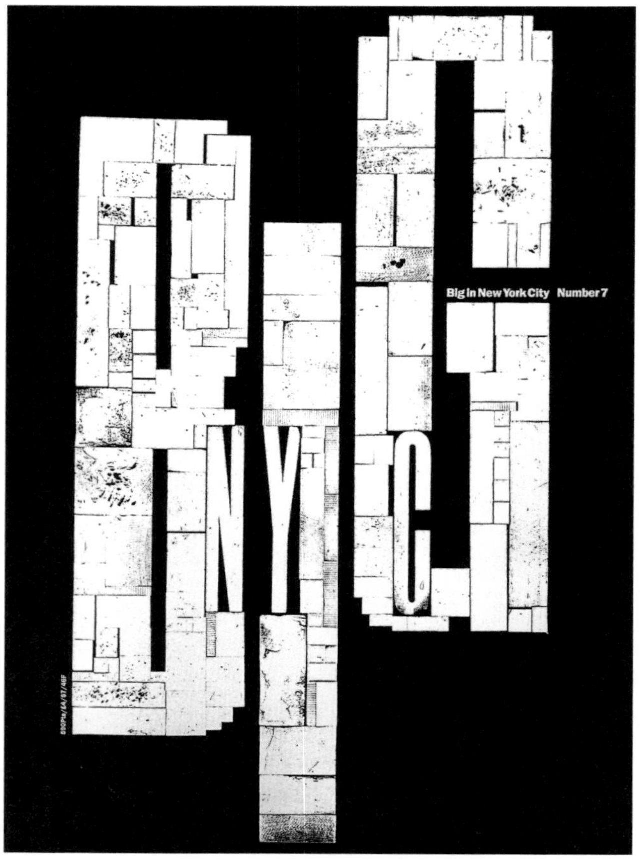

● **1994–1998 . BIG MAGAZINE .** Magazine / Newspaper . Vince Frost
"Big in New York City," No. 7, 1994

→ p.495

EXCEPTIONAL SUPPORT FOR THE 1995-1996 SEASON HAS BEEN PROVIDED LuESTHER T. MERTZ CHARITABLE TRUST.
THE PUBLIC THEATER
95 96 SEASON
BRING IN 'DA NOISE, BRING IN 'DA FUNK
BY SAVION GLOVER, REG.E. GAINES AND GEORGE C. WOLFE
WASP AND OTHER PLAYS
WRITTEN BY STEVE MARTIN DIRECTED BY BARRY EDELSTEIN
2 WOMEN IN REP
ANDREA MARTIN & MARGA GOMEZ
BY HAN ONG DIRECTED BY MARCUS STERN
THE CHANG FRAGMENTS
KING LEAR
WRITTEN BY WILLIAM SHAKESPEARE
DIRECTED BY ADRIAN HALL
VENUS
WRITTEN BY SUZAN-LORI PARKS DIRECTED BY RICHARD FOREMAN
DANCING ON HER KNEES
WRITTEN BY NILO CRUZ
DIRECTED BY GRACIELA DANIELE
212-260-2400
425 LAFAYETTE STREET
SPECIAL ADD-ON PRODUCTION
WAKE UP CALL FEATURING CAMRYN MANHEIM
THE SKRIKER
WRITTEN BY CARYL CHURCHILL DIRECTED BY MARK WING-DAVEY
MEMBERSHIP IS EASY! CALL 212-260-2400

● **1995 . PUBLIC THEATER .** Poster . Paula Scher

→ p.495

● **1995/2002 . S,M,L,XL, BY REM KOOLHAAS .** Book . Bruce Mau

→ p.496

● **1995–PRESENT . FOUND FONT .** Typeface . Paul Elliman

→ p.496

● **1995–PRESENT . BASELINE .** Magazine / Newspaper . Mike Daines, Hans Dieter Reichert, Veronika Reichert
HDR Visual Communication, No. 40, 2003

→ p.496

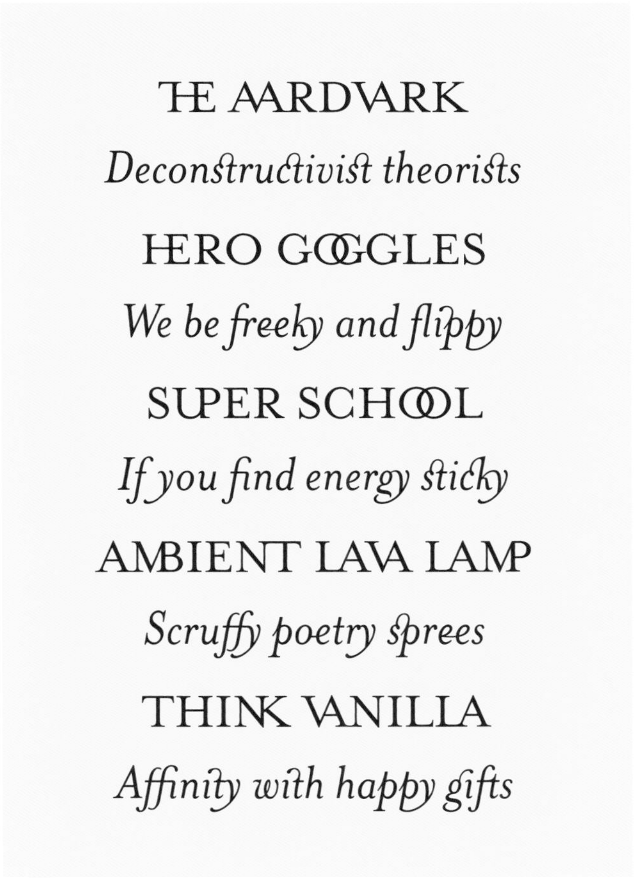

● **1996 . MRS EAVES .** Typeface . Zuzana Licko

→ p.497

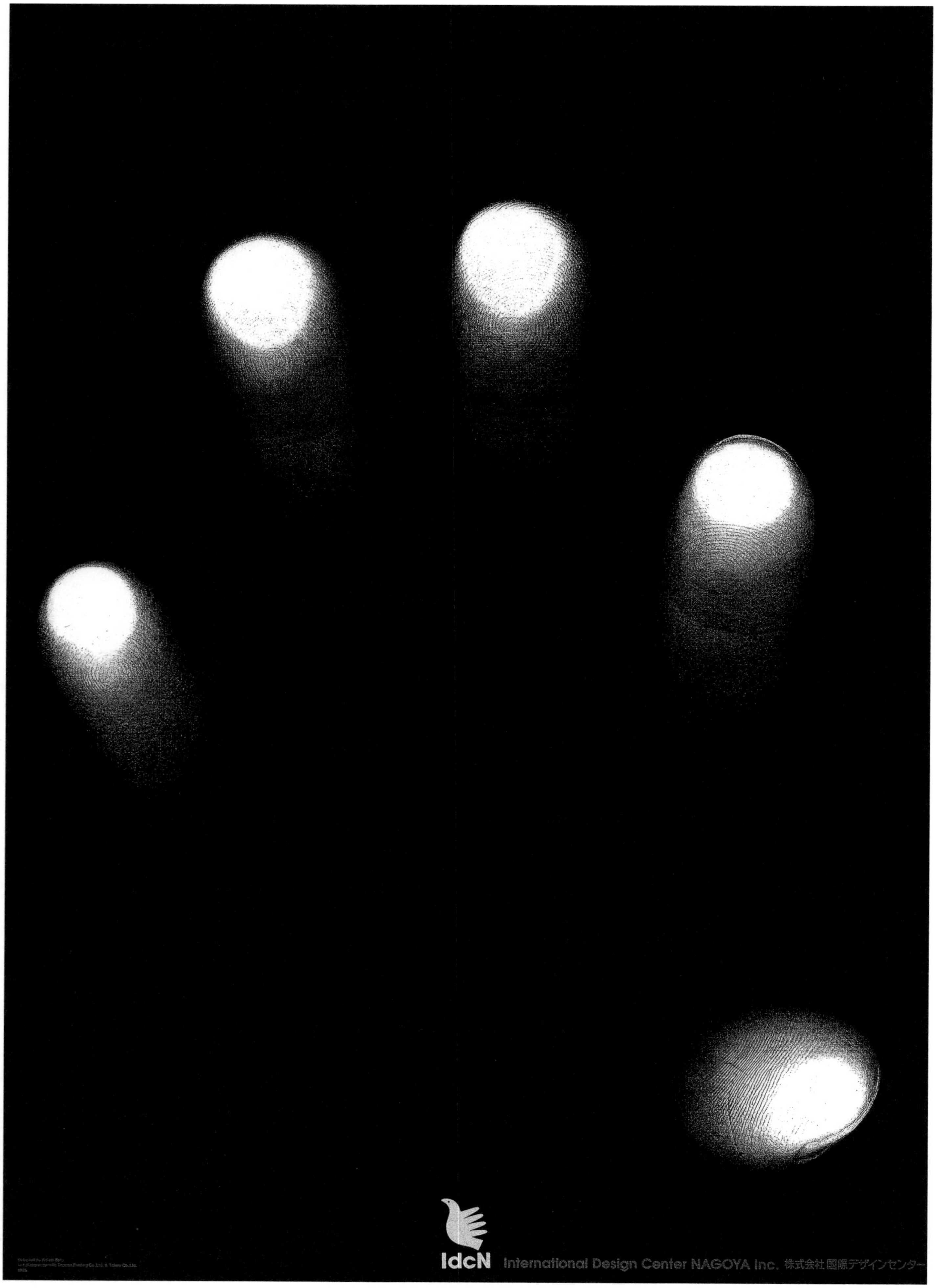

● **1996 . IDCN .** Poster . Koichi Sato

→ p.497

● **1996 . HOKUSETSU .** Poster . Ken Miki & Associates

→ p.497

Georgia
Latin ABCDEFGHIJKLMNO
PQRSTUVWXYZ&abcdefghij
klmnopqrstuvwxyzæœfifl1234
567890$¢£ƒ¥@%.,-:;!?()*†‡
Greek ΑΒΓΔΕΖΗΘΙΚΛΜΝΞ
ΟΠΡΣΤΥΦΧΨΩαβγδεζηθικλμ
νξοπρσςτυφχψω
Cyrillic АБВГДЕЖЗИЙКЛМ
НОПРСТУФХЦЧШЩЪЫЬЭ
ЮЯабвгдежзийклмнопрсту
фхцчшщъыьэюя

● **1996 . GEORGIA .** Typeface . Matthew Carter, Thomas Rickner

→ p.498

● **1996 . THINKBOOK .** Book . Irma Boom

→ p.498

MILLER
AVAILABLE FROM FONT BUREAU AND ITS DISTRIBUTORS

CARDBOARD
DISPLAY SEMIBOLD

Boxes in strange dimensions
DISPLAY ITALIC

63 Cubits
DISPLAY LIGHT

ROLL OF CLEAR PACKING TAPE
DISPLAY ROMAN

POINTED KNIVES
DISPLAY ITALIC

Little Styrofoam Peanuts Were So Adorable
DISPLAY ITALIC SMALL CAPS

New Acquaintances
DISPLAY ROMAN SMALL CAPS

They became my most trusted confidantes
DISPLAY ROMAN

Late Practices
DISPLAY SEMIBOLD ITALIC

I taught them some dance routines
DISPLAY ITALIC

Let me tell you, getting them to listen carefully was difficult
DISPLAY ROMAN

SYNCHRONIZE
DISPLAY BOLD

Packing Material on Ice Opens on Broadway
DISPLAY ROMAN & ITALIC SMALL CAPS

Ecstatic Reviews
DISPLAY ROMAN

Miller, designed by Matthew Carter, is a 'Scotch Roman,' a class of sturdy, general purpose types of Scottish origin, widely used in the US in the last century, but neglected since & overdue for revival. Miller is faithful to the Scotch style – though not to any one historical example – and authentic in having both roman & italic small caps, a feature of the originals; Tobias Frere-Jones & Cyrus Highsmith added to the series; C&C, FB 1997–2000

15 STYLES: ROMAN, ROMAN SMALL CAPS, AND BOLD, ALL WITH ITALICS, IN TEXT SIZE;
LIGHT, ROMAN, ROMAN SMALL CAPS, AND SEMIBOLD, ALL WITH ITALICS, PLUS BOLD, IN DISPLAY SIZE
CONTACT FONT BUREAU FOR INFORMATION ABOUT ADDITIONAL STYLES

38

● **1997 . MILLER .** Typeface . Matthew Carter

→ p.498

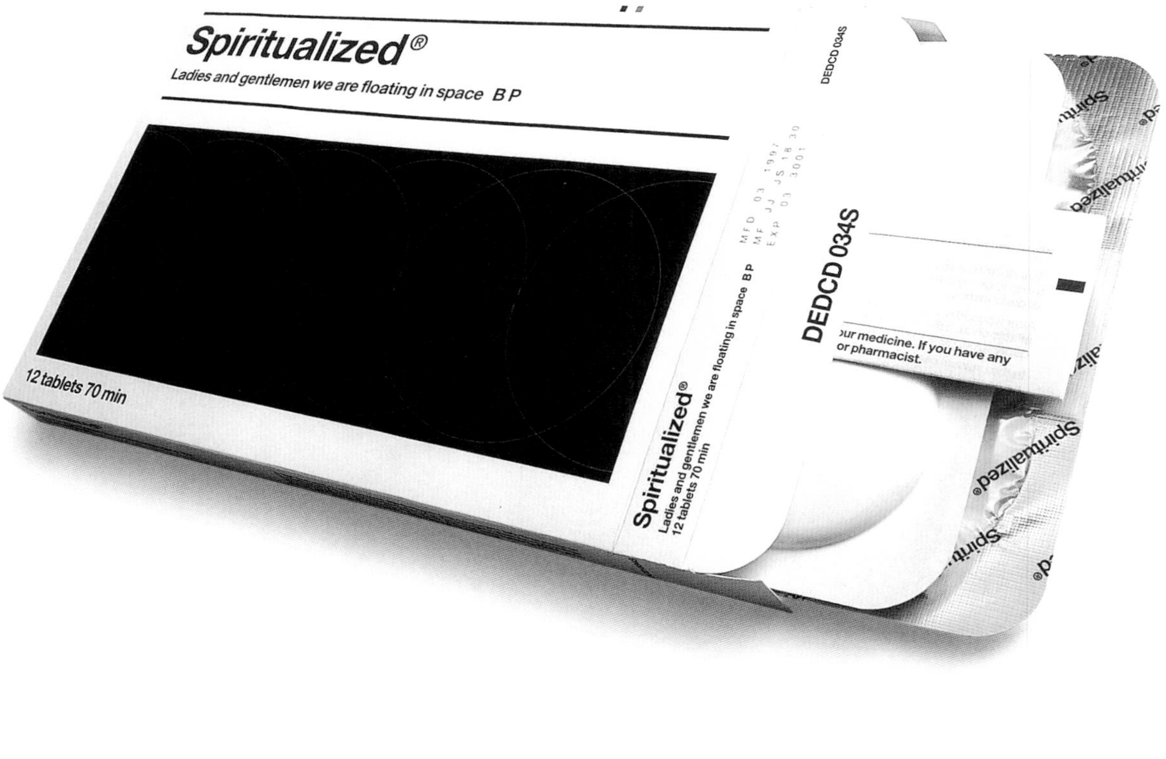

● **1997 . SPIRITUALIZED—LADIES AND GENTLEMEN WE ARE FLOATING IN SPACE .** Record / CD Cover . Mark Farrow

→ p.499

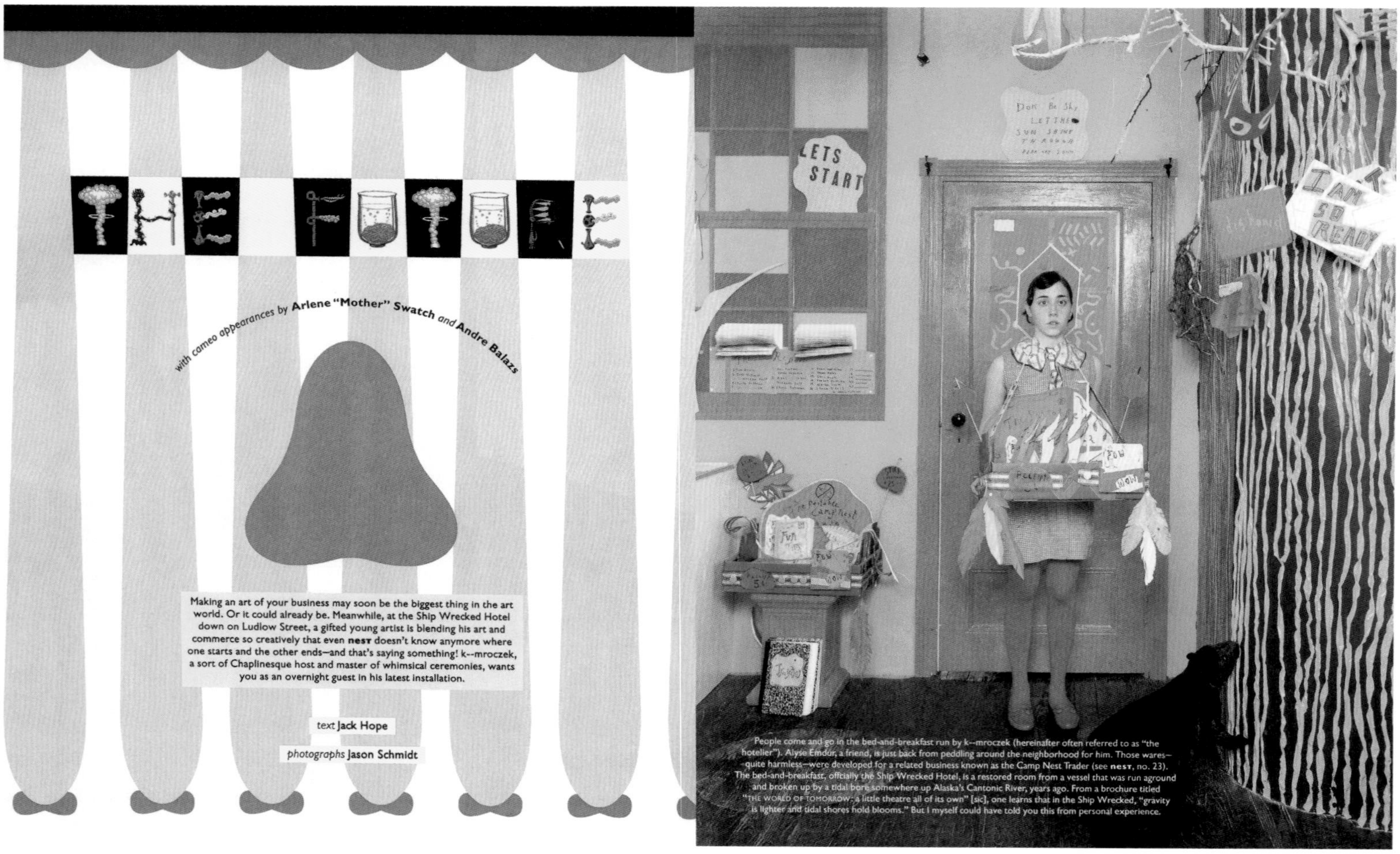
with cameo appearances by Arlene "Mother" Swatch and Andre Balazs
Making an art of your business may soon be the biggest thing in the art world. Or it could already be. Meanwhile, at the Ship Wrecked Hotel down on Ludlow Street, a gifted young artist is blending his art and commerce so creatively that even nest doesn't know anymore where one starts and the other ends—and that's saying something! k--mroczek, a sort of Chaplinesque host and master of whimsical ceremonies, wants you as an overnight guest in his latest installation.
text Jack Hope
photographs Jason Schmidt
LETS START
I AM SO READY
People come and go in the bed-and-breakfast run by k--mroczek (hereinafter often referred to as "the hotelier"). Alyse Emdur, a friend, is just back from peddling around the neighborhood for him. Those wares—quite harmless—were developed for a related business known as the Camp Nest Trader (see nest, no. 23). The bed-and-breakfast, officially the Ship Wrecked Hotel, is a restored room from a vessel that was run aground and broken up by a tidal bore somewhere up Alaska's Cantonic River, years ago. From a brochure titled "THE WORLD OF TOMORROW: a little theatre all of its own" [sic], one learns that in the Ship Wrecked, "gravity is lighter and tidal shores hold blooms." But I myself could have told you this from personal experience.

● **1997–2004 . NEST: A QUARTERLY OF INTERIORS .** Magazine / Newspaper . Joseph Holtzman
TOP LEFT: Photograph Langton Clay, No. 4, Spring 1999; TOP RIGHT: No. 16, Spring 2002; BOTTOM: Photograph Jason Schmidt, No. 26, Fall 2004

→ p.499

● **1997–2004 . RE-MAGAZINE .** Magazine / Newspaper . Jop van Bennekom
"The Boring Issue," No. 4, Summer 2000

→ p.499

● **1997 . TYPOUNDSO .** Book . Hans-Rudolf Lutz

→ p.500

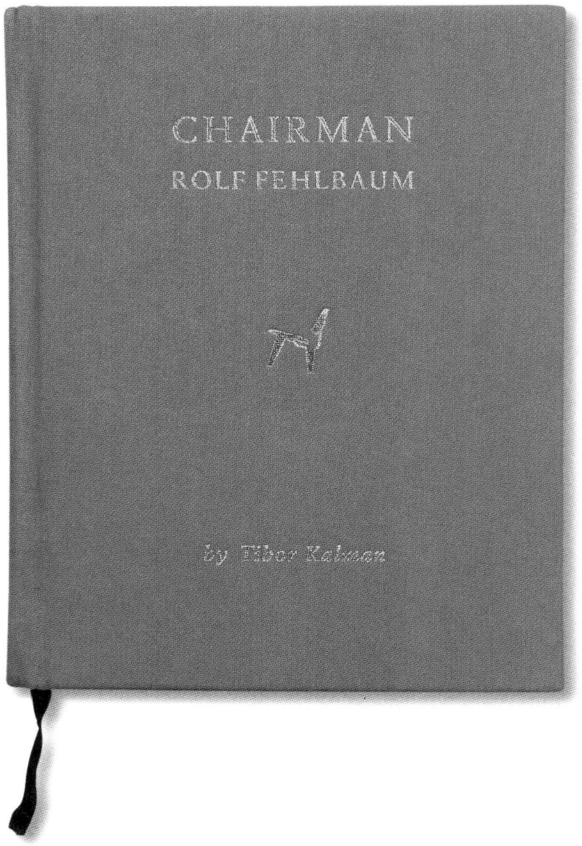

● **1997 . CHAIRMAN ROLF FEHLBAUM .** Book . Tibor Kalman

→ p.500

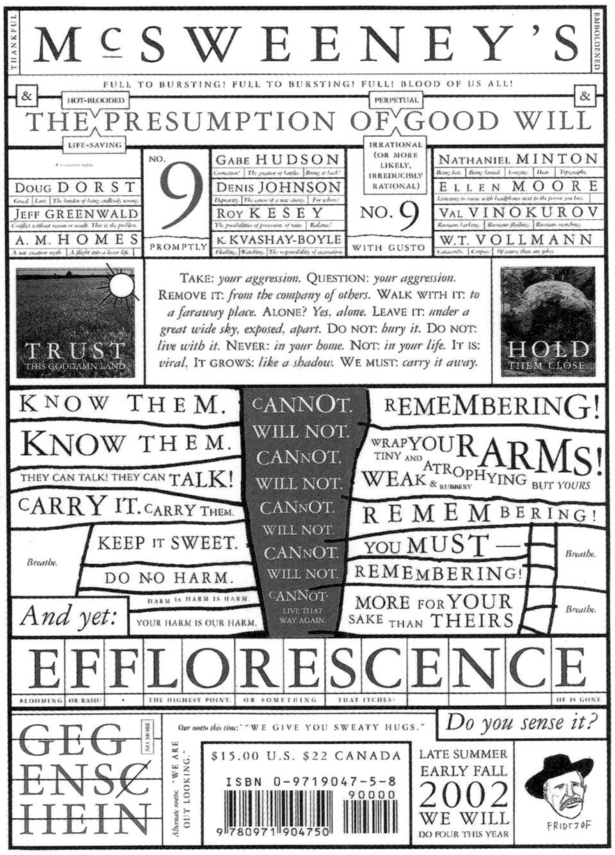

● **1998–PRESENT . TIMOTHY MCSWEENEY'S QUARTERLY CONCERN .** Magazine / Newspaper . Dave Eggers et al.
No. 9, 2002

→ p.500

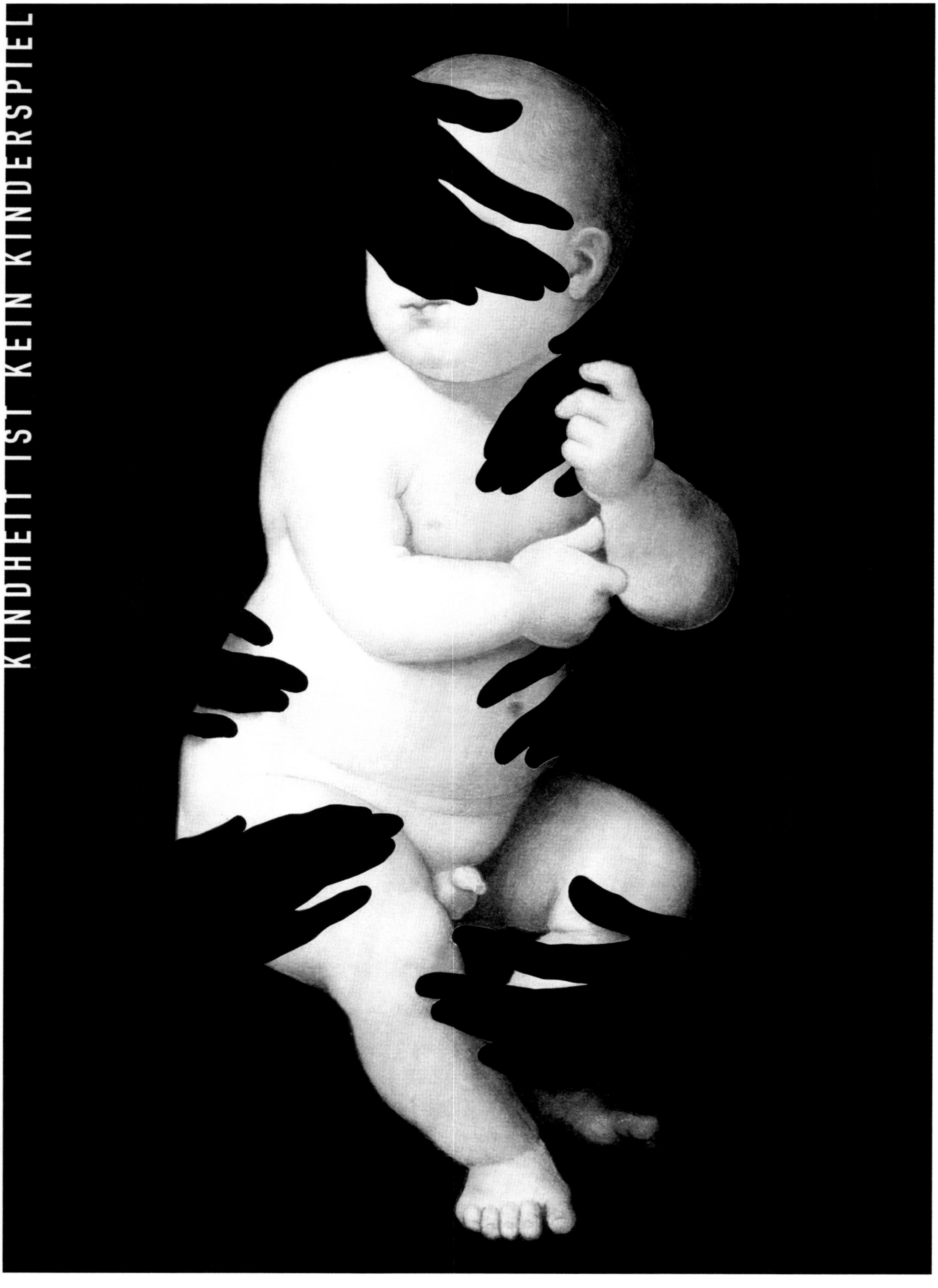

● **1998 . KINDHEIT IST KEIN KINDERSPIEL .** Poster . Alain Le Quernec

→ p.501

● **1998–PRESENT . YALE SCHOOL OF ARCHITECTURE .** Poster . Michael Bierut

→ p.501

● **1999–PRESENT . BRAND EINS .** Magazine / Newspaper . Mike Meiré
Vol. 8, No. 5, May 2006

→ p.501

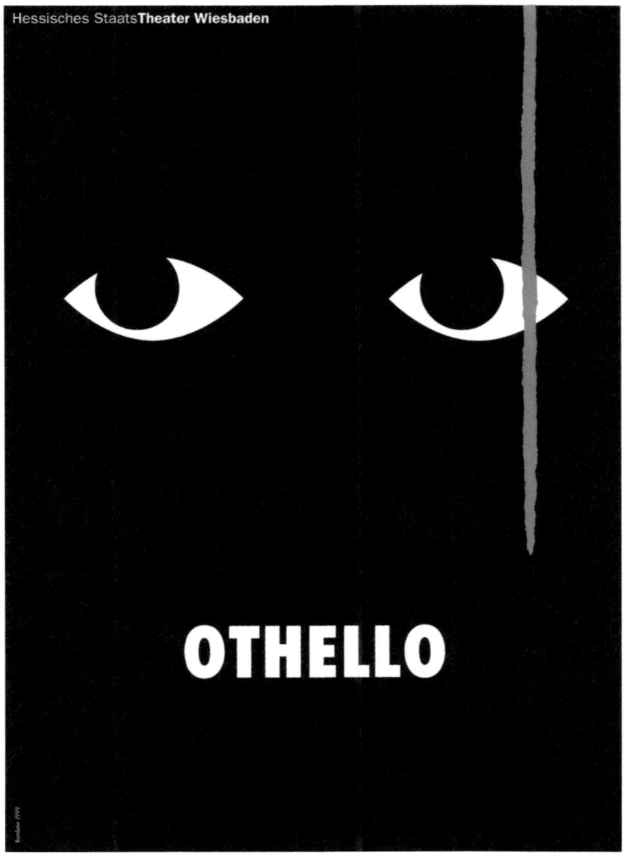

● **1999 . OTHELLO .**
Poster . Gunter Rambow

→ p.502

● **1999 . STEALING BEAUTY .** Book . Graphic Thought Facility

→ p.502

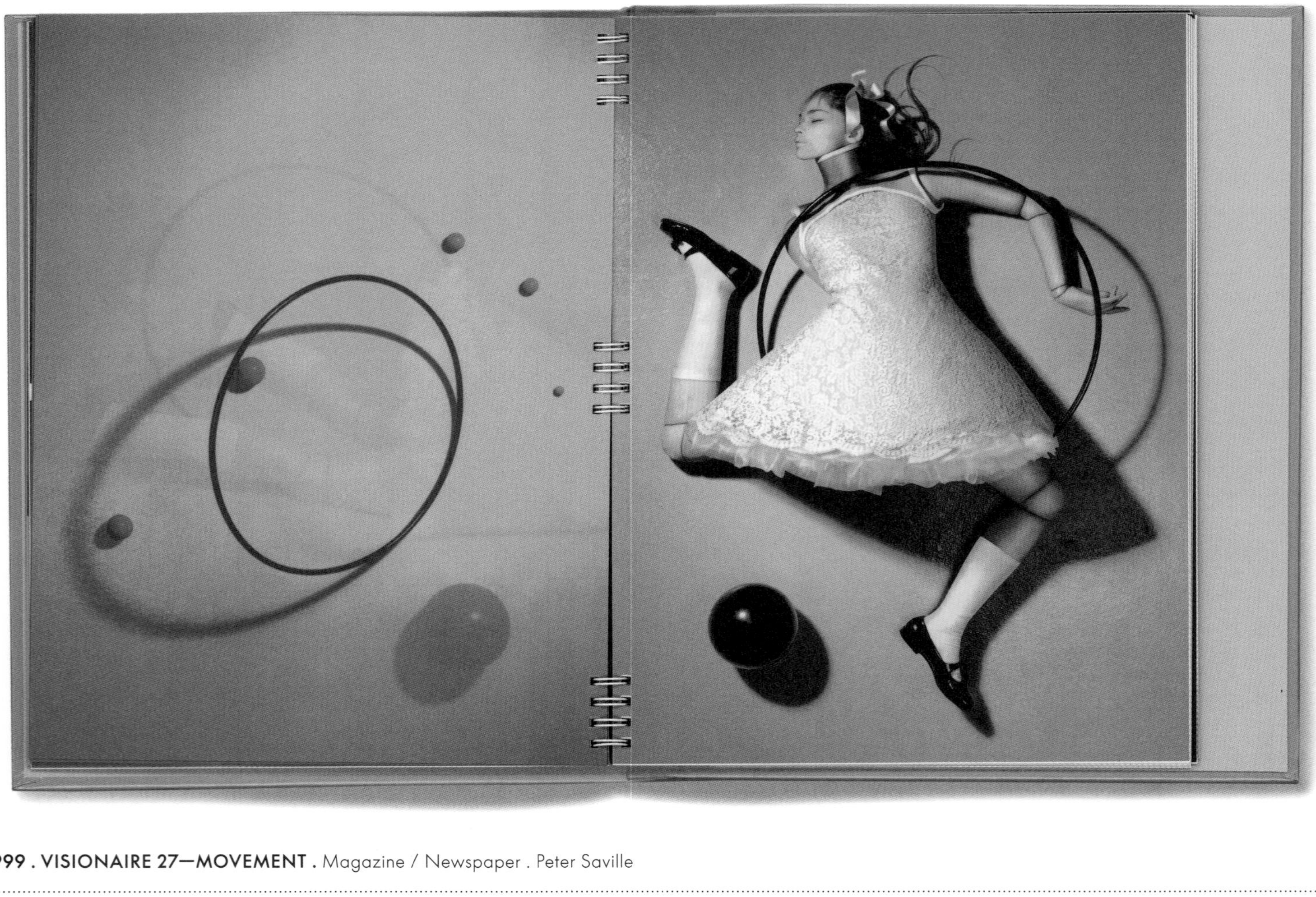

● **1999 . VISIONAIRE 27—MOVEMENT .** Magazine / Newspaper . Peter Saville

→ p.502

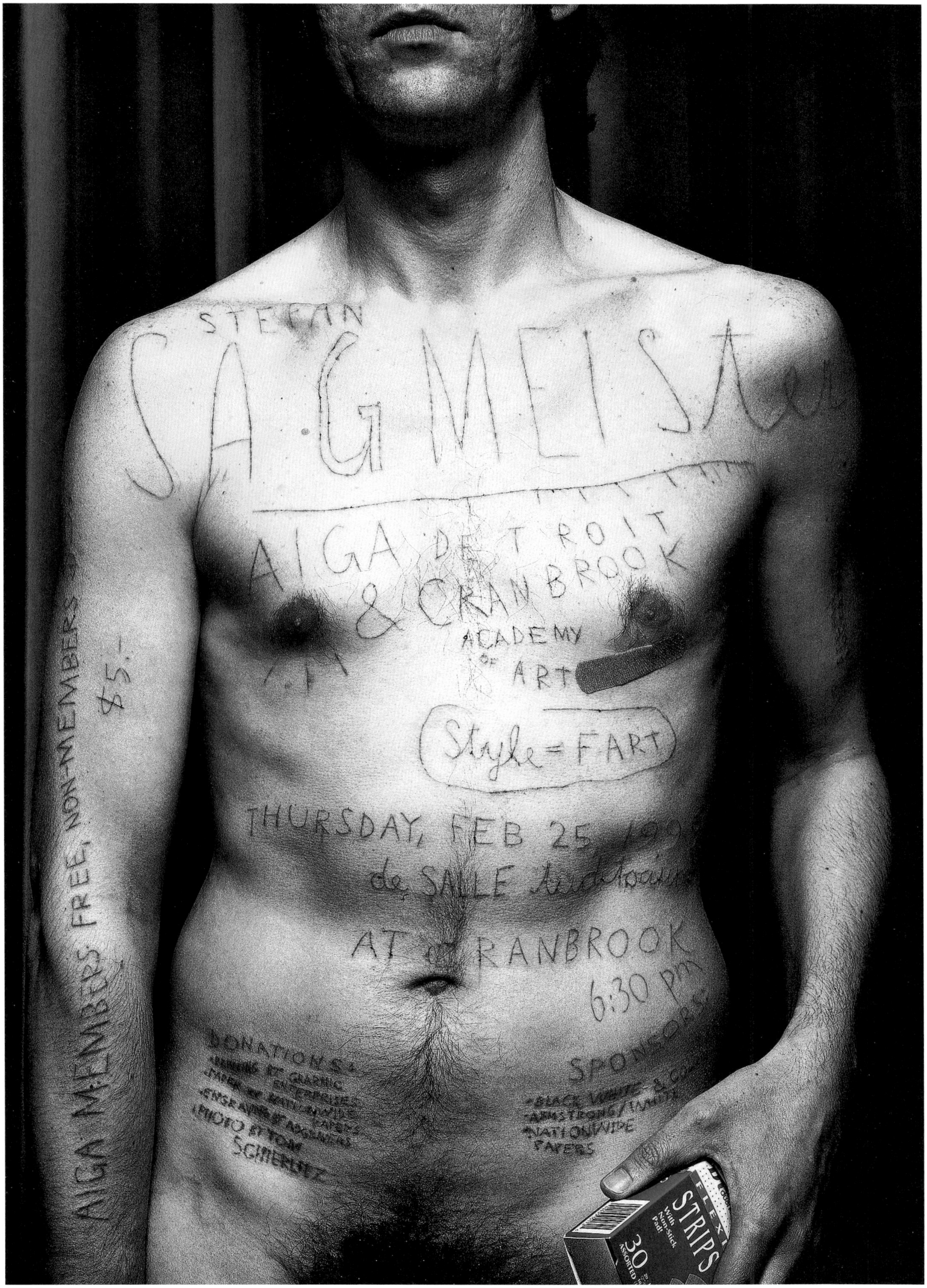

● **1999 . AIGA DETROIT LECTURE .** Poster . Stefan Sagmeister

→ p.503

RE
PIN

GOTHAM ULTRA

DING
PAWN
HORSE
MUSEUM

GOTHAM BOLD

MARGIN
DOGFISH
FUNCTION
POTPOURRI
FOSSILATION
BRAMBLEBUSH

GOTHAM MEDIUM

PI
HE

GOTHAM COND X-BLACK

FBI
CEO
NICE

GOTHAM COND BLACK

PIPE
MAUI
FINCH
DEMON

GOTHAM COND BOLD

EARN
DENIM
MICRON
RANDOM
NEUMANN

GOTHAM COND MEDIUM

ROUGH
PODIUM
KNUTSEN
CYMATIUM
HEADSTONE
CRENELATION

GOTHAM COND BOOK

STRINGER
RIVINGTON
STRICKLAND
HERTZBERGER
COLLABORATIVE
MAYFAIR THEATER
DONATO BRAMANTE
BUCKMINSTER FULLER

GOTHAM COND LIGHT

SIRIUS
GOTHAM THIN ITALIC

IMAGE
GOTHAM EXTRA LIGHT ITALIC

REIGN
GOTHAM LIGHT ITALIC

FOLIO
GOTHAM BOOK ITALIC

LOTUS
GOTHAM MEDIUM ITALIC

OXIDE
GOTHAM BOLD ITALIC

PRISM
GOTHAM BLACK ITALIC

SPIKE
GOTHAM ULTRA ITALIC

MILIEU
GOTHAM THIN

DENIM
GOTHAM EXTRA LIGHT

PATCH
GOTHAM LIGHT

ROBIN
GOTHAM BOOK

NINTH
GOTHAM MEDIUM

REIGN
GOTHAM BOLD

BIJOU
GOTHAM BLACK

PARIS
GOTHAM ULTRA

● **2000 . GOTHAM .** Typeface . Jonathan Hoefler, Tobias Frere-Jones

→ p.503

● **2000 . COMMON WORSHIP: SERVICES AND PRAYERS FOR THE CHURCH OF ENGLAND .** Book . Derek Birdsall, John Morgan

→ p.503

DOT DOT DOT 7
... uptight, optipessimistic art & design magazine ... pushing for a resolution ... in bleak midwinter ... with local and general aesthetics ... wound on an ever tightening coil[1] ...
GOD IS IN THE FOOT-NOTES
ISSN 1615 1968
Pay no more than 10 Euros

● **2000–2011 . DOT DOT DOT .** Magazine / Newspaper . Stuart Bailey, Peter Bil'ak, David Reinfurt
No. 7, 2004

→ p.504

● **2001 . RAIN .** Poster . Catherine Zask

→ p.504

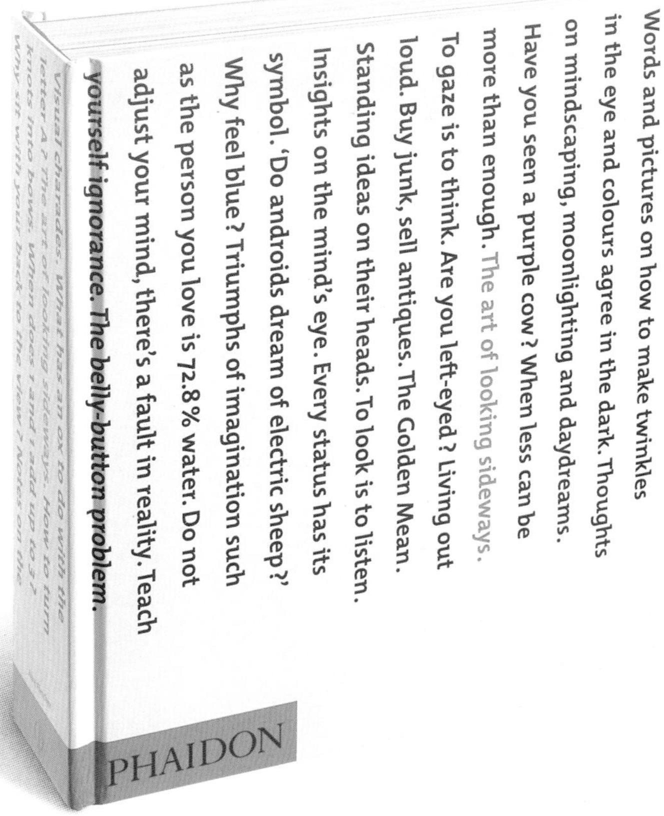
Words and pictures on how to make twinkles
in the eye and colours agree in the dark. Thoughts
on mindscaping, moonlighting and daydreams.
Have you seen a purple cow? When less can be
more than enough. The art of looking sideways.
To gaze is to think. Are you left-eyed? Living out
loud. Buy junk, sell antiques. The Golden Mean.
Standing ideas on their heads. To look is to listen.
Insights on the mind's eye. Every status has its
symbol. 'Do androids dream of electric sheep?'
Why feel blue? Triumphs of imagination such
as the person you love is 72.8% water. Do not
adjust your mind, there's a fault in reality. Teach
yourself ignorance. The belly-button problem.
PHAIDON

● **2001 . THE ART OF LOOKING SIDEWAYS .** Book . Alan Fletcher

→ p.504

PAINTING AT THE EDGE OF THE WORLD / DOUGLAS FOGLE / WALKER ART CENTER

● **2001 . PAINTING AT THE EDGE OF THE WORLD .** Book . Andrew Blauvelt, Santiago Piedrafita

→ p.505

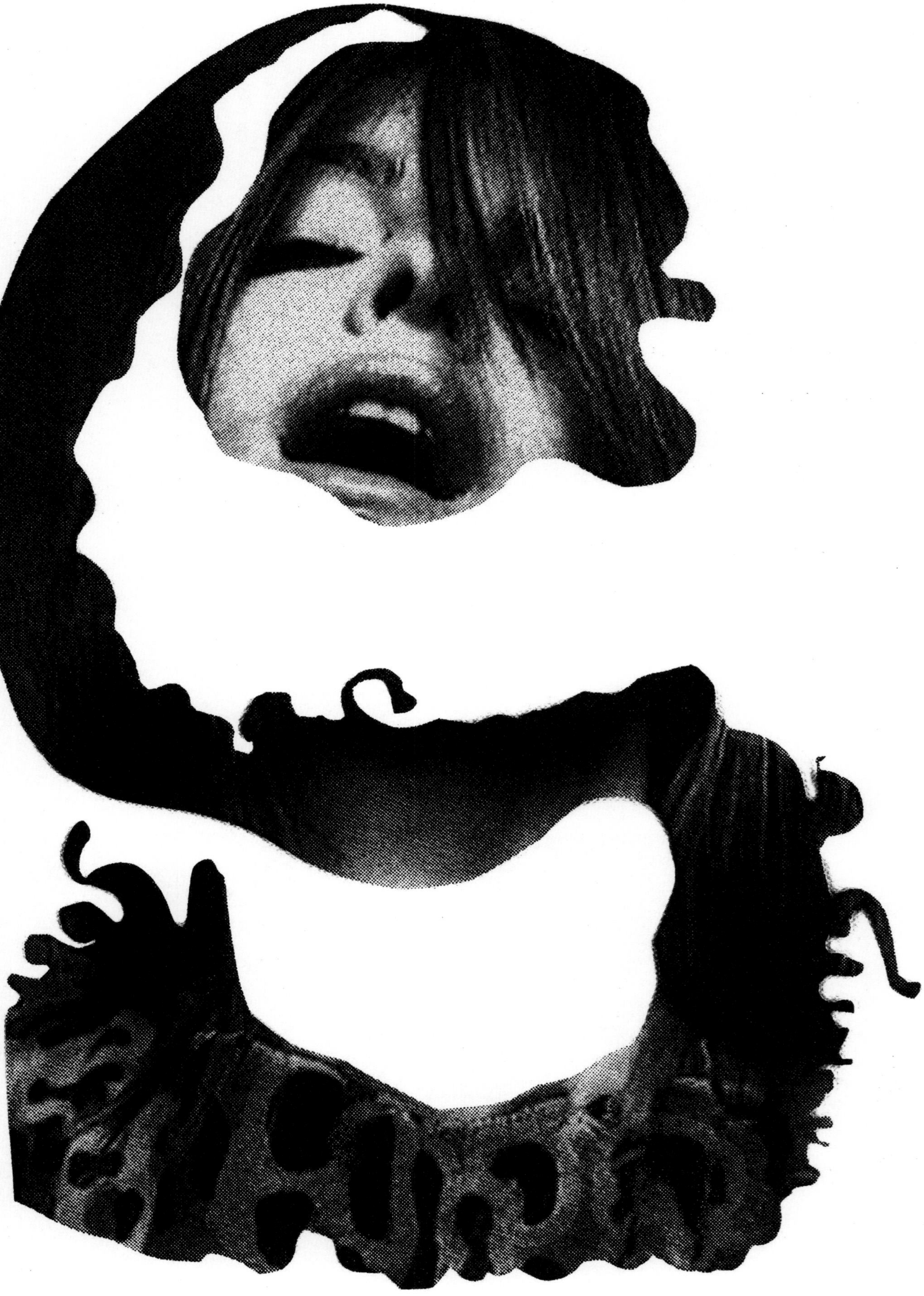

● **2001 . THE ALPHABET .** Poster . Michaël Amzalag, Mathias Augustyniak

→ p.505

● **2001–PRESENT . BUTT .** Magazine Cover . Jop van Bennekom
TOP LEFT: Photograph Wolfgang Tillmans, model Bernhard Willhelm, No. 1, Spring 2001; TOP RIGHT: Photograph Zac Bayly, model Emil Cañita, No. 33, Autumn 2023; BOTTOM LEFT: Photograph Andreas Larsson, model Jonjo, No. 12, Spring 2005; BOTTOM RIGHT: Photograph Clifford Prince King, *Sonny and David*, 2019, No. 30, Spring 2022

→ p.505

Courier Sans Light Regular Bold
ABCDEFGHIJKLMNOPQRSTUVWXYZ
abcdefghijklmnopqrstuvwxyz
1234567890@<$£€¢¥>§Æªßfifl
(åéîøü)ç*º→&%!?/#,;©®'‡:
Practise Alphabet
HELPFUL
Los Angeles County is seriously considering a new proposal where at least eight satellites operated by Hughes Electronics would be taxed to bring in more revenue for schools and other public amenities.
County assessor Rick Auerbach believes that the satellites, in a geostationary orbit some 22,000 miles above the earth's surface, ought to attract a tax because they are, in theory, within the tax jurisdiction of the county and therefore have significant value.
SWISS BEAUTIES
Basic Typography
****
HOBO
A, E, I, O, U
and sometimes Y
Courier Only
LineTo and how they've ruined my life:

2002 . COURIER SANS . Typeface . James Goggin

→ p.506

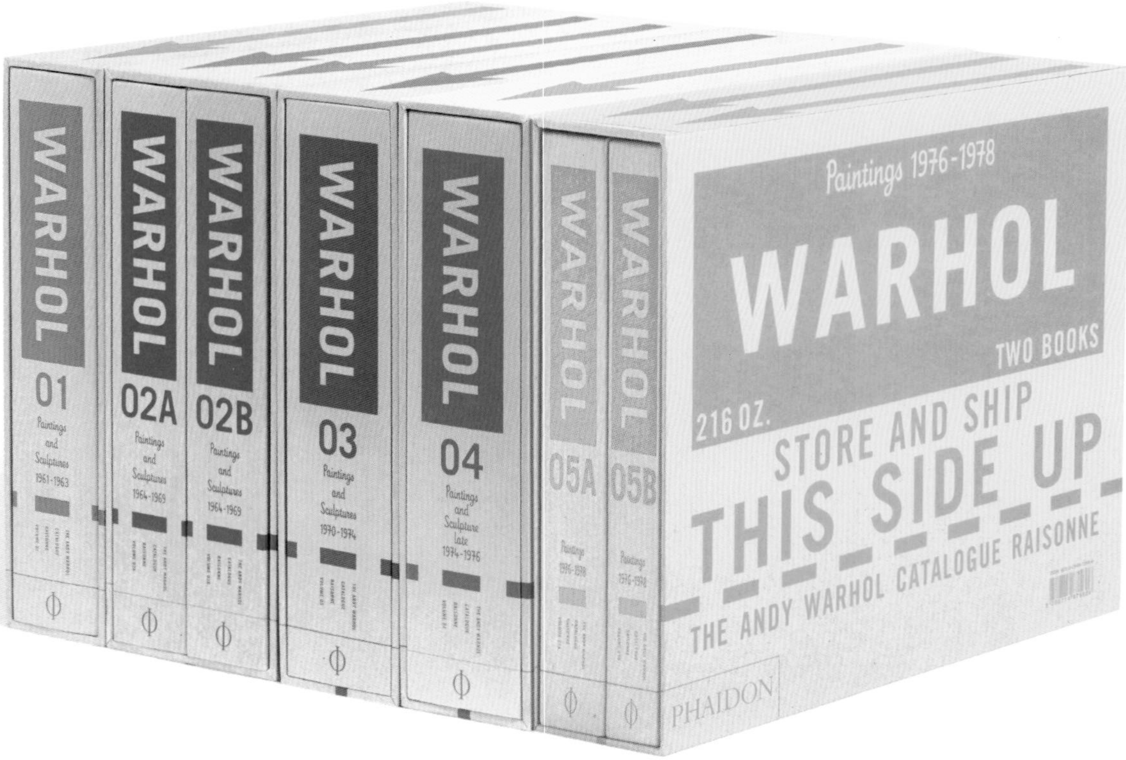

2002/2004/2010/2014/2018/2024 . ANDY WARHOL CATALOG RAISONNÉ . Book . Julia Hasting

→ p.506

ABCDEFGHIJKLM
NOPQRSTUVWXYZ
abcdefghijklm
nopqrstuvwxyz
1234567890

ABCDEFGHIJKLM
NOPQRSTUVWXYZ
abcdefghijklm
nopqrstuvwxyz
1234567890

● **2002 . ARNHEM .** Typeface . Fred Smeijers

→ p.506

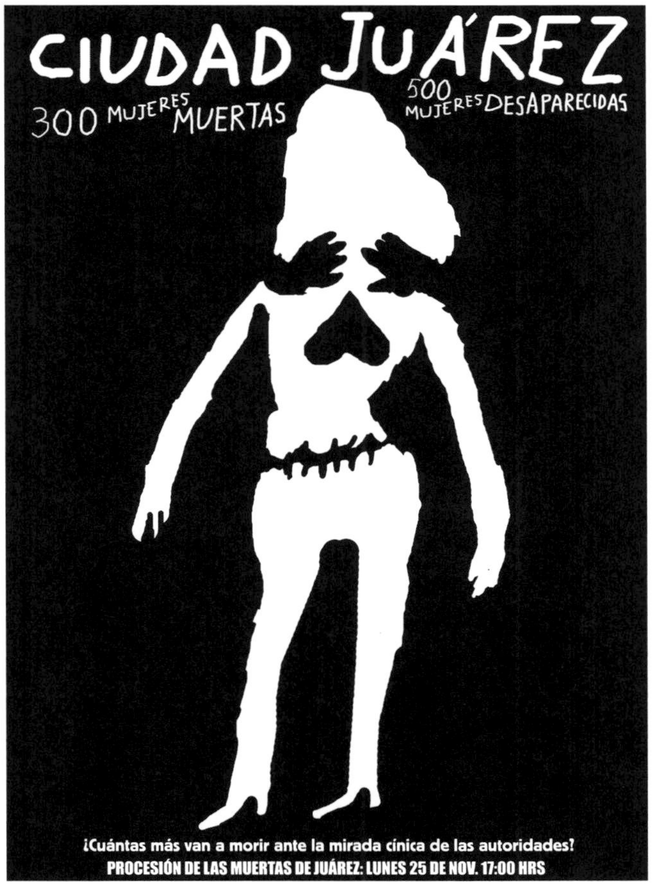

● **2002 . CIUDAD JUÁREZ: 300 DEAD WOMEN, 500 MISSING WOMEN .** Poster . Alejandro Magallanes

→ p.507

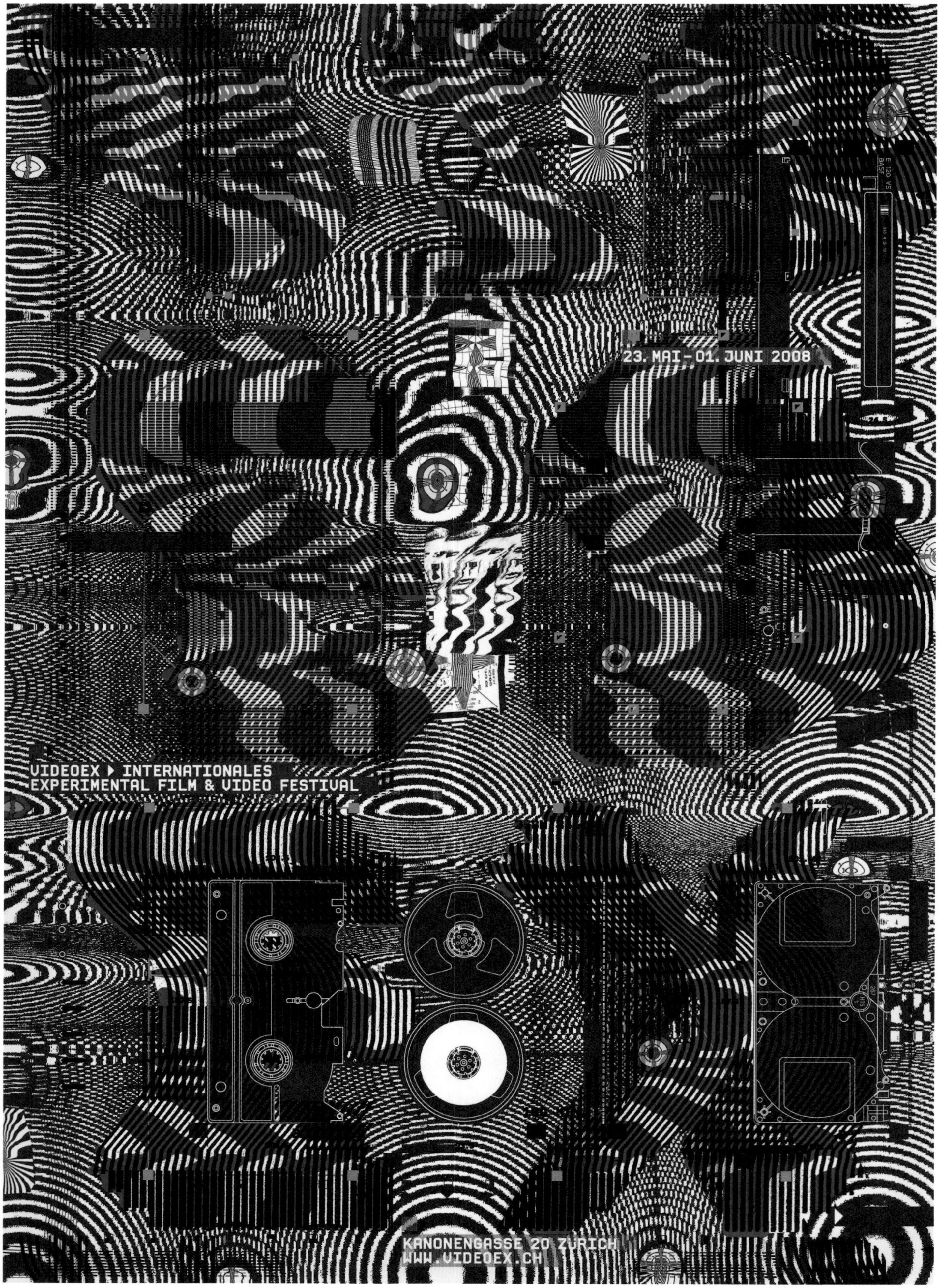

● **2003/2008/2010-PRESENT . VIDEOEX .** Poster . Martin Woodtli

→ p.507

● **2003 . PERSIAN TYPE AND TYPOGRAPHY .** Poster . Reza Abedini

→ p.507

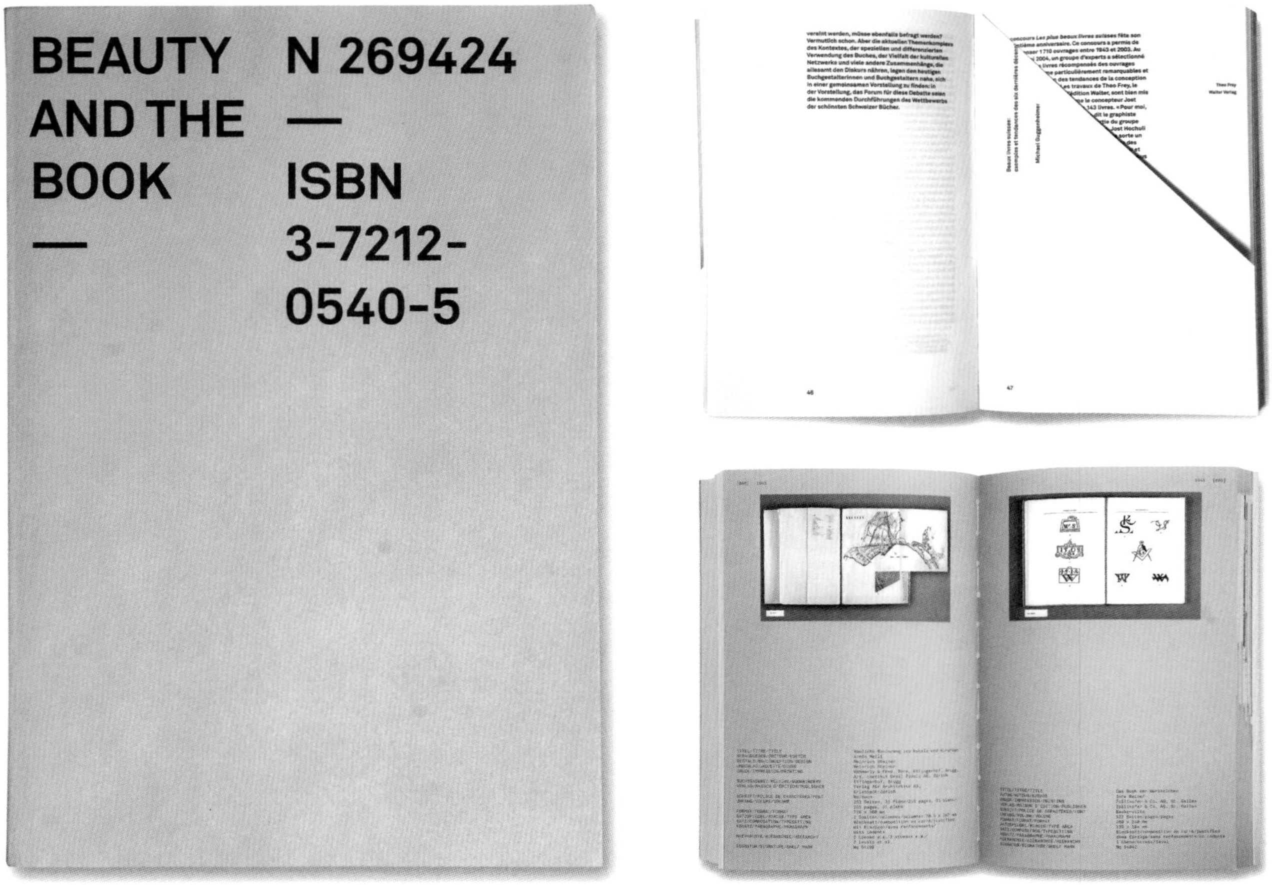

● **2004 . BEAUTY AND THE BOOK .** Book . Julia Born

→ p.508

BEAUTY
AND
THE
BEAST

● **2004–2005 . BEAUTY AND THE BEAST .** Identity . Frith Kerr, Amelia Noble

→ p.508

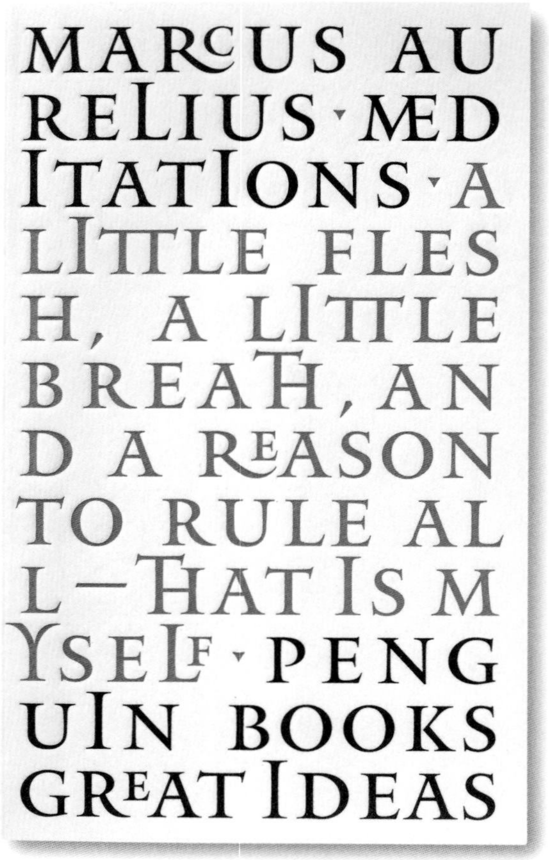
MARCUS AU
RELIUS · MED
ITATIONS · A
LITTLE FLES
H, A LITTLE
BREATH, AN
D A REASON
TO RULE AL
L—THAT IS M
YSELF · PENG
UIN BOOKS
GREAT IDEAS

● **2004–2010/2020 . GREAT IDEAS .** Book Cover . David Pearson et al.
Phil Baines, *Meditations*, by Marcus Aurelius, Vol. 1, No. 2, 2004

→ p.508

● **2005–2007 . ESTABLISHED & SONS .** Identity . Made Thought

→ p.509

A325 – slot car

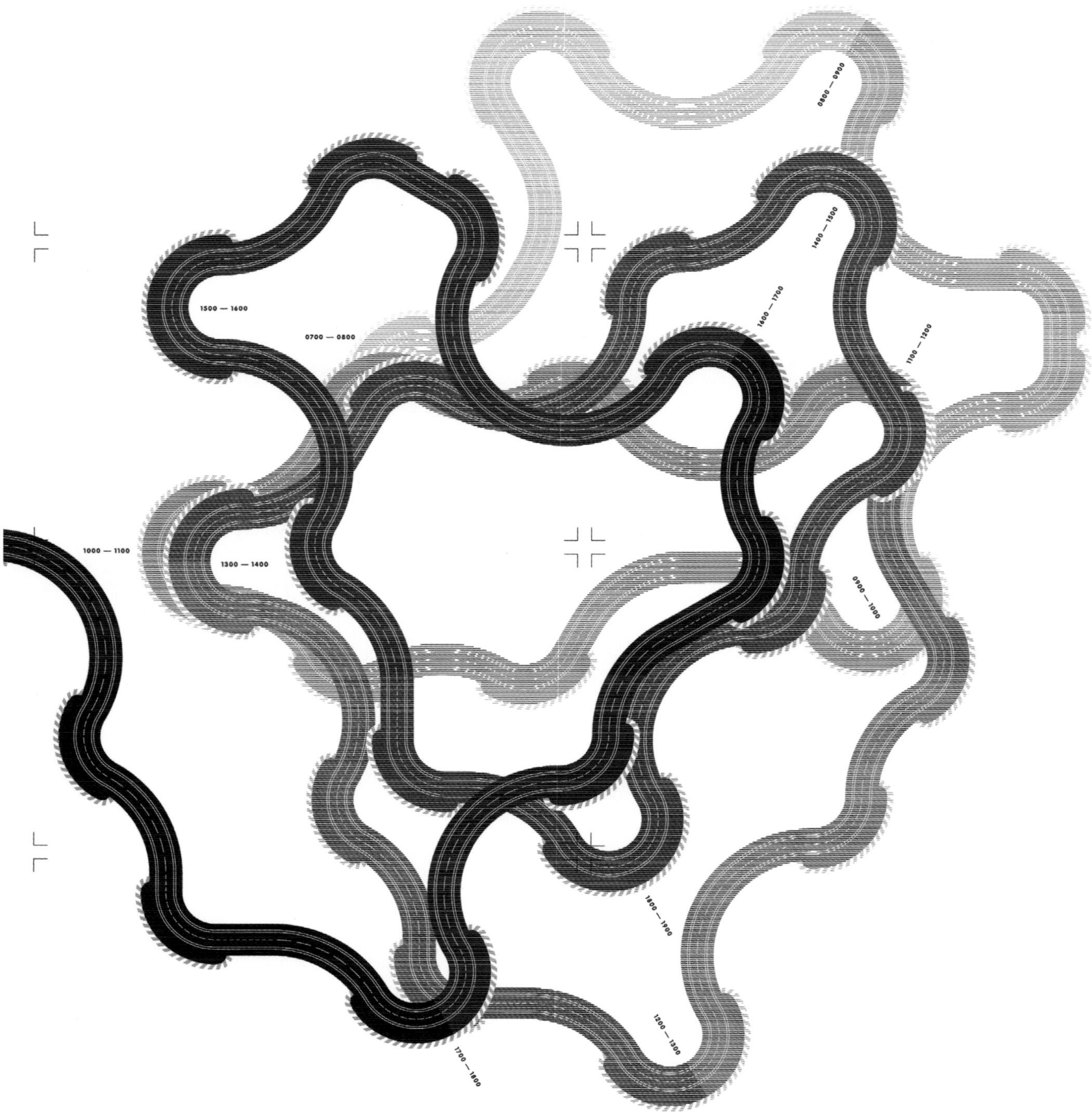

0700 — 0800

plaats	richting	auto's
1	7 (rechtsaf)	1649
2	6 (linksaf)	1261
3	8 (rechtdoor)	652
4	9 (linksaf)	575
5	2 (rechtdoor)	572
6	11 (rechtdoor)	470
7	5 (rechtdoor)	450
8	10 (rechtsaf)	347
9	1 (rechtsaf)	110
10	12 (linksaf)	65
11	3 (linksaf)	46
12	4 (rechtsaf)	11

0800 — 0900

plaats	richting	auto's
1	7 (rechtsaf)	1338
2	6 (linksaf)	1069
3	9 (linksaf)	741
4	8 (rechtdoor)	566
5	2 (rechtdoor)	559
6	10 (rechtsaf)	491
7	5 (rechtdoor)	472
8	11 (rechtdoor)	460
9	1 (rechtsaf)	124
10	12 (linksaf)	97
11	3 (linksaf)	89
12	4 (rechtsaf)	23

0900 — 1000

plaats	richting	auto's
1	7 (rechtsaf)	1139
2	6 (linksaf)	967
3	8 (rechtdoor)	549
4	2 (rechtdoor)	380
5	9 (linksaf)	369
6	5 (rechtdoor)	324
7	11 (rechtdoor)	322
8	10 (rechtsaf)	294
9	12 (linksaf)	118
10	1 (rechtsaf)	103
11	3 (linksaf)	73
12	4 (rechtsaf)	30

1000 — 1100

plaats	richting	auto's
1	7 (rechtsaf)	799
2	6 (linksaf)	701
3	8 (rechtdoor)	518
4	2 (rechtdoor)	436
5	11 (rechtdoor)	319
6	10 (rechtsaf)	298
7	5 (rechtdoor)	275
8	9 (linksaf)	210
9	1 (rechtsaf)	105
10	12 (linksaf)	83
11	3 (linksaf)	76
12	4 (rechtsaf)	46

1100 — 1200

plaats	richting	auto's
1	7 (rechtsaf)	783
2	6 (linksaf)	707
3	8 (rechtdoor)	464
4	2 (rechtdoor)	459
5	11 (rechtdoor)	325
6	5 (rechtdoor)	291
7	10 (rechtsaf)	247
8	9 (linksaf)	243
9	1 (rechtsaf)	124
10	3 (linksaf)	101
11	12 (linksaf)	77
12	4 (rechtsaf)	36

1200 — 1300

plaats	richting	auto's
1	7 (rechtsaf)	893
2	6 (linksaf)	804
3	8 (rechtdoor)	476
4	2 (rechtdoor)	466
5	11 (rechtdoor)	369
6	10 (rechtsaf)	296
7	5 (rechtdoor)	277
8	9 (linksaf)	230
9	1 (rechtsaf)	111
10	3 (linksaf)	72
11	12 (linksaf)	67
12	4 (rechtsaf)	34

1300 — 1400

plaats	richting	auto's
1	7 (rechtsaf)	970
2	6 (linksaf)	854
3	2 (rechtdoor)	512
4	8 (rechtdoor)	512
5	11 (rechtdoor)	451
6	10 (rechtsaf)	357
7	5 (rechtdoor)	290
8	9 (linksaf)	252
9	12 (linksaf)	140
10	1 (rechtsaf)	136
11	3 (linksaf)	108
12	4 (rechtsaf)	34

1400 — 1500

plaats	richting	auto's
1	7 (rechtsaf)	953
2	6 (linksaf)	916
3	2 (rechtdoor)	507
4	8 (rechtdoor)	506
5	11 (rechtdoor)	396
6	10 (rechtsaf)	375
7	5 (rechtdoor)	366
8	9 (linksaf)	275
9	1 (rechtsaf)	177
10	12 (linksaf)	128
11	3 (linksaf)	116
12	4 (rechtsaf)	43

1500 — 1600

plaats	richting	auto's
1	7 (rechtsaf)	1111
2	6 (linksaf)	918
3	2 (rechtdoor)	638
4	10 (rechtsaf)	536
5	8 (rechtdoor)	465
6	11 (rechtdoor)	460
7	5 (rechtdoor)	400
8	9 (linksaf)	279
9	1 (rechtsaf)	181
10	12 (linksaf)	139
11	3 (linksaf)	102
12	4 (rechtsaf)	46

1600 — 1700

plaats	richting	auto's
1	7 (rechtsaf)	1669
2	6 (linksaf)	1063
3	2 (rechtdoor)	833
4	10 (rechtsaf)	690
5	11 (rechtdoor)	644
6	8 (rechtdoor)	572
7	5 (rechtdoor)	482
8	1 (rechtsaf)	234
9	9 (linksaf)	223
10	12 (linksaf)	112
11	3 (linksaf)	107
12	4 (rechtsaf)	23

1700 — 1800

plaats	richting	auto's
1	7 (rechtsaf)	1549
2	6 (linksaf)	1301
3	10 (rechtsaf)	878
4	2 (rechtdoor)	821
5	8 (rechtdoor)	695
6	5 (rechtdoor)	608
7	11 (rechtdoor)	542
8	9 (linksaf)	356
9	1 (rechtsaf)	258
10	12 (linksaf)	118
11	3 (linksaf)	106
12	4 (rechtsaf)	22

1800 — 1900

plaats	richting	auto's
1	7 (rechtsaf)	1181
2	6 (linksaf)	969
3	8 (rechtdoor)	594
4	2 (rechtdoor)	590
5	5 (rechtdoor)	534
6	10 (rechtsaf)	534
7	11 (rechtdoor)	461
8	9 (linksaf)	347
9	1 (rechtsaf)	222
10	12 (linksaf)	154
11	3 (linksaf)	97
12	4 (rechtsaf)	38

Dit affiche is het achtste in een reeks van tien. Het maakt deel uit van 'VINEC', een project van Dziga een Plaatsmaken. Het diagram is gebaseerd op een verkeersmeting op het Nijmeegseplein. Van 07:00 tot 19:00 uur zijn hier op 23 september 2003 alle auto's afhankelijk van hun richtingen geteld. Volgende richtingen zijn mogelijk:

1 Nijmeegseweg (n) — Batavierenweg
2 Nijmeegseweg (n) — Nijmeegseweg (z)
3 Nijmeegseweg (n) — Pleijweg
4 Pleijweg — Nijmeegseweg (n)
5 Pleijweg — Batavierenweg
6 Pleijweg — Nijmeegseweg (z)
7 Nijmeegseweg (z) — Pleijweg
8 Nijmeegseweg (z) — Nijmeegseweg (n)
9 Nijmeegseweg (z) — Batavierenweg
10 Batavierenweg — Nijmeegseweg (z)
11 Batavierenweg — Pleijweg
12 Batavierenweg — Nijmeegseweg (n)

Voor het diagram boven zijn per uur alle richtingen gerangschikt op hun intensiteiten. Vaak gereden richtingen staan in deze top 12 bovenaan, weinig gereden richtingen onderaan. Iedere lijst dient als bouwplan voor één carrerabaan à 12 onderdelen. Vervolgens zijn deze deelstukken aan elkaar gevoegd tot één grote baan à 144 onderdelen. Het patroon ontstaat door veel verkeer in richting 7 en 6 en door weinig verkeer in richting 3 en 4.

Met dank aan: Ditmer Santema, Freek Peul en Hennie van der Horst
Ontwerp: www.catalogtree.net
Druk: Plaatsmaken Arnhem Oplage: 100

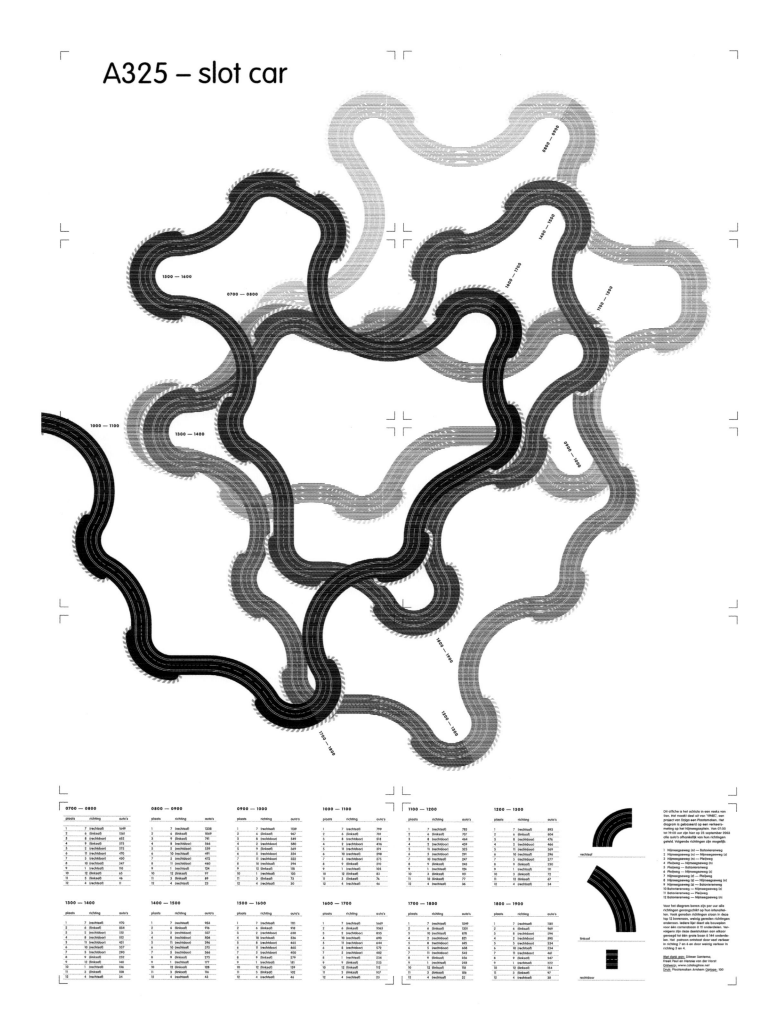

● **2005–2006 . A325 .** Poster . Catalogtree

→ p.509

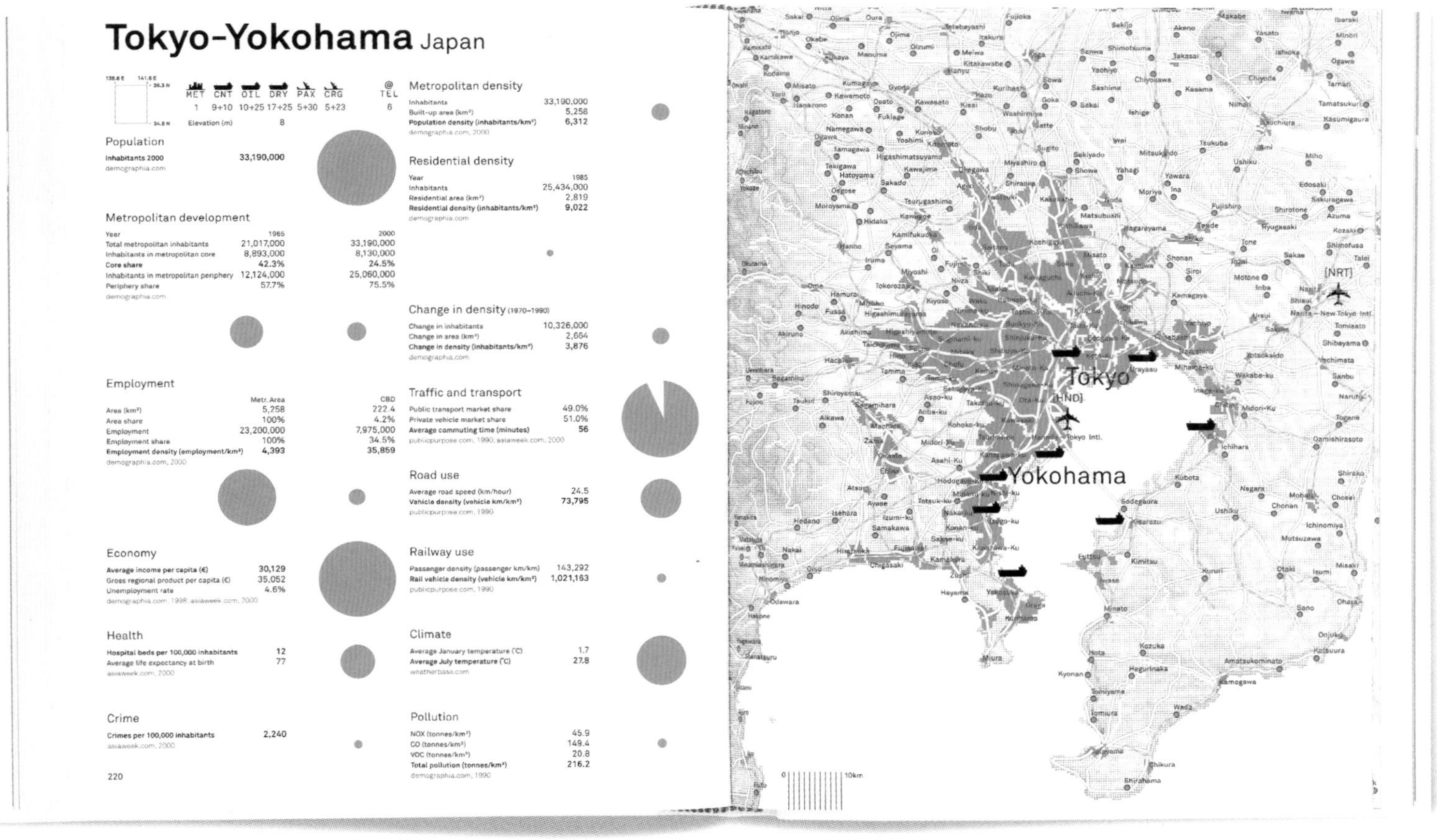

● **2005 . METROPOLITAN WORLD ATLAS .** Book . Joost Grootens

→ p.509

● **2006 . 21ST QURAN NATIONAL FESTIVAL FOR STUDENTS OF IRAN .** Poster . Iman Raad

→ p.510

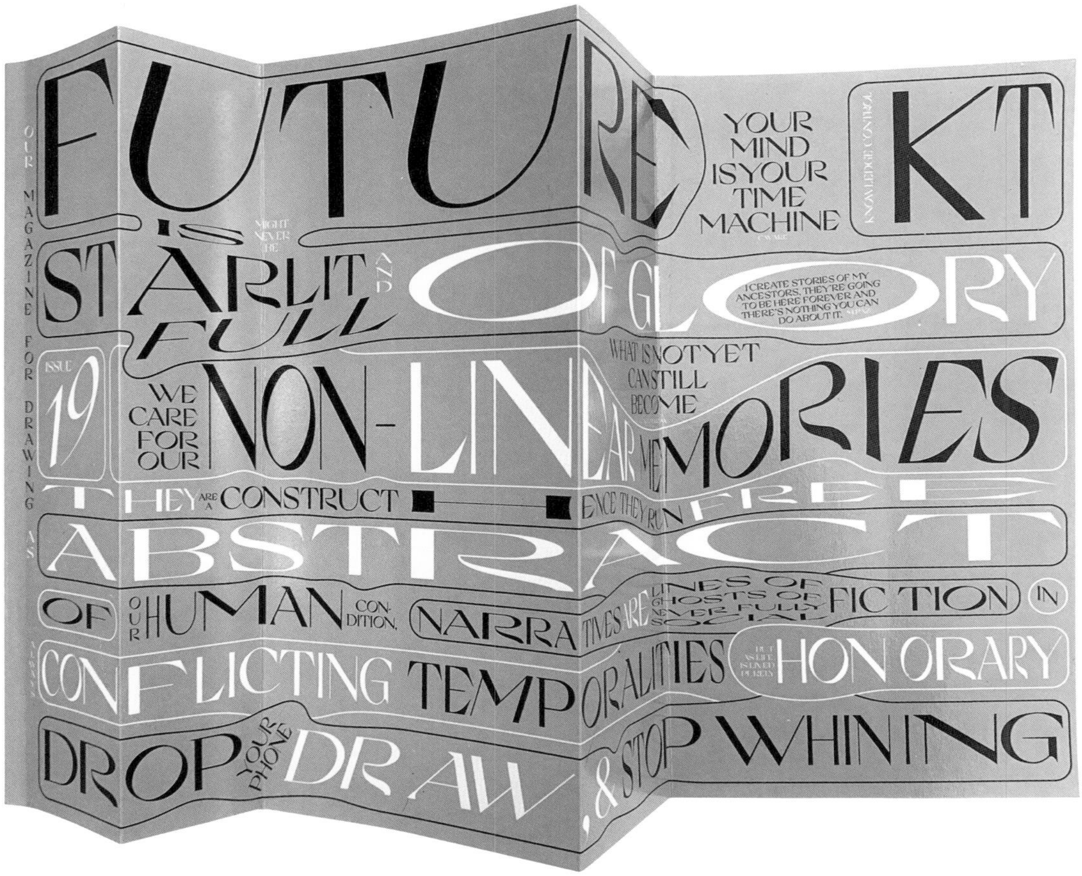

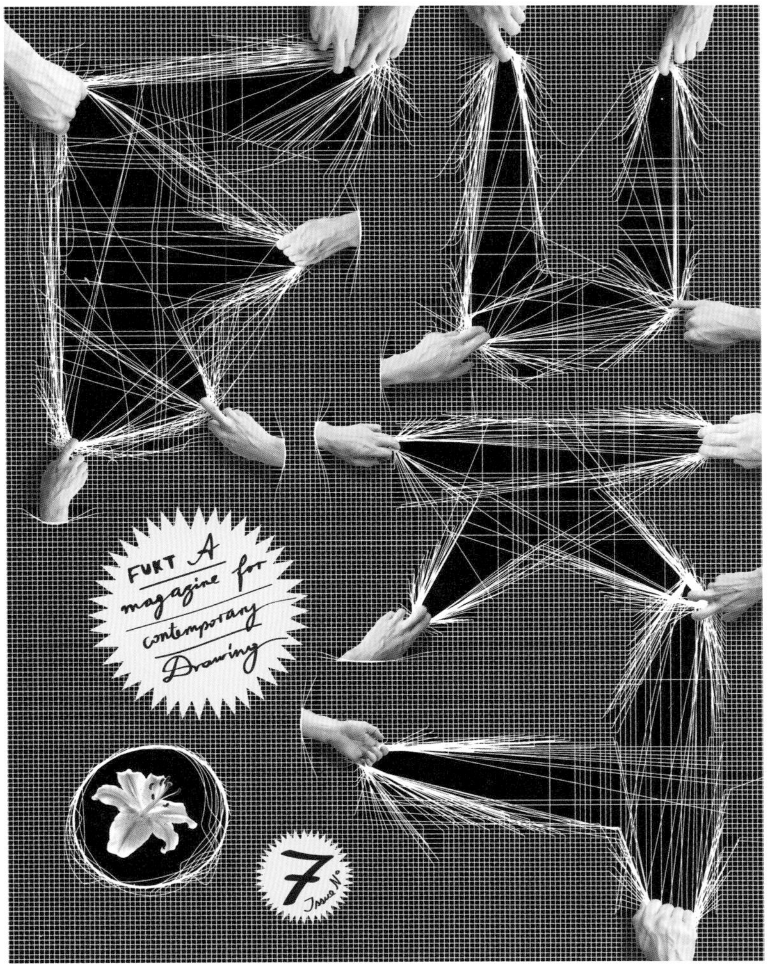

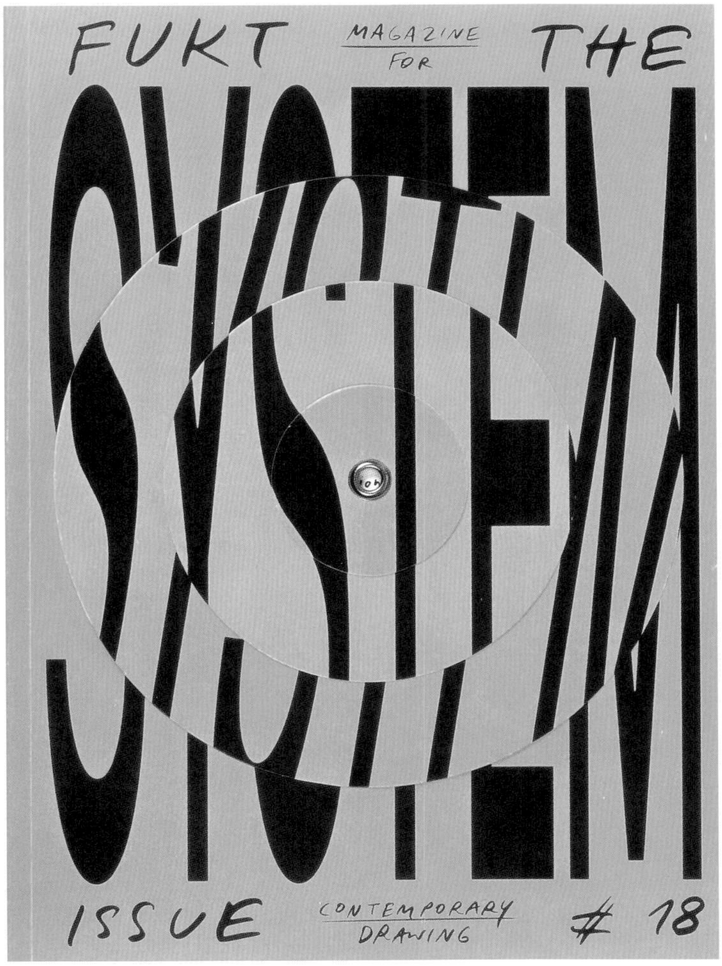

● **2006–PRESENT . FUKT .** Magazine Cover . Ariane Spanier
TOP: "The Storylines Issue," No. 19, 2020–1; BOTTOM LEFT: No. 7, 2008; BOTTOM RIGHT: "The System Issue," No. 18, 2019

→ p.510

● **2006 . BECK—THE INFORMATION .** Record / CD Cover . Big Active

→ p.510

● **2007 . DESIGNING DESIGN .** Book . Kenya Hara

→ p.511

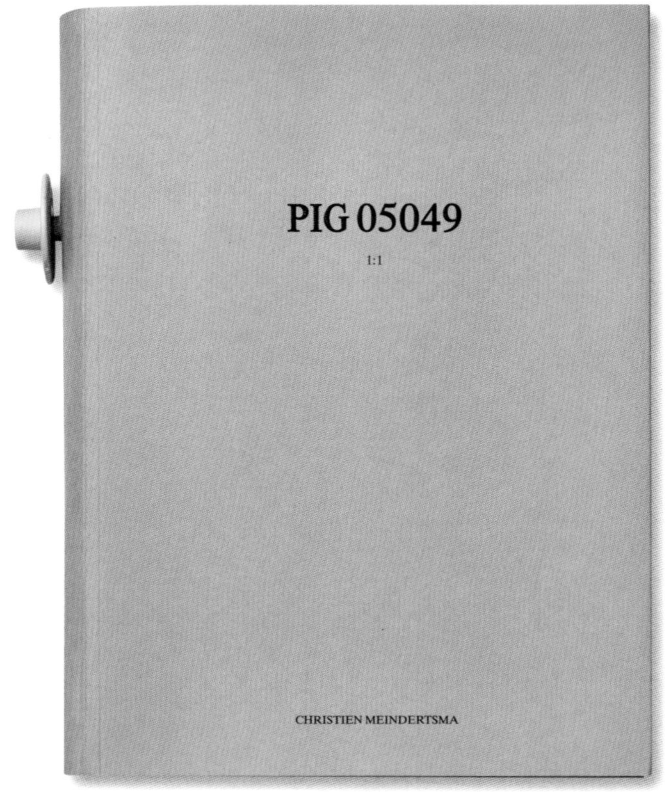

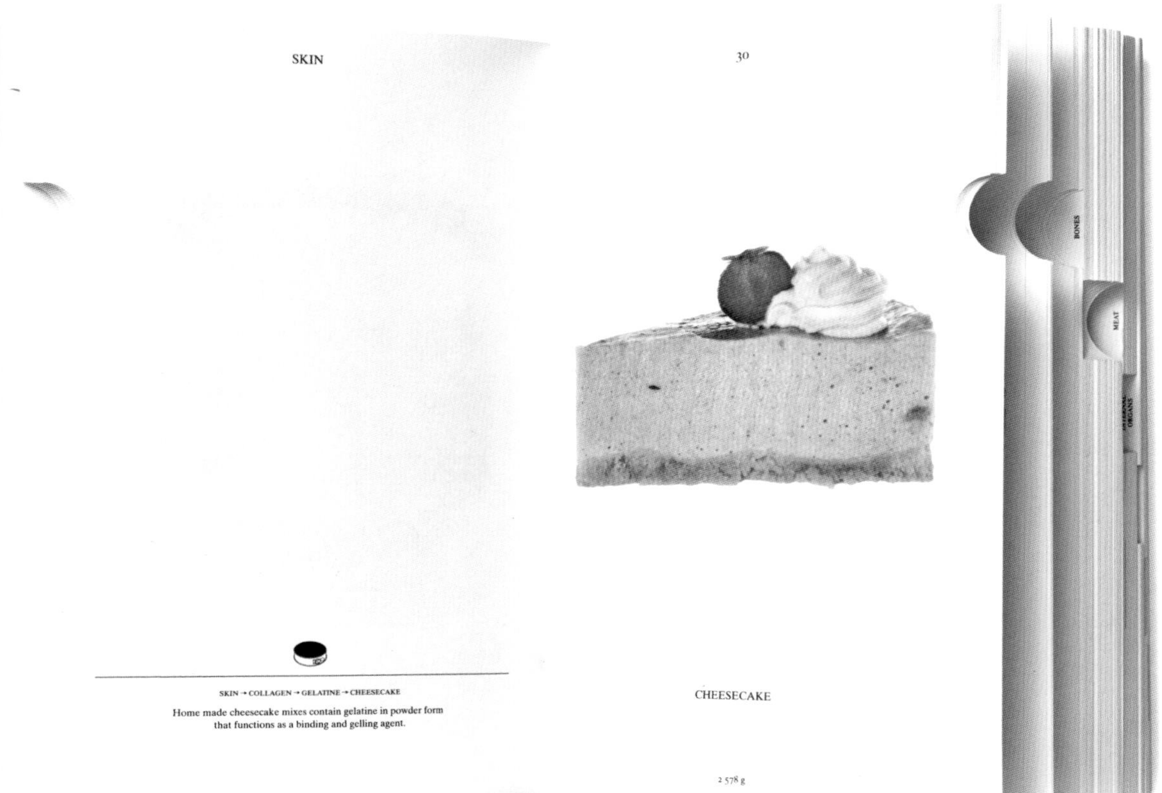

● **2007 . PIG 05049, BY CHRISTIEN MEINDERTSMA .** Book . Julie Joliat, Christien Meindertsma

→ p.511

Lettera	**Lettera-Txt**
Lettera	***Lettera-Txt***
Lettera	Lettera-Txt
Lettera	*Lettera-Txt*
Lettera	Lettera-Txt
Lettera	*Lettera-Txt*

Quickest	**Expeditious**
Brownest	***Sententious***
Foxy-est	Ambitious
Jumpiest	*Factitious*
Slackest	Delicious
Caninest	*Seditious*

ABCDEFGHIJKLMNOPQRSTUVWXYZ
abcdefghijklmnopqrstuvwxyz
1234567890©®℗™*∗fifl¤$$££¥¢€
…_\!?¡¿&@¶†‡|;:.,“”‘’„‚‘”•
([{‹«-–—›»}])←↑→↓↖↗↘↙

ABCDEFGHIJKLMNOPQRSTUVWXYZ
abcdefghijklmnopqrstuvwxyz
1234567890 1234567890 ©®℗™*∗fifl
¤$$$£££¥¥¢¢€€…_\!?¡¿&@¶†‡|;:.,“”‘’„‚‘”•
([{‹«-–—›»}])←↑→↓↖↗↘↙

● **2008 . LETTERA .** Typeface . Kobi Benezri

→ p.511

● **2008 . OBAMA—PROGRESS/HOPE .** Poster . Shepard Fairey

→ p.512

VERTICAL AND HORIZONTAL STEMS /GAUGE BALLS

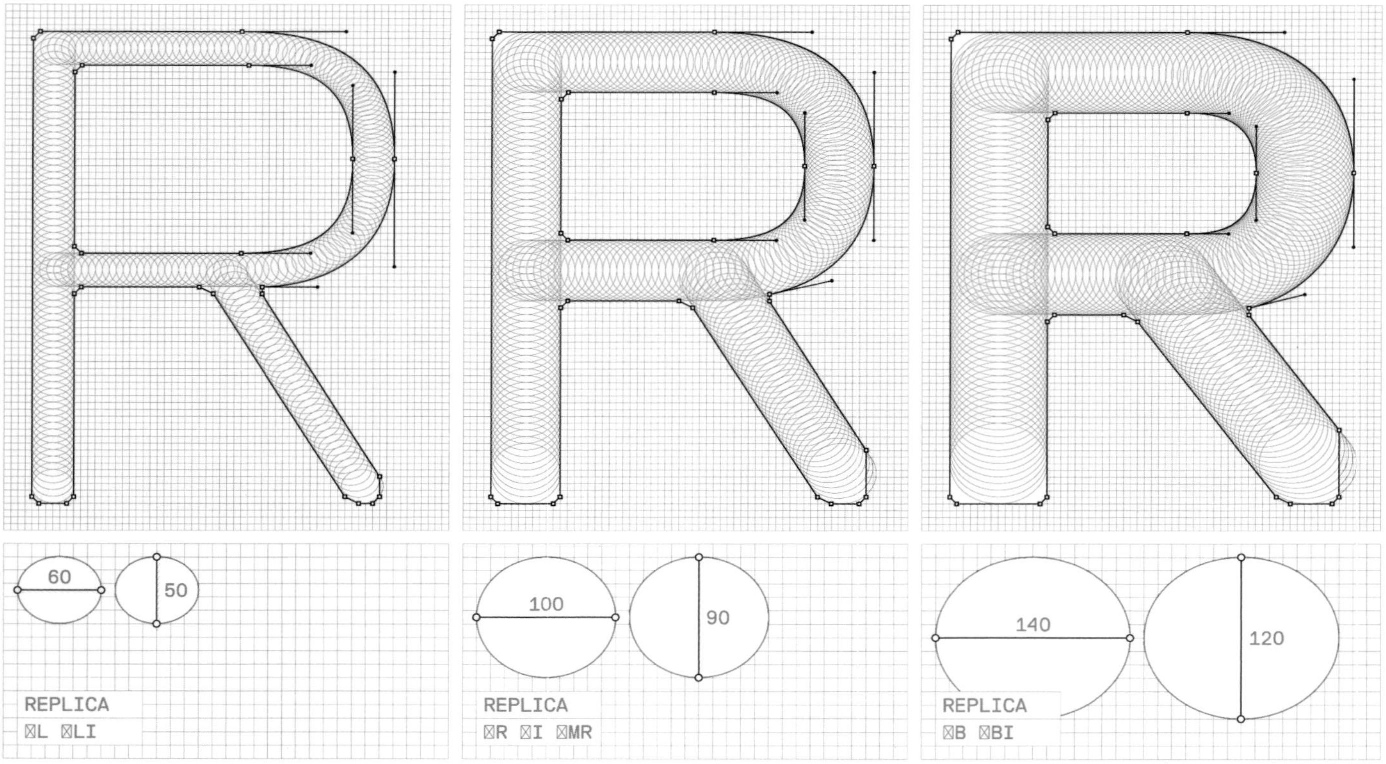

DECIMAL GRID /■WIDTH /■SIDE BEARINGS /■KERNING

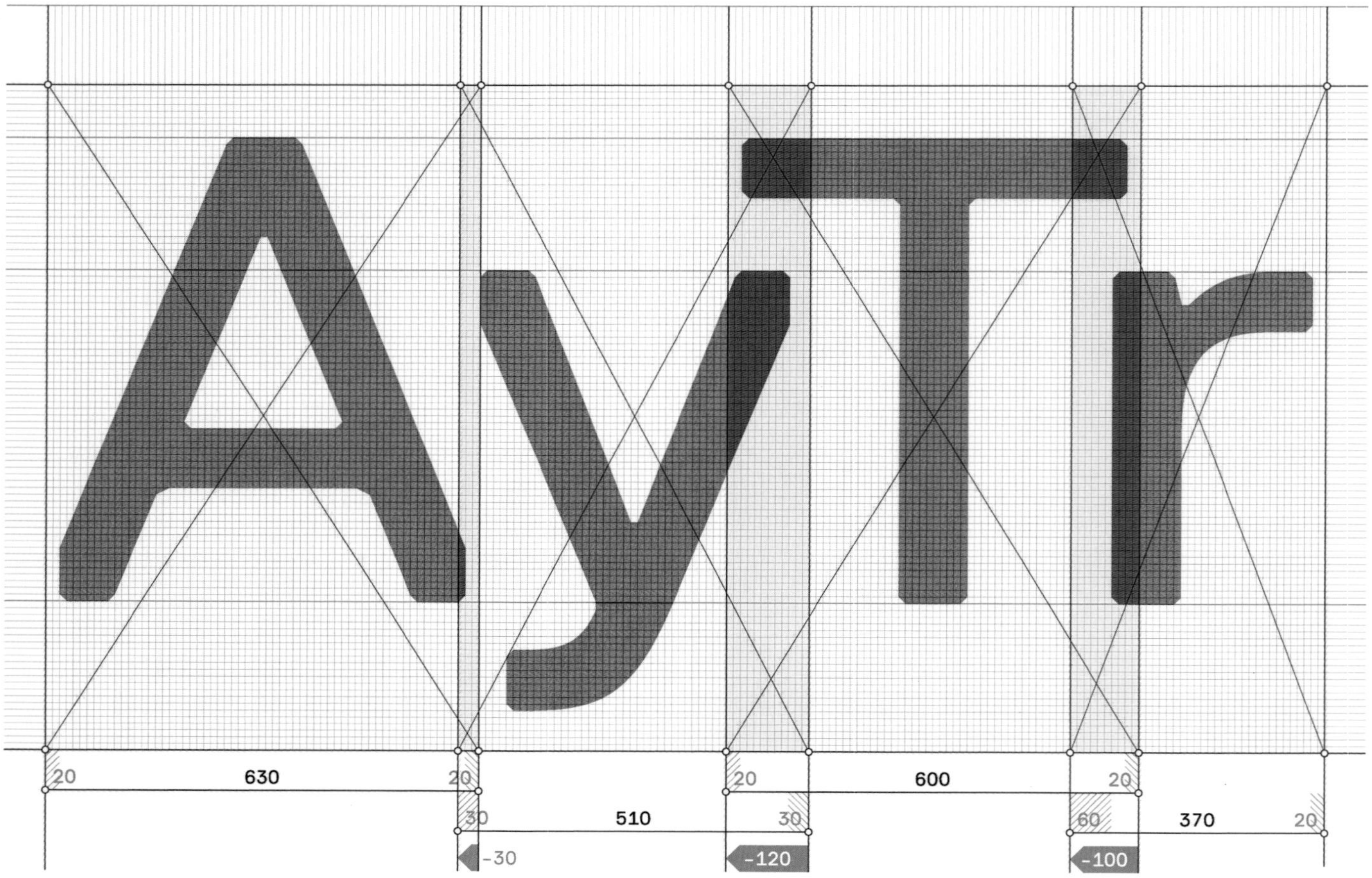

● **2008 . REPLICA .** Typeface . Norm

→ p.512

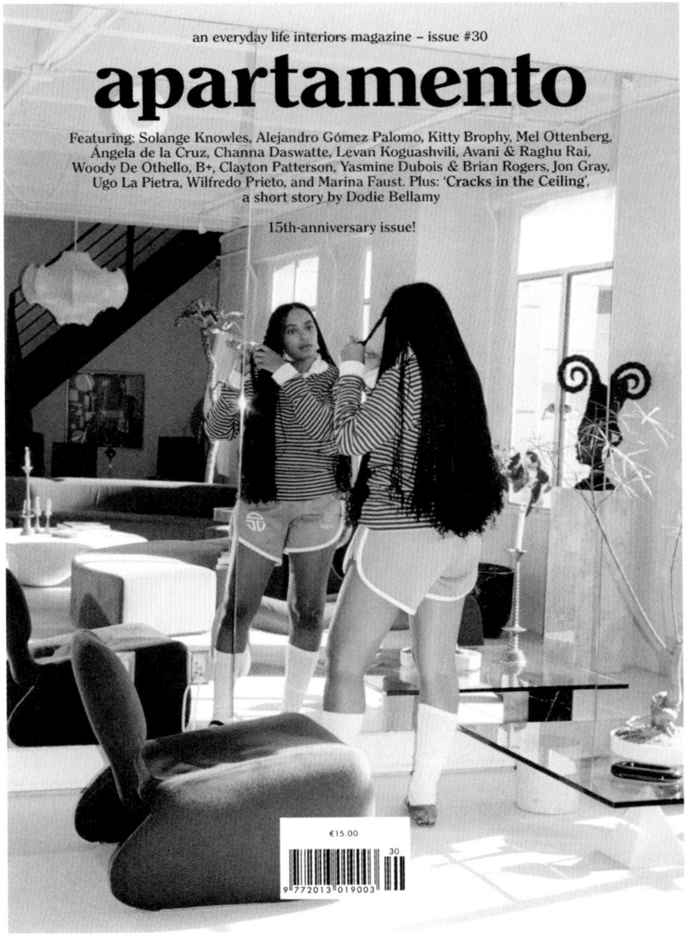

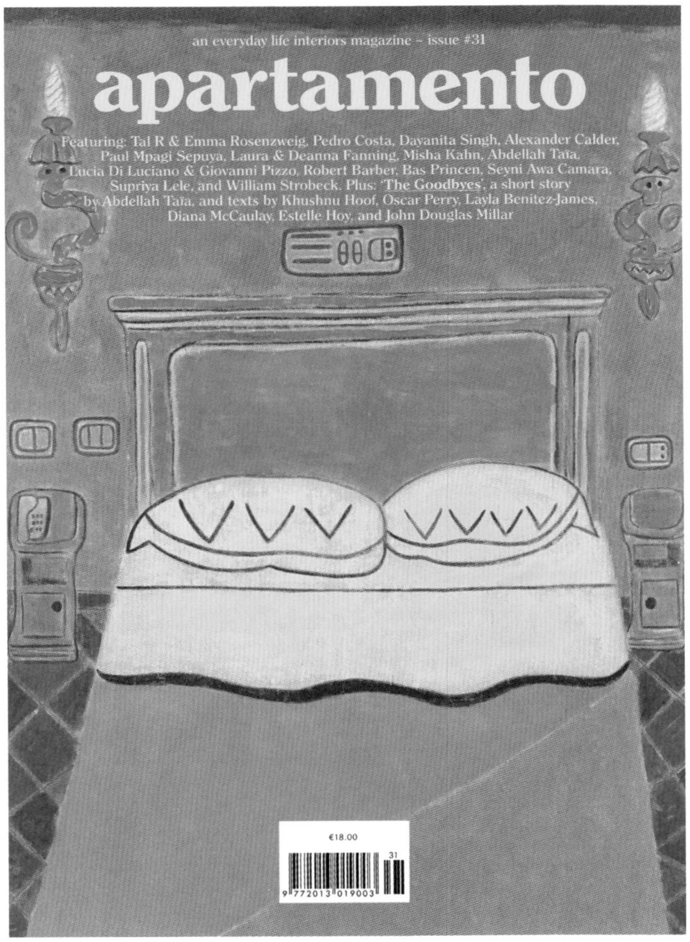

● **2008–PRESENT . APARTAMENTO .** Magazine Cover . Apartamento
TOP LEFT: Photograph Jeremy Liebman, No. 10. Autumn/Winter 2012–13; TOP RIGHT: Photograph Laurent Condominas, No. Autumn/Winter 2021–2; BOTTOM LEFT: Photograph Jody Rogac, No. 30, Autumn/Winter 2022–3; BOTTOM RIGHT: Artwork Tal R, *Venice Bed*, 2015, No. 31, Spring/Summer 2023

→ p.512

● **2010 . ACCESSIBLE ICON PROJECT .** Information Design . Sara Hendren, Brian Glenney, Tim Ferguson Sauder

→ p.513

● **2010 . WERK NO. 17: ELEY KISHIMOTO .** Magazine / Newspaper . Theseus Chan, Joanne Lim

→ p.513

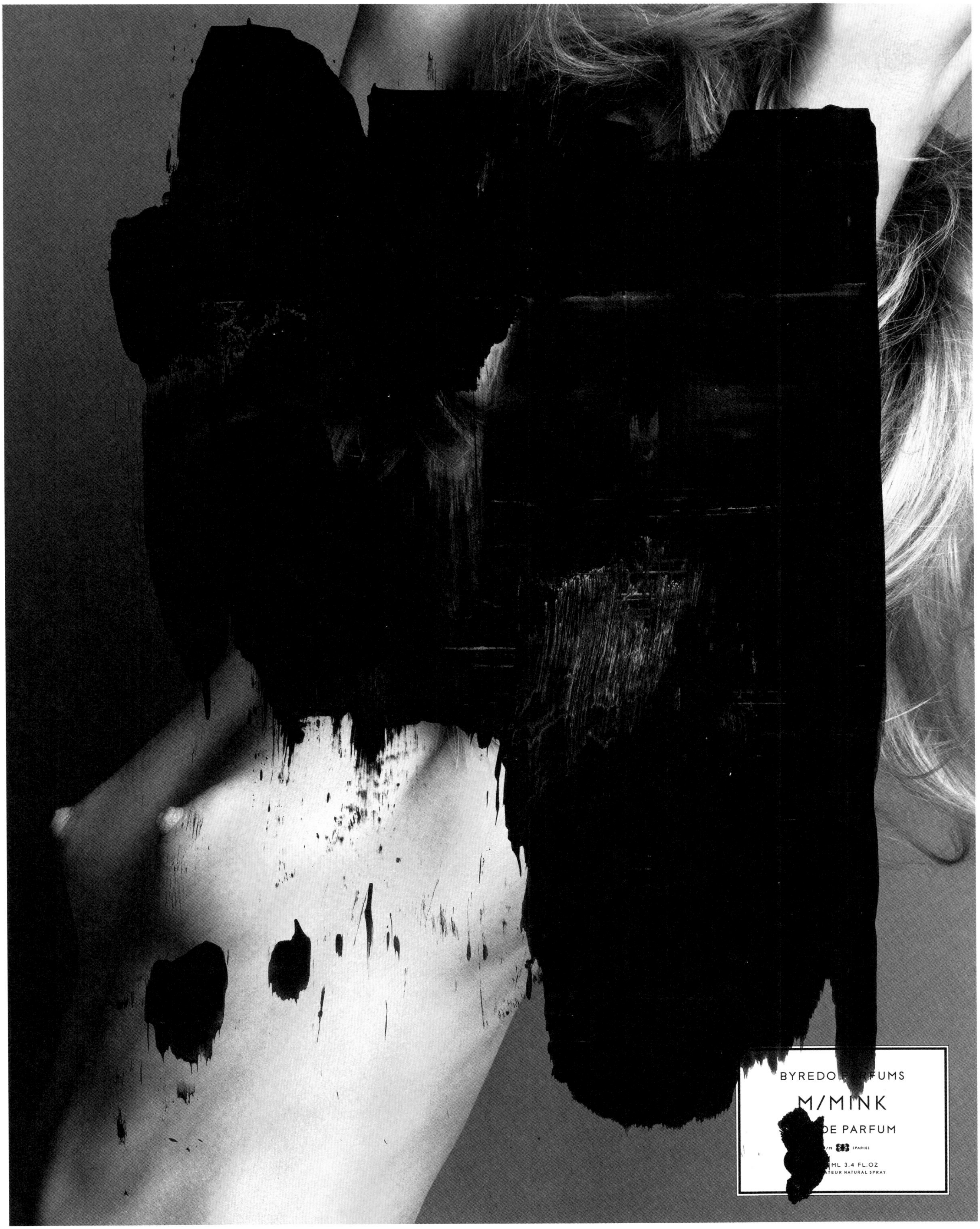

2010 . M/MINK . Advertising . Michaël Amzalag, Mathias Augustyniak

→ p.513

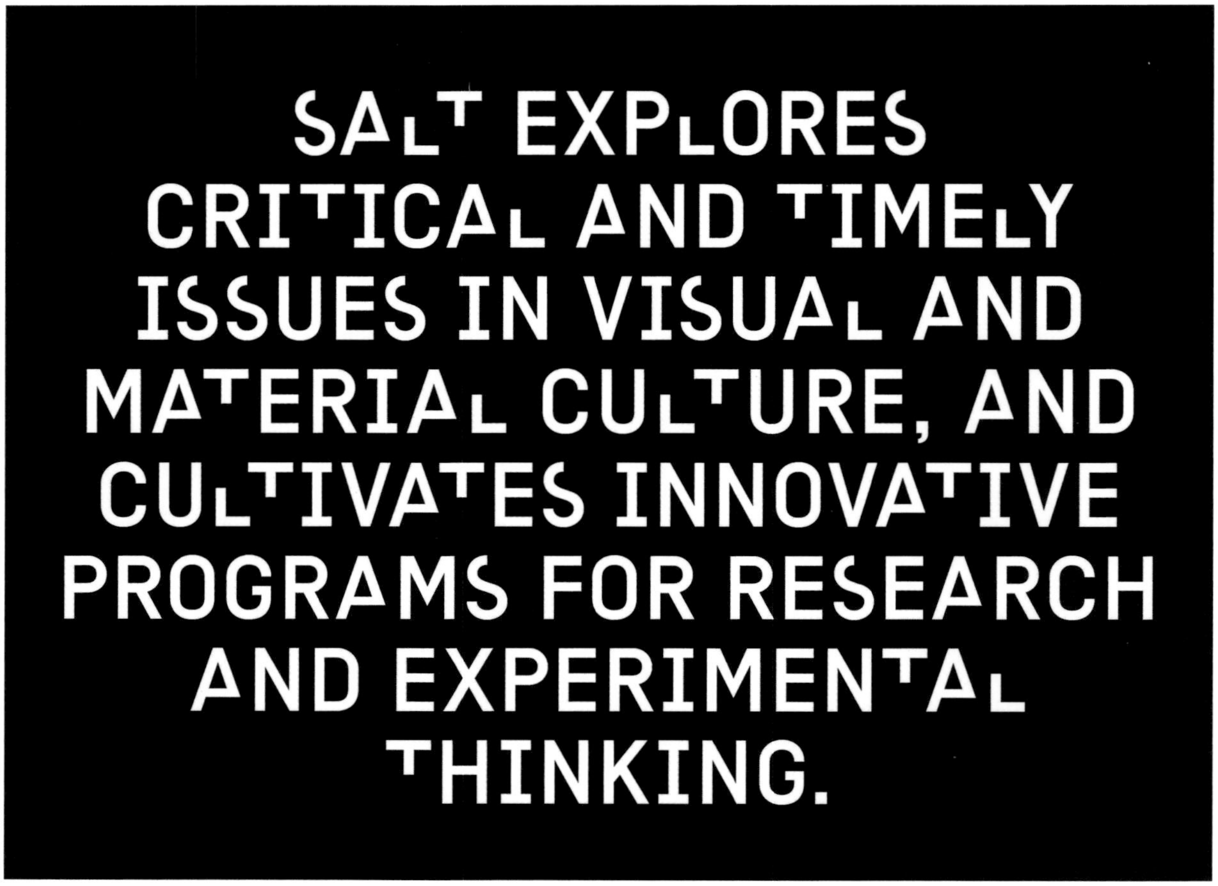
SALT EXPLORES
CRITICAL AND TIMELY
ISSUES IN VISUAL AND
MATERIAL CULTURE, AND
CULTIVATES INNOVATIVE
PROGRAMS FOR RESEARCH
AND EXPERIMENTAL
THINKING.

● **2011–PRESENT . SALT .** Identity . Project Projects

→ p.514

Nº001
Nº015
Paul
Nº017
Kenneth
Goldsmith
Nº003
Nº011
Jalal
Nº012
Vandana
Shiva
Nº013
G. M.
Nº010
Christoph
Menke

● **2011–2012 . 100 NOTES—100 THOUGHTS .** Book . Leftloft

→ p.514

BLACK
LIVES
MATTER

2013 . BLACK LIVES MATTER . Logo . Design Action Collective

→ p.514

Circular Poster
Circular Extra Black
Circular Black
Circular Bold
Circular Medium
Circular Book
Circular Regular
Circular Light
Circular Thin

Circular Mono

● **2013 . CIRCULAR .** Typeface . Laurenz Brunner

→ p.515

● **2013 . DAVID BOWIE—THE NEXT DAY .** Record / CD Cover . Barnbrook

→ p.515

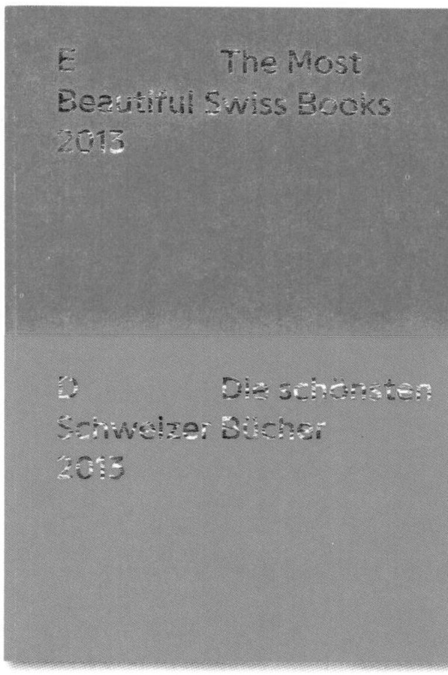

● **2014 . MOST BEAUTIFUL SWISS BOOKS 2013 .** Book . Maximage

→ p.515

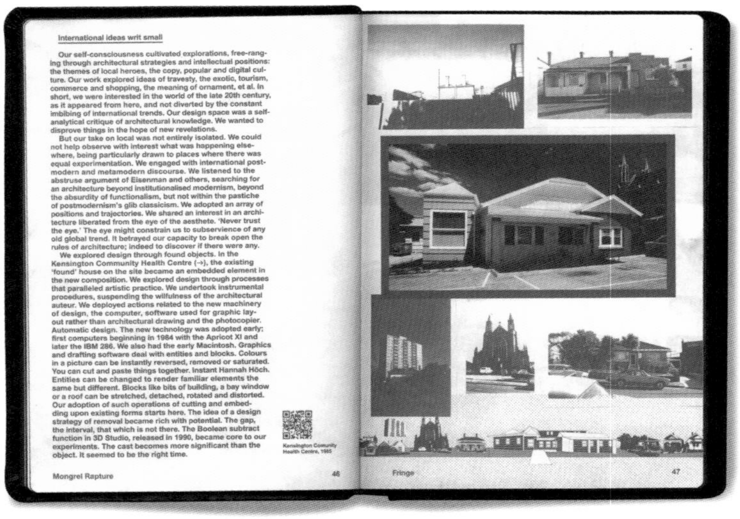

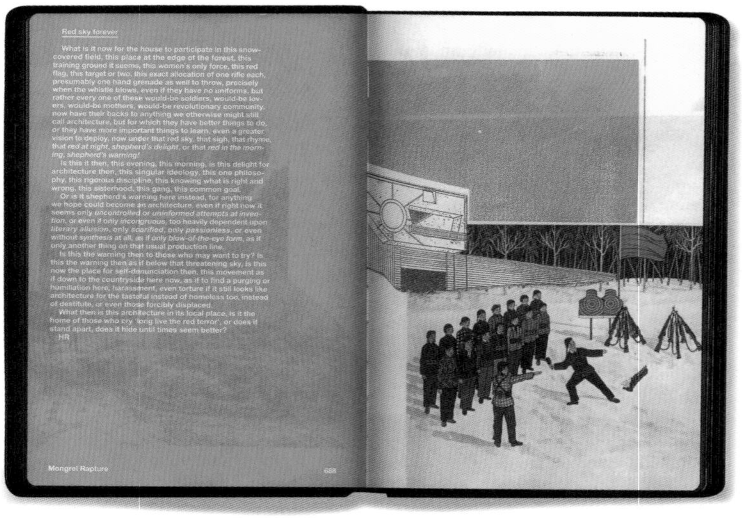

● **2015 . MONGREL RAPTURE: THE ARCHITECTURE OF ASHTON RAGGATT MCDOUGALL .** Book . Stuart Geddes, ARM Architecture

→ p.516

● **2017–PRESENT . MOLD .** Magazine / Newspaper . Eric Hu, Matthew Tsang
"Designing for the Human Microbiome," No. 1, August 2017

→ p.516

2018 . DREAM CRAZY . Advertising . Weiden+Kennedy

→ p.516

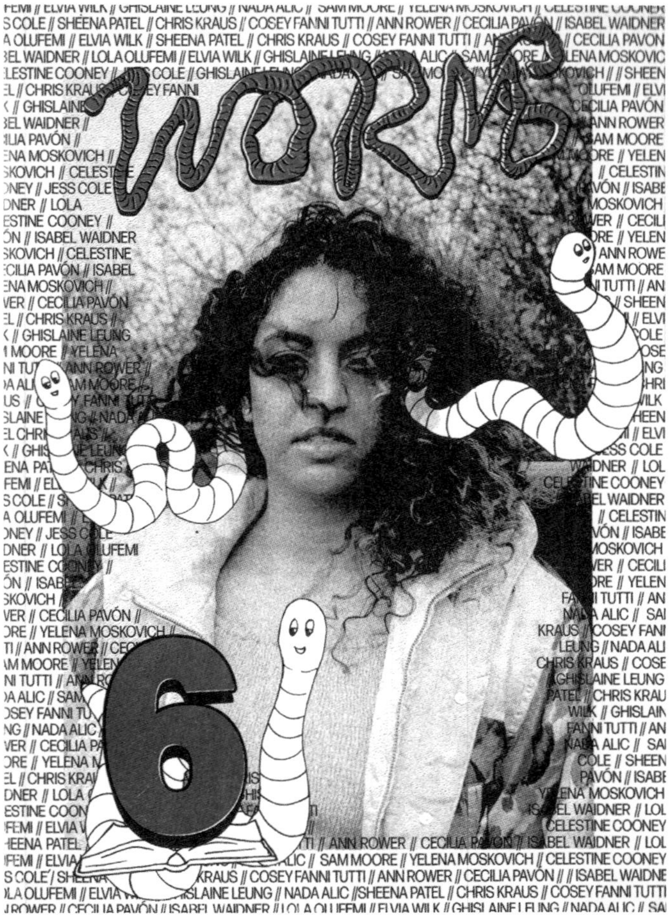

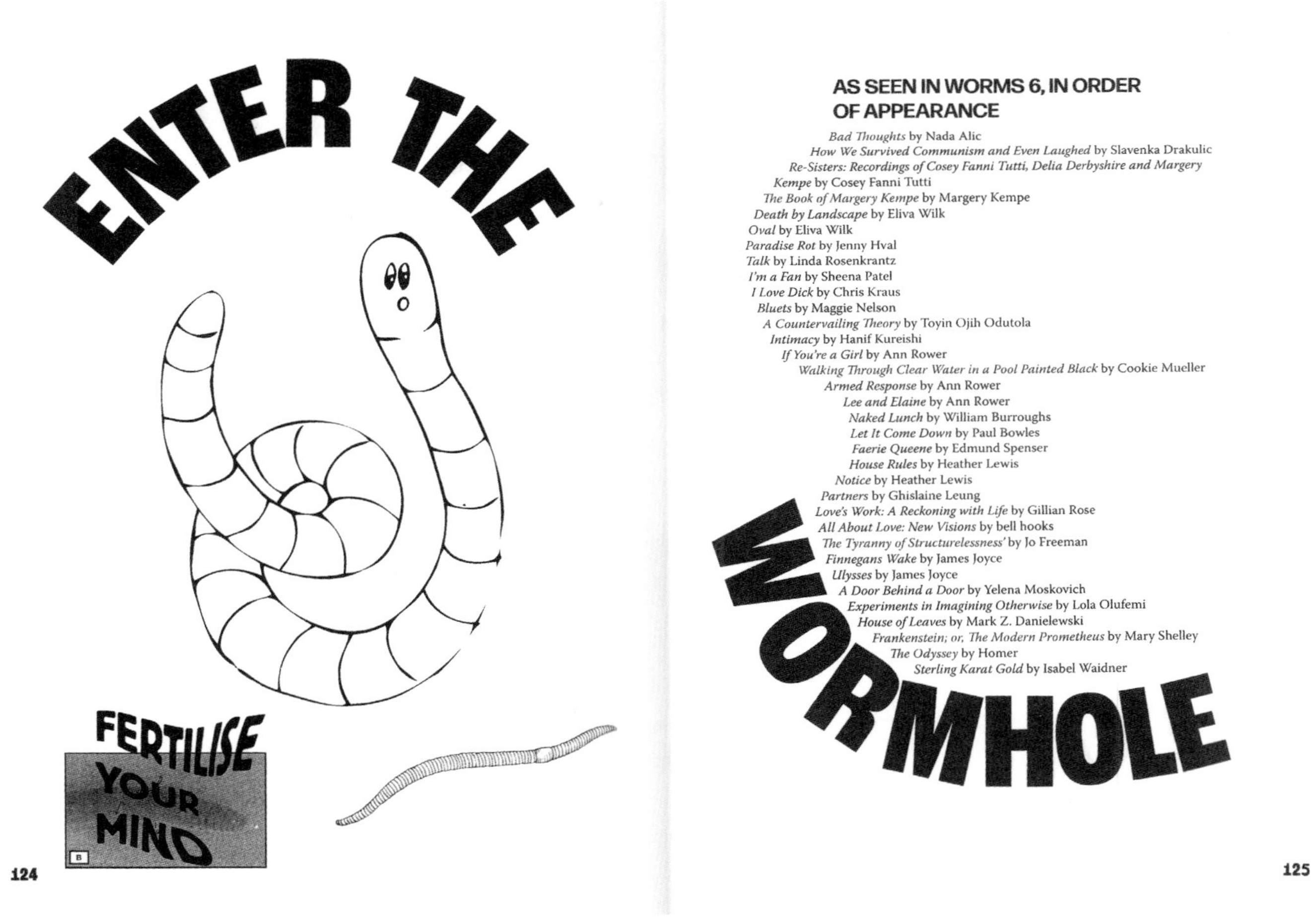

AS SEEN IN WORMS 6, IN ORDER OF APPEARANCE

Bad Thoughts by Nada Alic
How We Survived Communism and Even Laughed by Slavenka Drakulic
Re-Sisters: Recordings of Cosey Fanni Tutti, Delia Derbyshire and Margery Kempe by Cosey Fanni Tutti
The Book of Margery Kempe by Margery Kempe
Death by Landscape by Eliva Wilk
Oval by Eliva Wilk
Paradise Rot by Jenny Hval
Talk by Linda Rosenkrantz
I'm a Fan by Sheena Patel
I Love Dick by Chris Kraus
Bluets by Maggie Nelson
A Countervailing Theory by Toyin Ojih Odutola
Intimacy by Hanif Kureishi
If You're a Girl by Ann Rower
Walking Through Clear Water in a Pool Painted Black by Cookie Mueller
Armed Response by Ann Rower
Lee and Elaine by Ann Rower
Naked Lunch by William Burroughs
Let It Come Down by Paul Bowles
Faerie Queene by Edmund Spenser
House Rules by Heather Lewis
Notice by Heather Lewis
Partners by Ghislaine Leung
Love's Work: A Reckoning with Life by Gillian Rose
All About Love: New Visions by bell hooks
The Tyranny of Structurelessness' by Jo Freeman
Finnegans Wake by James Joyce
Ulysses by James Joyce
A Door Behind a Door by Yelena Moskovich
Experiments in Imagining Otherwise by Lola Olufemi
House of Leaves by Mark Z. Danielewski
Frankenstein; or, The Modern Prometheus by Mary Shelley
The Odyssey by Homer
Sterling Karat Gold by Isabel Waidner

● **2019–PRESENT . WORMS .** Magazine / Newspaper . Clem MacLeod, Caitlin McLoughlin
TOP LEFT: Rifke Sadleir, photograph courtesy Moyra Davey, "Biomythography," No. 3, 2021; TOP RIGHT: Clem MacLeod and Caitlin McLoughlin, photograph Isabel MacCarthy, "The Relatability Issue," No. 6, 2023; BOTTOM: Caitlin McLoughlin, "The Relatability Issue," No. 6, 2023

→ p.517

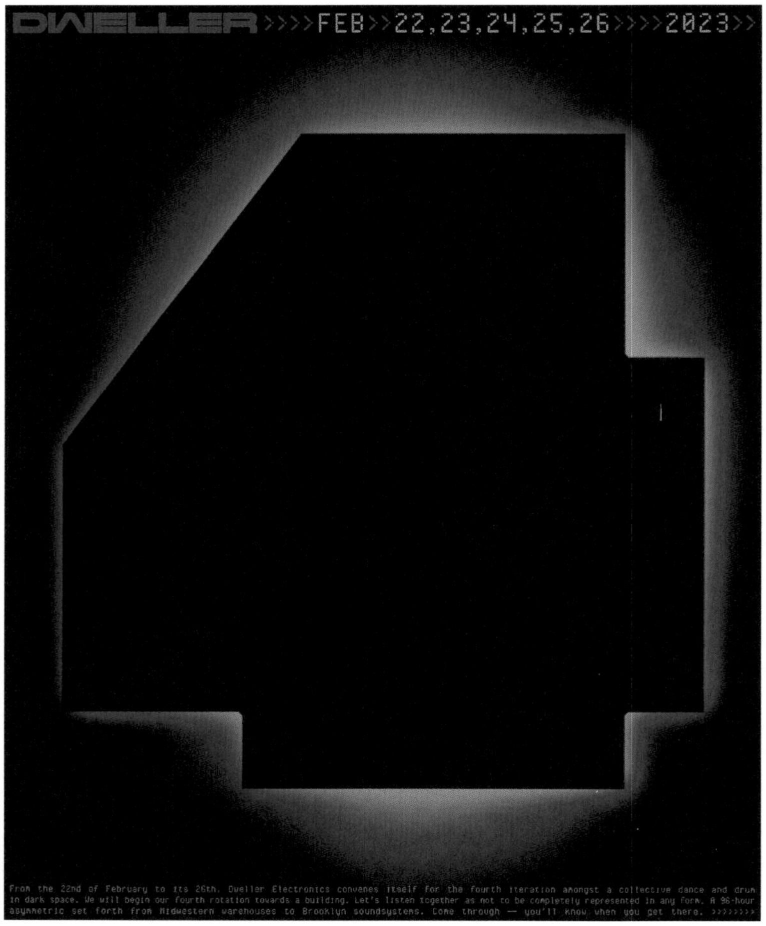

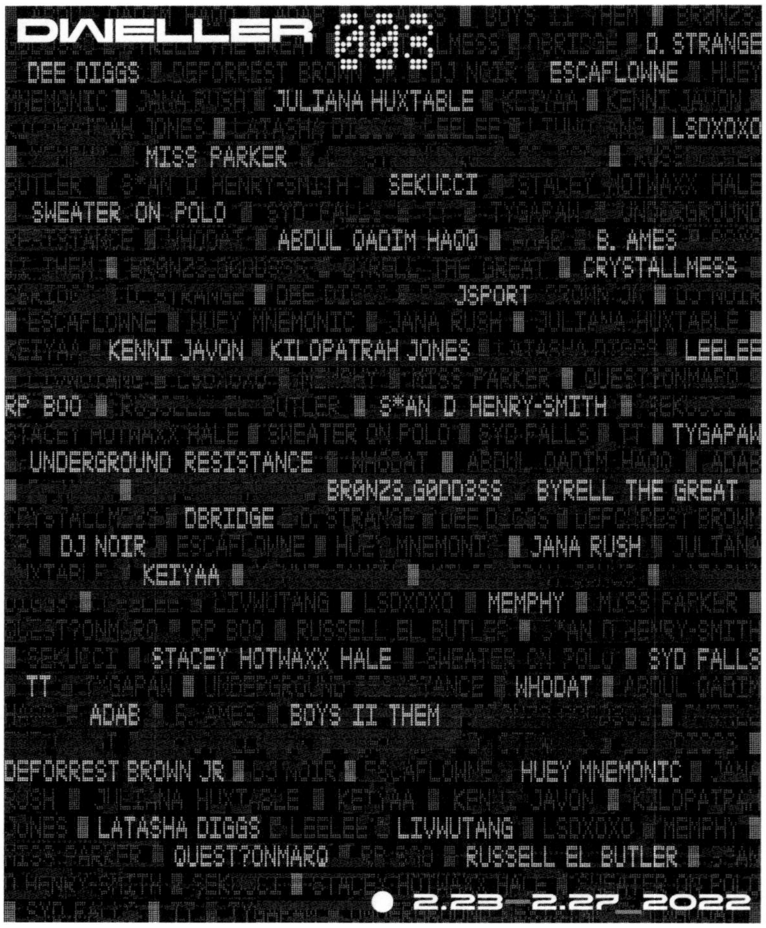

● **2019–PRESENT . DWELLER .** Poster . Hassan Rahim, Bryant Wells, David Lee

→ p.517

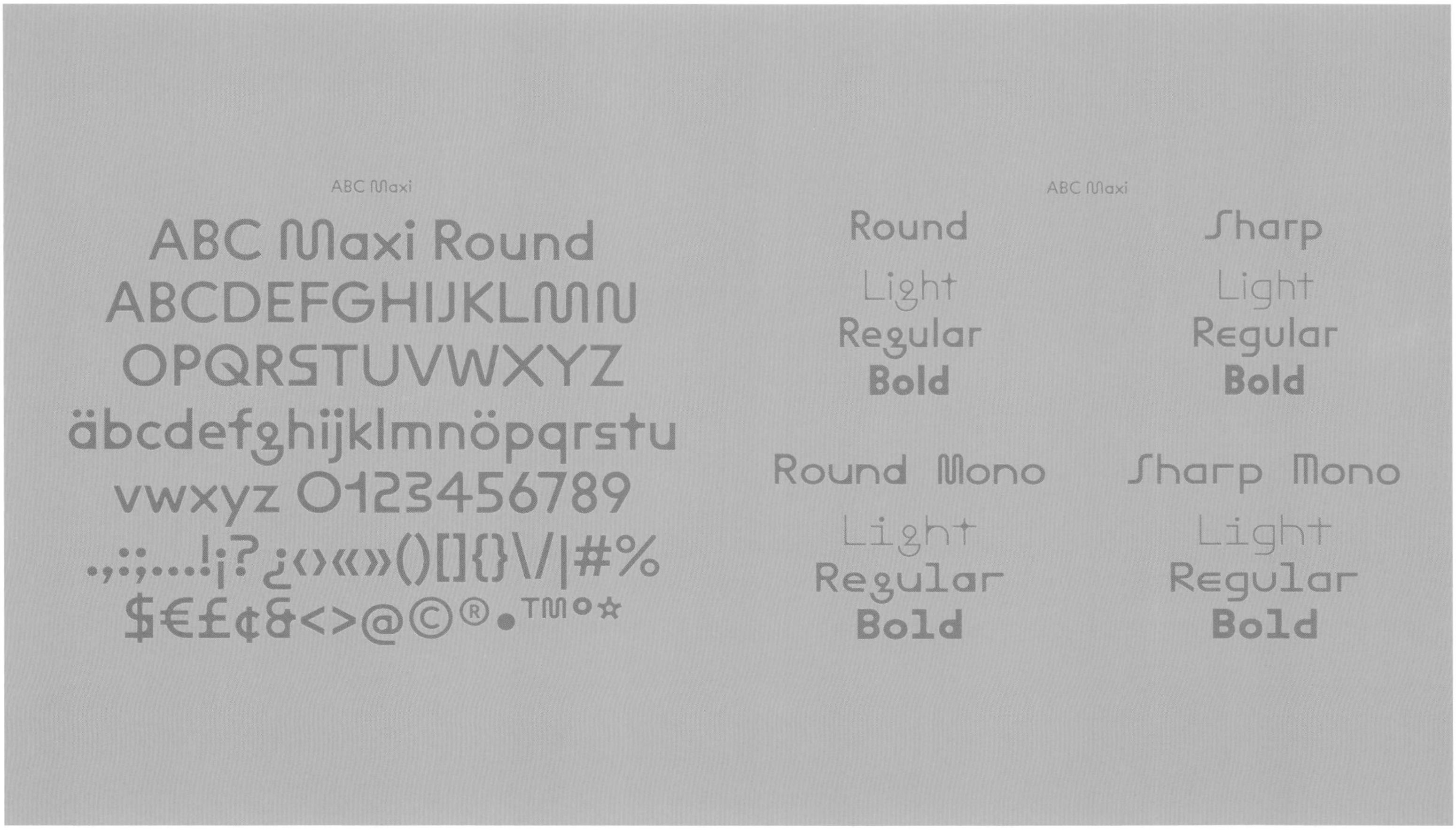

● **2020 . ABC MAXI .** Typeface . Dinamo

→ p.517

● **2020–PRESENT . MSCHF MAG .** Magazine / Newspaper . Shira Inbar, MSCHF
FROM LEFT: “Vs,” Vol. 3, 2020; “People,” Vol. 4, 2021; “Eat More Meat, Watch More Fox, Stop Printing the Bible, Stick Your Hands in Your Mouth,” Vol. 6, 2022; “MSCHF Mag 360,” 2023; “XXX,” Vol. 7, guest editors Dirty Magazine, 2023

→ p.518

● **2021 . KUSINA MAI / KUSINA MAI FUTI .** Poster . Nontsikelelo Mutiti

→ p.518

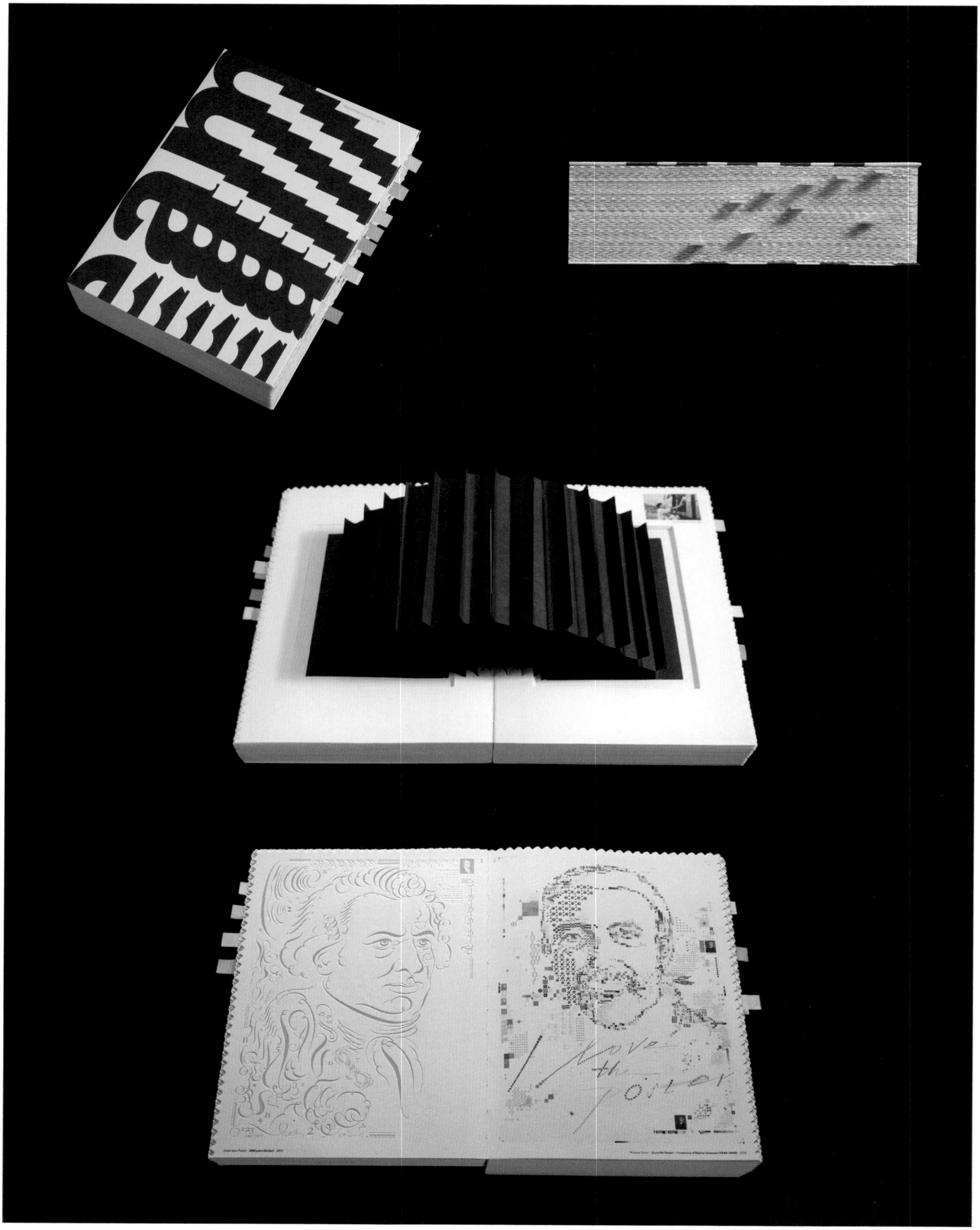

● **2021 . DAYDREAM: JUMPING HE .** Book . Jianping He

→ p.518

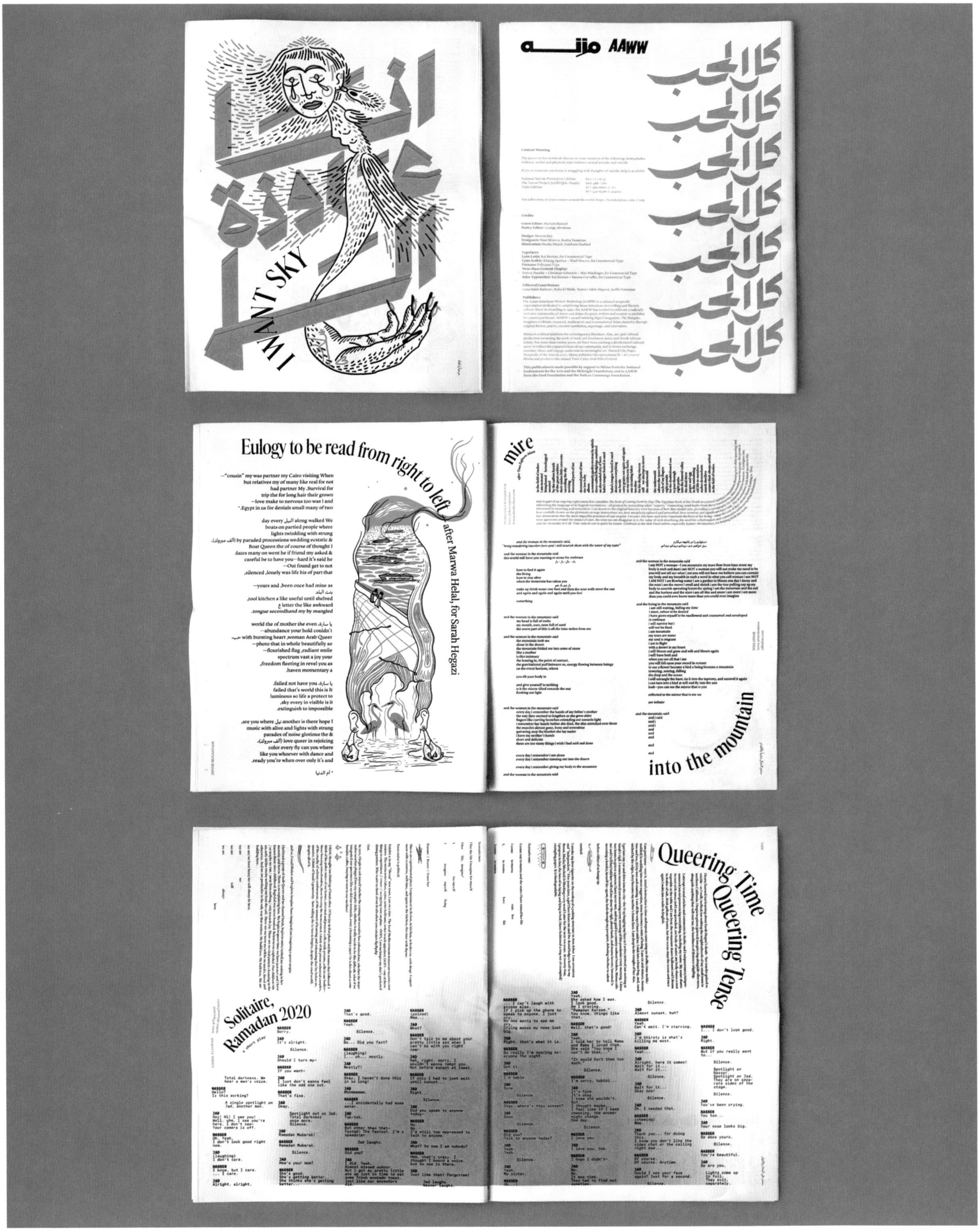

● **2021 . I WANT SKY .** Magazine / Newspaper . Wael Morcos, Rouba Yammine, Haitham Haddad

→ p.519

Environmental taxes

Tax revenue from environmentally related taxes

The visualization shows tax revenues from environmental taxes, calculated as a percentage of total tax revenues, from 2000 to 2020 for 20 countries.
The countries indicated are the top 20 by GDP in 2021, selected from those with data on environmental taxes available from 2000 to 2020.
An environmental tax is defined as «a tax whose tax base is a physical unit (or a proxy of it) that has a proven specific negative impact on the environment. Four subsets of environmental taxes are distinguished: energy taxes, transport taxes, pollution taxes and resources taxes»

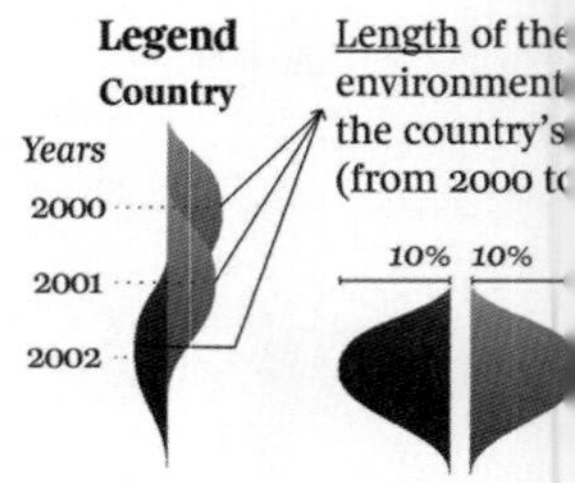

The top 20 countries by GDP in 2021, selected from those with data on environmental taxes available from 2000 to 2020

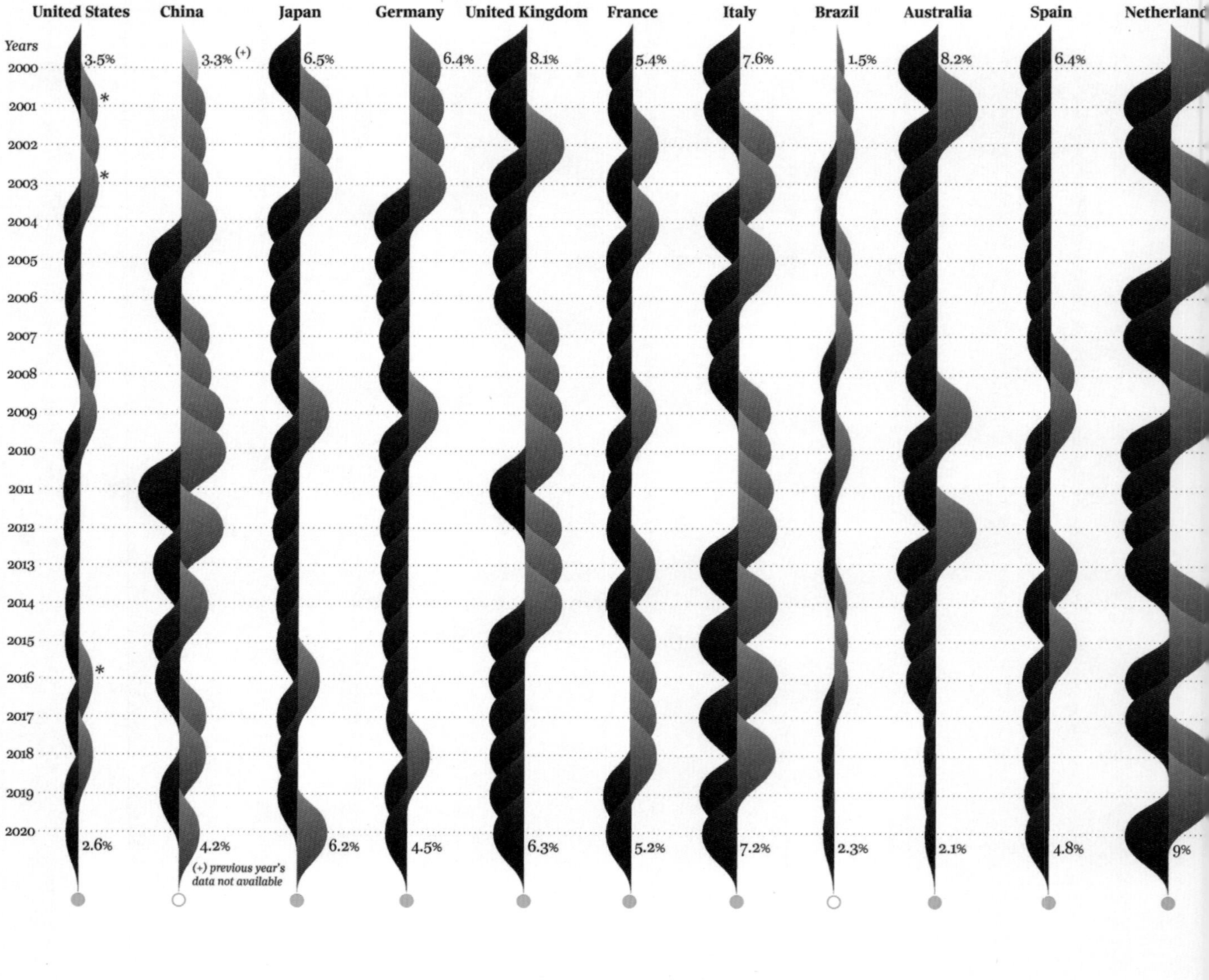

→ p.519

es = tax revenue from
es, as a percentage of
tax revenue
)

5% 5% 2% 2%

Direction and color of the shapes = change over the previous year

shape pointing to the left = the percentage of revenue from environmental taxes has decreased compared to the previous year

shape pointing to the right = the percentage of revenues from environmental taxes has increased compared to the previous year

* *the percentage has not changed since the previous year*

Symbol = change in data from 2000 to 2020

● = *the percentage of revenue from environmental taxes in 2020 has decreased compared to 2000*

○ = *the percentage of revenue from environmental taxes in 2020 has increased compared to 2000*

Source: *data.oecd.org*

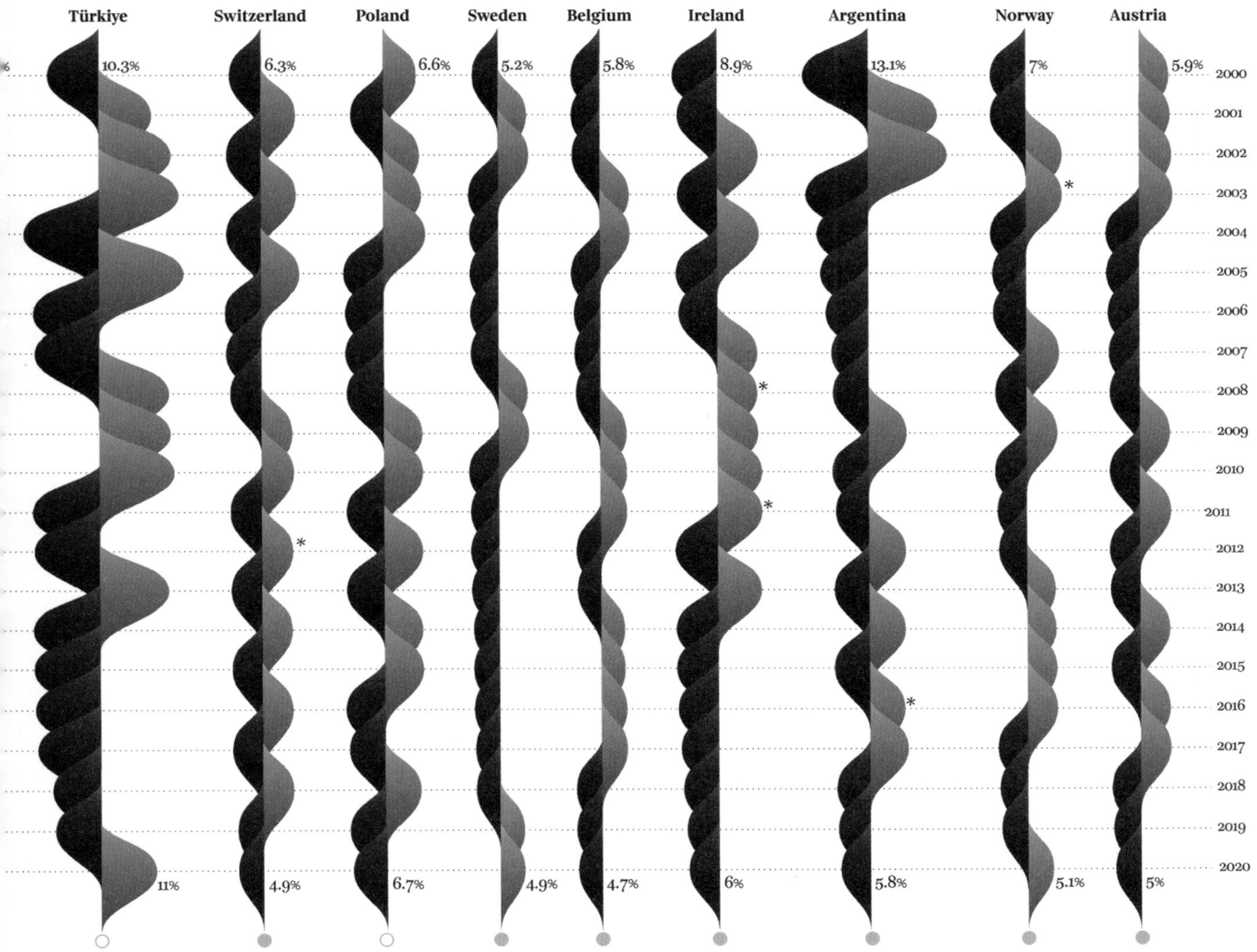

● **2022 . EYES ON IRAN .** Poster . Mahvash Mostala, Hank Willis Thomas, et al.

→ p.519

● **2023 . THE POSTMODERN CHILD (PART 2) .** Poster . Everyday Practice

→ p.520

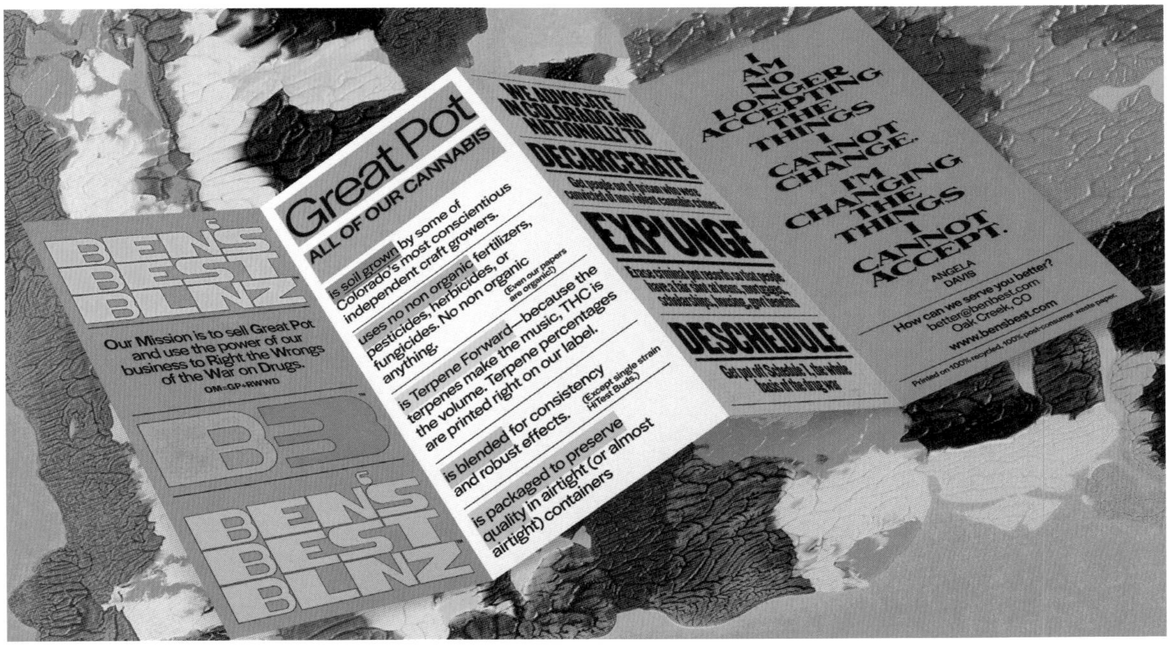

● **2023 . BEN'S BEST BLNZ (B3) .** Identity . Eddie Opara, Pentagram

→ p.520

GRAPHIC CLASSICS

← P.6

1377

BAEGUN HWASANG CHOROK BULJO JIKJI SIMCHE YOJEOL

Book

Various

Heungdeok-sa Temple, South Korea

The first book to be printed with metal movable type, *Baegun Hwasang Chorok Buljo Jikji Simche Yojeol (Anthology of Great Buddhist Priests' Zen Teachings)* is a collection of essential Zen Buddhist texts that was published during the Goryeo Dynasty, at Heungdeok-sa Temple in the Chungcheong Province of South Korea. The text is made up of Chinese characters—the only written script used in Korea during the Goryeo period, before Hangul, the official Korean script, had been created—and reflects the influence of Chinese Zen Buddhism on Korea; in 2001 the book was registered in the UNESCO Memory of the World program. The original *Jikji* consisted of two volumes, made up of 370 chapters. However, only the last volume, which is held in France's Bibliothèque Nationale, minus its first page, has survived.

The manuscript was printed on delicate white paper, probably *xuan*, an absorbent paper commonly used in traditional Chinese calligraphy and painting. Resembling Chinese books printed with woodblocks, the manuscript contains flaws typically associated with early metal type, such as irregular edges, inconsistent type weight, and lines written in reverse or sometimes incompletely printed. The pages were printed with two pages on each sheet, then folded in half (a method known today as French folding) and bound by a traditional Chinese technique using doubled silk string, with the knot hidden in the spine.

UNESCO's recognition of the *Jikji* has led Korea to claim credit for the invention of movable type printing, although, in fact, China first developed the method in 1040, when a movable-type system using baked clay was created by Bi Sheng. China had also led the ancient world in devising earlier printing technologies, such as xylography, where the reverse of an image is carved into a woodblock, which first emerged as early as AD 600. By 1215, during the era of the Song Dynasty (960–1279), movable copper-block printing was used to print *Jiaozi*, the world's first paper money. As a vassal state of several Chinese dynasties from 1271 to 1911, Korea has a lengthy history of Chinese influence, and some Chinese experts have questioned the Korean origin of the *Jikji*. What is less controversial is the manuscript's important contribution to the preservation of both nations' cultural heritage.

← P.6

c. 1453–1455

THE GUTENBERG BIBLE

Book

Johannes Gutenberg (c. 1398–1468)

Self-commissioned, Germany

The Gutenberg Bible was the first book using Latin letterforms to be printed from movable type (earlier technologies in China and Korea failed to survive or spread), and represented a turning point in the history of the printed word. Johannes Gutenberg, a goldsmith from Mainz, Germany, spent almost twenty years perfecting his invention, finishing his forty-two-line Bible in about 1453–55. Only forty-eight copies are known to exist today.

The Gutenberg Bible is celebrated as much for its beauty as for its historical importance. In appearance the books look like the finest handwritten manuscripts, although their words were composed from metal letters, first inked then pressed onto the page by machine. Headings and sections in different colors were added by hand, making every copy of the Bible an individual work of art. Copies for important monasteries were printed on vellum and elaborately illuminated.

Gutenberg's press allowed a printer to produce in a single day what had previously taken a scribe an entire year. His basic process remained unchanged for more than three hundred fifty years: first, a letter would be carved on a steel stick called a punch; second, the punch was hammered onto a soft, "blank" piece of copper or brass, which became the matrix or casing, and in turn was placed into a mold for casting. The mold was adjustable on two sides, allowing the letters to have varying widths. Molten metal was then poured into the mold, and the individual letters, when removed, were assembled using a compositor's stick. To ensure that his Bible resembled calligraphy, Gutenberg created a set of 290 alternate characters; this allowed him to use different letter widths as a way of justifying columns without having to adjust their spacing. He also developed a new kind of ink that would adhere to the metal and transfer effectively to vellum or paper. This process was accomplished using a screw press, possibly adapted from wine presses.

Gutenberg's innovations enabled books to be duplicated quickly and inexpensively, producing a rapid surge in literacy as printing technology proliferated throughout Europe. Even though new technologies have now long superseded those used by Gutenberg, his Bible remains a "gold standard" for beauty in book design and production.

← P.7

1493

THE NUREMBERG CHRONICLE

Book

Michael Wolgemut (1434–1519), Wilhelm Pleydenwurff (c. 1450–1494), Albrecht Dürer (1471–1528)

Sebald Schreyer and Sebastian Kammermeister, Germany

One of the most important examples of early printing, *The Nuremberg Chronicle* (as it is known in English) is an illustrated world history written by the physician and humanist scholar Hermann Schedel. Although the book dates from the Renaissance, it follows the narrative tradition of medieval universal chronicles, telling the story of seven ages, and interweaving biblical and nonbiblical historical events with other subject matter. First published in June 1493 in Latin in the city of Nuremberg, and known in the academic world as *Liber Chronicarum*, the book was translated into German later that year.

Michael Wolgemut and Wilhelm Pleydenwurff, who oversaw the design and illustration of the book, were leading artists who specialized in the new art of book illustration, employing draughtspeople to transfer artists' designs onto woodblocks and cutters to carve the blocks. The young Albrecht Dürer apprenticed under Wolgemut and may have been involved with producing the early designs, which consist of 1,804 colored illustrations. Most famous are the thirty-two illustrated landscapes that record the early appearance of many German cities, including Nuremberg itself. Other images vary in format, depicting narrative and genre scenes from the Gospels, as well as contemporary people mentioned in the narratives. While some illustrations are spread across two pages, others appear alongside the text, breaking it up into irregular shapes. Altogether, the book contains fourteen basic page layouts, with many woodblocks used more than once, and around 1,164 instances of repetition. To reflect the different readerships of the book, the Latin edition, aimed at the imperial, theological, and academic markets, was printed in Antiqua Rotunda, whereas the German version, targeting the upper-middle classes, used Bastarda Schwabacher.

The *Chronicle* is valued for its graphic layouts, integrated text and images, and the quality of its illustrations, many of which, due to the book's oversized format (approx. 18¼ × 12½ inches [46 × 32 cm]), are large and highly detailed. Of the estimated 1,400–1,500 Latin and 700–1,000 German copies printed, roughly 400 and 300, respectively, have survived.

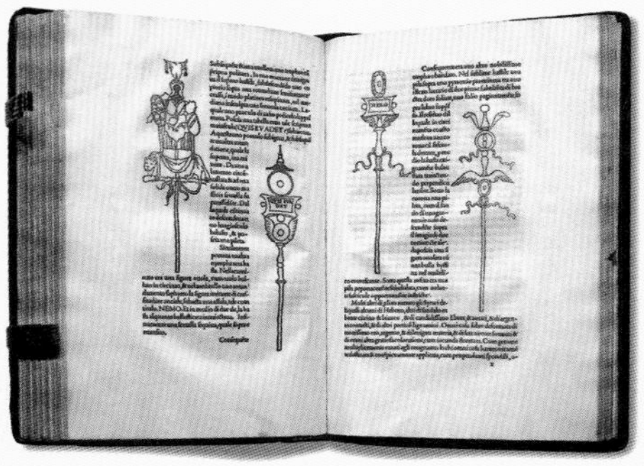

← P.8

1499

HYPNEROTOMACHIA POLIPHILI

Book

Aldus Manutius (1449–1515)

Leonardo Crassus, Italy

Hypnerotomachia Poliphili (*Poliphilus's Strife of Love in a Dream*) is a particularly fine example of a woodcut-illustrated book produced during the incunabula (early typographic) period, and the most famous work published by the Venetian Aldine Press.

Aldus Manutius set up his press in Venice in 1495 primarily to print classic Greek and Latin texts, earning a reputation for scholarly works such as his five-volume edition of Aristotle (1495–98). Although he published few illustrated books, Manutius was commissioned by Leonardo Crassus of Verona to print Francesco Colonna's curious erotic and pagan tale of the quest of the young Poliphilus for his beloved, chaste Polia. Colonna was a Dominican friar, as revealed in the book by the sentence POLIAM FRATER FRANCISCUS COLVMNA PERAMAVIT, which is formed by the first letter of each successive chapter. The colophon records the date of the novel as 1467.

Hypnerotomachia Poliphili contains 234 leaves and 172 variously sized woodcut illustrations. The latter depict Poliphilus's journey through classical landscapes and architecture; one of them, showing a dolphin and an anchor, inspired the famous Aldine Press trademark. Although the artist of the illustrations is unknown, they are an outstanding example of Venetian-style outline cuts of the period, in which even, delicate tone and exceptional use of white space function in perfect harmony with the weight and texture of the type and unusually shaped blocks of text, several of which taper inward toward the base. The type itself was an improved version of the roman Bembo font, cut by Francesco Griffo for Manutius's 1495 publication of Pietro Bembo's *De Aetna*, and included Griffo's newly designed capitals. This orderly print style, along with wide margins, starlike ornaments, and floriated, outlined initials, all contributed to a new lightness of page. Griffo also produced the first italic type for use in Aldine classics printed from 1501. Ever the shrewd businessman, Manutius recognized that italics used less space in octavos (small books), and could therefore help to make large editions more affordable.

Hypnerotomachia Poliphili was not a commercial success, but remains Manutius's masterpiece due to its visual harmony and grace.

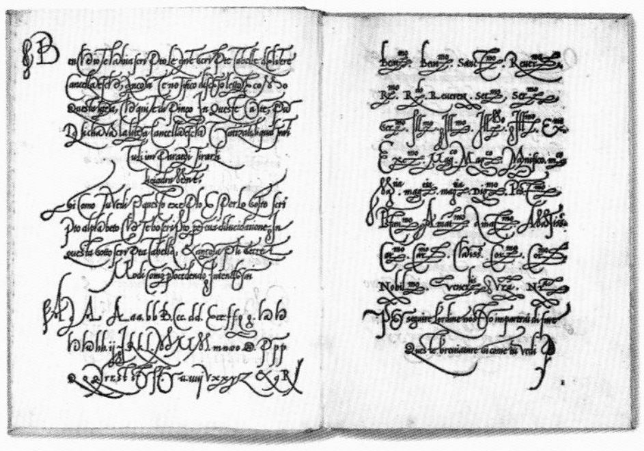

← P.8

1524

LO PRESENTE LIBRO

Book

Giovanni Antonio Tagliente (c. 1465–1528)

Self-commissioned, Italy

A distant forerunner of Hermann Zapf's *Manuale Typographicum* (1954), which illustrated typographical compositions, *Lo Presente Libro* is a tribute to the art of calligraphy and the joy of creating beautiful letterforms. Venice-born Giovanni Antonio Tagliente was one of the most celebrated calligraphers of the Renaissance, who wrote and set out *Lo Presente Libro* to showcase his work and instruct others in the skill of fine handwriting.

A slender, pocketbook-sized guide, *Lo Presente Libro* contains forty-eight irregularly numbered pages printed on paper of varying density, each of which is a composition in its own right, with its own rules of space, balance, and interplay of contrasts. It opens with an illustration of writing implements—a penman's *vanitas*, reminding us perhaps of the stability of words among the uncertainties of life. The book goes on to present examples of decorative letters interspersed with passages of text; letters (but very few numbers) are shown in italic, roman, and even backslope versions in a multiplicity of possible arrangements, and the texts provide commentary on the letterforms' history and recommendations for use. Flourishes and ligatures fill awkward spaces and change the pace, the occasional fleuron or "difficult" character is highlighted and resolved by minute adjustments, black pages are filled with tiny white dots such as stars and white letters of different sizes to form complex patterns, and elsewhere there are occasional excursions into Hebraic and blackletter.

The book was printed from woodblocks, which Tagliente described as "not printing the usual way, but by a new method." In fact, this method, xylography, was not new and had long predated the invention of movable metal type of c. 1450. As metal type became popular, it made xylography largely obsolete, but it also regularized typographic arrangements, and would have made Tagliente's graceful and exuberant layout impossible. His book could therefore be seen as an early example of a designer ignoring prevailing technical trends to produce a highly personal work.

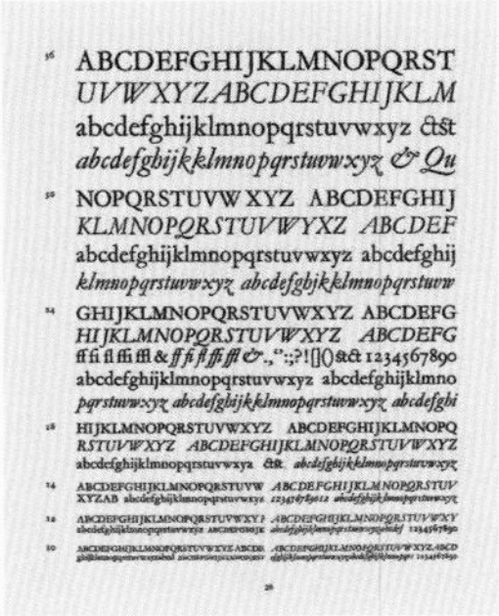

← P.9

1530

GARAMOND

Typeface

Claude Garamond (c. 1480–1561)

Self-commissioned, France

The typefaces produced by Claude Garamond between 1530 and 1545 are considered among the typographical highlights of the sixteenth century. His fonts were widely accepted at the time of their creation, have been extensively copied, and are still produced, remaining in popular use today.

Claude Garamond was a French type founder, publisher, punch cutter, and type designer who trained in 1510 first with Simon de Colines in Paris, then with Geoffroy Tory. Garamond's first typeface appeared in 1530 in an edition of Erasmus's *Paraphrasis in Elegantiarum Libros Laurentii Vallae*. From 1545 onward Garamond worked as a publisher, initially with Pierre Gaultier and later with Jean Barbe. His first book was David Chambellan's *Pia et Religiosa Meditatio*, which was composed using a roman typeface designed by Garamond himself.

Garamond had probably seen Venetian old-style typefaces from the printing shops of Aldus Manutius, and he based his own roman characters on Manutius's font De Aetna, cut in 1455. He based much of the design of his lowercase letters on the handwriting of Angelo Vergecio, librarian to the French King Francis I. Garamond's letterforms convey a sense of fluidity and consistency, along with some unique characteristics, such as the small bowl of the lowercase "a" and the small eye of the lowercase "e." Long extenders and top serifs have a downward slope, and the uppercase "T" is the most notable spot character, with its inclining left-hand serif. The court of Francis I adopted Garamond's roman types, and the characters influenced printing typefaces across France and Western Europe.

After Garamond's death, a large portion of his original punches and matrices was acquired by Christophe Plantin in Belgium, the Le Bé type foundry in France, and Egenolff-Bermer in Germany. Today the only complete set of original Garamond type is in the Plantin-Moretus Museum, Antwerp. In the 1920s Stanley Morison and the Monotype Corporation successfully designed a family of fonts based on the original matrices, giving Garamond a new lease of life. So popular is the typeface that virtually every font publisher in the world has now published Garamond in both physical and digital form.

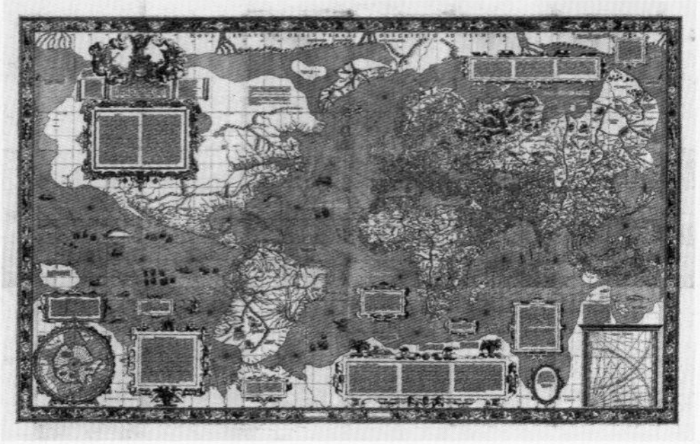

← P.10

1569

MERCATOR PROJECTION

Information Design

Gerardus Mercator (1512–1594)

Duke Wilhelm of Cleve, Belgium

Since 1569, the Mercator projection has defined our idea of the Earth. Although planned as a purely maritime navigational aid, and despite four centuries of adaptations, criticism, and misuse, the map has become one of our planet's primary cartographic representations. Today, it is still in use for Google Maps.

The projection was originally published as a set of eighteen sheets by the sixteenth-century Flemish mathematician and geographer Gerardus Mercator. Although neither the first world map nor the first instance of cylindrical projection, Mercator's achievement revolutionized navigation. His whole-world maritime chart and simpler, more accurate navigational method meant that for the first time sailors could plot their course on a flat surface with a straight line. However, like any method used to translate the surface of a sphere onto a flat surface, Mercator's system involved distortion, resulting in an exaggeration of the poles at the expense of the equator. Hence, Greenland seems to be the same size as Africa, and Brazil appears equal to Alaska. Despite this, the success of the projection with sailors ensured its adoption by other cartographers. Edmund Halley mapped the trade winds using the system in 1686, and Benjamin Franklin used it as the basis for his Gulf Stream map in 1769.

The ubiquity of Mercator's projection was challenged in 1973 by the historian Arnold Peters, who claimed that the diminished size of developing nations was imperialistic. Peters promoted a revision of the 1855 Gall projection, which provided a more accurate reflection of area by stretching land at the equator. Peters's projection was championed by organizations such as Oxfam, Christian Aid, and the United Nations Development Program, although it, too, proved to be distorted. Most cartographic institutions, including the National Geographic, favor modified azimuthal projections, which replicate the Earth's curvature more realistically.

The popularity of the Mercator projection testifies to its author's aim to make the world "look right." Sinusoidal projections represent land masses more correctly, but their nonrectangular form is both unappealing to the layman and less practical for the mariner. There is no truly accurate world map, but Mercator's projection has outlasted all others.

A SPECIMEN
By WILLIAM CASLON, Letter-Founder, in Chiswell-Street, LONDON.

← P.10

1734

CASLON

Typeface

William Caslon (1692–1766)

Self-commissioned, UK

A typeface epitomizing grace, harmony, and warmth while upholding the highest standards of legibility, Caslon was immediately successful and remains enduringly popular today.

The name Caslon refers to a family of serif typefaces created by the English type designer William Caslon, of which the earliest is his famous 1734 specimen sheet. Characterized by a larger x-height than preceding Dutch types, short ascenders and descenders, bracketed serifs, moderate-to-high contrast, and a robust overall appearance, Caslon made a significant contribution to the art and design of printing and proved immediately superior to existing Dutch typefaces; it has been often said that one cannot "go wrong" by setting a text in Caslon. Among the unique features of this typeface is the concave hollow at the apex of the uppercase "A," and the absence of a spur in the uppercase "G." Caslon Italic is rhythmic and decorative, with a particularly ornate ampersand; the design of this symbol may be a reflection of William Caslon's background in engraving flourishes on gun barrels.

Caslon took particular care to preserve the uniformity of his letterforms when producing different sizes, which effectively brought to an end the dominance of Dutch type foundries. Caslon types were distributed throughout the British Empire and quickly developed an international following, appearing in many historic documents, including the U.S. Declaration of Independence. Twentieth-century digital revivals of Caslon include Adobe Caslon, designed by Carol Twombly and released in 1990 (now available as Adobe Caslon Pro), and ITC Founders Caslon, created by Justin Howes in 1998. A display version of Caslon, Big Caslon CC, designed by Matthew Carter in 1994, exaggerates the contrast between thick and thin strokes, giving it a vibrant look. With its combination of liveliness and classicism, Caslon is ideally suited to a wide range of contemporary design uses.

← P.10

c. 1750

MUSIC NOTATION (FIVE-LINE STAVE)

Information Design

Unknown

Unknown

Employed ubiquitously for the notation of Western music, the five-line stave became popular with the increase in polyphonic music around 1200, developing from a four-line stave commonly used for plainchant manuscripts. Although four-, six-, and seven-line staves were also in use, the five-line stave emerged as the most common. In 1756 Pierre-Simon Fournier published a specimen of a new character font for music to appear as if printed by copperplate engraving but instead using movable type. It was by this point that music notation started to appear as it does today.

There are several notations located at the beginning of a stave that govern how a piece of music should be performed: a clef—either a G-clef (treble clef), a C-clef (alto or tenor clef) or an F-clef (bass clef), which developed from the letters "G," "C," and "F," respectively—and its location on the stave is used to indicate the range of pitches. Accidentals (flats, sharps, and natural symbols), which were developed in Germany during the fifteenth century, indicate whether a note should be played a semitone lower or higher than normal. The flat symbol was represented by a rounded lowercase "B," similar to the way it looks today, whereas a square lower-case "B" indicated a sharp, or a note to be played a semitone above the pitch of the adjacent note.

The time signature is a symbol or set of numbers marked vertically on the stave and follows the clef and key signatures, with a "C" sometimes used to indicate 4/4 time or "common time," or a "C" with a vertical line drawn through it to indicate 2/2 time. Other notations include rests, which can take a variety of forms and are placed between or across the lines to indicate a pause in performance.

Although the many musical notations originated hundreds of years ago, their appearance in sheet music today remains largely unchanged, a fact that testifies to the success of these early models in establishing a comprehensible and universal system.

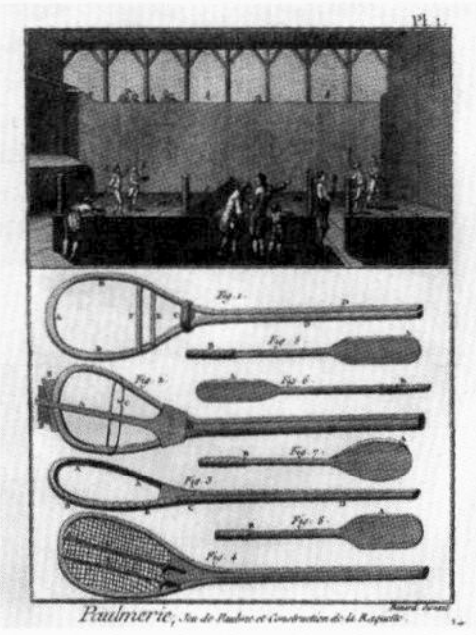

← P.11

← P.11

A
SPECIMEN
By JOHN BASKERVILLE of Birmingham.

← P.12

1752–1772

L'ENCYCLOPÉDIE

Book

Denis Diderot (1713–1784), Jean Le Rond d'Alembert (1717–1783), Louis-Jacques Goussier (1722–1799)

André le Breton, France

A Herculean task, this twenty-eight-volume French encyclopedia—the first comprehensive collection of scientific, technical, philosophical, and artistic knowledge available at the time—was the collaborative achievement of three individuals. Viewed as contentious, even subversive, because of the dangerous nature of Denis Diderot's enquiries, the *Encyclopédie* was an extraordinary and highly innovative scientific and visual adventure for its authors.

The work's main author and instigator, Diderot, is remembered as a philosopher, yet approached the ambitious project of compiling and organizing the entries as an editor and art director. The graphic artist Louis-Jacques Goussier, however, who worked closely with Diderot, is seldom mentioned. Mathematician Jean Le Rond d'Alembert, on the other hand, is named as coauthor on the frontispiece, even though he resigned in 1759 to distance himself from the controversy surrounding the enterprise.

The *Encyclopédie* contains eleven volumes of original engravings, which Goussier researched and carefully logged while canvassing France to collect firsthand information. He noted carefully how artisans practiced their *métier*, and which instruments, tools, and machines they used (such as for button-, lace-, and silk-making), creating a huge archive that documented in detail the techniques and mechanical devices developed in France during the early days of the Industrial Age. The resulting drawings were a source of pride for Diderot, who acknowledged in writing that glancing at the pictorial data conveyed more information to readers than a page of written explanations.

Treated as a freestanding source of knowledge rather than mere illustrations, the plates of the *Encyclopédie* were published separately from the main text, and often delayed because of opposition from religious authorities. Meanwhile, the publisher, André le Breton, was surreptitiously deleting pages that he thought might irk conservative critics. Goussier's work, by contrast, was usually received enthusiastically. The narrative quality of his diagrammatic layouts, which demonstrated the best way to build and operate various machines, show evidence of a truly enlightened mind.

1754

JOIN, OR DIE

Information Design

Benjamin Franklin (1706–1790)

Self-commissioned, U.S.

A classic example of early American political iconography, and considered by many to be the first political cartoon, Benjamin Franklin's wood engraving was a timely cry for the unity of British colonies in America prior to the start of the French and Indian War (1754–63). When it was made, the British and French battled for control of the New World, individual colonies had their own militias, and confederation was a concept not necessarily appreciated by all.

Franklin—a writer, politician, scientist, wit, and printer and publisher of the *Pennsylvania Gazette*—had already created the concept of the indigenous rattlesnake as a symbol of revolution in 1751, when he argued that the colonies should send rattlesnakes to infest the British in return for their sending of convicts. In 1754, also in the *Gazette*, he gave the symbol graphic expression by printing the cartoon "Join, or Die." The device soon spread to other newspapers throughout the colonies, redrawn or modified and with different slogans.

By 1775, on the brink of demanding independence from Britain, colonial flags, banners, and militia drums began carrying an even more threatening flag image: a coiled rattlesnake accompanied by the motto "Don't Tread on Me." The most famous of these flags was the "Gadsden," named after Continental Army Colonel Christopher Gadsden, who placed the symbol and motto on a flag carried at the head of the first Continental Navy Fleet. Along with a wide range of other symbols such as pine trees and variations on the word "Liberty," the rattlesnake persisted in various guises and was flown by military units throughout the Revolutionary War.

"Join, or Die" retains its graphic impact even today. The directness of its accompanying motto has resonated down the centuries, although such slogans are now more likely to be used on T-shirts. Examples include British fashion designer Katharine Hamnett's "Clean Up or Die" environmental campaign line of 1989, now in the permanent collection of the Victoria and Albert Museum, London.

1757

BASKERVILLE

Typeface

John Baskerville (1706–1775)

Baskerville Type Foundry, UK

Baskerville is a transitional serif typeface, positioned between the old-style faces of Caslon and the modern styles of Bodoni and Didot. Simple yet visually eloquent, and conveying both dignity and tradition, it belongs to a small handful of historical typefaces, which, because of their stellar design characteristics and impeccable legibility, remain in wide use today. Due to its quiet refinement, Baskerville is often pressed into service for typographic purposes as diverse as poetry and scientific literature.

Baskerville is the result of its creator's desire to improve upon the types of William Caslon. Its author's advancements in printing technology allowed the precision of the punch cutter's skill to be more evident, exhibiting greater contrast between thick and thin strokes. Baskerville spent seven years perfecting his typeface, inventing a hot-press technique (pressing each sheet through heated copper plates) and improving printing inks—innovations that greatly enhanced the readability and crisp appearance of the type: serifs became flatter, sharper, and more tapered, and the axis, or stress, of rounded letters became more vertical, while curved strokes were made more circular and characters more regular. All of these changes contributed to greater consistency in size and form. One of Baskerville's unique features is the distinctive swash tail on the uppercase "Q"; another is the open loop and swash-like tapered tail of the lowercase "g." The cursive serifs in the italic font are also noteworthy.

The Baskerville typeface fell out of use with the advent of Bodoni and Didot, but was revived in 1919 by Bruce Rogers for Harvard University Press. Twentieth-century digital revivals include ITC New Baskerville, designed in 1978 by Matthew Carter and John Quaranda, and Berthold Baskerville Book, devised in 1980 by Günter Gerhard Lange. In 1996 Baskerville was used as the basis for the Mrs Eaves typeface, designed by Zuzana Licko and named after Baskerville's longtime mistress, whom he eventually married.

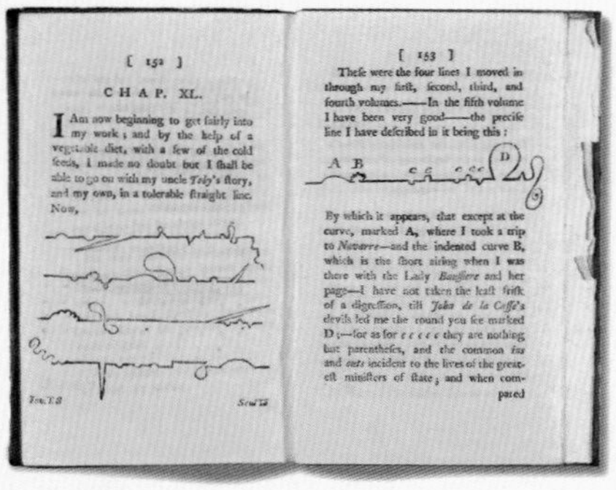

← P.13

1759–1767

THE LIFE AND OPINIONS OF TRISTRAM SHANDY

Book

Laurence Sterne (1713–1768)

Self-commissioned, UK

Laurence Sterne's satirical novel, *The Life and Opinions of Tristram Shandy*, was not only groundbreaking in literary terms, foreshadowing modernist literature by almost two centuries; in its use of exaggerated (and sometimes understated) punctuation and format, radical approach to typography, and at times seamless integration of image and text, the book constituted a graphic revolution.

Sterne, who worked as a clergyman in his early career, had already produced a number of minor publications (mostly sermons) by the time he published the first two volumes of *Tristram Shandy* in 1759. Sterne oversaw the publication of each of the nine volumes, paying meticulous attention to format, paper, type, and layout, and using numerous unusual devices to enable the protagonist to narrate his life story. Dashes of varying lengths and asterisks denote pauses or omissions of text and speech, blank pages invite readers to illustrate the text for themselves or, when black, mourn the death of a character, while effects of marbling and line drawings map out the storyline. More radical still, misplaced chapters and page numbers disrupt the traditional linear narrative, language switches from English to Latin, and typefaces are mixed together or interspersed with pictograms. All of these devices demonstrate Sterne's belief that the abstract can be made concrete through visual representation.

Tristram Shandy overturned the conventions of literature and printing in the name of literary expression, and was one of the earliest examples of typographic experimentation. The book demonstrates that letters, words, and imagery can all be molded to communicate meaning beyond that of the words themselves, and in this sense truly foresaw the potential of what would ultimately become graphic design.

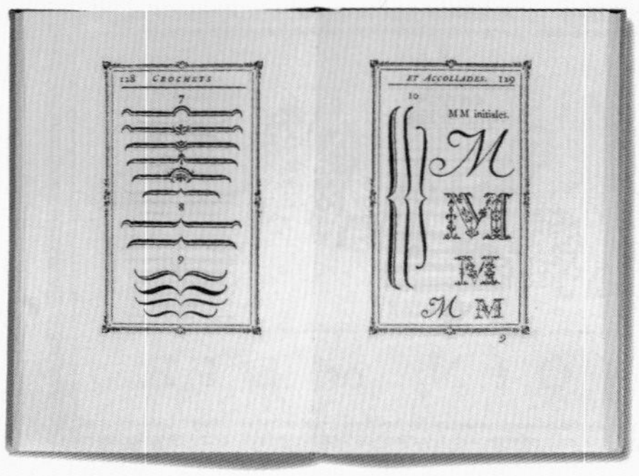

← P.13

1764–1766

MANUEL TYPOGRAPHIQUE

Book

Pierre-Simon Fournier (1712–1768)

Jean-Joseph Barbou, France

Ornately decorated in sextodecimo format (a sheet folded to form sixteen leaves or thirty-two pages), Pierre-Simon Fournier's *Manuel Typographique* was the crowning work of his career, and an outstanding example of rococo book production. The book planned to encompass the whole of typography in four volumes, but Fournier's death in 1768 left the work incomplete, and only two volumes were published: *Type, Its Cutting and Founding* (1764), and *Type Specimens* (1766), which included examples of exotic alphabets.

Fournier was a one-man showcase of the printing arts—a type designer, punch cutter, and founder who set and made his own specimen pages, and was an enthusiastic exponent of the practicalities of printing and its history. Intended for "men of letters and for those who are practitioners in the different branches of the Art of Printing," as its subtitle indicates, *Manuel Typographique* was the first book to discuss the type cutter's art. The first volume is devoted to punch cutting, matrix making, type founding, molds, the caster's furnace and dressing block, font schemes, and typography, while the second volume repeats much of the material that Fournier produced for the 170-page specimen book of 1764, *Les Caractères de l'imprimerie*, but with many more font sizes—eighty-two body types in total are illustrated. *Manuel Typographique* also testifies to Fournier's extraordinary innovation. As well as devising the first point system, enabling type size to be measured, he designed 377 varieties of flower vignettes—cast type-metal floral ornaments—at thirteen different sizes, for the creation of patterns, along with numerous garlands, sunbursts, medallions, and pictorial brackets. All of these floral illustrations are displayed in the book's pages, as are the various implements of the type cutter's craft—tables, presses, cutting tools, matrices, and so on—and numerous foreign and regional alphabets, ancient and modern (many no doubt fanciful), such as Hebrew, Babylonian, and Armenian. Fournier also devised two innovative systems for printing musical notation.

Despite his greatest efforts, Fournier was never granted the right by the monopoly of Parisian master printers to own a printing press or to print his own material. His great work was printed by Jean-Joseph Barbou.

← P.14

c. 1784

DIDOT

Typeface

Firmin Didot (1764–1836)

Didot Foundry, France

The stylish elegance of the Didot typeface has made it an enduring classic, a milestone in the evolution of typography that is as fresh today as when it was created in the eighteenth century.

The name Didot refers to a group of typefaces designed by Firmin Didot, a member of the French printing-and-type-founding family, around 1784. Although a similarly modern typeface was devised by Didot's contemporary, Giambattista Bodoni, Didot's faces are considered the first to have defined the unmistakably modern style known as Didone. Didone is characterized by strong, clear forms, a distinctly vertical emphasis, and a high contrast value between thick and thin areas of the letterforms, with flat, unbracketed hairline serifs. Both the Bodoni and Didot typefaces took inspiration from John Baskerville's experimentation with increased contrast in letterforms and more vertical stress. Didot is used for a wide variety of design purposes, especially in the fields of fashion and culture, and is often selected as a display typeface due to its highly etched hairlines.

In its rational and objective character, Didot embodied the spirit of the Enlightenment, although, partly owing to a dearth of Didot fonts, it was ultimately Bodoni that came to dominate the modern typographic landscape. The greater availability and slightly more robust weight of Bodoni, which was produced by various foundries, made it more popular for text settings. In 1991, however, Adrian Frutiger designed a successful digital revival of the roman display cut of Didot for Linotype and, one year later, Fabien Baron, then creative director of *Harper's Bazaar* magazine, commissioned the Hoefler type foundry in New York to create a digital version that would serve as the linchpin of the magazine's dramatic new visual vocabulary. Jonathan Hoefler designed HTF Didot with a matrix of different styles, each for a specific point size, ranging from six to ninety-six, which enabled greater fidelity to Didot's very thin, sharp serifs. His graceful interpretation can be seen in fashionable advertisements, shop window displays, cosmetics packaging, and magazine mastheads.

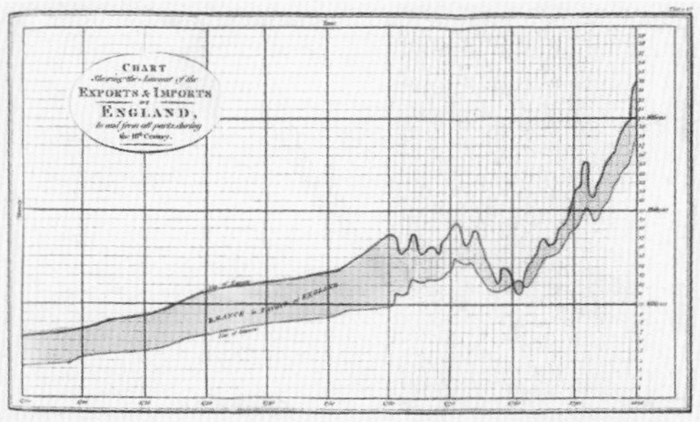

← P.14

← P.15

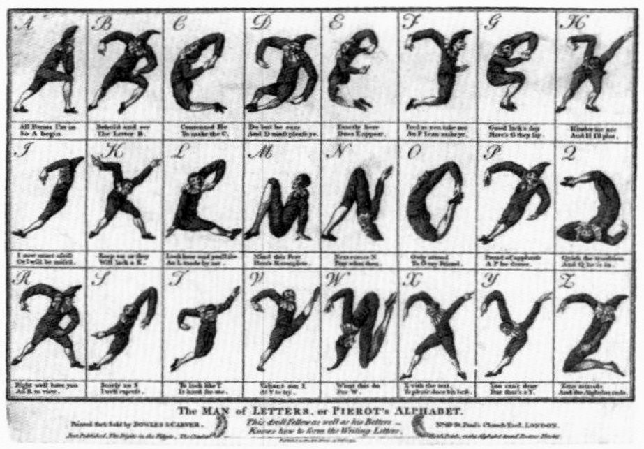

← P.16

1786

THE COMMERCIAL AND POLITICAL ATLAS

Book

William Playfair (1759–1823)

Self-commissioned, UK

William Playfair, a Scottish writer on business affairs and economics, is considered by many to be the founder of graphic statistics—a claim largely based on two of his many publications: *The Commercial and Political Atlas* and *The Statistical Breviary* (1801). In these two books, Playfair set out new ways of presenting information graphically: by means of the line graph and bar chart in the former, and through the use of the area or pie chart in the latter.

The Commercial and Political Atlas mainly documented England's commerce with other nations during the course of the eighteenth century. The forty hand-colored copper-engraved plates included in the first edition were all of line graphs, with the exception of one bar chart. In displaying this information, Playfair argued that the line graph had an advantage over figures in that it gave a simpler and more permanent idea of progress over time, and was easier and quicker to remember than figures alone. In an example showing the national debt of Britain from 1688, time is represented on the horizontal axis, and the amount of debt on the vertical. In his accompanying observations on the chart, Playfair argued that the exponential rise in the national debt—seen so clearly and immediately in the steep gradient of the red line on his graph—was a result of irresponsible "perpetual loans" for wars, which would continue to spiral out of control if not repaid. Playfair's graph summed up this argument in a single visual image and was clearly intended as a tool of persuasion rather than analysis.

If Playfair's works were largely forgotten for most of the nineteenth century, his rhetorical use of graphic statistics became an important tool in the promotion of reform, particularly in public health, as seen in the work of Edwin Chadwick, John Snow, and Florence Nightingale. Today, the line graph is omnipresent, commonly employed in newspapers, journals, television, and film, one example being the use of the Keeling Curve (a graph showing concentrations of carbon dioxide in the Earth's atmosphere since 1958) in Al Gore's polemical film on climate change, *An Inconvenient Truth* (2006).

1789–1794

SONGS OF INNOCENCE AND OF EXPERIENCE

Book

William Blake (1757–1827)

Self-commissioned, UK

William Blake's intensely idiosyncratic artistic and literary work came together in his "illuminated" books, which simultaneously harked back to pretypeset models and reinforced the role of bookmaker as auteur (as indicated on the title page: "The Author and Printer W. Blake"). *Songs of Innocence* and the subsequent augmented edition, *Songs of Innocence and of Experience*, are syncretic masterpieces whose originality long concealed the progressive printing techniques that went into their creation.

Ostensibly a children's book, *Songs of Innocence and of Experience* is pervaded, lyrically and symbolically, by Blake's eccentric Christian mysticism. Pastoral images of trees, vines, and other vegetal designs, representing complex and obscure philosophies, create borders and entwine with the text. In other instances human figures—portrayed in Blake's individual neoclassical style—are enclosed in brambles, positing the journey through dangerous and painful experiences. The poems are similarly often enclosed by natural motifs, and rendered in handwritten script that includes both flowing italics and more upright letterforms, which defy typesetting convention. To compose a whole page—text and image—from a single copper plate, Blake introduced advances to the relief-etching process, reversing the areas that were traditionally bitten (eroded with acid) and stopped. Blake may have known of this technique from *Valuable Secrets Concerning Arts and Trades*, a translation of a French book that appeared in 1758 in English, but his experimentation overcame major chemical and technical obstacles. Although color could now be printed directly from the plate, he went over the pages by hand to refine the effects of different pigments, and continued to print copies until late in life. No two exemplars are identical.

Blake's techniques derived partly from metaphysical beliefs (such as that his deceased brother Robert revealed secrets to him in a spiritual visitation), and partly as an answer to his struggles with money (that his pioneering printing method had considerable financial potential). More importantly, they seemed to promise artistic control of his work, and ultimately enabled a fusion of text and image that changed how books could be produced and interpreted.

1794

THE MAN OF LETTERS, OR PIERROT'S ALPHABET

Typeface

Unknown

Bowles & Carver, UK

The Man of Letters, or Pierrot's Alphabet depicts the unfortunate clown from the Commedia dell'Arte, Pierrot (whose name can also appear as Pierot and Perot), contorted into a twenty-four-letter alphabet. Ornamented letterforms have existed since the Renaissance, some of them originating as illuminated manuscripts. Although animal and plant motifs are particularly common themes, human alphabets became popular in the anthropocentric era of the Enlightenment. As the Dutch design critic Max Bruinsma wrote in his essay "The Erotics of Type": "Far from forgetting that letters once were pictograms, typographers of all times have sought to compensate for the letter's growing level of abstraction with ever more vivid pictorial renderings of the alphabet, foremost of which is, of course, the anthropomorphic alphabet."

By the eighteenth century, popular prints became available as broadsheets. Produced in print shops by largely anonymous engravers and sold on the streets by ballad mongers, in format and eventually content these sheets were the precursors to the modern newspaper. At the end of the eighteenth century and beginning of the nineteenth, the London print firm Bowles & Carver produced a broad range of such sheets, often known as "catchpennies," printed from metal plates, which were devoted to subjects that included urban and rural scenes, miscellanies, satirical reversals of the natural and social hierarchy ("the world turned upside down"), allegories (of the seasons, nature, vices, and virtues, etc.), historical figures, and literary (often Shakespearean) characters. This alphabet and its brief rhyming couplets took on a nominally didactic function, while also referencing Pierrot's association with pantomime and acrobatics to create a particularly exuberant set.

Anthropomorphic alphabets continue to haunt the visual arts. In 1926 the Czech avant-garde designer Karel Teige worked with the dancer Milca Mayerová to synthesize photographs of her in gestural poses with typeforms in order to create a Constructivist "typophoto" letterset. Letters composed of naked human figures and explicitly erotic compositions have also regularly been produced as far back as the sixteenth century, and have endured in the modern era with the development of photography.

← P.16

1798

BODONI

Typeface

Giambattista Bodoni (1740–1813)

Ferdinand I, Duke of Parma, Italy

One of Giambattista Bodoni's eponymous serif typefaces, classified as "didone" or "modern," Bodoni is an elegant and highly stylized noncalligraphic font that represented its neoclassical era.

In creating Bodoni, the Italian type designer and printer was undoubtedly influenced by the slightly earlier type designs of the Didot family, possibly the first truly modern typeface design; but Bodoni was from the outset more widely used, probably because its forms were extensively circulated and replicated. Although "modern" type styles have been criticized as the least legible faces for text settings, Bodoni continues to be in wide demand today, and has been imitated in countless revivals and redrawings. Both Bodoni and Didot advanced the ideas of John Baskerville, whose typeface had a heavier vertical stroke in contrast with its horizontals and flatter serifs, by pushing their typefaces to extremes of thick and thin, and using flat, unbracketed serifs. However, Bodoni's construction is more substantial than Didot's, with a slightly narrower set width, which adds to its legibility and usefulness. Much has also been made of the font's "dazzle," the visual effect caused by its high stroke contrast within a block of text, which is at once the great appeal of Bodoni's design and its ultimate weakness. Because Bodoni worked on his typeface over the course of his lifetime, constantly refining the letterforms, its design details vary, and it could be argued that there is no definitive version.

Popular and successful revivals of Bodoni's typeface include: Morris Fuller Benton's 1911 release from American Type Founders, ATF Bodoni; Heinrich Jost's version, Bauer Bodoni, brought out in 1926, which features even more exaggerated contrasts; and, in 1983, the release of G.G. Lange's Bodoni Old Face. In 1991 the International Typeface Corporation undertook a major digital revival of Bodoni, after intensive study of the original specimens and metal punches housed in the Museo Bodoniana in Parma, and in 1996 Zuzana Licko released Filosofia, a more geometric version, which had a strong vertical feel. More than two centuries after its release, Bodoni continues to be favored by modern designers, and is found today on innumerable products and in a wide range of media.

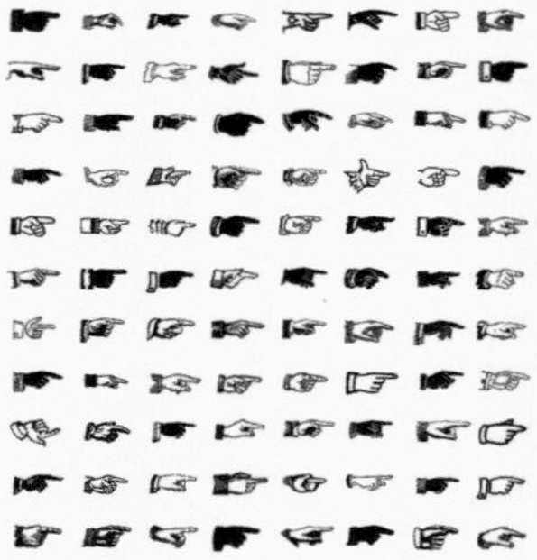

← P.17

c. 1800

PRINTERS' FIST

Information Design

Various

International

Printers' ornaments have existed since the introduction of printing, and are the precursors of dry-transfer images and computer clip art. One of the earliest ornaments was a "mutton fist," an index mark used by printers, which predates the advent of publishing. Title deeds and other secular manuscripts from as early as the thirteenth century contained pointing hands that drew attention to important passages.

Although the main function of mutton fists was to highlight information, they have also been used for other purposes such as astronomical entries, or simply for decoration. Prior to the nineteenth century, all type founders' and printers' specimens included fists among the special signs that lay outside the normal range of a type font. Early fists appeared in outline only, and many had fancy frilled cuffs. In the nineteenth century, fists developed further embellishments, and their use, size, and importance grew in parallel with the increase in display and jobbing printing: one printer's specimen book shows mutton fists up to 9¾ inch (25 cm) wide.

Theater and music-hall bills made great use of fists: it was not unusual to find more than twenty different typefaces and a row of half a dozen or more fists pointing downward to the headline artist's name. One nineteenth-century printer who deserves a mention because of his lively printing is Andrew White Tuer of the Leadenhall Press, who commissioned the wood engraver Joseph Crawhall to cut four extravagant mutton fists. Although anonymous artists were usually behind the creation of printers' ornaments, designer Eric Gill produced a range of mutton fists for the Monotype Corporation. His cuffed hand was used on the program of the Conference of the Federation of Master Printers in 1928, which also contained the first example of Gill's sans serif type.

The mutton fist fell out of fashion with the demise of metal composition, although Letraset produced sheets of such fists until dry-transfer letters were usurped by desktop publishing techniques in the 1990s. Today, the printers' fist is still occasionally seen in use, often in advertising for special effects, usually for humor, or to create an impression of a bygone era.

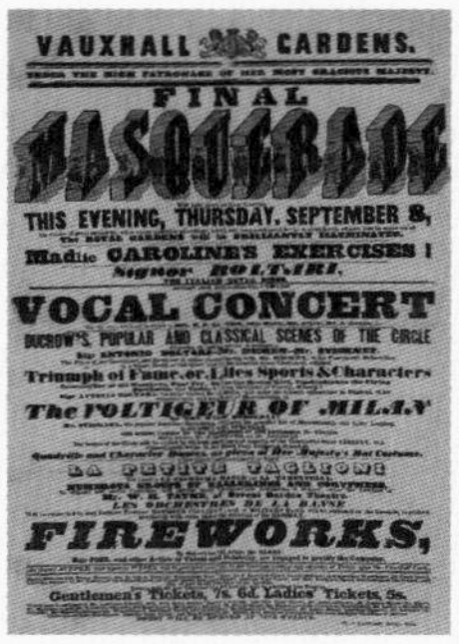

← P.18

c. 1800–1900

BILL POSTERS

Poster

Various

International

Produced by mostly unknown designers and printers, nineteenth-century bill posters were used to advertise commercial products and events, to promote political or religious ideas, or simply to disseminate public notices—by anyone with a message to convey. For those who created them, they offered a valuable opportunity to experiment with methods of attracting public attention.

Posters existed before the 1820s, but they tended to be relatively small and visually conservative, modeled largely on books. However, in a world that was increasingly cluttered visually, posters needed to stand out. Changes in technology during the nineteenth century made it possible to print on larger surfaces and in a greater number of editions, and the explosion of new typefaces, particularly sans serif after about 1810, produced more eye-catching designs, often by increasing the amount of black ink visible on the page. Most posters included a variety of typefaces, sizes, and weights, reflecting both the limitations of printers' cases and the need to add emphasis, as can be seen in the example pictured. For much of the nineteenth century, posters also remained linear in format, although eventually it became possible to integrate text and image more easily; by the 1870s color printing was also feasible, but relatively expensive.

Posters tended to be displayed mainly in urban areas, where there was greater potential readership, pasted onto buildings and hoardings that were quickly covered. In Berlin, this problem was mitigated after 1850 by the provision of *Litfasssäulen*—tall pillars specifically for the display of posters. So great was the demand for these that by 1900 there were more than 1,500 such pillars in the city. In London, too, posters were an intrinsic part of daily life, seen and read by millions. Charles Knight's 1843 multivolume encyclopedia of London devoted a chapter to advertising posters, noting their size, typography, and color. In their pioneering typographic layouts, aimed at a mass audience that was not necessarily looking for information, bill posters represented an important graphic development of the nineteenth century, and made the printed word an integral part of urban life.

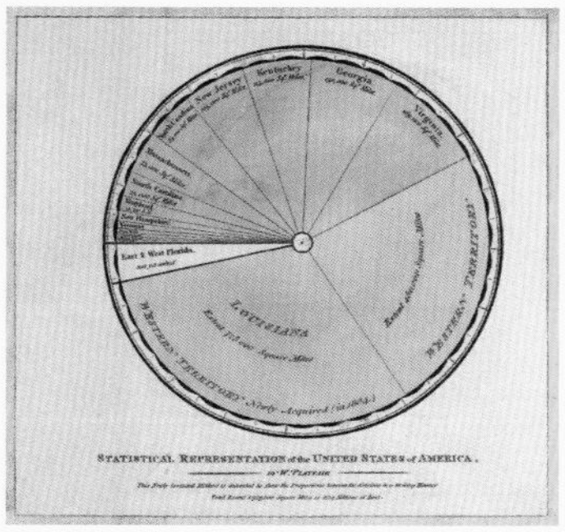

← P.19

1801

PIE CHART

Information Design

William Playfair (1759–1823)

Self-commissioned, UK

The first modern circle graph or pie chart appeared in William Playfair's *The Statistical Breviary,* published in 1801. Playfair was a political economist as well as a trained engineer and draughtsman, whose combination of skills helped him devise the many diagrammatic forms we use today to represent empirical and social data. These also include the line and bar chart, introduced in *The Commercial and Political Atlas* of 1786.

The Breviary was Playfair's most theoretical book on graphic representation, and employed diagrams as visual metaphors rather than as analogies to the physical world. Circle charts, which appear as four plates showing the tax burdens of different countries in Europe as functions of land and population, are used to embody data in simplified form to allow for quick visual comparison, and employ many standard features, such as consistent color coding. Crucially, the pie chart is easy to understand without reference to numerical data, making it accessible to a wide variety of people without specialist training. Aside from *The Breviary,* Playfair used the pie chart in two other publications. The one found in his translation of Denis François Donnant's *Statistical Account of the United States of America* of 1805 is notable for its carefully labeled segments.

Like many of Playfair's graphic forms, the pie chart was slow to be adopted in his own country, England, and first gained popularity in continental Europe. During the nineteenth century, his graphic innovations would continue to evolve—as, for example, with Florence Nightingale's landmark "coxcomb" charts of 1858, and again in the twentieth century through the work of Otto Neurath and others interested in conveying social-science data in accessible graphic form for the general public. Since World War II, "infographics," including the pie chart, have become standard fare in newspapers, magazines, and other popular media. They are also frequently found on maps, to show distributions and comparisons over an area, despite the potential for misunderstanding quantities displayed in multiple circles.

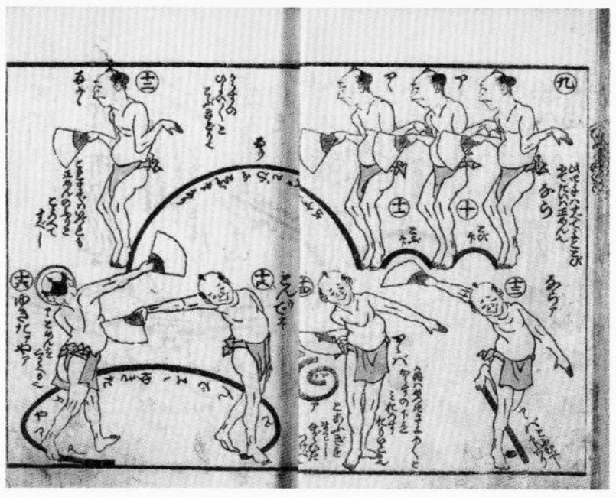

← P.19

1814–1878

HOKUSAI MANGA

Book

Katsushika Hokusai (1760–1849)

Self-commissioned, Japan

One of the masterpieces of Japanese graphic art, Katsushika Hokusai's fifteen-volume *Denshin kaishu Hokusai Manga* (*Education of Beginners Through the Spirit of Things, Random Sketches by Hokusai*) contains some forty thousand individual drawings of people, plants, animals, landscapes, buildings, and mythical creatures, arranged in a seemingly haphazard fashion. A scene of athletes training is followed by a meditation on the forms of grasses; a set of caricatures by architectural plans; studies of insects by expansive landscapes.

Although originally produced as instructional books for students of drawing, the *manga* became best-sellers (demand was such that three volumes were produced after the artist's death), appealing to a wide audience with their gently mocking depiction of life in Edo (now Tokyo), and precision and economy of form. Hokusai was already a successful artist by the time he released the first volume, as famous in Edo for his eccentric behaviour as for his woodblock prints. Originally part of the *ukiyo-e* ("pictures of the floating world") school, which produced popular images of the pleasure-seeking lifestyle of the time, he soon forged his own creative path, distilling subjects to their essence with the fewest possible brushstrokes.

Although predominantly Hokusai's work, the *manga* were also, by necessity, a collaborative effort, equally dependent on the skill of the carver who cut the woodblock. Unique among *ukiyo-e* artists, however, Hokusai had carving experience and made sure that his drawings were reproduced accurately. It is hard to know how far Hokusai was involved in the layout of his books, but the decreased quality of posthumous volumes suggests that his forceful personality held sway here, too.

Hokusai is now best known in the West for his *Thirty-six Views of Mount Fuji*, particularly *The Great Wave*, but at the time of their creation it was the *manga* that caused most waves internationally. At once realistic and revealing a deeper psychological truth, his drawings captivated the French nineteenth-century avant-garde in particular, influencing artists such as Degas, Manet, and Toulouse-Lautrec. Today, these records of a lost and beguiling world still exert a unique charm.

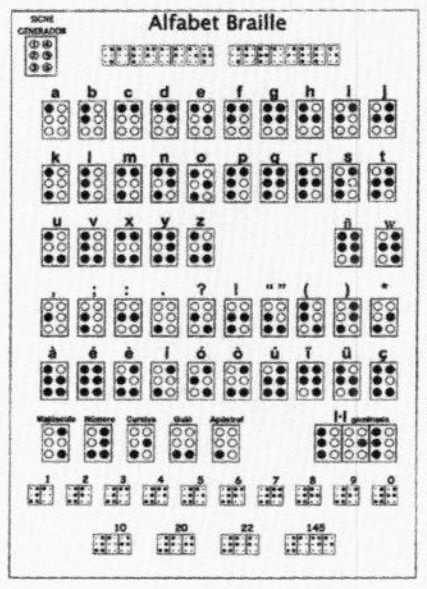

← P.20

1829

BRAILLE

Information Design

Louis Braille (1809–1852)

Self-commissioned, France

Braille is a tactile binary encoding system that represents written characters as embossed dots on a page, and enables the blind to read and write. An early version was developed by Charles Barbier, a captain in Napoleon's army, in an attempt to develop a method of communicating silently in the dark. However, Barbier's system was based on a twelve-dot cell, representing words according to their phonetic spelling, and was deemed too complex. After his system was rejected by the military, Barbier presented the idea to the Paris National Institute for the Blind in 1821, where a pupil, Louis Braille, who was twelve at the time, saw the potential of Barbier's idea. Braille set out to improve the design, first reducing the size of the cell, after realizing that the original cell did not allow the finger to cover the whole symbol without moving, which slowed down the reading process.

In 1829 Braille published an explanation of the system we know today, based on normal spelling and using a six-dot cell. The rectangular cell is arranged in a grid of two dots horizontally by three dots vertically, offering a possible sixty-four permutations of dots, with each character allocated a particular formation. Although the size of each dot is tiny, approximately 0.5 mm, typically each page of Braille accommodates only twenty-five lines of forty cells. This equates to one thousand characters, in contrast with the thirty-five hundred characters that fit on a standard typed page. The use of the thick paper for the embossing and the greater space each character takes means that the translation of a typeset book into Braille would require several volumes. To help increase the amount of words per page and reading speed, Braille also includes "contractions," in which one character or a combination of several characters represent a regularly occurring letter grouping or word.

Separate Braille codes are now available for other notational systems, such as mathematics, music, and computer programming. Computers and synthetic speech devices have to some extent reduced its use, but Braille has yet to be wholly replaced by new technologies.

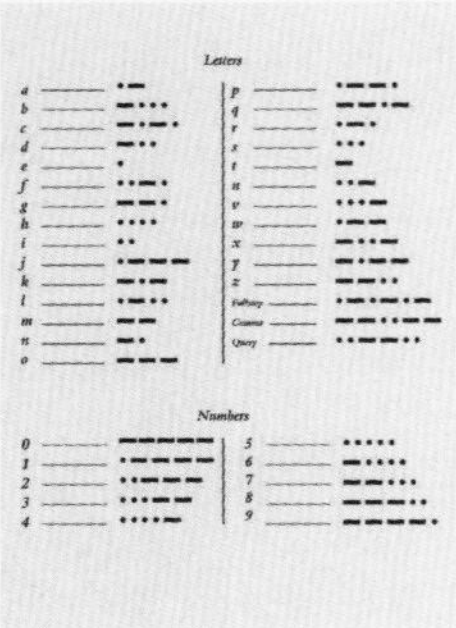

← P.21

← P.22

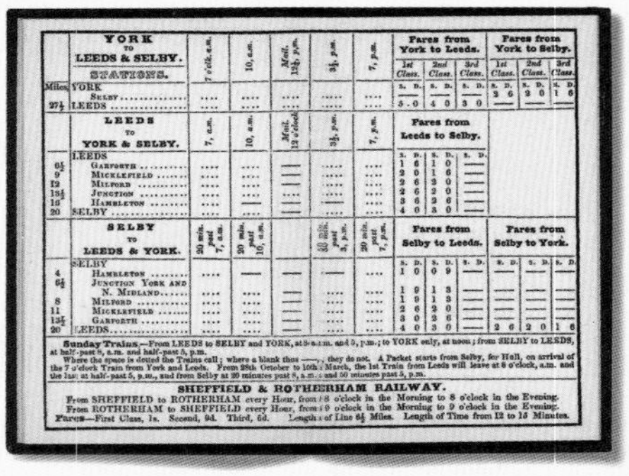

← P.23

1838

MORSE CODE

Information Design

Samuel Finley Breese Morse (1791–1872)

Self-commissioned, U.S.

Morse code, named after its inventor, Samuel Finley Breese Morse, is a system of electronically transmitted dots and dashes, which was once the primary method for sending telegraphic information throughout the world. The system derives from the keen interest in telegraphy that Morse developed in 1832, when he realized that the pulses of electric current could be used to convey messages.

The first telegraph was built in 1774, but was impractical, using a wire for each letter of the alphabet. Morse was convinced this could be reduced to a single wire. In 1837 Morse and his partners, Alfred Vail and Leonard Gale, unveiled a single wire device that generated an undulating line on ticker tape, which then had to be decoded. This proved to be an inaccurate method of communication, and in 1838 Morse (though some credit Vail) developed a dot-and-dash code that represented the numbers and letters of the English alphabet. The burgeoning success of the code was in part due to the simplicity of its system, which assigned the shortest sequences to the most frequently used characters in the English language. Employing traditional printed typography, Morse based his data on the quantities of type found in a printer's office, with "E" being the most frequent and "Z" the least; therefore "E" is represented as one dot, and "Z" by two dashes and two dots. This method enabled the international spread of the code, which was suitable for radio transmissions as sound, or even improvised visual sources such as a flashlight.

Morse code was standardized throughout the world in 1851, and was used internationally for maritime communication until 1999. The code has since been replaced by systems, such as ASCII, for the majority of electronic communications; its most popular users today are amateur radio operators.

1841–2002

PUNCH

Magazine / Newspaper

Mark Lemon (1809–1870) et al.

Self-commissioned, UK

Put together by its editor, Mark Lemon, and various other radical writers, illustrators, journalists (such as cofounder Henry Mayhew), and cartoonists (John Leech, Richard Doyle, and cofounder Ebenezer Landells), the first issue of *Punch* was published on July 17, 1841. The publication came at a time of great change in the production and reception of popular periodicals: with the *Penny Magazine* (1832–45) and the *Illustrated London News* (1842–2003), *Punch* led the way in opening up a new metropolitan mass readership by establishing a weekly journal that used visual images (wood engravings) alongside text. The first eleven-page issue contained only one large cartoon; by 1922, its twenty pages had no less than thirteen sketches, occupying far more space than the accompanying text. In its early years, *Punch* was known for its astringent satirizing of figures of authority, including the monarchy and leading politicians, and for its pronounced defence of the interests of the poor and oppressed.

By the time Doyle produced the cover illustration that would define the journal in 1849, *Punch* had already lost much of its radical content, especially after the departure of Mayhew in 1845. The engraving was used as the journal's masthead until 1956, and depicts Mr. Punch making a satirical portrait of his dog, Toby, surrounded by a garland composed of a host of mischievous figures. At the top and bottom of the page, advertisements are introduced—a common means by which mass-produced periodicals gathered revenue. Despite shedding its radical origins, *Punch* published some of the most provocative and shocking images of the nineteenth century, such as "The 'Silent Highway'-Man," which depicted Death as a Thames boatman during the notorious Great Stink of 1858, when the smell of the River Thames became a national concern. On the whole, though, the cartoons poked gentle fun at social mores, while offering rich insights into everyday life in London, from riding in cabs and omnibuses to filling out forms, as seen in "Filling up the Census Paper" of April 12, 1851.

Punch's influence was felt most strongly in the world of satire, providing a regular outlet for writers and artists, and popularizing cartoons as a form of satirical drawing.

1841–1961

BRADSHAW'S MONTHLY RAILWAY GUIDE

Information Design

George Bradshaw (1801–1853)

Self-commissioned, UK

The pioneering nineteenth-century publication *Bradshaw's Monthly Railway Guide* made the name of its producer, George Bradshaw, synonymous with railway travel. The guide provided for the first time a complete listing of all British railway services, enabling passengers to find in a single publication details of any journey they wished to make. By simplifying the logistics of railway travel, *Bradshaw's* also helped people to see the individual lines as an integrated national railway network.

Bradshaw's was an expanded version of previous timetables produced by the author since 1839, and remained consistent in design throughout its life: a tabular arrangement for each route (often split over several pages), with stations listed vertically and train times horizontally. Initially portable, by 1912 the monthly issue had grown to more than nine hundred pages, reflecting the development of the network. In time, *Bradshaw's* also became known for its illegibility: a small print size was used to fit increasing amounts of information into the smallest possible space, which, combined with thin paper, made it difficult to read. Another problem was comprehensibility: symbols informing passengers of exceptions to the printed services (explained in footnotes) littered the tables, and a single page could feature tables set at ninety degrees to each other.

Despite these difficulties, *Bradshaw's* remained in use for 120 years, and was widely and rapidly imitated. When the guide finally ceased publication in 1961, its passing was noted in the national press, where it was felt that an institution had been lost. Since then, Internet- and telephone-based enquiries systems have brought the national printed timetable in Britain to an end, although printed versions for individual train companies live on and bear many of the design features that Bradshaw popularized. In recent years, legibility has also been improved by removing column rules, including more white space and highlighting exceptions to services in different colors. The essential structure of the modern timetable, however, remains similar to that used by the original guide, a testament to the longevity of its tabular design.

← P.23

1845 ●

CLARENDON

Typeface

Robert Besley (1794–1876)

Fann Street Foundry, UK

Attributed to the Fann Street Foundry's owner, Robert Besley, in collaboration with his punch cutter Benjamin Fox, Clarendon was the first typeface in England to be registered for copyright protection (though the law did little to discourage other founders from imitating the font). The typeface's success may be due to its immediate utility as an "emphasiser" (as termed by the English type designer Walter Tracy) in text settings. Prior to this, italics were the only style available for highlighting words; Clarendon offered an alternative that was especially useful for references, such as dictionary entries, and was so effective that the Clarendon name became synonymous with bold type.

Formally, Clarendon is considered a modified Egyptian typeface and, like others of this genre, uses slab serifs. Unlike Egyptian faces, however, its serifs are bracketed (gradual, rather than right-angled, in their transition to the stems of letters). This bracketing, as well as the contrast in its stroke weights, made Clarendon compatible with roman faces at a time when type families did not include bold variations. Early versions were rather narrowly proportioned, making them suitable for tightly set text. Whether narrow or, as in some later variants, round, Clarendon typefaces tend to have a large x-height and short ascenders and descenders. Sometimes called Ionic, the style that Clarendon made popular was later adopted for use in newspapers because of its sturdy legibility.

Clarendon's style may have developed from the truncated serifs of poster type or, as in the case of Egyptian faces, from architectural lettering. In either context, its enduring appeal and distinction lie in its text-face display attributes. Egyptian faces, designed to call attention to the contents of printed ephemera, fell out of favor at the end of the nineteenth century, but Clarendon's practicality as a text face kept its newspaper variants in use into the twentieth century. In the 1950s Clarendon was revived by English and U.S. type foundries and, although it fared badly in the phototype era, its unique mix of curved transitions and blunt ends, of solid fit and lively color, have brought it back into fashion in digital form.

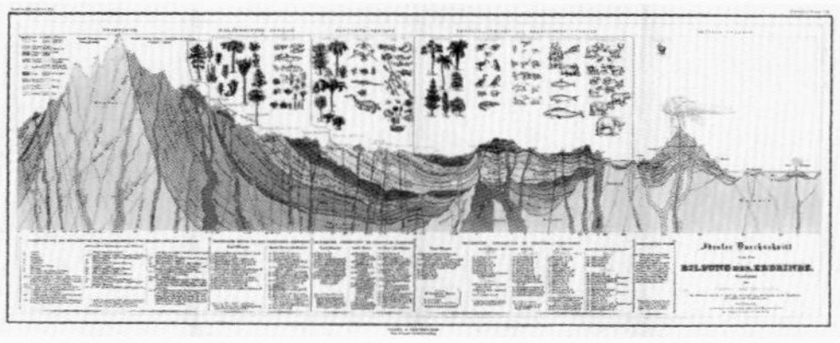

← P.24

1845/1848 ●

PHYSIKALISCHER ATLAS

Book

Heinrich Berghaus (1797–1884)

Self-commissioned, Germany

Considered the first comprehensive physical atlas of the world, Heinrich Berghaus's *Physikalischer Atlas* (*Physical Atlas*), which appeared in two volumes in 1845 and 1848, was the first to communicate scientific and geographic data through the graphic language of cartography. Immediately influential, Berghaus's work would serve as the basis for atlases throughout Europe, becoming a major sourcebook for both designers and scientists who were interested in the visual communication of complex physical information.

The *Physikalischer Atlas* had its origins in the advances in natural sciences that began in the mid-eighteenth century. The new emphasis on the collection of large quantities of data made it necessary to find a way of transmitting such information. At the same time, the breakdown of natural phenomena into scientific categories, such as climate, geology, botany, zoology, and ethnography, created an opportunity to reconceive the atlas as a map of new areas of scientific research. Berghaus's work is broken into sections devoted to these new disciplines, with maps, graphs, and drawings all used to chart specific facts, measurements, and details. Through specific visual codes, Berghaus was able to give complex information a legible graphic form, using overlays of hard lines, color fields, texts, and images to create relationships between data sets. The atlas's significance originated in this graphic superimposition of otherwise discrete sets of information; the juxtaposition opened up new possibilities for the atlas format and continues to be a standard that information designers strive to achieve. Printed drawings were then intricately finished in color by hand, and the two volumes bound in green cloth boards with the title of the work and its author stamped in gold on the cover and spine.

As a young man, Berghaus had worked on the Prussian Trigonometrical Survey in 1816 and, later in his career, he helped with the reissue of Adolf Stieler's *Handatlas*, the leading world atlas of late-nineteenth-century and early-twentieth-century geography. The *Physikalischer Atlas*—an essential reference work for contemporary scientists, cartographers, and practitioners of information design—remains his greatest achievement.

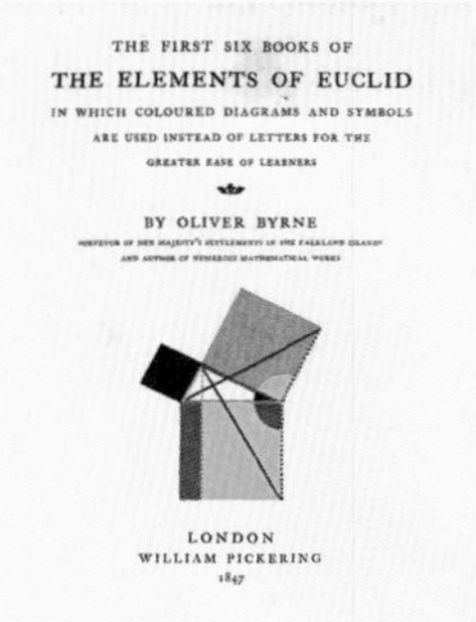

← P.24

1847 ●

THE ELEMENTS OF EUCLID

Book

Oliver Byrne (c. 1810–1880)

William Pickering, UK

Oliver Byrne's edition of Euclid's *Elements of Geometry* is a striking and highly unusual example of Victorian typesetting and book design, in which color and layout are used to express mathematical proofs. According to Byrne, the book presents "The First Six Books of the Elements of Euclid in which colored diagrams and symbols are used instead of letters for the greater ease of learners." Byrne was a surveyor, mathematician, and teacher, and the book covers topics that made up the basic school mathematics curriculum at the time.

Printed in London by the highly regarded Chiswick Press, the volume was innovative in its use of color, shape, and orientation, departing from the standard letter-based coding system used for Euclidean proofs. The aim was to reduce the sheer quantity of text by presenting the information in visual form, resulting in a surprisingly modern layout: a combination of bright blue, red, and yellow woodblock-printed shapes, integrated with black type and rules. The only hint of the book's true age, on certain pages, lies in the odd Victorian flourish or drop cap, and the cover of embossed and gilt red cloth.

On the surface, the saturated primary colors of Byrne's *Euclid* make it a forerunner of modernist design and of the archetypal De Stijl color palette, although arguably of greater significance to the history of information design is its use of visual metaphor. The volume also reflects developments in printing during the nineteenth century, a period in which the use of color increased radically through multiple advances in the productivity of the (by then) centuries-old press. The book's rediscovery and popularity today has been driven by the rise of information-design scholarship since the 1980s.

← P.25

← P.25

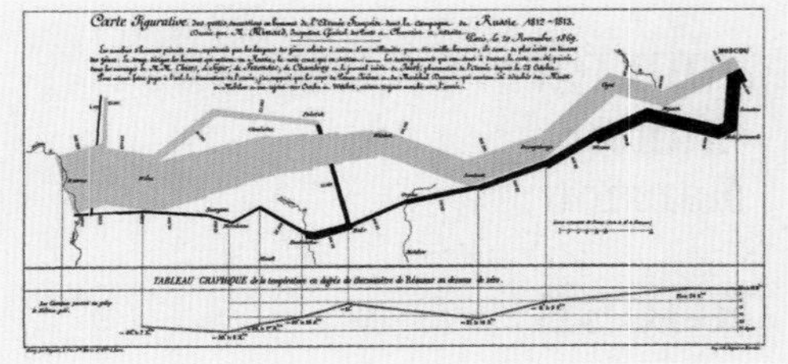

← P.26

1850

FETTE FRAKTUR

Typeface

Johann Christian Bauer (1802–1867)

Englische Schriftschneiderei und Gravieranstalt, Germany

Part of the Fraktur family of typefaces, Fette Fraktur is a blackletter script that was designed by Johann Christian Bauer in the mid-nineteenth century. Although closely associated with the Third Reich, Fraktur has seen a renaissance in recent times across diverse genres, becoming a popular choice for graphic design within musical subcultures, from punk rock to hip-hop.

Bauer was a German punch cutter and type founder, who in 1837 established the Bauer Foundry in Frankfurt. In 1839 he moved to Edinburgh to perfect his skills at the firm of P. A. Wilson, returning to Germany in 1847 to manage his company, run under the name Englische Schriftschneiderei und Gravieranstalt (English Type-cutting and Engraving Works).

Fette Fraktur (meaning "bold" Fraktur) was developed primarily for use in advertising, a task at which it was well suited and successful. The typeface is characterized by its integration of round and broken forms, and refined detail. Delicate lowercase letters have forked ascenders, whereas the broad capitals are marked by elegant flourishes that give the face its hallmark intricacy. Although legibility was an issue, Fraktur was a prevailing text face in German-speaking Europe and parts of Scandinavia over a period of nearly a century. The Nazi regime initially endorsed the use of Fraktur, when the propaganda minister, Joseph Goebbels, outlawed modern sans serif type due to its identification with the Bauhaus and Bolshevism. By 1941, however, Fraktur was deemed questionable in its origins and the typeface was banned.

The *New York Times* has long used Fraktur for its masthead. As evidence of the current revival of Fraktur, Matthew Carter was commissioned in 2005 to design a typeface derived from the masthead lettering, which is used in its Sunday *Style* magazine. A much bolder version of the elaborate uppercase "T" graces each cover, creating a recognizable and elegant identity linked with that of the main paper.

1856

THE GRAMMAR OF ORNAMENT

Book

Owen Jones (1809–1874)

Day & Son, UK

The Grammar of Ornament, Owen Jones's sumptuous encyclopedia of visual design ranging from the Stone Age to nineteenth-century Europe, was one of the most influential source books of the 1800s for the production of wallpaper, furniture, architectural decoration, and textiles. The book's one hundred beautifully illustrated plates are based on ornamental designs and patterns selected from nineteen different cultures, including Oceania, Ancient Greece and Rome, Byzantium, Renaissance Italy, and Moorish Spain.

Jones believed that the nineteenth century should produce a recognizable style of its own, based not only on the study of past trends but on a combination of historical research alongside the adoption of new materials. He advocated that ornament should be abstracted in a logical, geometric manner, resulting in stylized, flattened patterns; this was an antithesis to the existing and widely accepted practice of directly copying from original sources. Jones demonstrated this concept throughout the book, organizing his ideas into thirty-seven propositions of design.

Jones's work as an architect, theorist and designer strongly influenced British design in the nineteenth century. His explorations through Greece, Turkey, Egypt, and Spain in the early 1830s led to a passion for Classical, Islamic, and Hispano-Moresque polychrome architecture and arts. His trip to Spain resulted in *Plans, Elevations, Sections and Details of the Alhambra* (two volumes, self-published, London 1842–45), which was the first significant example of chromolithography to appear in Britain.

Today, *The Grammar of Ornament* is widely regarded as the classic reference book on Victorian aesthetics, and stands as an important visual guide to the major forms of decoration in both architecture and design during the period. Many leading artists, designers, and curators drew inspiration from its pages, including William Morris, the Arts and Crafts movement, and the Victoria & Albert Museum. Jones was also a key figure in the decoration of the Crystal Palace, which housed the Great Exhibition of 1851, where he designed the Egyptian, Grecian, Roman, and Hispano-Moresque courts.

1861

NAPOLEON'S MARCH

Information Design

Charles Joseph Minard (1781–1870)

Self-commissioned, France

If the simple display of complex data makes for successful information design, the flow map of Napoleon's fateful Russian campaign may be one of the finest ever drawn. Designed by French engineer Charles Joseph Minard, the diagram depicts Napoleon's epic losses so succinctly that the French historian E. J. Marey wrote in 1878 that it "[defies] the pen of the historian by its brutal eloquence."

A proportional brown line shows the diminishing size of Napoleon's Grande Armée of 1812 (from 422,000 to 100,000 men), as it moved from the Polish-Russian border toward Moscow. Finding the city deserted, Napoleon retreated across the Ural plain for supplies in a bitterly cold winter. Minard's genius was to link the plummeting temperature to Napoleon's dwindling forces, with a temperature line in Celsius that runs beneath the main graph, revealing with grim statistical clarity the calamitous crossing of the Berezina river, and attempts to defend the retreating army's flanks from the Russians. Only ten thousand men returned to Poland in 1813—a defeat that precipitated the collapse of Napoleon's empire.

Minard's diagram combines a number of variables into a single graphic image, including the army's size, speed, position, and direction, along with the temperature. Given the refinement and elegance of this combination, it seems surprising that Minard received no formal graphic training, and was sixty-five when he published his first map. Minard had also previously charted the exports of French wine, the movement of ancient languages throughout Europe, and the effects of the American Civil War on the global cotton trade. His work was so highly regarded that from 1850 until 1860 all French Ministers of Public Works had their portraits painted with a Minard work in the background, and in 1861 a collection of his works was presented to Emperor Napoleon III.

"The best graphics are about life and death, about the universe. Beautiful graphics do not traffic with the trivial," wrote the American statistician Edward Tufte. Minard's Napoleonic diagram was a dramatic illustration of tragic circumstances, and laid bare the futility of hubris.

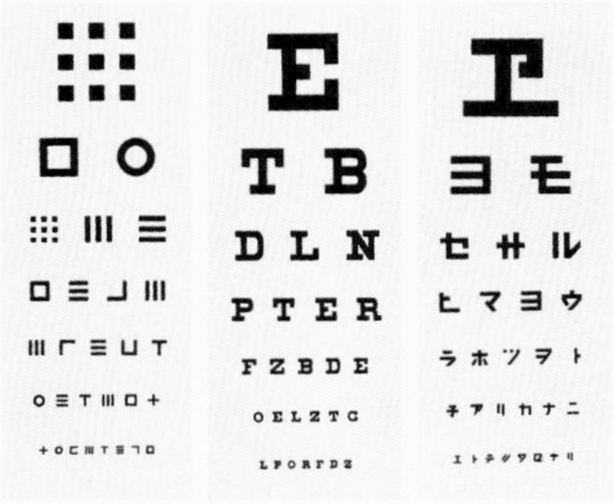

← P.26

← P.27

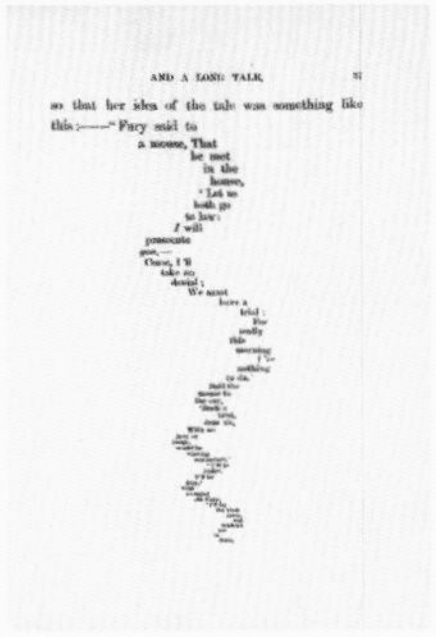

← P.27

1862

SNELLEN CHART

Information Design

Herman Snellen (1834–1908)

Self-commissioned, the Netherlands

The design of Dutch ophthalmologist Herman Snellen's eponymous eye chart was a major breakthrough in measuring acuity of vision, and has yet to be superseded, being the most commonly used chart to date.

In 1854 Eduard von Jaeger developed a set of reading samples in Vienna. The samples used both upper- and lowercase type and were printed in several languages, applying locally available typefaces. These contained drawbacks in terms of consistency of size, but the main omission was that they failed to test distance vision. In 1861 Franciscus Cornelis Donders developed a formula defining "visual acuity" or sharpness of vision, and Herman Snellen, his colleague and successor, devised his eye chart as a standardized measuring tool for Donders's formula. Initially, Snellen experimented with abstract shapes, but he later decided that letters would be more appropriate. The letters are commonly mistaken for a slab-serif typeface, such as Rockwell, but have, in fact, each been designed separately, based on their geometry, to standardize the chart. Known as "optotypes," the letters are five times higher and wider than the line width, which in turn equates to the gap between the lines in characters such as "C." In a traditional Snellen chart only the letters "C," "D," "E," "F," "L," "N," "O," "P," "T," and "Z" are used, with the first line consisting of one large letter and the following ten lines containing an increasing number of letters of a decreasing size.

Since Snellen produced his eye chart, few major developments in measuring visual acuity have been made. The chart has been adopted worldwide with modifications, such as the "Tumbling E" or the "Broken Wheel," introduced to test children or adults unable to read. Although rarely discussed in a typographic context, the Snellen test is a clear example of form following function, and in the systematic, geometric precision of his letterforms, Snellen could also be seen as a very early precursor to Paul Renner and Herbert Bayer.

1863

THE RED CROSS

Information Design

Dr. Louis Appia (1818–1898), Gen. Henri Dufour (1787–1875)

International Committee of the Red Cross, Switzerland

Formulated as part of the First Geneva Convention (adopted in 1864), the iconic "red cross on a field of white" symbol embodies the ideals of a humanitarian movement—its very use can mean the difference between life and death. Equally important, it also denotes the neutrality of medical personnel on and off the battlefield, and acts as a sign of help and hope during times of disaster.

The International Committee of the Red Cross (ICRC) was formed in 1863 by Henri Dunant after he witnessed the suffering of wounded soldiers at the Battle of Solferino in 1859. In an effort to establish in law the principle that wounded personnel and humanitarian workers should be protected, an international meeting was held in Geneva resulting in an agreement that has now been signed by 194 countries. The symbol enshrined in the treaty is a reversal of the Swiss national flag (a white cross on a red background), and was chosen in acknowledgment of Switzerland's permanent neutral status, and perhaps to honor Dunant, a Swiss national. The white background also indicates neutrality. Although officially the symbol is composed of five red squares, any red cross on a white background will suffice as a protective symbol, which means that it can be easily reproduced when needed on a battlefield. The symbol also has an important role as the logo of humanitarian organizations around the world that are part of the Red Cross movement.

Even though Dunant is often credited with the symbol's origin, the design is believed to be the work of Dr. Louis Appia and General Henri Dufour, who as founding members of the ICRC conceptualized the need for a high-contrast graphic marker for uniforms and flags that was unique and visible from a distance. Due to the need for a universally recognized emblem, the ICRC has resisted calls for a greater diversity of symbols, but has sanctioned the use of the red crescent and red lion in Muslim countries. The demand for new symbols also resulted in a resolution in 2005 to adopt a third symbol—a red crystal. The red crystal allows any other symbol to be placed inside or alongside it, enabling member states to tailor-make an emblem according to their cultural needs.

1865

ALICE'S ADVENTURES IN WONDERLAND, BY LEWIS CARROLL

Book

Sir John Tenniel (1820–1914)

Lewis Carroll, UK

Lewis Carroll—pen name of the Oxford mathematician Charles Lutwidge Dodgson—was inspired to write *Alice's Adventures in Wonderland* by ten-year old Alice Liddell, daughter of his friend Henry Liddell, who was then Dean at Christ Church, Oxford. In 1865, the year the book was finished, Carroll asked Sir John Tenniel, a well-known satirist, to produce the illustrations, many of which were based on his own sketches. The book became more widespread when in 1887 an affordable edition, called the "People's Edition" (pictured), was printed. The extraordinary appeal of the book lies as much in Tenniel's surreal and compelling images as it does in Carroll's ability to combine satire, verbal wit, logic, and fantasy, which together have succeeded in engaging audiences of all ages for well over a century.

Visually, *Alice* is very much of its time, with the wood-engraved illustrations and letterpress text exhibiting a typically Victorian eclecticism. Tenniel, however, had a tendency to assume a somewhat scholarly style of caricature, and his detailed, slightly stylized drawings beautifully match Carroll's fantastical story. In common with certain other illustrations of the 1860s, they also deliberately parodied the prevailing Pre-Raphaelite movement, a practice seen most commonly in illustrations for the satirical magazine *Punch* (many by Tenniel himself), which probably also influenced Carroll's sketches. Tenniel exploits this humorous convention by basing the figures of his kings, queens, and knaves on playing cards designed by Thomas De La Rue in the 1830s. *Alice* is also distinctive for Carroll's experiments with typography, particularly his arrangement of passages of text to play with and express meaning (or subvert it). Hence, the words of a mouse's *tale*, for example, are laid out in the shape of a *tail*, while a column of tall, thin text describing Alice's extreme growth is designed to mimic the illustration.

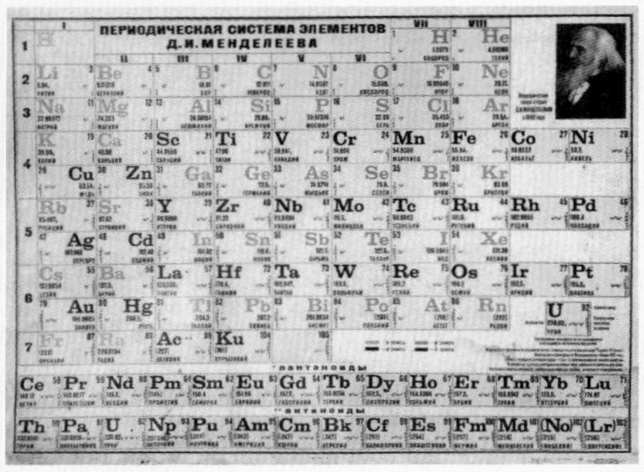

← P.27

1869

PERIODIC TABLE OF ELEMENTS

Information Design

Dmitri Mendeleev (1834–1907)

Self-commissioned, Russia

From dusty high-school wall charts to a Damien Hirst monograph, the Periodic Table has become ubiquitous in visual culture, even though its meaning is little understood by those outside the field of chemistry. A brilliant piece of information design, it is perhaps the only example of a single graphic solution that encapsulates an entire field of human knowledge. More than just an orderly arrangement, its visual structure reflects the fundamental laws underlying the chemical properties of matter.

The nineteenth century saw an explosion in the field of chemistry. By the 1850s, more than sixty elements and their atomic weights had been discovered. Chemists had long known that certain elements shared common properties, but it was only when the Russian scientist Dmitri Mendeleev sketched out the initial Periodic Table, and began mapping properties against their atomic weight, that significant progress was made in deciphering these qualities. When arranged sequentially, a pattern (or periodicity) began to emerge, with similar characteristics appearing at regular intervals. This pattern would not be fully understood until the development of quantum mechanics in the twentieth century. From 1869 to 1871 Mendeleev expanded his table, adding to its initial thirty-odd elements. He found that the integrity of the repeating structure could only be maintained by leaving blank spaces, and was bold enough to suggest that new elements would be discovered to fill them. He even anticipated the weight and properties of the missing elements, based on which column they fell under in the table. In just a few years Mendeleev's confidence was vindicated when gallium, then scandium and germanium, were discovered and found to accord with his predictions. The power of the table lay in its visualization of unseen interpretations of the world. Today, the Periodic Table accommodates 117 elements, encompassing a century and a half of scientific revolution, but it remains true to Mendeleev's original vision.

← P.28

1874

ORPHÉE AUX ENFERS

Poster

Jules Chéret (1836–1932)

Théâtre de la Gaîté, France

This poster by Jules Chéret, one of the earliest he produced during his long career as a poster artist, marks the birth of the form of pictorial poster that was to become fashionable in *fin-de-siècle* Paris. By liberating color lithography from its reputation as a process used mainly for mass production to that of a creative artistic medium, Chéret set a new benchmark in poster design for others to follow.

Chéret was apprenticed at an early age as a lithographer, and in 1858 received a commission to design a poster for Jacques Offenbach's operetta *Orphée aux Enfers* (*Orpheus in the Underworld*). Eight years later, with the help of the perfume manufacturer Eugène Rimmel, for whom he produced decorative labels and brochures, Chéret set up his own printing works in Paris, producing posters for theater, opera, and manufacturing companies.

In 1874 he designed a second poster of *Orphée aux Enfers* (pictured) for a play at the Théâtre de la Gaîté, which Offenbach had adapted from the original operetta. The poster shows the main characters framing the tableaulike scene, drawn in an assured black outline and highlighted in a rich red color. The style is reminiscent of the work of Alfred Grévin, who was known for his popular drawings and paintings of Parisian life. The lithographic medium of the poster gives the letters of the title and composer's name, with their freely drawn outlines and shadow effects, a freedom that was unprecedented in contemporary letterpress advertising, which contrasts with the more restrained treatment of the rest of the text. Chéret's mastery of the lithographic printing process also enhanced his capacity to capture the gaiety and movement of the dancers and actresses that his theatrical posters advertised. His works were to have a profound influence on many artists of the time, including Degas and Seurat, and inspired Toulouse-Lautrec to try his hand at poster art in the 1890s.

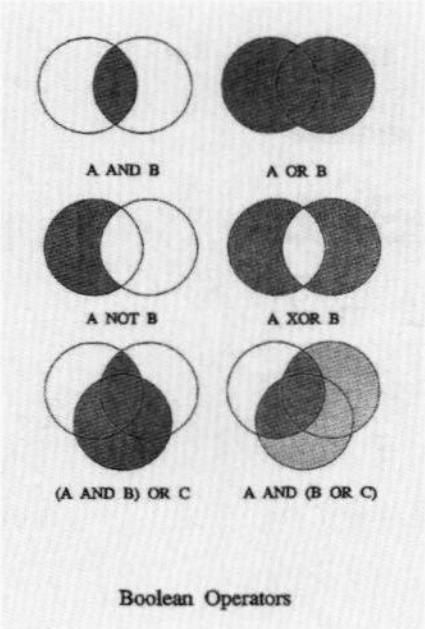

← P.29

1880

VENN DIAGRAM

Information Design

John Venn (1834–1923)

Self-commissioned, UK

The Venn diagram is one of the best-known examples of how a simple form can be used to convey complex information. Devised to represent the similarities and differences between things and how they relate to one another, Venn diagrams appeal as much to the general public as to scholars.

The area inside each shape of a Venn diagram represents a different mathematical or logical set, with each shape arranged so that it intersects once with all the other shapes. The areas where the shapes overlap represent where the sets meet. In a simple example using two sets, one of the circles could represent "birds" and the other "hunters." The area where the circles intersect represents all the birds that hunt, and could therefore include owls. A sheep, on the other hand, which is neither a bird nor a hunter, would fit into the space outside both circles. In this way, everything on a Venn diagram has a correct place.

The philosopher and mathematician John Venn was a fellow at Gonville and Caius College, Cambridge, and published his work on diagrams in a paper of 1880. The most famous version of his diagram, three interlinking circles, was not new, and had been used as a symbol to represent the Holy Trinity in medieval times. Similar diagrams had been made before to illustrate the relationships between certain categories (such as Euler circles, invented by Leonard Euler), but Venn proposed creating a diagram with all possible combinations of a certain number of sets first, and then applying them to specific problems, sometimes blacking out areas that did not exist. He found that circles could be used to create two-set and three-set diagrams, and that ellipses could be arranged to make four-set ones. It was only in the 1980s that A. W. F. Edwards worked out a method for drawing Venn diagrams with any number of sets, which uses ever more complicated combinations of shapes as the number of sets increases.

← P.29

1886

COCA-COLA

Logo

Frank Mason Robinson (1845–1923)

The Coca-Cola Company, U.S.

Coca-Cola's distinctive red-and-white cursive trademark is one of the most recognized in the world, regularly appropriated, adapted, and parodied by other manufacturers hoping to grab a slice of the drink's vast global market.

Coca-Cola was invented as a medicinal beverage by a pharmacist, Dr. John Pemberton, of Atlanta, Georgia. His business associate Frank Mason Robinson conceived the product identity, including the memorable, repetitive name. The swirling Coca-Cola logo was written in Spencerian script, a widely used form of handwriting at the time and consequently familiar to potential consumers, while the choice of red-and-white coloring was intended to add to the emblem's impact, enabling it to stand out in a crowded visual environment. Although the colors are an important element of the original design, the drink's brand identity is now so powerful that color variations are used in different versions, such as silver in Diet Coke graphics, and in certain contexts the logo has even been reduced to fragments: consumers will automatically associate a white curve on a bright red background (or vice versa) with the product.

The Coca-Cola logo has been the subject of numerous urban myths, such as the suggestion that in reverse it carries an Arabic phrase, and that it is the origin of the red-and-white costume of Father Christmas, who featured in early advertisements. T-shirts are regularly printed with spoof Coke logos, and Pop artist Andy Warhol, who saw Coca-Cola as the quintessential American product, created a famous series of screen prints containing repetitive images of the bottle. Ultimately, Coca-Cola's extraordinary success may owe as much to its logo as it does to the drink, the bottle, or its advertising.

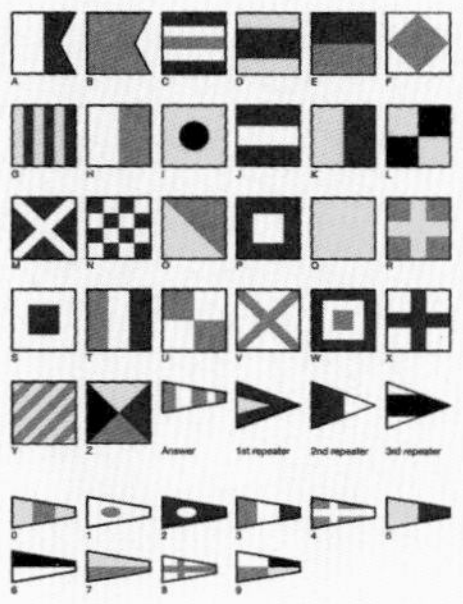

← P.30

1887

INTERNATIONAL CODE OF SYMBOLS AND INTERNATIONAL MARITIME FLAGS

Information Design

Unknown

British Board of Trade, UK

Before radio, communication between sea vessels was achieved with flags, which were used to indicate a ship's nationality and function ("colors of distinction"). Although there had been earlier vexillological signaling systems, the introduction of the International Code of Symbols (INTERCO) provided the first internationally recognized language of flag signals, which is still used by ships today.

By the nineteenth century, the need for a universal system of maritime communication was becoming urgent, and in 1855 the International Code of Signals, consisting of eighteen flags that could be combined into seventy thousand signals, was drawn up by the British Board of Trade and published two years later. Since its introduction, the code has been administered by several organizations, reflecting its global patronage, but in 1947 an international conference accorded overall authority to the Inter-Governmental Maritime Consultative Organization, now the International Maritime Organization (IMO). The code includes signals deliverable by flag, blinker light, semaphore, Morse code, and radio, but it is the maritime signal flags that are of greatest interest graphically. Today, the set consists of twenty-six flags (one for each letter of the alphabet), ten numerical pennants, three substitutes, and an answering pennant. Unlike semaphore flags, which are handheld, signal flag messages are conspicuously hoisted and lowered in alternate transmissions between vessels. Single-flag messages reflect broad status and certain forms of distress, two-flag series convey emergencies, and three or more flags are used for general or more complex messages. The flags themselves are configurations of basic geometrical units using the colors black, white, blue, red, and yellow. By combining contrasting colors in bars, squares, crosses, "X"s, and diagonals (rarely circles, and only the letter "Q" is in the form of a single, uninterrupted color), each is a discrete symbol visible at a distance even under challenging conditions.

As a purely functional system of translingual communication, signal flags perform a vital function; as examples of design, they are compelling models of how a limited set of colors and shapes can produce a vast array of potential meanings.

← P.31

c. 1890–1913

CALAVERAS

Magazine / Newspaper

José Guadalupe Posada (1852–1913)

Antonio Vanegas Arroyo, Mexico

Calaveras—traditionally, skulls or skeletons in contemporary dress with maniacal grins who drink, laugh, sing, dance, ride bikes or horses, smoke cigars, and woo women—were produced to be sold during the festivities of the Mexican "Day of the Dead" (November 2), an annual celebration of life, when barriers between worlds are transgressed and the living and dead coexist. Among the most memorable and influential were those created by José Guadalupe Posada, the Mexican etcher and engraver who illustrated poems, ballads, and news stories for the "penny press"—cheaply produced broadsheets aimed at the lower classes, which were sold at fairs and festivals.

Often mistaken for a self-taught artist, Posada in fact attended a trade school, becoming a highly skilled draughtsman, printmaker, and commercial artist who worked under commission for publishers. His most renowned prints and illustrations, particularly the *calaveras*, were produced for the small-scale publisher Antonio Vanegas Arroyo in Mexico City, where Posada started work in the early 1890s. His illustrations of contemporary events or crimes and humorous, gossipy stories, characterized by sensational, gory images, communicated directly to his near-illiterate readers. Posada died not long after the start of the Mexican Revolution (1910), and is best seen as an artist who caught the spirit and reality of the country's prerevolutionary society. As well as chronicling the interests of common people—murders, suicides, executions, and natural disasters, along with recipes and stories about heroes of the day—his work revealed the deep social divisions that existed between the rich and the poor.

Posada received little acclaim during his lifetime, but was made a legend by a later generation of Mexican artists, including Diego Rivera, who were eager to reject European or Spanish art and return to authentic Mexican and pre-Columbian artistic and folk traditions. Posada's influence can be seen in the work of the late political printmaker Paul Peter Piech and the American graphic designer Seymour Chwast.

← P.31

1892

GENERAL ELECTRIC

Logo

Unknown

General Electric, U.S.

With its curling, vinelike forms, the General Electric (GE) logo is a surviving example of Art Nouveau, which has remained virtually consistent for more than one hundred years. In that time, the mark has helped to turn GE into one of the most recognizable brands in the world.

In 1878 Thomas Alva Edison founded the Edison Electric Light Company to manufacture and sell his new invention, the incandescent electric lamp, later renaming his business the General Electric Company after it had merged with the Thomson-Houston Electric Company in 1892. Considered to be a stylized depiction of the eye of an electric stove, the logo (the designer of which is disputed to this day) was created for the new company and made its first-known appearance in 1898 on a pendant attached to one of GE's first electric ceiling fans. In 1986 Landor Associates introduced some small adjustments to the trademark, reducing the "tendrils" and making the GE calligraphy more compact, to bring the design into alignment with contemporary fashion. The current iteration was commissioned in 2004, with the arrival of Jeffrey Immelt as chief executive of the company, to be redesigned by the British partnership Wolff Olins. The studio subtly referenced its Art Nouveau character by emphasizing the roundness of the forms, to underline GE's century-long history. At the same time, a fresh corporate palette, which cast the logo in fourteen different colors, and the GE Inspira advertising font were also introduced to unify the company's visual identity across other aspects of the business.

GE's reputation is founded on ingenuity, which persists to this day, with initiatives such as "Ecomagination," devoted to the development of energy-efficient technology. Over the years, GE has diversified its portfolio of interests, introducing divisions such as GE Money, GE Healthcare, and the entertainment company NBC Universal. Despite these developments, the company trademark has undergone only minor modifications, emphasizing the essentially unchanged nature of GE's original identity and mission.

← P.32

1892–1893

ARISTIDE BRUANT

Poster

Henri de Toulouse-Lautrec (1864–1901)

Aristide Bruant, France

Jules Chéret had been responsible for advancing the lithographic printing process for the production of illustrated posters, but it was Henri de Toulouse-Lautrec who revolutionized their design.

In 1892 Toulouse-Lautrec produced a striking pair of posters of the celebrated Parisian cabaret singer Aristide Bruant. The first of these was used to publicize Bruant's guest appearance at the Ambassadeurs, one of the foremost cabaret clubs of the period. The resulting poster met with disapproval from the manager, but Bruant threatened to stop performing unless it was displayed onstage and throughout Paris. When Bruant commissioned a second poster for an engagement at the equally renowned Eldorado cabaret club, Toulouse-Lautrec used the same image again, but reversed. Both posters are notable for the way in which the close-up of Bruant's bulky body and profile has been boldly cropped and framed. Appearing as a cavalier character wearing a large felt hat, long red scarf, and dark blue cloak, Bruant has been drawn using broad brushstrokes for the outlines and *crachis* (ink-spattered) texture for the hair, glove, and stick.

Toulouse-Lautrec's first ever poster design (1891) was for the popular cabaret the Moulin Rouge. The two key figures in the poster represent Louise Weber, known as "La Goulue" (the glutton), and her partner Jacques Renaudin, known as "Valentin le Désossé" (the boneless), dancing the quadrille. What makes the work seminal is its simplicity. The flattened perspective, emphasized by the row of silhouetted spectators in the background, owed much to Toulouse-Lautrec's fascination with the spatial illusion of Japanese woodcuts. The lettering (not by Toulouse-Lautrec) is crude, yet it does not detract from the overall appeal. It was common for posters of this period to be printed across a number of sheets because of their scale, but unusually, "Moulin Rouge, La Goulue" was printed on two sheets of equal size with an added narrow strip at the top to complete the headline lettering.

By embracing the commercial restrictions imposed by the poster format and treating the graphics and imagery of poster design as a complete entity, Toulouse-Lautrec's oeuvre became a touchstone for future generations.

← P.33

1894–1898

THE CHAP-BOOK

Magazine Cover

William H. Bradley (1868–1962)

Stone & Kimball, U.S.

William H. Bradley's posters and covers for the Chicago-based literary magazine the *Chap-Book* are regarded as the first examples of American Art Nouveau. They drew heavily on the aesthetics of the Arts and Crafts movement and Japanese prints. Bradley designed numerous covers for the publication, in both color and black and white; as it became famous, the publishers began to reprint these as posters, which served as advertisements and images for readers to collect.

Bradley's technique has also been compared to that of the English illustrator Aubrey Beardsley, and to the pioneering French poster artists Henri de Toulouse-Lautrec and Jules Chéret. However, Bradley also maximized the potential of emerging print technology, using effects of repetition, variations in scale, and overlapping imagery, as seen in a poster known as "The Twins," created for the *Chap-Book*'s August 1894 issue. The design uses a limited range of bold colors and repeated curving lines, which create a powerful rhythmic and decorative image, in which the two female figures carrying flower bouquets become dynamic, quasi-abstract elements tied to the picture surface. Bradley's typography was also innovative in the way that it functioned as an integral element of the design and contributed a spatial dimension. In another example from 1895, the letters of the title are interwoven among a dense red-and-black pattern of flying horses. Although Bradley's work set the standard for American graphics, "The Twins" received a lukewarm reception on publication, provoking criticism that he had styled the women directly on Beardsley's the *Yellow Book*, while a review in the *American Printer* likened the figures to a turkey.

Overall, however, Bradley's posters were enormously popular during his lifetime and, as demand grew, they were among a small number of American graphic works that were able to command equal attention with those of European artists.

← P.33

1894

LA REVUE BLANCHE

Poster

Pierre Bonnard (1867–1947)

La Revue Blanche, France

With its flat shapes and almost abstract design, this lithographic poster for *La Revue Blanche*, one of the very few that Pierre Bonnard produced, epitomized the philosophy of the Nabis group, to which the artist belonged.

Owned and edited by three brothers—Thadée, Alexandre, and Alfred Natanson—*La Revue Blanche* was a monthly arts and letters magazine that published literary works by important writers of the period (including Leo Tolstoy, Anton Chekhov, Oscar Wilde, Émile Zola, and André Gide) and illustrations by artists such as Henri de Toulouse-Lautrec and Édouard Vuillard, as well as Bonnard. The poster was commissioned by Thadée Natanson, who admired Bonnard's striking poster "France-Champagne" of 1891. The identity of the fashionably dressed woman is thought to be Thadée's Russian wife, Misia Godebska, who is seen here wearing a flower-bedecked hat and manteau around her shoulders, and clutching a copy of the journal. Godebska was at the center of the magazine's activities and became a regular model for Bonnard and other artists, particularly Toulouse-Lautrec, who included her in his own poster for the journal in 1895. The significance of the character pointing his thumb toward the magazine is not known, but critics of the time thought that the shadowy shape in the background was a man in a cloak with the collar turned up, looking at a wall of *La Revue Blanche* magazines. Even to audiences of the day the poster's enigmatic message was unclear, but the directness of its line and somber coloring, especially when compared with the vibrancy of *fin-de-siècle* posters by artists such as Jules Chéret and Bonnard's own intensely colored paintings, makes it highly distinctive. The free-flowing lettering of the masthead, with its elongated "l," "b," and "h," and unfinished "a" of "a" (different in construction from the "a" in "blanche"), which appears to wrap around the woman's leg, is particularly unusual.

Bonnard also produced many book illustrations and lithographic prints, but he was acclaimed mainly for his colorful paintings featuring Marthe de Méligny, his lifelong companion and muse, portrayed in intimate domestic interiors bathed in sunlight.

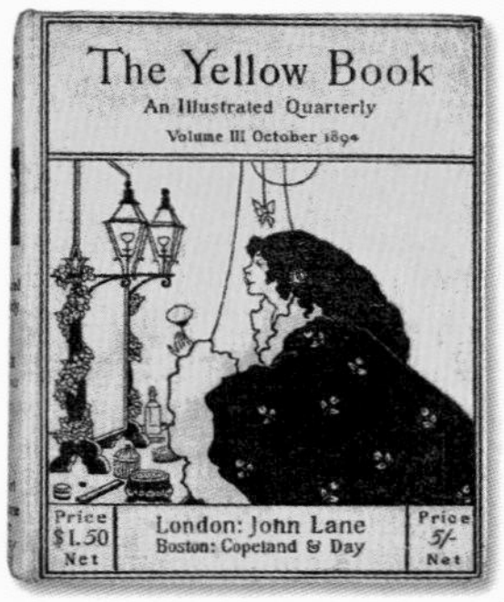

← P.33

1894–1895

THE YELLOW BOOK

Magazine / Newspaper

Aubrey Beardsley (1872–1898)

Elkin Mathews and John Lane, UK

A highbrow literary periodical associated with the 1890s Aesthetic and Decadent movements, the *Yellow Book* was daring, ambitious, and an immediate success. Edited by Henry Harland and published in thirteen quarterly volumes, it aimed from the outset to deliver the best art and writing of the day, including poetry, short stories, and essays, along with reproductions of prints, drawings, and paintings, without resorting to the serial fiction typical of magazines at the time. It also carried no advertising (a risky decision, considering the relatively high cover price of five shillings), while its clothbound, booklike format in bold yellow, based on contemporary French novels, also underlined its distinctiveness. As art editor, Aubrey Beardsley defined the magazine's vision, although his work was included only in the first four editions.

As well as choosing the periodical cover's distinctive color, Beardsley provided numerous black-and-white illustrations, mostly of theatrical performances and their audiences, with players in elaborate costumes of different periods, articulated by effects of sinuous line, decorative pattern, shallow pictorial space, and large areas of flat tone. Such features reflected the stylistic influence of Art Nouveau (also known as Jugendstil), which Beardsley helped to shape, and Japanese prints, which he collected, and made maximum use of the new technique of line-block printing to create uniform tonalities. Beardsley's era-defining images also appeared in Oscar Wilde's *Salome* (1893), a connection that proved disastrous for his career. When the scandal surrounding Wilde's homosexuality broke, the publisher of the the *Yellow Book*, John Lane, came under pressure to dismiss his art director, which he duly did in 1895, and the periodical continued to publish without him until 1897. Beardsley went on briefly to produce a rival magazine, the *Savoy* (1895–96), but died not long afterward at the age of twenty-five. His influence throughout the twentieth century was substantial, particularly on the design of 1960s posters, such as those by Wes Wilson, and continues to resonate in the work of graphic designers and illustrators today.

← P.34

1894

TOURNÉE DU CHAT NOIR

Poster

Théophile-Alexandre Steinlen (1859–1923)

Rodolphe Salis, France

This stylishly evocative poster is an enduring symbol of turn-of-the-century French bohemia. Based on a color lithograph and signed with a monogram, the poster is thought to have first been displayed in 1894. Théophile-Alexandre Steinlen loved cats and often depicted them. The black cat, which was inspired by Édouard Manet's 1868 illustration for Champfleury's book *Les Chats*, evokes the city streets without literally depicting the prostitutes and performers that made Paris infamous.

Among Steinlen's earliest works was an imposing scene based on the *vendange* (grape harvest) festival at Vevey in his native Switzerland, painted for the local town-hall gymnasium. All his imagery reflected his fascination with humanity and his feel for the zeitgeist, but his understanding of composition, two-dimensional design, and flat patterning evolved more fully around 1878, when he began creating textile prints. In 1879 Steinlen moved to Montmartre, the heart of bohemian Paris, where, under the name Jean Caillou, he collaborated with the satirical performer Aristide Bruant on the cabaret magazine *Le Mirliton*. He also worked with Henri de Toulouse-Lautrec, who used the anagrammatic pseudonym Treclau.

In 1882 Steinlen met Rodolphe Salis, an unsuccessful artist who opened a cabaret on the Boulevard Rochecouart. Between 1883 and 1895, Salis published Steinlen's drawings in *Le Chat Noir*, a journal linked to his cabaret. When Salis relocated to Rue de Laval, Steinlen not only produced the now-famous poster, but also decorated the exterior signage and ground-floor chimney with a large cat motif. The cat silhouette refers to the Chat Noir's popular Chinese-inspired shadow-theater performances that took place upstairs; black cats were painted above the stage and along the walls, among them a panel entitled *Apothéose des chats* (Quintessence of Cats) .

The poster design was heavily influenced by Japanese woodblock prints, in which strong outlines and flat expanses of color predominated. Steinlen produced two later versions, both advertisements, in 1896 and 1898, adapting the basic format and reworking the text: the first for the reopening of the café and concert hall, and the second for one of Salis's drawing, painting, and watercolor sales.

← P.35

1894

HAMLET

Poster

The Beggarstaffs: James Pryde (1866–1941), William Nicholson (1872–1949)

W. S. Hardy, UK

When first exhibited at the International Artistic Poster Exhibition in London in 1894, the Beggarstaffs' poster of "Hamlet," made for W.S. Hardy's theatrical company, was described by one critic as "the great sensation of the show." Artists such as Henri de Toulouse-Lautrec had made extensive use of the silhouette, but the uncompromising boldness of the figure, with its static composition, restricted color palette, and absence of background detail or perspective, was unprecedented.

Brothers-in-law James Pryde and William Nicholson, who worked under the pseudonym the "Beggarstaffs," based their design on drawings by Aubrey Beardsley of cast members of a production of *Becket* (1893) by the actor Henry Irving, but it was probably equally influenced by Japanese wood-block prints and contemporary shadow portraits. The forms were cut from colored paper and transferred to stencils, then handprinted on brown wrapping paper to provide a midtone. The artists went on to make numerous posters, although only seven ever reached the hoardings. In addition to those commissioned by specific advertisers (e.g., "Rowntree's Elect Cocoa," 1896), many were produced speculatively ("Kassama Corn Flour," 1894) and included imagery that could be adapted for a variety of commercial purposes. Later, they worked on much larger, even monumental, scales (up to 11½ feet [3.5 m] high), printed by a lithographic printer from a stencilled original, with certain editions reproduced exclusively for collectors. However, the radical simplicity of their designs and harmonious relation of lettering to imagery—which in "Hamlet" provides a visual base for the figure—were, it seems, hard-won, and production was slow.

By 1895 the Beggarstaffs were recognized as pioneers of the modern advertisement, but their success seems to have been more critical than commercial. Despite the revolutionary character of their work, their posters were relatively ineffective as selling tools and were often unpopular with advertisers. They remained sought after, however, by collectors, particularly abroad, and were to have a major influence on a later generation of graphic artists working in the 1920s, when the pictorial poster entered its golden age.

← P.36

1894

THE STORY OF THE GLITTERING PLAIN OR THE LAND OF LIVING MEN

Book

William Morris (1834–1896), Walter Crane (1845–1915)

Kelmscott Press, UK

William Morris's *The Story of the Glittering Plain or The Land of Living Men* was the first book produced by the Kelmscott Press, the publishing company he founded in Hammersmith, London, in 1891. Already an accomplished designer, calligrapher, and illuminator, Morris became interested in book design after attending a lecture in 1888 by the printer Emery Walker on the design unity of incunabula (early typographic books) and type. Morris launched his new venture to improve what he saw as the low standards of contemporary book production.

The Story of the Glittering Plain contained Morris's own designs for decorative borders and initials, and illustrations by Walter Crane. William Harcourt Hooper, a master wood-engraver, was employed to cut the blocks from which the designs were printed. Morris considered the opening two-page spread fundamental to establishing a book's typographic design, and designed three typefaces, all based on incunabula fonts: the roman Golden and two, more successful, Gothic faces—Troy and Chaucer. Legibility for Morris was a key concern, and these fonts were intended as subtle improvements on the originals. This was particularly important in relation to the typically dense character of the Kelmscott page, with its intricate floral motifs and dazzling tonal contrasts. In his aim to emulate the beauty of incunabula books, Morris also insisted on the finest materials: handmade paper from Joseph Batchelor in Kent, less-than-six-week-old calfskin vellum, and ink from Jaenecke of Hannover, Germany. The earliest Kelmscott books were bound in "half-holland"—canvas-backed board—later standardized to limp vellum with silk ties. Only twenty copies were planned, but, after unexpected interest, two hundred were produced and sold.

This book set the standard for others produced by Kelmscott, including the *Works of Geoffrey Chaucer* in 1896, regarded by some as the greatest of all. Altogether, the press produced more than 18,000 copies of fifty-three different titles and continued production for two years after Morris's death. His ideas about craftsmanship, if not his historicist aesthetic, would inspire a fifty-year revival in fine book printing through the private-press movement.

← P.37

1896

AKZIDENZ-GROTESK

Typeface

Unknown

H. Berthold AG, Germany

Akzidenz-Grotesk is a typeface whose cool, seemingly modernist design belies its original date of inception and its complicated journey to the face we know today.

Akzidenz's roots, and those of the sans serif generally, are found in the mid-nineteenth century, and more specifically the latter stages of the British Industrial Revolution, when the rise in advertising created greater demand for display faces. Early fonts were available in uppercase only, and usually in bold. Akzidenz, whose name comes from the German word "Akzidenzschrift," which means "display face" or "jobbing type," was released in 1896 by the Berthold Type Foundry of Berlin, and came in a single weight. During the following years, Berthold began to add weights, although, rather than designing them, it simply added different weights of "jobbing types" as they were acquired from other foundries. This gave the original Akzidenz series an inconsistent feel.

Although a product of the nineteenth century, Akzidenz started to make its mark as a typeface through the emergence of the "Swiss school" (also known as the International Typographic Style), which developed in Switzerland after World War II. The "Swiss school" built upon previous modernist typographic innovations and relied heavily on the use of a grid and sans serif type. Its popularity among designers, such as Max Bill, led Berthold to release a partially recut series with extended character sets in 1957 and 1958 under the direction of Günter Gerhard Lange. Akzidenz is credited as the model and inspiration for the design of Neue Haas Grotesk by Max Miedinger and Edouard Hoffmann, now known as Helvetica. The two faces can be hard to distinguish; key features to note are Akzidenz's smaller x-height, and the almost forty-five-degree terminal of the curved letters, such as "C" and "S," in contrast with the horizontal terminals of Helvetica.

Akzidenz is still used and widely available, but has lost much of the profile it had in the 1940s and '50s; its heritage continues to live on, however, through the ubiquitous Helvetica.

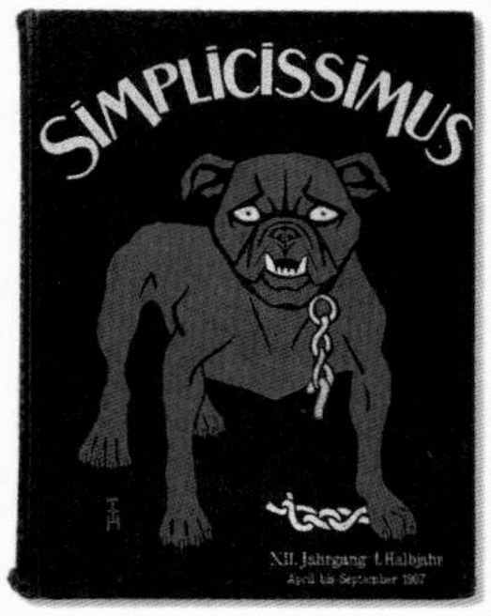

← P.38

1896–1944

SIMPLICISSIMUS

Magazine / Newspaper

Thomas Theodor Heine (1867–1948) et al.

Self-commissioned, Germany

Simplicissimus, or *Der Simpl* for short, was a satirical weekly tabloid cofounded in Munich by artist Thomas Theodor Heine and publisher/editor Albert Langen. Expressing youthful rebellion against materialism, nationalism, and the ruling classes, *Der Simpl* was known for its pioneering graphic minimalism, bold cover art by Heine, and savage satirical cartoons, which provoked censorship, fines, and even prison sentences.

Der Simpl was named after Simplicissimus, a character from the 1668 picaresque novel *Der Abenteuerliche Simplicissimus Teutsch* (The Adventurous Simplicissimus Teutsch) by Hans Jakob Christoffel von Grimmelshausen, which exposed the vices and hypocrisies of the aristocracy. The publication's mission was to advocate tolerance and justice, and, while eschewing specific ideologies or styles, champion a simple style for polemic purposes, as reflected in the magazine's title. Its contributors included major artists and writers, such as the cartoonists Bruno Paul, Karl Arnold, Eduard Thöny, Olaf Gulbransson, and Rudolf Wilke, who were free to work in whatever way they wished, often over a full page. Overall, the publication's style was Expressionistic and diverse, though in the tabloid's push toward Minimalism, it veered into Abstractionism. Heine's covers, in particular, were notable for their simplicity, with artworks stripped to essentials to intensify the satirical impact of the caricatures.

Der Simpl influenced public opinion as much as it did modern German illustration and design. During World War I, the publication supported the war effort with propaganda, but gradually lost its bite and, despite criticizing right-wing militias during the 1920s and '30s, finally became a Nazi publication in 1933. Heine, who was of Jewish heritage, fled to Norway. The magazine ceased publication in 1944, reappearing in name only from 1954 to 1967.

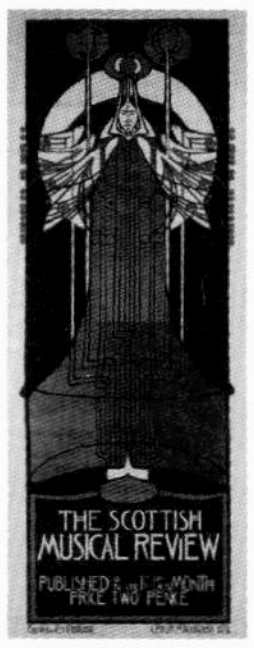

← P.39

1896

THE SCOTTISH MUSICAL REVIEW

Poster

Charles Rennie Mackintosh (1868–1928)

The Scottish Musical Review, UK

With its angular geometry, Charles Rennie Mackintosh's poster for the *Scottish Musical Review*, a monthly magazine published in Glasgow, heralds the twentieth century, yet remains bound to the nineteenth by its allegorical imagery.

A contemporary of Frank Lloyd Wright, Mackintosh was a prolific architect, designer, and graphic artist, who was greatly influenced by the work of Margaret Macdonald, a Symbolist and Art Nouveau muralist, who eventually became his wife. The unusually tall poster represents a winged woman standing on a pedestal, her statuesque figure accentuated by a large halo, and resembles both Macdonald's elongated decorative panels and his celebrated neo-medieval facade of the Glasgow School of Art. A complex network of vertical lines branches out from her figure, forming the outline of a tree in which four birds are nestled. The work of a draughtsman more than a painter, the poster was nevertheless steeped in mysticism. The unexpected combination of stylized organic and Celtic forms caused a scandal among members of Glasgow's art community, whose hostile criticisms revealed their provincial perspective. However, the poster was reproduced in the international art magazine, the *Studio*, and was hailed as a breakthrough outside England, particularly in Germany and Austria.

The critical acclaim received by the poster in Europe helped to publicize the work of Mackintosh and other members of the Glasgow Four: Mackintosh's wife Margaret, his wife's sister Frances Macdonald, and James Herbert McNair, Frances's husband. The Four designed distinctive interiors, which borrowed from a range of design idioms, including Japanese and medieval motifs. Essential to these interiors were Mackintosh's radical works of furniture, including his high-backed Argyle Chair of 1897. In its proportions, pattern, and stylistic details, the chair replicates the design of the *Musical Review* poster.

← P.40

1896–1940

JUGEND

Magazine / Newspaper

Various

Georg Hirth, Germany

Jugend, the magazine that gave its name to Jugendstil—the distinctively German form of Art Nouveau—was started in 1896 by Georg Hirth in Munich, and contained a heavily illustrated *mélange* of texts, caricatures, folk tales, songs, and nostalgic paeans to childhood.

"Jugend" means "youth," and despite its unconventional nature, championing of the avant-garde and erotica, and forays into eccentric anti-Christian and Aryan paganism, the magazine's influence extended to Berlin and Darmstadt as it sold throughout Germany. Subtitled the "Illustrated Weekly Munich Magazine for Art and Life," *Jugend* evidently connected with the concerns of the German public, occasionally reaching up to two-hundred thousand readers in its early life, and included many important artists among its contributors, such as Otto Eckmann, Peter Behrens, Hans Christiansen, Franz von Stuck, Ludwig Hohlwein, and the English artist Charles Shannon. The magazine's design was far from consistent, yet its variety gave it authority and a voice of its own. Most issues were produced by different designers or illustrators, with cover illustrations ranging from old-fashioned pastoral scenes and typical Jugendstil subjects, such as young girls and sinuous floral motifs, to a newer, more vivid graphic style suggestive of later *Sachplakat* (object poster) and the work of the French Fauves. Holding all of this together was the magazine's name, but although this featured prominently at the top of the cover, the typography was highly varied: from joyously hand-drawn lettering to subdued typesetting, at times echoing colors used in illustrations, the appearance of the text was never predictable and provided an early object lesson in how to distort a design identity without compromising its integrity.

Despite notable competitors such as *Pan* and the modernistic *Simplicissimus*, *Jugend* enjoyed a long period of success. Ultimately, however, its innocent, idiosyncratic, and occasionally chaotic production and nature proved out of place in the new world being forged at the beginning of the twentieth century. Although it continued until 1940, it was at its most iconic before the outbreak of World War I.

← P.41

1896/1898

JOB CIGARETTE PAPERS

Poster

Alphonse Mucha (1860–1939)

Job, France

Alphonse Mucha's two advertising posters for Job cigarette papers were exemplars of his Art Nouveau style and approach, contributing to his status as one of the pre-eminent poster artists of his day.

While working as a lithographer at the printer Lemercier in the early 1890s, Mucha was asked to create a poster promoting a performance by the actress Sarah Bernhardt. Presenting her as luxurious, bejeweled, and above all iconic, the poster (and Mucha) achieved overnight popularity and success. At a time when most poster artists drew their imagery directly onto stone as part of the lithographic printing process, Mucha proved himself an exquisite draughtsman, creating compositions of flowing forms, rich colors, and intense patterns that threaten to spill out of the picture frame.

Many of Mucha's posters were produced for the French publisher Champenois, who set him an exhausting pace in designing posters and other advertising material for Job, Nestlé, and Cycles Waverley, among other companies. They are distinguished by the sensual stance, grace, and cascading hair of his trademark female figures. Lettering was fully integrated, whether merged with the figure in the foreground or functioning as patterns or motifs in the background, and sometimes even doubling as a piece of jewelry. Apparently, Mucha also occasionally worked from photographs to capture the pose of a model or the flow and drape of material.

The 1896 Job poster (pictured) has remained the classic Mucha image, retaining its popularity through the decades with its glowing color, fluid movement, and sexual innuendo. It was particularly fashionable during the American peace-and-love movement of the 1960s, when a youth-inspired, decorative poster movement was heavily inspired by Art Nouveau.

← P.42

1898

TROPON: L'ALIMENT LE PLUS CONCENTRÉ

Identity

Henry van de Velde (1863–1957)

Tropon, Germany

One of Art Nouveau's most revered practitioners, the Belgian artist, architect, and designer Henry van de Velde is probably best remembered today for his poster and packaging design for a German powdered food product. While adhering to the pervasive style of Art Nouveau, van de Velde's design signaled a shift toward a modernist aesthetic, and avoided the standard practice of using a female figure to sell household goods. Here, the product is evoked by an abstracted illustration of egg whites being separated from yolks, in which curvilinear arabesques spill from beaklike motifs to merge gradually with an organic border design like that of Art Nouveau metalwork and architecture. Although the text is also decorative, the company name, surrounded by a linear pattern, is presented in a simpler style characterized by the exaggerated descending strokes of the "T," "R," and "P."

Van de Velde studied painting in Antwerp before moving to Paris, where he became involved with the neo-Impressionist movement known as Pointillism. In 1892 he abandoned painting to focus on the applied arts, believing, like William Morris, that his work would enhance people's lives. After receiving a commission to design interiors from Siegfried Bing, entrepreneur and proprietor of the Art Nouveau gallery in Paris, he was asked to devise a poster and a range of packaging and promotional items for the Tropon company based in Mülheim am Rhein (later part of Cologne). Van de Velde's designs for the packaging of children's food, cocoa, and other products manufactured by the company were less distinctive in appearance than his poster, and displayed a more generic Art Nouveau style.

← P.43

1898–1903

VER SACRUM

Magazine / Newspaper

Alfred Roller (1864–1935) et al.

Vienna Secession, Austria

The dedicated journal of the Vienna Secession (founded in 1897), *Ver Sacrum* (*Sacred Spring*) immediately established itself as one of the most important publications of its day, printing the work of Secession members and that of leading artists and literary figures across Europe.

Alfred Roller, a founding member of the Secession, was appointed the magazine's first editor, and designed the cover for the inaugural issue of January 1898. His illustration of a tree in bloom with its roots bursting free from a wooden container was symbolic of Secessionist thinking, which dictated that art should draw its strength from nature and free itself from the conservatism of traditional Viennese imagery. The three blank shields superimposed onto the illustration, similar to the masks representing painting, architecture, and sculpture that hung over the door of their exhibition building, acted as a heraldic emblem for the group and featured on many of its exhibition posters and catalog covers. Roller continued to play a significant role as editor, designer, and illustrator of the publication.

Ver Sacrum was renowned for setting high aesthetic and design standards, reflecting the distinctive and evolving Viennese Art Nouveau style. Apart from the creative use of page layout and typography, with the main body of text set in an old-face serif surrounded by wide margins, the almost square-shaped journal often used different paper stocks and special inks. It was richly illustrated, publishing more than fifty original lithographs and more than two hundred woodcuts during its five years of publication. Works by other European artists, such as Walter Crane and Aubrey Beardsley, complemented the line drawings, etchings, colored woodcuts, and chromo-lithographs by Secession founder members, who included Josef Hoffmann, Koloman Moser, and Gustav Klimt, while decorative borders framed literary contributions by important contemporary poets and essayists. Illustrated calendars, such as those designed by the Art Nouveau poster artist Alphonse Mucha for the November 1898 issue, were also a recurrent theme.

The journal ceased publication in 1903 due to dwindling subscribers. In the same year, Hoffmann and Moser left the Secession to form the Wiener Werkstätte (Viennese Workshop).

← P.44

1898

MICHELIN MAN

Logo

Marius Rossillon (1867–1946)

Michelin, France

One of the world's oldest trademarks, the chubby "Michelin Man," or "Bibendum," was originally designed to look like a stack of bicycle tires. The figure owed his nickname to a Latin inscription in the first poster to feature him—"*Nunc est bibendum*!" ("Now is the time to drink!"). Standing at a banquet table giving a toast, he holds aloft a goblet filled not with champagne but with glass debris and nails, which he apparently knows will not puncture his stomach or the tough inner tube of Michelin tires. This somewhat convoluted advertising claim is then spelled out below: "To your health. The Michelin tire swallows the obstacle!"

Drawn by Marius Rossillon, a satirical illustrator, animator, and later a filmmaker, who signed his work "O'Galop," Bibendum was the brainchild of one of the two owners of the company—André Michelin, a *bon vivant* who infused the company mascot with a personality as expansive as his own. According to the Michelin Guide website, the figure first appeared as a cardboard cutout at a Paris exposition in 1898, when a cabaret comedian was hired to crouch behind it and provide in-character repartee extolling the virtues of Michelin tires. In advertising campaigns, newspaper articles, and promotional brochures, Bibendum was cast as an authoritative character, an expert on car maintenance who could show you how to negotiate obstacles on the road, figure out the shortest distance from A to B, and who knew what to order at the best local restaurants (thereby already anticipating the company's second great enterprise—the Michelin hotel and restaurant guide—for which it would become equally famous).

The original Bibendum, whose girth, *pince-nez*, and cigar were considered upper-class attributes, was not only a lady's man, he was also a good father. He was always portrayed as white, the color of rubber tires before carbon was added to them to improve their resistance. Only once, in a 1965 poster by Raymond Savignac, was his color black. In the 1930s, as car ownership became less elitist, Bibendum lost his aristocratic props, but kept his pneumatic midriff for a further two decades. In the 1990s he lost weight to become merely barrel-chested, thus appearing more virile and perhaps more in keeping with the sensibility of an increasingly sedentary public, who equated the portly figure with ill-health.

← P.44

1899

HIS MASTER'S VOICE

Logo

Francis Barraud (1856–1924)

Gramophone Company, UK

The endurance and evolution of the His Master's Voice (HMV) logo, which has undergone a number of redesigns and refinements since its first appearance more than a century ago, is testament to the extraordinary power of its symbolism and narrative.

The symbol originally derives from Francis Barraud's painting of his late brother's dog, Nipper, who would allegedly listen to recordings of his dead owner's voice through a phonograph. Originally entitled *Dog Looking at and Listening to a Phonograph*, the painting was bought for £50 by the Gramophone Company in London after being renamed *His Master's Voice*, and the original black horn changed to one of the company's modern brass gramophones. In January 1900 the image appeared for the first time on the company's advertising literature. Soon afterward, Emile Berliner, the German-born American inventor of the gramophone and founder of the corporation, asked Barraud to make a copy of the painting (the first of many), which he passed, along with a trademark, to the Victor Talking Machine Company, the American gramophone firm founded by Eldridge Johnson in 1901. With the copyright now fragmented between the U.S. and Britain, the image began to acquire various modifications (in the U.S. it appears above the RCA Victor logo), which were to multiply throughout the twentieth century as it was distributed among different companies and countries. In the UK, HMV (as the Gramophone Company became known from 1910, due to the use of the trademark on its records) would ultimately become EMI.
The work's popularity was such that Barraud was employed until his death on producing copies (twenty-four in total), a tradition continued by other artists until 1930.

The success of Barraud's image and its use as a trademark are due to its sentimental appeal and its play on the concept of fidelity, the dog's fascination with the machine highlighting the high quality of the recording. Visually, the symbol displays a remarkable symmetry, with the dog and gramophone creating two sides of an arch. Later iterations of the symbol have included a temporary stand-in for Nipper on children's DVD posters featuring Nick Park's Gromit.

← P.45

1899

FROMME'S KALENDER

Poster

Koloman Moser (1868–1918)

Carl Fromme, Austria

With its clean forms, quiet expressive mood, and subtle geometry, Koloman Moser's idealized Art Nouveau-style image for 'Fromme's Kalender' is emblematic of the pioneering spirit of the Vienna Secession. The poster, which shows a goddess holding a snake ring and an hourglass (symbols of time's eternal cycle), was highly popular and was reprinted every year from 1899 to 1914 in different color combinations, to promote Albert Berger, a Viennese printer.

As the background was altered from one unmodulated shade to another, the colors of the different elements were adjusted, creating unexpected changes of mood. This dynamism was emphasized by the diagonal composition of the square image, with its dark silhouette on one side, and illuminated profile and sacred implements on the other.
The poster's striking character is also partly due to its proportions, which are formed by a perfect square above a rectangular panel, on which is inscribed, in capital letters, the name of the calendar.
The typography, with its handsome capital letterforms, is reminiscent of the stylized handwriting used by architects, such as Frank Lloyd Wright and Charles Rennie Mackintosh, and indicates the influence of these figures over Vienna Secession artists.

In comparison with Henri de Toulouse-Lautrec's famous 1893 poster "Aristide Bruant," with which it shares certain features (the black silhouette, strong profile, and vigorous sense of line), Moser's work is considerably more formalized and abstract—a prelude to modernism rather than a product of nineteenth-century pictorial tradition. Even though it is not necessarily the most innovative poster designed by Moser and other Secession artists, such as Josef Hoffmann, Alfred Roller, or Gustav Klimt, 'Fromme's Kalender' endures to this day as a beloved cultural icon.

← P.46

1900

ECKMANNSCHRIFT

Typeface

Otto Eckmann (1865–1902)

Rudhard Type Foundry, Germany

Otto Eckmann designed Eckmannschrift for Karl Klingspor at the Rudhard Type Foundry, the first German foundry to commission original typefaces by contemporary artists. Issued in 1900, the typeface extended lettering experiments begun by Eckmann in his book-cover designs and display work for Jugendstil journals, such as *Jugend*, *Pan* and *Die Woche*, and was immediately adopted by printers for a range of decorative uses.

Like many of his contemporaries who were inspired by modern modes of production to seek new forms of art, Eckmann had renounced painting in order to focus on graphic and typographic design. Drawn with a brush, the letterforms he prepared for the Rudhard Type Foundry recast a medieval construction in the organic shapes of Art Nouveau. At a time when German designers and critics were defending the symbolism of their nation's continued use of Fraktur (a German variant of blackletter) and debating its aesthetic and functional values relative to those of roman typefaces, Eckmann's design sought to combine and refresh the two sources.

Eliminating customary flourishes, Eckmann's letters retain Fraktur's calligraphic expression, which enlivens their otherwise consistent simplicity. In this respect, his design may seem to echo William Morris's Troy typeface (1892), which surrounds the openness of roman letterforms with simplified Gothic strokes. More specifically, Eckmannschrift's hearty rhythm exemplifies Art Nouveau's tendency to vary in style according to the different national and folk traditions to which it laid claim, even as its flowing forms proclaimed a freedom from academic or historical precedent.

Eckmann died of tuberculosis just two years after Eckmannschrift was issued. With the transition to modernism, Eckmannschrift's aesthetic response to industrial production was soon replaced by more streamlined (sans serif) forms. Yet its expressive bends and flares have survived several technological generations, to be rendered, most recently, in digital form.

← P.46

1900–present

MICHELIN GUIDE

Book

André Michelin (1853–1931)

Michelin, France

With its *Guide Michelin*, the French tire company pioneered the concept of "service." Conceived as a marketing tool that for the first twenty years was distributed free of charge, the little red handbook listed more than two thousand French towns, indiscriminately logging tire dealers, mechanics, gasoline stations, bicycle shops, hardware stores (where you could buy replacement parts), hotels (one per town only), post offices and railway stations. It also featured a dozen key city maps, a forty-page car and tire maintenance manual with scores of technical drawings, and a comprehensive roster of regulations and ordinances concerning motor vehicles.

The layout was smartly conceived. The many small headings, set in Bodoni extra bold extended, stood in sharp contrast to the wide letter spacing of the roman body type. The text was a landmark accomplishment in terms of legibility, a necessity given the reading conditions in which the guide was intended for use. Prominently displayed on the cover of the first issue was a drawing of what looked like a large badge. In fact, it was the cross section of a tire with a removable inner tube, a Michelin invention patented in 1891 for bicycles and adapted to cars four years later. Michelin claimed that it took hours to repair ordinary tires, whereas theirs took only three minutes. In reality, removing the inner tube from its casing and replacing it inside was so painstaking that each step had to be explained with exacting precision inside the guide. These illustrated diagrams, in the tradition of Denis Diderot's *Encyclopédie*, were detailed engravings of amazing elegance.

Even though the content of the early red guides was prosaic, it nevertheless helped to pave the way for what they would later become. Indeed, once French roads were better surfaced and travel became easier, the Michelin editors turned their attention, with the same punctiliousness, toward the evaluation of levels of comfort, excellence of cuisine, pleasantness of view, and price ranges of roadside facilities and services. From being not much larger than a passport, the *Guide Michelin* has grown to acquire the size, bulk and, for serious travelers, the authority of a bible.

← P.47

c. 1900

COMBINAISONS ORNEMENTALES

Book

Alphonse Mucha (1860–1939), Maurice-Pillard Verneuil (1869–1942), Georges Auriol (1863–1938)

Librairie Centrale des Beaux-Arts, France

A *fin-de-siècle* pattern book, *Combinaisons Ornementales* aims to celebrate Art Nouveau's versatility by demonstrating how its sumptuous visual language can be connected to real life. The book offers quick, straightforward and practical solutions for contemporary decorators under increasing pressure to offer new motifs and designs. The images provided can be customized, then traced or copied and applied to everyday decorative needs. The key to the book's purpose lies in the diagram at the beginning, which explains how to use hinged mirrors to create unexpected combinations and variations of shape, geometry, color, and scale; indeed, the book is often subtitled "se multipliant à l'infini à l'aide du miroir" (infinite multiplication with the aid of a mirror). Hence, the pages' contents are not particularly useful until liberated and transformed by mirrors.

With no supporting text apart from the instructions at the beginning, the book consists essentially of fifty-eight full-page, three-color lithographic plates, the majority of which are by Maurice-Pillard Verneuil, with others by Georges Auriol and Alphonse Mucha. It is generally hard to distinguish between the artists' works, although broadly speaking, Auriol's shapes are more graceful and Mucha's more intricate than those of the less inhibited Verneuil. All three were Art Nouveau painters, designers, and writers, whereas Auriol was also a typographer and typeface designer. Each plate has a different frame and page-number style, and most motifs are discernibly natural, if fanciful: peacock feathers in unlikely combinations, stylized wildflowers among frames of berries and leaves, beetles, sea horses, birds, and butterflies, as well as abstract swirling lines and the occasional satyr. In largely muted tones of brown, orange, sage, mustard, gray, blue, black, red, yellow, and green, the book's samples are a delightful treasury of potential.

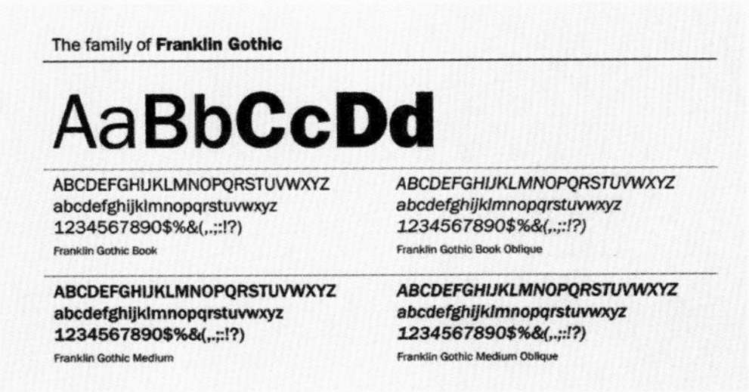

← P.48

← P.48

CITROËN

← P.49

1902

FRANKLIN GOTHIC

Typeface

Morris Fuller Benton (1872–1948)

American Type Founders, U.S.

By the time Morris Fuller Benton was appointed chief designer in 1901, the American Type Founders (ATF) was already the largest commercial foundry in the world. Established in 1892 from the incorporation of twenty-three small foundries dedicated to the manufacture and distribution of metal type, the ATF sold some of the most popular typefaces of the twentieth century, many of them commonly used today.

Franklin Gothic, often referred to as "the patriarch of American Gothics," is one of the ATF's best-known faces. Named after American president Benjamin Franklin and designed by Benton in 1902, it joined the foundry's specimen books in 1905. Despite possibly drawing inspiration from the Berthold Type Foundry's 1896 Akzidenz-Grotesk (Franklin Gothic's European counterpart in terms of fame and enduring use), it is considered in its own right as a successful, modernized version of early traditional wood letters. Capturing the bulky, monotone look of nineteenth-century American typefaces—with its round, thick strokes and subtly contrasting narrow stems—its letterforms maintain a calligraphic, individual quality, as expressed in its wide, square capitals, and its roman lowercase letters transformed into sans serif faces, such as its signature two-story "a" and "g."

The designer of more than 220 typefaces for the ATF, Benton is both one of the U.S.'s most prolific type designers and one of its unsung heroes. His many Gothics and sans serifs—which included News and Alternate Gothic—catered to the growing demand for display advertising typefaces. Franklin Gothic was no exception, and proved to be so popular at the time that Benton soon cut other weights—condensed (1905), extended (1906), and italic (1913)—to add to the typeface's versatility and to meet customer demand.

Franklin Gothic later survived the impact of geometric sans serifs, such as Futura, which dominated commercial design and advertising from the mid-1920s to the 1950s. The font is still widely used today, and is favored by newspaper and magazine designers for its charismatic headline appeal and no-nonsense legibility.

1903

PERRIER

Logo

St. John Harmsworth (1876–c. 1932)

Société des Eaux Minérales, Boissons et Produits Hygiéniques de Vergèze, France

Perrier's distinctive logo embodies both an iconic mineral-water brand and a certain idea of France itself. Unchanged since its first appearance, the trademark has been a constant presence in print and television advertising and, more recently, in Internet campaigns, where it has often played with its own history.

Perrier was named after Dr. Louis Perrier, who bought a small spa in which patients could recuperate by drinking mineral waters. In 1903 the spa was sold to St. John Harmsworth, a British investor whose ties to England and its colonies opened the way for Perrier's export around the world. Eager to link the water to its French origins, Harmsworth maintained the name of the product and developed a design for the logo using typography typical of French advertisements—lowercase serif letters in white with an embellished initial "P," forming a gentle arc, the whole set off against the green of the label, which is held by downward-curving arms to accentuate the shape of the bottle. The bottle itself was inspired by clubs used in India for strength training, which were popular in Victorian England. Harmsworth, who exercised with the clubs, hoped that the shape would link the drink in consumers' minds with wellbeing and health. The green glass bottles are produced in the same town of Vergèze, southern France, where the water itself is sourced, leading some to call the color "Perrier green."

The subsidiary text on the label, yellow to contrast with the green, has changed over time, according to different advertising campaigns (such as "Perrier, c'est fou," [Perrier, It's Crazy] or "l'eau, l'air, la vie" [Water, Air, Life]), and the logo itself has been periodically reworked: in the 1930s and '40s by French illustrators such as Luc-Albert Moreau and Jean-Gabriel Domergue, and by Salvador Dalí in 1969 for a full-page advertisement in *Le Figaro*. In 2006, an Internet campaign launched by Ogilvy & Mather substituted the "Perrier" text on the label with words such as "Sexier," "Crazier," and "Flirtier." These tactics reveal advertisers' faith in the enduring power of the label to withstand such interventions.

1903

CITROËN

Logo

André Citroën (1878–1935)

Citroën, France

The Citroën double chevron has provided France's best-known automobile company with a logo that is both inseparable from the brand and exceptional for its versatility. The current red-and-white version, which dates to 1985, is just one of numerous incarnations that have appeared since Engrenages Citroën, a small gear manufacturing factory in Paris, adopted a blue-and-yellow herringbone as its trademark in 1903.

Central to the story is the discovery, by André Citroën, that a particular double-helical gear design used in Poland to grind flour, vastly improved the gearboxes of engines, particularly in cars. In 1900, at only twenty-two years of age, André immediately applied for a patent, and today, thanks to the slanted angle of its gear teeth, the clutch used not only in Citroën cars but in most vehicles on the road can be changed smoothly and effortlessly. What is not clear, however, is why the chevrons point upward. One theory is that Citroën was a Freemason, and that the herringbone was an allusion to the Masonic compass, one of the two architect's tools represented on the Masonic icon. As official-looking as sergeant stripes, the two triangular forms featured prominently on the front of early Citroën models, such as the Traction Avant (1934) and the 2CV (1948), whereas 1950s classics, like the sleek DS series, sported only two small gilded chevrons on the back, leaving the cars' curvaceous hoods as smooth and unblemished as pebbles.

Today, the trademark is integrated into the design of Citroën cars, its distinctive dented profile merging with the aerodynamic lines of the bodywork. On the 2007 C-Crossover model, the "winged" chevrons look like two slender chrome handlebars separating the hood from the air intake, which requires that each chevron is mounted onto a different car part, one hot (next to the engine) and the other cold (next to the venting system). Such innovations demonstrate the lengths to which Citroën designers are prepared to go to keep the company's famous chevron symbol perennially alive and fresh.

← P.49

← P.50

← P.51

1903–1905

DOVES PRESS BIBLE

Book

Thomas James Cobden-Sanderson (1840–1922), Edward Johnston (1872–1944)

Doves Press, UK

With their famous Bible, Thomas James Cobden-Sanderson and the engraver and typographer Emery Walker of the Doves Press set out to create a book whose beauty was dependent on typography alone. Having already established the Doves Bindery, they set up the Doves Press in Hammersmith, London, in 1900, along similar lines to William Morris's Kelmscott Press situated close by, with the aim of restoring the relationship between typography and calligraphy. From 1900 to 1917 the Doves Press produced some fifty titles, all in a similar layout, but the Bible was their masterpiece.

For this edition, Cobden-Sanderson cut a new roman typeface, known as Doves Type, based on a fifteenth-century Venetian model used by Nicolas Jenson, and took on the calligrapher Edward Johnston to hand-draw some initial letters. In the final publication the words are printed with immense care on handmade paper, with no ornaments or illustrations to detract from the beauty of the words. The justified text was positioned within classically proportioned margins and closely set. To regulate color, ampersands were employed, when required, to even out spacing between words, along with paragraph marks rather than indents to rid the text of horizontal white space. Moreover, to compensate for Jenson's overly large capitals, each chapter begins with one of Johnston's initial letters, such as the extended "I" that opens Genesis, which have a beautiful form and color, and an enlarged, all-uppercase opening line followed by four lines set in text-size capitals. The overall result is a page of great beauty and control that has the austerity of Baskerville or Bodoni. The five large quarto volumes that comprise the total publication are a monument to dignity and restraint, and were influential in reforming typography during the early twentieth century in both Europe and the U.S.

Predominant among those who drew inspiration from the Doves Press were Bernard Henry Newdigate of the Arden Press and C. H. St. John Hornby at the Ashendene Press. In Germany, the Doves Press model influenced public presses such as Leipzig's Insel Verlag, which produced inexpensive yet well-printed editions of German classics, with calligraphy by Johnston and Eric Gill.

1903

SECESSION 16. AUSSTELLUNG

Poster

Alfred Roller (1864–1935)

Vienna Secession, Austria

Alfred Roller's poster for the sixteenth Vienna Secession exhibition, like many designed by members of the Secession group, pushed the boundaries of abstraction to extremes, particularly in its use of stylistic letterforms. Roller was an important figure of the Vienna Secession, producing murals and exhibition settings, editing and illustrating its journal, *Ver Sacrum* (*Sacred Spring*), and designing posters for four exhibitions. As the newly elected president, he used a fragment of his own mural decoration, *Sinking Night*, as the basis for his 1902 poster design for the fourteenth Secession exhibition.

Founded in April 1897, the Vienna Secession consisted of like-minded artists, including Gustav Klimt, Koloman Moser, Joseph Maria Olbrich, and Roller himself, who formed the group in protest against the artistic conservatism of the Künstlerhaus, the Viennese Fine Arts Academy. Klimt, the group's first president, designed the poster for the first Secession exhibition of March 1898, heralding a long series of similar events, each publicized by a poster created by a Secession member. A new purpose-built exhibition gallery, designed by Olbrich, housed their second show, and also featured in the poster in the form of a drawing.

The exhibition this poster advertises was the Secession artists' most ambitious to date, and brought together a large collection of French Impressionist and Post-Impressionist works. However, Roller's long narrow notice makes no reference to the exhibition theme, instead taking the form of an abstract design dominated by vigorous stylized lettering. The three "S"s from the word "Secession" sweep down in a dramatic whiplash through a space entirely filled with the group's heraldic emblem of three blank shields, underpinned at the base by an area of ornamental black text announcing details of opening times. Although almost indecipherable, the letterform is simple and skillfully crafted, and echoes contemporary Art Nouveau typefaces.

In later years Roller's poster would become a major influence on 1960s psychedelic posters produced by San Francisco designers, particularly Wes Wilson. Roller also established a reputation as a theatrical set designer, forming a close association with Gustav Mahler.

1903

WIENER WERKSTÄTTE

Logo

Josef Hoffmann (1870–1956), Koloman Moser (1868–1918)

Wiener Werkstätte, Austria

Launched in 1903 by Josef Hoffmann and Koloman Moser, the Wiener Werkstätte (Viennese Workshop) emphasized utility, symmetry, and authenticity in materials—values clearly embodied in the organization's two trademarks. As objects of graphic design, the marks helped to promulgate the Wiener Werkstätte's philosophy, borrowed from William Morris, of placing art and craft on an even plane; they are heavily reminiscent of traditional woodblock prints, a craft that the Werkstätte promoted and supported.

Originally members of the Wiener Künstlerhaus (the Viennese Creative Artists' Association), Hoffmann and Moser, along with fellow artist Gustav Klimt and the architect Joseph Maria Olbrich, resigned from the association because of ideological disagreements with its leaders, subsequently establishing the Sezessionstil, or Vienna Secession, in 1897. Like the Glasgow School, the Secession offered a counterpoint to French and German Art Nouveau, based on sans serif lettering and rectilinear, geometric design.

The first emblem designed to represent the organization, a rectangle divided into two squares, which in turn are subdivided into further geometrical shapes, served as the Werkstätte's registered trademark. The lower square evoked the essential geometry of a flower, relating the natural world to that of logic, craft, and business. The Werkstätte's second trademark (pictured in the poster here) was applied to its products. The design plays with formal relationships, interlocking the two "W"s of the organization's name to form a third "W." The design can therefore be read as a symbol for the merging of Hoffmann and Moser's work to create a third and greater enterprise. The sign particularly recalls Moser's personal monogram, thus binding his personal and professional interests.

The significance of the Wiener Werkstätte logos lies in both the simplicity and elegance of the designs and in their representation of a highly influential institution that played an important role in promoting graphic design. Among other things, the Werkstätte designed postcards, bookplates, menus, logos, and advertising, lending new visual standards to these previously uninspired products.

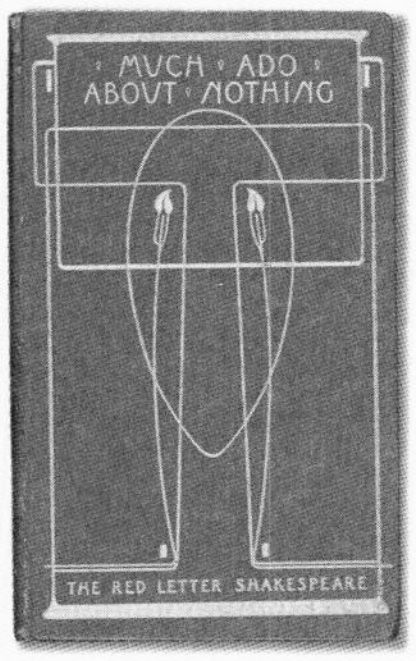

← P.52

← P.53

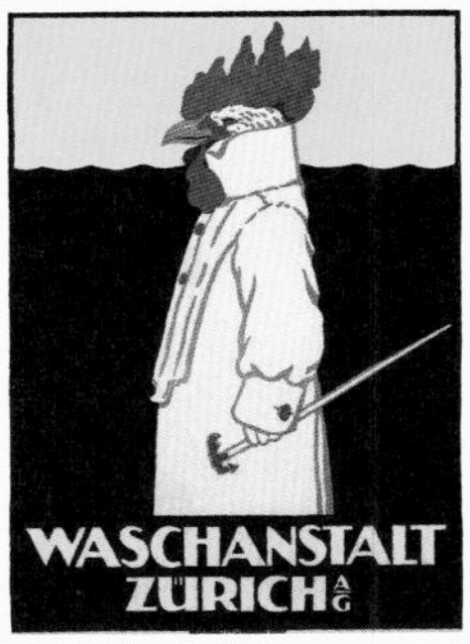

← P.53

1904–1908

THE RED LETTER SHAKESPEARE

Book

Talwin Morris (1865–1911)

Blackie & Son Ltd., UK

Blackie & Son launched the Red Letter Shakespeare series at a time when increasing levels of literacy—and corresponding rises in demand for affordable editions of the classics—coincided with technological developments that enabled well-made books to be produced more economically.

Appointed art director at Blackie's to develop the artistic image of their books, Talwin Morris, an associate of Charles Rennie Mackintosh and an acclaimed designer in his own right, was uniquely placed to challenge traditional taste and provide a mass audience with ordinary pocket books designed to be objects of beauty. Beauty, in terms of the Glasgow Style, was expressed in a graceful arrangement of space, based on a strong framework of fluid, linear verticals, often combined with organic forms or mystical Celtic symbols. In the Red Letter Shakespeare series these elements are intrinsic to the basic pattern reiterated throughout each book. The cover, spine, endpapers, half-title, and title pages, and even the rubricated initial capital of the introduction, are all decorated with variations of an ellipse, which usually consists of an egg shape intertwined with curved stems, suspended within a sinuous architectural outline of overlapping panels.

The unity of the series' covers was enhanced by Morris's idiosyncratic hand-lettering and the fixed proportions of the pattern's upper panel, which allow for titles of different lengths, providing a visually pleasing and commercially effective design solution. Three variants were published: a red leatherette binding stamped in gold, a red cloth binding, and a white cloth binding blocked in sage and vermilion published by Blackie's subsidiary, the Gresham Publishing Company. The version illustrated here, produced for a wealthier market, retained only some of the design elements; the title page is as orthodox as the tastes of the customers at which the Gresham editions were aimed.

The standardized format—used with much success for the World's Classics (Oxford University Press, from 1901) and Everyman's Library (Dent, from 1906)—both facilitated cheaper production and strengthened visual identity. In Morris's hands, however, it also familiarized the book-buying public with good design.

c. 1904

BAYER

Logo

Disputed

Farbenfabriken vormals Friedrich Bayer & Co., Germany

One of the oldest trademarks still in use today, the Bayer logo—a cross composed of the letters of the company name inside a circle—is a powerful example of a simple and functional graphic design that creates an immediate association with the brand and its product.

According to one account, the mark was created by one Hans Schneider, an employee in Bayer's scientific department, who wrote "Bayer" twice on a sheet of paper, the two words intersecting at the "Y," during a meeting in 1900. Another holds that a Dr. Schweizer, who sold Bayer products in the U.S. during the 1890s, devised a stamp with the mark for use on letterheads because the full company name, Farbenfabriken vormals Friedrich Bayer & Co., impeded business. The first explanation is generally thought to be more plausible. Whatever the truth of its origin, the new trademark gradually replaced the original logo, which depicted a lion with the grid on which Saint Lawrence was martyred, a design based on the coat of arms of Elberfeld, Germany, where Bayer was based at the time. From 1910, the logo was embossed on Bayer's aspirin tablets, which were sold unpackaged through pharmacists and doctors. After World War I, Bayer's assets, including the rights to its name and trademark, were confiscated, but by the mid-twentieth century the company had reappeared, and in 1994 it reclaimed the rights to the Bayer name and cross (modernized and adapted to their present form in 1919).

An illuminated version of the logo (236 feet 3 inches [72 m] in diameter) sits on top of Bayer's headquarters in Leverkusen, Germany, where it was originally installed in 1933, demonstrating that, unlike many trademarks, the design works equally well at widely divergent scales. Despite the longevity and adaptability of the trademark, in 2002 an updated version was introduced, adding two colors—blue and green—to the circle, to create a more three-dimensional effect, particularly on packaging. Although it is common practice for trademarks to adapt as production technology changes, it is ironic that this highly successful logo should have lost its original clarity.

1905

WASCHANSTALT ZÜRICH AG

Poster

Robert Hardmeyer (1876–1919)

Waschanstalt Zürich AG, Switzerland

A cockerel prepares to strut his stuff for a night out on the town. Aiming to impress the hens, he dons a smart, freshly laundered and starched tuxedo shirt with a high collar, its red buttons matching his fiery comb. This highly surreal poster for Waschanstalt Zürich, a Swiss laundry firm, was a sensation on its launch, and its designer, Robert Hardmeyer, was credited with a key role in the revival of Swiss poster design.

However, Hardmeyer's contribution to Swiss graphic design almost passed unnoticed. Originally trained as a landscape painter, Hardmeyer took commercial jobs to supplement his work illustrating children's books, designing posters only when he needed to eke out a living. Indeed, his image of a cockerel carrying a walking stick was never specifically designed for Waschanstalt Zürich. Johann E. Wolfensberger, the poster's printer, has related how Hardmeyer came into his studio in 1904 with a rough watercolor sketch from which he created a lithographic print, after adding several features to the image, including black and yellow bands to the background.

It is likely that Wolfensberger bought Hardmeyer's drawing for use in future projects. Some time after the original print was made, Waschanstalt Zürich commissioned Wolfensberger to create a poster advertisement. The laundry company selected Hardmeyer's image, possibly for the stark whiteness of the cockerel's shirt against the dark background. The printer cropped the shirt, tightened up the outlines, and added the firm's name below the picture. This practice was not unusual. Lithographic printers had an enormous influence on the design of their products, altering posters as they saw fit, and the printer's imprint held precedence over any designer's signature. Indeed, Hardmeyer's signature was omitted from the final design, and his death was largely unremarked upon.

Despite this, Hardmeyer's striking design became so strongly etched in the public memory that, forty years after his death, he was hailed as a "master of poster design" at a poster exhibition in the Museum of Applied Arts in Zurich in 1959. Hardmeyer's image of the gentleman cockerel was used as an emblem by Waschanstalt Zürich for well over a century.

← P.54

1905

PRIESTER

Poster

Lucian Bernhard (1883–1972)

Priester, Germany

In this exceptionally sparse poster consisting of just two matchsticks and a brand name, the elements are realized with the simplest of means: four flat colors to render basic, somewhat abstracted, shapes. In its reduced character, the design recalls the earlier work of the Beggarstaffs, who also rendered objects as flat color shapes.

Bernhard's original intention was to become a poet, and the poster, rather than being the outcome of a lengthy development process, was a hastily completed entry for a competition. The original sketches were considerably more detailed (including a cigar and dancing girls), but when a friend mistook the poster for an advertisement for cigars, Bernhard began removing its superfluous elements. His final solution communicates its message swiftly and efficiently, regardless of culture or language. Indeed, it could be seen as a demonstration of the principle of Occam's razor—the notion that (other things being equal) simplicity is always preferable to complexity. When translated into the sphere of graphic design, such an approach (prevalent through much of the twentieth century) embodies the belief that the less "visual noise," the clearer and more effective the message.

Compositionally, the heads of the two matches, with their bright coloring and tone, are the most salient parts of the poster, drawing the viewer's attention toward the brand name in a manner similar to Bernhard's later poster for Stiller, designed in 1912. This simple juxtaposition of object and word became known as *Sachplakat* (object poster), and was explored by other designers such as Hans Rudi Erdt. Both Bernhard and Erdt were under contract to the Berlin printing firm Hollerbaum and Schmidt; their work provided the impetus for what has since been termed *Plakatstil* (poster style), of which Bernhard's "Priester" was the first example.

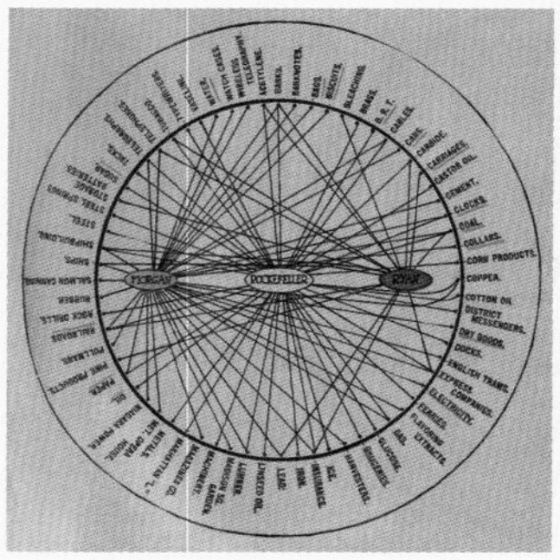

← P.55

1906

WHO GETS YOUR MONEY ("RING OF POWER")

Information Design

John Campbell Cory (1867–1925)

Joseph Pulitzer, U.S.

In John Campbell Cory's 1912 book, *The Cartoonist's Art*, he exhorted aspiring illustrators to use a strong central subject "to bring home your point at a glance." Contrary to his advice, in this diagram from the June 24, 1906 edition of the *New York World* newspaper, Campbell delivered a multifocal, muckraking information graphic.

As an illustrator, a designer, and a headline letterer for Joseph Pulitzer's hugely popular periodical, Cory fully subscribed to the paper's anticorruption and populist agenda. The names inside the diagram belong to the reigning American industrial titans of the day: J. P. Morgan, John D. Rockefeller, and Thomas F. Ryan. Every manner of contemporary product and service, including biscuits, collars, and wireless telegraphy, rings the outside of the circle. Each is connected to at least one—sometimes all three—of the moguls, indicating a monopolistic web that the common man (Citizen Jones, in the paper's accompanying narrative) cannot go through his day without incessantly paying out to in terms of his consumption patterns.

The information-design yield in this illustration is high, inscribing a complex series of associations into a dense circle. In today's detailed taxonomies of information schema, this is a radial diagram in form and a network diagram in function. Strictly relational, it also avoids any indications of quantity. In his cartoons, Campbell was a traditional, though talented, caricaturist. In this unique specimen of economic diagramming, he presaged more sophisticated directions for information design, staking out formal and conceptual territory for much later artists, such as Mark Lombardi, who created intricate models of geopolitical and economic influence. Cory's expression of the same concerns from his era feels remarkably modern.

The author Nicholson Baker and his wife Margaret Brentano rescued this graphic, and many other treasures from the *New York World* that would otherwise have been lost to obscurity, in their book *The World on Sunday*, published in 2005.

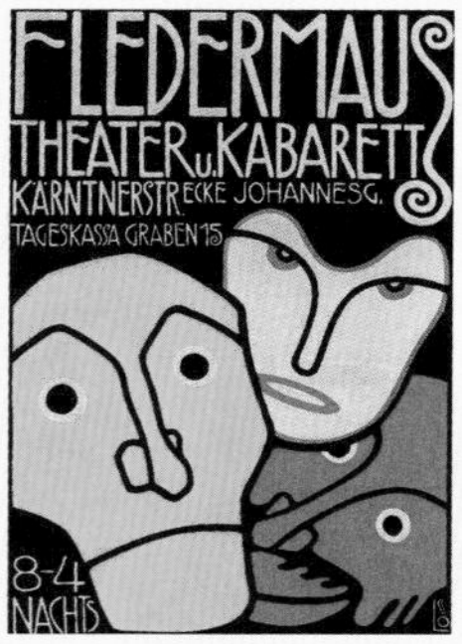

← P.56

1907

DIE FLEDERMAUS

Poster

Berthold Löffler (1874–1960)

Cabaret Fledermaus, Austria

The Cabaret Fledermaus, at Kärtnerstrasse 33 in Vienna, opened in 1907 with the goal of reviving the "nearly forgotten original conception of cabaret, by using artistic principles of its very own, to refurbish this conception, extend it, and develop it without paying any attention to the many ways in which it has been misapplied ever since it made its first appearance..." The cabaret was viewed as an integral work of art by the Wiener Werkstätte (Viennese Workshop)—whose major patron, Fritz Wärndorfer, instigated the opening of the cabaret—with all elements from the building to its lighting and tableware specially designed. Josef Hoffmann was responsible for the theater, auditorium, and tableware, while Berthold Löffler designed two colored panels for the auditorium and with Michael Powolny (his partner in the Wiener Keramik) created a wall mosaic of nearly seven thousand majolica tiles.

Löffler's brochure cover and poster for the opening of the Cabaret Fledermaus, with its areas of simple flat color defined by thick black lines, was a radical departure from the ornately decorative posters of the Vienna Secession. The lettering is sans serif, although it is not particularly organic or free-flowing—with the exception of the "E," "F," and most notably the "S" in "FLEDERMAUS." The crossbars of the "E" and "F" are subtly curved, while the "S" descends in a spiral that not only helps the long word fit into the space as a single line but also draws the eye toward the pair of masks. The poster was subsequently reproduced as a Wiener Werkstätte postcard.

Löffler's "Die Fledermaus" poster differed from the contemporary *Sachplakat* (object posters) of German expressionist designers, such as Lucian Bernhard and Ludwig Hohlwein. However, it had equally broken away from the solemn symbolism entrenched in the Vienna Secession, functioning in its simplicity as an important bridge between these movements.

← P.57

1907

AEG

Identity

Peter Behrens (1868–1940)

Allgemeine Elektricitäts-Gesellschaft, Germany

Peter Behrens's original honeycomb logo for the electronics company Allgemeine Elektricitäts-Gesellschaft (AEG) combined a sense of beehive activity and complexity with order, rationalism, and prudence. Although the trademark has since changed, the typeface remains in use today.

In 1907 Emil Rathenau, visionary director of AEG, hired Behrens to be the company's artistic advisor. Behrens was a founding member of the newly created Deutscher Werkbund, an association of designers, architects, and industrialists that advocated "the marriage of art with technology," a philosophy that formed part of their belief in *Gesamtkultur* (complete culture)—a new and universal man-made culture. Instead of confining themselves to one object at a time, Werkbund members sought to rationalize design into systems that would unite multiple ingredients into an orderly and coherent whole.

Behrens's work for AEG put the Werkbund's philosophy of unification to the test. Behrens redesigned the AEG logo surrounded by the honeycomb motif and, instead of the Art Nouveau type styles popular in his day, chose roman serif capitals to convey clarity and stability. Under the influence of J. L. Mathieu Lauweriks's studies in geometric composition, Behrens also created what is now known as the "grid," the underlying geometrical structure that orders the arrangement of graphic materials. He would redesign the logo again in 1912 using the same type, but stripped the design of its hexagonal format and laid the initials out on a horizontal plane.

Behrens's influence went beyond the company's trademark, however. As advisor to AEG, he was also responsible for advertising campaigns, product designs, and architecture. The advertisements he created, such as his 1910 "AEG Metallfadenlampe" poster (pictured), combined with his revisions of the logo, constituted what may have been the earliest known corporate identity program. Fifty years later, his achievement in harmonizing all aspects of AEG's visual identity helped to establish the basic elements of such programs: a logo, uniform typeface, and standardized formats. By unifying AEG's communications, Behrens, perhaps more than anyone, can be said to have invented corporate design.

← P.58

1908

CONFECTION KEHL

Poster

Ludwig Hohlwein (1874–1949)

PKZ, Switzerland

At the time Ludwig Hohlwein designed the masterful poster (pictured) for the Swiss men's clothing company PKZ (an acronym for Paul Kehl, the company founder, and Zurich, the city where the clothes were produced), he was just beginning to establish a reputation as a poster artist in his native Munich. Like his German contemporary Lucian Bernhard, Hohlwein's formative influence was the pioneering advertising work of the English graphic designers the Beggarstaffs, whose posters were renowned for their bold flat shapes. The decorative character of the three shadowy figures in the poster was to become the hallmark of Hohlwein's future work.

The scene implies that the smartly dressed man in the foreground—with a sporty style, sturdy footwear, and leather strap across the chest suggesting he is at a racetrack—is wearing clothes purchased from the PKZ store in Lucerne. The driver of the horse-drawn carriage is also wearing a PKZ outfit. Both figures are dressed in a suit and coat shown as flat patterned shapes, with tailoring absent. Their facial features are radically simplified, accentuated by the shadows cast by the hats of the wearers—all characteristics of Hohlwein's work in the period. The text is confined to a box, allowing it to be changed without affecting the design as a whole. This was one of the first posters commissioned by the company, heralding a fertile period when PKZ patronized emerging European artistic talent.

Hohlwein, who is known to have been a keen horseman and often included horses in his designs, began his career as an interior designer and architect, but subsequently turned to graphic art, making his mark as one of the most prolific and influential poster artists of the twentieth century. In 1913 *Das Plakat*, a journal devoted to poster design, dedicated an entire issue to his work.

← P.58

1908

ALSO SPRACH ZARATHUSTRA

Book

Henry van de Velde (1863–1957)

Insel Verlag, Germany

Henry van de Velde's title page for a new edition of Nietzsche's *Also Sprach Zarathustra* (*Thus Spoke Zarathustra*) is an outstanding example of Art Nouveau graphic design by one of the movement's founders. The book's design represented an attempt to reconcile traditional arts and crafts with modern industry and commerce, one of the missions of the Deutscher Werkbund, an association of artists, architects, and manufacturers to which van de Velde belonged.

Influenced by William Morris and the English Arts and Crafts movement, van de Velde, a Belgian architect, sought to rediscover the skill and beauty of the decorative arts in all spheres, and to establish a new style that championed ornamental patterns. As a member of the Werkbund, however, he aimed to combine this aesthetic with contemporary mechanical printing technologies. His design for *Also Sprach Zarathustra*, a seminal work that presented Nietzsche's ideas on morality, religion, and other philosophical topics, amalgamated van de Velde's own Art Nouveau style with a mass-produced publication. Van de Velde conceived the project as a *Gesamtkunstwerk*, or total work of art, designing not only the title page but also the binding, endpapers, and a series of gold ornaments on the inside pages. In its final form, the publication was reminiscent of medieval illuminated manuscripts; the title page in particular, with its elaborate geometries, rich color palette, and integral title composed of serif capitals, celebrated the values of pattern and ornamental complexity in book design.

The importance of Nietzsche's text, which was already well established, added to the impact of the design and helped disseminate van de Velde's graphic style throughout Europe.

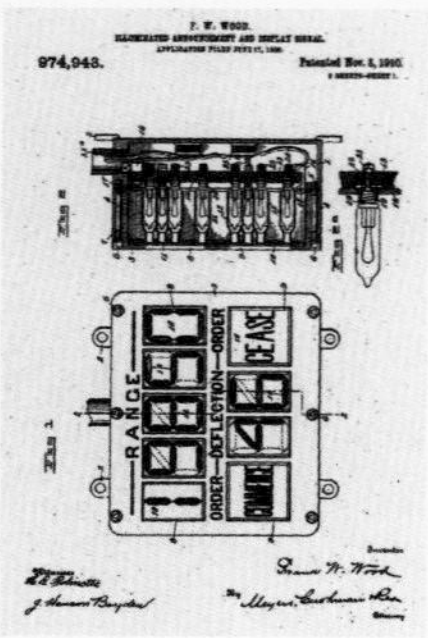

← P.58

← P.59

← P.60

1908

SEVEN-SEGMENT DISPLAY

Typeface

Frank W. Wood (n.d.)

Self-commissioned, U.S.

Ubiquitous in the 1970s and still prevalent today, seven-segment display technology is a method of showing Arabic numerals and is a precursor to dot-matrix systems. These recognizable digital forms have been used in a wide range of everyday mechanical devices, from timepieces and calculators to train-station flip-disc boards and electromagnetic vane indicators at gas stations. As the name indicates, ciphers are formed by seven elements which, when positioned at right angles to each other, can be turned on and off to form the numerals 0–9, as well as the uppercase ("A," "B," "C," "E," "F," "H," "I," "J," "L," "O," "P," "S," "U," "Y," "Z") and lowercase ("a," "b," "c," "d," "e," "g," "h," "i," "n," "ñ," "o," "q," "r," "t," "u") letters of the Latin alphabet.

First filed for patent in 1908 by the inventor Frank W. Wood as an eight-segment display (where an extra diagonal bar was included as the number four) for use in military devices, the more common seven-segment display was not widely used for another fifty years, appearing only on analog electromagnetic vane indicators. From 1965 Monsanto continued the development of light-emitting diodes (LEDs), which became commercially available in consumer electronics in 1968, marking the point at which the world saw the full cultural impact of seven-segment display. Early computers switched from complex Dekatron (1940s) and Nixie (1952) glass tube displays to the new system, and in the 1970s, with the further development of liquid crystal displays (LCDs) and vacuum fluorescent displays (VFDs), seven-segment display appeared on all kinds of personal electronics.

Today, seven-segment display represents one of the most functional and legible uses of type. Although antiquated, the style is still used by typographers as a point of inspiration, most notably the British type designer Alan Birch, who created the "LCD" font family in 1981. In doing so, he revived the eighth-line segment from the 1908 patent. The fact that, despite technological advancements, seven-segment is still in use as a graphic display today testifies to its functional legacy.

1908

BAUMWOLLPFLÜCKERIN

Poster

Oskar Kokoschka (1886–1980)

Kunstschau, Austria

The *Kunstschau* (Art Show) exhibition of 1908 in Vienna presented a mixture of art and design, including paintings, interior design, and theater arts. This combination of different media was reflected in the prolific career of Oskar Kokoschka, who designed this poster for the event while he was still a student at Vienna's Kunstgewerbeschule (School of Arts and Crafts).

Prior to World War I, Vienna was a flourishing cultural center, home to artists, composers, and pioneering figures such as Sigmund Freud. The Symbolist painter Gustav Klimt, an important influence on Kokoschka at the time, displayed some of his best-known works in the *Kunstschau*, most notably *The Kiss* (1907–8). Kokoschka's poster for the exhibition, entitled "Baumwollpflückerin" (The Cotton Picker), is designed in a bold Jugendstil manner, distinguished by its use of angular lines and integration of figure and strong sans serif lettering into the decorative picture surface, both of which reflect the mosaiclike style of Klimt. The poster was printed as a color lithograph, a widely used medium at the time that was particularly suitable for creating vibrant designs.

The cotton picker herself, made up of a series of jutting lines that nevertheless suggest a dreamy and tender quality as she reaches for a ball of cotton, conveys tranquility against a busy backdrop. In this respect the poster makes a stark contrast with the poster for Kokoschka's play "Murderer, Hope of Women," shown in the following year's *Internationale Kunstschau*. Here, the anguished, morbid central figure echoes the classic subject of the *Pietà*, anticipating the work of later artists, such as Francis Bacon.

Kokoschka's "Baumwollpflückerin" poster captures an early moment in the artist's career when he was starting to build an independent visual language and experimenting with different styles and imagery.

1908

ZERMATT MATTERHORN

Poster

Emil Cardinaux (1877–1936)

Zermatt Tourist Board, Switzerland

Emil Cardinaux's commanding image of Zermatt's famous Matterhorn is widely considered to be the first truly modern Swiss poster, the one that marked the beginning of that country's long and esteemed tradition in the genre.

During his formative years as a landscape painter Cardinaux had absorbed the "national art" ideals of the Swiss artist Ferdinand Hodler, and in 1904 was introduced to the printer Johann Edwin Wolfensberger, from whom he received a thorough education in the craft of lithography. Cardinaux then turned his hand to poster design, creating in 1906 a memorable poster for Bern, along with six mono-cards, a small collectible form of advertisement. One of these, commissioned by the Zermatt tourist office, was this design of the Matterhorn. The poster's power derives from its simplicity: the triangular form of the mountain, with its perspective reduced to strengthen the outline, dominates the composition, while the color scheme of orange and mauve suggests the seductive glow of early morning light. Cardinaux's understanding of lithography, which involved drawing directly onto the stone, is evident in the subtle effects of modeling: the snow-covered slopes in mixed tones of yellow and white, the green and black marks overlaying brown to convey the soft shadows of the foothills, and the speckled *crachis* gray border suggestive of stone. Beneath the image, the sans serif lettering, which typified the artist's posters from 1915 onward, set in orange and black, unifies the title and minimal text with the rest of the composition.

Even though Cardinaux had a thorough understanding of nineteenth-century poster art, his bold, reductive design shows more affinity with the German *Sachplakat* (object poster), emerging at the time in German Plakatstil, and therefore looks ahead to the pictorial forms of the new century. The work's importance was immediately recognized and adorned the walls of many a schoolroom and government office, with deluxe versions printed on higher quality paper to satisfy popular demand. Cardinaux designed more than a hundred posters for commercial and political purposes during his career, but most memorably for tourism.

← P.61

1909

COPYRIGHT

Information Design

Unknown

Unknown, U.S.

The copyright symbol, used to indicate the existence of copyright on authored creative and artistic works other than sound recordings (which are indicated by a "P" in a circle), is one of the most recognized in the world, although the origins of its best-known format—a plain sans serif "C" enclosed within a circle of the same width—are obscure.

The symbol originated in U.S. copyright law, which was first enacted by Congress in 1790. The act protected the rights of authors to publish "maps, charts, and books" for a period of fourteen years, with the option of renewal for a further fourteen-year term if the author remained alive. The act did not govern works of music, newspapers, or those of foreign authors, and only a very small number of published titles were ever registered. Strictly speaking, a work was only protected by US copyright law if it had a copyright notice, which consisted of three elements: the © symbol (or the word "Copyright" or abbreviation "Copr."), the year of first publication, and the name or other designation of the copyright owner. Since 1988, when the U.S. became a signatory to the Berne Convention, copyright has been automatic.

The copyright symbol was first mentioned in a 1909 revision of the U.S. copyright law, where it states that for various classes of artwork "... the notice may consist of the letter 'C' enclosed within a circle...." The symbol came into use because certain types of artwork were so small that including the full copyright term was impractical. Although the law prohibits deviations from this basic format, it does not specify a particular font, and the symbol can theoretically be created in any typeface. Moreover, in situations where it is not possible to create the correct format, the symbol is sometimes substituted by an upper- or lowercase "C" in brackets, but it is not clear whether the law recognizes such alternatives as legally valid. The classic form of the symbol as a sans serif "C" appears to be a convention that has developed over time. Its simplicity, clarity, and proportionality, especially when compared with other renderings, amply demonstrate why this version remains the standard and most popular.

← P.61

1911

OPEL

Poster

Hans Rudi Erdt (1883–1918)

Opel, Germany

A striking example of the German *Sachplakat* (object poster) style, practiced in Germany from the beginning of the twentieth century until the start of World War I, this poster achieves its effect through deceptively simple means.

With its mixture of implicit and explicit visual and verbal messages, the image has a beguiling ambiguity. The product itself—the car—appears almost incidental, and there are no demands or exhortations. Instead, the product is referenced by its large and dominant name, while the stern, almost disdainful, yet simultaneously melancholy, expression of the well-dressed chauffeur, whose collar and coat are adroitly suggested by the deeply colored background, acts as a subtle but powerful reminder of the status of Opel cars. The conceit of merging the driver with the poster's fabric is further underpinned by the capital "O," which has been subverted into the perfect circle of a car's tire. Overall, the design is anchored by its triangular composition, emphasized by the scattered touches of white and the powerful horizontal line of letters at the base, whereas the tick marks created by the chauffeur's collar provide a further subliminal endorsement of the product in the viewer's mind.

Sachplakat means "object poster," which was characterized by the simple arrangement of a minimal number of graphic elements—usually just a picture of the product and its name—with flat colors and prominent lettering. The style, whose celebrated practitioners included Erdt, Lucian Bernhard, and Ludwig Hohlwein, among others, reinvigorated German advertising. As there were no design agencies in Germany before about 1920, these posters were produced mostly by printers (in this case the celebrated lithographers Hollerbaum & Schmidt), who commissioned the designer on behalf of the client. *The Studio* magazine's assessment of the style in 1912 as "sane, sober and concise in effect" underplayed the complexity of its approach, which treated the viewer as a sophisticated consumer capable of choice. In this respect, the style bridged the work of the late-nineteenth-century Beggarstaffs in England, and the "Maximum Meaning, Minimum Means" of the mid-twentieth-century graphic designer Abram Games.

← P.62

1911

VOTES FOR WOMEN

Poster

B. M. Boye (1883–1930)

College Equal Suffrage League, U.S.

B. M. (Bertha Margaret) Boye was born in Oakland, California, in 1883. She studied art in San Francisco at the Mark Hopkins Art Institute and was a resident there until 1915. Later she moved to Calais, France, to further her art studies, and died there in 1930. Women's suffrage was an ongoing issue during Boye's lifetime, one in which she was regularly involved. Throughout the nineteenth century, calls for women to be given the right to vote had been gathering strength; by the dawn of the twentieth, the calls were beginning to be heard, both in the United States and internationally, with the first four states—Wyoming, Colorado, Idaho, and Utah—having already granted the right.

In Boye's home state of California the first attempt for women's suffrage, in the 1896 general election, was unsuccessful, plagued by problems during the eight-month campaign, including insufficient financial resources. However, local activist groups persisted in their efforts, and in 1910 managed to persuade the governor of California, James Norris Gillett, to include the question, "Should women be allowed to vote?" on the 1911 ballot. In support of the drive, the northern California chapter of the College Equal Suffrage League sponsored an illustration contest. Boye's design won first place and was chosen as the image to be used on cards, flyers, and publicity stamps for the campaign. The effort was successful, with California becoming the sixth state where women could vote, and Boye's design was produced through 1913.

The work features a suffragist draped in an ornamental yellow cloth, holding a scroll that reads "Votes for Women," foregrounded against the Golden Gate Straight. In the middle of the straight is a deep orange sun, which forms a halo around the figure's head. With her flowing garments and poised expression, she appears as a quasi-religious figure, devout in her commitment to the women's suffrage movement. The lithograph also nods to California's expanding Arts and Crafts movement, which regularly depicted the state's verdant landscapes. Composed in a relatively minimal style, and bearing a simple yet recognizable message, Boye's poster became an enduring image among women's rights groups and continues to inspire artistic protest signage.

← P.63

1912

INSEL-BÜCHEREI

Book Cover

Anton Kippenberg (1874–1950), Gotthard de Beauclair (1907–1992)

Insel Verlag, Germany

Established in 1901, Insel Verlag was part of the revolution in modern publishing that took place in Leipzig, the historical center of the German book industry. Here, the publishers Reclam and Tauchnitz had already started to address the needs of urban, literate consumers for inexpensive, easily available books, by publishing paperbacks in cheaply bound standard formats.

By the time Anton Kippenberg joined Insel Verlag in 1906 to become its director, the publisher already had a reputation for using legible typography and considered design in its finely bound books. However, when Kippenberg published Rainer Maria Rilke's *Die Weise von Liebe und Tod des Cornets Christoph Rilke* (*The Lay of the Love and Death of Cornet Christoph Rilke*) in 1912, a new concept in European publishing was born: the Insel-Bücherei (Island Library) collection. With sales exceeding thirty thousand by the time of Rilke's death in 1926, the book was a true success.

This unique series of attractive and collectible volumes was distinguished by its internal illustrations, and the decorative hardcover bindings created by Kippenberg and Gotthard de Beauclair, Insel Verlag's artistic director. Printed in crown octavo format (a sheet folded to form eight leaves or sixteen pages), each edition ran to between ten thousand and thirty thousand copies. A typographic label—indicating author, title, and series number—was directly printed or separately mounted on the cover, and from 1915 the book's short title and number were also printed on a small label on the spine. Both labels and inside text were set in the same Gothic typeface. Whereas most patterned cover papers were sourced from eighteenth- and nineteenth-century Italian wood-block prints, some were commissioned from artists and were often used many times. Insel-Bücherei's distinctive look was paramount to its appeal.

The series was published in hardcover until war-time restrictions forced the adoption of the paperback format in 1941. The Frankfurt-based Insel Verlag reinstated hardcover binding in 1951, occasionally making use of illustration on its covers, whereas the East German branch, which remained in Leipzig, continued to use only decorated papers. Both were reunited in 1991 and returned to Leipzig, where the Insel-Bücherei series is still published today.

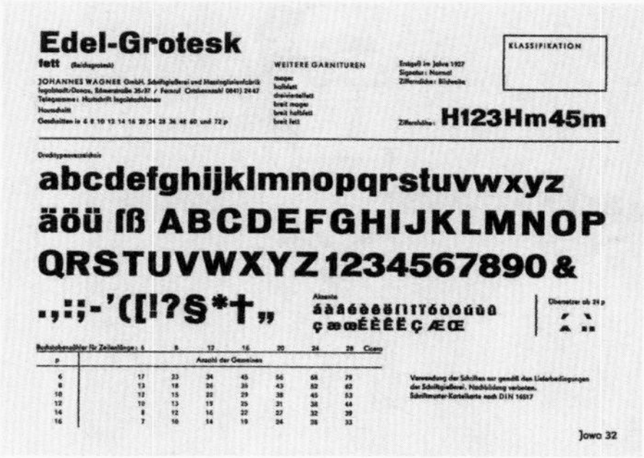

← P.63

1912–1914

EDEL-GROTESK

Typeface

Wagner & Schmidt

Self-commissioned, Germany

Sans serif typefaces such as Futura and DIN Engschrift rose to popularity during the period of the Bauhaus (1919–33), favored by leading designers for their modern design and utility. The lesser-known Edel-Grotesk face also percolated throughout Europe at this time, and designers used it with great frequency until it disappeared into obscurity with the rise of phototypesetting and digitization.

The type foundry Wagner & Schmidt opened in 1875 in Leipzig, the center of typographic design before World War II, where it manufactured matrices for companies to use in casting their own typefaces. Under the leadership of Ludwig Wagner, Wagner & Schmidt designed the Edel-Grotesk matrices between 1912 and 1914, but as they also manufactured matrices for other foundries, it is unclear how Edel-Grotesk factors into the design and distribution of various almost identical sans serif fonts of this era. As far back as 1907, the C. E. Weber foundry produced the remarkably similar Aurora-Grotesk in Stuttgart, and some sources have credited Wagner & Schmidt with its creation.

In 1921 the brothers Ludwig and Johannes Wagner, and Johannes's brother-in-law Willy Jahr, established the Norddeutsche Schriftgießerei (North German Type Foundry) in Berlin, and in 1927 they made the decision to cast Edel-Grotesk. They quickly distributed it for use in hand setting, and it became an ideal choice for small print products. Advertisements by the Dutch designer Piet Zwart appear to be set in Edel-Grotesk, as well as a wealth of advertising, business cards, and stationery produced in the 1930s and 1940s.

In 1949 Johannes Wagner moved the business to Ingolstadt, where it was also known as Letternservice Ingolstadt or Johannes Wagner Schriftgiesserei Messinglinienfabrik, and where it continued to cast typography for a number of leading foundries. By 1971, Wagner obtained some of C. E. Weber's typefaces, and a rare specimen sheet joins two of their typefaces by name as Edel (Aurora)-Grotesk. Unfortunately, Wagner's company did not make the transition to phototypesetting and digital media that would soon dominate the market, and in 1999 the firm closed.

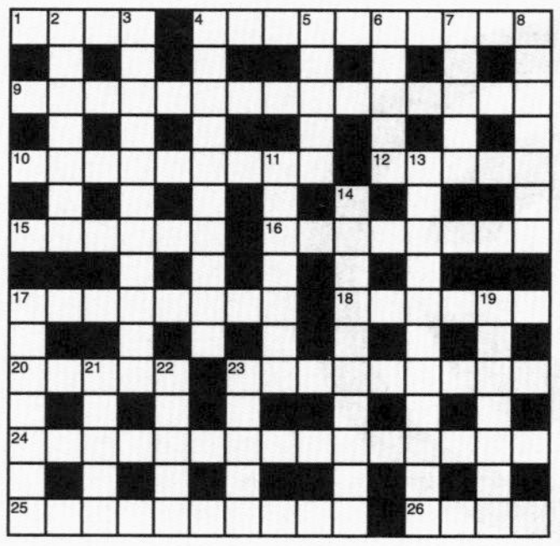

← P.64

1913

CROSSWORD PUZZLE

Information Design

Arthur Wynne (1862–1945)

New York World, U.S.

The crossword puzzle was introduced to the world on December 21, 1913 by Arthur Wynne, a Liverpool journalist working in New York. Wynne is said to have developed the idea from the popular Victorian parlor game Magic Square, which he had played with his grandfather, in which participants were required to fill a square with words that read both vertically and horizontally. Published in the entertainment section of *New York World*, for which Wynne was the "Fun" editor, the simple grid in the shape of a hollow diamond required readers to enter their answers to thirty-two clues. The demand for the puzzle immediately swept the U.S., and in 1924 the first book of crossword puzzles was published, which within weeks ran into many printings. A few months later, the now-familiar grid began to appear in advertising, as the subject of popular songs on sheet music, and on postcards. The crossword even inspired dedicated magazines, such as *Fad*, *Cross Word Puzzle Magazine*, and *Dell Crossword Puzzles*.

In Britain, the first puzzle appeared in *Pearson's Magazine* in February 1922, with *The Times* publishing an example for the first time on February 1, 1930. By 1925 Britain had produced a variation, the cryptic crossword puzzle, with devious and challenging clues that used quotations, metaphors, general knowledge, puns, and other wordplay. Many postcard publishers in both Britain and the U.S. (such as Raphael Tuck & Sons, Valentine & Sons, and Bamforth & Co.) featured on their cards artist-drawn comments on the craze, which by this time had spread to mainland Europe.

Crosswords have retained their popularity, the original simple clues of 1913 having spawned many specialist variants, from philately to the London Underground. Crossword championships and timed competitions have also sprung up, and the familiar box, conventionally fifteen by fifteen squares in size, may now appear as a "gigantic" puzzle or take the shape of a circle, triangle, or another complex shape to increase the difficulty of solving the puzzle. The crossword, that curious teasing grid, has now become a standard feature of newspapers and magazines around the world.

← P.64

PLANTIN
ABCDEFGHIJKLM
NOPQRSTUVWXY
Z&abcdefghijklmnopq
rstuvwxyz1234567890!
ABCDEFGHIJKLM
NOPQRSTUVWXY
ZŒÆabcdefghijklmnop
qrstuvwxyz1234567890
ABCDEFGHIJKLM
NOPQRSTUVWX
YZŒÆ&abcdefghij
klmnopqrstuvwxyz?
1234567890£œæ'.,?!

← P.65

LACERBA
DICHIARAZIONE
LACERBA

← P.65

1913

OLYMPIC RINGS

Logo

Pierre Frédy, Baron de Coubertin (1863–1937)

International Olympic Committee

The five-ring Olympic logo has become a highly effective visual emblem for an event that embraces almost every country and culture in the world. More than a century after its first creation, the symbol is now so recognizable that it can be toyed with, altered, or just hinted at, allowing designers to produce unique versions without losing its fundamental identity.

Pierre Frédy, Baron de Coubertin, the "father" and champion of the modern Olympics, had a keen interest in visual communication and was eager for the event to have a strong unifying symbol. In 1913 he conceived the five-ring Olympic logo, using the colors most often displayed on national flags. Although interpretations vary, the rings and their colors are usually taken to represent the five continents, while their interlocking design is thought to suggest eternity and unity. The logo first appeared on a white flag flown at the Antwerp Olympics of 1920, later appearing on posters for the St. Moritz Games in 1928. Since then, graphic designers have used the symbol in increasingly innovative ways: one Winter Olympics poster showed the five-ring logo skiing down a snowy hill, and in Per Arnoldi's poster design for the 1996 Danish Paralympics Association, the rings became transformed into shapes such as triangles and squares, still clinging together as a group but also conveying the diversity and independence that underline the Paralympic movement.

The importance of graphic design for advertising the Olympics, particularly during its early days, cannot be underestimated: distributed in public areas, such as train stations throughout the world, Olympic posters allowed different graphic styles and messages to spread as designers took the opportunity to promote not only the event but also the host nation and its political agenda. The five-ring symbol provides a neat visual shorthand for the Olympic movement as a whole, combining visual efficiency with flexibility and multiplicity of meaning.

1913

PLANTIN

Typeface

F. H. Pierpont (1860–1937), after Christophe Plantin (c. 1520–1589)

Monotype Corporation, U.S.

The launch in 1913 of Plantin—a font available in bold, italic, and condensed variants, with lining and non-lining numerals—was a landmark event, which presaged Monotype's major 1922 program to expand type families, adapt old faces, make new commissions, and revive classics. Plantin was an adaptation, but its meticulous cutting meant that the face could be equally well printed on coated and uncoated paper. At the time, coated paper was associated with commercial work, and Plantin's understated yet robust dignity bestowed quality on jobbing printing, while its versatility made it suitable for other processes, such as offset, stereotyping, and gravure.

Christophe Plantin was a sixteenth-century French printer based in Antwerp, whose expansive font range included designs by Garamond and Granjon. Monotype's cutting was based on a font originally acquired after Plantin's death, but never used by him. Under the direction of F. H. Pierpont, the foundry strengthened the original, reduced its extenders, and gave it a large x-height, making it a space-saving font that looks best in small sizes. Plantin also works well with tight leading and narrow measures, and accompanies illustrations well due to its even color (resulting from its reduced thick-and-thin contrast), which needs only light inking and never becomes spindly or tiring to read on high-quality stock. The weights of the roman, bold, and light variants are intelligently graded and create an integrity that helps to solve complex typographic problems without resorting to clumsy font mixes. Plantin Light is an excellent choice for the discerning poetry designer: its discreet capitals avoid unpleasant emphasis of the left-hand edge of text, while its tight set reduces turnover lines, thus helping to maintain a poem's overall shape on the page.

1913–1915

LACERBA

Magazine / Newspaper

Giovanni Papini (1881–1956), Ardengo Soffici (1879–1964)

Attilio Vallecchi, Italy

Even though it was not the Futurist's official mouthpiece, *Lacerba* played a major role in spreading the movement's highly charged poetry and revolutionary ideas on art and typography.

First published in Florence on January 1, 1913, *Lacerba* was founded by the writer Giovanni Papini and the painter-critic Ardengo Soffici, who had previously collaborated on other antiestablishment periodicals. Their uneasy relationship with the Milanese Futurists meant that the group's contributions did not appear until the edition of March 15, 1913, but during the following year the journal became closely linked with the movement, heralding an aggressive redesign of the magazine. This included a new, pitch-black masthead, 59 inches (15 cm) high—which would directly influence other journals, such as *Blast*, produced by the English Vorticists—and radical experimental typography on its inner sixteen pages. Using the concept of *parole in libertà* (words in freedom), the Futurists welded emotions, ideas, and typography together on the printed page to create complex, visually kinetic poems. Their chaotic but striking, nonlinear compositions, which used different fonts, type sizes, and inks, were achieved by pasting words and letters into place and then reproducing them by photo-engraving. Brutal defiance of typographic taste, as well as of the rules of syntax and grammar, expressed in visual and verbal terms their call for the destruction of traditional society. Meanwhile, provocative essays, such as "In Praise of Prostitution," reinforced this bold idea, causing regular scandal and censorship. Despite threats of prosecution, *Lacerba*'s publisher, Attilio Vallecchi, stood by the magazine's mix of anarchic art, poetry, and politics, and set a low cover price to make it affordable to Italian workers.

Published fortnightly, then as a weekly, *Lacerba* achieved a peak circulation figure of twenty thousand and ran for seventy issues. The publication finally closed on May 22, 1915, when the goal of Italy's entrance into World War I was realized, although Futurist poets continued to find an outlet for their ideas in the less well-known journal *L'Italia Futurista*, from 1916 to 1918.

← P.66

1914

ZANG TUMB TUMB

Book

Filippo T. Marinetti (1876–1944)

Edizioni Futuriste di "Poesia," Italy

Zang Tumb Tumb represents a seminal moment in both the history of Italian Futurism and the development of typography, ushering in significant changes in the design and technology of the printed page.

Using texts that included Filippo T. Marinetti's *The Technical Manifesto of Futurist Literature* (1912) and *Destruction of Syntax/Imagination without Strings/Words-in-Freedom* (1913), *Zang Tumb Tumb* tells the story of the Battle of Adrianapole in the Balkan War, one of the first occasions that aerial bombing was used. In seeking to develop a new visual typographic language to reflect the times, Marinetti attacked the harmony of the classical page, espousing a multitude of colors and typefaces, rejecting the use of conventional grammar, syntax, and punctuation, and exaggerating verbs, nouns, and onomatopoeia. In this respect, *Zang Tumb Tumb* was the first book to exemplify Marinetti's concept of *parole in libertá* (words in freedom), whereby typography conveys the sights and sounds of battles, with explosions and machine-gun fire depicted through type of different weights, styles, and sizes positioned dynamically across the page. In shattering the symmetrical order of the printed page, Marinetti affected the way in which type was read, treating texts as images. This typographic revolution also led to a change of process in the print industry and the use of photo engraving to create page layouts.

Marinetti's typographic ideas spread across Europe through the publication of his manifestos, influencing the work of the Dada, Constructivist, and Vorticist groups, among others. His legacy was also clearly seen in the late 1980s and early 1990s with the advent of the Apple Mac, which gave designers the typographic freedom to explore the expressive possibilities of the printed page in new ways.

← P.66

1914–1915

BLAST

Magazine / Newspaper

Wyndham Lewis (1882–1957)

Self-commissioned, UK

Conceived by the Anglo-American artist and writer Wyndham Lewis, *Blast* was a short-lived journal that appeared in only two editions—as a review and manifesto for Vorticism, England's main contribution to the emerging European avant-garde during the early years of the twentieth century.

In celebrating the disruptive energies of a new Machine Age, Vorticism shared much of its ideology with the Italian Futurists, and, like Futurism, was a literary as well as an artistic movement. Vorticism, however, reflected the influence of the poet Ezra Pound and the philosopher T. E. Hulme, and its approach to typography was less Expressionistic and more ordered. As well as Lewis's manifesto, *Blast* contained poems and prose by Pound, T. S. Elliot, and Ford Madox Ford, and reproduced the work of key modernist artists, such as David Bomberg, Edward Wadsworth, Henri Gaudier-Brzeska, and Jacob Epstein. Under the headings "Blast" and "Bless," the manifesto identified aspects of English bourgeois culture for attack, and examples of nonconformity and radical practice to be "blessed." Provocative and satirical, *Blast*'s pages shared with other modernist manifestos a concern for the integration of language and visual form, and are a landmark of avant-garde typography. Hand-set in wood type using a condensed nineteenth-century grotesque font, Lewis's design rejected the decorative idioms of the Art and Crafts movement, instead borrowing the vernacular rhetoric of advertisements and handbills, and the asymmetric structural experiments of modernist poetry. For the front cover of the first issue, referred to as "the Puce monster," the title was set in black sans serif capitals on a vivid pink paper, whereas the second edition's cover combined text with an abstracted angular image in a typically Vorticist style by Wyndham Lewis.

Blast came to an end during World War I, in which several Vorticist members were killed. Like many modernist experiments, its influence was felt throughout the twentieth century in the integration of design and writing, while the use of a commercial jobbing typeface and asymmetrical layout anticipated values later developed by Jan Tschichold in the New Typography of the late 1920s.

← P.66

1916

BATAVIER LIJN, ROTTERDAM–LONDEN

Poster

Bart van der Leck (1876–1958)

Wm H. Müller & Co., the Netherlands

Bart van der Leck's advertisement for the Batavier steamship line epitomizes many of the qualities of geometry and flatness that would become defining features of twentieth-century poster language.

In its simple, naive character, the poster deliberately opposed earlier Victorian travel narratives, which portrayed bright, ocean-sprayed steamships inhabited by well-off travelers enjoying the "full night's rest" that the company offered. The toylike simplicity of van der Leck's vessel, the ancient-Egyptian friezelike pose of the figures, and the plain, unmodulated colors distance the poster from popular, naturalistic designs, while splitting the scenes into rectangular compartments to evoke the character of comic strips or stained-glass windows. Nearly a decade before attending the State School of Arts and Crafts in Amsterdam and the State Academy of Fine Arts, van der Leck had worked as an apprentice in an Utrecht stained-glass workshop. The experience was crucial: strong, bright colors were used to provide contrast, details were eliminated, and shapes were surrounded by large areas of empty space. In its treatment of figures as graphic shapes against a flat white background, the poster also suggests an architectural surface, reflecting van der Leck's view that art was related to architecture. The poster's rudimentary lettering style was initially rejected by the shipping company, which pasted it over with new panels of text.

In its two-dimensionality and division into geometric shapes, van der Leck's design exhibits many of the stylistic ingredients for which Piet Mondrian and the De Stijl movement would become known. The image had a significant influence on contemporary poster design and set new visual standards for promoting international mass travel.

← P.67

1916–1917

NEUE JUGEND

Magazine / Newspaper

John Heartfield (1891–1968)

Malik Verlag, Germany

The final incarnation of the antiwar periodical *Neue Jugend* (New Youth) marked the beginning of John Heartfield's career as a radical monteur, when he embraced the Dada ideal of anti-art as a means for social protest and propaganda.

Born Helmut Herzfeld, Heartfield changed his name in 1916 in protest at German militarism and anti-English sentiment, and joined the Berlin Dada group, whose members included George Grosz, Raoul Hausmann, Hannah Höch, and Otto Dix. In 1916 Heartfield and his brother, the poet Wieland Herzfelde (who added the "e" to his last name in 1913), took over the monthly magazine *Neue Jugend,* running it for a year as an outlet for leading progressive German authors, such as Franz Kafka, and so-called "enemy foreigners," such as Walt Whitman and Arthur Rimbaud. Following a printing ban, the brothers established the Malik Verlag publishing house in March 1917, and continued to print the paper, primarily as an outlet for Grosz's political satires. However, the magazine quickly succumbed to censors. In May 1917, with Wieland Herzfelde called back to the front, Heartfield resumed publication, radically changing the format and eradicating the staid-looking quarto magazine with justified print columns in favor of a larger scale based on American journals. The sharp political satire was also now combined with highly unorthodox typography, including different fonts and line arrangements in varying sizes and colors, to reflect the chaos of the world as seen by the pacifist left wing. In the June edition, a quarter page was devoted to an advertisement for Grosz lithographs, and the unconventional use of lowercase and capital letters was further mystified by the addition of printed crossbones, a coffin, black index fingers, and roguish-looking characters, such as a lady with a mask.

Before Heartfield could bring out the third edition, which he planned to print in white ink on black mourning crepe, publication ceased again and was never resumed. In its brief lifetime *Neue Jugend* helped to launch a typographic revolution that would influence many more German Dada publications, as well as the work of the Russian Constructivists and De Stijl group.

← P.68

1916

PEOPLE'S CHARITY FOR GERMAN PRISONERS OF WAR AND CIVILIAN INTERNEES

Poster

Ludwig Hohlwein (1874–1949)

German Government, Germany

Ludwig Hohlwein designed for commercial and propaganda purposes in a career that covered two world wars, but that was ultimately tainted by his association with Nazism. He is perhaps best known for the poignant fund-raising posters he created during World War I.

In the 1890s, Hohlwein studied architecture in Munich, and in his early career he designed posters and other printed ephemera for cafés, restaurants, and shops. The bold, simplified image-making he employed quickly earned him a reputation as a major exponent of the lithographic *Sachplakat* (object poster) in Germany. This was exemplified by the posters he designed for various men's outfitters, which revealed the influence of the English Beggarstaff brothers in their use of flat decorative pattern, but are imbued with a greater sense of compositional balance and realism.

Hohlwein's spare, elegant advertising style evolved during World War I through the assimilation of increasingly naturalistic imagery. It reached its most affecting in a series of emotive fundraising posters, which included "Exhibition of Work by German Prisoners of War Interned in Switzerland," "The Ludendorff Appeal for the War-Disabled," and "People's Charity for German Prisoners of War and Civilian Internees" (pictured). The last in particular demonstrates the synthesis of his early and maturing traits in the block of heavy lettering, strong tonal contrasts, and flat areas of color, and a design framed, in this case, by prison bars. Graphic symbols of compassion, such as the red cross and heart, were also common motifs, but it is the economy of means with which Hohlwein depicts complex human emotions that lends these posters their pathos.

Later regimes, however, were scathing about the ability of such avant-garde pictorialism to communicate to a large enough audience. In the 1930s Hohlwein adapted his fluid manner to the demands of Nazi propaganda. The increased use of photographs and airbrushing led to a militaristic style of tight forms, severe contrasts, and dark sentiments, which was in marked contrast to the compassion and sincerity of his earlier "humanitarian" works.

← P.69

1917–1932

DE STIJL

Magazine / Newspaper

Theo van Doesburg (1883–1931), Vilmos Huszár (1884–1960)

Self-commissioned, the Netherlands

De Stijl magazine ushered in changes in graphic design that would resonate through much of the twentieth century, paring down visual language to its abstract minimum and rejecting natural forms in favor of geometric purity.

Emerging out of World War I, the De Stijl movement was part of a larger modernist response to the tragedy of European conflict, which sought a new visual language that would embody transformation. De Stijl (the style) coalesced around the magazine of the same name founded by the Dutch artist Theo van Doesburg, in 1917, and appeared under his editorship until his death in 1931, after which a final commemorative issue was published. Contributors included important figures of Dutch modernism, such as the painters Piet Mondrian, Vilmos Huszár, and Bart van der Leck, and the architects Gerrit Rietveld, Jan Wils, and J. J. P. Oud.

One of the most influential examples of the De Stijl sensibility was the magazine's original masthead. Created in 1917 by Huszár, the abstract woodcut consisted of a field of different-sized black rectangles on a white background. In this arrangement, the negative white space between the cubic forms takes on its own configuration, interlocking with the black shapes to create a charged composition. Below, a fully justified block of text in uppercase letters announces the magazine and its editor to the public, while above, a mass of fragmented rectangles is grouped into letters that spell out the words "DE STIJL." The cover remained unchanged until 1921, when van Doesburg abandoned Huszár's fragmented, mosaiclike typography in favor of a horizontal format with a bold sans serif font (pictured).

De Stijl magazine never sold more than three hundred copies and was printed on cheap stock, with illustrations reproduced on inserted leaflets of coated paper, and covers in light green or gray. Despite such poor quality materials, the magazine's influence was felt across Europe, continuing long after publication had ceased. The impact of De Stijl continues to be seen today in disciplines that range from architecture to typography and graphic design.

← P.69

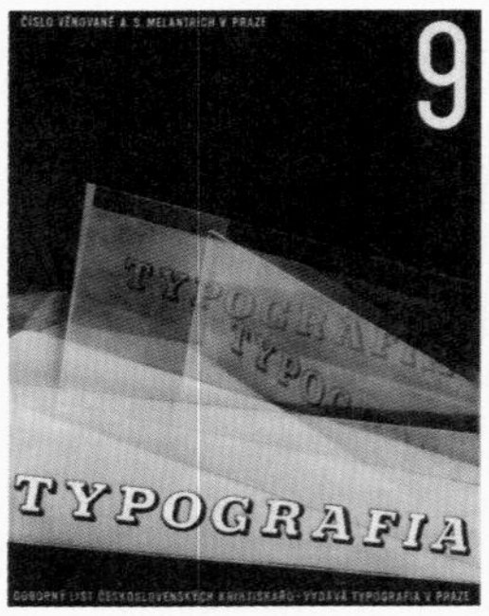

← P.70

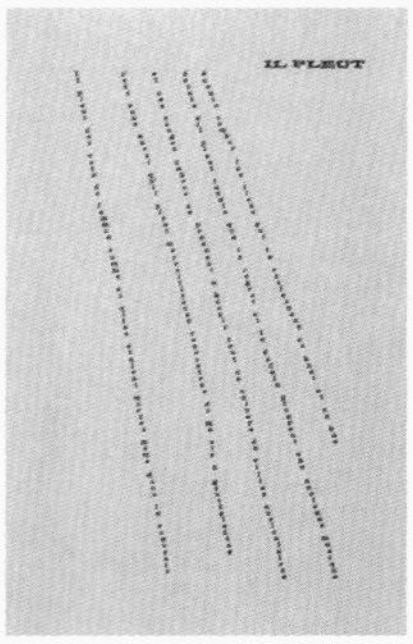

← P.71

1917–1920

DADA

Magazine / Newspaper

Francis Picabia (1879–1953), Tristan Tzara (1896–1963), Marcel Janco (1895–1984)

Administration Mouvement Dada, Switzerland and France

Edited in Zurich by Tristan Tzara and conceived as a gesture of defiance, *Dada 3* was a graphic design landmark that broke all existing typographical and editorial rules, ushering in an entirely new sensibility that helped to define the European avant-garde.

Dada 1 and *2* (1917) were laid out conventionally, but in *Dada 3*, in which he published his manifesto (a virulent condemnation of moral platitudes and conventions), Tzara decided to experiment. Futurist publications such as Filippo T. Marinetti's *Parole in Libertà*, published in Italy in 1915, had been visually provocative and innovative, but their layouts belonged to a typographical tradition in which letterforms were treated as beautiful objects. Here, by contrast, little attention is given to typefaces, their size, or spacing. For Dada artists, any form of seduction was suspect, a manifestation of bourgeois values. The publication also disrupted the relation between words and images, and even between words and sense. The woodcut by Marcel Janco and a quote by Descartes—"Je ne veux même pas savoir s'il y a eu des hommes avant moi" (I don't even want to know if there have been men before me)—had been brought together by chance, exemplifying the Dada predilection for absurd titles and accidental design decisions, and type was set diagonally across the page, making the words difficult to read. From this moment onward, the dynamic diagonal became a standard feature of avant-garde graphic compositions, not only in Dada photo collages later developed by Raoul Hausmann and John Heartfield for magazines such as *AIZ*, but also in the work of the De Stijl and Russian Constructivist movements.

For the publication's remaining three issues, Tzara was assisted by the Spanish artist Francis Picabia, who, despite being a better typographer, maintained Tzara's approach. *Dada 4–5* (1919) was published in Zurich, and *Bulletin Dada 6* and *Dadaphone 7* (1920) were produced in Paris following Tzara's move to the city.

1918–1939

TYPOGRAFIA

Magazine / Newspaper

Various

Typografia, Czech Republic

Typografia features a variety of styles on its cover and in its pages, as might be expected of a monthly printer's journal showcasing design work over such a long period. While the interior spreads regularly reproduced samples of classic typography, including book covers, advertisements, and letterheads—along with a 1923 issue celebrating the fiftieth birthday of Czech typographer Vojtech Preissig—the design of the publication itself became more and more modernist, reflecting much of the other work found in the journal's pages. Meanwhile, the cover designs exhibited a range of experimentation and graphic techniques, such as type-only constructions, illustration, and photomontage, with no set masthead to l ink them. They are rarely more than two colors, but their development and diversity exhibit a collective vibrancy that speaks to a country and industry in motion.

Although the establishment of *Typografia* predates Czechoslovakian independence (1918), the publication's design is most relevant to the period of the Czech avant-garde, a time and movement defined by the establishment of the republic of Czechoslovakia and its subsequent invasion by Hitler in 1939. This era of intense creativity was tied to the optimism of the nation's new identity, as Constructivism and the New Typography were synthesized by many of the country's artists and designers, including Karel Teige and Ladislav Sutnar. Teige built on the theories of Czech typographers, such as Karel Dyrynk, and critics like F. X. Salda, in essays that included "Moderní typo" (Modern Typography, 1927), and was soon introducing the ideas of László Moholy-Nagy, Jan Tschichold, and El Lissitzky. Before emigrating to New York in 1939, Sutnar designed a number of covers for *Typografia*, utilizing the same balance of sans serif type, negative space and photography seen in cover designs for his book *Nejmenší dům* (The Minimum House, 1931) and the periodical *Žijeme* (We Live, 1931). The involvement of figures like Teige and Sutnar in both the design and content of *Typografia* assured the spread of modernist design and typography to a larger audience, and in this respect the journal played an emissary role, similar to *Gebrauchsgrafik* in Germany and *Blok* in Poland.

1918

IL PLEUT

Book

Guillaume Apollinaire (1880–1918)

Self-commissioned, France

With its five long fingers of type meandering diagonally across the page, "Il pleut" (It's raining) is one of the most evocative of all calligrams, suggesting raindrops drizzling down a windowpane to create an eloquent visual equivalent for the melancholy character of the poem.

Although a literary genre popular with writers since antiquity, the term "calligram" (meaning "beautiful literature," from the Greek prefix *calli-*, of calligraphy, for "beauty," and *gramma*, of ideogram, for "letter"), denoting verses laid out to form a picture or image, was first coined by the French poet Guillaume Apollinaire. His posthumous book, *Calligrammes, poèmes de la paix et de la guerre*, published in 1918, contained traditionally laid-out and pictorial texts, with the latter including "La cravate et la montre" (The tie and the watch) and "Il pleut".

Apollinaire was influenced by the Italian Futurist poet and artist Filippo T. Marinetti, whose aggressive ideas he both condoned and embraced. Intent on subverting traditional classifications and blurring the line between poetry and the fine arts, Apollinaire (perhaps driven by his friendship with Pablo Picasso) created a series entitled "I, too, am a painter!" in which the works were designed for reproduction in color. In fact, the poet aspired to be a musician as well as a graphic artist. "Il pleut" can also be interpreted as a sheet of music, with each letter signifying a note. Words like "voices," "auricular," "music," and "listen" (repeated twice), encourage readers to keep their ears open. Best read aloud, the words conjure up the pitter-patter of rain on Paris rooftops:

It's raining women's voices as if they had died even in memory
And it's raining you as well, marvelous encounters of my life
O little drops
Those rearing clouds begin to neigh a whole universe of auricular cities
Listen if it rains, while regret and disdain weep to an ancient music
Listen to the bonds fall off, which hold you above and below

← P.72

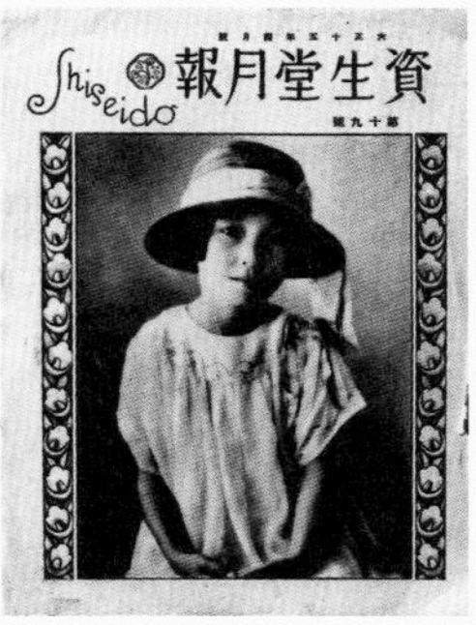

← P.72

← P.73

1918

LONDON UNDERGROUND

Logo

Edward Johnston (1872–1944)

London Underground, UK

Unchanged since Edward Johnston's adaptation of the original in 1918, the London Underground roundel has become one of the most famous and enduring company symbols ever created.

In 1908 Frank Pick, chief executive of London Underground, was given responsibility for the Underground system's publicity and signage system. He immediately set about improving its public image by introducing illustrated posters, ensuring that they were displayed in an orderly and regimented fashion, and commissioning a standard typeface and logotype for all signs and printed material. That role fell to the eminent calligrapher Edward Johnston, who in June 1916 delivered a design for an uppercase block-letter version of what was to become Johnston Sans, followed by a complete lowercase version the following month. Over subsequent years, Johnston continued to refine and modify the typeface, adding a bold version in 1929. The typeface was immediately put to use on all of the Underground's text-based posters, but was employed more sparingly on illustrated posters, with some artists preferring to draw their own lettering.

Pick also asked Johnston to redesign the company's corporate logo, which since 1907 had consisted of a red disc crossed by a central blue bar, bearing the names of stations in a plain, white sans serif typeface, and make it adaptable for other uses. The original logo, by an unknown designer, was pioneering in its simple, bold geometry and coloring. Johnston responded by changing the red disc to a red ring with a dark blue bar dissecting it, and by substituting the existing Underground logotype with his own typeface, Johnston Sans, and enlarging the "U" and "D." The new typeface, which was slightly heavier than other print-based sans serif typefaces, including the logo's original, also proved admirably suited to the Underground's signage system. Later, it would be modified for use on station nameplates and tram and bus-stop signs.

1918

SHISEIDO

Logo

Shinzo Fukuhara (1883–1948)

Shiseido, Japan

Shiseido's camellia logo, based on the flower indigenous to Japan and many parts of Asia, marked the introduction of Western-style commercial culture to Japan. With its associations of nature and femininity, however, it also strongly appealed to traditional Japanese sensibilities and helped to define the brand and its demographic.

Founded in 1872 by Arinobu Fukuhara, a pharmacist, Shiseido is Japan's leading cosmetics company, which began as an American-style pharmacy in the busy commercial neighborhood of Ginza, Tokyo. At first, Shiseido sold Western products as well as Japanese remedies, but slowly began producing its own line of medicines, and cosmetics. Due to the success of its toothpaste (a new product it introduced to Japan), the company's emblem was initially the hawk featured on its packaging. When Fukuhara's son and president of Shiseido, Shinzo Fukuhara, along with his business partner, Noburu Matsumoto, established a design department for the company, their American education exerted a strong influence. In addition to shifting Shiseido's focus from pharmaceuticals to cosmetics, the pair focused on the packaging and advertising of the company, which necessitated a rebranding. Shiseido's best-selling product at the time was Camellia Hair Oil, which led the company to adopt the flower as its trademark, originally using a nine-leaf version designed by Fukuhara and Matsumoto in 1915. By 1918, this was reduced to a seven-leaf design, similar to the one used today, enclosed by three irregular rings, with the innermost ring the same line weight as the flower and petals, and slightly thicker than the outer rings. The design has since been adjusted to only two rings, with the thicker on the outside.

The simple lines of Shiseido's emblem reveal the assimilation of European and American influences, and provide a symbol that aptly reflects the company's Japanese identity. Today, Shiseido branding focuses more heavily on the logotype of the company name, but the camellia still functions as a recognizable trademark.

1919

LA FIN DU MONDE, BY BLAISE CENDRARS

Book

Fernand Léger (1881–1955)

Editions de la Sirène, France

La Fin du Monde (*To The End of the World*), written by the Swiss poet, novelist, and journalist Blaise Cendrars (otherwise known as Frédéric Sauser) and illustrated by the French painter Fernand Léger, was originally conceived as a screenplay. However, when funding for the project was withdrawn, the proposal was transformed into a novel, which reads like the script for a film. Through the design of the book, Léger began to identify his fascination with mechanization, which he would later refine in his paintings. The project also led to his long association with cinema, particularly in regard to experimental works such as *Ballet Méchanique*, and his design, illustration, and pacing of the book reflect many of the techniques of film.

The book's theme portrays God as an anxious, cigar-chewing American businessman who is intent on satisfying the god Mars by initiating world war, whereby escalating death and destruction will increase income. Both Cendrars and Léger took pleasure in the character of the urban environment, especially in advertising displays, which Cendrars famously described as "a flower of contemporary life." Léger's illustrations contain fragments of advertising slogans, numbers, and posters, and converge with heavy mechanical typography to express the frantic pace and intensity of the city, as well as the insanity of the story. Densely layered compositions, in which space and form are given equal value, combine with primary colors that contrast with dense black letters, creating a pulsating visual experience that highlights Léger's interest in the relationship between typography and imagery. His concern for the overall impact of each page can be seen in the design of the bold typography used for the main text, which confronts the reader with continuous mechanical noise.

Cendrars had collaborated in 1913 on another project with a painter—*La Prose du Transsibérien*, illustrated by Sonia Delaunay—where the integration of type, illustration, and color creates an effect of simultaneity for the reader. In *La Fin du Monde*, Léger extends this concept by creating a visual sensation of time, space, and motion that tries to capture some of the experience of viewing a film.

← P.74

← P.75

← P.75

1919

FLIGHT

Poster

Edward McKnight Kauffer (1890–1954)

Daily Herald, UK

Edward McKnight Kauffer's poster for the *Daily Herald* newspaper is the most iconic of his prolific output and one of the most seminal works of graphic design of its time. The sheer scale of the poster (117¼ × 60 inches [298 × 152 cm], printed on three sheets), with its geometric forms of eight swiftlike birds in flight against a large expanse of flat yellow, must have made a considerable impact on the British public, who were more used to the whimsical style of artists such as John Hassall ("Skegness is So Bracing"). Its modernist appearance was not entirely of McKnight Kauffer's making, however. An original small design of eight birds in flight, published in the January 1917 issue of *Colour*, a monthly arts magazine, on a page entitled "Our Poster Gallery," was bought by Francis Meynell, a director and typographical designer of the *Daily Herald*. Meynell later had the image adapted by a printing house to incorporate the newspaper masthead (designed by Meynell) and the "Soaring to Success!—the Early Bird" caption. The poster was issued to coincide with the relaunching of the newspaper as a daily publication in 1919.

Kauffer's work at the time owed much to the artistic influences he had assimilated during the years he spent in Paris (1913–14); although Futurist in appearance, the design is more likely to have been inspired by an 1820 illustration of a flock of birds by the Japanese artist Sato Suiseki. According to Kauffer, Winston Churchill, then Secretary of State for War and Air, was so impressed by the poster that he thought of having the image adapted as an emblem for the newly formed Royal Air Force, although this project was never realized.

Only one complete version of this version of the poster exists, which is held in the Victoria & Albert Museum's extensive collection of works by the artist. An American émigré, McKnight Kauffer progressed from this early venture in commercial art to become the most celebrated poster designer of the interwar years in Britain.

1920

PRO DVA KVADRATA

Book

El Lissitzky (1890–1941)

UNOVIS, Russia

A story told in just six pages, El Lissitzky's children's book, *Pro Dva Kvadrata* (*About Two Squares*) concerns the struggle for control over a new world, between two forces in the form of a red and a black square. The red square ultimately defeats the black, dispels chaos, and installs order and harmony. The book was heavily influenced by Malevich's Suprematist theory of art and Lissitzky's own Proun works (dynamic compositions involving three-dimensional abstract forms), and uses basic geometric shapes and a reduced color palette of red, black, and white to communicate simple ideas concerning politics and morality.

In creating the book, Lissitzky was as preoccupied with sound as he was with visual effects, enlarging and repeating certain letters: these include "P" (the Russian "R" for *rebyatka*, or children); "C" ("S") in *skaz* (story); and the "A"s in *dva* (two) and *kvadrata* (squares), highlighting the letters' sounds as well as varying the graphics. Similarly, the instructions, which appear on the fourth page, emphasize activity ("don't read ... take, fold, color, build"), immediately progressing to construction and three dimensions from the more passive, two-dimensional act of reading. Even the format of this instruction page and of the title page, which links words through a long, slender, zigzag line, forces the eye to jump suddenly from one place to another. When the squares appear, the red is set at a dynamic angle, in contrast to the more static black, which echoes the framework of the page, a relationship also reflected in the horizontal and diagonal alignment of the text below. This dichotomy continues throughout the book, expressed by the illustrations, with their combination of rectangles, circles, and simple color contrasts, and by the limited but constantly varied layout of the text. Beautifully designed and set in a range of fonts, sizes, and weights, the type is as expressive and animated as the imagery to which it refers.

Highly sophisticated in execution and concept, *Pro Dva Kvadrata* demonstrates the potential within even the simplest of graphic effects to communicate meaning and narrative. The book was reprinted by Theo van Doesburg in Dutch for *De Stijl* magazine in 1922.

1920–1924

BROOM

Magazine / Newspaper

Various

Alfred Kreymborg, Harold Loeb, U.S.

Broom was a typical 1920s American "little" magazine that published largely experimental and obscure literature, criticism, and illustration by figures such as Ezra Pound, Gertrude Stein, Henri Matisse, and Pablo Picasso. Founded and originally edited by the poet and critic Alfred Kreymborg and the writer Harold Loeb, the journal might have taken its name from a typically enigmatic and cryptic reference to a broom sweeping the decks in a passage from *Moby-Dick*, printed on the back cover of the first edition.

Broom's whimsical covers and title pages were produced by a variety of avant-garde artists and designers, including El Lissitzky, Natalia Goncharova, László Moholy-Nagy, and Man Ray. Lettering varied from imaginative hand-drawn forms to abstract typographic compositions, in which characters overlapped, appeared upside down and back to front, or were integrated into Expressionist or Constructivist designs, in color schemes that ranged from the restrained to the vibrant. Imagery was equally diverse, and included the cameraless experiments of Moholy-Nagy's photograms and Man Ray's Rayographs, along with woodcuts and Cubist-looking abstractions. This eclectic, avant-garde style contrasted with the magazine's interior, which was much more understated, characterized by justified texts set in graceful serif fonts such as Old Style. Images were usually small in scale and integrated conventionally with the text, appearing either at the end or the middle of an article. Aimed at knowledgeable readers, the internal design provided a neutral setting rather than a visual expression of the contents.

Broom was like a luxurious book, with good-quality typesetting, binding, and printing on Fabbriano paper, and although published in the U.S., it was originally produced in Italy for cost reasons. Toward the end of its life, *Broom* returned to New York, but was perceived as too radical and folded after only five issues. The combination of avant-garde material with traditional graphic language may, ironically, have highlighted the experimental nature of the content enough to bring about its demise.

← P.76

1921

COOPER BLACK

Typeface

Oswald Cooper (1879–1940)

Barnhart Brothers & Spindler, U.S.

Cooper Black is a truly twentieth-century type and the most demonstrative of the so-called fat faces. Used for advertising and editorial display, it is as eye-catching as a charging bull.

Oswald Cooper was one of the progenitors of the Chicago style of graphic design. As a student at the Frank Holme School of Illustration, Cooper came under the influence of his teacher, the type designer Frederic W. Goudy, and met Fred Bertsch, who ran an art-service agency. Cooper and Bertsch formed a partnership—Bertsch & Cooper—in 1904, a type shop offering typesetting, copywriting, and design. A brilliant craftsman, Cooper had an instinctual distrust of things modish and strained, instead creating letterforms that evoked "free and friendly balance." In 1913 Barnhart Brothers & Spindler Type Foundry (BB&S), America's second-largest foundry, approached him to design a complete family based on his lettering, which was released in 1918 and named Cooper (later renamed Cooper Old Style).

BB&S popularized Cooper's first normal-weight roman (Cooper) and made it the basis for a continuing family. The second in the series, Cooper Black, billed as the "the selling type supreme, the multibillionaire sales type," was the most novel of early-twentieth-century superbolds and caused commotion in conservative circles. But the design quickly caught on. Other related type designs followed in quick succession—Cooper Italic (1924), Cooper Hilite (1925), Cooper Black Italic (1926), and Cooper Black Condensed (1926)—in what became known as "the black blitz."

Cooper's designs initiated trends, but he refused to take part in "the itch of the times." Nor was he a fan of what in 1928 he called "the balmy wing of modernism." However, his last face, designed in 1929 for BB&S, originally called Cooper Fullface and later changed in ATF catalogs to Cooper Modern, was, in fact, consistent with dominant styles, a display type described by Cooper as reflecting the "sparkling contrasts of Bodoni." Before his death in 1940, Cooper turned his attention to the fight for copyright protection for designers, at the same time chiding his colleagues for copying: "There was never a great imitator—not even in vaudeville. The way to become a master is by cultivating your own talent."

← P.76

1921

CHANEL

Identity

Gabrielle "Coco" Chanel (1883–1971)

Chanel, France

The success of the Chanel brand owes as much to its logo—two back-to-back interlocking "C"s—as it does to its signature fashion style and relaxed, informal conception of women's clothing.

Gabrielle Chanel opened her first couture shop in 1913, just prior to World War I. By the 1920s, Chanel was fully realizing her vision, pioneering a new vocabulary for women's fashion that would establish the "little black dress" and the "jersey suit" as wardrobe staples. Chanel created designs that reflected a glamorous, independent lifestyle and encapsulated a functionalism that echoed the era's modernist principles. During the same period Chanel conceived a house logo, based on the two "C"s of her nickname, "Coco," thereby forever connecting the brand with its founder.

The innovation of the Chanel logo is matched by that of the products and packaging. The Chanel N° 5 package, with its stark black lines and plain sans serif lettering, is one of the most iconic in the world—an example of minimalist aesthetics that has remained virtually unchanged for almost a century and is now inseparable from the product itself.

In conceiving the product and the packaging, Chanel may have been inspired by the rectilinear shape and unornamented labels of the laboratory bottles in which the French perfumer who created the perfume, Ernest Beaux, mixed his samples.

In testament to the Chanel logo's power as an emblem of glamour, examples are held in many museum collections, and in the 1980s Andy Warhol used the packaging as the subject of a set of silkscreens.

← P.77

1922–1931

BAUHAUS PROGRAMS

Book

László Moholy-Nagy (1895–1946), Herbert Bayer (1900–1985), Walter Gropius (1883–1969)

Bauhaus, Germany

Students and directors at the world-famous design school Staatliches Bauhaus have produced a multitude of magazines, books, and catalogs that have become graphic design landmarks.

Edited by Bauhaus founder Walter Gropius and László Moholy-Nagy, *Staatliches Bauhaus Weimar 1919–1923* was a catalog produced to accompany the Bauhaus's first exhibition of 1923. Herbert Bayer, then a student, designed the cover, while its interior and radical format (9¾ × 10 inches [25 x 25.5 cm]) was created by Moholy-Nagy, who had joined the Bauhaus that year to run its photography and typography courses. The catalog was a showcase for the Bauhaus itself, announcing its shift in emphasis from fine art to applied art.

In 1925, two years after becoming a Bauhaus master, Moholy-Nagy, along with Gropius, produced *Bauhausbücher*, a series of fourteen books to promote the institution. The prospectus used to promote volume fourteen (pictured) has become a symbol of the Bauhaus philosophy of combining craft and technology, as well as a manifestation of "typophoto" (the term Moholy-Nagy used to describe photograms combined with sans serif type).

Moholy-Nagy and Gropius also edited the first issues of the Bauhaus magazine, *Bauhaus: Zeitschrift für Gestaltung*. Bayer's cover for the fifth issue, published in 1928, has become an icon of twentieth-century design: a photograph represents various items of stationery, which cast their shadows over a previous issue of the journal folded at the corner. The radical composition would be the only cover that relied solely on a photographic image.

In 1926 Bayer, now director of the school's Druck and Reklame (printing and advertising) workshops, established a modernist approach to typography in printed material. Bayer's new approach is apparent in his 1926 *Staatliches Bauhaus in Dessau*'s catalog cover with its sharp angles, simple lowercase text, and clean use of color.

The emigration of many of the Bauhaus's important members, including Gropius, Moholy-Nagy, and Bayer, to the U.S. in the 1930s, disseminated Bauhaus ideas in a new context. Today, graphic design continues to look back to Bauhaus as one of the first modernist visions of the discipline.

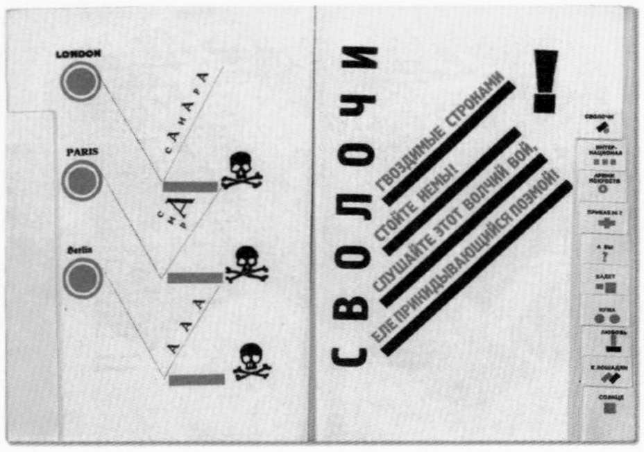

← P.78

← P.79

← P.80

1923

DLYA GOLOSA, BY VLADIMIR MAYAKOVSKY

Book

El Lissitzky (1890–1941)

Gosizdat (State Publishing House), Germany

El Lissitzky's design of *Dlya Golosa* (For the Voice), published by the Berlin office of the Moscow State Publishing House, made an outstanding contribution to the Constructivist project of forging a dynamic visual language, and of revolutionizing conventional forms, such as the book. A singular graphic achievement, the work, like a modern building, approaches space and materials with a fresh eye on their potential to be meaningfully organized and expressively structured.

Trained as an architectural engineer, Lissitzky taught at the state-run Soviet VKhUTEMAS (Higher State Artistic and Technical Workshops) schools of art and design, before moving to Berlin in 1921 to establish cultural ties with Russia's Western neighbors. Vladimir Mayakovsky, who was also in Germany at the time, commissioned Lissitzky to be the "constructor" of a collection of thirteen of his most popular poems. These poems were often read in public, and their collection into one volume was meant to facilitate such readings. Lissitzky's design includes a tabbed index that directs the reader to a chosen poem, and a typographic treatment of the poem's title that portrays its tone and meaning.

Using only the elements available in a compositor's type case, the red-and-black compositions incorporate abstract figuration (a red circle for the sun), concrete construction (an "A" made of rule), prefabricated representation (a pointing hand), and stylistic reference (a blackletter typeface for the word "Berlin"). Together, such devices involve the reader in graphic performances of Mayakovsky's exclamatory texts. For instance, "Our March" opens with a red square representing a city space overtaken by the Communist army. Below, large and small letters offer two possible imperatives: "BoY" (fight) or "BeY" (beat them). On the opposite page, "March" is printed in black, whereas "Our," in red, resonates with the square, reinforcing the claim of Communist gains. Letters shared by the two words are superimposed, creating a sense of depth, while all the letters, placed at varying angles, seem to swing with a forward movement.

With *Dlya Golosa*, Lissitzky expanded type's role in the visual interpretation of texts, setting a new standard for the expressive use of typographic scale, contrast, negative space, and layering.

1923–1925/1927–1929

LEF AND NOVYI LEF

Magazine / Newspaper

Aleksandr Rodchenko (1891–1956)

Gosizdat (State Publishing House), Russia

Edited by the poet Vladimir Mayakovsky, the aesthetics journal *LEF* (Left Front of the Arts), later renamed *Novyi LEF* (New Left Front of the Arts), created the perfect platform for communicating avant-garde ideology. In the first edition, published in March 1923, Ossip Brik, writer, critic, and cofounder of the magazine, condemned artists who adopted Constructivist principles yet still produced the "same old landscapes and portraits," while lavishing praise on Aleksandr Rodchenko for his pursuit of "productivism"—the design and production of utilitarian objects. Rodchenko epitomized the concept of the "artist engineer," who prioritized function over conventional aesthetics.

The publication took its name from the LEF group, an association of radical poets, writers, filmmakers, and artists. As designer of the magazine, Rodchenko articulated its aims through a bold design statement. Functional typography and dynamic composition, integrated with solid color, bold rules, and photocollage, formed distinctive wrap-around letterpress covers, positioning *LEF* at the apex of art and politics. Withdrawal of state funding in 1925 ended publication until 1927, when the association regrouped. In an attempt to reconcile internal divisions and combat mounting criticism of modernism, Rodchenko implemented fundamental changes: asymmetrical design, lowercase type for the masthead, and documentary photography.

In 1928 an anonymous letter in the photographic journal *Sovetskoe Foto* accused Rodchenko of "petty bourgeois formalism," and with Socialist Realism in the ascendant and internal factions within Novyi LEF intensifying, Mayakovsky resigned from the editorial board the same year. When Rodchenko was again criticized for indulging in technique rather than subject matter in the final issue of *Novyi LEF*, he too left, later becoming an official government photojournalist in an attempt at rehabilitation. This would culminate with his notorious but brilliantly inventive documentation in 1933 of the construction of the White Sea-Baltic Sea Canal, which used "corrective labor," for the propaganda publication *USSR in Construction*. Rodchenko's photographic layouts for that title use many of the graphic effects developed for *LEF* and *Novyi LEF*, and remain influential to this day.

1923–1926

THE NEXT CALL

Magazine / Newspaper

Hendrik Nicolaas Werkman (1882–1945)

Self-commissioned, the Netherlands

Only rarely do publications with just nine issues and a print run of forty copies become cultural icons. *The Next Call*, published in the provincial town of Groningen in the Netherlands, and unaffiliated with any of the avant-garde art movements of the day (Dada, De Stijl, Bauhaus, etc.), is such an oddity. Its author, the painter and small printer Hendrik Nicolaas Werkman, manipulated his 1850 German hand press as if it were a paintbrush, assembling scraps of lumber into blocks of wood type and experimenting with various pressures, ink textures, colors, and overlays, with the result that no two copies of the same run were ever the same. Considered by many a failed painter, Werkmann received no recognition during his lifetime.

Issues of *The Next Call* were essentially posters folded into modest eight-page booklets that Werkman would mail out free to fellow painters, colleagues, and acquaintances. The often-cryptic text, written by Werkman with contributions from the painter Job Hansen, was reminiscent of a Tristan Tzara, but owed nothing in presentation to any individual or group. Shunning the asymmetrical collages and patchworks of words and images favored by Dadaists, *The Next Call* featured elegant typographical compositions that Werkman called *druksels*, meaning "impressions."

The magazine's most intriguing characteristic is the monumental, almost architectural quality of its covers, spreads, and foldouts. Strong vertical motifs act as pillars against which graphic elements seem to lean (*The Next Call* 2, 5, 9); stacks of display letters rise as tall as skyscrapers (*The Next Call* 4, 9); piled on top of each other, words and numbers form a ladder for the eye (*The Next Call* 7, 8). A recurring theme is the jagged silhouette of a lock plate, a flat piece of metal that Werkman probably removed from a door and used on his press as if it were a giant letter (*The Next Call* 1, 2, 5). In the middle is a rectangular aperture, an evocation, perhaps, of the narrow window of opportunity between the wars when all artists, even those living like Werkman in remote corners of Europe, could hear "the next call"—the call of modernity.

← P.80

1923 ●

LIDANTIU FARAM

Book

Ilia Zdanevich (1894–1975)

Editions 41°, France

Ilia Zdanevich's *Lidantiu Faram* (Lidantiu as a Beacon) stands alone among the first modern works of experimental poetry, not only as an idiosyncratic literary creation but also as a typographic system unmatched in its elaboration. The culmination of a cycle of five *Zaum* plays, *Lidantiu* memorializes a friend of the author's youth, the painter Mikhail Lidantiu, and allegorizes the triumph of nonrepresentational over conventional art through an invented phonetic language (*Zaum*).

Like other Russian poets experimenting with *Zaum* ("transrational") language, Zdanevich rejected everyday speech as incapable of poetic meaning. But unlike his peers, he dismissed *all* conventional linguistic forms, turning instead to the bare sounds of the Russian language, which he believed could express deeply personal, emotional, and bodily experience, and devising graphic rules (of placement, style coding, scale variation) and typographic forms that re-created rather than replicated his verbal compositions.

Zdanevich's combination of conceptual, technical, and formal ingenuity in *Lidantiu* set the stage for a virtuoso performance in which each character is assigned a distinct range of sounds and typographic possibilities. Like Lissitzky's *Dlya Golosa* (*For the Voice*), which appeared in the same year, Zdanevich's design draws attention to its own means of physical production—visibly piecing large letters together from printers' ornaments, for example—and thereby involves the viewer actively in the (re)produced, constructed, and construed text, through a reading of its graphic terms. The first time that a letter assembled from decorative pieces appears, its height marks a word ("Mum's") that fills a page, lending primacy to the individual cry it embodies, in contrast with a choral text set in small, regular characters on the page opposite.

Like other avant-garde works by Zdanevich, *Lidantiu* occupied a cultural margin. Yet his work shared with early modern design an interest in the possibility of purely visual typographic meaning. *Lidantiu* represents a rare degree of thoroughness in the exploration of this possibility, and has come to be seen as a model of twentieth-century typographic innovation.

← P.80

1923–1932 ●

MERZ

Magazine / Newspaper

Kurt Schwitters (1887–1948) et al.

Merzverlag, Germany

The word "Merz," allegedly a meaningless fragment taken from "Commerz," was used by Kurt Schwitters in 1919 for his abstract compositions, and became the title of one of the most important avant-garde publications of the early twentieth century. The first issue was published in January 1923 and, in conjunction with artists and designers, such as El Lissitzky and Jan Tschichold, Schwitters went on to produce a further twenty-three issues before the magazine's demise in 1932. During a period of tumultuous change in Europe, with scientific, technological, and political developments all feeding an upsurge of cultural activity embodied by movements such as Futurism, Dadaism, and Constructivism, Merz provided a vehicle for driving forward modernist ideas and theories.

The layout of each issue of the magazine changed according to its theme and designer, although Schwitters retained the role of editor. The design principles, however, remained consistent, with sans serif type and asymmetric layouts epitomizing the publication's ideals. *Merz 8–9*, a double issue entitled "Nasci" (Nature), published in the spring of 1924, designed and jointly edited by Lissitzky, draws on Constructivist typographic principles and injects these with a playful sense of Dada disruption and experimentation. Also published in 1924, Issue 11—"TYpo REklame"—uses Schwitters's commercial design work for Pelikan ink to showcase his ideas for typography and advertising, in which colors (black and deep orange) are applied in blocks, while contrasts of size and color create dynamic space within an asymmetrical layout. "Ursonate," the twenty-fourth and final issue published in 1932, based on a sound performance piece of the same name by Schwitters and designed by Tschichold, had phonetic text set typographically as a form of concrete poetry.

Merz belongs to a history of radical publications that have challenged accepted social and cultural norms; its influence can still be seen in later publications such as *Émigré* and *Speak*, and in the DIY culture of the fanzine.

← P.81

1923 ●

LUCHSHIKH SOSOK NE BYLO I NET

Poster

Aleksandr Rodchenko (1891–1956)

Rezinotrest, Russia

This advertisement for babies' pacifiers, with text by Vladimir Mayakovsky, shows a grinning, bright green-and-red figure, whose wide mouth holds a row of pacifiers. The red, green, and black text translates approximately as: "There are no better pacifiers. Suck them 'til old age. Sold everywhere."

In 1923 Aleksandr Rodchenko was struggling with the copy for an advertisement he had been commissioned to produce for Dobrolet, the Soviet Aviation society. Mocked by his colleagues, who assumed that the jingle was the work of a bad poet, the artist turned to his friend and "national poet" Mayakovsky for help, thereby initiating their long and fruitful partnership as "Advertisement Constructors" for various state enterprises and organizations, usually known as "trusts." This example was produced for Rezinotrest—the rubber trust. Rather than representing a Western-style fantasy of acquisition, the posters tended to display products in action, using bold, colorful designs (usually two colors only in addition to black) of simple abstract shapes that avoided superfluous details. In contrast to the more sophisticated language of Rodchenko's photomontages, the posters' style was crude and direct, and had a wry humor that conveyed its message in a quick and easily understood way. This approach was essential for the largely illiterate audience at whom the advertisements were aimed, and was also well suited to the quick and inexpensive printing techniques that Rodchenko used. While some designs were displayed as single painted signs in store windows, others were reproduced by lithography or offset printing, often with the assistance of Rodchenko's students at the VkHUTEMAS (Higher State Artistic and Technical Workshops). The whole of Moscow, according to the designer, was decorated with their output.

Mayakovsky saw the work as a form of political agitation rather than advertising; in this case, he believed they were promoting health on the grounds that pacifiers were healthier to suck than dirty rags.

← P.82

1923–present

TIME

Magazine / Newspaper

Various

Time Inc., U.S.

The weekly news magazine *Time*, conceived by Briton Hadden and Henry Robinson Luce, was launched on March 3, 1923, with a cover designed by art director Gordon Aymar, who was then working at the J. Walter Thompson advertising agency. The cover image featured an illustration of the former U.S. Speaker of the House Joseph G. Cannon by the commercial artist William Oberhardt. Aymar also designed the first *Time* logotype, positioned across the top of the cover, as well as the scroll patterning that appeared on both sides of the image.

Early in 1927 another distinctive feature, the red border, made its first appearance, and in 1928 the magazine introduced the first color cover, replacing its previous black-and-white photographs and drawings. In the 1940s and '50s, illustrators Boris Artzybasheff and Boris Chaliapin's renowned photorealist covers revolutionized *Time*'s look, with the duo creating more than six hundred designs between them. The 1950s also saw an inanimate object featured on the cover for the first time, and assistant managing editor Otto Fuerbringer introduced a new format that superimposed the logotype over the image. Some twenty years later, in 1977, art director Walter Bernard changed the headline type to Franklin Gothic for texts printed underneath the masthead, a font that became widely used by other magazines and newspapers, and introduced the folding corner flap on the top right corner to alert readers to stories inside. Bernard's redesign also gave more prominence to the maps, charts, and diagrams used inside the magazine to illustrate world events, which have endured throughout *Time*'s history, and were designed from 1937 to 1970 chiefly by Robert Chapin. *Time*'s redesign in 2007 was overseen by Luke Hayman of Pentagram, who brought a cleaner, simpler style to the internal pages, with bold titles to introduce the magazine's various sections. Hayman's design also integrated the magazine's appearance more closely with that of its website, Time.com.

More than one hundred years since its first appearance, *Time* remains iconic, with a design heritage that continues to be hugely influential on international magazine publishing.

← P.83

1924

KINO GLAZ

Poster

Aleksandr Rodchenko (1891–1956)

Goskino (State Committee of the Council of Ministers on Cinematography), Russia

Aleksandr Rodchenko's poster for a film directed by Dziga Vertov—an avant-garde filmmaker who pioneered the use of documentary montage in film—marked an important step in the artistic development of film posters in the USSR. In 1924 the film industry was centralized under the aegis of the Russian state, endowed with its own publicity department responsible for commissioning posters. Before this, film posters were mediocre and produced largely by unknown artists. Rodchenko's hand-drawn design (using lithographic crayon) and his understanding of the lithographic printing process established a trend that was to be adopted by the Stenberg brothers, whose colorful film posters adorned the streets of Moscow throughout the 1920s.

The poster design for *Kino Glaz* reflects Vertov's pronouncement, made in *LEF*, the journal of the progressive group of artists known as the Left Front of the Arts: "I am kino-eye. I am a mechanical eye. I the machine show you the world as only I can see it." The all-seeing eye is representative of the camera gazing at its intended audience. In placing the mirror-image drawings of the handheld cameras and boy's head squinting into the light at a steep angle, Rodchenko echoes Vertov's use of high-angle shots, a strategy the artist himself was later to employ in his photographs. Although Rodchenko was already experimenting with photomontage as an aid to his commercial work, it was unusual to include photographic images on large-scale designs such as posters. The drawings of the camera and the boy's head are based on his own photographs. At the same time, the bold symmetrical arrangement of the sans serif lettering, with the film's title placed in the center, adds a mechanical feel that reflects the Constructivist ideology that Rodchenko helped to formulate.

Although Rodchenko was to produce only two further film posters, his work in photography and graphics exerted a major influence on other Russian poster artists such as the Stenbergs, as well as on numerous future generations of graphic designers.

← P.84

1924

PELIKAN INK

Advertising

El Lissitzky (1890–1941)

Günther Wagner, Germany

El Lissitzky's atmospheric sepia-colored photogram for Pelikan ink belongs to a series that he produced when he was making increasing use of photographic techniques, such as double exposures and photograms, to create effects of overlapping layers in portraiture and other works.

Although Lissitzky may well have discovered the photogram through the work of Man Ray, his use of the technique in graphic design as well as advertising was to be highly influential, particularly the positioning of type and photography within the same visual space, which is known as "typophoto." In this photogram the objects are lit from the side, casting long shadows, that provide a sense of depth and contrast sharply with the white "TINTE" that glides over the image on a separate plane. The image itself is evocative of an X-ray, penetrating the surface to reveal internal structures underneath. At the time of creating his typophotos, Lissitzky was being treated for tuberculosis in a sanatorium and may well have been X-rayed there; the Pelikan advertisements were conceived as a way of paying for his medical expenses.

Visually, the Pelikan ink photogram presents a number of contrasting elements: the crisp white lettering of "TINTE" contrasts with the softer, blurred Pelikan logotype and almost-black ink bottle; at the same time, the horizontal alignment of the letters and front face of the ink bottle counteract the more dynamic slanted forms of the pen and logotype. Variations in opacity also imbue the objects with different degrees of materiality. Similar themes were addressed in other designs promoting Pelikan carbon paper, although the stencil lettering has greater relevance to the product.

The photogram was produced in the same year as one of Lissitzky's most famous works, his self-portrait known as *The Constructor*, which shares its iconography with another Pelikan advertisement. The latter features a hand and a compass, similar to those in *The Constructor*, with a bottle of Pelikan ink held in the palm of the hand. Such crossovers illustrate Lissitzky's approach to the Constructivist project, which re-cast the relationship between art and more utilitarian forms of visual communication.

← P.84

← P.85

← P.85

1924

KNIGI

Poster

Aleksandr Rodchenko (1891–1956)

Gosizdat (State Publishing House), Russia

One of Aleksandr Rodchenko's best-known and most important works, this design for a poster, commissioned by the state publishing house Gosizdat, features a photograph of the actress Lilya Brik shouting the word "knigi" ("books"), with a subtitle reading, "for all forms of knowledge," surrounded by a powerful Constructivist design. It was commissioned as part of a program to democratize literacy by announcing that books would be freely available to all. Rodchenko created the original design in 1924, although it was not immediately reproduced in poster form.

One of the founders of Constructivism, Rodchenko was inspired by the photomontage works of the German Dadaists, and began his own experiments with photography in the 1920s, first using found images and then shooting his own work from 1924. Lilya Brik, wife of the critic and creative theorist Osip Brik, was something of a muse to the Russian avant-garde, particularly the poet-painter Vladimir Mayakovsky, a longtime associate of Rodchenko. With its bold colors, abstract shapes, sharp angles, dynamic energy, and sans serif lettering, all combined using the technique of photomontage, the design is typical of the visual style Rodchenko developed in his graphic work of these years, when large numbers of the population were semiliterate and propaganda messages had to be communicated simply for maximum impact. For Rodchenko, basic abstract forms, photographic imagery, and plain, rudimentary lettering corresponded to the language of the streets, belonging to the same family as public spectacles, news announcements, and modern machinery, as well as to the nascent Soviet film industry. Even though Rodchenko was not alone in using these elements, he harnessed them with particular mastery for propaganda purposes.

An icon of Soviet revolutionary graphics, "Knigi" inspired numerous imitations in the late twentieth century, particularly in cover designs for music albums. These include a series of six 7-inch (17.7-cm) vinyl singles for the influential Dutch punk band, the Ex, each of which contained a variation on the Lilya Brik portrait (1991), and the cover of the Franz Ferdinand album, *You Could Have It So Much Better* (2005).

1924–1944

GEBRAUCHSGRAPHIK

Magazine / Newspaper

Various

Phönix Illustrationsdruck und Verlag GmbH, Germany

The Berlin-based *Gebrauchsgraphik* (Commercial Graphics), subtitled *Monatschrift zur Förderung künstlerischer Reklame* (Monthly Magazine for Promoting Art in Advertising), published in German and English, showcased advertising art from around the world. The successor to the German poster magazine *Das Plakat*, it presented more diverse media than its progenitor and was international in scope.

Gebrauchsgraphik promoted major German names, such as Herbert Bayer, but, in reflection of the open-minded vision of its founder and editor H. K. Frenzel, it also featured a wide range of modernist styles from throughout Europe, such as Art Deco, Surrealism, Futurism, De Stijl, Constructivism, and Dutch typography, as well as the work of American designers. Frenzel, who worked on the magazine until his death in 1937, employed an array of cover designers, including Stephan Schwarz, Herbert Bayer, Uli Huber, and Joseph Binder. Rather than maintaining a strict house style, as *Neue Grafik* did, Frenzel allowed each artist to pursue an individual approach in terms of both imagery and typography. Covers of the 1920s were mostly inspired by the Bauhaus or Art Deco movements, although montaged designs (as seen in the extraordinary combination of buildings in the August 1926 issue) and Surrealist and neoclassical covers began to appear in the 1930s. From the late 1920s, when the magazine started to be distributed in the U.S. through the Book Service Company, these ideas became more accessible to American readers, and contributed in 1939 to Binder receiving the commission to design the poster for the New York World's Fair. The magazine was unusual in using high-end printing technologies for its reproductions, including bound-ins and foldouts, rarely seen in publications of the day.

Gebrauchsgraphik ceased publication in 1944 due to paper shortages (although political repression had already ended its focus on the avant-garde), but resumed in 1950 under the publisher Bruckmann Verlag (Munich). In format, design, and editorial policy, the periodical influenced numerous contemporary magazines, such as *Graphis*, *Advertising Arts*, and *Portfolio*. In 1972 it was relaunched as *Novum Gebrauchsgraphik*, which continued until 2021.

1925

BOCHUMER VEREIN

Advertising

Max Burchartz (1887–1961)

Bochumer Verein für Bergbau und Gusstahlfabrikation, Germany

The graphic artist and photographer Max Burchartz briefly attended the Weimar Bauhaus in the 1920s and co-signed the Weimar Manifesto of International Constructivists. Both these experiences were fundamental to his artistic practice and belief in the principles of universality and systematization.

In 1924 Burchartz and Johannis Canis founded Werbebau, Germany's first modern advertising agency, in the heart of the Ruhr, the country's heavy-industry region. Based in Bochum, Werbebau's first commission was a portfolio of brochures for the Bochumer Verein für Bergbau und Gusstahlfabrikation, the region's main association for industrial mining and cast-steel equipment manufacturing.

Each consisting of about a dozen A4 separate pages, these brochures were the visual equivalent of a modern, up-to-date production system; they showcased the firm's products (such as locomotive wheels, springs, rails, bolts, and nuts), but also their modern, efficient construction techniques. On each lithographed page, Burchartz also explored his notion of "optical efficiency," whereby the human eye is able to read text only after registering and comprehending the accompanying images. By isolating, grouping, and layering information in text and image groups, he attempted to achieve an efficient, universal method of communication while raising photomontage to the status of a truly "contemporary means of expression." Exploring the power of the photographic image, these brochures display complex dynamic compositions of images and text—written by Canis—set in sans serif type and arranged in boxes according to an abstract grid. Color is used throughout—in backgrounds, images, or geometric shapes—to express contrast.

Unlike other modernist materials designed for newer technology manufacturers, such as AEG, Burchartz's avant-garde work for Bochumer Verein was atypical in this kind of metallurgical industry: little is known of its print run, circulation, impact on sales, or relevance. The brochures were, however, a pioneering commercial application of an abstract Constructivist-inspired visual language—here set free from the political or polemic charge of other more widely distributed and influential artistic examples.

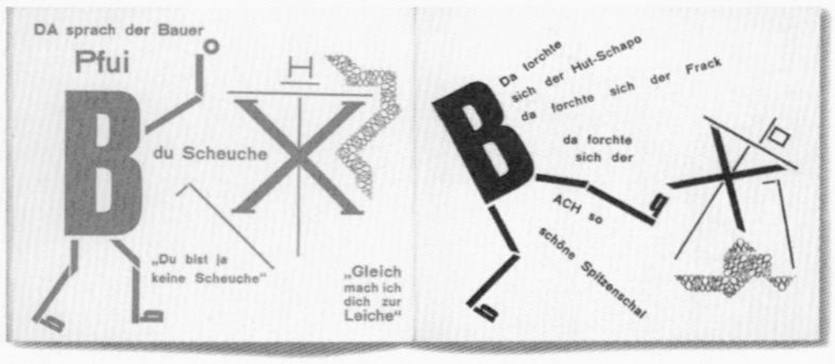

← P.86

1925

MERZ 14/15: DIE SCHEUCHE MÄRCHEN

Book

Kurt Schwitters (1887–1948), Theo van Doesburg (1883–1931)

Aposs-Verlag, Germany

Die Scheuche Märchen (The Scarecrow), conceived by Kurt Schwitters and illustrated by Theo van Doesburg with the aid of matchsticks, represents a considerable achievement in its merging of art and design, type and image. Schwitters subsequently designated a number of copies of the book for an issue of his modernist periodical Merz (no. 14/15) by pasting printed labels on to the front cover.

Based on an earlier collaboration between Schwitters and Kate Steinitz, *Der Hahnpeter* (Peter the Rooster), in which type and printers' ornaments had been used in unconventional ways—*Die Scheuche Märchen* represents a more radical expression of the same idea. Here, however, drawings have been replaced by images built entirely from typographic forms. The story itself, which is essentially an allegory, revolves around the downfall of a scarecrow adorned with the accoutrements of bourgeois society whose empty posturing is ridiculed and undermined by a rooster. The end of the story seems to usher in a new world as the scarecrow's belongings are reclaimed by their ghostly former owners.

Visually, the publication reflects both the destructive tendencies of the Dadaists, who hoped to destabilize the status quo through shocking and nonsensical acts, and the constructive tendencies of the De Stijl group, which sought unification through the inculcation of a universal style. The page containing publishing information employs a sans serif, uppercase setting, whereby type is cast in blocks that stress horizontal and vertical axes (all typical of the De Stijl movement), while many of the illustrations display the playful, less constrained approach associated with Dada. Similarly, the use of type to create both word and image is consistent with the reductive approach of De Stijl, whereas the construction of fresh visual forms and meanings that use preexisting elements resonates with the Merz assemblages created by Schwitters. It is known above all for its use of type as image, however, and the fact that it provides another landmark in the liberation of the letter from its role as signifier of phonological content that *Die Scheuche Märchen* is best remembered by graphic designers.

← P.86

1925

ELEMENTARE TYPOGRAPHIE

Magazine / Newspaper

Jan Tschichold (1902–1974)

Bildungsverband der Deutschen Buchdrucker, Germany

Elementare Typographie (Elemental Typography), published as a twenty-four-page insert in the October 1925 issue of the Leipzig printing-trade journal *Typographische Mitteilungen* (Typographic News), was one of the most influential early writings on modernist typography. In this special issue, practitioners of the New Typography expounded on the principles of asymmetric "elemental" typographic design to German typographers and printers. It included illustrations by avant-garde designers Herbert Bayer, Max Burchartz, El Lissitzky, Johannes Molzahn, László Moholy-Nagy, Kurt Schwitters, the Swiss poster designer Otto Baumberger, and Jan Tschichold himself, with each example accompanied by a brief commentary by Tschichold.

In addition to typographic examples, the publication included a series of articles, including two pieces by Tschichold. The first, "Die Neue Gestaltung" (The New Design), is a concise overview of the origins and development of the New Typography, illustrated with images from Lissitzky's "Mär von Zwei Quadraten" (March of Two Squares) from a 1922 issue of *De Stijl* magazine. These images exemplify Tschichold's Constructivist objectives and a compositional system based on the arrangement of geometric shapes. Tschichold's second article, a manifesto for the new style, introduced asymmetric typographic design based on the principles of functionality, communication, and simplification, and emphasized the importance of photography as a basic element of the New Typography.

Twenty thousand copies of *Elementare Typographie* were distributed to typographers and book printers. Although Tschichold's advocacy of asymmetrical layout and sans serif type caused controversy among its readership, within just a few years the publication had generated much-improved design results in the German printing trade. It also served as a precursor to Tschichold's 1928 handbook, *Die Neue Typographie* (*The New Typography*), and his 1935 textbook *Typographische Gestaltung* (Typographic Design), and established Tschichold as the chief spokesperson of the new style, known throughout the German-speaking design world.

← P.87

1925

DIE KUNSTISMEN/LES ISMES DE L'ART/ THE ISMS OF ART

Book

El Lissitzky (1890–1941), Hans Arp (1886–1966)

Eugen Rentsch Verlag, Germany

A collaboration between El Lissitzky and Hans Arp in Switzerland, the trilingual publication *Die Kunstismen/Les Ismes de l'art/The Isms of Art* was key to the development of the New Typography.

While at art school in Vitebsk in 1920, Lissitzky cofounded the UNOVIS group (an acronym for Affirmers of the New Art), headed by Kazimir Malevich. The seventh tenet of the group's manifesto advocated "the creation of a contemporary form of book and other advancements in printing," an exhortation fulfilled by *Die Kunstismen*. Lissitzky's training as an architect and his contact with avant-garde groups, such as Dada, De Stijl, and the Bauhaus, would all influence his conception of book design as an act of creation, rather than as a manipulation of graphic content; on the title page of the book he designed for Vladimir Mayakovsky, *Dlya Golosa* (1923), he credits himself as a "constructor."

In 1924, having recently collaborated with Kurt Schwitters on a combined issue of Schwitters's journal *Merz*, Lissitzky suggested devoting the final volume to a "last parade" of the era's significant art movements. When Schwitters demurred, Lissitzky approached the Dada artist Hans Arp. The resulting fifteen entries of *Die Kunstismen* include Abstract Film, Dada, Cubism, Futurism, and Lissitzky's own abstraction series, Proun, all of which are listed on the cover in an assertive, placard-like composition and bold Constructivist red-and-black palette. Inside, a brief all-text section introduces each movement with a quote or epigram set in parallel columns of French, German, and English, while the subsequent illustrated gallery is characterized by asymmetrical compositions of artworks and artist portraits set in fields of blank space, and exaggerated figure numbers. This valorizing of traditionally recessive graphic elements and novel structural approaches demonstrated Lissitzky's aim to develop a more conceptual basis for book design, in which graphics and layout attained equal stature with content.

While the New Typographic aesthetic would eventually pass, Lissitzky's liberation of the page as a field of graphic possibility, and his elevation of the designer to the status of creator, would irrevocably alter the trajectory of design history.

← P.87

← P.88

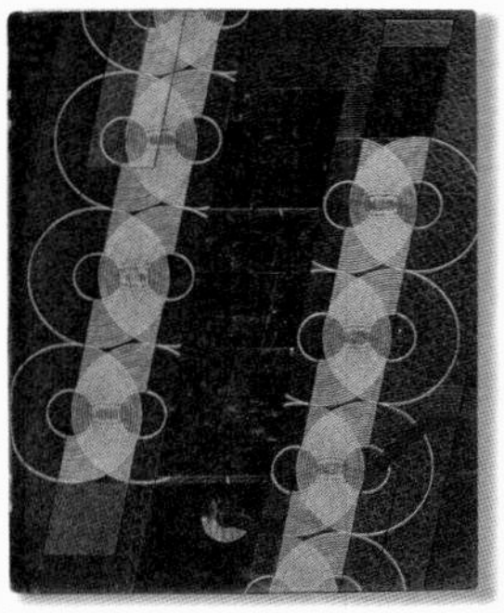

← P.89

1925

BAYER UNIVERSAL

Typeface

Herbert Bayer (1900–1985)

Bauhaus, Germany

Bayer Universal is a classic example of design reflecting the social, cultural, and political climate of its historical moment. Herbert Bayer was director of the typography and advertising department at the Bauhaus from 1925 to 1928 and, as a modernist, found the prevailing typographic style in use at the time in Germany—blackletter—antiquated and unrepresentative of the Machine Age. Convinced that sans serif type was more synonymous with the contemporary era, he set out to explore the possibilities of typography and language in a more theoretical manner. Bayer argued that as the spoken word did not distinguish between uppercase and lowercase, typography did not need two symbols for each letterform. In the case of German, which uses a high number of capitals, this was a particularly radical stance. This approach, he believed, would not only be more widely understood but also more economical for printing. Bayer designed his Universal alphabet to this end, and from 1925 the Bauhaus abandoned capital letters.

Bayer Universal is a sans serif unicase face that employs geometry as its inspiration and guide, rather than the stroke of the pen or cut of the chisel. This rationalized approach, in which the "blueprint" for the design consists of circles, arcs, three angles, and horizontal and vertical lines, with construction limited to essential elements and multiple characters, such as the "b," "d," "p," and "q" rotated or mirrored, calls to mind the efficiency and organization of Henry Ford's automobile production line. Bayer saw Universal as not just a typeface but as an all-encompassing writing system that would include typewriters and handwriting. Unfortunately for Bayer, his ideas were not released commercially, although a more conservative version, Bayer Type, was published by Berthold in 1935. Digital fonts, inspired by the original design, have since been produced by major foundries.

Bayer's legacy is, in part, the continued theoretical exploration of typography and language. Further experiments regarding the potential of a combined unicase typeface, such as Alphabet 26 by Bradbury Thompson, echo his efforts, while typefaces such as Read Regular by Natascha Frensch unravel the structural norm, seeking to help dyslexic individuals distinguish between characters.

1925–present

THE NEW YORKER

Magazine / Newspaper

Various

Condé Nast Publications, U.S.

Despite reflecting on the cultural developments of the day, the interior of the *New Yorker* has remained virtually unchanged for over nine decades. While the cover has served as an ever-shifting canvas, the simplicity and clarity of the interior has stayed constant, marking it as one of the most successful magazine designs of the twentieth century. The original three-column grid of the interior was crafted by the first art editor, Rea Irvin, who wanted nothing to come between reader and text.

The *New Yorker*'s strong tradition of cover illustration has also been carefully nurtured. Art editor Françoise Mouly describes the covers as a "portrait... of what urban sophisticates chuckled about, and [their] attitudes, prejudices." Saul Steinberg's cover illustrations (eighty-seven published during his lifetime and six posthumously) are the best known since the publication's inception. "View of the World from Ninth Avenue" (also known as "A Parochial New Yorker's View of the World"), created for the issue of March 29, 1976, and showing a self-absorbed New Yorker's perspective of the nation and the world from the vantage point of New York City's west side, is the most famous of all and has been reproduced many times. Other than Steinberg, the best-known and most provocative cover artist was Art Spiegelman, whose designs (from 1992 to 2003) often featured caricatures. An image of the cartoonist Jack Cole, for example, showed him dressed as his creation Plastic Man, with an absurdly elongated neck, examining a distorted portrait by Picasso. Spiegelman's most famous was his 9/11 cover, which portrayed a pair of barely visible black rectangles against an all-black background—an image that attempted to convey the meaning of the disaster without describing its horror. The magazine often featured Christoph Niemann's simple, brightly colored illustrations spotlighting cultural and political issues: a cover featuring a toy army of paper airplanes, tanks, and battleships made from American tax returns reflected on the cost of war. By giving artists a prominent platform, the *New Yorker* has demonstrated its belief in the continuing relevance of illustration. Both Spiegelman and Niemann have used the practice to combine gravitas with astute social and political commentary.

c. 1925

PIERRE LEGRAIN BINDING

Book Cover

Pierre Legrain (1889–1929)

Mercure de France, France

With their conspicuous geometric patterns and complex abstraction, Pierre Legrain's binding designs of contemporary literature and poetry (frequently of erotic subject matter for private clients) embody his mastery of Art Deco design. Whether or not the style was appropriate to the subject (and many critics felt it was not), his work reveals his ability to combine sumptuous materials with striking graphic motifs that captured the decorative power of the style.

A designer, furniture maker, and decorator, whose originality in binding has been credited to his inexperience in this particular art, Legrain was first employed as a binder by the French fashion designer and art collector Jacques Doucet when the latter was renewing his library. Many contemporary bibliophiles with a taste for modern design would get their books re-bound, and Legrain was associated with progressive, nontraditional binding and the rejection of conservative styles. Given *carte blanche* by Doucet, Legrain articulated his philosophy thus: "Each binding is the frontispiece to each book; it synthesizes the work, it is the frame which should embellish and give value to it." The opulent character of his designs, particularly that for *Daphnis et Chloé* (1925), one of his most famous, is distinguished by its clarity and boldness, and in most cases depended on working a limited range of colors into a febrile richness of abstract forms and lines.

Legrain also bound editions of André Gide, Guillaume Apollinaire, Charles Baudelaire, and Paul Verlaine. Although his approach was not always popular, for some he elevated binding from a minor craft to an art form. The great binder Rose Adler considered him peerless, while one commentator simply declared, "Pierre Legrain *is* contemporary binding."

← P.90

1926

U.S. ROUTE SHIELD

Information Design

Frank F. Rogers (1858–1942) et al.

Federal Government, U.S.

Rather than evolving through a coherent design program (as the British system did), American numbered highway signs developed haphazardly, with no coordinated scheme ever implemented nationwide. Although the black-and-white route shield is often thought of as the classic version, in reality variations across the country are common, with many states using the signs as an opportunity to add their own identifying characteristics.

The United States Numbered Highways (U.S. Highways) system numbers the roads and highways of the U.S. within a nationwide grid first introduced in 1926. The famous shield designed to mark them derived from a sketch by Frank F. Rogers, the Michigan State Highway Commissioner, which he based on the shield of the Great Seal of the United States. Originally, the letters "U.S." appeared above the number, with a horizontal line and the name of the state at the top. The typeface used for the numerals was taken from a hand-drawn font that appeared in the *Manual on Uniform Traffic Control Devices*, first published in 1935. Since then, this typeface has been revised several times, and today highway signs typically use the Series D version of Highway Gothic. The design specified in the manual also includes the black-and-white shield with rounded corners, but on the large green signs now used on major highways most states omit the black background, while California applies a simple black-line border in the shape of the shield and retains the letters "U.S." in a hybrid version of the original. In the 1940s in particular, many states introduced additional symbols and pictograms, as well as map-shaped signs, creating numerous variations, and as the Interstate Highway System has gradually superseded the U.S. Highways, the classic black-and-white road sign has grown increasingly scarce.

With its appealing retro character (and now rarity), the original numbered road shield has become one of America's most treasured national symbols, evoking the romance of the long-distance road trip, which holds a special place in modern U.S. mythology. Today, however, the sign is more likely to be found on items such as menus and albums than on the nation's roads.

← P.91

1926

ABECEDA

Book

Karel Teige (1900–1951)

J. Otto, Czech Republic

Bringing together poetry, photography, dance, and typography in an elegant whole, *Abeceda* is a prime example of typophoto: the integration of typeforms and photographic imagery. This was a technique popular among several of Czech designer Karel Teige's contemporaries, including László Moholy-Nagy, Jan Tschichold, Piet Zwart, and El Lissitzky, but Teige's combined use of graphic and photographic forms to express individual letters marked a new way of exploring the relationship between letterforms and the human body.

Teige collaborated on *Abeceda* with the poet Vítězslav Nezval, the dancer Milča Mayerová, and the photographer Karel Paspa. Such collaboration suggests synthesis, a process that is conveyed stylistically in the book by blending the approches of Constructivism and Surrealism. Teige's Surrealist influence is more apparent in some letter designs than others. The "M," for example, which depicts Mayerová superimposed over an outstretched hand with the letter inscribed in the creases of the palm, is more suggestive of the unconscious than other letter designs, many of which address the Constructivist theme of the body in motion. The combination of graphic letterforms and Mayerová's poses can also be seen as responses to Nezval's poem. This uses visual associations based on letterforms (as seen between the letter "C" and the moon), which are integrated visually through the use of black bars. Sometimes, the bars are extensions of letter strokes, sometimes they are treated as planes that intersect with one another, often they frame, or partially frame, the photographs. In other cases, the bars appear to be part of the photographic scene itself so that Mayerová is standing inside, atop, or in front of them (as with the "I," "R," and "T"). Viewed in its entirety, the alphabet is almost filmic in quality, with each of Mayerová's poses acting like a keyframe and inviting us to imagine the kind of transitional movements that might constitute a whole ballet.

Abeceda occupies a place within a rich tradition of constructing letterforms from images of the body and human proportions—a tradition encompassing typographic designs ranging from Geofroy Tory's *Champ Fleury* (1529) to Anthon Beeke's *Naked Ladies Alphabet* (1970).

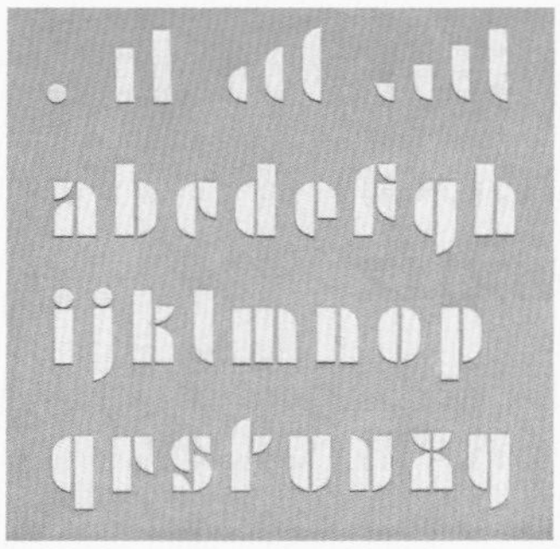

← P.92

1926–1931

KOMBINATIONSSCHRIFT

Typeface

Josef Albers (1888–1976)

Bauhaus, Germany

Kombinationsschrift resulted from typographic experiments with stencil lettering performed from 1926 by the German artist, designer, printmaker, and educator Josef Albers during his professorship at the Bauhaus in Dessau. The typeface was modified slightly over time, resulting in the third (definitive) version.

Albers's teaching was based on empirical knowledge of physical properties and visual characteristics, involving structural models in paper and card, as well as communication and perception. In the mid-1920s he explored designs for stencil lettering that could be used for posters and large-scale signs, aiming to retain legibility despite increased viewing distances. Kombinationsschrift was developed using a limited number of basic shapes and was partly inspired by Egyptienne and Grotesk, each coincidentally based on geometric forms. The elements employed are rationally constructed, and the counters and strokes of the typeface are based on a rigorous geometry of thirds. The same geometry is also applied to the area between the letters, which are intended to be mono-spaced.

Designed for easy legibility, the resulting letterforms were, above all, the visual expression of an increasingly industrial modern society. A firm adherent of Bauhaus ideas and theories, Albers regarded design to be in the service of the masses, and this typeface typifies these rationalist values. Kombinationsschrift is easily produced by machines (therefore suitable for mass production) and is highly legible, making it widely accessible.

In recent times the geometric aspect evident in Albers's typeface has come back into vogue within contemporary design typography. An example of its influence is Michael Bierut's 2008 graphic identity for New York's Museum of Arts and Design, the lettering for which develops the geometrical construction principles of Kombinationsschrift to the point of purism (the "o" consisting of a solid perfect circle) and virtual illegibility. Although this geometric approach proliferated rapidly during the early 2000s, it seems that Albers's dedication to the user and functionality has not been mimicked with the same vigor.

← P.93

1926

FANGHUANG, BY LU XUN

Book Cover

Tao Yuan-qing (1893–1929)

Beijing Beixin Book Company, China

Authored by one of the most influential writers and scholars in modern Chinese literature, *Fanghuang* (Wandering) was devised by Lu Xun's favorite collaborator and Chinese graphic design pioneer, Tao Yuan-qing, and reflects the latter's fusion of traditional Chinese aesthetics with modern artistic styles from the West.

Around the turn of the twentieth century, examples of Western art and design began to infiltrate China through imported books and journals intended for the country's foreign population. Lu and his associates were concerned that these influences would diminish China's own artistic identity, and encouraged young designers to consider forgotten native sources of inspiration, such as patterns on ancient Chinese clay pottery, bronze objects, and stone carvings. Tao Yuan-qing's long collaboration with Lu Xun began with his cover design for *Kumen de Xiangzheng* (Symbol of Depression), published in 1924, which was followed by the book pictured designed in a deliberately crude style, with black figures inspired by prehistoric carvings. Although criticized by other Chinese artists, the angular lines and dark, heavy shapes are symbolic of the book's theme, which involves the suppression of emotions. Flat shapes seen in profile are typical of Tao's work, and evoke stone transfers or rubbings used in China's ancient carved tablets. Executed in delicate brush-strokes, his compositions also reflect his training in traditional Chinese painting and Western water-color techniques.

Most Chinese book-cover design during this period consisted of hand-painted calligraphic titles and minimal color; any other graphic details present usually bore no relationship to the book's contents. Lu and Tao's collaboration pioneered the concept of viewing each book as a unity, including cover, illustration, text, layout, paper, and binding, each of which was considered in the light of the finished work. Their partnership would inspire renewed appreciation of China's native aesthetic traditions, and helped to develop a national identity for modern Chinese graphic design.

← P.93

1927

DEPERO FUTURISTA

Book

Fortunato Depero (1892–1960)

Dinamo-Azari, Italy

Secured with heavy-duty aluminum bolts, and, indeed, often referred to as "the bolted book," Fortunato Depero's monograph *Depero Futurista*, published by his friend Fedele Azari, announces on the cover its homage to technology. A ray of light (a favorite Futurist device), with its corresponding shadow, spreads diagonally downward from the top bolt (turning it into a light bulb) and splits the letters of the title into a shifting pattern of gray and black. The preface describes the work as "bolted like a motor ... unclassifiable ... original, invasive and assailing, like Depero and his art." It is estimated that just four or five copies were bound in tin plate, a material also used for Filippo T. Marinetti's *Parole in Libertà* five years later.

Depero, who was responsible for applying Futurist ideology to graphics, created the book largely as an exercise in self-promotion, setting out a selection of his paintings, advertisements, typographical experiments, theater designs, and life events, from 1913 to 1927. Both in content and design, the book declares assertively his alignment with the modernist avant-garde, particularly designers who had experimented with radical typography, such as László Moholy-Nagy, Theo van Doesburg, El Lissitzky, and Kurt Schwitters, and pays tribute to a host of other artists, creators, and heroes approved by the Futurists. These include writers, thinkers, poets, musicians, famous sportspeople, manufacturers (especially pioneers of the automobile, such as Fiat, Pirelli, and Alfa Romeo), and politicians, such as Benito Mussolini. With many versos (left-hand pages) left blank, and page weights ranging from tissue-thin to almost cardboard-thick, the design freely mixes fonts of different sizes, weights, colors, and styles in numerous unique formats. Texts are printed in constantly changing positions, stretched across the page or squashed together into tight blocks, and in multiple combinations. Languages (Italian, French, Spanish, English, and Polish) also change, and typefaces are interspersed with handwritten-style annotations.

A forerunner of the artist's book, *Depero Futurista* is more than just a celebration of typographic freedom. Treating type and layout, above all, as tools for expressing content, the book proclaims its love of energy and dynamism on every page.

← P.94

1927

NORD EXPRESS

Poster

A. M. Cassandre (1901–1968)

Compagnie des Wagons-Lits, Belgium

A. M. Cassandre's posters for the Chemin de Fer du Nord railway company marked a turning point in his career, beginning a new phase of posters on the theme of rail and sea travel, and giving him an international reputation. Commissioned by Maurice Moyrand, whose father was one of the directors of the company, "Nord Express" depicts a close-up view of a speeding locomotive on a trans-European route.

The modular structure of the design acts as an underlying framework for the rhythmic composition, in which an exaggerated linear perspective with a vanishing point in the bottom right corner of the image draws the viewer into the poster. The locomotive is given a solid metallic form that contrasts with the flattened treatment of the telegraph wires and porcelain insulators. As if to emphasize this contrast, the gradation of sky color in between the wires, achieved through the use of an airbrush, has been reversed, nullifying the illusion of depth. Cassandre, like other artists of his generation, found that the airbrush gave a smooth mechanical and ethereal quality to his work, which was characteristic of a contemporary modernist aesthetic. The sponged effect of the engine's billowing smoke and the thin intersecting lines connecting its wheels contribute to an illusion of great speed.

From the outset of his career, Cassandre recognized the importance of lettering in poster design, believing that text should be integral to the concept. However, in contrast to Bauhaus doctrine of the period, he preferred to use only uppercase letterforms. Hence, the two words "Nord Express" have been integrated into the illustration itself and reversed out of the blue background color, with small areas of red added at the extremities to ensure legibility. The train's journeys from Paris or London to destinations in Warsaw and Riga have also been woven into the design, appearing as railway tracks, with the remaining text surrounding the image acting as a frame. At a time when most travel posters illustrated the final destination, Cassandre was unusual in focusing on the locomotive as a glorification of the Machine Age.

← P.95

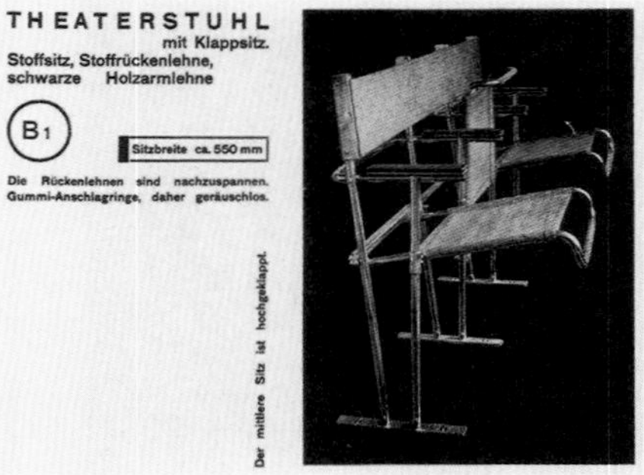

← P.96

← P.97

1927

FUTURA

Typeface

Paul Renner (1878–1956)

Bauersche Giesserei, Germany

Issued by the Bauersche Giesserei type foundry in Frankfurt, Futura was a key typeface that helped to create a paradigm shift in typography. Renner was a member of the Deutscher Werkbund, which, along with other modernist practices, offered a utopian alternative to the unstable political and economic realities of post-World War I Germany. In keeping with these ideals, Renner felt the typographic forms of the past were no longer relevant; indeed, he regarded Gothic letters as decadent and unsuitable for everyday use.

Along with contemporaries such as Jan Tschichold (New Typography, 1928) and Herbert Bayer (Universal typeface, 1925), Renner set about revolutionizing typographic practice, adopting sans serif as the letterform most in keeping with the spirit of the times. His initial designs for Futura were based on three forms—the triangle, square, and circle—leading to radically constructed letterforms that ultimately proved problematic in terms of legibility. The Futura we use today has none of these idiosyncrasies, and manages to combine the modernist aesthetic of functionalism with the classic proportions of roman characters. Although geometric in inspiration and seemingly entirely regular in construction, many letters have subtle variations of stroke width and proportion. In Germany, the introduction of Futura established the switch from blackletter by encouraging Western graphic designers to move from antique to sans serif typefaces.

Futura was one of the first sans serif faces to be widely accepted and used, becoming a staple of the advertising industry; the campaigns for Volkswagen from the 1950s and '60s are a classic example. With its roots so clearly reflecting its time, and the graceful cut of its characters, Futura has an ageless quality. As its name suggests, it could be seen as a prescient piece of modern-day branding—an established classic, while being ever-ready for the next typographic challenge.

1927

BREUER METALLMÖBEL

Book

Herbert Bayer (1900–1985)

Standard-Möbel, Germany

Designed to promote the furniture designs of Marcel Breuer, this catalog highlights a number of the seminal design philosophies of the Bauhaus and brings together two of its key exponents.

First as a student and later as a director, Herbert Bayer was central to the emergence of a Bauhaus graphic identity and a distinctive typographic style. After completing his studies, he was appointed head of the newly created workshop for print and advertising at the Dessau Bauhaus. Marcel Breuer is best known for the 1925 design of the tubular steel "Wassily" chair (named for the artist Wassily Kandinsky) and the application of engineering principles to furniture manufacture. Like Bayer, he was first a student and then a "young master" at the Bauhaus, and was an important figure in the school's development toward a pragmatic engagement with industry and production.

Bayer's catalog cover shows many defining characteristics of the emerging Bauhaus graphic style, including the setting of the title in geometric sans serif capitals and the use of a negative photographic image, which reflects the Constructivist approach to photography as a graphic medium rather than a documentary form. Together, the image and title demonstrate the shift from expressive and decorative graphics toward a more functional view of design as an organizational discipline concerned with the clear presentation of information.

During the period that Bayer and Breuer worked at the Bauhaus, the school developed a strong influence on European architecture, graphics, textiles, and product design. Bayer continued to promote Bauhaus principles for more than sixty years, working in Berlin, Paris, and the U.S., and applying avant-garde innovations to the needs of an emerging industrial culture. As a cross-disciplinary "total artist," his work encompassed painting, sculpture, environmental works, industrial design, typography, architecture, and photography.

1927

KABEL

Typeface

Rudolf Koch (1876–1934)

Klingspor Foundry, Germany

Like Paul Renner's Futura of the same year, Kabel embodies the geometric ideals of the Bauhaus and other modern design influences. Unlike Futura, however, Kabel exhibits idiosyncrasies of style and character that betray the inclinations of its maker, Rudolf Koch.

Born in Nuremberg, Germany, Koch was a master calligrapher and type designer at the Klingspor Foundry in Offenbach. Even though many of his designs for blackletter, roman, and display faces were developed from his own handwriting, for Kabel he constructed letterforms with the tools of the engineer: the straight edge and compass. Koch began work on Kabel just after finishing one of his most famous blackletter faces, Wilhelm Klingspor Schrift. Whereas the latter was deeply identified with German nationalism, the abstraction of Kabel was universal. Koch later said that he had relished the challenge of designing letterforms based on rational principles rather than impulse, although he also admitted that he had not altogether met the challenge. Indeed, the details that make Kabel more intriguing than Futura are precisely those that defy systematic logic.

The geometric paradigm of sans serifs designed in the spirit of Germany's New Typography called for a radical reconstruction of letterforms, and thus a departure from nineteenth-century grotesques, which had essentially reiterated roman models minus the serifs. In this respect, Kabel does not adhere to the predominant paradigm of its time: some of its letters adopt a roman structure, with the lowercase "a," "g," and "t," in particular reading as stylizations, rather than revisions, of their roman counterparts. Another objective of the New Typography was standardization and, here too, Kabel deviates: the lowercase "e," with its slanted bar, and several other letters have unique attributes. But, above all, it is perhaps the angled stroke endings of many of Kabel's letters that give the typeface its unique character.

Often called Cable in English, and known only as Sans Serif in its Lanston Monotype Company imitation, Kabel competed respectably with its more innovative rival Futura, and continues to be used where Machine Age forms are required to have a distinctive rhythm.

← P.97

1927–1929

OPEL

Poster

Max Bittrof (1890–1972)

Adam Opel AG, Germany

Max Bittrof's designs for posters, advertisements, and brochures for Opel cars, all based on the letter "O," provided the company with an integral corporate identity that helped consolidate its place at the forefront of Germany's car industry and identified it with avant-garde design.

Opel began as a manufacturer of sewing machines in 1862 before gradually diversifying into bicycles, motorcycles, and, finally, automobiles in 1902. Over the years it had sported a number of logos, the majority of which from 1910 to 1935 used an eye with the word "Opel" as the pupil. Eschewing the eye logo for his advertisements and other corporate designs, Bittrof instead devised a sans serif wordmark that subtly stressed the "O" of the company name to suggest the steering wheel and tires, combined with stylized illustrations and simple geometric forms.

Bittrof's designs shared many of the visual traits of the New Typography of the late 1920s, but his use of hand-lettering and illustration set his work apart from that of figures such as Jan Tschichold or Herbert Bayer. Before the release of commercial sans serifs, Bittrof drew his own letterforms; once other typefaces became available, he then combined these with his own lettering, which was still needed for large formats. However, his illustrations had more in common with the German commercial "modernism" of Karl Schulpig and Wilhelm Deffke than with the photography-driven New Typography, though Bittrof appears to have been moving toward Typophoto (as coined by Moholy-Nagy) toward the end of his employment with Opel. Certain advertisements of the late 1920s use photographs combined with line illustrations, while others, such as one for bicycles of 1928, are purely photographic. The latter also displays Constructivist influences in its use of a diagonal axis and red-and-black color scheme.

Unlike many of New Typography's adherents, Bittrof had trained in the applied arts rather than fine art (he was one of the founders of BDG—Bund Deutscher Gebrauchsgraphiker). Although brief, his work for Opel was widely seen throughout Germany and Europe, thus spreading his design approach.

← P.98

1927

DENTIFRICES GELLÉ FRÈRES

Poster

Jean Carlu (1900–1997)

Gellé Frères, France

This innovative poster for toothpaste, manufactured by Gellé Frères, an established Parisian perfume and toiletries company, is notable for its sophisticated yet minimal design. It was common for most commodity advertisements of the era to show the product, but in Carlu's poster the toothpaste is simply denoted by a gleaming smile indicated by a wedge shape of white in an otherwise featureless profile of a mannequin-like head. The vibrancy of the poster has been achieved through the startling vermilion red color of the silhouetted head, enhanced by a subtle sponged effect set against a geometric shadow form, while the stylized contemporary typeface gives further emphasis to the overall Art Deco appearance.

Jean Carlu studied architecture in Paris, until he was forced to abandon the course after losing his right arm in a trolley bus accident. Inspired by the innovative posters of the Italian émigré Leonetto Cappiello, he subsequently began working as a publicity artist. During the early years of his career he was influenced by Cubism, especially the works of Albert Gleizes and Juan Gris, and endeavored to apply their ideologies and geometric systems to his poster designs. He was a fervent believer that a poster should be "the graphic expression of an idea."

By the mid-1920s, Carlu was recognized as a master poster artist on a par with A. M. Cassandre, Paul Colin, and Charles Loupot. One of Carlu's most notable posters of this period was for the French soap manufacturer Monsavon, "Mon Savon C'est 'Monsavon,'" 1925; it received universal acclaim, enhancing his reputation still further. At the end of the decade Carlu became a political activist, founding the Agency of Graphic Propaganda for Peace in the 1930s, for which he produced a series of striking images advocating military disarmament. He spent the war years in New York, returning to France in 1953, where he re-established his career as a successful poster artist, working for major clients such as Perrier, Cinzano, and Air France.

← P.98

1927

GABA

Poster

Niklaus Stöcklin (1896–1982)

Goldene Apotheke Basel, Switzerland

Niklaus Stöcklin's poster for Gaba throat lozenges exhibits a harmonious combination of symbolism and economy of means to communicate a single, unified message. Best known for his hyper-realistic designs for products such as Binaca toothpaste and Meta-Meta fuel briquettes, Stöcklin here demonstrates his wide stylistic range.

Invented by the Swiss physician Dr. Emanuel Wybert in 1896, the liquorice-flavored Wybert cough drops were commercially mass-produced by 1917 by Gaba, a contraction standing for Goldene Apotheke Basel, a Swiss pharmaceutical company. The brand grew increasingly successful, and in 1927 Gaba commissioned Stöcklin, a Basel-based painter and designer, to produce an advertising poster. Previous advertisements tended to overemphasize the logo, showing it surrounded by a multitude of realistic-looking tablets. Rejecting the conventional route and recognizing the potential of the cough drop's lozenge shape as a branding tool, Stöcklin chose to feature the distinctive diamond shape and dark color of the throat pastille itself. By enlarging the tablet to several times its actual size, with the shape of the diamond mimicked by the open mouth that receives it like an eager baby bird, Stöcklin emphasized the familiar shape of the lozenge and its purpose (a cough drop to be swallowed), and created a simple geometric composition. The design was printed entirely by linocut blocks.

The Gaba image was extremely popular with the Swiss public, which chose it as their favorite Swiss poster of the previous decade in a vote at the first *Graphische Fachausstellung* (Printing Trades Exhibition) in Zurich in 1934. Although everyone knew the little Gaba throat lozenges by their peculiar shape and color, the poster underlined their role and reminded you to take them.

← P.98

← P.99

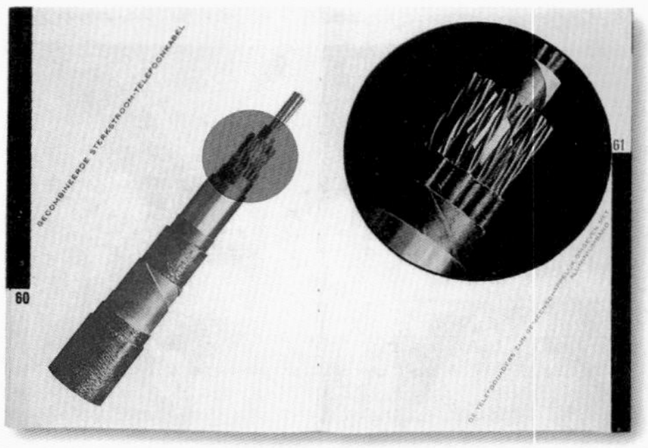

← P.100

1927–1932

BERKEL

Advertising

Paul Schuitema (1897–1973)

U.S. Slicing Machine Company, U.S.

The graphic identity for W.A. Van Berkel's patented food slicer was one of the first designs that Paul Schuitema produced using "typophoto," a combination of type and photography originally pioneered by the Russian Constructivist El Lissitzky. Trained as a portrait painter, Schuitema turned to advertising design in 1924 as an artform that expressed the spirit of the times. His first poster for Opbouw, an association of architects and designers, was designed in a style inspired by the typography of the Dutch Art Deco magazine *Wendingen*. Through Opbouw, Schuitema also became acquainted with Piet Zwart and Gerard Kiljan, pioneers of the New Typography and New Photography, and under their influence started using photography instead of pencil or gouache.

Van Berkel, a former butcher and firm believer in technology, had invented the world's first mechanical food slicer in 1898 and, after obtaining a patent, immediately began mass-producing the machine for an international market. Realizing that he needed to establish the brand name, he commissioned Schuitema in the mid-1920s to produce company advertisements and brochures. To make his advertisements effective, Schuitema developed a style based on strong contrasts: black-and-white photographic images of objects in combination with bold uppercase, sans serif text and other graphic figures set in a mixture of thick and thin type; to strengthen the composition he also used a combination of horizontal and diagonal axes, and bold colors such as red and black against white. Rather than illustrations, Schuitema treated photographs as constructive elements similar to letters.

In addition to advertisements, Schuitema designed books and furniture, and became internationally recognized as one of the main protagonists of the new graphic design, later practiced at the Bauhaus. From 1930 until 1962 he taught in the department of advertising design at the Royal Academy for Fine Arts in the Hague, exerting an important influence on future generations of Dutch designers.

1927–1939

ARTS ET MÉTIERS GRAPHIQUES

Magazine / Newspaper

Various

Deberny & Peignot, France

Published by the Deberny & Peignot type foundry, *Arts et Métiers Graphiques* showcased the emerging modernist design aesthetic and its innovations in the fields of printing, photography, film, and animation, although it was careful not to overtly promote its publisher's interests.

Charles Peignot, director of the foundry and the force behind the publication, was assisted by the designer, typographer, and publicist Maximilien Vox, along with a coterie of avant-garde designers. The format and editorial direction established in the first issue remained constant, but the magazine continually surprised with its varied page layouts and sections of experimental typography, which added to its sophisticated and mature look, achieved partly through impeccable production standards. The designs were mostly uncredited, although some can be ascribed to the photographer and graphic designer Alexey Brodovitch and to the photographer Herbert Matter. A.M. Cassandre contributed cover designs.

In terms of content, *Arts et Métiers Graphiques* offered articles on contemporary typographic developments, as well as on printing history. It promoted the French book trade, illustration, and design, giving prominence to the work of designers of the Alliance Graphique Internationale, such as Cassandre, Jean Carlu, and Charles Loupot. Later issues included articles about advertising and publicity, and the remit was extended to introduce new ideas from abroad by luminaries such as Herbert Bayer, Lester Beall, Herbert Matter, Edward McKnight Kauffer, Jan Tschichold, and Piet Zwart. The magazine ran to sixty-eight issues; the sixty-ninth was abandoned with the outbreak of World War II.

Arts et Métiers Graphiques's widespread influence can be seen in publications such as Lund Humphries's *Typographic* and *Penrose Annual*, and *Alphabet*, published for the Kynoch Press, all of which picked up the themes of technical and design innovation. The British typographer Ruari McLean cites *Arts et Métiers Graphiques* as one of the most entertaining and visually satisfying graphic arts magazines ever published, for being visually alert, inquiring, amusing, and open-minded.

1928

N. V. NEDERLANDSCHE KABELFABRIEK 1927–1928

Book

Piet Zwart (1885–1977)

Nederlandsche Kabelfabriek, the Netherlands

Over a ten-year period, Piet Zwart produced 275 press advertisements and information booklets, including this classic catalog for the Delft cable manufacturer Nederlandsche Kabelfabriek (NKF), noted for establishing a link between the principles of modernist design and commercial interests.

Zwart was thirty-six before he produced his first typographic design, a monogram and letterhead for the architect Jan Wils, in whose studio he worked, designing fabric patterns, wallpapers, and interiors. Together with an identity for Laga, a rubber floor manufacturer, this highlights the early influence of De Stijl in the arrangement of monochrome letterforms into a square format. Zwart's architectural ambitions appeared close to fulfillment after he had accepted a position with the prestigious architect H. P. Berlage. Unexpectedly, this proved to be the catalyst for an intense period of graphic and typographic experimentation, following an introduction to Berlage's son-in-law, a director of NKF.

The eighty-page catalog for NKF, published in Dutch and English, is an exceptional example of coordinated communication. The design features dramatic contrasts: structure and balance alongside rhythmic repetition of typography, primary colors, geometric shapes, asymmetry, and photomontage. The clarity and directness of the product photography is outstanding. Close-up framing illustrates cross sections of cables alongside manufacturing processes, punctuated by sequential imagery and extended Gothic sans serif typography. Each double-page spread is conceived as a single layout, which constantly challenges the viewer with shifts in emphasis and pace, through enlarged inserts and transparent, colored overlays that transform the mundane into a remarkable visual experience. The result is a distinctive visual identity and positive representation of a modern, progressive company.

Zwart resigned from the NKF project in 1933 to concentrate on industrial, interior, and furniture design. However, his experimental designs for commercial clients, including the Dutch Post Office, a brochure for the city of Rotterdam, and a series of twelve photomontage book covers on the art of film, were pivotal in establishing the Netherlands as a hub for graphic design and typography.

← P.101

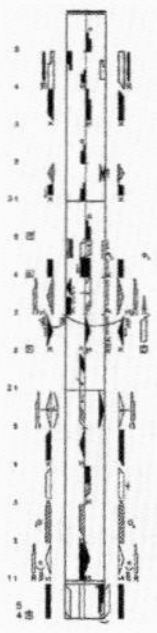

← P.102

← P.103

1928

SIMFONIA BOLSHOGO GORODA

Poster

Georgii Stenberg (1900–1933), Vladimir Stenberg (1899–1982)

Sovkino, Russia

"Simfonia Bolshogo Goroda" (Symphony of a Big City) was designed during an astonishingly productive period for the brothers Georgii and Vladimir Stenberg. Produced to promote the film of the same title directed by Walter Ruttman in 1927, the poster portrays the direction of an office scene in which desks, pens, and a typewriter are all assembled into the torso and arms of a cameraman.

Originally trained as theater designers, the Stenbergs were founding members of OBMOKhU, a society of young artists who devised street art, official festivals, and propaganda posters supporting the revolution. In 1921 they began work for the Free State Art Studios (SVOMAS) designing posters for films produced by the state-controlled studio, SOVKINO. Cinema was highly valued by the Communist regime as a propaganda mechanism, particularly for persuading a largely illiterate population of the benefits of Soviet society. After the industry was nationalized in 1919, all posters were required to obtain formal state approval, and in this context the Stenbergs' production of more than three hundred film posters during the 1920s is a remarkable achievement. Building on the pioneering works of Constructivist artists, the Stenbergs employed a range of graphic devices, including dramatic angles, magnified inserts, and montages to reflect contemporary film techniques. Characters fall from above or tumble into a downward spiral of concentric circles, creating powerful compositions and dynamic action; at a time when films were shot in black and white, the use of composite illustration with color lithography (sometimes combined with photography) also helped to generate drama.

By injecting filmic devices and imagery into the typographic techniques developed by the Constructivists, the Stenbergs captured the nature of the cinematic experience, and set a precedent for the future design of the promotional poster. Toward the end of the decade, Stalin's preference for Socialist Realism weakened the influence of modernism on Soviet graphic communication, and from 1928 the Stenbergs were engaged mainly in designing decorations for Red Square anniversary celebrations. Their creative partnership ended abruptly with Georgii's accidental death in 1933.

1928

LABANOTATION

Information Design

Rudolf von Laban (1879–1958)

Self-commissioned, Hungary

Developed by the Austro-Hungarian dancer and choreographer Rudolf von Laban, Labanotation is a graphical system for recording movement, similar to a musical score for the human body. Unlike other notation systems, however, it is not tied to a particular style of dance; instead, it aims to capture any physical movement, and has been described as "specific enough to record the flutter of an eyelid." Laban first became interested in the spatial components of human motion when studying architecture as a young man at the École des Beaux-Arts in Paris. He later became involved in dance and choreography, and grew concerned that an art form based largely on oral tradition had little chance of developing into "an equal among the arts." He consequently began work on a notation system for human movement, finally publishing it as *Schrifttanz* (*Written Dance*) in 1928. Now known generally as Labanotation, it has become one of the most commonly used dance notation methods in the world.

Rather than documenting dance as a series of poses and floor patterns, Laban's system focuses on motion, referencing symbolically even the smallest and most discreet movement. Notations are made on three vertical lines, with the spaces in between corresponding to the two sides of the human body, and time represented vertically from bottom to top. A series of symbols refer to nine different directions in space, and specify steps (weight-bearing movement) and gesture (non-weight-bearing). Their position on the staff indicates a body part, while their shading refers to the "level" or type of movement and its duration. Additional groups of signs indicate minor body parts and adjustments to the primary action.

The strength of Labanotation, and the key to its long-lasting success, is its versatility, its ability to analyse and record the smallest of movements, regardless of context, which has seen it adopted in fields as diverse as industrial work analysis, physiotherapy, occupational therapy, and sports. Labanotation has even been extended beyond the human body, with zoologists using it to record the courtship and mating rituals of the Cape Barren goose.

1928

BÜRO

Poster

Theo Ballmer (1902–1965)

Internationale Bürofachausstellung, Switzerland

The hallmarks of Theo Ballmer's work, whether as a photographer, typographer, or commercial designer, are accuracy and precision of execution. In relation to typography, this is manifested in the application of a pure geometry—constructing typefaces over graph paper and juxtaposing lettering with basic geometric shapes. Such work displays an affinity with the design ethos of the Bauhaus, which Ballmer attended from 1928 to 1930, having previously trained in Zurich under Ernst Keller, one of the driving forces behind Swiss graphic design. Ballmer went on to influence a new generation of Swiss designers and photographers by teaching photography at the Basel Allgemeine Gewerbeschule from 1931 to 1965. His precise, geometric approach is echoed in the work of such designers as Armin Hofmann and Emil Ruder.

This poster, designed for an international office exhibition in 1928, employs many of the characteristics typical of Ballmer's style: geometric, lowercase lettering, flat red and black colors, and the simple arrangement of a minimal number of elements. The mirrored red "büro" suggests a print reproduction process reminiscent of an office copying machine, as well as the propagation of ideas promoted by the exhibition itself. At the same time, this flawless reflection also suggests the aesthetic of the age by evoking the clean-lined, highly polished look of materials such as glass and steel. The poster engenders a sense of light, order and, somewhat surprisingly, space, even though the typography pushes against all four sides of the sheet.

In sympathy with much Dadaist and Constructivist work of the period, the poster also achieves an admirable balancing of visual forces: the ascender of the black "b," for example, is extended to offset the lettering in the top right corner, while the reflected red "büro" bleeds off the bottom, reducing the white space in the lower right corner. This subtlety and simplicity of composition, together with its geometric approach, combine to impart a timelessness that sets this poster apart from many others produced in the same era.

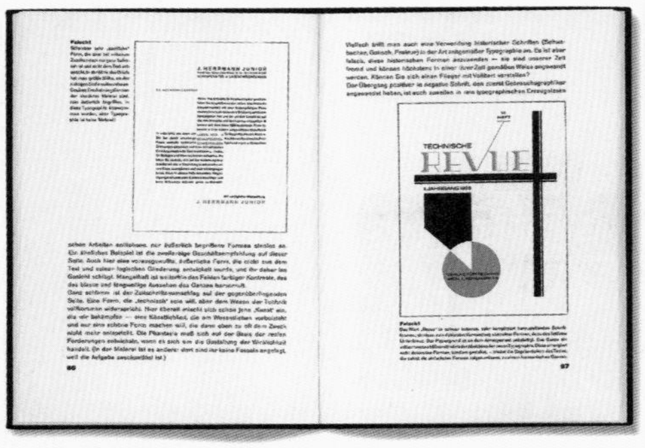

← P.104

← P.104

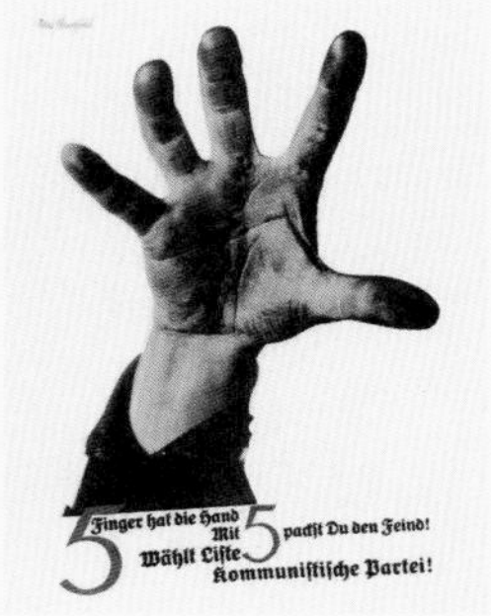

← P.105

1928

DIE NEUE TYPOGRAPHIE

Book

Jan Tschichold (1902–1974)

Bildungsverband der Deutschen Buchdrucker, Germany

Die Neue Typographie (*The New Typography*) was Jan Tschichold's most important written work on modernist graphic design, expressing the spirit and visual sensibility of the day and setting the standard for asymmetrical typography. *Die Neue Typographie* (a term first used by László Moholy-Nagy in his essay for the 1923 Weimar Bauhaus exhibition catalog) was divided into two parts: the philosophy and history of the New Typography, and a basic reference manual for designers working with compositors under the metric-based DIN (Deutsche Industrie-Normen) standards.

Although the New Typography represented a departure from his classical roots, Tschichold had been the unyielding voice and leading practitioner of the style since writing on sans serif typography, asymmetrical layouts, and Constructivist typographic methods for the October 1925 special edition of the printing trade journal *Typographische Mitteilungen* (*Typographic Notes*), in an article entitled *Elementare Typographie* (*Elemental Typography*). Believing that the new typography should express movement, as well as legibility and clarity, he recommended asymmetry over centered layout, simplicity over ornamentation, and machine- over hand-produced composition. In Tschichold's opinion, sans serif was the typeface "in spiritual accordance with our time."

Die Neue Typographie is a beautiful example of design and production, printed in red and black on coated paper with rounded corners, black linen binding, silver lettering on the spine, and text set in the sans serif Akzidenz-Grotesk. The book featured diagrams and illustrations, as well as examples of both classical and avant-garde modernist design, including works by Tschichold, Herbert Bayer, Theo van Doesburg, El Lissitzky, Filippo T. Marinetti, Man Ray, and members of the Ring Neue Werbegestalter (Circle of New Advertising Designers). With a print run of just five thousand copies, the book had sold out by 1931. Out of print until 1987, it was republished in facsimile by Brinkmann & Bose in Berlin; the first English language version was published in 1998. Today, graphic designers recognize *Die Neue Typographie* as the definitive text on modernist typography.

1928

CHRYSLER

Advertising

Ashley Havinden (1903–1973)

Chrysler, U.S.

As two cars roar past in opposite directions, cheered by a group of onlookers, the poster's German copy line urges viewers to raise their hats to the new Chrysler 65. This advertisement was one of a number that Ashley Havinden designed for the American car company and continued his radical overhaul of the car-advertisement genre, which involved stripping away descriptive paragraphs and realistic product illustrations and replacing them with modern geometric forms and a reduced color palette.

In this composition, Havinden flattens the pictorial space to a single plane, emphasized by the series of horizontal lines that stretch from one side to the other. The strong linear emphasis reinforces the powerful sense of dynamism, confirming the Chrysler model to be a thrilling modern machine, while the skillfully arranged copy line, with its colored, sans serif lettering, is suggestive of roadside advertising. In its visual economy and reductive graphic style, the poster reflects the influence of the French designers Jean Carlu and A. M. Cassandre, as well as emerging German modernists such as Jan Tschichold, Josef Albers, and Herbert Bayer.

Havinden spent his entire career with the London-based advertising agency W. S. Crawford Ltd., a forward-thinking studio strongly drawn to the commercial work disseminated through the Berlin-based magazine *Gebrauchsgraphik*. When William Crawford opened a branch in Berlin in 1926, Havinden moved there as art director of Chrysler's European account, enabling him to meet many of the designers and artists of *Gebrauchsgraphik* and raising his profile through the magazine's advertising for Chrysler. Although his later work adopted a more conservative approach, he was one of the first British designers to recognize and explore the significance of modernism to advertising design, demonstrated most successfully by his work on this campaign.

1928

5 FINGER HAT DIE HAND

Poster

John Heartfield (1891–1968)

German Communist Party, Germany

John Heartfield's powerful and dramatic poster "5 Finger Hat Die Hand" is a variation on a cover produced for the German Communist Party's newspaper *Die Rote Fahne* (The Red Flag), and is a call to arms aimed at garnering votes for the Communists in a forthcoming election, five being the number of the Communist electoral list. It translates as "A hand has five fingers. With five seize the enemy! Vote List Five Communist Party!" The hand, with its five fingers, thus becomes a useful *aide-mémoire* for the casting of votes, a weapon to seize the enemy, and a mechanism for literally grabbing the attention of the viewer. The poster's considerable illocutionary force is achieved by the visual projection of the hand as it reaches over the typographic elements below. On the cover of *Die Rote Fahne* this effect was further enhanced by the hand obscuring part of the text beneath the newspaper's masthead, seeming to reach through the newspaper toward the reader. Another possible interpretation, therefore, is that the target of the reaching hand is the viewer rather than the enemy, whose conscience is being pulled toward the electoral booth.

In addition to the psychological responses it provokes, the poster also demonstrates a sophisticated balance of visual forces. The axis formed by the thumb and little finger provides a counterpoint to the diagonal orientation of the typography. Detached from its background, the hand seems concerned less with documenting an event than with fulfilling a rhetorical purpose, functioning as a dramatic but convincing visual expression of an idea. The enduring qualities of the image were demonstrated in the 1998 eponymous debut album of the band System of a Down, where it appears unsupported by typography, leaving the meaning of the gesture open: a disconcerting experience in which we are left to speculate about the significance of the outstretched hand.

← P.106

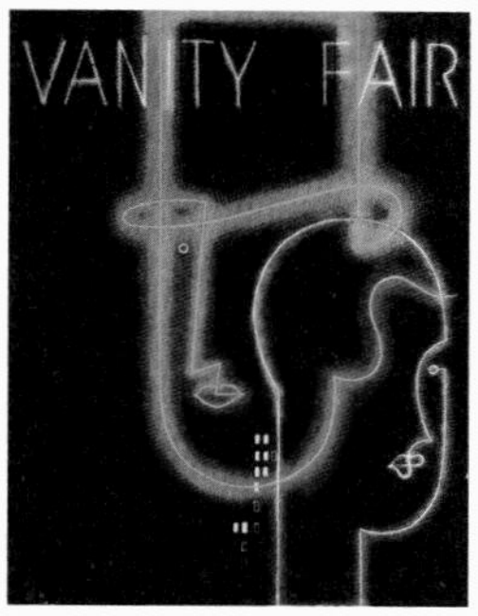

← P.107

← P.108

1928–present

DOMUS

Magazine / Newspaper

Gio Ponti (1891–1979) et al.

Editoriale Domus, Italy

Although primarily an architecture magazine, since its launch in 1928 *Domus* has chronicled the evolution of modernist design worldwide in all its forms "from spoon to city." With its commitment to graphic excellence, the design of the publication is as relevant today as it was eight decades ago, and its iconic semi-abstract covers, in which the lowercase, sans serif logo is often the only typographical intrusion, are as graphically arresting as posters. The most original feature of *Domus*, however, has always been its internal layout. Despite undergoing a compulsory redesign by a new editor every few years, the magazine's interior has maintained a unique visual signature.

Domus's first editor and art director, Gio Ponti, was an architect as well as a painter, poet, craftsman, and industrial designer, who treated the pages of the magazine as he would blueprints—complex documents of information that described every aspect of a project. Long views, close-ups, plans, and details in an array of scales and sizes, were combined on the same spread, while tall and narrow columns of dense text (in Italian and English) emphasized the magazine's vertical grid, making its large format (12⅝ × 9⅝ inches [32.5 × 24.5 cm]) appear slender and elegant. Ponti never segregated design disciplines into different sections, instead presenting images as an amalgam of information. He also eschewed the cinematographic sequencing pioneered by the Constructivists and later lionized by art directors such as Alexey Brodovitch, and never tried to adhere to a linear visual narrative. Hence, an office building on one spread might be followed by a dance performance on the next, rich black-and-white photogravure would often be inserted between highly stylized color photographs, and at times the magazine had to be turned sideways to view a wide-angle shot or read a headline.

After Ponti retired from the magazine in 1941, his vision was preserved by subsequent editors and designers, such as Alessandro Mendini, Mario Bellini, and Stefano Boeri. Today, *Domus* remains a highly respected design magazine, and although many art directors have tried to emulate its layout, none have so far been able to replicate its graphic impact or match its cultural influence.

1929–1936

VANITY FAIR

Magazine Cover

Mehemed Fehmy Agha (1896–1978)

Condé Nast Publications, U.S.

An American periodical dedicated to art and culture, *Vanity Fair* was published by Condé Nast, which had purchased *Dress* magazine in 1913. The magazine was originally named *Dress and Vanity Fair* before being relaunched in 1914 as *Vanity Fair* under the editorship of Frank Crowninshield, a member of the organizing committee for the Museum of Modern Art in New York. As the premier publication to focus on modern art, the magazine's cover design reflected its content, reproducing the works of Cubist, Futurist, and Expressionist artists, and, later, the Art Deco movement.

The magazine's links with Europe were strengthened by the arrival in 1929 of the Russian-born Mehemed Fehmy Agha, previously art director of German *Vogue*, when he took over the art directorship of *Vanity Fair*, *Vogue*, and *House and Garden*. With a thorough understanding of print and production techniques, as well as the ability to spot truly avant-garde work, Agha brought a mixture of Parisian style and German practicality to the cover designs of *Vanity Fair*, and introduced groundbreaking illustrative and photographic imagery. Drawing from European modernism, he commissioned artists such as the French Fauve painter Raoul Dufy, illustrators Georges Lepape and Paolo Garretto, the ex-architect-turned-graphic designer Jean Carlu, photographers Cecil Beaton, Edward Weston, and Edward Steichen, and the Italian Futurist painter and designer Fortunato Depero, to create fashionable, sleek, and original illustrations. Above all, Agha understood how to use symbolism and graphic nuance to represent the magazine's content without resorting to overt display. The masthead was generally set in large sans serif capitals, but occasionally appeared in outline or as decorative letters embellished with flags or flowers.

Along with those of *Vogue* in the same era, *Vanity Fair* covers brought a wide range of European art and design to an American audience, and are testament to the mutually fertile relationship of Europe and the U.S. that existed between the two world wars. *Vanity Fair* was relaunched by Condé Nast in 1983.

1928

MODIANO

Poster

Róbert Berény (1887–1953)

Modiano, Italy

One of a series of poster commissions undertaken by the Hungarian painter Róbert Berény, this design for the cigarette paper manufacturer Modiano reflects his interest in the Cubist and Purist movements of the early twentieth century, and reveals a strong graphic wit.

From around 1889, Saul D. Modiano sold booklets of rolling papers made in factories based in Trieste and Bologna. As the company grew, producing more than one hundred different booklets for sale in Eastern Europe and the Middle East, there were increasing opportunities for marketing and publicity. In 1928 Modiano recruited a number of contemporary Hungarian artists for his advertising campaigns, including Berény, Sandor Bortnyik, Lajos Kassack, and Janos Tabor. Berény had studied under Tivadar Zemplényi, a Hungarian nature artist associated with the Munich Realism movement, before moving to Paris in 1905, where he came under the influence of avant-garde French groups such as the Fauves and Cubists. The effect of this began to appear in both his paintings and posters after his return to Hungary in 1911, as can be seen in "To Arms!" of 1918, which he produced for the new National Council following Hungary's independence from the Austro-Hungarian monarchy. Threatened with imprisonment during World War I, Berény moved to Berlin in 1919, returning to Hungary under an amnesty in 1926. This design for Modiano, produced two years after his release, represents Berény's stripped-down Cubist approach, combined with the clean lines and simple geometric shapes of Purism. With its use of just five colors and the repeated motif of the circle representing the cigarette tip, the man's mouth and monocle, and the "O" of the brand name, the design also suggests the influence of the French poster designer A. M. Cassandre.

Simple, amusing, and stylish, "Modiano" reveals Berény's understanding of how to adapt the principles of modernist pictorial language and typography to the needs of twentieth-century commerce. Possibly influenced also by the *Sachplakat* (object poster) style Berény would have encountered in Germany, the design presents Modiano as the accessory of the modern urban sophisticate.

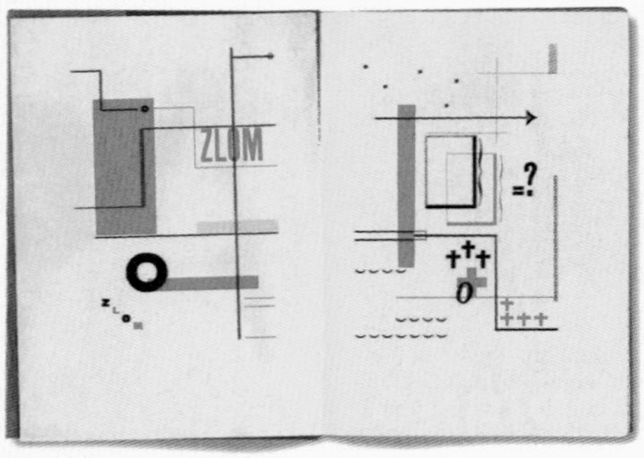

← P.109

1928

ZLOM, BY KONSTANTIN BIEBL

Book

Karel Teige (1900–1951)

Odeon, Czech Republic

Karel Teige's designs for the two volumes of Konstantin Biebl's poetry are among the most highly prized examples of this Czech designer's work. In addition to their functionalist covers, title pages, and layouts, *Zlom* (The Break) and *S lodí jež dováží caj a kávu* (With the Ship that Brings Tea and Coffee) featured Teige's striking "typomontage" pages, which were intended to act as a visual parallel to Biebl's poetry rather than as illustrations. For this second, expanded edition of *Zlom* (the first of 1925 had an entirely different design by Cyril Bouda and Otakar Fuchs), four pages of typomontage featured abstract arrangements of lines, blocks, typographic symbols, and occasional letters in red and black on yellow paper.

A poet, critic, artist, and designer, as well as a leading theorist, Teige epitomized Czechoslovakia's distinctive approach to graphic design between the wars. Characterized by a vigorous cross-fertilization among the arts, Teige's vision of "Poetism," as formulated in his *Poetist Manifesto* (1924), proclaimed itself to be the culmination of the modernist experiment and represented an expanded creativity free from the old hierarchies of artistic expression, which would achieve a universal, absolute poetry for all of the senses. In design terms, this translated into a sensitive but often playful reinterpretation of Bauhaus and Russian Constructivist principles, maintaining their geometrical layouts, emphasis on clarity, and use of photomontage, but enlarging on their vocabulary of colors and type forms to offer a more expressive response to the text.

As it develops through the book, *Zlom*'s design goes beyond the functional purity of Constructivist graphics—illustrated by the book's relatively austere blue-and-red front and back covers—toward a more poetic graphic style that embraced unexpected, allusive, or even exotic forms. In this respect, the book heralded the means by which Teige would later reconcile the disciplines of functionalism and Surrealism, and remains a classic example of Czech avant-garde design and its distinctive reinterpretation of the modernist idiom.

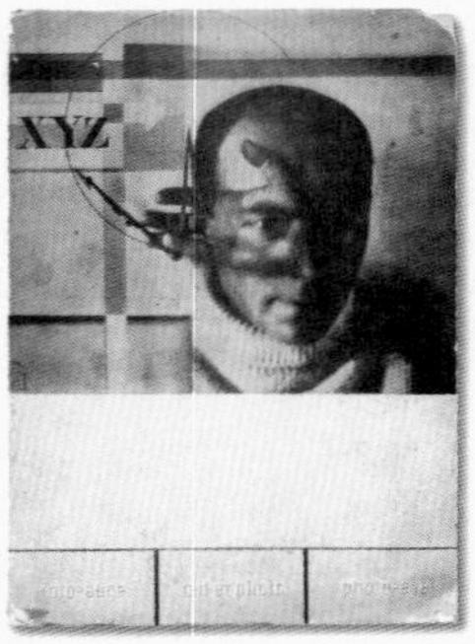

← P.109

1929

FOTO-AUGE

Book

Franz Roh (1890–1965), Jan Tschichold (1902–1974)

Akademischer Verlag Dr. Fritz Wedekind & Co., Germany

Presenting work from *Fifo* (an abbreviation of "Film und Foto"), a major photography exhibition that opened in Stuttgart in May 1929, Franz Roh and Jan Tschichold's collection of photographs, which bears El Lissitzky's *The Constructor* on the cover, explores the relationship between the artist, the camera, and the photograph.

Roh and Tschichold's association began after the latter relocated to Borstei, Munich, in 1929. The two men shared an interest in photography and photomontage, and would regularly meet as part of a circle of friends. Tschichold also sat on the selection committee for *Fifo*, which offered a platform to promote the kind of film, photography, and typographic work that interested him. Although not the exhibition catalog, *Foto-Auge* (Photo-Eye) illustrated work that promoted the idea of the camera as an extension of the body, enhancing the ability of the eye to capture detail, freeze motion, and penetrate surfaces—a view of photography elegantly expressed by Lissitzky's image. A range of meanings has been attributed to this self-portrait montage, with some critics seeing it as a rejection of painting and of the artist as creator, and others perceiving it as the juxtaposition of two complementary modes of making (the rational/scientific and the creative/artistic). *The Constructor* appears to deal with new relationships emerging between the artistic and the technical, the handmade and the machine-made. In the context of *Foto-Auge*, this Constructivist preoccupation seems especially pertinent.

In addition to Lissitzky's cover, the book contained work from Herbert Bayer, George Grosz, Hannah Höch, John Heartfield, László Moholy-Nagy, Jan Tschichold, and Piet Zwart. Tschichold's cover design was printed in sans serif, blind-embossed type for the title, and repeated in three languages, while the front and back were divided into rectangular sections, comprising blocks of color, typographic rules, and the photomontage itself. Internally, the pages were printed on one side only and folded, with the open edges bound into the spine.

Foto-Auge was an immediate critical success, but achieved poor sales, perhaps due to the onset of the Great Depression.

← P.109

1929–1938

DIE NEUE LINIE

Magazine Cover

Herbert Bayer (1900–1985), László Moholy-Nagy (1895–1946)

Leipziger Beyer-Verlag, Germany

The first German lifestyle magazine, *Die Neue Linie* (The New Line) was aimed at the country's fashion-conscious and intellectual elite, although its readership was predominantly female. Herbert Bayer's photomontage covers and lowercase masthead, a version of the Universal Alphabet that he unveiled in 1925, were based on experimental typography and graphic design carried out at the Bauhaus.

After Bayer left the school in 1928, he worked for the Berlin branch of the Dorland advertising agency, where he took over the account for *Die Neue Linie*. The first cover was designed by his fellow Bauhaus member László Moholy-Nagy (who created another nine covers before leaving Germany in 1934) and featured the title printed with large dots over the "i"s. Thereafter, the masthead remained unchanged, apart from variations in the weight and color of the typeface, or the occasional shift to an outline or shadowed version. Bayer's own covers—twenty-six produced between March 1930 and August 1938—consisted of imaginative, enigmatic, and often Surrealist photomontages: a Roman bust wearing a crown of laurel leaves with a tiny skier on its cheek, or a mountain town seen through the soles of a pair of shoes (his last design). His images often dissolved or faded, or were combined with additional vignettes and collages to create varied effects. Although Bayer and Moholy-Nagy were not the only cover designers, they established the dominant conceit of a close-up figure in front of a distant background scene, whether achieved through typophoto, Surrealist collage, or realist illustration. The magazine's interior was relentlessly modern throughout its publication, using black-and-white photographs rather than illustrations, with headlines set in Futura typeface.

Die Neue Linie survived intact under the Nazi regime until 1937, when it was forced to focus exclusively on German products and ideals. Facing increasing restrictions, Bayer resigned as art director and emigrated to the U.S. in 1938, even though the magazine itself continued to publish until 1943. Contrary to many assumptions about the period, Bayer and Moholy-Nagy's work on *Die Neue Linie* demonstrates that pockets of avant-garde graphic design continued to operate in Nazi Germany.

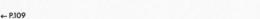

← P.110

← P.111

← P.112

1929–1939

YOU CAN BE SURE OF SHELL

Poster

Edward McKnight Kauffer (1890–1954)

Shell, UK

From 1933 until the outbreak of World War II, the Shell petroleum company produced lorry bills on the theme of trades and professions encouraging motorists to visit Britain's landmarks and beauty spots. The posters reinforced the middle-class image projected by the company's advertising by claiming that those "preferring Shell" included antiquaries, architects, doctors, judges, and scientists.

Shell had been using lorry bills as a means of advertising throughout the 1920s, but when Jack Beddington was appointed publicity manager in 1929, the campaign entered a new era. Beddington visited art exhibitions with a view to commissioning works from aspiring young artists and enhancing the aesthetic qualities of their advertising. McKnight Kauffer, however, was one of the few established poster artists who already had a reputation for the inventiveness of his designs, especially those produced for London Underground, and became Shell's most prolific artist during the 1930s, designing thirty-six lorry bills and numerous black-and-white press advertisements.

Most Shell lorry bills adhered to a standard format, with text appearing above and below the illustration, but McKnight Kauffer rarely conformed to a house style, insisting on designing the entire poster including text. "Magicians Prefer Shell" is almost entirely abstract, except for a stylized pair of gloved hands, possibly denoting a magician's sleight of hand, while the sans serif letterforms, expertly drawn with the assistance of the young studio assistant Sidney Garrad, act as a device to integrate the design elements. The lettering on "Actors Prefer Shell," on the other hand, is less assured; here, McKnight Kauffer has opted for a condensed typeface, with "Actors" rendered in an outlined slab serif. The Cubist-style "face" represents a theatrical mask hiding the shadowy head of the actor. "Magicians" and "Actors" are among the most radical and modernist of McKnight Kauffer's oeuvre. Others in the series include "Merchants Prefer Shell" (1933) and "Explorers Prefer Shell" (1935).

1929

THE MAN WITH THE MOVIE CAMERA

Poster

Georgii Stenberg (1900–1933), Vladimir Stenberg (1899–1982)

Reklam Film, Russia

With its dynamic forms and dramatic perspective, this poster for Dziga Vertov's film *The Man with the Movie Camera*, designed by Russia's foremost film-poster artists, reflects the highly innovative and experimental nature of Soviet avant-garde filmmaking in the 1920s.

The originality of the Stenbergs' designs derived from their ability to translate many of the techniques of filmmaking into a static image, frequently using montage that combined disparate hand-drawn elements to create new and witty meanings. In the making of his film about the energy of modern urban life, Vertov himself had used a host of pioneering methods, including multiple exposures, variable frame rates, split-screen imagery, freeze frames, and unusual camera angles.

The Stenbergs conveyed emotional and dramatic force in their posters through devices such as brilliant colors, extreme close-ups of faces or hands, disorientating perspectives, disembodied body parts, and abstract shapes or patterns. While other film-poster designers used similar techniques, the Stenbergs were more successful in engaging the viewer's imagination. Here, the woman's body is bent into a deep arch, and her arms, legs, and head flail in different directions while the buildings in the background, seen from various perspectives, clash to form sharp angles. By contrast, the circles formed by words (containing the film title and credits) become a swirling vortex that replicates the camera eye. All of these elements conspire to create a sense of dizzying movement akin to vertigo.

Many of the Stenbergs' posters were designed with tight deadlines, often overnight, using traditional lithographic techniques. Their creative partnership, marked by the signature "2 Stenberg 2," ended suddenly when Georgii died in a car accident at the age of thirty-three. Together, they had produced approximately three hundred posters, which continue to inspire students of graphic design and film today.

1929–1955

VOGUE

Magazine / Newspaper

Mehemed Fehmy Agha (1896–1978), Alexander Liberman (1912–1999), et al.

Condé Nast Publications, U.S.

First launched on December 17, 1892, as a weekly gazette for New York's social elite, then purchased in 1909 by Condé Nast, *Vogue* went on to become the most famous fashion magazine of its generation.

From 1909 until the 1940s, covers incorporated the title into the composition, a distinguishing feature that linked *Vogue* with all manner of modern pictorial-and-fine-art styles, as seen in the Surrealist cover by Salvador Dalí (June 1939). Mehemed Fehmy Agha, who became art director in 1929, introduced many important features, pioneering the use of duotone, color photographs, and full-bleed images. He commissioned now-legendary photographers, including Horst, Edward Weston, Toni Frissell, and Louise Dahl-Wolfe, and published the work of international artists such as Matisse and Picasso. Agha also increased the magazine's impact by replacing italics with sans serif typefaces, enlarging headlines, and incorporating double-page spreads.

Between 1941 and 1955, *Vogue* embarked on a campaign to outclass *Harper's Bazaar*, at the time considered the arbiter of style. *Vogue*'s art director during this period, Alexander Liberman, was a fierce competitor of Alexey Brodovitch, his counterpart at *Harper's Bazaar*. Both Russian émigrés, they shared a Constructivist heritage, but Liberman claimed that he approached his work as a journalist, not as an art director. Liberman's layouts were graphically understated compared with those of *Harper's Bazaar*, yet seemed more inventive, thanks to the striking photographs of exuberant young women.

Characteristics of the postwar period in *Vogue* were fashion photographs by Clifford Coffin, Toni Frissell, and John Rawlings, who shot outdoor settings for casual clothing. After 1947, when Dior's New Look reintroduced a formal fashion style, Liberman used photographers Bert Stern, Erwin Blumenfeld, Irving Penn, Norman Parkinson, and William Klein, whom he encouraged to "Americanize" the Paris couture craze.

After 1962, when Liberman was promoted to editorial director of all Condé Nast titles, and until his retirement in 1994, he taught each art director to act as a journalist on the forefront of fashion and culture.

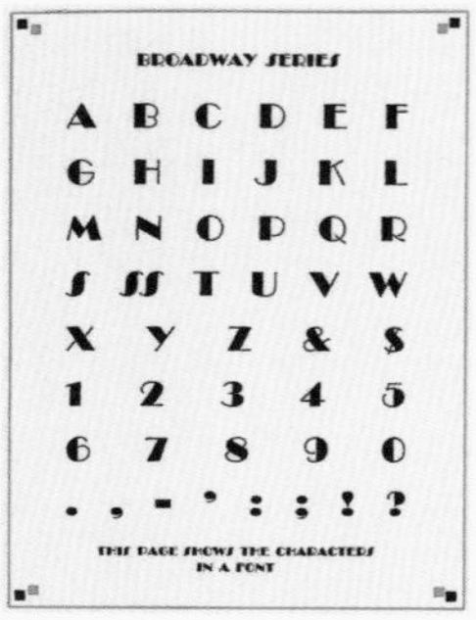

← P.113

1929

BROADWAY

Typeface

Morris Fuller Benton (1872–1948)

American Type Founders, U.S.

A popular Art Deco typeface produced by one of the world's most prolific designers, Broadway remains, even now, the display typeface of choice for impresarios, restaurateurs, and boutique owners, seen on theater posters, store fronts, and hotel exteriors. Quite literally a typeface for the "man in the street," if not the typographic connoisseur, Broadway remains as commonplace today as it was when first released.

Designed by Morris Fuller Benton, chief typeface designer at American Type Founders (ATF) from 1900 to 1937, Broadway was a tongue-in-cheek font born during the Great Depression, which in name and appearance aimed to bring glamor and glitz to the dark days of the economic crash. Benton probably drew inspiration from the explosion of creative energy in the fields of art, architecture, and fashion, much of which required advertising, including typefaces that embodied contemporary modernist styles. Benton was particularly adept at absorbing the styles of other genres and adapting them to the needs of a typeface. Combining the characteristics of a fat face with those of a sans serif, Broadway was an early hybrid typeface. In most of the letters only the main strokes are fat, with the thin strokes taking over the remainder of the character, while the thick and the thin strokes meet at an angle rather than in the curve. Since the advent of metal composition, Broadway has been much digitized and revived by foundries around the world, including the International Typeface Corporation and Font Bureau.

Broadway has also been the inspiration for many other typefaces, including Capitol, designed by K. H. Schäfer for Schriftguss in 1931; and Trio, designed by H. R. Möller, also for Schriftguss, in 1936. The thick strokes and hairlines of Trio emulate those of Broadway.

← P.113

1930–1933

GEORGE BERNARD SHAW SERIES

Book Cover

Ladislav Sutnar (1897–1976)

Družstevní Práce, Czech Republic

Inspired by film production of the period, Ladislav Sutnar's designs for a series of books by George Bernard Shaw are unusual in their playful use of photography combined with systematic design principles that immediately capture the eye.

The covers were designed for the Prague-based Družstevní Práce (Cooperative Work) publishing house, which Sutnar had joined as design director in 1929; three years later he also became director of the State School of Graphic Art, where he had been teaching since 1923. Dominated by a clear functional structure, the designs use a striking diagonal and asymmetrical orientation typical of Constructivist principles, in conjunction with a reduced and contained palette: black-and-white photographs on a warm, cream background, highlighted by abstract forms in brick red and black that serve as focal points. Essential to the designs' memorability are the characteristic photographs of Shaw himself, by then a well-established playwright and winner of the Nobel Prize for Literature (1925). Sutnar experiments with the author's tall, elegant figure, integrating his profile into the composition and playing with pose and scale.

A highly versatile designer, Sutnar believed in the Constructivist ideal of applying quality to everyday life; he became the leading supporter of functional design in Czechoslovakia, creating a wealth of objects, including toys, furniture, and dishes. His book covers demonstrate his ability to employ modernist design principles for effects of clarity and quirky humor. Sutnar also designed other covers for Družstevní Práce that use a similar approach, including books by Upton Sinclair and Emil Vachek.

← P.114

1930–1938

AIZ

Magazine / Newspaper

John Heartfield (1891–1968)

William Münzenberg, Germany

John Heartfield's creation of more than two-hundred anti-Nazi images for the German working-class magazine *Arbeiter-Illustrierte Zeitung* (Workers' Illustrated Paper, renamed *Volks Illustrierte* [People's Illustrated] after 1936) represents the artist's most radical contribution to the medium of photomontage.

A pioneer of photomontage as a weapon of political attack, Heartfield had been a member of the German Communist Party since its foundation, and throughout the 1920s gradually focused his energies on targeting the emergence of the Nazis. During the 1930s, his period working for the *AIZ* mirrored that of the party's rise to power, and this leading mass-market weekly provided an audience of up to half a million for his biting confrontational images. Heartfield's skill lay in manipulating found or specially commissioned photographs, usually of key Nazi personalities (above all, Hitler). His understanding of the radical potential of print media had been honed during the years of Berlin Dada (1918–20), and the black humor of his work for *AIZ* echoed the movement's aggressive cultural critique. Used as front or back covers, or as single- or double-page inner spreads, Heartfield's meticulously executed images brought together current affairs, word play, horror, and humor with layers of additional detail and text that captured the repugnance he felt toward the events that he saw happening around him. "Goering the Executioner of the Third Reich" (1933), for example, showed the creator of the Gestapo as a monstrous blood-stained butcher with the Reichstag burning behind him, while "The Meaning of the Hitler Salute" ridiculed a tin-pot dictator in the pay of big business.

Following Hitler's seizure of power in 1933, both *AIZ* and Heartfield were forced into exile in Prague, from where the paper continued to publish with a severely reduced distribution. Heartfield's *AIZ* photomontages are an exceptional example of graphic communication applied to political necessity, and highlight the case of a designer for whom work and life belonged to the same ethical imperative.

← P.114

1930–1939

ADVERTISING ARTS

Magazine Cover

Various

Advertising and Selling, U.S.

First published as a monthly supplement to the weekly trade journal *Advertising and Selling*, *Advertising Arts* aimed to integrate modern art into mainstream culture through the promotion of new and increasingly sophisticated advances in graphic art and design. Despite being launched at the height of the Great Depression, the publication was seen as a means not only of encouraging innovation in design but also boosting the economy—if progressive approaches in advertising could increase sales, further financial downfall might be averted.

By bringing an avant-garde European aesthetic to the more commercial markets of the U.S., the magazine soon gathered a responsive readership, although, as a trade publication, it spoke mainly to advertising artists and designers. However, *Advertising Arts* was careful not to promote all aspects of modern design; the work featured was included primarily for its ability to sell and was mostly decorative in style. Through its cover designs, each designed by a prominent graphic artist, the publication promoted a wide variety of approaches, including the home-grown Streamline Style, based on aerodynamic shapes symbolizing speed and motion. Other covers looked toward Cubist collage, particularly the work of John Atherton and Vladimir Bobri, or championed photographic images—often running images that bled off the cover on all four sides. Meanwhile, the typography of the masthead ranged from standard serif and sans serif fonts to distinctive styles that reflected the aesthetic character of the cover image (such as Bobri's issue of May 1932, Brodovitch's of March 1931, or Warren Chappell's of May 1933).

With its progressive look and feel, *Advertising Arts* sent a green light to other publishers that more inventive and creative design was a valid sales tool. By the time it folded, prior to the 1939 New York World's Fair, the magazine had succeeded in raising the level of print sophistication. It remains an important document in defining the evolution from everyday commercial art to modern graphic design.

← P.115

1930

VYPOLNIM PLAN, VELIKIKH RABOT

Poster

Gustav Klutsis (1895–1938)

Soviet Government, Russia

"Let's Fulfill the Plan of Great Works" was one of a pair of posters designed by Gustav Klutsis in 1930 as part of the celebrations for the thirteenth anniversary of the October Revolution. The second work, "Male and Female Workers All to the Election of the Soviets," featured a smaller text and a more irregular arrangement of hands and faces. Both, however, used photomontage, although Klutsis originally intended to produce the images by photogram, using double exposures in the darkroom.

The imagery in this poster was created in stages and started off as a photographic self-portrait of Klutsis with his arm outstretched, in which the open palm partially obscured his face. In an early preparatory collage, Klutsis removed his face and replaced it with that of a worker, whereas in the final image only the hand remains, repeated in a pyramid of decreasing size that runs diagonally across the page. These changes reflected a desire for anonymity in Klutsis's work as he attempted to move away from individuality toward a more collective meaning. In this case, the hands represent the workers but also symbolize the artist's service to the people. Meanwhile, the diagonal composition, which creates movement and tension, together with the red, white, and black coloring and sans serif lettering, are all typical graphic features of the era pioneered by Constructivist artists such as Aleksandr Rodchenko and El Lissitzky in the 1920s.

"Let's Fulfill the Plan of Great Works" is one of Klutsis's best-known images. Although other posters of the same period, such as László Moholy-Nagy's "The Law of Series" of 1925, included the repeated motif of the open hand, Klutsis's design is unusual in its application of the hand to represent collective solidarity. Thirty-five years later, "Let's Fulfill the Plan" was echoed in reverse in Saul Bass's 1960 poster for the film *Exodus*.

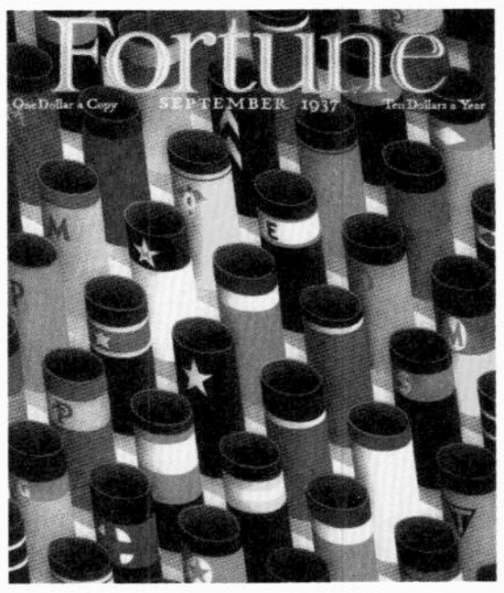

← P.116

1930–1962

FORTUNE

Magazine Cover

Various

Time Inc., U.S.

Arriving on the newsstands only four months after the Wall Street crash of 1929, *Fortune* magazine was published by the farsighted publisher Henry R. Luce. Although an inauspicious time to launch a magazine on trade and commerce, in terms of new design ideas, the moment was ideal. In response to the turbulence of Europe, the early 1930s saw the beginning of the large-scale influx of European designers into the U.S. As well as becoming a bastion of American business, *Fortune* played a central role in fusing the idealism of European design with the hard-nosed demands of commerce.

Published in a generous 11 x 14-inch (28 x 36-cm) format, *Fortune*'s cover became a ready-made canvas for such artists as Diego Rivera, Fernand Léger, and Ben Shahn. Internally, the magazine also benefited from the inspired vision of photographers Walker Evans (associate editor, 1945–65) and Margaret Bourke-White. Under the creative directorship of Eleanor Treacy, followed by Francis "Hank" Brennan and then Peter Piening, *Fortune*'s covers and double-page photographic spreads captured the machinery, produce, and people that drove the recovery of American industries throughout the 1930s and '40s. During World War II, *Fortune* identified itself with the U.S. government's message that the war was a battle for a just and noble cause. In its avoidance of clichéd war imagery and favoring of avant-garde graphics by designers such as Herbert Matter, Alvin Lustig, and Herbert Bayer, *Fortune* often generated a more effective form of propaganda than its more literal-minded competitors.

In 1945 Piening was replaced as art director by the German émigré designer Will Burtin, who introduced a wide range of new visual motifs to communicate key information on industrial productivity, pioneering technologies, or financial developments. From eloquent maps and charts to the instructive use of color in diagrams and graphs, Burtin's art direction enabled *Fortune*'s readership to gain a deeper understanding of the increasingly global reach of postwar American business. Burtin was succeeded by Leo Lionni in 1949, who served as art director until 1962, although Lionni's directorship never exhibited the consistent level of invention and originality of his predecessor.

← P.117

← P.118

← P.119

1931

MISE EN PAGE: THE THEORY AND PRACTICE OF LAYOUT

Book

Alfred Tolmer (1876–1957)

Self-commissioned, UK

Alfred Tolmer's *Mise en Page: The Theory and Practice of Layout*—a 120-page, quarto-format book (with the text in English and French), which was written, designed, and printed in Tolmer's small-scale workshop in Paris—was an inspiration to designers of its time, and continues to be an influential primer for modern graphic arts. It was published in 1931 by The Studio Ltd. in London and by William Rudge in New York.

Crammed with a dazzling array of imagery, the book combines lavish illustrations and striking photographic prints with unconventional typographic layouts—Black Garamond throughout, with headings in blue Futura, and thick blue rules arranged differently on each page. The pages are produced with every imaginable printing technique and material: the cover is made from illustrated paper-wrapped boards encased in a decorative slipcase, while the colorful insides consist of ten or more different paper stocks. Each edition has been painstakingly hand-finished with screen-printed and hand-painted tip-ins, gold and silver foil-blocking, and occasional scatterings of glued-in sequins, all applied with a loving attention to detail that reflects Tolmer's passion for his work. Perhaps most impressive is the way in which the pages function as artworks in their own right yet are anchored together as a whole with great elegance.

The content reflects the book's design. "The art of layout is the art of balance," explained Tolmer. "It cannot, however, be expressed merely as a mathematical calculation." Tolmer guides his readers chronologically, using reproductions of medieval woodcuts, manuscripts, calligraphy, musical compositions, paintings, and a variety of photographic techniques, but he opposes a historical approach to design, arguing that "one could never put together a complete historical evolution." He criticizes traditional book design, stating, "The layout of books at the present day ... is characterized by a respect for convention which amounts to timidity." *Mise en Page* is, of course, a reaction to such conventions; but published three years after Jan Tschichold's seminal handbook, *Die Neue Typographie* (*The New Typography*), it owes much to the ideas expressed there.

1930–1941

USSR IN CONSTRUCTION

Magazine / Newspaper

El Lissitzky (1890–1941), Aleksandr Rodchenko (1891–1956)

Moscow: State Publishing Union of RSFSR, Russia

USSR in Construction was created in the former Soviet Union to promote the nation's activities abroad. By the time that it ceased publication in 1941, the magazine had evolved an original visual style that used avant-garde design to communicate socialist ideology.

Designed by Aleksandr Rodchenko and El Lissitzky with the help of their spouses Varvara Stepanova and Sophie Lissitzky, *USSR in Construction* emphasized the importance of imagery in the delivery of information, with photography, diagrams, maps, and photomontage all employed to make powerful visual points. The designers worked with some of the most talented photographers of the time—Arkadii Shaikhet, Georgi Zelma, Max Alpert, Boris Ignatovich, and Georgii Petrusov. Lissitzky was inspired by the work of the documentary filmmaker Dziga Vertov to build cinematic narratives through photography that focused on each issue's specific theme. Varying scales, visual metaphors, and careful placement of imagery all contributed to creating a coherent visual flow of information. By contrast, Rodchenko and Stepanova were less engaged with narrative but produced dynamic layouts that combined geometric shapes with photomontage. Using a range of techniques, such as die-cutting, gatefolds, and complex triangular foldout panels, they experimented freely with visual textures and colors, while remaining true to the avant-garde palette of red, black, and white. This approach was particularly successful in an issue on Kazakhstan, which contrasted the new and old aspects of the country by linking gatefolds and peepholes. Such strategies forced readers to become active participants, discovering the information for themselves rather than absorbing it passively.

During the Stalinist purges, Lissitzky continued to use the material imposed on him to formulate powerful scenarios, but Rodchenko and Stepanova adapted less happily to the new constraints. *USSR in Construction* was forced to close when Germany invaded Russia, but it remains important for showcasing some of the most innovative magazine designs of the twentieth century. Its influence can be seen everywhere from Neville Brody's geometrical layouts for *The Face* in the 1980s to *Life* magazine.

1931–1933

FILM: SERIE MONOGRAFIEËN OVER FILMKUNST

Magazine Cover

Piet Zwart (1885–1977)

W. L. & J. Brusse N.V., the Netherlands

Piet Zwart's series of covers for *Film: Serie Monografieën over Filmkunst* (Monographs on Cinematography) marks one of the high points of his career as a designer, when he brought the dynamic principles of Constructivist graphic design to the subject of film, reflecting the movement and fluidity of the medium itself.

In seeking a design that would reproduce film's essential transparency and simultaneity, Zwart dispensed with the central alignment of typographic and visual elements, replacing it with a more dynamic "field of tension" in which different elements achieve balance through complex interaction. In keeping with Theo van Doesburg's innovations for De Stijl, dynamic tension is primarily achieved by the diagonal, with lines of type acting as vectors that pivot, counterbalance, and provide leverage. Photographic stills and film clips are also arranged diagonally, in ways that are reminiscent of the films of the Russian director Dziga Vertov, while three-dimensional space is conveyed through overlapping and semitransparent planes. The word "film," for example, is overprinted in red tint, creating the illusion that we are looking through it to other graphic and photographic elements. On the cover of the first issue, Zwart playfully positioned a lens that appears to sit atop the typography and orients the viewer, suggesting an overhead viewpoint consistent with that of the designer creating montages of objects on the baseboard of a photographic enlarger.

Despite the playful and dynamic character of the covers, information is hierarchically arranged into different categories, with the same rational system of typographic labeling used across the range of covers. Each issue deals with a different theme, such as "Russian filmmaking," and it is this title—appearing in uppercase letters on a white strip—that is perhaps the most salient typographical feature, despite being smaller than the word "film" that overprints it. This framework establishes a clear logic for the reader: the series title is set in the largest font size, while the subject title is distinguished by its high level of tonal contrast. In its balancing of dynamic spontaneity with control and order, the series is a masterful example of 1930s graphic design.

← P.120

1931–1935

ŽIJEME

Magazine / Newspaper

Ladislav Sutnar (1897–1976)

Družstevní Práce, Czech Republic

With its emphasis on photomontage and the New Typography, the arts journal *Žijeme* (We Live), designed by Ladislav Sutnar, is an important example of avant-garde Czech graphic design of the 1930s, which perfectly mirrored the spirit of its times.

Dedicated to subjects that ranged from lifestyle, sport, and housing to theater, dance, cinema, photography, literature, and music, including new techniques, such as phonograph recordings, *Žijeme* was best summarized by its strapline "An Illustrated Magazine of Modern Times," and by the inclusion of the current year in its masthead, which emphasized its focus on the contemporary.

As art director of Družstevní Práce, *Žijeme*'s publisher, from 1927, Sutnar was responsible for both book jackets and magazine covers. Throughout his time at *Žijeme*, Sutnar made extensive use of photography—the ultimate medium for documenting reality—and photomontage, publishing works by Helmar Lerski, Man Ray, and Josef Sudek, and adopting many of the techniques of Russian Constructivism and other European avant-garde movements, such as diagonal compositional arrangements and a strong use of perspective. For example, a 1931 cover shows a repeated image of Charlie Chaplin placed on a grid that recedes into the top-left corner of the page, whereas other early covers contain photographic figures isolated against graphic backgrounds. From 1932 Sutnar abandoned Constructivism in favor of a more functional design style, embracing strict typographic grids, a two-column layout, and sans serif typeface under the influence of the New Typography, which had emerged in Switzerland during the 1930s. Photographs were now juxtaposed with solid blocks of color, often yellow or orange, although the influence of Constructivism could still be seen in the choice of images with strong diagonals and figures shot from below.

Sutnar's work on *Žijeme*, which ran for twenty-nine issues, was the most important disseminator of the New Typography in the Czech Republic and was celebrated in 1934 at the exhibition *Ladislav Sutnar and the New Typography* in Prague. In 1939 Sutnar moved to the U.S. as designer of the Czech Pavilion at the New York World's Fair, later becoming a key figure in the advance of information design.

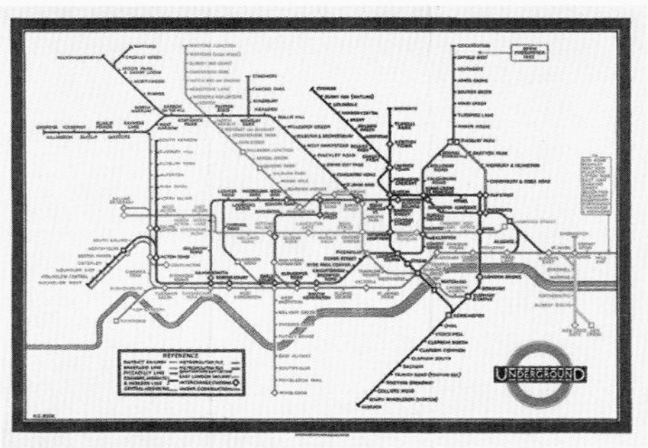

← P.121

1931

LONDON UNDERGROUND MAP

Information Design

Henry C. Beck (1902–1974)

London Underground, UK

With its clear and functional design principles, Henry C. Beck's London Underground map brought order to the chaotic sprawl of London and went on to become a quintessential symbol of the city, along with the Underground logo, the red Routemaster bus, and the black cab.

In 1931 the engineering draughtsman Henry C. Beck, known as Harry, first presented his diagram of the London underground railway system (which he had produced as an experiment in his spare time) to its governing body, London Underground. After initial scepticism, the governors officially commissioned Beck to design a map for the complete system and, two years later, in January 1933, the first trial print run of seven-hundred-fifty thousand copies was issued under the title, "A new design for an old map. We should welcome your comments." Beck's map was an element of a larger social design program led by Frank Pick, who, along with Lord Ashfield, founded the London Passenger Transport Board in 1933 and was central to ensuring design excellence. The map was an exemplar of this strategy and was well received by the public, even though its functionalist aesthetic was more representative of European architecture and design than British. More than seventy-five years later its popularity remains intact, with a MORI poll in 2001 voting it among the top ten designs of the century—a true classic.

Technically the design is more of a schema than a map, being evocative of electrical circuit diagrams: lines are color-coded to distinguish them, and drawn only as horizontals, verticals, or diagonals, whereas the Thames acts as a visual anchor. Although the essential design has remained unchanged, the diagram has been periodically reworked as the London Underground network expanded, bringing in a wider range of colors and adding pictograms.

Beck's design has been referenced a number of times for application around the world, and he himself designed a new diagram for the Paris Métro in 1951, which was never implemented. In 1972 Massimo Vignelli reworked the New York subway under the influence of Beck's diagrammatic approach, but his design was withdrawn in 1979 following public demand for a geographically correct map.

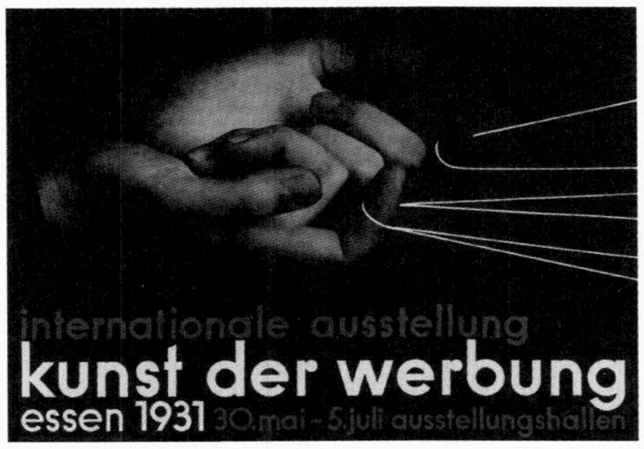

← P.121

1931

INTERNATIONALE AUSSTELLUNG KUNST DER WERBUNG

Poster

Max Burchartz (1887–1961)

Unknown, Germany

The *Internationale Ausstellung Kunst der Werbung* (International Exhibition of Advertising Art), held in 1931, displayed practical advertising projects carried out by students of the arts academy Folkwangschule in Essen, where the German designer Max Burchartz, creator of this poster, was a teacher. The event emphasized the importance he and other Constructivist artists placed on artists working in industry.

Initially a follower of Impressionist and Expressionist painting techniques, Burchartz adopted a more modernist aesthetic during the early 1920s, and later joined the Bauhaus in Weimar, where he taught alongside Theo van Doesburg, embracing the methods of De Stijl and Constructivism. In 1924 he opened his own design studio, Werbe-bau (Advertising-Construction), first in Weimar and then in the Ruhr area of Germany, a key industrial center, close to potential manufacturing clients. During the same period, Burchartz set out his philosophy in a manifesto that echoed many of the ideas of the emerging New Typography, particularly with regard to corporate advertising and identity. The document summarized what Burchartz considered to be the qualities of good advertising: objectivity, clarity, economy, modern techniques, strong design, and affordability. For this poster and other exhibition publicity material, Burchartz applied the rules he had established: geometric, lowercase text and strong colors that highlight the message against a contrasting background, combined with a powerful image—in this case a pair of hands pulling yellow strings across the paper—to add drama. Although deliberately ambiguous in meaning, the poster suggests a designer manipulating and controlling the elements of his work.

Burchartz would go on to become an important exponent of the Constructivists' "art into life" ethic, producing advertising designs characterized by dramatic imagery and simple functional typography for industrial engineering companies. For clients such as these, Burchartz's dynamic approach was unusual and gave them a distinctive and robust image.

← P.122

1931–1937

A. C. DOCUMENTOS DE ACTIVIDAD CONTEMPORÁNEA

Magazine / Newspaper

GATEPAC

Self-commissioned, Spain

A. C. Documentos de Actividad Contemporánea was designed and published by GATEPAC (Grupo de Artistas y Técnicos Españoles para el Progreso de la Arquitectura Contemporánea), a group of young Spanish architects that included Josep Lluís Sert and Josep Torres i Clavé, who had formed the original Catalan group, together with architects from central Spain and the Basque country.

Remaining active until just after the outbreak of the Spanish Civil War in 1936, the group promoted, via the magazine, modernist architectural ideals in Spain, including articles about innovative projects being carried out by the group, as well as work by other modern architects, such as Le Corbusier and Mies van der Rohe. In addition to focusing on social, economic, and political issues—exemplified by an article criticizing the terrible conditions in the Barcelona slums, as documented by the photographer Margaret Michaelis—the journal covered art, film, and culture, and provided a voice for the new republic. The magazine's design echoed the utopian ideals of its content: rational and modernist, with stark black-and-white photography, it is marked by clean, functional layouts with no extraneous ornamentation and sans serif typefaces. Classical and decorative architecture or failed modernist attempts were denounced, signaled by single red lines struck through the images.

Just as *A. C. Documentos de Actividad Contemporánea* had begun publication during the year in which the Second Spanish Republic was formed, its activities dwindled when the Civil War broke out. Torres i Clavé was killed, while many other members of the group, including Sert, went into exile after the war. However, although the magazine was short-lived, the modernist principles of its design lived on. Although the overall look of the magazine now appears dated, many of its graphic precepts remain in use.

← P.123

1931/1980/1995

DIN AND FF DIN

Typeface

Unknown, Albert-Jan Pool (1960–)

Deutsches Institut für Normung, FontShop, Germany

DIN 1451 is the standard for German typefaces, the name being derived from the Deutsches Institut für Normung (DIN), or German Institute for Standardisation. The "DIN" prefix accompanies each DIN standard: DIN 476, for example, refers to paper sizes.

In 1924 the DIN Committee of Type set out to create DIN 1451. The intention was to promote a similarity of design between printing typefaces (in the style of Akzidenz Grotesk), lettering on technical drawings (as defined in the earlier DIN 16), mechanical engraving, stenciling, and sign-making (as for Prussian Railways) by defining the basic proportions of the letters on a coarse grid. Released for use in 1931, the sans serif typeface known as DIN 1451 had its roots in the Royal Prussian Railways, where it had been used as far back as 1905 on trains and railroad cars. It had a more engineered than hand-drawn quality, giving it geometric properties with a much narrower setting than the likes of Futura.

As the head of the Committee of Type, Ludwig Goller championed the use of DIN 1451 by authoring a brochure to explain its usage. The graphic trade did not readily adopt the face, but in 1938 Temporary Order No. 10 required DIN 1451 to be used on all German motorways. This and other similar regulations resulted in the typeface dominating German public lettering, as it still does. The typeface was redrawn and digitized in 1980, and in 1990 it was released by Adobe/Linotype as the PostScript DIN Mittelschrift (Medium) and DIN Engschrift (Condensed). Leading designers began using both versions, making DIN a popular alternative to other sans serif faces.

In 1994 the Dutch type designer Albert-Jan Pool was asked to design a more functional version of DIN 1451. Pool created a revised face for FontShop's FontFont label, incorporating alternate characters and a wider range of weights; his new design, released in 1995, offered a regular weight of lighter color. FF DIN Condensed and FF DIN Italic were released in 2000, and by 2005 FF DIN was one of the best-selling FontFont typefaces. The release of FF DIN Round in 2010 transformed FF DIN into a superfamily, and Pool has continued to work on additional styles to extend it in new directions.

← P.124

1931–1938/1947–1948

RONINGYO

Magazine Cover

Takashi Kono (1906–1999)

Roningyosha, Japan

Directed by the poet, children's songwriter, and English literature specialist Yaso Saijo, *Roningyo* (Wax Doll) was a monthly children's journal of short musical pieces, *tanka* poems, ballads, and nursery rhymes. Takashi Kono, a leading figure in Japanese graphic design from the 1930s onward, designed and illustrated ninety-six covers for *Roningyo* over more than eight of its fourteen years of publication from April 1931 to February 1938, and again from March 1947 through November 1948. These mark the transition in Japanese graphic design toward modernism and away from the romanticism of the Taisho era, exemplified by the illustrations of *Roningyo*'s original art director, the poet and artist Yumeji Takehisa.

Under the influence of European design, Kono's simple and colorful covers for *Roningyo* combine geometric and abstract imagery with prominent typography, while simultaneously referencing traditional Japanese motifs and symbols. Kono was adept at identifying cultural crossovers—as with the issue of February 1938 featuring horses, and that of July 1937 depicting an accordion—and excelled at evoking seasonal storylines with just a few elements. Kono enlivened his covers with lighthearted combinations of decorative colors, simple motifs—ships, planes, circles, street lamps, games—and type, using a variety of styles, including hand-lettering and manufactured fonts, as well as different languages to expand the journal's international flavor, although the title was always displayed prominently in Japanese. Even abstract covers, such as the June 1934 issue featuring an array of white circles on a gray background, still succeeded in presenting the magazine's underlying poetic sensibility. Between 1944 and 1946 *Roningyo* ceased publication, but was subsequently rereleased by the children's book publisher Futaba Shoten. After World War II, Kono's covers revealed stronger Western influences: the title now read from left to right, and the images were largely Western in origin, although Kono continued to maintain the Japanese palette and texture.

Under Kono's guidance, *Roningyo* introduced subtly integrated images that included both traditional and Western icons, while the broad range of artwork and type expressed a dreamlike, optimistic vision for a new generation

← P.125

← P.126

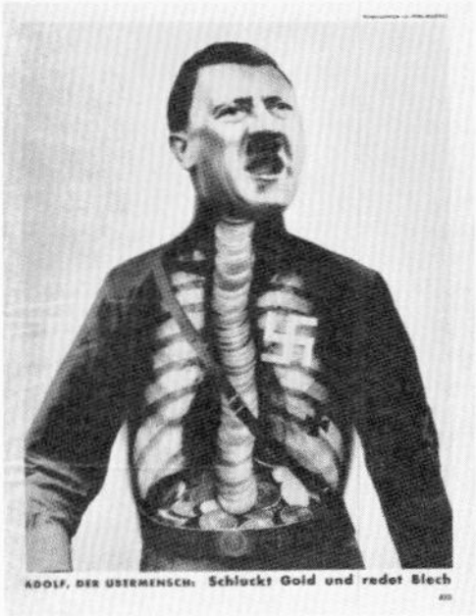

← P.126

1931

AUSSTELLUNGEN WALTER GROPIUS, RATIONELLE BEBAUUNGSWEISEN

Poster

Ernst Keller (1891–1968)

Kunstgewerbemuseum Zurich, Switzerland

A hand holding a trowel is transformed into a symbol of strength and forward thinking in Ernst Keller's elegant poster advertising two exhibitions at the Kunstgewerbemuseum Zurich—one on Walter Gropius's architectural work and one on "Rational Building Construction." The economical and meticulous use of imagery and typography are typical of Keller's designs, and were precursors of the International Typographic or "Swiss school" of the 1950s.

Initially trained in lithography and lettering, Keller first gained experience as a book and poster designer, and then began teaching at Zurich's pioneering Kunstgewerbeschule (School of Applied Arts) in 1918. By the time he stepped down in 1956, a generation of young designers had passed under his supervision, including Josef Müller-Brockmann, Richard Paul Lohse, Armin Hofmann, and Gérard Miedinger. This poster shows all the hallmarks of the International Style that Keller's students would go on to develop further: asymmetry, the use of a grid, and sans serif text. Keller believed in breaking down an image into its simplest forms, rationalizing it to produce an instantly recognizable sign, with text and graphics arranged methodically to create a logical whole. Keller cut the letters used here by hand, in a slightly elongated sans serif style that bears the stamp of his authorship. The diagonal placing of the arm attracts the eye and creates a sense of movement, almost as if the tool is a weapon about to be used. Keller often used the symbol of a clenched fist, but never so effectively as in this work. A year earlier, Keller produced "Schuelerarbeiten," another poster for the museum, in which a near-identical arm is placed horizontally. When comparing the two, the dynamic power of the angle used in "Ausstellungen Walter Gropius" becomes evident.

The exhibition posters made for galleries and museums during the interwar period set a standard for Swiss design. Keller's poster stands alongside Theo Ballmer's "100 Jahre Lichtbild" (1927) and Alfred Willimann's "Das Licht in Heim, Büro, Werkstatt" (1932) in heralding a breakthrough in graphic design. The impact of Keller's work continues to be felt in visual culture today.

1932

DUBO DUBON DUBONNET

Poster

A. M. Cassandre (1901–1968)

Dubonnet, France

Known all over the world for his travel posters, A.M. Cassandre is revered in France as the designer of the Dubonnet man. Created in 1932, the cult campaign shows the Chaplinesque figure of a bistro customer becoming progressively animated (and inebriated) as he admires and tastes the sweet tonic wine in his glass before pouring himself a refill. Using the drink's brand name as the narrative for this image sequencing, Cassandre played with the sounds of BO (a phononym for *beau*, beautiful) and BON (good). The gradually warming color palette of the three images, and the increasing blocks of shading formed by the typography, visually promote the cumulative virtues of the drink: first its beauty, then its taste, and finally its vivifying effect on the drinker. The campaign lasted twenty years, with sometimes only the "DUBO DUBON DUBONNET" slogan, in big capital letters, painted inside tunnels or on blank walls, acting as a teaser for passengers of speeding cars. For Cassandre, being able to decipher advertising messages quickly from a fast-moving vehicle was paramount. He wanted his posters to function like ticker tapes dispatching information with telegraphic speed in the urban jungle. A 1934 photograph by André Kertész documents the kinetic triple-punch sequencing of the Dubonnet posters on a Paris boulevard.

Cassandre's obsession with velocity was symptomatic of the late Art Deco style of Streamline Moderne, an American phenomenon pioneered by the likes of Raymond Loewy and Walter Dorwin Teague. The silhouette of the Dubonnet man, with his bowler hat, curvy elbows, and airbrushed anatomy, is as aesthetically pleasing as that of a chrome cocktail shaker designed by Norman Bel Geddes, or an enameled steel carafe by Henry Dreyfuss. Intoxicated, like many of his contemporaries, with the idea of modernity, Cassandre wanted his Dubonnet man to be a spirited mixture of mechanical perfection and lyrical expression.

1932

ADOLF DER ÜBERMENSCH SCHLUCKT GOLD UND REDET BLECH

Poster

John Heartfield (1891–1968)

Self-commissioned, Germany

One of the earliest and most powerful anti-Nazi images ever produced, "Adolf der Übermensch Schluckt Gold und Redet Blech" (Adolf the superman swallows gold and spouts trash) was created at the beginning of Hitler's rise to power, when few perceived the sinister reality that lay beneath the public oratory. John Heartfield's poster, which was used in the German election of 1932, savagely exposed what he saw as the hypocrisy behind the future dictator's words.

Born Helmut Herzfeld, Heartfield later anglicized his name—in itself a brave act of rebellion in Germany at the time. Like his Dada colleagues George Grosz, Raoul Hausmann, and Hannah Höch, Heartfield thought of himself as a "monteur," or mechanic, who questioned traditional techniques of illustration and painting, instead freely composing with disparate photographs to build a new image. A committed Communist, Heartfield worked for the Communist journal *Arbeiter-Illustrierte Zeitung* (Workers Illustrated Newspaper—*AIZ*) in the 1930s, where this image first appeared as an illustration, as did many of his finest pieces. Published from 1930 until 1938, the journal later succumbed to Nazi threats. Heartfield produced the work soon after Hitler gave a speech extolling Nazi goals for a classless society, a socialist promise Heartfield must have found particularly provocative.

Heartfield used a variety of techniques to produce his photomontages, cutting and pasting existing photographs, taking his own multiple exposures, and sometimes drawing on a photograph's surface, toiling for hours in the darkroom. This image seems to portray an X-ray image of Hitler, until one notices that the spine and oesophagus have been substituted with a column of gold coins, his heart with a swastika and his stomach with a collecting bowl. With a head too big for his slumping shoulders, suggesting a man of little physical strength or stature, Hitler is presented as an automaton, mechanically "swallowing" party donations while uttering empty slogans. As a work of propaganda, "Adolf the Superman" is notable for its bitter irony, at a time when satirical attacks of this kind were both rare and desperately needed.

← P.127

1932

TIMES NEW ROMAN

Typeface

Stanley Morison (1889–1967), Victor Lardent (1905–1968)

The Times, UK

Times New Roman is one of the most widely used and best known of serif typefaces, and the first to be designed exclusively for a newspaper. In its effortless lucidity and precision, the design is, however, a pastiche, drawing inspiration from Robert Granjon's Gros Cicero (c. 1569) and Frank Hinman Pierpoint's Plantin typeface (1913)—the latter an interpretation of Granjon's late roman. In the words of the type historian and poet Robert Bringhurst, Times New Roman has a "humanist axis but Mannerist proportions, Baroque weight, and a sharp neoclassical finish."

The font has traditionally been attributed to the designer, typographer, and historian Stanley Morison, who from 1929 to 1944 was typographical advisor to *The Times*. Faced with a deeply traditional readership, Morison considered the publication's typography antiquated and difficult to read. He believed a new version was essential, but also that any design should be "masculine, English, direct, simple ... and absolutely free from faddishness and frivolity."

In Morison's book *A Tally of Types* (1953), he maintains that he "pencilled the original drawings" in 1931 and then passed the typeface to Victor Lardent, a draughtsman at *The Times*, to finish. However, contrasting accounts have claimed that Starling Burgess, a successful yacht designer from Boston, Massachusetts, created an unused Times Roman typeface in 1904 for the American Lanston Monotype Company that found its way to the UK Monotype Company, where Morison had been an advisor since 1922. Through a series of minor alterations, Morison is alleged to have reworked the design to "create" the Times New Roman we know today, although little evidence exists to support this claim.

Times New Roman made its debut on October 3, 1932. Overnight, Morison had created a publication with improved legibility and that made efficient use of limited space, marking a significant development in newspaper design. A year later, the typeface was made commercially available through Monotype. The font's simplicity of form and suitability for a diverse range of applications has persisted into the digital age, where it remains the default serif typeface on most computer operating systems.

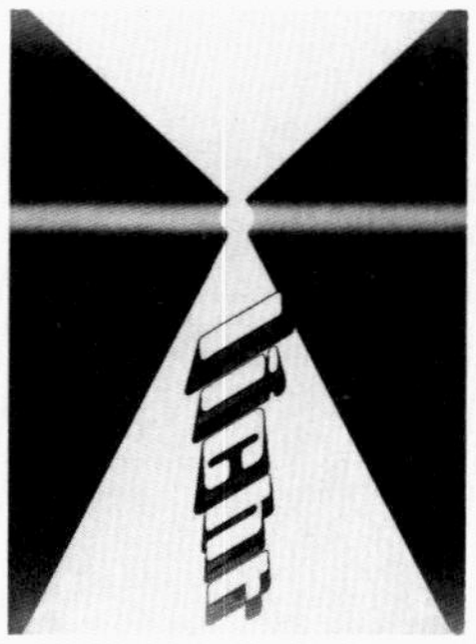

← P.128

1932

LICHT

Poster

Alfred Willimann (1900–1957)

Kunstgewerbeschule Zurich, Switzerland

Alfred Willimann's poster for the Zurich Kunstgewerbeschule's *Das Licht in Heim, Büro, Werkstatt* (Light in Home, Office, Workshop) exhibition is an intelligent study of the intangible qualities of light, as well as an exemplary illustration of the pioneering and modernizing ethos projected by shows in Switzerland at the time.

During the 1930s, the Swiss government realized the value of using exhibitions as a means of disseminating public information. Progressive architects and designers were commissioned to create exhibitions along the themes of "Die Praktische Küche" (The Practical Kitchen) and "Form ohne Ornament" (Design without Ornamentation) to challenge conventional ideas and present radical alternatives to traditional domestic life. The exhibition *Light in Home, Office, Workshop* was no exception, featuring illuminated lettering and signs by the Swiss designer Max Bill, and showcasing new and innovative approaches to lighting.

Willimann, a German designer and teacher at the Zurich Kunstgewerbeschule, was probably best known as a tutor of the typeface designer Adrian Frutiger and the graphic designer Armin Hofmann. Identifying with the principles of the Bauhaus, Willimann sought new forms of expression through the use of functional typography and photography. His "Licht" poster is a strikingly graphic expression of the exhibition theme. A ray of light emanates from a central source, casting shadows onto the vertically arranged letters of the exhibition title. Reproduced in black and white, the poster even incorporates a vignette effect and fogging, as though an errant light has managed to seep into the design process. Willimann's approach hints at an alternative to the rigorous graphic formalism preferred by modernist designers at the time. The Swiss designer Theo Ballmer produced a poster for the same exhibition, although his work, which uses a strict grid, lacks the ingenuity and wit of Willimann's.

Such posters played a significant role in promoting progressive ideas about modernism, providing information about exhibitions but propagating a new graphic language in the process. Well-designed posters such as Willimann's, were at the forefront of making avant-garde ideas accessible to the general public.

← P.129

1932–1934

FUTURISMO

Magazine / Newspaper

Enrico Prampolini (1894–1956)

Self-commissioned, Italy

Edited by Mino Somenzi and Filippo T. Marinetti, *Futurismo*, a weekly newspaper published between 1932 and 1934, emerged following a period of heated debate and division between Mussolini's Fascists and the Futurists, the group of avant-garde artists founded by Marinetti in 1909. Hitler's attack on German "degenerate art" influenced cultural policy in Fascist Italy and increased scepticism about Marinetti's political credibility and continuing support for modernism.

A scenographer, painter, and designer, Enrico Prampolini was a leading figure in the movement's synthetic phase, "Second Futurism" (1922–44). He helped to establish the Futurist periodicals *Noi* (Us) and *Stile Futurista* (Futurist Style) and was awarded the Grand Prix d'Arte Théâtrale in 1925 for *Magnetic Theatre*, a performance that employed the use of light in place of actors. *Futurismo*'s covers dictated that the illustration be stamped in translucent red ink over the copy, a conscious and anarchic act that challenged accepted conventions of publishing. This practice also reflected Marinetti's theory of *parole in libertá* (words in freedom), a concept involving the liberation of text from the formal layout of the page, to create a pivotal role for typography in expressing Futurist ideology. Prampolini's portrait of Mussolini (No. 8, Vol. 1), which is executed in his characteristically bold linear style, is designed to unify Marinetti and Mussolini's support of Fascism by adding the prefix "W" to the words "Marinetti" and "il Fascismo." "W" in Italian is used to abbreviate the word "Evviva!" ("Long Live," mirroring the double "V"); it appears here in the headline praising the "Futurist genius" of Mussolini: placed in front of a name it indicates allegiance, while inverted it signifies dislike or rejection. This symbolic prefix is still in use today, particularly with reference to political parties.

In another issue of *Futurismo* (No. 41, Vol. 2), an illustration by Giacomo Balla is used in a similar way to promote a lead article about Boccioni. Through such practices, the Futurists not only highlighted their irreverence for established views but also helped to revolutionize approaches to typography and graphic design in the twentieth century.

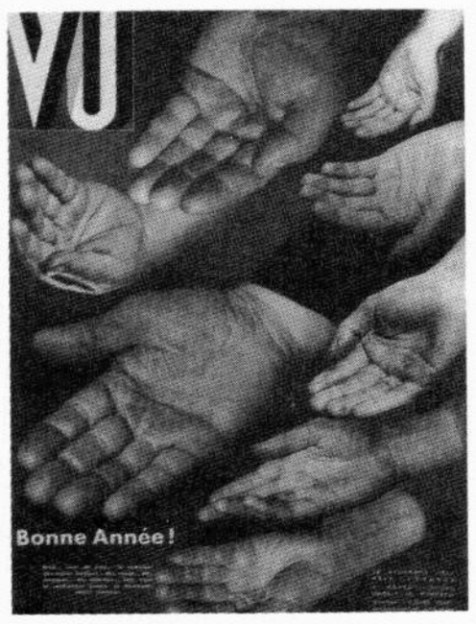

← P.129

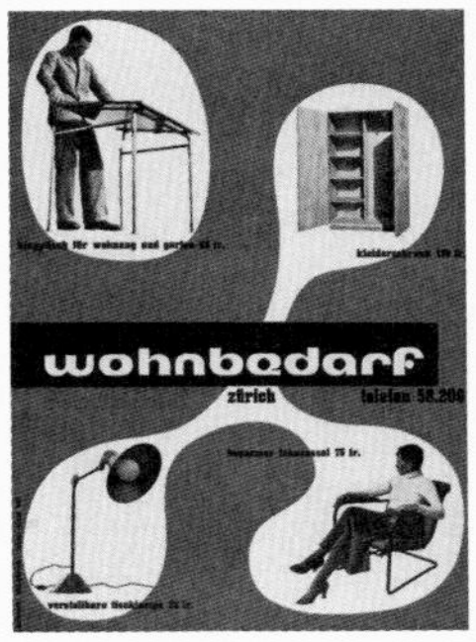

← P.129

← P.130

1932–1937

VU

Magazine / Newspaper

Alexander Liberman (1912–1999)

Lucien Vogel, France

The weekly news magazine *Vu*, abundantly illustrated with photography and with a logo designed by A. M. Cassandre, was founded in 1928 by Lucien Vogel; it ran for 638 issues, from March 21, 1928 to June 5, 1940. It quickly became the model for numerous magazines of the 1930s, and was an inspiration for *Life* magazine in 1936. *Vu*'s novelty was due not simply to the presence of photography on all its pages but also to its rotogravure printing technique, a method better suited to reproducing photographic tones and gradations. The process involved placing all graphic elements of the page, including positives and texts, on transparent film, which could then be cut out and stuck together to produce a montage based on a template. Titles were often drawn rather than typeset, with great freedom, and text columns would occasionally be given a nonrectangular format.

Vu's mode of production completely transformed magazine graphics and allowed for enormous flexibility in combining, arranging, and overlapping images. The double-page spread, central or not, sketched out from assembled photographs, provided the magazine's graphic unity. Hence, the arrangement of images determined the graphic treatment of individual topics, which in a daily publication would have been controlled by the material arriving each day. Photomontages—photographic fragments grouped together to form a new image—appeared from 1930, and again owed more to rotogravure printing than to the influence of groups such as Dada.

Alexander Liberman, a former collaborator of Cassandre, and director of *Vu* from 1932 to 1937, took full advantage of these technical opportunities, particularly when conceiving covers or internal spreads, and under his direction *Vu* graphics became more dynamic and oblique, less concerned with the legibility of each photograph and more with the coherence of the whole. Other innovations included full-bleed cover photographs and photomontages used to reveal unexpected meanings and ideas, especially those of a political or social nature that went beyond the purely aesthetic. Today, *Vu* remains a model of graphic innovation resulting from its redefinition of photographic media.

1932

WOHNBEDARF

Identity

Max Bill (1908–1994)

Wohnbedarf, Switzerland

Max Bill's corporate identity for the Swiss furniture company Wohnbedarf represents an integral stage in the development of graphic design and typography in Switzerland during the mid-twentieth century. Siegfried Giedion, Wohnbedarf's cofounder, as well as an art historian and engineer, took a keen interest in the publicity for the store. By hiring Bill and other graphic designers, such as Herbert Bayer, he helped to spread the message of modernism more widely across Europe.

Essentially unchanged to this day, Bill's logo and other components were clearly influenced by Bayer, his former teacher and director at the Dessau Bauhaus, particularly in their use of lowercase typography and letterforms with circle and line construction reminiscent of Bayer's Universal typeface (1925). To this Bill added his distinct, elongated "o," a near-exact, but rotated version of the one he used in his posters for the Neubühl estate of 1931. His design work for the company also included stationery, advertising, posters, and leaflets, wherein Bill drew from his Bauhaus roots and the principles of the New Typography, in the process helping to establish the foundations for the "Swiss school." This is evident in the ragged-right, sans serif text used in the publicity material, and the objective photography that shows Bill and his wife, Binia, interacting with Wohnbedarf furniture. Although these images seem almost stoic, they contrast with biomorphic forms reminiscent of the Dada artist Hans Arp, as well as with shots of nature and athletic figures in motion, encouraging the perception of a Wohnbedarf "lifestyle." Such designs also suggest Bill's steady movement toward more functionalist typography and layout, with fewer occurrences of thick rules than in his advertising work of the same period for the Zett-Haus. Just as the "Swiss school" was later developed and refined by designers such as Emil Ruder, Armin Hofmann, and Josef Müller-Brockmann, Bill's designs also evolved, growing simpler and more sophisticated in later years. However, his work for Wohnbedarf remains an outstanding example of the early steps in the journey undertaken by Bill and much of the European design community.

1933

BRAUN

Logo

Will Münch (n.d.)

Braun, Germany

The distinctive industrial and geometric character of the Braun word-mark, which employs a consistent line thickness and corner radius in every letter, is a design rooted in the philosophy of the Bauhaus. Although Max Braun founded his electronics company in 1921, the familiar Constructivist logotype with its signature raised "A," did not emerge until 1933, making its first appearance on a product brochure. Braun has at times been credited with designing the logo, however, it was created by graphic designer Will Münch.

Following Braun's death in 1951, his sons, Artur and Erwin, took over the company, leading to a more thorough espousal of the modernism born during the interwar period and a rejection of the romanticism preferred by Nazi Germany. This shift created the necessary environment for the birth of the classic forms of Braun design, and the approach to production that would define the company for the next thirty years. A slightly modified version of the logo was introduced in 1952, produced by freelancer Wolfgang Schmittel, ready to appear alongside Braun's redesigned line of radios at the 1955 Düsseldorf Broadcast Exhibition. Schmittel would go on to lead Braun's advertising design department, leaving the company in 1980.

The same functional design philosophy and aesthetic embodied in the logotype was eventually stamped into the industrial design of all Braun products by Dr. Fritz Eichler and Dieter Rams, both luminaries of the Ulm School. Here, the design of the product was an integral component of the engineering and production process rather than an afterthought, an approach that would be influential for an entire generation of product designers, such as Jonathan Ive at Apple. The Braun logotype was a perfect reflection of this functionalist design ethos in its formal construction and careful placement on the products themselves: always central and visible, but subtle in appearance.

Braun was recognized as one of the "Brands of the Century" by German Standards 2007, and the Braun logotype, which has seen only minor changes since its original inception, is still associated with this reputation. Today, the sleek geometry of the logotype still references the company's history and functional design values.

← P.130

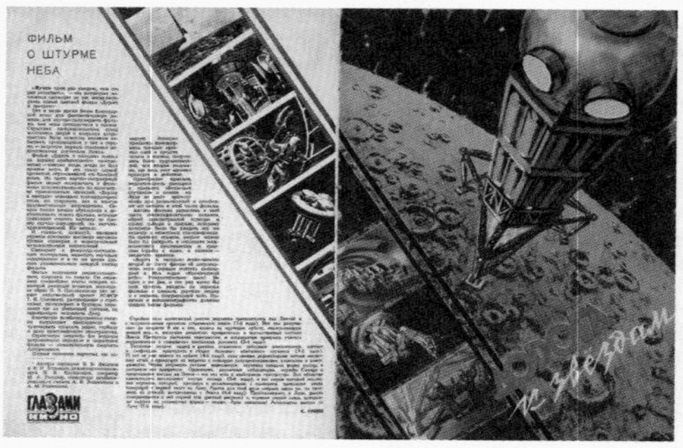

← P.131

← P.131

1933

ESSO

Logo

Unknown

Standard Oil Co. of New Jersey, U.S.

With its colors based on the American flag, oval format, and hand-drawn font, the Esso logo shares a number of features with other U.S. industrial and commercial symbols, such as Ford and Dupont. Developed in-house in 1933 by an unknown designer, and first used commercially in 1934, the trademark has remained unchanged since it first appeared, although it is now used mainly outside the U.S.

The brand name "Esso" is derived from the phonetic pronunciation of Standard Oil's initials, and was first registered in the U.S. in 1926, after John D. Rockefeller's Standard Oil was broken up into regional companies in 1911. Currently owned by ExxonMobil, the trademark Esso has largely been replaced in the U.S. by the Exxon brand name. From 1926 to 1933 the logo consisted of a slanting, cursive, joined-up font in blue inside a circular red border. In the later version, the letters were simplified and straightened, the color relationships reversed, and the framework made thicker as well as elliptical in shape. Bold, simple, and attractive, the design depends for its strength on both its coloring and rhythmic curves.

In the early 2000s, Greenpeace gave the logo a subversive twist when it replaced the double "ss" with dollar signs as part of its "Don't buy Esso, Don't buy ExxonMobil" consumer boycott. Esso France began legal action, claiming that the parody damaged Esso's reputation by associating the brand with the Nazi SS, but lost the case in 2004 when a court in Paris ruled that the pastiche was "within acceptable limits of freedom of expression."

1933–present

TEKHNIKA—MOLODEZHI

Magazine / Newspaper

Various

Central Committee of the All-Union Leninist Communist League of Youth, Russia

Founded in 1933, the monthly popular-science journal *Tekhnika—Molodezhi* (Technology for the Youth) remains a source of inspiration for its celebration of pioneering Soviet and Russian scientific advancements. Narrating significant breakthroughs, such as the development of nuclear energy, it originally won attention for factual reportage. Yet its embrace of the burgeoning Western genre of science-fiction writing is what the journal is now most widely known for, as well as its presence and role in the public consciousness during the feverish years of the Space Race.

Led by chief editor Vasilii Zakharchenko from 1949 to 1984, considered the magazine's peak creative period, *Tekhnika—Molodezhi*'s engaging blend of scholarship and cultural interpretation had widespread appeal. The journal commissioned writing and interviews from leading scientists and authors, which included local and international greats, such as Anatoly Alexandrov, Arthur C. Clarke, Paul Dirac, Enrico Fermi, Otto Hahn, Sergei Korolev, Robert Oppenheimer, Ivan Pavlov, and Nikolay Zelinsky.

The radical writing was matched by equally inspired illustrations depicting imagined worlds above, below, and beyond life on Earth. Hypothetical space stations, spacecraft, and new galaxies were rendered in full-color, highly detailed and large-scale. Modest mastheads and issue numbers did little to distract from the compelling imagery. Inside, the world-building continued: technical drawings and futuristic scenes captured the gleam and progress of technological advancements, complementing the popular-science focus. Illustrations were sometimes commissioned from scientists, including Georgy Pokrovsky, who developed a captivating style that combined technical accuracy with artistic license.

Along with other Soviet titles such as *Nauka i Zhizn* (Science and Life) or *Znanie—Sila* (Knowledge is Power), *Tekhnika—Molodezhi* held a prominence during the Space Race years that cannot be underestimated. At its height, the magazine reached a circulation of about one-hundred-fifty thousand copies. In this way, it contributed to the wider cultural progression and social cohesion of the USSR, sharing its hopes and dreams for international success by breaking interstellar frontiers.

1934–1942

PM/A-D

Magazine / Newspaper

Various

PM/A-D, U.S.

Although only a modest operation, relying on donated paper and reduced-rate presswork, *PM* (later renamed *A-D*) was among the most influential art and design publications in the U.S. prior to World War II. Over a span of nine years, the magazine chronicled the work of some of the period's most influential modern artists and designers, including many who had fled the prewar chaos in Europe.

PM was founded by Dr. Robert Lincoln Leslie, a retired physician who left medicine to return to the world of printing, which had fascinated him as a teenager. Leslie, who ran a small typesetting shop, had been the American editor of *Gebrauchsgraphik*, a German art and design periodical. When it folded, he and coeditor Percy Seitlin created *PM*, "an intimate journal for production managers, art directors, and their associates." From the outset, Leslie used the publication as a vehicle for talented European émigrés, although *PM* also featured the work of many American artists and designers, including Lester Beall. In 1936 Leslie established the A-D Gallery, the first in New York dedicated to exhibiting graphic and typographical design, further increasing the exposure and opportunities for contributors to the magazine. It was not unusual for a *PM* feature to become a gallery show, or for A-D exhibitions to be featured in the magazine's pages. In 1941 the *PM* name was sold (to avoid confusion with the evening newspaper of the same name) and the publication adopted the name of the gallery.

During the early years of modernism in the U.S., *PM* and *A-D* showcased the work of graphic arts luminaries M. F. Agha, Josef Albers, Herbert Bayer, Lester Beall, Will Burtin, A. M. Cassandre, Frederic W. Goudy, Edward McKnight Kauffer, Herbert Matter, and Paul Rand, among others. Over the course of its sixty-six-issue run, only four designers created more than one *PM/A-D* cover, evidence of the publication's—and founder's—egalitarian nature. *A-D* ceased publication in 1942, as the U.S. entered World War II. In 1969 the American Institute of Graphic Arts awarded Leslie its prestigious AIGA medal.

← P.131

1934–1944

NIPPON

Magazine Cover

Nihon Kobo

Self-commissioned, Japan

A high-quality magazine published in six languages (Japanese, German, English, French, Spanish, and Italian), *Nippon* was designed to attract overseas readers and increase tourism, while also serving as a quasi-governmental, state-supported tool to enhance Japan's image among international audiences.

Launched and produced by Nihon Kobo (Japan Studio), *Nippon* was partly funded by the cotton producer and exporter Kanebo, a competitor with Chinese mills in Manchuria with a vested interest in compiling a positive image of colonial power. Nihon Kobo had been founded in 1933 by early adopters of the Bauhaus philosophy: designers Hiromu Hara and Sozo Okada, photographer Ihei Kimura, and at its head photojournalist Yonosuke Natori, who had worked for *Berliner Illustrated News* (BIZ), known for its modern photo-reportage. In 1939 the studio's name was changed to the International News Company. Designers of the magazine alternated as art directors, integrating realist photography, symbolic graphics, typography, and text to narrate stories that presented an idealistic image of Japan as a benevolent imperialist power with a heightened appreciation of aesthetics. Issues focusing on Manchuria, Japanese handicraft, Japanese women, and other subjects were created by designers such as Yusaku Kamekura, Ayao Yamana, and Takashi Kono, and photographers such as Ken Domon and Shihachi Fujimoto. Covers used symbolism and montage to engage the viewer in interpreting the message: on the cover of Issue 20 (1939) by Jinjiro Takamatsu, a Shinto shrine's *torii* (gate) dominates a collection of national symbols (Mount Fuji, skyscrapers, farms, and modern roads); the reader is meant to understand Shinto as the backbone of a modern power strengthened by traditional culture. Kono's cover for Issue 15 (1938) on Japanese handicraft features a pair of hands gracefully holding taut a number of thin white threads against a lacquer-red background, extolling Japan's skill in the arts.

A grand exercise in the visual presentation of a nation in flux, *Nippon* attempted to re-create and promote itself worldwide through a medium that was itself in a state of creation and re-creation. Today, it provides a unique record of the nation and its aspirations at a key period in its history.

← P.132

1934

ST. MORITZ

Identity

Walter Herdeg (1908–1995)

St. Moritz Tourist Office, Switzerland

As with other designs by Walter Herdeg, this poster juxtaposes a photomontage technique, in this case two black-and-white photographic images, with brilliantly colored details—the sun symbol and wordmark—added by airbrush. At a time when the majority of graphic designers continued to favor an exclusively hand-drawn approach to poster design, this use of photomontage and mixing of graphic styles can be seen as pioneering, pre-dating Herbert Matter's iconic Swiss tourist posters.

In 1930 Walter Herdeg, only twenty-two, was commissioned by Dr. Walter Amstutz—an accomplished skier and mountaineer employed by the St. Moritz Tourist Office—to create a corporate identity for the famed St. Moritz winter holiday resort. Herdeg designed the decorative sun trademark and cursive script logotype at the outset of their partnership, and both are still in use today. The ensuing promotional campaign included travel brochures with inventive covers and page layouts that used photomontage images, and bold posters that focused on the emblematic sun, blue sky, and distinctive logotype as their central theme. The smiling sun was an important symbol, reflecting the winter resort's claim of three hundred days of sunshine, a message reinforced here by the gloved policeman in the foreground, who shields his eyes from its powerful rays. At the same time, the colorful sun motif lends a lighthearted touch to an otherwise unadorned scene of two skiers photographed on the Alpine ski run. The only wording on the poster, the red St. Moritz logotype placed at the same oblique angle as the figure of the policeman, emphasizes the sense of movement conveyed by the skiers, thus acting as an integral part of the image and helping to bring it to life.

In 1938 the St. Moritz Tourist Office made changes to its promotional strategies and ceased to employ Herdeg and Amstutz. The two continued to work together, however, by setting up their own advertising business specializing in the design of labels, brochures, and books. In 1944 Herdeg created *Graphis,* a unique international graphic design magazine that he presided over as owner, editor, and designer for forty-two years.

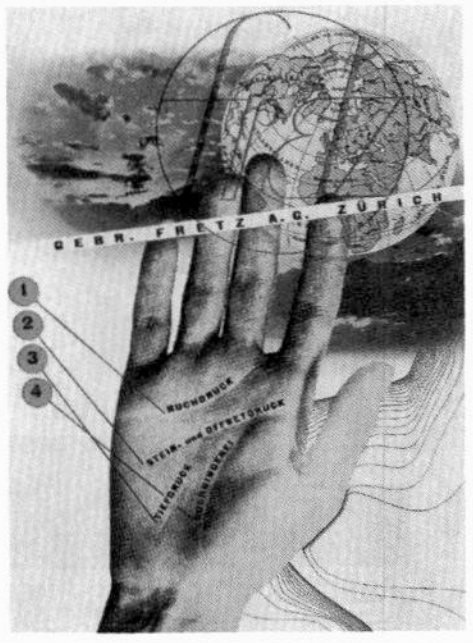

← P.133

1934

GEBRÜDER FRETZ AG

Book

Herbert Matter (1907–1984)

Gebrüder Fretz AG, Switzerland

Herbert Matter's eight-page brochure for the printing company Gebrüder Fretz AG provided a sourcebook of print examples, demonstrating how recent advances in offset lithography and gravure could allow complex arrangements of graphic and pictorial elements. Such compositions of imagery and text had been impracticable with letterpress printing. Now photographic images could be masked, framed, and arranged in new ways, and combined with textual and other graphic features. New print technology recognized the power of the image, as well as the possibilities of the fresh visual language that emerged in the 1920s and '30s, in which the spatial organization of elements provided structure and dynamism. This synthesis of qualities reflected Matter's own broad range of experiences; a photographer, painter, and filmmaker, as well as a graphic designer, Matter had worked alongside leading figures in art and design, including Fernand Léger and A.M.Cassandre.

What is immediately striking about the brochure is that images determine where the text is placed, rather than the layout being dominated by columns of text (the norm at the time). We progress through the printing processes via a sequence of black-and-white images that winds its way through the brochure, leading the eye to blocks of text. In addition to skewed frames, some images are rotated so that they no longer align with the vertical or horizontal axis, and many are masked or dropped out of their background. A number are also displayed as vignettes, which fade out into the white of the page, and black-and-white photographs or line drawings occasionally overprint monochrome images, producing a layered effect. Rather than being just an exercise in hollow virtuosity, such interventions reveal the connections that could be made between images.

Matter's exploration of the potential of print to frame and blend photographic imagery resonates with work produced some five decades later, when the arrival of digital technology made these effects still easier to achieve.

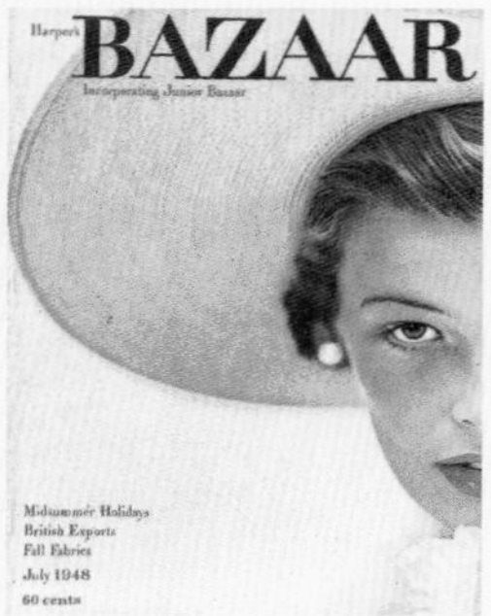

← P.133

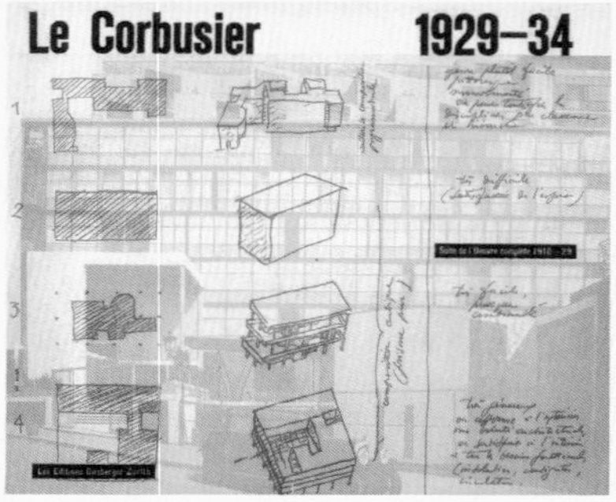

← P.133

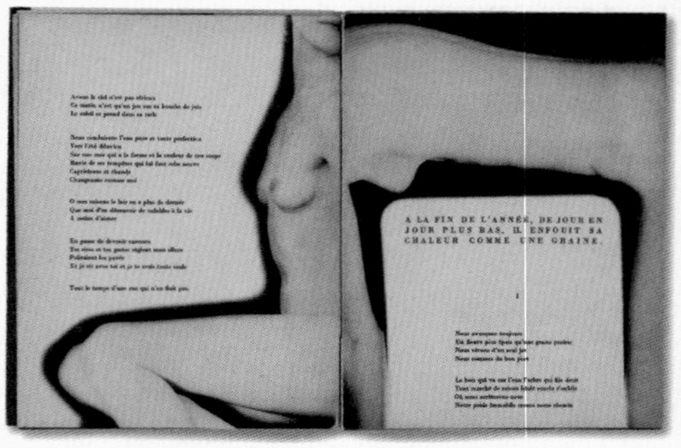

← P.134

1934–1958

HARPER'S BAZAAR

Magazine / Newspaper

Alexey Brodovitch (1898–1971)

Hearst Corporation, U.S.

The twenty-four years that Alexey Brodovitch spent at *Harper's Bazaar* mark one of the graphic highpoints of twentieth-century magazine culture. Throughout the 1920s and '30s, American fashion magazines treated the photograph in much the same way as a painting or illustration, and were largely devoid of innovation. Placed within ornamental frames and boxes, pictures of models draped in the latest creations from Paris or New York served as visual aids for the authors' words, and rather than being fully integrated into the overall page design, illustrations were clearly demarcated from the text by wide white margins.

Recognizing that conventional fashion photography and magazine design were no longer relevant to the modern woman, in 1934 the celebrated editor of *Harper's Bazaar*, Carmel Snow, hired numerous photographers not directly associated with fashion, such as the Hungarian photojournalist Martin Munkacsi, to bring freshness and vitality to the magazine's pages. Her most significant find was the Russian émigré designer Alexey Brodovitch, who had arrived in the U.S. only four years previously.

For his opening issue, Brodovitch commissioned the American photographer Man Ray, who was one of the first to exploit for fashion a technique usually reserved for news photographs, resulting in an elongated image of a woman leaning sharply to the left. Brodovitch integrated the image into the page by mirroring Man Ray's graphic expression in his treatment of the accompanying text, which duplicates the flow of the image.

Meanwhile, images by photographers such as Richard Avedon, Herbert Matter, Lillian Bassman, and André Kertész were no longer boxed in but had the freedom to run, jump, and dance across the page, whereas covers by A. M. Cassandre or double-page color spreads by Erwin Blumenfeld were enhanced by Brodovitch's fusion of image and text within the same graphic space. Such innovations became the norm during Brodovitch's tenure at *Harper's Bazaar*, bringing inventiveness and originality to a magazine that had hitherto looked staid and uninspired, and transforming it into a powerful rival of the more celebrated *Vogue*.

1935–1939

LE CORBUSIER & PIERRE JEANNERET: OEUVRE COMPLÈTE

Book

Max Bill (1908–1994)

Les Éditions Girsberger, Switzerland

Max Bill's work on *Le Corbusier & Pierre Jeanneret: Oeuvre Complète* epitomizes the outstanding graphic design produced in Switzerland in the mid-twentieth century, and demonstrates the designer's admiration and understanding of the work of Le Corbusier (Charles-Édouard Jeanneret).

An integral member of the Concrete art group, established in 1930, which endorsed the Constructivist concept of art as a tool for social order, Bill was one of the prime creators of the Swiss aesthetic, applying the principles he had learnt at the Bauhaus under Kandinsky and Klee to architectural and book design, advertisements, and typography. For Bill, art did not derive from nature but was an independent composition of color and form.

As a student in the 1920s, Bill had been deeply moved by his compatriot Le Corbusier's Pavilion de l'Esprit Nouveau in Paris, a utopian vision of a housing unit built for the Exposition des Arts Décoratifs, and became a staunch admirer of his architecture. In 1935 Bill was asked to design the book jacket for the second of an eight-volume series on the entire works of Le Corbusier and his cousin and collaborator Pierre Jeanneret. He went on to create a new cover for the reissued first volume in 1937, and to publish and completely design the third volume in 1939. Bill's graphics for these tomes employed architectural drawings and photographs sourced from Le Corbusier's sketchbooks, along with bold blocks of color and a stencil-like font to create the illusion of a third dimension. This complemented the stark modernism of the buildings illustrated and added vitality and movement to the images. At the same time, his method of breaking up large slabs of text with small images referenced both the functionalist aesthetic of the Bauhaus and the graphic techniques of the popular press, while the use of a gridlike system that reflects Le Corbusier's modular architecture orders geometric elements with mathematical precision.

1935

FACILE, BY PAUL ÉLUARD

Book

Guy Lévis-Mano (1904–1980), Man Ray (1890–1976)

Bibliothèque des Introuvables, France

Paul Éluard's pamphlet of love poems, *Facile*, dedicated to his wife, the German actress known as "Nusch," is illustrated with photographs of her by Man Ray and designed by the typographer Guy Lévis-Mano. The latter brought together words and images with a minimalist yet masterful sensibility. Although the book's title, *Facile*, means "easy," this in no way reflects the process that went into making the publication. In fact, the cover image, a photograph of metal letterforms casting a harsh shadow on a steely surface, deliberately contradicts any implication of effortlessness.

In the Surrealist tradition, nude images in the book are severely cropped to "defamiliarize" their subject, transforming the model's feminine curves into disconcerting abstract shapes. Some of the images are solarized, as if to create an afterimage, while others are overexposed, silhouetted, or layered on top of one another. The design pits black against white and positive forms against negatives ones, suggesting that the poems are about absence as much as presence. In the center of one spread, an exposed pelvis is laid bare, whereas elsewhere a standing black torso is shown intersecting with an ethereal one. Opposite, two gloves luxuriate in erotic abandon (perhaps a reference to the famous "pale blue glove" of Lise Deharme, the subject of André Breton's 1928 Surrealist novel, *Nadja*). On every page, the elusive Nusch seems to be engaged in a languorous shadow play.

For the Surrealists, women's bodies were a vital subject of exploration, their representation an opportunity to investigate the deepest recesses of the unconscious. Nusch's delicate features, lithe figure, and nymphlike presence made her a favorite model of artists, including Picasso, who painted numerous portraits of her in the mid-1930s, although she also inspired female photographers, such as Lee Miller and Dora Maar. Man Ray was one of her most attentive admirers, and it was his nude photographs of her taken in 1935 that prompted Éluard to write *Facile*. With only twelve photographs, this small volume is one of the first iconic French photo books.

← P.135

← P.135

← P.136

1935

PENGUIN BOOKS

Book Cover

Edward Young (1913–2003)

The Bodley Head, UK

Penguin Books's startlingly simple horizontal-striped cover design by Edward Young, then just a twenty-one-year-old office junior, announced an entirely novel way of selling and presenting books to a mass market. The covers had a tremendous impact, appearing fresh and modern and attracting a new type of customer to book buying.

Penguin was founded by Allen Lane and his brothers, Richard and John, in 1935, all three then directors of The Bodley Head, who funded the venture themselves. The first titles were all reprints of existing literature produced in runs of no less than seventeen thousand five hundred copies to keep the cost low (sixpence, equal to 2½ modern pence). The design—three horizontal stripes, the upper and lower of which were color-coded orange for fiction, green for crime, dark blue for biography, cerise for travel and adventure, and red for plays, with a central white panel containing the author name and title in black Gill sans serif type—was a reaction to the illustrative whimsy that was typical of most books of the period. In the upper colored panel was a cartouche, or "quartic," with the words "Penguin Books" set in Bodoni Ultra Bold, while the lower panel contained a logo, also drawn by Young. This "classic" look was partly derived from the German-English Albatross series of 1932, whose simple typography and color coding had been designed by Hans Mardersteig. Penguin also adopted its use of the golden section rectangle (7⅛ × 4⅜ inches [18.1 × 11.1 cm])—a format favored by printers, publishers, and book designers since medieval times.

With minor variations, the three-stripe design was used for the main (fiction) series for fifteen years. Other stripes were applied for series such as Pelican, Shakespeare, and Specials, whereas imprints, such as King Penguin, Puffin, and Penguin Classics, were given different designs. The stripes became so synonymous with the company that when Jan Tschichold redesigned Penguin's printed matter in 1947–49 he was only allowed to give the main series a typographic facelift. Young's design continued to be used until marketing dictated the inclusion of illustrations, when the stripes were reset vertically to provide a framing device.

1935

ALL ROADS LEAD TO SWITZERLAND

Poster

Herbert Matter (1907–1984)

Schweizerische Verkehrszentrale, Switzerland

Herbert Matter's well-known series of promotional posters, pamphlets, and magazine covers for the Swiss resorts of Pontresina, Engelberg, and Interlaken, created from 1934 to 1935 on behalf of the SVZ (Schweizerische Verkehrszentrale—Swiss National Tourist Office), are among the most celebrated works of twentieth-century graphic design ever produced.

In "All Roads Lead to Switzerland," one of the most daring and groundbreaking tourist posters of the period, Matter created a comparatively austere work composed of four principal elements: a whitened photograph of the Doldenhorn mountain set against a rich azure sky; a darkened image of a winding mountain road; a dynamic shot of a single road that occupies two thirds of the poster space, bleeding off at the sides and the base; and, finally, mirroring the gradient of the twisting road above, the words of the title printed in semitranslucent red. This montage has an immediate impact: at first glance, the eye is drawn to the title of the work, but moving on, attention is enveloped by the road, suggesting the start of an exciting journey. The impression of movement generated by the tire marks further emphasizes the trajectory of the road, and establishes a fictional dialogue between the ideal spectator and the proposed destination.

All of Matter's posters for the SVZ were made with both a Swiss and European audience in mind. Each work was widely reproduced, with the titles set in a variety of languages, from Czech to English, a requirement that made it essential to use symbols and imagery that could be readily understood by the foreign public. Like other Swiss poster designers, Matter was compelled to incorporate motifs of the alpine landscape and culture, and it is a testament to his skill that he was able to include this iconography while also introducing modern graphic devices that would attract the eye of the passer-by. In its deceptively effortless marriage of type, image, and color, the design was so successful that Matter repeated its main themes on numerous occasions.

1936–1939

TYPOGRAPHY

Magazine / Newspaper

Robert Harling (1910–2008)

Shenval Press, UK

Unparalleled both editorially and visually among other British typographic journals of its day, *Typography* explored the juncture of popular and high culture, and made an important contribution to the graphic industry by covering contemporary typographic developments and publishing unusual historical articles. The aim of the magazine was to illustrate the typography of everyday objects, including newspaper pages, transport timetables, and tea labels, alongside more serious traditional and modern type design, and included innovative features, such as bound-in mounted insets, gatefolds, and decorative colored paper.

Under the editorial and design leadership of Robert Harling, a writer and advertising art director, *Typography* offered critical reviews and articles on letter specimens and designers, type founding and setting, and books and ephemera by well-known names, such as Francis Meynell, Eric Gill, and Jan Tschichold. The publication's sparse paper covers mirrored the subject matter within its pages, often juxtaposing simple geometric forms with classical typefaces. Printed in either black and white or two colors, the magazine was set in a variety of Monotype faces, including Garamond, Plantin, Baskerville, Imprint, and Modern, and was meticulously illustrated with a range of images united harmoniously with the text. Its medium-format size and bulky extent (forty-eight pages) were intended to be functional and easy to access, whereas the plastic-comb binding, a new technique at the time, allowed for flat opening and for leaflets, subscription renewal forms, and insets to be bound in with the main body of the book. Although the print run never exceeded two thousand copies, its exceptional design and writing ensured that *Typography* had a loyal readership.

Typography closed suddenly after only eight issues with the outbreak of World War II, but its editors resumed publication after the war with two new titles, *Alphabet and Image* (1946–48) and *Image* (1949–52), which were similar in content and style.

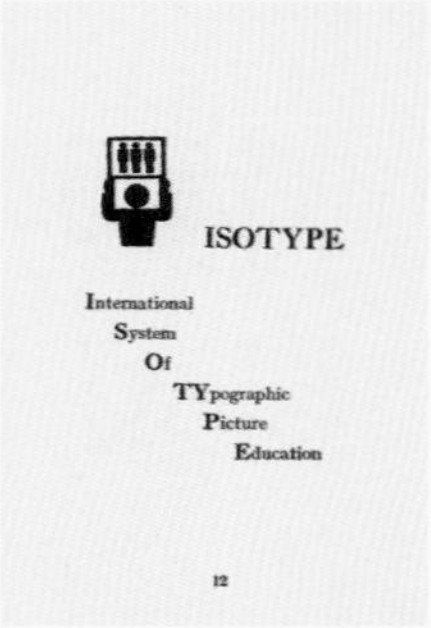

← P.136

1936

INTERNATIONAL PICTURE LANGUAGE

Information Design

Otto Neurath (1882–1945)

Self-commissioned, UK and Germany

"Every new picture is a step forward," wrote Viennese social scientist Otto Neurath in *International Picture Language: The First Rules of Isotype*, the primer of his new pictographic system. Neurath devised and promoted Isotype (an acronym for International System of Typographic Picture Education coined by his wife, Marie Reidemeister) in between the world wars, when European business and politics were increasingly conducted in multiple languages. As a pedagogical method designed to facilitate international communication, Isotype was a key precursor to standardized graphics across the world.

Published in the UK and printed in two colors in 1936, *International Picture Language* set out a rationale and a methodology to govern an expanding stock of pictographs. The book's illustrations were primarily by Gerd Arntz, whose simple and functional graphic approach paralleled that of the decorative arts and typography workshops of the Bauhaus and the New Typography. Figures were cast in easily understood silhouettes and were rigidly consistent: a symbol always represented the same thing regardless of context; multiplication of graphic units denoted quantity, not an increase or decrease in scale. Number, color, texture, and sequences were all manipulated to create a more complex and universal pictorial grammar.

To ensure the pictograms were consistent in standard and development, Neurath declared that a body of experts was needed to devise, propagate, and regulate his system (his International Foundation for the Promotion of Visual Education, with headquarters then located in the Hague). He emphasized that it was not self-sufficient but "a helping language" to supplement writing, although despite the spirit of egalitarianism and intercultural communication in which it was created, cultural biases are evident, especially in the depiction of people as men.

Neurath's wife and collaborator, Marie, continued to promote Isotype after his death, believing that "no one has made statistics as easy to comprehend instantly as ... Isotype," and establishing a continuum between Neurath's work and the modern pictographic vocabularies to which designers today are indebted.

← P.137

1936

SPRATT'S

Logo

Max Field-Bush (n.d.)

Spratt's, UK

With the company letterforms shaped into the form of a tail-wagging Scottie dog, the Spratt's logo established a winning design formula that lodged the name of this early-twentieth-century dog-food manufacturer firmly in the public mind. The Spratt's trademark is everything a successful logo should be—witty, engaging, and memorable. The company went on to issue a similar logo for Spratt's cat food, featuring an image of a cat also shaped from the letters of its name.

After World War I, with rising industrial production and increased prosperity for many sectors of the population, particularly the burgeoning middle class, manufacturers looked for new ways to win business and attract the attention of customers. In an increasingly competitive market, it was no longer sufficient to identify a company with a typeset name; products needed to be branded and rendered memorable, using strong images and powerful slogans. When Spratt's founder, James Spratt, arrived in England from Cincinnati in 1860 to sell lightning rods, he noticed dogs on the docks fighting over discarded ships' biscuits, and decided to go into trade, making specialty dog biscuits. The business grew and soon needed a recognizable brand identity, which Max Field-Bush's logo provides.

The Spratt's logo embodies some of the qualities of the *Sachplakat* (object poster). Simple and clear communication of the subject matter was of utmost importance to this style, with entire posters sometimes consisting of a lone coal briquette, a light bulb, or a spark plug. In 1927 Walter Kach took the idea further with his poster design for the exhibition *Form Without Ornament*, in which type is set in the shape of a hammer and pliers. Similarly, the Spratt's trademark blends type and image into a single unified form. The logo was discontinued when Spratts became part of General Mills in the 1950s, although many of the characteristic enameled signs remained in existence.

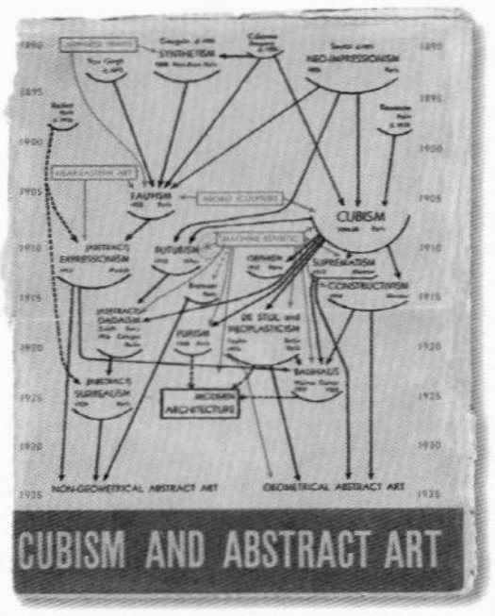

← P.138

1936

CUBISM AND ABSTRACT ART

Book Cover

Alfred H. Barr, Jr. (1902–1981)

Museum of Modern Art, New York, U.S.

This cover design for the catalog to the exhibition *Cubism and Abstract Art*, which traveled to many other U.S. cities after being originally held at the Museum of Modern Art (MoMA), New York, served as a shorthand explanation of the relationships between the various art movements represented by the exhibits, and has been admired and debated ever since its creation. Alfred H. Barr studied art history at Princeton and Harvard universities, and was the first person to teach an undergraduate course in twentieth-century art, at Wellesley College in 1926. In 1929 Barr became director of MoMA, and within ten years had organized seminal exhibitions of Van Gogh and Picasso. By the time he left the museum in 1967, he had helped to establish modern art as an accepted field of art history.

In this design Barr uses color, type (the geometric, Bauhaus-influenced, sans serif Futura), and line to tell the story of early-twentieth-century art. Whereas the names of Western art movements are in black, Asian and African art, and the date line, are in red to highlight their influential but complementary role. By recalling scientific diagrams, the map also lends weight to the view of the museum as an academic institution for discovering and analyzing the history of art, as well as a place for viewing its artifacts. The chart has often been criticized as overselective and lacking in context, and for failing to mention individual artists, but it has also been praised for its simplicity and for acting as a visual manifesto of the new museum. In his book *Beautiful Evidence* (2006), Edward Tufte analyzes the work, praising the use of color, size, and typeface but criticizing the lack of double-headed arrows, for instance, which would symbolize simultaneous mutual influence as naive.

Although Barr's diagram is far from scientific in its method, it nevertheless provides a compelling illustration of modern art as a rich, vital, and complex subject. As the century progressed, the relationships he outlined would become increasingly well documented and understood, but at the time of its creation it offered a fresh way of looking at a cultural phenomenon that many still found strange and alienating.

← P.138

1936–2000

LIFE

Magazine / Newspaper

Various

Time Inc., U.S.

Life was the first American weekly news magazine to focus heavily on photography, allocating equal space to images and text. Strongly influenced by German photojournalism publications, such as *Berliner Illustrierte Zeitung* (*BIZ*), it was produced by publisher and editor Henry Luce, who had previously launched *Time* in 1923 and *Fortune* in 1930.

Life had been in existence since 1883, but it was acquired by Luce in 1936 for Time Inc. The first issue of Luce's magazine, published on November 23, 1936, for a loss-making ten cents per issue, contained fifty pages of photographs and condensed captions. It featured a cover photograph of the Fort Peck Dam by Margaret Bourke-White, accompanied by a striking red rectangle in the upper left corner, containing the title in simple, white sans serif capitals. The magazine was rescued from early financial ruin by its controversial issue of April 11, 1938, which ran a five-page article on *Birth of a Baby*, a banned film that depicted the complete process of childbirth.

Life published the work of many World War II reportage photographers, including Robert Capa, who documented the Normandy D-Day landings. Their coverage was so successful that enemy propaganda copied the magazine's layout and emphasis on photography. Luce hired many renowned photographers and artists for *Life*'s covers, although the most famous cover image remains Alfred Eisenstaedt's photograph of a nurse swept off her feet by a sailor's kiss during V-J Day celebrations in New York's Times Square. When the magazine began to publish theater and film reviews, it adopted a traffic-light coding system, with good reviews marked by a green point, bad reviews by red, and mixed by yellow. The only time that the red-and-white title changed was in November and December 1963, when it was printed in white on black to mark the assassination of President Kennedy.

Life spawned many other photography magazines, such as *Look*, *Focused*, and *Pic*, all of which lost out to television in the 1960s. In 1972 the magazine ceased to publish weekly, and, after a series of biannual issues, reemerged as a monthly title in 1978.

← P.138

1936

LONDON A TO Z

Book

Phyllis Pearsall (1906–1996)

Geographers' Map Co. Ltd., UK

At one time, no London resident, employee, or visitor could survive without the *A to Z* street atlas, a brilliant piece of cartography that makes sense of the labyrinth of roads, cul-de-sacs, alleyways, railway lines, canals, and parks that make up Britain's capital.

The brainchild of artist Phyllis Pearsall, the first *A to Z Atlas and Guide to London and Suburbs* was published in 1936 and remains one of the most ingenious examples of early, twentieth-century information design. The previous year Pearsall had lost her way navigating the London streets using a twenty-year-old Ordnance Survey map. She set about mapping the city's twenty-three thousand streets, working eighteen hours per day and walking three thousand miles (4,828 km).

Too vast to be laid out on a cumbersome flat plan, London was divided by Pearsall into different sections, each of which was coded by an index. Once they were drawn and labelled, both the maps and index required meticulous checking for errors, inaccuracies, or omissions. For the *A to Z*'s visual identity, Pearsall chose Gill Sans, which gave a contemporary British look to a particularly British concept: the font was a typographic solution that was regarded as among the most exciting and innovative of its day. The title was an inspired choice, based on its all-important index. On completion the guide met with complete indifference from the book trade, so Pearsall published it herself, printing ten thousand copies and persuading the chain newsagent W. H. Smith to take two-hundred-fifty on a sale or return basis. Her *A to Z* was a runaway success.

The *London A to Z* was later made available on CD with a searchable index containing more than ninety thousand streets and places of interest. A to Z satellite navigation and maps for mobile phones are also available. These continuing innovations testify to Pearsall's vision and determination. The original *A to Z* is a model of modern information design that has been used to map virtually every city and town in the United Kingdom, and has been imitated in countries across the world. A household name, the *A to Z* addressed the real everyday needs of city dwellers everywhere.

← P.139

1936

VAN GOGH

Book

Béla Horovitz (1898–1955)

Phaidon Press, Austria

Publishing history was made in 1936 when Phaidon Press published a monograph of the work of Dutch artist Vincent van Gogh, entitled simply *Van Gogh*. The founders of Phaidon, Béla Horovitz and Ludwig Goldscheider, provided the impetus for publishing the large-format volume, with Horovitz handling the production processes and Goldscheider curating the plate selection. *Van Gogh*'s success was a major contributor to the popularity of art books from then onward.

Up until this point, Phaidon's books were printed on sheets that were folded three times to form sets of sixteen pages. But Horovitz investigated the printing press, determining the largest possible size that each page could be, and based the format of the book on that. In the case of *Van Gogh*, the sheets that had previously been folded three times were now folded twice to form sets of eight larger pages.

At 10⅝ × 14⅛ inches (27 × 36 cm), *Van Gogh* is not only substantial in size but, with a linen-bound hard cover, also feels solid. The typeface of the interior is bold and sans serif, based on a clean, clear, and modern Bauhaus aesthetic. The monotone images were printed using photogravure, which transfers a photographic negative to a metal plate and etches it in, resulting in images with a precise detail suitable for art reproduction. In addition, color images were glued into the book in the form of tipped-in plates. Part of the reason for the quality of the book was the close relationship that Horovitz established with his printers. His enthusiasm for printing techniques and close contact with those who worked the printing machines ensured a fine result.

Although Béla Horovitz was not the first to come up with the idea of the large-format, generously illustrated monograph, he realized that this kind of book could be popular if it was priced reasonably, which could be achieved by risking the production of a large print-run. The gamble paid off. A day or two after the launch of *Van Gogh*, Horovitz went to his Viennese printers to check the stock, where exhausted staff told him that all fifty-five thousand copies had been sold and dispatched. Three further editions were also produced in 1936.

With the publication of *Van Gogh*, Phaidon Press secured its position as a leading art publisher.

← P.140

← P.141

← P.141

1937

RURAL ELECTRIFICATION ADMINISTRATION

Poster

Lester Beall (1903–1969)

Department of Agriculture/Rural Electrification Administration, U.S.

Lester Beall's posters for the Rural Electrification Administration (REA) are a striking example of avant-garde design applied to public service. The REA program was established by the United States Department of Agriculture in collaboration with utilities companies to improve general services and living standards in rural areas of the U.S. It was also intended as a stimulus to the economy in the after-math of the 1929 stock-market crash.

REA posters were large format (40 × 30 inches [102 × 76 cm]) and acted as an information platform for the work of the organization. In this, the first of three poster campaigns, Beall established a color palette of only four colors—black and the primary colors, applied in flat blocks and combined with simple graphic motifs such as arrows, a limited number of words, and objects reduced to basic shapes. This approach aimed to increase impact and strengthen communication to an audience that was often illiterate. The poster for "Radio," for example, uses arrows to draw the viewer's eye toward the house in the center, emphasizing the delivery of radio communications to rural households, whereas in "Farm Work" and "Wash Day," machinery is reduced to silhouettes. Beall's deliberately rudimentary compositions, which depended on a partly abstract modernist language, were important in democratizing graphic design, making visual communication accessible to the most deprived sectors of the population and providing information about issues that directly affected people's daily lives. Two further sets of posters, using a different style that combined naturalistic imagery with abstract elements, were published in 1939 and 1941.

Despite being largely self-taught, Beall had a prolific career, particularly in corporate design, working for organizations such as the U.S. Post Office, Eastman Kodak, and the American Red Cross. His talent was recognized in an exhibition of his work held at the Museum of Modern Art in New York in 1937, the same year in which these posters were produced.

1937

PEIGNOT

Typeface

A. M. Cassandre (1901–1968)

Deberny & Peignot, France

Admired for its elegance and versatility, Peignot was one of the most popular letterforms of the 1930s and '40s, and the emblem of a modern age. This distinctive sans serif is notable for its thick-and-thin body, and the quirky use of uppercase letters in its lowercase form.

Peignot has two spiritual parents: the Bauhaus and the Middle Ages. German experimental typography of the 1920s had placed sans serif lettering at the forefront of design, as seen in Paul Renner's Futura (1927) and Herbert Bayer's Universal alphabet (1925, available only in lowercase form). In an attempt to create an equally daring and original sans serif, Cassandre, after many false starts, found inspiration in an unlikely source: Medieval half-uncial calligraphy, which mixed capital and lowercase letterforms, and combined rounded letter forms with elongated ascenders and descenders. Whereas Cassandre is widely recognized for his contributions to poster design, little is known of the man who gave the face its name. Charles Peignot was an establisher of the Parisian type foundry Deberny & Peignot, and a visionary who employed leading European designers of the era, such as Herbert Matter, Alexey Brodovitch, and Charles Loupot, as well as Cassandre. More than just the proprietor of a successful type business, Peignot embodied French typography for more than five decades, and was known as an arbiter of taste, a courageous experimenter, and an adventurous publisher.

Peignot was launched spectacularly in 1937 as the "official" typeface of the Paris World's Fair, when it was chosen by Paul Valéry for inscriptions on the two towers of the Palais de Chaillot. A fabricator produced cardboard stencils for making complete alphabets, which were then used for mural inscriptions on the exhibition stands. The face provoked a powerful response among designers and consumers, and was adopted for many magazines and advertisements. Although a reflection of the Parisian modernist style of the interwar period, Peignot retained its flair well into the 1960s, inspiring Art Deco revivals in the U.S. and Europe.

1937

MERCEDES-BENZ

Logo

Gottlieb Daimler (1834–1900)

Daimler Motoren Gesellschaft, Germany

Sleek, simple, and elegant, the Mercedes trademark star has become synonymous with high-quality automobile design and manufacture, whether luxury private cars or solid working vehicles, such as coaches and trucks. Indeed, the logo represents the concept of top class, from the German word *Spitzenklasse*, which means peak or pinnacle class, an idea conveyed by the upward-thrusting point.

According to legend, Mercedes-Benz's three-pointed star derives from a mark that Gottlieb Daimler, founder of Daimler Motoren Gesellschaft (DMG), scribbled on a postcard to his wife in the 1870s to mark the position of his house in a photograph of his hometown Cologne, saying that it would one day appear over his factory. In 1900, shortly after Daimler's death, the company produced its first car, commissioned by Emil Jellinek, a Daimler distributor, who named it after his daughter, Mercedes. Some years later, Daimler's sons, Paul and Adolf, who were by then senior executives of the company, suggested that Gottfried's sign be used as a trademark, with the three points indicating their ambition of universal motorization on land, water, and in the air. The emblem first appeared on a car in 1909 and was officially registered in 1910. In 1916 it was surrounded by a circle, and in 1921 became three-dimensional as a symbol for placing on or above car radiators; further slight variations were introduced in subsequent years until the merging of DMG and Benz & Cie., in 1926 resulted in a final design incorporating the trade names Mercedes and Benz, connected by Benz's characteristic laurel wreaths.

In 1937 the Mercedes emblem was streamlined, reducing the width of the points and enclosing the star in a simple, slender circle devoid of motif or lettering—a distillation of the original that now endures as a timeless classic. In the 1980s the logos on cars became a cult item frequently stolen by teenagers for use as a fashion accessory, prompting the company to manufacture spare stars for deprived owners from 1987.

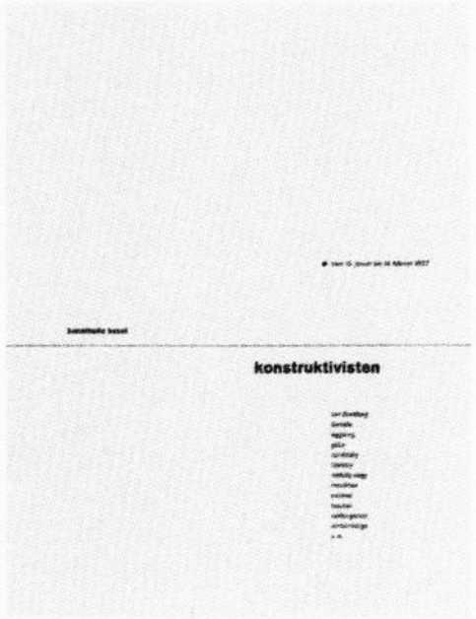

← P.142

← P.143

← P.144

1937

KONSTRUKTIVISTEN

Poster

Jan Tschichold (1902–1974)

Kunsthalle Basel, Switzerland

Designed for the *Konstruktivisten* (*Constructivism*) exhibition at the Kunsthalle Basel, this poster by Jan Tschichold reflects the peak of his allegiance to the Neue Typographie (New Typography) and to the principles of Constructivist and asymmetrical typography. Tschichold also demonstrates his use of classical proportions to create a harmonious balance between symmetry and asymmetry.

In August 1923 Tschichold encountered the work of the Hungarian Constructivist designer László Moholy-Nagy at the first Bauhaus exhibition in Weimar, which he found a revelation. Shortly afterward, he was also introduced to the work of the Russian Constructivists El Lissitzky and Aleksandr Rodchenko, as well as to the Dutch graphic designer Piet Zwart, and soon began to incorporate their methods into his work. For this design, Tschichold has stripped the typography to its basic elementary shapes, and set the lettering into a graceful arrangement of horizontal and vertical axes, while the asymmetrical layout, white space, and changes of scale provide contrast. The circle, horizontal line, and bullet also illustrate his preference for rudimentary geometric forms that establish subtle relationships with the whole.

The work of Constructivist artists in Germany was declared *Entartete Kunst* (Degenerate Art) by the Third Reich, and in March 1933 Tschichold and his wife were arrested. He designed this poster four years after fleeing to Switzerland, and two years after publishing his landmark text *Typographische Gestaltung* (Typographic Design), which elaborated on the principles of his earlier handbook *Die Neue Typographie* (1928). "Konstruktivisten" is one of his last posters to use asymmetrical typography, and along with "Der Berufsphotograph" (The Professional Photographer), designed in 1938, brought to completion Tschichold's poster oeuvre. His work as a whole would continue to influence future generations, particularly leading Swiss designers who followed the New Typography and used sans serif type (at the time referred to as Grotesque typefaces) with asymmetrical arrangements of geometric forms.

1937

IL POEMA DEL VESTITO DI LATTE

Book

Bruno Munari (1907–1998)

Snia Viscosa, Italy

The extraordinary title *Il Poema del Vestito di Latte* (The Poem of Milk Clothing) on the brochure for the Italian textiles company Snia Viscosa owes more to developments in textile production than to its author Filippo T. Marinetti's radical concept of *parole in libertá* (words in freedom). In fact, Marinetti is celebrating the invention in 1935 of Lanital, a synthetic woolen fiber made from the casein protein found in milk. Bruno Munari's design, on the other hand, bears many of the hallmarks of modernist graphics.

Combining figurative with abstract forms and linear overlay, Munari's cover reflects his ironic attitude toward the subject and captures the Surrealist character of the title, represented here by the curious juxtaposition of the cow's outlined head and textile sample. In a more direct reference, the design also echoes Enrico Prampolini's 1933 cover for the Futurist newspaper *Futurismo*. The aerial photograph at the top is probably of one of the sixteen factories operated by the company in Italy, while the sharp sans serif letters of the heading and author credit complete the red-and-green-against-white color scheme representative of the national colors of Italy, and reinforce the graphic clarity of the design as a whole. Internal spreads continue the theme of transparency, with overlapping photographs, body text superimposed on images, and transparent inserts adding to the flow of information.

A painter, sculptor, photographer, designer, filmmaker, and writer, Munari was an influential and controversial figure. His constant inventiveness with materials and technology, and interest in abstract form, led to a series of nonobjective sculptures ("Useless Machines") in the 1930s. After World War II, he operated a design studio, conducting radical experiments in graphics and typography, designing *Tempo* magazine and producing advertisements for corporate clients, such as Campari and Olivetti.

1937–1960

SAINT-RAPHAËL QUINQUINA

Advertising

Charles Loupot (1892–1962)

Saint-Raphaël, France

Pasted up in every French city as well as on country roads, Charles Loupot's abstract posters and murals for the French aperitif Saint-Raphaël, with their ubiquitous red, black, and white logo, were a familiar part of the French landscape in the 1950s. Expressed in a bold calligraphic style, the product name was split into three parts—St. Ra/pha/ël—and collaged in multiple directions to create a dynamic patchwork. Although not easily legible, the logo was instantly recognizable from a distance.

The stylized design had a long evolution. Loupot, a perfectionist, began working on the logotype in 1937, and kept improving it until his death, sustained by the ever-changing legal status of advertisements for alcoholic beverages in France. Between 1941 and 1951, only the logo, not the product, could be shown, and was restricted to a small portion of the image. Loupot turned this prohibitive regulation to his advantage, celebrating the spirit of the brand rather than its name. Following World War II, he hired a young Swiss graphic typographer, Werner Häschler, to trace the logo carefully, and help control the way in which it would be used in all its serendipitous permutations.

Loupot's achievement was aided by the support of the visionary Max Augier, head of advertising at Saint-Raphaël and a staunch supporter of graphic excellence, who knew how to promote innovation without alienating his audience. After 1951, he allowed Loupot to transform the company's mascots—two traditional French waiters shown in profile against a black background, one thin, the other rotund, which had been popular since the 1930s—into hieroglyphic symbols both elegant and playful. Even though the abstracted white-and-red figures were rigorously plotted as a series of intersecting circles and diagonals, they were as endearing to the public as their more figurative incarnations, and endowed with a very French *pince-sans-rire*, deadpan sense of humor. Today, Saint-Raphaël ancillary products, from wall clocks to ice buckets, stamped with the red-and-white "twins" and/or the abstract logo, are prized collectors' items.

← P.144

← P.145

← P.145

1938–1940

MATCH

Magazine Cover

Unknown

Jean Prouvost, France

Launched in Paris by the newspaper proprietor Jean Prouvost in 1938, *Match* halted publication with the German invasion in World War II. Among the many magazines emulating Henry Luce's celebrated *Life* magazine, *Match* was one of the most intriguing, and might have become a showcase for great photojournalism, like England's *Picture Post*, had its existence not been so brief.

Match—its name held over from its previous life as a sports journal—is remembered mostly for its striking red logo, stuck on the cover like a hot button. Few magazines before or since have tried fitting their titles inside discs, despite the eye-catching possibilities. During the late 1930s, at the time of *Match*'s launch, it seems that the most famous circular emblems were red—the Coca-Cola bottle cap, the Lucky Strike cigarette seal, and the London Underground symbol—all of which had found a typographical solution to a tricky problem. *Match*'s approach was just as creative: to negotiate the circle, the five letters of the name, set in Akzidenz-Grotesk Condensed, were enlarged and reduced in size, with the symmetrical "T" marking the center.

When Prouvost bought *Match*, he transformed it into a *Life* magazine copycat. In fact, the classic combination of black-and-white photography, dynamic composition, and red typography, which was emblematic of *Life*'s early covers, had originally been introduced by Rodchenko on the covers of *LEF* magazine in the 1920s. Luce had shamelessly appropriated a Russian revolution's graphic formula and put it at the service of a conservative U.S. magazine. In 1949 Prouvost resuscitated *Match* as *Paris-Match*, which is still going strong, its logo a red rectangle that is identical to the trademark of the now defunct *Life*.

1938

LONDON TRANSPORT—KEEPS LONDON GOING

Poster

Man Ray (1890–1976)

London Transport, UK

During the interwar years, London Transport gained a reputation for innovative poster design, but this pair of posters by the Surrealist artist and photographer Man Ray (Emmanuel Radnitzky), is particularly unorthodox—among the most revolutionary travel posters of all time.

Paired London Transport posters such as these were intended to be displayed side by side or in close proximity, and usually comprised complementary designs. However, Man Ray's image of the planet Saturn and the iconic bar-and-circle logo is repeated in both, while the asymmetrical arrangement of the strips of white on the left-hand side is another unusual facet. The concept of using the corporate symbol as the basis of the design was not uncommon, but the bleak emptiness of these black-and-white images contrasts starkly with the decorative character of works by other artists of the period. Man Ray was renowned for what he referred to as "rayographs," photographic prints produced without the use of a camera, but in this instance he may have photographed models of Saturn and the roundel against a black background. Johnston Sans, London Transport's own corporate typeface, has been used for the headline text.

The circumstances of the commission are not known, although it is almost certain that Man Ray was introduced to Frank Pick, vice-chairman of London Transport, by the graphic designer Edward McKnight Kauffer, who had mounted an exhibition of Man Ray's work at the Lund Humphries gallery in 1934. The following year, Man Ray returned for a brief period to work at Lund Humphries's photographic studios, where he may have produced this poster. As a patron of contemporary art, Pick had commissioned many prominent artists and graphic designers, including László Moholy-Nagy, Paul Nash, and Edward Wadsworth, but Man Ray was his most radical choice. The posters (1,375 were printed) were displayed on Underground station sites in January 1939.

c. 1938

VOLKSWAGEN

Logo

Franz Reimspiess (1900–1979)

Volkswagenwerk, GmbH, Germany

The classic Volkswagen logo is rooted in the fame of the Beetle (or Bug), a vehicle born out of Nazi social planning but popularized in the West as a symbol of flower power. The VW logo thus gained fame just as much for its placement on these revolutionary vehicles as for its striking geometric form.

The origin of the logo's design has been the subject of speculation, with rumors that even Hitler penned the original logotype, and a long-standing lawsuit (only recently settled) over copyright. It is generally believed to have been produced in 1937 or 1938 by Franz Reimspiess, an Austrian engine designer working for Ferdinand Porsche, who created the symbol on his own initiative.

The prewar logo featured the familiar stacked "V" and "W" in a simple circle. By the time the first Beetle rolled off the assembly line in 1938, the logo was surrounded by a cog similar to that found in the symbol of the DAF, the National Socialist German Worker's Party, which had built the original cars. The British took over responsibility for production in 1945, with copyright for the final logo filed in 1948.

On postwar Beetles the VW roundel was not prominent, appearing as a small chrome emblem at the base of the windscreen and stamped on the protruding hubcaps. When the Type 2 VW Microbus was introduced in 1950, it featured a much larger VW symbol on its nose, occasionally replaced with a peace symbol as the vehicle became an icon for counterculture. This central placement on the vehicle suited the symmetry of the logo's interlocking letters, and helped to give this already distinctive logotype legendary status in visual identity design.

Today, the logo is also associated with sleek German engineering, following MetaDesign's overhaul of the Volkswagen corporate identity program in 1995. This involved a "road identity strategy," which removed the Volkswagen name from the exterior of the cars altogether and replaced it with prominent VW emblems on the front and rear. The final modification of the logo appeared in 2000 with the introduction of a blue-and-white three-dimensional version, a minor change that maintains its classic form and recognizable configuration.

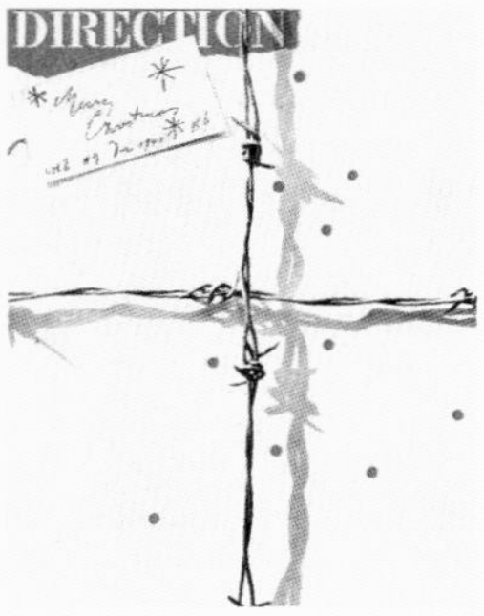

← P.146

1938–1945

DIRECTION

Magazine Cover

Paul Rand (1914–1996)

Marguerite Tjader Harris, U.S.

Paul Rand's covers for *Direction* magazine define his transition from boy wonder to creative force. A bimonthly, anti-Fascist cultural magazine, *Direction* was published and edited by Marguerite Tjader Harris, who actively recruited Rand, then art director for *Apparel Arts* and *Esquire*. With limited funds, all that Harris could offer by way of payment was creative understanding and freedom, but this was just the kind of patronage Rand needed to explore and develop his ideas. Later, he was paid in Le Corbusier watercolors, and felt that he had received the better deal.

Even though Rand credited his *Direction* covers to the influence of Picasso, Fernand Léger, and Theo van Doesberg, as well as to magazines such as *Verve* and *Minotaure,* he was already transforming these sources into his own distinctive style, based not on visual components alone, but on the fusion of form and idea. Taken as a whole, the covers exhibit a combination of wit and metaphor—a series of collages characterized by a DIY sensibility that have an all-inclusive approach without the disconnection that such eclecticism can sometimes suggest. Yet the covers are also individual works of art, notable not only for their visual range, but also for their variety of subject matter and mood: one distinctive design features a present wrapped with barbed wire; another includes a swastika split apart by a slab-serifed "v" for victory. Such imagery reflected Rand's sense of the artistic and geopolitical upheaval in the world, as well as an interest in content generation and design authorship, all of which was enhanced by his unique style.

A direct line can be drawn from Rand's *Direction* covers to his subsequent advertising and promotional work for Coronet Brandy (1945–48), Kaufmann's (1947–48), and El Producto (1952–57). In all of these designs, Rand added his actual signature to the stylistic one that was by then becoming widely recognized.

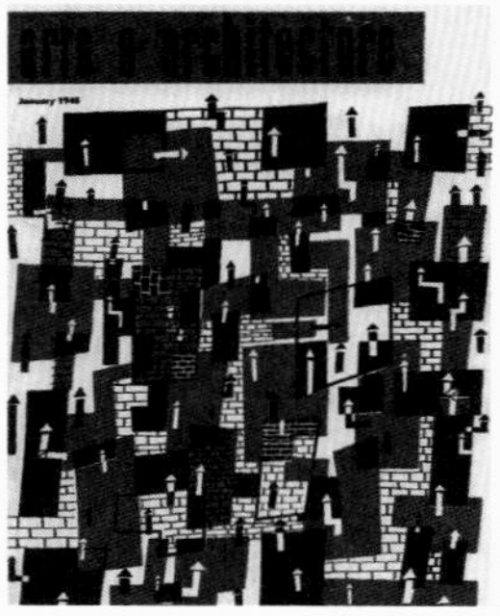

← P.146

1938–1962

ARTS & ARCHITECTURE

Magazine Cover

Various

John Entenza, U.S.

The mission of the architecture magazine *Arts & Architecture*, one of the most important publications for the promotion of American mid-century design, was to embrace modernism as popularized through residential projects.

In 1938 editor John Entenza revitalized the decade-old *California Arts & Architecture* magazine, shortening the name to *Arts & Architecture*. Focusing on the new modern architecture of southern California, the magazine brought attention to the region's designers, and demonstrated that domestic building could be innovative and affordable. It became renowned for its Case Study Program, through which it commissioned and published revolutionary (but accessible), low-cost residential designs by architects ranging from Richard Neutra to Eero Saarinen.

Reflecting the magazine's shift toward more social goals, Entenza commissioned artists belonging to the current design movement to create its inventive covers. Many were designed by graphic design masters Herbert Matter and John Follis. Other contributors, whose work also featured on the inside pages, included architectural photographer Julius Shulman, sculptor Isamu Noguchi, and architect Le Corbusier, as well as designers Saul Bass, Paul Rand, Alvin Lustig, and Ray Eames (whose own home, designed with her husband Charles, was No. 8 in the Case Study House Program).

Rather than reflect the magazine's contents, the covers of *Arts & Architecture* were almost always abstract—combinations of meandering lines and organic shapes that nodded to the natural world yet also included overtly constructed elements. Some incorporated pastiche, often using architectural photography. The masthead also lent itself to experimentation, broken into two lines, or highlighted with different colors, but always keeping the same letter style to create a unified identity. Free of any other text, the cover was a canvas on which designers could truly experiment.

← P.147

1939

WAIT! COUNT 15 SLOWLY BEFORE MOVING IN THE BLACKOUT

Poster

G. R. Morris (n.d.)

National Safety First Association, UK

The blackout as a precaution against air raids was a frightening experience for millions of Britons during the early years of World War II. In this public safety poster for the National Safety First Association G. R. Morris clearly targets a specific audience considered to be the most vulnerable in these circumstances—young, working women.

The design intelligently combines a tense, dramatic atmosphere with a calm, stable composition. In a moment of potential panic, Morris's poster underlines the need for clear, coordinated thought, expressed through the link between the sculpted profile and the stocking-clad, high-heeled foot by means of a lipstick-red, wandering, broken line. Concise copywriting and irregular typographic layout, combined with the somewhat crude drawing, give the image a playful, informal quality that makes it approachable, emphasizing safety rather than danger. Meanwhile, the word "slowly," picked out in red, highlights the most important aspect of the message. Morris was known for his slightly Surrealist style and imagery; used here, it reflects a sensitive, progressive approach to design and the avoidance of elements likely to shock or disturb.

This is one of two known posters that Morris designed for safety prevention in the blackout. The second—"Wear Something Light, Carry Something White"—was targeted more directly at men but employed similar visual devices: a split figure, red directional lines, integrated typography, and a dark, dramatic background. Morris continued to work for the Royal Society for the Prevention of Accidents (RoSPA), formed in 1941, designing numerous posters for them, as well as for organizations such as London Transport, and was a member of the Society of Industrial Artists. After the war, he was employed by several publishing houses, including Longman and The Bodley Head, but he disappeared into obscurity in the early 1950s.

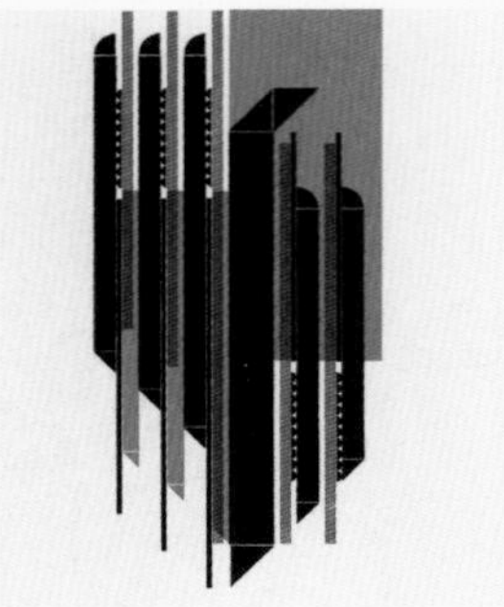

← P.148

1940

THE GHOST IN THE UNDERBLOWS, BY ALFRED YOUNG FISHER

Book

Alvin Lustig (1915–1955)

Ward Ritchie Press, U.S.

Alvin Lustig's book design for Alfred Young Fisher's 304-page poem fragment *The Ghost in the Underblows* is an unfortunate victim of its subject's obscurity and impenetrability. However, for such a difficult, multilayered piece of verse, Lustig's experimental style proved fitting. His abstract cover, title page, and chapter dividers were designed as modernism was making its first steps in the U.S, and in style and process resemble Constructivist, Futurist, and Bauhaus typographic designs and experiments of the previous two decades.

Not unlike El Lissitzky and Aleksandr Rodchenko before him, Lustig fashioned these illustrations from hot-metal rules and ornaments, or "furniture" taken from the typecases of his own print shop early in his career. The results were inventive and attractive, presenting form and content as one. Lustig's overlapping, Abstract black-and-red shapes suggest section titles, as seen in the avian illustration for "The Dying Phoenix," and the complexity of the whole work, with its multilayered biblical structure and many allusions. These illustrations are tied visually to the text pages through the use of bold, geometric sans serif folios.

Although Lustig had studied modernist design, it was the brief time that he spent with Frank Lloyd Wright at Taliesin East—which allowed him to appreciate the architect's pencil sketches for stained glass windows—that inspired him to experiment. First came designs for holiday cards, business papers, and other ephemera, one of which came to the attention of the publisher Ward Ritchie. With Ritchie's encouragement, Lustig then undertook book design, applying his ornamental abstract style to *Ghost* and other titles, such as *Robinson Jeffers* (1938). He moved on to create more organic layouts for the New Directions "New Classics" series in cover designs such as *The Man Who Died* (1950). Toward the end of his brief career he came full circle, creating largely typographic covers, such as *Keats* (1953), for which he used ornate and slab-serif typefaces to devise solutions reminiscent of *Ghost*, without the typographic furniture.

← P.148

1940–1947

VIEW

Magazine Cover

Parker Tyler (1904–1974) et al.

Charles Henri Ford, U.S.

With a circulation of just three thousand, *View* was a cultural magazine with eclectic interests, which ranged from art, poetry, and critical writing to folk and indigenous art forms, jazz, and work by and for children. Nevertheless, the intellectual current dominating the magazine was primarily European Surrealism. Presented in a glossy format featuring lavish illustration and color covers, the publication served to rally and popularize the work and ideas of European and American avant-garde artists and writers during and immediately after World War II.

View's remit and graphic identity—edited by Charles Henri Ford and designed by his associate editor, Parker Tyler—owed much to the recently discontinued French luxury arts magazine *Minotaure*, in being led by its arresting artist-designed covers. These provided a roll call of high-profile European émigrés resident in the U.S, including Max Ernst, André Masson, Wifredo Lam, and Fernand Léger. American artists who contributed cover designs, such as Man Ray, Alexander Calder, or Joseph Cornell, were also those essentially in tune with *View*'s Surrealist sympathies. In layouts and typography Tyler steered a course between the playful and the sophisticated, creating a look closer to upscale fashion journals than the "little magazines" typical of the literary avant-garde. *View*'s covers were a key part of this strategy, balancing visual complexity with poetic ambiguity, and occasionally featuring a special masthead, such as when the sculptor Isamu Noguchi turned its four letters into spatial forms. The most celebrated cover (pictured) was designed by Marcel Duchamp—a meticulously set-up photograph of a wine bottle leaking smoke into the night sky, delicately hinting at both the cosmic and the everyday, the serious and whimsical, and conveying *View*'s editorial vision of poetry for a mainstream audience.

View's circulation eventually proved too small to sustain it, and by 1947 the Surrealist currents represented by many of its European contributors had begun to look outdated. It was not until the 1960s, and the rise of American Pop art, that *View* became once again appreciated as a bridge between the avant-garde and the popular.

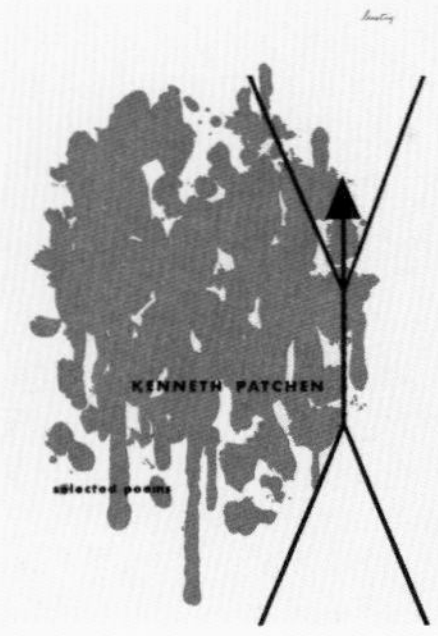

← P.148

1940–1952

NEW CLASSICS

Book Cover

Alvin Lustig (1915–1955)

New Directions, U.S.

Alvin Lustig's book-jacket designs for the New Directions "New Classics" series have come to epitomize modern American postwar design. In addition to their commercial success (they dramatically increased sales of the previously slow-moving volumes), they also showcased, in an uncommonly public and accessible forum, the experimental approach then being undertaken by modern designers.

Lustig's interest in modernism can be traced to his high-school days in Los Angeles, when he was introduced to the posters of A. M. Cassandre and Edward McKnight Kauffer, an experience that forever changed his way of seeing. During the 1930s, Lustig was inspired by the innovative techniques "imported" by the many designers and architects fleeing increasingly turbulent conditions in Europe. He was especially influenced by tendencies toward the unconventional ordering of space, asymmetrical composition, and the use of large type and photomontage.

Lustig's work for New Directions began in 1940 and continued until 1952, during which time publisher James Laughlin granted him complete creative freedom. For each jacket design, Lustig, for whom form and content were so inextricably linked as to be indistinguishable, began by reading the text. Once he had a sense of the author's intent, he set out to create visual representations of the book's essence, sometimes literal reflections of the subject of the story and at other times highly subjective and abstract interpretations. What ties the series together is not so much a recognizable treatment—indeed, each jacket design is distinctive—but Lustig's approach to representing the "spirit" of each book. Although the "New Classics" series reflects his unapologetically modern sensibilities, Lustig saw his contribution as restoring a visual richness that was an essential part of the tradition of book-making.

Lustig's output would have been more extensive had his career not been cut tragically short. For the last year or so of his life, he was virtually blind, but he continued to work with the help of his wife and assistants until he died.

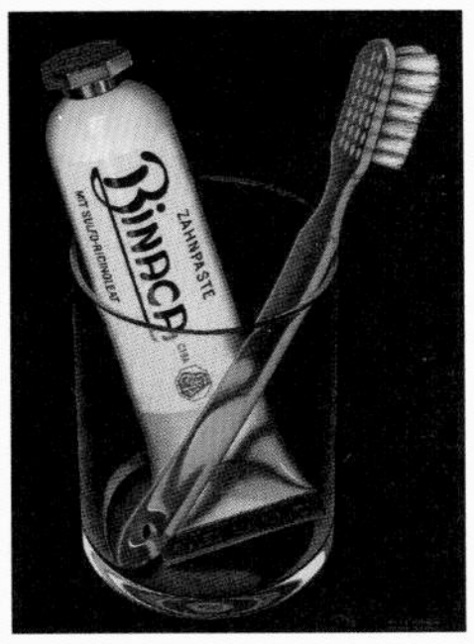

← P.149

1941

BINACA

Poster

Niklaus Stöcklin (1896–1982)

Binaca, Switzerland

Niklaus Stöcklin's poster for Binaca is one of the most celebrated examples of the hyper-realistic variety of *Sachplakat* (object poster) style that dominated Swiss advertising from the 1920s to the '50s. Designed in 1941, it features a tube of Binaca toothpaste standing upright in a clear glass with a pink translucent toothbrush leaning in the opposite direction. Featuring no text other than the brand name, it could be understood by everyone—which was no small task in a country with four national languages.

Stöcklin's poster owes much to the *Sachplakat* style initiated in 1906 by the Berlin designer Lucian Bernhard. Stöcklin, leader of the Basel group of advertising designers, started from Bernhard's principle of stripping extraneous details from advertisements as a rejection of unnecessary ornamentation, but arrived at a singularly different result. The heavy, bold colors and the flat geometry that characterize the German style were replaced with a pioneering new approach, distinctive for its expression of volume, lightness, and sheer richness of detail.

"Binaca" is remarkable not so much for its economy of message but for its technical virtuosity. This was made possible by advancements in lithographic printing technology especially suited to the *Sachplakat* approach, in that brilliant colors and textures could be applied to make otherwise mundane and prosaic objects look realistic. Lithographic posters from Switzerland, including Stöcklin's advertisements for Bi-Oro sunscreen and Meta-Meta fuel briquettes (both produced in 1941), were admired the world over for their wealth of detail.

By the 1950s, the lithographic process was superseded by the more popular four-color printing process, and other Basel designers, including Herbert Leupin and Donald Brun, adopted a more humorous graphic language that was less reliant on the rich color and textures associated with lithography. Of the hundreds of posters produced in the hyper-realistic style, however, few manage to surpass the glossy surfaces and subtle highlights of Stöcklin's precisely rendered still-life of the Binaca toothpaste tube, which effortlessly conjures up an image of cleanliness and purity.

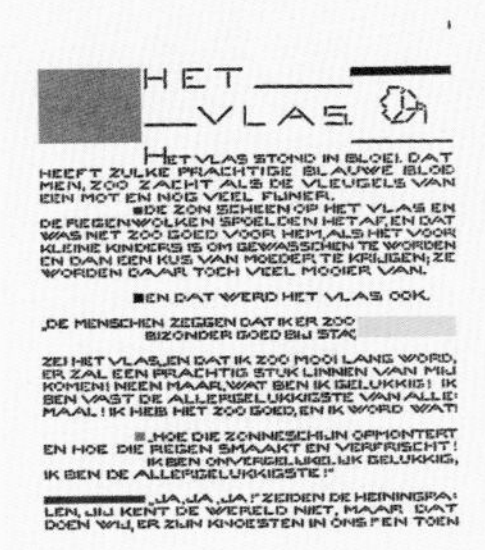

← P.150

1941

HET VLAS

Book

Bart van der Leck (1876–1958)

De Spieghel, the Netherlands

Het Vlas (The Flax) is a perfect example of De Stijl aesthetics, which sought to express both the standardization of the machine age and the balance of the natural world through a rigorous but harmonious abstract visual language. The story, based on a tale by Hans Christian Andersen, tells of a flax flower (blue) being made into paper (white) before being burned (red) and drifting up to the sun (yellow); each page is a carefully orchestrated symphony of primary colors and geometric shapes that hold the content in place.

Both text and pictures of *Het Vlas* are composed of black dots and straight lines, meaning there are no curves. Specially designed by Bart van der Leck, the font consists entirely of square-shaped, broken sans serif capitals, while the text is justified throughout and tightly leaded. Although far from easy to read, the text is made more manageable by being broken into chunks and by generous indents and line breaks. These breaks are managed by incorporating different-size, primary-colored blocks that range from squares and rectangles to short, thick lines, and are governed by a grid that pushes the texts into a variety of shapes. The colored shapes are also balanced by areas of white space and by simple black-and-white figure drawings, which, rather than explaining the story, serve to enhance the sense of positive and negative space.

Even though it is scarcely suitable for children, Van der Leck's *Het Vlas* nevertheless succeeded in humanizing De Stijl's austere geometry, and is recognized as the only significant illustrated publication to emerge from the movement.

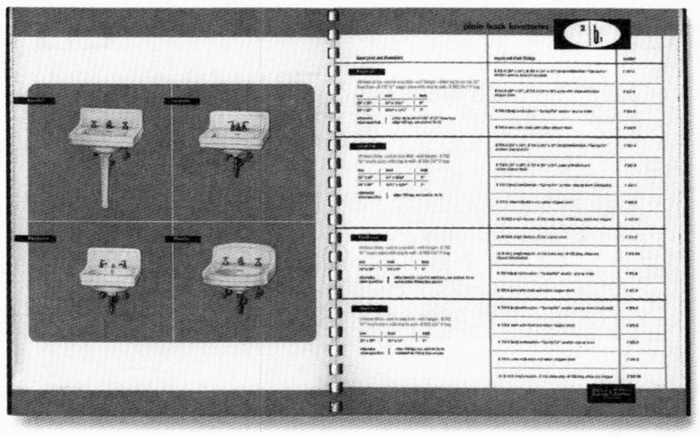

← P.150

1941–1960

SWEET'S FILES

Book

Ladislav Sutnar (1897–1976)

McGraw-Hill, U.S.

Known for his functional approach to typography and layout, Ladislav Sutnar believed that graphic design should be produced with the user in mind, and be a tool for facilitating the transmission of information regardless of how technical or unappealing it was. His design for *Sweet's Files*, a catalog of materials, products, and manufacturers for the construction industry, which contained large amounts of administrative and corporate material, demonstrates his logical and systematic approach to this type of challenge.

The Czech-born Sutnar belonged, with Karel Teige, to the avant-garde Devetsil group in his native country before emigrating to the U.S. in 1939, bringing with him the principles of De Stijl, Constructivism, and the Bauhaus. When Sutnar began work on *Sweet's Files* in 1941, one commentator observed that the files' "only organizational device was the overall binder." Sutnar instituted a practical typography in a post-Bauhaus modernist style, and carefully arranged imagery, at times using second and third color blocks, boxes, and tints in addition to black. The main text was generally a black sans serif, but by using other colors for subheads and decorative fonts for brand names, he created a textured, if controlled, richness. The flexible but methodical grids work closely with the color blocks, dividing the information into manageable quantities and assimilating uneven amounts of text, awkward shapes, and helpful page divisions. Sutnar disliked design based on nostalgia or popularity, or design that put styling above measurable results, believing that "good visual design is serious in purpose." While some felt his view of the designer as an interpreter of information was unnecessarily authoritative, his commitment to reducing time and misunderstanding by helping readers to navigate their way through disparate information demonstrated respect for the consumer.

Sutnar's work for clients such as Sweet helped transform American corporate graphics in the postwar period. His use of well-engineered channels of information that ease progression from one level to another and treat readers as unpredictable but attentive could be seen as a precursor to today's sound-bites, interactive media, and hypertext.

← P.151

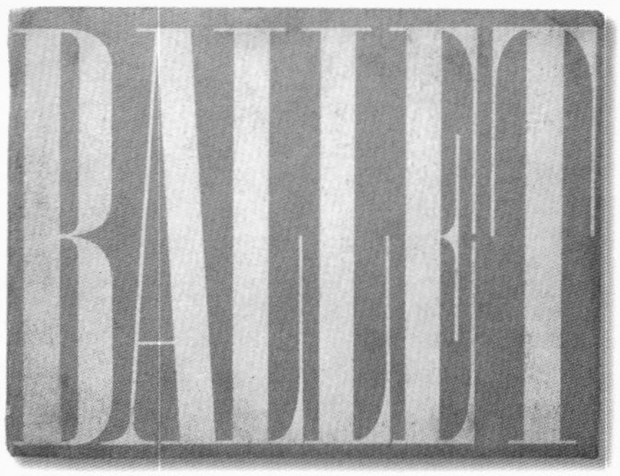

← P.152

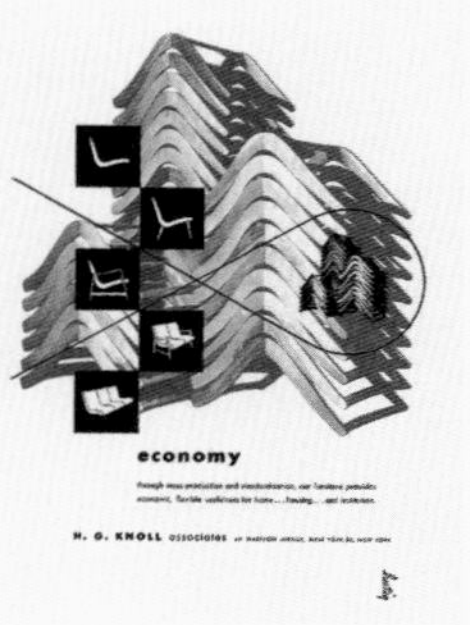

← P.153

1944–1951 ●

SCOPE

Magazine / Newspaper

Lester Beall (1903–1969)

Upjohn Co., U.S.

Some of the most inventive visual communication and information design in the U.S. during the mid-twentieth century was created not for mainstream consumer publications, but for *Scope*, the monthly in-house magazine published by the Upjohn Company "for the medical profession and other health workers." From 1944 to 1951, Lester Beall was responsible for the look and feel of *Scope*, from its legendary covers to its editorial and advertising content.

Although he had little formal design education, Beall was well established in the advertising business by 1944, with an impressive and diverse portfolio. Like so many American designers, he was intrigued by the broad range of European avant-garde experimentation, from the rigid structure of Jan Tschichold's New Typography to the Dadaists' fascination with chaos and László Moholy-Nagy's ghostly photograms. Beall had also been influenced by the Bauhaus when early in his career he worked with Fred Hauck (art director for Chicago advertising agency Batten, Barton, Durstine & Osborne), who had visited the seminal design school, and had studied with the modernist artist Hans Hofmann.

Beall's responsibilities for *Scope* extended well beyond layout duties, and included overseeing typesetting, purchasing engravings, and approving printers' proofs. Beall was granted remarkable creative freedom by Upjohn, at times sending issues of the magazine to the printer without first seeking the management's approval. Inside the magazine, Beall's innovations included two-page spreads designed as contiguous layouts, sometimes combining editorial and advertising content. It was his covers, however, that drew the most praise. Through his use of form, color, and multilayered texture—often created by combining photography, illustration, and type of differing styles and periods—Beall created an unexpected depth and richness.

Beall's work for *Scope* attracted praise from the pharmaceutical industry for its easily understood information graphics, and from the graphic arts community for its cutting-edge layout and type treatments. His legacy of sophisticated yet unpretentious modern design was continued for many years under the direction of Will Burtin.

1945 ●

BALLET

Book

Alexey Brodovitch (1898–1971)

J. J. Augustin, U.S.

Ballet revealed for the first time Alexey Brodovitch's unique brand of photographic narrative and his determination to release photography from the stranglehold of commerce.

From 1920, Brodovitch worked in Paris as a magazine and advertising designer before moving to the U.S. in 1930 to develop an advertising design course at the newly established Philadelphia Museum School. In 1934 he joined *Harper's Bazaar* as art director, where until 1958 his work in magazine design outclassed that of all his contemporaries. Each issue presented the reader with a feast of sumptuously cropped photography, sophisticated typography, asymmetrical layout, and elegant use of white space. In *Ballet*, which Brodovitch produced at the height of his career at *Harper's*, he developed an intimate photographic documentary style to record the dance rehearsals of several ballet companies performing in New York. What began as a private photographic study gradually evolved into a radical departure from photographic convention by experimenting with slow shutter speeds and high contrast to create blurred sequences of movement. Applying bold darkroom techniques, Brodovitch bleached and filtered the images to enhance and reinforce his sense of the vibrancy of dance. His design signature was economy of white space, but in *Ballet* close-up composition and severe cropping allow images to bleed off the page, or combine to form dynamic sequences across double-page spreads. For the cover, however, Brodovitch relied on typography alone, using a dramatic, extra-condensed modern typeface to cover the entire space and create a sense of expectation and drama. The title page lists the names of the ballets in an assortment of slab-serif and modern display fonts embellished with drop shadows, a reference to his earlier advertising and poster designs as a young Russian émigré in Paris, and are designed to reflect the characteristics of each performance.

Brodovitch's revolutionary approach to image-making in *Ballet* and his unique method of interpreting movement represented a pivotal moment in the history of photography, encouraging young designers and photographers, such as Richard Avedon and Irving Penn, to treat the form as a vital creative element in print media.

1945 ●

H. G. KNOLL ASSOCIATES

Advertising

Alvin Lustig (1915–1955)

H. G. Knoll Associates, U.S.

Prior to the "creative revolution" of the 1950s and '60s, sophisticated advertising was a rarity in American publications. The series of print advertisements that Alvin Lustig created for H. G. Knoll Associates in 1945, with their conceptual, almost Surreal, aesthetic was a notable exception that anticipated a burgeoning trend.

Lustig never worked for an advertising agency and, unlike some of his contemporaries, did not produce mass-market campaigns. However, in common with many Los Angeles designers at the time, Lustig's livelihood depended on his ability to diversify. Advertising was just one part of his broad portfolio, which spanned architecture, interior design, and product design. Lustig never sought out advertising commissions—clients came to him and, as a result, he generally enjoyed unfettered artistic freedom.

Lustig's series of Knoll advertisements represent a convergence of three entities with much in common, each in its own way giving voice to the modern movement then taking root in the U.S. Founded in 1938, H. G. Knoll Associates was among the first large-scale manufacturers of modern furniture in the country. *Arts & Architecture*, the magazine in which the advertisements appeared, was instrumental in promoting the virtues of modern housing, first to Californians and then to a national readership. For Lustig, the challenges of the publisher, the furniture designer, and the graphic designer were largely the same: creating design solutions that addressed the essential elements of a particular demand. In a treatment that reflects his keen interest in the work of the Bauhaus and Jan Tschichold, Lustig's Knoll advertisements promote the furniture's form, structure, and economy—modern tenets echoed in his sensitive use of photography, illustration, unobtrusive typography, ample white space, and simple color palette of black and red; they are constructed as compositions of pieces of furniture, abstract architectural forms, and directional lines.

Lustig's work for Knoll is representative of the immediate postwar period, a more innocent age of "soft-sell" experimentation that preceded the era of "the big idea." From 1946, Knoll began to undertake its advertising design work in-house, under the direction of Herbert Matter.

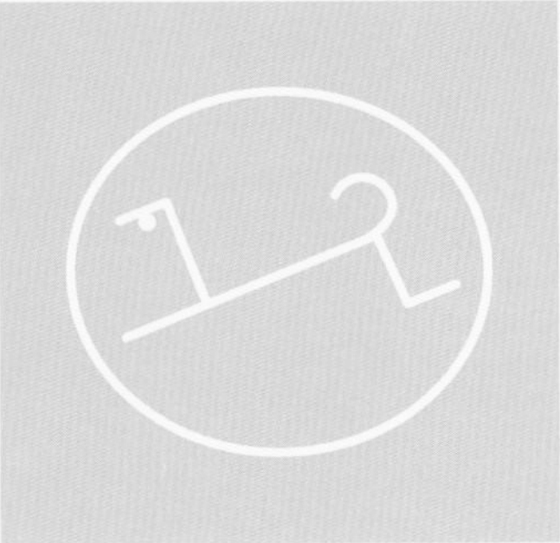

← P.153

← P.153

← P.154

1945

BORZOI

Logo

Paul Rand (1914–1996)

Alfred A. Knopf, U.S.

Before Paul Rand became known for his many iconic logos, he was asked to redesign the trademark of the venerable American publishing company Alfred A. Knopf. Rather than a rebrand, this exercise was an initiation undertaken by all Knopf designers at the behest of the publisher, who saw the presence of the borzoi (a Russian dog) on the cover and title page of every book as a promise of quality both in form and content. First created by Rudolph Ruzicka in 1922, the borzoi emblem had already been reworked by a number of designers, including classic names, such as W. A. Dwiggins, as well as more experimental ones like Ernest Reichl.

Most designers delivered a classical interpretation of the Russian dog, either with pen and ink or woodcut, but Rand employed the same modernist reductivism to every cover that he designed for Knopf. While the subject of the logo was predetermined, the question of what the company represented was open to interpretation. Rand distilled the borzoi into its simplest geometric form: five straight lines, a dot, and a semicircle, all in white, set inside a slightly ovoid bright-yellow frame. Despite being composed of the most basic graphic ingredients (elements that could be found on almost any printed page), the image manages to avoid specificity (representing a number of possible animals), while also conveying energy, optimism, and forward movement. The motif also suggests a seal of approval, extending Knopf's promise to his readers, but updated for future generations. Although there have been other borzoi marks, Rand's is the simplest, defined by an extraordinary economy that recalls his streamlined (but unused) revision of the Ford logo twenty years later. Rand knew the value of abstraction and innovation: how far he could alter a design without changing it, and how to locate the new in the old. His borzoi speaks to the past, but in its treatment points to the future, a combination that ultimately looks timeless.

1946

RADIATION

Information Design

Bill Ray (1898–1972), George Warlick (1902–1989)

Berkeley Radiation Laboratory, U.S.

Commonly known as the trefoil, the international radiation symbol was a "doodle" produced by a group of people at the Berkeley Radiation Laboratory, University of California, who were keen to develop a warning symbol for this new type of dangerous material. The trefoil represents the activity of an atom.

The symbol was first designed in magenta on a blue background. However, the blue proved to be unpopular and, in 1948, Bill Ray and George Warlick, who worked for the renowned health physicist K. Z. Morgan at the Oak Ridge National Laboratory in Tennessee, cut out the magenta symbols and stapled them on to cards of different colors, then looked at them from a distance outdoors. They decided that magenta on yellow best conveyed the idea of danger, and this became the standard design in early 1948. The image is drawn with a central circle of radius R, an internal radius of 1.5 R, and an external radius of 5 R for the blades, which are separated from each other by sixty degrees. Since then, the use of a yellow background has come to be a general indication of "hazard," as defined by the International Organization for Standardization (ISO), which decides on criteria for worldwide signs; outside the U.S. the magenta trefoil is often printed in black (pictured).

In 2001, when it was learned that, in certain parts of the world, people who did not understand the meaning of the trefoil were touching and disassembling lethal material, the International Atomic Energy Agency (IAEA) announced its intention to create a new radiation symbol for the most dangerous categories of ionizing radiation. Released by the IAEA and the ISO in 2007, the new symbol features a stick figure running from a skull and waves radiating from a small trefoil, set against a red background. The trefoil remains the international symbol of radiation, but this new pictogram acts as an additional sign to alert those unaware of the symbol to the dangers of radioactivity.

1946–1966

KNOLL ASSOCIATES

Advertising

Herbert Matter (1907–1984)

Knoll Associates, U.S.

Herbert Matter's advertisements for the furniture designers Knoll Associates represent one of the longest and most fruitful relationships between a designer and client in the history of design. At Knoll, Matter was lucky enough to find two individuals, Florence and Hans Knoll, eager to allow him to realize design solutions on his own terms, resulting in an array of works and a logo that testify to his indefatigable imagination.

Nearly all of Matter's advertisements for Knoll were originally published in either the *New Yorker* or *Interiors* magazine. Of these, one of the most celebrated appeared in the *New Yorker* of November 29, 1958, and was built around two images presented on successive pages. On the first, we see an enigmatic object wrapped in brown paper, which on the next is revealed to be a woman sitting on an Eero Saarinen pedestal chair. Exceptional for its time, the advertisement was situated halfway between photography and film, crafting a narrative from two single images to establish a dialogue between the viewer and the design. At the same time, Matter's decision to use no text apart from the company details and logo acknowledged the increasingly international market at which Knoll was aiming. As the company expanded to become Knoll International in the mid-1950s, Matter's advertisements presaged the development of global advertising campaigns that relied on the dominance of images to convey a commercial message.

The use of a white backdrop to isolate the furniture was a *mise-en-scène* that Matter favored throughout the majority of his Knoll designs. Similar to the pure, snowy Alpine vistas of his homeland, the studio became a blank canvas, a place where he could control the relationship between objects on the surface with no distracting intrusions. Another favorite motif was children or performers, often seen cavorting around tables or juggling chairs. As well as lending a whimsical optimism to his designs, these figures signified the durability of the products. With their minimal text, Matter's Knoll advertisements typified his ability to build a design around a single powerful image, calling on the viewer to make sense of its meaning.

PIRELLI

← P.155

1946

PIRELLI

Logo

Unknown

Pirelli, Italy

The Pirelli logotype, with its distinctive elongated "P" stretched across the length of the word, conveys with elegance and economy the essential qualities of its best-known product—elasticity and stability. Although certain early iterations were considerably less streamlined and the fonts more decorative, a stretched "P" has remained constant since the logo's first appearance at the beginning of the twentieth century.

Italy's famous tire company was founded in Milan in 1872 by Giovanni Battista Pirelli, a young engineer, for the production of tires and cables. According to most accounts, the trademark was proposed by a company representative, who, on arriving in New York around 1908, was asked to devise a design that would stand out amid the plethora of signs in the city. Pirelli had recently supplied the tires used in an overland car journey from Peking to Paris, and the sign seemed an appropriate way of suggesting the product's properties of speed and softness. Hence, in early versions the "P" was fatter and rounder, but gradually the typeface was simplified to a plain sans serif, and the loop of the "P" was lengthened and flattened until the letter finally settled into its classic form in 1946—a strong upright "P" with pronounced vertical and horizontal axes.

In the 1960s Pirelli introduced calendars of nudes as a promotional tool (discontinued in 1974), deliberately playing on the male association of women's bodies with cars. For both its calendars and advertising campaigns the company employed many leading artists and photographers, such as Max Huber, Bruno Munari, Armando Testa, the British Pop artist Allen Jones, and the American photographer Annie Leibovitz. In 1994 Leibovitz produced perhaps the most iconic of all Pirelli advertisements—an image of the Olympic runner Carl Lewis in red high-heeled shoes. As an Italian company with a sophisticated appreciation of aesthetics, Pirelli has always known the value of good art and design, which is evidenced as much by its signature trademark as by its striking advertising.

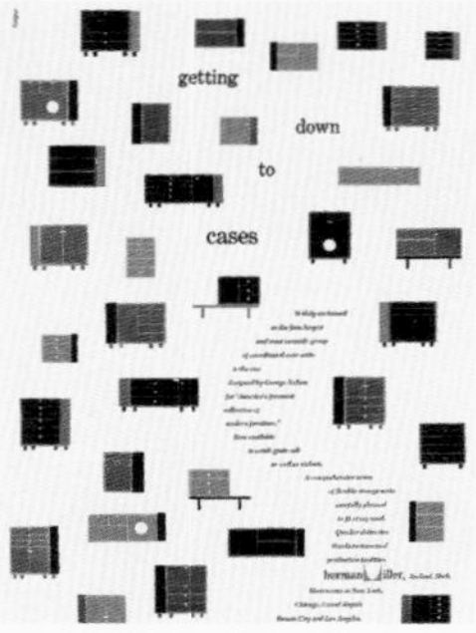

← P.155

1947

HERMAN MILLER

Identity

Irving Harper (1916–2015) et al.

Herman Miller, U.S.

Irving Harper's corporate identity for the furniture manufacturer Herman Miller, founded in 1923, efficiently summarized the company's aesthetic and promoted the brand's image as a designer and manufacturer of groundbreaking modern furniture.

Under the direction of the designer Gilbert Rohde, Herman Miller managed to beat the financial threats posed by the Great Depression by selling home and office "living solutions" that used the latest manufacturing techniques and materials. Rohde's place was taken in 1945 by George Nelson. Over a period of twenty-five years, Nelson turned this small furniture maker into one of the most influential companies in American home and office furniture design.

Irving Harper, who had worked at Rohde's office before World War II, was hired shortly after Nelson took over as Herman Miller's design director. His highly stylized "M" symbol was first applied to advertisements that featured no products, only the new graphic device and the company's name. Harper later perfected the "M" by making it narrower and taller.

In 1953, Nelson hired George Tscherny, a Hungarian-born German, to work on advertisements. Among them was "Herman Miller Comes to Dallas," a masterful poster that advertises the opening of a new furniture showroom. Employing only three colors, the poster shows a chair with gleaming white legs and a cowboy hat lying on the seat. In addition to conveying a strong graphic vision, the poster captures the spirit of postwar optimism and consumerism, as well as a moment of American culture when the traditions of its pioneering cowboy past morphed with corporate entrepreneurship.

Armin Hofmann's poster for the Herman Miller Collection (pictured) is one of his supreme achievements in poster work. It is marked by a preference for black and white, a reliance on hand-lettering or hand-altered typefaces, the use of photographs or drawings derived from photographs, and a minimal number of elements arranged in an intuitive though rigorous manner. The composite image resembles the vertebrae of a spinal column, evoking a sense of timelessness, as well as alluding to the ergonomic comfort of the furniture.

← P.155

1947–1950

SEVENTEEN

Magazine / Newspaper

Cipe Pineles (1908–1991)

Condé Nast Publications, U.S.

The first magazine for teenage girls, *Seventeen* was art-directed for a short but crucial period by Cipe Pineles, who, along with its founder and editor Helen Valentine, recognized the importance of offering serious journalism in an unpatronizing manner to a young female audience.

Pineles had honed her skills under the watchful eye of Dr M. F. Agha, Condé Nast's renowned art director, going on to become art director of *Glamour* in 1937, followed by *Seventeen* a decade later. Her true innovation in the magazine's design was her unique illustration program, for which she commissioned the best artists of the time—a first for mass-market publications. For her inaugural issue, she hired Richard Lindner to illustrate a fiction selection and continued to introduce teenage girls to artists they might not know: Ben Shahn, Bernarda Bryson, Dong Kingman, Jacob Lawrence, Reginald Marsh, and John Sloan, to name a few. Pineles gave artists complete freedom, stipulating only that the illustrations should be as good as their gallery work.

Pineles's typographic approach also proved to be prescient, using a different treatment for each section. The type selected for fiction was the most traditional and reserved, while feature articles were treated in a more inventive way, with initial capitals and playful headlines. Indeed, there are moments of typographic expressionism (letterforms made from paper clips and staples for an article about secretarial training), which may have inspired Herb Lubalin's conceptual approach.

Seventeen's covers illustrate Pineles's great facility with graphic language. The July 1949 issue (pictured) features a young swimsuit model sitting with an umbrella and what appears to be a mirror image below. However, if you look carefully, you see that this is not the case. Such nuances demonstrate extraordinary attention to detail, and were executed before the days of digital manipulation.

Pineles's editorial direction at *Seventeen* remained in evidence for decades to come. Her influence extended not just to design concept and implementation but also to marketing and content, and was widely felt throughout her lifetime. She also pioneered the teaching of editorial design, and in 1948 became the first female member of the New York Art Directors Club.

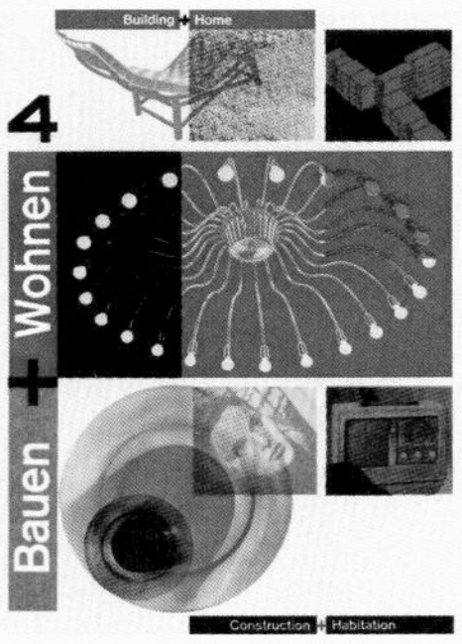

← P.156

← P.157

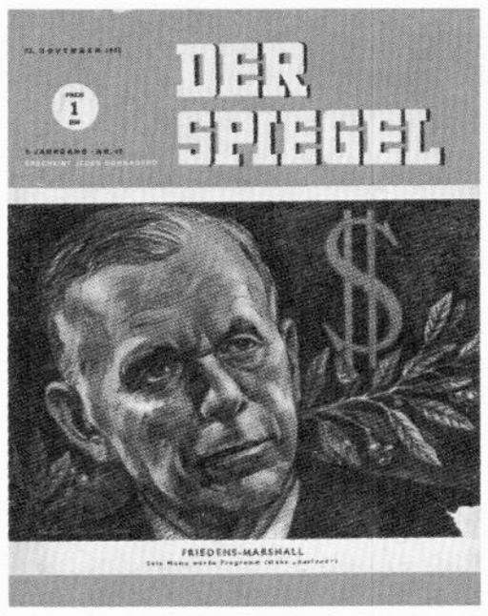

← P.157

1947–1956

BAUEN + WOHNEN

Magazine / Newspaper

Richard Paul Lohse (1902–1988)

Bauen + Wohnen, Switzerland

First published in Zurich in 1947, *Bauen + Wohnen* (*Building + Living*) was initially intended as a conservative publication covering architecture and interiors. After just one issue, however, it was transformed into a collaborative manifesto representing the beliefs of its designer, Richard Paul Lohse, and the architect Jacques Schader. Lohse had been drawn to architecture since becoming a member of an association called Friends of New Architecture in Zurich in 1934. Working on *Bauen + Wohnen* gave this interest a context for expression.

Lohse worked on the design from the second issue, creating the logo and introducing a flexible twelve-column grid for the inside pages. For the masthead, he chose sans serif Akzidenz-Grotesk, a forerunner of Helvetica, which expressed the aesthetic that Lohse would later develop in the magazine *Neue Grafik*, set inside two equal black and purple rectangles separated by a plus sign. From the third issue, Lohse took over the design of the entire magazine, applying the grid system to the cover to convey what he saw as the close relationship between graphic design and architecture, particularly the parallel between modular building design and page layout. Issue 4 illustrated these principles particularly clearly: the logo appeared in three languages, the largest of which, in German, ran up the left-hand side of the page; a palette of different-sized overlapping images was set within a three-column horizontal and vertical grid; and the cover's structure reflected the hierarchical relationship of the various topics featured on the inside pages. Squares were a recurrent theme in Lohse's work, and represented the modernist ideal of pure geometric form.

As one of the earliest publications to cover the modern movement, *Bauen + Wohnen* provided Swiss architecture and graphic design with an international platform. However, more than any other magazine of the time, it succeeded in matching design with content, introducing both architects and lay readers to new techniques for building and design in an exciting and accessible way. *Bauen + Wohnen* continued to be published until 1972, although Lohse left the magazine in 1956 to found *Neue Grafik* with Josef Müller-Brockmann, Hans Neuburg, and Carlo Vivarelli.

1947

WIEDERAUFBAU

Poster

Otl Aicher (1922–1991)

Volkshochschule Ulm, Germany

The "Wiederaufbau" (Rebuilding) poster represents an important period in the evolution of Otl Aicher's design style and corresponds to his active role in supporting Germany's postwar redevelopment—the "rebuilding" of the poster's headline. The design was one of dozens produced by Aicher for the public lectures held on Thursdays at the Volkshochschule Ulm, the people's college founded by Aicher and his future wife, Inge Scholl, in 1946. The school focused on practical and social issues, and was closely tied to the goals of the American postwar reeducation program, providing a gathering place and forum for those who had resisted the influence of the Third Reich.

Aicher was responsible for all of the school's designs, which, until this poster, he executed with the uncertainty of a man who was still considering sculpture as a possible career path. Prior to this, his lecture posters had usually been A4 in size with hand-drawn type, and swerved unevenly in style. "Wiederaufbau," on the other hand, reveals the effect of Aicher's meeting the previous year with Max Bill. Aicher now standardized the poster formats and made them distinctly modernist, using Bauhaus-inspired letterforms combined with semiabstract illustrations suggestive of the artworks of Henri Matisse. The strong, upward-thrusting arm meeting a horizontal bar suggests a builder hoisting a beam, strongly evoking the poster's title. While the series continued in this vein for several years, by 1950 Aicher's work was fully immersed in modernist typesetting, patterns, and geometric forms.

"Wiederaufbau" thus marks the beginning of Aicher's transition from artist to designer, from purely aesthetic considerations to practicality, and from hand-lettering to typesetting. Although the title is still hand-drawn, the type shows the influence of Josef Albers's Universal typeface; more important, its hybridization of serif and sans serif letterforms can be seen as the start of the forty-year process that resulted in Aicher's influential typeface Rotis (1988). His major identity projects for Lufthansa and the 1972 Munich Olympics, with their painstaking attention to detail, were as yet a long way off, but the design philosophy that Aicher established during this period paved the way for their realization.

1947–present

DER SPIEGEL

Magazine Cover

Various

Spiegel-Gruppe, Germany

The covers of *Der Spiegel* are like a family album for the German people. For more than fifty years, from the postwar *Wirtschaftswunder* ("economic miracle") to the fall of the Berlin Wall, the weekly title that sells over one million copies across 172 countries has visually defined Teutonic current affairs.

Der Spiegel was initially funded by the occupying British forces after World War II, and the magazine's cover design owes much to its English-language forebears, *Time* and the *Economist*. Like *Time*, its cover is distinguished by a red border that frames the lead image, and, like the *Economist*, it has frequently used illustration to "make the visible understandable, and the invisible visible," in the words of the German art critic Walter Grasskamp. The red border and illustration were introduced by Eberhard Wachsmuth, the magazine's art director from 1954 to 1985. Before Wachsmuth, the magazine featured red banners on the cover's header and footer, and a closely cropped monochromic photograph of a well-known person. Although this "man of the moment" format proved popular and gave the magazine a clear identity, Wachsmuth felt it was inflexible, so from 1956 he used illustration, after having expanded the red bands to a four-sided red border in 1955. Over the next three decades, Wachsmuth developed *Der Spiegel*'s cover into a showcase for the world's best illustrators, including Boris Artzybasheff and Michael Prechtl. But he also allowed for experimentation and a more radical use of photography, such as a playful duplication of the *Time* cover within the *Spiegel* frame (1961), or a photograph of two topless, white German parents holding a Black baby (1982), two years before Benetton's famous "Colors" campaign.

Der Spiegel's covers have won popular acclaim and numerous art-direction awards, and in 2005 the magazine's legacy was showcased in the exhibition *The Art of Der Spiegel*, shown at galleries in Germany, Austria, and Switzerland, and at New York's Museum of American Illustration. Each cover was juxtaposed against the original drawing or painting, forming a comprehensive and unique chronological survey.

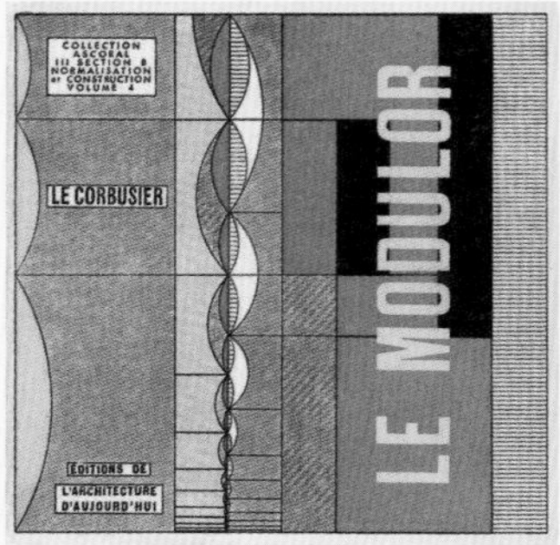

← P.158

1948

LE MODULOR

Book

Le Corbusier (1887–1965)

L'Architecture d'Aujord'hui, France

Inspired by the use of the Golden Section and the proportional schemes of architects, such as Vitruvius and Leon Battista Alberti, Le Corbusier's *Le Modulor*, in which he set out his system described as "a measuring tool based on the human body and on mathematics," was designed to provide a standardized system of proportions for the contemporary world. Le Corbusier (Charles Édouard Jeanneret) hoped the use of such a structure would create harmony and beauty without compromising utility.

The influential modernist architect first began developing his mathematical system of proportions, Le Modulor, around 1943. In 1948, in the book of the same name, Le Corbusier fully explained the system, illustrating the mathematical breakdown in relation to human scale through the use of the Modular Man, a hand-drawn man with his left arm raised above his head to represent the average man's height. Two sets of Fibonacci numbers (a sequence in which each number is the sum of the previous two) are used to convey the system itself: a blue set measuring the full height of the figure (85 inches [216 cm]), and a red set measuring the navel height (42½ inches [108 cm]). These figures and measurements are then divided on the basis of the value of pi (3.14) or the Golden Ratio (roughly 1.1618). The book also includes hand-drawn diagrams along with notes and sketches to explain the need for and development of the Modulor in the modern world, and illustrates applications of the system.

The Modulor system was first used by Le Corbusier in the design for the Unité d'Habitation in Marseille (1945), which features a casting of the Modular Man in the concrete wall of the building. He continued to use it in several other projects, including his late expressionist work Notre Dame du Haut, also known as the Chapelle de Ronchamp (1954). In subsequent years, Le Corbusier further developed his system and published a second edition, *Modulor 2* (1955), in which he refined his previous treatise.

Le Modulor, as represented by the Modular Man with its Fibonacci numbers, has become an iconic architectural emblem, as well as an important modern contribution to the architectural tradition of proportional treatises.

← P.158

1948

HALAG

Logo

Hermann Eidenbenz (1902–1993)

Halag, Switzerland

This stylish logo for Halag, the Basel linen and hemp trading company, illustrates the economy of modernist design. By means of a single line, the company name is simplified and drawn out in a cursive script (a condensed version of the font Latenische Ausgangsschrift), from an old-fashioned reel, eloquently expressing the fluidity and continuity of the product. Simple and effective, the concept typifies Eidenbenz's solution to design problems: reductive functionality allied with craftsmanship, demonstrated through his ability to capture the unique aspects of a commission and the beautifully executed integration of text and image.

A graphic artist, typographer, and teacher, Eidenbenz initially trained in lithography under Ernst Keller at Zurich's famous Kunstgewerbeschule, and subsequently worked for graphic design agencies in Berlin prior to opening his own studio in 1932. One of the first Swiss designers to embrace modernist principles of geometric structure, asymmetric layout, and photographic imagery, he was an acknowledged influence in the design philosophy that later developed into the "Swiss school." However, Eidenbenz was also capable of delivering more traditional work and, as an accomplished typographer, was just as comfortable working with Fraktur as with Akzidenz-Grotesk. Later in his career he designed two condensed display fonts for Haas, the Swiss type foundry that published Helvetica—Graphique Pro (1945) and Graphique-AR (1946). He is also well-known for the Clarendon font (1956), and for posters designed for a range of commercial uses and public service purposes, such as "Swissair" (1948), "Ein Freies Volk Braucht Freie Frauen" (Women's Right to Vote, 1946), and a campaign to promote reading.

Eidenbenz's adaptable, problem-solving approach to design defies easy categorization. The Halag logo, although no longer in use, is one of a number of monograms that he produced for corporate and civic clients, including the University of Basel, the town of Brunswick, and the publishing arm of the Bauer Type Foundry. In every case, his mission was to create appropriate, optically balanced design solutions rather than to adhere rigidly to dogma or style.

← P.159

1948

GRAN PREMIO DELL'AUTODROMO

Poster

Max Huber (1919–1992)

Autodromo Nazionale di Monza, Italy

Predating photocomposition and even digital (typo) graphic manipulation, Max Huber's poster for the 1948 Gran Premio dell'Autodromo gave an early indication of his future impact on Swiss and Italian design, both on a generation of graphic designers and on the postwar visual landscape.

Following his education as a graphic artist and photographer in Zurich, Huber worked during 1940–41 with the pioneering graphic designer Antonio Boggeri at his Studio Boggeri in Milan. During World War II Huber returned to Switzerland, joining the international group of architects, designers, and artists who were to make Zurich the unofficial center of international modern design, particularly the so-called Swiss school of graphic design. After the war, Huber reestablished himself in Milan, introducing a completely new visual language to Italy, blending his own craft-informed, naturalist sensibility with the constrained forms of the abstract Constructivist-inspired Swiss school. Thereafter, Huber worked for a wide range of industrial, commercial, and cultural clients, exploring his signature style of vibrant, elegant compositions that incorporated color, typography, and photography.

One of the first examples of his groundbreaking style is evident in the pictured poster, part of a longtime collaboration with the Autodromo Nazionale di Monza, the motorsports racetrack north of Milan, best known for hosting the Formula One Italian Grand Prix. Maximizing effects caused by the transparent quality of printing inks, Huber masterfully creates the illusion of depth and movement by juxtaposing layers of color and hand-drawn, sans serif type. The perspective is distorted almost to the point of visual chaos. However, this dramatic integration of text and arrows never fails to lose the balance and alignment that make this design a successful marriage between Swiss and Italian modernity, from Max Bill to Marinetti: rational Constructivist order meets "the need for speed."

← P.160

← P.160

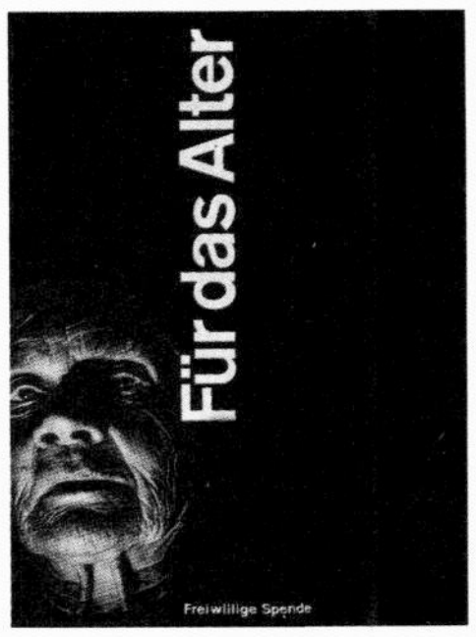

← P.161

1948–present

STERN

Magazine / Newspaper

Various

Henri Nannen, Germany

Founded in 1948 by its first editor, Henri Nannen, *Stern* has become one of the most influential news magazines in Germany, renowned for its controversial content and provocative art direction.

Nannen began the magazine during the Allied occupation of West Berlin after World War II. Having obtained a license to publish the German youth magazine *Zick-Zack* a few months before the end of the war, Nannen went to the British military government, seeking to relaunch it under the name *Der Stern* (Star). After an inaugural sixteen-page issue featuring the actress Hildegard Knef, the publication went on to trace the currents of postwar German politics and society, eventually reaching a weekly readership of almost eight million.

Stern's independent, risk-taking stance is immediately conveyed by its logo: a six-point asymmetrical white star on a red background. The star recalls comic-book explosions, whereas the italicized, lowercase masthead letters suggest a forward-looking, aggressive spirit. For its covers, *Stern* was one of the first magazines to use photomontage, often reinforcing an editorial position through the use of carefully selected and juxtaposed images. A classic cover from 1977 shows the naked chancellor, Helmut Schmidt. The same image was reproduced in 2002, this time for an article on Gerhard Schroeder, in which the former chancellor appears paunchy and grim-faced, covered only by a red-and-green fig leaf (representing the colors of his governing coalition). In a deliberate reference to the fairy-tale "The Emperor's New Clothes," the caption asks: "The naked truth—can Schroeder still win?" In another haunting cover image for an article on airline hijacking (April 1988), a precise drawing of a skull is grafted onto a photograph of a Kuwait Airways 747 aircraft. In fusing together disparate elements, often mixing the sophisticated with the crude, *Stern*'s editors produced memorable images that have played a part in shaping the political and social landscape of contemporary Germany.

1949

ZEBRA CROSSING

Information Design

Unknown

Road Research Laboratory, UK

The zebra crossing is an example of life-saving graphic design. Simple for councils to install, pedestrians to use and motorists to see, the painted road-marking has made an invaluable contribution to road safety. With their unmistakable bold black-and-white stripes, which are also easily seen at night, zebra crossings aim for maximum visibility.

The first zebra crossings were designed in the 1940s by the British government's Road Research Laboratory (RRL), although pedestrian crossings had existed in the United Kingdom since 1934, marked by pole-mounted orange spheres and parallel rows of studs in the road. Growth in postwar traffic and the continued disregard of studded crossings by pedestrians and motorists led the RRL to develop a more visible alternative. RRL experiments demonstrated that longitudinal stripes 15⅝–23 ⅝ inches (40–60cm) wide contrasted best with oncoming vehicles, and these were initially tested in combinations of blue and yellow, and red and white. After a limited number of trials, black-and-white crossings were introduced to one thousand locations in the UK in 1949, and in 1951 they were installed nationwide. Before long, the zebra crossing had been adopted across the world. In Britain the design spawned four variations, incorporating traffic lights, pedestrian controls, and lanes for cyclists or horse riders. In the U.S., just two of the six types of pedestrian crossings are striped, although a 1965 report found pedestrians use the striped more than the non-striped versions. The effectiveness of zebra crossings has at times made them a popular campaign issue in British locations where they were lacking; cases have even been reported of people painting their own, and a Russian design studio has developed a zebra crossing-style aerial strip-light for places where snow obscures the road surface in winter. However, parts of northern Europe are currently beginning to adopt "shared space" roads, where pedestrians and motorists have equal right of way, which may threaten the future of zebra crossings.

One of the simplest graphic devices, and a ubiquitous sight on urban roads, the zebra crossing has perhaps been unique in its impact on people's daily lives.

1949

FÜR DAS ALTER

Poster

Carlo Vivarelli (1919–1986)

Für das Alter, Switzerland

Judged to be Best Poster of the Year in 1949 by the Swiss Federal Department of Home Affairs, Carlo Vivarelli's poster for the "Für das Alter" (Help the Aged) campaign communicates with a powerful simplicity the vulnerability of the elderly.

Vivarelli was an important member of the "Swiss school" that emerged after 1945. After studying with the French graphic designer Paul Colin, he joined and briefly directed (1946–7) Studio Boggeri in Milan, which championed the prewar New Typography and New Objectivity in photography. Although his interest in the principles of Constructivist design was already evident in a 1940 photographic poster for the winter sports resort of Flums, "Für das Alter" reveals a maturing of approach and contains many traits that would epitomize "Swiss school" in the 1950s. The dramatically lit image of the old woman was supplied by the Zurich-based Swiss photographer Werner Bischof, a member of the Magnum photo agency. Through clever positioning of the stark perpendicular sans serif type, Vivarelli reinforces the image of candlelit impoverishment by squeezing her face into the bottom left corner of the design. Before the advent of Univers and Helvetica, Vivarelli, like many Swiss designers, favored the Akzidenz-Grotesk typeface and designed his posters to be printed in more than one language, in this case German, French, and Italian. In the Italian version, the extra characters needed for the main slogan "Per la Vecchiaia" extend further down the composition, so the words "dono volontario" (voluntary donation), the Italian equivalent of "Freiwillige Spende," are repositioned to the right-hand side, in line with the subject's eyes. However, by using an implied unifying grid, Vivarelli was able to maintain a consistent visual elegance in his asymmetric design across these different versions.

Vivarelli continued to play an important role in the Neue Grafik movement in the 1950s, producing exhibition posters and logotypes for Therma (1958), Swiss TV (1958), and Electrolux (1962), and becoming a founding coeditor of the hugely influential *Neue Grafik* magazine. In the 1960s he gradually turned away from commercial design to focus on fine art, but he continues to be best known for his photographic posters.

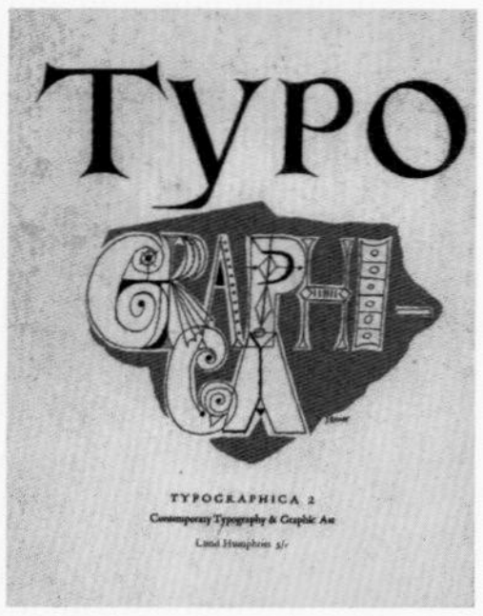

← P.162

1949–1967

TYPOGRAPHICA

Magazine / Newspaper

Herbert Spencer (1924–2002)

Lund Humphries, UK

The 1950s were a period of uncertainty and change in the graphic-arts industry: the transition from letterpress to offset lithography, and from metal composition to computer-generated type, with new processes, papers, and principles, all influenced design solutions. For the emerging generation of designers, the visual arts magazine *Typographica* did more than any other title to lead them through this uncharted territory, with its boundary-blurring, visually sumptuous, and graphically tactile covers, which merged past prints with modern experimentation in type and image.

Launched in 1949 by the British publisher Lund Humphries, *Typographica* was the brainchild of Herbert Spencer, a twenty-five-year-old designer, editor, and writer, who guided the publication for eighteen years. The magazine was produced in two series—the "Old Series" and the "New Series," each published in sixteen issues—and had modernist intentions, seen most dynamically in its cover designs. The inaugural issue was aggressively asymmetrical in layout and Constructivist in its choice of bright, solid colors: green, red, orange, and black. Fascinated with the typographic contingents discovered by the early modernists, Spencer wanted *Typographica* to record the experimental work of designers of the 1920s and '30s who helped to establish a new aesthetic, and to define the vocabulary of modern type. Although Spencer designed most of the covers, others were produced by luminaries that included the English artist and designer Edward Wright, the Italian Franco Grignani, and the Swiss-German Dieter Roth; among the contributors were leading designers John Tarr, Hans Schleger, Max Bill, and Anthony Froshaug.

Practitioners influenced by *Typographica*'s news, discoveries, and teaching were inspired to incorporate new energy and ideas into their artworks, which helped to create a genuinely contemporary genre of design.

← P.163

1950–1951

PORTFOLIO

Magazine / Newspaper

Alexey Brodovitch (1898–1971), Frank Zachary (1914–2015)

Zebra Press, U.S.

The idea for a publication that focused entirely on art and design, and would itself be an outstanding example of both, came from the art director Frank Zachary. His desire to produce not just a magazine but an example of great design would have instant appeal to Alexey Brodovitch, who craved the opportunity to create a magazine in totality and to display to the fullest his capacity for experimentation and invention.

To realize his vision, Zachary collaborated with friend and publisher George S. Rosenthal (whose family owned Zebra Press), who was highly sympathetic to Zachary's ideas and those of the New Bauhaus. Rosenthal spared no expense, buying the finest paper and permitting Zachary to include special inserts, such as shopping bags and wallpaper. He also had no hesitation in accepting Brodovitch as the only suitable candidate for art director of the publication. In the first issue of *Portfolio* (Winter 1950), Brodovitch circumvented the common practice of using a photograph on the cover, instead using a technique from his early days at *Harper's Bazaar*. Applying two color filters to the magazine title, which is set against a black back-drop, Brodovitch created a simple but strong intro-ductory design, which, like his treatment of the magazine as a whole, Zachary recognized as "cinematic." Internally, *Portfolio* demonstrated Brodovitch's disregard for any calculated distinction of high and low culture, promoting both vernacular American artifacts and the products of recognized artists and designers. Photographs were cropped, enlarged, and arranged to create stunning layouts that illustrated a diversity of topics.

Even though its no-expense-spared ethos and rejection of all forms of advertising resulted in the title folding after just three issues, *Portfolio* represented the extensive visual influences that informed Brodovitch's design philosophy. With articles on figures such as Jackson Pollock, images by Henri Cartier-Bresson, sketches by Saul Steinberg, and poetry by Guillaume Apollinaire, *Portfolio* was a luminous example of content, production, and design in perfect synthesis. More than fifty years after the magazine's demise, its capacity to surprise and astonish still endures.

← P.163

1950s

OVOMALTINE

Advertising

Carlo Vivarelli (1919–1986)

Ovomaltine, Switzerland

Carlo Vivarelli's advertisements for Ovomaltine, a malt-flavored milk drink, were designed in collaboration with advertising consultant Ernst Baenziger in Zurich. The series marked the application of modernist methods to commercial objectives, and relied on the stylized use of image as symbol, the text being secondary to the design's visual dynamic.

Vivarelli's work in the 1950s reflected the assimilation of Swiss modernism into the commercial mainstream of postwar European graphics. He had studied at Zurich's Kunstgewerberschule, setting up his own practice and becoming cofounder and editor of the influential design journal *Neue Grafik*, working alongside Josef Müller-Brockmann, Richard Paul Lohse, and Hans Neuburg. The advertisement pictured is characteristic of postwar modernist graphic design, in that it is compositionally dynamic but deliberately impersonal and objective, making no use of visual rhetoric, narrative, or metaphor. Monochrome photographic elements are juxtaposed against abstract fields of flat color, an approach that reveals the continuing influence of Russian Constructivism, and the imagery is radically cropped: in contrast to the conventions of advertising at the time, we do not see the subjects' faces, and although photographic, the figures are treated as symbols rather than as a personalized narrative device. The design is based on a four-column grid, which divides the composition equally into four vertical sections and three horizontal, although this rigid geometric structure is balanced at the center by the vivid diagonal formed by the arm and hand of the mother and child. The grid also determines the areas of flat color and the alignment of the type at the base of the page, and creates breaks in the functional sans serif text, introducing dramatic pauses and establishing a link between the dynamics of the copy and the overall visual composition. Certain advertisements were produced in color but could be adapted for black-and-white use in newspapers.

The principles of objective design formulated by the Zurich school became increasingly attractive to commercial enterprises, as the consumer culture of the postwar decades gained momentum and, in turn, influenced a new generation of U.S. designers, including Paul Rand and Massimo Vignelli.

← P.163

1950–1951

FLAIR

Magazine / Newspaper

Federico Pallavicini (Federico von Berzeviczy-Pallavicini) (1909–1989)

Fleur Cowles, U.S.

The story of *Flair* magazine begins with American editor Fleur Cowles, who in 1946 had married Gardner "Mike" Cowles, owner of a media conglomerate that included *Look* magazine, the *Des Moines Register*, the *Minneapolis Star*, and several radio stations. Created to support the standing of sister publication *Look* in the advertising world, *Flair* was Cowles's most beloved project. There were only twelve issues published between 1950 and 1951.

Cowles's aim was to create a magazine that was an homage to literature and to the arts. Inspired by the printing and handcrafted beauty of European publications, she spent three months in Europe researching printing techniques to bring to America. It was during this trip that she met Swiss-Italian designer Federico Pallavicini, who was subsequently appointed art director of *Flair*.

Based on his experience as a decorative artist and set designer, Pallavicini's approach is ornamental. His illustrations appear frequently in the magazine, and his style is rich and imaginative. The standpoint that he (together with Cowles) took was that of creating each issue as an art book in its own right.

The covers frequently incorporate cutouts, which reveal the pages below. Throughout the magazine, with its thick, tactile pages, appear other cutouts, half pages, fold-outs, postcard inserts, tipped-in brochures, and minibooks, all devised to add value to the content. For example, half pages in a feature containing fashion illustrations allow the reader to see different combinations of outfits. The magazine's typographic layout is simple, with headlines and body text in a serif typeface. Each article has a different layout, with text often interspersed with illustrations and images, or with a background color.

In 1951 the magazine closed for financial reasons—the production costs were too high and advertisers were cautious to commit themselves. Despite its short life, *Flair* was highly influential, inspiring designers and magazine-makers for years to come. It was so popular with readers that the magazines have become treasured collectors' items, and in 1996, Rizzoli published *The Best of Flair*, which reproduced a selection of the magazine's innovative material.

← P.164

1951

CBS

Logo

William Golden (1911–1959)

CBS Broadcasting, Inc., U.S.

William Golden's universally distinguishable and iconic CBS trademark, known simply as "the eye," was initially intended for use during only one season, but has remained the CBS mark for over half a century. Golden was the creative director of CBS Television's advertising and sales promotion department, and maintained that while driving through Pennsylvania Dutch country he was captivated by the hex symbols painted on barns to ward off evil spirits, some of which resembled human eyes. He researched the symbols further and enlisted CBS graphic artist Kurt Weihs to draw the first eye logo.

In the book *The Visual Craft of William Golden*, Golden describes the eye as being "originally conceived as a symbol in motion. It consisted of several concentric 'eyes.' The camera dollies in to reveal the 'pupil' as an iris diaphragm shutter which clicked open to show the network identification and clicked shut." However, in early designs the image appeared "as a still composite photograph of the 'eye' and a cloud formation photographed from an abandoned Coast Guard tower." CBS president Frank Stanton had the clouds removed and applied the symbol extensively to a variety of objects and print, recognizing its memorable quality. He insisted on keeping the symbol in use, although Golden was already preparing a new one for the next season.

Golden died suddenly of a heart attack, at age forty-nine, in 1959. His successor was his protégé Lou Dorfsman, who, over the course of the next thirty years as guardian of the CBS eye, paired it with an elegantly restyled and hand-lettered monogram in a proprietary version of the typeface Didot (called CBS Didot), standardizing its use. It is largely through Dorfsman's efforts that the CBS trademark has maintained its integrity. Even though over the years the eye has been animated in a variety of ways and used in many colors and sizes, its basic design has remained unchanged, making it one of the most widely recognized corporate symbols in history.

← P.164

1951–1954

Interiors

Magazine Cover

Andy Warhol (1928–1987)

Whitney Publications, Inc., U.S.

Before Andy Warhol achieved global success with his prints of Marilyn Monroe and Campbell's Soup cans, he had a successful career working as a commercial artist in New York. As well as producing illustrations for magazines such as *Vogue*, *Harper's Bazaar*, and the *New Yorker*, advertising images for the I. Miller shoe company, and album sleeves for RCA Records, he worked for the influential New York-based periodical *Interiors*, published by Charles E. Whitney. This high-quality magazine showcased mid-century interior design, profiling trends and practitioners, and was also famous for its covers by well-known artists and designers, such as Alvin Lustig, Bruno Munari, and Warhol himself.

Warhol's drawings and illustrative works during this period consisted of extremely fanciful ink drawings. His loose, whimsical style was dubbed "blotted ink" for its wavering, disconnected lines that seemed to issue from an unreliable fountain pen. In fact, these drawings were produced as mono-prints, but their broken lines and mottled appearance gave them the character of batik. Using the magazine's standard masthead to evoke typewriter lettering, his simple, low-key covers stand in sharp contrast to the photographic images of picture-perfect homes that fill the magazine's inside pages. For example, the cover of May 1951 features a scratchy drawing of a grand antique mantel clock over a mottled pink background; that of May 1953 depicts a tea set in a similar style. For other covers, he used photographic collage: the February 1954 issue portrayed a blotted-ink cage over photographic images of birds, while the cover for September 1954 includes a small photograph of a living room overlaid with decorative lines and an illustration of a lamp emitting light.
At a time when mainstream magazines such as *Harper's Bazaar* and *Vogue* were becoming increasingly identified with the glamorous cover shot, Warhol's quirky *Interiors* covers offered a modest and charming alternative, a reminder of the days when both publishing and art were less driven by the need for visibility and impact.

← P.165

1951–1959

The Financial Times

Advertising

Abram Games (1914–1996)

Financial Times, UK

The 1950s was Abram Games's most successful decade as a freelance graphic designer. His symbol design for the 1951 Festival of Britain had been chosen and applied to a multitude of publicity items and souvenirs, and in the same year his career as a poster artist took off. An important commission to design a poster advertising the *Financial Times* led to a fruitful relationship with the newspaper's publicity agency, which resulted in his designing a series of eight posters. Games's idea of creating a "manewspaper" character was seen as radical at the time, but soon became a huge success. The character's main body was formed by an illustration of an elongated version of the pink newspaper, adding only pinstriped legs to symbolize the city businessman. The first in the series, "Men who mean business read the *Financial Times* every day," depicts the businessman striding forth carrying a rolled umbrella and briefcase. Although designed to fit standard poster sites, it also appeared as an extra-large hoarding and as a freestanding model positioned outside London Bridge station.

The first five versions of the character featured the businessman in different work-related situations, but in 1958–9, for the last three in the series, Games took a more lighthearted approach. Whereas the earlier versions were drawn with geometric precision, he now used a sketchy, more cartoonlike, style: the businessman is shown in his pinstriped pajamas, as a dapper golfer sporting plus fours, and as a cricketer. He was to develop this freer, jagged-edged style of drawing much further over the course of his career, as can also be seen in a series of posters for *The Times*.

As a freelance designer, Games worked on a wide range of commissions, including logotypes and corporate identities, most notably for the engineering company GKN in 1968. He stayed true to his craft, however, carrying on the tradition of poster art in Britain during the postwar years. In 1958 he was awarded an OBE, and in the following year received the prestigious appointment of Royal Designer for Industry (RDI), established by the Royal Society of Arts.

← P.166

1952

NIE!

Poster

Tadeusz Trepkowski (1914–1954)

Polish Government, Poland

Originally pasted along streets darkened by the miseries of war and occupation, Tadeusz Trepkowski's "Nie!" (No!) presents a falling bomb whose silhouette contains the ruins of a building: a reminder of the object's destructive power to those who had survived the war, and an urgent call to join the cry of "Nie!"

The poster was commissioned in 1952, the year that America began testing the hydrogen bomb, and a period in which Socialist Realism dominated all forms of visual practice in countries of the Eastern bloc. Rather than concede to the demand for images of cheery workers, a number of Polish designers fought for creative freedom, finding favor with the authorities. This group, which later became known as the Polish Poster School, included the self-taught Trepkowski, Tadeusz Gronowski, and Henryk Tomaszewski. Aware that the street offered little time for passing viewers to read or consider his posters, Trepkowski strove for the direct and memorable, an approach that is evident in "Nie!," where subtlety and nuance are stripped away to concentrate on the "The Bomb" as a symbol of annihilation. In the context of the Cold War, the bomb no longer drops as one of many but as a single object capable of utter devastation—which, rather than falling, hangs ominously over the architectural forms of the lean, sans serif lettering.

The humanitarian cry of "Nie!" found global resonance when it was reproduced for a Western audience in *Graphis* magazine. It also confirmed the existence of a fresh and dynamic group of Polish designers somehow flourishing under Communism's oppressive rule. Sadly, Trepkowski was unable to enjoy his recognition, dying at the age of forty, two years after the poster was produced.

← P.167

1953

SCHÜTZT DAS KIND!

Poster

Josef Müller-Brockmann (1914–1996)

Swiss Automobile Club, Switzerland

This poster was commissioned by the Swiss Automobile Club, and was one of a number of powerful photomontages that Swiss designer Josef Müller-Brockmann created for the organization to promote road safety during the 1950s.

Often integrating photomontages and light paintings into his work, Müller-Brockmann produced a large number of poster designs, which he considered to be "barometers of social, economic, political, and cultural events, as well as mirrors of intellectual and practical activities." These ranged from the typographically led posters with abstract lines that he created for the Tonhalle-Orchester Zurich and Musica Viva, to the series pictured, which incorporates the photography of E. A. Heiniger. The poster, produced as both "Protégez l'enfant!" and "Schützt das Kind!" for multilingual Switzerland, is a striking visual composition with a diagonal emphasis, the image featuring a huge motorcycle bearing down in a menacing fashion on a child playing. The influence of Constructivism and the graphic work of Aleksandr Rodchenko can be seen clearly in the dramatic juxtaposition of scale between the images and the powerful use of composition. The various elements are accentuated and framed by the reduced color palette of the yellow strip across the bottom of the image and the minimal red text at the top. Overlaid onto the motorcycle, the latter also suggests the threat the vehicle presents, while the yellow further highlights the drama and links the boy with the threatening motorcycle.

During the 1960s and '70s, Müller-Brockmann established himself as one of the most important and prolific voices of graphic design. He is perhaps best known today as the foremost proponent of grid systems, which allowed him to organize disparate elements into functional, objective designs and to structure the complex variety of design decisions. The system is discussed in his books *The Graphic Artist and His Design Problems* (1961) and *Grid Systems in Graphic Design* (1981).

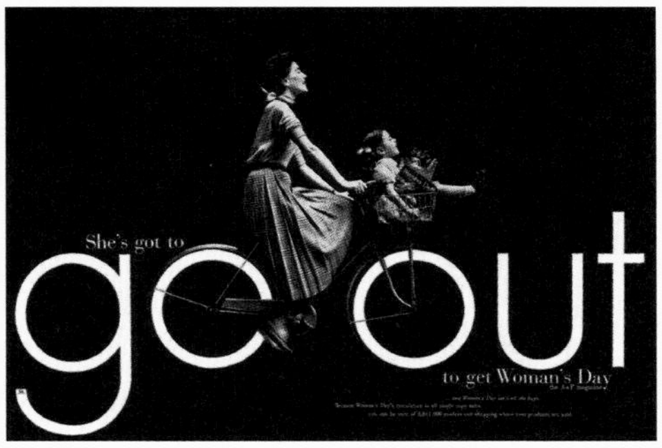

← P.168

1953

SHE'S GOT TO GO OUT TO GET WOMAN'S DAY

Advertising

Gene Federico (1918–1999)

Woman's Day, U.S.

Gene Federico produced this double-page advertisement for *Woman's Day* for the *New Yorker* magazine when he was working as art director at the then recently formed Doyle Dane Bernbach advertising agency.

Federico often introduced visual puns into his work, and in some cases relied on the integration of typographical and pictorial elements. In the 1950s and '60s many designers experimented with what has since been termed "figurative typography," in which text and image are blended into one "communicative act," rather than presenting these elements as separate modes of communication. Such experiments challenged more commonplace treatments of images as illustrations of text, or of type as a way to anchor the meaning of images through captions, headlines, or annotations. In such configurations, text or image is assigned a dominant role, but here neither predominantly carries the message, and rather than being scanned sequentially the two are perceived simultaneously. Moreover, although the advertisement still contains distinct pictorial and typographic forms, certain elements—the two Futura "O"s, which double as the bicycle wheels—serve as both image and text. Hence, the meaning we attribute to the words "go out" are mediated by the uplifting feelings evoked by the woman and child on the bicycle. The necessity to "go out" is therefore conceived of as a happy and liberating event in which both mother and child are swept up in the same adventure, a message that highlights the magazine's success in getting women to seek out and purchase copies. Indeed, according to contemporary statistics, the publication was bought by more than three million readers, a fact the poster aimed to communicate to potential advertisers.

← P.168

1953–present

IDEA

Magazine / Newspaper

Various

Seibundo Shinkosha, Japan

An important sourcebook of design and information, the bimonthly title *Idea* was launched primarily to introduce modern Western graphic design to Japan, but developed to present Japanese design to a global audience. As first editor and designer, respectively, Takashi Miyayama (editor of its prewar ancestor, *Kokoku-kai—Advertising World*) and Hiroshi Ohchi formed important ties with European and U.S. design magazines. These have been expanded and deepened by successive editors and designers, and continue to inform the magazine today.

For its stellar information, graphics, and design, the magazine depends on prominent outside designers who take on particular articles about themselves or others. Hence, each issue is marked by its own style and emphasis, although all are united by the simple bilingual logo designed by Yusaku Kamekura. *Idea* is now edited by Kiyonori Muroga and, since the fiftieth anniversary issue (September 2003), the renowned book designer Yoshihisa Shirai has acted as art director, even though he never intervenes in guest designers' pages. For example, Issue 326 (January 2008), called "Visual Communication," begins with sixteen color pages of an illusionary special project by the Japanese designer Kazunari Hattori; Issue 333 (March 2009) by the German designer Helmut Schmid focuses on the philosophy and typography of his former instructor Emil Ruder, reproducing Ruder's work and writings, and including eighteen lines of the master's handwriting on the cover; the clean text pages, which are set in Ruder's favored Univers and make full use of empty space, also echo his work. Issue 306 (September 2009), marked by a blank white cover, was designed by and focuses on the work of Kenya Hara, well-known art director of the household store Muji and producer of several philosophical design exhibitions. The issue's interior pages progress through Hara's body of work and theory, much of which hinges on the concepts of white and the empty vessel, as presented on the cover.

Since 1953, when advertising and graphic design were first recognized in Japan as professions, *Idea* has showcased the communication methods of different eras and industries, focusing specifically on individual creators.

← P.169

1953

PAUSE—TRINK COCA-COLA

Poster

Herbert Leupin (1916–1999)

The Coca-Cola Company, U.S.

Designed during a period of expansion for the Coca-Cola company, Herbert Leupin's poster "Pause—Trink Coca-Cola" was part of the brand's effort to establish itself in Europe, and to downplay its associations with American postwar prosperity of which it had become a symbol.

Coca-Cola excelled at marketing and took every opportunity to promote the brand, with staff photographers regularly snapping statesmen and celebrities caught holding the classic curvy bottle. After World War II, however, certain parts of the world were resisting what was perceived as Coke's cultural colonization, with campaigns against the company and its product springing up in many countries, including Switzerland, where this poster was produced, and where the law prohibited the use of the phosphoric acid contained in the product. At the time he produced this poster, Leupin had already established himself as an advertising designer, creating posters for the Swiss newspaper *Die Weltwoche* and for products such as toothpaste and shoes. Leupin's simple visual style was considerably less austere than that of his Swiss contemporaries, particularly those associated with the Neue Grafik approach, displaying wit and lightness of touch.

A billboard-sized poster (50⅜ × 35⅜ inches [128 × 90 cm]), "Pause—Trink Coca-Cola" packs a strong visual punch with its brightly colored background and scratchy, naive drawing combined with its clever use of photomontage to represent the company logo and bottle. Subtle and low-key, the poster successfully draws the eye to the product and its name without compromising the simplicity and charm of its visual effect, while the motifs of trumpet and music stand suggest the occasion of a Coke break taken by a jazz player. This association with music and pop culture has long been a part of the company's advertising campaigns, particularly those made for television, which have helped to launch hit records and created an association with youth and fashion.

At a time when Coca-Cola was struggling to establish itself across the globe, Leupin's deceptively persuasive approach helped the brand to cement its reach and its worldwide place in the popular imagination.

← P.170

1953

SHELTERED WEAKLINGS—JAPAN

Poster

Takashi Kono (1906–1999)

Self-commissioned, Japan

"Sheltered Weaklings" was a highly controversial work produced at a sensitive time in international politics. While at first glance the image looks colorful and almost childlike in its characterization, it in fact expresses a blatant attack on what Takashi Kono believed to be the political, social, and cultural influence of the U.S. on Japan during the era of the Cold War.

By the time he produced this poster, Kono was already established as a leading Japanese designer, with a portfolio that included seminal logo, book, and magazine designs, as well as posters. Having started his career well before World War II, Kono witnessed the influx of Western—particularly American—culture that occurred as a result of the Allied occupation of his country. "Sheltered Weaklings" illustrates his opposition to Japan's assimilation of this culture, and demonizes American influence as an essentially aggressive force that dominates Japanese sensibility. The main political players in Kono's scenario are clearly identified by their national flags, whereas the Communist Chinese are symbolized by the red fish in the background swimming in the opposite direction. The sharp angles of the figures and the solid black background also contribute to the aggressive character of the image, and the use of English rather than Japanese for the text reinforces the message of national humiliation. Kono's interest in exploring a modern representation of traditional Japanese subjects manifests itself in the simple color palette, clean geometric shapes, and depiction of nature.

Kono was a founding member of the Japanese Advertising Artists Club (JAAC), established in 1951, which encouraged the exploration of more artistic forms of graphic design, and mounted annual exhibitions, at first featuring mostly posters. Known for voicing his strong political opinions in noncommercial work, Kono created this poster as part of his work with JAAC, and it was probably included in one of the group's exhibitions. The poster reflects Japan's deep sense of nationalism, which, during the period of its creation, seemed to be profoundly under threat, a perspective that is illustrated here in particularly forceful terms.

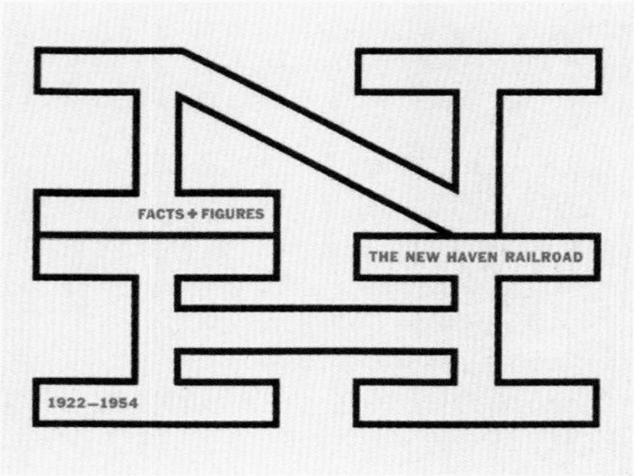

← P.170

1954

THE NEW HAVEN RAILROAD

Identity

Herbert Matter (1907–1984) et al.

New Haven Railroad, U.S.

One of the most recognizable trademarks of postwar America, the New Haven Railroad logotype formed part of a comprehensive corporate identity program led by the Swiss-born designer Herbert Matter, which endowed the company with a muscular industrial image appropriate to its role in the modern world.

In 1954, when Patrick McGinnis took over management of the New York, New Haven, and Hartford Railroad Company, as it was then known, he was faced with lagging schedules, unsatisfied customers, and legal disputes. McGinnis saw a comprehensive corporate redesign program as a way to breathe new life into the firm. Under its abbreviated name, the New Haven Railroad would become a modern passenger and freight transport corporation, with trains, stations, advertising, and many other elements all bearing a new identity created by some of the most distinguished design professionals of their time. In addition to Matter, the team of consultants included Florence Knoll (interiors), Marcel Breuer (train designs and prototypes), and Minoru Yamasaki (new stations and shelters).

Matter's elongated logotype, which replaced the previously elaborate script-based symbol, consisted of the two letters "NH" set in an old-letter expanded Egyptian serif typeface. As such, it conveyed brevity and simplicity while also suggesting heavy-duty railway tracks and sleepers. Assisted by Norman Ives, Matter maintained consistency for the program as a whole by changing the company's green-and-gold trim to a robust color scheme of red, white, and black in varying combinations. Painted on the sides of passenger-train cars and freight gondolas from 1955, the logotype, colors, and a series of striking geometric compositions addressing safety and identity issues turned trains into moving billboards. In the space of a year, the mark was also applied to posters, train schedules, signage, brochures, and menus.

Unfortunately, McGinnis's administration of the company was less successful, and by 1961 the New Haven Railroad was bankrupt. The logo, however, remains one of the most admired in corporate design history, and continues to be used by the Metro-North Railroad on its New Haven line.

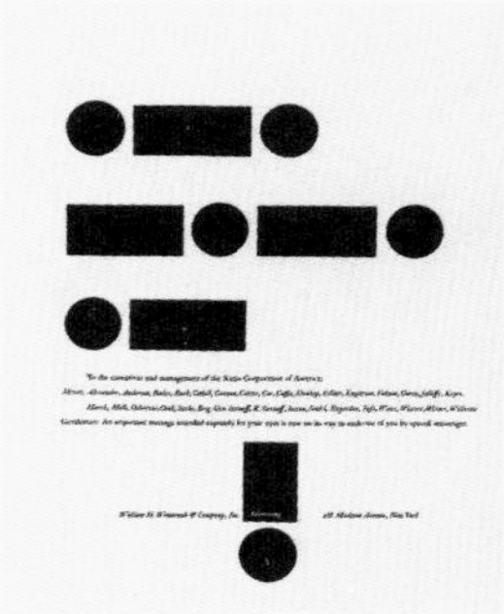

← P.171

1954

RCA

Advertising

Paul Rand (1914–1996)

William H. Weintraub & Company, Inc., U.S.

In an audacious attempt to elicit business for the advertising agency William H. Weintraub & Company, Paul Rand sent this Morse code message via a full-page *New York Times* advertisement. The message read "RCA" and was aimed at the Radio Corporation of America, which he hoped to win as a client.

Influenced by European modernism, Rand's design philosophy emphasized simplicity and restraint, as well as the use of symbolic association, innuendo, and humor, and he is credited with transforming the prewar "commercial artist" into the modern-day business-focused art director and graphic designer. As art director at Weintraub & Company from 1941 to 1954, Rand developed a reputation for ingenious conceptual advertising, pioneering the "big idea" and breathing life into the staid relationship between copy and art departments. His bold strategy for the RCA advertisement reflected his knowledge that David Sarnoff, CEO of RCA, had been a Morse code operator who would understand this highly public yet personal message. Rand's design embodied his belief that persuasive communication is enhanced by an appropriate application of aesthetics, with the heavy dots and dashes of the code contrasting with the elegant application of the Caslon typeface to convey a serious tone. The "sign-off" upends a dot-dash into an exclamation mark containing the word "Advertising," emphasizing the service on offer. Sarnoff was not persuaded to give Weintraub RCA's business, preferring to employ an agency commensurate with RCA's corporate status, but Rand's innovative approach was widely acknowledged and won a Gold Medal from the Art Directors Club of America.

Resigning as Weintraub's art director in 1954 to work as an independent design consultant, Rand went on to acquire an impressive portfolio of corporate clients. Highly critical of superficial trends in design, he was a profound thinker regarding graphic communication, arguing his position in three key publications: *Thoughts on Design* (1943); *Design, Form, and Chaos* (1993); and *From Lascaux to Brooklyn* (1996).

← P.172

1954–1957

UNIVERS

Typeface

Adrian Frutiger (1928–2015)

Deberny & Peignot, France

Adrian Frutiger's crowning achievement, Univers, continues to be an alternative to classic sans serif faces, such as Akzidenz-Grotesque and Neue Haas Grotesk (later known as the ever-popular Helvetica). Although regarded as a Swiss typeface, Univers—originally called Monde—was completed while Frutiger was living in France, where he was employed by the foundry Deberny & Peignot, for which he had recently produced Meridien. Technological advances in printing, production, and typography required Deberny & Peignot to create type designs that could function on France's soon-to-be popular Lumitype photosetters.

Using research from his student days in Zurich under Professor Walter Käch, Frutiger transformed his early hand-drawn renderings into an inventive and concise system, with twenty-one type styles given numerals to indicate different stroke weights and proportions—of which Univers 55 was the roman (or regular) typeface. Through this visual and numerical classification system, designers and composers could easily measure differences between one style and the next, across light, regular, bold, and heavy weights, where odd numbers represented roman styles and even numbers indicated italics. In addition to Lumitype media, Univers became available in hot metal and transfer lettering to give designers and compositors a plenitude of media to choose from. Not only did the numerical system and wide availability further its popularity, but the font's larger x-height gave it a more statuesque, taller appearance, in which lowercase letters were close in size to their uppercase peers.

During the late 1950s, sans serif typography populated the Swiss design landscape, and later the Americas, with Helvetica, Folio, Akzidenz-Grotesque, and Univers among the most widely used. At first sight, Univers and Helvetica appear eerily similar to each other, although some have argued that Helvetica's ease of access on computer hardware helped to turn it into a generic and somewhat clichéd typeface. The designers who remain loyal to Univers insist that its formal unity and classification system make it a smarter, more logical alternative to its sans serif competitors.

← P.172

1955

COURIER

Typeface

Howard Kettler (1919–1999)

IBM, U.S.

Courier is one of the most recognizable typefaces of the twentieth century—a surprising achievement for a face whose trademark is its air of anonymous officialdom and bureaucratic efficiency.

Howard Kettler was originally commissioned by IBM to design a face for use on their typewriters. However, IBM failed to secure exclusive rights to Courier, and it rapidly became the industry-wide standard. Courier's design, which is "mono-spaced"—each character takes up the same width on a line regardless of whether it is an "i" or an "m"—stems directly from its original use. This uniformity was necessary for typewriters due to the manual correction process, and for setting out tabular information. However, if set as extended text, Courier looks anything but uniform, with runs of characters that seem to have been kerned too tightly or loosely together.

The advent of the personal computer might have spelled the end for Courier, but because of its design it took little memory and was included as a system font; indeed, its typographic continuity may have helped to ensure a smooth transition from typewriter to new technology. Kettler originally named the typeface "Messenger," but ultimately chose "Courier" as he felt this conveyed greater prestige. He may have been right, as Courier was redrawn as Courier New by Adrian Frutiger during the 1960s and went on to become the chosen typeface of officialdom, used regularly within the legal profession and as the U.S. State Department's standard typeface.

In the 1990s Courier also spawned a new generation of postmodern, ironic typefaces such as Trixie, designed by Erik van Blokland in 1991, a distressed digital homage to a typewriter font. However, the State Department's replacement of Courier with Times New Roman in 2004, together with Microsoft's decision to use Consolas as its primary mono-spaced font for the Vista operating system, may have marked the beginning of the typeface's demise. However, Courier may survive yet, since it is frequently the laser printer's default choice when it cannot find the correct font.

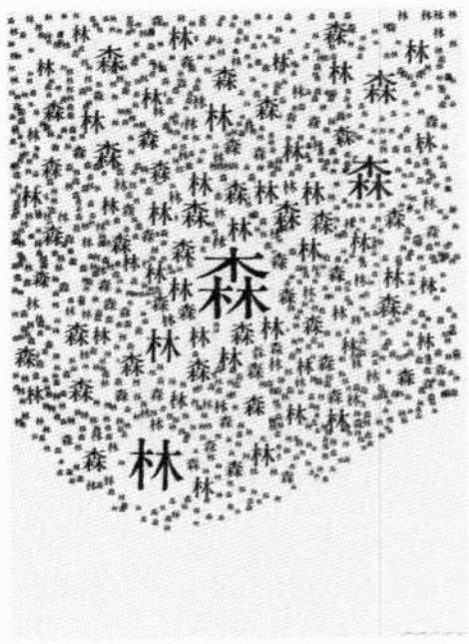

← P.173

1955

HAYASHI-MORI

Poster

Ryuichi Yamashiro (1920–1997)

Forest Protection Movement, Japan

This poster was designed by Ryuichi Yamashiro for the *Graphic '55* exhibition, and was later presented in the Japanese Pavilion of the 1958 International Exhibition in Brussels. It represents the forested slope of a snow-covered mountain, which appears to be depicted either from a bird's-eye view or looking up from below. The image is composed of a scattering of two Japanese ideograms—林 (grove) and 森 (forest), composed from the word 木 (*ki*), meaning tree, which is doubled to create the word *hayashi* (grove), and tripled to create the word *mori* (forest). The changing size and weight of the letters creates the perspective and mountainous topography.

The poster was chosen to represent Japan because its graphic qualities are similar to those of Zen paintings, in which the spaces between marks of black ink are designed to be filled by the viewer's imagination. These images are also characterized by asymmetrical compositions that can be perceived from numerous perspectives, as well as by a deliberate flatness that is distinctly graphic. Additionally, the poster emblematizes the special character and double function of Japanese writing: in Japan, each letter functions not only as part of a text but as a pictogram with an independent structure and message. In Zen compositions featuring painting and calligraphy there is a deliberate blurring of the boundaries between text and image, which allows for a double reading of the ideogram; this dual message could not be communicated by either a regular word or a simple visual image. Hence, the poster presents an image of a forest both to viewers who read Japanese and those with no knowledge of the language.

This type of graphic design was prevalent in Japan during the 1950s, when Constructivism was adopted and infused with Japanese characteristics. It was a style intended to represent the country abroad, yet was also well received at home, addressing the need for a lost "Japaneseness" in a country that had suffered a blow to its cultural pride under American occupation.

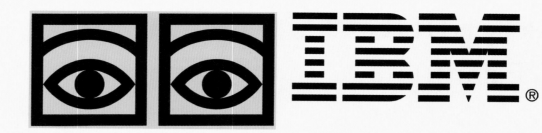

← P.174

← P.175

← P.175

1955

BEETHOVEN

Poster

Josef Müller-Brockmann (1914–1996)

Tonhalle-Orchester Zürich, Switzerland

Josef Müller-Brockmann's posters, produced for the Tonhalle-Orchester Zürich over a period of twenty-five years, mark a high point in the visualization of music via graphic forms, and set a new benchmark in the history of poster design in terms of invention and originality. His most celebrated design is this poster for a performance of Beethoven's "Coriolan Overture."

Throughout the nineteenth and early part of the twentieth centuries the music poster was composed of dense blocks of type with little or no illustration, and gave only the bare details of date, time, and location of a performance. Aiming to bring balance and order to these typographically congested notices, Müller-Brockmann punctuated the type with elegant geometric illustrations. Working on small grid pages, and beginning with a single square, he would sketch out rough shapes and lines signifying the text. From there, he looked for a "logical connection" between the marks on the page and the music, attempting to develop feelings of "rhythm" and "transparency," and to discover a particular ordering of geometric elements. In the case of the Beethoven poster, this process took more than two months. Beginning with a series of concentric circles flowing outward in waves, Müller-Brockmann decided to fragment the circles into arcs, which emanate from a first circle at the center according to the mathematical sequence of "1, 2, 4, 8, 16, 32." The main body of text is positioned at the center of the first circle, with the text's left border acting as a vertical axis for the design. Key information detailing the composer, location, and performers is situated on the other side of this divide.

The finished work is a carefully honed visual sound: a graphic harmony rendered in the most meticulous and rhythmic manner. Along with all of his music posters, including the equally renowned "Musica Viva" series, the design reveals Müller-Brockmann's intelligent use of geometric forms to symbolize the full repertoire of classical works performed at the Tonhalle.

1956

MAZETTI

Identity

Olle Eksell (1918–2007)

Mazetti, Sweden

Olle Eksell's simple, bold monolithic pictogram created for the Swedish confectioner Mazetti was known affectionately as "cocoa eyes" and was one of the most important commissions of the designer's career, which spanned nearly seventy years. His stylish trademark gave the company a strong and popular identity, seen as a first for the country, and was applied to the entire range of its products.

Eksell was given considerable freedom in developing the mark by the firm, which launched a competition in 1955 to modernize their old symbol. After it was selected as winner, Eksell's passion for craft and preference for thinking small helped to determine the charm of the design and its scale, which he produced at matchbox size, suggesting a direct reference to the chocolate pieces it would later adorn. Two lozenge shapes enclosed in squares evoke the eyes of a child looking through the panes of a shop window at the delights inside, and are also reminiscent of the stamped squares of a chocolate bar. Before long, the mark was applied to every aspect of the company's business and beyond, from chocolate and packaging to letterheads, stamps, trucks, and even railway freight wagons. The mark also referenced a number of other graphic symbols associated with the era, such as William Golden's eye logo for CBS television. Meanwhile, George Orwell's novel *Nineteen Eighty-Four*, published six years prior, and a growing awareness of the surveillance associated with the Cold War, increased the popularity of the eye as icon. Eksell was also influenced by his professional education at the Art Center College of Design in Pasadena under Tink Adams, and the work of design luminaries such as Paul Rand, who greatly extended the possibilities of brand design.

Despite the identity's success, Eksell's relationship with Mazetti ended in the 1960s, although his design was retained by the new owners of the company when it was sold in 1975. The experience of creating the identity would go on to define his later design and business activities, which included further commercial identity work alongside advertising, books, posters, and illustrations.

1956–1991

IBM

Identity

Paul Rand (1914–1996)

IBM, U.S.

When the eminent architect and designer Eliot Noyes was made director of the International Business Machines Corporation (IBM) design program in 1956, the high-tech company looked decidedly old-fashioned. With the aim of creating an integrated modern identity similar to that of European companies, such as Olivetti, Noyes hired Paul Rand—famous for his witty yet stylish advertising, magazine, and book design since the early 1940s—to work on the graphics.

The designer's first act was to adapt the slab-serif logo introduced in 1947, written in the Beton Bold Condensed font, to the more modern-looking City Medium (devised by Georg Trump). For the design of packaging and company literature he carried out more radical work, rejecting what he felt was austere Swiss modernism by liberally sprinkling the new logo across the material and using bright colors and his own handwriting. His overhaul of the annual reports set a new standard, transforming what was merely a legal requirement into a powerful branding tool, with photography, drawings, and the new logo all employed to give an editorial look to the covers.

Rand was not satisfied with the trademark, however, feeling the overall shape was awkward (a thin letter followed by two wide ones with square counters in the "B"). During the 1970s he introduced stripes, unifying the design and obscuring its idiosyncrasies. Rand believed that a logo on its own was incapable of personifying the products or ethos of a company; rather, a logo that was authoritative, timeless, and striking would come to embody the values of the company simply by association. His IBM trademark exemplifies this principle: there is nothing about stripes in themselves that relates to computing, but for millions they have come to acquire this meaning.

Over the decades, Rand used his logo in myriad ways, inspired by Noyes's attitude that "good design" in all its forms would embody IBM's identity, and that there should be no unbreakable rules and regulations. The 1981 rebus poster (Eye, Bee, M) shows that Rand's essential playfulness had not been stifled by working in what Noyes termed "corporate design."

← P.176

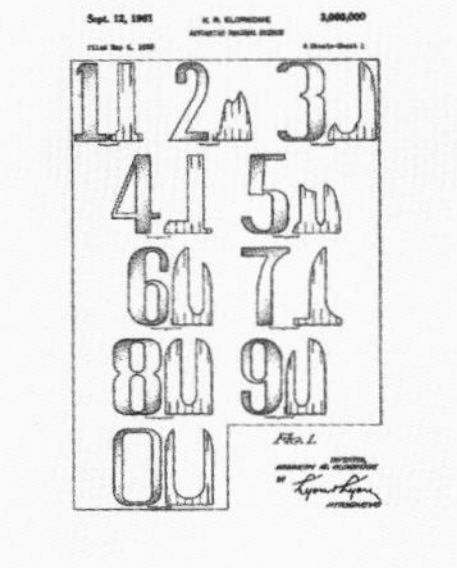

← P.177

← P.177

1956

OLIVETTI

Advertising

Giovanni Pintori (1912–1999)

Olivetti, Italy

Among the most recognizable advertising graphics of the 1940s and '50s are those that Giovanni Pintori produced for Olivetti, the Italian manufacturer of typewriters and calculators. Their bold, colorful illustrations and rhythmic type reflect the light touch that would become a Pintori trademark and link his name inexorably with the company.

In 1936, at the age of only twenty-four, Pintori was hired by Adriano Olivetti, the son of the company's founder, to be art director of Olivetti's advertising office. For thirty-one years he helped to define the Olivetti style, thriving in an environment of artistic freedom and rich collaboration. Olivetti was among the first of the large corporations to embrace design as a core value, and demanded design excellence not only in the company's finished products but in every aspect of its business, from promotional materials to offices and factories (many of which were designed by prominent architects).

In order to convey this message to the widest possible audience, Pintori relied on strong images, which he felt were more immediate and accessible than clever copy. Drawing inspiration from various Olivetti machines, he created simple, striking forms to represent their function (a series of typewriter keys in silhouette, for example, suggesting motion). In other instances (such as that of the Elettro-summa 22 calculator) he used highly abstract forms, only hinting at the device's character and function. Pintori's vibrant, poetic graphics presented Olivetti's products as technologically advanced but at the same time easy—even pleasurable—to use. Unlike the more rigid design programs employed by other companies, Olivetti's was highly expressive, reflecting an uncommon degree of individualism. For Olivetti and Pintori, promotional graphics were an art form, and therefore made an important cultural contribution, as well as helping to increase sales.

Pintori's award-winning work was included in the 1952 exhibition *Olivetti: Design in Industry* at the Museum of Modern Art in New York. In addition to his innumerable contributions to the company's advertising campaigns, Pintori also designed typewriters and typefaces, as well as the interior of Olivetti's Milan showroom in 1969.

1956

MAGNETIC INK CHARACTER RECOGNITION

Typeface

Stanford Research Institute

General Electric, U.S.

Magnetic Ink Character Recognition (MICR) characters are familiar to us as the figures that run along the bottom of checks, generally specifying check number, sort code, and account number. These figures are in fact printed in magnetic ink, allowing electronic sensors as well as human beings to read them and process the checks.

The character-recognition technology was demonstrated to the American Bankers Association in 1956, and was almost universally employed in the U.S. by 1963. The system is now also commonly used by British banks.

By the early 1960s, computers were performing complex tasks in the service of humanity, and it became obvious that an alphabet was needed that was intelligible to both man and machine. In answer to this problem, the Stanford Research Institute developed MICR, and went on to be awarded the patent for the invention in 1961. With magnetic material incorporated in the printing ink, the MICR reader sensed the magnetic properties rather than the optical ones intended for the human reader. To avoid scanning errors due to the relative lack of sensitivity of the contemporary electromagnetic detector heads, the precision of magnetic ink characters had to be superior to that of normal characters.

The Stanford Research Institute font, known as E-13B or ABA (as it was sponsored by the American Bankers Association), was composed of horizontal and vertical features, each character comprising ten horizontal stripes and seven vertical stripes. The points of intersection of these stripes yield a total of seventy possible positions. The electronic reader senses whether each of these positions is black or white, and notifies the control unit accordingly. The control unit then compares the sensed pattern with the expected reading for each character and thereby identifies it. As the pattern for each character was designed to be as different as possible from any other, an E-13B character could be correctly identified even when it had been subject to considerable distortion or overprinted with other marks.

During the 1960s, the association of MICR fonts with modernity and computer aesthetics led to the creation of a number of imitations.

1956–1962

DESIGN

Magazine / Newspaper

Ken Garland (1929–2021)

Council of Industrial Design, UK

Drawing on a strong contemporary aesthetic, Garland's directorship of *Design* magazine brought a fresh approach to the way in which design in industry was presented, and endowed the publication with a distinctive visual identity.

In a brave move for an untested and unknown designer, Garland took on the art direction of *Design* magazine in 1956, just one year after graduating from London's Central School of Arts and Crafts. The magazine had been launched in 1949 by the Council of Industrial Design—renamed the Design Council in 1972—with a remit to "help industry in its task of raising standards of design." By his own admission, Garland took time to stamp his vision on the publication. The first three covers under his leadership (beginning with issue 81 of October 1955) were designed by F.H.K. Henrion, who had worked for the previous art editor, Peter Hatch. By 1959, Garland's cover designs had begun to come into their own: confident, bold, and playful, they injected a personality and confidence into the publication that had not previously been seen. They also departed refreshingly from the norm in their combination of simple graphic images and icons with bold photographic elements; images were juxtaposed and overlaid, with abstract shapes formed, cropped, and bled to give dramatic visual impact. For the first time, *Design* had a human face, capturing issues within design and the optimism of the late 1950s and early '60s.

In January 1962 *Design* emerged with a new Garland-designed masthead that cleverly conveyed his vision for the magazine, softening the overall feel of the publication and giving it a more accessible and contemporary edge. The logotype, with its rounded, sans serif letterforms, hinted at a new era of graphic design based on a more youthful and expressive aesthetic. Although Garland left the magazine two issues later in March 1962, the masthead would remain untouched for a further twenty-five years—a testament to his enduring contribution.

DANESE
MILANO

← P.178

← P.178

← P.179

1957

DANESE

Logo

Franco Meneguzzo (1924–2008)

Danese, Italy

The Danese logo by Franco Meneguzzo created a strong and highly distinctive brand identity for this Italian furniture and lighting company, appearing on all of its printed and publicity material.

Originally called DEM (for Danese e Meneguzzo), Danese was founded in 1955 by Meneguzzo and Bruno Danese. Meneguzzo, who designed ceramics for the company, produced the logo two years later when Danese took over full ownership. At the time the concept of "design" was still developing in Italy and, rather than creating mass-produced industrial objects, the company manufactured small editions of handmade items and furniture for the home and office. From the beginning, packaging, display, and marketing were highly considered. The fact that a painter or ceramicist designed the logo was far from unusual at a time when architects, artists, and designers often switched roles and a multidisciplinary approach was standard practice. In creating the logo, Meneguzzo drew upon his experience as a ceramicist and his interest in paleontology (his grandfather and great grandfather were geologists who discovered important fossils) and tribal and archaic art. This is evident in the simple black-and-white rectangular emblem at the center, which resembles an archaic stone carving. The shapes inside the rectangle refer to Danese's initials (BD), whereas the words "Danese Milano," in a simple uppercase sans serif font above and below, locate it firmly in the modern age.

More than fifty years later, Meneguzzo's well-judged design has retained its relevance, and lives up to the Danese philosophy of creating designs that stand the test of time. The hand-drawn, slightly quirky symbol marks the company as individualistic and unusual, setting it apart from the values associated with classic Italian modernism.

1957

SCHIFF NACH EUROPA, BY MARKUS KUTTER

Book

Karl Gerstner (1930–2017)

Verlag Arthur Niggli, Switzerland

Schiff nach Europa (Ship to Europe) is considered to be one of the most innovative book designs of the twentieth century and an outstanding example of "Integral Typography," which Karl Gerstner outlined in his 1963 publication, *Designing Programmes*.

Written by Markus Kutter, *Schiff nach Europa* is an experimental novel that describes the journey of the *Andrea Doria* ocean liner from New York to the French port of Le Havre. The book was pioneering in its use of the grid, which depends on a rigid set of divisions—squares (2 × 3), units (7 × 7) and body size (3 × 3), based on the smallest typographical measurements: type size and leading. This system provided a format into which type could be integrated with almost limitless freedom. Using the two sans serif faces Akzidenz-Grotesk (for larger, hand-set type) and Monotype Grotesque (for the machine-set copy), Gerstner plays with a wide variety of print styles, combining traditional narrative formats with those of play scripts and newspaper journalism, and manipulating type size, column widths, and orientation to convey the individual voices of the ship's passengers. The work was a collaboration between Gerstner and Kutter, and, in a prefatory note to the book, the latter acknowledges his good fortune in working with a designer who understands format, and wonders why writers are not more interested in the way their work is presented.

Gerstner and Kutter met in the late 1950s, when they worked together on publications to mark the Geigy Chemical Corporation's two-hundredth anniversary, such as *Geigy Today*. After the success of *Schiff nach Europa*, Gerstner and Kutter went on to establish their own design practice in 1959—GGK—which became the largest and best-known advertising agency in Switzerland. Although Gerstner belonged to the modernist European tradition, he also followed the American New Advertising style, in which message and form are inseparable. Integral typography was his response to this concept, while his emphasis on the grid helped to shape and popularize a system that is today synonymous with Swiss graphic design. A leading pioneer in advertising, corporate identities, and typography, Gerstner also created his own eponymous font in 1987 for the Berthold Type Foundry.

1957–1967

BRITISH MOTORWAY AND ROAD SIGNAGE SYSTEM

Information Design

Jock Kinneir (1917–1994), Margaret Calvert (1936–)

Ministry of Transport, UK

After meeting at Chelsea College of Art, where Margaret Calvert was an illustration student and Jock Kinneir a visiting design teacher, Kinneir invited Calvert to join him on a commission: to design a signage system for the London Gatwick airport. The work was a success, and Calvert was hired as Kinneir's full-time design assistant.

The next assignment came from the Ministry of Transport in 1957, which hired Kinneir as a design consultant to the Anderson Committee, responsible for proposing new signage for Britain's first motorways. With increasing numbers taking to the roads, the existing network proved inadequate and in need of an upgrade. This was followed in 1963 by an even bigger project: to help redesign the national road-sign system. The original signage had been commissioned by several different bodies and was thus muddled and inconsistent; a more cohesive solution was needed to keep motorists and pedestrians safe.

Kinneir and Calvert were meticulous in designing graphics that were immediately identifiable and understandable. In addition to the iconography, the legibility of any text-based elements was key, and required rigorous testing. Part of this process involved putting the signs on cars and driving at high speeds toward test subjects—a group of volunteer airmen—sitting on a platform to verify at what distance the prototypes were readable. Full-size road signs were later tested in situ by the Road Research Laboratory. The result was Transport, a typeface that utilized upper- and lowercase letters (rather than all capitals) to ensure coherence in high-speed contexts.

The project also produced Calvert's now-ubiquitous "school children crossing" and "road works" pictograms, the former of which she based on herself as a child. The signs were coded by color and shape: triangles were used for warnings, circles for orders, and rectangles for information. Startling in their simplicity yet universal in their communication, the pictograms characterize a large part of British culture today. Although Kinneir passed away in 1994, Calvert's contributions to typography and road safety were recognized with an OBE in 2016 and an exhibition at London's Design Museum in 2020.

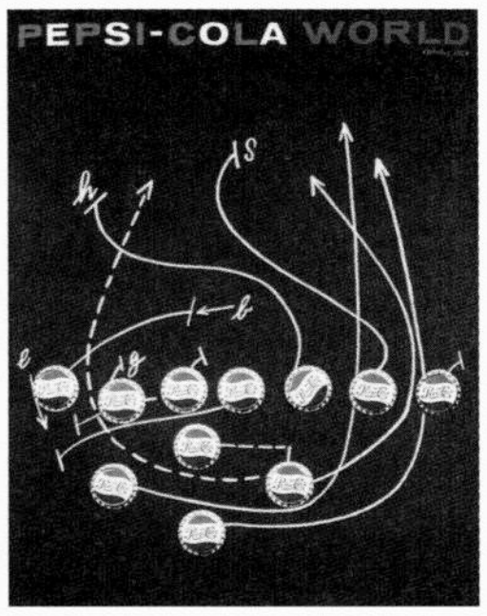

← P.180

1957–1959

PEPSI-COLA WORLD

Magazine Cover

Robert Brownjohn (1925–1970) et al.

Pepsi-Cola, U.S.

A monthly in-house magazine distributed to Pepsi-Cola bottling plants across the U.S., *Pepsi-Cola World* changed the way in which company publications communicated with their employees.

From 1957 to 1959, the magazine's most seminal period, *Pepsi-Cola World* was designed inside and out by design firm Brownjohn, Chermayeff & Geismar (BCG). However, the cover ideas were credited largely to Robert Brownjohn, who was known for a trademark design approach that included giddy graphic puns. *Pepsi-Cola World* covers played upon a timely, seasonal theme, often employing the iconic Pepsi bottle-caps as the predominant visual device. These were used to depict an event at which Pepsi might be enjoyed—perhaps a football game in the autumn or a golf game in the summer; or something more universal, such as bottle-caps raining down on an umbrella for the month of April. Above all, *Pepsi-Cola World* portrayed a wholesome vision of Americana, executed with a sweep of nostalgia: a still-life of bottle-caps with toys and trash, as if the contents of a boy's pockets had been emptied and photographed; or, for a summer issue, the bottle-cap as bait on a fishing hook, streaming through a deep blue background. The designers also experimented with more upscale iterations of the Pepsi brand, using the scripted "P" to replace the "P" in New York's Park Avenue street sign, or filling the Waldorf Astoria's check-in registry with guests all named "Pepsi-Cola World."

Known for its witty visual style, BCG demonstrated through its provocative work for Pepsi that this approach could be used appropriately for a corporate as well as a more mainstream audience. The success of *Pepsi-Cola World* was responsible for boosting the agency's business and for grabbing the attention of future clients, such as the U.S. broadcast network NBC.

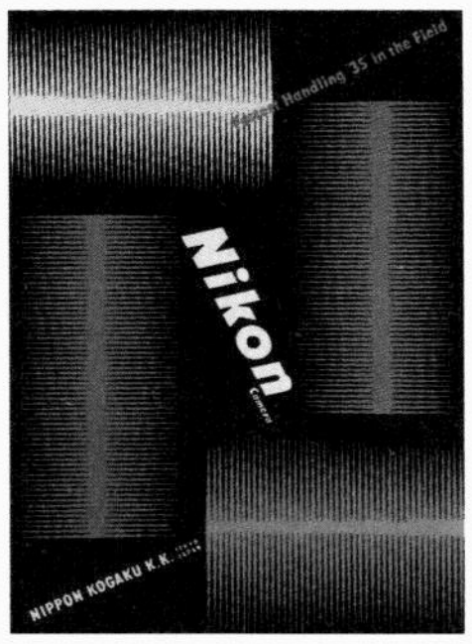

← P.181

1957

NIKON CAMERA

Poster

Yusaku Kamekura (1915–1997)

Nippon Kogaku Ltd., Japan

Yusaku Kamekura's "Nikon Camera" poster reveals the increasing influence of modernism on Japanese design after World War II. Having learned about the New Typography at Japanese art institutions in the 1930s, Kamekura art-directed and edited several cultural magazines, such as the English-language *Nippon* (from 1937 onward), and in 1951 founded the Japan Advertising Artists Club, which brought a new level of professionalism to graphic design.

In 1954 Kamekura began working for Nippon Kogaku Ltd., manufacturers of Nikon cameras, producing various promotional and packaging designs. His series of posters for the company vary in style from the use of abstract pictorial motifs to purely typographic designs, though all are characterized by their bold central focus, inspired by the *katachi* tradition of Japanese art, with its emphasis on concentrated and direct yet perfectly drawn graphic form. In the brightly colored design pictured, with its kinetic, diagonally aligned type, Kamekura achieved a perfect synthesis of modernist and Japanese ideas, which suggests the prismatic qualities of photography. The sharp, intricate pattern reflects not only the precision of the products but also Kamekura's understanding of the technical discipline involved in printing such designs, and was a variation of an effect used in his celebrated poster of 1956, "Peaceful use of atomic energy"—the first piece of graphic design to be included in the *Japan Art Annual*. With this work, however, which was reproduced in the 1957 *Graphis Annual*, Kamekura felt that he had finally established a style of his own.

Kamekura's Nikon posters also show an affiliation with the graphic styles of Western designers, such as Alvin Lustig, Giovanni Pintori, and Josef Müller-Brockmann. Comparisons with the last named became even more pronounced in the 1960s through Kamekura's increased use of dramatic photography, particularly in designs for ski resorts and the Tokyo Olympics, which helped to forge his reputation internationally. Affectionately known as the "Boss" among postwar generations of Japanese designers, for helping to set up and run initiatives such as the Nippon Design Center in 1960, Kamekura played a vital role in introducing Western visual ideas to his country.

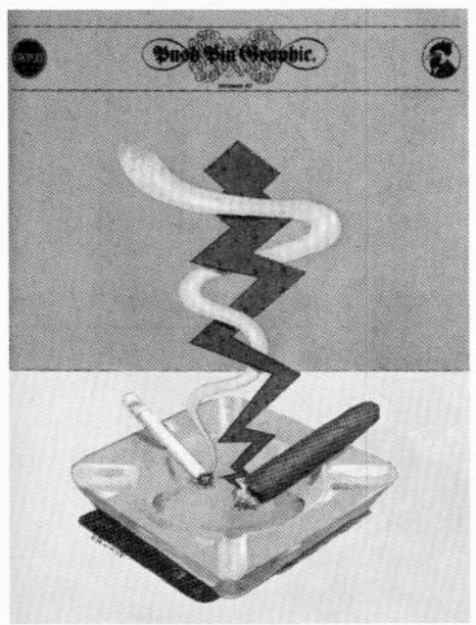

← P.182

1957–1980

THE PUSH PIN GRAPHIC

Magazine / Newspaper

Seymour Chwast (1931–) et al.

Push Pin Studio, U.S.

The *Push Pin Graphic* was the second incarnation of a formula that Seymour Chwast, director of the Push Pin Studio in New York, had first tested in 1953 with the *Push Pin Almanack*. A promotional magazine, available by subscription only, it was renamed the *Monthly Graphic* in 1957. With the establishment of the studio, the publication was relaunched as *Push Pin Graphic* to showcase the work of studio members, as well as that of guest artists whose sensibility resonated with Chwast, and soon became a cultural reference for designers in the U.S. and Europe.

An exceptionally inventive and tireless illustrator, Chwast had a treasure hunter's mentality when it came to graphic design, sourcing obscure pictorial references from Chinese anatomical plates to vernacular Art Deco typographica, and reinterpreting them with insolence and wit to serve fresh purposes. The logo of the magazine, displayed in nineteenth-century Fette Fraktur laid over ornate Victorian calligraphy pen scrolls, was typical of Chwast's ability to quote the old to invent the new. Each issue had a theme (clowns, dreams, hell, chickens, mothers) that gave its editor an opportunity to hunt for intriguing visual specimens. However, this medley of tidbits was primarily an excuse to show off the talents of the artists involved, who in the early days included Milton Glaser, Paul Davis, Edward Sorel, and Barry Zaid, and, after Glaser's departure, John Collier, Haruo Miyauchi, and Barbara Sandler. Occasionally, photographs by Benno Friedman served as counterpoints to the illustrations. Yet, despite the profusion of images, Chwast's layouts were skilfully paced to surprise and amuse. Inspired by the work of typographer and designer Herb Lubalin, Chwast pitted dense text against white space, and elegant letterforms against boisterous line drawings. Contributors were encouraged to experiment with new techniques or styles, and advertisers were coaxed into allowing the studio to redesign their advertisements.

More than just a promotional vehicle, the magazine was an essential outlet for creativity and remained relevant for decades. In 1997, continuing this tradition, Chwast launched a further publication, the *Nose*.

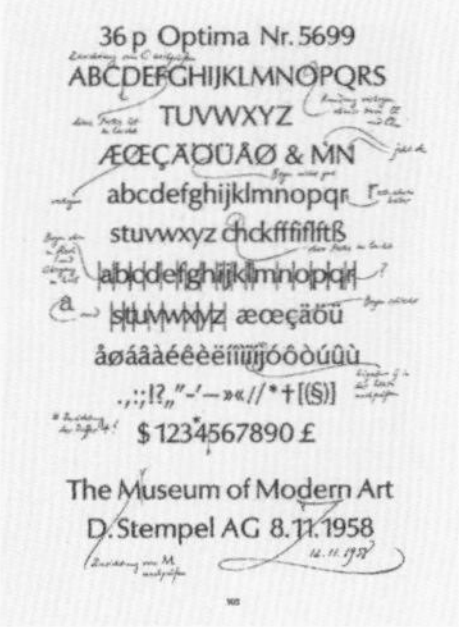

← P.182

← P.182

← P.183

1958

OPTIMA

Typeface

Hermann Zapf (1918–2015)

D. Stempel AG, Germany

Optima is a humanist sans serif typeface designed by the prolific and renowned German typographer Hermann Zapf, who began work on the style in 1952. The type foundry D. Stempel AG released Optima Roman, Italic, and Bold in 1958. Although Zapf wanted to name his font Neu Antiqua (New Roman), marketing executives insisted on Optima.

Humanist sans serifs were a response to the criticism that sans serif letterforms were cold, mechanical, and difficult to read. Humanist forms incorporate aspects of fifteenth-century handwritten letterforms and incised roman capital letters, and are characterized by variable stroke width and a sloping axis.

Zapf's typefaces all exhibit to some degree his background as one of the world's most accomplished calligraphers. His predisposition is to imbue his letterforms with the slight but unmistakable touches of handmade shapes. No exception, Optima is a graceful and elegant typeface with tapering stems that swell slightly at their terminal points, suggesting a bridge between serif fonts and mono-line sans serif type. Zapf's goal was to design a face that would be legible at standard text sizes and also work well at display dimensions. Although additions to the Optima family have been released over the years, Zapf's ultimate realization of Optima was the result of a collaborative redesign with the noted type designer Akira Kobayashi. Called Optima Nova, it was released in 2002 and contains seven weights and a titling capitals variant.

Optima has proved to be a highly regarded and enduring typeface. Widely admired, it has also been widely plagiarized, along with other typefaces designed by Zapf, especially his equally popular Palatino. Zapf, who has long been an active proponent of copyright protection for type designs, resigned his membership of the Association Typographique Internationale in 1993, in protest of the organization's disregard of unauthorized copying by prominent corporate members.

Optima's modernism tempered with its warmth has made it useful for a wide variety of products, media, and companies. Notably, it was chosen by the architect Maya Lin for Washington D.C.'s Vietnam Veterans' Memorial Wall.

1958

CAMPAIGN FOR NUCLEAR DISARMAMENT

Information Design

Gerald Holtom (1914–1985)

Self-commissioned, UK

Printed or painted on banners, badges, bodies, or walls, the peace symbol became one of the most important and visible indicators of dissent throughout the latter part of the twentieth century.

The emblem was originally conceived by British graphic artist Gerald Holtom as a symbol for nuclear disarmament, and encompassed the semaphore (flag-waving) signals for the letters "N" and "D." Holtom also suggested symbolic readings of the shaft or broken cross as the death of man, and the surrounding circle as the unborn child, together representing the threat to existing humanity as well as the unborn. Such symbolism may have been inspired by Rudolf Koch's *The Book of Signs* (1930), a collection of medieval symbols that was highly influential in art and design education and professional practice at the time. The most significant characteristic of the peace symbol, however, was its distinctive yet simple form, which could be easily drawn or reproduced, thereby assuring its widespread use.

The peace symbol appeared in a decade that felt the constant threat of nuclear war as the Cold War locked the U.S. and the Soviet Union in an arms race where peace was maintained by deterrence via "mutually assured destruction." The resulting nuclear-bomb testing led to the founding of Britain's Campaign for Nuclear Disarmament (CND) and its adoption of the antinuclear or peace symbol in 1958. Protest marches and peace camps of the 1980s often displayed the symbol in posters and other graphics, including the popular photomontages of political artist Peter Kennard, though, significantly, CND never claimed copyright of the symbol. The symbol was also adopted in the 1960s by the hippie movement and by the U.S. public at large as a call for peace, particularly in protests against the Vietnam War, and accompanied a wide range of antiwar statements, even appearing on the Zippo lighters and helmets of American soldiers in Vietnam. Today, the peace symbol continues to maintain an international presence in the world of twenty-first century protest, and is a graphic reminder of how debates regarding nuclear weapons and armed conflict continue to resonate with new generations.

1958–1978

UOMO E MITO

Book Cover

Anita Klinz (1923–2013)

Il Saggiatore, Italy

Largely unacknowledged in the history of graphic design, at least during her lifetime, Anita Klinz was in fact a prolific and remarkable talent of the Italian design canon. Born in 1923 in the resort town of Opatija, once part of Italy but now in Croatia, Klinz, after high school, moved with her family to Prague, where she studied economics and, later, graphic design. The 1939 German occupation of Prague forced her to move once more, this time to Milan, where she eventually got her professional start, first as an illustrator and artworker at a women's weekly, then at Mondadori, designing advertisements for *Epoca* magazine.

It was there that Klinz really developed her craft, mentored by none other than Bruno Munari, a maverick of Italian design and then *Epoca*'s art director. She also benefited from working with the publisher Alberto Mondadori, whose attention to both content and aesthetics drove an especially high quality of work. In 1958 Mondadori set up a new publishing house, Il Saggiatore, and invited Klinz to join as art director. The new imprint intended to publish the "greatest writers in the history of Western thought," and under Klinz's skilled eye became known for its stand-out covers.

Uomo e Mito (Man and Mythology) was among the first series of books she designed, which featured works on ancient cultures, including Donald Harden's *The Phoenicians*. For the covers, Klinz playfully collaged cut-outs of black-and-white archival photographs with brightly colored, condensed sans-serif titles ensconced in tight black boxes. This treatment pushes the letters forward in the hierarchy of the design, allowing the creatively cropped images to form a graphic backdrop. The designs harness the best of the mid-century modernist tradition while expanding readers' preconceived notions of this style (as Italians are wont to do).

It goes without saying that Klinz's legacy suffered the same underappreciation as her female counterparts; her name is often overshadowed by Munari's. Luckily her contributions were finally recognized in a volume by Luca Pitoni, *Ostinata Belleza* (translated as *Stubborn Beauty*), published in 2022, which brought long-overdue praise from design critics Alice Rawsthorn and Steven Heller.

← P.184

1958

VERTIGO

Poster

Saul Bass (1920–1996)

Paramount Pictures, U.S.

Alfred Hitchcock's 1958 thriller *Vertigo* was his first and most complete collaboration with the graphic designer Saul Bass, who was renowned for rejecting the uninspired conventions that then prevailed in film poster and title-sequence design, and for pioneering the use of minimal lettering and symbolic imagery. Bass's poster campaign and opening credits for *Vertigo* typify this innovative avant-garde style.

Bass aimed to set the scene for the film from the very first frame, treating titles as a prologue, a miniature film within the film, rather than simply a list of credits. He identified one emblem in particular—the spiraling circle—as conveying the atmosphere of the film. An extreme close-up of a woman's face, eventually focusing on one eye, generates an uncomfortable sensation, which is intensified when the screen is suddenly bathed in red. Gradually, the eye is replaced by spirals of color on a black background, which spin to create a dizzying sensation that mirrors the main character's fear of heights. The whirling shape also signifies various aspects of the plot—the lack of control felt by the protagonist, the inner workings of his fevered mind, and even the heroine's hairstyle.

Bass repeated many of these symbolic features for the film poster, allowing the circling vortex to dominate much of the page and to emphasize the film's unsettling ambience. Falling into the vortex is the silhouette of a man reminiscent of those drawn by police at a murder scene, which looms over the outline of a woman. The font is nervous and asymmetric, expressive of the unstable mind of the central character, while the red color implies danger and warning.

Bass's work for *Vertigo* would establish him as the foremost film designer of his generation. With its ability to convey an impressive range of mood and emotion, his graphic style continues to influence designers working today.

← P.185

1958

DIE ZEITUNG

Poster

Emil Ruder (1914–1970)

Gewerbemuseum Basel, Switzerland

Emil Ruder's 1958 exhibition poster "Die Zeitung" (Newspaper) embodied his influential ideas on graphic design and the "Swiss school" that emerged in the second half of the twentieth century.

After serving an apprenticeship as a compositor from 1929 until 1933, and studying print at the Kunstgewerbeschule Zürich (1941–42), Ruder became a typography instructor at the Allgemeine Gewerbeschule in Basel, where he developed the curriculum in partnership with Armin Hofmann. This poster put into practice many of the key ideas concerning effective visual communication through legibility that he advocated in his teaching, particularly in its use of sans serif lettering and asymmetric composition. From 1946, Ruder had made important contributions to the debate surrounding Jan Tschichold's renunciation of the New Typography, through his involvement with a number of influential professional journals, such as *Typografische Monatsblätter*. In an article published there in 1961, he demonstrated the design potential of the new Univers font, which he had explored extensively with his students. While systematic in its application of a unifying grid structure, Ruder's approach allowed for variety, manifested here by the negative spaces in and around letterforms, and the use of striking compositional and tonal contrasts. His dedication to the craft of the letterpress is also demonstrated by the coarse, half-tone "news" image, which was meticulously hand-cut into lino, a process he would repeat in another exhibition poster for "Abstract Photography" in 1960.

In 1967 Ruder set out his philosophy of design and education in *Typographie*, a seminal manual published in English, French, and German. Prior to this, his article "The Typography of Order," printed in the September/October 1959 issue of *Graphis*, had introduced the "Swiss school"to a foreign audience.

← P.185

1958–1968

ULM

Magazine / Newspaper

Anthony Froshaug (1920–1984), Tomás Gonda (1926–1988)

Hochschule für Gestaltung Ulm, Germany

A masterpiece of modernist design, *Ulm* started life as the new school journal for the Hochschule für Gestaltung Ulm. Taking its name from the town in which the school was based, it was initiated by Anthony Froshaug as one of the many activities connected with his newly established visual methodology course. Froshaug, who had accepted a teaching position at the Hochschule in 1957, was to make a major contribution to the institution's development, introducing students to graph theories and applying mathematics to design.

Froshaug was involved in the first five issues of *Ulm*, which had been set up to promote general school interests and to cover its research projects, with Froshaug also publishing one of his texts on visual methodology. The magazine's design reflects an encounter between two different typographic cultures: Froshaug's conceptual approach and the ordered typography of Swiss-German graphic design. The large, 11 × 11⅝ inch (28 × 30 cm) format is based on a four-column grid system that is able to carry text in three languages alongside visual material, with the column width defined by the line length of the language that occupies most space. This language also determines the line breaks for the other two languages. Akzidenz-Grotesk was the only typeface used across the magazine as a whole, appearing in two type sizes, and represented a turning point for Froshaug, who until then had favored Gill Sans.

Ulm went on to attract an international readership, while the Hochschule für Gestaltung Ulm became one of the most important European schools of design since the Bauhaus. In its sixth issue, *Ulm* dramatically assumed an A4 format at the hands of Tomás Gonda, who taught in the Visual Communication department of the school. He maintained the use of Akzidenz-Grotesk in the masthead and throughout the main text, but transformed the pages into a three-column grid, allowing only German and English communication. The publication continued production until the school closed in 1968 due to a lack of funding.

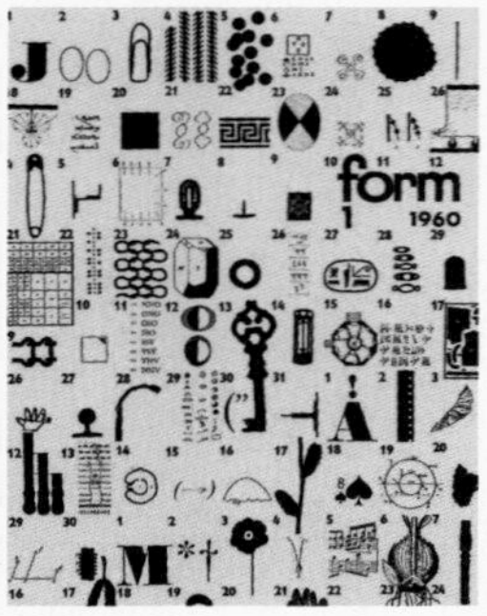

← P.186

← P.186

← P.187

1959–1961

FORM

Magazine Cover

John Melin (1921–1992), Anders Österlin (1926–2011)

Svenska Slöjdföreningen, Sweden

Since it was first published in 1904, *Form* has showcased the applied arts, but in the late 1950s and early '60s John Melin and Anders Österlin produced a particularly adventurous series of graphic covers using typography and graphic symbols. Although working for the large advertising agency Svenska Telegrambryån at the time, Melin and Österlin formed an independent creative partnership, for many years (1955–66) signing their work "M&Ö."

The covers for Issues 1 and 7 of 1959 and Issue 1 of 1960 follow a similar template, consisting of abstract shapes and limited colors that require interpretation on the part of the viewer. For example, the black-and-white cover of 1/1959, entitled "Typografiskt experiment," appears to be an abstract cityscape buzzing with people and cars, but on looking closer it becomes clear that the shapes are formed by typewriter letters and the spaces inside them; the urban character of the design echoes the modern tools for living explored in the magazine's pages. Cover No 7, 1959, in red and black, is made up of circles and squares built into increasingly elaborate structures that act as a metaphor for the creative process of the magazine—an object blossoming out of small beginnings; cover No. 1, 1960 (pictured), uses elements from a calendar for the NK Inredning department store in Stockholm as symbols for each day of the month: a key, paperclip, safety pin, snowflake, seashell, and music notes, thereby placing human designs on a par with those created by nature. Issue No. 2, 1961, differs from the others in its use of multiple colors, which turn out to be magnified cutouts from product packaging arranged to suggest supermarket shelving.

Although dense and busy, these designs reveal the extraordinary variety of modern graphic language and its capacity to communicate meanings for which it may not have been originally intended. Melin and Österlin have been widely recognized for their work and awarded with prizes and exhibitions in Sweden and abroad.

1959

RHEINBRÜCKE

Advertising

Karl Gerstner (1930–2017)

Rheinbrücke, Switzerland

The beginnings of Karl Gerstner's systematic and methodical approach to design are visible in this series of advertisements created early in his career for the Rheinbrücke department store in Basel. Appearing serially in local newspapers, the advertisements were designed to inform customers about construction taking place in the store over a period of seven weeks. The pieces describe in sequence the closing of the store for renovation and the process involved, and attempts to assuage any public concerns provoked.

One of the proponents of the so-called "Swiss school," Gerstner was well-known for his development of strict grids and use of grotesque lettering, as well as for applying to Swiss graphic design the innovative conceptual approach to advertising emerging in the U.S. Formally, the advertisements are a daring study in abstraction, balance, and surprise. Typified by the use of tightly cropped images of the archetypal customer in the bottom third of the page and an illustration in the top two-thirds, they range from typographic solutions to abstracted product shots, and are related and consistent in their simple beauty. Printed in black and white, the advertisements use scale and composition to great effect, in some cases relying on clever visual puns, such as type, to illustrate steam rising from a coffee cup. Their true originality, however, lies in their narrative quality and the engagement of the audience in a prolonged conversation over the course of the advertisements' lifespan. This aspect prefigures Gerstner's future exploration of computational systems and the recent impulse to interpret branding in terms of storytelling—a conceit that has been adopted by modern practitioners, such as Brian Collins.

1959

THINK SMALL

Advertising

Helmut Krone (1925–1996)

Volkswagenwerk GmbH, Germany

Volkswagen's "Think Small" campaign, designed by Helmut Krone of the DD&B studio, marked a new departure in advertising, relying on simplicity, honesty, and wit, and subverting audience expectations rather than selling products through passive imagery and glamour. Equally innovative was the campaign's boldness in attacking one of the ideals of American consumption; in a culture where big always meant better, these were advertisements that made a virtue out of being small and understated.

Although revolutionary in their simplicity, advertisements such as "Think Small" and "Lemon" were also the result of a twisted convention. The template of two-thirds picture, one-third copy had evolved over time, passing through the hands of many designers and art directors. Krone, who claimed to hate advertising and set out to redefine it, stripped out anything that was not part of the core message, distilling it to an essence of precision and clarity. By employing mostly empty space with a very small image, what came to be considered a "humble little car" took on a mythical status. Krone wanted people to stop on his pages, and sometimes went as far as removing the Volkswagen logo, arguing that "Logos say 'I'm an ad. Turn the page.'" He also became famous for his use of full stops in headlines. Although Krone was responsible for the layout of "Think Small," it was Julian Koenig's copywriting that steered the concept in this particular direction. The slogan was taken from the last line of Koenig's copy.

Other headlines in the series included: "It makes your house look bigger," "Live below your means," and "The '51 '52 '53 '54 '55 '56 '57 '58 '59 '60 '61 Volkswagen." Krone's rigorous, uncompromising approach, combined with Koenig's and other DD&B copywriters' deprecating wit, resulted in a new benchmark of visual communication. One of the most important advertising directors of the twentieth century, Krone won numerous awards for his work and is represented in the collections of the Museum of Modern Art in New York and the Smithsonian Institution in Washington D.C.

← P.188

← P.189

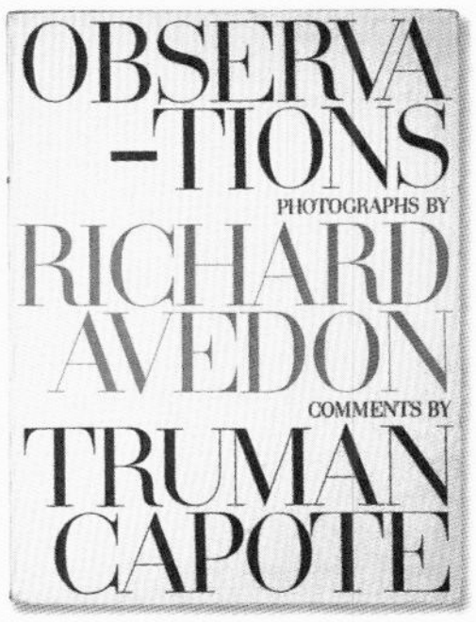

← P.190

1959

WORLD GRAPHIC DESIGN EXHIBITION

Poster

Ikko Tanaka (1930–2002)

World Design Conference Committee, Japan

Like many artists of his generation, in the 1950s the Japanese designer Ikko Tanaka was concerned with how to combine Western and modernist graphic idioms with traditional Japanese culture and aesthetics. An early work, this poster for the World Graphic Design Exhibition, held at the Mitsukoshi department store in Tokyo in 1960, uses the abstract motif of different-sized arrows to convey the idea of multiple relationships contained in the theme of the exhibition. Even though the arrow is a Western graphic device, the repetition of the form and the simple black-and-white palette also recall Japanese writing and calligraphy, thereby adding a twist to a traditional art form. Tanaka is known for his use of powerful colors, but here the minimal scheme creates a sense of cohesion that unifies the diversity of the shapes.

In its simplicity and abstraction, the poster reflects Tanaka's absorption of modern European design principles into his work a few years earlier. After working in textile design and the newspaper industry as a young man in Kyoto and Osaka, where he steeped himself in traditional Japanese values and styles, Tanaka moved to Tokyo in 1957, where he came into contact with Western design theories and practices. Unlike the prewar generation of Japanese designers, who attempted to emulate the West, Tanaka sought to integrate Western influence with Japanese cultural tradition. A highly diverse designer, Tanaka has developed a body of work that resists easy definition, and often uses styles associated with Japanese crafts, such as masks, Kabuki theater, kimono textiles, *ukiyo-e* prints, and calligraphy, which he reinterprets and revitalizes through a rational modernist language. In 1963 Tanaka established his own design studio in Tokyo, subsequently undertaking important commissions for major Japanese clients, such as the logotype and pictograms for the 1964 Tokyo Olympics, and corporate identity projects for the fashion houses Kenzo and Issey Miyake. His work has served as an important example to young designers seeking ways to reconcile their identity and artistic legacy with the commercial imperatives of the modern world.

1959–1961

ALMANAQUE

Magazine Cover

Sebastião Rodrigues (1929–1997)

Grupo de Publicações Periódicas, Portugal

Sebastião Rodrigues was one of the most adventurous yet overlooked graphic talents of twentieth-century Portugal. Although he was prolific across a wide range of printed matter since his apprenticeship at *A Voz* newspaper and Electrolux from age thirteen, it wasn't until 1991 that his work was recognized internationally with an Award of Excellence from the International Council of Graphic Design Associations (ICOGRADA).

Born and raised in Lisbon, Rodrigues based his design practice in his hometown his entire life, as he famously despised travel. His work is identified by its interpretation of Portuguese culture in a style that balances joyful expression with graphic parsimony. Spanning books, posters, graphic identities, and advertising campaigns—notably for the National Information Secretariat (SNI), the propaganda arm of the Portuguese regime (1933–74)—all of his projects transmit the geometric, colorful, and playful mode for which he has become known.

But it is *Almanaque*, a monthly magazine published between 1959 and 1961, that epitomizes his oeuvre. While only eighteen issues were ever produced, they have become shorthand for Rodrigues's design approach. Adopting an abstract and figurative style, his compositions are a masterclass in uniting painting, illustration, photography, and collage through the medium of print. The covers alone speak volumes: a cat silhouette poised on cobbled setts splashed with colored confetti; fleshy watermelons printed out of register. Each translates humor, simplicity, context, and the poetry of Portuguese cultural traditions.

An avid illustrator, Rodrigues drew much of his catalog of Portuguese symbols from regular visits to Lisbon's museums of art and archaeology. Later, despite his travel aversion, he expanded his lexicon in northern Portugal, during a fellowship with the Calouste Gulbenkian Foundation, for which he would later design an entire graphic identity.

Rodrigues was faithful to analog production methods until the end, eschewing computerized processes and instead working by hand. In 1995 he received the medal of Grand Officer of the Order of Merit, a national prize of Portugal, which belatedly acknowledged his lifetime contribution to communicate the spirit of Portuguese identity.

1959

OBSERVATIONS

Book

Alexey Brodovitch (1898–1971),
Richard Avedon (1923–2004)

C. J. Bucher, Switzerland

One of the most important photographic monographs ever published, *Observations* united two central figures in design history on a project that would define their respective careers. Although Alexey Brodovitch was already well known for his work on *Harper's Bazaar*, the book cemented Richard Avedon's reputation as the portraitist of his generation.

Avedon's images began appearing in *Junior Bazaar* in 1945, a year after he enrolled in Brodovitch's legendary Design Laboratory at the New School in New York; shortly afterward, he was made a staff photographer on the main title. For his part, Brodovitch had always taken a keen interest in photography, and published a collection of his own work, *Ballet*, in 1945. In Avedon, however, Brodovitch found the photographer he would never be, and of the three people involved (Truman Capote wrote the text), Avedon arguably wielded the most influence. According to some accounts, Brodovitch pushed Avedon to include his most expressive work and to view the book as a graphic artifact in its own right rather than a catalog. Brodovitch's direction treated the images of actors, musicians, singers, and directors as a cinematic experience that takes the reader through a crisp white landscape punctuated with black-and-white bursts of energy and intensity. The layout has been described as "fiercely anarchic," but in reality it is highly considered, allowing the verve inherent in the images and words to spill forth. The book's modern yet romantic tone is also evident on the cover: the wonderfully large characters, set in Bodoni typeface, cut through the crispness of the white ground, while the slightly awkward breaking of the title hints at a modernist's respect for the grid and the great stone inscriptions of classical Rome. This play of classicism and modernism is further emphasized by the clear, crisp, space-age acetate dust jacket the original edition was wrapped in.

In an era when American graphic design tended toward the ultra-efficiency of Helvetica on the one hand, and early Pop art on the other, Brodovitch created a superbly elegant design that is beholden to neither, and that looks as fresh today as when it was first printed.

← P.191

← P.191

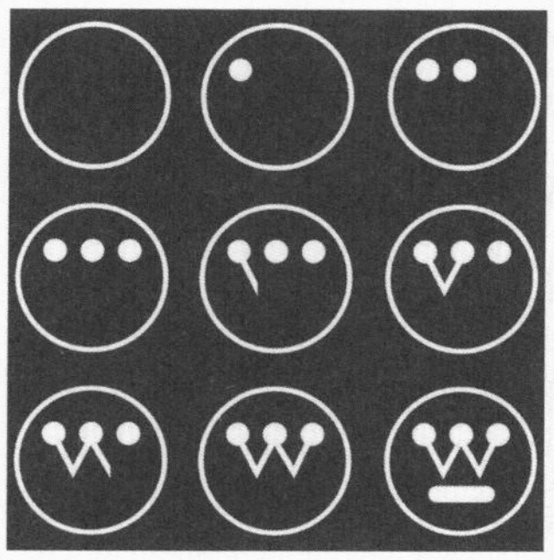

← P.192

1959–1971

TWEN

Magazine / Newspaper

Willy Fleckhaus (1925–1983)

Adolf Theobald and Stephan Wolf, Germany

Twen is one of several titles that marked the reemergence of glossy European magazine design after the austerity of the 1950s. An abbreviation of "twenty," *Twen* was targeted at Germany's burgeoning youth market through an eclectic mixture of subject matter ranging from entertainment to art to politics. Noted for its startling use of photography, *Twen*'s pages often confronted the viewer with extreme blow-ups cropped in unconventional and dramatic ways.

In terms of typography, *Twen* displays a precision more commonly associated with the digital age. Tight letter-spacing, kerning, reverse leading, and often the smallest of margins between photographs and the trim edge of the magazine add to the impression of immediacy and of an assault on the senses. A twelve-column grid accommodates a diverse range of layouts, providing great flexibility in cropping photography. The apparent simplicity of the layouts—often consisting of a handful of elements, of which photography is the most prominent component, belies the intricacy of this supporting grid. Willy Fleckhaus selected and commissioned work from many great photographers, including Will McBride, Art Kane, and Richard Avedon. Photographs are treated with the same clarity as the typography, any extraneous detail being edited out, whereas tight cropping focuses on the object, providing just enough context to make the image meaningful. In many cases, the crop activates background negative space, similar to the way in which the spaces between letters are emphasized by tight kerning. On the cover, the white-on-black lowercase extended masthead is often complemented by the condensed capitals used to announce articles and is also, in some issues, treated as an object with the same material weight as the photographic subject (usually a young, attractive woman), enabling it to be held or obscured by the featured person.

One of the most innovative magazines of the postwar era, *Twen* influenced the designs of *Queen*, the *Sunday Times Magazine* and *Nova*, especially in its exciting high-contrast visual qualities established through major shifts in scale, and through the tension between the white of the page and dense blacks of printed image and text.

1959–1962

TY I JA

Magazine / Newspaper

Roman Cieslewicz (1930–1996)

RSW Prasa, Poland

Roman Cieslewicz's career as art director of the Polish cultural review *Ty i Ja* (*You and I*) began shortly after he had produced his first photo-montage in 1958—an activity he claimed to have undertaken to keep his mind off posters. As the only one of its kind in Poland, this highly popular monthly title allowed Cieslewicz to hone his newly found technique and to lay a strong foundation for personal success at home and abroad.

In direct contrast to the "Swiss school" prevalent at the time, Cieslewicz and other members of the Polish School, such as Jan Lenica and Franciszek Starowiejski, sought to forge a national visual identity built largely around bold, visceral, and experimental imagery. In Cieslewicz's case, this involved linking text to image and experimenting with processes such as enlarged half-tone patterns. His covers for *Ty i Ja*, like his designs for posters such as "Vertigo" (1958), drew from a varied avant-garde palette. While elements of Dada, Surrealism, Constructivism (particularly the Polish group Blok), and the Bauhaus were clearly visible, a cover could just as easily be influenced by Pop art. This approach was carried over to the illustrations inside the magazine, the layout of which exhibited many characteristics of its French cousin *Elle*. Unconventional layouts featured rough yet well-organized typography arranged in narrow, justified columns and juxtaposed with a friendlier, more open brand of fashion photography. Pages such as these illustrated the degree to which Cieslewicz was inspired by Western publications and culture.

When he left Poland—and *Ty i Ja*—for Paris in 1963, Cieslewicz took what he had learned from working on the magazine and went on to influence generations of French designers, particularly the 1970s design collaboration Grapus. Cieslewicz's work for *Ty i Ja* also led *Elle's* art director, Peter Knapp, to commission a series of photomontages, which would ultimately lead Cieslewicz to become the magazine's designer, and then art director. Here, and in the pages of other titles, such as *Vogue* and *Opus International*, Cieslewicz refined the style that began with his first photomontage, while continuing to create designs for Polish cultural organizations and covers for *Ty i Ja*.

1959

WESTINGHOUSE

Logo

Paul Rand (1914–1996)

Westinghouse, U.S.

The Westinghouse "Circle W" symbol is as simple as it is versatile, and demonstrates Paul Rand's unique ability to combine rigor and geometry with humor and humanity.

Founded in 1886, the Westinghouse Electric Corporation, based in Pittsburgh, Pennsylvania, was one of the twentieth century's first truly multinational conglomerates. By the 1950s, its products ranged from lightbulbs and portable radios to jet engines and nuclear power plants, but its trademark—originally created by founder George Westinghouse himself and last updated in 1953 into a circle containing a block "W" underlined by a lozenge-shaped bar bearing its founder's surname—looked decidedly old-fashioned. In 1959 the company appointed Eliot Noyes as consultant director of design, following his success as director of IBM's design program. Noyes hired Rand, with whom he had worked at IBM, to redesign Westinghouse's graphic identity, packaging, and advertising.

Rand adapted Westinghouse's trademark, which still evoked the electric era of the nineteenth century, bringing it into the modern electronic age: the circle, lines, and dots of the logo were designed to suggest interlinked points of a circuit board. On its opening pages, the Westinghouse corporate identity manual featured an animated version of the mark as a sequence of interlinked elements, and went on to illustrate its implementation across myriad applications. This playful yet logical exploration of form highlights Rand's inventiveness, as well as his demand for tight quality control of the corporation's overall visual identity, qualities that have ensured the timeless nature of much of his work. His Westinghouse logo has remained untouched, and contributes to his reputation as one of the most influential and revered of modern designers.

← P.192

← P.193

← P.193

1959

NORTH BY NORTHWEST

Identity

Saul Bass (1920–1996)

Metro-Goldwyn-Mayer, Inc., U.S.

In his title sequence for Alfred Hitchcock's *North by Northwest*, Saul Bass seamlessly integrated the film's credits, opening scene, overarching theme, and general mood. From the very first frame, the audience is drawn into the psychological thriller through Bass's skilful use of stylish motion graphics.

Bass was among a small group of designers who in the late 1940s brought the sensibilities of the New York School, with its less rigid, more pragmatic interpretations of European modernism, to Los Angeles. He opened his own studio there in 1952, and two years later began applying his graphic design talents to the motion picture industry, quickly establishing himself as the master of film-title sequences. Prior to Bass's contributions, opening credits were largely considered a "necessary evil" and treated as an element entirely separate from the picture itself. Bass saw an opportunity to use title sequences to project, often in provocative or humorous ways, the very essence of the film. By applying his approach across all the graphics associated with a film—from letterheads and posters to, in some cases, the shooting of the movie itself—Bass created a unified, comprehensive package.

In his sequence for *North by Northwest* Bass wastes no time establishing the film's mood. First, a series of lines glide across the screen to create an angled grid against which the credits soon appear, each one moving up and down, pausing only long enough to be read—mimicking the motion of the elevator out of which the story's main character will shortly emerge. The grid then dissolves into the steel-and-glass skin of a New York skyscraper reflecting the busy street below. Bass's criss-crossing lines, in addition to their apparent purpose of aligning type, also suggest the tracks of the trains that play an important role in the film and, on a more abstract level, the "intersections" of the main characters.

Although Bass is often recognized for his logo and corporate-identity designs, he created, often in close collaboration with his wife, Elaine, more than fifty title sequences and accompanying advertising campaigns over a period of almost forty years in the film business.

1960

WASSER

Advertising

Siegfried Odermatt (1926–2017)

Neuenburger Versicherungen, Switzerland

Siegfried Odermatt's dynamic and evocative advertisements for the insurance firm Neuenburger Versicherungen demonstrate the power of both image and typography to animate the meaning of a word.

After first working as a photographer for several years, Odermatt turned his attention to design and typography, opening his own design studio in 1950. Producing trademarks, informational graphics, advertising, and packaging for corporate clients, he is considered to have played an important role in the development of the "Swiss school," although his approach did not rigidly adhere to its tenets. Odermatt believed that through careful consideration of concept, space, form, and tone, a one-color typographic solution could be as effective as a multicolor one. His work also tended toward the playful and uninhibited.

Odermatt's predilection for abstraction and playfulness are clearly evident in his project for Neuenburger Versicherungen, for which the strapline translates as "Between you and adversity, put Neuenburger Insurance." Describing the dangers of water, accident, fire, car, glass, liability, and burglary, each image uses abstracted, tightly cropped photography together with expressive, illustrative typography, to reinforce the message of risk, as well as a restricted color palette that identifies the series as a set. The advertisements also anticipate the direction that Odermatt was to take in the future, leading Swiss design away from its rigorous, systematic program.

During the early 1960s Odermatt was joined by Rosmarie Tissi, establishing their Odermatt & Tissi partnership in 1968. The team further loosened the constraints of the "Swiss school," introducing elements of surprise that in some ways presaged the postmodernist work of designers such as Steff Geissbuhler and Wolfgang Weingart.

1960s

MCGRAW-HILL PAPERBACKS

Book Cover

Rudolph de Harak (1924–2002)

McGraw-Hill, U.S.

In the 1960s the graphic designer Rudolph de Harak produced nearly four hundred covers for McGraw-Hill Paperbacks. The challenge of visually representing the fields of philosophy, anthropology, sociology, and psychology inspired an experimental visual style that integrated the principles of Dada, op art, and Abstract Expressionism.

De Harak's influential cover-design opus is widely considered to be one of the earliest examples of purist visual communication in the U.S. Influenced by the "Swiss school," notably the work of the Swiss modernist Max Bill, de Harak created engaging covers that avoided extraneous elements. A rigid compositional system was developed in which the typeface Akzidenz-Grotesk was used for the title and author lines, which appeared in one or two colors aligned at the top left of the book, while a single bold image in the center of the white cover—either high-contrast black-and-white photographs or pure graphics—communicated the theme of the publication. In *A Preface to History* (1955), for example, an image of an old wheel in motion suggests the evolution of mankind and time, while the cover of *Units, Dimensions, and Dimensionless Numbers* (1960) is filled with intersecting brightly colored cubes. Each McGraw-Hill cover is an economical blend of expressive imagery and systematic typography. These qualities would mark the subsequent years of de Harak's career, as would his rejection of overtly symbolic typography and his use of a limited number of typefaces.

De Harak continued to explore color, optical illusion, photography, and type in his other designs, such as the Metropolitan Museum of Art's bold shopping bags and the photographic timeline and information signs of its Egyptian Wing. His ability to simplify complex ideas without sacrificing meaning has provided an important model for later generations of graphic designers.

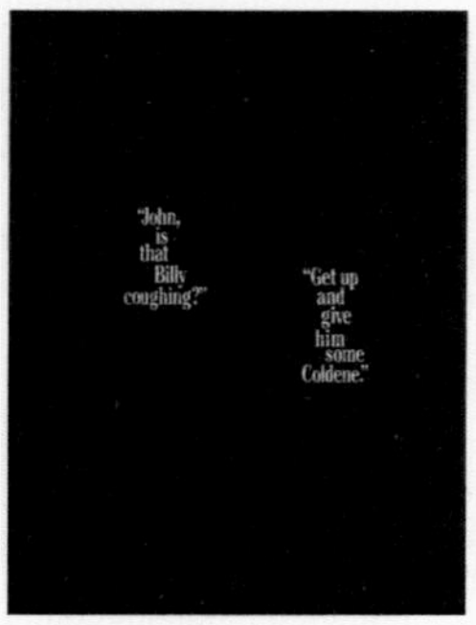
"John, is that Billy coughing?"
"Get up and give him some Coldene."

← P.194

1960

COLDENE

Advertising

Papert Koenig Lois

Coldene, U.S.

When a full-page advertisement for Coldene cold medicine first appeared in *Life* and *Look* magazines, it created a considerable stir within the advertising industry. Lacking nearly all of the elements commonly associated with consumer advertising, most notably an image of the product and a logo, the advertisement instead focused on the very human experience of parents concerned for a sick child.

The unconventional advertisement was the work of Papert Koenig Lois (PKL), a start-up agency formed by Fred Papert, Julian Koenig, and George Lois. Papert recruited Koenig and Lois from Doyle Dane Bernbach (DDB), a highly successful New York agency known for combining powerful visuals and no-nonsense copy. Unlike those employed by the more established firms of the period, DDB's art directors and copywriters worked directly with one another in small teams—an approach that was adopted from the outset at PKL.

Conventional advertisements for over-the-counter medicines emphasized the product's active ingredients and their benefits, often accompanied by vaguely anatomical illustrations. PKL reframed the subject, eliminating the medical connotations entirely and replacing them with everyday dialogue that would resonate with readers. The blacked-out page, in addition to suggesting a darkened bedroom, serves to focus the viewer's attention on the message.

Even though the exact origins of the advertisement have been a point of controversy for almost fifty years—with both Koenig and Lois claiming credit—there is no disputing its impact. Its radical nature quickly attracted the attention of the advertising world, and helped to establish the agency's reputation for doing exciting, provocative work. Over the years, PKL worked with a number of major clients, including Xerox, Peugeot, and Ronson, playing a significant role in the "Creative Revolution" of the 1950s and '60s.

In 1970 the firm's partners went their separate ways, each continuing to use his talent for "selling" in different ways. Papert was instrumental in saving New York's Grand Central Terminal from demolition, Koenig helped to establish Earth Day, and Lois continued his successful career in advertising and graphic design, receiving numerous accolades.

PUNT E MES
APERITIVO
un punto di amaro e mezzo di dolce

← P.195

1960

PUNT E MES

Poster

Armando Testa (1917–1992)

Carpano, Italy

Armando Testa's poster design for Carpano's vermouth Punt e Mes (a Piedmontese expression literally meaning "point and a half") is one of the most unusual images in Italian advertising and graphic design. The campaign coincided with an energetic period for Italy, which, against the background of an economic boom, hosted the Olympics in Rome (1960), saw the release of the film *La Dolce Vita* and witnessed a flourishing of innovation in the visual arts.

The impact of "Punt e Mes" lies in the simplicity of a subtle semantic play that synthesizes word and image, visually translating the dialectical expression "punt e mes" into a universal message. The sphere and half-sphere dominate the white space, enhanced by shadow and the use of red, in a reference to the drink's color. In contrast to Testa's previous representational advertisements for Carpano, this new design does not show the actual product, and in its abstraction it marks the climax of his work on the series.

Testa began his career during the late 1930s, but was interrupted by World War II and had to relaunch it in 1946, with the opening of his advertising agency, Studio Testa, in Turin. In his early work he adopted several styles, elaborating on the influences of Erberto Carboni and Bruno Munari, among others, and combining them with the graphic language of the Bauhaus and late Futurism. During the 1950s he started to develop a more personal visual language defined by a constant search for synthesis and the introduction of an evocative, fantastic element—evident, for instance, in his Pirelli elephant, which had a tire in place of a trunk.

Testa's Surrealism often blurred into a brand of Minimalist art, which was emerging around the time "Punt e Mes" appeared; he thus introduced the new language of Minimalism to the public realm even before it appeared in galleries. What probably made Testa so successful in advertising was his capacity to capture, if not anticipate, the latest innovations in art, merging them with business acumen—an ability illustrated perfectly by "Punt e Mes."

← P.196

1960

CHASE MANHATTAN BANK

Logo

Ivan Chermayeff (1932–2017), Tom Geismar (1931–)

Chase Manhattan Bank, U.S.

A precursor of what has since become one of the largest sectors of the graphic design industry—corporate design—the Chase Manhattan Bank logotype is among the world's most recognizable and enduring trademarks.

First introduced in November 1960, the logo was designed following the 1955 merger of Chase National Bank and the Bank of the Manhattan Company, signaling a significant change in the bank's self-perception and public image. Prior to this, banks were content to be known purely by their name and address. It was David Rockefeller, president of Chase Manhattan in the 1960s, who saw the potential of adopting a trademark and who opened the door to the innovation of Ivan Chermayeff. The era was an exciting time for corporate design in the U.S., when modernist idealism combined with capitalist pragmatism to create a new field of corporate identity. In 1958, Chermayeff and Robert Brownjohn teamed up with Tom Geismar to establish the Brownjohn, Chermayeff & Geismar design agency in the middle of what is commonly described as the graphics revolution. Brownjohn left the company to move to London in 1960. The Chase logo stands out for its cool simplicity, clean, strong lines, and proven timelessness—all intended to present the bank as a symbol of strength. These features reflected the design firm's avoidance of the more dogmatic aspects of 1950s Swiss graphics, characterized by strict adherence to the grid and exclusive use of sans serif typefaces. Instead, the agency followed the approach of the designer Paul Rand, known for his experiments with quirky forms, playful colors, and imaginative ideas, as a means to explore visual boundaries and communicate a client's message.

When first introduced, there were three versions of the Chase logotype, one in brown, blue, green, and black, another in solid blue, and black, and a third design comprised of parallel lines. Variations in the color and typeface have been adopted over the years, but the octagon remains the enduring symbol.

← P.197

1960

CANADIAN NATIONAL RAILWAY

Logo

Allan Fleming (1929–1977) et al.

Canadian National Railway, Canada

Often referred to as the "wet noodle," the now iconic CN logo is usually attributed to the Canadian graphic designer Allan Fleming, although the mark was in fact a product of collaboration. In 1959 Dick Wright, public relations officer of Canadian National Railways (CNR), hired New York industrial designer James Valkus to create a trademark that would position the company as a "customer-friendly, technologically advanced railroad." Valkus convinced CNR that it needed a complete overhaul of its visual image, from locomotive paint schemes and building exteriors to the sugar packets on its passenger trains. Valkus gave the job of designing the trademark to Fleming, who, according to myth, came up with the sinuous CN logo while sitting on a New York-bound airplane, sketching it out on a cocktail napkin.

The true story is more complex. Although Fleming recommended shortening the company's bilingual name to CN from Canadian National/Canadien National, it was Valkus who drew the initial logo sketches. Some used slab-serif letters, in an obvious nod to Herbert Matter's 1956 logo for the New York, New Haven, and Hartford Railroad, whereas others were based on gestural letters that combined the "C" and the "N" into a single mark. Fleming continued the gestural approach, adding an arrow to the "C," but it was Carl Ramirez, one of Valkus's employees, who conceived the more geometric, typographic "CN," when he sketched an elongated sans serif "C" joined to an "N." Fleming refined the proportions of the design, transforming the letters into "a single, bending, flowing line of uniform weight." Valkus, however, felt that the weight was too heavy, and wrote on the sketch, "make it thinner and we've got it."

Fleming was credited with the design of the logo mainly because he was responsible for selling it to both CNR management and the Canadian public, likening it to the Christian cross, the CBS eye, and Paul Rand's IBM logo. The new CN logo, combined with a bold color scheme for all of the company's equipment, buildings, and signage, was an immediate sensation, described by a critic as "one of the most thorough, consistent, and high-profile corporate identity programs in history."

← P.197

1961

THE GRAPHIC ARTIST AND HIS DESIGN PROBLEMS

Book

Josef Müller-Brockmann (1914–1996)

Verlag Arthur Niggli, Switzerland

With *The Graphic Artist and His Design Problems* the Swiss graphic designer and teacher Josef Müller-Brockmann crystallized his design ethos, which was based on the notion of the social responsibility of the designer.

Modern and reductive from the outset, with a distinctive deep orange cover adorned with the title in giant white Akzidenz-Grotesk letters, the volume emphasized the need for a well-rounded training in design based on both technical and artistic considerations, and a more organized approach to design for "publicity." The essay "Sans Serif as the expression of our age" is a classic call for modernist functionalism. Müller-Brockmann also explores copy in advertising and the use of the grid, advocating a more flexible approach than in his later *Grid Systems in Graphic Design* (1981).

These messages are reflected in the book's design—a landscape-format volume in which the layout alternates between pages full of black-and-white images (with a few sections in color), and trilingual texts set out in narrow columns of German, English, and French. The book is extensively illustrated and includes the author's own famous posters for public safety and the Tonhalle-Orchester Zürich; overall, it serves as a catalog of Müller-Brockmann's work as much as an educational design primer. In a more critical vein, the manual also contains theories on "science and communication," a chapter on semiotics, communication, and information theory and their relevance to practice, and proposals for graphic design training with reference to the program that Müller-Brockmann set up at the Zürcher Hochschule der Künst (Zurich School of Applied Arts). A basic exercise that involves organizing and visualizing a series of proportionally related circles is described in detail as an example.

The Graphic Designer and His Design Problems is deceptively slim, but it provides a valuable account of some of the key principles of Swiss design by a central figure of the movement.

← P.198

1961

YVES SAINT LAURENT

Logo

A. M. Cassandre (1901–1968)

Yves Saint Laurent, France

A. M. Cassandre's logo for the Yves Saint Laurent label, with its vertically aligned, interconnecting letters, has provided France's famous fashion house with an elegant and sophisticated identity that evokes the timeless dress style for which it has become known.

The commission from Yves Saint Laurent came at a significant point in Cassandre's life when he had abandoned his successful prewar career as a graphic artist and poster designer to focus on his original vocation of painting and theater design. In 1958, however, Olivetti had commissioned him to design several typefaces for their typewriters. When one of these was rejected, Cassandre developed a much freer letter style, possibly influenced by his painting, which contrasted with the more geometrical character of his earlier typographic work. Inspired by the proportions of roman capitals, the design went on to be used for the Yves Saint Laurent logo; the letters' bold sloping lines and sharp edges, offset by sumptuous curves, manage to suggest both the sweep of drapery and the clarity of characters cut in stone.

In 1961 Saint Laurent had recently lost his job as head designer of Dior and was hoping to make a fresh start under his own name. An instant classic, the trademark he commissioned has remained unchanged for almost half a century, and has helped the company grow into one of the world's most recognizable brands. It would be the last logo Cassandre designed before his suicide in 1968.

← P.198

1961–1964

SHOW

Magazine / Newspaper

Henry Wolf (1925–2005), Sam Antupit (1932–2003)

Hartford Publications, U.S.

For a short period of time, one extraordinary magazine, *Show*, captured the mystique of the Kennedy era. With its strikingly beautiful covers, bold use of portraiture, well-tempered typography, uncluttered layouts, and smart visual editing, it reflected the prevalent optimistic mood in the U.S. and Western Europe, and a belief in the primacy of talent and intelligence.

A progressive arts monthly, *Show* was published by George Huntington Hartford II, owner and developer of the Bahamas' Paradise Island and one of the richest men of the time. Between 1961 and 1964, under the art direction of Austrian-born Henry Wolf, assisted by the talented designer Sam Antupit, the magazine was as sophisticated and witty as what came to be known as "the spirit of Camelot." A large-format periodical (10¼ × 13 inches [26 × 33 cm]), it showcased some of the most celebrated artists and celebrities of the Kennedy era, an eclectic list that included Leonard Bernstein, Sophia Loren, Henry Moore, Hubert de Givenchy, Rudolf Nureyev, and Marguerite Duras, photographed by the likes of Irving Penn, Diane Arbus, and Duane Michals. Also featured were Wolf's favorite serif typefaces—Didot, Bodoni, Garamond, Baskerville, and Clarendon—which he combined with modernist flair on a clean, simple grid.

Show's covers demonstrated Wolf's brilliant capacity for what he called "visual thinking." Borrowing from the vocabulary of twentieth-century graphic artists ranging from Herbert Bayer to Andy Warhol, or inspired by the works of painters such as René Magritte and Barnett Newman, he created covers that referenced these universal cultural icons, sometimes even beating the artists at their own game. For the April 1963 cover, for instance, he devised a Warhol hybrid, from which Warhol himself created a pastiche. Inspired by the 1962 *Marilyn Diptych*, Wolf made an assemblage of the U.S. flag from portraits of JFK, Jackie, and Caroline, as the perfect accompaniment to a cover story by Alistair Cooke entitled "Too Many Kennedys?" After Kennedy's assassination, Warhol reused the same image of the former First Lady for some of his famous *Jackie* silkscreens. Wolf eventually moved on, leaving Antupit to pursue a career in advertising.

← P.199

1961

HELVETICA

Typeface

Edouard Hoffmann (1892–1980), Max Miedinger (1910–1980)

Haas Type Foundry, Switzerland

The typeface we know as Helvetica is largely credited to Edouard Hoffmann and Max Miedinger, who were employed by the Haas Type Foundry in Münchenstein, Switzerland. Together, they worked on a font originally known as Neue Haas Grotesk, which addressed the problems of the Akzidenz-Grotesk typeface.

Neue Haas earned the name Helvetica (derived from Helvetia, the Latin name for Switzerland) during its production at the D. Stempel AG type foundry in 1961. This grotesque sans serif, which falls under the Lineal domain in the Vox-ATypI classification, was used religiously by those who followed the tenets of the "Swiss school." During the 1960s and '70s, Helvetica became the most specified typeface as a result of its clean appearance and various styles, but lacked unity because so many different typographers designed variants.

The tall x-height popularized by Univers and Helvetica would become models for other type foundries, such as the International Typeface Corporation, which developed almost one hundred typefaces during its first ten years. In 1983 Linotype introduced a cohesive Neue Helvetica in a system comparable to Univers, with its numerical identification and varying weight, applied to extended, condensed, and oblique versions. Over time, the typeface has starred in thousands of corporate identities and communication systems, including the Unigrid system developed by Vignelli Associates in 1977 for the United States Park Service. Helvetica became even more pervasive during the computer revolution, owing to its inclusion in the Apple Macintosh operating system in 1984. Indistinguishable to some users, but frequently adopted by default in word processors, email programs, and design software, Helvetica is avoided by many, possibly due to its corporate associations and conventional appearance.

Helvetica is often confused with Arial, but the feature-length film about the face, produced and directed by Gary Hustwit in 2007, separated it from the pack and elevated it to stardom. The general public, however, still has difficulty appreciating such eccentricities as its oval counter-forms and square dots over the "i" and "j."

← P.199

1962

MCDONALD'S

Logo

Jim Schindler (n.d.)

McDonald's, U.S.

One of the most recognizable and iconic designs in the world, the McDonald's logo was more the product of serendipity and opportunism than deliberate design.

The first McDonald's restaurant opened in May 1940 in San Bernardino, California, and catered to drive-in customers. In 1948 brothers Richard and Maurice McDonald ditched the carhops, reduced the offerings to take-out food, instituted an assembly-line process called the Speedee Service System, and delivered the world's first fast-food burgers. Some years later, in 1953, Richard McDonald, with the help of sign-maker George Dexter, designed a pair of golden arches as an eye-catching architectural flourish for a second McDonald's restaurant in Phoenix, Arizona, that is still in business.

In 1961 McDonald's, which by now had become a small franchise, was bought out by Ray Kroc, an entrepreneur from Oak Park, Illinois. In the 1960s the company decided to modernize the logo, which until then had been the Speedee chef, and to remove the arches from the buildings designed by Richard McDonald, but was advised against this action by design consultant and psychologist Louis Cheskin. Instead, Fred Turner, a McDonald's employee and later CEO, sketched a "V" for the new logo, which was subsequently altered by James Schindler, head of engineering and design, to an "M," consisting of two golden arches pierced by the slash of the building's roofline. In 1968 the slash was eliminated and the McDonald's name was added. The company then tore down the restaurants designed by Richard McDonald and replaced them with red-brick buildings with mansard roofs.

By 1968 McDonald's operated one thousand restaurants, a figure that by 2008 had reached more than thirty thousand worldwide. McDonald's spends more money on advertising and marketing than any other company, and has now replaced Coca-Cola as the world's most famous brand. Signifying more than fast food, the McDonald's logo has come to symbolize global corporate culture itself.

← P.200

← P.201

← P.201

1962

MODERNA MUSEET

Poster

John Melin (1921–1992), Anders Österlin (1926–2011)

Moderna Museet, Sweden

John Melin and Anders Österlin's poster promoting Stockholm's Moderna Museet belongs to what is now regarded as a legendary era in the development of the contemporary art museum. The design's clean-cut "M" and grid structure act as a cipher for both the museum and the exhibition, and illustrate the postwar fascination with the modern.

Melin and Österlin both worked at the advertising agency Svenska Telegrambyrån in Malmö, where Melin was creative director and Österlin was a freelance illustrator. The two formed a close collaboration that lasted for more than forty years (informally referred to as a pairing of "anden" and "handen"—the spirit and the hand) and resulted in groundbreaking work that attracted new customers and accounts. Pontus Hultén, director of Moderna Museet and friend of Melin, offered a working climate free from the demands of marketing, and collaborated conceptually with the design team.

This poster conducts a playful visual experiment with the sans serif initial "M" of the museum's name, which appears to dodge in and out of view across a grid framework made up of nine squares. In each square the full "M" is never quite revealed, suggesting a wry commentary on the exhibition the poster advertised, which was one of a series showing a selection of the modern works held by the gallery. Just as all the works could not be seen at once, so the public face of the museum is incomplete, while the fragmented design as a whole might also gesture toward the selective and varied aesthetic of modern art. The poster also offers an inventive take on the graphic structures canonized more than a decade earlier in Le Corbusier's *Le Modulor*. Essentially, however, the poster depicts the museum as a playful and diverse institution whose image is constantly changing.

Melin and Österlin's partnership with Hultén proved a highly fertile one for Moderna Museet, significantly raising the gallery's international reputation. The designers went on to produce more radical work for Hultén, such as their "growing" poster, in which the museum's name was sown with seeds and became gradually obscured by plants.

1962–1972

ESQUIRE

Magazine Cover

George Lois (1931–2022)

Esquire, U.S.

In June 1962 Harold Hayes, editor of *Esquire* magazine, called George Lois, then a high-profile advertising creative director, to ask for advice about covers. Hayes was producing stellar editorial content, but circulation was stagnant and the magazine needed a financial boost. Lois agreed to art-direct *Esquire*'s October cover, persuading Hayes to run a shot of a sprawled-out Floyd Patterson look-alike in an empty boxing ring. The issue came out a few days before Patterson's fight against Sonny Liston, which most experts had predicted Patterson would win. Instead, Liston (and *Esquire*) won: the prescient cover was a huge hit on the newsstand, and Lois went on to art-direct every subsequent *Esquire* cover for the next ten years, until Hayes left in 1972. Lois credits the success and freedom that he had at *Esquire* to the trust and respect between him and Hayes.

Lois's covers were about "the big idea," using images that were simple and direct, concise, and crisply defined. But they were also hard-hitting, controversial, and memorable—instant classics that remain an essential reference for magazine art directors and editors. Collectively, they represent an era when magazines mattered most, when the power of mass-circulation publications forced readers to confront racism, sexism, and the Vietnam War. The timeline of Lois's *Esquire* covers coincides with one of America's most turbulent periods.

Not all the covers were serious. There was Andy Warhol "drowning" in a giant can of Campbell's soup, and Richard Nixon ("Tricky Dick") having lipstick applied in a makeup artist's chair (a not-so-veiled reference to his visible sweating during a televised presidential debate). But Lois took a stance on racial and social injustice, and many of his covers were deliberately provocative: he posed Muhammad Ali as the martyred Saint Sebastian, put a Santa hat on a glowering Liston for a "Christmassy" cover, and combined a grinning Lieutenant William Calley (who ordered the My Lai massacre) with pictures of four Vietnamese children. The covers typically had few words, using the images to tell the story. The October 1968 cover had no text at all, just three figures standing amid receding gravestones: John F. Kennedy, Robert Kennedy, and Martin Luther King, Jr., all assassinated within a few short years of each other.

1962

PIRELLI SLIPPERS

Advertising

Fletcher/Forbes/Gill

Pirelli, Italy

This witty advertisement for Pirelli slippers, with its inspired use of site, is typical of the work produced in the 1960s by Fletcher/Forbes/Gill (Alan Fletcher, Colin Forbes, and Bob Gill), forerunner of the Pentagram design studio. Inventive designs of this kind ushered in a new mood of irreverence and fun that helped to transform the austerity of postwar Britain.

The most striking feature of the design is its relationship between word and image, in which words are given material substance and treated as physical objects for figures to sit on, and photography is allowed to partially obscure and interrupt the text. What makes it particularly unusual, however, is the poster's exploitation of the side of a double-decker bus, a traditional location for conventional advertising. By contrast, this poster recruits visual elements beyond the poster's boundaries to make a single visual statement so that the entire upper story of the bus and its passengers contribute unwittingly to the advertising message, providing rich opportunities for humor as travelers become paired with incongruous sets of legs. At the time, such inventiveness was seen as a radical and welcome departure from the norm.

Fletcher/Forbes/Gill found an important client in Pirelli, particularly in the practice's early years, an association that resulted from the company's connection with Alan Fletcher. After graduating from Yale University School of Architecture and Design, Fletcher traveled to various countries and cities (with his Italian wife, Paola), including Milan, where he worked briefly at the Pirelli design studio. "Pirelli Slippers" follows his earlier work for Pirelli, such as a 1961 poster advertisement for tires that displays a similar playfulness with typography.

A more recent juxtaposition of type and image, similar in certain ways to Fletcher's "Pirelli Slippers," can be seen in Alexander Isley's 1987 cover for *Spy* magazine, where the typographic structure on which Donald Trump sits is shown to collapse and shatter into its constituent elements.

← P.202

← P.202

← P.203

1962

EROS

Magazine / Newspaper

Herb Lubalin (1918–1981)

Ralph Ginzburg, U.S.

Ralph Ginzburg has the dubious honor of being the first American publisher to be sentenced to a federal prison term for producing and distributing a magazine judged to have abrogated the moral values of society. However, *Eros*, a subscription-only quarterly that ran for just four issues, was neither a tawdry porn mag nor a faux-artistic nudist journal but one of the most beautifully designed magazines produced at the time. Herb Lubalin, the designer, infused *Eros*'s pages with exquisite typography, and his sensual letterforms and type-image compositions were as enticing as the magazine's contents.

Unlike *Playboy* and other magazines of the period aimed at men, *Eros* did not directly exploit or objectify women; there were no playmates, pinups or gatefolds, and no gratuitous nudity. Instead, sex and eroticism were addressed as integral facts of life undivorced from love and without pandering to voyeuristic appetites. The magazine, however, did not take the name Eros, the god of love, in vain, and in its pages the whole spectrum of erotic behavior was explored—from passion to humor, both past and present. *Eros* was also the first national magazine to feature intimacy between a Black man and a white woman, and the first to publish photographs by Bert Stern of America's greatest sex goddess, Marilyn Monroe.

In 1963 Ginzburg was charged with violating federal obscenity laws and sentenced to five years in prison (serving eight months), although this did not stop him and Lubalin from continuing to collaborate on controversial publications, such as *Fact:* and *Avant Garde* in the years following *Eros*'s demise. Lubalin used *Eros* as a hothouse for his unique blend of modern and eclectic typography, wedding expressive letter compositions, photography, and illustration into a seamless whole. Although the courts viewed *Eros* as a scourge, even today it remains one of the most elegant magazines ever created.

1963

PROGRAMME ENTWERFEN

Book

Karl Gerstner (1930–2017)

Verlag Arthur Niggli, Switzerland

Programme Entwerfen (*Designing Programmes*) is possibly Karl Gerstner's most significant achievement, marking the culmination of the design professional's transition from individual freelance artist to member of a studio whose role was defined by collective activity, rationality, logic, and systems.

First published in German in 1963 and then in English in 1964, *Programme Entwerfen* is a collection of essays that analyze typography, imagery, and method in terms of morphology, logic, mathematical grids, photography, literature, and music. Gerstner's slogan, "Instead of solutions for problems, programs for solutions," is a possible rejoinder to Josef Müller-Brockmann's *The Graphic Artist and His Design Problems* (1961). The essay "The Old Berthold Sans Serif on a New Basis" details Gerstner's attempt to turn the hodgepodge of types grouped together as Berthold Akzidenz-Grotesk into a consistent, harmonious, and logical family that would surpass Adrian Frutiger's recently designed Univers. "Integral Typography" describes an approach that strives for a new unity of language and type beyond the dichotomies—sans serif versus roman, symmetrical versus asymmetrical layout, flush-left and ragged-right versus justified text—created by the 1920s New Typography. "Making Pictures Today?" and "Structure and Movement" concern the origins and extension of Concrete painting, a particularly Swiss variety of Constructivist art. As well as describing the problem as part of the solution, *Designing Programmes* promoted the idea that the interval is an essential part of a program; that there are no absolute solutions because there are limitless possibilities; and that a program is an open-ended system. Gerstner's concept liberated designers from thinking based on typeface, image, and page, and allowed them to see their work as part of a continuum operating together with literature, music, painting, architecture, and urban planning.

In *Programme Entwerfen* Gerstner put into practice his principles of integral typography and the grid. More importantly, the book's many iterations have since incorporated extra material and changes, making the publication itself an excellent example of Gerstner's concept of the open-ended program.

1963

WILHELM TELL

Poster

Armin Hofmann (1920–2020)

Basler Freilichtspiele, Switzerland

This poster exemplifies Armin Hofmann's, and to some degree the "Swiss school's," fascination with the abstract visual qualities of graphic design. It advertises an open-air performance of *William Tell*, without foregrounding a particular set of performers, a venue, or a period in history, but with emphasis on one word: "TELL." What for a moment appears to be three abstract black shapes resolves into an apple as we identify the small, dislocated black shape at the top of the poster as an apple stalk. The typographic treatment of "TELL" utilizes similar compositional strategies as it oscillates between two virtual interpretations. In one the letters trace the path of a crossbow bolt or arrow as it travels into the poster toward the apple; in the other it forms the flat, triangular shape of an arrowhead that cuts across it.

In his book *Graphic Design Manual: Principles and Practice* (1965), Hofmann describes the synchronization of word and image as a confrontation between very different kinds of things. This confrontation is elegantly expressed in "Wilhelm Tell," where Hofmann contrasts the crisp, mechanical qualities of the text with the hazy image target. The use of silhouettes, the balancing of white and black soft shapes, and the use of whole tone are all characteristic of his work. The result is a piece of visual communication that fulfills all the practical demands of a poster—communicating in an instant, across distances with elegance and economy of means.

Hofmann continued to be influential as a practicing designer, and through his work and writings as an educator. The simplicity of his poster would seem perfectly at home on any design site today, yet it captures much of the spirit of mid-century modernism.

← P.204

1963

KLM

Logo

F. H. K. Henrion (1914–1990)

KLM Royal Dutch Airlines, the Netherlands

KLM's clean, simple logo with its abstract crown hovering over a bold sans serif letterhead epitomized the strong, modernist style of corporate design for which F. H. K. Henrion became known. With its simplicity and readability, the logo pays homage to the so-called "Swiss school" pioneered in Switzerland after World War II.

An influential German designer, Henrion had already created KLM's former postwar logo in 1948, nicknamed the "stripes and dots," which showed the company's initials in stark italic capitals inscribed on a circle, which, in turn, was superimposed over a rectangle filled with diagonal black-and-white stripes. Essentially a transitional trademark, Henrion's design also contained the company's older "winged" sign of the 1920s. Toward the end of the 1950s, however, the influence of the "Swiss school" started to gain momentum, with grid-based designs and sans serif faces, such as Helvetica and Univers, recognized as ideal vehicles for corporate communication. Henrion had emigrated to Britain in 1939, where he established his reputation as a poster designer during the war years for Britain's Ministry of Information and the United States Office of War. In 1951 he founded Henrion Design Associates to distance his profession from the image of freelance practice, at the same time developing a rational and systematic design approach where all elements of a program shared similar characteristics and could be produced by a team. In the early 1960s Henrion worked with the mathematician Alan Parkin to apply these principles to the identity program of KLM, a company undergoing rapid growth. The airline's shiny new aircraft were painted in a fresh sky blue with dark blue stripes and accents that were carried through to the interiors and staff uniforms, while the tail fins were emblazoned with Henrion's new logo: a plain company signature in black and white surmounted by a crown made up of a horizontal bar, four dots, and a cross.

The fact that KLM chose a British design studio to undertake its corporate identity was cause for concern among Dutch designers, leading Wim Crouwel to establish Total Design, Holland's first multidisciplinary studio, in 1963.

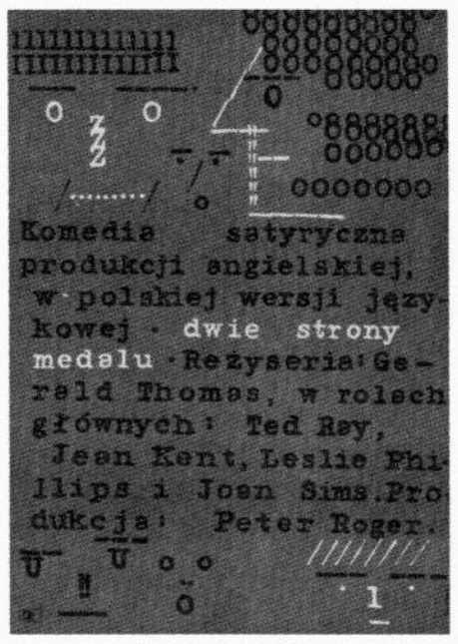

← P.204

1963

DWIE STRONY MEDALU

Poster

Waldemar Swierzy (1931–2013)

Zespół Filmowy Kamera, Poland

With its crude typewritten text, Waldemar Swierzy's stippled aquamarine poster advertising the Polish television series *Dwie Strony Medalu* (*Two Sides of the Coin*) has an improvised quality that suggests a jaunty, lighthearted look at life. Using an aesthetic reminiscent of binary code, punctuation marks, letters, and zeros surround the names of cast and crew members, suggesting human faces that seem variously puzzled, blank, or surprised.

One of the most prolific poster designers of the twentieth century and an important member of the Polish Poster School, Swierzy often brings a painterly quality to his work by breaking forms into brightly colored fragments and brushstrokes. He tends to eschew metaphor and subterfuge, focusing instead on textural and visual effects that express the character of the subject. In addition to a body of two thousand posters, Swierzy has created book covers, illustrations, and record sleeves that have been widely exhibited and won many prizes. He also paints commissioned portraits, particularly of musicians, and pastiches of icons and Renaissance portraits, often substituting the faces of his wife and daughter for those in the original paintings. Although most of his graphic and illustrative work has been for specific cultural events, some of his poster images, such as those of the Beatles and Jimi Hendrix, have become part of the cultural fabric of our times. In general, however, Swierzy's work is highly diverse, and this is one of only a few posters he produced in this typewritten style.

← P.205

1964

WOZZECK

Poster

Jan Lenica (1928–2001)

Warsaw Opera, Poland

Jan Lenica's poster for a revival of the opera *Wozzeck*, which won the Grand Prix at the Poster Biennale in Warsaw in 1966, epitomizes his highly Expressionistic style. The opera was originally composed by the Austrian composer Alban Berg between 1914 and 1922. Drenched in an intense and lurid red, rhythmic concentric lines reverberate like waves around a screaming head and encircle a wide-open mouth, in an evocation of the anguish of the opera's principal character. It was this aggressive imagery that built Lenica's reputation and led him to be identified with the "angry young men" of the 1960s.

An artist, filmmaker, and art critic who received no formal training in graphic art (having studied music and architecture), Lenica was responsible for creating (alongside others) Poland's famed postwar Polish Poster School, and for coining its name in the Swiss journal *Graphis*. In early caricatures, posters, or animated films, Lenica's work depicts a grim reality, although his deliberate naivete and crudeness softens themes of fear and demoralization. "Wozzeck" dates toward the end of a fifteen-year period during which Lenica developed a distinct artistic language for theater posters, producing more than two hundred designs that use flowing wavy lines and simplified two-dimensional forms, executed in gouache, watercolor, and tempera. Lenica excelled at combining techniques across the various genres of his artistic practice.

During the 1950s and '60s, advertisements by the Polish Poster School for cultural events dominated Poland's cityscapes and brought artistic ideas to wide audiences. Unlike Western counterparts, the posters rarely used photographs of movie stars and were more likely to draw on a wide range of graphic interpretations and styles. Equally important, the work of Lenica and his fellow artists became a vehicle for cultural expression and pride, following Poland's losses in the war and the subsequent rise of the Communist government. The posters were widely admired outside Poland, appearing in magazines and exhibition spaces in the West.

← P.206

← P.207

← P.207

1964

LA CANTATRICE CHAUVE, BY EUGÈNE IONESCO

Book

Robert Massin (1925–2020)

Editions Gallimard, France

Robert Massin's legendary design of Eugène Ionesco's *La Cantatrice Chauve* (*The Bald Soprano* [America] and *The Bald Prima Donna* [UK]) transformed this somewhat absurd comedy into a living, breathing, albeit printed, performance through frenetic typography.

Ionesco's play, first performed in 1950, examined context, interpretation, and semantics through the lives of two married couples who interact with maids, fire chiefs, and public figures. Their argumentative confrontations set the stage for a playful romp, where logic, philosophy, and modern-day communication get turned upside down. Massin adored Ionesco's play, and reportedly saw it more than twenty times until he decided to make his own surrealistic attempt at directing the characters, setting, dialogue, and pacing. Could the printed page do a better job of delivering Ionesco's script in all its chaotic glory?

Massin's design took Ionesco's atypical dialogue and made it perform in print the way in which professional actors would play the work on stage. Part comic book, part stage direction, Massin's graphically theatrical experiment used high-contrast, photographic illustrations by Henry Cohen to document the characters, and then matched each one with a specific typeface, bringing the dialogue to life with each characterization. The characters become caught up in a battle between hopeless situations, meaningless wordplay, and ongoing cliché.

Completed in 1964, the book arrived in readers' hands three years before Fiore and McLuhan's *The Medium Is the Massage*, and twenty years before the advent of digital design, which would have made Massin's physical labor of love a more immediate exercise. The typographic language that Massin created became an underground sensation, and many designers began to mimic its experimental style, which echoed that of Dada and Futurism. Today, designers continue to play with typography, but few credit Massin as the first to bring the theater of the absurd to life through typographic form.

1964

WOOLMARK

Logo

Franco Grignani (1908–1999)

International Wool Secretariat and Australian Wool Board, Australia

The result of a competition for a symbol that would demonstrate what an Australian publication, the *Weekly Times*, called "wool's inherent quality and superiority," the Woolmark logo continues to be one of the most recognized in the world. The mark was selected from eighty-six entries by the Australian Wool Board and the International Wool Secretariat to advertise all-wool products, and by 1997 more than AU $1 billion had been spent on its promotion.

Working in an Italian advertising agency in Milan at the time of the competition, Franco Grignani (whose entry was submitted under the pseudonym Franceso Saroglia) took inspiration from the unnaturally sharp angles that he saw reflected in glass when wool yarn touched its surface. The design also makes reference to op art—still nascent in 1964—although unlike op art's mind-bending patterns, the symbol was intended to express meaning rather than induce psychedelic effect. In his classic text *Visual Thinking: A Grammar of Form*, Rudolf Arnheim describes the Woolmark as using avant-garde aesthetics to counteract the reputation of stodgy tweeds, focusing instead on wool's properties as a soft and supple material, in a visually tangible and concentrated form.

In 1999 a second mark, the Woolmark Blend logo, was developed from Saroglia's design, to promote fabrics containing 30–50 per cent new wool. Thirty-five years after its launch, Saroglia's symbol was still seen as an undeniable mark of quality, partly due to its reference to modern art, which lent it a note of sophistication. At the same time, subsequent manifestations, such as the Woolmark Blend trademark, have demonstrated its ability to evolve with the times and adapt to new purposes.

1964

CAMPARI

Poster

Bruno Munari (1907–1998)

Campari, Italy

When the Italian brand Campari asked Bruno Munari to design an advertisement in 1960 for display in Milan's newly opened metro system, he came up with a poster that would greet commuters with its lively invention.

Composing a collage of Campari logos taken from previous advertisements, Munari designed a poster in various versions that could be seen from a speeding train and contemplated for longer periods by waiting travelers. However, Munari did not show the product itself, basing his design solely on what was most recognizable—the brand's name and the use of red that refers to the aperitif's distinctive color. His solution, a combination of synthesis and wit, is an approach more likely to be found in the advertising of today than in the more descriptive style of the 1960s. The collage technique in particular is very unusual for consumer advertising of the time, being closer to the languages of early avant-garde movements, such as Futurism, the second generation of which Munari was involved with from the late 1920s.

Although Munari began his career as an artist, he became one of the most "complete" designers of the last century, constantly concerned with human progress and the improvement of our surroundings. His output spanned literature, poetry, and innovations in learning, as well as the visual arts in a broader sense. All of his interventions were based on a meticulous methodology, combining rigor and imagination with the desire to observe the world. Munari's approach to design was both open and analytical, illustrating a willingness to incorporate the error as an integral part of the process. If the reading of a static image from a moving train produces a new image, Munari asks, "Can we design that image?"

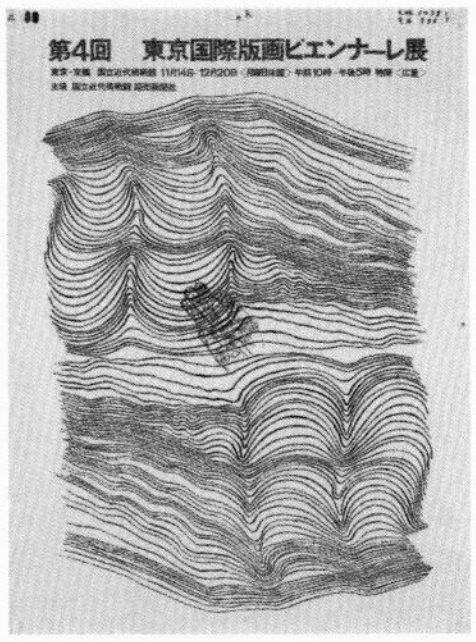

← P.208

← P.209

← P.210

1964

4TH INTERNATIONAL BIENNIAL EXHIBITION OF PRINTS IN TOKYO

Poster

Kiyoshi Awazu (1929–2009)

National Museum of Modern Art, Tokyo, Japan

Since the 1950s, Kiyoshi Awazu has worked with lines as a major graphic motif, using them as a method of creating shape and drawing attention to the process of printing. In this poster promoting an important print exhibition in Tokyo, which included a special exhibit of the work of the nineteenth-century *ukiyo*-e artist Hiroshige, best known for his landscapes, the background lines evoke both a topographical landscape drawing and the texture of wood grain. The hand motif was first used in 1959 in a poster called "Jigao" (True Selves), and is comprised of the imprints of Japanese family seals, which stand in for manual signatures. This combination of graphic elements is designed to highlight the conflict between the repetition involved in the printing process and the individualism of an original artwork, particularly the differences between printed copies.

One of the pioneers of graphic design in Japan during its formative postwar period, Awazu used his practice to explore images and motifs that interested him, often adapting these features to the needs of clients. Under the influence of the American Socialist Realist painter, photographer, and printmaker Ben Shahn in the 1950s, he began producing line drawings. In the 1960s and '70s, Awazu expressed this interest in psychedelic color, using lines to imply vast undulating landscapes or details such as a womb or a face, as well as waves of water or sand in architectural and sculptural works.

This poster, one of many pieces that explored the line/palm/fingerprint/seal theme in Awazu's personal quest, makes an important distinction between the client-driven nature of Western graphic design and the more indirect, designer-led tradition of Japanese graphic art. The image also marks the shift in his work from figurative to abstract representation, and combines his interest in the history of printing with what he calls "the hardness of lines." For Awazu, a hard line is like a sharply focused photograph and must tell the truth. This is useful even when revealing those things seen in the mind's eye but that have no physical reality.

1964–1966

GRAFISK REVY

Magazine Cover

Helmut Schmid (1942–2018)

Grafisk Revy, Sweden

Helmut Schmid's early 1960s covers for *Grafisk Revy*, a Swedish print trade magazine, demonstrate the eloquent power of abstract, minimalist typography, and the effects that can be achieved through experimentation with modest printing technology.

Schmid describes the thinking behind the covers as "applications of elementary ... exercises, using the name of the magazine." The covers divide into two types: black on white and white on black. The themes of the former type are the four dimensions of "dot," or dimensionless "line, plane, space, and movement," whereas the latter type explores "horizontal, vertical, and diagonal." Rather than depending upon the then-emerging technology of photo-typesetting or pasted-up artwork from typeset proofs, the dynamism of the repeats and overlays was produced on a modest, hand-operated proofing-press using traditional metal type. Each time a pull from the press was taken, the type block was moved and the same sheet of paper reprinted, with the curved "movement" cover going through forty-three times. The result was a single image for each cover, used as a one-off original to be reproduced, printed, and then bound as the cover of the magazine. Achieving white on black, however, is very difficult using letterpress, so Schmid produced black on white originals like the others, but reversed the film for the final printing blocks at the prepress stage.

Using only basic resources, with the same wording and type limited to a single size, color, and font (sans serifs such as Univers and Akzidenz-Grotesk being among his favorites), Schmid therefore achieved his effects by experimenting with the basic characteristics of "Swiss school" typography. Seeing—and even feeling—the build-up of ink as one image overprints another, and the constant repeats of the title, endows the letterpress process with a compelling magic. The covers work as well close up, where the detail is absorbing, as from various distances at which different patterns and densities emerge. The randomness of the compositions presaged the grunge typography of David Carson's *Ray Gun* (1992–2000) by almost thirty years.

1964

1964 TOKYO OLYMPICS

Identity

Yusaku Kamekura (1915–1997), Masaru Katsumi (1909–1983)

Japanese Olympic Committee, Japan

When Tokyo became host to the XVIII Olympiad in 1964, it marked a series of firsts: the first Olympics hosted by a non-Western nation, the first use of computers to record statistics, and the first comprehensive identity program, which set a standard for all subsequent Games.

As art director and graphic designer, respectively, Masaru Katsumi and Yusaku Kamekura were concerned with both the social importance of the graphic program and with creating a standardized signage system. Deciding that simple pictographs would be the most effective means of communicating information to a global audience, they created twenty comprehensive multisport symbols and thirty-nine general information pictograms, which were drawn using a grid on a square field. Each geometrically stylized pictogram accentuated the bodily movement of the athletes and was designed to enable instant identification by a multilingual audience. This system has since become a template for international events and universal visual design systems, influencing Lance Wyman for the 1968 Mexico City Olympics and Otl Aicher for the 1972 Munich Olympics.

With the assistance of the photographers Osamu Hayasaki and Jo Murakoshi, Kamekura also designed the four Olympic Games posters, which are unified by the Games' emblem. Three of the posters included carefully orchestrated photographs, with the athletes' movements frozen in time. Their unique perspective and dramatic lighting served to reinforce the advertising campaign and symbolize the competitive spirit of the Olympics. With its three basic elements—the red "rising sun" of the Japanese flag, the Olympic rings, and the words "Tokyo 1964" set in gold Helvetica type—the logo is one of Kamekura's most iconic works, and evokes the subtle and precise use of line and space seen in traditional Japanese art.

Simultaneously reflecting aspects of European modernism (the Bauhaus, Constructivism, and the "Swiss school") and the grace and beauty of traditional Japanese art, Kamekura's work for the Tokyo Olympics exerted a significant influence on subsequent Olympic identity systems, as well as on contemporary Japanese graphic design.

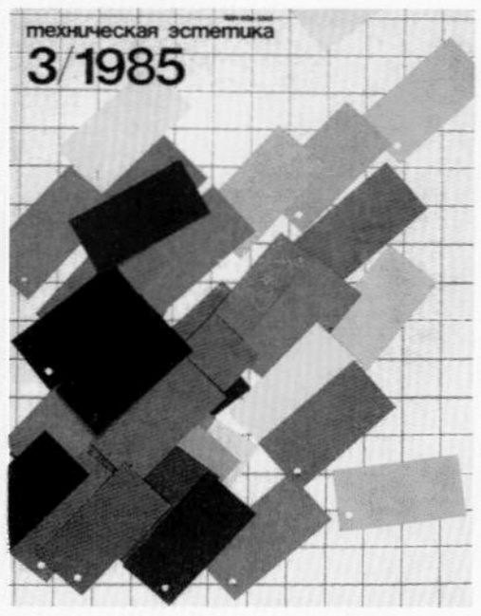

← P.211

MoMA

The Museum of Modern Art

← P.211

← P.212

1964–1992

TEKHNICHESKAYA ESTETIKA

Magazine Cover

Various

VNIITE, USSR

Under the auspices of the Soviet Union, a state-run center for design—the All-Union Scientific Research Institute of Industrial Design (VNIITE)—was formed in 1962. Its role was to develop a design framework that could address industrial-design challenges ranging from urban planning and public transport to modular buildings and home appliances. Headed by designer Yuri Soloviev, the VNIITE initiative was ambitious in its scope, with a Moscow headquarters supported by ten branches across the USSR, as well as hundreds of design bureaus connected to Soviet industries.

To promote its design theories and practices, VNIITE established in 1964 a monthly journal, *Tekhnicheskaya Estetika* (Technical Aesthetics), which became a natural extension of the institute's work, encompassing its broad focus, from advancements in engineering to toy manufacturing. Reflecting the forward-thinking nature of the organization, the publication's graphics were bold and experimental, graduating from largely monotone covers in the late 1960s to four-color printing from the late 1970s. Similarly, its evolving graphic language denoted shifts in design and production techniques.

Early geometric designs that relied on punchy contrasts of white and black linework on gray background gave way to brightly colored diagrams and detailed product shots of new technology and domestic goods and furniture. Generous displays of children's toys, laminates, or plastic stools imply an awareness of capitalist consumerism in the West, beyond the Iron Curtain. Yet the abundance they suggest failed to materialize.

In reality the production of VNIITE's progressive ideas struggled against the controlled economic conditions and a resistance against change for design's sake. Often its visionary, homegrown works were sidelined in favor of Western knock-offs. While the "Vniitians" output was prodigious, they were ultimately unable to make effective progress for societal good. The fall of the Soviet Union in 1991 also signaled the institute's end. Its relatively unknown output has received renewed interest through the tireless archival and promotional efforts of the Moscow Design Museum, including two catalogs: *Designed in the USSR: 1950–1989* (Phaidon) and *VNIITE: Discovering Utopia—Lost Archives of Soviet Design* (Unit Editions), both published in 2018.

1964/2004

MOMA

Logo

Ivan Chermayeff (1932–2017), Matthew Carter (1937–)

Museum of Modern Art, New York, U.S.

For an institution whose mission is to be modern and contemporary, the history of the Museum of Modern Art (MoMA) logotype may seem surprisingly prudent and practical, although to think so risks confusing the modern with the trendy. Over a forty-year development period, the discretion of Ivan Chermayeff, Bruce Mau, and Matthew Carter has helped the image of this modernist institution keep pace with changing times.

When the Museum of Modern Art approached Chermayeff & Geismar Associates in 1964, the firm was still relatively young but had already produced some of its most identifiable marks, including Mobil (1964) and Chase Manhattan (1959). Chermayeff's approach was to replace the museum's geometric, Bauhaus-inspired typeface with Franklin Gothic No. 2, a classic, sturdy "modern Gothic" with just the right touch of humanity. While the fully spelled-out name had previously always had a place, time and familiarity led to the increased use of the acronym MOMA, and finally to the more recognizable and distinct MoMA. Adaptable and functional, it was a mark that could survive both dissection—as in the case of the multiplanar supergraphic above the museum's satellite location in Queens, New York—and addition, as in constructions such as MoMA Store and MoMA QNS. Nevertheless, to mark its 2004 reopening, MoMA wanted a new logotype, and looked to Bruce Mau, whose firm was handling the revised signage system, to choose a new typeface. His response was to retain Franklin Gothic.

The museum then approached Carter, whose career had seen the evolution of typography from punch-cutting to Fontographer, and who had produced the practical Bell Centennial (1978) and the playful Walker (1995) fonts. His view was that Franklin had lost its character: the distinct letterforms had been brutalized and made squat by being enlarged and converted to digital type. Using the original metal type, Carter went about redrawing every character, creating a new logo and two complete alphabets for signage and text. The result was a revision so subtle that few noticed it, but for the museum, Carter, and the typographic community, it was a reunion with an old friend, which improved upon the original by making it true to its roots.

1965

YOU DON'T HAVE TO BE JEWISH TO LOVE LEVY'S

Advertising

Doyle Dane Bernbach

Whitey Ruben, U.S.

Rye bread has long been associated in American culture with Jewish bakeries, and in the early 1960s Levy's Real Rye was no exception. When Whitey Ruben, the businessman who had bought the almost bankrupt Levy's bakery, called New York advertising agency Doyle Dane Bernbach for help, the first thing founder and creative director Bill Bernbach did was to change the name of the product. No longer called Levy's Real Rye, Levy's Real Jewish Rye boasted its "Jewishness," not only to its natural consumer group but also to a much larger audience.

Under Bernbach's creative direction, Bill Taubin and Judy Protas produced a visually simple yet memorable campaign using a multiethnic, all-American cast that explored racial and social stereotypes of both product and consumer. The advertisements featured an American Indian railway engineer, a white police officer and children, and adults from other ethnic backgrounds.

A single color photograph portrayed each of the campaign's smiling subjects directly after their first bite into a Levy's Real Jewish Rye sandwich. The headline and product name remained the same throughout the campaign and translated the humor of the image through the use of the chunky, generous Cooper Black typeface, which displays curves that echo the sandwich's shape.

The campaign, which ran for decades in New York City's subway trains, not only influenced ethnic consciousness in America but also became part of a revolution in modern advertising. By bringing ideas and concepts to the forefront and addressing its potential clients as sophisticated consumers, the pioneering agency Doyle Dane Bernbach created many unforgettable messages through words and images that have grabbed and retained the attention of their viewers, becoming part of popular culture.

← P.213

← P.214

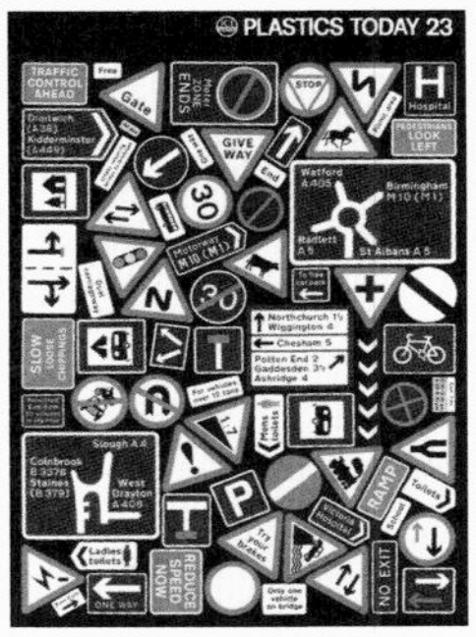

← P.215

1965–1975

NOVA

Magazine / Newspaper

Harri Peccinotti (1938–) et al.

Self-commissioned, UK

A dynamic and innovative lifestyle magazine, *Nova* was launched in March 1965 when Britain was undergoing rapid cultural and social change. From the outset, it was known for its provocative approach to gender roles, sexuality, and reproductive health, and its unflinching engagement with racial issues.

Partly driven by art director Herb Lubalin, previously known for his work on the short-lived *Eros*, *Nova* set a precedent in confronting controversial subject matter through image and text: a famous photo story by John Minshall focused on childbirth (October 1965), and cover stories ran under such headings as "Inside every woman there's a stripper longing to get out" (January 1970), or "How to undress in front of your husband" (May 1971), accompanied by provocative images. A January 1966 cover, featuring a young Black girl in a lace-trimmed dress, white gloves, and Mary Jane shoes, was accompanied by the headline "You may think I look cute but would you live next door to my mummy and daddy?" Meanwhile, the August 1968 issue, depicting an Asian family of five, asked, "Why can't they stay at home?" Bold writing and imagery became a platform for the complex realities beneath the social changes taking place in women's rights and the lives of ethnic minorities, capturing the excitement and anxiety of the time.

Under *Nova*'s first editor, Harry Fieldhouse, the publication struggled to find a receptive audience, but when directed by Dennis Hackett, it sharpened in editorial scope. Harri Peccinotti, *Nova*'s founding designer and art director, developed the magazine's fresh, vibrant style through the influence of Alexey Brodovitch and Henry Wolf's *Harper's Bazaar* and the German magazine *Twen*. Designed by Willy Fleckhaus, *Twen* originated as a student project of Christa Peters, later a *Nova* photographer, and was characterized by eye-catching covers often featuring nudes or close-ups of women's faces. When David Hillman held the position of art editor in 1969-75, *Nova*'s texts and images were integrated in dynamic ways to document the rapidly changing culture of music, sexuality, fashion, and world affairs.

Nova was briefly relaunched in June 2000, but is primarily remembered as a product of the 1960s.

1965

ASAHI STINY BEER

Poster

Kazumasa Nagai (1929–)

Asahi Breweries Ltd., Japan

Kazumasa Nagai's poster for Asahi beer was commissioned to celebrate the brand's success, specifically the sale of three hundred million beer bottles in 1965, as signaled in the advertisement's caption. Seen from a bird's-eye perspective, the image features an Asahi beer bottle standing at the head of a crowd of caps, suggesting a peacock showing off his tail. The bottle caps are covered with the rising-sun emblem of the Imperial flag that was used during World War II, and thus also evoke another image—a commander leading a battalion of soldiers. The poster embodies the story of Japan's appropriation of many aspects of Western culture.

Western alcoholic beverages, such as beer and whisky, arrived in Japan in the nineteenth century (during the Meiji period), but became particularly popular after the war. The rise in beer sales led Asahi to rebrand its beer as an original Japanese drink, stamping a logo of the rising sun on the caps, as designed by Walter Landor. With beer growing in popularity throughout the 1960s and '70s, sales of traditional Japanese *sake* plummeted, prompting its producers to rebrand this, too, as a young and modern drink—values that were synonymous with the West. Nagai's poster thus led to a complex process that transformed beer into an original Japanese drink, and *sake* into a Western drink, making the poster emblematic of the adoption of Western-style advertising by Japanese companies as a means of transforming brand image, and of the competition between *sake* and beer. On a deeper level, it represents the struggle between Japanese tradition and Western culture in postwar Japan, a tension that is embodied in the subtitle of the poster: "Drinking at my pace." The phrase "my pace" is written in *katagana* letters, which are used for foreign words, and thus also refers to the West, as well as to the rising concept of individuality in Japanese consumer culture.

A graduate in sculpture from Tokyo University, Nagai worked as a graphic designer for the Daiwa Spinning Company, and in the 1970s and '80s as president of the Nippon Design Center.

1965

PLASTICS TODAY

Magazine / Newspaper

Colin Forbes (1928–2022)

Kynoch Press, for Imperial Chemical Industries, UK

First published in the late 1950s, *Plastics Today* was produced by the Kynoch Press on behalf of the Plastics Division of ICI (Imperial Chemical Industries). Edited by K. B. Bartlet and an editorial board of four, it was published quarterly and aimed to keep readers abreast of developments in the technology and application of the wide range of plastics made by ICI.

Typographically advanced, *Plastics Today* was originally conceived by Kynoch's head of design, Roger Denning. The design of a number of issues was placed with the London agency Fletcher/Forbes/Gill (headed by Alan Fletcher, Colin Forbes, and Bob Gill), who the press briefly retained as advisors. The magazine is an early model of the use of the newly introduced international ISO standard of paper sizes, and fully exploited the A4 format by abandoning proportional in favor of equal margins, thus producing a page emphasizing depth rather than width. The publication's modernity was reinforced by the use of the newly released Univers typeface, which was applied across text and display setting in a single size, with only weight and space used to give it prominence. Published in seven languages, *Plastics Today* was a rare example of a multilingual publication produced at a time when only a small proportion of print was devoted to foreign-language work or overseas readership.

The title's covers were also innovative, featuring inventive displays of ICI's flexible plastic substrates, as well as fresh graphic techniques. On the cover of Issue 23 (1965), for instance, the designers presented a montage of British road signs, which reflected the topical fascination with Britain's new road-signage system and involved a graphic repetition that was to become the hallmark of Pentagram, the agency's later incarnation.

Shorn of all extraneous typographic devices, *Plastics Today* was pared down to the necessities of communication, displaying a typographic egalitarianism seldom seen in other magazines of the period.

← P.215

1965

MOBIL

Identity

Ivan Chermayeff (1932–2017), Tom Geismar (1931–)

Mobil Oil Corporation, U.S.

Ivan Chermayeff and Tom Geismar's redesigned identity system for Mobil Oil was notable for bringing clarity, simplicity, and cohesion to all levels of the company's graphic program, resuscitating its future at a tenuous time and reintroducing the brand to the world. In the 1950s, in the context of a booming economy and increasing suburban growth, gas stations in the U.S. were rapidly falling out of favor with developers due to their unsightly visual presence. Fearing exclusion, Mobil Oil was quick to commission the Chermayeff & Geismar studio to redesign the company's corporate identity.

The original prewar trademark, first implemented in 1933, featured a shield-shaped sign containing the red Pegasus illustration, accompanied by the word "Mobilgas" in bold, dark blue lettering. Although simple in design, the elements were disjointed, the typography unrefined, and the two core elements unnaturally coerced into an awkward geometric shape. Chermayeff & Geismar effectively streamlined the previous logo, while simultaneously adjusting its mode of communication. The logotype and Pegasus were redrawn, with letterforms simplified and the clunky strokes around the Pegasus eliminated, and the name of the company now identified as the primary component; in future, Pegasus would be relegated to a secondary role on different surfaces. In 1965, the letter "o" in "Mobil" was infused with red, which not only created a focal point for passers-by but also served as a visual link between the logotype and the red-winged horse.

Mobil's association with Chermayeff & Geismar was not limited just to corporate design. Over a period of thirty-five years, the partnership also resulted in a series of posters for television programs sponsored by the company, such as *Winston Churchill: The Wilderness Years* (1983). Chermayeff's design for the eight-part PBS series, which dramatized Churchill's period out of office in the 1930s, manages to convey both the politician's strong character and his loss of stature and influence during these years: Churchill is clearly recognizable from his trademark cigar and homburg, but the dense cloud of white lines obscuring his face implies that he has literally been scrubbed out in a crude act of censorship.

← P.216

1965

TADANORI YOKOO: HAVING REACHED A CLIMAX AT THE AGE OF 29, I WAS DEAD

Poster

Tadanori Yokoo (1936–)

Matsuya, Japan

Tadanori Yokoo's entry for the "Persona" exhibition, held at Tokyo's Matsuya department store, marked the beginning of his independent career as an artist, as well as the entrance of Pop art and psychedelic imagery into Japanese graphic design.

The poster depicts a young man in Western dress and holding a wilted rose hanging from a noose against the background of a rising sun. In the lower left-hand corner he is shown as a baby in a photograph stamped with his age—a year and a half—while on the opposite side he appears again as a teenager in a class photograph, overlaid by a crude hand gesture meaning "sex." Meanwhile, in the upper corners two drawings of Mt. Fuji—one of which provides a backdrop for Japan's new bullet train, introduced in the early 1960s—are set above a banner displaying the artist's name in English. Above, in an overt allusion to Pop art, the caption "Made in Japan" implies that the artist, along with the other objects depicted, is no more than a Japanese product. At the bottom, the inscription "Having reached a climax at the age of 29, I was dead" refers to the theme of the exhibition, which celebrated Japan's leading artists. However, in a negation of his previous achievements, the artist has metaphorically killed himself, setting out like a baby on a new artistic path. The exhibition was accompanied by a performance involving a mock funeral performed by Yokoo and his friends at a Tokyo cemetery and later documented in a book, *The Posthumous Work of Tadanori Yokoo* (1968).

With its bitter humor, psychedelic palette, and iconoclastic references to sacred Japanese symbols, the poster is emblematic of Yokoo's fusion of modernist graphic design with traditional Japanese motifs. During this period a number of experimental, subversive Japanese movements, such as *Buto*, *Gutai*, and *Mono-ha*, proposed a new creative agenda, pushing forward the country's long-dormant artistic discourse. In the same spirit, Yokoo forged a personal style, in which the values of Pop art were transformed into an original and innovative Japanese idiom.

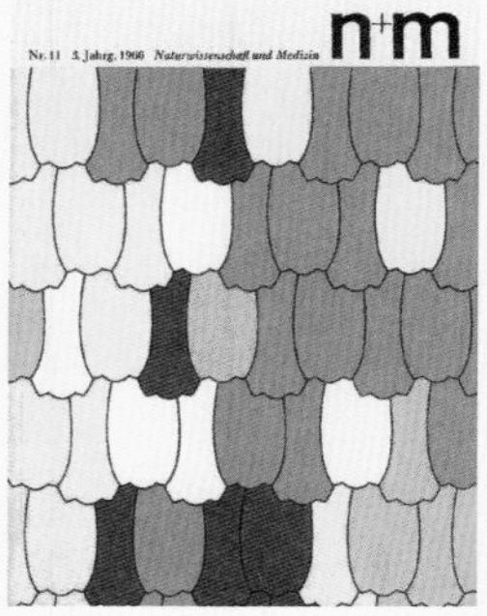

← P.217

1965–1972

N+M

Magazine Cover

Erwin Poell (1930–)

Boehringer Mannheim, Germany

Erwin Poell's work on *n+m*, an acronym for "Naturwissenschaft und Medizin" (Natural Science and Medicine), transforms what could have been a lackluster science journal into a collection of exciting and desirable volumes. Bold, flat colors and black lines make up the charts and schematic diagrams that grace the covers, turning information into abstract patterns and bringing a touch of psychedelia to the science world.

Published every two months, the journal was the brainchild of the physician Hoimar von Ditfurth, who worked for the Boehringer Mannheim pharmaceutical company and wanted to produce a journal that covered the latest developments in all areas of science for the medical profession. Poell already had a long-standing working relationship with Boehringer, having designed its logo in 1957 and developed its integrated corporate identity. The designs on the cover of each issue relate to an article featured inside, and could range from a graph of the world's changing population to the structure of a neuron cell or the movements of a bird in flight. Poell was following a long tradition of science and statistical graphics, but his stylized work was designed to be beautiful as well as informative (there is an explanation of what the design represents on each title page), with colors carefully chosen to complement one another. Although the covers are an example of the 1960s fashion for bold geometry, the design scheme inside is restrained, with a plain, two-column grid and ample white space. The use of a bold, lowercase sans serif on the masthead reflects the dominant "Swiss school" of the period.

Essentially a generalist, Poell had designed hundreds of stamps, books, and logos, but after the success of *n+m*, he found a niche producing diagrams and charts. Other journals and textbooks followed. Being able to translate difficult concepts and complex biological structures into a clear graphic form is a skill that is crucial to understanding and communicating science. Poell makes the result both accessible and pleasing to the eye. In 1972, *n+m* was replaced by an annual called *Mannheimer Forum*.

← P.218

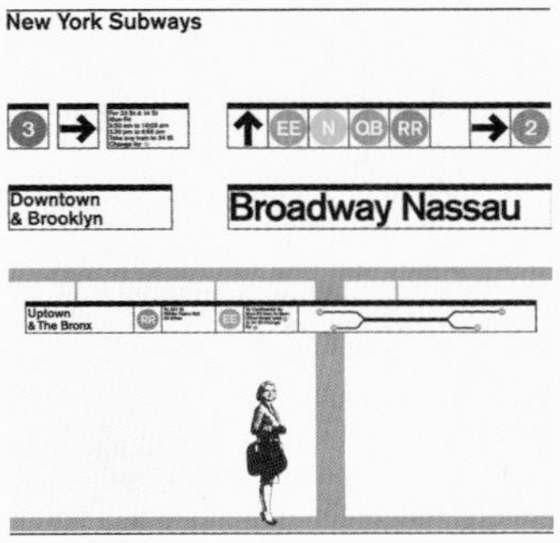

← P.219

← P.220

1966–1972

1972 MUNICH OLYMPICS

Identity

Otl Aicher (1922–1991) et al.

National Olympic Committee, Germany

The logo and pictorial information system of the 1972 Munich Olympics is an impressive example of the large-scale international graphic identity systems that arose during the twentieth century, particularly those used to promote global cultural and sporting events. Practical and efficient, the various designs provide an eloquent solution to untangling complex visual communications for international users.

Led by Otl Aicher, the design team worked in consultation with Germany's National Olympic Committee (NOC) to develop a standardized identity program marked by an orderly yet adaptable design. Aicher and his colleagues at Büro Aicher (among them Rolf Müller, Alfred Kern, Gerhard Joksch, Ian McLaren, Thomas Nittner, and Elena Winschermann) created around 180 pictographic symbols that could be easily recognized by a multilingual audience. Drawn on a diagonal and orthogonal grid at 45- and 90-degree angles, the symbols depict both the athletic events and general information. Their distinctive styling follows the pictograms developed by Masaru Katsumi for the 1964 Tokyo Olympics, with whom Aicher had consulted in 1966, and were so successful that they were reused for the Montreal Olympics in 1976.

The Munich Olympics' main logo resulted from a collaboration between Aicher and the designer Coordt von Mannstein. The NOC had rejected Aicher's original design—a sunburst logo—on the basis that it would have been difficult to copyright. Von Mannstein modified Aicher's design, creating an energetic helix symbol derived from a mathematical computation. In developing the Games's posters, Aicher worked with Ian McLaren, dividing them into two categories—athletic and cultural—with one distinguished by a "posterization" style and minimal type, and the other an information series based on type and horizontal bars. The "posterization" effect was produced by separating the tonal grades of monochrome photographic images and adapting them to the official color scheme through manual retouching. The palette and typeface (Univers) established a contemporary image of Germany that moved beyond lingering memories of nationalism associated with the 1936 Berlin Olympics.

1966–1972

NEW YORK SUBWAY SIGN SYSTEM AND MAP

Information Design

Massimo Vignelli (1931–2014), Bob Noorda (1927–2010)

New York City Transit Authority, U.S.

Despite being in use for only seven years, Massimo Vignelli's radical New York subway map and sign system is considered by many to be a classic due to its uniquely gridded style.

When the design firm Unimark was commissioned in 1966 to undertake the project, Vignelli and Bob Noorda (previously art director of Pirelli in Milan and a designer of the Milan subway information graphics) developed a system of black support bars to hold signs containing directions, locations, and line names, based on a 1-foot- (0.3 m) square matrix, with each component displayed in a different size according to its information level. For the typeface, they chose Standard Medium (known today as Akzidenz-Grotesk), combined with color-coded circular badges to identify line direction and destination. The scheme was intended to operate as a tightly woven system, enabling passengers to find the information they needed quickly and easily.

Several years later, Vignelli left Unimark to establish Vignelli & Associates and Vignelli Design, and in 1972 the firm was asked by the New York City Transit Authority to create a new subway map. Vignelli transformed the existing geographically accurate system into something similar to Henry Beck's London Underground map of 1933. Instead of drawing the subway routes and city to scale, Vignelli ran lines at forty-five- and ninety-degree angles, using color to differentiate the lines, and dots to denote stations and terminal points. He also broke the subway lines into easily recognizable sections, enabling commuters to see how to get from Brooklyn to Manhattan by glancing at a single series of colors, letters or symbols. Although this reduced the rectangular Central Park to a square, the map succeeded in untangling a web of subway lines, helping commuters to get easily from A to B, and sometimes literally taking lines "A" and "B" to do so.

Vignelli's design, however, was replaced in 1979 by a more conventional map after new research concluded the former distorted the landscape beyond recognition. Even though the new version is more accurate, Vignelli's remains highly prized for the clarity and simplicity of its grid system. In 2011 Vignelli was asked to reinterpret the map once more for use on New York's MTA website.

1966–1979

EPICUREAN

Magazine Cover

Les Mason (1924–2009)

Lawrence Publishing, Australia

One of Australia's most esteemed designers, Les Mason was the art director of *Epicurean*, a magazine for "lovers of good living." Across thirteen years and seventy-seven issues, his work would shape the country's first dedicated food and wine magazine into a prestigious journal for connoisseurs. *Epicurean* united Mason's graphic vision and his strong friendship with founder and publisher Alan Holdsworth. Together the two worked, and drank, convivially, from Mason's first issue in 1966 until the founder's death in 1977.

A Chouinard Art Institute graduate, Mason emigrated from California to Melbourne in 1961, establishing his design studio a year later. *Epicurean* provided a channel for his joie de vivre. As his daring grew, the bimonthly magazine gradually developed its bold aesthetic, with absurdist compositions worked up from Mason's precisely drawn 2B pencil concepts on oilskin paper. Created from bromides and paste-up, the experimental covers nodded to Mason's broad art references, notably Surrealism, Pop and Op art, Neo Realism, and Arte Povera.

The cover for Issue 17, for instance, sports a Magritte-esque portrait in tones of pink and orange: a glistening fish dangles, held between the model's teeth. The fishy theme continues with Issue 63, which presents a book sandwiching a limp-looking catch of the day between its pages, with an upright wine bottle puncturing its cover. Self-taught and armed with a Hasselblad camera, Mason captured unlikely *natura morte*: an army of cyclopean, rubber-gloved hands offering up grapes and wine; a carpet of green bananas framing a Keith Haring-style illustration. Props were found, painted, cut, collaged, and repurposed, recalling the readymades of Marcel Duchamp or Joseph Cornell. The title treatment was also in flux, loosened from a traditional repeating banner; Mason experimented with many fonts, from classic serifs to decorative faces. By contrast, the shoestring budget meant one-color interiors were simply set in Times on a uniform grid.

Mason's fascination with design psychology shaped his career, conveying to how graphic language can elicit emotional responses. Considered Australia's "father of graphic design," Mason was recognized with a solo exhibition at the National Gallery of Victoria in 2015.

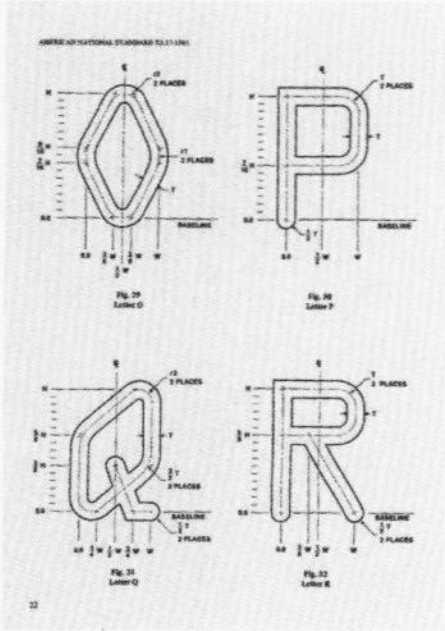

← P.221

1966/1968

OCR—A and B

Typeface

Adrian Frutiger (1928–2015)

Monotype Corporation, UK

The OCR-A typeface was developed to meet specifications set by the American National Standards Institute for processing documents by banks, credit card companies, and other businesses. It was designed specifically to be "read" by scanning devices—hence OCR (Optical Character Recognition)—and could be used to process large quantities of forms by machine. The font is distinguished by the letters' uniform width (known as mono-spacing) and the use of simple, thick strokes.

OCR-A was deemed inappropriate for use in Europe, and in 1968 Monotype commissioned Adrian Frutiger to design a variation of the typeface to meet the standards of the European Computer Manufacturers' Association for use on products to be scanned by electronic devices, as well as those read by people. Combining strict mathematical criteria with typographic tradition, Frutiger resolved both technical and aesthetic issues to create letterforms that are more legible to the human eye than most other OCR fonts. The resulting OCR-B typeface was made a world standard in 1973.

Mono-spaced and grid-based fonts have long been popular with graphic designers, and OCR has proved to be a source of inspiration for such fonts as Data 70 (1970), Fiber Eno and Carbon C6 (both 2006), and Tephra (2008). Most notable, however, are the fonts designed by Wim Crouwel: New Alphabet (1967) and Gridnik (1976). New Alphabet is distinguished by having neither curves nor diagonal lines, and was appropriated and adapted by Peter Saville and Brett Wickens of Pentagram in 1987 for use on Joy Division's *Substance* cover—thereby inspiring a whole new generation of younger designers.

Although optical character recognition technology has now advanced to the point where such simple fonts are no longer necessary, both OCR-A and -B fonts have remained in use, particularly on checks and credit cards. Some utility companies also insist that the account number and amount owed on a bill return form are printed in OCR.

← P.221

1967

SABON

Typeface

Jan Tschichold (1902–1974)

D. Stempel AG, Germany

A graceful, stately typeface in the tradition of old-style French Renaissance typefaces, Sabon is a direct descendant of the sixteenth-century designs of Claude Garamond, which were in turn inspired by the types cut by Francesco Griffo for Aldus Manutius in Venice.

The typeface is named after Jacob Sabon, a punchcutter who acquired Garamond's matrices and punches when they were sold to the printer Christophe Plantin after Garamond's death. Sabon was commissioned to meet the need for a typeface that would work equally well, whether set in metal type using a mechanical composition, or hand-set as a foundry type.

Eminently legible, Sabon was intended to be an all-purpose book typeface and to that end has a moderately large x-height and open counter spaces, with a slightly heavier stroke weight than its Renaissance forebears. It also differs from Garamond in its flatter, sharper, and heavier serifs and the ball terminals of its descenders. Other differences include a truncated descender on the lowercase italic "*f*," a tapered crossbar on its roman counterpart, and the lack of a serif on the leg of the uppercase "K." For economy's sake, it is also slightly narrower, a difference that might seem infinitesimal in a short text but saves a significant amount of space over an entire book in comparison with Garamond, without sacrificing elegance or style. Jan Tschichold was primarily a book designer who designed just a few typefaces. Sabon is his best-known face, and in sensibility reveals his early training in calligraphy.

Sabon has proved to be a useful typeface for text, with an enduring and robust life, although it is less graceful at larger sizes. It was one of the first typefaces to be digitized in the 1980s, and has been revived by type designer Jean François Porchez for Linotype in OpenType format as Sabon Next.

← P.222

1967

THE MEDIUM IS THE MASSAGE

Book

Quentin Fiore (1920–2019), Marshall McLuhan (1911–1980)

Bantam Books, U.S.

In 1967 Quentin Fiore teamed up with Marshall McLuhan and Jerome Agel (coordinator) to create an experiential book characterized by bold language and cinematic graphics. Through cutting and pasting imagery from multiple sources, with varied typography and layout, Fiore helped McLuhan's text to reach an audience of millions. Due to a typesetting error, the intended title, *The Medium Is the Message*, became *The Medium Is the Massage*. (The book addressed theories about the relationship between the sender, medium, and receiver that were orginally expounded in McLuhan's 1964 book *Understanding Media: The Extensions of Man*). When McLuhan saw the typo, he was amused by the accidental double entendre and decided to leave it unchanged.

The Medium Is the Massage bombarded readers with brash statements about culture and how the world would be changed by the dawn of the electronic age. Typeset in the highly functional, modern Helvetica typeface, the book communicated McLuhan's popular theories on technology, communication, politics, and television via Fiore's erratic photographic and typographic design. Although a largely self-taught designer, Fiore studied art under the German graphic artists George Grosz and Hans Hofmann, later working as a typographer for Lester Beall. Like McLuhan, Fiore sensed the coming of a new age when designers and artists would translate their ideas using computer technology. Lacking these tools himself, he juxtaposed everything from stock photography and magazine clippings to vernacular and fine art, all cut, pasted, and sequenced into an assault on the senses. The resulting visual/verbal hybridization was created without a concrete manuscript, since the author and designer worked by reviewing Fiore's concepts, most of which passed McLuhan's inspection. Each new spread offered readers a glimpse into the future, making them ponder the phenomenon that McLuhan called the "global village."

The metaphoric, bombastic, and cinematic qualities of the book continue to make it one of the most sought-after design resources of the twentieth century.

← P.222

1967

TYPOGRAPHIE

Book

Emil Ruder (1914–1970)

Verlag Arthur Niggli, Switzerland

Typographie focuses on the New Typography championed by designers such as Max Bill and Josef Müller-Brockmann, which sought to clarify the discipline's functional responsibilities. Despite this, the book reveals a warmth and playfulness not always associated with Swiss modernism.

First published by Arthur Niggli in 1967, the publication represented the culmination of a lifetime of teaching and exploration by its author, Emil Ruder. He had trained as a compositor before taking up a position at the Allgemeine Gewerbeschule Basel in 1942, where he taught typography on the four-year program, and then set up an advanced one-year course. Examples of student work reproduced in *Typographie* suggest that he created a laboratory-like environment—a protected space for controlled testing and experimentation. Investigation of the design properties of proportion, rhythm, form, and counterform are detailed in dedicated chapters, each presenting examples captioned with Ruder's observations, which reveal a Zen-like sensitivity to the equality of positive and negative space. Carefully framed in generous quantities of white space, the text advances many of the ideas explored a decade earlier in a series of four articles entitled "Wesentliches" (Fundamentals) that Ruder had written for the journal *Typographische Monatsblätter*: "The Plane," "The Line," "The Word," and "Rhythm." Although working purely with typographic arrangements, Ruder constantly sought affirmation for these ideas in modern art and architecture, referring particularly to the work of Paul Klee, Piet Mondrian, and Le Corbusier. As a result, the book was accessible and relevant to designers from any discipline.

By the time *Typographie* was published, Ruder had become director of the Kunstgewerbeschule Basel (formerly the Allgemeine Gewerbeschule). The following year, Wolfgang Weingart took responsibility for the advanced course, steering it toward a more intuitive and graphic approach that eventually flowered into the postmodernism of the "New Wave." Yet for many designers, Ruder's publication remains an essential, timeless reflection on typography.

← P.223

1967–1973

OZ

Magazine / Newspaper

Martin Sharp (1942–2013) et al.

Oz Publications Ink Ltd., UK

Oz magazine was one of the most visually exciting publications of its time and a massive hit. The chief organ of the British underground press movement, Oz was antiestablishment, filled with anger, radical ideas, and left-wing politics.

Although certain issues were designed by Hapshash and the Coloured Coat, the majority were the work of the Australian artist Martin Sharp, whose posters of Bob Dylan and others are considered classics of the genre. Sharp experimented with LSD, and his stunning *Oz* covers were a testament to its mind-expanding effects: Issue 3, featuring a joint-smoking Mona Lisa framed by peeled bananas, and the graphic "Magic Theatre edition," produced in collaboration with Philippe Mora, have been described by British author Jonathon Green as "arguably the greatest achievement of the entire British underground press." Perhaps the most famous of all was Sharp's Dylan cover for Issue 7, its success ensured by virtue of its psychedelic beauty and Dylan's worldwide popularity. But not all Oz covers were dependent on psychedelic design; some became show-stoppers simply by virtue of their powerful imagery, as in the case of Issue 10's blood-splattered depiction of a man shot in the head, or the controversial and explicit sexual imagery of Issues 25 and 28.

Keen to encourage more democratic values in design, Oz intermittently handed creative control to different groups. The most notorious was the "School Kids Issue" featuring sexually explicit articles and artworks by twenty teenage readers, and a cover depicting scenes of lesbian sex and bestiality. The issue provoked the authorities into raiding Oz's printing works, leading to the arrest and imprisonment of its three editors, Richard Neville, Jim Anderson, and Felix Dennis. The three were later released after pressure on the government.

Oz gained notoriety for its graphic invention. While early issues appeared in an A4 format, others were produced as foldout posters or as long, thin publications printed on high-gloss stock or newsprint, and exploited new technologies, such as metallic foils, fluorescent inks, and offset lithography. The magazine's liberal approach paved the way for other magazines (*Time Out, Private Eye, New Statesman,* and *Viz*) to throw off the shackles of tradition.

← P.224

1967–1980

THE BLACK PANTHER

Magazine / Newspaper

Emory Douglas (1943–)

Black Panther Party, U.S.

In 1967 Emory Douglas first met Huey P. Newton and Bobby Seale, political activists and cofounders of the Black Panther Party for Self-Defense. Douglas was young but well-versed in the workings of the printshop, and Newton and Seale put him in charge of the group's newspaper, the *Black Panther.*

The weekly paper's intention was to spread news within the Black community for the purposes of protection, organization, education, and mutual support. It was important that printing costs be kept low to maximize the number of copies printed. This decision created design constraints, such as the requirement that only one color be used in addition to black and white. Douglas successfully exploited these restrictions to produce a visual language that was striking and urgent. He used a marker pen to mimic a linocut-style print and created powerful photomontages with recycled imagery to visually communicate the week's headlines. Symbolism was also key to *Black Panther*'s appeal: police were depicted as uniformed pigs (a metaphor that has lasted to this day) to counteract the strength of the panther representing the party. These impactful symbols allowed the community to see themselves reflected in the paper—an uncommon experience for working-class people at the time—and to identify with leading party figures, such as Angela Davis and Fred Hampton.

As literacy rates in the Black community were low due to inadequate access to good education, Douglas's image-first communication style was a vital catalyst in the growth of the movement. From 1968 to 1971, the *Black Panther* was the most widely read newspaper in the United States and peaked at a weekly circulation of 300,000, despite the desperate attempts by the Federal Bureau of Investigations (FBI) to shut it down.

The September 21, 1974, issue of the paper demonstrates Douglas's masterful skill with photomontage, depicting the thirty-eighth U.S. president, Gerald Ford, as a puppet controlled by corporate giants, such as PepsiCo, Exxon, Gulf, and Ford.

After the party disbanded in the 1980s, Douglas continued to create activist artwork. He was awarded an AIGA medal in 2019, ensuring that his work will enter the design canon and reach new audiences for generations to come.

← P.225

1967

BLACK POWER / WHITE POWER

Poster

Tomi Ungerer (1931–2019)

Self-commissioned, U.S.

This powerful image of interlocking cannibalistic figures, which seems to portray Black and white militancy as equally destructive forces, demonstrates Tomi Ungerer's unfashionably skeptical attitude to the potential for social change.

In the early 1960s the Black Power movement, in alliance with the Black Panther Party (BPP), was in the ascendant and strongly supported by the Student Non-violent Coordinating Committee (SNCC). Produced as a poster in 1967, "Black Power/White Power" was initially conceived as a cover for the satirical journal *Monocle* (edited by Victor Navasky) in 1963, the same year in which the D'Arcy Gallery in New York held an exhibition of Ungerer's satirical paintings. At the time, Ungerer formed part of a vibrant cohort of cartoonists based in New York that included Bob Blechman, David Levine, and Jules Feiffer, and his image offered a potent alternative to contemporary civil-rights posters and their left-wing messages. With its attempt at balance seldom seen in 1960s propaganda posters, "Black Power/White Power" seeks to address the complexity of contemporary race relations—their tensions and contradictions—which contrasted with the heroic, Socialist Realist-style posters promoting the struggle of African Americans, produced by artists such as Emory Douglas, a prolific graphic designer and Minister of Culture for the BPP. Ungerer's work, usually produced in pen, ink, and colored dye, and rarely reworked or corrected, relied on a similar immediacy and directness, but failed to share the optimistic view that prevailed. The message of "Black Power/White Power" is deliberately ambiguous, refusing to endorse any form of racial supremacy.

Ungerer spent his childhood under the spectre of the Nazi regime in Alsace and, although he was an advocate of nonviolence and peaceful coexistence (as can be seen clearly in his anti-Vietnam War posters), he aimed to avoid extreme points of view. The simplicity and power of his imagery has also been linked to fellow children's book illustrators Shel Silverstein and Maurice Sendak.

← P.226

1967

THE BEATLES—SGT. PEPPER'S LONELY HEARTS CLUB BAND

Record / CD Cover

Peter Blake (1932–), Jann Haworth (1942–)

EMI, UK

For the postwar generation that came of age in the 1960s, there was no more influential band than the Beatles. The most iconic of their works, the 1967 *Sgt. Pepper's Lonely Hearts Club Band* album, forever altered the content and style of rock and pop music. Not coincidentally, Peter Blake and Jann Haworth's Grammy-award-winning album cover was also a breakthrough in terms of launching the popular trend of "concept cover" art.

The cover was conceived by art director Robert Fraser in collaboration with Paul McCartney, who originally wanted to use a painting entitled *The Fool*. Fraser persuaded McCartney to abandon the idea, instead proposing that Blake, an acclaimed artist at the time, should design the cover. Blake has recorded that the original concept was to create a scene showing the Beatles as the fictional Sgt. Pepper band performing in a beautiful, flower-strewn setting (photographed by Michael Cooper); this evolved into a view of the group surrounded by an assortment of their heroes (as well as Madame Tussaud's wax-work versions of their younger selves), as life-size, cutout figures. Ultimately, the collage depicted more than seventy famous people, including writers, musicians, film stars, and Indian gurus and, at John Lennon's insistence, an image of the original Beatles bass player, Stuart Sutcliffe. The word "Beatles" in the foreground of the image, spelled out in flowers, simulated a grave, which led to speculation that the biographical tableau symbolized their transition from mop-tops to serious composers. Inside, the album, which was designed as a gatefold, opened up to reveal a large color photograph of the Beatles as the Sgt. Pepper band against a yellow background, and an additional page of cutouts of Sgt. Pepper regalia. Blake's imagery drew on the influences of Dada, Surrealism, and, of course, psychedelia (which was a composite of the two earlier styles).

The album's Pop sensibility inspired many subsequent record covers, including the Rolling Stones's *Their Satanic Majesties Request*. Years later, it also prompted numerous parodies, such as Ed Lamm's 1999 *New York Times Book Review* illustration entitled "Clinton," showing all of the players in President Clinton's Monica Lewinsky scandal.

← P.226

1967

THE VELVET UNDERGROUND AND NICO

Record / CD Cover

Andy Warhol (1928–1987)

Verve Records, U.S.

Andy Warhol's philosophy of art is crystallized in this debut record cover of the Velvet Underground, which manages to turn a meaningless object into a symbol as recognizable and easily reproduced as Marilyn Monroe's face or a soft-drink can.

Warhol was at the peak of his creative powers when he designed the record sleeve, and already widely known for his brightly colored silkscreen prints depicting famous faces and newspaper clippings, produced at his "Silver Factory" (later known as the "Factory"). Before becoming an independent artist, Warhol was an established commercial designer of promotional graphics, including record sleeve designs. The Velvet Underground were members of the cultural scene that surrounded him, but their music was only modestly successful. Although this album, *The Velvet Underground and Nico*, was not a hit on its release, it gained in influence and reputation as the band's musical influence grew and as the record sleeve itself gradually acquired a following of its own.

The importance attributed to the relationship between Warhol and the emerging band is conveyed by the design, which features Warhol's name prominently, but neglects to mention that of the band—it was only on later reissues that the group was added to the sleeve. Moreover, the original sleeve included a banana that could be peeled to reveal a second—pink—banana underneath. Warhol's interest in the mass-produced and the banal is clearly evident here: the banana looks like any other, a mundane object writ large, and echoes the artist's images of famous commercial objects, such as Coca-Cola cans, which represented for him the ultimate symbol of American consumer democracy. The banana is now so famous that it is regularly printed on T-shirts and other merchandise, completing its elevation to consumer icon.

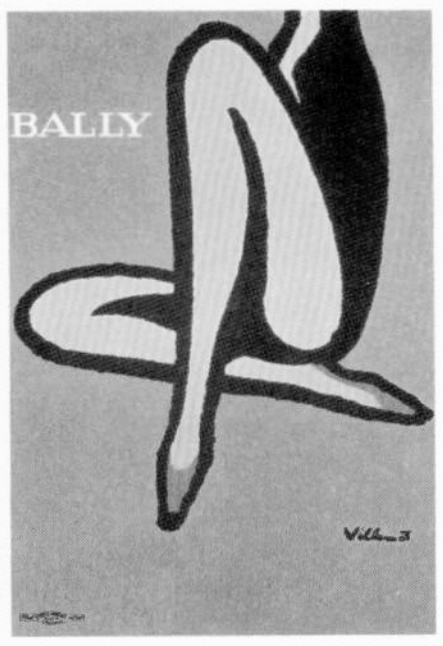

← P.227

1967–1989

BALLY

Poster

Bernard Villemot (1911–1989)

Bally, Switzerland

This poster for the Swiss footwear company Bally formed part of a series that Bernard Villemot designed for the company over a period of fifteen years. All of his designs are characterized by vivid color, extreme economy of line and form, and minimal text.

Villemot gained a reputation in postwar France for creating vibrant posters advertising household products and commodities, continuing the tradition that had been established by Jules Chéret and other poster artists in the latter part of the nineteenth century. As a student, Villemot had attended Paul Colin's design school, and later came under the influence of major Parisian poster designers of the time, including A. M. Cassandre, Leonetto Cappiello, and Jean Carlu, as well as artists such as Matisse and Nicolas de Staël. In 1967, having already designed successful advertisements for the soft-drink companies Orangina and Perrier, he was asked by Bally's publicity director to revive their advertising campaign. His first poster for the company, known as "legs," was an immediate hit with the public and went on to win the Martini *grand prix*. In this audacious design reminiscent of Matisse's paper cutout *Nu Bleu* of 1952 Villemot has sectioned off the girl's body at the neck, focusing on her legs and bright red Bally shoes. Meanwhile, her arms have become subsumed into the blackness of the silhouetted torso.

Numerous other striking posters followed, such as the 1973 "les femmes fleurs" design in which two female torsos form a giant lotus blossom, with the shoes almost an afterthought. In 1989, the year of his death, Villemot produced one of his finest posters, "Bally Ballon"—like all his designs, containing very few features. Here, however, a blue-and-white globe adds a symbolic note, indicating the appeal of the shoes to a worldwide audience.

Villemot's contribution to poster art was recognized by two retrospective exhibitions and numerous prestigious awards.

← P.228

1967–1982

ROLLING STONE

Magazine Cover

Various

Jann S. Wenner, U.S.

The covers of *Rolling Stone* magazine were so influential on popular culture in the 1970s and early 1980s that they became the subject of a hit record from 1972, "The Cover of the Rolling Stone," by Dr. Hook and the Medicine Show (written by Shel Silverstein).

The genesis of the publication's cover, as recounted by founder Jann Wenner, whose imprimatur is still on every page, was a "wonderful, revealing accident." In an account of the inaugural cover of November 9, 1967 (printed in *Rolling Stone: The Complete Covers*), which pictured John Lennon in a publicity still from a "mostly forgotten film" by Richard Lester called *How I Won the War*, Wenner says, "The *Rolling Stone* logo was an unfinished draft of a design by San Francisco psychedelic-poster artist Rick Griffin, who was planning to refine it until I used his sketch in order to get it to the printer on time." Wenner admits that for the first ten years the covers were not driven by newsstand considerations, and were allowed to be adventurous. Wenner commissioned several West Coast photographers to shoot the performers, including his friend Baron Wolman, *Rolling Stone*'s first staff photographer. In 1970 Wenner hired Annie Leibovitz to become the magazine's second staff photographer, and she brought a more naturalistic sensibility to the covers. One of her most unforgettable cover images was a portrait of John Lennon and Yoko Ono, with Lennon curled up nude against a fully clothed Ono. Several hours after the photo session ended, Lennon was murdered.

In February 1973 *Rolling Stone* began publishing four-color covers and, several months later, acquired a tabloid format. At the same time, Wenner hired the magazine's first "professional" art director, Mike Salisbury, who introduced concept covers and illustration. In the 1970s, under the art direction of Tony Lane, the covers developed a cleaner, poster-type look that relied on Leibovitz's now more formal portraits, but with the irreverent *Rolling Stone* spirit still alive. Now over forty years old, *Rolling Stone* continues its reign as a beacon of pop culture.

Knoll

← P.229

1967

KNOLL

Logo

Massimo Vignelli (1931–2014)

Knoll Associates, U.S.

Designed at the outset of Helvetica's popularity in the 1960s, the spare Knoll logotype epitomizes both the rational principles of the "Swiss school" and the modernist tenets embodied in the company's furniture.

Founded in 1938 by the German-born Hans Knoll, Knoll is renowned for its iconic designs by Mies van der Rohe, Jens Risom, Eero Saarinen, Harry Bertoia, Isamu Noguchi, and Niels Diffrient. The company's original logo, a wordmark set in French Clarendon capitals, was designed by Herbert Matter in the 1940s, who later reduced it to the single letter "K" around 1952, and then revised it again to a double "K" during the early 1960s. When Massimo Vignelli succeeded Matter as graphic design consultant to Knoll in 1967, he standardized all of the company's printed material from its stationery to price lists and posters; he imposed a grid and a consistent type style, and introduced a wordmark tightly set in an upper- and a lowercase Helvetica Medium (although Matter's "K" logo continued to be used alongside the marks). Vignelli's graphic program for Knoll was so successful that by the mid-1970s it had been copied by many of the firm's competitors.

Along with Vignelli's 1967 logo for American Airlines, the Knoll wordmark paved the way for Helvetica to become the preferred typeface for corporate logos in the late 1960s and '70s. Rather than a mark that expressed the personality of a business, the logo functioned as a neutral element in a broader identity system. However, in posters, where it features as the main motif, variations in color and scale have made it considerably more playful and decorative. Many companies have now abandoned the minimal approach represented by Helvetica, but in Knoll's case the logo's simple sans serif letters continue to capture the essence of the company's style.

← P.229

1967

NEW ALPHABET

Typeface

Wim Crouwel (1928–2019)

Self-commissioned, the Netherlands

Four years after opening the multidisciplinary Total Design offices with four partners, Wim Crouwel created the New Alphabet with the intention of using cathode-ray tubes to render its letterforms. Conceived for the publication *Nieuw Alfabet*—a magazine that examined typographic similarities and differences through the lens of high technology—Crouwel's typeface, like the magazine, asked similar questions to those Bauhaus designers, such as Herbert Bayer, had posed thirty years previously: can one system of letterforms do the job of both upper and lowercase?

To create a universal, single-case letter system, the typeface was drawn with a series of only horizontal and vertical lines, and very few angular or Bézier curves. Radical approaches such as these where function took precedence over form, typified the Dutch design movement of the mid- to later-twentieth century, which placed as much emphasis on tools, process, and media as on the final product. The New Alphabet's mechanical anatomy and rigid construction from a five-by-nine gridded matrix lent a scientific personality to the typeface. Like Univers and Frutiger, it had a numerical naming system that helped to differentiate between normal, bold, condensed, and extended weights. Fortunately, the unique and quirky face earned Total Design a wealth of publicity, helping the studio to win a number of new clients, although many criticized Crouwel's New Alphabet for being overambitious and cryptic. Although it is easy to dismiss some of its letters as otherworldly and alien, Crouwel has insisted that even the unrecognizable ones have a basis in typographic history.

As indecipherable as it was ingenious, Crouwel's typeface foreshadowed technological advancements that would take designers, mass media, and culture by storm almost twenty years later. As a typographer, graphic designer, and educator, Crouwel remains an influential figurehead and, popular or not, his New Alphabet looks as fresh today as when it was first designed.

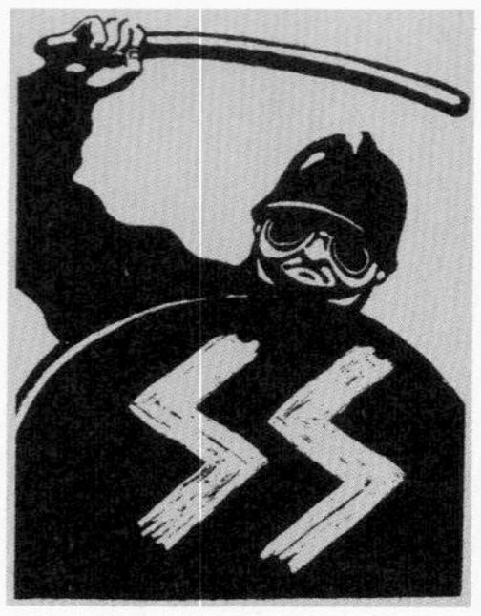

← P.230

1968

ATELIER POPULAIRE

Poster

Atelier Populaire

Self-commissioned, France

Numbering some three hundred different designs, and printed by cheap, "homemade" silkscreen processes, the posters created by Atelier Populaire were among the most enduring achievements of the 1968 student and worker uprising in Paris.

Established by students of the École Nationale Supérieure des Beaux-Arts, who occupied university buildings during the general strike against President de Gaulle's suppression of civil and working rights, Atelier Populaire was a democratically run print studio, with slogans and designs selected by committee. In one of their most famous images, printed on May 18, 1968, a baton-wielding riot policeman of the French Compagnies Républicaines de Securité holds a shield bearing the letters "SS," a reference to the Nazi SS (Schutzstaffel). Another design shows de Gaulle—a soldier during World War II, who later led the Free French government-in-exile—with a mask slipping off his face to reveal that of Adolf Hitler. On his armband, de Gaulle carries the double-barred Cross of Lorraine, emblem of the French Resistance and of his own birthplace. This subversion of the Lorraine Cross was to become a symbol of the government's malfeasance, appearing in another poster on a ballot-box-shaped coffin. Capitalism was a further favorite target. In one of the simplest designs, which refers to the French education system and its tradition of rote conjugation of verbs, a hand writes out the verb "to participate," culminating with the final line for third person plural, "They profit." The posters are characterized by bold, easily reproducible images—usually two-tone black on white—in which recurrent symbols, such as the fist of protest, the armed policeman, or the factory chimney stack, could be incorporated into different designs. Their somewhat crude appearance is a testament to the urgency with which they were produced and displayed.

Although short-lived, Atelier Populaire spawned other socially conscious French graphic collectives, such as Grapus (1970–91), the UK's See Red Women's Workshop (1974–84), and the American Red Dragon Print Collective (1973–77). More recently, their rough-and-ready youth-culture aesthetic has even permeated commercial graphics, including the 2005 album cover *Push the Button* for the Chemical Brothers.

← P.231

1968–1975

WHOLE EARTH CATALOG: ACCESS TO TOOLS

Book

Stewart Brand (1938–)

Self-commissioned, U.S.

The *Whole Earth Catalog* is a unique example of the visionary thinking associated with U.S. counterculture of the 1960s. A vast compendium of books, maps, experiments, and other "tools" for thinking, it encouraged readers to question the power systems and attitudes of the time while sharing information as a route to self-education and empowerment.

Founded, edited, and designed by Stewart Brand, the *Whole Earth Catalog* was divided into sections that ranged from "Understanding Whole Systems" to "Nomadics"; entries included information about building materials, cybernetics, solar energy, beekeeping, camping and survival, self-hypnotism, yoga, and Tantra art—all accompanied by evaluative commentary and sources. A best-seller with many editions and permutations, the first *Whole Earth Catalog* (Fall 1968) was sixty-four pages long and cost five dollars, whereas *The Last Whole Earth Catalog*, released before research was stopped "permanently" in 1971, stretched to more than three hundred pages. However, the publication started again, and *The (Updated) Last Whole Earth Catalog* appeared in 1975 with more than four hundred pages. Other variants of the publication included the *Whole Earth Epilog* (Volume II of the "updated" *Catalog)* and *The Co-Evolution Quarterly*. In 1985 it became *Whole Earth Review* and later *Whole Earth*.

A contributing factor to the *Catalog*'s status as the "handbook of the counterculture" was its design. The publication was large and unwieldy (approximately 14⅛ × 11 inches [36 × 28 cm]), but its bulk and weight only added to its appeal, and it always had a vibrant feel. The cheap, "instant" production methods that came into use at the time were responsible for the *Catalog's* many images, headings, and fonts, while the absence of a clear pathway enabled the reader to make surprising connections between different worlds of information, leading some to see it as a forerunner of the Internet. The front and back covers bear the final lasting sentiment: a photograph taken from outer space of the "whole Earth" poised in all its beauty and fragility in blackness, and the concluding comment: "We can't put it together. It is together."

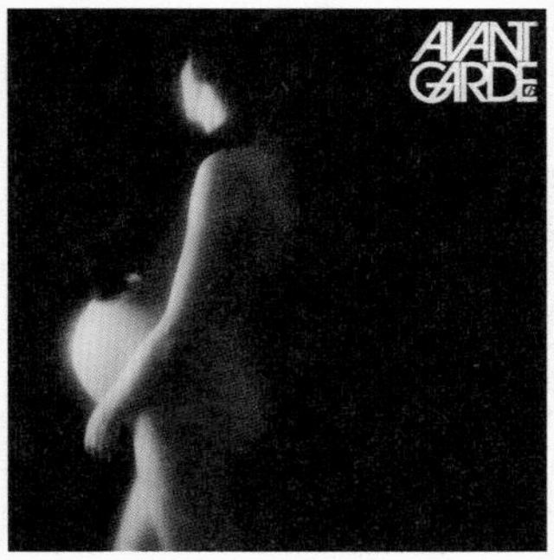

← P.231

← P.232

← P.233

1968–1971 ●

AVANT GARDE

Magazine / Newspaper

Herb Lubalin (1918–1981)

Ralph Ginzburg, U.S.

A magazine centered on art and politics, *Avant Garde* was Herb Lubalin's third collaboration with the independent publisher Ralph Ginzburg (the previous two being *Eros* and *Fact:*). Despite having only a modest circulation and a brief lifespan (fourteen issues), the title was high-profile and popular and, with its critical stance on American politics and society and provocative sexual imagery, it quickly established a reputation for controversy. Art director Lubalin brought an inspired look to the magazine, producing outstanding spreads and the magazine's own dedicated and noteworthy typeface.

Considered an intellectual equal by Ginzburg, Lubalin was given a free hand in the design: intricate illustrations were blended with lengthy photographic essays, often printed on a variety of paper stock with the occasional blast of Day-Glo inks, while drama was created by contrasts in scale, pacing, and flow. Covers were strong single images, unfettered by titles apart from the logo, and often tending toward the bizarre and fantastic. No less important for its reputation, the magazine's generous square format (11 x 11 inches [27.9 x 27.9 cm]) and many full-page headlines provided a sizable canvas for typographic expression—a relatively new idea at the time that has now become commonplace. After developing the magazine's innovative masthead, with its distinctive sloping "V" and "A" (inspired by Ginzburg's wife, Shoshanna, who told him to "imagine a jet taking off of a runway into the future"), Lubalin turned his attention to the typeface. Specifying a full set of capitals for the internal headlines, he asked three assistants from his firm to hand-draw all twenty-six characters. Tom Carnase, one of Lubalin's partners, created many additional tightly fitted pairs of letters with negative spacing, or kerning. These pairs, called "ligatures," became the hallmark of the typeface. The full set of characters was released by the International Typeface Corporation (of which Lubalin was a partner) in 1970.

Avant Garde perfectly framed the uncertain zeitgeist of the 1960s, and remains a testimonial to Lubalin's genius as an editorial graphic designer. Both the magazine and its eponymous typeface are landmarks in their fields.

1968 ●

VORMGEVERS

Poster

Wim Crouwel (1928–2019)

Stedelijk Museum, the Netherlands

Created for an exhibition at the Stedelijk Museum in Amsterdam, Wim Crouwel's poster "Vormgevers" (Designers) famously made the grid visible, turning a previously hidden tool of the graphic designer into an explicit device. Here, the underlying framework for layout and lettering is transformed into a formal element, providing a memorable piece of communication that reflected the theme of the show.

Crouwel's studio, Total Design, founded in 1963, oversaw the production of printed matter for the Stedelijk from 1964 and had a particular approach to the grid; it even had its own grid sheets printed in advance, which enabled this high-contrast composition to be created. The poster also marked another step in Crouwel's experimentation with constructed, modular typography, and recalls the architectural lettering of early-twentieth-century Dutch designers, such as H. P. Berlage and Gerrit Rietveld, as well as the 1950s "Swiss school" developed by, among others, Karl Gerstner and Armin Hofmann.

Although created by hand with a ruler and compass, the poster's basic geometric shapes and reversals of color anticipate the typography of early computer displays, as well as trends in pixilation and digital typography of the 1990s. The type can be compared to the typography Crouwel composed from dots, as seen in his Job Hansen exhibition poster for the Fodor Museum, which anticipates dot matrix and LED lettering, and his modular New Alphabet, a typeface system inspired by the technological constraints of the photographic typesetter he encountered in 1965. "Vormgevers" is an archetypal example of Crouwel's work: abstract and unorthodox yet still precise, calculated, and made up of only rational forms.

1968 ●

FRUTIGER

Typeface

Adrian Frutiger (1928–2015)

Charles de Gaulle International Airport, France

Swiss type designer Adrian Frutiger's eponymous typeface was originally designed for the signage system for the Charles de Gaulle International Airport at Roissy, France, which opened in 1974. Frutiger, already well known for the design of Univers in 1957, and for the modern signage systems of the Paris Métro and Orly Airport, wanted to design a typeface that would suit the architecture of the terminal building and be legible from various angles and at various sizes and distances while driving and walking. He took his inspiration from the neo-grotesque clarity of Univers and the humanistic forms of roman typefaces, such as Gill Sans. Consequently, Frutiger is neither completely geometric nor completely humanist in style, which is perhaps what gives it a distinctive character.

As a typeface, Frutiger is characterized by its variations in width and in the proportions of its letterforms, many of which are open and rounded with almost classical proportions. It has prominent ascenders and descenders, with the ascenders taller than the capitals. The design of each character was drawn by hand and rigorously tested by Frutiger for legibility in poor light and at speed, including even unfocused letters. Originally named "Roissy" after the airport, Frutiger was finally released commercially in 1976 by the D. Stempel AG type foundry, and is now available in an extended family, using the same two-digit system as Univers to differentiate between weights and styles. Although the face was designed for signage and use at a large scale, Frutiger also works well at the much smaller scale of body copy in books or magazines, and is used within the corporate identity of the UK's National Health Service and the Royal Navy.

Frutiger's distinctive, legible design continues to evolve, going from strength to strength. In 2003 a revised version, ASTRA Frutiger, was produced for use in Swiss road signage.

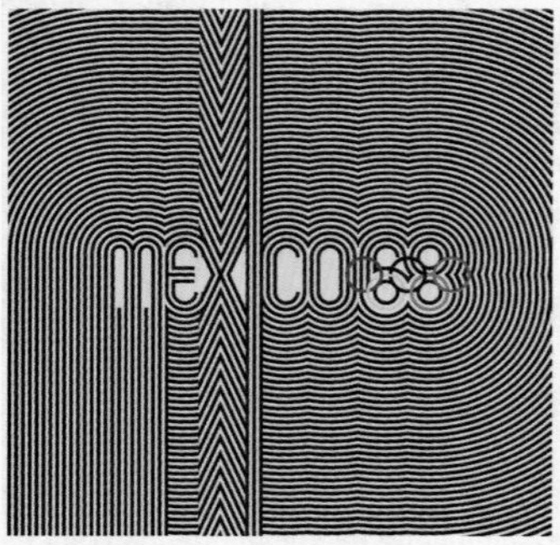

← P.233

1968

1968 MEXICO CITY OLYMPICS

Identity

Lance Wyman (1937–), Peter Murdoch (1940–), et al.

Mexico City Olympic Committee, Mexico

The Nineteenth Olympiad in Mexico City is remembered for, among other things, the graphic originality and sophisticated implementation of its design system. The comprehensive scheme derived from visual references to Mexican culture and had broad multilingual applications.

In 1966 the chair of the organizing committee, Mexican architect Pedro Ramirez Vazquez, set out to assemble a multicultural, multidisciplinary team to design an effective information system for the event based on the theme of "the young of the world united in friendship through understanding." The team of five design directors, which included American graphic designer Lance Wyman and British industrial designer Peter Murdoch, produced wayfinding systems, environmental signage, pictographs, visual identities, and publicity materials. For the logotype, Wyman studied Aztec artifacts and Mexican folk art to create a look that would not only define the Olympic event, but also evoke Latin cultural heritage in the 1960s.

Next to the word "Mexico," Wyman laid Olympic rings over the numerals 68, creating a pattern of repeated lines suggestive of pre-Hispanic Mexican art. Like a black-and-white op art design, the vibrating stripes spelled out the words "Mexico 68" before exploding outward. The radiating lines were easily adaptable to a wide range of graphic media, such as posters and the helium-filled balloons that floated above the entrance to each event, and Wyman ultimately applied the extended typeface to everything from tickets and billboards to uniforms. Also integral to the scheme was the use of rich hues evocative of Latino festival culture, which, as well as adding vibrancy, provided a universal coding system for organizing information. For example, a rainbow of colors along the major routes referred to those on the official map, making it practically impossible to get lost when traveling between arenas.

Wyman's identity for the 1968 Mexico City Olympics, particularly the logotype, marked a high-water line in graphic design for the Olympics, and remains one of the standards by which other Games are measured.

← P.234

1968

DAY OF THE HEROIC GUERRILLA

Poster

Elena Serrano (1934–)

OSPAAAL, Cuba

In Cuba, October 8 marks the Day of the Heroic Guerrilla, which commemorates the life of Che Guevara, executed in Bolivia on October 9, 1967. Elena Serrano's poster for the Organización de Solidaridad con los Pueblos de Asia, África y América Latina (OSPAAAL) observes the first anniversary of Che's capture, and hints at his impending rise to becoming a symbol of the revolution.

Cuban posters, especially those produced by OSPAAAL, played an important part in disseminating revolutionary messages across the globe. OSPAAAL was set up in 1966 with the intention of promoting anti-imperialist struggles throughout the world. Through the pages of *Tricontinental* magazine, OSPAAAL became one of the largest publishers of "third world" perspectives on international politics. Initially published in English, Spanish, French, and Arabic, *Tricontinental* brought together the theories of radical thinkers under a single framework, featuring contributors as diverse as Vietnam's Ho Chi Minh, Frantz Fanon from Martinique, and North Korea's Kim Jong-il.

In *Tricontinental*'s early issues, a poster was folded and placed between its pages. At its peak, the publication reached eighty-seven countries, constituting one of the largest poster-distribution networks in the world. The overarching concept behind OSPAAAL posters was to raise awareness of oppressed people in their struggle against imperialism. The designers developed a common graphic language that could be assimilated by different cultures and languages, using simple, strong images that conveyed meaning without words.

Serrano's poster is an early example of the use of Alberto Korda's famous photograph. Serrano superimposes Korda's image of the freedom fighter over a map of South America. The square surrounding Che's face increases outward, reverberating throughout Latin America, until Che and the continent appear to merge. Serrano's depiction blends the legend of Che with the Latin America that Cuban leaders believed would eventually submit to similar revolutions. His myth did indeed spread worldwide but, ironically, instead of giving impetus to further revolutions, Che's image became a universal and commercial symbol of the romantic freedom fighter—partly through posters such as Serrano's.

← P.235

1969–1971

KUNST DER SECHZIGER JAHRE

Book

Wolf Vostell (1932–1998)

Wallraf-Richartz Museum, Germany

As much an artwork as a book, this museum catalog embodies the playfulness and subversion of the 1960s art scene. A bundle of pages encased in a clear plastic cover and held together by screws, its high production values and unique design system make it an object that demands to be picked up and explored. The book showcases the extensive collection of 1960s works loaned by Peter and Irene Ludwig to Cologne's Wallraf-Richartz Museum in 1969, and was designed by one of the artists featured, Wolf Vostell. Five editions were made, each updated as further items were added to the collection.

The book's extraordinary construction begins with the cover, which is made up of four layers of different materials, all overlapping to produce a tangled mess of images that become clearer as each page is turned. Two of the collection's works—*Miss America* by Vostell and *M-Maybe* (*A Girl's Picture*) by Roy Lichtenstein—are placed on top of each other to create a third, hybrid image. Inside, various paper stocks are used. The introduction is printed on thin sheets of styrofoam and graph paper, but the bulk of the catalog is made up of thick brown paper, with plates of the artworks tipped in. Between these pages are inserted individual, transparent plastic sheets printed with photographs of the artists.

Vostell, one of the pioneers of the Fluxus movement, was obsessed with the processes of destruction and construction, creating collages and assemblages full of juxtaposing themes and overlapping images. The blending of artworks and photographs in this book is sometimes beautiful, but at other times it can be awkward and confusing, making no concession to the varying quality and size of pictures: strict rules govern the design, but they are allowed to produce chaotic results.

In the book's introduction, Gert von der Osten, director of the museum, declares that the 1960s was the first period in which art could no longer be judged in terms of "good taste." This ostentatious book embodies this shift, which, rather than being pretty or usable, is designed to be iconoclastic and to provoke a reaction from the reader.

← P.235

1969–1987

INTERVIEW

Magazine / Newspaper

Andy Warhol (1928–1987), Richard Bernstein (1939–2002)

Andy Warhol and John Wilcock, U.S.

At the intersection of two phenomena—the celebrity cult and DIY culture—*Interview* magazine was originally an amateurish black-and-white, quarter-folded tabloid, printed on cheap newsprint. Launched by Andy Warhol and the British journalist John Wilcock, it was conceived as a subterfuge for Warhol to gain access to the New York Film Festival underground scene. Since he was already famous as an artist and founder of The Factory, Warhol's latest ambition was to become an avant-garde filmmaker, focusing on interviews with stars. Even though it was dilettantish, the magazine became idolized; to be featured on the cover of *Interview* was soon perceived as the ultimate consecration.

Much of the credit for *Interview*'s success is owed to Richard Bernstein, the retouching artist who from 1972 designed all the publication's covers. In the May issue of that year, the old *Interview* logo and strapline "Andy Warhol's Film Magazine" were replaced by a script title, *Andy Warhol's Interview*, scribbled over a color portrait of Donna Jordan, a young actress featured in Warhol's film *L'Amour*. Using colored pencils, airbrush, and pastels, he knew how to bring out the best in a face, intensifying its beauty and erasing its flaws, and had a unique ability to empathize with his subjects. During his fifteen years at the magazine, Bernstein created more than one-hundred-twenty of these posterlike covers, refining his graphic enhancement techniques to keep the magazine looking fresh, as exemplified in the 1977 cover featuring Jodie Foster (pictured).

The layout of the magazine itself was unmemorable, its typography deliberately neutral so as not to detract from the photographs. In design terms,it remained true to its DIY roots, and even after Warhol's death did not disown its alternative-culture, avant-garde beginnings. In the 1990s, however, *Interview* was transformed into a glossy contemporary fashion-and-art tabloid, its oversized pages a vehicle for displaying the talents of famous art directors, such as Fabien Baron and Tibor Kalman. Today, its editorial serves only as a pretext to feature celebrities of the moment—the actors, sports heroes, and top models who endorse advertisements for luxury products.

← P.236

1969

VALENTINE

Poster

Milton Glaser (1929–2020)

Olivetti, Italy

Milton Glaser's curious poster for the Olivetti Valentine typewriter was an attempt to create a sophisticated advertising image that avoided overtly commercial imagery or slogans. Olivetti was a particularly progressive company with regard to design and advertising, and in Giorgio Soavi, Olivetti's design director, a poet, novelist, and art lover, Glaser found a kindred soul. Given carte blanche, Glaser seized the opportunity to indulge two passions: his love of animals and affinity with Renaissance painting.

Olivetti's bright red portable Valentine typewriter, designed in 1969 by Ettore Sottsass, was a precursor of the laptop computer in terms of mobility and style. Conceived as a personal fashion accessory rather than an office machine, it came with a case and handle, and was essentially a lifestyle statement. Glaser took this concept of portability to another dimension. Transposing the typewriter to the past, he set it in a Renaissance landscape, specifically a scene from *The Death of Procris*, a fifteenth-century work by Piero di Cosimo that hangs in London's National Gallery. But instead of the whole image, Glaser focused on a detail—the doleful portrait of a dog, which in the original watches intently as a satyr comforts a wounded nymph. In Glaser's version, only the feet of the reclining figure are visible, and the dog, now center-stage, sits strangely bemused over the distinctive silhouette of the typewriter, set down in the grass. But most divergent from the painting is the dog's scale in relation to the whole and its place within the frame. Reminiscent of comic books, the cropped image seems to be part of a longer narrative sequence in which the dog is perhaps a reporter who will, in the next frame, turn to the typewriter and write a quick dispatch.

Executed in colored pen and ink using a cross-etching technique, the poster showcases Neo Futura bold, a new stencil typeface designed by Glaser in the early 1970s. With its ambiguity and dreamlike mood, the poster also appears to be yet another example of the growing influence of Surrealism on advertising arts during the second half of the twentieth century.

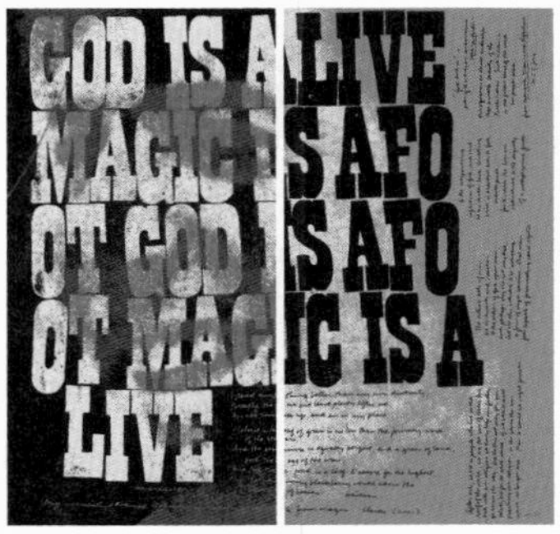

← P.237

1969

GOD IS ALIVE (PARTS 1 AND 2)

Poster

Corita Kent (1918–1986)

Self-commissioned, U.S.

Corita Kent, formerly Sister Mary Corita, was only eighteen years old when she joined the Immaculate Heart of Mary (IHM) in 1936 in Los Angeles, despite having no apparent religious bent. Joining the Catholic order enabled her to pursue training in art and art history at the University of Southern California. Her subsequent teaching at Immaculate Heart College drew on her own work, which focused on traditional religious representations and heavily layered techniques.

It wasn't until the 1960s that Kent's memorable artistic voice emerged. The era was stained by turbulent hallmarks of political and social upheaval. In response, Kent began stripping back her approach, looking outside the Catholic canon to Pop art, advertising, pop culture, and secular literature and lyrics. By the time she left the IHM in 1968, John F. Kennedy and Martin Luther King, Jr. had been assassinated, the civil rights movement had formally dissolved, Black voting rights were enshrined in the U.S. Constitution, and foreign tensions had escalated through the Cold War, the Space Race, and the Vietnam War.

Kent's series of twenty-nine posters, "Heroes to Sheroes," reflects the unsettled national mood and marked an artistic turning point. Experimenting with a mash-up of uppercase fonts and strident imagery, she produced serigraphs with conventional half-tone print methods, but their compositions were anything but predictable. Inverted imagery and bold ink choices, such as red, white, and blue, or fluorescent overprinting, met with jarring, irregular typographic line breaks that conveyed slogans, verses, philosophical phrases, and inspirational quotes. Together, the posters were a strident call to action that embedded the language of advertising with messages of hope.

Kent never returned to IHM and actively practiced as an artist until her death in 1986. Although often overlooked, her legacy includes hundreds of screenprint editions, countless watercolors, and commissions for clients, such as Amnesty International, IBM, and Westinghouse. Her work is held in the collections of the Los Angeles County Museum of Art, and the Metropolitan Museum of Art and Museum of Modern Art, both in New York.

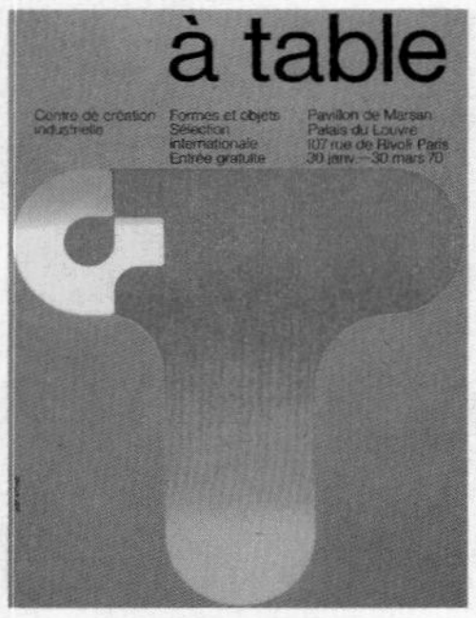

← P.238

1969–1972

CENTRE DE CRÉATION INDUSTRIELLE

Poster

Jean Widmer (1929–)

Centre de Création Industrielle, France

With their fluorescent colors and bold, abstract, almost childlike shapes, Jean Widmer's posters might at first seem inappropriately lively for the Centre de Création Industrielle (CCI). This diligent organization, set up in 1969 and later subsumed into the Centre du Pompidou in Paris, produced exhibitions, publications, and discourse around a wide range of design practices. However, Widmer counted these posters among his favorite works, and felt that the "visual coherence" of their forms was complemented by a Minimalist style, creating a distinctive and immediately recognizable identity for CCI.

The Swiss-born Widmer trained under the former Bauhaus color theorist Johannes Itten. The latter tempered his sternly objective design approach with a philosophical and, at times, mystical mind-set, which may explain Widmer's apparently contradictory combinations of visual language. The posters' backgrounds are plain and even, and the typography is a classic example of the "Swiss school"—consistently sans serif, minimal in size and uniform in weight, ranged left across three columns, with the heading uniting the two on the right. However, despite (or perhaps because of) this uncompromising approach, the neatly balanced columns of text form an assured presence alongside the whimsical and strongly contoured shapes, which evoke heavy-duty industrial components but also temper the austerity of the design.

Widmer is sometimes said to have introduced the "Swiss school" to France at the expense of its traditionally more spirited practice, yet these posters also reinforce that tradition: there is a blithe wit in the graceful poise of the abstract shapes, which sets them in a pleasing counterpoint to the rigid typography. With its contrasting effects, Widmer's sophisticated, streamlined design brings a sensitive, imaginative touch to an organization with an identity that could be easily misconstrued, enabling viewers to imagine its name and remit as essentially human and creative.

← P.239

1969–1970

GAY POWER

Magazine / Newspaper

John Heys (1948–) et al.

Joel Fabricant, U.S.

The 1969 Stonewall Uprising in New York saw the city's LGBTQ+ community clash with local police for five consecutive nights after the latter violently raided a gay bar in Greenwich Village. The events that unfolded brought into sharp focus the human-rights abuses routinely suffered by the queer community and helped advance the worldwide movement for LGBTQ+ rights. In turn, the protests sparked the creation of a series of periodicals, disseminated within various underground publishing scenes, that aimed to spotlight and celebrate queer culture. Among them was *Gay Power*, spearheaded by editor John Heys and publisher Joel Fabricant, which grew to become one of the most popular queer periodicals of the era.

Bearing the tagline "New York's first homosexual newspaper," *Gay Power* featured a wide array of content, combining political news, calls for activism, short stories, personal ads, and a selection of commissioned artworks and photographs. Its creators' far-reaching network and influence brought in prominent writers and artists as contributors, including Pudgy Roberts, Tom of Finland, Arthur Bell, Charles Ludlam, and Robert Mapplethorpe—the last of whom contributed a photograph that is purported to be his first-ever published image. Adorning the front cover of Volume 1, Issue 16, Mapplethorpe's artwork exhibits the kind of erotic (and at the time controversial) subject matter that he soon became known for.

This cover typifies the publication's visual approach, which embraced the dominant psychedelic styles of the period. At the top of page, the *Gay Power* wordmark is rendered in a "groovy," hand-drawn font composed of warped, expressive letterforms. Beneath it is Mapplethorpe's iconic photo collage, titled *Bull's Eye*, which shows a naked male figure in knee-high leather boots, framed by various geometric forms. At the center is a transparent yellow rectangle containing a single red circle that serves to censor the nudity in a playful way. A black stripe covers the figure's face, obscuring his identity and introducing a layer of mystery and intrigue to an otherwise completely exposed subject.

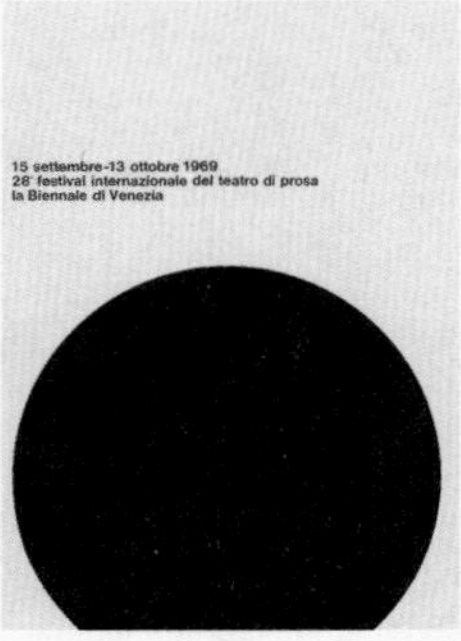

← P.240

1969

LA BIENNALE DI VENEZIA

Poster

A. G. Fronzoni (1923–2002)

La Biennale di Venezia, Italy

In 1969, Italian graphic designer A. G. Fronzoni completed a series of powerful, black-and-white posters for the Venice Biennale. These posters, like many that Fronzoni did for other cultural events and organizations, are striking in their simplicity. Two in particular—"28 Festival Internazionale del Teatro di Prosa" and "32 Festival Internazionale di Musica Contemporanea"—are important examples. The first (pictured) has a large, round, black dot placed in the lower two-thirds of the completely white background. Above this to the left are three lines of text—the minimum required to communicate the sense—in a bold sans serif font with minimal capitalization. The second poster features the same white background with a black dot and three lines of text, though this time the dot is markedly smaller.

The powerful simplicity of these posters is a result of Fronzoni's interest in the Modernism of Le Corbusier and the Bauhaus. Part of a late wave of Modernism that emerged in the 1960s, Fronzoni has been credited with being the initiator of Minimalism in Italy. He was also known for using only black and white in his work as well as in his everyday life: the furniture and furnishings that he designed were black and white, and he wore black and white clothes for most of the year.

The relative lack of text in these two posters is also significant. Unlike his contemporaries, for whom writing about their designs was a key part of their practice, Fronzoni almost never wrote about his work. Indeed, when asked by Giorgio Camuffo in 1997 to write an essay about design, Fronzoni submitted forty-two lines of text written in a tiny Futura font. On closer inspection, the main text is made up of characters that look like words but are nonsense, while the title reads "*Che vergogna scrivere*" (How shameful it is to write).

Despite the fact that Fronzoni was largely silent about his own work, the stark efficacy of the images themselves has meant that he is increasingly named by graphic designers as a crucial influence.

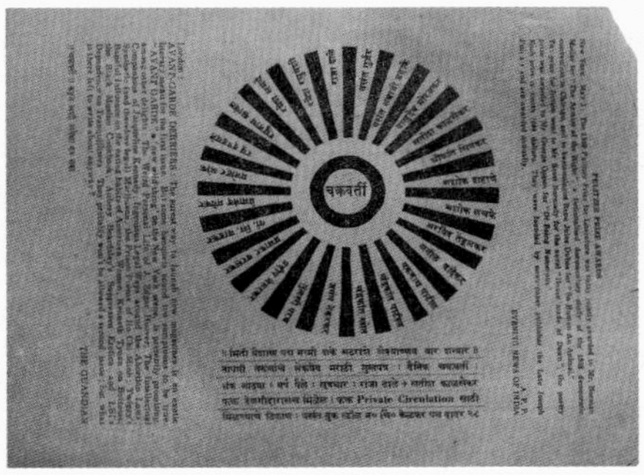

← P.241

1970s

CHAKRAVARTY

Magazine / Newspaper

Raja Dhale (1940–2019)

Dalit Panthers, India

The caste system has dominated South Asia for thousands of years, creating an oppressive social hierarchy by dividing the population into four categories. Brahmins, the priests and academics, sit at the top, while Shudras, the manual laborers, are at the bottom. Dalits (which in Sanskrit means "oppressed" or "broken"), known in India as Scheduled Castes, are those who are left out of the system entirely. In the early 1970s, a revolutionary movement called the Dalit Panthers (which took inspiration from the Black Panther Party in the United States) organized to fight against the system that had marginalized them for so long.

One of the key stakeholders in the Dalit Panthers was the artist, publisher, and activist Raja Dhale, who produced a small literary magazine called *Chakravarty* for thirteen consecutive days. In an industry that is controlled by the upper castes, self-publishing has historically been a way for the voices of oppressed communities to be heard. *Chakravarty* gave members a platform to raise awareness about anti-caste ideology, a concept that advanced the region's little magazine movement.

The *Chakravarty* title is framed by a circle from which the names of the movement's editors and writers fan outward, creating an image reminiscent of rays of light. In a feature in AIGA's *Eye on Design*, Ritupriya Basu notes that "the circle, with no definite start or end, nodded to ideas of equality ... it posed an antithesis to the pyramidal structure of the caste system that they were bent on tearing apart." Issue 8 features an essay on the impossibilities of language and writing, as well as a satirical gossip column by Dhale, proving that wit in revolutionary movements is as vital as critique.

Today, much of the archiving and sharing of this movement is done via an Instagram account called the Dalit Panther Archive, run by illustrator Shrujana Shridhar, who painstakingly documents and translates the magazines she can find. The difficulty Shridhar experienced in sourcing these historical works illuminates the oppressive structures of institutional archiving: whose stories get to be remembered? With this grassroots initiative, Shridhar is correcting historical narratives and keeping the spirit of the Dalit Panthers alive.

← P.241

1970

RECYCLING

Information Design

Gary Anderson (1947–)

Container Corporation of America, U.S.

Since its design in 1970, the universal recycling symbol has become one of the twentieth century's most widely recognized emblems. However, the triangle of three curved arrows has also been a victim of its own success, reproduced in so many forms around the world that it now no longer has a consistent meaning and even varies between industries.

The icon was the outcome of a nationwide competition held by the Container Corporation of America (CCA), the nation's largest paper recycler, which required a recycling symbol for its cardboard boxes, and roughly coincided with the first Earth Day. CCA's history of graphic patronage stretched back to World War II, when it commissioned the Bauhaus typography master Herbert Bayer and French poster artist Jean Carlu to create anti-Nazi posters. Gary Anderson, who won the contest, was a twenty-three-year-old architecture student at the University of Southern California. His hand-drawn design was inspired by the Möbius strip, while the arrows were intended as both a representation of the recycling process and a metaphorical reference to the constancy of matter. Anderson's original design was rotated by CCA so that the space inside the three arrows could resemble a tree, and licensed to other paper companies for a nominal fee. When CCA attempted to register it as a trademark, however, this was challenged by an environmental group on the grounds that it would force other companies to design their own symbols. This happened anyway, and by the 1980s the American Paper Institute alone was promoting four different versions.

Anderson's recycling symbol has since been adapted for aluminum, steel, glass, and plastic recycling, as well as for paper. In addition to its official commercial redesigns, amateur politicized versions have appeared, such as a map showing North and South America looping into each other, with a question mark formed by rotating one of the arrows downward. Despite its multiplicity, however, the recycling symbol is broadly recognized internationally, if not always clearly understood. The adoption of the icon as a Unicode computer character has further helped to enshrine its place in popular consciousness.

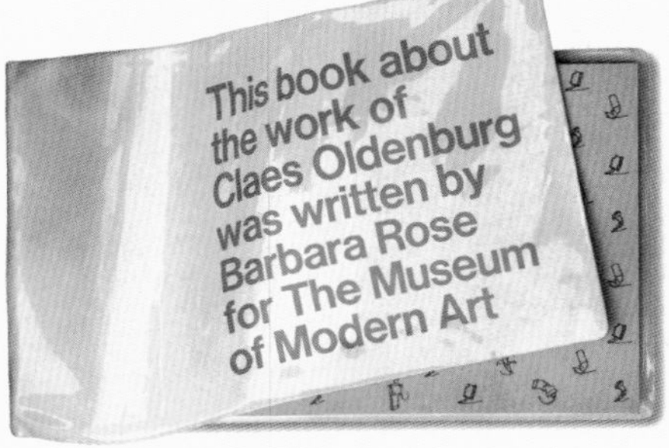

← P.242

1970

CLAES OLDENBURG

Book

Ivan Chermayeff (1932–2017), Tom Geismar (1931–)

Museum of Modern Art, New York, U.S.

After designing the identity and publicity material for the Museum of Modern Art (MoMA) in New York during the 1960s, Ivan Chermayeff and Tom Geismar were asked to create the catalog for an exhibition of Claes Oldenburg, the Swedish-born American Pop art sculptor. The agency produced this "soft" book, which shares many of the features of the exhibits.

By 1969, Oldenburg had established a reputation for monumental sculptures of banal, everyday objects, culminating in the controversial installation of *Lipstick (Ascending) on Caterpillar Tracks* at Yale University. His first major retrospective was held at MoMA later that year, and included drawing proposals for monuments and sculptures in hard, soft, and "ghost" representations. The soft versions were sewn together from vinyl and filled with kapok (a silky fiber obtained from the seeds of a tropical tree) to appear lacking in form, deliberately denying sculpture's traditional monumentality and three-dimensionality. Chermayeff and Geismar had always taken an uncompromising approach to design, viewing their role as that of problem solvers, and rejecting style in favor of appropriate solutions to specific communication problems, laced with humor and invention. The result in this case was a book with a textural, foam-filled vinyl cover, printed with a long and prosaic title set in Helvetica. On the flyleaf inside are miniature repetitions of Oldenburg drawings in red on a pink background, which evoke wallpaper or wrapping paper. The effect, combined with the yellow vinyl cover and blue-green typography, is reminiscent of a children's book, contrasting simplicity with comic disorientation. Inside, the catalog is divided into two sections that echo the cover-print style of large simple letters and a plain layout.

Chermayeff and Geismar met at the Yale School of Art and Architecture in 1957, and shared a passion for typography, which they later expressed in the brochure *That New York* (1959). Incorporated in 1960, their agency has since produced numerous major identity programs for companies, including Mobil, Chase Manhattan, PanAm, Xerox, and Time Warner. In 2003 designer Sagi Haviv joined the firm and was subsequently made partner.

← P.242

← P.243

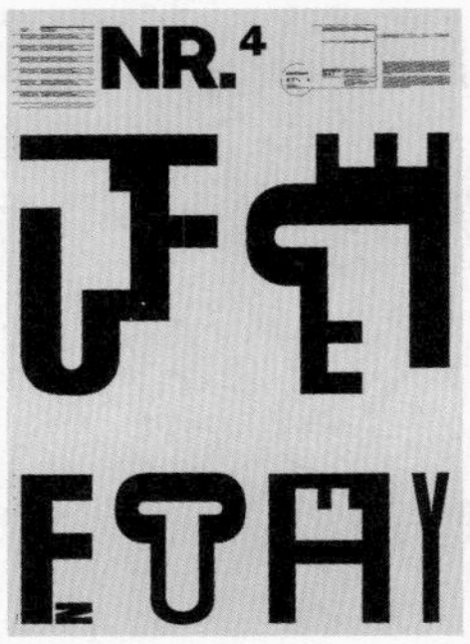

← P.243

1970–1976

CASABELLA

Magazine Cover

Alessandro Mendini (1931–2019)

Studio Editoriale Milanese, Italy

Originally founded by Guido Marangoni in 1928 as *La Casa Bella* (Beautiful Home), this long-standing architecture, interiors, and design magazine has garnered prestige for its notable directors and editors, including Ernesto Rogers, Franco Albini, and Vittorio Gregotti. After several masthead rebrands, the title was changed to *Casabella* in the mid-1960s, and by 1970 the provocative Milanese designer Alessandro Mendini was appointed art director.

Under Mendini's tenure, *Casabella* entered a period of progressive experimentation that drew on his interest in radical art practices of the time, provoked by global political and social tensions. Questioning the status quo of polite interiors and good taste, Mendini positioned the title as a beacon for avant-garde design thinkers. This cultural frame found expression in Italy and beyond through the radical design movement. Under Mendini's direction, the magazine introduced work by pioneers such as Superstudio, Gaetano Pesce, and Ettore Sottsass, as well as the Arte Povera and Situationist artists.

In addition to driving its countercultural content, Mendini translated its subversive attitude through thought-provoking covers. The June 1973 issue displays a detail of *Exodus, or the Voluntary Prisoners of Architecture*, a series of drawings about Cold War–era Berlin by architects Rem Koolhaas and Elia Zenghelis and artists Madelon Vriesendorp and Zoe Zenghelis. August/September 1974 features Mendini's "suitcase for the last journey": a forebidding gray valise stamped, sealed, and cast on a muddy ground. Perhaps Mendini's most famous cover is from July 1972 (pictured), which depicts a Godzilla-scaled gorilla beating its chest, emblazoned with the words "Radical Design" in blood-red Helvetica. Superseded by Tomás Maldonado in 1977, Mendini continued his brave and brilliant art direction at *Modo* magazine (1977–79) and Italian design bible *Domus* (1979–85).

Alongside his publishing career, Mendini worked as a curator, artist, architect, and designer, notably collaborating as part of Studio Alchimia with Sottsass and Michele De Lucchi, and advising brands such as Swatch and Alessi through the 1980s. He was awarded the prestigious Compasso d'Oro three times and was honored with the French Chevalier de l'Ordre des Arts et des Lettres.

1970–1976

AVALANCHE

Magazine / Newspaper

Willoughby Sharp (1936–2008)

Self-commissioned, U.S.

One of the first fine-art magazines to feature portraits of artists on its covers rather than works of art, *Avalanche* reflected the growing importance of the artist's personality in the international art world of the 1970s.

Two years in development, *Avalanche* was launched in SoHo, New York, in October 1970 by Willoughby Sharp (who as Boris Wall Gruphy, an anagram of his real name, also designed the magazine) and Liza Béar, and soon became an important reference point for the city's art scene. The magazine's location meant that it could directly access leading figures in contemporary art, such as Robert Smithson, Bruce Nauman, and William Wegman, who in turn were allowed to speak about their work unmediated by critics. Close-ups of the artists' faces in grainy black-and-white photographs, which gazed out from the covers, were intended to convey the magazine's informal approach to interviewing and to bring the audience into closer contact with the individuals behind the works, starting a dialogue that would continue through the publication's pages. At the same time, the use of Helvetica for the masthead (the only text to appear on the cover) aimed to reference the neutral, understated aesthetics of the conceptual and performance artists to whom the magazine was largely devoted. Joseph Beuys, an artist perfectly allied with the concept of the magazine and the art it represented, was an ideal choice to illustrate the first issue.

As its name suggests, *Avalanche* signaled the momentous changes that were taking place in the art world during the period. The magazine continued publishing until 1976, when the rise of Expressionist painting challenged the artistic counterculture that *Avalanche* promoted, and in the end Béar and Sharp were unable to secure the funding to continue printing (the final cover featured a photograph of their accounts ledger). Although it survived for only thirteen issues, *Avalanche* anticipated the rise of the artist as celebrity that was to emerge in the 1990s, and has had a direct influence on current publications, such as *Flash Art* and *Art Review*, which place the artist and the interview at the forefront of their coverage of artistic trends.

1971–1974

TYPOGRAPHIC PROCESS

Poster

Wolfgang Weingart (1941–2021) et al.

Self-commissioned, Switzerland

Wolfgang Weingart's limited-edition "Typographic Process" series of posters presented the work of his design and typography students at the Basel School of Design, where he began teaching in 1968. As well as testifying to Weingart's passion for learning and teaching, which are nearly inseparable in his mind, the posters were published to coincide with his 1972–73 lecture tour of American schools on the topic "How Can One Make Swiss Typography?" in which he presented his nascent ideas about typographic education.

The posters' design showcases both Weingart's roots in reductive Swiss typography and his attempts to question and build on that foundation through experimentation and exploitation of process. While he is known for his postmodern layouts for posters such as "Das Schweizer Plakat" (1984) and the "Kunstkredit" series (1976–77), as well as for the New Wave style he spawned through students such as April Greiman and Dan Friedman, such work is the by-product of the approach documented in these posters.

Weingart set the masthead and descriptive text in his favorite Akzidenz-Grotesk typeface, but the student work illustrated is as diverse as that of any class, and represents the curiosity and questioning of standards that Weingart encouraged at Basel. On one poster the viewer is treated to unexpected solutions for advertisements for the Swiss Post, Telegram and Telegraph Service, whereas others include "Typo-signs," where the nature of letters is explored and challenged, and "Typography as Painting," in which students were encouraged to fill an empty space and make it dynamic. In each case, traditional typographic skills are learned, broken down, and built upon.

Weingart "retired" from teaching at Basel in 2004, but continued working there as a summer lecturer. These posters were followed a decade later by a supplement to the magazine *Typografische Monatsblätter*—also called *Typographic Process*—in which outstanding students at Basel documented long-term research projects, for which Weingart also designed the layout.

← P.244

← P.245

← P.245

1971–present

OKIKE: AN AFRICAN JOURNAL OF NEW WRITING

Magazine Cover

Obiora Udechukwu (1946–)

Chinua Achebe, U.S. and Nigeria

Founded in 1971 by Nigerian novelist, poet, and literary critic Chinua Achebe, *Okike: An African Journal of New Writing* was developed to platform the work of new and established writers from the African continent and diaspora. Achebe, who published his first novel, *Things Fall Apart*, in 1958, is widely credited as being the founding father of African fiction. He spent much of his career challenging European stereotypes of Africa and African art and literature, and promoting the culture and perspectives of its people. *Okike* allowed African literature to be critiqued and celebrated outside of a Western framework.

At the time of *Okike*'s founding, Achebe was working as a senior research fellow at the University of Nigeria, Nsukka. It was here that he met the artist and poet Obiora Udechukwu, who was commissioned to design the cover for the journal. The design centers on an illustration of Ala, the Igbo earth goddess and patroness of the arts, which was reproduced from a photograph showing the deity in an Mbari house, an architectural artwork built in her honor. Udechukwu hand-drew the title, *Okike*, in a decorative style that reflects the expressive, ink-black linework in the image. In addition to defining the journal's external appearance, Udechukwu served on *Okike*'s editorial board and contributed both art and literary works throughout its publication. He later relocated to the United States, where he became professor of fine arts at St. Lawrence University, New York.

In 1972 Achebe also temporarily moved to the U.S. to teach African literature at the University of Massachusetts, Amherst, but continued as editor of *Okike*. Each issue featured a range of pieces, including essays, fiction, poetry, literary reviews, and letters to the editor, as well as drawings that often played on the narrative themes. Contributors included Kofi Akoonor, Dennis Brutus, Prospère Pierre-Louis, Wole Soyinka, and Ekwueme Michael Thelwell. *Okike*'s adroit combination of literature and art recalled publications from America's Black literary canon, including the Harlem Renaissance–era *Fire!! Devoted to Younger Negro Artists* (1926). Achebe continued to write and lecture until his death in 2013, having received numerous accolades and more than thirty honorary doctorates.

1971

NIKE

Logo

Carolyn Davidson (1943–)

Nike, U.S.

In 1971, Phil Knight's Blue Ribbon Sports shoe company required some statistics and marketing graphics for a business presentation, so he commissioned Portland State University art student Carolyn Davidson. Davidson did not realize that her charts-and-graphs assignment would deliver her a more substantial project at a later date—designing the iconic Nike "swoosh." Knight was not completely happy with Davidson's early rendering, but decided to use the logo in order to meet a string of deadlines.

Track coach and Nike cofounder Bill Bowerman felt the symbol resembled a foot pushing off the ground, but thanks to employee Jeff Johnson's suggestion that the company be called Nike, we associate it with one of the Greek goddess's wings. Davidson invoiced Nike $35 for her design work, and would maintain her position as Nike designer by creating a complete range of corporate communication material, advertisements, and packaging, until the volume of work became too much for one person to manage.

The logo has evolved since the 1970s, when the shape had "Nike" written over it with a script typeface. Subsequent iterations include "Nike" in oblique sans serif lettering stacked above (1978), the lockup contained within a red box (1985), and the symbol on its own without any text. As early as 1986, Nike began to abandon the swoosh on certain shoe styles, most surprisingly the Air Jordan II, the popular successor to the first Air Jordan. This marketing decision raised a lot of eyebrows, but it was a move in the right direction, allowing the Air Jordan brand to survive and demonstrating the power of star athletes' endorsements—in this case, basketball player Michael Jordan. Nike became even more serious about dropping the symbol in 1996–97, when corporate executives identified it in the company's annual report as over-dominant. Despite this, the Nike logo has become indelibly associated in the public mind with the athletic-goods industry, making sports virtually synonymous with the Nike name.

1971

SHELL

Logo

Raymond Loewy (1893–1986)

Royal Dutch Shell Co., UK

Over the course of more than a century, Shell has changed its logo ten times, although always repeating the same basic idea. The scallop shell, or "pecten" motif, was periodically adapted to reflect contemporary styles and tastes, but it would be Raymond Loewy who established the iconic identity associated with the company today.

Royal Dutch Shell Company, or Shell as it is known, resulted from the merging of two companies in 1907. Previously, the British company Shell Transport and Trading imported and exported antiques and seashells, among other goods, to and from the Far East—hence the company's name. The first version of the logo was a black-and-white mussel shell, with very little surface area, which was replaced by the pecten shell in 1904. Further changes were made to the emblem in 1909 and 1930, and in 1948 the word "shell" in an uppercase sans serif type was introduced along with the red and yellow coloring to provide greater definition. In the 1950s and '60s the graphics were further simplified and refined, until the design reached its final incarnation by Loewy in 1971. Loewy, who had by this time established himself as a successful industrial and graphic designer, is known for creating some of the most memorable corporate logos. Shell is one of many enduring Loewy designs.

With its straight lines and strong, semicircular red border, Loewy's clear, simple symbol has given Shell's corporate identity a longevity and recognizability that it previously lacked, as testified by the removal in the early 2000s of the "Shell" logotype. More than fifty years later, the logo continues to be one of the best known in the world, as well as appropriate for the company's changing role. Recently, Shell has tried to identify itself with a wider range of energy sources, including more environmentally and socially responsible methods of extraction and delivery, a program the symbol is also highly suited to promoting.

← P.245

← P.246

← P.246

1971

Rolling Stones

Logo

John Pasche (1945–)

Rolling Stones, UK

John Pasche's career was just dawning when the Rolling Stones commissioned him to design a symbol for the band's own record label. The lolling tongue that is now synonymous with the group first made its appearance on the inner sleeve of the 1971 album *Sticky Fingers*, and since then has featured prominently in the Rolling Stones's promotional graphics.

The visual appeal of the lips and tongue is based on the bright simplicity and sexy suggestiveness of the design, which, with its plump lines and gloss, owes a debt to cartoons and Pop art. Over the years, the design has proved a highly versatile emblem, used for Rolling Stones's marketing campaigns, record sleeves, and tour merchandise. The "She's So Cold" single sleeve of 1980, for example, appropriately showed the tongue with icicles, whereas the U.S. tour of 1981 depicted it flying above a stylized American landscape. Today, the logo is licensed to appear on a wide variety of products, including clothing, accessories, and wine.

One factor in the trademark's success is undoubtedly the longevity of the band it represents. The group's regular tours and huge stadium shows provide ample opportunities for the easily reproduced logo to play a starring role. Another is the ideal marriage of the symbol and the product it represents; based on the famous lips of Mick Jagger, the design evokes the history of the Rolling Stones itself, with its emphasis on sexuality, excess, and danger. Indeed, the logo encapsulates all that a rock band should be: cheeky, visceral, and uncomplicated. Pasche has since sold the copyright of his design, and in 2008 the original gouache artwork was acquired by London's Victoria and Albert Museum.

1972

KIELER WOCHE

Poster

Rolf Müller (1940–2015)

Kieler Woche, Germany

With its letters bending and curving in space, Rolf Müller's poster communicates with elegant simplicity the essence of an annual sailing event, Kieler Woche (Kiel Week). The typography evokes a sail billowing in the wind as effectively as any figurative image.

Kieler Woche has been celebrated in the port of Kiel in northern Germany since the turn of the twentieth century, and since 1948 has involved a poster competition; winners have included some of the best graphic designers in Europe, including Anton Stankowski, Christof Gassner, and Wim Crouwel, whose contributions have chronicled changing styles and ideas in graphic design. Early Kieler Woche posters of the 1950s tended to involve pictorial images of boats and sails with varying degrees of abstraction. By the 1960s, the style had become even more abstract, with water and sails given geometric interpretations. In 1972 Rolf Müller broke this tradition by designing a poster without an image, using typography alone to express the visual character of the event. Experiments involving curving and bending of type in space had been carried out in the 1960s: George Tscherny in 1962 had used undulating type to evoke the sculpture of José de Rivera for an exhibition catalog cover, and in 1965 Steff Geissbuhler used a reflective mylar cone to create the illusion of type spiraling down a tunnel in a Geigy brochure. However, in treating type as an image, Müller's poster took the idea to a new level. In addition to the typography, his design uses the blue ground of the poster to evoke both water and sky, while the dates of the races are set horizontally in green type to allude to the sailboats' ties to land.

Müller graduated from the Hochschule für Gestaltung in Ulm in 1965 and spent a year working as an apprentice at the studio of Josef Müller-Brockmann. In 1967 he joined the design team of Otl Aicher, where he helped create the graphics and signage for the XX Olympiad in Munich. He later designed and edited *HQ (High Quality)* magazine, which ran from 1985 to 1999.

1972

RENAULT

Logo

Victor Vasarely (1908–1997)

Renault, France

Victor Vasarely's redesigned Renault logo is an apparently three-dimensional diamond that in reality could never be constructed. Best known for his contribution to op art, Vasarely transformed the original symbol, suggestive of a radiator, into a clean, sharp, and distinctive sign evocative of energy and rhythm.

Renault was founded by two brothers at the turn of the twentieth century, when its cars were sold for the equivalent of ten years' salary. The 1972 logo marked the apex of a successful streak for the company, when it released a range of innovative car models. The original Renault logo had begun life as a circular bonnet emblem with the uppercase logotype across the center; because it also acted as a cover for the car's horn, it was slotted to allow the sound to escape. In 1924 the logo was given its distinctive diamond shape but retained the horizontal slots. When approached by Renault in 1972 to update the identity, Vasarely converted the badge into a purely graphic emblem, with the diamond interpreted as a twisting three-dimensional band and the slots turned into stripes laid vertically along the band's inner and outer surfaces like a Möbius strip, greatly enhancing the illusion of movement.

Vasarely studied graphic art and typography at the Muhely Academy in Budapest before working as a graphic designer and poster artist in Paris in the 1930s. For the next three decades he also pursued his own experimental geometric and kinetic art, exploring effects of perspective, light and dark contrasts, and simulated movement while maintaining a link with his design work. Vasarely developed a fruitful collaboration through his work for Renault, going on to produce motorway approach signage that used enameled metal recommended by the Renault paint laboratory.

Vasarely's Renault logo remained in place until 1992, when it was changed to a plain silver diamond without stripes. Although the overall shape is essentially unchanged, the complex spatial relationships created by the black-and-white stripes of the original have now been altered, causing the new emblem to lose much of the teasingly ambiguous character it once possessed.

← P.246

1972

ADIDAS

Logo

Various

Adidas Aktiengesellschaft, Germany

The three-stripe logo on sports apparel and equipment has been synonymous with the Adidas brand since it first appeared on the company's footwear in 1949. Over the years, the appearance and use of the three stripes has varied, but the company's slogan, "Die Weltmarke mit den Drei Streifen" (The brand with the three stripes), is a testament to its importance for the brand's identity.

The name "Adidas" comes from the founder, Adolf "Adi" Dassler. Dassler began designing training shoes shortly after returning from World War I, and in 1924 he and his brother, Rudolf, formed Gebrüder Dassler Schuhfabrik (Dassler Brothers Shoe Factory). Despite the company's rapid growth, the partnership ended in 1948, with Rudolf going on to found a competing sports shoe company, Puma. Adolf formally registered Adidas AG in the same year, and added the trademark three stripes to his shoe designs for the first time, combined with the bold, sans serif, lowercase logotype. In 1962 the company began producing its now-iconic tracksuits, featuring three stripes running down the length of the arms and legs, but it had yet to develop the three stripes into a single graphic representation. Finally, in 1972 the company began using the trefoil as its corporate logo, with three horizontal stripes running through it to maintain the three-stripe corporate identity. This logo, which represents the diversity of the growing brand, is used today as the identity of the Originals collection, consisting of classic Adidas designs. Although not introduced as the corporate logo until 1997, the current "mountain" emblem was designed by the then creative director Peter Moore in 1990, the year after the company established itself as the Adidas Aktiengesellschaft. The A-shape of the three parallel bars is intended to embody an athlete's focused, goal-oriented mentality, and was initially used solely on sports equipment.

Today, Adidas continues to be one of the largest athletic and leisurewear companies in the world, a position the three-stripe logo, in all its incarnations, has played a significant part in helping to achieve.

← P.247

1972–1993

SPARE RIB

Magazine / Newspaper

Kate Hepburn (1947–), Sally Doust (1944–), et al.

Spare Rib Limited, UK

Spare Rib was founded in 1972 by Marsha Rowe and Rosie Boycott at the outset of second-wave feminism. Rowe was an Australian transplant, who had been a secretary at radical magazine Oz; Boycott was a privately educated college dropout from Jersey, United Kingdom. Having been part of the underground press, Rowe and Boycott were tired of supporting publications run by men and wanted to set up their own to confront the issues facing women in the 1970s. *Spare Rib* quickly gained traction and was soon selling twenty thousand copies per month and being stocked in national newsstand chains, such as W. H. Smith and Menzies.

A key voice within the women's liberation movement, *Spare Rib* gave a platform to articles on sexism in the workplace, motherhood, domestic abuse, racism, anticapitalism, sexual liberation, and more. One of its most contentious issues delved into the female orgasm, with the woman on the front cover seemingly in the middle of one. Contributors included well-known feminist writers and activists such as Nawal El Saadawi and Angela Carter, but there were also pieces from readers around the world. As a result, a dedicated community grew around the magazine.

Spare Rib's design was considered particularly forward-facing for its time; clothed in a tongue-in-cheek aesthetic that modeled itself on other women's magazines of the period, it also revealed a more playful DIY side, using paste-up methods. Its principal designers, Kate Hepburn and Sally Doust, called on friends and acquaintances to produce illustrations for its pages, where black-and-white-only sections were mixed with colored inks on colored paper. Crucially, *Spare Rib*'s look was dictated by financial challenges, which restricted the palette to just two colors plus black and white. These considerations also played out in the advertising, which was necessary to build revenue but also risked pandering to corporate requirements.

Spare Rib's appearance transformed quite drastically over its twenty-plus year run, with subsequent redesigns watering down its early irreverence in favor of gaining widespread appeal, a move that also reflected discontent within the team. It dissolved in 1993, but its innovative and unapologetic intent set a benchmark for British feminist publishing.

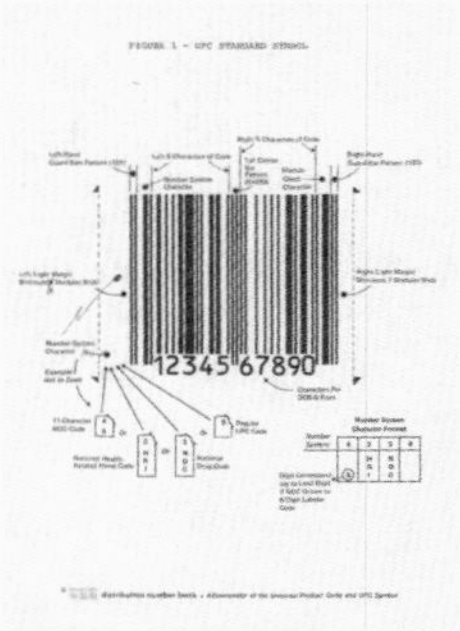

← P.248

1973

The Universal Product Code

Information Design

George J. Laurer (1925–2019)

National Association of Food Chains, U.S.

The Universal Product Code (UPC) is a barcode system originally used in North America that was invented for grocery checkouts. The first UPC-scanned item was a pack of Wrigley's chewing gum, purchased on June 26, 1974 in Troy, Ohio.

The Uniform Grocery Product Code Council was formed in the early 1970s to create a barcode that could be used with automated checkout systems to achieve greater efficiency. Even though automated checkouts were introduced in the early 1930s with the invention of a punch card, followed by a bull's eye system patented in 1952, these ultimately proved impractical. The council hired consultants McKinsey & Company to define the UPC's numerical format, and technology firms including IBM, Pitney Bowes-Alpex, and Singer to propose alternative ways of presenting the data in a symbolic form. In 1973 IBM's design, created by one of its engineers, George J. Laurer, was selected as standard.

The UPC has twelve numerals (though variants, such as the international EAN barcode shown above, have between eleven and thirteen) and consists of a pair of left guard bars, a pair of right guard bars, and two standard guard bars in the center. Each numeral is represented by two bars and two spaces that vary in width according to the number coded, making a total of thirty bars and twenty-nine spaces. The first number on the left is always a system character—for example 0 (zero) denotes grocery items—with the remaining five numbers on the left identifying the manufacturer. The number on the far right is a check character, while those preceding it are specific to the product itself. The nominal symbol height of a UPC is 1 inch (2.59 cm), but this can be reduced or magnified by values ranging from 80 to 200 percent. In order to obtain optimum reliability in scanning, the bit pattern for each numeral is designed to be unique and requires blank areas on both sides.

Today, the UPC is widely employed for other applications, in addition to its use in the retail industry. With its insistent stripes and digital numerals, the product has become an indispensable part of the modern world and is regularly appropriated as a symbol of the digital age.

← P.248

← P.248

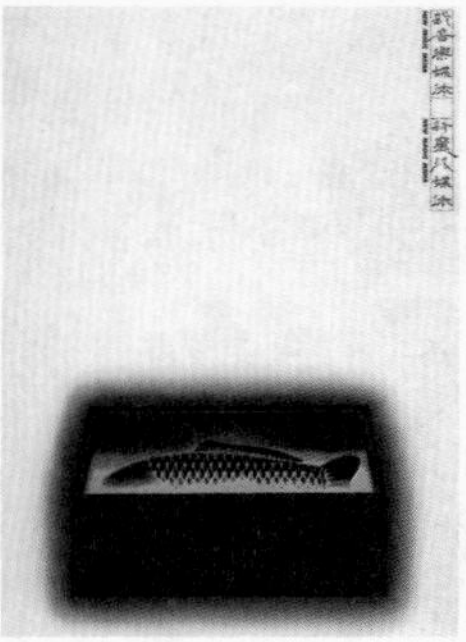

← P.249

1973–1999

U&LC

Magazine / Newspaper

Herb Lubalin (1918–1981), Aaron Burns (1922–1991), Ed Rondthaler (1905–2009)

International Typographic Corporation, U.S.

U&lc (shorthand for "upper & lowercase") magazine, a typographic journal and sales tool, was a platform for progress in the development of expressive typography, and one of the first magazines to use spreads comprised wholly of typographic experiments. The publication also provided a model for other typographic showcases, such as *Emigre*.

Established with the support of the International Typographic Corporation (ITC), which Herb Lubalin, along with Aaron Burns and Ed Rondthaler, helped found, *U&lc* served as a vehicle for promoting ITC-designed typefaces and typographic illustrations by Lubalin. The typefaces were "soft marketed" (using sophisticated content and design rather than an overt sales pitch) to those who would be using them, via the hands of a master typographer—a progressive form of salesmanship in the design community. Colleagues of Lubalin, such as Lou Dorfsman, Ernie Smith, and Seymour Chwast, also contributed to the content and look of the magazine.

U&lc's playful and challenging typographic voice was evident from its inception. On the opening spread of the first issue (No. 1, Vol. 1) a mission statement entitled "Why U&lc?" provided an insight into the magazine's point of view: thoughtful content given loving typographic attention. After his death in 1981, Lubalin was succeeded by a number of art directors and editors, including Ellen Shapiro, Bob Farber, and Margaret Richardson. Under Richardson's editorship, a single designer or studio would be responsible for an entire issue, which led to some fruitful pairings: Roger Black's 1994 issue on type, and P. Scott Makela and Laurie Haycock Makela's "Creative Collaboration" in 1997.

A subscription-only magazine, with a circulation at its peak of roughly two-hundred thousand, *U&lc* finally ceased publication in 1999, when it was sold by the Swiss owner of ITC (Esselte). In its distinct typographic voice, *U&lc* illustrates the intersection of pop culture and design in the second half of the twentieth century and has left a lasting impression on the canon of graphic design. It continues to influence the work of designers today, such as that of Fred Woodward in *Rolling Stone*.

c. 1974

CHURCHWARD ROUNDSQUARE

Typeface

Joseph Churchward (1933–2013)

Churchward Type, New Zealand

Joseph Churchward was New Zealand's most industrious type designer, with more than six hundred different typefaces to his name. The author of internationally recognized fonts, such as Churchward Brush Italic and Churchward Marianna, he called on his rich heritage of Chinese, Scottish, English, Tongan, and Samoan ancestry, and a steadfast devotion to letter craft. Born in Samoa, Churchward emigrated to New Zealand's capital city, Wellington, at age thirteen. His artistic flair was recognized early on, leading to hand-lettering training at a local technical college. A subsequent apprenticeship at the Charles Haines Advertising Agency honed his agility with pencil and ink; drawing headline lettering for hours and weeks, he refined his technique during twelve years of service.

In 1962 Churchward established his own business. Seven years later a commission for the national Woolworths supermarket chain—Churchward 69—made his name. But it was a coincidental meeting with a Berthold salesperson in the late 1960s that led to his breakthrough. Encouraged by the visit, he sent fonts to Berthold, which licensed and distributed them internationally. This introduced his work to other clients, including Mecanorma-Polyvroom, Magictype, and Zipatone.

Designed in the 1970s, Churchward Roundsquare is indicative of his playful, experimental approach. The typeface includes five styles: Solid, Outline, Fill-in, Deep Shadow, and Setback Shadow. Its circular counterspaces and blocky vertical strokes speak to an architectural language—perhaps a reflection of the era's postmodern excess. As with all of his typefaces, Churchward designed Roundsquare by hand. He favored analog processes and rejected the arrival of the Apple Macintosh computer in 1984, believing it to be a Disney "cartoon machine." Ultimately, the ubiquity of computerized work rendered his business obsolete, though he never stopped designing by hand.

Although Churchward's work was overlooked locally, interest in his prolific output was revived by graphic designer David Bennewith through a mono-graph published in 2009. His work is now in the permanent collection of the Museum of New Zealand, Te Papa Tongarewa, and is becoming more widely known through an agreement with MyFonts to translate his analog originals to the digital platform.

1974

NEW MUSIC MEDIA, NEW MAGIC MEDIA

Poster

Koichi Sato (1944–2016)

Mei Corporation, Japan

"New Music Media, New Magic Media" exemplifies Koichi Sato's ethereal, quasi-mystical design style in which color gradients and soft tones emanate from simple objects and forms. His vision represents a significant episode in Japanese graphic design when the country was experiencing a manufacturing boom and designers felt the need to establish a more indigenous aesthetic.

After graduating from Tokyo National University of Fine Arts and Music, Sato worked briefly in the advertising department of the cosmetics company Shiseido before becoming a freelance graphic designer. Sato's approach is distinguished by his unusual choice of forms, often deliberately obscure in meaning, and the expressive effects he creates from the way in which objects are depicted. In this poster advertising a music concert, a plain white space forms the background to a black, boxlike shape—a neutral form that lacks national and cultural associations—at the center of which lies a carp, a common East Asian fish. Apart from the strange combination of objects, the image is distinct for its forms' softened edges, which give them an aura and suggest a third dimension. The overall simplicity of the design, with its narrow black border, has an austere character, but the ambiguity of the objects and their surrounding glow evoke a more mysterious atmosphere that contrasts with the geometric framework. This relationship is to some degree also represented by the juxtaposition of traditional Japanese calligraphy and modern English type in the bilingual text of the upper right-hand corner.

Sato's style—a combination of rational design redolent of modernist Western graphics and elements that evoke the mysticism of the East—is highly individual among Japanese designers. Used in posters for commercial clients as well as for independent designs, Sato's design aesthetic maintains the simplicity and purity of the Japanese style and includes references to nature, a favorite Japanese subject, while suggesting a futuristic or celestial vision.

ABCDEFGHI
JKLMNOPQR
STUVWXYZ
abcdefghijkl
mnopqrstuv
wxyzæœß/&
Ø(–).:;!?€¥£§
1234567890

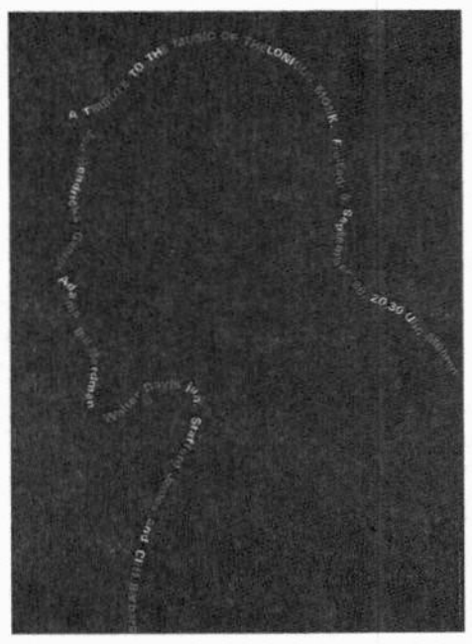

← P.250

← P.250

← P.251

1974

DEUTSCHE BANK

Logo

Anton Stankowski (1906–1998), Karl Duschek (1947–2011)

Deutsche Bank, Germany

Deutsche Bank's trademark exemplifies corporate design at its most archetypal: the diagonal line symbolizes growth and development, while the surrounding square represents security and control—two qualities the bank was keen to stress even during the increasingly turbulent financial world of the 1970s. The design is bold without being strident, and simple without being anonymous.

Deutsche Bank's identity had evolved from an imperious Teutonic eagle in 1870, through sixteen equally bland monograms; choosing this dynamic modernist symbol, with its echoes of Russian Constructivism, over more conventional alternatives represented a radical break with tradition. Anton Stankowski and Karl Duschek's emblem was the winning entry in a competition involving eight graphic designers who had been invited to rebrand the company. Diagonals had been a constant reference point for Stankowski, as seen in his logo for Berlin (the city's first comprehensive corporate identity) and the paintings he exhibited at Stuttgart Airport shortly before the Deutsche Bank commission. Aside from designing the logo, Stankowski produced detailed guidelines on how it should be used. The mark was set in a precisely configured DeuBa Blue color, with the company name in DeuBa Univers, a bespoke version of the popular sans serif typeface. These principles still underpin the identity today.

The emblem's concise summary of capitalist principles, albeit in abstracted form, has cemented its totemic importance to Deutsche Bank. In 2005 the company rolled out a global advertising campaign called "Winning with the Logo," which featured giant computer-generated 3-D logos that mimicked the glass-and-steel idiom of Norman Foster's buildings. In 2007 the bank unveiled a 3-D logo (32¾ feet [10 m] tall and built from 20 tons of steel) at Berlin Tegel Airport in the German capital. Deutsche Bank's trademark is one of the few graphic identities to have received such a validation of permanence.

1975

DEMOS

Typeface

Gerard Unger (1942–2018)

Dr.-Ing Rudolf Hell GmbH, Germany

Demos is an ancient Greek word meaning "people," in the sense of the populace of a city; it forms the root of the word "democracy," literally "rule by the people." As such, it is a fitting name for this practical and functional typeface, which has gone on to be used for government communications.

Rudolf Hell first commissioned Gerard Unger to develop the typeface that came to be known as Demos, stipulating that Unger had to use the Digiset, an early digital typography composing tool produced by Hell's company, Dr.-Ing Rudolf Hell. (In 1990 the firm merged with Linotype AG to form Linotype-Hell AG, known today as Linotype GmbH.) This made Demos one of the first digital typefaces, and allowed Unger to adjust the characters' nuances pixel by pixel. Each letter was formed by a cathode-ray tube, with coarse pixels creating outlines and fill. In traditional type design, a typeface would have versions cut for small and large sizes, but many of the early digital typefaces had only one master, which was enlarged or reduced to fit the size required. This resulted in letter distortions that reduced overall quality. Unger solved this problem by giving Demos a reduced stroke contrast, producing very little differentiation between horizontal and vertical strokes. The resulting typeface possesses angular letterforms and blunt but sturdy serifs. Unger also designed a sans serif companion to Demos entitled "Praxis," with each typeface boasting open counters and a tall x-height.

Demos works well for text typography, especially short columns with tightly spaced lines as used in newspapers—one of the uses for which it was originally conceived—but it has also been used for other applications, such as government publications. The German government adopted Univers, Praxis, and Demos in 2001 after Unger and Linotype GmbH adapted it to meet official communication design standards. Since then, further modifications have been made, with Neue Demos and Neue Praxis designed to meet the requirements of Germany's thirteen federal ministries, the Chancellor's Office, and the Press and Information Bureau.

1975–present

JAZZ

Poster

Niklaus Troxler (1947–)

Self-commissioned, Switzerland

As both graphic designer and organizer of the Willisau Jazz Festival, one of the longest-running and best-known festivals of its kind, Niklaus Troxler has an enthusiasm for every aspect of the project that is clearly evident in his energetic and inventive poster designs.

After training in typography and graphic design and working in Paris for several years, Troxler returned to his native Willisau in 1973 to open his own design studio. Beginning in 1966, he organized a series of jazz concerts, which in 1975 he expanded into the Willisau Jazz Festival, coordinating all aspects of the event, including designing the posters. Always produced by the same local printing company, the festival posters are eclectic in style, offering a sketch of recent design history through the lens of one man's viewpoint. Troxler references every school of aesthetic thought in his designs, from Swiss postmodernism to Californian grunge, and he acknowledges early career influences as diverse as American and British Pop art, and Cuban and Polish revolutionary posters.

Dynamic and unpredictable, the posters play with ideas of rhythm, scale, and contrast, occasionally displaying a macabre sense of humor or mirroring the musical forms they celebrate. Many are purely typographic, often in crudely stamped or printed letters that suggest musical sequences, such as the poster for Schulldogs (2006) or Jandeln (2004). Others have featured body parts, such as a row of chopped-off hands in a poster of 1973 advertising a concert that featured the pianist Irene Schweizer; she is also part of a design in which clothes and shoes perform music of their own accord (1977). Although Troxler also works on other design projects, mainly for arts organizations, the festival posters always come first. Few designers have been able to so completely fuse personal passion with professional practice.

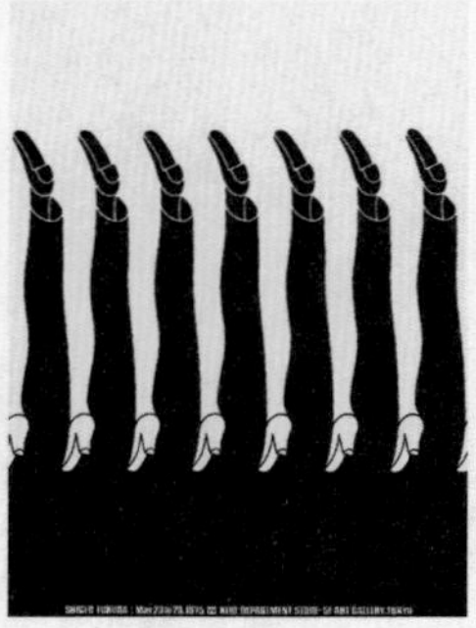

← P.251

1975

SHIGEO FUKUDA

Poster

Shigeo Fukuda (1932–2009)

Keio Department Store, Japan

Shigeo Fukuda's work has been driven by a fascination with the magic of visual illusion and the power of implied meaning. Optical illusion, whimsy, humor, and puns are central themes used to delight and captivate the audience, challenge assumptions, and provoke new ideas. This poster advertising an exhibition of his work at the Keio Department Store contains many of Fukuda's hallmark features, including illusionary devices and figure-ground reversal.

Fukuda began working when other Japanese designers, such as Takashi Kono and Tadanori Yokoo, were beginning to rebel against traditional Japanese idioms, and to experiment with Western techniques and styles including collage, Pop art, and comic-book drawing. Like that of Yokoo, Fukuda's graphic style has been inspired by the work of the New York-based Push Pin studio, but his merging of illusion, whimsy, and satire is highly individual. During the mid-1960s, Fukuda's work came to the attention of the designer Paul Rand, who arranged an exhibition of his wooden toys and illustrated books, and in the late 1960s Fukuda was selected to design the *Japan Expo '70* poster, which brought his work to a global audience.

In the image pictured the repetitive black-and-white, male and female legs fight for dominance in a visual war of the sexes. The illustration's simple shapes, minimal details, and strong tonal contrasts result in an intriguing play of fluctuating space, causing the legs to advance and recede and the eye to move toward the center. In this context, attention is entirely absorbed by the illusion, and the single line of uppercase text at the base becomes an irrelevance. Starkly simple in its graphic elements, the poster demonstrates Fukuda's ability to tease the viewer, visually and conceptually with glimpses of meanings and images that remain tantalizingly unresolved.

← P.252

1976

LONDON ZOO

Poster

Abram Games (1914–1996)

London Transport, UK

The last and possibly the best of the eighteen posters that Abram Games designed for London Transport between 1937 and 1976, this work was very different in style and subject from the war imagery that had established his reputation. Instead of the soft airbrush and hard message of "Your Talk May Kill Your Comrades" (1942), here Games uses crisp, straight lines and bold contrasts to create an amusing multilayered image with very little copy, which perfectly reflects his philosophy of "maximum meaning, minimum means." Games's relationship with London Transport was highly rewarding for both parties and spanned a large part of his long and prolific career.

The poster also demonstrates the visual puzzles and influences of Surrealism and Cubism that permeate much of Games's work. As well as evoking a tiger and the bars of its cage, the horizontal black-and-yellow stripes suggest a series of energetic fragments seen from a moving train, including a number of deconstructed logos. The image worked well even at 1 inch (2.5 cm)—a test Games applied to gauge the immediacy of his designs and to ensure that they could be seen from a distance. However, the simplicity of the design belies the many hours he spent sketching zebras and giraffes before settling on the subject of the tiger. In each sketch, Games built up the animal from elements of the London Transport roundel, which in the final version were also used to construct the word "zoo" in different colors. Moving in closer, the viewer finds one last puzzle: four tiny Hebrew symbols spread vertically down the tiger's tail; they spell out "Revital," which was the name of Games's first granddaughter.

Although Games also designed logos and book covers, posters were his first and greatest love. This last design for London Transport is an example of not only the thought that went into each of his works, but also the simple abstract style for which he would become known, and which would characterize his work for the remainder of his career.

← P.253

1976

APPLE

Logo

Rob Janoff (1948–)

Apple Inc., U.S.

The Apple logo is one of the world's most recognizable corporate symbols and has spawned numerous (apocryphal) interpretations among its legions of fans.

Apple Computer's original logo, devised by one of Apple's founders, Ron Gerald Wayne (he opted out of the partnership with Steve Jobs and Steve Wozniak after eleven days), depicted Sir Isaac Newton sitting under an apple tree. However, the image was deemed too intricate, and Jobs and Wozniak asked Regis McKenna Advertising in Palo Alto, California, to produce a simpler version. Art director Rob Janoff created a design using the basic graphic shape of an apple, adding a bite to give it scale and to prevent it being misconstrued as just a fruit; Janoff also felt the bite suggested a twist on the idea of a worm coming out of an apple. Inspired by the Beatles film *Yellow Submarine*, he gave the apple rainbow stripes to endow it with a happy look and to remind him of his hippie days. The stripes also demonstrated that the Apple screen displayed color, a rarity at the time, and suggested a friendly personality, rather than a "hard, techy thing," that was likely to appeal to children, a market Jobs hoped to attract. Some have seen the logo as a symbol of interconnectivity and knowledge, while others attribute to it qualities of lust and hope. It has been said that the bite represents temptation, or a "byte," and that it contains an oblique reference to the seduction of the marketplace. Janoff says that, sadly, none of this is true—it was designed purely for utilitarian reasons on the basis of the company's name.

Janoff attributes the symbol's longevity to the excellence of the products it represents and to the friendliness of the image, which encourages a cultlike attachment. Janoff's original shape, more asymmetrical and natural than the current iteration, was tweaked by Landor Associates a few years after it first appeared, making it simpler and more streamlined. In 1997 Jobs decided to abandon the rainbow colors in favor of a monochrome logo, first used on the Powerbook G3 in 1998. In 2003, with the launch of Apple's Panther operating system, the emblem acquired its current sophisticated silver-chrome finish, bringing it more in line with the ultra-sleek style of the company's products.

← P.253

← P.254

← P.255

1976

NASA GRAPHICS STANDARDS MANUAL

Identity

Danne & Blackburn

NASA, U.S.

After NASA's famous Apollo program ended in 1972, having achieved its goal of putting the first human on the moon a few years prior, the agency was uncertain how to maintain its now-iconic image. Its next move was prompted by a 1971 directive from President Richard Nixon for federal agencies to improve the quality of their design and visual communications. To aid in this venture, the U.S. government set up the Federal Design Improvement Program. Keen to take advantage, NASA partnered with emerging New York–based studio Danne & Blackburn to completely redesign its visual identity. Richard Danne had made his name in the film industry, having created the iconic poster for *Rosemary's Baby* (1968); Bruce Blackburn had a background in corporate branding, and in 1971 was chosen to design the official logo for the United States Bicentennial.

The duo's extensive work was laid out in a ring binder called the *NASA Graphics Standards Manual*, which presented in detail the many different applications of the identity. At the heart of the new system was the "Worm," a sleek, futuristic logotype set in bright red. This replaced the original "Meatball" logo, now reserved for legacy occasions. The manual also specified treatments for NASA's mission patches, symbols, stationery, forms, and publications. Key to the overhaul was a strict visual consistency, with Danne & Blackburn insisting that "the logotype should never be altered or distorted in any way. It must not be re-drawn, but rather reproduced photographically from reproduction artwork."

Another important aspect of the identity was the color palette, featuring the crucial NASA red, and including a dark blue, cool gray, warm gray, and black. The red and blue were taken from NASA's previous logo, ensuring a continuity of branding and recognition of the agency's heritage. Much like the new logo, the color palette aimed to evoke notions of unity and progress, reestablishing NASA as the world's foremost space agency and an enduring symbol of technological advancement at home and abroad. In homage to its continued appeal, the NASA manual was re-issued in 2015 in facsimile form by Jesse Reed and Hamish Smyth of the Standards Manual publishing imprint.

1976–1979

S. FISCHER-VERLAG

Poster

Gunter Rambow (1938–)

S. Fischer-Verlag, Germany

The S. Fischer-Verlag poster series represents one of Gunter Rambow's most innovative photographic applications, particularly his use of Surrealistic montage. Created in 1976 and 1979 for the Frankfurt publishing house, the advertising campaign comprised eleven black-and-white posters, each bearing a photograph of a book interwoven with other images.

In each poster, Rambow seamlessly combined different photographs to create a single image in which books and other objects are displaced from their normal surroundings and set against a background of undefined space, transforming their identity. In each case, the manipulation of photographic imagery is designed to impart a message about books: the book as transmitter of knowledge, a window or door to the world, transportability, the power of the written word. Rambow created the photographs by taking multiple exposures, sometimes producing a series in a day, and often cutting and recombining photographs to create the final image. The posters were printed at traditional German poster size (46¾ × 33 inches [119 × 84 cm]) and displayed on advertising pillars.

Rambow's command of photomontage and ironic juxtaposition recalls the methods of both Dada and Surrealism, particularly the pioneering photo collages of fellow German artists Hannah Höch, Raoul Hausmann, and John Heartfield. Experimental photography also played a role in later works by Rambow, notably the poster series he created for S. Fischer-Verlag's centennial in 1986. Similar to his earlier series, these images portray a single book, now fused with the background plane, but are colored and have more reduced forms.

One of his most important advertising campaigns, the S. Fischer-Verlag posters exemplify Rambow's understanding of the expressive and symbolic potential of photomontage to create powerful imagery and meaning. As such, they also embody a further irony: a series of advertisements for books that are entirely without words.

1977

I ♥ NY

Logo

Milton Glaser (1929–2020)

New York State, U.S.

Milton Glaser designed the I ♥ NY logo *pro bono*, to help the state of New York with its tourism campaign. It was designed to raise the spirits of New Yorkers, who were suffering spiraling decline in their quality of life, and to produce an atmosphere that would attract visitors and business to the city. The mark was freely distributed for about fifteen years to any enterprise that wished to use it. Later, the state decided to trademark it and control its use. Little did Glaser—or anyone for that matter— know how incredibly popular it would be. "The universal acceptance and ongoing reinterpretation of the I ♥ NY logo continues to astonish me," he said. In addition to aiding the campaign, the logo became an icon, both for New York and numerous other cities and towns throughout the world, and is the most borrowed visual idea since Grant Wood's *American Gothic* or Saul Steinberg's 1976 *New Yorker* cover "View of the World from 9th Avenue."

After the events of September 11, 2001, the slogan took on an entirely new and unexpected relevance, becoming the seal of a city (and nation). Within hours of the tragedy, Glaser decided to inject even greater emotion into the symbol: to I ♥ NY he added the words "more than ever," and bruised a corner of the heart. Although the state of New York objected, Glaser explained that the symbol—old and new—had become an emotional touchstone, and that the extra features made its relevance incalculable. Curiously, the city had no interest in using this new variant, feeling that anything that acknowledged 9/11 might be interpreted as weakness. Glaser nonetheless emailed it to a friend on the *Daily News*, whose editor, Ed Kosner, promised to publish it in two days' time. "The following morning I was awakened by a call from a local radio show," Glaser recalled, "asking me why I designed the logo, which went from an inside page to the front and back cover of the paper. Evidently, Kosner had decided to use it earlier and more dramatically than I could have imagined." Glaser's instinct had proved sound: as before, the logo resonated with the public, who now felt the need for a symbol that reflected both the tragedy visited on the city and their own defiant response.

3M

← P.255

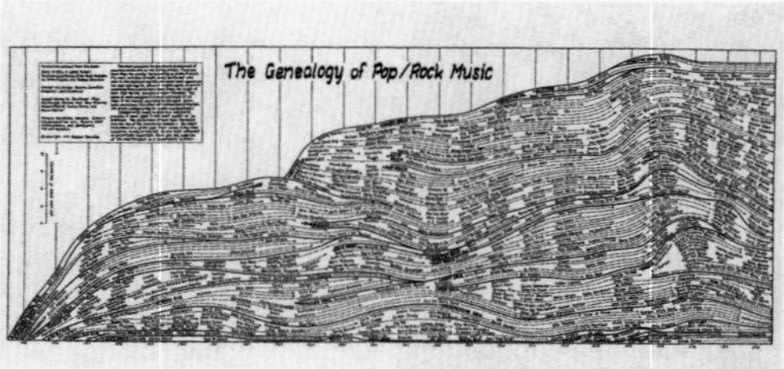

← P.256

← P.258

1977

3M

Logo

Siegel+Gale

3M, U.S.

One of the most ubiquitous brands in the world, 3M currently markets over fifty thousand products, including many stalwarts of the home and office, such as Post-it notes and Scotch tape. With its straightforward, can-do approach, the company's bold, simple logo is a statement of confidence in its ability to let a single red ensign speak for a century of quality and innovation.

3M's success as a business is built on the application of its technologies to the widespread needs of consumers. From humble beginnings as the Minnesota, Mining and Manufacturing Company, the brand has evolved into a "diversified technology" enterprise, with six business divisions and operations in more than sixty countries. In the early days diversification was a challenge to the guardians of 3M's corporate image, so it is perhaps unsurprising that the logo underwent several iterations before Siegel+Gale (S+G) was appointed to re-brand the company in 1977. Fashion aside, the slimness of the S+G design can be attributed to the need for clarity and coherence in reinforcing a single corporate voice across a range of sectors, countries, and industries.

Consisting of nothing more than the 3M name, the 1977 logo brings to a logical conclusion the reductive design process that began with the company's first complex trademark in 1906. With its bespoke font, color, and character spacing, the mark has a strong utilitarian look that retains its integrity at extremes of scale, and works well alongside other symbols. As 3M's most important visual signifier, this is crucial, since it is often seen with other graphic devices—including established secondary trademarks, such as the Scotch tartan ribbon—and has an almost infinite number of applications, from packaging to corporate communication. The product of a designer whose ethos is "simple is smart," 3M's logo continues to look fresh and contemporary more than thirty years after its launch.

1977

THE GENEALOGY OF POP/ROCK MUSIC

Information Design

Reebee Garofalo (1944–), Damon Rarey (1944–2002)

Burnham Inc., U.S.

"The Genealogy of Pop/Rock Music" by the music scholar Reebee Garofalo with artwork by Damon Rarey charts commercial hits over a twenty-year period (from 1955 to 1974) and is renowned among both designers and music lovers.

The chart illustrates more than seven hundred artists, representing over thirty styles of music, including virtually every performer who sells in the pop/rock market and whose name appears on the annual top fifty album or single charts. The names and genres form undulating streams that map the connections between various musical styles, with arrows extending from the performers' names to indicate the length of time that they remained popular. The width of each category indicates a rough approximation of its share of the market.

Published in several different versions, the first edition (called "Marketing Trends and Stylistic Patterns in Pop/Rock Music") was created in 1974 and published in 1977 as a foldout poster in a book on which Garofalo collaborated with Steve Chappell: *Rock 'n' Roll is Here to Pay*. The chart was updated in 1978, and it is this second edition that is most widely distributed today. In 2004 artist Dave Muller created an enlarged reproduction of the chart as the centerpiece of his installation for the Whitney Biennial in New York.

The information design guru Edward Tufte, who reproduced the original 1974 version in his book *Visual Explanations* (1997), described the illustration as an example of richly detailed information design that engages the viewer with its view of music as belonging to a shared history. Unusually, the diagram helps audiences to understand the complex network of determinants that operate within the music industry. Through its curving forms and movement, the map also captures the rhythms and cadences of music itself, suggesting a series of constantly shifting patterns and relations.

1977

SEX PISTOLS—GOD SAVE THE QUEEN

Record / CD Cover

Jamie Reid (1947–2023)

Virgin Records, UK

Although the exact genesis of punk music is vague, the enormously provocative work of its most famous graphic artist, Jamie Reid—sometime lyricist, hanger-on, and designer for the Sex Pistols—represented a major milestone in the history of graphic art.

British and American graphic art of the late 1970s shared the subversive Dada spirit of the early twentieth century, as well as the improvisational approach of its techniques, particularly collage and photomontage. As an untrained designer ignorant of paste-up or typesetting, Reid used methods that were considerably more crude: a Xerox machine and scissors, which he used to cut and paste existing letters onto the page in a style reminiscent of a ransom note in which the author's handwriting has been deliberately obscured. However, Reid's deceptively amateurish graphics perfectly reflected the music itself, which was based on simple four-chord progressions and was often played by inexperienced musicians.

Released in 1977, the year in which England celebrated Queen Elizabeth's Silver Jubilee, the single "God Save the Queen" not surprisingly created controversy, as much for the graphics of its poster and record cover as for the song itself. Concealing the Queen's eyes with the title implied her refusal to see or understand the circumstances of an increasingly disgruntled youth, and pasting the band's name across her mouth suggested a sexual assault that reflected punk's own dalliance with violence and destruction. In just a few simple strokes, Reid's work succeeded in encapsulating the underlying theme of all punk culture: to offend the establishment and draw attention to the dissatisfaction of youth with their social, political, and economic condition.

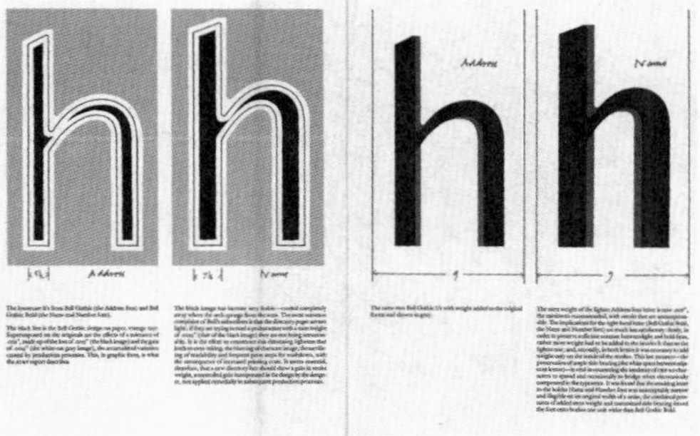

← P.259

← P.259

← P.260

1977

FESTAC '77

Identity

Unknown

International Festival Committee, Nigeria

In the 1960s the tide of independence had washed over much of Africa, and the arts were seen as a way to reclaim African identity from damaging colonial stereotypes. Pan-Africanism allowed newly freed populations to bask in the wealth of their shared culture, leading to the World Festival of Negro Arts (FESMAN) in Dakar in 1966.

In 1977 the month-long Second World Black and African Festival of Arts and Culture (FESTAC) brought together thousands of luminaries from across Africa and the African diaspora. Writers, artists, musicians, activists, scholars, and others traveled to Lagos, Nigeria, to represent and give expression to pan-African culture. Art and politics were deeply entwined in the ethos of those who attended: South African singer-songwriter Miriam Makeba rallied alongside musician Gilberto Gil, Brazil's future minister of culture, while writer and poet Audre Lorde traveled from the United States, along with jazz legend Sun Ra and Louis Farrakhan, the controversial leader of the Nation of Islam. Any tendencies toward nationalism were suspended.

The festival's official emblem is a bronze replica of the ivory mask of Queen Idia, sculpted by Nigerian artist Erhabor Emokpae. Queen Idia was the first Iyoba, or Queen Mother, of the Benin Empire in the 1500s, and the original mask was looted by the British in the late 1800s. Choosing a vital part of African history was essential to establishing a powerful identity for the festival. The delicate typeface surrounding the emblem balances out the fuller-formed lettering of the FESTAC '77 wordmark. Adopting a tri-color palette of gold, black, and white, the visual language of the identity fuses modern and traditional aspects of African culture and also incorporates the design of a flag.

The legacy of FESTAC '77 has since been archived in multiple ways, including a 2019 book and mixtape by the pan-African media platform Chimurenga, in partnership with Afterall Books. The book took almost ten years to make and required in-person visits to Nigeria's Centre for Black and African Arts and Civilization, which holds the event archive. It also drew on less tangible forms of documentation, such as the many music albums that captured the monumentality of the FESTAC experience.

1978

BELL CENTENNIAL

Typeface

Matthew Carter (1937–)

AT&T, U.S.

Bell Centennial was commissioned to mark the Bell company's one-hundredth birthday, as a typeface that would work at a six-point size and address the legibility shortcomings of Bell Gothic. Veteran typographer Matthew Carter took on the task with ease, going so far as to expand the style into four variants, and adding useful names to aid application: Bell Centennial Name and Number, Address, Bold Listing, and Sub-Caption.

Carter's Bell Centennial has appeared on computer screens, in art museums, and within the telephone book. When the Linotype foundry's Chauncey Griffith designed its predecessor, Bell Gothic, for the telephone company in 1937, it fulfilled existing technological standards for hot-metal production, delivering an able-bodied typeface for general use. However, when printing technology moved to high-speed presses with cathode-ray typesetting, the face proved to be unfit for the purpose: text turned blobby and illegible, with adjacent letters running together and numbers becoming distorted. Moreover, it lacked variety, offering only two weights to the designer, who had to distinguish between name, telephone number, address, and paid advertisers' names and addresses.

The success of Carter's redesign owed much to his relationship with technology, including obsolete devices, such as the metal punch, and to his willingness to experiment with different rendering techniques. During the development phases, Carter drew Bell Centennial entirely by hand with both pencil and ink on vellum, then cut the letters out one by one and redrew them in pixilated form for the computer. These renderings were transferred to a digital typesetter, where Carter identified and adjusted lines that filled with excess ink, distorting the letters' shapes.

With Bell Centennial, Carter designed a typeface for a specific purpose by experimenting with traditional media and modern technology. In doing so, he prepared himself for another media revolution—the computer screen—and would later apply its principles to other type designs, such as Microsoft's Verdana, also a quadrille-grid face.

1978

SWISSAIR

Identity

Karl Gerstner (1930–2017)

Swissair, Switzerland

A leading figure of twentieth-century Swiss design, Karl Gerstner produced work that was deeply rooted in the postwar modernism of the Bauhaus—a design ethos that relied on geometric abstract composition. Although the notion of a "Swiss school" has been rejected by many practitioners, the sensibility that Gerstner and his compatriots developed became a calling card for the nation.

Nowhere is this more visible than in Gerstner's redesign of the corporate identity for Swissair, the country's former national airline carrier. Gerstner had been working on advertising campaigns for the company for nearly twelve years when a simple assignment to consult on new colors for Swissair planes turned into a redesign of the logo and a united advertising campaign. Swissair had a long history of promoting progressive design, commissioning work by groundbreaking Swiss designers, such as Kurt Wirth, Donald Brun, Fritz Buhler, and Siegfried Odermatt, over its sixty-year history. Gerstner's new logo consisted of the Swissair name in all lowercase Futura typeface, a font chosen for its efficient geometric character, in a warm cinnabar red that was a subtle change from the fire-engine red used previously. While Futura served as the font for all text larger than twelve point used in the advertising campaign, smaller type was set in Times to provide contrast. To accompany the logo, Gerstner abandoned the directional arrows that had served the airline since the 1950s, and adopted the white cross on a red field of the Swiss flag, which already marked the tail fins of the airline's planes.

Gerstner's use of typefaces demonstrates his interest in "integral" typography, according to which message and form are inseparable and interdependent, representing a move away from the more functionalist notions of the Bauhaus under the influence of American postwar advertising campaigns. Indeed, Gerstner's design for the Swissair logo became linked with certain ideas associated with the Swiss nation itself—the notion that luxury could be delivered with efficiency and discretion. In 2001, when the company was forced to reorganize, pleas from the design world not to abandon the Gerstner logo led the new national carrier, Swiss, to adopt a corporate identity similar to that of its predecessor.

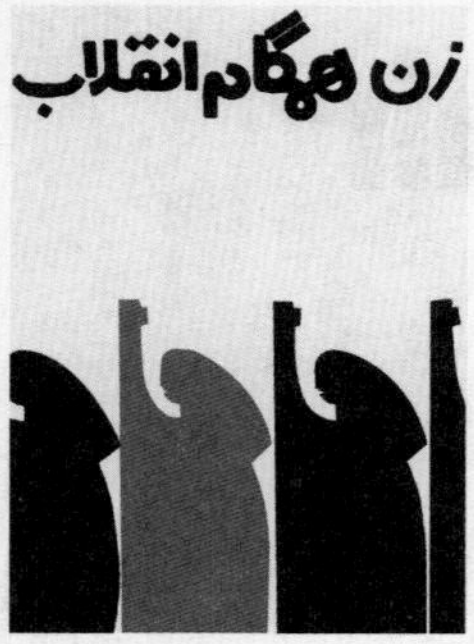

← P.260

1979

WOMEN OF THE REVOLUTION

Poster

Morteza Momayez (1935–2005)

Unknown, Iran

Designed to celebrate International Women's Day in 1979, when Iranian women marched in support of the revolution then sweeping the country, Morteza Momayez's strong, simple poster combines streamlined Western graphics with traditional Islamic script and motifs. Although the verbal message is clearly articulated as "Women are the companions of the revolution," its visual message is more subtle and ambiguous.

A designer, illustrator, animator, and teacher, Momayez has often been described as the father of contemporary Iranian graphic design, urging his students to look outward and forward while also remembering their traditions and heritage. He was particularly concerned that calligraphy, in his view a "sign of knowledge and intellectualism," should not be marginalized by new design methods. This philosophy is illustrated here by the abstracted shapes of the draped women (the *chador* is a significant Shiite motif), whose raised hands look like rifle barrels, the simplified Iranian writing of the slogan, and the bold color scheme, which evokes both revolution and the blood of martyrs. Despite such obvious cultural references, the poster's style also suggests essentially international design styles, such as Isotypes and Olympic symbols, while the simple horizontal composition establishes continuity between the figures on the left- and right-hand sides: the woman on the far left could be completed by the arm of the one on the far right, implying an infinite number of identical fighters.

Many Iranian posters produced at the time were relatively amateurish, characterized by lurid figurative details, which no doubt provided familiar associations during a period of crisis. By contrast, Momayez's insistence on a more international graphic style has decontextualized the subject, giving it a universal and modern resonance, and erased the emotional language that made other posters look clumsy and parochial. Balancing the traditional with the radical, and the tested with the unknown, is a common problem for designers; with this work Momayez has taken a popular theme and given it a sophisticated and modern treatment, retaining Iranian women's cultural identity while evoking the struggle of women around the world.

← P.261

1979

JOY DIVISION—UNKNOWN PLEASURES

Record / CD Cover

Peter Saville (1955–)

Factory Records, UK

Although seemingly ambigious, the album sleeve for *Unknown Pleasures* by Joy Division is, paradoxically, perfectly suited to the music and band it serves. The design was conceived by Peter Saville, art director of Factory Records, for the group's debut LP after drummer Stephen Morris gave him a selection of images, including the one used as the central motif. Chosen by Morris's fellow band member Bernard Sumner from the *Cambridge Encyclopedia of Astronomy*, the sharp waves represent the radio pulses transmitted by a collapsing star. With the original colors reversed and surrounded by a large area of black, the radiowave graphic creates an effect of minimalist elegance and is deliberately enigmatic, interpretable as a mountain landscape, a medical diagram, or the magnified surface of human skin. Inside the sleeve a photograph of a hand reaching for a door handle by the American photographer Ralph Gibson is similarly evocative.

Joy Division was known for such songs as "New Dawn Fades" and "Love Will Tear Us Apart," and cultivated a dark aesthetic, often captured in black-and-white photographs of the band amid stark surroundings. Before MTV (broadcast from 1981) and the Internet, music packaging acted as an important promotional vehicle for recording artists, who were otherwise limited to communicating with their audience through weekly music publications and occasional television appearances. Music graphics provided a way of conveying the atmosphere contained in their music. After the lead singer Ian Curtis committed suicide in 1980, Saville continued to design for the new group, New Order, formed by Curtis's band members, as well as a diverse range of musicians over the next two decades.

Unknown Pleasures served as the opening act of Saville's career and the springboard for his unique visual language. The forty-plus years since the release of the album have seen Saville become one of the most significant figures not only in music graphics but in contemporary design. Yet in the three decades since it was produced, and despite its ambiguous meaning, *Unknown Pleasures* has retained its fresh and otherworldly appearance, and continues to invite curiosity and fascination—a difficult achievement in the fast-moving and ephemeral universe of pop graphics.

← P.262

1980–present

ABSOLUT VODKA

Advertising

TBWA

Absolut, Sweden

Absolut's highly successful advertising campaign of the 1980s, with its famous two-word baseline, helped transform the company from relative obscurity into a leading market brand.

With Geoff Hayes and Graham Turner of the American agency TBWA as art director and copywriter respectively, the design brief was to focus on the bottle, creating an image that would be both timeless and contemporary. With its short neck and round shoulders, which echoed traditional Swedish medicine bottles (subtly linking vodka with its origins as a pharmaceutical tonic), and the medallion of Lars Olsson Smith (the Swedish inventor of a process to improve vodka's taste), the bottle had already established itself as a distinctive product, representing a combination of tradition and innovation. Despite this, Absolut had achieved relatively little brand recognition. The campaign would help to lodge the bottle's profile firmly in the public mind.

The first Absolut advertisement, "Absolut Perfection," shown with a halo hovering over the bottle, was conceived in 1980 and shot by advertising photographer Steve Bronstein, who solved the problem of eliminating glare from the glass by using a backdrop of matte Plexiglas. This practical solution foregrounded Absolut's future approach, in which even the most detailed advertisements were created in the studio with minimal postproduction retouching. The "Absolut Perfection" advertisement was released in 1981, and was followed by "Absolut Heaven," "Absolut Gem," and "Absolut Temptation."

Thereafter, TBWA found increasingly creative means of varying the theme. In 1985 Andy Warhol was commissioned to create "Absolut Warhol," the first of many images by contemporary artists and designers, while the lesser known "Absolut Stardom" (1987) was the first in the series to suggest the iconic bottle shape without depicting the product. This process was continued to great effect in the international cities series (with Tom McManus as art director and Dave Warren as writer), which began with "Absolut LA" in 1988—an aerial view of a sumptuous bottle-shaped swimming pool—and "Absolut Manhattan," featuring Central Park. The new format underlined the reason for Absolut's advertising supremacy: shifting the focus from the consumers' view of the product to how they were defined by it.

← P.262

← P.262

← P.263

1980–present

I-D

Magazine / Newspaper

Terry Jones (1945–) et al.

Terry Jones, UK

Launched in 1980 as a cheaply printed fanzine (fan magazine), *i-D* celebrated the fashion and lifestyle of a New Romantic post-punk movement, taking the idea of the "identity" of youth culture to its full potential, and providing a vehicle for the commodity display of the ordinary. Founded by the entrepreneur and photographer Terry Jones, the publication sought to break away from the clichéd approach to design and imagery of mainstream fashion magazines, such as British *Vogue*, where Jones had worked as art director in the 1970s. Now almost forty-five years old, *i-D* has outlived many of its glossy competitors, including *Blitz*, the *Face*, and *Sleazenation*.

Early issues of *i-D* were a composite of photographic collage, grainy images, stenciling, hand-drawn lettering, typewritten texts, and chaotic layouts, which set out to popularize a design aesthetic first seen in late 1970s punk fanzines. Jones would later call his approach "instant design"—a method that captured the immediacy of its fashion style by means of "cut-and-paste" graphics. This was echoed by the pioneering use of "straight-up" photography—a hybrid fashion/documentary approach that combined imagery and interviews, and brought what was happening on the street into mainstream fashion consciousness. Early covers were typographic and printed on fluorescent stock with the bold *i-D* logo turned on its side to resemble a wink and a smile—an expression echoed by cover models. Although its first issue sold only fifty copies, *i-D* went on to become a bestselling "style bible," selling more than sixty-seven thousand copies per month. It has been praised as a maker and a mirror of subcultural fashion, as well as a training ground for talented young designers, journalists, and photographers, including editor Dylan Jones, designers Moira Bogue and Malcolm Garrett, and photographers Nick Knight, Mark Lebon, and Ellen von Unwerth.

With its bold graphic style, *i-D* established an international brand based on innovative approaches to typography and photography, and has had a powerful influence on subsequent magazines, including capturing ordinary street fashion in "As Seen" sections.

1981–1986

THE FACE

Magazine / Newspaper

Neville Brody (1957–)

Wagadon, UK

Styled by British graphic and record-sleeve designer Neville Brody, the *Face* pioneered a new visual language for magazines during the 1980s that was extensively copied.

Initially published on a small budget, the magazine cut across music, fashion, film, and visual culture in general to become a street-wise style bible. Talented image-makers, such as Ray Petri, who created the look of the sulky eight-year-old Felix Howard for the March 1985 cover, brought underground and London street designs, such as the Buffalo fashions seen on the young Howard, to mass audiences. Brody's groundbreaking art direction introduced different typefaces on the same page, and used dynamic typography and strong visual accents to enhance the impact of the magazine's photography. While some pages were drenched in color, others remained starkly black and white, and certain covers—unusually for a style publication—featured only text without imagery. Brody also took images to the edges of the page, deliberately cropping and cutting into the photographs.

After Brody's departure in 1986, the *Face* continued publication until 2004, when dwindling sales forced the publisher, by then Emap, to close the magazine. Over the years, the *Face*'s graphic look had evolved into something less pioneering, and in its last decade it relied less on innovative graphics and more on photography for visual impact. The *Face* nevertheless had an enormous influence on the graphic environment of its time, and its signature trademarks of cropped photographs, bold styling, and models with attitude are now firmly established in the contemporary visual vernacular. Attempting to recapture some of that trailblazing spirit, the *Face* relaunched in 2019, with Stuart Brumfitt as editor and Alex O'Brien as art director.

1982

EXPO '85

Poster

Takenobu Igarashi (1944–)

Organizing Committee for the International Exposition of 1985, Japan

This poster promoting the International Exposition of 1985, which Takenobu Igarashi created several years ahead of the event, is an example of the designer's axonometric typography, in which letters are treated as three-dimensional forms without the use of perspective. Here, both two- and three-dimensional letter shapes are organized into a series of layers, with the middle layer extended to create a sense of depth. The complexity of the central row, with its varied range of shapes and colors, suggests a series of mechanical parts, evoking technology as much as typography, and alludes to the theme of scientific exploration and innovation celebrated by the exhibition.

Unlike earlier generations of Japanese designers, who were preoccupied with updating the traditional forms of Japanese art and culture by means of modernist Western idioms, Igarashi, who studied design in the U.S. as well as in Japan, is comfortable working with many of the more technical elements of Western graphic language, including grids and isometric projection. In addition to the lettering, the faint background lines in this image suggest the language of geometry and technical drawings, while the color blue evokes logic and reason. Igarashi maintains that all his work is underpinned by basic geometric and graphic shapes—circles, triangles and squares—which he organizes by means of flat or three-dimensional grids. Igarashi's axonometric alphabets also anticipated his later interest in "architectural alphabets," which are sculptures that have been used for signage and applied by architects as a mechanism for modeling the built environment.

As well as this poster, Igarashi created advertising for Habitat's exhibit at Expo '85, which continued his exploration of the structural potential of letterforms, and designed a series of posters and other products for the Museum of Modern Art in New York during the 1980s. The designer has received a number of awards, including one from the Art Directors Club of Los Angeles and the Japan Design Committee's Masaru Katsumi Award.

← P.264

← P.265

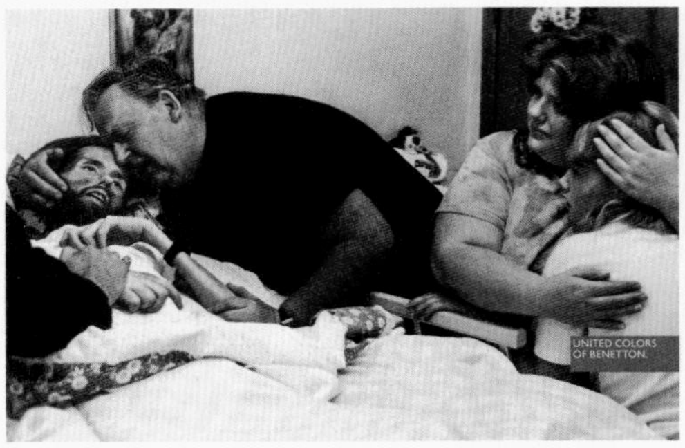

← P.265

1982

GRAPUS

Poster

Grapus

Musée de l'Affiche, France

Hailed as the *enfant terrible* of design for its outlandish sense of humor, the Grapus collective introduced radical politics and a vibrant, explosive visual style to the staid and heavily commercialized world of 1970s graphic design.

With a vision based on the uprising of May 1968, Grapus was founded in 1970 by Pierre Bernard, Gérard Paris-Clavel, and François Miehe, who were later joined by Jean-Paul Bachollet and Alex Jordan. All were members of the French Communist Party (PCF), and, having rejected commercial advertising, were determined to devote themselves to social, economic, and political causes. They signed their posters simply "Grapus," as the product of collaborative teamwork.

The group's distinctive image-making was an energetic and joyous but shocking and subversive mix of montage, frenzied scrawls, primary colors, handwriting, and minimal use of type. These trademark elements are at their most volatile in a poster for their exhibition at Paris's Musée de l'Affiche. The bastardized "smiley face" has one eye bearing the Communist emblem, and the other a thickly painted *cocarde*—the ribboned emblem worn by French revolutionaries and a play on the word *coquard* (black eye). A few black brush strokes suggest Hitler's forelock and mustache. The portrait represents a mass of politics, contradictions, and pleasures. Other well-known posters include "Apartheid Racisme," created in 1986 to denounce the racial segregation practiced in South Africa at that time. The silhouette of the African continent, omitting South Africa, is turned into a skull using two maps for eye sockets.

As the years passed, Grapus grew to around twenty members, and its work became more ambitious in scale, including corporate identities for the Parc de la Villette and the Musée du Louvre. The members disbanded in 1991, each moving on to pursue new creative interests.

Grapus had a huge influence on the international graphic design profession. The group's desire to merge politics and the spirit of change with lively images lives on in politicized design studios all over the world including El Fantasma de Heredia in Buenos Aires and the agitational groups La Corriente Eléctrica and Fuera de Registro in Mexico City.

1982

FABER & FABER

Logo

John McConnell (1939–)

Faber & Faber, UK

When asked to revise Faber & Faber's logo in 1982, John McConnell set out to create a distinctive identity that would reflect the company's illustrious publishing heritage, which had included designs by Eric Gill and William Morris. A member of Pentagram, McConnell joined Faber as an external consultant (later becoming a board member), and for the next ten years oversaw the design of all the company's book covers, instigating a style that drew upon the publisher's classical traditions.

When Faber & Faber was first established, there was only one Faber involved (Geoffrey Faber, who founded the company in 1929), but the double name was deemed to display more authority. However, it also fit uneasily onto the spines of books, a problem that led McConnell to shorten the name to just the initials, which he adapted from an existing font. The ligature effect used in the two lowercase letters derives from traditional printing, thereby also reflecting the origins of the company. In fact, McConnell designed two different logos, one each for the company's publishing and music arms—a roman "f" for the publishing division and an italic "*f*" for Faber Music, due to its similarity to a treble clef.

As well as reflecting the publisher's traditional heritage, the logo has grown to symbolize the elegant design of Faber & Faber's books. With its old-fashioned appearance, the double "f" has a strong literary character, but the lowercase monogram also conveys modesty and friendliness, an effect enhanced by the enlarged rounded curves of the heads and the stroke uniting them at the center. A beloved symbol among Faber's readers, the trademark is immediately recognizable on the books' spines.

1982–2000

BENETTON

Advertising

Oliviero Toscani (1942–)

United Colors of Benetton, Italy

Oliviero Toscani's advertisements, produced over eighteen years for the United Colors of Benetton campaign, shattered conventional perceptions of the role of advertising. The Italian clothing company, established by Luciano Benetton in 1965, had always been committed to creative advertising, but Toscani's appointment in 1982 was to place Benetton among the most recognizable brands in the world.

Required to create a campaign that would appeal to a global audience and address universal themes, Toscani had a difficult task. The first campaign, dubbed "All the Colors of the World," offered a vision of racial harmony, featuring images of young, culturally diverse people in Benetton clothing. Over time, the advertisements became more adventurous, confronting controversial issues intended to promote social awareness and debate. In 1989 an image of a Black woman breast-feeding a white baby, designed to represent an unorthodox view of racial equality, was banned in the U.S. because of connotations of slavery. Despite this controversy, the image won many awards.

Subsequently, Toscani continued to use provocative images to raise public awareness of racism, war, religion, and capital punishment, but now he removed all reference to Benetton products, apart from a small green logo. Probably the most famous is the 1990 photograph of a man dying of AIDS, surrounded by his mourning family. This caused a storm of debate over its comparison to the Christian tradition of the *pietà* (the Virgin Mary cradling the dead body of Christ), and is typical of Toscani's reinterpretation of the advertising image as art. Criticized by many for trivializing genuine human issues, the advertisements were immediately recognizable as belonging to Benetton, despite not promoting products, and proved highly successful in counteracting cultural standardization.

Toscani's work for Benetton brought an alternative form of brand promotion to the foreground, and proved influential in demonstrating that controversy could be a valuable tool in the advertising world.

← P.266

1983

HIROSHIMA APPEALS

Poster

Yusaku Kamekura (1915–1997)

Hiroshima International Cultural Foundation and Japan Graphic Designers Association, Japan

As founding president of the Japan Graphic Designers Association (JAGDA, established in 1978), Yusaku Kamekura set the bar high with this entry for the Hiroshima Appeals poster competition, creating one of the most powerful antiwar and antinuclear images in history.

Kamekura was uniquely situated to help shape Japanese design and turn it into a vehicle for culture and commerce. After working with Yonosuke Natori at *Nippon* magazine, he helped to found the Japan Advertising Artists Club, as well as JAGDA, and persuaded Japan's presidents of industry to establish the house agency, Nippon Design Center (NDC), for corporations such as Asahi Beer, Toyota, Japan Railways, and Toshiba. Uncompromising in his pursuit of clarity and beauty in graphic design, Kamekura also took seriously the designer's role, believing that it should tackle important issues of the day—in this case the painful subject of Hiroshima's destruction. Realizing that images of skeletons and nuclear mushroom clouds were unlikely to be hung on walls, he proposed an altogether different solution: a shocking image of burning butterflies, gorgeously multicolored but painfully so: flames steal their flight, sending them plummeting downward, underscoring the fragility of all life and the suffering inflicted by the atomic bomb. Kamekura, however, remained unsatisfied with the design until the third color proof, when he trimmed the edges, slicing through a single butterfly to make the composition appear more random and highlighting the arbitrary nature of those caught by the attack.

For the next six years, the Hiroshima Appeals posters—the first in a series of Japanese poster campaigns promoting peace—were produced by some of Japan's most important graphic designers: Kiyoshi Awazu, Shigeo Fukuda, Yoshio Hayakawa, Kazumasa Nagai, Ikko Tanaka, and Mitsuo Katsui. As an undisputed master in his later years, Kamekura edited the internationally distributed and bilingual *Creation* magazine, which presented the work of artists and designers that Kamekura felt deserved wider attention. His most important message, however, is contained in this poster—that designers should speak the truth to those in power.

← P.267

1984

ORIGINAL MACINTOSH ICONS

Information Design

Susan Kare (1954–)

Apple, Inc., U.S.

Both the Apple Mac screen icons and the Chicago typeface were designed in the early days of Apple computers, when they had to comply with the screen-resolution limitations that then existed. Despite this, they have remained an important part of the Apple brand identity. Designed by Susan Kare during her tenure as creative director of Apple, the set includes some of the most recognizable computer icons ever created—the trash can, watch, and bomb, among others.

Owing to the restrictions of the early Macintosh screens, artwork had to be presented in a coarse bitmapped format, while the monochromatic structure of the display meant that shadings were handled as varying densities of atonal pixels (lighter shades were simulated by using fewer pixels). In the mid-1990s small, independent type foundries took up the challenge of this coarse-display medium by designing pixel-perfect typefaces (those without anti-alias shading), which could be clearly read at astoundingly small point sizes. By contrast, graphic designers and collectives, such as eboy and Delaware, capitalized on the limitations of 72 dpi screen resolutions by purposefully adapting, as Kare had done, to the coarse-graphic screen grid, testifying to the lasting appeal of the original aesthetic.

Also designed by Susan Kare, Chicago belonged to a series of basic system fonts created for Apple, all named after major world cities, and included only a twelve-point bitmap version. The type lacks the traditional character sets of roman and italic styles, and remains legible on screen even in "gray" mode. Chicago was eventually turned into a scalable TrueType font by the type designers Charles Bigelow and Kris Holmes, and when Mac OS 8 was introduced in 1997, Apple replaced Chicago with Charcoal as the default font. Chicago, however, was still distributed with the system as a foundation for other screen types, and is available in a wide variety of media, particularly for signage and printed work, without regard to its original purpose. More recently, Chicago was resurrected for use in the screen interface of a third-generation iPod, and there are also copies available for Windows-based systems, with names such as "Chicane" and "Mac Type."

← P.267

1984

CYCLE OF FILMS BY JEAN-LUC GODARD

Poster

Werner Jeker (1944–)

Cinémathèque Suisse, Switzerland

Werner Jeker is a key figure in the history of Swiss poster design, which is known for its balanced composition, clean typography, and technical precision. All of Jeker's posters were created in the same format, and most are in black and white. As he said, "Black and white is the simplest and the most radical expression."

Jeker almost always used photography as a key element in his posters. Incorporating unusual crops, jagged distortion, multiplication of images, and the superimposition of text or graphics over photography, Jeker reinterpreted the photographs he used and gave them new meanings. For a poster of French film director Jean-Luc Godard created for the Cinémathèque Suisse in Lausanne, Jeker began with a portrait photograph of the film-maker in black and white. He extended the black space above Godard's head and cropped the face below the eyes, repeating the eyes twice more. Jeker may have manipulated the photo to create multiple pairs of eyes in order to express the idea that Godard sees more than others, reflecting the experimental, avant-garde nature of his films. Alternatively, it may be a literal reference to the repetition of an image that appears in successive frames of a strip of film. A white line extending from the filmmaker's head to the right side of the poster is also repeated, continuing up the entire length of the right-hand side of the poster and suggesting the format of a film reel. Across the top of the page, the words "Cinémathèque Suisse" in uppercase form a neat line, with three lines of smaller text about this particular poster completing the line at the far right.

A master of photography, Jeker's manipulation of images in his posters resulted in strong visuals that communicate in powerful and thought-provoking ways.

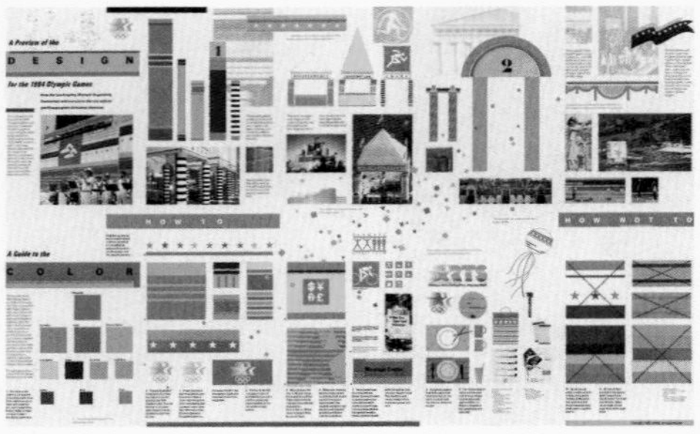

← P.268

1984

1984 LOS ANGELES OLYMPICS

Identity

Sussman/Prejza & Company

Los Angeles County Arts Commission, U.S.

The XXIII Olympiad was a breakthrough for Los Angeles: its first chance to host the event after many failed bids. The County Arts Commission saw the starry international sporting arena as a chance to rebrand clichéd perceptions of the city. Yet, while the event needed to be memorable, its limited budget didn't match the usual expectation for hosts to build new venues. Instead, the Los Angeles Olympic Organizing Committee (LAOOC) sought a creative way to revive and unite the county's twenty-eight existing facilities and to visually express a sense of optimism.

Designer-architect team Deborah Sussman and Paul Prejza, together with architecture and urban-planning firm Jerde, were tasked with the challenge, and they saw an opportunity to link the different sites using a vibrant "visual alphabet" that could be applied to wayfinding, banners, ephemera, and the venues themselves. The backbone of the design scheme hinged on an energetic color palette that included magenta, vermillion, yellow, and aqua, rather than a predictable patriotic response of red, white, and blue. This breakthrough approach drew on Sussman's earlier experiences working at the Eames Office and with Alexander Girard, all masterful designers of form and color.

Sussman's proposed palette came by way of a stack of collage paper. Those same hues of paper stock, while chromatically dynamic, nodded to the richness of Hispanic and Asian cultures in the Californian region. From this unexpected start, Sussman/Prejza and the Jerde team developed a hardworking and adaptable design language based on a star, circle, square, and triangle. Rescaled and combined, this kit of parts was extended to include additions and alterations to venues with star-shaped monoliths, rainbow-hued scaffolding towers, and enormous cylindrical columns. Although temporary and inexpensive, their united festive identity translated well onscreen and off, with its bold hues, punchy motifs, and the event's catchy moniker, LA84.

By Sussman's account, the fresh approach for LA84 came down to the trust and enthusiasm of the LAOOC general manager, Harry Usher. But it is the Sussman team's graphic legacy that remains the star of the games.

← P.270

1984–2005

EMIGRE

Magazine / Newspaper

Rudy VanderLans (1955–), Zuzana Licko (1961–)

Emigre Inc., U.S.

Emigre magazine, a showcase for creative type, arrived before the Apple Macintosh computer gained widespread acceptance. With the first issue, subtitled "A Magazine for Exiles," Rudy VanderLans and his wife, Zuzana Licko, aimed to display the work of émigré artists and designers like themselves—poets, writers, journalists, graphic designers, photographers, architects, and artists—at a time when digital tools were beginnning to transform the nature of creativity.

As the magazine gained momentum, the typefaces (most of them designed by Licko), including coarse, fixed-sized bitmap fonts, such as Oakland, were made available for purchase. *Emigre*'s earliest typefaces functioned on non-Postscript printers of the day, but in 1986 the magazine released Citizen and Matrix for three hundred dpi printers. By this time, *Emigre* had evolved into a format similar to what the foundry ITC offered in the magazine *U&lc* (*Upper and lowercase*). In 1991 *Emigre* also released the quintessential grunge font and one of the most defining typefaces of the 1990s, Template Gothic, designed by Barry Deck.

Despite the continuing success of their Emigre Graphics Studio, VanderLans and Licko gave up designing for clients and proceeded to push the limits of design in the magazine. As one of the forerunners of grunge typography—later popularized in the 1990s by David Carson—*Emigre* went on to exhibit highly experimental work, often produced for the designer and without any client at the receiving end. Special issues, such as "Design as Content" and "Fanzines," empowered designers, who began to position themselves at the forefront of visual culture rather than merely as service providers.

Having exhausted the graphic landscape, *Emigre* ventured into the audiovisual realm with a series of musically inspired issues equipped with their own compact discs. Its partnership with the Princeton Architectural Press in 2003 marked the shift from magazine to pocketbook format, while the focus on more writing and discussion about visual culture encouraged practitioners to look critically at their own work and the art world that surrounded them.

← P.271

1984

MUSÉE D'ORSAY

Logo

Bruno Monguzzi (1941–), Jean Widmer (1929–)

Musée d'Orsay, France

The strongly typographic logo designed by Bruno Monguzzi and Jean Widmer for the Musée d'Orsay in Paris recalls the Didot typeface in its classical, elegant appeal and exaggerated thick and thin strokes. Bleeding out of the top and bottom of a black square, the two half-formed letters invite viewers to complete their shapes, whereas the "d" is conspicuous through its absence, suggested only by the apostrophe. Overall, the composition has the character of a film sequence and suggests a dynamic, flexible institution moving between the traditional and the modern.

During the early 1980s, the Direction des Musées de France implemented plans for the Gare d'Orsay to be transformed from a railway station into a national museum that would unite Paris's nineteenth-century art collections, previously scattered between the Louvre, the Musée d'Art Moderne, and the Jeu de Paume. As a major national landmark, the new museum required an identity that would reflect its cultural status and give it a global profile. Jean Widmer of the Swiss graphic design studio, Visuel Design, together with the Milanese designer and typographer Bruno Monguzzi, won the ensuing commission in 1983. Widmer, who trained under the Bauhaus artist and designer Johannes Itten, had already established a reputation in France, having worked on signage for several new museums in Paris, including the Centre de Création Industrielle, and raised the international reputation of French graphic design. Monguzzi, who trained in typography, had worked at the Studio Boggeri in Milan with designers such as Max Huber, and was known for his precise yet lyrical typographic compositions.

Today, the Musée d'Orsay identity looks as fresh as when it first appeared, and is used for both exhibition posters and print materials, occasionally in brilliant color, as well as with the letters in full view without cropping.

← P.271

1985

YALE UNIVERSITY PRESS

Logo

Paul Rand (1914–1996)

Yale University Press, U.S.

Lux et veritas—light and truth: the Yale University motto could be a mantra for Paul Rand's logo designs, including the one he produced late in his career for the university at which he had taught for almost forty years. Rand was a natural choice to redesign the Yale University Press (YUP) logo—over seventy-five years into the Press's storied existence.

Although Rand created the logo toward the end of a long line of successes, including IBM (1956), UPS (1961), NeXT (1986), and Morningstar (1991), the design is as fresh, clean, and distinct as its closest cousin in the Rand oeuvre, the Borzoi Books logo that he produced for Alfred A. Knopf in 1945. Like the linear hound, the YUP emblem is a playful representation of an august institution based on a balance of abstraction and recognition, although with its many ligatures, the publisher's mark seems to flirt deliberately with illegibility. Typeface and application seem inseparable, with the slab serifs contributing significantly to the balance of its four entwined characters.

As with all Rand logos, validity and meaning are heavily dependent on the client organization, although a large amount of interpretation is left to the viewer. The former is assured through Yale's place in American academia, with the university (which published three of Rand's books) placing its imprimatur on the designer even as he placed his on them. The latter is evident in the subjective interpretation of the design's allusions, although comparisons with the workings of a printing press, or references to the values of dialogue, inquiry, and debate extolled in YUP's mission statement, might all be valid. That is to say, the logo could be about the workings of the press or the press itself. ...ver, Rand himself believed that a logo could ... mpany or its product; its role ... orable, to function and ... es, and, above all, ... s of how many

← P.272

1985–1991

J.D.s

Magazine / Newspaper

G.B. Jones (1965–), Bruce LaBruce (1964–)

Self-commissioned, U.S.

J.D.s was a zine created by Canadian artists Bruce LaBruce and G. B. Jones that ran from 1985 to 1991, comprising eight issues in total. Its name an abbreviation of "Juvenile Delinquents," the zine contained a mix of personal stories, photographs, collages, artwork, and manifestos that addressed issues surrounding the queer community, rising homophobia within punk culture, the AIDS crisis, and social and political activism. *J.D.s* was renowned for its unfiltered and unapologetic content, and is widely credited as the catalyst behind the queercore music subculture. LaBruce and Jones used the zine as a space to collaborate with friends and other artists, and to "call for a return to the roots of punk, which were much more sexually revolutionary and experimental and of course homosexual."

Aesthetically, the zine embraced the punk and DIY sensibilities of the era, utilizing a scrapbook approach that highlighted the grittiness of its editorial content. Handwritten text and pornographic collages in chaotic compositions rejected common graphic design principles. The photography and illustrations were equally subversive, often presenting out-of-focus and distorted subjects. Jones's emerging *Tom Girls* drawing series presented an all-female reimagining of Tom of Finland's hypermasculine characters. The layout changed drastically from one page to the next, ranging from comic-strip-like spreads to typewritten letters, offering a freeform approach that reflected the diverse and frequently confrontational nature of the zine's content.

Across its black-and-white xeroxed pages, *J.D.s* reflected the interests and pursuits of LaBruce, Jones, and their collaborators, no matter how provocative. It featured ads for their friends' Super-8 movies, art, and porn, as well as personal playlists, erotica, and cartoons. Together this creation and reproduction of ephemera built a scene, and a significant following, that far surpassed its originators' expectations. At the close of the final issue, LaBruce had fully entered the world of filmmaking while Jones continued to pursue her dual focuses of art and music. Today *J.D.s* is cited as one of the most influential early queer zines and was included in an exhibition at the Brooklyn Museum, entitled *Copy Machine Manifestos: Artists Who Make Zines*.

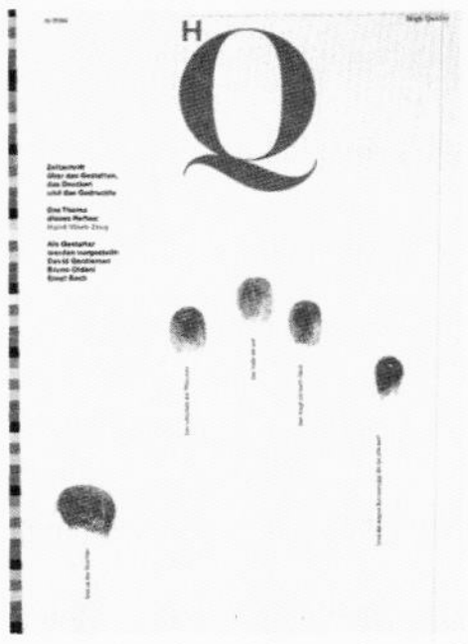

← P.272

1985–1998

HQ (HIGH QUALITY)

Magazine / Newspaper

Rolf Müller (1940–2015)

Heidelberger Druckmaschinen, Germany

HQ (High Quality) magazine was a publication designed and edited by Munich-based designer Rolf Müller between 1985 and 1998 for publisher Heidelberger Druckmaschinen, a German company that manufactures printers. The readership comprised mainly graphic designers and printers.

As editor and designer of *HQ*, Müller had full artistic control over the magazine, including decisions regarding the density of content and form. A member of the old school of design, Müller prefers to work without computers for at least some of the time; for a period he provided only two computers for three designers in his studio, forcing them to interact with each other without reference to a screen. Designs were not judged on screen but were printed before being critiqued.

A noncommercial magazine, *HQ* had no need to chase advertisers or commercial support, meaning the content could be truthful and authentic, as well as experimental. Each issue had a theme around which the subject matter revolved. Photographer David Paul Lyon recalls that *HQ* was searching for material on the theme of "remains" or "leftovers" when he contacted them to suggest a series on the Palermo mummies photographed using a new process. He was surprised that Müller agreed right away without hesitation, but these sorts of experimental ideas were part of the magazine's manifesto.

The *HQ* cover featured a strip of colors that is reminiscent of the CMYK model used in process color printing, which gave the magazine continuity and made it easy to identify. Designed like a poster, the cover used one key image that summarized the theme of that particular issue. Inside, the main typefaces used were Univers 55 and 65; the layout grid was based on the proportions of these typefaces.

Because *HQ*'s sole intention was to show off the high quality that could be achieved by graphic designers and printers, the magazine had the freedom to experiment with fluid content and ideas, while presenting beautiful design and production values.

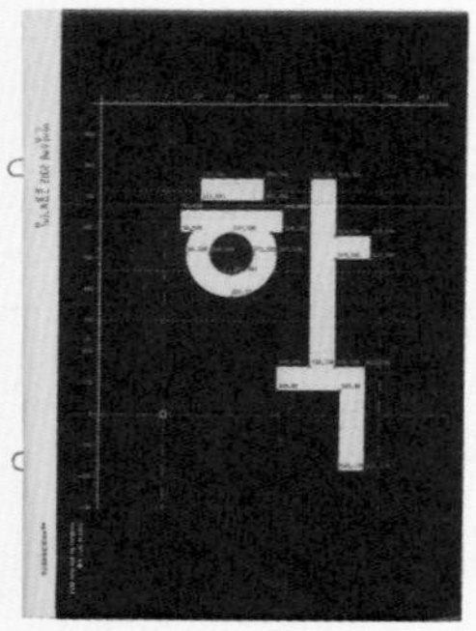

← P.273

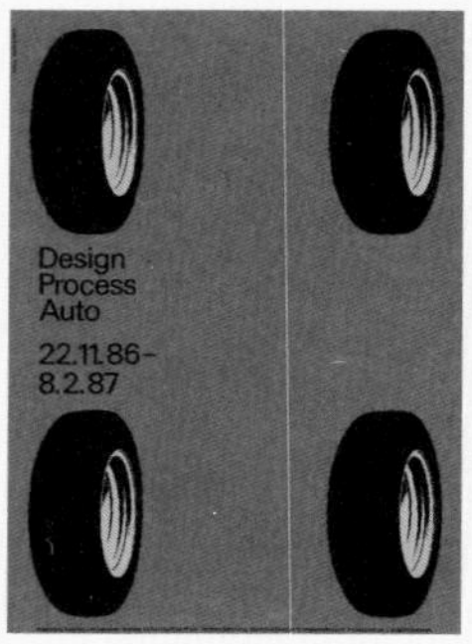

← P.274

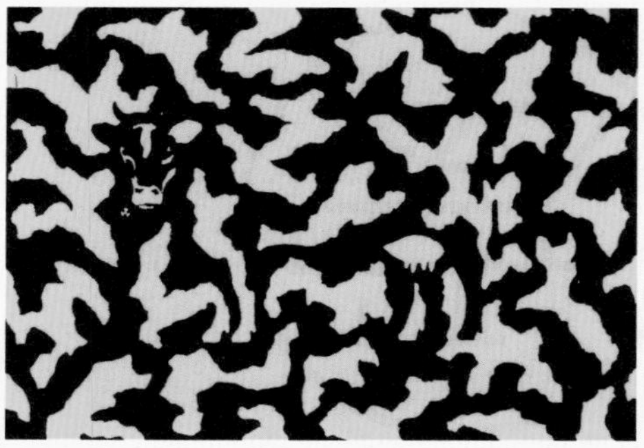

← P.275

1985

AHNSANGSOO

Typeface

Ahn Sang-soo (1952–)

Self-commissioned, South Korea

A love letter to his nation's Hangul alphabet, Korean designer Ahn Sang-soo's reinterpretation of the fifteenth-century system in 1985 was motivated by his curiosity about the relationship between written language and culture. He believes Hangul is central to Korea's culture, noting: "If Hangul had not been invented, would Korea even exist? Korean culture maybe would not have developed."

Trained at Hongik University in Seoul, Ahn Sang-soo has a love for letterforms that is broad but runs especially deep for Hangul. This phonetic Korean alphabet was introduced in 1446 as a simplified expression of Chinese Mandarin characters. Developed by King Sejong and his court during the Joseon dynasty, Hangul was intended to give everyday citizens access to reading and to expand literacy beyond the country's educated elite.

Centuries later, it seems fitting that Ahn Sang-soo has revived the alphabet in a way that is both modern and accessible. His eponymous font innovates the traditional representation of Korean letters by breaking the orthogonal grid system of each letter (*jamo*). The groundbreaking change is in translating the old square-based characters into a modern system with bold geometries, such as circles, squares, and triangles, that seem to "jump" outside the box. Ahn Sang-soo describes this playful act of design (*meotjium*) as central to his process: he tests and applies spirited logic across all his endeavors, including exhibitions, books, writing, research—and even the iron gates of his home.

His subsequent alphabet, Leesang—named for the Surrealist writer Lee Sang—extends the design logic that breaks Hangul rules. Developed between 1988 and 2013, its *jamo* follow a diagonal pattern, read top to bottom for each first consonant (*choseong*), central vowel (*jungseong*), and final consonant (*jongseong*). This format creates a cadence akin to music notation that gives space and pause between each letter.

The significance of Ahn Sang-soo's revised Hangul typeface won him the 2007 Gutenberg Prize. In 2012 he founded the AG Typography Institute type foundry, and he was previously a professor of graphic design at Hongik University, Seoul.

1986

DESIGN PROCESS AUTO

Poster

Pierre Mendell (1929–2008)

Die Neue Sammlung, Germany

Pierre Mendell's poster for the *Design Process Auto* exhibition, held at Die Neue Sammlung (Munich's international design museum), demonstrates clearly and concisely that all car design starts from a single basic principle: four wheels.

Born in Germany, Mendell worked in his family's textile factory in France during the 1950s, before studying graphic design at the Basel Schüle für Gestaltung under the Swiss designer Armin Hofmann. After finishing his training, he moved to Munich, where in 1961 he set up the Mendell & Oberer studio with Klaus Oberer, a fellow student from Basel. The *Design Process Auto* exhibition featured models and sketches of ideas for cars, illustrating how designs are progressively refined until they reach a final solution. This process of simplification is mirrored by Mendell's poster and reflects his work as a whole, which involved distilling subjects to their barest essence to create striking designs. His work is also characterized by strong geometric forms, bold color, and unexpected juxtapositions or missing elements, which need to be completed by the viewer to identify the message.

In *Design Process Auto*, Mendell gives us little more than the first stage of car design, inviting us to supply our own imaginative thoughts by filling in the details. The left-aligned typography encourages this interpretative process, leaving the center of the poster as a bright red ground to emphasize the limitless field of design possibility. Mendell's process of reduction provided the basis for a truly individual signature, but it also incorporated and acknowledged the role of the viewer. With characteristic obliqueness, however, he refused to ever articulate this approach: when asked for his design philosophy, Mendell replied, "I have none."

1986

IQ

Poster

Uwe Loesch (1943–)

Self-commissioned, Germany

Uwe Loesch's stereographic poster "IQ," produced after the meltdown of the Chernobyl nuclear reactor in 1986, protested the radioactive damage the disaster caused to vegetation and wildlife throughout Europe. Initially covered up by the Soviet government, the event later sparked uproar within the international community over how it had been handled.

From 1968 to 1986, Loesch produced hundreds of nonprofit posters for charities and protest events, but 'IQ' is a particularly biting representation of the environmental cost of the Chernobyl disaster. The field of irregular, bright yellow shapes against a black background expresses the breakdown and mutations on all scales, cellular and human, caused by radioactive emissions. Within this field, a stereographic cow is just visible, its body camouflaged by the irregular shapes around it. The accident had a particularly destructive effect on European livestock, especially grazing animals, such as cows and sheep, whose meat and milk were rendered poisonous for many years. An animal that often has a mottled coat, the cow was also a particularly suitable vehicle for the poster's graphic language and style. The livid yellow echoes that of the nuclear-hazard sign, and the trefoil symbol itself appears in miniature just to the left of the cow's face.

This simultaneously beautiful and disturbing design has also been made into wallpaper, covering an entire space with its unsettling pattern. Whether presented as a single poster or multiplied over a large surface, the image communicates a powerful message and, similar to many other works by Loesch such as his exhibition poster "... nur Fliegen ist schöner" (... only flying is more beautiful, 2003) is characterized by a fascination with visu

← P.275

1986–1992

OCTAVO

Magazine / Newspaper

Mark Holt (1958–), Hamish Muir (1957–), Simon Johnston (1959–)

8vo, UK

A limited-edition typogaphy magazine, published in only eight issues, *Octavo* rebelled against the fashionable, surface-driven design trends of the 1980s that were inspired by new computer technologies. Its belief in a rational, functional, and restrained approach to graphic communication, which placed typography at the forefront, earned it a place in history, alongside *Merz* and *Emigre*.

Mark Holt, Hamish Muir, and Simon Johnston situated the design workshop Octavo (aka 8vo) in Johnston's London apartment after the trio decided to go into business (and later publishing) together. With a firm design ideology, the consultancy expanded into a team of five and developed an expansive client base. *Octavo*'s lack of extraneous ornamentation, decoration, or illustrative renderings reflected the studio's utilitarian approach to graphic design. Less concerned with trends and more with timeless aesthetics, 8vo rejected over-manipulated typography, preferring a more direct transmission of information locked into interwoven grid structures and set with sans serif typography. Each issue became a stylistic experiment in and of itself. The black/gray Issue 87.4, for example, possessed an economy of means, allowing body type to drape in wispy columns with systematic high-contrast thumbnail images popping up from the paper's dark ground. By contrast, Issue 88.5 was understated, with lowercase letters starting sentences; at the same time it erupted with electric yellows bound together by an angular grid system, as exemplified on its cover.

8vo continued to publish the magazine sporadically until its eighth and final publication—a CD-Rom—released in 1992. In 2005 the studio released *8vo: On the Outside*, a book that chronicles the workshop's inception, vision, clientele, and ideology.

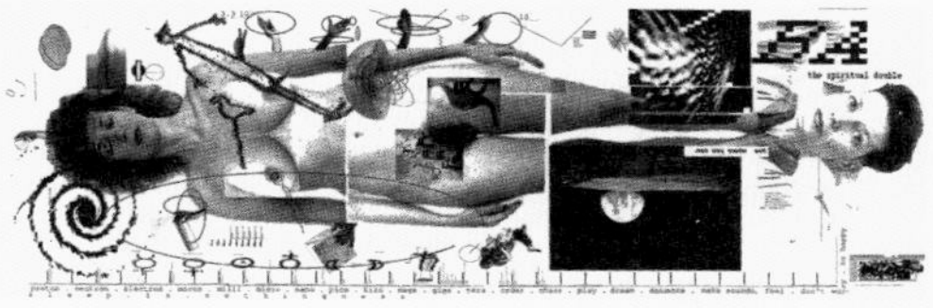

← P.276

1986

DOES IT MAKE SENSE?

Magazine / Newspaper

April Greiman (1948–)

MIT Press, Walker Art Center, U.S.

In 1986 the designer April Greiman was commissioned by the Walker Art Center in Minneapolis to design Issue 133 of its *Design Quarterly* journal. Greiman had built a reputation on her experimental approach and was one of the first in the field to adopt the use of the Macintosh computer, released only two years earlier. Departing from the journal's usual editorial-led stance, "Does it Make Sense?" took the thirty-two pages of the magazine as a framework and turned them into a two-by-six-foot, double-sided, fold-out poster. Greiman used MacDraw software to create both the type and image compositions; spliced graphic and photographic elements were united in a postmodern aesthetic. The press dubbed Greiman "Queen of New Wave," and although she later denounced the moniker, her unorthodox use of technology disrupted the modernist dogma that had dominated the industry for so long.

A life-size, segmented self-portrait of Greiman dominates the front of the poster, encircled and overlaid with a maelstrom of images that evoke the origins of life on Earth, such as a dinosaur, scientific elements, and a timeline that ranges from the birth of the solar system to the invention of the Macintosh and beyond. In a self-referential turn, the back of the poster documents the work's process, inviting readers behind a curtain that is usually closed. By questioning the point of sensemaking, Greiman plays with the purpose of graphic design: In a discipline concerned with communication, should we prioritize sense or expression?

Today, Greiman runs her Los Angeles–based design consultancy, Made in Space, and the rebellious language of her style continues to push the envelope. During her brief stint as director of the graphic-design program at California Institute of the Arts, from 1982 to 1984, Greiman's work was unfairly disparaged by a largely male faculty. In an interview for AIGA's *Eye on Design*, she recalled one critic saying, "She takes a bunch of typesetting and stands at the top of the stairs and throws it down, and where it lands is her design." "Does it Make Sense?" acts as Greiman's visual rebuttal. Paraphrasing Ludwig Wittgenstein, she often retorts, "It makes sense if you give it sense."

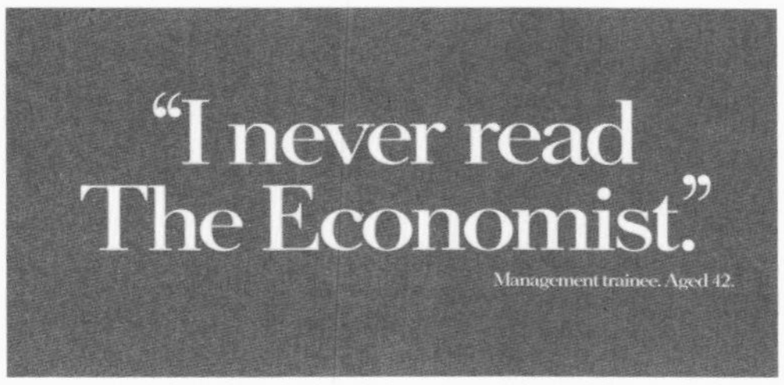

← P.278

1986–2006

THE ECONOMIST

Advertising

Abbott Mead Vickers BBDO

The Economist Group, UK

Originally founded in 1843, the *Economist* owes much of its recent commercial success to one of the longest-running poster campaigns in graphic design history. The series has been admired for its powerful unadorned style, tight creative constraints, and rejection of some of the cardinal rules of advertising.

The distinctive red advertising posters for Britain's stalwart news and current affairs title grew out of a need for the magazine, then read by a somewhat esoteric group of financiers and economists, to increase its readership as the UK economy slid into recession at the end of the 1980s. At a time when millions of pounds were being pumped into television advertising, the *Economist* adorned billboards with a predominantly print campaign (using the journal's own Headline typeface), showing that outdoor media can be just as successful in promoting brand recognition at a fraction of the cost.

As well as concentrating on the bold color of the masthead, the London-based advertising agency Abbott Mead Vickers BBDO integrated research with the creative process to find its hook for the campaign: the belief among informed readers of the *Economist* that the title gave them a competitive edge and membership of an exclusive club. The decoding of straplines, visual puns, and wordplay reinforces this sense of superiority, while other viewers are teased into curiosity and a sense of inferiority. The longevity of the campaign has helped to bolster its recognition, enabling subsequent style developments to push the boundaries still further. One poster omitted the masthead altogether, featuring just an image of the character Brains from the television series *Thunderbirds*, set against a red background. However, this was deemed too oblique even for readers in the know.

Despite its wide variety of adaptations and creative executions, the campaign has managed to maintain consistency while staying true to the magazine's central brand proposition as a provider of essential political and economic information. This message has also been promoted by other media, such as Virgin Atlantic's eye masks, which in the early 2000s carried the strapline "Don't stay in the dark for long."

← P.279

1987

SILENCE = DEATH

Poster

Avram Finkelstein (1952–) et al.

ACT UP NY, U.S.

The HIV and AIDS epidemic began in the United States from an unknown yet deadly virus, with the first official cases recorded in 1981. Initially there was little information about the disease, but six years later it was spreading like wildfire. People, mostly gay men, were dying in large numbers, and the lengthy Food and Drug Administration approval process for medicines, coupled with widespread ignorance and prejudice over who was susceptible to infection, delayed the development of experimental drugs that might allow those with HIV to live longer.

It was amid this atmosphere of palpable urgency that Avram Finkelstein cofounded the "Silence = Death" project in 1986, alongside Jorge Socarrás, Chris Lione, Charles Kreloff, Oliver Johnston, and Brian Howard. To raise awareness and protest government inaction, the group collectively designed a poster. They chose a pink triangle as their emblem—a symbol that had been forcibly used to identify gay men in Nazi Germany—and paired it with the slogan.

A message was born that would define the fight against HIV/AIDS for decades to come. By subverting a symbol of historical persecution, the collective reclaimed the narrative while powerfully communicating the necessity of their cause and the imminent consequences of inaction. The slogan called for the opposite of silence: for action, for the power to speak out and be heard, in order to hold onto life for as long as possible. Addressing mainstream audiences was key to tackling the misinformation perpetuated by politicians and mass media—that the virus affected only gay men, or that it was transmitted simply through kissing—so the simplicity of the messaging was crucial.

The collective eventually gave the rights to the poster to the direct-action advocacy group, the AIDS Coalition to Unleash Power (ACT UP), known for its large-scale protests, and it became the central image of the movement. It would be more than a decade before the United States recorded its first substantial decline in deaths, and the battle against the virus continues worldwide, but there is no doubt that Finkelstein and the activists who followed helped to curb the spread, making this poster one of the most important graphic outputs of the twentieth century.

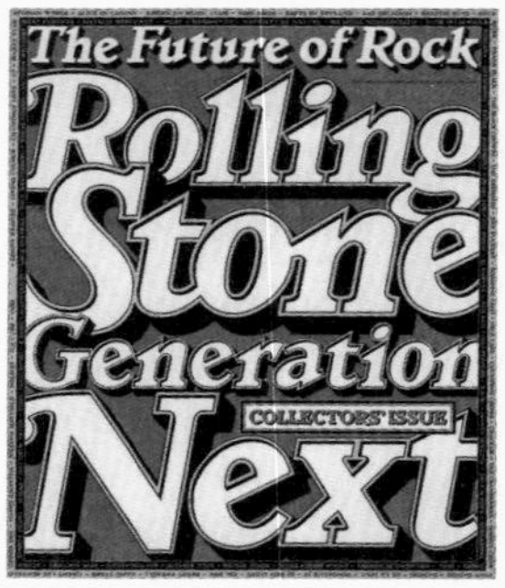

← P.280

1987–2001

ROLLING STONE

Magazine / Newspaper

Fred Woodward (1953–)

Jann S. Wenner, U.S.

Rolling Stone, the biweekly rock and roll "bible," was launched in 1967 and already had a substantial design legacy when Fred Woodward signed on as art director in 1987. The magazine's founding art director was Robert Kingsbury, who was joined in 1970 by the then-unknown Annie Leibovitz as a staff photographer, the latter becoming chief photographer in 1973. Mike Salisbury and Roger Black then built on the magazine's reputation by introducing conceptual covers and illustration, along with customized typography.

Mindful of *Rolling Stone*'s profile and its origins in San Francisco, Woodward reinstated some original design features, such as the Oxford border. This device helped the reader distinguish between editorial and advertising content, becoming part of the magazine's immediately recognizable visual identity, along with a classical approach to the body copy, which was rigorously contained by column rules. These served as a stabilizing counterpoint to Woodward's wildly expressive and unpredictable feature openers, which have become icons of magazine design.

Woodward says that it took him two or three years to reach a "mature period" at *Rolling Stone*. Often taking his cues from the photography, he devised tightly integrated typographic responses to the images. But while his signature style often embraced American vernacular, his typography was also wide-ranging, and included experiments with ornamental woodblock display typefaces.

Woodward, who left *Rolling Stone* in 2001 to become art director of Condé Nast's *GQ* magazine, claims he enjoyed the speed of its execution, which exploited spontaneity rather than over-planning. He also took full advantage of *Rolling Stone*'s oversize format, creating innovative and astonishing layouts that won awards from every major design organization and inspired a generation of publication designers. During his tenure, which spanned almost four hundred issues, Woodward mentored many designers who went on to become prominent art directors in their own right. In 1996 he was recognized by the Art Directors Club Hall of Fame, the youngest inductee in its history.

ABCDEFGHIJKLMN
OPQRSTUVWXYZ&
abcdefghijklmnopqrs
tuvwxyzß1234567890
You may ask w
hy so many differen
t typefaces. They all serve the
same purpose but they express man's di

← P.280

1988

AVENIR

Typeface

Adrian Frutiger (1928–2015)

Linotype-Hell AG, Germany

At the close of the twentieth century, sixty years after Paul Renner designed Futura, a geometric font inspired by the Bauhaus design style, Adrian Frutiger created a typeface that would also symbolize the aesthetic zeitgeist. Avenir is French for "future," and so forms a link to Futura by way of form, name, and concept. In Avenir, Frutiger married the geometry of Futura with the humanism of Gill Sans. Both of those qualify as Constructivist typefaces—that is, built on geometric principles—and Frutiger challenged himself to create a similar typeface that while inspired by them, possessed qualities unique to itself. Letters such as "f," "r," "t," and "a" give Avenir a humanistic quality that sets it apart from properly geometric typefaces. The similarity of Avenir to geometrics, such as Futura and Century Gothic, is clear at first glance, but Avenir lacks true geometric shapes: the "o" is not a circle, for example. Italic letters are sloped at an angle, as in so many of Frutiger's designs, and the typeface uses a numeric system to identify regular, bold, condensed, and italic styles. It works well for text or display type, owing to its bookish qualities and even typographic color.

After its initial release, Avenir did not earn the attention that Futura had, in part because it offered only six weights. In 2004 Frutiger worked with Akira Kobayashi, the type director of Linotype GmbH, to rework the font; the result, Avenir Next, now has condensed versions of the face to give it a total of twenty-four weights, in addition to small caps and Old Style figures. The new Avenir typeface has gained popularity throughout Europe; a very playful application was for the city of Amsterdam's "I amsterdam" visual identity. Avenir has also been used by the AltaVista search engine, Dallas-Fort Worth airport in the U.S., and the American insurance company Blue Cross Blue Shield.

The Guardian
Top officers face fresh RUC inquiry
Scotland Yard queries legal aid claims
US colonel kidnapped

← P.281

1988–2005

THE GUARDIAN

Magazine / Newspaper

David Hillman (1943–)

The Guardian, UK

David Hillman's redesign of the *Guardian* transformed this previously sullen socialist title into one of the most iconic and successful brands on the newsstand, placing it at the forefront of editorial design.

In 1988, when he was asked to overhaul the *Guardian's* layout, Hillman had already redesigned newspapers in Paris, Bilbao, and Milan, and served as art director of *Nova* magazine during its most successful period of the late 1960s. Hillman's revamp, which at first shocked a public used to the traditional, staid appearance of the broadsheet, comprised two major innovations to distinguish it from its main rivals: a dual-font title and a subsidiary section that was further developed into the daily tabloid "G2" supplement in 1992. "The," spelled out in playful ITC Garamond Italic on the masthead, together with the more severe Helvetica Black "Guardian," created a striking mix of typefaces that signified the diverse nature of the reportage inside. The relaunch campaign played on this unusual application of typography with advertisements declaring "The Nous" and "The Wit" of the font juxtaposition. Although this typographic approach had been used previously for album covers, its appropriation for a long-established, mainstream publication was groundbreaking. Hillman may have been influenced by another newspaper, the *Minneapolis Star*, which used Helvetica for both text and title. Hillman also considered reducing the paper to tabloid size, with a foldout, broadsheet-style cover, but eventually decided this was unnecessary; instead, he imposed a strict grid system on the text—a format that often required editors to cut down or pad out copy to fit the framework.

In 2005 the *Guardian* was redesigned a second time by Mark Porter, who introduced the highly successful Berliner format and a new single-font, dual-color masthead. The fundamental changes, however, had been made by Hillman's revolutionary design, which were on a par with Neville Brody's proto-minimalist designs for *Arena* magazine a few years earlier, and set a new standard for the newspaper industry.

← P.282

1989–1992

Beach Culture

Magazine / Newspaper

David Carson (1956–)

Surfer Publishing Group, U.S.

On rare occasions, a magazine rises above design clichés and captures the zeitgeist. In 1990, *Beach Culture*, a journal devoted to West Coast water sports, became the cult publication of the moment. The magazine set a benchmark for 1990s design when the art director, the largely self-taught David Carson, turned it into a showcase for radical typography and design experimentation.

Beach Culture was born out of an advertorial called *Surf Style*, which Carson helped transform into a magazine. This former art director of *Skateboard* and *Musician* magazines had studied typography with designer Jean Robert in Switzerland, where he learned the power of vernacular forms and abstract type. After the inaugural issue of *Beach Culture*, many advertisers left, confused by its mix of sports, popular art—including Surrealism and *art brut*—and media culture; but enough remained for five more issues to be published. Following the lead of contemporary design progressives, such as Wolfgang Weingart, Rudy VanderLans, Rick Valicenti, and Neville Brody, Carson began using new, and often illegible, forms of visual presentation.

Carson's typographic anarchy differed from that of his contemporaries, embracing wit and irony, and celebrating the magazine page's ephemerality. In one issue he ran a story that read horizontally across three columns of type, while in another he designed page numbers larger than the main headline. When the editor changed the order of the pages, Carson kept the original numbering, saying, "I just happened to like it there." In the final issue, page numbers were eliminated altogether, with jump lines simply saying "continued." Elsewhere, letterforms overlap, collide, and abstract themselves to the point of incomprehensibility, forcing readers to find their own way. With *Beach Culture*, Carson allowed the audience to become part of the process.

The typographic language that emerged from *Beach Culture* was an attack on readability and legibility, and was criticized by advocates of modernism, but it was essentially a blip in the continuum of graphic design. Although its experimental veneer had begun to fade by the late 1990s, it continued to inspire many exponents of postmodernism.

← P.283

1989

WORKSHOP: Y'S FOR MEN

Book

Yasuhiro Sawada (1961–)

Yohji Yamamoto, Japan

Yasuhiro Sawada had only recently graduated from the Tokyo National University of Fine Arts and Music when he was hired in 1989 by the fashion designer Yohji Yamamoto's brand, Y's for Men, to design the winter catalog for its Workshop line of casual leisurewear.

Since the early 1970s, Yamamoto had impressed the fashion world and wider creative community with his exploration of Japanese aesthetics through a focus on asymmetry, multiple textures, layering, and irregularity. In the mid-1980s, recognizing that Japan was experiencing a wave of anticorporate sentiment among the younger generation, he decided to introduce a casual brand that would appeal to the global youth market. Yamamoto made no demands on Sawada other than asking him to show the five pieces in the collection. Judging that, compared with Yamamoto's signature haute couture, the design of the Workshop line was more orthodox, Sawada chose to visually amplify the elements of each garment by cramming them into a handmade white plaster box with a sliding glass top, photographing them in natural light, then printing the resulting images on a B2-sized sheet (19⅝ × 27¾ inches [50 × 70.7 cm]). The box is only 5⅞ inches (15 cm) deep, so every coat and jumper appears ready to burst out, or as Sawada says, like so many faces pressing against the glass. The life-size presentation forces the viewer to concentrate on the details of its simple construction.

The catalog is simple but radical. Poring over its unbound sheets, received in a specially designed envelope, is like having five beautiful articles of clothing delivered by hand. Sawada says that his goal was to express the energy and vitality of the antiestablishment youth market for which the line was designed. He claims that, as a reckless youth himself, he enjoyed expressing the prevailing nonchalant attitude—clothes shown wrinkled rather than hanging neatly on a model—as much as the challenge of showcasing one of Yamamoto's lines.

← P.284

← P.284

← P.285

1989

V&A

Logo

Alan Fletcher (1931–2006)

Victoria and Albert Museum, UK

Simultaneously novel and timeless, the Victoria and Albert (V&A) museum logo created by Alan Fletcher for Pentagram—the London design agency that he cofounded in 1972—is one of the most memorable of its era and remains in use today.

Inspired by the elegant eighteenth-century typeface of Giambattista Bodoni, Fletcher formed a single unit from the museum's abbreviated name (V&A), a typographic marriage that allows the serif of the ampersand to stand in for the bridge of the "A." Although such a traditional typeface was unusual in Fletcher's work of this time, when he opted mostly for sans serifs, the strength and idiosyncrasy of the idea is consistent with his approach in general. His design turned the organization's colloquial name into a formal but friendly logo characterized by simplicity, economy, and brevity. Rigorous and restrained yet fresh and original, the monogram is wholly appropriate for the institution, reflecting its position as a bastion of the establishment and speaking eloquently of its past, while giving a passing nod to the museum's experimental, forward-looking attitude.

Fletcher's simple, witty, and accessible design summarizes his work as one of the most influential figures in British graphic history, and is characteristic of the Pentagram style of the late 1980s.

1989

TRAJAN

Typeface

Carol Twombly (1959–)

Adobe Systems, Inc., US

Carol Twombly joined Adobe Systems in 1988 as a designer in the Adobe Originals program, where in 1989 and 1990 she, along with the firm's design team, created Adobe's first display faces: Trajan, Charlemagne, and Lithos. Each of these typefaces has historical significance: Lithos is based on ancient Greek letterforms, Charlemagne on classical Roman epigraphy, and Trajan on the letters inscribed on Trajan's Column (AD 113) in Rome. Trajan contains only uppercase letters, an acknowledgement of the lack of lowercase letters in Roman inscriptions.

The Reverend Edward Catich documented the Trajan's Column inscriptions in rubbings and tracings published in *The Trajan Inscription in Rome* (1961). In his seminal 1968 book *The Origin of the Serif*, he proposed that the first typographic serifs dated back to early Rome. Twombly used Catich's reproductions for Adobe's Trajan in the late 1980s, a time when designers, illustrators, and typographers were in the process of moving from physical tools to digital ones. A small number of digital typefaces were created in the late 1970s and early 1980s, but Twombly's work on Trajan represents a fundamental shift to an entirely digital platform. With Trajan, she succeeded in bringing the look and feel of ancient typography from the physical world into the digital one, and Adobe went on to create a number of digital typefaces based on classical lettering and calligraphy in what became known as the Adobe Modern Ancients Collection. Trajan has never gone out of style; it has become a popular movie-poster typeface, for example, on the poster for the 1997 blockbuster *Titanic*. Adobe continues to advance the Trajan typeface, seen in OpenType Trajan Pro (2000), with its added support for European languages, as well as small caps. In 2011 Robert Slimbach developed Trajan Pro 3, with four additional weights, as well as support for Greek and Cyrillic. Carol Twombly was consulted by Adobe's design team on both occasions.

Twombly honed her type design skills under Charles Bigelow (designer of Lucida and Wingdings fonts, among others) at the Rhode Island School of Design, and later at Stanford University. In 1994 she became the first woman and only the second American to be awarded the prestigious Prix Charles Peignot, given to outstanding type designers under the age of thirty-five.

1989–2006

CINEMAFRICA

Poster

Ralph Schraivogel (1960–)

Filmpodium, Switzerland

Ralph Schraivogel's series of posters for CinemAfrica, the Stockholm-based film festival that presents work by filmmakers of African origin, highlights his experimental approach to visual communication, demonstrating how far he has distanced himself from the understated, rational approach of the "Swiss school."

Schraivogel, who trained at the Hochschule für Gestaltung und Kunst in Zurich, primarily produces posters that promote art, film, photography, and new media for cultural organizations such as Zurich's Filmpodium and Theater Neumarkt, as well as CinemAfrica. For the last, Schraivogel broke the traditional mold of the conventional film poster, creating graphics that build layers of color, line, and pattern to create dynamic, hallucinatory images. Schraivogel incorporates typography into these compositions, sometimes allowing words to undulate into quasi-dimensional hills and valleys or to shimmer and vibrate on the surface. His designs call to mind the collage work of Robert Rauschenberg and the graphic experiments of op artists such as Victor Vasarely, who toyed with optical perception and illusion. Schraivogel's design process is a laborious one; he often produces multiple iterations before arriving at the final layered work, as when he printed and reprinted the 2002 zebra-patterned poster. With each CinemAfrica edition, he succeeds in alluding to African culture and the festival films without resorting to cliché, enthralling viewers with hypnotic designs that present African film as a vibrantly creative industry. Schraivogel's work can also be compared to that of Wolfgang Weingart, who similarly challenged the established rules of Swiss design with his three-dimensional, typographic cube experiments.

Despite his dissociation from the "Swiss school," Schraivogel was one of the most revered graphic designers to emerge from Switzerland during the twentieth century. An overview of his oeuvre, however, reveals that his style and means of expression are as mobile and flexible as these images, regularly changing to reinvigorate his approach.

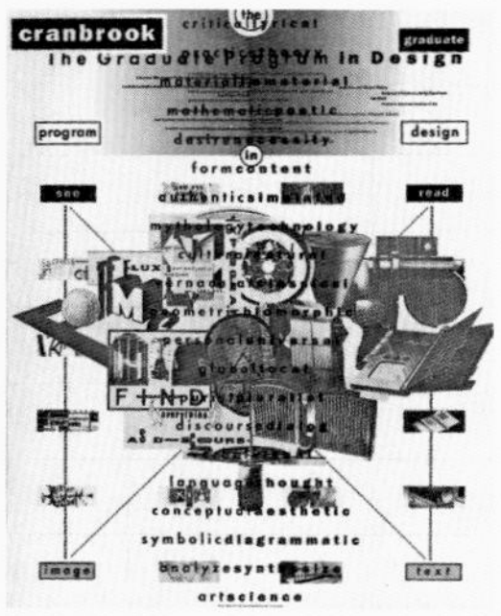

← P.286

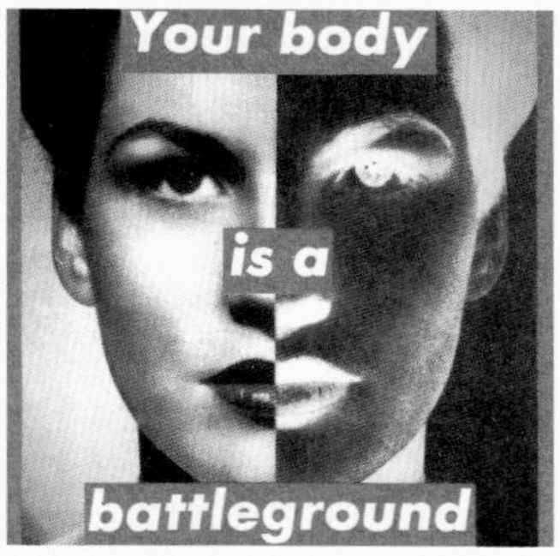

← P.287

← P.288

1989

CRANBROOK: THE GRADUATE PROGRAM IN DESIGN

Poster

Katherine McCoy (1945–)

Cranbrook Academy of Arts, U.S.

Katherine McCoy's poster "Cranbrook: The Graduate Program in Design" represents the shift away from functionalist ideas about information design in the postmodern era toward a more oblique and ambiguous form of presentation. From 1971 to 1995, McCoy and her husband, Michael, a product designer, co-chaired the small postgraduate design school the Cranbrook Academy of Arts near Detroit, Michigan. The school had a long-established reputation for excellence and experimentation in design that at the time the McCoys took over could be characterized as late-modernist. By the late 1970s, the school was beginning to embrace postmodern ideas about graphic design, due partly to the "new wave" influence of visiting lecturer Wolfgang Weingart; in the 1980s French structuralist texts were introduced into the curriculum. This background in critical cultural theory informed 1980s design semantics, in which Cranbrook played a leading role, in terms of developing both product and graphic design.

This concept is immediately evident in the poster's photographic collage, which features student-designed prototypes exploring "product semantics." While the mix of photomontage and linear forms has its roots in modernist design, the eclectic typography and layering show a more postmodern attitude. Set against a red-blue divided background, the composition is loosely held together by an overlaid communications diagram, and a central, misaligned list of unusually paired terms that require deciphering by the viewer. In this way, by using what Katherine McCoy called her theory of "typography as discourse," the viewer is engaged in a kind of "conversation" rather than simply being fed the information, as is the case in more conventional modernist design.

This interactivity was further enhanced by perforated sections that could be used as reply postcards. Through complex semantic layering, the problem of the "authored" message has been circumvented, and McCoy's recruitment poster is transformed into an unconventional and challenging visual puzzle through which viewers negotiate their own path.

1989

UNTITLED (YOUR BODY IS A BATTLEGROUND)

Poster

Barbara Kruger (1945–)

Self-commissioned, U.S.

Subverting tactics often adopted by mid-twentieth-century advertising campaigns, the artwork of Barbara Kruger is known for taking on controversial topics, such as this bold poster that speaks to women's abortion rights in the United States. The punchy aesthetic and anti-patriarchal tone of *Your Body is a Battleground* are indicative of the critical lens that Kruger's work typically wields. She urges viewers to resist falling victim to wishful thinking through statements that are arresting in their directness, their call to action, and their bold graphic language.

A graduate of Syracuse University and Parsons School of Design, where she studied with Diane Arbus and Marvin Israel, Kruger shaped her artistic voice as a graphic designer at Condé Nast in the 1960s, working on the magazines *Mademoiselle* and *House & Garden*. Designing with paste-up techniques, she began to see how imagery held the power to convey and challenge ideas and feelings and to influence people.

Kruger's work is underpinned by an immediacy that draws on the attention-grabbing appeals of consumerism, and its success builds on the tension she creates through the starkness of her compositions. Adopting Futura Bold Oblique and Helvetica Ultra Compressed typefaces, Kruger amplifies her messages with a raw typographic palette of black, white, and red.

The graphic medium of her work is heightened by the choice of images. Primarily using found photographs, Kruger typically abstracts images by stripping their color to create mono- or duotones, sometimes amplifying print effects to create moiré-dot constellations. This combination creates a powerful, confronting visual language that maintains her critique of mainstream media and its manipulation of what female bodies and behaviors should look like.

Such is the power of Kruger's work that when Roe v. Wade was overturned in 2022, the *New York Times Magazine* featured this poster—then more than thirty years old—on its cover, to highlight the abolition of women's reproductive freedom. Her highly recognizable text treatment of white Futura on a red background also reached a whole new generation of consumers when it was adopted for the logo of U.S. skateboarding brand, Supreme.

1990–present

OASE JOURNAL FOR ARCHITECTURE

Magazine / Newspaper

Karel Martens (1939–)

SUN, the Netherlands

In design, content, and editorial position, *OASE Journal for Architecture* differs significantly from other magazines dedicated to building design. Whereas most such publications cover the latest design trends and are heavily illustrated with photographs of buildings and interiors, *OASE* tries to encourage debate by stressing the relationship between design practice, criticism, history, and theory. The journal is also intimately connected with the work of its art director, Karel Martens, and with the Werkplaats Typografie studio and educational program that he founded in Arnhem.

OASE was originally launched as a student publication in 1981 by a group of young architects in the Faculty of Architecture at Delft University of Technology as a way of bringing them together with researchers and academics, and it has remained a collective project to this day. In 1990 the journal found an ally and a publisher in SUN, the socialist publishing house in Nijmegen, whose critical perspective on society and culture in general, and architecture in particular, connected with the interests of *OASE*'s founders. SUN also recruited Martens to take over the graphics of the journal. The designer chose a smaller, booklike format and opted for lettering and typographical elements as the journal's main medium of communication, stating, "Because the magazine was mostly filled with words and intellectual debate, my choice for type was self-evident." In this respect, *OASE* profits greatly from the typographical experiments and noncommissioned work that Martens has carried out over the years, particularly a large collection of found images and cuttings, printers' registration marks, color charts, and odd bits of typography. This landscape of ephemera has informed his commissioned work and is showcased in *OASE*. Covers are typically characterized by strong lettering, usually as part of a dynamic composition, which can include layered and abstracted type and three-dimensional space.

Martens's work has been influenced by the early-twentieth-century German artist and designer Kurt Schwitters, as well as by the experimental Dutch printer Hendrik Nicolaas Werkman. Martens was awarded the H. N. Werkmanprijs in 1993 for his design of *OASE*.

← P.288

1990s–present

LETTERPRESS POSTERS (VARIOUS)

Poster

Kennedy Prints

Various, U.S.

Amos Kennedy, Jr.'s design output has grown exponentially since he started producing hand-set letterpress posters in the early 1990s. Retiring from his career at AT&T to pursue his passion for printmaking and its power to connect people, Kennedy, Jr., creates works that are as much political statements as visions of the world he wants to see. This has led to a prolific collection that is widely celebrated for its direct messaging and bold, imperfect aesthetic that intentionally disrupts classic print rules.

Kennedy, Jr., describes himself as "the humble negro printer" and makes clear that his motives are commercial, not artistic. Such proclamations come readily; he has no qualms in challenging the status quo and being blunt. His poster topics run the gamut from the heinous to the inspirational: Black murders, Black voting rights, civil rights struggles, and rousing quotes by prominent Black figures, such as Rosa Parks or Frederick Douglass. Despite the often oppressive and painful events they draw from, the posters are intended as messages of hope that connect with different audiences and share universal values of humanity and joy.

Kennedy, Jr.'s enthusiastic mash-up of metal and wooden type gives his posters their characteristic hard and soft edges, and glyphs are readily adopted in place of "correct" letterforms as necessary. Multilayered printing brings in different colors and ink saturations, forming a riotous backdrop to the distinctive black-ink typography. More bricoleur than purist, Kennedy, Jr., celebrates the accidental mark of the maker's hand and overtly adopts "mistakes," such as off-register leading and kerning or unevenly inked print blocks.

The posters' accessible format and freedom of speech facilitate the printer's overarching intent to reach as many people as possible. Kennedy, Jr., is equally deliberate in his move away from the idea of art production, which he sees as a capitalist construct that is increasingly limited to privileged elites. As such, his works are modestly priced and sometimes even distributed freely at bookstores, food trucks, or community events.

The social significance of Kennedy, Jr.'s posters means that they are now held in collections at the Library of Congress and the Metropolitan Museum of Art, New York.

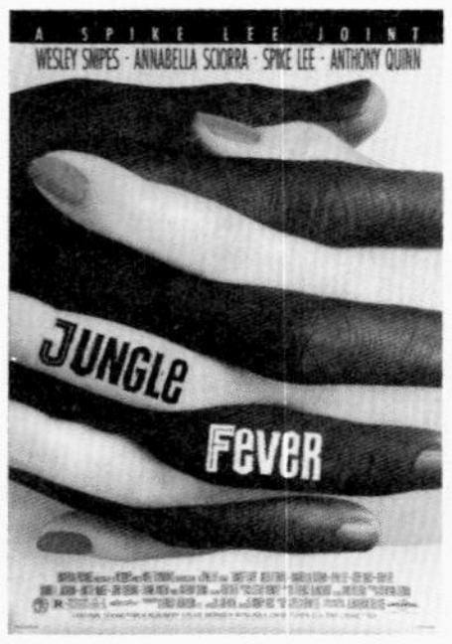

← P.289

1991

JUNGLE FEVER

Poster

Art Sims (1954–)

Universal Pictures, U.S.

The poster for *Jungle Fever*, a 1991 film by renowned director Spike Lee, artfully sets the tone for the romantic drama without giving too much away to the viewer. Intertwined Black and white hands indicate a level of intimacy while putting front and center the film's premise of an interracial romance. The title immediately introduces the provocation that Lee's films never shy away from; the term *jungle fever*, slang for a non-Black person being attracted to someone who is Black, acts as an instant critique of the relationship between the hands before the story has even begun. The playful treatment of the typeface presents "trembling" letters, suggesting a feverish state of mind that could lead to a loss of control.

The poster's designer, Art Sims, is a close collaborator of Lee, having worked with him on the visuals for a number of films, including *Do the Right Thing* (1989), *Malcolm X* (1992), and *Bamboozled* (2000). Hailing from Detroit, Sims gained a scholarship to study art at Michigan State University in 1971 and went on to work at Columbia Records in New York City. He soon set up his company 11:24 Design Advertising in Los Angeles, dedicated to the promotion of African American art and culture. Sims's agency boasts an impressive entertainment-based client list, having worked with everyone from Stevie Wonder to Steven Spielberg.

After more than three decades of partnership with Lee, Sims is an expert at visually communicating the filmmaker's directorial style. Bright color palettes are splashed behind photographs of the films' main characters, who often interact with the witty typography, appearing almost as cocreators of the design. The consistent declaration that this is a "Spike Lee joint" lets the audience know that they're in for a great time. In 2010 Sims was recognized by the AIGA in an exhibition and online archive series entitled *Design Journeys*, which showcased the work of leading creatives of color—an apt reward for a designer who is responsible for defining a large proportion of the visual languages prevalent in Black film, culture, and beyond.

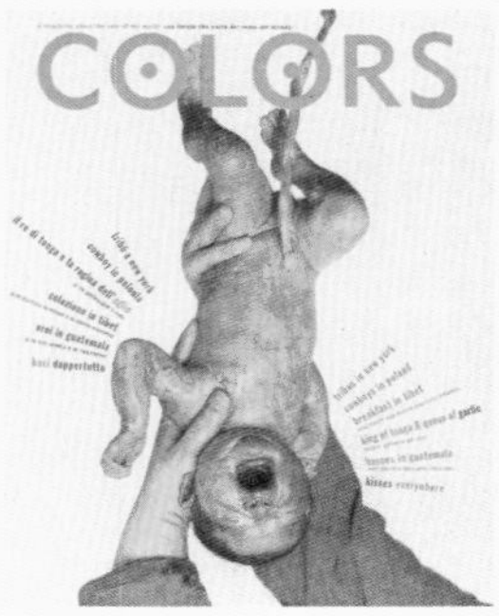

← P.290

1991–1995

COLORS

Magazine / Newspaper

Tibor Kalman (1949–1999)

Benetton Group, Italy

Published by the Italian fashion brand Benetton, *Colors* was one of the first magazines to promote a brand without advertising products for sale. From the outset, its overt editorial intent was to fight bigotry by celebrating the universality of human experience and the beauty of different skin colors, a promise fulfilled by a combination of bold photography and a few carefully chosen words.

Edited by the maverick graphic designer Tibor Kalman, the magazine initially lacked a specific format, appearing as an oversize tabloid (and then as a smart publication) with a clean sans serif typographical signature: red-and-black headings in Franklin Gothic Bold Condensed contrasted with the comfortably leaded Futura Light body copy. However, the most distinctive visual innovation was the upbeat mood and questionable coloring of the photographs by Oliviero Toscani, director of the controversial "United Colors of Benetton" billboards. Even when dealing with depressing (or distressing) subject matter, images were illuminated to erase deep shadows, brighten up faces, and enhance ambient colors, making refugee-camp or Amazon rainforest dwellers look as personable as Benetton models. Their clothes, although worn out, never looked completely shabby, and they were invariably depicted under a serene blue sky.

Over the years, the issues have confronted a range of themes: racism (4), AIDS (7), war (14), weight issues (25), religion (37), immigration (41), madness (47), and violence (56), printed in multilingual editions (English, Italian, Spanish, or French) that were distinctive because of the shock value of their visuals. In Issue 4, Kalman doctored a portrait of Queen Elizabeth II to make her look like a Black woman; in Issue 28, Toscani asked actors to impersonate an interracial homosexual couple kissing. However, the editorial tone remained steadfastly nonjudgmental, leading to criticism that *Colors* was capitalizing on suffering and idiosyncrasy to promote what was essentially a fashion label.

In 1995, after only thirteen issues, Kalman left *Colors*, followed five years later by Toscani, who had come under attack for a photo essay and advertising campaign featuring death-row inmates. Since then, the publication has changed formats and editors, but its original point of view prevails.

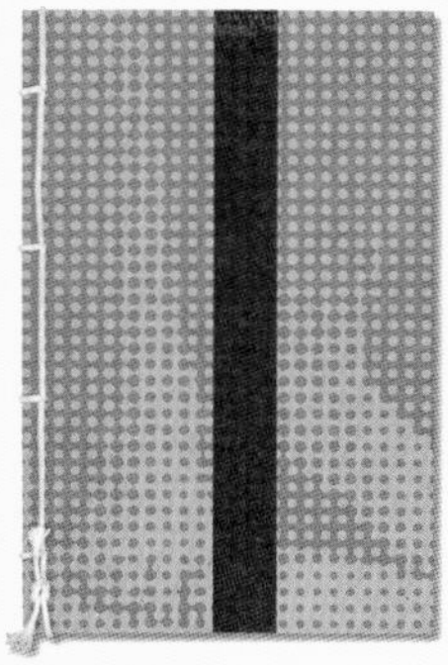

← P.291

← P.291

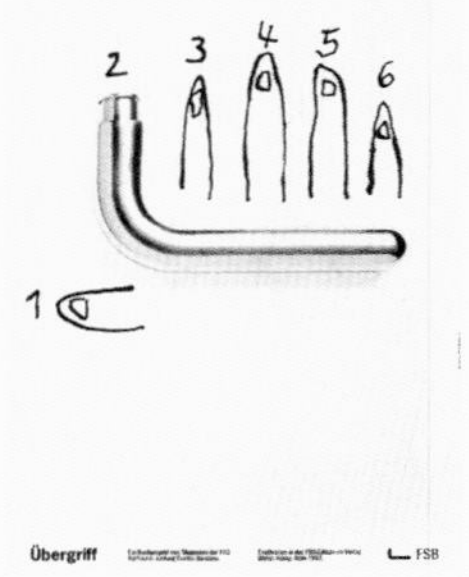

← P.292

1991–1995

FORM + ZWECK

Magazine / Newspaper

Cyan

Form + Zweck, Germany

Form + Zweck (Form + Purpose) was founded in 1956 as a state-run design journal in East Germany. After the fall of the Berlin Wall, the title was in need of revision, a project undertaken by Daniela Haufe and Detlef Fiedler (who had formalized their design partnership as Cyan in 1992, after leaving East Berlin's Grappa studio) in collaboration with editors Angelika and Jörg Petruschat.

Cyan's radical, clever, and humorous use of typography and photography makes *Form + Zweck* a fresh and enticing object, as well as a vehicle for serious articles. Separating each feature—whether concerning a design or a philosophical look at the nature of contemporary graphics—is a photographic double-page spread, either specially shot by Cyan or using archive images sourced from libraries. Photographs are also featured within the articles, often layered between or wrapped by text. Typographic treatment changes from page to page, and is playfully referential: in an article about Art Deco, the text is printed in diagonal shafts, whereas in an issue devoted to dance, intertwined slices of text and photography create a choreographic rhythm of their own. Disregarding design convention, each issue—printed in runs of three thousand—also presents a completely new cover design and even a different method of binding. Issue 6, for instance, was hole-punched, and came with a piece of string and instructions on how to bind it in the Japanese style.

In a bid to avoid becoming another disposable object in a throwaway culture, *Form + Zweck* carried no advertising and was not consumer-driven. This principle was also carried through in the visual richness and experimentation of the magazine's design, which treated each issue of *Form + Zweck* as a unique object.

1992

THE NEW YORK TIMES OP-ED

Magazine / Newspaper

Mirko Ilić (1956–)

The New York Times, U.S.

Mirko Ilić's designs for the "op-ed" page (opposite the editorial page, and typically devoted to personal opinion and commentary) of the *New York Times* are startling for their visual communication of complex, sometimes controversial topics.

During the 1970s, Ilić was involved in producing comics, magazine illustrations, and album covers for the underground culture of Zagreb, Croatia, and for international comics, such as *Heavy Metal* and *Alter Alter*. Abandoning comics in 1980, he subsequently concentrated on illustration and graphic design before moving to New York in 1986, where he became art director of *Time International* in 1991, and art director of the *New York Times* op-ed page the following year.

Characterized by Milton Glaser as "an illustrator who thinks and a graphic designer who can draw," Ilić produces almost exclusively conceptual works, each of which aims to communicate a single powerful idea, almost to the point of rejecting style. His approach has been described as "in your face" or even brutal, but this may be the result of his engagement with highly topical issues. Bold and over-the-top, his op-ed pages often consist of only one or two columns, but in his hands they become a full-page design, enhancing the article and strengthening its thesis. One of the best examples was a page with articles that presented conflicting religious views in which the Jewish star was used to support both arguments, through being the container for text (a dense black star) in the first article, and the negative space around which the text is wrapped (a white star) in the second. Before reading a single word on the page, the viewer has grasped the juxtaposition and become aware of the duality it represents. Although other topics that Ilić has addressed, such as famine in Zimbabwe, have been equally serious, many, such as "Pafko at the Wall" and "Broadway Book War," have focused on cultural and sports issues.

Ilić has much in common with designers such as Michael Bierut, Bob Gill, and Stefan Sagmeister, who are known for their conceptual approaches, but only Ilić has successfully applied this method to the textual design of one of the most important pages of a major international newspaper.

1992

ÜBERGRIFF

Advertising

Julia Hasting (1970–)

Franz Schneider Brakel, Germany

This award-winning poster by Julia Hasting was one of six commissioned by Franz Schneider Brakel (FSB), a company that manufactures door handles. Simple and witty, the design consists of a cartoon-like ink drawing of numbered fingers overlaying a photograph of the handle, in which the handle acts as an additional digit, implying that it works in perfect harmony with the hand.

In 1992 FSB invited a group of students (including Hasting) from the Staatliche Hochschule für Gestaltung Karlsruhe to design their annual book of products and design philosophy, which from 1987 to 1991 had been art-directed by the German designer Otl Aicher. FSB has continued to publish a book annually, partly in homage to Aicher's work.

The students designed the book in the form of a catalog, with each handle in the FSB range shown in a life-size photograph. Each photographic page was then overlaid with a semitransparent page containing the students' creative statements. Titled *Übergriff*—which means intervention, crossover, or overlap, but also plays with the idea of *über* (over) and *griff* (grip or handle)—the book studies the intricacies of grasping, gripping, and feeling—treating man as "an animal that can marvel with its hands." An immediate success, the annual won awards at the Frankfurt Book Fair and Leipzig Book Fair in 1993, prompting FSB to commission six posters for advertising and promotion. Hasting's poster appeared on the cover of *Form* magazine in 1993, announcing a nineteen-page feature about the book and the campaign.

The posters were awarded a series of prizes in the same year, including an award for Communication Design from the Design Zentrum Nordrhein Westfalen and another at the Triennale of the Deutsches Plakat Museum Essen.

← P.293

1992

LEXICON

Typeface

Bram de Does (1934–2015)

The Enschedé Font Foundry, the Netherlands

In 1989 Bernard C. van Bercum, designer of Van Dale's *Dictionary of the Dutch Language*, approached Bram de Does about using the Trinité typeface from The Enschedé Font Foundry (TEFF) for the book's text—at a meager seven-point size. The research and experimentation that Bercum enabled de Does to undertake would change the world of newspaper design.

Rather than licensing Trinité, de Does offered to create a new typeface for use at small sizes, which would become Lexicon. De Does—who like many type designers is also interested in the history of typography—looked at small typefaces from the 1500s, including Galliarde romans. He made his first drawings using physical design tools, such as a felt-tip pen, then photographed and reduced the sketches in order to see how the text would appear at smaller sizes. The temporary font and test page made for Van Dale's dictionary proved successful, and de Does worked with Peter Matthias Noordzij to digitize the hundreds of working drawings using Ikarus typography software. The Van Dale dictionary was released in 1992, and the font was further improved for release as part of the TEFF library. De Does's attention to detail and Noordzij's technological skill helped make Lexicon a typeface suitable for small sizes, low-quality printing, and general use.

When the Netherlands's *NRC Handelsblad* newspaper decided to replace its Times typeface with Lexicon, it signaled a paradigm shift. Consummate perfectionists, de Does and Noordzij expanded the Lexicon family to serve all the functions that Times did, including making changes to the descenders, kerning pairs, and a new version of bold for headlines. Lexicon No. 1 has short ascenders and descenders, allowing more type to be set vertically on a page, while Lexicon No. 2 has longer stems, but both are the same width so that column widths remain the same. Lexicon's use in the *NRC Handelsblad* sent a message to other news media outlets: thanks to new technologies, designers could improve upon many of the conventions that printers and the media had heretofore relied on. The possibility of each newspaper having its own typeface looked well within reach.

← P.293

1992–1999

HARPER'S BAZAAR

Magazine / Newspaper

Fabien Baron (1959–)

Hearst Corporation, U.S.

One of the oldest American fashion magazines, *Harper's Bazaar*, founded in 1867, has maintained a unique sense of elegance and flair due to the contribution of its visionary image-makers and designers. Directed by Alexey Brodovitch from the 1930s to the 1950s, the publication was reinvented in the early 1990s by the French-born art director Fabien Baron, who transformed it into a balancing act of understatement, energy, and glamor.

While honoring his predecessor's signature use of white space and refreshing the masthead, Baron created a new design ethos that combined stripped-down with savvy, classical with contemporary, and tasteful with borderline outrageous. "I was passionate about the beauty of design, but I was also passionate about writing .... It's not enough to only do pretty things," said Baron in an interview with *Graphis* magazine in 2003. Baron's layouts are dynamic in a cinematic fashion: in a deliberate attempt to contrast word and image, his type is blown up, stacked, multicolored, or abstracted, while across the page are striking, serene photographs (by the likes of Patrick DeMarchelier, Peter Lindbergh, David Sims, Craig McDean, and Mario Sorrenti), featuring dramatic Richard Avedon-like poses, surrounded by ample white space, which together produce a graphic composition of the utmost elegance. At the same time, the cool classicism of the Didot typeface used for the masthead and texts (a modernized version specially commissioned from the Hoefler and Frere-Jones foundry in 1992) would become part of *Harper's* trademark. This high-contrast font with its crisp serifs perfectly embodied Baron's pursuit of purity and clarity.

Few art directors have had so great an influence on graphic designers, photographers, and typographers. Baron successfully inspired them with a refreshing sense of how word and image can coexist harmoniously yet expressively on the same page.

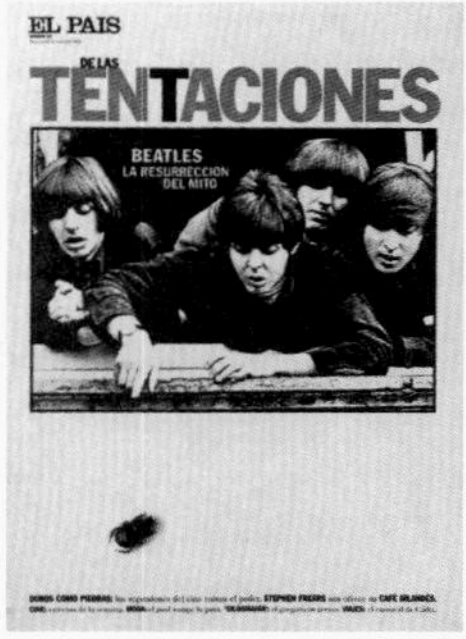

← P.293

1993–present

TENTACIONES

Magazine / Newspaper

Fernando Gutiérrez (1963–)

El Pais, Spain

Commissioned by parent newspaper *El Pais*, the first issue of *Tentaciones* was launched on October 29, 1993 by editor Joaquin Stephanie and graphic designer Fernando Gutiérrez. This weekly supplement to the national newspaper, created to attract a youth market, each Friday reports on shows, television, travel, movies, and games. *Tentaciones*'s full name is *El Pais de las Tentaciones*, "the Country of Temptations."

Much of the design of *Tentaciones* was driven by its relationship with *El Pais*. While being the same size and format as the newspaper, the supplement was in full color, a striking contrast to the black-and-white *El Pais*. However, for technical reasons it was impossible to print full bleed (i.e. beyond the edge of the sheet), a constraint that also affected the design. So that the cover would achieve maximum impact, Gutiérrez featured one main image on a white background, giving the impression of a fully bled image.

The cover design was often arrived at through a process of lateral thinking. For example, for a cover featuring the film *Interview with the Vampire* (1994), the design incorporated a representation of two small holes dripping blood. In a similar play with verisimilitude, Gutiérrez placed a color photograph of a real beetle in the corner of a 1960s black-and-white image of the Beatles looking down at something from a window at a time when the three remaining Beatles were talking about getting together for a world tour. The effect was so convincing that readers thought an actual beetle was scuttling across their morning paper.

Inside *Tentaciones*, Gutiérrez used a standard grid and restricted the typefaces to just two—Franklin Gothic Condensed for titles and Baskerville for text. Even within these self-imposed limitations, the designer was able to create a dynamic layout.

The enduring quality of *Tentaciones*'s design is partly due to the graphic designer's engagement with the rest of the magazine's contributors. Gutiérrez spent long hours collaborating with writers, photographers, and illustrators, adjusting text, thinking about ideas, reworking titles, switching or pulling stories, and having pieces rephotographed. Immediately mimicked by advertising agencies, the design was also quickly adopted by other media groups.

← P.294

1994

THE ART BOOK

Book

Alan Fletcher (1931–2006)

Phaidon Press, UK

When British designer Alan Fletcher was first hired by Phaidon Press, it quickly became evident to publisher Richard Schlagman that he could not just give Fletcher a brief and expect immediate results. Each time Fletcher worked on a book he came back with numerous questions, asking what it was about and why it was being created. Schlagman explains: "[Fletcher] was a true editorial designer—concerned with ideas, content, and communication."

Soon Fletcher became involved in coming up with ideas for new projects as well as designing them, one of the best examples of which was *The Art Book*. He realized that Phaidon's vast archive of photographic slides could be reproduced in very simple layouts with just one image and a short caption. Instead of categorizing the works of art by date or movement, Fletcher proposed to organize them alphabetically. This approach created striking layouts that juxtaposed the minimalist work of Donald Judd with Frida Kahlo's surrealist paintings, for instance, and the photorealist paintings of Gerhard Richter with the seventeenth-century realism of Jusepe Ribera.

The cover is a Fletcher masterpiece of invention, which made the book an instantly recognizable object. The large-format cover features the three words "THE ART BOOK" in huge capital letters occupying the whole of the front, Phaidon's logo being the only other element. Fletcher gave each letter of the book's title an individual hand-drawn treatment, using different materials and colors, including cutout paper, black ink, dripping paint, and watercolor. These various techniques were often used in combination by the designer, creating a signature style. The method illustrates Fletcher's belief that letters are fundamentally different from typefaces: one of his well-known aphorisms was "A typeface is an alphabet in a straitjacket."

The success of *The Art Book*, originally published in 1994, led to a miniature, more portable version, followed by *The Photography Book* in 1997, *The American Art Book* in 1999, plus their mini versions, and in 2005 *The Art Book for Children*. These books, all designed by Fletcher, are variations on the theme, with the cover taking the form once again of large colorful letters on a blank background.

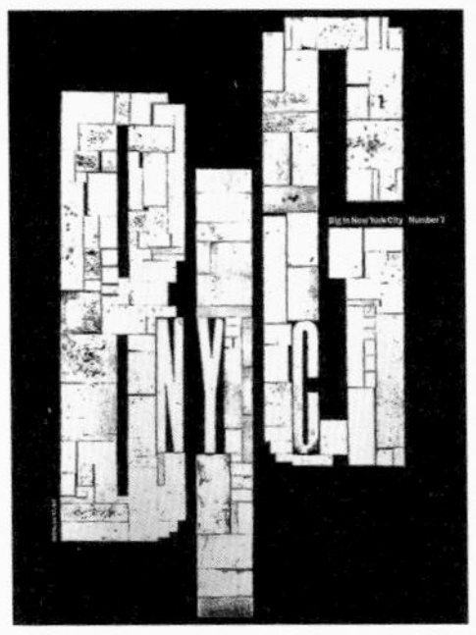

← P.294

1994–1998

BIG MAGAZINE

Magazine / Newspaper

Vince Frost (1964–)

Location Printing Big, S. L., Spain

Invited to become art director of the Madrid-based fashion and photography title *Big* by its editor, Marcelo Jünemann, in 1994, Vince Frost designed six issues, transforming it from a fledgling publication into a quality magazine. Despite poor material and a limited budget, Frost was given free creative rein; the only predetermined factors were the publication's rather unconventional A3 size and the black-and-white format. Each issue explored a specific theme, such as "New York," "London," and "Action and Direction," with covers adopting a simple approach. For the "New York" issue, Frost's first and arguably his most distinctive, the word "Big" was constructed by arranging a large collection of woodblock letters. Collectively, the blocks make up the letters of the title, but only one in each letterform is turned correctly to print the abbreviation for New York City, "NYC." For other covers, a single intriguing or dramatic black-and-white photograph was used with the magazine's title positioned irregularly, often at a dramatic angle.

Taking inspiration from the gritty qualities of the photography and from the publication's title, Frost turned to the rawness and scale of letterpress typography, experimenting at the typographer Alan Kitching's workshop in London with large woodblock letters to compose boldly printed headlines. Frost wrote many of the headlines himself, which he set in enormous block letters, sometimes at odd angles to reflect the meaning of words. For example, in one issue the letters of the headline "Closeup" are set in bold sans serif wood type and printed as close together as possible. He also made dramatic use of grainy black-and-white imagery: a photographic story about motorcycle couriers is entitled "Deliverance" with the word set in huge, condensed sans serif letters, over which he placed a photograph of a tattooed arm holding up a wheel brace, in the way an evangelical priest might hold up a cross.

A labor of love, Frost's work for *Big* magazine played a major role in raising his own profile and reputation as a designer and won him numerous awards, while bringing the publication itself to the attention of a broad, design-conscious audience.

← P.295

1995

PUBLIC THEATER

Poster

Paula Scher (1948–)

Public Theater, U.S.

Paula Scher's campaign for the 1994 summer season of the New York Shakespeare Festival presaged the radical transformation that she and George C. Wolfe, the Public Theater's newly appointed director, would bring to the theater over subsequent years.

Faced with dwindling attendances and membership, Wolfe wished to capture a younger, multicultural audience and take the-then fifty-year-old institution "closer to the street." Scher did so by rejecting the use of standard advertising slogans, promotional photography, and elaborate logos, and finding in the American woodcut typography of the late 1800s a bold, illustrative vocabulary that would completely change the paradigm of visual identity for the theater. Her comprehensive redesign of the Public Theater brand successfully united its several entities and performing spaces under what would be known as "The Public," at the same time making the most of consistently tight budgets.

The most visible expression of this identity was the series of posters that Scher designed for individual plays each season, of which the one for the 1995–96 street-tap musical *Bring in 'Da Noise, Bring in 'Da Funk* became the most memorable. For what was one of the company's most successful productions, Scher took her own typographical vocabulary to a new extreme, creating a dynamic composition of bold typographic forms in multiple weights and sizes, tightly wrapping a black-and-white photograph of one of the show's actor-dancers and displaying information in horizontal, vertical, and oblique orientations.

Scher sourced her unique vocabulary of "bold, free type" in subway posters, billboards, street paintings, and even from the side of a New York water tower. Later, this style would be routinely imitated, re-created in magazines, advertising layouts, and other Broadway campaigns, becoming not only the new image of the Public Theater but also the face of the city and its time.

← P.296

1995/2002

S,M,L,XL, BY REM KOOLHAAS

Book

Bruce Mau (1959–)

Office for Metropolitan Architecture, the Netherlands

This extensive, multidisciplinary book—documenting the work of the Dutch architectural studio Office of Metropolitan Architecture (OMA) and its principal, Rem Koolhaas—generated something of a cult following on its publication in 1995, and marked the reinvention of the traditional architect's monograph. At its core, the volume is a collaborative work that reflects Toronto-based designer Bruce Mau's approach to design and authorship.

The book's considerable length (some thirteen hundred pages) and modest page size give it a massive appearance—the starting point of its construction. The introduction presents OMA's approach and ethos: architecture is a "chaotic adventure," and accordingly the book is presented as an assemblage rather than as a linear text. The title reflects its only organizational principle: projects and texts are sorted on the basis of size only, in four parts—Small, Medium, Large, and Extra Large.

Koolhaas expresses the studio's approach in his statement that the scale of a work "generates its own logic." His essay "Bigness: or the problem of Large" is typeset in giant letters, which grow incrementally smaller over the course of about twenty pages. This is typical of the fanciful approach to layout found throughout the book, which can be summarized as a cinematic succession of essays and manifestos—"a cycle of meditations on the modern city." It also includes a variety of complex overlaid illustrations and other images on themes of modernity, density, and the advent of mega-cities. Interwoven through all of this visual material is the "Alphabet," a series of text entries that extends over the entire volume.

Overall, the picture *S,M,L,XL* presents of OMA is somewhat postmodern in its lack of distinctness; it can be picked up and read in any order, as the collection of projects and texts only subtly links theory and practice. Criticized by some for its sprawling size, the work nevertheless remains a seminal text on a contemporary architectural practice and its outlook.

← P.296

1995–present

FOUND FONT

Typeface

Paul Elliman (1961–)

Self-commissioned, UK

One of the more enduring typeface designs of the 1990s, the Found Font has been described as the first vernacular typeface, mindful of how it refuses universality, remaining partial and constantly evolving. More provocatively it has also been called the last typeface, with reference to its use of discarded, broken, or worn-out forms.

Found Font began as a collection of objects that Elliman gathered while traveling in 1989. The typographical focus of the project coalesced through a series of photograms in 1993–4, with the objects grouped according to shape as if to convey structural components of letters. A full character set appeared in the electronic type publication *FUSE* (Issue 15, called "Cities") in 1995, and the Found Font has continued to evolve, with no character ever being used more than once.

There is a rich tradition of incorporating the found object into art and design practice, ranging from Kurt Schwitters's Merz works and Claes Oldenburg's "ray guns" to examples of other "found" letterforms, perhaps most notably Mervyn Kurlansky's 1977 alphabet constructed from studio tools and objects. However, the Found Font differs in that Elliman's use of these shards indicates a perceived clash between technology and language, and explores a relationship to the social and object world around us based on a more primal need to cohere to a common language. He is also preoccupied with the idea of "the collection" and the ways it might be used to create narratives. The Found Font is archived not by alphabetical categories but according to other attributes. These include the sources for letter shapes (scissor handles, broken bicycle locks, paste jewelry, for instance); specific materials (die-cut cardboard, black polyethylene, steel, and aluminum section); or even places biographically linked to the artist (Birkenhead, Detroit, Cupertino, among others), where the objects were gathered.

In 2001, the project was included in the London section of Tate Modern's inaugural exhibition, *Century City*. In the catalog essay, Elliman is quoted as preferring the idea that the Found Font defies being useful, "as if it came from a depressed but still beautiful part of the city."

← P.297

1995–present

BASELINE

Magazine / Newspaper

Mike Daines (1947–), Hans Dieter Reichert (1959–), Veronika Reichert (1964–)

Bradbourne Publishing, UK

Baseline, an authoritative international magazine devoted to type design, lettering, calligraphy, book binding, and the history of the graphic arts, has contributed significantly to the development of graphic design as a scholarly discipline.

First published as an annual in 1979, the magazine was originally launched to promote new typeface designs for use under license, rapidly winning recognition for its eclectic content and careful selection of source material. For example, the *Baseline* lexicon series, found in the back pages, included a recurring index of type designers, typographers, foundries, and technical terms, and its international team—including Milton Glaser (New York), Ed Cleary (Canada), Mo Lebowitz, and Darrell Ireland (London)—contributed new material to its early development and helped to increase worldwide readership. Today, the magazine's focus has shifted to historical and research-based articles, which are reflected in the design, with color scheme, paper, typeface, and page layout all carefully adapted to the subject matter. At the same time, the unity of the design emphasizes the coherence and interdependence of the various elements. *Baseline* uses high-quality production techniques, as demonstrated by its large-format color printing on specially selected papers, and frequent use of rare images.

In 1995, with its original owner, Letraset, facing hard times, the magazine was purchased by Mike and Jenny Daines, and Veronika and Hans Dieter Reichert (director since 1993 and editor from 1995), who gradually modified the design, introducing a new cover, masthead, and "banner," which resulted in a more coordinated and unique appearance over the next twelve years. In 2007, with the departure of Mike and Jenny Daines, the team again undertook a complete redesign, introducing a fresh grid, typefaces (Akkurat and Kingfisher), and masthead (a stencil design based on Akkurat Schwarz), reducing the size of the banner (in order to expose the new masthead) and replacing the lexicon series with an innovative educational section. Back issues of *Baseline* have become collectors' items for their design quality and their value as a resource on typographic history.

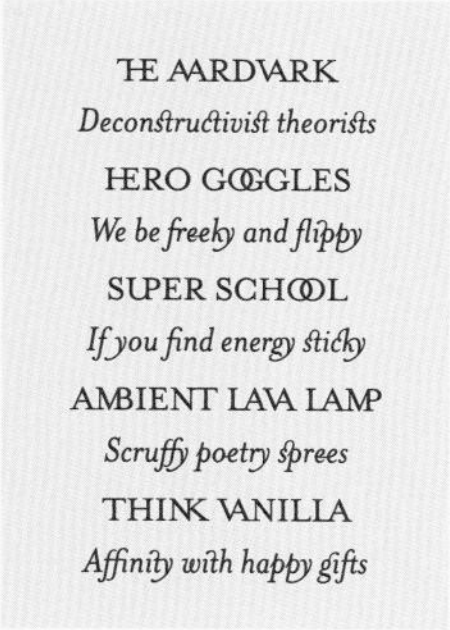

← P.297

1996

MRS EAVES

Typeface

Zuzana Licko (1961–)

Emigre Inc., U.S.

Although often referred to as a Baskerville revival, Zuzana Licko's typeface Mrs Eaves is actually an interpretation of the classic eighteenth-century face. In the course of this re-imagining, Licko, who first made her name in the 1980s as one half of the Emigré publishing and type-designing team, also wrote a new chapter in her own career.

The faces Licko designed in the mid-1980s won her both praise and derision. Exploiting the new technology of the Apple Mac, she created original, postmodern designs, such as Lo-Res (1985) and Citizen (1986), which some dismissed as unreadable, ugly or worse. As font software became more sophisticated and *Emigre* magazine began to publish more design criticism in the mid-1990s, Licko felt the need to create a typeface that would set well for body text, and turned to Baskerville and Bodoni. Starting with rough transcriptions of each face's proportions rather than exact copies, she filtered these classics through her own instincts, as if she were designing an original face. The Bodoni interpretation, Filosofia (1996), was successful, but Mrs Eaves caused a true stir in the design community, thanks to a quirkiness and character that made it both familiar and exciting: a softer alternative to Baskerville's revered transitional face, with less contrast and more gradual brackets, which suggested letterpress printing. Licko also crafted seventy-one ligatures for each face in the family, ranging from the standard ("fi") to the sublime ("ggy"). These add to the personality of the face and the responsibility of the individual designer setting the type.

Named after Sarah Ruston Eaves, who was first John Baskerville's housekeeper, then his wife and collaborator, Mrs Eaves has been called both feminine and feminist, giving credit to the woman who completed her deceased husband's work. Unlike Baskerville and his wife, who never lived to see the well-deserved respect that his elegant types eventually received, Licko created a bestseller, used by designers for everything from annual reports to books of poetry.

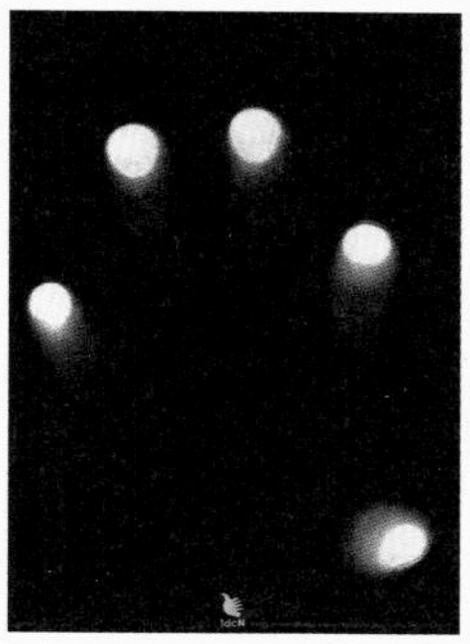

← P.298

1996

IDCN

Poster

Koichi Sato (1944–2016)

International Design Center Nagoya, Japan

The Japanese designer Koichi Sato is renowned for his graceful and poetic poster designs, which combine traditional Japanese motifs with Western influences. Sato worked for the Japanese cosmetics brand Shiseido before becoming a freelance designer in 1971. Since then, the main focus of his practice has been producing posters for cultural institutions and museums, such as the work pictured here for the International Design Center in Nagoya (IdcN), designed the year in which the building opened.

Sato's posters have often been described as closer to works of art than designs, and this example is typical of his mystical, reductive style. The image relates to an earlier poster of 1988 for a musical play that featured a handprint taken from his own hand, to which he added color washes to create an ethereal, otherworldly quality. The metaphysical atmosphere is even more apparent here, where only the fingertips can be seen, looming out of the black background. Typical, too, of Sato's work are the softened, blurred edges of the forms, which suggest movement and depth. Although the finger spots could evoke stage lights, the meaning is essentially ambiguous, drawing the viewer in with its subtlety and mystery.

Sato has also designed posters for commercial clients such as Matsushita, now the electronics company Panasonic, for which he created an advertisement for a television set that linked the beauty of modern industrial technology with haiku poetry and imagery of the moon. He has won many prizes for his work and has been included in important international exhibitions, such as UNESCO's "20 Best Japanese Posters" in 1986.

← P.299

1996

HOKUSETSU

Poster

Ken Miki & Associates

Heiwa Paper Company, Japan

Ken Miki's promotional poster for the Heiwa Paper Company, a wholesale distributor of high-quality print paper, is typical of his work: simple in logic but complex in execution. Heiwa Paper wished to promote their product Hokusetsu (meaning "northern snow"), a fine, uncoated paper with a superior level of whiteness that they associated with snow. Miki used Illustrator to build up a glistening mountain range spelling the word "SNOW" at its peaks, which are left free of ink so that the paper's unadulterated dazzling white shines out while the mountains darken progressively toward pitch black at their bases. Miki likens the image to a digital version of an ink-and-wash (*sumi-e*) painting, in which gradations in color and line are achieved through varying types of brush and concentrations of ink. The tranquil beauty of the image, frigid white in a silent space, conveys a graceful dignity.

Miki also created a sample book to accompany the poster. Its gate-folded cover, a flattened version of the poster image, opens up to reveal more vertical gradation, intended to conjure the mesmerizing image of a heavy night of snowfall, where the light of the moon reveals the white of the snow. Along the snow-white bottom of the page runs the text: "an endlessly expanding plain, a wind blowing in the distance, the fullness of a void, poetry of emptiness." In the final spread, technical information is displayed against three symmetrical images. In one case the background grows from light at the bottom to dark at the top, punctuated by an array of tiny circles—white and full at the top right and black like a void at the bottom left, like phases of the moon.

As a child growing up in Kobe, Miki was transfixed by topographic maps and created his own dioramic landscapes. Today, most of his designs incorporate a three-dimensional quality, which, like his imagery, is intended to engage the viewer in a sensual world.

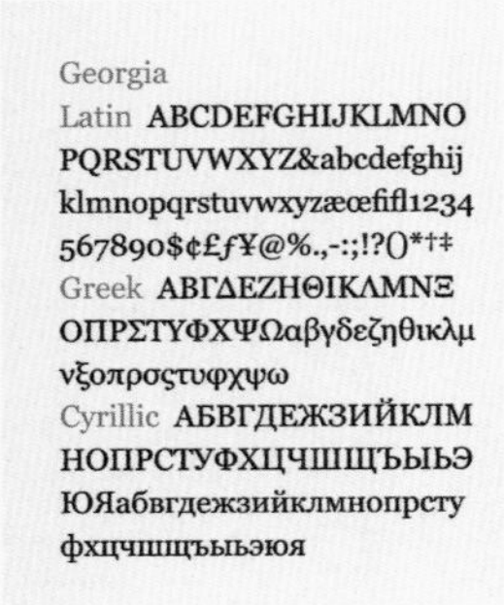

← P.300

1996 ●

GEORGIA

Typeface

Matthew Carter (1937–), Thomas Rickner (1966–)

Microsoft Corporation, U.S.

Georgia is a serif typeface in the Scotch Roman style. It was commissioned in 1995 and released on November 1, 1996 as one of Microsoft's core fonts for the World Wide Web, a set of screen-optimized typefaces made available as free downloads, and later included with the Windows and Mac operating systems. Microsoft program manager Virginia Howlett named the font Georgia O'Keefe, after her favorite artist.

Georgia is considered the serif companion to Microsoft's Verdana typeface, also designed by Carter (although they do not share the same proportions, and Georgia appears slightly smaller than Verdana at the same point size) and developed in the same way. In contrast to the usual practice of drawing fonts first as outlines, Carter started by creating bitmap letterforms in a range of sizes, and then drew outlines to match the bitmaps. Rickner then added computer codes, known as hints, to each font, to produce bitmap shapes matching Carter's original designs. The result is a typeface family ideally suited to displays on screen at small sizes but still perfectly rendered at larger sizes and in print.

Georgia was not as popular as Verdana on its release, partly due to its more limited distribution, and partly due to the conventional reaction of web designers against serif type. Unlike the sans serif Verdana, Georgia was perceived as too similar to Times New Roman (the text default of most web browsers), despite its structural differences. However, over the years Georgia has grown in popularity, especially with text-heavy sites and those aiming for a more upmarket and classic design.

The current Georgia fonts support Latin, Greek, and Cyrillic characters, and have hardly changed since their initial release. Adjustments were made, however, to the numerals; Carter describes the original figures as "hybrid," situated between a "modern" alignment with capitals and "old style" figures resembling the lowercase. This visual ambiguity was deemed too confusing by Microsoft's type director Robert Norton, who introduced a set of old-style (nonlining) figures that conform authentically to those of other Scotch Roman faces.

← P.300

1996 ●

THINKBOOK

Book

Irma Boom (1960–)

Steenkolen Handels Vereniging, the Netherlands

Thinkbook, commissioned by the Dutch energy company Steenkolen Handels-Vereeniging (SHV) to celebrate its centenary and designed by Irma Boom, was published in a limited edition of forty-five hundred copies for private distribution. As much a beautiful object as a book, this monumental 7-pound 15-ounce (3.6 kg), 2,136-page volume loudly proclaimed the demise of legibility.

To fully experience *Thinkbook*, one must handle it and flick through the pages. The cover is a plain, blank surface, while the edges of the delicate pages present a rainbow of subtly varied colors. Crack it open at random, for there are no headings, no page numbers or index, no beginning or end: pages unfurl as if springing from the deep furrow of the binding.

At first glance, *Thinkbook*'s images seem upstaged by their spectacular setting. However, their juxtaposition creates a surprisingly entertaining slideshow. You discover, haphazardly, vintage photographs, old advertisements, company documents, family pictures, transcripts of speeches, memos, poems, sales reports, letters from employees, and official portraits of executives. A hidden title, die-cut holes, mysterious watermarks, cryptic messages, dangling silk bookmarks, and questions scattered throughout the pages add even more excitement to the process of exploration and deciphering.

It took three-and-a-half years for Boom to gather material from the company's archives, and another eighteen months to design this opus, often working around the clock. During the process she had absolute creative control, no budget limit, and the unconditional support of SHV's president. Among the greatest challenges she encountered was inventing a new kind of paper for the book—and meeting her May 1996 deadline. Not at any point during those five years did she think about her audience, strongly believing that if the result pleased her it would please others.

← P.301

1997 ●

MILLER

Typeface

Matthew Carter (1937–)

Self-commissioned, U.S.

In the Miller typeface, Matthew Carter designed a font that has its roots in nineteenth-century broadsheets, updated with practical refinements that make it suitable for today's printed newspapers. Miller takes its name from William Miller, an early-nineteenth-century Edinburgh typefounder. Carter, who trained in the Netherlands under P.H. Rädisch, a punch cutter with the Jan Van Krimpen press, wanted to design a contemporary version of the Scotch Roman font that had been created by the British type designer Richard Austin and produced by Miller & Richard, the foundry run by William Miller and his son-in-law Walter Richard. Carter fused a knowledge and practice of traditional typographic rendering techniques with digital tools that had made their way into design studios during the 1980s. Rather than directly reproducing the Scotch Roman letterforms digitally, he captured the tone and modeling of the originals in an updated font, maintaining their vertical stress and large x-height for added readability.

Carter & Cone Type, Inc. (Carter's Cambridge, Massachusetts, studio), in conjunction with Tobias Frere-Jones and Cyrus Highsmith, designed Miller to be a utilitarian typeface for long-form reading. The type family has been expanded with bold and italics for text use, and it includes graded weights, which allow publishers and printers to choose the best reproduction of the typeface for the inking and printing methods they use. Miller has been further augmented with Miller Headline and Miller Daily, the latter of which has been refined and redesigned specifically for use in newspaper texts, with more open counters and even proportions between its stroke widths. In the United Kingdom, the *Guardian* newspaper commissioned an adaptation of the font, and it is used in the *Hindustan Times* and the *Boston Globe*. In 2011, the Museum of Modern Art in New York acquired Miller for its permanent collection.

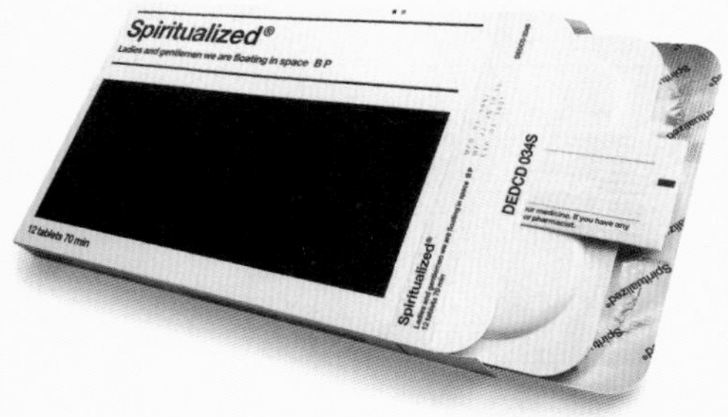

← P.301

1997

SPIRITUALIZED—LADIES AND GENTLEMEN WE ARE FLOATING IN SPACE

Record / CD Cover

Mark Farrow (1960–)

Dedicated Records, UK

Mark Farrow's packaging for the limited-edition, boxed version of "Ladies and Gentlemen We Are Floating in Space," the third studio album by the British rock band Spiritualized, introduced a completely new artistic and marketing concept. The inspiration was a statement made by the band leader, Jason Pierce, when he and the designer first met: "Music is medicine for the soul."

In its physical form and graphics, the album's packaging emulated a medicine packet. The box's contents were indicated by the text on the front cover, "1 tablet 70 min," which referred to the disc included inside and the running time of the album as a whole. Pierce purposely manipulated the latter, editing out several minutes of music in order to have a round number for the sake of concise typography. The disc was contained in a blister pack, which had to be pushed through the foil like a pill. As well as being released as a standard-size CD, one thousand extra albums were produced that each held twelve 3-inch (76-mm) CDs.

Imperatives such as "For aural administration only" and "Store out of reach of children" peppered the information enclosed, formatted like a prescription leaflet, and the predominance of white space and sans serif navy blue type emphasized the clinical, sterile tone.

Until this point, there had been few alternatives to the standard plastic packaging of CDs, and none had employed such a strong and inventive metaphor. Although the playback of twelve individual discs was cumbersome, the medicinal packaging altered the way in which the listener related to the record, drawing attention to the act of consumption. It also heightened the meaning of the music itself, suggesting that it had some sort of healing power. The original packaging was produced in a pharmaceutical factory, paid for in part by Pierce, and won several design awards. This was the first of several collaborations between the band and the designer, including the artwork for "Let It Come Down," which features a vacuum-formed girl's face.

← P.302

1997–2004

NEST: A QUARTERLY OF INTERIORS

Magazine / Newspaper

Joseph Holtzman (1957–)

Self-commissioned, U.S.

To describe *Nest* as simply "A Quarterly of Interiors" is to overlook the bombastic appeal of this American design magazine published from 1997 to 2004 and devised by editor-in-chief and art director Joseph Holtzman. An alternative to the era's ultra-sleek and tasteful lifestyles portrayed in popular titles such as *Wallpaper**, *Nest* translated Holtzman's untrained but confident eye to present exotic, strange, and overlooked spaces around the world. Through its style and content, *Nest* expanded the relatively narrow concept of what interiors should look like, disrupting the expected with stories that were wildly diverse. Content ricocheted from a Brazilian Amazonian longhouse with earthen floors, to Liberace's Las Vegas living room with its gilded surfaces and masses of mirrored sparkle, to André Leon Talley's hospital room, or a shelter in Harlem trimly built from Coca-Cola crates.

Twenty-six issues were published in total, and the magazine's design was as diverse as its content. Its theatrical graphics reflected Holtzman's eccentric sensibility and his love of set design and painting. *Nest's* pages were vibrant, patterned, and over the top. Its covers were daring and never the same: they often employed special finishes, inks, embossing, and die-cutting that set the scene for the wild interiors.

Nest originated with a provocation from Holtzman's friend, the British photographer Henry Dermot Ponsonby Moore, twelfth Earl of Drogheda—or Derry—for whom he had created a book.

Drawing in enthusiastic collaborators, such as fashion designer Todd Oldham and graphic designer Alex Castro, *Nest* excelled in presenting a riot of color, theater, and provocation. This was amplified by a roster of high-profile photographers, including Candida Höfer, Horst P. Horst, Nan Goldin, Jan Groover, and David Seidner. As Oldham describes, the nonconformist approach was as if the magazine had been "put together by someone who has never seen a magazine before." Despite this naivete, it won two National Magazine Awards, but seven years after it began, *Nest* closed. By going out on a high, it avoided Holtzman's fear of boredom and the maga-zine becoming "repetitive." Its issues are now coveted and attract cult-like collectability. In 2020 *Nest* was immortalized in *The Best of Nest* (Phaidon), which reproduced sixteen-page portfolios of each issue.

← P.303

1997–2004

RE-MAGAZINE

Magazine / Newspaper

Jop van Bennekom (1970–)

Self-commissioned, the Netherlands

Jop van Bennekom started producing *Re-Magazine* while studying at the Jan van Eyck Academie in Maastricht, the Netherlands. A self-initiated and personal magazine, it is highly experimental, questioning the very idea of the magazine itself.

Acting as author as well as designer, van Bennekom created the magazine, writing all the text and taking all the photographs, for at least the first issue, as well as conceiving all the graphic design. The first number, called "The Home Issue," com-prised interviews with friends in which he explored in detail the minutiae of their everyday existence.

The first eight issues examined aspects of life not usually tackled by magazines—boredom, home, or connecting with one's past, for instance—focusing on the lives of regular people. By the third issue, van Bennekom was collaborating with writers and photographers; later, an editorial board was set up. From Issue 9, the approach shifted once more. Now the focus for each edition was on one fictional person, with each article telling a story related to him or her. Rather than publishing something fake said by a real person, van Bennekom attempted to access the truth through the words of a fictional character.

Re-Magazine's intention is to describe life from a personal perspective, rejecting the idea that a magazine should be about celebrities and advertising, or that it be beautiful or glossy. Articles feature seemingly banal subjects, such as an ashtray on a table: where does it come from and how did it get here?

The design of the magazine is similarly radical—photographs appear as snapshots and are arranged in informal photo essays. The layout and typography are simple, including only headings, body text, rules, and folios. The format changes to suit the subject matter. Issue 9 is about John, whose boring personality is represented by the A4 format, while Issue 10 features Claudia, an unusually tall woman, encapsulated by the A3 newsprint.

Re-Magazine is evidence that magazines can flout commercialism or celebrity, and provide a vehicle for graphic designers to experiment.

← P.304

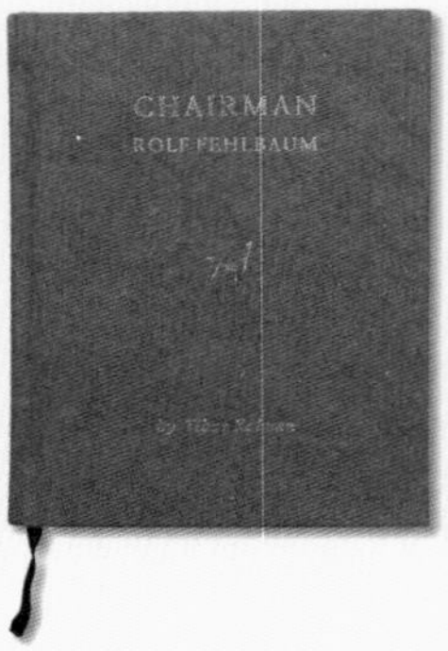

← P.305

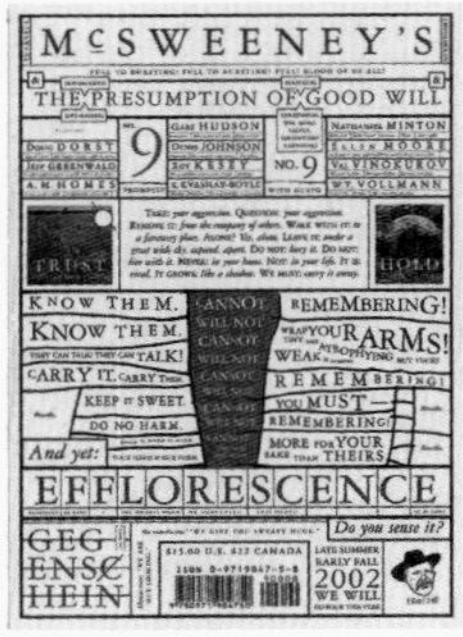

← P.305

1997

TYPOUNDSO

Book

Hans-Rudolf Lutz (1939–1998)

Self-commissioned, Switzerland

Typoundso is one of nine books that Hans-Rudolf Lutz wrote, illustrated, designed, typeset, and produced under his own imprint, Lutz Verlag. Together with *Ausbildung in typografischer Gestaltung* (Training in Typographic Design), *Typoundso* chronicles Lutz's own work over the previous forty years together with that of his students. At four-hundred forty pages, *Typoundso* contains a huge amount of information and, with over two thousand illustrations, is visually dense.

The book's title came about when Lutz was asked what the book was about; he replied, "Typography and so on," which became fused into one word. The texts, all written by Lutz himself, are short and to the point, relating to the images. He wrote and rewrote each text at least six times, making sure that it did not simply describe what was already being communicated in the images but provided further insight.

Typoundso communicates Lutz's approach to typography from a social, political, and personal perspective: for instance, his belief that typography can never be free from context, that there is no such thing as typography that says nothing. The silver dust jacket acts as a mirror, so if you pick up the book, you immediately see an image of yourself reflected in it; if there is a second person present, it becomes an object of communication. The book was originally published without an ISBN, as Lutz thought it was a shame that everything should be cataloged, calling it "this dreadful efficiency."

Known for his role as a design educator, Lutz saw the influence of his work as being primarily through the communication of ideas—through the push and pull of critique. Always questioning the norms presented in the world of graphic design, he saw this subversion and approach to ideas as his legacy: "If students derive inspiration from me, it is because of my attitude, not a particular style."

1997

CHAIRMAN ROLF FEHLBAUM

Book

Tibor Kalman (1949–1999)

German Design Council and Lars Müller Publishers, Switzerland

Tibor Kalman's *Chairman Rolf Fehlbaum*—published to celebrate Fehlbaum's German Design Council Award—reflects Kalman's characteristic wit and eclecticism: small and red, it references the 1970s *Little Red Schoolbook* and the 1960s "Little Red Book" of China's Chairman Mao. With six hundred pages, the book is a long but compact photo essay, occasionally punctuated by short, simple statements set in cream sans serif type against a blue double-page-spread background. Starting with a whimsical introduction to human posture, the book illustrates various modes of sitting and chairs found around the world, then continues with a visual biography of Fehlbaum, celebrating his fixation with chairs, such as the Eames Lounge Chair and Ottoman, and progressing to his design influences and philosophy.

With nearly all the images in *Chairman* fully bled, Kalman makes little use of white space, preferring instead to use sequence, contrast, and scale in the design. Images—mostly photographs, but with some illustrations, cartoons, and diagrams—include politicians, acrobats, dogs, houses, cars, and bicycles, with Kalman breezily mixing together film stills, reportage, the bizarre, humorous, exotic, and absurd, as well as black and white with color. Some are a provocative mix (one sequence has toilet bowls followed by disabled wheelchair sprinters, followed by the death penalty's electric chair), reflecting the social commentary that characterized Kalman's work on *Colors* magazine. Kalman also connects themes by juxtaposing images that have common visual elements, such as a pope and an African who exhibit the same posture, and a portrait of Frank Gehry alongside a sketch of the Vitra Center.

The book won Kalman a Graphis Prize, with some commentators praising its "chunk-factor," whereas others felt it was lightweight. The work is nevertheless a masterpiece of picture research, cropping, and sequencing, demonstrating what can be achieved using only found imagery.

1998–present

TIMOTHY MCSWEENEY'S QUARTERLY CONCERN

Magazine / Newspaper

Dave Eggers (1970–) et al.

McSweeney's Publishing, U.S.

Timothy McSweeney's Quarterly Concern is a literary journal that had achieved cult status by its fourth issue—a boxed set of fourteen booklets, with cover images chosen by the author of each—for its eclectic and unclassifiable style; each number is distinguished by an entirely different design and editorial focus.

The approach of *McSweeney's* editor, Dave Eggers, is to rediscover lost aesthetics and techniques from a variety of historical sources, and inventively apply the design elements. Archaic typographic treatments used rarely before the mid-1990s are now enjoying a renaissance: centered layouts, reminiscent of early broadsheets, and eccentric mixes of upper- and lowercase type within a single font. The same approach is taken with other design features: pseudo-Victorian clipart (Issue 1), block-printed board covers (Issues 15 and 16), pulp art, parodied classified advertisements (Issue 10), and die-cuts (Issue 27). Eggers has admitted to valuing experimentation above all, and to being obsessed by form: whether a jacket that folds out to become a poster, as designed by Chris Ware for an issue devoted to comics and the graphic novel; printing three sections that fit inside a magnetized cover decorated with Kara Walker-like silhouettes; or even making the whole journal resemble a pile of junk mail. *McSweeney's* heterogeneous look has exerted a wide-ranging influence and has been reinterpreted in advertising campaigns, corporate publications, and book design.

Coherence is provided by text set consistently in Garamond 3 and carefully laid-out pages, with the intermittent use of page borders and rules, and a refusal to ignore the design potential of the spine, the copyright page, or the barcode. More importantly, each issue carries the hallmarks of a self-aware inventiveness and egalitarian idealism, cut with irony and underscored by a genuine love of words. There is substance underpinning this emphasis on style: the writing is generally well reviewed and is often by respected mainstream authors.

McSweeney's graphic and textual tricks are motivated by a desire to make good literature look great, and have, in the process, challenged and changed design, earning the title a place in history.

← P.306

← P.307

← P.307

1998

KINDHEIT IST KEIN KINDERSPIEL

Poster

Alain Le Quernec (1944–)

Deutsches Plakat Museum, Germany

With a text that reads "Childhood is not child's play," this poster highlighting the dangers of child abuse carries a bleak message, but the image, although disturbing, deliberately avoids the sensational or predictably graphic. The design was produced for a competition organized by the Folkwang Museum in Essen, Germany; its slogan is the title of the theme song for DKSB (Deutsche Kinderschutzbund), Germany's child-protection agency.

Alain Le Quernec, whose work often involves social campaigning, believes that poster art should engage directly with the public and be subtle in meaning. This view is manifested here by the discreet positioning of the text and the cherubic child, whose plump, soft flesh, delicate coloring, and innocent genitals all contribute to the suggestion of vulnerability. Le Quernec maintains that he originally appropriated the image of the baby from a Renaissance painting of a Madonna and Child for a hospital poster campaign on sudden infant death. After removing the mother's hands and photocopying the image, he felt that it made the child's body look as though [illegible] had been partly eaten, a memory that provided
[illegible] the concept for this poster. By locating the
[illegible] ditional art rather than in contemporary
[illegible] illustration, he also creates an
[illegible] babies in the world. Meanwhile,
[illegible] d, which mutates into hands that
[illegible], acts as a metaphor for child
[illegible] hat often accompanies it.
[illegible] of the hands suggests a
[illegible] ack of obvious harm that
[illegible] the damage caused.
[illegible] painting and the
[illegible] round, Le Quernec's
[illegible] enced by the
[illegible] quently referenced
[illegible] art movements.
[illegible] ticed design
[illegible] d to producing
[illegible] motivated.

1998–present

YALE SCHOOL OF ARCHITECTURE

Poster

Michael Bierut (1957–)

Yale School of Architecture, U.S.

This ongoing series of posters announcing events at the Yale School of Architecture is the most visible representation of its reinvented identity under the architect Robert A. M. Stern, who served as dean from 1998 to 2016. For the rebrand, Stern turned to Michael Bierut, a partner at the New York office of the design firm Pentagram, who had lectured at Yale since 1993. A designer with a long professional association with architecture, Bierut had designed graphics for New York's Architecture League from 1982, and a series of Stern monographs while working at the Massimo Vignelli studio.

The posters serve one of three purposes: to announce the semester's lectures, exhibitions, and symposia, to invite potential students to attend an "open house," or to advertise a special symposium. Each measures 22 x 34 inches (56 x 86.5 cm) and can be folded down for posting, and each, with one exception, is printed in black. Bierut's approach to the brief began by looking at a precedent—Willi Kunz's design program at Columbia University in New York, which used the Univers typeface throughout. Bierut decided to do the opposite at Yale, never using the same typeface twice; the only constant is the trademark "Y" within a circle. His concept demonstrates that typographic diversity could represent its own form of consistency. Although Bierut remains the series designer, others have collaborated with him on specific posters and, despite their cacophony of typefaces, the designs retain a strong identity. The series now numbers more than fifty, and many have won industry awards, but they are most exceptional as a total body of work.

A constant presence on campus, Bierut's poster series succeeds in capturing and reinforcing the intellectual spirit and style of the school, and in transmitting complex and serious information in an evolving, playful, and inventive manner.

1999–present

BRAND EINS

Magazine / Newspaper

Mike Meiré (1964–)

Brand Eins, Germany

German designer Mike Meiré, of Berlin-based Meiré und Meiré, has broken all the rules since he originally created the design of German financial magazine *Brand Eins* in 1999. The cover treatment changes with each issue and can feature full-bleed images or framed ones, illustration, handwritten lettering, or Photoshopped creations. The only element that remains constant is the lowercase serif masthead, which stands quietly in the top left corner.

On the inside pages, with no set layout, there is the same degree of invention. Many spreads feature stunning photography, surrounded by different margins each time, the images being allowed to occupy their own space without being constrained by a layout. A spread might bear a number of different images arranged apparently at random, or a cartoonlike line drawing, or scrawled handwriting. The page might even be turned sideways. Often, text or images are laid over photographs to create another layer of meaning.

The magazine includes many deliberate "mistakes": awkward crops, pictures zoomed in too closely, images and text running in different directions, illustrations placed in the spine. These are part of Meiré's approach and show his interest in creating a rhythmic disjuncture that he describes as "harmony/break/harmony." He explains, "During this period of getting the issue together I like being silly on the computer, behaving like a dilettante just to make sure we are able to bring in ideas out of the blue, to create interesting backward- and forward-looking designs."

Meiré also believes that each of his magazines requires its own graphic voice, responding directly to the content. This means that he treats each title differently: "I am interested in the changing identities from magazine to magazine. To me it seems much more exciting to slip into various characters. For example, I behave differently when I do *Brand Eins* or *032c*. I listen to different music and prefer to work at night when it's time again for *032c*. It's a kind of method acting."

← P.307

← P.308

← P.308

1999

OTHELLO

Poster

Gunter Rambow (1938–)

Hessisches Staatstheater, Germany

Designed to promote Shakespeare's play at the Hessisches Staatstheater in Wiesbaden, and one of around eighty posters that he produced for the theater, Gunter Rambow's "Othello" demonstrates a radical transformation of style, in which the play's themes of jealousy, betrayal, and murder are expressed by a starkly minimal design.

Motionless and represented only by the geometric shapes of his eyes, the figure looks slightly to the left, as if in fear or suspicion, while the red line that runs vertically down the page suggests a stream of blood and brings an element of depth to the picture plane. Most posters belonging to the series convey little or no textual information, except for the plays' titles and the unobtrusive theater logo in the corner. Meanwhile, the typography, which often takes on a pictorial role (possibly representing a mouth in this image), is generally set in uppercase sans serif black or white lettering. The posters were printed at double A0 format, twice the usual German poster size, to attract maximum attention.

Whereas photography and images of material objects and physical structures had played an important role in Rambow's designs of the mid-1960s to late-1980s, the simple shapes and colors of these posters are reminiscent of the black-and-white images he created in the early 1960s while studying poster design at the Hochschule für Bildende Künste in Kassel. "Othello" was designed shortly after a single-color poster series entitled "Rambow Back to Black" (1997–8), which referred to his Bauhaus-style education at the Hochschule, where he was taught by Ernst Röttger, who had himself studied at the Bauhaus. The course exerted an important influence on the Staatstheater series.

In contrast to the greater complexity of previous posters, Rambow's "Othello" reduces the drama and emotional darkness of the play to its simplest graphic form, and marked the designer's return to a strictly modernist language.

1999

STEALING BEAUTY

Book

Graphic Thought Facility

Institute of Contemporary Arts, UK

Designers are often faced with the question of how much of a message should be explicitly stated and how much left to the viewer to construct. The cover for the catalog of the *Stealing Beauty* exhibition at the Institute of Contemporary Arts in London, produced after a period when designers focused greater attention on the personal and expressive potential of graphic design, acknowledges the importance of the viewer in the meaning-making process by presenting evidence that needs to be connected to achieve understanding. What appears at first glance to be a purely aesthetic and abstract response to the notion of beauty turns out to be a masterful explication of the principles behind the exhibition: for example, the book's binding method determines the size and shape of the punched-paper fragments that appear on the cover.

Graphic Thought Facility (GTF) was founded by Paul Neale, Andrew Stevens, and Nigel Robinson in 1990. Robinson left in 1993 and GTF was later joined by Huw Morgan. During the 1990s the practice developed a reputation for simplicity and innovation based on a rational appraisal of clients' needs. *Stealing Beauty* focused on raising the ordinary to a state of beauty through design that engages with the "detail of our own lives." This commitment to the fabric of everyday existence is reflected in the layout of the book's inside pages, which vary in size and material, with postcard-size sheets occasionally inserted. The first of these smaller pages, a Perrier-Jouët Champagne label, deftly identifies the sponsor. This incorporation of different page sizes adds to the feeling of an accumulation of cast-offs and pieces of scrap.

The power of the design comes not from the way in which visual elements are arranged, however admirably this is achieved, but through making and reasoning. This message is communicated in the book not by telling us about the phenomenon in question but by providing the evidence and allowing us to come to our own conclusions—an approach that would be explored by many designers in the years that followed.

1999

VISIONAIRE 27—MOVEMENT

Magazine / Newspaper

Peter Saville (1955–)

Visionaire Publishing, U.S.

The New York-based magazine *Visionaire* has been a fertile ground for groundbreaking explorations in fashion, photography, and image-making since its inception in 1991. Called an "album of inspiration" by its founders—Stephen Gan, James Kaliardos, and Cecilia Dean—the title has been crafted by some of the fashion, design, and art worlds' most celebrated creative influences. Appearing at intervals of four months, each issue is a collection of commissioned work gathered around a broad theme, such as "Woman," "Man," "Power," or "The Bible," often produced in collaboration with guest editors, art directors, and fashion houses. With a print run of six thousand numbered copies, unconventional formats, and lavish production values, the issues are complex and coveted collectors' items.

For instance, Number 27, one of the simplest issues of *Visionaire* published so far, is a hardback, spiral-bound book. Art-directed by the British designer Peter Saville, the front and back covers are engaging and surprising explorations of motion and depth made possible through the use of lenticular printing. Working closely with the British fashion photographer Nick Knight, Saville
beyond the usual set of two alternate
provided by this motion-capturing te
cover contains a groundbreaking
shots of model Kate Moss captur
an Alexander McQueen dress.

Beyond the covers, the insid
by *Visionaire*, continue to e
of movement by masterful
revelation and concealm
of vellum paper. This tr
the possibility for laye
paper also allows for
the successions of im
such as fashion des
Hussein Chalayan,
phers Steven Mei

Other *Visiona*
innovations in th
an area of des
to have inspir
Japanese des

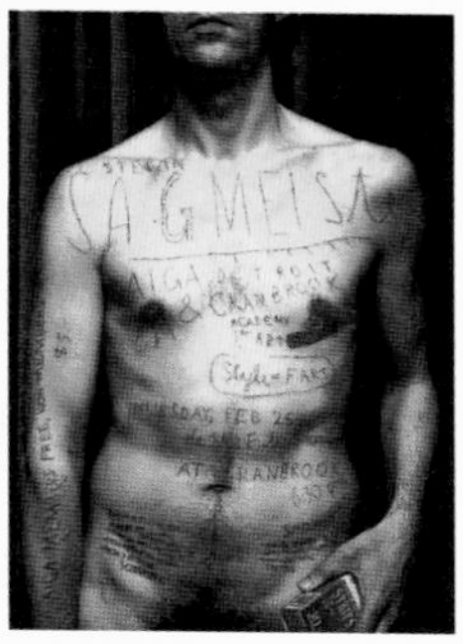

← P.309

← P.310

← P.311

1999

AIGA DETROIT LECTURE

Poster

Stefan Sagmeister (1962–)

Sagmeister Inc., U.S.

Stefan Sagmeister's deliberately shocking poster produced for the AIGA Detroit lecture was devised to depict, quite literally, the blood, sweat, and tears of the design process. Treating his own body as a canvas, and having the typography cut directly into his skin, Sagmeister places maximum emphasis on the most physical and tactile aspect of design—the designer.

During the late 1980s and '90s, graphic design underwent a substantial shift in self-assessment, fueled by new technology, legibility debates, and postmodernism; it was a time when rules were swept aside. This transformation was particularly identified with the Cranbrook Academy of Art, at which Sagmeister's lecture was held; in many ways the poster represents the culmination of a decade of inquiry. For his part, Sagmeister pushed this period of experimentation even further by intentionally rejecting the then-popular convention of computerized perfection and overtly embracing the personal mark as handmade and visceral, producing an effect [illegible]t is consciously crude. Equally important, the [illegible]tched into his skin stand as a painfully [illegible]ustration of the industry's increasing [illegible] itself. By making himself the center- [illegible] is not only referring to graphic [illegible] with the "designer as author" [illegible]ncept to include "designer [illegible]designer as subject." [illegible]ed's *Set the Twilight Reeling* [illegible] analogy: with lyrics from [illegible]ger's highly recognizable, [illegible]pital letters, the text [illegible] words amplified by [illegible]g a seething texture [illegible] songs. [illegible] closed his office [illegible] develop a more [illegible]as begun to yield [illegible] graphic design's

2000

GOTHAM

Typeface

Jonathan Hoefler (1970–), Tobias Frere-Jones (1970–)

GQ, U.S.

Gotham was commissioned by the men's magazine GQ, with a brief that demanded a font that was "masculine, new, and fresh." It quickly became a quintessential twenty-first-century American typeface, and one of the most widely used in the world, employed for everything from entertainment promotions and soft-drink advertising to television program identities and even, in 2008, for Barack Obama's U.S. presidential campaign.

Working together from 1999 as the type foundry Hoefler & Frere-Jones in lower Manhattan, the designers Jonathan Hoefler and Tobias Frere-Jones took inspiration for Gotham from their everyday urban environment. Much like DIN 1451, which was used throughout Germany and Poland during the early twentieth century on everything from railroad cars to road signage, Gotham's connection to visual culture comes from the lettering on old New York City buildings. The designers were initially inspired by the vernacular lettering above the New York Port Authority Bus Terminal entrance. As Frere-Jones said, it's "not the kind of letter a type designer would make. It's the kind of letter an engineer would make." Attracted by its muscular sturdiness and unself-conscious masculinity, they expanded their research throughout the city, discovering other buildings, mostly dating from the 1930s through the 1960s, with similar typographic attributes—many of them scheduled for demolition. Their race to document the lettering and ultimately transform it into the new Gotham was part of a desire to preserve the typographic history of a multicultural city where different national styles have intersected for centuries.

Although Gotham has its roots in early twentieth-century American letter design, it has become a mainstay of twenty-first-century typography. In 2004 the face was chosen for the engraving at the 9/11 Memorial of nearly three thousand names of those who lost their lives on September 9, 2001.

2000

COMMON WORSHIP: SERVICES AND PRAYERS FOR THE CHURCH OF ENGLAND

Book

Derek Birdsall (1934–), John Morgan (1973–)

Church Publishing House, UK

Common Worship: Services and Prayers for the Church of England, published in 2000, is the culmination of the most complex and significant project ever undertaken by the Church Publishing House. The work represents the Church of England's new liturgy—a revised version of the *Alternative Service Book* of 1980 for use alongside the 1662 *Book of Common Prayer*.

In terms of production, the prayer book was a mammoth operation: an initial print run of 910,000 copies, using 2,485 miles (4,000 km) of paper, 186 miles (300 km) of ribbon, and enough binding material to cover 4½ soccer pitches. Moreover, the book was typographically challenging. The Church Publishing House brief required *Common Worship* to fuse traditional and modern elements of worship and, therefore, to be designed for use as well as appearance, taking into account the varying circumstances of users, some with disabilities. As befits the prayer book's purpose, the design had to be timeless and convey quality while adhering to clearly defined protocols.

Derek Birdsall and John Morgan of Omnific design studio were commissioned in 1999 and proved themselves to be a proficient and sensitive design team, guided by principles of practicality, clarity, and poetry. Research and trial proofs indicated Gill Sans to be the clearest typeface. This may seem surprising, but the font was also selected because of its English origins and humanist qualities, and because each weight functions as a typeface in its own right.

Common Worship represents a masterful handling of typography and is a triumph of clarity, logic, function, and spacing. More than any other book, it is testimony to Birdsall's claim that his approach to book design is based less on inspiration than on simple, discoverable facts about books themselves.

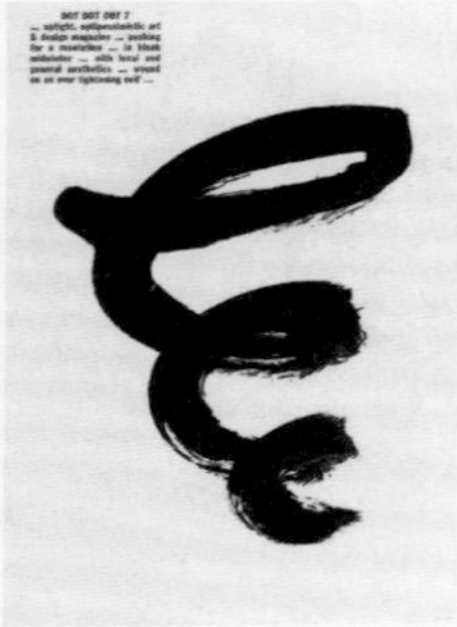

← P.311

← P.312

← P.313

2000–2011

DOT DOT DOT

Magazine / Newspaper

Stuart Bailey (1973–), Peter Bil'ak (1973–), David Reinfurt (1971–)

Self-commissioned, U.S.

An alternative magazine of visual culture, *Dot Dot Dot* quickly distinguished itself from the usual array of design publications with its eclectic, experimental, and highly cross-disciplinary approach to design a nd content. Each issue incorporated a broad range of elements, written, pictorial, and diagrammatic, as well as combinations of these, and often included work that falls outside standard boundaries of writing. The diversity of the journal's material was one of its defining characteristics, along with its austere, experimental digital and craft aesthetic.

Originally produced and edited by designers Stuart Bailey and Peter Bil'ak, *Dot Dot Dot* was directed by Bailey and David Reinfurt from Issue 13 onward; from its new base in New York, it continued to experiment with content and formats. The editorial policy was intentionally open: each issue possessed its own internal logic, driven largely by content and a particular approach to design and construction, which reflected the multidisciplinary tastes and interests of its contributors. That said, a subtly modernist approach underlay the magazine's identity, which reflected the backgrounds of its founders—Bailey's training in typography and his roots in the tradition of British and Dutch typography, and Bil'ak's association with Dutch design. In the final issues, the journal saw the development of Bailey and Reinfurt's application of "just in time" production to *Dot Dot Dot*, a responsive production model popularized by the car company Toyota in which orders for goods prompt the creation of the product. Although the magazine was not exactly printed to order, their production method economized on storage and emphasized spontaneity, and was reflective of the journal's consistent explorations in construction and distribution.

One of the most distinguished alternative design and culture journals of its time, *Dot Dot Dot* ended in 2011. Its status as an established design journal was consistently challenged by its own development and by the editors' enthusiasm for experimentation.

2001

RAIN

Poster

Catherine Zask (1961–)

Hippodrome de Douai, France

Catherine Zask's poster for *Rain*, a contemporary dance performance by the Belgian choreographer Anne Teresa De Keersmaeker, captures the formal elements of the dance through a linear, typographical exploration of space and movement. Situated at Douai's theater, dance, and concert venue, the Hippodrome, *Rain* was performed by ten dancers to the accompaniment of a musical score by Steve Reich, and a stage set by Jan Versweyveld, consisting of metal ropes that shimmered on contact, creating a sensation of liquidity.

An independent French graphic artist, Zask works mainly in the arena of educational and cultural promotion, within which she has developed a group of collaborative partnerships with clients that include the Society of Multimedia Artists in Paris, the universities of Franche-Comté and Paris Diderot, and the French Ministry of Culture. Like an architect or, indeed, a choreographer, Zask activates dormant spaces to enhance visual communication and provide meaning and interpretation. Her typographic poster designs reconfigure the hierarchy of visual language by radical experimentation: letterforms overlap, sway, repeat, splinter, collide, and stretch, offering insight into the emotional meanings and creative concepts underlying dance or theater productions. Here, wildly extended letterforms pour through the top of the frame to follow a meandering route via the forms of words, as they strive to communicate the elements of the dance. Despite this questioning of the nature of written text, Zask maintains legibility. She has also developed a personal visual language of three-dimensional, animated, and deconstructed letterforms, which she calls "Alfabetempo," derived from a research project based on the letter "R" in "Rome." An enigmatic version of the structure was used as the dominant typographic element in a poster promoting the choreography of Merce Cunningham in 2002.

As well as being a member of the Alliance Graphique Internationale, Zask has exhibited at the Centre du Pompidou in Paris and received numerous awards for her work in design and typography, including the Grand Prix at the Brno Graphic Design Biennale in 2000 for this glittering silver-and-black silk-screen print.

2001

THE ART OF LOOKING SIDEWAYS

Book

Alan Fletcher (1931–2006)

Phaidon Press, UK

This personal and idiosyncratic book was described by Alan Fletcher as a "cross between a collage and a box of goodies." A celebration of Fletcher's unique methods as a graphic designer, it is about opening up possibilities by providing stimulating and engaging starting points, rather than closing down inquiry by supplying answers. Such investigation for Fletcher was primarily concerned with looking: he privileged vision over the other senses, recognizing that we use words like "seeing" metaphorically, to mean such things as "understanding." In *The Art of Looking Sideways*, his approach is eclectic, drawing together visual and written fragments from a diverse range of sources.

Each discrete piece of information resonates with its neighbors in the same way as different visual elements in a collage. The idea of collage is also conveyed through the use of many different typefaces, papers, and layouts, yet the book still achieves a coherent and consistent quality. Fletcher thought about the design of the book in cinematographic terms, where changes of pace equivalent to cuts across scenes are brought about throug [illegible] page turns (one page number designates a [illegible] spread) and the use of scale and white [illegible] also challenged conventional ways o [illegible] so that periodically the reader is re [illegible] it sideways or even upside down t [illegible] The work's appeal and relevance e [illegible] the boundaries of graphic design [illegible] suggested that it might require i [illegible] bookshop), but the use of graph [illegible] tool to arrange and integrate [illegible] as well as to capture and visu [illegible] was central to its success.

The Art of Looking Sideways provided a fre [illegible] approach to making books and gave an idea of what it might be like to occupy Fletcher's mind. Dealing with profound topics, such as "thinking," "perception," and "aesthetics" via conundrums, puns, and diverse visual material, the book is inflected with Fletcher's characteristic wit and lack of pretension.

← P.313

2001

PAINTING AT THE EDGE OF THE WORLD

Book

Andrew Blauvelt (1964–), Santiago Piedrafita (n.d.)

Walker Art Center, U.S.

Published to accompany the exhibition of the same name held at the Walker Art Center in Minneapolis, *Painting at the Edge of the World*—created by the Walker's design director, Andrew Blauvelt, and senior graphic designer Santiago Piedrafita—brings together critical essays on painting from a diverse array of disciplines, including the visual arts, film, architecture, design, and music. The catalog addresses the practice and relevance of painting in the contemporary world, asking where the canvas ends and the world begins.

The book's essays are presented on French-folded sheets that literalize the exhibition's title, allowing images to wrap around the page, while texts are interspersed with film stills and color photographs of artworks, exhibition spaces, and urban landscapes. The second section contains thirty large, gate-folded pages, one for each artist, with reproductions of an exhibited piece of work, a short profile, documentation, and examination of his or her artistic approach. Paintings bleed off the pages, and the frontispiece to each essay, laid out in a landscape format on tinted paper in a range of type weights, sizes, and tones, adds pace and variety. The total makes for a n impressively international survey of contemporary painting, sympathetically presented—with artists representing countries as diverse as Belgium, Brazil, Ethiopia, Germany, Iran, Italy, Japan, Scotland, South Africa, and the U.S. Some familiar international names are also featured, including Mike Kelley, John Currin, Marlene Dumas, Takashi Murakami, and Chris Ofili.

Regarded as a model of best design practice, the Walker Art Center's design studio has won more than one hundred awards and was nominated in 2001 for the Chrysler Award for Innovation. At its head, Blauvelt is one of the most influential figures in graphic design in the U.S., both as a practicing designer and as a director of other designers' work.

← P.314

2001

THE ALPHABET

Poster

Michaël Amzalag (1968–), Mathias Augustyniak (1967–)

Self-commissioned, France

"The Alphabet" poster series, designed by Michaël Amzalag and Mathias Augustyniak of M/M (Paris), derived from an ambition to prove that typefaces are essentially emotional, driven by the same figurative and semiotic influences that govern the visual language of fashion photography. "The Alphabet," which was published by the New York-based *VMagazine*, was initiated by M/M together with photographers Inez van Lamsweerde and Vinoodh Matadin, who used their experience of the fashion world to demonstrate that even a typeface could be crafted from fashion imagery.

Prior to 2001, when the posters were designed, M/M (Paris) had made its name directing advertising and brand campaigns for fashion designers Yohji Yamamoto and Balenciaga, in collaboration with van Lamsweerde and Matadin. In the 1990s, the group began to wonder whether a relationship could be developed between typography and fashion photography. If, as an embodiment of certain desirable female qualities, a model could be a signifier of a type of beauty or a particular brand, could she not also be a typographic symbol? "The Alphabet" consists of van Lamsweerde and Matadin's portraits of twenty-six models, most of which illustrate the initial letter of each one's first name. The letters question the way the viewer relates to the person in the image and their reaction to the human form as a symbol or a sign. The first series explores notions of female beauty and femininity by using sensuous letter shapes, whereas in the subsequent male series, "The Alphamen," the letters are depicted as masculine, angular, and strong. Although they appear to be freehand, the typefaces were hand-crafted to conform with typographic rules of balance, weight, and height, and were also suitable for large-scale formats.

"The Alphabet" received plenty of interest, but, adhering to their professional policy, the designers decided not to license its use in order to preserve the integrity of the concept. They did, however, use a large-scale version in oversized labels for the *Translation* exhibition of contemporary art at the Palais de Tokyo in 2005.

← P.315

2001–present

BUTT

Magazine Cover

Jop van Bennekom (1970–)

Top Publishers, the Netherlands

Founded in Amsterdam in 2001 by Dutch art director Jop van Bennekom and journalist Gert Jonkers, legendary magazine *BUTT* made its name through spotlighting the ideas, work, and sex lives of gay men in a straightforward, accessible way. This focus on the mundane and quotidian was in itself revolutionary, being a side of queer life that was rarely seen in print, and *BUTT* quickly garnered a loyal following. Between 2001 and 2011, twenty-nine issues of the magazine were released before *BUTT* took a sudden and lengthy hiatus, eventually returning in the spring of 2022, with its pocket-size, strawberry-pink-washed package in top form. Since then, the magazine's scope has expanded to include perspectives from the wider queer community, including lesbian and transgender contributors.

From the very first issue, *BUTT* has championed male sexuality on its front covers, each one featuring a different male model expressing vulnerability, desire, and playfulness. These honest depictions of gay men seek to normalize their experiences and to break down the binaries so often associated with gender and sexuality. Cover photographers—including Wolfgang Tillmans, Hedi Slimane, and, for the thirtieth issue, Clifford Prince King—employ a range of creative approaches: from documentary-style unadorned portraits to shots involving role-playing and performance, and from black-and-white photographs to brightly lit, studio-like setups.

On the cover *BUTT*'s wordmark is treated as a mutable, dynamic element. Consistently rendered in the magazine's signature bold Compacta typeface, in either black or knocked out to the pink of the background, its positioning and size are in constant flux. The placement and dimensions of imagery are also up for grabs. Inside, the design language is more defined and rigorous, creating a familiar space for readers to return to. Prior to founding *BUTT*, van Bennekom authored and designed *Re-Magazine*, which, though similarly preoccupied with the everyday, took a more experimental and freeform design approach. *BUTT*'s successor was *Fantastic Man*, launched in 2005, followed by companion title *The Gentlewoman* five years later. These narrowed van Bennekom's and Jonkers's focus further toward fashion while still maintaining the trademark intimacy the duo had so skillfully honed at *BUTT*.

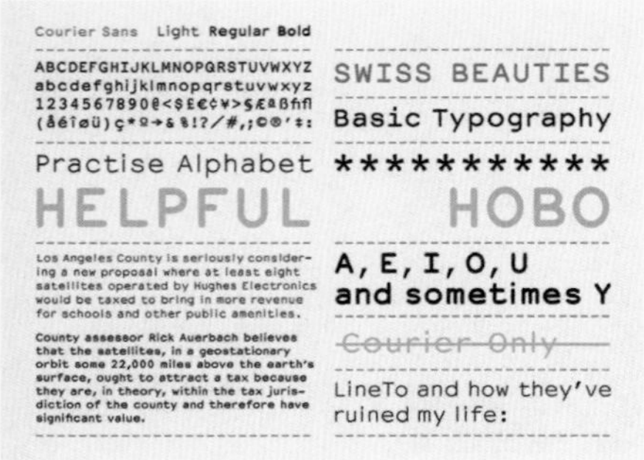

← P.316

2002

COURIER SANS

Typeface

James Goggin (1975–)

Self-commissioned, UK

By the 1980s, IBM's Courier font had become nearly anonymous due to its use on typewriters, and by the 1990s its inclusion in the Windows and Macintosh operating systems furthered its prevalence. Such utility and familiarity have made Courier fodder for typographic innovations.

The typeface that became known as Courier Sans is a benchmark design of the late 1990s, when experimentation with typography was thriving. During that time, other designers who took note of graphic designer James Goggin's unorthodox approach to typography began to view type design as approachable and viable. Faced with a seemingly illogical "Courier Only" rule during a first-year design college typography exercise in 1994, Goggin took it upon himself to circumvent the restriction with an unexpected variant. He deftly cut the slab serifs off Howard "Bud" Kettler's seminal 1955 IBM typewriter font to create a handmade typeface all his own—so-called "Courier Sans"—and the result would pave the way for other typographic experimentation, including his modular elaboration of German typographer Rudolf Koch's 1931 Prisma typeface, titled Prismaset (2017).

Upon graduation from London's Royal College of Art in 1999, Goggin rediscovered the Courier experiment he began years ago, and set out to complete the font. Through using the typeface in his own designs, it was noticed by designer Cornel Windlin, cofounder of the Swiss type foundry Lineto. After Windlin typeset the 2000 publication *Die schönsten Schweizer Büche* (*The Most Beautiful Swiss Books*) in Courier Sans, the font earned so much attention and requests for availability that Goggin was encouraged to redraw many of the typeface's intricate details and respace it proportionally, in direct contrast to the mono-spaced characters of the Courier original. The resulting three-weight typeface was released for commercial sale through the Lineto foundry in 2002.

Goggin has applied Courier Sans to his own clothing label, All-Weather, in addition to several book design and identity projects. Courier Sans's utilitarian properties have given design projects a distinctiveness that few typefaces possess, and its oddly familiar aesthetic makes it friendly and inviting.

← P.316

2002/2004/2010/2014/2018/2024

ANDY WARHOL CATALOG RAISONNÉ

Book

Julia Hasting (1970–)

Phaidon Press, UK

The term "catalog raisonné" is usually associated with lengthy, dense, dry books that provide a text-heavy listing of a single artist's entire creative output. However, when collating the body of work produced by such a prolific artist as Andy Warhol (and bearing in mind that he referred to his studio as "the Factory"), a traditional catalog raisonné would have possessed the length and heft, not to mention the visual flair, of a dictionary.

When faced with such a challenge, Julia Hasting, design director of Phaidon Press, first decided that it was necessary to redefine visually the conventional catalog raisonné. Her aim was to present a complete record of Warhol's works in an elegant and engaging layout. The catalog needed to serve both as a book for art lovers and as a professional reference for collectors, galleries, and museums.

Hasting devised a system in which groups of the artist's works could be reproduced in a large format and in full color over consecutive spreads uninterrupted by textual information. Captions, which included descriptions, provenance, complete listings of exhibitions, and bibliographic history, together with hundreds of comparative images, were interspersed between the illustrations in discrete spreads. The immense amount of information is assembled deftly, and the long sequences of image-only pages provide the reader with a thorough overview of Warhol's various styles and techniques. The book's visual narrative is deeply rooted in Warhol's eccentricity and wit, and the typography gives another hint to his style.

The volumes are packaged in a slipcase laminated with silk-screened brown craft paper, inspired by Warhol's box sculptures. The bold consumerist typography of the slipcase displays the information about the book as if it were a product in a cardboard box, including its weight and its directional graphics. Warhol's iconic *Heinz Tomato Ketchup* box sculptures inspired the colors for the first volume, while the *Kellogg's Cornflakes* boxes and the *Del Monte Peach Halves* boxes inspired the blue and green of the following two volumes, respectively.

The design won several awards, including a gold medal at the Art Directors Club New York and the Golden Bee in Moscow.

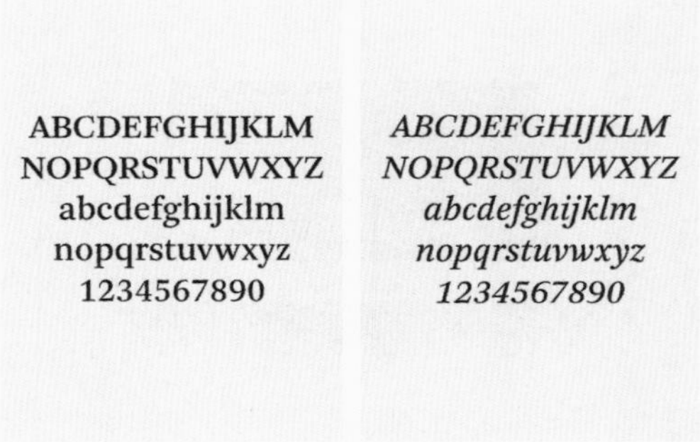

← P.317

2002

ARNHEM

Typeface

Fred Smeijers (1961–)

Self-commissioned, the Netherlands

In 1999, while acting as consultant to the Werkplaats Typografie (Typography Workshop), a design practice-cum-postgraduate course at the Academie voor Beeldende Kunsten (Academy of Fine Arts) in Arnhem in the eastern Netherlands, Fred Smeijers showed some early prototypes of a typeface he had been working on. The workshop had been offered the opportunity to redesign the Dutch state's daily newspaper *Nederlandse Staatscourant*, and Smeijers's embryonic Arnhem letterface seemed suitable for the job.

As part of the *Nederlandse Staatscourant* project, Smeijers tested a number of type designs in print, comparing letterforms to decide which nuances in their design would enable ideal legibility. This user-centered approach was unusual at a time when many designers were generating nonfunctional, experimental typefaces and typographic layouts. Smeijers developed his initial renderings into a face appropriate for headline use, now called Arnhem Fine. Then he began to work on an accompanying text face, incorporating strong color and a large x-height to make it dark enough and large enough to read easily.

In the end, Arnhem was not chosen for use in the *Nederlandse Staatscourant*, but writers such as Robin Kinross championed it for books, such as those published by the Hyphen Press. Smeijers and Rudy Geeraerts released Arnhem in 2002 with the launch of the OurType foundry, along with Fresco, Sansa, and Monitor. Arnhem then had four weights of roman and italic letters, including Arnhem Blond, Normal, Bold, and Black. Arnhem Blond is a visually distinctive font: it is not a true lightweight face, but it does deliver less color than Arnhem Normal. Years later, Smeijers expanded Arnhem to include Arnhem SemiBold, and its PRO character set now gives Arnhem a fuller range of uppercase letters and numerals, as well as accents for all Latin script-based Western, Central, and Eastern languages. This range of characters, including but not limited to mathematical and monetary symbols and ligatures, makes Arnhem a strong candidate for any newspaper or book, especially one where statistical figures play a prominent role.

← P.317

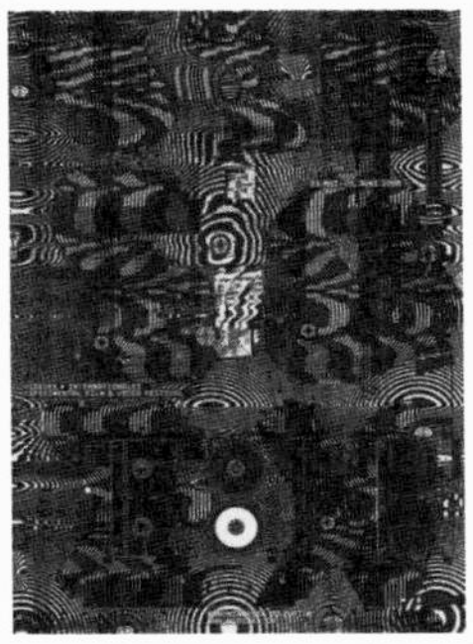

← P.318

← P.319

2002

CIUDAD JUÁREZ: 300 DEAD WOMEN, 500 MISSING WOMEN

Poster

Alejandro Magallanes (1971–)

Self-commissioned, Mexico

Ciudad Juárez, Mexico, sits on the United States border, across the Rio Grande from El Paso, Texas. The city's proximity to the U.S., and the establishment of foreign investment and free-trade deals between the two countries, dating back to the 1960s, saw the rapid, largely unregulated development of *maquilas* (duty-free manufacturing plants), followed by a huge influx of people. In 2023 Juárez's population was just over 1.5 million, of which an estimated 32 percent were migrants.

These conditions have enabled an equally steep increase in drug trafficking and gang violence. Historically, a significant proportion of this violence —whether gang-related or otherwise—has been inflicted upon women, a trend that, many argue, reflects the patriarchal government and economic imbalance in the country. The ten years between 1993 and 2003 saw a particularly devastating rise in femicide cases, with more than 300 women recorded as being kidnapped and murdered, in the most brutal circumstances, and dozens of others missing, presumed dead. Despite these shocking statistics, the vast majority of cases remain unsolved.

In response to perceived institutional apathy at the deaths, a large-scale demonstration was held in Mexico City on November 25, 2002, coinciding with the International Day for the Elimination of Violence Against Women. Designer Alejandro Magallanes created this poster in support of the action.

Its design is chilling: a female body is depicted through the use of negative space, her head and neck shaped by a pair of hands poised to strangle, her waist spliced by barbed wire. Together, the various cutouts that compose her anatomy form a skull-like face, personifying death. The stark black-and-white color palette and hand-lettering add an urgent, anarchic tone to the poster, making clear its central purpose as a symbol of protest. At the base a line reads: "How many more will die under the cynical gaze of our authorities?"

The sociopolitical topic is typical of Magallanes's work, which has been lauded internationally with awards from "The 4th Block" Eco-Poster Triennial, Ukraine, and the Political Poster Triennial, Belgium. This poster won the silver medal at the International Poster Biennale, Warsaw, in 2004.

2003/2008/2010–present

VIDEOEX

Poster

Martin Woodtli (1971–)

Kunstraum Walcheturm, Switzerland

Since 2003, Martin Woodtli has designed the posters for the VideoEx experimental music, film, and video festival, which is celebrated annually in his hometown of Zurich, Switzerland.

Woodtli's work is highly detailed—possibly the result of an obsessive personality. He spends a huge amount of time on each image, building layer upon layer to create something so painstakingly detailed that it becomes a highly original creation. Rather than using one set of principles for all his work, Woodtli finds the method for each project from within its own particular spirit and format.

Woodtli is a master of computer-aided design, highly proficient in the use of computer programs. Designer Stefan Sagmeister, in whose studio Woodtli was an intern at the beginning of his career, has commented, "He is the only person I know who can actually think with the keyboard. His proficiency in various programs is such that he sketches with the keyboard as quickly and uninhibitedly as with pencil and paper." In addition to exploiting computer-aided design as part of the design process, Woodtli uses a photocopying machine, producing prints on glossy sheets and sliding images on top of one another.

Woodtli designed the VideoEx posters over a number of years. The subject matter of the film and video festival, which is heavily aligned with new technologies and a vision of the future, fits perfectly with his aesthetic style.

For the VideoEx series, Woodlti based his designs on video test patterns, faxes, and computer coding, creating intricate screenprints in four colors. Embedded in the posters are illustrations of video cassettes and tape spools that hide among the variegated colored backgrounds. Meanwhile, the heading text is created by shifting elements of the pattern to create the letters, rather than by laying a typeface over a background. Layering creates highly detailed digital images on a comparatively massive scale: these posters each measure about 47¼ × 35⅜ inches (120 × 90 cm). The finished result is a riot of color and detail that perfectly captures the age of computer technology.

Woodtli's highly recognizable signature style has been well received in the international design community as well as in Switzerland.

2003

PERSIAN TYPE AND TYPOGRAPHY

Poster

Reza Abedini (1967–)

Academic Center for Education, Culture and Research (ACECR), Iran

Reza Abedini has played a seminal role in introducing Iranian graphic design to the wider world. This poster, designed for a lecture at the Iranian Academic Center, demonstrates the skill with which he merges Persian culture with Western design principles. The text appearing inside Abedini's silhouette is a mixture of Farsi script and English. Also included are words written in a hybrid of Farsi and English commonly used in Iran for SMS texting and referred to as "Pinglish." This fascination with merging both the historic and contemporary, and Eastern and Western cultures, permeates Abedini's work.

His use of typography is based on the belief that historic literature, particularly poetry, is the gateway to Persian culture. For example, the typographic layout of this poster was influenced by an Iranian calligraphic composition written in Arabic, based on different typographic ways to express one's relationship with God. But this and Abedini's seemingly minimal approach to composition and color belie the complexity behind the work. He has an expert command of Farsi typographical structures, which are highly complex and traditionally used as decorative devices as well as to convey meaning. When written, Farsi consists only of letters attached to one another; that is, letters are not used independently and only find meaning according to their relationship with the letters that precede and follow them. This presents a number of challenges when creating a design that combines Farsi with Western roman lettering. Abedini's work often bridges the differences between these writing systems.

A prolific body of work is testimony to his personal exploration of past and present, and to an awareness of the broader perception of Iranian culture, particularly the "negative history of [Iranian] art as the Westerners wrote it." Rather than succumbing to Western design trends, he has succeeded in creating a unique hybrid style that conveys the relationship between Persian and Western type and references his own cultural heritage. In doing so, Abedini has brought world recognition to Iranian typography and design.

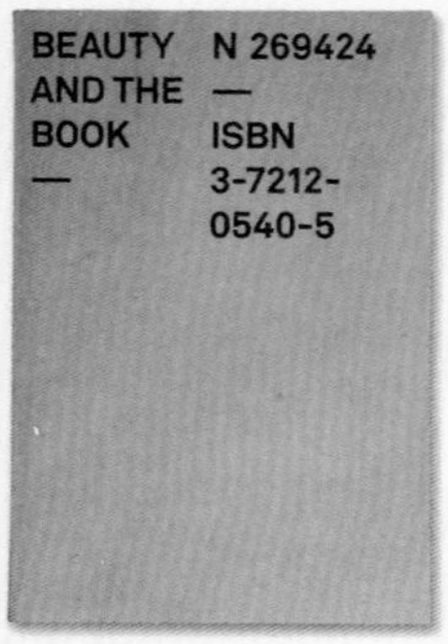
BEAUTY AND THE BOOK
—
N 269424
—
ISBN
3-7212-
0540-5

← P.319

2004

BEAUTY AND THE BOOK

Book

Julia Born (1975–)

Swiss Federal Office of Culture, Switzerland

In 1943 Jan Tschichold initiated The Most Beautiful Swiss Books, an annual award for achievements in Swiss book production, which he saw not only as an exercise in value but a means of encouraging good practice in all aspects of book-making. Sixty years later, the award was celebrated by the exhibition *Beauty and the Book: 60 Years of The Most Beautiful Swiss Books* and its accompanying catalog.

The emerging Swiss designer Julia Born was commissioned to design *Beauty and the Book*, which, as well as documenting the highlights of the award's history, features essays from leading experts in the field. The book initially appears austere, quietly referencing the history of Swiss design it is intended to cover: for example, the text is set in Laurenz Brunner's Akkurat, a brand-new typeface that continues the tradition of Swiss sans serifs. The design, appropriately for a book about books, represents an almost archetypal idea of the book, intended as an object as much as a record of knowledge or expression.

This approach is reflected by the variety of materials used and by the subtle choices that Born has made for the volume's different sections. The cover is printed on a buff manila stock, which suggests an archival feel, whereas the rest of the book uses a paper similar to that used for novels. By listing the publishing number and ISBN on the cover alongside the title and with equal importance, Born emphasizes the idea of the book as an object in context. Inside, the start of a different language (German, French, or English) is marked by a turned-down page, and important parts of the chronology are highlighted by printed text, which simulates handwritten notes made in pencil. Through these interventions, Born contrasts the design with the methods that we adopt when we read and handle a book.

Beauty and the Book, as befits such a project, deserves to be featured as a "most beautiful Swiss book," and confirms Born's status as one of the most interesting Swiss designers working today.

BEAUTY
AND
THE
BEAST

← P.320

2004–2005

BEAUTY AND THE BEAST

Identity

Frith Kerr (1973–), Amelia Noble (1973–)

Crafts Council, UK

Frith Kerr and Amelia Noble, of the graphic design firm Kerr | Noble, were commissioned by the Crafts Council of the United Kingdom to design the graphic identity for *Beauty and the Beast*, an exhibition of new Swedish design held in 2004–5 at the Crafts Council Gallery in London. Kerr and Noble are highly conceptual designers who devote a great deal of time to research and the development of ideas before starting work on any visuals, and this practice applied to the *Beauty and the Beast* commission. Given one month to come up with a visual identity for the exhibition, they spent three and a half weeks on research, with nothing to show for it until the last few days before the deadline. They comment: "It is quite hard to trust this process. Sometimes it takes a long time and you don't know where you are going."

As part of their research, rather than looking at Swedish design, they decided to explore everything else about Sweden—the country, its people, its climate. They learned that many Swedish people have a second home in the forest, where, surrounded by trees, they spend a lot of time chopping firewood. With the Scandinavian woods as inspiration, the shape of logs became the starting point for a font. Straight lines recall the shape of long logs, while curved elements are based on the semicircular cross sections that result when a log is split lengthways. The "T," which consists of one long shape with two semicircular shapes above, is a good example. The text is black on either a plain white or pale pink background. Full of character and created just for this exhibition, the font became the key feature of the graphic identity for *Beauty and the Beast*, with the other illustrative elements—photographs of craftspeople and their work—taking a back seat.

Kerr | Noble was dissolved in 2008, after 11 years in practice, though both designers continue to work independently.

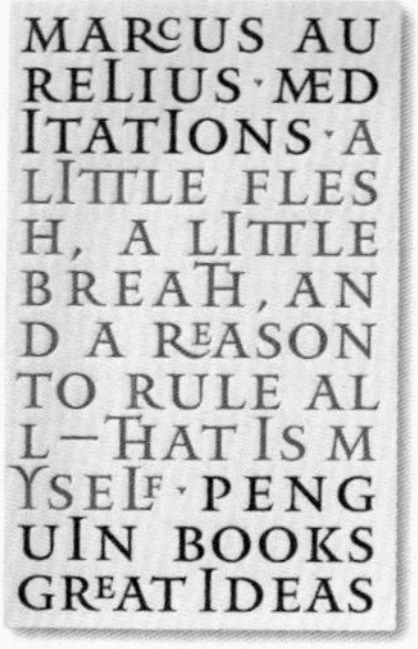
MARCUS AU
RELIUS·MED
ITATIONS·A
LITTLE FLES
H, A LITTLE
BREATH, AN
D A REASON
TO RULE AL
L—THAT IS M
YSELF·PENG
UIN BOOKS
GREAT IDEAS

← P.320

2004–2010/2020

GREAT IDEAS

Book Cover

David Pearson (1978–) et al.

Penguin Books, UK

Carefully selected from Penguin's own Classics and Modern Classics back catalog, "Great Ideas" is a series of nonfiction books radically repackaged in three sets of twenty, published in 2004, 2005, and 2008. Covering subjects such as art, philosophy, politics, science, sociology, and war, each title is recognized as being of highly influential, world-changing importance. During a trip to Italy, Penguin editor Simon Winder noticed bookstands stocked a surprising number of philosophical texts, which sparked the idea of re-presenting important works to a broad contemporary readership.

The striking cover design of each title created a stir when the first set appeared. The conventional approach for such a series might be to devise a consistent grid structure, differentiated on each cover by imagery. However, David Pearson, with Alistair Hall from the design studio We Made This, and their former tutors Catherine Dixon and Phil Baines from the Central St. Martins College of Art and Design, developed a more innovative approach. Printed in just red and black on a white cover, the restricted color palette and use of debossing and tactile material gave the series a unifying identity and a strong presence, strengthened by a consistent layout for the spine and back cover. An entirely individual, typographically led front-cover design was developed for each book, inspired by the text's subject or its historical context. The cover for Marcus Aurelius's *Meditations*, for instance, takes its cue from Roman inscription by spreading the title and publisher name across a line break. A similar effect was used for Plato's *Symposium* to combine these texts' classical heritage with a fresh and modern look.

The first series in particular soon became the subject of much publicity, especially in the design press, and the designers received a number of award nominations, including one for the Design Museum's Designer of the Year in 2005. That year an additional series appeared, this time with covers in blue and black but otherwise in the same design. The final series was published with green-and-black covers and a more modern choice of texts.

← P.321

2005–2007

ESTABLISHED & SONS

Identity

Made Thought

Established & Sons, UK

When the graphic design partnership Made Thought was commissioned to produce an identity for the contemporary furniture designers and makers Established & Sons, their intention was to "create a brand vocabulary that reflects both the solid values of traditional British manufacturing and cutting-edge contemporary design."

The basic logo is purely typographic, white out of black, the words "Established" and "British Made" appearing in a robust sans serif, the ampersand elaborate and calligraphic, and the word "Sons" in bold serif capitals. However, the identity of the fonts is less important than their neat and well-resolved arrangement, which shifts the focus away from specifics of font choice to displays of typographic finesse and a sense of delight in letterforms.

Made Thought's range of applications for Established & Sons is demanding in its variety of content, setting, and scale, and extends from boxes to exhibition displays, invitations, and signage. The ampersand sometimes dominates; the logo itself is occasionally italicized; huge outline serif lettering is used on walls; welcome messages in sans serif wrap around corners and text can be vertical or horizontal, or sometimes embossed. Whole walls are emblazoned with quotations and comments in different sizes: arrangements and fonts make careful use of spaces, contrast values, and type weights, creating a textured experience that can be read and reread, offering endless variation. The typographic design has been carefully thought out for each application, with well-controlled color schemes generally featuring the type in black or white with flat backgrounds—there are no tints, since depth of color is achieved by font variation.

Innovative and versatile, the typography has a strength that reflects the furniture, but rather than representing the products in any technical or visual sense, the identity simply celebrates the joys of good design—an ethos that in turn becomes easily associated with the furniture itself.

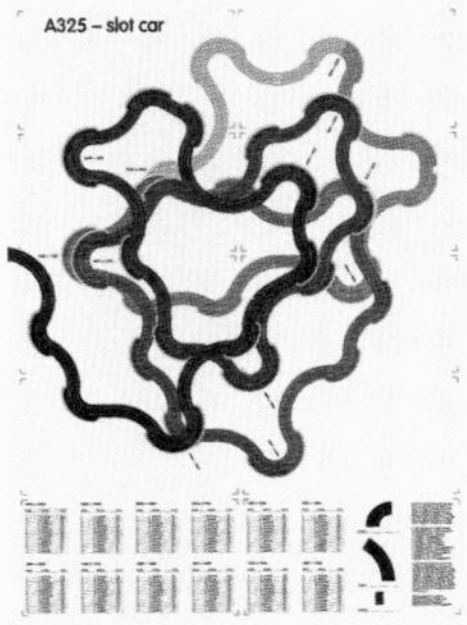

← P.322

2005–2006

A325

Poster

Catalogtree

Self-commissioned, the Netherlands

The "A325" poster series by Dutch design studio Catalogtree (Joris Maltha and Daniel Gross) aimed to visualize the growth and possible future amalgamation of Arnhem and Nijmegen. Catalogtree did this by focusing on the A325, the main road that connects the two cities. The nine posters feature infographics that Catalogtree created using data provided by the local council. The council staff were so excited by the project that they even carried out extra traffic counts.

Catalogtree's love of facts and figures, and its creative use of the infographics medium, can be seen in the series. The graphics include a circular graph that compares average speeds in two directions during twenty-four hours; a green-and-white grid with linear black lines that represent ten thousand cars passing a bridge, categorized by time, speed, and distance; a diagram made up of many lines coming off a spine that illustrates all accidents that happened between 1998 and 2003; and a series of the road depicted as overlapping aerial images in sepia tones.

The process is an integral part of Catalogtree's work. The designers collect their data, knowing that the more dense the information, the better. Then they discuss how to use the results to represent the idea at hand. Using a formal approach and their own self-written computer programs, they establish a set of rules by which to represent the data as a whole, rather than deciding how to deal with each individual fact. By creating information-based images, Catalogtree have made it possible to visualize the complex content provided, creating a striking and thought-provoking series of posters.

← P.323

2005

METROPOLITAN WORLD ATLAS

Book

Joost Grootens (1971–)

010 Publishers, the Netherlands

The *Metropolitan World Atlas* documents a total of 101 metropolises, from Anchorage to Beijing, which it analyzes through a unique combination of same-scale ground plans and statistics ranging from data traffic to air pollution.

To enable readers to understand the information intuitively, Dutch designer Joost Grootens developed a system of orange dots, which vary in size according to how a particular city compares with others in a given category. Combined with world data maps of statistics that offer additional comparisons, this system allows the differences between individual cities to be understood at a glance. The city map appears on the recto, whereas the verso carries data about social and economic issues, such as metropolitan development and employment, set out in simple graphics and clean typography (LL Akkurat and LL Akkurat Mono). The book is printed in five colors, including a Day-Glo orange that indicates population density on the city maps. A clear, accessible design that eschews the traditional atlas format of unwieldy columns of text and overelaborate keys, and provides information about each city on a single spread, the *Metropolitan World Atlas* literally changes the way in which we see the world.

Grootens spent two years designing the book, working closely with 010 Publishers to produce a work that epitomizes his idea of a contemporary atlas: a collection of data made accessible through trim size, choice of paper, and the integration of color and typography. The book has won several prizes, including the Red Dot: Grand Prix and a Gold Medal in the Schönste Bücher aus aller Welt, both awarded in 2006. Trained as an architect, Grootens has since 2000 almost exclusively designed books in the fields of architecture, urban space, and art, and has also worked on other atlases, such as the *Atlas of Conflict: Israel–Palestine* (2010).

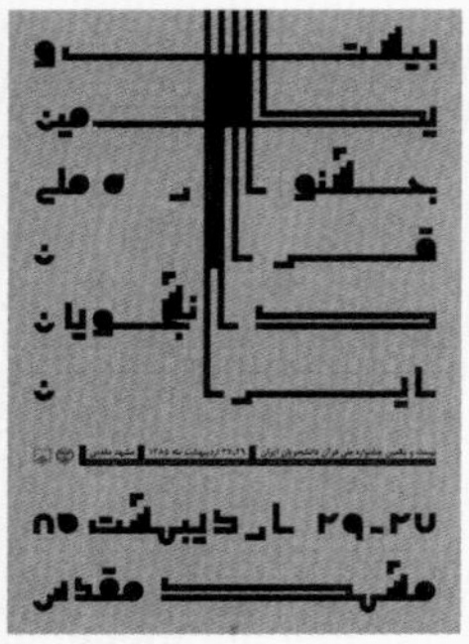

← P.324

2006

21ST QURAN NATIONAL FESTIVAL FOR STUDENTS OF IRAN

Poster

Iman Raad (1979–)

Academic Center for Education, Culture and Research (ACECR), Iran

In this poster for a student Quran competition, angular black script runs across an ornate gold-and-brown-patterned background. Although strikingly modern, the use of ancient techniques marks this as part of the contemporary Persian graphic design movement, which seeks to produce a new and wholly Iranian aesthetic.

Fascinated by the folklore and crafts of his country, Iman Raad uses a wide variety of techniques, ranging from computer-generated 3-D text to faux-naïf watercolor illustration. Here, he combines the two most highly prized art forms of Persian culture: calligraphy and carpet weaving. Beautiful writing is valued throughout the Muslim world because of the central place of the word of God in the Muslim faith. Iran uses the Arabic writing system, modified to suit the Farsi language, which in this poster is characterized by the use of right angles in the typography. Although, to a Western eye, this evokes the modernist obsession with geometry and clean lines, it in fact recalls the classical Arabic calligraphy style, Kufic. This script was used almost exclusively in the Quran until the end of the tenth century, but an Iranian adaptation of this, known as Banna'i or "Square Kufic," was also an inspiration. Used for inscriptions on brick or tiled buildings, the script has a built-in grid system that makes it even straighter than other Kufic styles, and it has undergone a renaissance due to its suitability for computer-based fonts. Carpets have also long held a special place in the culture, religion, and economy of Iran, and are evoked in this poster in the background pattern of medallions and arabesques, which create a soft geometry that contrasts with the bold linear style of the typography. The gold of the background is considered a holy color in Islam.

Although Raad has combined many elements and motifs associated with the Quran in this poster, it is by no means a traditional design. A beautiful and stylish arrangement of lines, curves, and color, the image also represents a typographic experiment by an acclaimed designer working in a country with a new sense of openness.

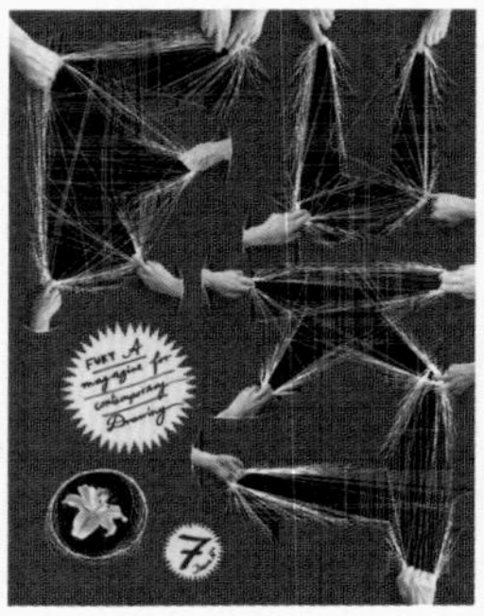

← P.325

2006–present

FUKT

Magazine Cover

Ariane Spanier (1978–)

FUKT, Germany and Norway

FUKT was founded in Norway in 1999 by Norwegian-Swedish visual artist and publisher Björn Hegardt, with the intention of exploring the world of contemporary illustration and drawing. In 2006 Hegardt was joined by coeditor and designer Ariane Spanier, who is responsible for shaping the experimental visual direction and who, as of 2023, serves as *FUKT*'s creative director. Through essays, featured works, and interviews, the magazine examines drawing's endless permutations and expressions, and how it continues to be a challenging medium, serving as a platform for artists and illustrators to showcase their work. In Norwegian, *fukt* can mean moisture, humidity, or dampness; its use as a title perhaps suggests the conditions for something to grow.

Over the years, the magazine has earned a loyal following for its ever-changing cover designs and layouts, and has accrued a number of awards, including a Stack Award in 2019 and a D&AD Graphite Pencil in 2020. Notably, *FUKT* contains no advertising. Conceptually driven, each cover pushes the boundaries of traditional editorial design and is often used to bridge the gap between design and content, reinforcing the theme of the issue. Primarily typography-focused, the covers use a range of hand-drawn and custom fonts for the *FUKT* wordmark, the cover lines, and other textual information. Spanier's type experiments have utilized such unconventional sources as hair, paper, tape, graphite powder, clay, and mice.

The designs not only break convention in terms of layout and composition but also experiment with new formats entirely. Issue 18, for example, features an interactive puzzle wheel on the front that can be turned to align and misalign text that reads "Fukt the System"—playing on the issue's theme of systems (in the form of rules, schedules, structures, or otherwise) and how these are employed within drawing and the creative process. Issue 19 (pictured) delves into the world of narrative drawing, which plays out in a concertina-style fold-out cover reminiscent of a storyboard. It is this kind of thoughtful innovation that separates *FUKT* from its competitors and keeps it ahead of the curve, even in the continually innovating independent-publishing scene.

← P.326

2006

BECK—THE INFORMATION

Record / CD Cover

Big Active

Beck Hansen, U.S.

The CD packaging for Beck Hansen's seventh studio album, *The Information*, is distinctive in handing over control of its visual identity to the audience.

With increasing access to music online, Beck's brief to the London-based designers Big Active was to distinguish the pleasures of owning a physical CD album from the experience of simply downloading files. The solution was to present the CD's front and back cover as gridded graph paper, the back cover bearing a discreet track list, barcode, and copyright information, and the front cover left entirely blank. The clear case bears a single "Beck" logo sticker. Inside, a loose sheet of stickers—one of four possible sets—leaves it to owners to create their own cover art, so that no two copies of *The Information* are ever the same. A total of two hundred fifty stickers, commissioned from twenty different artists, provide an eclectic mix of graphics, illustrations, and logos from which each self-appointed designer can choose.

Although playfully undermining the standard cover design elements—images of the artist and band—this novel approach is also entirely in keeping with Beck's ethos. With a pedigree in the visual and performing arts (his grandfather is the Fluxus artist Al Hansen), Beck had always been keenly aware of the visual possibilities surrounding the production, performance, and promotion of his work. The packaging kit for *The Information* mirrors the magpie montage technique of his music, which blends inspirations such as folk, hip-hop, and 1970s rock with the aid of loops, samples, and cross-genre references—a style whose often casual air is belied by reports that this album took three years to make. *The Information*, widely regarded as a successful integration of Beck's playful dance-inspired music and his more serious and understated work, could be regarded as his own DIY collage of an entire career, presented to his audience for further collaboration.

← P.326

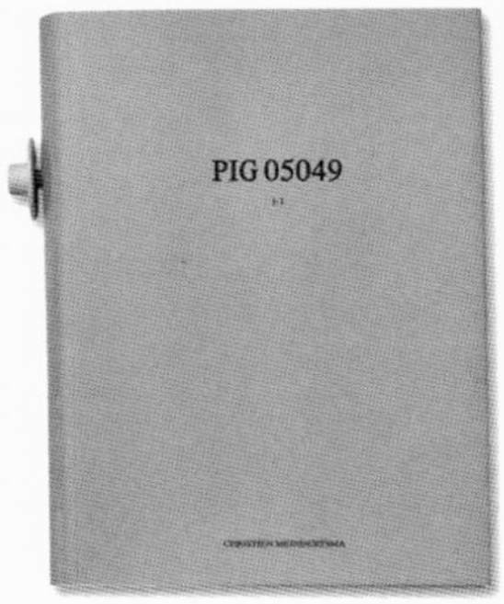

← P.327

← P.328

2007

DESIGNING DESIGN

Book

Kenya Hara (1958–)

Self-commissioned, Japan

Designing Design is a 474-page fully illustrated hardcover book designed and written by Kenya Hara, a Japanese designer and academic who runs his own design studio, is a professor at Musashino Art University, and is both a board member and the art director for the Japanese brand MUJI.

Although the book could be described loosely as a monograph, it is probably more accurate to call it a manifesto. *Designing Design*, Hara's first book in English, attempts to explain to a Western audience the Japanese design aesthetic. This includes notions such as "emptiness" as it is understood in Japan's visual, spiritual, and philosophical tradition—a concept that should not be confused with the Western idea of simplicity.

Hara carefully selected a collection of images and texts, which are arranged into sections: Re-design, Haptic (Awakening the Senses), Senseware, White, Muni (Nothing, yet Everything), Viewing the World from the Tip of Asia, Exformation (Rivers, Resorts), and What is Design? Although much of the work presented is his own, Hara has also chosen to illuminate these themes with the work of others. For example, the first section features images from a series of exhibitions, curated by Hara, in which designers were invited to provide solutions to his questions, including one that asked architects to redesign pasta.

Hara explains and explores pertinent concepts through essays written by both himself and others. He acknowledges in the preface that the texts themselves are their own form of design communication: "Verbalizing design is another act of design. I realized this while writing this book."

However, while the texts in *Designing Design* are important, it is the illustrations that are the most powerful communicators. The images have a sense of quiet and are treated simply on white backgrounds. The hardback cover itself is plain white, with title and author in two harmonious lines of black capitals. Inside, the first page of text is reached only after three blank endpapers, the third of which is a slightly smaller leaf of hand-made paper.

As one of the key living proponents of the Japanese design aesthetic, Hara succeeds with *Designing Design* in communicating this philosophy to a Western audience.

2007

PIG 05049, BY CHRISTIEN MEINDERTSMA

Book

Julie Joliat (1979–), Christien Meindertsma (1980)

Self-commissioned, the Netherlands

This book is an exercise in rigor and conservation, charting the path of every single part used from a single pig, number 05049, raised on a commercial Dutch farm. Designed by Christien Meindertsma, in collaboration with Julie Joliat, and later published by Thomas Eyck, its single-page photos appear on a spartan grid and are cataloged in a restrained graphic language that compels the viewer to ponder uncomfortable questions about food production, waste, and animal welfare.

Printed on white stock, the success of the design hinges on its arresting use of negative space that frames an unfussy portfolio of 185 objects and products. Without passing judgment, its unflinching information is similarly spartan, adopting a serif font to describe animal-part usage, paired with a simple icon of each pig-derived element. The book is organized according to the essential body parts, and—recalling the traditional technique for dictionaries—each chapter is marked by a crisp half-circle thumb index. The unbleached craft-paper cover bears one adornment: a pig's earmark affixed to the spine.

The range of materials that pig 05049 creates is astonishing. The "Bones" section charts how gelatin from pig collagen is used to transform gunpowder into a gleaming ammunition casing; "Blood" describes the nascent use of pig's hemoglobin in cigarette filters; "Skin" catalogs gelatin found in many cheesecake mixes. Both revolting and enlightening, the book's effects suggest readers will never think about deer figurines in the same way again.

This kind of forensic graphic language has become Meindertsma's hallmark since graduating from the Design Academy Eindhoven in 2004 with her publication *Checked Baggage*, which documented every item from a week's confiscated objects at Amsterdam Airport Schiphol. In *Pig* and subsequent books, *Flax Project* (2012) and *Bottom Ash Observatory* (2015), Meindertsma leads readers to look at the life cycle of raw materials. By demystifying commercial production processes, she lays bare information that would otherwise be hidden or lost.

Pig 05049 won a Dutch Design Award in 2008 and an Index Award in 2009. Meindertsma's work is held in collections at the Museum of Modern Art, New York; the Victoria and Albert Museum, London; and the Vitra Design Museum, Weil am Rein, Germany.

2008

LETTERA

Typeface

Kobi Benezri (1976–)

Lineto, Switzerland

The Italian industrial design company Olivetti produced Josef Müller-Brockmann's Candia typeface for use in their typewriter golf balls and daisy wheels in the mid-1970s, discontinuing it shortly thereafter. In 2006 Kobi Benezri found early drawings of the font's basic specimen. Captivated by its honesty and unusual properties, he began redrawing it, producing a typewriter-inspired font during a time when typewriters were becoming extinct.

Benezri worked from the low-quality specimen scans of the Müller-Brockmann characters and glyphs. When he enlarged the scans, many of the letterforms were distorted, and thick crotches, which resembled reversed ink traps, began to appear where the letterform lines intersected, caused by a swelling of the ink. Benezri systematically included these crotches in his design, and it was only later, having found a more complete specimen of Candia in an Olivetti catalog, that he discovered the ink traps did not exist. Nevertheless, he decided to include them in his design, as they allowed the font to perform well at a small size. When it came to naming his typeface, he was inspired by the 1950 Lettera 22, Marcello Nizzoli's laptop-style Olivetti portable typewriter, for reporters on the go.

Benezri drew Lettera for Phaidon's 2005 book *AREA 2*, designed by Julia Hasting. He then proceeded to work with Cornel Windlin and Stephan Müller at the Swiss foundry Lineto to develop Lettera for release in 2008 as a mono-spaced typeface in four cuts. At small sizes, text set in Lettera looked clean and crisp, and the font was adopted by many designers for books, branding, and web projects, as well as in various publications such as *Grafik* and *Wallpaper** magazines. Shortly after its release there was clear demand for a proportional version of the font. Benezri began designing Lettera Proportional in 2008, based on his original design of Lettera, carefully balancing between a legible sans serif text font and the tone of Lettera.

While working on Phaidon's *Dieter Rams: As Little Design as Possible* (2011), Benezri completed his development of Lettera Proportional as the new Lettera-Txt, testing its delicate and clean simplicity in the book. In 2012, Lettera-Txt was released by Lineto.

← P.329

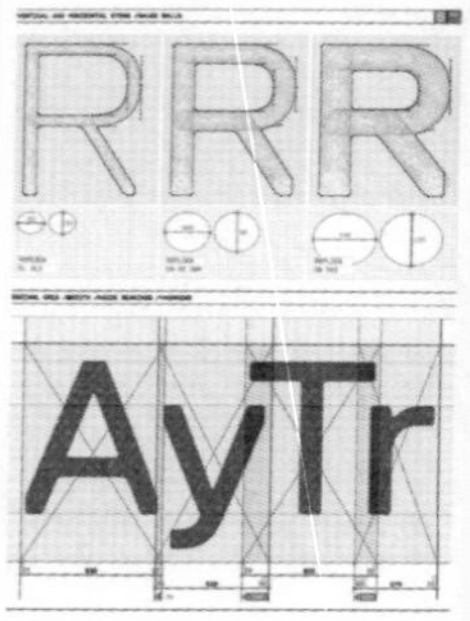

← P.330

← P.331

2008

OBAMA—PROGRESS/HOPE

Poster

Shepard Fairey (1970–)

Self-commissioned, U.S.

In a very short period of time Shepard Fairey's Obama poster, produced to demonstrate his allegiance to Barack Obama's 2008 presidential election campaign, has become an icon of twenty-first-century graphic design. Displaying a stylized illustration of the presidential candidate (based on a found image), coupled with the one-word text, the poster can be compared with the Pop art portraits of Andy Warhol or the conceptual works of Barbara Kruger. Allying a powerful simplicity to an optimistic message, the poster achieves a perfect synthesis of image and text to communicate the essence of the Obama vision.

Fairey is best known for his stenciled "Obey the Giant" posters and stickers, based on a photograph of a French wrestler, and other street-art and guerrilla-marketing techniques he originated in 1989. For this poster, Fairey began by selecting a suitable news photograph of Obama, looking, as the artist states, "wise but not intimidating." The image was then cropped and simplified by eliminating facial lines and background details, and red, white, and blue colors were added to emphasize its patriotic nature. The original edition, bearing the word "Progress," depicts Obama wearing one of Fairey's "Obey Giant" logos on his lapel. It was produced at Fairey's own expense and pasted up around Los Angeles, where he lived, and on his website. The response to the image was immense. Although wary of Fairey's notoriety as a street artist, the Obama campaign team asked for a new version carrying the word "Hope" to tie in with their campaign slogan, of which around three-hundred thousand copies were ultimately printed. Fairey later donated two more portraits of Obama to the campaign, bearing the words "Change" and "Vote."

Such was the popularity of the Obama poster that the National Portrait Gallery in Washington D.C. acquired a large (4 feet 11 inches [1.5 m] high) mixed-media stenciled collage version, and *Time* magazine commissioned Fairey to produce a portrait of the president-to-be for the cover of its 2008 "Person of the Year" issue.

2008

REPLICA

Typeface

Norm

Self-commissioned, Switzerland

Replica is a sans serif typeface created by Dimitri Bruni and Manuel Krebs of Zurich-based design studio Norm in 2008. Produced for text as well as for headlines and sign writing, the typeface is based on a technical concept that is not immediately obvious. This is partly why, in the same year, Lineto type foundry published the *Replica Specimen* booklet as a guide to understanding its characteristics.

Using FontLab, a standard piece of software for drawing typefaces, Norm mathematically limited Replica's grid. In place of seven hundred units as the standard height for capital letters, the grid was reduced to seventy units. Consequently, when drawing the typeface, Norm had fewer options for placing Bézier control points—anchor points used to create Bézier curves in vector graphics. This means, on a plane that would normally have one hundred points, they had only four. This arbitrary restriction affected the shape of each glyph, artificially simplifying the form of the typeface. A second, formal decision that affected the final typeface concerns the bevel. All the characters are cut off at the corners to eliminate right angles, with the result that when the typeface is small, it looks slightly damaged. The decision was taken to make the grid visible, as the corners are exactly the same width as a unit in the larger grid. Third, all the diagonals are cut vertically at the corners so that there are no pointed ends. This was done to make the letters more compact.

The name "Replica" has two important aspects. The first is the idea of a copy—when viewed in smaller sizes, the typeface looks familiar, but when enlarged its differences appear. The second meaning is a reference to the French word "réplique," which means a retort. In this case, Norm sees Replica as a sharp response to Helvetica, Univers, and Unica. The trend for many years had been in the opposite direction—to increase, using software, the detail and malleability of a drawing—and the restriction of drawing through the enlarging of the grid is a significant departure.

2008–present

APARTAMENTO

Magazine Cover

Apartamento

Apartamento Publishing, Spain

When *Apartamento* launched in 2008, it extended a theme that Joseph Holtzman's *Nest* had introduced more than a decade earlier. Like *Nest*, the Barcelona-based magazine is more interested in showing the modest homes of interesting people than the glamorous but vapid ones of wealthy, dull homeowners. The emphasis is on capturing behind-the-scenes glimpses into the lives of creative people and the places they eat and sleep in.

Founded by the Italian-Spanish trio Marco Velardi, Nacho Alegre, and Omar Sosa, the magazine began not as a commercial venture but rather as a hobby that called on their respective talents as editor-in-chief, creative director, and art director. Partly in reaction against a slick publishing culture that warns, "Look, but don't touch," *Apartamento* steers readers toward places they want to reach out and feel.

Connecting homes with their owners, the magazine embraces the clutter and chaos of normal life. It doesn't shy away from showing unmade beds, grubby kitchens, tangled hi-fi wires, or the jumbled contents of a medicine cabinet. Of course, it doesn't hurt that the homes on show are often owned by admired figures from the worlds of music, film, fashion, design, and art. Readers are presented Solange Knowles in her earth-toned downtown Hollywood loft, Molly Goddard breezing through her mid-century London pad, or Alessandro Mendini opening up the door to his Milanese atelier. Each issue is a piquant mix of voyeurism and style: nothing is for sale, but all is on show.

As such, the design relies on the images to convey character. On the cover sits a full-bleed photograph or illustration; text elements comprise the lowercase wordmark centered at the top, followed by a list of the issue's contributors, sometimes set in color. Inside, the simple grid accommodates the photographic imagery on a white background; occasional tinted pages are used to highlight thematic colors. Copy is largely narrated in fonts of Futura, interspersed with Clearface titles and accents of Plantin.

Still mostly a team of three, *Apartamento's* tight enterprise belies the devoted anticipation for each issue and consequent side projects, including books, film collaborations, and a survey volume by Abrams in 2018.

← P.332

2010

ACCESSIBLE ICON PROJECT

Information Design

Sara Hendren (1973–), Brian Glenney (1974–), Tim Ferguson Sauder (1972–)

Triangle, U.S.

The Accessible Icon Project, initiated by Sara Hendren and Brian Glenney, represents a practical yet significant step in graphic design focused on social change. This project reimagined the traditional symbol for disability—depicting a passive figure in a wheelchair—into a dynamic, forward-leaning one. The new icon advocates for a broader understanding and representation of disability.

Hendren and Glenney's approach blends graphic design with elements of street art and activism. They began by altering existing wheelchair-accessible-parking signs. This act of redesign was not solely focused on aesthetic enhancement; it also aimed to challenge and redefine the representation of people with disabilities in public signage.

Following some press coverage of the project, the designers were contacted by members of the public, who advocated for formalizing the icon. To achieve this, Hendren and Glenney partnered with graphic designer Tim Ferguson Sauder, who helped to transform the symbol from its grassroots origins into something refined and universally recognizable. This ensured not only that the icon would exist beyond a passing gesture but also that it would meet high design standards and could be applied in formal contexts. The team—none of whom is disabled—worked to validate its approach through involving people with disabilities in its development, thus ensuring that the icon authentically communicated the experiences of those it intended to represent.

Importantly, the project was available through an open-source model. By placing the icon in the public domain, the team encouraged its widespread adoption and adaptation, allowing it to evolve within different contexts worldwide. This approach demystifies the notion of design ownership, emphasizing community and inclusivity over proprietary interests. The project's success is evident in the symbol's global adoption and its inclusion in the permanent collection of the Museum of Modern Art, New York. However, it's crucial to reflect on the icon's focus on the wheelchair: while it is symbolic for mobility challenges, it does not fully represent the diversity of disabilities, which raises an ongoing conversation in the design community about inclusivity and representation.

← P.332

2010

WERK NO. 17: ELEY KISHIMOTO

Magazine / Newspaper

Theseus Chan (1961–), Joanne Lim (1982–)

WORK, Singapore

This special issue of *WERK* magazine, designed and published by Theseus Chan of the Singapore graphic design studio WORK, was a collaboration with Mark Eley and Wakako Kishimoto, of the UK-based fashion design studio Eley Kishimoto. Issue 17 was the latest of several collaborations with other fashion designer firms and artists, including Comme des Garçons, Colette, Adidas Originals, and the British artist Joe Magee. Each of the one thousand copies of Issue 17 had a unique cover: four pieces of fabric for the front and four for the back. Taken from Eley Kishimoto's collection, the sections of fabric were stapled to the front pages of the magazine and then fastened together with dressmakers' pins. According to Eley and Kishimoto, this gives the magazine the feeling of being a "textile work-in-progress." The result is a singular and highly tactile publication. Loose threads and other imperfections give the magazine a sense of the "perfect imperfect" to which Eley Kishimoto and Theseus Chan are both drawn.

Each copy was shrink-wrapped in plastic with a notice on the front in one of four colors (red, blue, yellow, or green), giving the title and specifications of the issue (336 pages, 8¾ × 12 inches [220 × 305 mm], etc.), as well as a warning to keep out of the reach of children. It cautions readers that the fabric will fray and alerts them to the pins, stating that "the impermanence is part of the process of the design."

Inside, the magazine begins with family photos from the childhoods of Eley and Kishimoto and carries on through to their wedding pictures. After this, the focus shifts to the pair's fashion-design work over the years up to their current collection at the time. Photographs and sketches dominate, from inspiration to screen artwork to finished product. There is very little text; when it appears it is brief and often in the form of an interview. The result is a unique magazine full of character that gives an insight into the lives and work of Eley and Kishimoto, including their love of fabrics and prints.

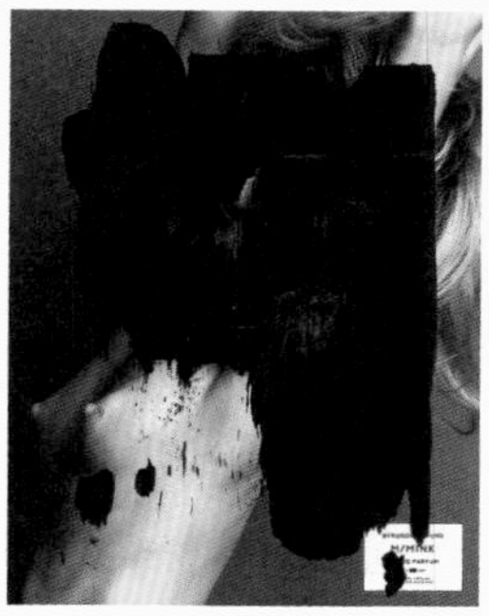

← P.333

2010

M/MINK

Advertising

Michaël Amzalag (1968–), Mathias Augustyniak (1967–)

Self-commissioned, France

The M/MINK project turns on its head the relationship between designer, client, and product. A perfumer would usually engage a graphic designer to produce packaging and advertising once a fragrance had been created. However, in this case the process was reversed, with Paris-based graphic design studio M/M approaching Stockholm-based Byredo fragrance house with a concept and a visual identity for a perfume, the result of which is M/MINK.

M/M's Michaël Amzalag and Mathias Augustyniak reappropriated a group of photographs by Inez van Lamsweerde and Vinoodh Matadin to create a series of striking promotional images. These high-fashion photos of beautiful men and women are partially obscured by black ink rolled over the surface, which evokes the look, feel, and even the smell of fresh ink. Although central to the product, these images (now available to download as iPhone, iPod Touch, and iPad wallpaper) arose at the end of an unusual process.

When Amzalag and Augustyniak first invited Byredo's founder, Ben Gorham, known for inventing abstract and extreme fragrances, to explore their concept, they presented him with only three objects to represent the materiality of their idea. A photograph showed a Japanese calligraphy master immersed in his art; an illustration set out their oversize fantastical formula for the creation of the new perfume, drawn on traditional Korean paper; and a stone that is ground and mixed with water to create ink, and that has its own particular scent.

Gorham agreed to the collaboration and, with the help of fellow perfumer Jérôme Epinette, translated these three items into a fragrance that matched the designers' original notion. Amzalag describes his first encounter with the scent: "In a restaurant before ordering lunch, [Gorham] sprayed us with what is now called M/MINK, and we had not one comment—it was perfect, surprising, beyond everything we had dreamt about."

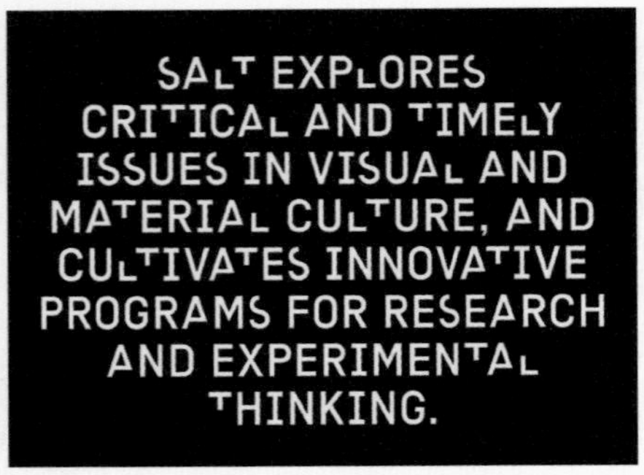

SALT EXPLORES CRITICAL AND TIMELY ISSUES IN VISUAL AND MATERIAL CULTURE, AND CULTIVATES INNOVATIVE PROGRAMS FOR RESEARCH AND EXPERIMENTAL THINKING.

← P.334

2011–present

SALT

Identity

Project Projects

SALT, Turkey

In 2011, New York design studio Project Projects, founded by Prem Krishnamurthy and Adam Michaels in 2004, and joined by Rob Giampietro in 2010, created an identity for Istanbul-based cultural institution SALT. Based on the idea of flux and temporality, it was created as an entity that would change with the passing of time.

Rather than create a logo that would remain static, Project Projects created a typeface called Kraliçe: anyone who asked for the institution's logo would be given the typeface and asked to type something with it. Kraliçe was based on a typeface called Queen by Berlin-based typographer Timo Gaessner. Gaessner and Project Projects collaborated on creating the new typeface, formed by removing parts of each letter of Queen.

In addition to this first version of the typeface, Project Projects arranged for certain letters to be replaced by new typefaces designed by special guest typographers. Each iteration retains the name Kraliçe but is followed by a new qualifying word. At the time of this book's publication, there were three versions: Kraliçe Open, the original version made with Gaessner; Kraliçe Marble with Dries Wiewauters; and Kraliçe Uncertain with Sulki & Min. By producing SALT's identity in this way, it is not only an evolving graphic marker but also a way of creating a community, with a new designer or design studio invited to participate every four months.

In order to control how the identity is applied, there is a manual that describes how to use grids, how to typeset and how the system will change over time. Integral to this system, SALT's website has also been designed to be flexible and to evolve. It is ordered according to page and tag, and organized without a strict hierarchy, while a modular system allows administrators a fluid layout.

By basing the SALT identity on a changing typeface as opposed to a static one, Project Projects has invented a way for graphic designers to engage with their clients while creating their graphic identity.

← P.334

2011–2012

100 NOTES—100 THOUGHTS

Book

Leftloft

Documenta, Germany

The "100 Notes—100 Thoughts" project represents a near-perfect marriage of form to content and concept. This series of one hundred notebooks served both to expand the reach of and build anticipation for the *dOCUMENTA (13)* art exhibition in Kassel, Germany, in June 2012.

Commissioned by Documenta's artistic director Carolyn Christov-Bakargiev, with Chus Martínez and Bettina Funcke, the series was designed by Italian design company Leftloft, utilizing the same visual grammar that the firm brought to the exhibition's "nonidentity" and website. The repetition and consistency of typeface and layout from the cover of one notebook to the next created a rigid structure, which was offset by the use of differently colored paper, and contrasted with the variety of form and content within each notebook. This fitting treatment for a variety of ideas in an information age also acted as an embodiment of the notes' call—as defined by the organizers—"to suspend analysis in favor of skeptical speculation." The variety of authors, from fields as diverse as art, science, philosophy, anthropology, political theory, and poetry, were thus represented simply by their names in a light slab serif and a number on one of the projects' three cover sizes. Inside, however, readers experienced a wealth of ideas and jumping-off points—facsimiles of existing notebooks, commissioned essays, collaborations, and conversations—all meant to capture a process-based view of art, set in or supported by straightforward typography and photography.

The notebooks were published by Hatje Cantz, mostly in sixteen- to forty-eight-page print and e-book editions, and released in five rounds of approximately twenty notebooks per round, between April 2011 and May 2012. Venues in Cairo, New York, Buenos Aires, Thessaloniki, Paris, Oslo, and other cities hosted launch events. A natural step from five years earlier, when ninety diverse publications explored the motifs and themes of *documenta 12*, the range of ideas and broad nature of the *dOCUMENTA (13)* notebooks ensured that the themes would carry through over the next five years to the exhibition's fourteenth iteration.

← P.335

2013

BLACK LIVES MATTER

Logo

Design Action Collective

Alicia Garza, U.S.

Black Lives Matter (BLM), a slogan now synonymous with worldwide calls for racial and social justice, and an end to police brutality, originates from the movement of the same name, which began in 2013 after a neighborhood-watch coordinator, George Zimmerman, fatally shot an unarmed Black teenager, Trayvon Martin. The founders of the movement, Alicia Garza, Patrisse Cullors, and Opal Tometi, initially set up BLM as a hashtag and call to action, but over the following three years—as incidents of racial profiling and police violence against Black people increased—they expanded the premise to form a nationwide network of more than thirty local chapters.

As with many other social movements, the visual manifestation of BLM is rooted in protest imagery and signage. The original branding for the movement was created by a California-based design studio, Design Action Collective, which partners with socially minded groups and organizations. Asked to come up with an identity in just three days, the team devised a straightforward logo that was legible, instantly identifiable, and easily reproduced. Their main concern was creating something that people within the movement could also paint or draw by hand, to apply it to ephemera, such as placards, leaflets, and other protest signage.

The simple wordmark uses Anton—a new take on a traditional advertising sans-serif typeface—and renders all letters uppercase. Although the wordmark is often seen in black and white, the original version features black letters against a yellow background, creating what team designer Josh Warren-White has referred to as a "bold, strong, and militant" impression. The very first iteration of the logo also included an illustration of a person holding a dandelion seed head, with blown seeds symbolizing the origins of a movement.

More than a decade later, as the movement has moved from grassroots to mainstream, there is still significant work to be done. For BLM's founders, the slogan and symbol—adopted by individuals and corporations alike—must not ring hollow; it necessitates decisive action and a commitment to change at all levels. As cofounder Garza explains, "If we don't say what we mean and mean what we say, what are we actually fighting for?"

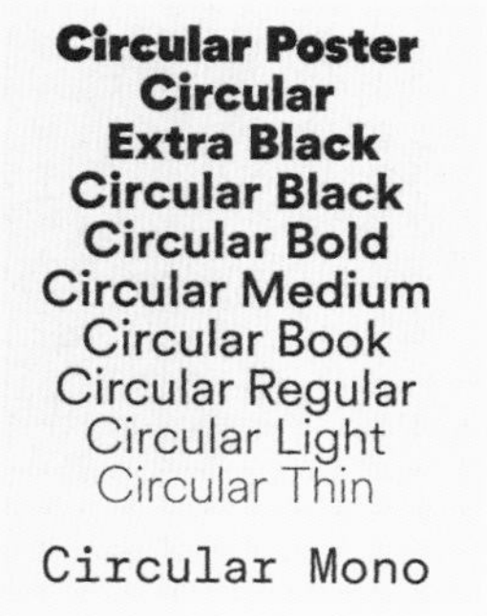

← P.336

2013

CIRCULAR

Typeface

Laurenz Brunner (1980–)

Lineto, Switzerland

Developed over a seven-year period and released in 2013, Circular was Laurenz Brunner's second published sans-serif typeface, following his celebrated Akkurat of 2004. Circular is a contemporary take on classic geometric sans serifs, such as Paul Renner's iconic Futura, but, as Brunner describes it, "with a less dogmatic approach." The effect echoes the Swiss Design Award jury's observation that Brunner's work sits "exactly between tradition and modernization."

The Circular font is issued in a family of eight weights that graduate from the whispered nuance of Circular Thin to the chunky application of Extra Black. Its elegant and adaptable character allows for varied design applications that flex from brand identities to editorial uses, indie films, fanzines, or packaging. Typical of a classic grotesque letterform treatment, all strokes of Circular share a similar width that gives the family a spare, rhythmic look and feel.

The Swiss designer cut his teeth studying at Central Saint Martins in the early 2000s, where he crafted his breakthrough typeface Akkurat, which won a 2006 Swiss Federal Design Award. He later graduated from Amsterdam's Rietveld Academie, soon after designing a catalog trilogy for *The Most Beautiful Swiss Books*, based on the themes of past, present, and future. His approach has been honed through a career working with some of the world's leading fine-art institutions, such as Tate Modern and documenta, as well as clients of design and popular culture, including *Fantastic Man* magazine and the *New York Times*.

Brunner's Swiss heritage is reflected in his graphic aesthetic and his ability to design a large font family in a rational way. This lends itself to Circular's likable rounded character and its legibility, characteristics that have seen the typeface used by companies including Spotify, AirBnB, and Alphabet, Google's parent company. Brunner has released three typefaces, including Bradford (2018), through Swiss type foundry Lineto, of which he is a member.
In 2022 he launched Source Type, a platform for typographic research and visual literacy, through which he has published Rapid (2022), Karl (2022), and Reform (2023). He is now based in Zurich and leads his eponymous studio.

← P.336

2013

DAVID BOWIE—THE NEXT DAY

Record / CD Cover

Barnbrook

Sony Music Entertainment, U.S.

Acclaimed British graphic designer Jonathan Barnbrook had a long working relationship with music icon David Bowie, collaborating with him on four album covers and other visual branding associated with Bowie's music and persona. These albums span from 2002 to 2016 and include *Heathen*, *Reality*, *The Next Day*, and *Blackstar*. Each one visually pushed the envelope of record-cover design, proving divisive among critics and fans but staying true to Bowie's avant-garde approach to music. Of the covers that Barnbrook worked on with Bowie, he says that *The Next Day*, released in 2013 and marking Bowie's return from a ten-year recording hiatus, proved to be the most polarizing.

The cover features an altered version of the artwork used for Bowie's 1977 album *"Heroes"*, with a white square obscuring the artist's face. The *"Heroes"* title is also crossed out, leaving only Bowie's name in the upper-right-hand corner and the new album's title in the middle of the white square, rendered in Barnbrook's own sans serif typeface, Doctrine. The design as a whole is minimal yet striking, with the conscious act of "defacing" the old artwork, posing questions about the nature of art, identity, reinvention, and the passage of time.

Created in the strictest secrecy, the album design was accompanied by a viral marketing campaign, disseminated in guerrilla-like style. Wheat-pasted posters and billboards popped-up in cities worldwide, customized to their individual markets; obscure ads featuring out-of-context song lyrics appeared in daily newspapers. The white-box motif became an instant internet meme, with fans applying it to their self-portraits circulated online.

The album cover is rendered in black-and-white, hinting at notions of erasure and obscurity, which is offset by an inner sleeve in color. Inside the record, a contemporary portrait of Bowie is also covered by a white square and accompanied by the words, "And the next day. And the next. And another day." Barnbrook says these artworks play with "image expectation," subverting the accepted formula of an updated portrait of the artist. It is a fitting riposte from an artist who has consistently fought against societal trends and expectations, and it marked a triumphant return for one of pop music's most enigmatic and beloved creators.

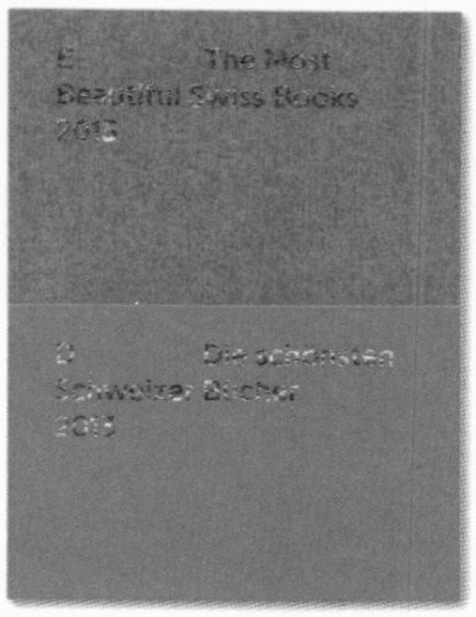

← P.337

2014

THE MOST BEAUTIFUL SWISS BOOKS 2013

Book

Maximage

Federal Office of Culture, Switzerland

The Most Beautiful Swiss Books is a celebrated annual award from the Swiss Federal Office of Culture (FOC) that recognizes exemplary publications designed, produced, or published in Switzerland. Further celebrating the art of bookmaking, the FOC publishes the prize-winning works in a catalog, which in 2013 was designed by Swiss studio Maximage.

Employing a heavily exploratory approach, Maximage sought to innovate the typical catalog design, treating the book as one large test print that could function as a guide for other designers and printers. The processes on display range from CMYK and Sixplex printing to varnishes and manipulated or enhanced image screens, such as halftone. Printed offset, the book's experimental color combinations and graphic interventions push the limits of reprographic techniques. This strategy not only harnessed the possibilities of print production but also reanimated the form and content of each featured title, enabling an entirely different reading of the work.

Such experimentation is entirely characteristic of the studio, which was cofounded by Julien Tavelli and David Keshavjee in 2009, upon graduating from the École cantonale d'art de Lausanne (ECAL). The duo have previously described their outlook as combining "emotions and technology": being technically skilled as well as embracing human error and creative sensitivity. To achieve this, they sometimes adopt tricks of the trade; at other times they create their own tools to produce the graphic language they seek for a project.

Interrupting the usual linear process that runs from computer to printing plate has become their signature, as has the pairing of high and low technology, which can be traced back to their early work. One example is *Typeface as Program* (2009), a book that evolved from their graduate project and explored type design through both digital and analog (woodcut) methods. Maximage's investigative design sensibility carries through in subsequent publications, including *Color Library* (2018), an homage to the craft of color printing, and *Salutary Failures* (2021), a monograph on the work of Swiss artist Raphael Hefti. In recognition of the studio's contribution to graphic design, it has received multiple Swiss Design Awards and was honored with the prestigious Jan Tschichold Award in 2020.

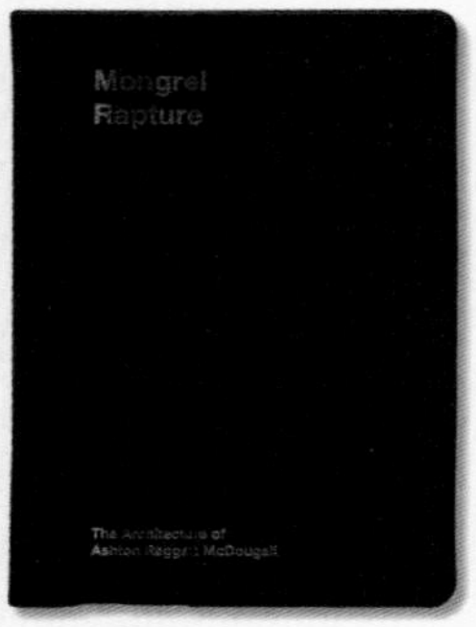

← P.338

← P.339

← P.340

2015

MONGREL RAPTURE: THE ARCHITECTURE OF ASHTON RAGGATT MCDOUGALL

Book

Stuart Geddes (1975–), ARM Architecture

Uro Publications, Australia

This volume—part manifesto, part archive—charts the work of Ashton Raggatt McDougall (ARM), Australian architecture's *enfants terribles*. Published by Uro in 2015, *Mongrel Rapture* marks the firm's Australian Institute of Architects Gold Medal win and riffs on the idea of the "good book" with a hefty tome of 1,616 pages wrapped in a floppy black-leather cover and printed on wafer-thin paper stock.

ARM commissioned Stuart Geddes to translate their survey opus into print. Melbourne-based Geddes is a leading Australian designer with a distinguished graphic language, *Mongrel Rapture* being a case in point. This doorstopper of a book took three years to create and is delivered in "stealth" mode, disguised by its 11⅞ × 6⅞-inches (250 × 175 mm) format and innovative production methods.

Geddes and ARM's team, led by director Mark Raggatt, sought an alternative to a generic architecture monograph that would also make the vast content legible. A genius move was to employ ivory-colored bible paper (*scritta*) to convey the dense information without adding unwieldy bulk. The paper stock was fine-tuned on press to achieve its saturated finish without compromising the delicate pages.

A single thumb-index tab aids navigation through the book's mass; similarly, rainbow backgrounds organize the seven chapters and range from ultraviolet to blood red. The colors share analogies with the content—blue for building blueprints, for instance—while more oblique connections are underpinned by the hues of ARM's buildings. An oil slick of foil on the cover reinterprets the classic gilt finish of a Bible.

Wrangling more than thirty years of prolific practice across images, interventions, text, and drawings, Geddes exercises graphic restraint—from limited typefaces to image rules for inset, spliced, and threshold treatments—that provides design structure across the quantity of material and pages. *Mongrel Rapture* is predominantly set in Union and Larish Neue, with essays in Stanley, but Geddes created a new font to annotate drawings by the three founders, resulting in the "Not Ashton's, Raggatt's, nor McDougall's Handwriting" typeface.

Mongrel Rapture won Geddes a Pinnacle award from the Australian Graphic Design Association and two 2016 Australian Book Design Awards.

2017–present

MOLD

Magazine / Newspaper

Eric Hu (1989–), Matthew Tsang (1986–)

MOLD, U.S.

Founded and launched online by LinYee Yuan in 2013, *MOLD* explores the busy intersection of food and design. Known for its "anti-foodie" approach to the subject, the magazine seeks to provide a new framework for understanding and engaging with the things that we eat, particularly through the lens of food security. The first print issue of *MOLD* was released in 2017 following a successful Kickstarter campaign that appealed to the future of food: "By the year 2030, if we keep eating how we eat today, people around the world will be born into starvation," the pitch read. After securing funding, Yuan was keen to commission a designer whose work could reflect *MOLD*'s progressive approach; this search brought her to Eric Hu.

Based in New York, Hu has also worked as global design director at Nike and director of design at fashion retailer SSENSE. Thoughtful and forward-facing, his personal approach was a natural match for Yuan's vision. Hu was drawn to the project's subject; for him, as an Asian American, food and its representation of culture has always been inherently political. For *MOLD*'s first issue, themed "Designing for the Human Microbiome," Hu worked alongside his SSENSE colleague Matthew Tsang to create a memorable debut release. The cover features a layered, energetic design that sets the tone for the publication's experimental visual language. The decorative, twisting forms of the Gyrator typeface used for the title are countered with a clean Swiss sans serif for the subheadings, while the bold red of the polka-dot pattern pops against the darker, cooler aqua and gold tones beneath. The result feels like an expressive blend of science, art, and design, speaking to the emergent strains within *MOLD*'s study of food innovation.

Inside, features on fermentation sculptures, ingestible dyes, and a "Digestive Car" powered by methane gas provide the foundation for engaging layouts, where overscaled titles overlap and interact with imagery and text. The color palette is predominantly monochromatic, allowing the photography to take center stage, while the images feature a hypersaturated, Surrealist aesthetic, made popular by magazines such as the *Gourmand*, alongside more traditional documentary shots that complement the scientific and cultural rigor of *MOLD*'s editorial.

2018

DREAM CRAZY

Advertising

Weiden+Kennedy

Nike, U.S.

In 2018, to celebrate the thirtieth anniversary of Nike's famed "Just Do It" slogan, created by advertising agency Wieden+Kennedy (W+K) in 1988, the sportswear brand released a special campaign. Titled "Dream Crazy," it sought to spotlight athletes of all ages and abilities across the world who rose to prominence despite seemingly unrealistic ambitions. The campaign was primarily composed of a series of short films, produced by Park Pictures, as well as physical and digital posters created by W+K that each feature the profile of a different athlete from across the world of sports.

One of the key protagonists of the "Dream Crazy" message is Colin Kaepernick, a National Football League player and civil rights activist, who garnered worldwide attention in 2016 after he repeatedly knelt during the playing of the U.S. national anthem in protest against racial injustice and police brutality. Kaepernick's poster, as with others in the series, features an intimate portrait along with a tagline that alludes to his story, reading: "Believe in something, even if it means sacrificing everything." In line with Nike's trademark approach to its "Just Do It" campaigns, the visual style is powerfully simple: a punchy piece of messaging to accompany an equally evocative image and the brand's iconic "Swoosh" logo.

Predominantly captured in black and white, the photography for the posters speaks to the way in which history had been made by each of the athletes featured. Occasional color portraits expand the palette of the series while retaining a cinematic aesthetic. These are overlaid with white text rendered in the typeface Palatino Light. Originally drawn by German designer Hermann Zapf in 1949, Palatino is an old-style serif that has risen to prominence over the years due in part to its use as Nike's signature typeface. Here, its classic letterforms complement the poster's minimalist composition and humanist spirit, helping it to accentuate the athlete and their personal narrative of success, as well as offering a universal appeal to anyone whose dreams have ever been doubted.

← P.341

2019–present

WORMS

Magazine / Newspaper

Clem MacLeod (1995–), Caitlin McLoughlin (1996–)

Worms Magazine, UK

Founded by Clem MacLeod in 2019, Worms is a London-based print publisher that champions female, nonbinary, and underrepresented writers. It launched with *Worms* magazine, its main publication, which similarly aims to amplify and give access to marginalized voices and readers. With eight issues released between 2019 and 2023, *Worms* has featured the work of emerging talents, as well as more established authors, such as Olivia Laing, Chris Kraus, and Kathy Acker. In an interview with the fashion-education platform *1 Granary*, MacLeod explained, "On the surface *Worms* is a magazine about books and writing, but what it really explores is ideas of identity and the formation of the self."

Working alongside MacLeod is coeditor and designer Caitlin McLoughlin, who helped to evolve the DIY look that aligns with the magazine's roots in zine culture. Printed on a risograph, largely in black and white, the overall aesthetic is decidedly punky and handmade. The spare use of color is concentrated on the covers, where neons play off against grainy monochrome, and fuzzy portraits are framed by a quirky cast of characters and other playful elements. The scribbled *Worms* wordmark, in a whimsical hand-drawn font designed by Jonas Pequeno, constantly changes position across the front of the magazine.

Interiors receive the same lo-fi treatment; texts are animated through an unrestricted grid and a liberal use of pull quotes that—alongside illustrations, photography, and more hand-drawn fonts—make the content feel fluid and dynamic, like the movement of a worm. With each new issue breaking the irregular mold of the previous one, *Worms* subverts the characteristics of stuffiness and rigidity traditionally associated with literary magazines. The design is a fitting partner to the exploratory nature of the content. Themes range from psychogeography to humor, from biomythology to impurity. MacLeod has admitted that she, somewhat self-indulgently, uses each issue to dive into a subject that she wants to learn more about, educating herself and everyone else along the way.

In addition to the magazine, Worms publishes books, hosts book clubs, and has programmed a series of listening and writing events called "Ear Worms" at the Institute of Contemporary Art, London.

← P.342

2019–present

DWELLER

Poster

Hassan Rahim (1987–), Bryant Wells (1990–), David Lee (1996–)

Dweller, U.S.

Hassan Rahim is an artist, designer, and creative director from California who now lives and works in Brooklyn, New York. Collaborating with other artists, institutions, and various commercial clients, he draws on a broad range of influences and inspirations, including skateboarding, car culture, art, and hip hop, and his work is characterized by dark, esoteric imagery that seamlessly blends digital and physical media. Rahim describes his approach as slow, thoughtful, and "anti-disciplinary."

Dweller is a seminal techno festival that takes place each February in Brooklyn. Founded in 2019 by Frankie Decaiza Hutchinson—who also helped to set up Discwoman, a DJ-booking agent for female and nonbinary talent—Dweller platforms Black electronic artists working in a music genre that has traditionally lacked diversity or an acknowledgment of its Black origins. A statement on Dweller's website reads: "We strive to be a black lighthouse; a siren in the storm for those who know the isolating whitewaters of electronic all too well." Rahim joined forces with Dweller to create its visual identity, and has since spearheaded the graphic design for each festival.

Rahim worked alongside co-designers Bryant Wells and David Lee to craft an aesthetic that is excessively dark and digital. Exploring the frenetic visual language of dance scenes from across the diaspora, a series of posters dips between the informational and the cinematic. For the festival's third year, the design functions on a system of dots and dashes reminiscent of early computer-generated images and Morse code. This is complemented by the monospace typeface, recalling the pixelated lettering found on concert tickets and LED displays. The fourth year's design was sparer in its styling, with halos of light casting their surroundings into an abyss of blackness—a euphoric club moment. Although nodding to their pre-internet precedents, the posters are very much a product of the 2020s. The effect keeps step with Rahim's wider portfolio, which stealthily treads the lines between maximalist and refined, warmly nostalgic and piercingly futuristic. In this way he joins the anachronistic tradition of Black speculative fiction that techno itself is also a product of—a lineage that Detroit techno mainstays the Underground Resistance describe as "Hi-Tech Soul."

← P.343

2020

ABC MAXI

Typeface

Dinamo

Dinamo Typefaces, Germany

Dinamo is a Swiss type-design agency established in 2012 by Johannes Breyer and Fabian Harb. The Berlin-based studio has built a reputation for designing and licensing conceptually driven, characterful typefaces with the help of its sprawling network of global collaborators. Its ABC Maxi family, which the designers describe as "warm and witty," owes a debt to the teachings of Swiss architect and designer Max Bill, as well as interwar type developments, such as the "universal typography" systems that fascinated Herbert Bayer and Jan Tschichold. For them, the notion of a standard universal alphabet was an attempt to translate the spoken word graphically. By dispensing with the differentiations between majuscules and minuscules (upper and lower cases), they sought to simplify comprehension of the written word.

Maxi was designed with these strong precedents in mind. Created by Breyer and Harb, alongside Andree Paat, it began with the digitization of Bill's type experiments and since then has passed through four iterations that subtly altered the letter weights and expanded its font families. The alphabet now includes four subfamilies: Round, Round Mono, Sharp, and Sharp Mono, with three styles in each (Light, Regular, and Bold). This variety in letterform provides many playful combinations that can stretch and flex to animated effect. From the thin wriggling Round "M" to the chamfered edges of the Sharp "R," the typeface is alive with what Dinamo describes as "spaghetti movements and angular lines."

Of particular note are the vowel letterforms that translate Bill's linguistic theory, which suggested that a visual emphasis on vowels increased legibility in print. In this case, many of the font's counter spaces are small in comparison to the strokes, giving the letters a chunky appearance. Other sources of inspiration included Josef Müller-Brockmann's 1958 CWS wordmark and Marlyse Schmid and Bernard Müller's 1981 Swatch logo. ABC Maxi's inherent variability means it has been adopted for designs that range from Dinamo's branded packaging tape to the film titles of Joji Koyama's *Kuro* (2017) and the headlines of *Tate Etc.* magazine.

← P.343

2020–present

MSCHF MAG

Magazine / Newspaper

Shira Inbar (1988–), MSCHF

MSCHF, U.S.

MSCHF is a Brooklyn-based collective of self-proclaimed "mischief makers" and conversation starters that works across a range of mediums and outputs, including art, fashion, and publishing. Among the last is a quarterly publication titled *MSCHF Mag*, which serves as a space to share various cultural observations, as well as tips and tricks on exploiting power structures. The magazine is also a creative playground for the MSCHF members, bearing a visual style that draws on a wide range of their influences, from post-internet art to DIY zine culture.

Several of the past issues were designed by New York–based graphic designer and image maker Shira Inbar, who brought her bold, shape-shifting style to bear on the magazine. Never one to be tied down to a specific aesthetic, Inbar has an approach that naturally matched *MSCHF Mag's* quirky, rebellious spirit. Featuring the group's distorted, ever-changing logotype, which was designed by Christina Bull, Inbar's range of covers defy convention with their playful compositions and unruly use of color and texture. Volume 6 of the publication, for example, stands out through its holographic finish, whereas Volume 4 (pictured) provokes with a lurid green palette forming a backdrop for the Sims-like figures scattered like ants across the cover.

Inside, the magazine presents a smorgasbord of visual styles, surprising and amusing readers with each turn of the page. Treading a conscious line between editorial and advertorial, Inbar's spreads are packed with a dizzying mix of stock photography, high-gloss corporate imagery, and retro internet artwork. Tawdry typefaces draw attention to each word on the page and sit within busy layouts that highlight MSCHF's irreverent attitude. Nearly every element in the publication is big, bold, and more closely aligned with the visual language of billboard advertisements and TV infomercials than that of traditional magazine editorial style. As such, *MSCHF Mag* is able to wear the disguises of the very systems that it satirizes in its content.

← P.344

2021

KUSINA MAI / KUSINA MAI FUTI

Poster

Nontsikelelo Mutiti (1982–)

Self-commissioned, Zimbabwe

As a visual artist and educator, Nontsikelelo Mutiti has an interdisciplinary practice driven by an intention to elevate the practices of Black peoples past, present, and future. After graduating from Saki Mafundikwa's renowned Zimbabwe Institute of Vigital Arts, she received an MFA from Yale School of Art, where she became the director of graduate studies for graphic design in 2022. Mutiti explains that her work "traverses the boundaries of fine art, design, and public engagement." Applying this broad spectrum of expertise to her teaching is key, as she declared that Yale students "receive an education unrivalled in vision, breadth, and relevance—one that challenges them to exceed their own aspirations."

Mutiti has collaborated with the artist Simone Leigh, the Centre for Contemporary Art in Lagos, and New York's New Museum. Her self-commissioned *Kusina Mai / Kusina Mai Futi* diptych was produced at the community-led Robert Blackburn Printmaking Workshop in New York (the oldest such establishment in the United States). The print stands out for its meandering, experimental letterforms; the braided shapes were designed in a modular way to produce a range of patterns and characters. The work forms part of Mutiti's wider research project, "Ruka" (meaning to knit, braid, or weave, in the regional Shona language), which correlates the intricacies of African hair-braiding methodology with digital image-making and technology. This focus manifests in other projects, such as the website Morning 0, which displays the transcript of a hair-braiding appointment in Johannesburg.

The diptych's title comes from the phrase "Kusina Mai Hakuendwe" (roughly, "You do not go where your mother is not"), originating within the spiritual practice of Chivanhu. The expression speaks to the dangers of going somewhere without the support that a mother might offer, such as protection or wisdom, and reflects Mutiti's own experiences as an immigrant. The way the *Kusina Mai* letterforms fit together suggest that family can be constructed in different ways, as long as the value of culture and heritage is retained. The print was made in 2021, when the artist had spent pandemic-induced time away from her family, and it prompts the question: how can art connect us to home?

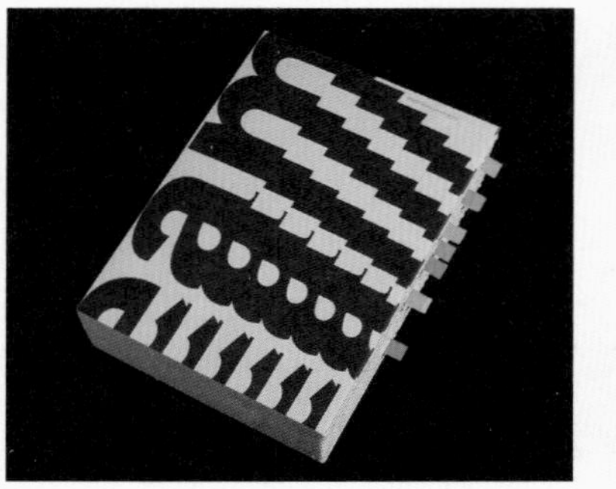

← P.346

2021

DAYDREAM: JUMPING HE

Book

Jianping He (1973–)

V&A Gallery at Design Society, Shenzhen, China

Jianping He, also known by his artist moniker, Jumping He, is a German-Chinese graphic designer, professor, and publisher. Based in Berlin, with a satellite office in Hangzhou, China, He has received numerous awards for his work, including a D&AD Yellow Pencil and a Gold Prize at the International Poster Biennial. Since 2005 he has also been a member of the Alliance Graphique Internationale (AGI). His works have been displayed around the world in more than fifty exhibitions, including at the V&A Museum in London and the Centre Pompidou in Paris. The output of his design studio, Hesign, spans publishing, graphic design, spatial design, and curation and is characterized by its melding of the zeitgeist of European culture with the traditions of Asian culture.

In 2021 He opened an exhibition in Shenzhen, China, to showcase a collection of works made between 1995 and 2020. The exhibition was divided into nine categories: montage, the indeterminate, mountains and water, faces, typography, art, reading, identity, and curation. Alongside the show, He produced a catalog titled *Daydream: Jumping He*, spread across 678 pages and following the same categorization. Like the exhibition, the book demonstrates He's expansive and prolific approach to design, exploring his thoughts and concepts, as well as his mixing of styles, forms, and content. Following its release, the book received an ADC award and a Red Dot Design Award.

Daydream plays with dimensions and materiality. Although its main purpose is to be a pragmatic guide to He's practice, it is also a work of art in and of itself. The deckle-edge pages create a rough and tactile object and are mirrored in the front cover's jagged letterforms, spread across like a deck of cards. As if applied by an eager student, fluorescent tabs protrude from the side of the book, marking the various sections and adding function, and each turn of the page offers something new: several inserts, tissue-paper fold-outs, and pop-ups, most strikingly. Combined, these elements make for a truly special experience, presenting He's oeuvre in a clever, multidimensional way while serving as proof of his masterful understanding of the book as an object.

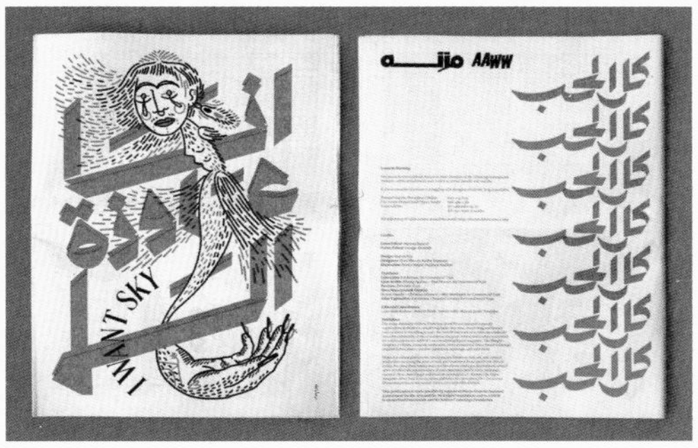

← P.347

2021

I WANT SKY

Magazine / Newspaper

Wael Morcos (1986–), Rouba Yammine (1993–), Haitham Haddad (1989–)

Mizna, Asian American Writers Workshop (AAWW), U.S.

In 2020 Egyptian activist Sarah Hegazi took her own life after being imprisoned and tortured by the Egyptian government as punishment for flying a rainbow Pride flag at a music event. The following year, nonprofit arts organization Mizna partnered with the Asian American Writers' Workshops to create *I Want Sky*, a book celebrating Hegazy's life and work as well as the lives of all LGBTQ+ Arabs and people of the Southwest Asian and North African (SWANA) region and its diaspora. The book comes in print and digital editions, and features prose and poems from a range of contributors and illustrations from Haitham Haddad of Palestinian graphic-design studio Mnjnk.

I Want Sky was designed by Jon Key and Wael Morcos of Brooklyn-based studio Morcos Key, whose practice specializes in creating "visual systems that demonstrate how thoughtful conversation and formal expression make for impactful design." Their approach to this project was no different, striking a balance between traditional editorial design and grid-breaking experimentalism. A key focus of the design was the formatting of the text, which was treated as a flexible, shape-shifting component. Contrasting typefaces of different sizes, colors, and languages—including Lyon Text in both Latin and Arabic, as well as custom lettering by Morcos—sit alongside one another, highlighting particular passages and helping the writing to flow not just figuratively but also literally. Many of the titles are displayed in rounded forms reminiscent of the rainbow symbol on Hegazi's flag. After graduating from Notre Dame University in Lebanon, Morcos spent three years specializing in the development of bilingual Latin-Arabic typefaces, making him the perfect partner for such an intimate and honest portrayal of the Arab experience.

Haddad's haunting and evocative illustrations use a strict color palette of red, green, black, and white—the colors of the Palestinian flag—to capture the stories, characters, and concepts found throughout *I Want Sky*. His style, characterized by bold lines and ethereal expressions, adds another rich layer of narrative to a publication already brimming with deeply personal writing and storytelling.

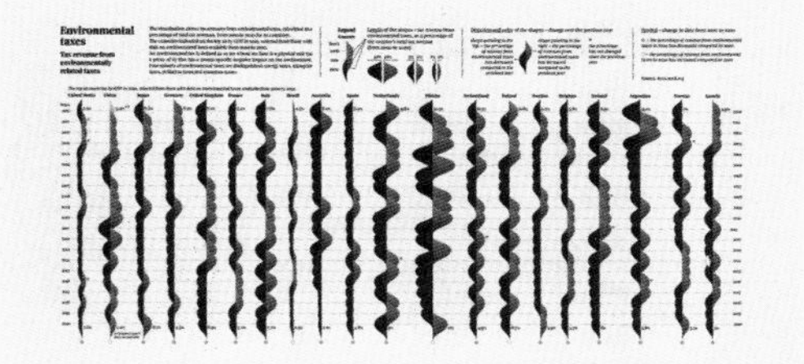

← P.348

2022

ENVIRONMENTAL TAXES

Information Design

Federica Fragapane (1988–)

La Lettura, Corriere della Sera, Italy

Federica Fragapane's "Environmental Taxes" represents in tax terms the negative impacts of climate change and environmental-resource stress, as registered by the world's wealthiest nations. Designed for Italian newspaper *Corriere della Sera*'s weekly cultural magazine *La Lettura*, this regular commission sees Fragapane propose and interpret topics that have ranged from literary villains in the manner of Dante to a catalog of famous paintings stolen since 1900.

Fragapane approaches data visualization as story-telling. Adopting refined graphic markers as tools, she aims to show how to interpret typically complex information. This example conveys how much each nation pays, as a percentage of total tax revenue, for its negative environmental impacts, which include energy, transport, pollution, and resources.

This data set from the Organization for Economic Cooperation and Development (OECD) is illustrated through a series of wriggling spines rendered in green hues. They show how much and when twenty nations with the highest gross domestic product (GDP), within a set of countries with available data, increased or reduced their tax revenue for environmental impacts. Organized vertically over a twenty-year period from 2000 to 2020, each nation's line bends right (light green) or swerves left (dark green) in response to positive or negative change, respectively. For example, Turkey's pronounced left-and-right oscillations hover at about 10 percent, whereas Brazil's register sits between 1.5 and 2.3 percent, which creates barely a ripple down its spine.

Rose-pink-colored circles below the green spines detail whether each country's environmental taxes have increased or decreased since 2000, and is respectively empty or full, representing this change over time. What these symbols indicate is that only four countries have increased their environmental-tax spending in this period: a sobering piece of data in our age of global warming.

Fragapane takes her role as a communicator seriously, placing it on a par with other forms of journalistic reporting. But, while a journalist uses words to describe events, her visualizations convey news through design. In this way we are reminded that there is a human hand and a subjectivity behind the numbers; they are not merely statistics.

← P.350

2022

EYES ON IRAN

Poster

Mahvash Mostala (1955–), Hank Willis Thomas (1976–), et al.

For Freedoms, Vital Voices, U.S.

In New York City on December 3, 2022, a banner flew amid the skyscrapers. Stemming from a collaboration between Hank Willis Thomas's non-profit, For Freedoms, the Iranian artists Shirin Neshat and Mahvash Mostala, and the French photographer and artist JR, among others, "Eyes on Iran" was an art activation project launched to coincide with the United Nation's campaign, "16 Days of Activism Against Gender-Based Violence."

The project was initiated after three months of worldwide protests, sparked by the death in custody of twenty-two-year-old Mahsa Amini, an Iranian woman who was arrested and detained in Tehran by the country's morality police for wearing her headscarf "incorrectly." The rules regarding the wearing of hijab were mandated under Iran's penal code following the 1979 Islamic revolution; any deviation from this can result in arrest or worse.

The series of installations happened in and around the Franklin D. Roosevelt Four Freedoms State Park and included a mural by Neshat of an eye looking toward the UN complex, urging the world to keep its eyes on Iran. Another installation saw aerial banners by Thomas and Mostala crisscross the city's skyline; Mostala's featured an eye underlined by the phrase, "Woman, Life, Freedom," the call-to-arms slogan of the protests. The eye's pupil reflected a self-portrait of Mostala and the Farsi word for "Woman" (زن). First presented above Miami during the Art Basel art fair, the flying billboards were brought to New York to raise awareness for the UN vote on Iran's membership on the Commission on the Status of Women.

On December 14, 2022, the UN passed a resolution to oust the Islamic Republic of Iran from the commission because it "continuously undermines and increasingly suppresses the human rights of women and girls." At a time when many protesters have been killed or are facing the death penalty, the UN's vote was critical in retracting support for the state.

As Mostala explained, "This piece is in solidarity with the Iranian Woman, especially the young generation, who have fiercely brought the voice of the Iranian Woman to the global stage. This moment in our history is a defining reflection of the strength of Iranian women all over the world."

← P.350

2023

THE POSTMODERN CHILD (PART 2)

Poster

Everyday Practice

Museum of Contemporary Art Busan, South Korea

Founded by Joonho Kwon, Kyung-chul Kim, and Eojin Kim, Everyday Practice is a studio that relates its design work to the realities of the modern world. When asked in December 2022 to design a visual identity for the *Postmodern Child* exhibition at the Museum of Contemporary Art Busan, which attempted to question the validity of universally accepted methods of child-rearing and development, the studio centered their approach on unconstrained typography to convey the idea of being freed from the established order.

The exhibition was split into two parts. The first was concerned with how being a child is inevitably connected with being subject to discipline, and it argued that the modern way of raising children denies the unique nature of each child. The second part posited that the multiplicities of existence can only be harnessed if we reject this point of view, thus freeing ourselves from the modern.

Everyday Practice reinforced the show's critique of universality with an identity that embraced a postmodern style, drawing on a lineage popularized by such practitioners as the Memphis Group and April Greiman. The designs for Part 1 were clothed in a witty visual language, replete with hand-drawn hearts and flowers and bubble lettering. The exaggerated typography aimed to, in the designers' words, "twist the rigor of modern perspectives," while a set of sticker shapes, which were sold separately, developed out of painting workshops with children.

The design for Part 2, shown here, is somewhat more grown-up: the hand-lettering is gone, and the set typography collapses in a heap. This is about freedom from constraints and leaving the constructs of modernism behind. Each poster acts as a mask, with children's eyes peeping through holes at the top. In animated versions, the eyes blink while lines wriggle above, bringing a childlike playfulness to the composition.

In 2023, the studio released a tenth-anniversary catalog of their projects. Leafing through the sheer variety of work, one can witness how Everyday Practice continues to push the boundaries of design into new realms of versatility.

← P.351

2023

BEN'S BEST BLNZ (B3)

Identity

Eddie Opara (1972–), Pentagram

Ben's Best Blnz (B3), U.S.

Ben's Best Blnz (B3) is a nonprofit cannabis company fronted by Ben Cohen, cofounder of the world-famous ice cream brand Ben & Jerry's. Created not only to offer "great pot" but also to "right the wrongs of the War on Drugs," B3 champions racial justice within the cannabis industry. Historically, Black people in the United States have been four times as likely as white people to be arrested for possession of cannabis, despite the two groups using it at roughly the same rate, and only a mere 4 percent of the country's cannabis companies are currently Black-owned. By investing 100 percent of its profits in Black cannabis entrepreneurs and groups advocating for criminal-justice reform, and aided by a protest-inspired visual identity, B3 hopes to change that.

Partnering with Pentagram's Eddie Opara, B3 developed a visual framework and style of packaging that draws attention to these ongoing issues while avoiding the conventional iconography of cannabis branding, such as marijuana leaves. Opara came up with an adaptable system that could not only flex to fit the ever-changing rules around cannabis marketing but also feature a diverse range of work by Black artists and designers. Expressive typefaces and artworks are paired with galvanizing quotes by contemporary and historical Black figures to form an identity rooted in protest culture and graphics.

The typography in particular plays a key part in the branding and visual appeal of the reusable, plastic-free packaging. Varied and characterful, it is drawn from a core group of fonts by Vocal Type that refer to key moments in the histories of underrepresented races, ethnicities, and genders. Meanwhile, the B3 wordmark is composed of dynamic letterforms that can change in size and scale to frame various types of imagery. Across the brand's website, social media, and packaging, these typefaces are accented in bold hues and are complemented by newly commissioned artworks by Opara and Brooklyn-based multimedia artist Dana Robinson. All of these elements are contained within maximalist compositions that spotlight key messaging from the brand, capturing its ethical ethos and providing thought-provoking reading material for users.

Index

Page numbers in *italics* refer to illustrations

Y

Z

Image credits

T = top; B = bottom; L = left; R = right

21st Century Museum of Contemporary Art, Kanazawa 208; Reza Abedini 319 (T); ACT-UP © 1987, courtesy Wellcome Collection 279; Adidas 246 (B); From *Adrian Frutiger—Typefaces. The Complete Works* 280 (B); © ag Typography Lab, all rights reserved 273; akg-images 28; Photo Albers Foundation/Art Resource, NY 92; Amherst College Library 109 (T); Gary Anderson 241 (B); Apartamento 331; Apple 253 (T); Arnoldo Mondadori Editore 242 (B); Collection of the Art of the Poster/theartofposter.com 166; The Arthur and Elizabeth Schlesinger Library on the History of Women in America, Radcliffe Institute for Advanced Study, Harvard University 62; Courtesy the Artist, the Broad Art Foundation, and Sprüth Magers 287; Australian Wool Innovation Limited, owner of The Woolmark Company 207 (T); Jean-Paul Bachollet 264; Baron & Baron Inc. 293 (BL); Bauhaus-Archiv Berlin 96 (B), 101; Kobi Benezri 328; Biblioteca Angelica 8 (B); Bibliothèque Nationale de France 6 (T); La Biennale di Venezia, ASAC 240; Michael Bierut/Pentagram 307 (T); BLX-Hemeroteca Municipal de Lisboa 189; Irma Boom 300 (B); Julia Born 319 (B); Stewart Brand 231 (T); © Braun GmbH, Kronberg 130 (T); Bruce Mau Design 296 (T); Laurenz Brunner 336 (T); *Bull's Eye*, 1970 © Robert Mapplethorpe Foundation. Used by permission 239; Courtesy Margaret Calvert 179; Canadian National Railway Company 197 (T); Matthew Carter 259 (B), 300 (T), 301 (T); Catalogtree 322; CBAAC, Lagos, Nigeria 259 (T); Theseus Chan 332 (B); Cheltenham Art Gallery & Museums, Gloucestershire, UK/The Bridgeman Art Library 49 (B); Chermayeff 180; Chermayeff and Geismar 196, 242 (T); Churchward Roundsquare Print Negative, New Zealand, by Joseph Churchward, … Te Papa (FE012198/1) 248 … Chwast 182 (TR); … Coca Cola … unication … Corita … (B); Everyday Practice 350 (B); Shepard Fairey/Obeygiant.com 329; Mark Farrow 301 (B); Lisa Federico 168 (T); Fondazione Arnoldo e Alberto Mondadori, Milano, 2022. Photo Louis De Belle, from the book *Ostinata Bellezza: Anita Klinz, La Prima Art Director Italiana*, by Luca Pitoni 183; Archivio Fondazione Primo Conti 65 (B); Colin Forbes 215 (T); Foundation Le Corbusier 133 (B), 158 (T); Foundation Pierre Bergé–Yves Saint Laurent 198 (T); Federica Fragapane 348–9; Collection of Marc J. Frattasio, author of *The New Haven Railroad in the McGinnis Era* 170 (B); Frost Design 294 (B); FUKT, editor in chief and founder: Björn Hegardt; creative director and designer: Ariane Spanier; junior and assistant editors: Alice Finney, Erika Clugston, Faye Campbell, Sarah Gretsch, and Page Wicks 325; Fukushima Prefectural Museum of Art © Miwa Natori 131 (BR); Hans Rudolf Gabathuler 126 (B); © Estate of Abram Games 165; © Estate of Abram Games and Transport for London 252; Ken Garland 177 (B); Reebee Garofalo 256–7; Stuart Geddes with ARM Architecture 338; Collection of the Gemeentemuseum den Haag 100, 119; Geographers' A–Z Map Company Limited 138 (B); Karl Gerstner 260 (T); Archives Karl Gerstner, Prints and Drawings Department, Swiss National Library/NL 178 (B); © Martyn Goddard/Corbis 90; James Goggin 316 (T); Gono LLC 116; Grabink Collection of Images 89; Graphic Design Collections, Special Collections, University of Amsterdam 293 (T); April Greiman 276–7; Joost Grootens 323; Fernando Gutiérrez 293 (BR); Kenya Hara 326 (B); Harvard University—Harvard Map Collection 24 (T); Michael Harvey 311 (T); Julia Hasting 292, 316 (B); Sara Hendren, Brian Glenney, and Tim Ferguson Sauder 332 (T); Herman Miller, Inc. 155 (BL); Hesign Inernational GmbH 346; Armin Hofmann 203; Idea 168 (BL); Mirko Ilić 291 (B); Shira Inbar and MSCHF 343 (B); Insel-Verlag 63 (T); International Poster Gallery 132; J.D.s No. 8, photo Jena von Brücker, 1990 272 (T); Werner Jeker 267 (B); John Frost Newspapers Ltd 127; Maira Kalman 290; Susan Kare LLC 267 (T); Ken Miki & Associates 299; … dy Prints 288 (B); Frifth Kerr … or Museum, … (T) 76 (BR); Zuzana Licko 297 (B); Uwe Loesch 275 (T); George Lois 194, 201 (T); Elaine Lustig-Cohen 148 (T, BR) 153 (T); Made Thought 321; Alejandro Magallanes 317 (B); MART Archivio del '900 93 (B); Karel Martens 288 (T); Mary Evans Picture Library 16 (T); Les Mason, courtesy Devine Contemporary Art 220; Katherine McCoy 286; McDonald's 199 (B); Michelin 44 (T), 46 (B); Meiré und Meiré 307 (BL); Abbott Miller/Pentagram 281; M/M (Paris) 314, 333; MOLD 339; Momayez Foundation 260 (B); Bruno Monguzzi 271 (T), Monotype Imaging Ltd. 199 (T); Morcos Key (Wael Morcos, Rouba Yammine, Haitham Haddad) 347; Moscow Design Museum Collection 131 (T), 211 (T); Most Beautiful Swiss Books 2013, published by the Swiss Federal Office of Culture (FOC), design Maximage 337; Mahvash Mostala 350 (T); © MOURON. CASSANDRE. Lic 2012-20-05-03 cassandre.fr 126 (T), 141 (T); Hamish Muir 275 (T); Rolf Müller 272 (B); © Josef Müller-Brockmann Archive 167, 174; © 1937, Bruno Munari. Licensed by Maurizio Corraini srl 143; Musée de l'Imprimerie de Lyon 14 (T); Museum of Decorative Arts, Prague 91, 113 (B); Museum für Gestaltung, Zürich, Poster Collection 128; Museum für Gestaltung Zürich, Design Collection. Franz Xaver Jaggy © ZHdK 105, 129 (BR), 185 (T); Museum for the Printing Arts Leipzig or Druckkunst Museum Leipzig 63 (B); © 2009. Digital Image, The Museum of Modern Art, New York/Scala, Florence 75 (T), 79, 96 (T), 121 (B), 243 (B); © 2012. Digital image, The Museum of Modern Art, New York/Scala, Florence 207 (B); Nontsikelelo Mutiti, 24 x 36 inches, one-color screenprint, published in an edition of 30 to raise funds for Stable, Washington D.C., printed at the Robert Blackburn Printshop, Elizabeth Foundation, New York 344–5; Kazumasa Nagai 214; The National Archives of Sweden 200; National Library of Australia, Canberra (ref 23525) 93 (T); Trustees of the National Library of Scotland 27 (T); National Széchényi Library of Hungary, Collection of Posters & Printed; Ephemera, inventory number PKG 1929/121 108; © Nike, courtesy Wieden+Kennedy 340; Norm 330; From The New York Public Library 47; Octavo Corp. and the Library of Congress Rare Book and Special Collections Division 8 (T); … fried Odermatt 192 (B); Okike … urnal, photo courtesy … Courtesy Todd … k Pentagram Archives 201 (B), 213, 284 (T); Perkins Library, Duke University 55; Phaidon Press Limited 139, 294 (T), 313 (T); Pirelli 155 (T); Albert-Jan Pool/Preliminary version © Copyright by DIN 123; Special Collections, J.B. Priestley Library, University of Bradford 192 (B); Private Collection 136 (B); Project Projects 334 (T); Alain Le Quernec 306; Iman Raad 324; Gunter Rambow 254, 307 (BR); Rare Book Collections, National Library of Scotland 19 (T); Marion Swannie Rand/Paul Rand Archives 146 (T), 153 (BL), 171, 192 (T); Rochester Institute of Technology/Archive Collections 99, 151; Randall Ross and Molly McCombs, modernism101.com 131 (BL), 136 (T), 146 (BL), 150 (B), 162, 163 (T); Stefan Sagmeister/Photo Tom Schierlitz, courtesy of Stefan Sagmeister Inc. 309; Koichi Sato 249, 298; © 2012. Photo Scala, Florence/BPK, Bildagentur fuer Kunst, Kultur und Geschichte, Berlin 114 (T); Paula Scher/Pentagram 295; Andrew Sclanders 223; Helmut Schmid 209; Ralph Schraivogel 285; Shiseido 72 (B); SilverScreen / Alamy Stock Photo 289; Spare Rib Collective 247; SRI International 177 (T); St Raphaël 144 (T); State Library of Queensland, Australia 24 (B), 58 (BL); Sussman/Prejza & Company 268–9; Svensk Form 186 (T); Swann Auction Galleries, NY 53 (B); Swiss Foundation Type and Typography 172 (T); Takenobu Igarashi 263; Armando Testa 195; © TfL/London Transport Museum 72 (T), 121 (T), 145 (T); © Niklaus Troxler 251 (T); Gerard Unger 250 (B); © Tomi Ungerer and Diogenes Verlag AG Zurich/All Rights Reserved 225; Top Publishers BV, Studio Jop van Bennekom 315; University of Glasgow Library/Department of Special Collections 13 (T); University of Reading Special Collections Service 115; Universitatsbibliothek Basel 10 (T); National Institute of Standards and Technology 221 (T); Miguel Valleri 122; © Verlag H. Schmidt, Mainz 86 (B); Vignelli Associates 219; Visionaire 308 (B); Kunstraum Walcheturm 318; Photos Rebecca Walker/from the collection of Elizabeth Philips/eprarebooks.com 80 (TR); Walker Art Centre 313 (B); © Copyright 2013 Warner Music Group, design Barnbrook 336 (B); Richard Weston 85 (B); Jean Widmer 238, 271 (T); Worms Magazine 341; Lance Wyman 233 (B); Yale University Press, New Haven 271 (B); Yasuhiro Sawada Design Studio 283; Shizuko Yoshikawa/Josef Müller-Brockmann Archive 197 (B); Catherine Zask 312

… ble effort has … owledge … for

Text credits

L = left; M = middle; R = right

Caroline Archer: 355 (R), 360 (M), 376 (L), 400 (M), 406 (L), 419 (M), 432 (L), 439 (M), 457 (R), 461 (M), 490 (L), 503 (R). Melanie Archer: 440 (M), 447 (R), 473 (R), 509 (R). Laura Aylett: 361 (M), 411 (L), 438 (R), 458 (R), 466 (R), 510 (L). Phil Baines: 417 (L). Alison Barnes: 361 (R), 362 (L), 365 (L), 370 (R), 384 (L), 391 (M), 395 (L), 398 (L), 437 (M), 465 (R). David Barringer: 371 (L), 450 (R). Ory Bartal: 437 (R), 458 (M), 457 (M). Nick Bell: 365 (M), 409 (M), 444 (R), 458 (L), 483 (M). Simon Bell: 355 (M), 371 (R), 374 (R), 381 (M), 383 (M), 388 (R), 395 (R), 425 (M), 425 (R), 455 (M), 468 (L), 480 (L), 500 (M), 501 (L), 509 (L). Amelia Black: 380 (L), 389 (M), 466 (L). Jody Boehnert: 354 (R), 395 (M), 427 (M), 453 (R), 478 (M). Mark Braddock: 445 (R). Chris Brown: 355 (L), 370 (M), 380 (R), 383 (R), 385 (M), 431 (R), 441 (M), 443 (M), 491 (L). Carol Choi: 356 (R), 379 (R), 387 (M), 430 (L), 436 (L), 471 (R), 473 (L), 474 (R), 486 (R), 499 (L). Line Hjorth Christensen: 385 (R). Bryan Clark: 438 (M). Maire Cox: 478 (L). Penny Craswell: 410 (L), 419 (R), 433 (L), 440 (L), 468 (R), 483 (R), 485 (R), 494 (R), 495 (L), 500 (L), 499 (R), 501 (R), 506 (M), 507 (M), 508 (M), 509 (M), 511 (L), 512 (M), 513 (M), 513 (R), 514 (L). Simon Daniels: 498 (L). Frank DeRose: 364 (L), 368 (R), 396 (R), 428 (R), 444 (M), 447 (M), 474 (L), 475 (R), 493 (M). Sony Devabhktuni: 363 (M), 375 (M), 385 (R), 431 (L), 479 (R). Valerio Di Lucente: 409 (L), 443 (R), 448 (M), 454 (R), 470 (M), 508 (L). Paul Dobraszczyk: 359 (L), 362 (M). Richard B. Doubleday: 394 (M), 402 (L), 417 (R), 421 (L), 455 (R), 459 (L), 477 (M), 496 (R), 502 (L). Frederico Duarte: 375 (L), 382 (L), 393 (R), 430 (R), 436 (M), 446 (R), 456 (R), 495 (R), 502 (R). Kimberly Elam: 418 (M), 472 (M), 476 (L). Mike Esbester: 360 (R), 362 (R). Krzysztof Fijalkowski: 404 (L), 406 (R), 424 (M), 510 (R). Kevin Finn: 503 (L), 507 (R). Michel Frizot: 413 (L). Katherine Gillieson: 361 (L), 363 (R), 413 (R), 422 (R), 449 (M), 465 (M), 496 (L), 504 (L). Steven Heller: 389 (L), 420 (M), 452 (L), 462 (M), 477 (R), 489 (M). Will Hill: 384 (M), 398 (M), 432 (R). Maggie Hohle: 410 (R), 415 (L), 418 (R), 435 (M), 455 (L), 483 (L), 489 (R), 497 (R). David Hyde: 393 (L), 434 (R), 451 (L), 460 (L). Natalia Ilyin: 368 (L), 376 (R), 379 (L), 454 (M). Phil Jones: 373 (M), 378 (L), 392 (R), 394 (L), 396 (M), 401 (R), 402 (R), 404 (M), 408 (R), 415 (R), 435 (L), 446 (L), 451 (R), 452 (R), 496 (M), 502 (M), 504 (R). Michael Kelly: 386 (M), 413 (M), 423 (L), 424 (L), 427 (L), 429 (M), 446 (M), 456 (M), 470 (R), 476 (M), 485 (L), 497 (L), 514 (M). Anoushka Khandwala: 440 (R), 442 (R), 461 (R), 469 (L), 471 (L), 479 (L), 487 (M), 488 (L), 492 (M), 507 (L), 518 (M), 519 (R), 520 (L). Riikka … tinen: 367 (L), 369 (M), 380 … (L), 389 (M), 420 (L), 428 … , 444 (L), 462 (R), 472 (L), 480 (M), 481 (M). Toon Lauwen: 400 (L), 453 (L), 491 (R). Jae Young Lee: 445 (L). Gina Lovett: 487 (R), 484 (R), 505 (M). Liz McQuiston: 357 (M), 367 (R), 372 (L), 405 (M), 442 (M), 464 (R), 482 (L). Emily McVarish: 363 (L), 374 (L), 390 (L), 391 (L), 398 (R). Helena Michaelson: 358 (M), 385 (L), 391 (R), 449 (R), 453 (M), 493 (L), 493 (R), 505 (L). Daniel Milroy Maher: 381 (R), 468 (M), 473 (M), 477 (L), 485 (M), 505 (R), 510 (M), 514 (R), 515 (M), 516 (M), 516 (R), 517 (L), 517 (M), 518 (L), 518 (R), 519 (L), 520 (R). Catrin Morgan: 407 (M), 408 (M), 429 (L). Christopher Mount: 411 (R), 478 (R). Anne Odling-Smee: 364 (M), 365 (R), 366 (R), 408 (L), 448 (R). Kerry William Purcell: 407 (R), 412 (L), 416 (L), 417 (M), 427 (R), 432 (M), 438 (L). Alan Rapp: 359 (M), 359 (R), 367 (M), 378 (M), 394 (R), 418 (L). Steve Rigley: 402 (M), 432 (M), 461 (L). Sebastian Röck: 513 (L). Rebecca Roke: 151 (R), 414 (M), 445 (M), 456 (L), 459 (R), 467 (R), 470 (L), 474 (M), 484 (L), 486 (L), 491 (M), 492 (L), 499 (M), 511 (M), 512 (R), 515 (L), 516 (L), 517 (R), 519 (M). Ina Saltz: 354 (M), 356 (M), 357 (R), 358 (R), 360 (L), 395 (M), 433 (M), 442 (L), 451 (M), 460 (M), 463 (M), 465 (L), 476 (R), 488 (R), 501 (M). Justine Sambrook: 416 (M), 443 (L), 482 (R), 489 (L). Aaron Seymour: 366 (L), 401 (M). Paul Shaw: 378 (R), 399 (L), 404 (R), 449 (L), 452 (M), 463 (R). Mike Sheedy: 387 (R), 390 (M), 400 (R), 401 (L), 412 (R), 421 (M), 423 (R), 426 (M), 430 (M), 436 (R), 469 (R), 504 (M). Deborah Sutherland: 377 (L), 388 (M), 500 (R). Amoret Tanner: 382 (R). Ben Terrett: 377 (M), 396 (L), 414 (L). Davina Thackara: 370 (L), 381 (L), 397 (M), 428 (L). Teal Triggs: 481 (L). Jason Tselentis: 382 (M), 393 (M), 410 (M), 437 (L), 450 (M), 454 (L), 459 (M), 460 (R), 464 (L), 471 (M), 475 (M), 479 (M), 484 (M), 487 (L), 488 (R), 490 (M), 490 (R), 494 (L), 498 (R), 503 (M), 506 (L), 506 (R), 511 (R). Graham Twemlow: 366 (M), 368 (M), 369 (L), 372 (M), 372 (R), 376 (M), 379 (M), 387 (L), 388 (L), 389 (R), 392 (M), 397 (R), 399 (M), 405 (L), 415 (M), 422 (M), 434 (L), 463 (L), 512 (L). Veronique Vienne: 357 (L), 371 (M), 373 (L), 373 (R), 374 (M), 375 (R), 386 (L), 386 (R), 390 (R), 403 (L), 411 (M), 416 (R), 421 (R), 422 (L), 441 (R), 450 (L), 467 (M), 467 (L), 492 (R), 498 (M). Alissa Walker: 423 (M), 433 (R), 441 (L). Daniel West: 356 (L), 364 (R), 429 (R), 431 (M), 469 (M), 475 (L). Richard Weston: 409 (R), 495 (M), 508 (R). Zoe Whitley: 369 (R), 405 (R), 419 (L), 457 (L), 462 (L), 464 (M), 480 (R). Eliza Williams: 392 (L), 482 (M), 497 (M). Thomas Wilson: 377 (R), 399 (R), 412 (M), 425 (L), 466 (M), 486 (M). Peter Wolf: 414 (R), 424 (R), 436 (L), 426 (R), 439 (L), 447 (L), 448 (L). Laetitia E. Wolff: 494 (M). Wendy Wong: 354 (L), 397 (L). Lawrence Zeegen: 403 (R), 403 (M), 407 (L), 439 (R), 472 (R).

Phaidon Press Limited
2 Cooperage Yard
London E15 2QR

Phaidon Press Inc.
111 Broadway, Suite 301
New York, NY 10006

phaidon.com

First published in 2012 as *The Phaidon Archive of Graphic Design*
Revised and updated in 2017 as *Graphic: 500 Designs That Matter*
Reprinted in this format in 2024 as *Graphic Classics*

ISBN 978 1 83866 842 6

A CIP catalogue record for this book is available from the British Library and the Library of Congress.

Commissioning Editor: Emilia Terragni
Project Editor: Robyn Taylor
Production Controller: Lily Rodgers
Design: Julia Hasting
Artworker: Cantina

Printed in China